THE
DICTIONARY
OF
NEEDLEWORK

THE
DICTIONARY
OF
NEEDLEWORK

by SOPHIA CAULFEILD and BLANCHE SAWARD

An
Encyclopedia of Artistic, Plain, and Fancy Needlework
Illustrated with more than 800 Wood Engravings

BLAKETON HALL LTD

Published 1989 reprinted
from the second edition of 1885

This is a facsimile edition of the second edition of
The Dictionary of Needlework published in
London, 1885. Copyright this impression 1989
Blaketon Hall Limited, Unit One, Devon Units,
Budlake Road, Marsh Barton, Exeter, England

ISBN 0 907854 10 9

Printed in Yugoslavia

TO HER ROYAL HIGHNESS

THE PRINCESS LOUISE, MARCHIONESS OF LORNE,

THIS BOOK IS, BY HER SPECIAL PERMISSION,

DEDICATED,

IN ACKNOWLEDGMENT OF THE GREAT SERVICES WHICH, BY MEANS OF HER CULTIVATED

TASTE AND CORDIAL PATRONAGE, SHE HAS RENDERED TO THE ARTS OF

PLAIN SEWING AND EMBROIDERY.

PREFACE TO FIRST EDITION.

JOHN TAYLOR, in Queen Elizabeth's time, wrote a poem entirely in praise of Needlework; we, in a less romantic age, do not publish a poem, but a Dictionary, not in praise, but in practice, of the Art. It is true that many books dealing with distinct varieties of both plain and fancy work have been published from time to time, but there has not been any that has dealt exhaustively with both subjects, and combined in one volume not only descriptions of ancient and modern Laces, plain and fancy stitches and work, and the manner of working, but also particulars of the various stuffs and materials used for the same.

It has been our object to produce such a comprehensive work—to bring within the compass of a single volume full instructions in working any and every kind of plain and fancy Needlework, to give information concerning the various materials and implements used, to explain the meaning of the terms and technical phrases which are now so generally employed in describing Needlework operations, and, in short, to make the DICTIONARY OF NEEDLEWORK so complete in all respects that any one may be certain of finding in its pages information on every point connected with Needlework.

To many who are not workers, the Lace portion of the Dictionary will, it is hoped, be especially interesting, as there will be found full particulars and numerous engravings of the various makes, both ancient and modern, and in very many instances the most minute instructions for working them—for even some of the most prized of old laces can be successfully copied by all who have patience, leisure, and eyesight.

It is not in the scheme of the present book to include other work than that done wholly, or in part, by the aid of the needle, and the materials used; and mere *patterns* of fancy work are also necessarily excluded—except so far as they be required as examples—as they are already multitudinous, and are being added to day by day, for they change with the fashion of the hour. Besides, anyone with THE DICTIONARY OF NEEDLEWORK at hand can readily master the principles and details of a given work, and can then at will apply that knowledge to any suitable design which may be possessed, or which may be given in the pages of the various journals which devote space to such matters. But beyond these two exceptions we have endeavoured to follow out Lord Brougham's maxim, that a good index can hardly be too prolix, and have introduced every possible stitch, work, and material; feeling with John Taylor of old, that

> All these are good, and these we must allow;
> And these are everywhere in practice now.

LONDON,
June, 1882.

S. F. A. C.
B. C. S.

MARKS AND SIGNS.

In Crochet, Knitting, and Tatting patterns, the same stitches are frequently repeated in the same round of the work. To save the recapitulation thus necessary, the following signs are adopted to indicate where the stitches already given are to be repeated or in any way used again:

The Asterisk or *.—Where an asterisk is put twice, with instructions between, they indicate that the part of the pattern enclosed between them is to be repeated from where the first asterisk is inserted, thus; 3 Chain, * 1 Double Crochet, 5 Chain, 2 Double Crochet, repeat from * twice. This, if written at full length, would read as follows: 3 Chain, 1 Double Crochet, 5 Chain, 2 Double Crochet, 1 Double Crochet, 5 Chain, 2 Double Crochet, 1 Double Crochet, 5 Chain, 2 Double Crochet.

The Square Cross or + is used in Knitting and Crochet to indicate the place to which a row is worked and then repeated backwards. For example: 1 Double Crochet, 5 Chain, 3 Treble Crochet, + ; if written at full length this would be—1 Double Crochet, 5 Chain, 6 Treble Crochet, 5 Chain, 1 Double Crochet. The letters A and B sometimes take the place of the cross, as follows: A, 1 Double Crochet, 5 Chain, 3 Treble Crochet, B.

The St. Andrew's Cross or × is used in instructions to help a worker in a difficult pattern, by enclosing a particular part of a design within two of these crosses, thus: 4 Chain, 5 Treble, × 12 Chain, 1 Purl, 12 Chain, 5 Double Crochet, 6 Treble, × 4 Chain.

The Long Cross or Dagger (†) is used in conjunction with the asterisk in instructions when a repetition within a repetition has to be made, as for example: 1 Chain, † 4 Double Crochet, 5 Chain, * 3 Chain, 5 Treble Crochet, 1 Purl, repeat from * twice, 4 Chain, 3 Double Crochet, repeat from †; if written out fully would be—1 Chain, 4 Double Crochet, 8 Chain, 5 Treble Crochet, 1 Purl, 3 Chain, 5 Treble Crochet, 1 Purl, 3 Chain, 5 Treble Crochet, 1 Purl, 4 Chain, 3 Double Crochet, 4 Double Crochet, 8 Chain, 5 Treble Crochet, 1 Purl, 3 Chain, 5 Treble Crochet, 1 Purl, 3 Chain, 5 Treble Crochet, 1 Purl, 4 Chain, 3 Double Crochet.

Words in Small Capital Letters.—In the explanations of the manner of working the various Embroideries, we have endeavoured to facilitate the references by printing in SMALL CAPITAL LETTERS the designation of any stitch or movement when first mentioned that is of sufficient importance as to require a separate heading. The worker will understand from this that she can, if necessary, refer to a fuller explanation of the stitch or movement than is supplied in that particular place. The same stitches being used in totally different branches of needlework, a description of them under one heading, once for all, does away with the necessity of continual repetitions. When a stitch or movement is only required in the particular work where it occurs, it is only referred to in the main part of the Dictionary, and is described in a separate paragraph, under the heading of the work it is used in.

ERRATA.

Art Embroidery on Needlework should be "Art Embroidery, or Needlework."
Brides and Brides Claires.—"*See* Bar" should be "*see* Bars."
Half Hitch.—The second heading should be "Half Stitch."

THE

Dictionary of Needlework.

A Practical Encyclopædia.

ABACA.—The native name for the Manilla hemp, produced by one of the Banana tribe. This fibre was introduced into France for the manufacture of dress materials, as well as of tapestry and articles of upholstery. In India it is made into the finest muslins and linen cloth. For these delicate stuffs, only the inner fibre of the leaf-stalk is employed; while canvas, as well as cordage, is produced from the coarser kind outside. The Abaca plant is a native of the East Indian Islands; and the well-known Manilla straw hats are plaited from its coarser fibres.

Abb. — From the Anglo-Saxon *ab-ob*. The yarn of which the warp of any textile is composed, of whatever material it may be. Thus the term "Abb-wool," as employed by weavers, signifies the wool of which the warp of any stuff may be woven.

A Bout.—A phrase denoting one complete round made in knitting. *See* KNITTING.

Abrasion.—A technical term denoting the figuring of textiles by means of weaving down the surface.

Adding Bobbins.—Extra Bobbins are often required in Pillow lace while in progress of making. To add: Hang them on in pairs to the pin nearest the working Bobbins, and the knot that joins them together cut close and wind out of the way to prevent the ends getting entangled with the Bobbin threads. The new thread pass under two working Bobbins, and continue as usual.

Adrianople Twill. — The French name synonymous with TURKEY RED TWILL, which *see*.

Aficôt.—French name of instrument for polishing lace, and removing small hard scraps of cotton or thread.

Agrafe.—The word is derived from the early Norman term *Aggrapes*, and is the modern French for a clasp or hook. It is also applied to gimp fastenings. The ancient Aggrapes included both the hook and eye which fastened mediæval armour.

Aida Canvas.—This material, introduced under the French name *Toile Colbert*, is a description of linen cloth. It is also called "Aida Cloth," and JAVA CANVAS (which see), as well as "Fancy Oatmeal." It is made in widths varying from 18 inches to 54 inches, and can be had in white, cream, grey, and gold colour; and is also produced in a woollen coloured material. A cotton cloth of the same make is known by different names, those most employed being BASKET CLOTH and CONNAUGHT.

Aigrette. — A French term employed in millinery, denoting an upright tuft of filaments, grapes, or feathers as a decoration to the headdress, hat, or bonnet.

Aiguille.—The French for needle.

Aiguillette. — A trimming of cords terminating in tags of gimp, silk, gold, silver, or black metal.

Alaska Seal Fur.—A comparatively inexpensive description of Seal-skin. It is of a pale brown or fawn colour, and is employed for tippets, muffs, and trimmings.

Albatross Cloth.—A soft fine bunting; it is known also as "Satin Moss," "Llama Croisé," "Vienna" (the stoutest make), "Snowflake" (which is flecked), "Antique Cloth," &c., 25 inches in width.

Albert Crape.—A variety of crape composed of a union of silk and cotton; that called Victoria Crape being of cotton only. The widths of all descriptions of crape run from 32 inches to 1 yard. *See* CRAPE.

Alençon Bar. A Needle Point Bar, chiefly used for filling up irregular spaces in Modern Point lace. To make, as shown in Fig. 1: Pass a thread backwards and forwards over the open space to be covered as a HERRINGBONE. Cover this thread with BUTTONHOLE, as shown in the illustration.

FIG. 1. ALENÇON BAR.

B*

Alençon Grounds.—These grounds were first made as Bride and then as Réseau. Those worked in Argentan lace were similar, except that Alençon excelled in the extreme fineness and regularity of its Réseau grounds, while Argentan was justly considered superior in its Bride. The Bride was the plain Bride, and the Bride Picotée or Bride Ornée. The Grande Bride was formed of a six-sided mesh covered with buttonhole. The Réseau was worked after the pattern, and served to join it. It was worked all one way with a kind of knotted stitch, the worker commencing always on the same side, and placing her needle between each stitch of the row just formed. Sometimes the plain ground was formed with a thread thrown across, and others intersecting it. The Alençon grounds are of the same hexagonal shaped mesh as the Brussels, but the Argentan are coarser. The Ecaille de Poisson ground is found in both laces. It is a Réseau ground very much resembling the overlapping scales of a fish.

edict, he established a small school of 200 workmen for the purpose of producing Point de Venice in France, and thus directing into French hands the money that was spent in foreign countries. The old Point Coupé workers at first rebelled against the monopoly of Colbert, but the lace was ordered to be worn at court, and soon became fashionable, as much on account of its intrinsic beauty as for royal favour. Enormous quantities were sold, and it was sent to Russia, Poland, and England, and even to Venice. At this period, Alençon was but a copy of Venetian and Spanish Point; the patterns were the same, and the stitch confined to the Buttonhole; the grounds were the Bride and the Bride Ornée, the flowers in relief, and trimmed with Picots and Fleurs Volantes. In 1678 a slight change appeared in the lace, the ground was dispensed with, and the patterns so formed that they connected themselves together with long stems and small branching sprays, but still in high relief, and chiefly made with Buttonhole stitch. During the reign of Louis XIV., Alençon was

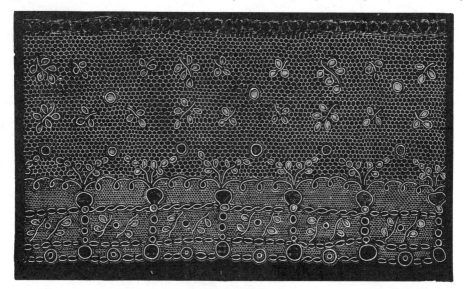

Fig. 2. ALENÇON POINT—EIGHTEENTH CENTURY.

Alençon Point.—This beautiful French lace is one of the glories of that nation. It is, with the exception of Argentan, which is allied to it, the only Needle Point lace executed in France. It was known in England as Point à l'Aiguille for many generations, while from the date of its manufacture in France, 1665 to 1720, it was there called Point de France. The chief seat of its manufacture at the present time is at Bayeux, but in olden times the making of the lace did not extend beyond a few miles round Alençon, and yet gave employment to from 8000 to 9000 hands, chiefly women and children, but old men also worked. The town of Alençon, before the time of Colbert, made the lace called Point Coupé, and when that energetic minister conceived the idea of establishing a Venetian school of lace in France, he fixed upon his chateau of Lonray, close to Alençon, as its seat. The enormous sums spent by the nation in the purchase of Venetian and Spanish points induced Colbert to take this step, and, obtaining a royal

made of these two descriptions; but after his death, and that of Colbert, a great change was introduced. The ground was made with a honeycomb mesh, called Réseau, and the pattern filled up with numerous open stitches, called Jours, Fellings, or Modes. In the first part of the eighteenth century, this Réseau ground was made of various sizes and thicknesses, and the pattern flowing and undulating; latterly, the lace patterns partook of the bizarre rage, and were stiff and formal. They then again changed to the Réseau ground, which was sewn over with small dots or sprays, and the pattern worked as a solid border (see Fig. 2). During the Revolution, the manufactory at Alençon became almost extinct; but Napoleon I. assembled the old workers that remained, and gave a new impetus with magnificent orders, amongst them the layette for the King of Rome and the bed hangings of Marie Louise. With the abdication of Napoleon the trade again almost disappeared, but was revived by Napoleon III., and still exists, although the greater part of its glory has departed. The Vrai Réseau ground, for which Alençon was so justly famous, is now rarely worked, and only for such orders as royal marriages, as its production by hand labour is so expensive, and the work is confined to the pattern formed with the needle and appliqué upon bobbin net. The use of Alençon during the reigns of Louis XIV. and XV. was universal, and it was then at the height of its fame. The prices given were enormous, and yet every article of attire was trimmed with it, and such large furniture as bed-hangings, and vallances to cover baths composed of it.

the pattern upon separate pieces of parchment, which number, so that no error in the joining occurs. These pieces of parchment prick with little holes along the outlines of the design, and follow the outline with a doubled thread, called FIL DE TRACE, caught down to the parchment at regular intervals, as shown in Fig. 3. The ground make either with the BRIDE—thus: Throw a thread across a space from one part of the pattern to another, and cover it with a line of BUTTONHOLE stitches worked close together—or with the HONEYCOMB RÉSEAU or ALENÇON GROUND, and finish by filling up the pattern either with

FIG. 3. ALENÇON LACE, showing Réseau Ground and Fil de Trace.

The lace hangings of the bed at the baptism of the Duke of York, 1763, cost £3783, and a single toilette 6801 livres. When we consider the time that Alençon took to make, and the number of hands it passed through, these prices are not surprising; and we must also take into account that the fine Lille thread of which it was composed cost 1800 livres the lb. The lace is made as follows: Draw the pattern upon copper, and print it off on to parchment, from the use of which its name Vilain is derived, that word being a corruption of vellum. Place small sections of

thick rows of POINT DE BRUXELLES or with POINT DE GRECQUE or other open FILLINGS. In the oldest specimens of this lace, these Fillings were all Buttonhole; in the more modern, they were remarkable for their lightness and beauty, the Alençon workwomen excelling all other lace makers in these fancy stitches. The CORDONNET, or outer edge, of the lace is always thick, and horsehair is introduced into it. This renders the lace firm and durable, but is heavy, and is the reason that Alençon is considered a winter lace. It also causes the Cor-

FIG. 4. ALOE THREAD EMBROIDERY.

donnet to shrink when cleaned. The FOOTING and PICOTS add after the piece of pattern is joined to the whole design. When the pattern is so far completed, it is unpicked from the parchment, and is joined by the cleverest workwomen. The lines of the joins are made to follow the pattern as far as possible, and form part of it. The finish to the lace give by polishing all the parts in relief with the AFICÔT, and adding the Picots and Footing. Each workwoman takes a separate portion of these protracted processes, and is known by one of the following names: Piqueuse, or pricker; traceuse, or outliner; réseleuse and fondeuse, ground makers; remplisseuse, the flat pattern worker; brodeuse, raised pattern maker; modeuse, those who work the fillings; assembleuse, the joiner; mignonneuse, those who add the footings; picoteuse, the picots; while the toucheuse, brideuse, boucleuse, gazeuse, help the joiners. The Alençon lace now made is not passed through so many hands, but is executed by one person, and the pieces joined together or APPLIQUÉ on to machine net. Two flounces made at Mons. Lefébure's, at Bayeux, and exhibited in 1867, are one of the finest examples of modern work. They cost £3400, and engaged forty women for seven years in their making. The ground is the VRAI RÉSEAU, hence the time spent over them. The price of the Alençon, upon machine net ground, now is about 6s. 6d. the yard, width 2in. to 2½in. In the Report of the Commissioners at the Great Exhibition, Alençon is classed fifth, Brussels, Mechlin, Valenciennes, and Lille being ranked above it. At the same exhibition a new kind of Alençon was exhibited, which was made and patented by a Madame Hubert. It consisted of flowers and fruit made with the needle, and so much in relief as to approach in form and outline to the natural ones; in fact, a perfect imitation of Nature without the colour.

Algerian Lace.—A gimp lace made of gold and silver threads. *See* GREEK LACES.

Algerian Stripe.—A mixed cream-coloured material, so called because made in imitation of the peculiar Moorish cloth, manufactured in alternate stripes of rough knotted cotton web, and one of a delicate, gauze-like character, composed of silk. It is employed for the making of women's burnouses, in imitation of those worn by the Arabs. It used to be produced in scarlet and cream-white, as well as in the latter only. The price varies from 6s. 6d. to 10s. 6d.; the width, 52 inches.

Algerian Work.—*See* ARABIAN EMBROIDERY.

Allah Haik.—The original Moorish striped material, a mixture of gauze and cotton, unbleached, and of a cream-white, made in stripes of silk gauze and cotton in equal widths, the former plain, the latter rough, with a knotted nap on the right side. It is employed for turbans, and measures about a yard wide. An imitation is made in England and elsewhere, of not quite so rough a make, which is much employed in making burnouses. The threads running the long way of the material are the knotted ones, and are much coarser than those running across them, which are but sufficiently strong to keep them together.

Alloa Wheeling.—A Scotch yarn, made in the town

of that name. It is to be had in black, drab, grey, and white, as well as in heather shades, and is employed for knitting men's thick riding gloves. The price in England varies from 3s. to 4s. per lb., but the fluctuations in the market must be allowed for in the purchase of these goods.

Aloe Thread Embroidery.—The peasants of Abbissola and the nuns of Oldivales were accustomed to make lace from the fibres of the aloe, and recently an embroidery with aloe threads, instead of silk, has been introduced into England. The colour of the thread is a pale straw, but, apart from the novelty of the material, the work has little to recommend it, although it is believed to retain its tint better than silk. To work, as shown in Fig. 4: Select an ordinary satin stitch embroidery pattern, and

chief amongst the varieties of cloth made of the wool are called alpacas, fancy alpacas, lustres, silk warp, alpaca lustres, twilled alpaca mixtures, alpaca and mohair linings, and umbrella and parasol cloth. What are mostly sold as alpacas now are really a fine make of Orleans cloth, which is a mixture of wool and cotton, dyed in all colours, and varying from 24 to 36 inches in width; but the first quality of real alpaca runs from 30 to 36 and up to 54 inches. Nearly all the wool is worked up at Bradford, and the several varieties are most commonly to be had in black, white, and grey. In its natural state it is black, white or brown, yet from these an almost endless variety is produced. The pure vigogne measures 48 inches in width.

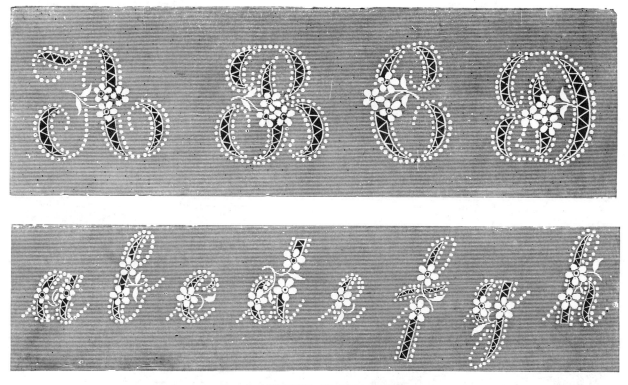

FIG. 5. ALPHABET IN EMBROIDERY.

trace it out upon silk or serge; lay down over the outline of the chief flowers, or other prominent parts of the design, a pad of wool, and work in SATIN STITCH over this padding with the aloe fibres.

Alpaca Cloth.—This name is derived from the original Spanish, denoting a species of llama or Peruvian goat, the *Vicuna* or *Vigonia*, producing the most expensive quality of hair. These animals are of the tribe *Camelina*, and are the camels of South America. The hair is fine, woolly, and longer and finer than that of the Cashmere goat. The manufacture of it into textiles was introduced into England by Sir Titus Salt. The wool is mixed with silk or cotton, producing a thin and durable cloth of various degrees of fineness, suitable for wearing apparel for men and women, as well as for other purposes. The

Alpaca Yarn.—A very valuable description of yarn, and much superior to the ordinary qualities of sheep's wool. In its natural state it is black, white, or brown, but a great variety of shades are produced from the three colours. It is spun so finely that the thread may be used either alone or in combination with silk or cashmere in the manufacture of fabrics of the lightest description. The seat of the English trade is at Bradford.

Alphabet.—The word alphabet is derived from Alpha and Beta, the first and second letters in the Greek language. The embroidery of letters entered largely into the instruction given in needlework in ancient days, no girl being considered a proficient in the art until she could work in cross stitch all the letters of the alphabet upon a sampler. In modern times this proficiency is not so much required, as linen marking is done with ink, but ornamental alphabets are still used. The Irish peasantry are celebrated for their skill in embroidering letters upon handkerchief corners, and French ladies display much taste in working with silk upon silk tablecloths and cushions. English ladies use alphabets more for initials upon saddle cloths, rugs, and cambric. The designs for these letters are taken from well-known characters, such as Gothic, Roman, Renaissance or Cuneiform, the preference being given to the letters that are clear in form, however much ornamented. To work: Trace the pattern upon stiff paper and lay it under such materials as allow of the lines showing through, or for thick stuffs iron it off. The letters look better placed across the material than straight. Embroider them with lace thread, embroidery cotton, silk, floss, gold and silver thread, or with human hair. For the stitches use SATIN, FEATHER, OVERCAST, and ROPE for solid thick materials; and POINT DE POIS, POINT RUSSE, POINT D'OR add to the first mentioned for cambrics, Japanese silks, and other light foundations. The illustrations (Fig. 5) show the capitals and small letters of an alphabet much used in embroidery; work these in Satin Stitch, Point de Pois, and HERRINGBONE. Where the dark lines of the illustrations are, cut out the material and BUTTONHOLE it over, and fill in the open space thus made with Herringbone stitches.

American Cloth.—A stouter material than the French *Toile cirée.* It is an enamelled oil-cloth much employed in needlework for travelling and toilet "necessaries," "housewives," and numerous other useful articles. It possesses much elasticity, and is sold in black, sky-blue, white, and green, silver and gold, by the yard. It is a yard and a half in width, and is enamelled on one side only.

FIG. 6. AMERICAN PATCHWORK.

American Patchwork.—A work well known in Canada under the name of "Loghouse Quilting," but only lately introduced into England. It is a variety of patchwork, into which strips of coloured ribbon are introduced. To work: Take a five-inch foundation of strong calico, tack to the centre of this a piece of silk or satin an inch and a half square. Round this centre square, run on seven rows of narrow ribbon, so that their edges overlap. Run on round two sides of the square dark shades of ribbon, and on the other sides light colours, and make the corners square — not dovetailed (*see* Fig. 6). Form several of these large five-inch squares, and then sew together like ordinary patchwork pieces, so that the light side of one square is next the light side of the next square, and the dark next the dark, giving the look of alternate squares of light and dark colour. The effect of this work depends upon the judicious selection of the narrow ribbon as to its shades of colour and their contrasts with each other. The centre squares of piece silk should always be of a dark shade, but not black.

Andalusian Wool.—This is also called Victoria Wool, and is a fine, soft, warm make of woollen thread or yarn, employed for knitting a superior description of stockings and socks. It is the same wool as the Shetland, but is thicker, being spun with four threads instead of two. It is to be had in all colours as well as white and black, and also ingrain; the price in Great Britain varies from 6s. 6d. to 8s. 6d. the lb.

Angleterre Bars.—These are used in Modern Point lace. To work: Fill in the space between the braids with lines of crossed threads, and at every junction make a spot, as shown in illustration (Fig. 7). To form these spots, run the thread along one of the horizontal lines until it comes to one of the upright cross lines, twist the thread over and under the two lines alternately until a

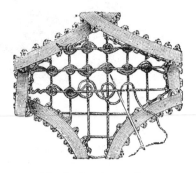

FIG. 7. ANGLETERRE BARS.

sufficiently handsome knot is formed, then carry it along the horizontal line until another upright cross line is gained, and repeat.

Angleterre Edge.—A Needle Point edging to braid or Cordonnet, and made with one line of POINT DE BRUXELLES loops. To work: Make a POINT DE BRUXELLES, and into it work a tight BUTTONHOLE, and repeat to the end of the space. Identical with POINT D'ANGLETERRE EDGING.

Anglo-Saxon Embroidery.—The earliest English embroidery known, consisting of patterns in outline, worked either with gold thread, silk, or beads, and used for borders to garments. The outlines were generally laid upon the surface of the material, and caught down, as in

FIG. 8. ANGLO-SAXON EMBROIDERY.

couching, while any fillings were of an open description, as shown in illustration (Fig. 8), which is a modern imitation. This embroidery must not be confounded with the celebrated Opus Anglicanum of a later date, or with the embroidery upon muslin with untwisted thread. For manner of working, *see* SAXON EMBROIDERY.

Angola Cashmere, or Angora Cloth.—Names employed in the trade to denote a certain cloth made in imitation of the camels' hair cloth; said to be made of the long white hair of the Angora goat of Asiatic Turkey, which rivals that of Cashmere. This cloth is of a light quality, and the widths run to 27, 48, and 54 inches.

Angola Cloth.—A pretty diaper-woven cotton cloth, with a fine rough face, somewhat resembling the character of Shagreen. It is of a cream colour, is 54 inches in width, and is employed for embroidery.

Angola Mendings.—So called from a semblance in quality to that of the wool of the Angora goat. This yarn is composed of a mixture of wool and cotton, and

may be had in many shades and tints of colour. It is sold on cards and reels, and also in skeins, and is designed for darning merino and woollen stockings.

Angora Cat Fur.—This fur is remarkable for its length and beauty, and is of a very light shade of grey, or white. The hair of the tail measures about five inches in length. A large trade is carried on in these skins.

Angora Goat Fur.—Otherwise called *Angona* and *Angola*. This fur comes from Asiatic Turkey, and the goat is called after a city of that name, in the neighbourhood of which it abounds. The size of the skin measures 27 inches by 36 inches, and is valued at from 18s. to 35s. It is employed for jackets, hats, and trimmings.

Angora Wool.—This wool is supplied by the goat after which it is named, grows long, is silky in appearance, and is employed in the making of shawls, braids, lace, and for other decorative purposes, besides dress materials of various makes. The Angora wool is also called mohair, and is now being extensively produced in California, as well as in the east.

Antwerp Edge.—A Needle Point edging to braid or Cordonnet, and made with a line of open Buttonhole caught with a knot in each loop. To work, as shown in

FIG. 9. ANTWERP EDGE.

Fig. 9: Make a Point de Bruxelles loop, and secure it with a BUTTONHOLE made as a knot round the lower part of it. Work each Point de Bruxelles ⅛ of an inch apart. It is identical with POINT DE BRUXELLES edge.

Antwerp Lace.—A manufactory was founded at Antwerp for the making of pillow lace in the seventeenth century, and the lace made was, with that of Mechlin, indifferently known as Flanders lace. Savary mentions that lace was made there of two kinds, one without ground and the other with patterns attached with Brides; but the Réseau ground was also made, and Antwerp lace had the effect of embroidery given to it, as that of Mechlin, by the plait thread that outlined the design. The Antwerp lace was larger as to design, and was chiefly exported into Spain; and, when the market for it ceased there, it would have quite decayed, had it not been for the lace shown in Fig. 10, which was used so much by the peasants as to buoy up the production for some time. This pattern is called Potten Kant, and is the sole remnant of a design once worked in lace, representing the Annunciation. The angel, the Virgin Mary, and the lilies were gradually omitted, until nothing but the vase for holding the flowers was worked. Antwerp at present produces Brussels lace. (*See* illustration on following page.)

Antwerp Lace.—A Needle Point edging identical with ESCALIER LACE, which *see*.

Appliqué.—A French term, signifying the sewing of one textile over another. This work was anciently known as

Opus Consutum or Cut work, *Passementerie*, and *Di Commesso*. Of these names, the first is the most ancient; but, as it is also used to denote some of the early laces, it has been succeeded by *Appliqué*, which is derived from the Latin *applicare*, to join or attach, and the French *appliquer*, to put on. The Di Commesso is a name given to the work by Vasari, who claims the invention of it for Sandro Botticelli, a Florentine; but, as some Appliqué is still in existence that dates back before Botticelli's birth, this is incorrect, and the origin of it is lost in antiquity. It was, however, most practised from the thirteenth to the seventeenth centuries, and numerous specimens of the early times are still extant. The work has been known in India and Persia for many hundreds of years, and was probably invented there; the Italians, Germans, and French use it largely for household decorations, the English more for altar cloths and vestments. The word Appliqué has a

century, destroyed in 1870; and the Blazonment of Cleves are the best known old examples. It is not unusual to find, amongst mediæval woven materials, spaces left open when weaving, into which figures of saints and other devices were inserted by the method known as Inlaid Appliqué and finished with fine needle stitching either in Opus Plumarium (or Feather stitch) or Opus Anglicanum (Split stitch). At other times the fine linen or canvas inserted for the faces and hands only of figures would be simply painted. Appliqué is divided into Inlaid and Onlaid, and from these heads spring many adaptations of the work, the best known being gold embroidery, used in ecclesiastical work; Appliqué proper, used for all ordinary purposes; Broderie Perse, or Appliqué with cretonne; and Appliqué upon muslin and net. Inlaid Appliqué has more the effect of woven brocade of various colours than of needlework, unless used, as described above, for letting in needlework into loom-made materials.

FIG. 10. ANTWERP LACE.

wide meaning, and many varieties of needlework come under its designation. Being originally introduced as an imitation of the earlier and more laborious raised embroidery, it embraces every description of work that is cut or stamped out, or embroidered, and then laid upon another material. It is therefore possible to Appliqué in almost every known material, as in feathers, skins of animals, gold and silver, mother o' pearl, and other foreign substances, the motive being to produce effect with varied and bold materials and without the labour of close embroidery. The most curious English example of the materials that may be artistically Appliqué together was exhibited in the Paris Exhibition in the Prince of Wales's Pavilion, and consisted of a series of Chinese fowling scenes, in which the human figures were clothed in silk and velvet, the animals in their own furs, and the birds in their own feathers. The Baldachino of Orsanmichele, worked in the fourteenth century; the Banner of Strasburg, worked in the fourteenth

To make: Carefully design the pattern upon a foundation material, and cut away from that the various flowers or *motifs* that make up the design. Replace these pieces by others of different colour and textures, accurately cut so as to fit into the places left vacant by the removal of the solid material, and lay these in to the foundation without a margin or selvedge overlapping either to the front or back of the work. Stitch them into position, and conceal the joins and lines of stitches by COUCHING down a line of gold cord, narrow ribbon, or floss silk over those places. Great nicety is required in the cutting out and fitting into place of the various pieces, and sewing them down. The materials used in Inlaid Appliqué should match as to substance, or a thinner one be backed with linen when used with a thicker, otherwise the finished work will strain and wrinkle. Inlaid Appliqué was much used in Italy during the eleventh century, and specimens of it can be seen at South Kensington; it is also used in Indian embroideries and Cashmere shawls, but it is not much worked by modern ladies. Onlaid Appliqué is the true Appliqué, and is divided into two descriptions of needlework—one where the solid pieces of stuff are laid down upon the material and secured with a cord stitched round them, and the other where materials of various kinds are laid down and enriched with many stitches and with gold embroideries. True Appliqué is formed by laying upon a rich foundation small pieces of materials, varied in shade, colour, and texture, and so arranged that a blended and coloured design is formed without the intervention of complicated needle stitches. The stuffs most suitable for the foundation are velvets, cloths, plush, cloth of gold and silver; for applying, satin, silk, plush, cloth of gold and silver, satin sheeting and velvet. Velvet and plush only make good foundations when gold embroidery is laid upon them, as they are too thick for lighter weights; but they are admirable for applying gold and silver cloth upon, but the cost of the latter precludes their being

most prominent shades of the work; if single, let them match the foundation colour; they should not contrast with the work, or be obtrusive by their colouring, they rather enrich by their beauty and depth of tone. Much of the beauty of Appliqué depends upon its design, but combination of colour is an important item in its success. Badly designed patterns are coloured with the aim of attracting attention by the brilliancy produced by contrasts between material and applied work, but such is not true art, and is never used by good designers, except when bold effects are to be produced, and large spaces covered; the brilliancy of the colouring is then lost in its breadth and richness. Smaller work requires to be restful in tone and harmonious in colour, and all violent contrasts avoided. Shades of the same colour, but of different materials, have a pleasing effect. Ancient work presents many examples of this variety of material and sameness of colour, but it consists chiefly in the amalgamation of two colours, and derives its effect from

FIG. 11. APPLIQUÉ UPON SATIN.

used with freedom. Velvet, plush, satin and silk are the materials chiefly employed for applying, the aim of this work being to lay one handsome material upon another as though it were a raised portion of the same. To work: It is necessary that each separate piece should lie flat and without a wrinkle, therefore the materials to be applied to the foundation must be first backed (*see* BACKING). Carefully cut out the pieces to be applied, after having traced their outline upon the Backing, and keep them ready, then stretch their background or foundation in a frame, and trace the outline of the pattern upon it by means of tracing and blue carbonised paper. Lay the cut-out pieces in position one at a time, and secure them by sewing down their edges. Conceal these sewn edges by a handsome gold or silk cord, which lay over them, and COUCH down by a stitch brought from the back of the material and returned to the back. Make these fastening stitches of a silk of a different colour to the cord they catch down. Lay on the cords either as single or double cords; if double, select the colours of the two

the difference of material used for the grounding and the applied. Numerous shades of colour and various tints are more the result of the revived Appliqué than strictly old work; but as long as these arrangements in colour are formed of soft harmonious tones, they are an advancement of the work. Fig. 11 is an Appliqué pattern one-third its original size. It represents a scroll, the centre of which is filled by a flower showing its back and front alternately. To work: Select a deep peacock blue or dark red-brown satin for background, pale blue plush for the turned-over flower, and citron coloured petals, with orange centre, for the fully opened one. Work over tendrils and stem in CREWEL STITCH and in brown shades, Appliqué leaves in green, and vein the flowers and leaves with SATIN STITCH. A less elaborate Appliqué is made with fine écru linen laid upon satin sheeting or silk grounds. This kind is generally continuous as to design, and the écru linen is cut out and applied to the ground as one piece. The linen is strong enough to

c

need no backing, and the groundwork only requires to be stretched in a frame while the two materials are stitched to each other. The écru linen is not pasted, but stitched to the foundation, and the stitches concealed by Feather or Buttonhole wide apart stitches worked over them. Of this kind is Fig. 12. Work the écru oranges round with a sober orange-tinted filoselle, the flowers with cream colour, and the leaves with pale green, the stalk with brown, and the veinings in satin stitch with pale green filoselle. Deep brown-red is the best foundation colour.

Fig. 12. ÉCRU APPLIQUÉ.

In Fig. 13 we have another design suitable for velvet application. The animals and scrolls, cut out in brown velvet and lay upon golden-coloured satin or sheeting, and secure their edges either with FEATHER STITCH or a plain gold cord of purse silk; the same design can be cut out of écru linen and laid upon an art blue background. The Feather stitching must then be in the same tinted blue silk. When the Appliqué materials of various shades and enriched with silk, floss, and gold threads, are laid down, the stitches used are chiefly FEATHER, LONG, BASKET, CUSHION, TENT, and all the various COUCHINGS. Being

the same. In true Appliqué plain self-coloured stuffs are amalgamated, and the effect obtained by the variety and beauty of these tints; in Broderie Perse the applied pieces are shaded and coloured pieces of chintz or cretonne, representing flowers, foliage, birds, and animals in their natural colours. These require no backing, and are simply pasted upon a coloured foundation and caught down with a Feather or open Buttonhole Stitch. Broderie Perse was practised 200 years ago, and then fell into disuse. It is capable of much improvement from the patterns ordinarily sold, and though, by reason of its attempting to imitate round objects in nature, it can never attain an art value, still it could be made a more harmonious decoration than it is at present. The faults of ordinary cretonne and chintz work are too great a contrast between background and design as to colours, and too lavish a use of brilliant flowers or birds in the pattern. The worker should bear in mind that the setting of one or two brilliant colours among several subdued ones will produce a much better effect than the crowding together of a number of equally bright shades. Much

Fig. 13. VELVET APPLIQUÉ.

worked as embroideries of gold and silver, and chiefly used for church purposes, the description of the latter will apply to this kind of Appliqué in the manner of design, colouring, and execution. *See* EMBROIDERY.

Appliqué, Baden. *See* BADEN EMBROIDERY.

Appliqué, Broderie Perse.—A modern work, founded upon ancient and true Appliqué, but differing from it in the nature of the material used and the labour bestowed; but the word Appliqué is common to both, as the essentials of the work, that of laying one material upon another, are

will depend upon the selection of flowers, &c. The best come from old pieces of chintz manufactured before the days of aniline dyes; their shades mix together without offence, and their outlines are generally clear and decided. When not procurable, select bold single modern chintz or cretonne flowers of quiet tone and conventional design. Avoid bright colours, and choose citron, lemon, red, red-browns, lavenders, and cream-whites. Sunflowers, tulips, hollyhocks, crown imperials, foxgloves, chrysanthemums, peonies, sweet peas, anemones, thistles, are all good flowers. Palm leaves or Virginia creeper leaves make good designs alone, but not amalgamated, and ferns are not used at all. Only one to three different kinds of flowers are grouped together. Backgrounds for Broderie Perse can be of any material but velvet, and should match the darker tints of the flowers applied to them. Black and white are never used, being too crude in colour and too great a contrast. If dark backgrounds are wished, invisible green, deep peacock blue, garnet brown, will give all the depth of black without its harshness; and if light, lemon and cream-whites will tone better than pure white. Sunflowers are applied upon brown-red, red hollyhocks upon deep red, peonies upon deep maroon. Before commencing to work, cut out the flowers and leaves that make the design, and group them upon a sheet of white paper; run a pencil round their outlines, and disturb them

Fig. 14. APPLIQUÉ, BRODERIE PERSE.

only when they are required. Stretch the background upon a frame or clothes horse, and paste the chintz flowers into position upon it. Transfer the outline of the design to the material with the aid of a carbonised tracing paper, if required. When the pasting is finished and dry, take the work out of the frame and BUTTONHOLE loosely all round the leaves and flowers. Make this Buttonholing as little visible as possible, and let the colours used for the filoselle or cotton match the medium tint of the flower or leaf that is secured. FEATHER STITCH can be used instead of Buttonhole. Enrich the veinings of the leaves and flowers with SATIN STITCH and sometimes work this enrichment so as to cover the larger part of the chintz, but the character of the work is much altered by so doing, and the filoselle enrichments make brighter what is already sufficiently prominent. The illustration

(Fig. 14) is a design for Broderie Perse of storks and water plants. To work: Cut out the storks from Cretonne materials and lightly BUTTONHOLE them round, also treat the bulrushes and flags in the same manner. Use CREWEL STITCH and LONG STITCH to form grasses and other portions of the design that are too minute to be APPLIQUÉ, and enrich the chief high lights and greatest depths in the plumage of the birds with filoselle, worked in in SATIN STITCH.

Appliqué, Broderie Suisse.—This is a modern variety of Appliqué, and consists of a design embroidered on white cambric or muslin laid upon satin or silk backgrounds. To work: Trace out a pattern upon pink calico, lay this under muslin or cambric, embroider the pattern lines seen through the muslin with CHAIN STITCH, and then cut out and lay the design upon a coloured background, to which affix it with an open BUTTONHOLE or FEATHER STITCH worked in coloured filoselles. The veinings of the sprigs in the embroidery, and any prominent parts in that work, fill and ornament with fancy embroidery stitches, such as HERRINGBONE, SATIN, TÊTE DE BŒUF. These fancy stitches work in coloured filoselles.

Appliqué Lace.—Much of real lace now being made is in two parts, the sprigs separate from the ground; it is therefore necessary to learn the method of joining them together. To work: The sprigs of lace being ready, draw a rough outline of the design upon paper, whose size is the width and breadth of the lace when finished. Upon the outline tack the sprigs loosely, right side downwards. The tacking should only be strong enough to prevent the sprigs turning up their edges before the net is laid on them. Cut the net length-ways of the material, lay it over the sprigs and tack down to the paper, so that no part drags or puckers. Sew the sprigs to this net with fine thread round all the outer and inner edges, OVERCASTING, and not Running them to it. Cut away the net from under the solid parts of the lace, Overcasting all the raw edges so made. All light fancy stitches in the lace require the net cut from under them, while outer edges or borders require a double Overcasting, as at those places there is more likelihood of the net tearing than in the body of the work. Then unpick the lace from the paper with care, the net foundation being neither cut nor dragged. Iron the lace on the wrong side, placing a piece of tissue paper between it and the iron. After ironing, pull up any raised part of the sprigs, such as FLEURS VOLANTES, with the small ivory hook used for that purpose in lace making.

Appliqué upon Net.—The manner of joining together two thin materials differs somewhat from that employed upon solid foundations, and forms a separate branch of fancy work. To Appliqué with net, muslin, or cambric was a favourite work in England during the latter part of the last century and the first years of the present, and the work so made was largely used in the place of lace, the foreign laces of that period being subject to so heavy a duty as to render them only within the reach of the wealthy. The embroidery is partly an imitation of Indian work and partly of lace; it is durable, gives scope for individual taste, has a soft and pleasing effect, and is again finding favour among fancy workers. The materials used are book or mull muslin or cambric, best Brussels net, and white embroidery cotton. In olden times, the foundation was generally muslin, and the net applied or let in ; but the reverse plan, though not so durable, has a better appearance. To work the pattern : When muslin is the foundation, trace upon the muslin ; when net, upon oiled paper. Strengthen both with a brown paper back. Tack the net to the muslin, or *vice versâ*, and run both materials together wherever the design indicates. Do this running carefully, and pass the threads well through the materials. Cut away the net wherever it is not run to the muslin, and in any centres of flowers that are to be filled,

few places. Darn these lace stitches into the net, and make the various tendrils and sprays by running lines about the net and OVERCASTING them. Work detached dots on the net. The edge is a narrow straight line of Buttonhole, with a bought lace edging as a finish. Another variety of cambric on net is, after the cambric is sewn down, to put a line of CHAIN STITCH in coloured silks round it, instead of Buttonhole, and to work with the coloured silk instead of the embroidery cotton. The illustration (Fig. 15) is of fine cambric applied upon net. To work: Trace the design upon the cambric, and surround that with the very finest BUTTONHOLE line, or with a line of CHAIN STITCH, and cut away both net

FIG: 15. APPLIQUÉ UPON NET.

make WHEELS. Surround the whole design with BUTTONHOLE, and scallop and Buttonhole the edge, adding PICOTS to enrich it. Finally untack the pattern from the brown paper, and cut away the muslin foundation from under the net wherever the net has been left, and cut away both materials from under the Wheels. When the net is the foundation and the cambric applied, a lace thread is run all around the cambric outlines and caught down with a finer thread firmly sewn, so that the cambric may not fray when cut away. The Buttonholing is of the lightest, but close, lace stitches are introduced in many parts of the design, but with the net always retained as foundation, as that is only cut in a

and cambric in two places ; fill in the one with a wheel, to form the centre of the flower, and leave the other entirely open. The thick filled-in part next the wheel make with SATIN STITCH, to give solidity to the work.

Appliqué Patchwork.—*See* PATCHWORK.

Apprêt.—A French term, used to signify the stiffening or duping employed in the finish of calicoes and other textiles. It is used to describe any finish to a head-dress.

Arabesque Designs.—Patterns in the style of the Arabian flat wall decorations, which originated in Egypt, where hieroglyphics were made a decoration for monuments and other buildings. Subsequently the idea was carried out by the Saracens, Moors, and Arabs, by whom it was introduced into Spain; and during the wars in Spain in Louis XIV.'s time it was adopted by the French, who gave the style the name Arabesque. Appliqué lace work is often executed in designs of this character.

Arabian Embroidery.—A work executed from time immemorial by the Arab women, and after the conquest of Algeria by the French known as *Ouvroir Mussulman.* It was brought prominently to European notice some forty years ago, when, for the purpose of relieving the destitute Algerian needlewomen, Madame Lucie, of Algiers, founded a school in that place, and reproduced there, from good Arabian patterns, this embroidery. The designs, like all Mussulman ones, are purely geometrical, are very elaborate, and are done with floss silk upon muslin or cloth. They are worked in a frame, and when the embroidery is upon

with gold and silver thread and floss silk upon velvet, satin, cashmere, or muslin, which has the peculiarity of presenting no wrong side, the pattern being equally good upon either. Like all oriental embroidery the work is distinguished for brilliancy of colouring, quaintness of design, and elaborate workmanship. Arabian embroidery and Algerian are of the same description.

Areophane, or Arophane.—A description of crape, but considerably thinner than the ordinary kind. It has been much used for bonnets, trimmings, and quillings, and also for ball dresses. It is made in most colours, and is cut, like crape, on the bias, width 27 inches. *See* CRAPE.

Argentan Point.—Although the date of the commencement of lace-making in Argentan is unknown, as its manufactory is mentioned in the Colbert Corre-

FIG. 16. ARGENTAN POINT.

muslin, only Satin Stitch is used; when executed upon cloth the design is traced upon the material, and all centres and fillings laid down with floss silk in a long satin stitch across the whole space, while over this foundation, wide apart, satin stitches in floss are taken at right angles to those first embroidered. These upper satin stitches are stitched or couched down to the material by securing threads that are taken right through the material, and this couching has to be executed with great precision and neatness. When the centres and thick parts are filled they are surrounded with Chain-Stitch outlines, and all stalks, tendrils, &c., are also done in chain stitch. The Arabian embroidery brought to England consists chiefly of the ornamental towels worn by Arab women on their heads when going to the baths, and these towels make excellent chairbacks. Besides this work there is another kind embroidered

spondence, we may conclude it was established about the same time as that of Alençon, and probably by some workers from that town. No royal edict protected it until 1708, but the lace obtained a good market, and rivalled, in some ways, that produced at Alençon. The two laces are often confounded together, and frequently sold as of the same manufacture, but they differ in many points, though both are needlepoints, and the only needlepoints produced in France. The patterns of the Argentan lace (Fig. 16) are bolder than those of Alençon, and are in higher relief, the fillings are less fanciful and much thicker, retaining much of the close buttonhole of Venice point; but the great difference between the laces lies in their grounds, that called grand bride being almost essentially Argentan. It was made by first forming a six-sided mesh with the needle, and then covering it on all sides with buttonhole, the effect of which was extremely bold, and which rendered the lace almost imperishable. This ground was also called bride épingle, and was marked out upon the parchment pattern, and pins put in upon every side to form the meshes exactly the same size throughout. Besides this grand bride, the bride picotée and the plain bride were made at Argentan, and from old patterns recently discovered at the same period. The art of making these brides grounds died out when the réseau, or net-patterned ground, took their place; but the lace flourished during the reigns of the Louis, and was only extinguished at the revolution, since which period efforts have been made to re-establish it, but without success, the peasantry having turned their attention to embroidery. In the old bills of lace Argentan is mentioned with Brussels and Alençon, and Madame du Barry, in 1772, gave 5740 francs for a set of it. At present it only exists as specimens, so much of it having been destroyed, and as it is no longer manufactured, its price is large, and only limited by the collector's eagerness. For grounds *see* ALENÇON GROUNDS.

Argentella Point.—A needle-made lace, of which but few specimens remain, and at one time considered to be of Genoese origin, but lately found to be a variety of Alençon. The beauty of this lace consists in a réseau ground resembling the Mayflower; the pattern of the lace is similar to Alençon.

Armazine, or Armozeen.—The name is derived from the French *Armosin*. It is a strong make of thick plain black corded silk, a kind of taffetá, employed for scholastic gowns, and for hatbands and scarves at funerals. It is 24 inches in width. From the time of Queen Elizabeth to that of George III. it was used for women's dresses and men's waistcoats.

Armorial Bearings.—*See* HERALDIC DEVICES.

Armure.—This is a silk textile; plain, striped, ribbed, or with a small design. Sometimes it is made of wool and silk. There is also Satin Armure and Armure Bosphore, this latter being a reversible material. The width run from 22 to 24 inches. *Armure* is a French term applied to either silk or wool, signifying a small pattern.

Armure Victoria.—A new and exceedingly delicate textile, semi-transparent, and made of pure wool, designed for summer or evening dresses. It is manufactured in Paris, on special steam power looms, and has delicate patterns woven in the cloth, which is black, and without lustre, whence it has been given the name Armure by its French manufacturers. The width of this beautiful material is 44 inches, and the price varies from 5s. to 6s. 6d. a yard. It is especially suited for mourning.

Arras.—In the capital of Artois, in the French Netherlands, one of the first looms was set up for weaving tapestries, and hence the word Arras became a common term for tapestry, and was applied to needle-made and loom-made tapestries indiscriminately. It is mentioned in Shakespeare's Hamlet.

Arras.—A lace made at Arras of the same description as that made at Lille and Mirecourt, but generally known as Lille lace. The factory was established in the latter part of the seventeenth century, and flourished until 1804. At present the lace made at Arras, though white and of good texture, cannot compete with that of Lille and Mirecourt, as the lace makers introduce no new designs, and are content with the simplest patterns. For illustration and description, *see* LILLE LACE.

Arrasene.—A kind of woollen, and likewise of silk chenille, employed for the purpose of embroidery. The wool is coarse, and the needle used has a large eye. Arrasene of both kinds is sold by the ounce. The centre cord of the arrasene is visible through the wool or silk covering.

Arrasene Embroidery.—A variation of Chenille embroidery of recent invention, and suitable for curtain borders, mantel borders, parasol covers, and other positions where

FIG. 17. ARRASENE EMBROIDERY.

the pile of the Arrasene is not injured by friction. Materials: Arrasene either of wool or silk, No. 1 Chenille needles, canvas, velvet, silk and serge. To work upon velvet or silk: Stretch the material in a frame and apply the Arrasene as in canvas work in TENT STITCH. Use short strands of Arrasene, and draw them backwards and forwards through the material without twisting. The chief part of the design work with the wool Arrasene, the silk use to indicate the bright lights, and work the fine lines of a flower or leaf in ordinary embroidery silks. Some workers prefer to treat the Arrasene as Chenille, and lay it along the surface, catching it down as in COUCHING, but the few shades that can be employed in this manner of working detract from its beauty. Arrasene can be worked upon serge and canvas without a frame; the material is then held in the hand, a Chenille needle used, and the work executed in STEM or CREWEL STITCH. When so done, great care is necessary in passing the Arrasene through the material so that it lies with its pile uppermost, and does not show the woven centre line from which the soft edges proceed. Broad and velvety effects are obtainable from Arrasene embroidery, and it is capable of good art work, as it gives scope for individual taste. Arrasene is not suitable for a background; these are made either of solid material or in Tent Stitch. To work Fig. 17: A group of forget-me-nots, worked upon a deep russet red

Arrasene. After the embroidery is completed, lay it face downwards on a cloth, and pass a warm iron over the back of the work.

Arrow Stitch.—So called from the slanting position of the threads forming it. Identical with STEM STITCH.

FIG. 18. AU PASSÉ STITCH ON SILK.

ground of cloth. Work the forget-me-nots with two shades of pale blue silk Arrasene, and fill in their centres with maize Arrasene; work the leaves and stalks with three shades of subdued greens in wool Arrasene, and the ornamental border surrounding the flowers in two shades of russet red colour, lighter than the ground, and of wool

Art Embroidery on Needlework.—A name recently introduced as a general term for all descriptions of needlework that spring from the application of a knowledge of design and colouring, with skill in fitting and executing. It is either executed by the worker from his or her design, or the patterns are drawn by a skilled artist, and much individual scope in execution and colouring is required from the embroiderer. The term is chiefly used to denote INLAID and ONLAID APPLIQUÉ, embroidery in silk and crewels for ordinary domestic purposes, and embroidery with gold, silver, and silk, for church work; but there is no limit to its application.

Artificial Flowers.—See flowers employed in millinery and evening dress, and in room decoration.

Asbestos.—A mineral substance, of a fibrous texture, of which there are several varieties; all alike resisting the action of fire. It is found in this country, in Canada, India, and various parts of Europe; the best being that obtained in Italy. The lumps of fibre require much soaking in water to separate them; and when moistened with oil and mixed with cotton, the filaments are spun and woven into cloth, and the latter subsequently fired to consume the oil and cotton. Thread, ropes, net, millboard, and flooring felt are likewise made of it, and woven sheeting, or "packing," and tape, are both produced in combination with indiarubber. The Italian Asbestos cloth (or packing) is sold in continuous rolls, up to 50yds. in length, and 36 inches or 40 inches wide, or else in sheets 1 yard or 40 inches square. The tape is sold in 50 feet or 100 feet rolls, from ¾ inch to 2½ inches wide. The cloth is employed for suits of clothing for the use of furnace and firemen.

Astrakhan Fur.—This fur is the wool of the sheep of the Russian province of Astrakhan. It is of a greyish brown, and is dyed black. It is erroneously supposed to be of two descriptions, one of the sheep and the other of the dog; but no furrier sells dog fur. It is also confounded with the curly wool of the Persian lamb, which is of a much softer and finer quality, and far more costly. The skins measure from about 12 by 14 inches, and are valued in London at from 1s. to 5s. Imitations of this fur are also made for trimmings, and are generally sold at from 3s. to 4s. a yard.

Attachments.—The adjuncts of the sewing machine, intended to serve various purposes, such as quilting, hemming, tucking, gauging, felling, buttonholing, binding, and braiding, &c. These names vary with different makers, as well as the method of their employment. Every one purchasing a sewing machine should take the trouble to become thoroughly acquainted with the attachments; the most simple in their application will be found the best. They are as follow: the tuck marker, spindle, cradle, or boat-shaped shuttle, which holds the bobbins (or spools), the bobbins, braider, hemmer, quilter, needles, and needle wrencher, screwdriver, spanner, and oilcan. To this list may be added "The English Embroiderer and Fancy Worker," a recently invented appliance of the sewing machine. Oriental and other artistic work may be produced by it—embroidery with gold and silver thread, beads, and jet bugles; and on net, to produce lace; also with wool, worked on canvas, for mats and rugs. The yarn is arranged on hooks, according to the design required, and then sewn down.

Attalea Cloth.—A washing material, much employed for the trimming of sailors' suits. It is twenty-seven inches in width.

Au Fuseau.—A term given to Réseau grounds when used in Pillow Lace making. *See* RÉSEAU and PILLOW GROUNDS.

Au Passé.—A flat Satin Stitch, worked across the material, with no raised foundation. This stitch is also called POINT PASSÉ, LONG STITCH and SATIN STITCH. It is used in all kinds of embroidery upon linen, silk, satin, and velvet, and is much employed in church work. Anything that can be threaded through a needle will embroider in AU PASSÉ. In Fig. 18 is given an illustration of embroidery upon silk, in which Au Passé forms the chief stitch, surrounded in some places by a border of STEM or CREWEL STITCH; in others it forms its own outline, but in all cases follows the curves and lines of the arabesque fruit and foliage it delineates; POINT DE RIZ is the other stitch used in this pattern. The following illustration (Fig. 19).

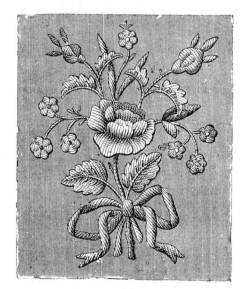

FIG. 19. AU PASSE.

represents a group of flowers embroidered in Au Passé, with coloured silks upon satin; it should be worked in a frame, and the satin backed with muslin. To work: The materials required are—a silk or satin foundation, and embroidery silks; colours—shades of olive green, art blues, and yellow pinks, with gold thread. Make the stitch by bringing the needle from back of the frame up in the centre of the leaf or inner part of petal, and putting it back again at the outer side. These long stitches must follow the curves of the leaf or flower.

Auriphrygium.—The earliest term applied to the gold fringes that bordered the garments of the ancients, and that are supposed to have given the idea of lace. The Phrygian embroiderers in gold and silver were world-famed, and hence the word, though the work was not necessarily executed by them. Canon Brock derives the more modern "Orphrey" from *Aurifrisia* and *Auriphrygia*, and considers that these borders to cope or alb were the combined work of goldsmith and embroiderer.

ALPHABET.

Austrian Pillow Lace.—At Vienna, in 1880, the Austrian Government opened a lace school partly to relieve the distress prevalent in Erzgebirge in the Tyrol, and partly to improve the manufacture. The lace made is an imitation of old Italian Pillow Lace, and the school is flourishing.

Ave Maria Lace.—A narrow kind of Valenciennes lace, made at Dieppe, and so designated by the peasants.

FIG. 20. AVE MARIA LACE.

The ground is a plaited ground, and the border a Cloth Stitch, with the threads running all the way. The waved line beyond the plaited ground is made with threads,

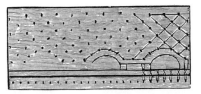

FIG. 21. AVE MARIA PATTERN. (Pricked Pattern for Fig. 20).

which are cut where not required (Fig. 20). The pricked pattern, as shown in Fig. 21, will indicate the manner of working. For stitches, *see* VALENCIENNES.

B.

Baby Lace.—An English Pillow Lace, formerly made in Bedfordshire and Buckinghamshire, and called English Lille, from its patterns being the same as those of LILLE (which *see*). The name Baby Lace was given, as, on account of the narrow width of the lace, it was chiefly used for trimming babies' caps.

Babylonian Embroidery.—The art of embroidery is believed to have been first known to the Phrygians, and from them imported into Egypt and India. Even before the time of Moses, embroidery was known to the Medes and Persians and to the Egyptians, and the work executed at Babylon was celebrated throughout the then known world. This Babylonian work maintained its pre-eminence until the end of the first century after Christ, when it gave way before that of other countries. Josephus mentions that the veils of the Temple were of Babylonian work. Pliny celebrated the Assyrian embroideries, and Metellus Scipio reproached Cæsar for his luxury in having furniture covered with it, although a kind of embroidery had been known in Rome in the time of Aristotle, 325 B.C. It was the thickness and richness of the embroidery, not the materials used, that made the work prized. This embroidery by hand must not be confounded with the cloths of divers colours that the Babylonians excelled in weaving.

Backing.—A method of strengthening Appliqué and other embroideries when the materials applied are not of the same texture and strength as the foundations they are to be laid upon. Backing is necessary for cloth of gold and silver, satin, silk, brocatines, and other slight materials, when they are to be laid upon heavy backgrounds. When velvet has to be richly embroidered it should be backed like other materials; when only laid upon ground work, it will be sufficient to back it with very fine linen or even tissue paper. To back: Unbleached linen and fine holland are the usual backing materials; stretch these in an embroidery frame, and firmly and evenly strain them. Then trace out, upon the wrong side of the framed holland, outlines of all the various pieces required. These pieces of the pattern need not be arranged with any symmetry, but all should go the same way of the stuff they are to be cut from, and sufficient space left between them to allow of a good margin. The holland being stretched, paste the material on to it. When cloth, serge, and plush are being backed with holland, they are made to adhere by paste, made as follows: Take three tablespoonfuls of flour, and as much powdered resin as will lie on a shilling. Mix them smoothly with half-a-pint of water, pour into an iron saucepan, and stir till it boils. Let it boil five minutes, and use cold. The cold paste is evenly laid over the holland on the right side, and the material laid upon it back downwards, and smoothed and pressed with a soft cloth to the holland. It should be allowed to dry gradually, and no haste used in commencing to cut out. To cut out, follow the lines traced at the back of the holland, and use a very sharp pair of scissors. Never go beyond the traced lines on the inside, rather keep a little on the outer side of them. Foundations are backed as above without the cutting out.

Background or Darned Embroidery.—*See* DARNED EMBROIDERY.

Back Stitch.—Knitting term, indentical with PEARL, RIB, SEAM, and TURN. *See* PEARL.

Back Stitch.—In making a running, a stitch is taken back into the material beyond where the thread was last drawn through, after the manner of stitching; but this method of strengthening a running is only adopted from every second stitch to greater intervals, as may be deemed expedient, in plain sewing.

Back Stitch.—It is identical with HEM STITCH, and is used for embroidery and Berlin wool work. Illustrated (Fig. 22). *See* HEM STITCH.

Back Stitch Embroidery.—One of the simplest kinds of work. Trace the design upon fine leather, silk, satin, cloth, or linen materials, and then follow it with BACK STITCH round every line; no filling in of pattern is necessary, as the work is done in outline. Illustrations (Figs. 22, 23) show the back stitching upon leather and upon silk, and are good samples of this kind of embroidery. This work is now often done with the sewing machine, and can be brought by this means to great perfection.

Baden Embroidery.—A species of APPLIQUÉ of modern invention. The design is traced upon one material, sewn to another, and the edges worked round

D

with CHAIN STITCH. The peculiarity of the work consists in the stitches worked on to connect the design to the background after the former has been attached by the CHAIN STITCHES and the superfluous material cut away. The stitches used are any long irregular kinds, the most effective are wide HERRINGBONE, DOUBLE CORAL, FEATHER, and SATIN STITCH. The spiky and irregular lines of these stitches blend the two materials used in the embroidery together. For the background and pattern materials, oatmeal cloth of all shades, red and blue Turkey twills, and sateens are employed; for the embroidery, flourishing thread, ingrain cottons, unbleached flax Luxemburg thread, and white flosette. The most effective patterns are made with dark blue laid on a red ground, or red upon écru grounds. To work: Upon a piece of blue twill, or oatmeal cloth, trace an outline design of a conventional flower spray, such as a sunflower and its leaves. Lay this piece of cloth, without cutting it, on to some red Turkey twill, and tack both together. With blue ingrain cotton, or white flourishing thread, work in CHAIN STITCH round all the outlines of the pattern, and mark out the divisions between petals and the veining of leaves in the same way. Stitch the two materials together with the CHAIN STITCHES. Cut away from beyond the outlines of the pattern the superfluous upper material and the centres of the sunflowers; but leave enough margin to prevent the material fraying out. Work stems,

FIG. 22. BACK STITCH EMBROIDERY.

tendrils, and light sprays on the background in CREWEL STITCH. Work cross bars in CHAIN STITCH in the centres of the sunflowers, and fill their spaces up with FRENCH KNOTS. Work all round every outline of the pattern with wide and pointed HERRINGBONE; work the stitch half on the pattern and half on the background.

Bagging.—The fabrics employed for the purpose of bag making comprise baize (green, blue, and black), black and unbleached linen (or holland), American cloth, gutta-percha, oiled silk, black alpaca, calico prints, twine, plaited rushes, leather, canvas, and coarse sacking.

Baize.—Possibly derived from *base*, of little value. A coarse, open-made woollen stuff, or flannel, having a long nap, and faced like a Lancashire flannel. First introduced into England by the Flemings. It is generally dyed green, blue, or red, but it can be obtained in other colours. It is used for linings, cuttings, floorcloths, bags, &c., and is made in various widths, from one yard to two. A superior quality has latterly been made which is employed for table-cloths.

Balayeuse, or Sweeper.—A French term to signify the frilling of material or lace which lines the extreme edge of a dress skirt to keep the train clean as it sweeps along the floor. The balayeuse is allowed to project beyond the edge of the dress, so as to form a decorative as well as a useful trimming.

FIG. 23. BACK STITCH EMBROIDERY.

Baleine.—The French word for whalebone, employed in the stiffening of stays and dresses. It is sold in strips of 1½yd. in length, and is also to be had cut into short lengths ready for the dressmakers' use. It is sold by the gross sets. That designed for stay makers is cut into suitable lengths, which varies between 3-16ths and 1½ inch. It is sold by the pound.

Balerino.—This is otherwise called a BALAYEUSE, or SWEEPER (which *see*). It is a frilling of material, muslin, or lace, either in white or black, sewn under the edge of a dress skirt to preserve it from wearing out, and from being soiled from sweeping the floor.

Ball Cottons.—These include the 2 drachm balls for tacking, and the ¼oz. balls for sewing, together with smaller ones for marking either red or blue. Some crochet cotton and Maltese thread are also wound in balls, occasionally taking the shape of eggs.

Balls.—Useful for using up skeins of wool left from single Berlin work, and made either with knitting or upon card. To make in KNITTING, use pins 14, and colours either 3, 6, or 9, as 18 sections make up the Ball, and the colours are repeated. Cast on 39 stitches, and work in the BRIOCHE STITCH, KNIT 1 row, and for the 2nd row Knit all but three stitches, leaving these on the needle, and putting in a white thread where left as a marker. Turn the work and Knit back until the 3 end stitches on that row are reached; leave these unknit, and mark as in 2nd row; continue to Knit, leaving each row with 3 stitches unknit on the needle, and carrying the marking thread along until the two threads come within 3 stitches of each other in the centre, and 7 distinct ridges appear on each pin. Turn and Knit all the stitches up, putting in a new colour for last stitch; continue to work in this way until the 18 sections are made, then cast off, draw up one end of the ball, and sew up the side; stuff the ball with shreds of wool, and sew up the last end. Larger Balls may be made by increasing the number of stitches Cast on, taking care that they divide by three; or smaller ones by decreasing. To make Balls of skeins of wool, cut 2 circles of cardboard with a hole in the centre. For a Ball 4 inches in diameter the cardboard should be 6 inches round, and centre hole 1½ inch; for a 3-inch Ball the cardboard should be 5 inches round, and the hole in the centre 1¼ inch. Place the two cardboards together, and wind your wool tightly round them until the centre hole is filled up; then cut the wool at the outer edge with sharp and large scissors, and pass a piece of fine, but strong, twine between the two cardboards, knotting it strongly; then cut the cardboard away and snip the wool with scissors until it is fluffy and the ball quite circular in shape.

Ball Silks.—Principally prepared for Knitting purposes, and include the French, Swiss, Chinese, and Imperial, &c.

Ball Wools.—These are prepared either for Crochet or Knitting, and are well known under the names of Rabbit, Orkney, Bonne Mère, French Pompadour, Connaught, and Burmah, &c. Besides these there are the crewels and the eis wool, in plain and parti-colours, tinselled, coral, &c.

Balzorine or Balzarine.—A French name for a light mixed material, composed of cotton and worsted; manufactured for women's dresses. It was succeeded by Barège, which superseded it likewise in public favour. It measures 40 inches in width.

Bandana Handkerchiefs.—Indian washing silk handkerchiefs, having white or coloured spots or diamonds on a red, yellow, blue, or dark ground. They were a yard square, and were both plain and twilled, and kept their colours to the last. Other patterns have long been introduced into their manufacture, and they are extensively imported plain and printed to this country, being solely manufactured for export to the United Kingdom. Imitation Bandanas are largely made in England and elsewhere, but are mostly composed of cotton. They can now be purchased by the yard, and are made into dresses, aprons, and caps.

Bande.—A French term for the English name, Band. Employed by dressmakers, and applied to any kind of material. *See* BANDS.

Bandeaux.—French. A term to denote arrangements of flowers or other materials in bands as a sort of diadem headdress. It is a term employed by milliners.

Bandoulière.—A French term to signify a scarf worn over one shoulder and under the other.

Bands.—(French *Bandes.*) A term employed to denote a strip, more or less narrow, of any material used in the making of any garment or other article, whether necessary to its completion or merely decorative, and whether of the same material or of another. Thus there are waist, neck, and wrist Bands, and Bands of insertion embroidery let into underclothing, and infants' dresses. In making linen Bands, the stuff should be cut by the thread, having previously drawn out a single strand. Bands may be made of either bias or straight material; if of the latter, they should be cut down the selvedge, as being the strongest way of the stuff. Bias Bands are sometimes used for the necks of dresses, but are more especially in vogue for trimmings, being sown on both sides with the sewing machine. Great care is requisite in cutting them at an exact angle of 45 degrees. The waist-bands of dress skirts are sometimes of Petersham, a strongly-made ribbon (which *see*). Bands sometimes require to be stiffened, in which case buckram, or stiff muslin, is used to back them.

Band Work.—A term used in Needle-made Laces to denote the open and fancy stitches that fill in the centres of lace. The word is identical in its meaning with FILLINGS, JOURS, MODES. The different stitches filling in these spaces are named after various laces, and described under their own headings. The illustrations are of two bandwork stitches, and are worked as follows : Fig. 24. — Work three rows of thirty-three close BUTTONHOLE, as a foundation. First row—work 15 Buttonhole, miss 3, work 15 close. Second row—12 Buttonhole, miss 3, work 3, miss 3, work 12. Third row—9 Buttonhole, miss 3, work 3, miss 3, work 3, miss 3, work 9. Fourth row—6 Buttonhole, miss 3, work 3, miss 3, work 3, miss 3, work 3, miss 3, work 6. Fifth row—9 Buttonhole, miss 3, work 3, work 9, miss 3, work 9. Sixth row—6 Buttonhole, miss 3, work 15, miss 3, work 6.

FIG. 24.
BAND WORK.

Work two rows of close Buttonhole, and repeat the pattern from first row. In Fig. 25, commence first pattern with three plain rows. First row—work 6 Buttonhole, miss 3, work 3, miss 3, work 9, miss 3, work 3, miss 3, work 6. Second row—9 Buttonhole, miss 3, work 9, miss 3, work 3, miss 3, work 9. Third row—6 Buttonhole, miss 3, work 3, miss 3, work 3, miss 3, work 3, miss 3, work 3, miss 3, work 6. Fourth row—15 Buttonhole, miss 3, work 3, miss 3, work 3, miss 3, work 9. Fifth row—6 Buttonhole, miss 3, work 3, miss 3, work 3, miss 3, work 3, miss 3, work 12. Sixth row—9 Buttonhole, miss 3, work 3, miss 3, work 3, miss 3, work 15. Seventh row—6 Buttonhole, miss 3, work 3, miss 3, work 3, miss 3, work 18. Eighth row—15 Buttonhole, miss 3, work 6, miss 3, work 12. Ninth row—6 Buttonhole miss 3, work 3, miss 3, work 6, miss 3, work 3, miss 3, work 9. Tenth row—9 Buttonhole, miss 3, work 12, miss 3, work 12. Eleventh row—6 Buttonhole, miss 3, work 3, miss 3, work 24. Work one row all Buttonhole, and repeat. The second pattern (Fig. 25) is worked thus : First row—24 Buttonhole, miss 3, work 15. Second row—miss 3, 3 Buttonhole, miss 3, work 12, miss 3, work 3, miss 3, work 3, miss 3, work 3, miss 3. Third row—3 Buttonhole, miss 3, work 12, miss 3, work 3, miss 3, work 9, miss 3, work 3. Fourth row—miss

FIG. 25. BAND WORK.

3, Buttonhole 3, miss 3, work 6, miss 3, work 3, miss 3, work 9, miss 3, work 3, miss 3. Fifth row—12 Buttonhole, miss 3, work 3, miss 3, work 21. Sixth row—miss 3, 3 Buttonhole, miss 3, work 6, miss 3, work 15, miss 3, work 3, miss 3. Seventh row—3 Buttonhole, miss 3, work 6, miss 3, work 21, miss 3, work 3. Eighth row—miss 3, 3 Buttonhole, miss 3, work 18, miss 3, work 3, miss 3, work 3, miss 3. Repeat the pattern from first row. In the illustration the open spaces are white, and the Buttonhole stitches black, as they are easier for the worker when so engraved.

Bar.—The connecting threads thrown across spaces in all Needle-point Laces, whether imitation or real, and known as Brides, Bride Claires, Coxcombs, Pearls, Legs, and Ties.

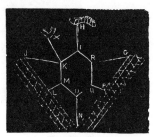

FIG. 26. BARS.

These threads are arranged so that they connect the various solid parts of the lace together, and are made by passing two or three strands across, and either cording them or covering them closely with Buttonhole. Bars can be made of any form, the ones shown in Fig. 26 being intended to fill in a large space, and to form a kind of wheel. To work: Throw a thread across from G to H, CORD this back to I, then take it to J, L, N, &c., and cord it back half way again until B is reached, when Cord the centre all round, and fasten the thread off at G.

Bar.—In Honiton and Pillow Laces, make these either by rolling the top bobbins round and round, drawing one up through the pinhole, passing a bobbin through the loop lower end first, and drawing up the loop, or else by working in CLOTH STITCH, when no pins are required, except where PIN WORK is added.

Bar.—Portions of the pattern of Macramé. Made of one to three threads, according as single, double, or treble Bar is required, and consisting of a succession of MA-CRAMÉ KNOTS worked alternately over right and left-hand threads. The number of knots depends upon the

length of Bar required, nine knots being the usual length made.

Bar.—Derived from the old English word *barre*, the Welsh *bar*, French *barre*. A term in plain work to signify the sewing made, in Buttonhole Stitch, across a buttonhole to prevent its being torn. *See* BUTTONHOLE STITCH.

Barathea.—A mixture of silk and worsted, with a diaper-like appearance. It is about 42 inches wide, and is used for mourning. This is one of the new designations under which bombazine is now known. There is a variety called Barathea cloth, a soft, durable, woollen textile, having a small diaper pattern. It is 24 inches in width. There is also a fancy Barathea, having a crape ground and brocaded spots, and a diagonal Barathea, which is woven with fancy stripes. The woollen kinds measure 42 inches in width.

Barcelona Kerchiefs.—So called from the Spanish province from which they originated. At present they are all made in England, and are of four kinds—in black, plain colours, checks, and fancy. The black measure from 26 inches square to seven quarters. Turban checks used originally to be made for head-dresses. They measure about 20 inches square.

Barcelona Lace. — This stitch is used in ancient Needle-point and in Modern Point. To make: First row—work 4 BUTTONHOLE STITCHES close together, then miss the space that would take 4 more, and make 4 others, leaving a loop between the close stitches; continue until the end of the row. Second row—work 3 But-

FIG. 27. BARCELONA LACE.

tonholes into the loops left in last row, and make loops under the close work of that row. These two rows, worked alternately, form the lace. *See* Fig. 27.

Barège.—A name derived from the valley so called in the Pyrenees, where the textile was first manufactured in the village of Arosons. It is now chiefly made at Bagnères di Bigorre. It is a kind of gauze, composed of silk and wool, or else of wool only, in warp and woof; and at first made in all colours. It has been called by many names as the manufacture has improved—such as woollen gauze, woollen grenadine, &c. The width of the material is 26in. The Barèges made in Paris have a warp of silk. Cheap sorts are made with a cotton warp.

Barège Yarn.—A hand-spun yarn employed in manufacture of a very fine gauze cloth, and chiefly for men's veils. The seat of industry is at Rheims, in France.

Barnsley Crash, or Linen.—A name indiscriminately used to denote the narrow crash employed for round towels. For the latter it is made in four different widths, viz., from 16 inches up to 25 inches. *See* CRASH.

Barnsley Linens.—A description of linen especially made for the purpose of embroidery. It is to be had both bleached and unbleached, and in different degrees of fineness and of width, from narrow to a double width of 80 inches. One kind of Barnsley Linen is designated Brand—a brown textile, 38 inches wide, and likewise made for crewel work decoration. These linens are commonly, but improperly, called "crash," arising from the fact that the first examples of crewel embroidery were worked on crash.

Barracan.—(Latin *Barracanus*, French *Bouracan*.) A coarse, thick, strong stuff, somewhat resembling camlet, used for external clothing. A garment made of camels' hair is called in the East "barak," "bârik" being a camel. It was formerly employed for cloaks. Barracan is now made with wool, silk, and goats' hair; the warp being of silk and wool twisted, and the woof the hair of the Angora goat, when purely oriental.

Barragon, or Moleskin.—A description of FUSTIAN (which *see*) of a coarse quality, strong and twilled, and shorn of the nap before dyed. It is a cotton textile, and is employed for the clothing of the labouring classes of men. The width of this material runs to 27 inches.

Barratee.—A silk stuff, being a variety of barathea, of 24 inches in width.

Basket Cloth, or Connaught.—A fancy cotton cloth, made after the manner of Aida Canvas, or *Toile Colbert*, the French name under which it was first introduced. It is employed as a foundation for Embroidery. *See* AIDA CANVAS and *Toile Colbert*.

Basket Stitch.—One of the handsomest stitches in embroidery, and much used in ancient and modern church needlework. It is

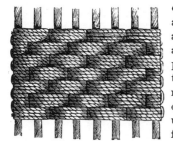

a variety of COUCHING, and its particular beauty arises from the raised appearance given to the threads composing it by rows of whipcord or cotton cord laid down upon the foundation before the work is commenced. *See* COUCHING.

FIG. 28. BASKET STITCH.

Basques.—A French term, designating that part of the dress bodice below the waist. They may be cut in one piece with the bodice, or added to it, all in one piece, or divided.

Basquine.—The French term to denote a bodice of a dress having a basque finish to it depending from the waist.

Basse Lisse.—The French for low warp; a term used in tapestry work.

Basting, otherwise called TACKING.—Derived from the old German *bastan*, to sew, or *besten*, to bind. This term is chiefly employed by tailors, while Tacking is used by women. The term is used to signify the light runnings made by taking up a stitch at long distances successively, to keep the separate portions of a garment or other article in position, preparatory to their being sewn together. A lining is said to be basted on the material for which it is designed. Knots may be used in Basting threads, as they are not for permanent use. *See* TACKING.

Bath Coating, or Duffl.—A light cloth or baize, with a long nap, which is generally made in wide widths, both coloured and white, and is used for thick flannel petticoats, and blankets for babies' cots. Bath blankets are also

made of it, embroidered at the edges. It is also used for men's greatcoats. It varies in width from 48 and 60 to 72 inches. *See* FLANNEL.

Batiste.—A description of cotton muslin, having a good deal of dress in it, to be had in all colours, as well as in white and black. Its chief use is for summer dresses, and it is also employed for linings and trimmings. The price varies with the quality, and it measures about a yard in width.

Batiste.—The French name for cambric. A fine linen muslin made in France, in various colours, and used for dresses, dress linings, and trimmings; so called from its inventor Baptista, at Cambray, who was a linen weaver in Flanders in the thirteenth century; or because this fine linen was used to wipe the heads of young infants who had just received baptism. The width runs from 18in. to 36in.

Batswing.—A thick, rough description of cloth of a grey colour, woven into the shape of a petticoat without a seam, and having only the band or the yoke, for the waist, and the binding to be handsewn. This material is a description of FELT (which *see*).

Battlemented.—A manner of embroidery upon white materials or ticking so as to form an indented line in imitation of the battlements that crowned ancient fortresses.

FIG. 29. BATTLEMENTED.

To work, as shown in Fig. 29: Trace the outlines of the design upon the material, and work in POINT RUSSE for the Battlemented line. Fill in the rest of the design with SATIN STITCH.

Battlemented.—The ornamentation of any border of a garment or other article, either by means of a trimming laid upon it, or by cutting out the material, in the pattern known in architecture by that term, and forming the parapet of a castle or church; the open portions being called embrasures.

Batuz Work.—A manner of ornamenting embroidery now obsolete, but much used by the earliest workers with the needle. It was technically known as "silk beaten with gold and silver," and was sometimes called "hammered-up gold." Batuz work was very prevalent in mediæval times, and often mentioned in ecclesiastical inventories and royal wills from the eleventh to the fifteenth centuries. It consisted of sewing upon silk, as a part of the pattern embroidered, very thin plates of gold, silver, or silver gilt. These plates were frequently hammered into low relief, and were formed either to represent animals, flowers, or heraldic devices. Batuz work was largely used in England, but was also known on the Continent, the banner of Strasbourg being so ornamented. At one time in Italy these costly gold and silver plates were imitated with metal ones, which were glued, not sewn, to the material; but the metal, not being pure, speedily turned black. A specimen of this work was seen when the tomb of Edward I. was opened in 1774, in the quarter-foils on his robe. The lions on the Glastonbury cope are in hammered-up silver.

Baum Skin Fur, or Pine Marten (*Mustela abietum*).

specimens of needlework extant in a good state of preservation, and is highly prized for the illustrations which it gives of the dress and customs of the times and the labour it must have entailed. It is 214 feet long and 20 inches wide, including a border top and bottom, and contains 530 figures. The material is fine linen, which has turned brown with age, and the stitches are CHAIN and LONG. It is not rightly tapestry, but rather embroidery with crewels, as

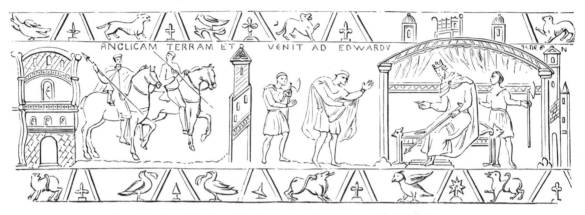

FIG. 30. HAROLD'S RETURN TO EDWARD THE CONFESSOR.

—A description of sable, imported under this name from the forests of Germany, of which the baum is a native, and is distinguished from the stone marten by the yellow colour of the throat, while the rest of the skin is brown. When dyed the fur rivals in appearance that of the best sable. It is the wood marten of British America, and is used for muffs, tippets, and trimmings. *See* PINE MARTEN.

Bayeux Tapestry.—This celebrated piece of needlework is believed to have been executed by Matilda, queen of

the material is left exposed in many parts, and the design indicated with Chain Stitch. Thus the faces of the figures are left bare, and the features rudely indicated with Chain-Stitch. The embroidery is in two-strand worsteds or crewels, and the colours of the wool limited to eight, two blue, two green, a buff, pink, red, and yellow. The embroiderers have not attempted to give the natural colouring to animals, &c., frequently working a yellow or blue horse with legs of a widely different colour, and from the limited

FIG. 30a. BURIAL OF EDWARD AT WESTMINSTER.

William the Conqueror, and her ladies, after the conquest of England, 1066. There is, however, no authentic record of the fact, and some maintain that it was worked by three Bayeux men in London during the reign of William, and sent by them as an offering to their native cathedral. This claim rests on the poorness of the materials used. Other authorities believe it to be the product of the twelfth, and not of the eleventh century. Whatever its exact origin, it is undoubtedly of great antiquity, and is one of the earliest

number of colours used there is little variety in the shading. The original, after being for many years hung in Bayeux cathedral, was removed to Paris in the time of the first Napoleon, and is now preserved in the public library at Bayeux. A coloured photograph of the whole is to be seen in the South Kensington Museum. The work is divided into compartments, the subjects of which are explained by an embroidered Latin inscription and commence with Harold swearing fealty to William of Normandy over the relics of saints, which is followed by Harold returning to England, the death and burial of Edward the Confessor in Westminster Abbey, the assumption of the crown by Harold, the landing of William, the battle of Hastings, and death of Harold. The border is chiefly occupied with grotesque animals, griffins, dragons, birds, except in the compartments devoted to the battle of

Bead Mosaic Work.—This work, popular in England in 1855, consists in uniting together beads without any foundation. The beads used are large, long, transparent ones, variously coloured, which are formed by this process into hanging baskets, lamp shades, and dinner rings. To work: Thread the beads upon linen cotton in order as to colour and pattern for the first row; in the next, and

Fɪɢ. 30b. **BATTLE OF HASTINGS.**

Hastings, where the bodies of the slain are worked instead. Part of this tapestry is shown in Figs. 30, 30a, 30b, and 30c.

Beaded or Jetted Stuffs.—These textiles are divided into two kinds, those hand-embroidered and those having the beads woven into the texture. The latter is an art newly discovered in France, and is accomplished by an ingenious adaptation of certain machinery. Beading was first applied to elastic cloths, but afterwards to silk grena-

in all other rows, thread each bead singly, and pass the cotton through the bead above and beyond it in the preceding row. No bead can be placed under this threaded one, so that only half the number of beads are used in the rows after the first one, and the work presents a battlemented appearance while in progress. Always commence the work in the centre of the pattern, whether the design is round or square; and,

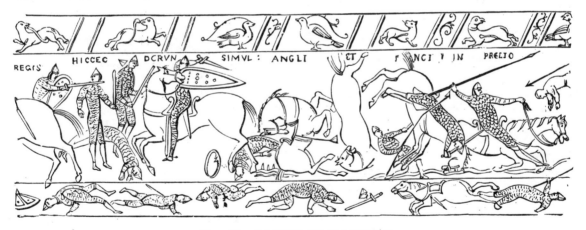

Fɪɢ. 30c. **BATTLE OF HASTINGS.**

dines, having stripes of brocaded velvet. These fabrics are exceedingly costly.

Beading, or Bead Edge.—A simple heading for Pillow Lace, and also known as Beading. To make it: Hang on seven pairs of bobbins and a Gɪᴍᴘ, the latter runs along the Pʟᴀɪɴ Eᴅɢᴇ side. Work in Cʟᴏᴛʜ Sᴛɪᴛᴄʜ, and, at the end of each bead-head, twist the gimp twice round all the bobbins excepting the two pairs lying at the plain edge. *See* illustration (Fig. 31).

one side finished, return to the middle, and from there work the other. The pattern is sometimes varied by holes or open spaces being left in the close lines; these manage by passing the needle and cotton through the same bead in a given place for several rows, with no beads attached. Make fringes to these pieces of bead-work of long loops of beads attached to the outside row of beads. The designs are all geometrical. Unless lined with velvet or other soft foundation, this work is not suitable for mats placed upon woodwork, as the beads scratch the varnish. In Germany and on the Continent, Mosaic Beadwork is executed with small and beautifully shaded beads, in designs representing flowers or landscapes. These elaborate pieces of work are large, and are made in a frame. The lines of beads are stretched

FIG. 31. BEAD EDGE.

across the frame from right to left, and supported by perpendicular lines of very fine silk, which are arranged close together and of a set number, and fastened tight to the top and bottom of the frame before the beads are inserted. The pattern, which is coloured and divided into squares like a Berlin wool pattern, clearly indicates the colouring of each bead in each square, and each bead when laid across rests between two perpendicular threads, not on one thread. To work: Count the number of squares in the work, and glue firmly to a piece of linen two more silk threads than there are squares. Stretch these threads and glue their other ends on to a second piece of linen, being careful to lay each thread in order and at even distances. Sew these prepared threads to a frame in an upright position. Fasten a thread of fine silk to the right side of the frame and thread on it a whole row of beads, putting the last bead on first. Lay this straight across the frame, so that each bead drops in between an upright thread. Secure the silk firmly on the left side, and recommence the work on the right side. Large pieces of work are used for fire and candle screens, small for bracelets. When working such narrow pieces as bracelets, instead of fastening the thread off every time on the left side, secure it firmly there and run it back through every bead to the right side, where fasten it before beginning a second line.

Beads.—These may be had for the purposes of decorative needlework in all varieties of colour, sold by the dozen bunches; and also in varieties of chalk, crystal, and alabaster, sold by the ounce.

Bead Watch Chains.—To form these chains, small shiny black beads are required, and black purse silk. A whole skein of silk is taken, and on to this a number of beads are threaded. A four chain Crochet is then worked and united, and rounds of double Crochet are made until the required length is attained, dropping a bead into every stitch as it is formed.

Bead Work.—(From the Anglo-Saxon *beade*, a prayer.)—The small globules or balls now called beads, either made of iron, pearl, garnet, amber, or crystal, were used as ornaments in pre-historic times, while glass beads were made almost as soon as the art of making glass was discovered. The Egyptians, Greeks, and Romans made use of them as ornaments, and the Druids, before the conquest of Britain, used annulets, or large perforated balls of glass, in their religious rites. The English name of bead

came from the practice of using these strung balls for telling off the number of prayers recited, but this custom is not exclusively a Roman Catholic one, as Mahommedans and some heathen tribes do the same. The greater number of beads used in Bead work are made at Murano, near Venice, but there are also manufactories in Germany and England. Large quantities of coarse beads are sold to the natives of America and Africa, for embroidering their garments, &c., and the taste these savages display over their work puts to shame that of more civilised nations. For a long time the beads used for needlework purposes were made with but a few varieties of colour, and could only be employed for groundings or simple patterns, as seen on the work of the time of Charles II.; but, during the last 100 years, many additional colours and sizes have been manufactured, thus giving great scope for ingenuity in their arrangement. Thirty years ago, the art on the Continent was carried to great perfection, the beads were beautifully coloured, most minute, and worked as flower patterns of great delicacy. These fine beads are difficult to procure in England. The beads are generally sewn upon canvas (*see* Fig. 32), but cloth, fine

FIG. 32. BEAD WORK.

leather, and velvet are also used as foundations. To work: Attach the beads singly to all materials with fine waxed sewing silk, in long straight lines, with a TENT STITCH across two threads of the canvas on the slant. For patterns, use the Berlin ones, which generally consist of large or small white flowers, worked with opal and opaque beads for high lights, and shading from black to grey for the darker portions, or the same in golden and amber beads, shading to brown. Work the leaves either in beads like the flowers, or in woolwork, and in CROSS STITCH; and make the groundings with beads of one shade, or with fine Berlin wool. The difficulty of all large pieces of Bead work is in procuring beads of a uniform size, as all irregularities show upon a smooth surface of glass. A great improvement in an art point of view would be gained if the patterns used in this work were geometrical instead of impossible florid ones, and the articles embroidered were of a kind suitable to the application of glass. The work is of a lasting kind, neither heat nor damp affects it, and the colours never fade, and it is easily cleaned with a damp sponge; therefore, with different execution, it could be raised from its present low position. Groundings in Bead work are not always attached bead by bead to the foundation canvas, though they are far stronger when so treated; but six or eight beads are strung upon a thread, which is laid along a line of the canvas and caught down at regular distances by a thread coming from the back of the material and returning to it; in fact, a species of Couching. The work so done is more raised and quicker of execution; but is not so lasting, and, unless well done, the rows of laid beads are not flat. Bead work, when used

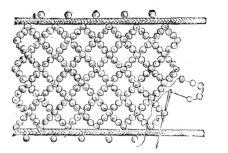

FIG. 33. BEAD TRIMMING FOR DRESSES, &c.

as a trimming, as shown in Fig. 33, is made of fine round black beads, selected all of the same size. The only foundation required is a narrow strip of braid upon each side. Thread five beads together, and pass a needle through the centre bead of the stitch above it in the preceding row. String together twenty-two beads for the first row, and commence the pattern by putting a needle and thread, on which five beads have been strung, through every sixth bead.

Bead Work on Net.—This work is largely used for trimmings, and looks well executed in white or black bugles, as well as with fine beads of any colour. A bold and well-defined arabesque pattern is the best to ornament. Mark the design out upon a strip of pink calico, which stiffen with a paper lining, and tack net, the colour of the beads, firmly over it. Thread the beads singly upon fine sewing silk, and sew upon the net so as to fill in the pattern under the net. When finished take the net off the pattern, and lay a fresh piece on the design.

Bead Work on Velvet.—For this work fine and well-shaped beads are required, and good velvet. The velvet is either stamped out with a stamping machine in scroll or ivy leaf patterns, or the same designs marked out with transfer patterns on to the material, and then cut out, and the fine beads thickly sewn over every part. The work is only used for trimmings, and is very laborious.

Bearskin Cloth.—A coarse thick woollen cloth, with a shaggy nap, manufactured for the making of overcoats, and very durable. A variety of this material is commonly called Dreadnought.

Bearskin Fur.—(*Ursus.*) The several furs of the black, brown, white, and grey bears are all employed for either clothing, trimmings, or rugs, &c. That of the brown, or Isabella bear, has often come much into fashion in this country for women's dress; that of the black bear is made into military caps and accoutrements, hammer cloths, wrappers, and rugs; that of the grey bear is used for trimmings and coat linings, and so is the skin of the

cub black bear, which, in Russia, is always very much esteemed.

Beaver Cloth.—A stout make of woollen cloth, milled, and compact, with only one face shorn. A kind of fustian, having a smooth surface, and resembling a west of England cloth, such as are manufactured in Gloucestershire (*see* FUSTIAN). It is of double width.

Beaver Fur.—(*Castor Americanus.*) This animal is a native of British America, as well as other parts of that continent. The fur is of a chestnut brown until plucked, when it is of a grey colour. It is beautifully fine, soft, and glossy. The long hairs are plucked from it and the surface cut smoothly, and it is much employed for hats, bonnets, muffs, tippets, cuffs, and trimmings, and also as linings, being warm and durable. The white fur underneath the body is largely exported to France, where it is employed for making bonnets. A medium-sized skin measures 18 by 22 inches. The skins are imported to this country by the Hudson's Bay Company. (Anglo-Saxon *Befor*, Danish *Bǽvor*.)

Beaverteen.—One of the varieties of fustian. It is a coarse twilled cotton, manufactured with a nap, and it is first dyed and then shorn. The chief seats of this manufacture are Bolton and Manchester. It was originally a mixture of cotton and linen, but is now made entirely of the former. Like all fustians it is both strong and durable. This material may be had in three different widths—27, 48, and 54 inches. *See* FUSTIAN.

Bedford Cloth.—A description of ribbed cloth, drab coloured, and of great strength; made as a dress material. It is a kind of Russel cord, all wool, and is a variety of French woollen poplin.

Bedford Cord.—A strong thick cloth, made for men's riding breeches. It is to be had in three sizes, the large, medium, and fine cord. The width is 27 inches.

Bedfordshire Lace.—Queen Catherine, of Arragon, is believed by some people to have introduced Pillow Lace making into England, and particularly into Bedfordshire, Buckinghamshire, and Northamptonshire; but, as pins were not known in England until 1543, and she died in 1536, it is more probable that the lace making she fostered was a Needle-made Lace, or a coarse lace made with fish bones instead of pins. It seems to be pretty well decided that Pillow Lace was brought to England in Elizabeth's reign by the French refugees from the persecutions of Alva (1568), as the patterns of the old laces are of Flemish origin, and the lace was often known as English Lille. Many pieces of it were presented to Queen Elizabeth, who encouraged its manufacture, and, in 1660, it obtained so large a sale that a mark was placed upon it when exported to foreign countries, to distinguish it from the true Lille. The ground was a Réseau, and the pattern a wavy description differing but little from Lille Lace. The manufactory flourished during the whole of the seventeenth and eighteenth centuries, and the character of the lace up to the earlier part of the present century did not materially alter. The Regency Point is a specimen of a more complicated

E

kind of Bedfordshire Lace with a thick edge (see illustration, Fig. 34), and was much made in the first part of the

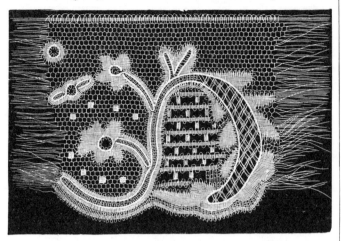

FIG. 34. BEDFORD REGENCY POINT.

nineteenth century, but was succeeded by lace of plaited instead of Réseau grounds, with raised patterns more resembling the old Maltese Laces than the Lille, and this last lace has destroyed the hands of the workers for the more delicate kinds. The demand for white lace having failed of late years, black lace is now taking its place; but the lace makers are so wretchedly paid for their work, that few are now learning the art, although specimens of the lace have been sent to the English exhibitions, and received praise from the judges, it, however, being remarked by them, that English lace failed in elegance and beauty when compared to those of foreign manufactories, and seemed rather to arrest by the apparent amount of labour bestowed upon it, than by the just lines of ornament and delicacy of design.

Bed Lace.—A description of binding, of white cotton, twilled or figured, and employed for binding dimities. It is likewise made in chintz colours, and in a diamond pattern for furniture prints, and striped with blue for bed ticking and palliasses. It is sold by the gross in two pieces of 72 yards each.

Beggars' Lace.—A name given to a braid lace, a species of Torchon, made at Guese. It was made in the sixteenth century, and was so called as it was cheap and easily executed. It is now obsolete.

Beginner's Stem.—In Honiton and other Pillow Laces, this stem is formed by plaiting together the threads that have been used to form detached leaves and flowers. To make: Divide into three the number of bobbins that have been employed in the leaf, and then plait these together for a short distance, so as to form a stem to the leaf. The illustration (Fig. 35) shows a finished leaf with its threads thus plaited up as a finish.

FIG. 35. BEGINNER'S STEM.

Beige, or Bège.—A French term to denote wool in its natural state. Beige is made of undyed wool, is an extremely soft textile, graceful in draping, and employed for morning and out-door wear. This material measures from 25 to 28 inches in width. There is a description of this textile, called Snowflake Beige, of a neutral ground, hairy in texture, to be had in grey-brown, light green, and drab; the wool being interwoven with threads of silk of a brightly contrasting colour.

Belgian Laces.—These include Brussels Lace, Mechlin, Antwerp, and Valenciennes, and all the varieties executed in the neighbouring towns. The manufacture of lace in Belgium dates back to the fifteenth century, and by some is considered to have been made there before the Italian laces. The making of lace in Belgium still continues, and is a flourishing trade. The chief employment is Pillow Lace making, with the exception of the modern needle Brussels Point Gaze, and at present the grounds are made of machine net, and the patterns on the pillow. *See* ANTWERP, BRUSSELS, MECHLIN, and VALENCIENNES LACES.

Belgian Tapestry.—A very stout handsome new cloth, to be had in every colour. It is made of jute, or with a mixture of linen, at the Glasgow jute manufactories, although given a foreign name. It has designs in colours, and is 52 inches in width. It is employed for covering furniture, and for hangings of all kinds.

Belgian Ticking.—These cloths are composed of linen and cotton, are stout, have a satin face, and are 64 inches in width. They are manufactured in various colours and patterns for purposes of upholstery, and especially for bedding.

Belgravian Embroidery.—This is a modern name given to braid and bugle work. Patterns of leaves, &c., are traced upon braid, and filled in with solid masses of bugles fastened to the braid with filoselle. The braid may be cut to represent leaves, with edges Overcast or turned down and then bugled. For trimmings this is handsomer than when the braid is left as a straight edge. To work: Take a piece of broad braid, lay over it an open design of leaves (such as ivy leaves) and their stems, and cut out the braid to that. OVERCAST over the raw edges of the braid, then cover every part of it over with bugles stitched firmly down.

Bell Pattern.—This is a design for a sleeve trimming, and is made of Damascene Lace. This lace is a modern adaptation of Honiton Pillow Lace. Draw the pattern upon pink calico, then tack the sprigs (which are bought ready made) into position, and run on the braid, which is either made on the pillow or by machine. Wherever the braid touches another piece of braid in its various curves OVERCAST the two together, and Overcast the whole outside edge. Nothing now remains to be done but to tack on a lace edging as a finish, and to connect the sprigs to the braid. Do this by means of CORDED BARS and WHEELS of various shapes, as shown in Fig. 36. For full description, *see* DAMASCENE LACE.

Belt.—(Anglo-Saxon *Belt*.) Derived from the Latin *balteus*, a girdle. The Belt may be made of leather, ribbon, silk, satin, or velvet, or of the material of the dress with which it is worn, and is fastened by either a band, rosette, or buckle. If made to match the dress, it must be made with buckram or stiff linen. Cricketing Belts are worn by gentlemen, and form a favourite present. There are several ways of making them, but the most general is embroidery applied to webbing, leather, cloth, or flannel. They may be also knitted or crocheted.

Bengal.—A thin stuff, made of silk and hair, originally brought from the Indian province of that name; also an imitation of striped muslin.

Bengaline.—A corded silk of Indian make, and possibly origin, slight in texture, manufactured in all colours, considered most appropriate for young ladies' wear in France.

Bengaline.—A French made silk textile, exceedingly soft, and made of silk and wool. It bears some resemblance to poplin, but has a much larger cord, and more silk in its composition. Different qualities are sold, but they all measure 24 inches in width.

Berlin Wool, otherwise called GERMAN WOOL and ZEPHYR MERINO.—Manufactured for the purpose of knitting and embroidery. It is to be had in two sizes, the single and the double. Keighley, in Yorkshire, is the chief seat of the manufacture, and the Wool is sold either in skeins or by weight. A quantity of real German Wool is brought into Great Britain in a raw state, and is combed, spun, and dyed, chiefly in Scotland, but that dyed here is less perfect and durable than that imported ready for use, excepting those dyed black, which are cleaner in working. The English-grown embroidery lambswool, though harsher, is in some respects superior, the scarlet dye quite equalling, if not surpassing, the German; as also several shades of all the other colours and neutral tints. It is best suited for use on coarse canvas. Berlin or German Wool is the finest of all descriptions, and is produced from the fleece of the Merino breed of Saxony sheep, and of neighbouring

FIG. 36. BELL PATTERN DAMASCENE LACE.

Bengal Stripes.—A kind of cotton cloth or gingham, woven with coloured stripes. It was so called after the cottons formerly imported from Bengal, the name referring only to the pattern, but is also to be had in a mixture of linen and cotton. It resembles the French PERCALE and MILLERAYÉS (which *see*), but is softer, and is made of English cotton, or cotton and wool. The cotton stripe measures 34in. inches in width, and linen stripe about 24 inches. It was first manufactured in this country at Paisley.

Bergamot.—A common description of Tapestry, produced from goat and ox hair, mixed with cotton or hemp. It derives its name from Bergamo, in Italy, where it is supposed to have been first manufactured.

Berlin Canvas.—Every two strands in this textile are drawn together, thus forming squares, and leaving open spaces for the wool, with which it may be embroidered. It is more easily counted and worked than the ordinary sorts, and is a great improvement upon the old Penelope canvas, the threads of which were woven in equal distances throughout, taking, of course, much more time to count and separate them. It may be procured in almost all

German States. The principal seat of its manufacture into thread for needlework is Gotha, whence it is sent to Berlin and elsewhere to be dyed. Wool of the same breed of the Merino is largely exported from Australia and Van Dieman's Land. Berlin Wool for embroidery may be had in all colours, also shaded and partridge-coloured, and ingrain at different prices, both by the skein and by weight.

Berlin Work.—A modern name given to the *Opus Pulvinarium* of the ancients, and also known as Cushion Style and Point de Marque. Opus pulvinarium was well known to the Phrygians and Egyptians, and its principal stitch (Cross Stitch) was used in the curtains of the Tabernacle. The work was prevalent during the thirteenth and following centuries, but then chiefly used for kneeling mats and cushions in churches, as it was more durable than embroidery. From this application it owed its name of Cushion style; but that it was not only confined to the baser uses is apparent in the fine example of a church vestment still left us, the Sion cope, date 1225, the border of which is worked in Cross Stitch upon canvas, exactly as the present Berlin work is done. During the fifteenth and sixteenth centuries Tent Stitch was more used than Cross

Stitch for this work, and it was called Canvas Work until the present century, when the production of Berlin coloured paper patterns, in 1804, procured for it the title of Berlin Work, though this last name was not finally adopted until 1820, the date of the introduction of Berlin wools, which took the place of the crewels, lambswools, and silks, that had been used up to that period. The patterns worked until the Berlin ones were printed were drawn directly on to the canvas, and the places to be coloured were painted in their various shades, so that but little variety could be marked out, and more was left to individual taste. The first coloured patterns upon paper were inferior in design and shading to the present ones, but in 1810 a printseller at Berlin, named Wittich, produced a series of these patterns, which were copies from celebrated pictures. These were drawn upon "point paper" by good artists, and cost £40 for the original. These picture patterns were first copied in Tent and Tapestry Stitches and in silks, then in beads, and finally with Berlin wool. The Berlin wool was superior in texture, and in the varieties of its dyes, to the English wool, but with it was introduced large-sized canvas and Cross Stitch, innovations that rendered the figured designs coarse and inartistic. These were gradually displaced by the impossible parrots, animals, and groups of flowers known in the present day as Berlin patterns, which have done so much to debase the public taste as far as fancy work is concerned. The work in itself is capable of good results, and is strong and lasting; but when it degenerates into the mere copying of patterns conceived in defiance of all true art principles, it helps to degrade, and not elevate, the mind. Happily, during the last few years the public have been taught to distinguish and appreciate good from false designs, and as long as this is so, there is no reason why Berlin work should not take its ancient position among needlework. The stitches formerly used were Cross, Cushion, Satin, Tapestry, and Tent, but these have been considerably added to in the last few years, and now include Back, Damask, German, Herringbone, Irish, Plush, Leviathan, Single, Double and Treble, Raised and Rep, and varieties of these known by the general name of Fancy Berlin Stitches. The size of the canvas used for Berlin wool work must depend upon whether single or double wool is to be used, the space to be covered, and whether the stitch is to be taken over one or two threads. The patterns state the number of stitches they cover, therefore there is no difficulty in fitting them. The canvas used is tightly stretched in a frame, so that the selvedges come on the braced sides. Commence the pattern, when a floral one, from the centre stitch; so that, should any errors in counting or working occur, the whole design will not be thrown out. In figures and landscapes, an accustomed worker will commence at the bottom and work upwards: the sky and lighter parts of the design are thus worked last, and kept unsoiled. The grounding requires to be as carefully done as the design, as uneven and pulled ground will destroy the good work of the rest. It is begun at the bottom of the canvas, on the left side, and is worked in rows, short needlefuls of wool being used, and the ends run in, not knotted. Care is taken before commencing to ground that sufficient wool is ready to

finish the whole, as nothing looks so bad as two shades in the grounding, and the exact tint is rarely dyed twice. The selection of shades of wool for the design that harmonise is essential to the success of Berlin Work, and the placing in juxtaposition of several brilliant and contrasting colours is especially to be avoided. Discard large double flowers, figure, and animal patterns, also coarse canvas. The best patterns are single flowers worked in TENT STITCH upon fine canvas, or with CROSS STITCH over one thread, also intricate geometrical designs. Berlin wool patterns, worked upon cloth or silk, are done by these materials being stretched in the frame under the canvas, and when the pattern is worked, the canvas either drawn out thread by thread, or cut short off close to the work. No grounding is required when the threads are thus drawn away, and only the few stitches left in the interstices between the work when they are cut away. Silk canvas is often used for Berlin work—it is a substitute for grounding; when used, the back of the work must be neatly finished off, and no loops of wool carried from one shade to another across open spaces, as they will be visible in the front. Silk canvas is backed with satin of its own colour when the work is completed. Before taking the ordinary filled Berlin Work from its frame, it requires to have a coat of embroidery paste or thin starch passed over it at the back, to keep the wool well stretched and in

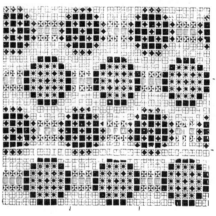

FIG. 37. BERLIN WORK.

its right position. In the illustration (Fig. 37) of Berlin wool work, the different shades used are marked with various shaped crosses and stars, so that the worker will have no difficulty in placing them in their right order. The pattern is a suitable one for a cushion, and is worked as follows: Work the ground, shown by the thin black cross upon a white square, in grey wool, and in CROSS STITCH; the bands across (shown by the white cross upon a black square, and squares filled with black lines) with two shades of old gold colour, the darkest outside; and the round bosses in three shades of deep crimson and two shades of violet. The following are the principal stitches used in Berlin wool work.

Back Stitch.—This stitch is made like the BACK STITCH (which *see*) used in plain needlework. See also *Back, Satin, and Raised* (Fig. 52), and *Slanting Gobelin, Back, and Satin* (Fig. 57).

Cross Stitch.—The principal stitch now used for Berlin wool work, and known as POINT DE MARQUE, GROS POINT, and KREUZSTICH, as well as Cross Stitch. It is used not only for working upon canvas with wools, but for embroidering with any material that will thread upon cloth, silk, satin, and velvet. It was much used in the Phrygian, Egyptian, and Hebrew embroideries, and is occasionally to be met with in the work done between the first and sixteenth centuries (the Sion cope being partly worked in Cross Stitch). In the middle of the nineteenth century, a few years after the printing of the Berlin patterns, they began to be solely executed with Cross Stitch, and that work is often called after the name of the stitch. Cross Stitch is worked either in a frame or upon the hand, the work in the frame generally turning out the best. The

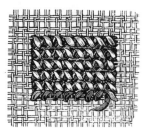

FIG. 38. CROSS STITCH.

stitch is a double one, taken over two threads of canvas in height and width, or more than two threads, the object being always to form a perfect square. To work, as shown in Fig. 38: Take the wool in a slanting direction across the square, from left to right. Bring the needle up on the lower left-hand corner, put it in at the upper right-hand corner, bring it up at the lower right-hand corner, and cross it back to the upper left-hand corner. When grounding in Cross Stitch, work the first part of the stitch in rows along the canvas, and cross these when returning. When working a pattern, finish each stitch at once, and commence from the bottom on the left-hand side.

Cross Stitch Double.—See Double Stitch.

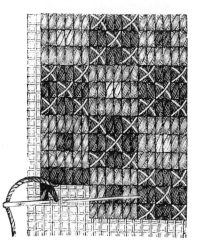

FIG. 39. LONG CROSS STITCH.

Cross (Long) Stitch.—This is a variation of Cross Stitch, the two stitches forming it not making a perfect square, as in ordinary Cross Stitch, but a Long Stitch crossed. To work: Take the wool over a greater number of threads in height than in width—four threads in height to two in width being the correct proportion. This stitch was more used in Berlin wool work thirty

years ago than at the present time; it is suitable for geometrical patterns. To work, as shown in Fig 39: Take a dark and light shade of the same coloured wool and some gold coloured filoselle. Work six LONG CROSS STITCHES with light wool and six with dark wool alternately to the end of the line, and repeat for two lines, putting a darker and a lighter shade in the centre of the light part in the middle line. Vary the design by altering the positions of the dark and light shades, so as to form alternate squares, and finish by working silk CROSS STITCHES over two Long Cross Stitches in the dark squares.

Cross (Persian) Stitch.—A variety of Cross Stitch, and

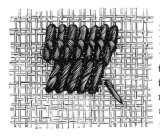

FIG. 40. PERSIAN CROSS STITCH.

known also by the name of Rep. To work: Make the first half of the stitch a LONG TENT STITCH, which take over six horizontal threads in a slanting direction, and two in height, and make the second part of the stitch like the last half of CROSS STITCH; take this over the two centre threads of the Long Tent Stitch

from right to left, as shown in Fig. 40.

Cross (Slanting) Stitch.—This is a variety of Cross Stitch, and is but little used in work. Make the first part of the stitch the same as CROSS STITCH, but make the return like a STRAIGHT GOBELIN. It can only be worked upon fine canvas, as the stitch, not being carried over the whole of the foundation, requires that foundation to be of the finest.

Cushion Stitch.—One of the ancient names for Cross Stitch. It must not be confounded with the Cushion Stitch used in embroidery.

Damask Stitch.—This is a variety of Long Stitch. Take it over four horizontal threads of canvas, or two stitches in a slanting direction and over two upright threads. The variety is, that all the remaining second lines of Damask Stitch are taken over the two lower threads of the upper line and two new threads, instead of all the threads being new.

Double Stitch.—This stitch is also known by the name of "Star Stitch," and is in reality but a variety of Tent Stitch as worked by the Germans. To work: Take a square composed of four threads of canvas; cross its centre with a TENT STITCH. Work from the bottom of the left-hand corner to the top of the right-hand corner of the square, then fill in on the right and left of this stitch with two smaller Tent Stitches. *Double Stitch*, as worked by the Italians, is a centre Cross surrounded by a square made with four stitches, each stitch crossing from point to point of the arms of the Cross. Double Stitch, worked in the Italian style, is used in Kreuzstich and in Russian embroidery more than in Berlin work. This stitch is only used with others in fancy patterns, and is illustrated in *Star, Cross, and Leviathan* (Fig. 55).

German Stitch.—This stitch is formed from a Tapestry

and a Tent Stitch being worked alternately in a diagonal line across the canvas. To work, as shown in Fig. 41:

FIG. 41. GERMAN STITCH.

Pass the TAPESTRY over four threads of canvas, the TENT over two. In the succeeding line, place the Tent under the Tapestry, and the Tapestry under the Tent, but so that the canvas shows. This stitch is only useful where the foundation material, like silk or gold canvas, can be left exposed, and is rarely employed for patterns. Is also employed when working in chenille upon silver and gold cardboard.

Gobelin Stitch.—A stitch that has derived its name from its use in ancient tapestries, being known also under the title of Tapestry Stitch. It is used in embroidery as well as in Berlin work. As shown in Fig. 42, the stitch is

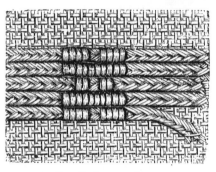

FIG. 42. GOBELIN STITCH.

raised from the canvas by means of a padding of braid; this padding is a great improvement to Gobelin, as otherwise it is quite a flat stitch, not being crossed. To work: Pass the wool over two horizontal threads of the canvas, and into every space left between the upright threads.

Herringbone Stitch.—See Plaited Stitch.

Irish Stitch.—This is used for groundings, or for patterns formed with shades of colour in vandykes crossing. Irish stitch is a long stitch, taken over five or more threads of canvas, in an upright direction, and it requires to be worked on fine canvas. Its only peculiarity consists in its being alternately started from the last row of canvas and from the third. This allows the stitches to end in one line where the centre of the next line comes, and gives a pleasing variety to ordinary groundings. To work: Make a LONG STITCH over five upright threads of canvas for the first stitch; for the second, commence the work two threads of canvas above the bottom part of first stitch, but cover five threads of canvas as before. Repeat these two stitches to the end of the row; and, for the second row, work in the same way, thus making an irregular line of stitches, but one that fills up the spaces left in the first row.

Leviathan Stitch.—A modern Berlin stitch, sometimes called Railway Stitch, because it is considered to cover the canvas quickly. It requires large-sized or leviathan

canvas, as is shown in Fig. 43. To work: Take four squares of canvas for one stitch, and make a CROSS STITCH into the four corners of this square; then carry the wool

FIG. 43. LEVIATHAN STITCH.

across the centre of the stitch from top to bottom, and then from left to right, so that it passes through all the outside holes of the square forming the stitch. Work all together, and make each stitch exactly the same as to crossings, or an even appearance to the whole will not be given. A greater quantity of wool is used in this stitch than in other grounding ones, but it is considered quicker in execution. Varieties of Leviathan are formed by working over six or eight threads in height, and as many in width; these require a double crossing at top and side for the six-thread, and a double crossing and a straight stitch top and side for the eight. They are called *Double Leviathan* and *Treble Leviathan Stitch.*

Leviathan (Double) Stitch.—A variety of Leviathan worked over eight square threads or four square stitches. To work: Make a CROSS STITCH into the four corners of the square, then a LONG CROSS STITCH to fill in the holes

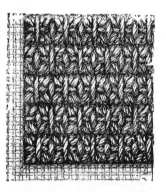

FIG. 44. DOUBLE LEVIATHAN STITCH.

on each side of the Cross Stitch, and lastly an upright Cross Stitch into the middle stitches in length and width of square. Fill in all the squares in the same order, or the uniformity of the pattern will be destroyed, and put a single Long Stitch between each square, to fill up the part of the canvas that is left bare. See illustration (Fig. 44). When commencing a new line of stitches on the canvas, make a half-stitch to begin, so that the centre of the second line of stitches does not come under the centre of the first line. Commence with a half stitch at each alternate row. Double Leviathan is worked upon leviathan canvas; it consumes more wool than plain Berlin stitches, but gives a raised appearance to the design. It is only used for geometrical designs, and is not suitable for groundings.

Leviathan (Treble) Stitch.—This stitch is worked upon leviathan canvas, and is used for covering large surfaces with a raised and showy pattern, but is not suitable for groundings. To work: A square of eight threads of four stitches is required. Commence from the centre, take the wool from there to one of the corners, passing, in so doing, over four upright threads and four lengthway ones in a slanting direction. Place the next two stitches one on each side of the first, crossing over four lengthway threads and two upright ones, and *vice versâ*, and finishing in centre hole. Work the four corners thus (*see* Fig. 45), and complete the stitch with a Cross Stitch over the centre hole, and one in the centre of each side of the square (*see* Fig. 46). When repeating the stitch only work these

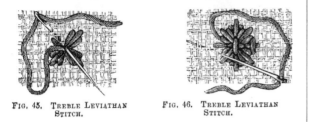

FIG. 45. TREBLE LEVIATHAN STITCH.　　FIG. 46. TREBLE LEVIATHAN STITCH.

outside Crosses in every alternate square of eight, as there is no room for them to every stitch. They should be worked with silk, or with a contrasting shade of wool.

Long Stitch.—See Satin Stitch.

Plaited Stitch.—This stitch is an imitation of the ordinary Herringbone, and is frequently called by that

FIG. 47. PLAITED STITCH.

name. To work as shown in Fig. 47: Take the wool over six threads of canvas or three stitches in height, and two

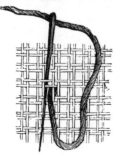

FIG. 48. BERLIN PLUSH STITCH.—DETAIL 1.

threads, or one stitch, in width, and repeat to the end of the row. The number of threads gone over can be enlarged

or decreased without detriment to the stitch, as long as the relative height and width are maintained.

Plush Stitch.—This stitch is chiefly used in raised wool work, but is also required to form borders or fringes to plain Berlin work. To work: Fasten the wool at the back of the canvas, bring it to the front and put the needle in again two threads above where it came out, and bring it back to the front in the same hole it started from (Fig. 48). Draw the wool up, but only so that it forms a loop of the length required, which is usually an inch (Fig. 49). Hold this loop in the left hand, and make a

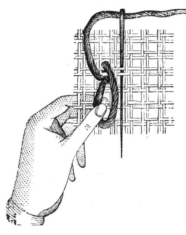

FIG. 49. BERLIN PLUSH STITCH.—DETAIL 2.

TENT STITCH. This completes the stitch. Work several rows in this manner (Fig. 50), commencing from the

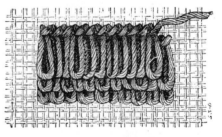

FIG. 50. BERLIN PLUSH STITCH.—DETAIL 3.

bottom of the canvas and working upward. Every loop is of the same length, and is passed over a mesh for this purpose if necessary. The stitch is cut and combed out in raised wool work, but it is generally left in loops for borders to mats, &c. RAISED and TASSEL STITCHES are but slight varieties of Plush.

Railway Stitch.—See Leviathan Stitch.

Raised Stitch.—This is sometimes called "Velvet," and is but a variety of Plush Stitch. It is suitable for raised wool work, and can be worked to any height by using various sized meshes, and then cutting and combing until the wool attains the softness of velvet pile. Any sized bone knitting-needles or wooden meshes are used, but a No. 4 knitting-needle is the most suitable. To work: Make the first stitch a TENT STITCH, then bring the needle up where the stitch commenced, push the knitting-needle over the Tent Stitch, and make a GOBELIN STITCH over it, the wool needle being put in two threads above the place it came out from. Bring it out at the bottom of the next stitch to be made, work a Tent Stitch, and repeat the process described above. The work is commenced from the bottom, and the knitting-needle left in the lowest row until the row above it is completed, to prevent any dragging of wool. Cut and comb out the loops when all the work is completed. The stitch is worked with the Gobelin over the knitting-needle, and without the securing Tent Stitch; but when this is done leave the knitting-needles in the rows, and paste a strong piece of ticking at the back of the work before they are withdrawn, and the stitches cut and combed.

Rep Stitch.—*See Cross (Persian) Stitch.*

Satin Stitch.—This stitch is used in embroidery as well as in wool work, and under the latter is equally called LONG and SLANTING. To work: Make a TENT STITCH in a diagonal direction across the canvas, the length being varied according to the design; the width, whatever number of threads of canvas, is covered with the wool. Shown in *Slanting Gobelin, Back, and Satin* (Fig. 57).

Slanting Gobelin Stitch.—A name sometimes given to LONG or SATIN STITCH.

Star Stitch.—*See Double Stitch.*

Tapestry Stitch.—*See Gobelin Stitch.*

Tassel Stitch.—This stitch is used in Berlin wool work for making fringes, and is but a variety of Plush. It requires to be worked with a mesh, and with the wool doubled. The stitch requires six threads of canvas in length, and four in height. To make: Pass two loops, formed of four strands of wool, over the mesh, and put the needle into the centre of four threads of canvas in height, and along six in width, and secure with a CROSS STITCH. Pass this Cross Stitch over them, and into the outer holes of the Stitch, binding the loops firmly down together with it. Paste the back of the canvas before these loops are cut, as they are not so secure as those made with real PLUSH STITCH.

Tent Stitch.—This stitch is also known as "Petit Point" and "Perlenstitch," and in all ancient needlework it was more used than Cross Stitch. Tent Stitch

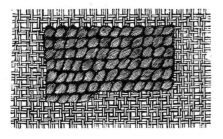

FIG. 51. TENT STITCH.

requires much finer canvas than that used in Cross Stitch, the wool being only laid on the canvas once instead of twice, necessitating a fine background, and

therefore more labour. To work, as shown in Fig. 51: Cross the wool over one or two threads of canvas in a diagonal direction from left to right.

Various Fancy Stitches (1).—In the fancy pattern given in Fig. 52 the stitches are Back, Satin, and Raised. The

FIG. 52. BACK, SATIN, AND RAISED STITCHES.

work covers a square of eight stitches, or sixteen threads, and when complete has the appearance of lines radiating from a centre rosette of raised work, the outer part of the design being surrounded with a line of Back Stitch. To work: Leave a centre square of eight threads, bring the wool up from the back, and pass it over three stitches, or six threads, in a straight upright direction, so that it finishes on the line that forms the outer square. Repeat this SATIN STITCH all round the four centre stitches that are left bare, place the wool once into every outer stitch of the square, and twice into every inner. Fill the four centre stitches with raised stitches. Wind the wool several times round a bone crochet-hook, and then, secure it by a needle run through the loops, while still on the hook, and pass it through the unworked canvas; these loops are made until the centre is well filled with them; they are cut or not, according to fancy. The lines of BACK STITCH in the pattern are worked in filoselle; two shades of crimson, or two of blue, with amber filoselle, are the best colours.

(2).—In the arrangement shown in Fig. 53, Cross Stitch is used to catch down upon the canvas hori-

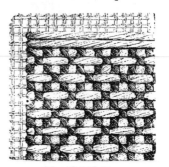

FIG. 53. CROSS STITCH.

zontal lines of wool. The Cross Stitches form diagonal lines, crossing each other at equal distances, while they catch down the wool in some rows at every other stitch, at others missing two stitches. The pattern is a very effective one and easily worked, as so much of it is only laid upon the surface. Work the Cross Stitches all in one shade

APPLIQUE UPON LINEN.

CLOTH APPLIQUE.

of colour, but vary the horizontal lines, three lines of each colour being sufficient. A pattern useful for any Berlin work that is not subject to hard wear, and upon which short lengths of wool can be turned to account.

(3).—A fancy pattern, showing how Cross and Long Cross and Leviathan stitches can be formed into a design. Form the groundwork of the pattern with CROSS STITCHES worked in one shade of colour; work the LONG CROSS over eight threads of canvas in height and two in width, and with five shades of one colour. Work each pattern or arrangement of Long Cross in distinct colours, the five shades of each being always necessary. Make with

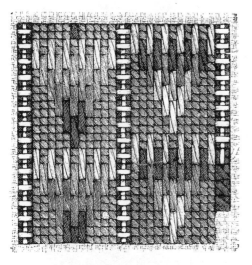

FIG. 54. CROSS, LONG CROSS, AND LEVIATHAN STITCH.

LEVIATHAN STITCH the dividing lines between the designs, using black wool, with the last two crossings formed of bright filoselle. *See* Fig. 54.

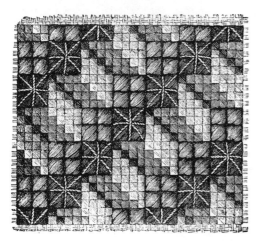

FIG. 55. STAR, CROSS, AND LEVIATHAN STITCH.

(4).—The design given in Fig. 55 is of a pattern formed by grouping together Double or Star Stitch and Cross, and by taking over four of the Double Stitches a

Leviathan Stitch made with purse silk. Make the plain Cross Stitches of four different shades of one colour, but any number of colours can be used about them, as long as four shades of each are worked. The Double Stitches not crossed with the Leviathan are all one colour throughout the pattern, the four crossed with the Leviathan are dark in colour, and of the same colour throughout the pattern, as is also the purse silk. The pattern is a good one for using up short lengths of wool, and is worked either upon a leviathan or plain canvas. To work: Commence by working the DOUBLE STITCHES, work the four that make a square and that are not crossed over with LEVIATHAN STITCH in pale blue wool, the four that are afterwards crossed in dark blue. Work the CROSS STITCHES in four shades of crimson, and finish by making the LEVIATHAN STITCHES with old gold filoselle.

(5).—This is a pattern showing the Plaited and Cross Stitch together. The Plaited Stitch is too heavy to work alone upon canvas, so is always arranged with some other stitch to lighten it. The illustration (Fig. 56) is on Berlin canvas, and the plaits are there separated with rows of Cross Stitch, the three centre ones of which are, when worked, covered with a light Herringboning in silk, the Herringbone being taken in every alternate stitch

FIG. 56. PLAITED, HERRINGBONE, AND CROSS STITCH.

of the two outer lines. To work: Make the first and fifth rows of CROSS STITCH in a dark wool, the three centre ones in a lighter shade of the same colour. The plaits are sometimes divided with one row of Cross Stitch, sometimes with three, and sometimes with five. Arrange the PLAITED STITCH lines as to colours, as two of one colour, and one of a lighter shade of the same; they should harmonise with the shade used for the Cross Stitch. Finish the pattern by HERRINGBONE STITCH lines in purse silk, which pass over three of the Cross Stitch lines.

(6).—In the pattern given in Fig. 57, the manner of grouping three Berlin Stitches together, to form a design, is shown. The stitches are Slanting Gobelin, Satin, and Back Stitch. To work: Divide the pattern

F

into strips of unequal breadth, the narrowest taking up six threads in width, or three stitches; the widest twelve threads, or six stitches. Fill in the latter strips with

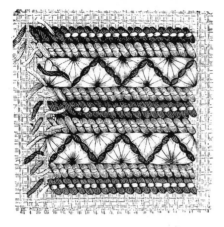

FIG. 57. SLANTING GOBELIN, BACK, AND SATIN STITCH.

three rows of SLANTING GOBELIN, taking each stitch over four threads. When the wool work is complete, BACK-STITCH these over with a bright filoselle. Form the narrower strip of SATIN STITCH arranged as rays of seven stitches to a ray; commence each ray from its centre, and let it cover six threads of canvas. When finished, outline with Back Stitch, formed with a contrasting colour. This design is worked upon leviathan or ordinary canvas, and is suitable for most Berlin work.

(7).—A pattern formed of Satin Stitch so as to make squares upon the canvas. (*See* Fig. 58). To work: Make the squares over six threads of canvas, or three stitches in length and breadth, and fill this in with unequal

FIG. 58. SATIN STITCH IN SQUARES.

length SATIN STITCHES. The direction of the stitches is altered in each alternate square. It makes a good design for cushions and footstools, and is worked with many shades of colour, or only one, according to the worker's fancy. Requires Berlin canvas.

(8).—A pattern illustrating Slanting Gobelin, or Long Stitch, and Back Stitch. It is used upon fine canvas, the wool not being crossed. The stitch, as shown in Fig. 59, can be varied in length, the longest SLANTING

GOBELIN being carried over six threads of canvas, the shortest over two; the width never varies. It should be worked in lines of colour that harmonise, and completed with a BACK STITCH in filoselle.

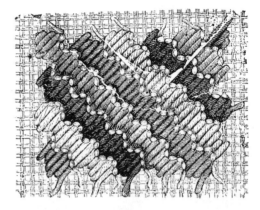

FIG. 59. SLANTING GOBELIN AND BACK STITCH.

(9).—A pattern illustrating an arrangement of Satin and Cross Stitch. It is worked with Berlin, single or double, or with fleecy wool, and upon Berlin canvas, and is suitable for footstools, and curtain and table borders. To work: Make the dark lines in the illustration (Fig. 60) in SATIN STITCH, which work over six threads of canvas, rising two threads a time and falling in the same manner,

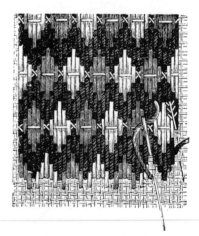

FIG. 60. SATIN AND CROSS STITCH.

to form the wavy line across the work. Divide the light lines in the middle, and pass over four threads each of canvas, excepting the two long middle ones, which pass over six threads. When completed, cross the centre light lines with a line of filoselle, purse silk, or gold cord, but leave the outside line on each side free, and work a CROSS STITCH beyond it over the junction of the dark wavy line.

Velvet Stitch.—*See* RAISED STITCH.

Berne Embroidery.—A work executed with white or gold beads, or silver or gold wire, upon black velvet. Berne Embroidery takes its name from the Canton of Berne, where it is used to ornament the gala dresses of the peasantry. The designs used are all small detached sprays of conventional flowers and leaves. The best embroidery is that where the centre part of the leaves or flowers is filled up with rows of beads, either raised over a stuffed foundation, or lying flat on the surface, and the outlines, tendrils, stalks, and ornaments too minute to be worked with beads, formed with gold thread. The second kind of patterns are made only of gold or silver thread. To work: Trace a small flower spray on black velvet, and fill in the petals of the flowers and the leaves with rows of beads laid flat across the space and very close together. The rows of beads are not caught down as carried over the space, but taken plainly across from side to side; they are, however, laid either slanting or straight, in the best way to follow the natural curve of the design. Work the gold thread outlines in SATIN STITCH, and the stems, tendrils, and buds in the same stitch.

Betweens.—A description of needle shorter than those called ground-downs, and longer than blunts. They are strong, and thicker made than the ordinary sewing needles known as sharps.

Bias.—A term derived from the French *biais*, used to denote a line taken, either in folding or cutting a material, diagonally across the web. To fold or cut a square handkerchief on the Bias, would mean from one corner to that opposite it, when folded shawlwise, so as to make three corners. To cut any stuff on the Bias is vulgarly called (Hampshire and Kent) "on the cater," but this is only a provincialism in use amongst the lower orders. It appears in Webster's (American) Dictionary, and may be in more general use in the United States.

Binche Lace.—At Binche, a town in Hainault, Brussels Lace has been made since the seventeenth century, and even in Savary's time obtained a high reputation. For some years Binche Lace was considered superior to that made at Brussels, and it is continually mentioned in the inventories of the eighteenth century, and called "Guipure de Binche." Another lace also made at Binche partook more of the heavy pattern of old Dutch Lace, while its ground, instead of being confined to the mesh pattern, was varied with the spider and rosettes grounds seen in old Valenciennes, and illustrated under VALENCIENNES LACE, but never the plait ground. The making of Binche Lace has now degenerated into sprigs of Pillow Lace, which are afterwards Appliqué on to machine net.

Binding.—(Derived from the Anglo-Saxon *bindan*.) A term used in plain sewing to denote the encasing of the edge of any material, garment, or article if made of a textile, in the folded band of tape, braid, ribbon, or of any other stuff cut on the bias, so as to hide a raw edge, or to strengthen or decorate the border of a dress, coat, or other article. It may be Backstitched through on both sides at once; run one side, and turned back over the edge on the inside and hemmed; or laid flat, and sewn on the inside of a skirt.

Binding.—A term used in KNITTING.

Bindings.—These consist of some fourteen different descriptions of braid, and ribbons of various materials respectively. The chief amongst them are as follow:—

Bag Strapping, a Binding employed by upholsterers, to preserve selvedges, and resembling very broad stay-tape. The widths are known as Nos. 1, 2, and super. The measure given is usually short; and there are twenty-four pieces, of 9 or 12 yards to the gross. Bed Lace is a twilled or figured white cotton binding, used for dimities. It is made in chintz colours for furniture, also in a diamond pattern, and in blue stripes for bed tick and palliasses. The piece runs to 72 yards, two pieces forming a gross. Carpet Bindings are made in plain and variegated colours to match with carpets. The best qualities are all of worsted; the cheaper are a mixture of cotton and worsted. The pieces measure 36 yards, four forming a gross. Cocoa Bindings are manufactured in two widths, $2\frac{1}{2}$ and 3 inches. They are used to bind cocoa-nut matting. The pieces contain from 18 to 24 yards. Cotton Ferrets are like unsized tape. Grey and black are principally used. They were originally intended to be stouter than tapes, but have sadly decreased in value. Italian Ferrets are made entirely of silk, and are used to bind flannels and dressing gowns. They are made in white, black, scarlet, blue, crimson, &c., of one width only, 36 yards going to the piece. Galloons were formerly used for boot bindings and shoe strings. They are now out of date for the former purpose. They are a mixture of cotton and silk, and are now chiefly in use for binding oilcloths, &c. Statute galloons are narrow ribbons employed for binding flannel, composed of cotton and silk. The piece consists of 36 yards. There are five widths, respectively called twopenny, fourpenny, sixpenny, eightpenny, and tenpenny. These old-fashioned names do not refer to the price of the galloon, but to the fact of the old penny piece having been taken as a gauge. This ancient plan is also still in use by ribbon maufacturers. Pads is the technical name for watered galloons, used for watch and eye-glass ribbons. Petershams are belt ribbons, used commonly for dresses. Prussian Bindings have a silk face and a cotton back. They are twilled diagonally, and are used for binding waterproofs, mantles, and sometimes for flannels, instead of the more suitable Italian ferret and statute galloon. The piece contains 36 yards, sold by the gross in four pieces. Stay Bindings are used for binding women's stays, and can be procured in black, grey, white, and drab. They are of widths, running from $\frac{3}{8}$, $\frac{1}{2}$, and $\frac{5}{8}$ of an inch; or from Nos. 10 to 30. They are sold by the gross in lengths of 12—12, 8—18, or 6—24. Venetians are used for several purposes in upholstery. Their chief use, however, is at present for Venetian blinds; they vary in width from $\frac{1}{2}$ to 1 inch, and from $1\frac{1}{4}$ to $1\frac{1}{2}$ inches. The colours are dyed ingrain, and are green, blue, yellow, and white; they are now sometimes used for embroidery. Worsted Bindings are employed by saddlers and upholsterers, and they have also come into use for embroidery, and can be had in many widths, and in nearly every colour. They are called by many people webbing, and as such are frequently named in descriptions of work. Binders and Bindings used in needlework may be either on the bias or the straight way of the material when they are placed round the necks and cuffs of garments or round the waists. They are usually sewn on, and then turned over and hemmed down on the wrong side. The gathered part should be held next to the worker. Binders should be cut the selvedge way of the material as being the strongest. Bias bindings are best sewn on with the machine when used to trim dresses and skirts.

Bird's-eye Diaper.—A cloth made both in linen and in cotton, named after the small design woven in its texture. *See* DIAPER.

Birds' Nest Mats.—These mats are made of Combed-out Work and Knitting. To make: Cast on sufficient stitches to make a width of five or six inches of Knitting, and cut a number of pieces of soft wool into 8-inch lengths. First row—PLAIN KNITTING; second row—KNIT the first stitch, * take one or two of the cut lengths, according to size of wool, and put them once round left-hand needle, hold so that their ends are equal, knit these with the next stitch, and bring their ends well to the front, knit one, and repeat from *; third row—Plain Knitting; fourth row—same as second, except commencing with two Plain Stitches rather than one, to allow of the inserted pieces mixing flatly with those on the second row; continue second and third rows until the length required is obtained, changing only the first stitches of the second row as shown. Cast off and join, and comb out the inserted pieces until they cover the whole of the Knitting with a soft and thick layer of wool, and sew this on to a round cardboard foundation by one of its edges, allowing the other to stand erect. Turn this edge inside, and catch it down to the back side of the Knitting at a depth of two inches. Shaded greens are the best colours for these mats. Wool—single or double Berlin, or fleecy.

Bisette Lace.—An ancient Pillow Lace, made in the villages round Paris during the whole of the seventeenth century. It was coarse and narrow, but it obtained a ready sale among the poorer classes. Some better kinds are mentioned in old inventories; these seem to have been made of gold and silver thread, or to have been ornamented with thin plates of these metals.

Black Mohair Cords.—These were formerly used for binding coat edges, but are now employed for looping up dress skirts. They are to be had of various sizes, but the most useful are numbered 2, 4, and 7. They are sold by the gross of four pieces of 36 yards each, but short lengths can be obtained. *See* CORDS.

Black Silk Cords.—Fine round Cords, employed for binding coat edges, making button loops, and for watch-guards and eyeglasses. There are many numbers, but the most useful sizes are 3, 5, and 7. They are made up in knots of 36 yards, and sold by the gross, but short lengths may be purchased. *See* CORDS.

Black Silk Stuffs.—These are to be had in many varieties of make and of richness for dresses. The quality of the plain kinds may be judged of by holding them up to the light and looking through them, when the evenness of the threads may be seen, and superior quality of the material shown by a certain green shade in the black dye. The widths vary from 22 to 26 inches.

Blanketing.—This name is derived from that of the first manufacturer of this description of woollen textile,

Thomas Blanket, who produced them at Bristol, temp. Edward III. Yorkshire Blankets, for servants, and to put under sheets, measure from 2 by 1½ yards to 3½ by 3 yards, so do the Witney. Austrian Blankets have gay coloured stripes, and are much used as *portières*; their size runs from 2 by 1½ yards to 3 by 2½ yards. Scarlet Blankets have the same proportions, as well as the grey and brown charity Blankets. Crib Blankets average from 1 by ¾ yards to 1¾ by 1¼ yards, and the very best bath make are not sold narrower than 2½ yards. The same name is applied to a kind of towelling in white cotton; the cloths measure 48 by 80 inches to 72 by 96 inches. Brown linen bath Blankets are manufactured only in the latter dimensions.

Blanket Stitch.—*See* EMBROIDERY STITCHES.

Bley.—A term especially used in Ireland to denote unbleached calico. *See* CALICO.

Blind Chintz.—These are printed cotton cloths, plain made, and calendered, produced in various colours and patterns, chiefly in stripes and designs resembling Venetian blinds. Their narrowest width is 36 inches, running upwards, by 2 inches, to 80 or 100 inches.

Blind Cords and Tassels.—These are made of linen or cotton thread, and of flax covered with worsted. They are sold in lengths of 72 yards, two pieces to the gross, and may be had in amber, blue, crimson, green, and scarlet. The Tassels are made of unbleached thread, to match the several colours of the Cords.

Blind Ticking.—This is a stout twilled material, made of a combination of linen and cotton in all colours and stripes, from 36 to 60 inches in width.

Block-printed Linen.—The art of printing linen owes its origin to Flanders, and dates back to the fourteenth century. Ancient specimens are rare; the earliest sample can be found in the Chapter Library, Durham, and a sample of Block Printing on a fine sheet wrapped round the body of a bishop in the cathedral was discovered in 1827. The Indian method of Block Printing has recently been revived in England, the blocks being lent for the purpose by the authorities of the India Museum to a firm in London, and used for printing on silk.

Blonde de Caen.—*See* BLONDE NET LACE.

Blonde de Fil.—A name sometimes applied to MIGNONETTE LACE, which *see*.

Blonde Net Lace.—A general term for black and white Pillow Laces made with a network ground. The best is made at Caen, Chantilly, Barcelona, and Catalonia. The patterns of Blonde Laces are generally heavy—thick flowers joined together with a wide meshed ground. The Blondes de Caen were celebrated for their delicate and soft appppearance. Blonde Laces were first produced in 1745 from unbleached silk, and were known as BLONDES. *See* CHANTILLY LACE.

Blond Quillings.—These resemble bobbin quillings, but are made of silk and highly sized and finished. Mechlins are also of silk, but are both unfinished and soft. Each of these Quillings is made in various widths; they are used for frills and ruffles.

Blue Bafts.—A description of coarse muslin, manufactured at Manchester, designed for wearing apparel, and for export to Africa.

Blunts.—A description of needle, short, thick, and strong, employed by staymakers as being the most suitable for stitching jean or coutille, especially when doubled; and used likewise by glovers and tailors.

Bobbin.—(French, *Bobine*.) A cotton cord employed by needlewomen for making a ribbed edge to any garment, or other article, by enclosing it in a strip of the material cut on the bias. Bobbin is likewise called cotton cord. It is to be had in white and black, varying in size, and done up in half bundles of 5lb., mixed sizes or otherwise, also in single pounds ready skeined. Bobbin is a term likewise employed to denote the small reel on which thread is wound in some sewing machines, and also a circular pin of wood, with a wide cutting round it, to receive linen, silk, or cotton thread for weaving.

Bobbin Lace.—Used to designate Pillow Lace, and to distinguish it from Needle-made Lace during the sixteenth century. It was a better kind than Bone Lace, and supposed to be of gold or silver plaited threads.

Bobbin Net.—A kind of Net made by machinery, the stocking frame being adapted to that purpose. The cotton of which it is made is chiefly spun in Lancashire, and the superior kinds are known by the elongation of the meshes near the selvedges. The first attempt to make Net by machinery was in 1770, when a stocking frame was employed, and success attained in 1810. The width of this Net runs from 30 to 72 inches. Quillings are made of it.

Bobbin Quillings.—Plain cotton net, made in various widths, and used for frills. Brussels Quillings are superior in quality, having an extra twist round the mesh.

Bobbins.—The thread that is used in Pillow Lace is wound upon a number of short ivory sticks, called Bobbins, and the making of the lace mainly consists in the proper interlacing of these threads. The Bobbins are always treated in pairs, with the exception of the Gimp Bobbins, and are divided into Working and Passive Bobbins. Hang the number required for the commencement of a pattern upon a lace pin into the top pinhole of the pattern, and unwind the thread from them four inches. Spread out the Passive Bobbins or Hangers in a fan shape, and allow them to fall down the pillow; work the Workers or Runners across these from side to side, alternately. Place no mark upon the Bobbins to distinguish them, as they change too often to allow of it, but number them in the mind from one to eight, &c., as used. Never look at the Bobbins when working, but watch the pattern forming, and use both hands at the same time. Wind the thread upon the Bobbins by holding them in the left hand, and wind with the right; keep the thread smooth, and never fill the Bobbin. When finished winding, secure the thread by holding the Bobbin in the left hand turned upwards, the thread in the right; place the middle finger of the left hand upon the thread, and turn the wrist to bring the thread round the finger; transfer the loop thus formed to the Bobbin by pulling with the right hand

while putting the loop over the head of the Bobbin with the left finger. This keeps the Bobbin from running down, and is called a ROLLING or HALF HITCH. Lengthen by tightening the threads, at the same time gently turning the Bobbin round towards the left, or shorten by lifting the loop with the needle pin, and winding up the Bobbin. When wound, tie the Bobbins in pairs by fastening the ends of the two threads together; cut off the ends of the knot as closely as possible, wind one Bobbin a little way up, and unwind the other in the same degree; this puts the knots out of the way for the commencement. Winding by a machine is preferable to hand-winding when the thread is very white, as the hand is apt to discolour it.

Bobbin Tape.—Made in cotton and in linen, both round and flat; the numbers being 5, 7, 9, 11, 13, 15, 17, 19, and 21. *See* TAPES.

Bobs.—These are used in Pillow and Needle Laces to ornament the connecting Bars between the lace patterns, and are identical with Crescents, Crowns, Spines, and Thorns. To make a Bob: Twist the thread six or seven times round the needle, draw it up tight, and make a loop with it upon the BAR or BRIDE ORNÉE.

Bocasine.—(Old French, *Boccasin*.) A kind of fine buckram or calamanco, made of wool.

Bocking.—A coarse woollen material, resembling baize or drugget, called after the town where it was manufactured.

Bodkin.—(Anglo-Saxon for a dagger; also designated tape needle.) A small metal instrument, combining in appearance a needle and a pin, having a knob at one end to prevent its piercing the hem through which it is passed to convey the ribbon, cord, or tape, and two eyes at the other end—one long, and one near the extremity, small and oval shape. They are sold by the gross or singly.

Body Linings.—These may be had in linen, union, and calico; in white, grey, black on one side, and grey the other; plain and figured materials. They usually measure about 34 inches in width; some plain made, and others with a satin face.

Bolting.—A kind of canvas, so called because made originally for the bolting or sifting of meal and flour. It is a very fine kind of woollen canvas, chiefly made in England, and employed for samplers. There is also an inferior description, of a yellow colour, known as sampler canvas. Bolting is woven after the manner of gauze of finely-spun yarn. It may be had also in silk, linen, and hair.

Bolton Sheeting.—Otherwise *Workhouse sheeting*, or *twill*. A thick coarse twilled cotton, of the colour technically called grey—really yellow, being unbleached; much employed for crewel embroidery, and washing better each time it is cleaned. A suitable material for ladies' and children's dresses and aprons, as well as for curtains and other room hangings. It is to be had in various widths, from 27 to 36 and 72 inches. There are two makes of this material, the plain and the snowflake. It is much employed for purposes of embroidery, and often in combination with Turkey-red twill.

Bombazet.—This is one of the family of textiles denominated Stuffs, or those worsted materials introduced into England by the Dutch settlers in the reign of Henry I. It is a plain, twilled, thin worsted fabric, with a warp of a single thread, pressed and finished without a glaze. The width varies from 21 to 22 inches.

Bombazine.—(Latin, *Bombacinium,* French *Bombasin.*) A combination of silk and worsted, the warp being of the former, and the weft of the latter; formerly made at Norwich and Spitalfields, &c., in various colours, but now chiefly black. A manufacture introduced by the Flemings in 1575, which has no glaze, and is manufactured both plain and twill, of about 18 inches in width. Nearly the same fabric is now sold in different widths, and under various names. It has a twilled appearance, as the worsted weft is thrown on the right side, is easily torn, and ravels out quickly. In the time of Queen Elizabeth it was also made of silk and cotton. Bombazine had its origin at Milan, and was then a twilled textile, so named from *bombyx,* the Latin for silkworm. It was first made of a mixture of cotton and wool at Norwich in 1575.

Bombé (French).—A term signifying puffed or rounded, and employed in dressmaking as well as in embroidery.

Bone-casing.—The covering made for strips of whalebone, designed for the stiffening of dresses and stays.

Bone Point.—The first Pillow Laces made in England in the sixteenth century were all called Bone, by reason of the bobbins being formed from the bones of animals, and sometimes the pins made of fish bones. The word Point is, however, an incorrect term to use for Pillow Laces.

Boning.—A term used by staymakers and dressmakers to signify the insertion of strips of whalebone into stays, or into casings in the bodices of dresses.

Bonnet Cotton.—A coarse kind of thread, consisting of eight to sixteen strands twisted together. Calico bonnets are made with it, and it is employed in upholstery. *See* Sewing Cottons.

Bonnet Wire, or Wire Piping.—A small, pliant wire, covered with silk—black, white, Leghorn, or straw colour, &c.; or with white cotton. The numbers are 2, 3, 4.

Boot Elastics.—This material may be had in silk, thread, cotton, or mohair, small cords of indiarubber being enclosed and woven into the fabric. They are made from 3 to 5 inches in width, and are sold in lengths to suit the purchaser. *See* Elastic Webbing.

Book Muslin, more correctly written buke muslin, is a plain, clear description of muslin. It is either "lawn buke," stiffened to imitate the French clear lawn; or hard, bluish, and much dressed; or else it is soft, in imitation of the Indian buke. It is woven for working in the tambour. *See* Swiss Muslin.

Bordé (French).—Edged with any description of trimming, and *Bordé à Cheval,* a binding of equal depth on both sides of the material.

Borders.—Any description of muslin, net, or lace frillings, whether embroidered or plain, employed for women's caps and bonnets, and the bodice of outer or inner garments, and usually attached to the neck and sleeves.

Borders.—That part of the pattern in lace that forms the rim or outer edge. In Needlepoints this edge is button-holed, and, when raised, called the cordonnet, and profusely trimmed with picots and couronnes. In Pillow Laces it forms part of the pattern, and in the working is ornamented with pinholes.

Botany Wool Cloth.—A fine woollen textile, having a small woven design on the surface like herringbone in appearance. It measures 25 inches in width, and is a new description of material for women's dresses.

Botany Yarn.—A description of worsted yarn employed for the knitting of coarse stockings.

Bourette (otherwise known as "Snowflake" and "Knickerbocker").—A French term employed to signify a method of weaving by which the small loops are thrown up to the face of the cloth. It measures 24 inches in width.

Bourré (French).—Stuffed or wadded. A term frequently applied to quilted articles; also used in embroidery.

Bourre de Soie, Filoselle.—A French term to denote that portion of the ravelled silk thrown on one side in the filature of silk cocoons, and afterwards carded and spun, like cotton or wool. It forms the spun silk of commerce.

Bowline Knot.—Useful for fringes, also for Netting and Knitting, Crochet, and for any work where double threads require joining together securely without raising a rib. To make: Take a loop of one thread, and hold it in the left hand, pick up the other thread in the right hand, pass one end of it under and through the loop, and out at the lower side, then under both the ends held in the left hand, then over them and under its own thread after it comes out of the loop, and before it goes under the threads held in the left hand. Pull tight right and left-hand threads at the same time. For fringes, the right-hand threads are arranged to fall down; for knots or joins, the ends will work in flat.

Bows.—Ornamental loopings of ribbon or other silk, satin, and other material. They are made in several forms, such as the "Alsatian," two large upright ones worn by the peasants as a headdress; the "Marquise," so called after Mme. de Pompadour, made with three loops and two ends, seen on the dresses of that period; the "Butterfly bow," made in imitation of that insect's wings; the well-known "True-lover's knot," "Nœuds flots," a succession of loops so placed as to fall one over the other, like waves, being one of the present modes of trimming dresses. For an ordinary Bow, two loops and two ends, three-quarters of a yard of two-inch ribbon will be found sufficient.

Box Cloths.—These are thick coarse Melton cloths, dyed in all colours, although usually in buff. They are designed for riding habiliments, measure 1½ yard in width, and vary in price.

Box Plait or **Pleat.**—Two Plaits made side by side, reversewise, so that the edges of the respective folds should meet, leaving a broad space of the double thickness between each such conjunction of the Plaits (or Pleats). The name is taken from the box-iron employed for pressing them.

Brabançon Lace.—A name given to Brussels Lace, so called because Brussels is the chief town of South Brabant.

Brabant Edge.—Used in ancient Needle Point and Modern Point. A combination of Brussels and Venetian edge worked alternately.

Braid (Anglo-Saxon *Bredan*).—A woven string, cord, or thread of any kind, employed for binding the edges of materials and articles of wear, or other use and for purposes of decoration.

Braiding.—(From the Saxon *bredon*, to braid or plait together.) Braiding has for many centuries been a form of ornamental needle-work, gold plaits having been found

FIG. 62. PLAIN BRAID UPON CLOTH.

in British barrows, and ornaments of braidwork are seen upon the pictured dresses of the ancient Danes. In the sixteenth century, in Italy, lace was formed of braids made upon pillows, and the Asiatics, Greeks, Turks, and Indians have always used it largely for decorations. Modern Braiding in England is confined to ornamenting dress materials, the simpler kind of antimacassars, and mats with mohair and silk braids; but the natives of India still embroider magnificently with gold and silver and silk braids. Braids, of whatever kind, can be laid upon velvet, leather, cloth, silk, or fancy materials, and are Backstitched to these materials with strong silk or thread. To work: Trace the pattern upon the material or draw it out upon tissue paper, which pull away when the design is worked. Thread a needle with silk and lay the braid upon the traced outlines, and BACKSTITCH it down to the foundation. The beauty of the work depends upon stitching the braid even and keeping the stitching to its centre, turning all corners snarp; either twisting the braid or carefully settling it; and in making the braid lie flat on the material without a pucker.

To prevent the latter fault, fasten one edge of the material to a weight cushion while working. Take both ends of the braid through to the back and fasten off there, as no joins or frayed edges are allowable to the

FIG. 61. FANCY BRAID ON WHITE.

FIG. 63. GOLD BRAID ON CLOTH.

front. Damp the material, and iron at the back, when the work is finished. Figs. 61, 62, and 63 are the ordinary Braiding patterns used in England. The first is worked with a fancy coloured braid on white mar-cella, or other washing ground, and is suitable for children's dress, nightgown cases, comb bags, &c. Fig. 62 is a black plain braid upon cloth, and is suitable for ladies' dresses and jackets. Fig. 63 is a gold braid upon cloth, useful for mats, tea cosies, and other small articles. Fig. 64 is an illustration of Indian Braiding, and is a much more elaborate and beautiful design than is attempted in England. It is entirely executed with gold and silver braid, and is worked upon cloth. This cloth is of different colours, joined as in Appliqué. The outside border is black, also the dark centre line; the rest of the ground is scarlet, except in the centres of the pine-shaped ornaments, which are pale buff and soft green alternately.

Braids.—(Derived from the old English *brede*, and the Anglo-Saxon *bredan*, to braid, bend, weave.) There are twelve or more varieties of Braid. The alpaca, mohair, and worsted Braids, for trimming dresses, may be had in many colours, as well as in black. These are sold in pieces of 36 yards each; also in small knots by the gross, and by the yard. Their numbers run 53, 57, 61, 65, 73, 77, 81, 89, 93, 97, and 101. The black glacé Braids, made of cotton, though pretty when new, are not durable. The numbers are 41, 53, 61, 65, 73, 81, 93, and 101; and there are four pieces of 36 yards each to the gross. Crochet Braids, also called Cordon, are very fully waved, and are used for work-

former being rarely more than 16 or 18 yards in length, instead of 24. Skirt Braids of alpaca and mohair are sold in lengths sufficient for the edge of the dress, and are tied in knots. In the "super" and "extra heavy," the numbers are 29, 41, and 53. The lengths vary from 4 to 5 yards, and are sold by the gross pieces. All black Braids should be shrunk before being put on the dress, by pouring boiling water on them, and hanging them up, to allow the water to drop from them until dry. Hercules Braid is a corded worsted Braid, made for trimming mantles and dresses, the cords running the lengthway, not across. Grecian Braid is a closely woven article, resembling a plait of eleven or thirteen. There are also waved white cotton Braids, used for trimming children's dress, which are sold by the gross, cut into lengths. The numbers are 11, 17, 21, 29, and 33. There are also waved worsted Braids for children's use, which are sold in knots of 4 to 5 yards each, and sold by

FIG. 64. INDIAN BRAIDING IN GOLD.

ing edges with crochet cotton: they are a heavy article. Fancy cotton Braids are made in different colours and patterns, and a chintz Braid in many colours is included amongst them, suitable for cuffs, collars, and children's dresses. There are also thin narrow ones, which are employed in hand-made lace. French cotton Braids, made more especially for infants' clothing, are loosely woven, plain, and fine. The numbers in most request are 13, 15, 17, 19, 21, and 39; but they run from 5 to 77. They are cut into short pieces, and sold by the gross. The mohair, Russia, or worsted Braid is to be had in black and in colours, and consists of two cords woven together. The numbers run from 0 to 8; they are cut into short lengths, and sold by the gross. The wide makes are in lengths of 36 yards each, four pieces to the gross. The Russian silk Braids are of similar make, and are employed for embroidering smoking caps, their colours being particularly bright. They are sold in skeins, six making the gross, the

the gross pieces. The numbers are 13, 17, and 21. White cotton Braids, employed for trimming print dresses, run in the same numbers as the worsted Braids. Gold and silver Braids, employed for uniforms and court and fancy dresses and liveries, &c., form a distinct variety, and are called lace. Every season produces new varieties, either designated by some fashionable name of the current time, or some distinct term connected with their make, such as basket, or mat braid. Church Lace, composed of silk, and sometimes with gold and silver thread, is another make of Braid. The real Cordon Braid is made without any wave, and is edged with picots. Most of the coloured cotton Braids will wash, excepting the pink, but they shrink. The broad are sold cheaper by the dozen yards, or piece of 36 yards; the narrow are sold by the knot. The STAR BRAID (which *see*) is coloured. To every sewing machine a braiding foot is attached, by which narrow Braid can be put on in a pattern. When wide ones are employed they

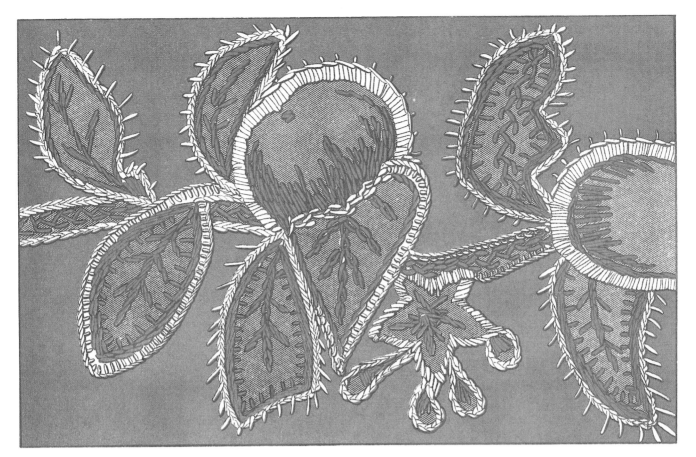

APPLIQUE.—SABRINA.

APPLIQUE.—BADEN.

APPLIQUE ON MUSLIN.

APPLIQUE ON NET.

need very careful tacking, to keep them flat during the process of sewing on. Since the introduction of machine sewing, wide Braids have been more extensively used than ever before.

Braid Work.—The variety of Braids used in Tape Guipures is great, and the manner of forming them is the first step to Pillow Lace making. They form the Engrelures and edgings, and are really the chief stitches in the lace; they are easier understood when learnt as a Braid, where all the various interruptions necessary to form patterns are laid aside, than in the regular patterns, until the stitch has been thoroughly mastered in straight rows.

Cloth or Whole Braid.—Some of the old Guipures are entirely worked with this Braid, the stitch of which resembles weaving. Rule two parallel lines on the PASSEMENT a quarter of an inch apart, and, with a fine needle, pierce an even row of holes on each line, about as wide apart as the width of a coarse needle (the pricking is guided by the coarseness of the thread used); the holes should be opposite each other, and quite even. Take twelve pairs of Bobbins, tie in a knot, put a pin through it, and pin it to the pillow, putting the pin in up to its head. Six of the Bobbins should have a distinguishing mark, and are called RUNNERS; they run from side to side, and answer to the woof of the cloth; the remaining eighteen are called HANGERS, and hang down upon the pillow without moving, and answer to the web. Run a pin into 1st hole of pattern of left hand side of pillow, and wind up all the bobbins to a distance of four inches from the pin to head of bobbin. Take two pairs of the runners, twist each pair three times outside the left hand pin, working with the left hand, and twisting towards the left; leave one pair of runners hanging behind the pin (and name the others 1st and 2nd, the 1st being on left hand),* take up 2nd, and pass it with the left hand over the 1st hanging bobbin towards the right hand; then take up the 1st hanging bobbin in the left hand between the thumb and first finger, and the 2nd hanging bobbin in the right hand between the thumb and first finger, and lift them to the left, so that each passes over one of the running bobbins; then take the 1st running bobbin and lift it to the right over the 2nd hanging bobbin; the two hangers will now be together; leave them resting by the left hand pin, and take up the 2nd runner, and pass it to the right over the 3rd hanger; take up the 3rd and 4th hangers, and pass them with both hands backwards to the left, each over one of the two runners; take the 1st runner and lift it over the 4th hanger to the right, bringing the hangers and runners together again; leave the 3rd and 4th hangers by the side of the 1st and 2nd hangers; take 2nd runner and pass it over the 5th hanger to the right; take the 1st and 2nd hangers in both hands, and pass them backwards, as before, to the left, over the 1st and 2nd runners; take the 1st runner and pass it over the 6th hanger to the right; leave the 5th and 6th hangers next to the 3rd and 4th on the left; take the 2nd runner and pass it over the 7th hanger to the right; take up the 5th and 6th hangers and pass them back to the left over the two runners; take the 1st runner and pass over the 8th

hanger to the right, and leave the 7th and 8th hangers by the 5th and 6th on the left hand; take 2nd runner and pass over 9th hanger to the right; take 9th and 10th hangers and pass backward to the left hand over the two runners; take 1st runner and pass over 10th hanger to the right; take 2nd runner and pass over 11th hanger to the right; take 11th and 12th hangers and pass backwards to the left, over the two runners; take 1st runner and pass over 12th hanger to the right, leave the 11th and 12th hanger by the side of the 9th and 10th; take 2nd runner and pass over 13th hanger to the right; take 13th and 14th hangers and pass backwards to the left, over the two runners; take 1st runner and pass over the 14th hanger to the right, leave 13th and 14th hangers by side of 11th and 12th, on the left side; take 2nd runner and pass over 15th hanger; take 15th and 16th hangers and pass backwards to the left, over the two runners; take 1st runner and pass over 16th hanger to the right, then leave the 15th and 16th hangers on the left, by the side of the 13th and 14th; take 2nd runner and pass over 17th hanger; take the 17th and 18th hangers and pass backwards to the left; take 1st runner and pass over 18th hanger to the right. Having now come to the end of the line, and worked in all the hangers, take the two runners in right hand quite across the pillow, put in a pin opposite to the one which was placed in pattern on left hand side, twist the two runners three times to the right. The 3rd pair of marked runners will now be hanging behind the pin which has just been placed in the pattern, twist these three times towards the left; then take the 2nd runner of the pair just brought across, and pass it to the right over the 1st runner of the pair found behind the right hand pin; take these two runners and pass them back to the left over those runners used in working across; take the 1st runner of those brought across, and pass it over the 1st runner of the new pair. The pair which has been brought across is now left behind the right hand pin, and those found must be twisted three times to the left and worked back the reverse way by taking the 1st hanger and passing it to the right over the 2nd runner; take the two hangers and pass over the 1st and 2nd hangers to the left; take the 2nd hanger and pass over 1st runner; leave 1st and 2nd hangers on the right, and take 4th hanger and pass over 2nd runner to the right; take the two runners and pass over 3rd and 4th hangers to the left; take 4th hanger and pass over 1st runner to the right; leave 3rd and 4th runners on the right, and take 5th hanger and pass over to the 2nd runner to the right; take both the runners and pass over 5th and 6th hangers to the left; take 6th hanger and pass over 1st runner to the right; leave 5th and 6th hangers by the side of 3rd and 4th on the right; take 7th hanger and pass over 2nd runner to the right, and take both the runners and pass over 7th and 8th runners to the left; take 8th hanger and pass over 1st runner to the right; leave 7th and 8th on right by 5th and 6th; take 9th hanger and pass over 2nd runner to left, and take both the runners and pass over 9th and 10th hangers to the left, and take 10th runner and pass over 1st runner to the right; leave 9th and 10th hangers on the right by 7th and 8th; take 13th hanger and pass over 2nd runner to the right; take both runners and pass over 13th and 14th hangers to

G

the left; take 14th hanger and pass over 1st runner to the right; leave 13th and 14th on the right by 11th and 12th; take 15th hanger and pass over 2nd runner to the right; take both runners and pass over 15th and 16th hangers to the left; take 16th hanger and pass over 1st runner to the right; leave 15th and 16th hangers on the right beside 13th and 14th hangers; take 17th hanger and pass over 2nd runner to the right; take both runners and pass over 17th and 18th hangers to the left; take 18th hanger and pass over 1st runner to the right; leave 17th and 18th on the right by the 16th and 17th; take the runners across the pillow, and put up pin in the pattern, Twist three times, and make the same stitch with the pair of runners which are waiting behind the left-hand pin; leave the pair just used in working across, and work back with the pair that has been waiting, commencing from *.

Cucumber Braid.—Rule the PASSEMENT to a quarter of an inch between two parallel lines, as before, and prick twelve pinholes to the inch. Put up six pairs of Bobbins, work two rows of CLOTH STITCH, putting up pins on right and left; divide the bobbins into fours, and begin with the four middle ones; make a Cloth Stitch, and pass the bobbin nearest the right hand over the next bobbin towards the left hand. Take up the right-hand pair of centre bobbins and make a Cloth Stitch, pass the left-hand RUNNER over towards the right-hand runner, make a Cloth Stitch, put in the pin, and TWIST each pair once, make a Cloth Stitch, and leave the right side. Take up the left-hand pair of the four middle bobbins, make a Cloth Stitch with the next pair towards left hand, pass the right-hand runner over the left-hand runner, make a CLOTH STITCH, set up the pin, make

FIG. 65. CUCUMBER BRAID.

a Cloth Stitch, and pass the right-hand bobbin over the left-hand bobbin. Now return to the middle four, and make a Cloth Stitch, pass the 1st right-hand bobbin over the 2nd towards the left-hand side; then pass the 3rd from the right hand over the 4th towards the left: work the right-hand pair back to right pin, as before, and the left-hand pair to the left-hand pin; continue to do this until perfect. *See Fig. 65.*

Cucumber Braid as an Edging with an Inner Pearl Edge.—Hang on the Bobbins in two sets, five pairs and a GIMP for the PLAIN EDGE side, four and a gimp for the

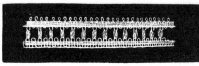

FIG. 66. CUCUMBER BRAID.

PEARL EDGE. Begin at the Plain Edge, work into the middle with CLOTH STITCH, pass the gimp, and make the inside pearl by Twisting the runners six times; stick a pin

into inside hole, and work back (*see* Fig. 66). Return to the middle, TWIST the runners twice, and work the other side the same, but adding the Pearl Edge. Fill the centre with a CUCUMBER PLAITING, then Twist 1st and 2nd runners twice; stick a pin in pillow to hold these threads, Twist 3rd and 4th runners, and work to the edge with them; then return, and take 1st and 2nd runners to other edge. Make Inside Pearl as before, and repeat.

Diamond Hole Braid.—Make a HOLE in centre of braid, then work two CLOTH STITCH rows, make a Hole upon each side, and PLAIT the four bobbins under the upper Hole with Cloth Stitch; work two Cloth Stitch rows, and make a Hole in the centre under the four bobbins which make the Cloth Stitch. Work Holes that go straight across the braid as follows: Begin from the left; having put up a pin in the left hand, bring one pair of bobbins towards the right hand, making a Cloth Stitch with the first pair, leave all four hanging; take the next four bobbins and make a Cloth Stitch; leave these four hanging, and take the next four and repeat; this brings the work up to the right-hand pin. Put up a pin, and work back to the left hand with Cloth Stitch, having thus formed three small holes across the braid.

Half or Shadow, or Lace Braid.—Prick the PASSEMENT as in Cloth Braid, and put up twelve pairs of bobbins. The Runners in this stitch are not brought in pairs across the braid. One goes straight across and the other slanting down the work. Put up six pairs of bobbins; work one row in CLOTH STITCH across from left to right and back again; make a Cloth Stitch, place the pair on one side, and give the running bobbins one TWIST to the left; take the next pair, which is already twisted, pass the centre left-hand bobbin over the centre right-hand bobbin; Twist both pairs once to the left; bring forward the next pair, centre left hand over centre right

FIG 67. HALF OR SHADOW, OR LACE BRAID.

one Twist with both pairs, and continue this to the last pair, when make a Cloth Stitch without Twisting; Twist three times, and put up pin for the PLAIN EDGE; return in the same way, making one Twist after the Cloth Stitch, as, unless the worker does this, and is very careful to bring only one runner across, the work will go wrong. This stitch is not drawn tightly, but a firm pull at the heads of all the bobbins must be occasionally given to keep the threads straight and even, and present a perfect open braid, as shown in Fig. 67.

Hole Braid, or Flemish Stitch.—Prick the PASSEMENT as in Cloth Braid, and put up twelve pairs of bobbins. The holes are always made in the same way, although their arrangement, and the number of bobbins used, can be varied. Work across from left to right in CLOTH STITCH six times, putting up the pins each side in holes pricked for them; then divide the bobbins equally, and put a pin in the centre, having six pairs on each side. Take up left-hand bobbins and work with six pairs in Cloth Stitch, which brings the work to the pin in the centre; then work back to the left, without twisting or putting up a pin, with the same six pairs, TWIST and put up a pin and leave the bobbins. Take up those on the right hand, and work up to the pin in Cloth Stitch, and back without Twist

FIG. 68. HOLE BRAID, OR FLEMISH STITCH.

or pin; put up a pin and work across the whole twelve bobbins to the left hand, and so enclose the centre pin, which thus makes the Hole the Braid is called after. A badly-shaped Hole will disfigure the lace, but a well-made one requires practice and care. To avoid making it too large, do not draw the bobbins tight after dividing them, and keep the hanging bobbin drawn towards the centre pin. *See* illustration (Fig. 68).

Ladder Braid.—Hang on twelve pairs of bobbins, divide the HANGERS in halves, leaving two pairs of RUNNERS on left-hand side of pillow, and one pair of runners on right-hand side. Begin from left-hand side, work in the pin, and work with CLOTH STITCH up to the middle of the hangers; TWIST the pair of runners twice,

FIG. 69. LADDER BRAID.

and work Cloth Stitch up to right-hand hangers; work in the pin on the right, and return to the middle of the hangers; Twist the pair of runners twice, and work Cloth Stitch to the left; repeat from side to side until the stitch is perfect, as shown in Fig. 69.

Lattice Braid.—Hang twelve pairs of bobbins on the pillow. Work in the pin on the right-hand side, and give one TWIST to each pair of bobbins; take the pair of RUNNERS and make a CLOTH STITCH with the 1st pair of HANGERS; then take the bobbin nearest the right-hand pin, and pass it over the bobbin towards the left-hand pin; then pass the 3rd bobbin over the 4th towards the left hand; make a Cloth Stitch with the next pair of hangers,

FIG. 70. LATTICE BRAID.

and pass the right-hand bobbin over the one next to it towards the left-hand pin; then the 3rd over the 4th to the left hand, and continue until the left hand of the Braid is reached. The same pair must work right across, and should be distinguished with a mark. *See* Fig. 70. In this stitch work the bobbins in a slanting direction

instead of taking them straight across. Fig. 71 will show their direction. One side has its pin put in three pins in advance of the other. In Fig. 71, the dots down the side are the pinholes, the square ones between are the finished stitches, the falling lines show the direction of the work. Keep the hangers tight down while working the pair of runners across, which manage by continually pulling the hangers, and pressing down their heads to keep them even, and to prevent the threads rising up when a pin is put in. This stitch is much used for the inside or centre of flowers.

FIG. 71. LATTICE BRAID.

Open Braid.—Hang on twelve pairs of bobbins. Make one row of STEM on each side, and keep the RUNNER bobbins at the inner edge; TWIST each pair twice, make a CLOTH STITCH, stick a pin in the centre hole, Twist twice,

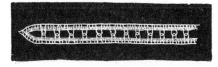

FIG. 72. OPEN BRAID.

and make the stitch about the pin, then Twist three times, and once more work Stem on each side for the space of two holes, and repeat centre stitch, as shown in Fig. 72.

Open Cross Braid.—Fig. 73 may be worked with different numbers of bobbins, but the illustration only requires eight pairs, and the usual size prickings on PASSEMENT. Stick in pin right and left; divide the eight pairs of bobbins into three sets—that is, leave two pairs in the centre, two pairs to the right and the left, one pair behind the left-hand pin, and another pair behind the right-hand pin. Make a CLOTH STITCH with the two

FIG. 73. OPEN CROSS BRAID.

centre pairs, cross the right-hand bobbin nearest the pin over the next bobbin towards the left hand, and cross the 3rd bobbin from the right over the 4th towards the left hand. Make a Cloth Stitch with the left-hand pair of the centre four; cross them as before; make a Cloth Stitch, crossing the pair only with which the Cloth Stitch is to be made; set up pin, cross each once, and make another Cross Stitch, crossing the runner once. Take the four middle bobbins, make a Cloth Stitch, and cross the bobbins as before, once; take up the pair on the right-hand side, and make a Cloth Stitch with the next pair, but crossing the one pair only that is required to set up the pins; having set up the pin, cross both pairs and make a Cloth Stitch; leave them, return to the middle bobbins and make a Cloth Stitch, cross, and return to the left, and so continue, always working from the centre alternately from left to right.

Plain Braid.—Made with eight pairs of bobbins in

FIG. 74. PLAIN BRAID.

CLOTH STITCH and a PLAIN EDGE, as shown in Fig. 74.

Slanting Hole Braid.—Begin from where the holes are to commence, immaterial which side; put in a pin, make a CLOTH STITCH and a half with the first two pairs of bobbins, work back to the pin and leave them; take up the bobbins from the place worked on the opposite side of Braid, put up a pin and work right across, tighten the bobbin with a twitch, and upon reaching the hole return with a Cloth Stitch right across, leave these and begin from opposite side; now work to the second set of four bobbins, make HALF STITCH and return; take up the bobbins as before and work to the opposite side, and return right across and back again; this must be repeated until the Braid is worked right across, taking four more bobbins from the side worked from each side, so that the holes are each time one stitch nearer the opposite side. A dice pattern, as shown in Fig. 75, can be formed by working from both sides of the Braid to form the hole; it requires twelve pairs of bobbins, and, when not formed as a Braid, is either used as open work to other stitches, or for the half of a Stem when the other half is in Cloth Stitch; take the four bobbins on the right hand, and work in the pin, leave them hanging, take the two 1st pair after the pin, TWIST these twice and leave; take the 2nd pair, twist thrice and leave, and continue in the same way up to the last pair on the left-hand side; now return to the right

FIG. 75. SLANTING HOLE BRAID, DICE PATTERN.

hand four behind the pin, work them over to the left side, give the runners a twist twice between each stitch until the pin is worked in, twist the pair in front of the pin twice and leave; twist each pair twice, then take up the left hand bobbin behind the pin, work in the pin, and, twisting the runners twice between each pair of bobbins, work back to the right hand. Fig. 75 illustrates this stitch as a square with Cloth Stitch. The square is begun from pair in the middle of the Braid, and increased each time until it reaches either side, then decreased until it becomes a single pair; the rest of the bobbins are used for Cloth Stitch. In working this Braid, each pair of bobbins must be Twisted the same number of times, so as to make the open work look in small squares. Sometimes the hangers are Twisted four or six times, and the runners only twice. This makes a long stitch, and is chiefly used for the stalks of flowers.

Branching Fibres.—In Honiton and Pillow Laces, where sprigs are formed separately from the ground, the sprigs are often diversified by adding to the chief stems

in the leaves some indication of the fibres that run to right and left. Fig. 76 gives an example of these Branching Fibres on a close worked leaf. In working from this illustration use No. 9 thread. Hang on six pairs of Bobbins, and commence with the stem and work to first fibre, then leave two pairs and work the fibre with four pairs, coming back with RETURN ROPE; continue the main stem, picking up the bobbins that were left, make

FIG. 76. LEAF WITH BRANCHING FIBRES IN CLOSE WORK.

another fibre with four pairs, coming back with Return Rope, do the opposite fibre in the same manner, and continue up the main stem, picking up the left bobbins. Work these double fibres three times, and the stem to the end of the leaf. HALF STITCH fills in the leaf, the tips of the fibres being connected to it as they touch; extra bobbins will be required for this part of the work. *See* HALF STITCH.

Brandenbourgs. — Synonymous with "Frogs." A button formed somewhat in the shape of a long and narrow barrel, smaller at the ends than the middle, and made of silk on a wooden foundation; also, according to Fairholt, "the ornamental facings to the breast of an officer's coat." So termed from the place where the fashion originated.

Brazil Lace.—Consists of two kinds, both probably remnants of the early Italian and Spanish Laces. The lace formed with drawn threads is good, but that made on the pillow has no pretension to beauty, and is only in use among the natives.

Breadth.—(Anglo-Saxon *Braed*, or broad; Old English *Bredth*, or *Bredethe*.) A term employed in drapery and dressmaking to denote an entire piece of textile of any description, measuring from one selvedge to the other. Thus a skirt or an under garment said to contain so many Breadths, means lengths of material running the width way that it was manufactured in the loom.

Bretelles.—A French term to signify an ornamental shoulder-strap.

Breton Lace, Imitation.—A lace made with machine net and lace cotton, in imitation of the Run Laces. To work: Draw out the design upon pink calico, and upon this tack a good open meshed net. Work the outlines

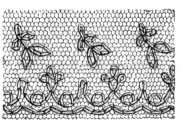

FIG. 77. BRETON LACE.

of design in SATIN STITCH or RUN, and fill in the thicker parts with STEM STITCH and POINT FESTON. To edge this Lace, lay a cord along it and OVER-

CAST it; ornament the cord with PICOTS, or finish it with the edging sold for MODERN POINT LACE. This edging must not be at all heavy, or it will detract

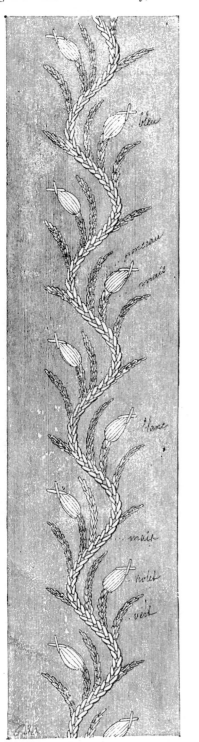

FIG. 78. BRETON WORK—FLOWER PATTERN.

from the light appearance of the Lace; it is frequently only Run with a double line of thread and the net cut straight beyond the running, as shown in Fig. 77, which

is only Breton Lace Run with silk without lace stitches. Breton Lace can be worked in coloured silks or floss, and the foundation made of coloured net, or it may be fabricated of good Brussels net and cream coloured lace thread.

Breton Work.—An ancient Embroidery, long practised in Brittany, and still to be found on the best garments of the peasants. Like most ancient work Chain Stitch forms the chief motif, but Satin Stitch, Point Lancé, Point Russe, &c., can also be introduced. The foundation material is either of cloth or silk, the embroidery in

FIG. 79. BRETON WORK—GEOMETRICAL PATTERN.

coloured silks and gold and silver thread. The work is usually made for borders to garments, and the two illustrations given are for that purpose. To work the flower one (Fig. 78): Trace out the outline upon cloth or silk, and go over every thick line with CHAIN STITCH, and make the buds with POINT LANCÉ and with bright-coloured silks. To work the geometrical pattern (Fig. 79): Trace the design upon cloth, and work it over with SATIN STITCH, POINT DE POIS, POINT RUSSE, and STEM STITCH, with gold and silver thread and coloured silks. Besides these border designs, Breton Work is also used for ornamenting necktie ends, book markers, &c., and then the patterns represent

Breton peasants. Draw these to size upon paper, and transfer to silk ribbon. Cut the faces of the figures out of cream silk or sticking plaister, and ink in the features, work them in Satin Stitch, as likewise the hands and legs; work the drapery in Chain Stitch. The costume of Breton women varies as to colour, but consists of a dark skirt or petticoat, with bright overskirt, white or black apron, embroidered with colour, dark body, with yellow, green, or scarlet handkerchief pinned across it, wide, but not high cap, with flapping sides, heavy gold earrings, chain and cross, sabots large and heavy, either of pale brown or black. Breton man—wide flapping black hat, short black jacket and breeches, ornamented with gold buttons and braid, bright waistcoat, white shirt, grey stockings, black sabots, and blue umbrella. The work is also known as Brittany embroidery.

Brick Stitch.—Used in Embroidery, but chiefly for Ecclesiastical work; a variety of Couching, and made with floss silk, Dacca silk, purse silk, or gold or silver

FIG. 80. BRICK STITCH.

thread. The name is derived from the appearance of the stitches, representing regular courses of brickwork, as in Fig. 80. *See* COUCHING.

Bridal Lace.—A Reticella, or Drawn Lace, fabricated during the sixteenth and commencement of the seventeenth centuries, in Italy. The peculiarity of this lace was that it was made for weddings, and the patterns were the coats of arms and other distinctive badges of the families about to be united.

Brides.—*See* BARS.

Brides Claires.—*See* BARS.

Brides Ornées.—These are Bars ornamented with Picots, Pin Works, Half Wheels, and used to connect

FIG. 81. BRIDE ORNÉE.

together the heavier portions of Needle-made Laces. These Brides Ornées can be made of any shape according to the spaces that require filling and the fancy of the worker.

FIG. 82. BRIDE ORNÉE.

The illustrations (Figs. 81, 82, and 83) are some of the most effective. To work: Make the Bars of BUTTON-

HOLES, and for the Picots wind the thread while making a Buttonhole eight times round the needle, and then draw it up tight; for the COURONNES make a loop from one part of the Bar to the other, and return the thread to the point started from; cover this loop with Button-

FIG. 83. BRIDE ORNÉE.

hole, and make Picots upon it where indicated in the pattern. *See* COURONNES and PICOTS.

Brighton Towelling Embroidery. — Modern work upon honeycomb, linen, or Java canvas, and upon

FIG. 84.

FIG. 85.    FIG. 86.

BRIGHTON TOWELLING. (DESIGNS FOR PANAMA CANVAS.)

such washing materials as are woven so that the threads cross each other at equal distances, and are coarse enough to be counted. Any fancy stitches can be embroidered, the square threads of the material being counted and used to keep the designs apart and even in size. To work: RUN lines in squares over the canvas, and fill in these squares with crosses or devices, as shown. Work Fig. 84 with darne lines only For Fig. 85 work a diamond with BACKSTITCHING and fill that in with DOTS. For Fig. 86 work another diamond pattern, cover the outside with DOTS, and fill in with SATIN STITCH. Form borders with DRAWN THREADS, and make fringes of the material by drawing out all the threads one way of the material together, and knotting together or BUTTONHOLING those left, to prevent the work fraying.

Brilliante Lace Work.—A manner of colouring and ornamenting black lace used as edgings to small tea tables, mantel borders, &c. The foundation is broad and coarse Yak lace, and this is ornamented with stitches made in coloured filoselles, and with black bugles. To work: Select a piece of Yak lace with a star, rose, or some decided pattern; tack this to a brown paper foundation. Stitch coloured beads, or small black beads, to the centre part of a flower, or ornament, and work in coloured filoselles, either in CREWEL STITCH, or RUN-NINGS, round all the outlines of the pattern. Make rosettes, crosses, and little devices on the lace with different coloured silks, and finish off the outer edges of both sides of the lace with BUTTONHOLE. Remove the lace from the paper back, and sew it on to crimson or blue cloth as a background to it.

Brilliantines.—Dress fabrics composed of mohair or goats' wool. They are to be had in all colours, and are called by various names, according to the fancy of the several firms producing or selling them. They are very silky looking, and are equally durable and light.

Brilliants.—Muslins with glazed face, and figured, lined, or crossbarred designs.

Brioche Stitch.—*See* KNITTING.

British Point Lace.—A Thread Lace, formerly made in and near London. Black Lace is the only variety now made, and that in very small quantities.

British Raised Work.—This is also known by the name of Cut Canvas Work, and is worked upon leviathan canvas with four-thread fleecy wool, and the wool cut and combed, giving it the appearance of velvet pile. To work: Trace the pattern with black wool and in CROSS STITCH Take a skein of wool, fold it three times, and cut; again fold each thread three times and cut, then tie once in the centre with fine string, whose ends pass through the canvas and firmly secure. When these tufts are thus made fast to the canvas, comb them out. The success of the work consists in completely filling up the canvas with tufts and in arranging them in pretty coloured patterns. British Raised Work differs but little from LEVIATHAN RAISED WORK.

Brittany Embroidery.—*See* BRETON WORK.

Broadcloths.—So called because exceeding 29 inches in width. The stoutest and best descriptions of woollen cloths. These, of course, vary in quality, and are termed superfine, second, and inferior. Broadcloth is seven quarters in width, NARROW CLOTHS being of half the width named. All our superfine cloths are made of either Saxon or Spanish wool, an inferior kind of superfine being manufactured from English wool, as well as the seconds, of which liveries are made, and all the coarser kinds of various quality and price. The texture should

not only be judged of by the fineness of the threads, but by the evenness in the felting, so that when the hand is passed over the surface against the lie of the nap there should be a silkiness of feeling, uninterrupted by roughness in any part. To judge of the quality, a considerable portion should be taken into the two hands, a fold pressed strongly between the thumb and forefinger of one hand, and a sudden pull given with the other, and according to the peculiar clearness and sharpness of the sound, produced by the escape of the fold, the goodness of the cloth may be judged. There should not be a very satin-like gloss upon it, or it would be spotted by rain. Broadcloths, single milled, run from 52 to 63 inches, in wool-dyed woaded colours (blue, black, medleys, Oxford, and other mixtures). In wool-dyed common colour and unwoaded there are black, medleys, Oxford, and other colours. Piece-dyed woaded colours are in black, blue, and fancy colours; and the piece-dyed unwoaded are in black, scarlet, gentian, and other colours, double milled, which run from 52 to 57 inches; medium cloths, from 54 to 63 inches; ladies' cloths, 54 to 63 inches (otherwise called habit cloths), which are of a light and thin make; Venetians, 54 to 58 inches; army cloth, 52 to 54 inches; beavers, pilots, mohair, 54 to 58 inches; cloakings, 54 to 58 inches; weeds (single, double, and treble milled), China striped cloths, piece-dyed, &c., 60 inches wide; India cloths, piece-dyed, 72 to 81 inches; elastic glove cloth, 54 to 70 inches; union cloths, cotton warps, piece-dyed, 52 to 54 inches wide; double colours, piece-dyed, 54 to 63 inches. *See* NARROW CLOTHS.

Broad Couching.—A variety of Couching. Floss silk, Dacca silk, sewing silk, purse silk, gold and silver cord, used for the laid lines, and purse silk of different shades of colour for the securing. The stitch is the same as Couching, and is illustrated in Fig. 87. *See* COUCHING.

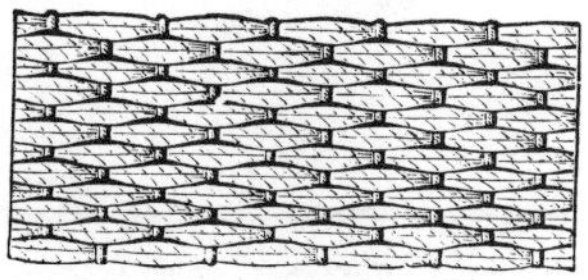

FIG. 87. BROAD COUCHING.

Brocade.—(Derived from the Latin *Brocare*, and French *Brocher*, to figure, prick, emboss, and stitch textiles.) In the present day all silk or stuff materials woven with a device are said to be brocaded; but in olden times this term was applied to a costly silken fabric of stout make, having an embossed design woven in it in gold or silver threads, and sometimes enriched with gems and otherwise. It is named in the inventory of the wardrobe of Charles II., where the price is given of different examples; the "white and gold brocade at two pounds three and sixpence per yard, and *Colure du Prince* at two pounds three shillings per yard." Chinese and Indian Brocade have been famous from very remote times. The richest varieties have been made in Italy, and there was a considerable manufactory of them at Lucca in the thirteenth century.

Brocade Embroidery.—Modern work, consisting in covering over or outlining the various flower or geometrical designs woven into brocaded materials. These patterns are outlined in Stem or Crewel Stitch, or a double piece of wool or silk cord is Couched along the chief edges of the design, as shown in illustration, Fig. 88. Greater effect may, however, be obtained by covering over the whole of the brocaded design, and leaving only the foundation material visible; when so treated Long or Satin Stitch is used, as in Satin Stitch Embroidery, for filling in the centres of the design, and gold or silver thread, or purse silk, to outline. Where the design is good and the colours judiciously blended, the work is mediæval in appearance. The brocades are of silk or stuff; the embroidery in crewel wools, floss silk, purse silk, and gold and silver thread. To work, as shown in Fig. 88: take a thick strand of wool or silk and lay it down, following the outline of the design. Couch this

Broché.—A French term denoting a velvet or silk textile, with a satin figure thrown up on the face.

Broder and Broderie.—French terms for embroidery.

Broderie Anglaise.—An open embroidery upon white linen or cambric, differing from Madeira work in being easier to execute, but of the same kind. True Broderie Anglaise patterns are outlines of various sized holes, arranged to make floral or geometrical devices. To work: Run embroidery cotton round the outlines, then pierce the holes with a stiletto, or cut with scissors and turn the edges under and Sew over with embroidery cotton. The art in the work consists in cutting and making all the holes that should be the same size to match, and in taking the Sewing over stitches closely and regularly, as shown in

FIG. 88. BROCADE EMBROIDERY.

strand to the material with small stitches made with purse silk, and put in at regular intervals. Work the stitches in the centre of the pattern with SATIN STITCH.

Brocat.—A variety of brocade of rich quality, composed of silk interwoven with threads of gold and silver.

Brocatelle.—A French term for linsey-woolsey. A silk material used for drapery, the linings of carriages, &c. It is also made of silk and cotton mixed, or of cotton only, after the manner of brocade.

Brocatine.—A term employed to signify broché; that is, a method of weaving by which a raised pattern is produced. Thus, there are silk Brocatines and woollen Brocatines, or textiles having a raised design thrown up in the weaving.

Fig. 90, on opposite page. When used as an edging, a

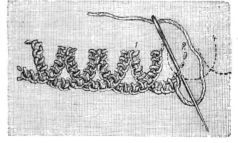

FIG. 89. BRODERIE ANGLAISE, SCALLOPED EDGE.

scalloped or vandyked border is worked in BUTTONHOLE

BERLIN CANVAS AND STITCHES.

STITCH, as shown in Fig. 89, the outer lines of the border being run in the same manner as the holes, and the centre frequently padded with strands of embroidery cotton. Do not cut away the waste linen outside the Buttonhole until the work has been once washed, as it will then wear longer, and there is less fear of cutting the embroidery cotton in the process. When Broderie Anglaise is used for an insertion, it requires no edging. The work is adapted for trimming washing dresses or underlinen.

Broderie de Malines.—A name given, in olden times, to Mechlin Lace, originating in the look of embroidery and draw the braid together at the edges to make them flat, as in MODERN POINT LACE. For thick portions of the work the stitches are in ESCALIER or close BUTTON-HOLE, while lighter parts require POINT DE BRUXELLES or POINT DE VENISE. BARS connect the braids together, as in real lace, when there is no filled pattern to be worked, while a twisted stitch, like POINT D'ALENÇON, fills up narrow spaces where greater lightness than that given by bars is required.

Broderie Perse.—*See* APPLIQUÉ.

Broderie Suisse.—*See* APPLIQUÉ.

FIG. 90. BRODERIE ANGLAISE.

given to the lace by the peculiar thread that was worked in it, and that surrounded all the outside of the pattern.

Broderie de Nancy.—Identical with DRAWN WORK and PUNTO TIRATO. *See* DRAWN WORK.

Broderie en Lacet.—An Embroidery upon satin with Silk Braid and Point Lace Stitches, useful for mantelpiece and table borders, &c. To work: Draw the pattern upon the satin, and stitch the braid on to the lines, a thread of silk drawn from the braid being the best to use for sewing it down, as it matches exactly. Wherever the braid ends or commences, draw the ends to the back of the satin, so that no joins show in front of the work. Fill in the rounds and centres made by the braid with POINT LACE STITCHES,

Broken Bobbins.—In Pillow Laces, when the runners or workers are broken, and require replacing, tie the new bobbins in close behind the pin nearest the runners, and work them into the lace before the knot joining them is cut close. Twist up broken hangers or passive bobbins behind the pin, and there tie.

Brown Holland.—A kind of linen, so called because it is only half or altogether unbleached, and also because the manufacture was at one time peculiar to Holland. The half-bleached kinds are sized and glazed. There are also Hollands in black and in slate colour, and there is a light make of the unbleached brown called Sussex lawn, much used for women's dress. The glazed are

H

employed for lining trunks and covering furniture. All linen textiles were anciently called Holland in England, as we learned the manufacture from that country, which was in advance of our people in the art. *See* LINEN.

Bruges Lace.—The Lace made at Bruges is of two kinds, one similar to Valenciennes, and the other called Guipure de Bruges. The former was not considered of much value, the Réseau ground being a round mesh, the bobbins of which were only twisted twice. The Guipure de Bruges is a species of Honiton Lace, with the sprig united with Brides Ornées. It is held in high esteem.

Brussels Dot Lace.—*See* BRUSSELS LACE.

Brussels Edge.—This stitch is used to ornament the Headings or Footings of Needle Laces, and also in Modern

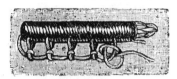

FIG. 91. BRUSSELS EDGE.

Point lace. Make it of a series of loose BUTTONHOLES, secured with a POINT DE BRUXELLES STITCH, as shown in Fig. 91.

Brussels Grounds.—In modern Brussels Lace the net ground is made by machinery, but in olden times this was worked by the hand, either for the Pillow or Needle Lace. The Needle Lace Grounds were of two kinds —the Bride and the Réseau. The Bride is formed of the connecting threads already described in Bars; the Réseau is a series of honeycomb-shaped hexagonals formed with the needle, or upon the pillow, with the pattern of the lace, the manner of working which is shown in Fig. 92, and which is used for most of the net grounds of old Needle Lace. The fine flax used for these Needle-made

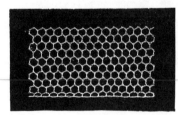

FIG. 92. BRUSSELS GROUND RÉSEAU.

Grounds often cost £240 per lb., and this rendered the lace very expensive. It required to be spun in a dark underground cellar, as air and light caused it to split, and the worker was obliged to feel, not see, the threads in the course of making. This fine flax is not used in machine net, a Scotch cotton thread being substituted, which renders the lace much cheaper, but not so durable. The Needle-made Ground is more expensive than the Pillow, as it takes four times longer to execute. The Pillow Réseau, introduced early in the eighteenth century, is called AU FUSEAU, and is made in narrow

strips upon the parchment pattern, and united together by an invisible stitch, known as RACCROC. This stitch requires a magnifying glass to detect it. The Au Fuseau most used is a Mechlin ground, and is made upon a parchment pattern, being a six-sided mesh, with pins inserted into the pattern at set distances, to form even meshes; round these pins the worker turns and twists the threads, over and round each other, until the desired mesh is formed, two sides of which are plaited and four twisted. The threads for Brussels Grounds are four in number, and the worker carries the line of mesh from side to side in a perpendicular line. Rosette and star grounds were also made like those used in Valenciennes and Normandy Laces; and, indeed, for variety of pattern and beauty of execution in ground work, Brussels Lace has no rival. *See* RÉSEAU. The Brussels wire ground is formed with silk, and is a partly arched, partly straight mesh; the pattern is worked with the needle separately.

Brussels Net.—Of this textile there are two kinds— BRUSSELS GROUND and BRUSSELS WIRE. The former is made of the finest flax, having a hexagonal mesh, four threads being twisted and plaited to a perpendicular line of mesh; the latter of silk, the mesh partly straight and partly arched. It is sold by the yard for women's evening dresses and other articles of wear, being double width, and the best description of net that is made.

Brussels Point, Imitation.—A lace formed with braid laid on net and ornamented with lace and darning stitches. The work is much easier of execution than most imitation laces, cleans well, and the worker has ample scope for taste from the number and variety of stitches with which the net can be adorned. The materials are: best cream-coloured net of a clear honeycomb, cream-coloured braids of various kinds, the usual lace thread, also cream-coloured lace edging. The different braids

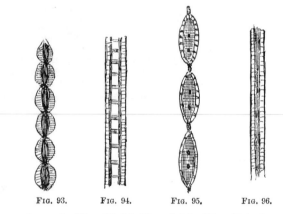

FIG. 93.   FIG. 94.   FIG. 95.   FIG. 96.

are shown in Figs. 93, 94, 95, and 96. Fig. 96 is foundation braid, and the one most used; Fig. 94 a variety of the same, generally put as the Engrelure; Fig. 93 for small flowers, Fig. 95 for larger. A variety of Fig. 95 is shown as forming the flowers in Fig. 97. The manner of working is as follows: Trace the pattern of the lace on pink calico, and back with brown paper. Take Fig. 97 as pattern (which is intended for a flounce, and reduced to half-size). Tack on to the pattern a straight piece of well-opened net, run on the top braid, and the braid forming the scallops, which narrow where so required by turning it under itself. Then tack on the braid that forms the heading. None of these braids are more than tacked to their places, and their ends are not cut, but rolled up, so that the flounce can be finished without joins. Cut the fancy braid (Fig. 95) where it narrows, and tack the pieces singly on to form the flowers. Now secure these braids, the single sprays first, by OVERCASTING their edges on to the net. Where cut at the points BUTTONHOLE them down, but only enough to prevent them from unravelling and to give a pointed finish. Give a little turn of the thread round one honeycomb of the net beyond their other points, to make them look light. After they are secure, DARN the thread in and out of the net to form stalks and tendrils, and make the DOTS that finish the work by Buttonholing round one honeycomb for the larger ones, and by thick

neater to sew it on after the lace has been unpicked from the pattern, but more difficult than when the lace is still in position.

Brussels Point Lace.—This name is given as a general term, with that of Brabant Laçe, Point d'Angleterre, and Point de Flandre, to the laces made at Brussels, classing together the Needle and the Pillow made Laces. Brussels is equally celebrated for her Needle and Pillow Laces, and for centuries has maintained without rivalry the highest position in lace making. Her Needle Laces are known as Point d'Aiguille, Point d'Angleterre, and Point Gaze, and her Pillows as Point Plat. The manufacture of these kinds of lace is carried on to the present time. The making of Brussels Lace seems to have commenced in the fifteenth century, when laces in imitation of Spanish and Venetian Point were made, as well as Genoese Guipures, and to have been upheld in the country through all its wars and persecutions during the following

FIG. 97. BRUSSELS IMITATION LACE.

Overcasting for the smaller ones. Then Overcast all the remaining braids, taking the stitches in their outer edges. Fill the interior of the scallops with fancy darning stitches, Buttonholed Spots, and lace Wheels. The darned stitches are easily made by taking advantage of the honeycomb of the net, and present a good field for the display of individual taste. Thus, the thread may be run across the net with an occasional loop round a honeycomb, or down it as a HERRINGBONE, or transverse, ending as a Spot, or a combination of lines, Herringbone, and Spots made. The lace stitches should be simple POINT DE BRUXELLES, POINT D'ALENÇON, and POINT D'ANGLETERRE, and should be worked adhering to the net. The little spots over the surface of the net work simply over and over until a sufficiently thick knob is made. They are a great help to the lace, and should never be omitted. The pearled edge is Overcast on the scallops when the rest of the work is finished; it is

three centuries. The Pillow Laces were manufactured under the supervision of the nuns, and were largely used as Bone laces on the Continent by those lace wearers who could not afford to purchase the more expensive Needle Lace. The Needle Lace, or Point d'Aiguille, made in Brussels during the sixteenth and seventeenth centuries, was so much imported into England, that in 1665 the native laces were protected by an Act of Parliament, and from that date Brussels lace was known as Point d'Angleterre, being smuggled to England and sold under that name, by which it was called in a few years' time all over the Continent. The earliest Point à l'Aiguille patterns were taken from the ancient Point de Venise, and were made like the earliest Alençon and Argentan Laces, with Raised Work, and a thick Cordonnet, except their grounds, which were simple open buttonholes, known as Point de Bruxelles, neither with Brides or net patterned meshes. The flowers of the patterns were fine, and the Fillings open, without many picots' all that were used being made on the Cordonnet. The net-patterned Réseau ground succeeded the earlier lace, and the patterns, like those of Alençon, followed the fashion of the age, changing from Renaissance to Rococo, and from that to dotted; in fact, they degenerated from their old beauty, although the workmanship was as excellent as ever. The illustration (Fig. 98) is of a Brussels needle point of the earliest part of the present century, and is taken from a piece formerly in possession of Queen Charlotte. The patterns of the lace have much improved of late years, and the kind that is worked with the Vrai Réseau ground is the most valuable lace that

together, as in Fig. 99; the grounds were made in narrow strips upon the pillow, joined together with the invisible Raccroc Stitch, and the sprigs finally attached; but, at the present day, the ground is machine-made net, and the sprigs only of real lace. Many specimens of Brussels Lace display flowers made both with the needle and on the pillow mingled together; and these patterns are remarkably good. The making of Brussels Lace, like that of Alençon, is not confined to a single worker, but many hands are engaged in forming one piece, a plan originally adopted to hasten the execution of the numerous orders for the work. With the pattern the real workers have no concern; their pieces are distinct, and are put together

FIG. 98. BRUSSELS NEEDLE POINT LACE.

can be obtained. The flowers are first made and the ground worked from one to the other, as in illustration, Fig. 3, page 3. The best lace is made at Binche and Brussels, although other towns also manufacture it, and one reason of its great cost is the fine flax thread, which is grown in Brabant, and spun by hand. The use of this thread for the grounds of Brussels Lace is now confined to orders for royal weddings, &c., and the ordinary Brussels Lace is made of sprigs which are laid upon machine net made of Scotch thread. The Brussels Pillow Lace, though not so good as that made with the needle, was more used on the continent, and a greater article of commerce than the Needle Lace. Pillow Lace was formerly made in one piece, flowers and ground

by the head of the establishment: thus the platteuse makes the pillow flowers, the pointeuse the needle-made ones, the drocheleuse the Vrai Réseau ground, the formeuse the open stitches, the dentelière the footings, the attacheuse unites the portions of lace together, and the striqueuse attaches the sprigs to the machine net. These machine nets have made a vast difference in the trade at Brussels, and with the exception of the modern Point Gaze, the lace makers now limit their work to the making of the needle or pillow flowers. Real Brussels Lace, with the Vrai Réseau, costs in England 42s. the yard, 2½ inches wide; the same, with machine ground, 2s. 6d. the yard. Point Gaze, the modern Brussels Lace, so called from its needle ground or Fond Gaze, which is an open gauze-like mesh, is made in small pieces, like the other Brussels Laces, the ground and flowers at one time, and the joins carefully arranged so as to be hidden by the pattern. The Cordonnet is not a Button-holed edging, but is a thread caught round by others.

mentioned by old writers. It received the first prize for Bone Laces in 1752. The Baby Lace before mentioned was chiefly made in Buckinghamshire, though it was not unknown in Bedfordshire. The grounds were the Réseau, net-patterned and wire, the design shown in Fig. 100

FIG. 99. BRUSSELS PILLOW LACE.

The stitches are varied and raised in some parts. It requires three people to make it—one to make the flowers and ground, another the fancy stitches, and the third the Cordonnet. The habit of whitening the Brussels Lace sprigs, after they are made, with a preparation of white lead, is most injurious, causing the lace to turn black when

being called Buckinghamshire Trolly, from the outline of the pattern being accented with a thick thread, known as trolly by the workers. The finer Réseau grounds have now been displaced by plaited Maltese patterns in black lace. These are the flat Maltese patterns, and are not raised like the black lace produced

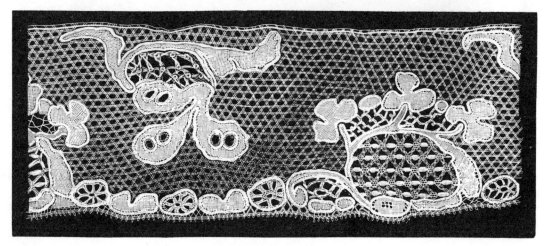

FIG. 100. BUCKINGHAM TROLLY.

put away near flannel or woollen materials, and producing a disease among the striqueuses.

Buckinghamshire Lace.—This is of the same date as Bedfordshire Lace, and shared with it the name of English Lille during the seventeenth and eighteenth centuries. The lace produced in Buckinghamshire was considered superior to that of Bedford, and was more

in Bedfordshire, the stitches being similar to those used in Honiton Lace. The industry is reviving, and some good specimens of modern Buckinghamshire were exhibited in 1884, at the Health Exhibition.

Buckle Braid.—*See* BRAIDS.

Buckle Stitch.—This stitch is used in Honiton and other Pillow Laces as an open braid, for open fibres down the leaves of sprays, or for stems. It requires eight pairs of bobbins—four workers or RUNNERS, and four passive or HANGERS, but the number of the latter can be increased according to the width required. To work: First row, work from left to right into the middle across the two pairs of hangers, TWIST the runners once, and also the next pair (which will now become the fourth working pair); make a CLOTH STITCH, Twist both pairs once, continue across to other side with the first workers, make the edge stitch, and bring them back into the middle, Twist once, and leave them. Take up fourth runners, work to the left edge, back into the middle, Twist once. Two pairs of runners will now be in the middle and both twisted; make a stitch with these pairs, Twist once then work with each of these to the edges, and back

luggage, and is called ticket-buckram. It was originally as costly as the richest silks, and in Louis XV.'s time was used for stays.

Buckskin.—A kerseymere cloth of very fine texture, embroidered with silk by children. It is remarkably beautiful, is designed for waistcoatings, and is manufactured at Bradford, Yorkshire. *See* KERSEYMERE.

Buckskin Cloth.—A species of closely-woven woollen cloth, designed to supply the place of buckskin leather, and of a cream-white colour. It is preferred to corded cloth for riding, being fine, smooth, thick, and firm in its texture, and measures 27 inches in width.

Buckskin Leather.—This leather is dressed with oil, after the method of chamois leather, and is employed for

FIG. 101. BUCKLE STITCH, CONVOLVULUS SPRAY.

into the middle. In the illustration of the convolvulus spray (Fig. 101), BUCKLE STITCH is shown as a braid to the flower, as stems to the leaves, and as open fibre down the centre of the leaves.

Buckram.—(Latin *Buchiranus*, French *Bouracan* or *Barracan*.) This textile was originally manufactured at Bokkara, in the Middle Ages, and was also called *Panus Tartaricus*, and afterwards *Bokeram*. It was then a fine and costly stuff, and much esteemed. The material now known as Buckram is a coarse linen or cotton cloth, stiffened with glue. It is strong, though loosely woven, and is used for the making of bonnet shapes. A variety of it is placed by tailors between the cloth and the lining of a garment in which some degree of stiffness is required. It is made both in white and black, and is sold in lengths of 10 or 12 yards. Buckram, with a highly-sized paper face, is employed for making labels for

the use of cavalry soldiers. It was substituted for woollen cloth by the selection of the Duke of Wellington, with the exception of the two regiments of Life Guards. The greater part of the deerskins employed are imported from the United States of America.

Budge.—(Old English). Lambskin, with the wool dressed outwards. Formerly used as an edging and decoration, more especially for scholastic habits. It is still employed as a trimming on the City liveries. Budge-row was so named after this fur, as the dressers of it used to reside there. It is mentioned by Chaucer, and also by Milton—

> " Oh, foolishness of men, that lend their ears
>   To those *budge* doctors of the Stoic fur! "

Buff Leather.—This is a preparation of the skin of the buffalo, so named from its colour. It is durable and strong, and is employed for military accoutrements and uniforms. In earlier times, it was used to supply the place of armour. Imitations are made of the skins of oxen.

Bugles.—(Latin, *Bugulus.*) An ornament worn by women, consisting of an elongated glass bead, sold in various colours, but chiefly in black, and much used for trimmings of bonnets, mantles, and dresses.

Buke Muslin.—*See* BOOK MUSLIN.

Bulgare Pleat.—A double box pleat, employed at the back of a dress skirt at the waistband, to produce an extra fulness.

Bulgarian Needlework.—A description of oriental needlework executed in Constantinople by the refugees from Bulgaria. The material upon which the embroidery is executed is worked in hand looms by the workers, and resembles coarse unstiffened black or white muslin. The embroidery is especially beautiful, being firm, compact, and even, and is the same on both sides. It is made with gold or silver thread and silks of different colours; both threads and silks are much finer in texture than those used in England, and are capable of being passed in and out of the work without raising the pattern from the muslin foundation. The stitches used are not named in England; the one most employed is a rem line worked over with a line of stitching, while lines of gold or silver thread are made by Overcasting in a slanting direction, and leaving no space between each stitch. The value of the work is judged, by the Bulgarians, by the amount of gold thread employed in each pattern, and very little attention is paid to the labour of the execution and the time spent over bringing it to perfection. The designs, before the Countess Dufferin took the work under her protection, were of no particular art value; but since a committee has been formed to help and encourage the development of the trade, good arabesques and oriental patterns are worked, and the result is much superior in execution and colouring to the ordinary oriental embroidery.

Bullion Embroidery.—As ancient as Embroidery with gold thread, and dates back to the time of the Phrygians. By early writers it is called embroidery with gold wire, and as such mentioned as being used about Aaron's garments. It was known to the Egyptians, Hebrews, and Romans in very early times, and by them embroidery, when wrought in solid gold wire or gold thread, was distinguished by the name of "Auriphrygium," even as embroidery with silk was called Phrygio or Phrygian work, from the first workers. From Auriphrygium the old English word "Orphrey" is derived. Much of the celebrated Opus Anglicanum of the eleventh and following centuries was ornamented with bullion work. It is now but sparingly used in ecclesiastical embroidery for monograms and work in relief, and is chiefly employed for ornamenting uniforms or for heraldic devices. The work is difficult of execution; the twisted gold wire being so formed that it will pull out to any length, and has therefore to be laid on with the greatest exactitude so as to fit the place it has to fill without being unduly drawn out or pressed together. The patterns are the same as used in ordinary ecclesiastical embroidery, and the bullion is laid on for stems, works in relief, and

letters. To work : For raised work and letters, cut a cardboard foundation to the design, and lay this over the holland backing; upon this sew down a stuffing of yellow carpet threads, and lay the bullion over all. The work is done in a frame and APPLIQUÉ to the proper foundation. First cut the lengths of bullion to their various sizes with a sharp pair of nail scissors, and lay them upon an extra piece of cloth, and place on the frame for the worker to select from; when required, pick them up with the needle without touching them with the hand. Use Walker's needle No. 9, and strong yellow sewing silk, waxed and doubled, for working with. Bring the sewing thread through from the back of the linen foundation, pick up the bullion and run it down like a bugle, and pass the needle through the linen on the opposite side to where it came out, leaving the bullion upon the raised surface. The hand, while working, keeps a strong and even hold of the silk, firmly drawing it through and laying down each twist of bullion side by side, regulating its position with the flat end of the piercer, but never touching it. The bullion is always better cut a little longer than required, so as to lay down without dragging over the raised surface, and so that it may completely cover the sides. The five sorts of bullion (rough, check, pearl, wire, and smooth) are often worked in together, and make a species of diaper pattern, with judicious intermixture. The check is all glitter, and should therefore be used with greater caution than the others, one line of check to three of rough being the right proportions. Bullion embroidery, when used for letters and large pieces, is applied to the material, as in APPLIQUÉ; but when worked upon a piece of silk embroidery that has already to be applied, it can be worked in the frame with it.

Bullion Knot.—Useful in Crewel and Silk embroideries, and largely employed in ancient embroideries for the foliage of trees and shrubs, and the hair of figures. It is made of a number of rings of silk or crewel, obtained by being rolled round the working needle, and this roll laid flat along the surface of the work, instead of being raised up and knotted together, as in French Knot. To make : Put the needle into the material where one end of the Bullion Knot is to come, and bring the point out at the other end, and round this point wind the silk and the wool ten or twelve times (according to the space to be covered) and then carefully draw the needle through, while keeping straight the knots or rolls upon it, by holding them down with the left thumb. Still holding down the rolls, insert the needle into the other end of the space where it was first put through, and gently pull the thread until the knots lie all along the intervening space as a long roll. A quantity of these long rolls laid together, and of various lengths, form a variety in the trees in ancient landscape embroideries with French Knots.

Bullion Lace.—A Lace made of gold and silver thread, and of great antiquity, the earliest laces being made of gold threads. The patterns are simple, and like Greek and Maltese Laces. It is much used in the East for ornamenting robes of state, and is found in Italian and French churches upon the priests' vestments and saints' robes. In England, owing to the climate, it is rarely seen. An inferior Bullion Lace is used for footmen's clothes, although such was the extravagance of the ancient nobility, that in the time of Queen Anne the most expensive kind was employed for this purpose.

Bullion Lace or Braid (Latin *Bullio*, a mass of gold or silver; old English *Bullyon*).—Officers' epaulettes are made of a large gold wire, which is called "bullion," a smaller kind is called "frisure," a flat gold ribbon is called "cliquant," and all are classed under the name of "cannetille."

Bundle, or Romal, Handkerchiefs.—These are made in dark blue plaids, in both cotton and linen. The former measure 34 inches by 39; the latter 37 inches by 41.

Bunting (German *Bunt*, *i.e.*, variegated, streaked, or of different colours).—A thin open-made kind of worsted stuff, employed for flags, and, of late years, for women's dresses. The width runs from 18 to 36 inches.

Burano Lace.—In this island a considerable quantity of lace was manufactured during the eighteenth century, and the art lingered in the nunneries until 1845. Within a few years the making of lace in Burano has revived, but the new patterns are not as delicate as the old ones. Burano Lace was a hand-made Venetian Point, with a Réseau and not Bride ground; it resembled both Alençon and Brussels Needle Laces. The thread used was fine, and of extreme delicacy.

FIG. 102. BUTTONHOLE, ORNAMENTAL.

Burden Stitch.—A variety of Cushion Stitch and Plain Couching, called "Burden," as it was used by a lady of that name, at the South Kensington Needlework School, for working flesh, but dating from the fourteenth and fifteenth centuries, when German, Flemish, and Italian schools used it for grounding, and for working flesh in embroidery. The beauty of the stitch consists in every thread being laid evenly down, and caught or secured in exact lengths. To work: Lay the floss silk forming the ground straight across the foundation, and bring a small fastening stitch through from the back, return it to the back, and there secure it. Keep these fastening stitches at even distances from each other, but do not begin at the same place for each row, but at every other row, as in PLAIN COUCHING.

Burlop.—An arrangement at the top of a dress improver, so termed in certain shops.

Busks.—Broad flat steels employed by staymakers to stiffen the fronts of stays. These are often covered with chamois leather before they are inserted in their outer casing. In former times these busks were made of wood.

Buttonhole, Ornamental.—The illustration (Fig. 102) is of an ornamental Buttonhole. Work the spray of leaves in raised SATIN STITCH, the stem and battlemented outline surrounding the Buttonhole in OVERCAST, and the dots in POINT DE POIS.

Buttonhole Stitch.—One of the chief stitches in all Needle-made Laces, and equally known as Close Stitch and Point Noné. It is used for the thickest parts of all patterns, and called Cordonnet when outlining or raised.

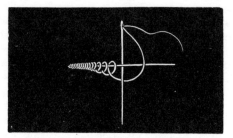

FIG. 103. BUTTONHOLE IN LACE WORK.

The manner of working is identical with Buttonhole Stitch; but, as a number of rows are required instead of the ordinary single Buttonhole, the loops of each row are used for the foundation of the next, and the needle is passed through every one of them. The effect of this is that no raised ridge is left on the surface of the stitch, but it has the appearance of a solid mass of upright close lines. Worked as follows: Throw a foundation thread across the space to be filled from right to left, and

FIG. 104. BUTTONHOLE STITCH FORMING THICK PART OF LACE.

firmly secure it; put the needle into the CORDONNET or other already made part of the lace, and then downwards behind the foundation thread; and pass the working thread to the right, under the needle, to form a loop upon the foundation thread when drawn up tight, as shown in Fig. 103. Continue these loops to the end of the space, and pull all up to the same tightness and work close, but do not overcrowd. At the end of the line secure the thread, then throw it back again to the left to form a foundation line, and repeat, using the raised edge of the buttonhole this time to pass the needle through instead of the Cordonnet or already formed lace. Fig. 104 shows the important part in lace that this stitch plays, all the solid part of the pattern being formed by it.

Buttonholes.—In linen or calico cut the hole with the thread of the material, using the proper scissors, exactly the diameter of the button; insert the needle four or five threads from the edge on the wrong side, and bring out on the right, holding the material so as to let the buttonhole lie along the forefinger (Fig. 105). When the thread is drawn through ready for use, hold it down with the left thumb, so as to make a loop at each stitch; and in passing the needle through the material, bring it likewise through the loop, leaving a sort of Chain Stitch along the edge. A bar of Buttonhole Stitching should be made across each end of the hole. This work must be done from left to right. One or two loose strands of thread should be kept along the edge, over which sew, and when the Buttonhole Stitching is finished, thread the loose strand on the needle and pull it slightly, and thus draw the hole even; then fasten off, darning in the ends of thread underneath. In working on thick cloth, cut the hole like an elongated V, the wide part at the edge. The silk employed is tailors' twist. The bar at each end of the Buttonhole is called by some a "bridge." The needle should be brought through the loop of thread, which the engraver has failed to do in the illustration. The bar at the end has not been given.

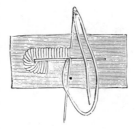

FIG. 105. BUTTONHOLE STITCH.

Buttonhole Twist.—This is employed to bind and strengthen buttonholes in cloth stuffs. It is sold by 1oz. and 2oz. reels, and by the yard wound in twelve strands.

Buttons.—(French *Bouton*, Welsh *Botwm*.) These substitutes for hooks are made in every variety of stuff, depending on the material of the garment or article of furniture requiring them. Linen ones, and those of silk and cotton, can be bought machine-made, but they can be hand-made by covering a wooden mould designed for the purpose, or a round flat bone foundation. The strongest fourfold linen buttons are sold by the dozen or the gross, and are measured by lines, from 6 to 36. Some kinds are covered in hand crochet, netting, and gimp. Other varieties can be had in ivory, bone, jet, mother-o'-pearl, leather, glass, and metals of all kinds—those of polished metal covered with a thin coating of gold or silver being the most durable. They are made with and without shanks, those of bone, horn, and mother-o'-pearl being drilled with holes necessary for their sewing on, when there is no shank, and when uncovered by any textile. The most ancient form of button was a short cylinder, which was sewn at the middle upon the garment.

Byzantine Embroidery.—A modern work, dating from 1878. It is a combination of Onlaid Appliqué, Couching outlines, and fancy stitches, and useful for ornamenting leather, cloth, and such materials as are too thick for the needle to be easily taken through them. Geometrical and arabesque outlines are traced upon cloth or fine leather, and strands of filoselle, double crewels, or worsted, laid down upon these lines, and secured by a fastening thread coming from the back of the material, and returning to it as in Appliqué and ecclesiastical embroidery. The beauty of the work consists in selecting suitable colours for these strands of filoselle, &c., upon their raised appearance, and upon the catching down threads being put in at regular distances. Their ends must be brought from the back, as in braiding. Byzantine Embroidery is enriched by applying to the design pieces of cloth, silk, or satin of varied colours. These are surrounded with a thick strand of filoselle or cord, as in Appliqué. Fancy stitches, such as Satin Stitch, Feather Stitch, Wheels, and French Knots, are worked over such applied pieces or on to the leather or cloth in vacant spaces. To work: Trace out the pattern upon fine cloth and cut this out. Lay the cloth upon a different coloured foundation, and slightly tack it down. Then take a strand of filoselle or some fine braid, and COUCH it down along the edge of the cloth, so as to connect that firmly to the material. Work in with filoselle and with SATIN STITCH any parts of the design that require filling in.

C.

Cable Knitting.—*See* KNITTING.

Caddis.—A variety of worsted lace or ribbon.

Cadis.—A kind of coarse serge.

Cadiz Lace.—A stitch used in old needle point and modern point laces. It takes two lines to make, and is one of the numerous varieties of Point de Bruxelles. It is worked as follows: First row—work 6 Point de Bruxelles close together, * miss the space that 2 would take up, work 2 Point de Bruxelles, miss the space of 2 and work 6, repeat from * to end of row. Second row—work 2 Point de Bruxelles into every loop left in first row, missing all the thick stitches of whatever number. Third row—work like the first, commencing with the 6 close Point de Bruxelles stitches. Fourth row as second. Repeat to end of space.

Caen and Bayeux Lace.—In the department of Calvados, Bayeux and Caen are justly celebrated for their black silk blonde laces, which are identical with those made at Chantilly. Before 1745 the lacemakers at Caen made a white thread lace of Venetian design, the needle point flowers being surrounded with a heavy thread called "fil de crin," instead of the ordinary thick cordonnet of Venice points. The Blondes de Caen were first made in 1745 from a silk of an écru colour brought from Nankin, which afterwards gave place to a beautiful white silk brought from Cevennes, and which established the reputation of the lace. Blonde de Caen was made of two descriptions of silk, one used for the pattern, and the other for the ground. The manufacture of this beautiful white blonde was destroyed by the machine blondes made at Nottingham and Calais. The Blonde Matte, which resembles Chantilly lace, is

I

described under that heading. At the present time, Caen, with Chantilly and Bayeux, produces black silk laces, and this city is considered to excel in the making of piece goods, such as veils, scarves, and dresses. (*See* Fig. 106.) These large pieces of lace are joined with the celebrated raccroc stitch, and so beautifully as to be almost imperceptible. The workers earn about 50 sous a day, and more than 25,000 are engaged in the trade.

Calamanco, or Callimanco. — (Spanish, *Calamaco*, a kind of worsted stuff; French *Calmande*.) This material

the art of printing upon cotton textiles. In 1712 the printing of these goods in England, exported plain from India (on account of a prohibitory Act passed at one time against the importation of printed cottons and chintzes), was introduced, and England now carries on the largest trade in the world. America produces the next in quantity, France and Switzerland follow, but produce goods far superior in quality to the American. The introduction of the manufacture of cotton into Europe was effected by the Arabs or Moors of Spain, who brought the cotton plant to

FIG. 106. BLACK LACE OF CAEN AND BAYEUX.

resembles Tammies and Durants. It is highly glazed, and can be had plain or twilled, raised in stripes or brocaded, the width ranging from 27 to 36 inches. It is employed for women's petticoats.

Calfskin. — Calfskins, which are imported from the Baltic, are taken from younger animals than those killed in this country, and are employed in the manufacture of gloves and ladies' shoes, as well as for bookbinding.

Calico. — The name of this textile is derived from Calicut, a seaport town on the coast of Malabar, the birthplace of

that country, from the fleecy wool of which the yarn for calico is spun. It is made into hanks containing 840 yards each. It was brought to England in the year 1631, but not manufactured here until 1772. The various makes of calico are known respectively under the following names: Cotton Cloth, Croydons, Derries, Double Warp, Dacca Twist, Longcloth, Loom Sheeting, Madapolams, Power-loom Sheetings, Swansdown Unions, and Wigans. There are also printed calicoes. The widths rarely measure above 36 inches, and those numbered 33 or 36 inches seldom reach that standard. "Fents" are ends of calicoes of different descriptions. Calico should have an even selvedge, fine and close in the woof and warp, without knots and flaws. Cheap sorts are dressed with a coating of lime and china clay, to detect which a corner should be rubbed together in the hands, when it will fall off in powder. Unbleached calico of a coarse description goes by the name of "bley" in Ireland. (*See* each make under its own heading.) The cotton plant is grown in Egypt, the United States, and Brazil, as well as in the East Indies.

Calico Prints.—*See* COTTON PRINTS.

Calico Shirting.—Otherwise known as Twine Cloth. A very evenly made cotton material, supplying a good imitation of linen, and employed for shirt making. It runs from 32 inches to 36 inches in width, and is made both in single and double warp.

Californian Embroidery.—The natives of California, before that land was discovered, in the sixteenth century, by the Spaniards, were unacquainted with silk and other ordinary embroidery materials; but they managed to twist into fine cords the entrails of whales, and covered their garments with needlework made with these threads. Their needles were shaped fishbones.

Cambric.—(German *Kammerich*; Dutch *Kammerack*; French *Toile de Cambrai* and *Batiste*.) The name of this textile is derived from Cambrai, a town in the department du Nord, France, whence the manufacture was originated by Baptista. It is a beautiful and delicate linen textile, of which there are several kinds. Its introduction into this country dates from the reign of Queen Elizabeth. That made in Lancashire is, perhaps, on a par with that made in Ireland and France. The Scotch are mere imitations in cotton. *See* FRENCH CAMBRIC.

> "Come, I would your *cambrick* were sensible as your finger,
>   That you might leave pricking it for pitie."
>   —*Coriolanus*, Act i., sc. 3.

Cambric Muslin.—This is an imitation of cambric, being made of cotton instead of flax. It may be had in most colours, as well as in black and white. These varieties are figured, striped, corded, and twilled, and sometimes have a glaze. Cambric muslin is much employed for linings. They run from 34 inches to a yard wide, at various prices.

Camelina.—A woollen material with very small basket pattern and loose upstanding hairs. It measures 25 inches in width, and is a species of the material called Vicuna.

Camelote.—A coarse kind of fustian of inferior quality, employed for the dress of labouring men. It is 27 inches in width. *See* FUSTIAN.

Camels' Hair. — This is long and silky hair spun into textiles, tents, ropes, shawls, carpets, fine stockings, &c. The hair clipped from the animal furnishes three qualities, distinguished by the colour. Black is the dearest, red the next, whilst grey fetches but half the value of the red.

Camels' Hair Cloth, or Puttoo.—Sometimes known as Cashgar cloth. This material is thick, warm, light,

full of electricity, and has a fine gloss. It is unshaved, and the long hairs are of a paler colour than the close substance of the cloth. The price varies according to its quality, and the widths are respectively from 42 to 48 inches. It is French made, and is employed for costumes, mantles, and other articles of dress. This material is generally considered to be manufactured from the inferior qualities of shawl wool in India, where the material is known as Puttoo.

Camera Work.—A modern embroidery of recent invention. It consists of Photographs expressly designed for the work, attached to linen or cream sheeting materials, and surrounded with sprays and groups of flowers. The photographs (Watteau landscape and figure subjects) are sold ready fixed to the material, and the worker is only required to embroider the already traced flower design.

Camlet.—The name of this textile was due to its manufacture of camels' hair, being of Eastern origin. By a strange coincidence, the subsequent manufacture of a similar kind of stuff had its rise in Montgomeryshire, and was named after the river Camlet in that locality. Subsequently to the employment in the East of camels' hair, that of the white glossy hair, growing in spiral ringlets, of the Angora goat of Asia Minor, has been substituted. In certain districts of that country the whole of the population is engaged in the manufacture and commerce of camlets. The best European article is made at Brussels, where woollen thread is mixed with the hair. The imitations are made of closely twisted worsted yarn or worsted and silk, hair being sometimes added. Camlet is thick and warm, and admirable for winter wear. It turns off rain better than any other unprepared article, and measures 25 inches in width. It is sold at various prices.

Campane Lace.—A narrow pillow lace made in France in the sixteenth century, which was used as an edging to wider laces. The Feston was ornamented with grelots and sonnettes.

Canada Lynx Fur.—(*Felix Canadensis*.) This fur is chiefly employed in British America and the States, but is prepared, as all furs are, in this country. The animal much resembles the cat, but has longer ears, and a short thick tail. The fur is long, soft, and of a greyish colour, and is sometimes covered with brown spots. Under the body it is white, silky, and at times spotted with black. It is dyed, and exported largely to America, and being very soft and light, it is well suited for cloaks, facings, and linings.

Canadian Embroidery.—The natives of Canada were at one time celebrated for their skill in embroidery with porcupine quills, and with the skins of reptiles and animals. Their skin work was particularly ingenious, as they cut the skins into minute pieces and formed from them designs representing trees, plants, and animals, using their own hair for thread. The porcupine quill work was of two kinds—a coarse kind, executed upon bark or leather, with split quills arranged in devices according to length and size, and sewn together; and a much more elaborate work, shown in Fig. 107, kept to ornament their dresses, tobacco pouches, &c. In these the quills were split so fine that they became flexible, and could be threaded through a coarse needle. They were dyed various colours, and worked upon scarlet and other bright toned cloths in the same way as Satin Stitch embroidery. The quills were dyed such pure colours as yellow, green, scarlet, blue, and amber, and great ingenuity was exercised in bending to shape them into flowers and leaves. The illustration is upon scarlet ground, the flowers are amber and white, the white being in the centre; the leaves, stems, and tendrils are of shaded greens, terminating in bright yellow. The design is part of a tobacco pouch, the whole of which is hand made, the scarlet cloth being sewn to a dark foundation, and the stitches concealed by a row of white quills couched down. At the present time Canadian embroidery is no longer worked by the natives, but is exclusively executed in the French nunneries, and the true spirit of the old designs is dying out, the nuns having introduced into the work many fancy stitches and dyes unknown

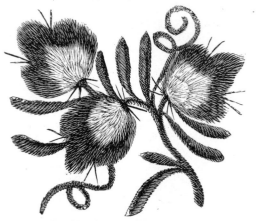

FIG. 107. CANADIAN EMBROIDERY.

to the real native patterns. The work made by the nuns can be recognised by the elaborate French Knots that form the chief part of the devices, by these devices being bad imitations of natural flowers, and not so conventional as the old ones, and also by the quills being dyed magenta, pink, mauve, and other aniline colours. Bundles of these split quills are procurable, and the work is easy of execution; therefore English ladies could embroider in Canadian work without much trouble, and it would form a pleasing variety to other fancy needlework. To work: Procure bundles of split quills. Trace out upon thin leather or scarlet cloth a design similar to the one given. Thread the quills upon a large-eyed needle, and work with them with irregular SATIN STITCHES to fill in the pattern. Change the colour of the quills used, so as to represent flowers, leaves, and stems, in their natural hues.

Canton Crape.—One of the many varieties of crape-woven fabrics. It is a dress material, measuring 27 inches in width, and is made in various plain colours.

Cantoon.—A kind of fustian, having a fine cord visible on one side, and a satiny surface of yarns, running at right angles to the cords, upon the other. This satiny side is sometimes made smooth by means of singeing. It is a strong stuff, has a good appearance, measuring 27 inches in width, and is employed for the dress of labouring men.

Canvas.—Derived from the Latin *Cannabis*, hemp; and the name literally means Hempen Cloth. There are four distinct kinds of Canvas—the silk, thread of flax or hemp, cotton, and woollen. They are to be distinguished by numbers corresponding to their several sizes.

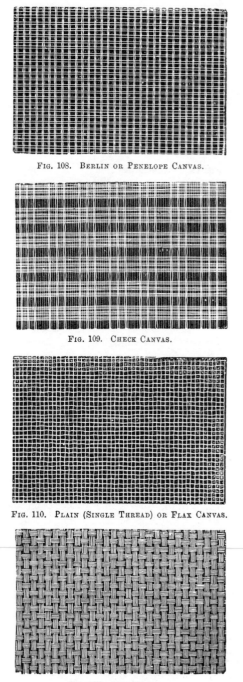

FIG. 108. BERLIN OR PENELOPE CANVAS.

FIG. 109. CHECK CANVAS.

FIG. 110. PLAIN (SINGLE THREAD) OR FLAX CANVAS.

FIG. 111. JAVA CANVAS.

The finest Canvas, whether of silk, thread, or cotton, is denominated Mosaic. Amongst those in use for embroidery are the Berlin or Penelope Canvas (Fig. 108), Check Canvas (Fig. 109), Flattened French and Flax Canvas (Fig. 110), the Java and Japanese (Fig. 111), Painters' Canvas, and coarse descriptions such as Scrim, made of hemp, for tent curtains and sails, upholstery, papering, and sieves. The seat of the home manufacture is at Dundee. (*See* BERLIN, BOLTING, COTTON, FLATTENED, SILK, THREAD, and WOOLLEN CANVAS.) With the exception of silk Canvas, four sizes only are generally manufactured, which number about twenty-one, twenty-nine, thirty-four, and forty threads to the inch respectively.

Canvas Work.—Before the introduction of Berlin patterns, in 1835, all wool work upon canvas was called by this name, which has now, however, become almost obsolete. Besides the Canvas Work described under Berlin Wool Work, there are four other kinds. For the first: Paint in shades matching the wools to be used; then take the wools and work in CROSS or TENT STITCH over the painted surface, commencing with the darkest shade and ending with the lightest. To work the second, in which the ground is of cloth or satin, and the pattern painted upon the canvas: Work in TENT STITCH, and pull away the threads when the design is finished. To work the third: Sew gold or silver braid upon canvas in outline patterns, and fill in the grounding with CROSS or TENT STITCH. The fourth is the Raised Canvas Work. Ancient Canvas Work was done upon very fine canvas in Tent Stitch, and was really Tapestry Work. The works of Miss Linwood, during the last century and the beginning of the present, are the most remarkable examples of modern Canvas Work. They are large copies of celebrated pictures, sixty-four in number, and were drawn upon closely woven canvas, or tammy, by that lady's own hand, and embroidered by herself in coloured worsteds, or what are now called crewels, dyed expressly for the purpose. These works were exhibited to the public, and one is now in the South Kensington collection. All the stitches enumerated in Berlin Wool Work are suitable for Canvas Work.

Raised Canvas Work.—This is a work that is executed from Berlin flower designs upon silk çanvas with Plush Stitch, and which, when completed, is raised above the foundation, and has the appearance of velvet pile. The Plush Stitches forming the pattern are made in single Berlin wool, taken over a mesh, as described in *Plush Stitch.* Begin the work from the bottom, and complete each line before the next is commenced, holding the mesh on the first line of stitches, until the second line is worked, when it is withdrawn, and ready for using in the third line. From this manner of working, a number of shades of wool are required at one time. To prevent delay, have them ready threaded and arranged before commencing. When the pattern is completed, cut the loops made on the surface by the withdrawal of the meshes, and be careful that they are cut quite evenly, and then turn the work, and paste a piece of tissue paper at the back of the Plush Stitches to prevent any of the cut threads coming out. Raised Canvas Work is only suitable for mantel boards and fire screens.

Cap.—Anglo-Saxon, *Cœppe*; Greek, *Skepo*, to cover. A generic term for a head covering. *See* MILLINERY.

Capitonné.—This is a French term, signifying drawn in at intervals, as a stuffed sofa, chair, or pincushion,

which is buttoned down at each attachment of the double material, at the front and back.

Cap Springs.—These appliances are made of steel, and in either round or flat form. They are sold by the gross.

Carbonised Linen and Paper.—These are required for tracing patterns upon thick materials, and are used in BRAIDING, CREWEL WORK, SILK, LINEN and CLOTH EMBROIDERIES. The best is the linen, which is sold in two colours, white and blue. It is durable and clean. The paper is sold in black, blue, white, orange, and red; but the black rubs off upon the material, and is not good. A new piece of linen or paper is either rubbed with bread or tissue paper laid between it and the work, as the carbon, when quite fresh, is liable to come off. The white is used when tracing on dark materials, the blue for light. To trace: Lay the material upon a sheet of plate glass, then place the carbonised linen, and then the pattern. See that the pattern is over the part it is to be traced upon, and pin all three together. Take a blunt bone crochet-hook or steel knitting-needle, and carefully go over every line of the pattern with a firm, even pressure upon the needle. Look under the carbonised linen now and then to see if the marks are right, and continue until the whole design is thus transferred. Carbonised linen is warmed with a moderately-heated iron, when, after much using, the marks are becoming faint; or it can be entirely renewed by the maker.

Carmelite.—A woollen textile, almost identical with beige. So called because adopted as the dress of the order of Carmelites. It is 25 inches in width.

Carnival Lace.—A Reticella Lace, used in Italy, Spain, and France, during the sixteenth century, and differing only in its pattern from the ordinary Reticella. This particular lace was ornamented with the badges of the families who possessed it, and was given as part of the trousseau to the bride, and worn by her during the wedding ceremonies and upon state occasions, such as carnivals, during her life. *See* BRIDAL LACE.

Carpet.—Derived from the Latin *Carpeta*, woollen cloth.

Carpet Bindings.—These are manufactured in different qualities, the best being made entirely of worsted, and the inferior kinds of a mixture of worsted and cotton thread. They are to be had in plain colours and also in chintz designs, so as to match carpets of every colour. They are sold by the gross, four pieces of 36 yards each. They may also be purchased by the yard from a few pence upwards, according to the width and quality.

Carpet Thread.—A heavy-made three-cord sewing thread. It may be had in black, drab, green, brown, yellow, and red, as well as unbleached, and is made with a soft and satin-like finish. Sold by the ounce and the pound.

Carpet Worsted.—A very coarse kind of sewing thread of worsted yarn, made in various bright colours, and done up in balls. Sold in paper bags containing 3lb. or 6lb. each, and used for darning and renewing carpets.

Carrickmacross Point.—A lace made in Ireland since the year 1820, Miss Reid, of Ahans, founding a school for instruction before. There are two kinds of lace known as

Carrickmacross, the first resembling Bruxelles Appliqué Lace, except that the design is cut out of fine cambric, and applied to net, with Point Lace stitches worked with a needle. The second lace is a Guipure, and is quite distinct from the first kind. A design is traced by a thread on cambric, and connected with Point Stitches, and worked round with Overcast. Brides and Brides Ornées connect the various parts of the pattern together.

Casbans.—Cotton textiles of similar make to jaconets, only of a stouter quality, some being twilled and having a finished surface, resembling sateen. They are chiefly used for linings, the widths running from 30 to 36 inches.

Cascade.—The method of laying down a trimming of lace folded in a zig-zag form, first one way and then back again, taking a broken diagonal descent down the front of a dress.

Casing.—A term used to denote a cover of material, of whatever description, through which a ribbon is to be passed, laid on separately from the foundation stuff.

Cashmere des Indes, or Goat Cloth.—A variety of casimir, made of the soft wool of the Thibet goat, mixed with Australian wool. It is exceedingly fine in texture and twilled, measuring 42 inches in width. The seat of the manufacture is at Rheims, and those French made are much superior to our own. Many imitations and varieties of this cloth are made in England. One description is produced at Bradford, the weft of which is spun from the fur of the Angola rabbit, which is an exceedingly soft material, and much resembles cashmere. There is also a variety made at Huddersfield, called the Tigré cashmere; a variegated cloth, having a cotton warp, figured, and shot with goats' hair. Ordinary French cashmere is sent to England unwashed and undyed, is of a delicate écru or cream colour, and is made entirely of wool, either of the finest Saxon or the Australian.

Casimer, or Cassimere, or Kerseymere.—A twilled woollen cloth, remarkable for its pliability, so that when pressed it does not become creased. One third of the warp is always above and two-thirds below each shoot of the weft. It is either single or double milled, and is usually woven of the width of 34 or 36 inches, and reduced by milling to 27 inches. Cassimerette is another variety of this stuff.

Cassinette.—A cloth made of cotton warp, and the woof of very fine wool, or wool and silk. It differs from toilinette and Valentia in having its twill thrown diagonally, and measures 27 inches in width.

Cast off.—A knitting term, used to describe the finishing of the work in any part.

Cast on.—A knitting term, used to describe the first putting of the wool upon the needle to form stitches.

Castor.—A heavy broadcloth, used for overcoats.

Cast over.—A knitting term, used when the cotton is brought over the needle and quite round it. Identical with "Round the Needle." *See* Knitting.

Caterpillar Point.—A Needle-made Lace, resembling flat Venetian point, made in Italy during the seventeenth century, and distinguished by this name from other varieties of Venetian Lace. The reason it was so called was the resemblance of the narrow, curling, and inter-

lacing sprig that formed its pattern to the bodies of caterpillars when in motion. These sprigs are surrounded with a fine Cordonnet closely Buttonholed, and are filled with a variety of thick stitches, such as Escalier and Brabaçon. They are connected together with fine Brides, trimmed with Cockscombs and Picots, and the effect of the whole design is peculiarly rich and delicate. A different kind of Caterpillar Lace has lately been made at Munich by a gentleman of that place, who has trained a large hairy species of caterpillar to unconsciously become lacemakers. The process is as follows: A paste is made of the food the caterpillars most like, which is thinly spread upon a smooth flat stone. A lace design is then traced upon this with oil, and the caterpillars arranged at the bottom of the stone, which is placed in an inclined position. The caterpillars eat their way from the bottom to the top of the stone, avoiding any parts touched with oil, and spinning a strong web as they go, which serves to connect the uneaten parts together. This lace finds a sale because of the peculiarity of its make, and it is distinguished from real lace by its extreme lightness, a square yard of it only weighing $4\frac{3}{4}$ grains, while the same quantity of net would weigh 262 grains.

Catherine Wheel.—This wheel is also known by the name of Spider Wheel or Spider Stitch, and is chiefly employed to fill up round holes in embroidery on muslin. It is made as follows: Outline the round to be filled by the Wheel with embroidery cotton, and closely Buttonhole;

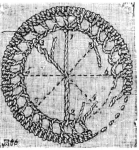

FIG. 112. CATHERINE OR SPIDER WHEEL.—DETAIL A.

then work a row of loose Buttonhole under it, and from this the cords that form the centre of the wheel proceed (*see* Fig. 112, Detail A). Take these across the space in the order shown; the figures 1 to 2 being the first line;

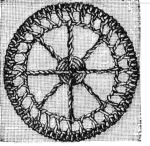

FIG. 113. CATHERINE OR SPIDER WHEEL.—DETAIL B.

Cord back 2 to the centre, and put the needle in at 3, which Cord back to the centre, and so on until all the lines are completed. Form the boss to pass the thread under and over the threads until a round is made of the size indicated in Fig. 113, Detail B, and Cord the thread up No. 1 to finish. Take a line of OVERCAST round the second line of Buttonhole when the branching lines are formed, which will tend to strengthen and to stiffen the work. Cut away the under muslin from the first Buttonhole line, when the Wheel is complete.

Catskin Fur (*Felis catus*).—The fur of the wild cat of Hungary is of a brownish grey, mottled, and spotted with black. It is soft and durable, and is employed for cloak linings and wrappers for carriages. The domestic cat of Holland is bred for its fur, fed on fish, and carefully tended until the coat has arrived at its full perfection. The fur is frequently dyed in imitation of Sable.

Caul Work.—The ancient name for.NETTING, which *see*.

Centre Fibre.—This Centre Fibre is required in Honiton Lace making and other Pillow Laces, when a raised appearance is to be given to the centre of the leaves. This is shown in Fig. 114, and worked as follows : Hang on five pairs of bobbins at the stem of the leaf; work up the middle of the first leaf, and when last pin is stuck, work to the TURNING Stitch and back; then, with the pair lying at the pins, make a ROPE SEWING, and this, which is termed a RETURN Rope, is made, not upon the stem, but at the back of it. Work the next two fibres in the same manner, the middle one last, and when each is finished, run a piece to its head in the end hole, and take out the rest. Now carry the RAISED WORK to the tip of the middle leaf, hang

FIG. 114. CENTRE FIBRE.

on two pairs, work back in CLOTH STITCH, and when the fibre is reached, take out the pin, stick it three or four holes lower down, insert the hook into the top hole, and make a SEWING with the centre stitch of the work to the cross strand; this will secure the fibre, and it can now be worked over. The other leaves are done in the same manner.

Ceylon Pillow Lace.—A lace of Maltese design, made in Ceylon by the native women, and probably imported there by early European settlers. It is of no commercial value, and only remarkable because of its semblance to that of European manufacture.

Chain Boulée.—A short rough cord, made in macramé lace with two threads. Hold one in each hand, and keep the left tight while looping the right-hand thread over it, and running it to the top of left-hand thread. The right-hand thread is then held tight, while the left-hand thread is looped over it. In this manner a rough cord of any length can be made. *See* MACRAMÉ.

Chain Fork.—This instrument is usually made of ivory, bone, or boxwood. It is shaped something like an ancient lyre, but flat, and the braid is fastened round the two horns, and when made into a chain is passed through the round hole in the middle of that portion of the fork which resembles the sounding-board.

Chain Stitch.—A stitch used in Embroidery, Tambour Work, and Crochet. The manner of working it for embroidery (shown in Fig. 115) is as follows : Bring the needle, threaded, from back of material, and form a loop on the right side, and keep this loop steady with the left thumb, return the needle close to where it came out;

bring the needle up again in the centre of. the loop, and pull the thread evenly up; then form another loop and return the needle as before, and so on for the whole of the pattern. Gold thread, silk, and cotton are all used for Chain Stitch.

Chain Stitch Crochet. See CROCHET.

Chain Stitch in Tambour Work (of which it is the only stitch) is formed with a crochet hook, and can only be worked upon fine linen, cambric, or muslin, that will allow of the work passing through it with ease. To work : Stretch the material in an open frame, draw the thread through from the back to the front by the hook in a succession of loops, the second loop formed catching or securing the first; and so on for the remainder.

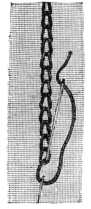

FIG. 115. CHAIN STITCH (EMBROIDERY).

Chain Stitch Embroidery.—One of the most ancient of embroideries, and first brought from the East, where it is still practised by the Persians, Indians, and Chinese. It was known to the workers in Europe of the Middle Ages, and much of the celebrated Opus Anglicanum was simply Chain Stitch. When worked with a hook, and not with a needle, it was known in later times as Tambour Work. The imitation of Chain Stitch Embroidery by machinery has caused it to fall into discredit; but although machinery may do much in reproducing the appearance of hand work, it can never give such an amount of varied shades and minute curves and embellishments as hand work. The embroidery is worked upon any material, and with anything that can be threaded; it is chiefly worked in filoselle or gold thread upon cloth or silk, or in bright-coloured washing silks and cottons upon white materials, for ornamenting washing dresses and household linen. Fig. 116, p. 64, is an example of this kind of embroidery, and is done with red ingrain cotton, upon flax or Kirriemuir twill, and used for a tea table cover. The same pattern would look well as a border to a Japanese silk tablecloth. The pattern is traced with the aid of carbonised paper and tracing linen, or ironed off. Chain Stitch Embroidery is now more used for embellishing Church linen than for anything else; the corporal, chalice veil and cloth, used at Communion, should all be embroidered with designs in Chain Stitch, either in white or coloured washing silks. The Communion cloth is generally of a fine damask woven expressly for the purpose, and is made so as to fall over the table to the depth of embroidery, should there be no super-frontal. The chalice veil is of fine cambric or silk, from 9 inches to 18 inches square; the corporal of fine lawn. The only colours allowed in this embroidery are red, blue, lilac, and green ; but the first two are the ones chiefly used. The Chain Stitch, though forming the chief part of the design, can be varied with Satin Stitch fillings, or with enrichments of Dots and Bosses worked in dotting cotton; but the character of the work should be that of an outline, or it will be too heavy for the purpose. To work, as shown in Fig. 116: Trace the outline of the design upon fine cambric. Thread a fine needle with scarlet ingrain cotton, and work with it the centre part of the design in CHAIN STITCH. Take blue ingrain cotton, and work the two borders with that, also in CHAIN STITCH.

Chain Work Cloth.—A peculiar style of textile, employed for tambouring and hosiery.

Challis, or Chalis.—A thin textile, made of silk and wool, and having a good lustre; employed for women's

whether Réseau or Bride. It is identical with Fond and Trielle. *See* FOND.

Chantilly Blonde Lace.—No other country can surpass France in its black and white silk Blonde Laces. They were first made at Chantilly, about the year 1740, and, though produced at Caen and Bayeux, the mother town was considered to manufacture finer patterns and textured laces, though it did not produce such large pieces. The old white and black Pillow Blondes were made of floss silk, with flowers of large size, and with a fine open

FIG. 116. CHAIN STITCH EMBROIDERY.

dresses. It is twilled and printed in coloured flowers on a white ground, which has the effect of velvet painting. The material was introduced into this country about the year 1832. It is made on a similar principle to the Norwich crape, but is thinner and softer, and without a gloss. The width measures about 30 inches.

Chamois Leather.—The skin of the Alpine goat of that name, which has been "efflowered" or deprived of the epidermis. It is dressed without tan, salt, or alum, and is brought to a state of pelt by liming and washing.

ground. These cost twenty guineas a yard, and were much used in the court of Marie Antoinette. Fig. 117 is an illustration of one of them, copied from one of the old order books of that date; but is much reduced in size, in order to take in its design. The flowers and ground of this lace are worked in the same silk, and the pattern has more open stitches than some of the laces. The manufactory at Chantilly was broken up during the French Revolution, and most of the lace-makers were guillotined, as the popular fury could not dis-

FIG. 117. CHANTILLY BLONDE LACE.

That dyed buff colour is dipped in tan ooze. The skin is strong, soft, elastic, and warm in wear, is used for tight riding breeches for both sexes, as it does not wrinkle, and is otherwise suitable for that purpose, as well as for under-vests, linings of petticoats, and other garments, which are perforated to make them more wholesome wear. Chamois leather is used by jewellers in cleaning trinkets and plate, and is also employed for cleaning carriages. It is sold by the skin. Much leather, improperly called chamois, and rightly named wash-leather, is the skin of deer, sheep, and ordinary goats prepared with oil.

Champ.—A term used, in lace work, for the ground,

tinguish between the wearers and makers of a costly fabric, and classed them both as royalists. It was, however, restored in 1805, when the white Blondes were eagerly bought, and the trade flourished more than at any other period of its history. The large-patterned Blondes Mattes were then made. The machine laces spoilt the trade in white Blondes, and black are now chiefly made. The flowers of the modern laces are not so heavy and so distinct as those of the old blondes; they are slighter in form, and thoroughly dispersed over the lace, and cannot be transferred from the ground like the ancient ones. Another variety has been brought to great beauty. It is a close pattern with deep borders of irregular outline, flowered

BERLIN WOOL WORK.

in most patterns, and contrasts with the fine filmy Réseau ground upon which it is worked. It is too expensive to be an article of commerce, and the Chantilly laces now in the market are nearly certain to be productions of either Caen or Bayeux. *See* CAEN.

Check-Mohair.—Dress material, so called from the pattern woven in it, and measuring 24 inches in width. It is much employed for children's dresses; the cross-bars being of small dimensions, like the shepherd's plaid and the "Louisine silks." The price varies according to the quality. It may be had in pink, blue, brown, red, and black "shepherd's plaid" checks; all on a white ground. It is plain made, *i.e.*, not produced in any fancy style of weaving.

Cheese Cloth.—An open-make of fine canvas, employed for drawn work embroidery. It is 42 inches in width, and is inexpensive, but varies in price in different shops.

Chemise.—A loose under-shirt of linen, longcloth, or calico, worn next to the vest; sometimes called Shift. *See* CUTTING OUT and DRESSMAKING.

Chemisette.—A plain or ornamental under-bodice, with fronts and backs unconnected at the sides. *See* CUTTING OUT and DRESSMAKING.

Chenille.—The French for Caterpillar. A beautiful description of cord employed for embroidery and decorative purposes. The name denotes the appearance of the material, which somewhat resembles that of a hairy caterpillar. It is usually made of silk, is sometimes a combination of silk and wool, and has been produced in wool only. There are two sizes; the coarse is called Chenille Ordinaire, the small Chenille à Broder. There is a new kind of Chenille called Pomponet, having a very long pile, boa-shaped, and employed for neckties. For the purposes of millinery it is mounted on fine wire; the fine soft silk Chenille is that used for embroidery, and sold in art colours.

Chenille Cloth.—Also known as Moss Bège. This material is made with a fringed silken thread used as weft in pile-weaving, in combination with silk, wool, or cotton. When woven, the fringed threads protrude through the interstices of the material, and produce a fur-like surface. Many varieties are made, since the recent great demand for the cloth, both in millinery, dress, and flower making. It was appropriately named by the French *Chenille* (caterpillar), from its great resemblance to the insect's velvety coat of fur. It is 27 inches in width.

Chenille Embroidery.—A work originating in France, and deriving its name from the resemblance its round fluffy threads have to the bodies of caterpillars. During the eighteenth century, Chenille Embroidery was the fashion at the French Court; and many specimens of it executed by Marie Antoinette and her ladies are still preserved. From France it passed over to England, and was popular for years, and never entirely disappeared in this country. The taste for the work has now revived; and, when well executed, it has all the softness and beauty of painting upon velvet, and well repays the time and money spent upon it. It looks particularly handsome when made up as curtain borders, in which form it has been lately employed at the South Kensington School of Art Needlework.

Chenille is of two kinds: Chenille à Broder, which is soft and not on wire, is the one used in old, and in the better sorts of modern, work. This Chenille à Broder comes from Paris, and is extremely fine in texture. The other kind is called Chenille Ordinaire, a coarser Chenille, adapted for being either COUCHED upon the surface of the material, or darned through large-holed silk canvas net, or gold and silver perforated cardboard. The fine Chenille costs about 3d. the yard, and the greater the number of shades required in the design the greater the expense. Simple Satin embroidery patterns are the best to work from.

To work: Outline the design upon the material before it is framed, and use a coloured pattern to work from. Use for the needles large-eyed, sharp-pointed rug needles, and thread the Chenille in short lengths, as every passing backwards and forwards deteriorates its pile. If the work is upon canvas, stretch it in a frame, and only work the design in Chenille; make the ground in CROSS or TENT STITCH with filoselle or wool. The stitch used is SATIN STITCH. Thread many needlefuls of various coloured Chenille before commencing the work, and put in each shade of colour following the line preceding it, not the

FIG. 118. CHENILLE EMBROIDERY.—DETAIL A.

whole of one shade before another is commenced. Fig. 118 (Detail A) is of fine Chenille worked upon thin silk. Frame the silk after the outline of the design is traced, and fill the needles with Chenille, bring these up from the back of the frame, and push them down again as in ordinary WOOL WORK. Each thread of the Chenille can also be laid on the surface in lines, and secured with silk of the same colour, as in COUCHING. When this is done at the commencement and end of the thread, make a hole through the material with a stiletto, and pull the Chenille through to the wrong side, and there secure it; but, unless the foundation is thick and heavy, the first manner of working is the best.

K

Chenille Ordinaire can be worked as shown in Fig. 119 (Detail B), upon large open-meshed canvas. To work: Pass the Chenille backwards and forwards through the open-meshed canvas. Use but few shades. The stitches for the rosebud are SATIN; for leaves and points of bud, TÊTE DE BŒUF; for the stem, CREWEL. Upon a closer

FIG. 119. CHENILLE EMBROIDERY UPON LARGE CANVAS.—DETAIL B.

material the Chenille is laid in lines close together for the leaves of a pattern, while loops of Chenille, mounted upon fine wire and sewn to the material with purse silk, make the flower petals. Make the centres to the flowers by loops sewn flat, and form the stems of Chenille plainly COUCHED down.

Fig. 120 (Detail C) is an illustration of Chenille Ordinaire used upon perforated gold and silver cardboard, and very pretty devices and patterns are worked by simple arrangements of the stitches to form crosses, stars, and wheels. The work is useful as an ornamentation for sachets, blotting cases, dinner rings, and other

FIG. 120. CHENILLE UPON GOLD CARDBOARD.—DETAIL C.

fancy articles suitable for bazaars. To work: Back the cardboard with linen, to prevent its breaking away in the process of working, and thread the Chenille into large-eyed needles, which pass backwards and forwards through the cardboard, as if it were canvas. Two or three distinct contrasting colours are the best to use for this kind of Chenille embroidery.

Chenille Lace.—A peculiar kind of Lace made during the eighteenth century, in France. The ground of this lace was silk honeycomb Réseau; the patterns were poor, and chiefly geometrical, filled with thick stitches, and outlined with fine white Chenille; hence the name.

Chenille Needles.—These Needles resemble in form the ordinary rug needle, but are sharp at their points, and to avoid rubbing the Chenille they are very wide in the eye.

Chenille Rolio.—A twisted silk Chenille cord stiffened

by wire; used, according to its width, either to surround glass shades for clocks, boxes, &c., or to be twisted into flowers. It is sold by the yard and by the piece. When passed through an iron tube the Chenille becomes the silky compact roll, appropriately nicknamed "rats' tails," employed in rich mantle fringes.

Chenille Travailleuse.—The French name to designate the fluffy silk thread employed in embroidery, fringes, and gimp ornaments.

Chequer Stitch. — This Stitch is used for working berries in Honiton Lace designs, and is illustrated in the *Poppy and Briony Design.* (*See* HONITON LACE.) To work: Hang on six pairs of bobbins, and begin at the base of the lower berry, work the STEM all round, leave the three outer pairs of bobbins to carry on the Stem afterwards, hang on six more pairs. There being Stem on both sides, there will be one pair of workers to pass backwards and forwards across eight pairs; work one, TWIST the workers thrice; work two, Twist thrice, work two, Twist thrice; work one, and SEW to the Stem. Repeat this row three times, then Sew the workers to the next pinhole, Twist all the passive pairs three times, and repeat the three rows; then Sew to two pinholes in succession, and Twist the passive pairs. Be careful to draw each stitch well up. This Stitch is used for fillings to flowers as well as berries.

Chequeté.—A French term employed in dressmaking, to denote "pinked out," or cut by means of scissors, or a stamping instrument having teeth, which produces a

FIG. 121. CHEQUÉTÉ.

decorative bordering in notched scallops, or diamond points, to a silk ribbon, flounce, or other trimming. *See* Fig. 121.

Chessboard Canvas.—A handsome thick white cotton Canvas, designed as a foundation for embroidery. Each chequer is upwards of an inch square, and made in alternate honeycomb pattern, and simple Egyptian cloth mat. The width is 26½ inches. *See* illustration (Fig. 122) on page 67.

Cheveril.—Soft leather, made of kid-skin.

Cheviot Cloth.—A rough description of Cloth, made both for men and women's dress, twilled, and coarser than what is known as Homespun. This Cloth is 27 inches in width. The Cheviot Homespun measures 25 inches in width, and Cheviot Tweed 27 inches.

Chiffon Work.—A modern variety of Patchwork, which consists of laying on to a foundation straight lines of black velvet alternately with stripes made of pieces of silk and satin. The advantage of Chiffon Work is that it uses up pieces of silk too small for ordinary Patchwork, and pieces that are cut upon the cross. To work: Cut out and arrange bits of silk as in PATCHWORK, but upon the cross; lay down a line of velvet, and then TACK a piece of silk to it, so that it will turn over on the right side. Continue to tack pieces of silk together cut into the forms of crosses, wedges, rounds, and other devices, but keep them within the margin of a broad straight band. Add more velvet and more coloured stripes until the foundation material is quite covered, then stuff the velvet with wadding to give it a raised appearance, and ornament the scraps of silk with CORAL, FEATHER, HERRINGBONE, and other fancy stitches in filoselle, after the rest of the work is finished. The foundation should be of ticking or coarse canvas.

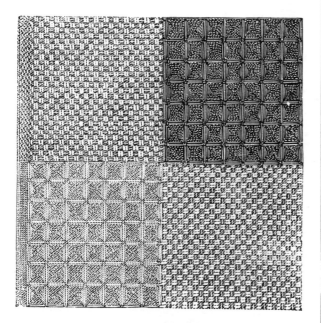

FIG. 122. CHESSBOARD CANVAS.

China Crape.—A beautiful variety of Crape, but thicker in texture than the ordinary kind, remarkably fine, but weighty in substance. It is generally sold at Indian warehouses, being made in white and various colours, exquisitely dyed, and is employed for women's dress. It is made of raw silk, gummed, and twisted on the mill, and woven without crossing. The width is 24 inches.

China Grass Cloth.—A beautiful and delicate, as well as a very coarse description of Cloth, having its origin in China. It is produced from the fibres of a species of nettle (*Urtica nivea*), which the natives split into lengths and unite together at the smaller ends. Exquisite handkerchiefs and fine linens are also made from China Grass, and of late years it has been united with silk and cotton for coloured textiles, having a brilliant appearance. It is employed in Canton, and has been utilised at Leeds with much success. Very beautiful textiles are produced in China Grass with a silk warp. One of the chief seats of the manufacture as a yarn is to be found at Leeds.

China Ribbon.—A very narrow Ribbon, of about one-eighth of an inch in width, woven with a plain edge, and to be had in one colour, or shaded gradually from a dark to a light tint of any colour. This description of Ribbon was much in fashion about forty years ago, but the best qualities are now only to be had at first-class embroidery shops in town, and sometimes in country places. Inferior kinds are procurable elsewhere. China Ribbon is often used for book markers in the best bound books (especially Prayer-books), being attached in the process of binding.

China Ribbon Embroidery.—This work was largely employed for decorative purposes during the earlier part of the present century, and has lately reappeared under the title of Rococo and Ribbon Embroidery. Ancient designs were floral and of the Renaissance style, and differed but little from those used at that period for silk embroidery upon dresses, waistcoats, &c. The materials required are China ribbon of various colours, shaded and self-coloured; thick cotton canvas, silk, satin, or velvet foundations, and embroidery silk. Shaded China ribbons, being now out of date, are sold only at some of the first class embroidery shops; but the plain can still be met with at linendrapers'.

The work, which is very durable, is done in a frame; the background being generally selected of a dark colour, as the ribbons look best upon dark foundations. When the material is stretched in a frame, trace the design upon it, and apply the ribbon to it as follows: For all sprays intended for leaves or grasses, thread shaded green China ribbon upon a large crewel needle, and work in SATIN STITCH. Bring the needle up from the back of the material at the outer line of the spray, hold the ribbon in the left hand, to prevent its twisting, and put the needle into the material in the centre of the spray or leaf in a rather slanting direction. Form all one side of the leaf, and then work the other side in the same manner, always bringing the ribbon from the outer edge and finishing in the centre. By this means the appearance of a centre vein is given to the leaves and sprays. The flowers are variously worked: small ones with unshaded ribbon in SATIN STITCH worked to their centres, and a knot of different coloured ribbon put over the Satin Stitch as a finish; while large ones make more raised, thus: Run the ribbon at one edge, and gather it closely together, and then sew it to the background in enlarging circles, so that the unrun edge of the ribbon stands up from the material in a thick round mass. Make the centres of these rounds of shaded ribbon, and of a different colour to the shaded ribbon used in the first part of the rounds. Make the buds of Satin Stitch, with ribbons of two colours, but not shaded; or all of the same tint, and finish with stitches of embroidery silk, and work the stems and other light parts of the work with the same silk in CHAIN, CREWEL, or LONG STITCH. The best patterns are those that introduce flowers of the forget-me-not size, small roses and bluebells, as, although this work does in no way attempt to be natural, it should never offend by being executed in large designs; when worked in small patterns, it has a quaint, old-fashioned look which it cannot retain when enlarged.

Fig. 123 is an illustration taken from a piece of work fifty years old, and intended for a sachet or hand-bag.

The foundation is of black satin, and the colours used are as follows: Commencing from the top left-hand corner, the spray there is formed of pink and white ribbon intermixed, the large flower, of amber-coloured shaded ribbon, with buds of a deeper tone, and the small bunch of flowers beneath it, blue with yellow centres. On the right hand, the small flowers at the top are yellow, the rose of gathered ribbon of a plain crimson shade, and the bunch of small flowers above it, white with pink centres. The rose in the centre is formed by the ribbon being closely gathered as before described, the colour a variegated deep red; the little two-petal flowers over it are rose

threads being drawn out easily, and is useful for table-cloths and chair backs, and very simple in execution. To work : Cut the material to the size, and then draw out its threads in wide lines at equal distances from each other, and wider than the width of the ribbon. Into these drawn lines run ribbon which has previously been threaded into a rug needle. DARN the ribbon down the space left by the Drawn Threads, going over six and under six of the threads still remaining. An inch and a half space is generally sufficient to leave between the lines, and this should be ornamented with a pattern in HOLBEIN or CROSS STITCH. Various coloured ribbons

FIG. 123. CHINA RIBBON EMBROIDERY

colour, and at its left side are yellow and white; the four-petal flowers underneath rose pink with white centres; leaves throughout of shaded yellow greens. Form all stems, rose thorns, and other fine parts of the pattern of green purse silk, and work in STEM or CREWEL STITCH. The above are the shades used upon this old piece of work, and, as none of them are produced from aniline dyes, they amalgamate extremely well.

China Ribbon Work.—A modern name given to a kind of Drawn Work, into which coloured China ribbons are run instead of crochet cotton. It is suitable for any linen or cotton materials coarse enough to allow of the

are used in one piece of work; their ends being allowed to form the fringe with the Drawn Threads of the material. Check and other drawn patterns are adapted to China Ribbon Work, the ribbons being crossed in the open spaces. The ribbons when forming check pattern are sewn on the wrong side of the material, to keep them from moving; and care is taken that they are run in flat and are not twisted. Letters forming the initials of the worker are made by darning the ribbon into the background, to form their outlines. These initials are placed in a corner.

Chinas.—Ribbon composed of a common kind of satin,

designed for rosettes, book markers, &c., and dyed in white, black, and all colours. They are made in narrow widths, and are trifling in price.

China Sewing Silk.—This Silk is of a pure white colour. One quality is much used by glove-makers, and a coarse two or three cord by stay-makers. The best Sewing Silk is sold on reels, containing one ounce.

China Stripe Cloth.—A description of BROADCLOTH (which *see*).

Chinchilla Fur. — Of the animal producing this Fur there are two varieties, both of South America.

broideries. But little of ancient needlework now remains, the dampness of the Chinese climate being injurious to the preservation of materials, and the long civil wars proving destructive to much that had escaped the action of the climate; but the ancient designs are continually reproduced with extreme fidelity, the Chinese mind being averse to novelty and change, and preferring what is already pronounced good to any innovations. Toochow was the ancient seat of embroidery, but at Canton and Ning-po a great deal is now worked, particularly large screens, fan cases, and robes, which are the

FIG. 124. CHINESE EMBROIDERY.

That giving the best Fur is a native of Buenos Ayres and Arica, and is of a silver grey, the darkest and best in colour coming from the latter place. Those from Lima are short in the Fur, and inferior in quality. The Fur is extremely soft and delicate, and lies as readily in one direction as another. The skins measure 6 inches by 9 inches.

Chinese Embroidery.—The Chinese appear to have learnt the art of embroidery from Persia at a very early date, and became celebrated for their productions, which display an amount of labour and delicacy of execution almost unsurpassed, save by the Japanese em-

principal articles in request. Men embroider as well as women, and the patience with which they entirely cover a state robe, curtain, or screen with elaborate needlework, is remarkable. Under the late dynasty, robes embroidered with floss silk, and with gold and silver thread, were worn much more universally than they are at the present time, as it is now considered sufficient to indicate a mandarin's rank by a small square of embroidery containing his device, instead of repeating the same, combined with dragons, ribbons, and flowers, all over the dress, as was universal during the Ming dynasty. Chinese ladies are also now content with embroidery in silk instead of floss about their dresses, and the costly floss and gold embroideries are found more upon screens and actors' costumes than upon ordinary wearing apparel. The Chinese embroider in several ways.

In one, both sides of the work are the same; this is done by painting the pattern upon transparent material, stretching it, and working in Satin Stitch backwards and forwards, so that there is no wrong side.

Another kind is crêpe work, as borders to crêpe shawls. In this, large showy flowers are worked in Long and Feather Stitch, or in Chain Stitch. The beauty of the last-named consists in the dexterity of its execution, the lights and shades of the pattern being shown, not by varying the shades of colour, but by working the Chain Stitch open and wide apart for light, and close and thick for dark parts, the effect being further enhanced by the soft tones of the oriental colours.

Feather work, in which real feathers are introduced, is another kind of embroidery they execute; the designs in the parts where the feathers are to be laid are stamped upon metal, to which the feathers are glued, and the rest of the pattern finished in silk work. But their most famous embroidery is with floss silk and gold and silver threads. The patterns for these, though numerous, exhibit but little variety, the sacred dragons, various monsters, figures, jars, ribbons, asters, and cherry blossom, mixed with birds and butterflies, being repeated and accurately copied as to colours in most of the designs. Pattern books for these are sold in China for a penny.

Fig. 124 is an example of this kind of embroidery. It is taken from the border of a mandarin's robe, which is covered from top to bottom with embroidery in floss silk, gold and silver thread, and purse silk, representing dragons, quaint animals, flowers, ribbons, and jars. It is worked as follows: The foundation material is of dark blue silk, and the dragons are constantly repeated all over it. Make these of gold thread, laid upon the surface and Couched down with coloured silks. Where the animal has scales, arrange these threads as half curves, but upon the head, feet, claws, and tail make the lines to follow the undulations of the parts they represent. Pad the eyes and make them very prominent, and work with coloured floss silk; decorate the mouths with long white moustaches, which allow to trail and curl over the background. The flower shown in Fig. 124 is taken from the border of the robe; surround every petal with a fine white silk cord, and fill with French Knots in purse silk, colour deep crimson, shading to pale silk in centres; make the half-opened flowers of the same colours, work them in Satin Stitch, with leaves of a deep green; finish the large centre one with veins of gold thread; work the ribbons in dark blue; where turned under in light blue, or green turned under yellow silk; the outline knot of ribbon with white cord, and fill with crimson French Knots. Work the animal at the side in red and white, without any intermediate shades. None of the colours blend imperceptibly into each other; all are sharply defined, and three distinct shades used when any shading is employed, but the greater part of the design is in Satin Stitch worked in one colour. The effect is in no way bright and vulgar, as the tints are all subdued and blend together.

Chinese Silks.—Although there are several varieties of Silk, satin, and brocaded textiles, the Silk stuff most known, and having a large sale in this country, is the Pongee. It is manufactured from the silkworm feeding on the leaves of the Ailanthus oak, and made in the mountain ranges of the province of Shantung, bordering on the Yellow Sea. *See* Shantung Pongee Silk.

Chinese Tape, India or Star.—This Tape is of superior strength, and is made both soft and sized. It is sold in any lengths desired, or on blocks. The numbers run from 00 to 12.

Chiné Silk.—So called because the patterns upon them have the appearance of having run from damp. The name is derived from the origin of the style in China. The threads are coloured in such a manner before being woven that when worked up into the silk textile, the peculiar appearance of the shading is produced. The silk measures 36 inches in width.

Chintz.—This word is the Persian for spotted, stained or variegated. It is a term employed in this country to denote a fast-printed calico, in which several, and generally five, different colours are applied to small designs and printed on a white or yellow ground, highly glazed. Originally of Indian manufacture, and known by the names of Kheetee and Calum-koaree, or firm colour, it is now made in this country, and is of great beauty. Chintzes measure from 30 inches to a yard in width.

Chintz Braid.—A cotton galloon resembling dimity binding, but having a minute chintz pattern, and printed in all kinds of colours to suit the dresses for which they are designed. They are much employed in the making of collars and cuffs. Chintz Braid is sold in pieces, or by the yard; and the price varies according to the width.

Chip.—Wood split into thin filaments, for bonnets. *See* Millinery.

Chromo Embroidery.—This is a modern work, invented by Mrs. Mee, and consists of coloured paper patterns of flowers or geometrical designs laid upon silk, satin, or coloured cloth foundations, and then worked over in Satin Stitch with filoselles or fine crewels, so that the colours on the pattern are reproduced upon the work. To work: Trace out a design upon thin coloured papers, cut this out, and then lay them upon the material. Work over them in Satin Stitch in the natural colours of the design until the whole is filled in. The paper pattern is entirely covered with the Satin Stitch, and need not be removed. Chromo embroidery is especially useful to workers who are diffident about their powers of shading leaves and flowers naturally; the design being so close to the eye, they cannot fail to match the colours painted upon it, and by following it out, line by line, need be under no apprehension about the result.

Church Embroidery.—Some of the finest specimens of needlework ever produced are those that were consecrated to the use of the Church during the centuries between the tenth and the sixteenth. In them are displayed both elaborate workmanship and good design, and we are the more impressed at their production when contrasting their excellence and refinement with our knowledge of the rude manners and customs of the times in which they were made. The work is, verily, picture painting, the colouring and the symbolical meaning attached to the ornaments depicted matching with the famous illuminations of the time. Many reasons combined to produce this perfection. Thus, artists were employed to sketch out the patterns (some of them lay claim to being those of St. Dunstan's), and an embroiderer was content to labour for a lifetime over one piece of work, which frequently was too elaborate to be finished even then, and was handed reverently down from one generation to another until completed. Such labour was looked upon as a service particularly pleasing to the Creator, nor was there any fear of its not being used when completed. In the gorgeous ritual prevailing before the Reformation, every altar required a different frontal and appendages for each festival or fast; and curtains, known as Tetravela, were placed at the sides of the altar and drawn in front of it, while priests and choristers had as many various vestments, and all required rich and elaborate embroidery. The Anglo-Saxons were not behind other nations in this particular, and mention is made of gifts of needlework to the Church as far back as 708; while Pope Innocent and Pope Adrian collected from England, for St. Peter's, much of the celebrated Opus Anglicanum; and a good deal of the old needlework now preserved on the Continent is undoubtedly of English make. William I. enriched Normandy with it, and it is constantly mentioned in the "Roman de Rose" and "De Garin;" and in 1345 the Bishop of Marseilles made a special bequest of his English alb to his church. The early Anglo-Saxon embroidery was distinguished by its lightness and freedom from overloaded ornaments. The designs were chiefly in outline, and worked as borders to garments, &c.; they were all symbolical, and conceived and executed under true art principles. These outlines were altered later, when more elaborate work was achieved. The work executed in Europe from the tenth to the twelfth centuries is of Eastern origin, and possesses many of the features of the early Phrygian and Babylonian embroideries; but the workers of Europe developed its sacerdotal character, and clothed each individual ornament with symbolical meanings, while they executed the designs with the minuteness and untiring patience that now only survives in Japanese and other oriental works. The magnificent embroidery produced was a mass of gold and silver threads, pearls, spangles, precious stones, and silks. A few specimens still remain; but at the time of the Reformation much was burnt for the sake of the gold, while copes and frontals were made into carpets and put to other base uses. The Sion cope (1250), the cope of St. Cuthbert, in Durham Cathedral, the maniple of St. Stephen and St. Blaise, the palls of the Vintners' and Fishmongers' Companies, are still in good preservation, and are the best-known specimens extant. In the earlier Anglo-Saxon works, which were chiefly in outline, the symbol of the Gammodian is frequently used, but it is not found often in later examples. It had the appearance of the Greek letter Gamma, and four of these letters are either entwined together, so as to form a square cross, or two of them, arranged to make the figure S, are used with Church roses and leaves as outline embroidery. This

Gammodian was of Indian origin, and was known to the worshippers of Buddha, 600 B.C.; it was brought by the Orientals to Rome, and adopted by the early Christians as an emblem of Christ crucified. The celebrated Opus Anglicanum of the twelfth and thirteenth centuries is not an outline embroidery, but consists of the most elaborate filled-in figure designs, the stitch used for the faces and garments being considered to be an invention of the English, and therefore its name. It is an exceedingly fine Split Stitch, which has the appearance of Chain Stitch, and it is so worked that it follows the curves and lines of the face and drapery, and gives the appearance of relief to a flat surface without any great change of colouring. This relief was further heightened by those parts that were intended for hollows in drapery or flesh, being depressed by a heated knob, thus throwing into bolder relief those places which were arranged to be in the light. Some fragments of this work can be seen at South Kensington, so carefully executed, and with such exactness, that we can understand the

FIG. 125. ALTAR CLOTH FROM STEEPLE ASTON, OXON.

admiration it gained from the whole world. The Opus Anglicanum is not confined only to this stitch; the Opus Plumarium, or Feather Stitch, is largely used; also Crewel Stitch, Long Stitch, and many varieties of Couching. Of the raised work formed with different kinds of Couching an example is shown in Fig. 125, taken from an altar cloth at Steeple Aston, Oxon, time Edward III. The grotesque animal (an emblem of power) would not be introduced in the present age upon such a covering, but figures of this description were not then considered irreverent; witness the representation of the Deity (Fig. 126) taken from the same cloth. To work Fig. 125: Form the chief parts of gold threads, which COUCH over various thicknesses of whipcord, and raise by this means above the level of the flat embroidery; the direction the gold threads take copy from the design. For Fig. 126, work the face of flesh-coloured silk, with the features rudely indicated, and surround the silk with a thick gold cord. Work the leaves above and below the face in floss silk embroidery, surround them by a dark cord, and clearly define the veins in the leaves. Raised work was not always in good taste when applied to faces of the Holy personages, as the embroiderer frequently imparted a grotesque expression to the figures instead of the agonised suffering intended to be conveyed by the contorted features; but nothing could exceed the beauty produced by the backgrounds formed with these raised Couchings or the flat floss embroideries of the figures and powderings. In Fig. 127, taken from a pulpit cloth at Forest Hill, is shown one of the favourite devices of early embroiderers. It is the winged and crowned angel resting upon a wheel, and is a symbol of eternity, power, and swiftness. This device is frequently scattered over altar frontals, and is found worked in every variety of colour; for this one, work the wings in shaded blues and crimsons and in floss silk. COUCH each leaf round with a thick cord; make the nimbus of silver or gold, outlined with a gold cord; the

although the figure scenes were varied, and ranged through incidents in both Old and New Testaments, and through the lives of numerous saints and martyrs, the symbols that surrounded the subject embroidered as a centre, or that were scattered separately over the foundation (and called powderings in that position), were almost limited to the following : Angels, with or without wheels, the Star of Bethlehem (the rays of which are waved like flames), fleur-de-lys, winged eagles, leopards, lions, white harts with crowns and gold chains, griffins, dragons, swans, peacocks, moons, crowns, lilypots, thistles, roses, and black trefoils. Secular subjects were not wholly excluded, and the coats of arms of the donor of the frontal are occasionally met with worked upon some part of it. Towards the close of the fifteenth century Church embroidery became overloaded with ornaments, and more mixed with secular subjects. The work may be said to have died out in England in

FIG. 126. ALTAR CLOTH FROM STEEPLE ASTON, OXON.

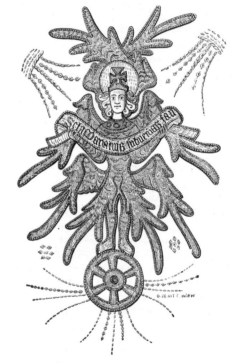

FIG. 127. PULPIT CLOTH FROM FOREST HILL.

wheel of silk, finished with gold cord; work the face and hair of the angel in floss silk. In the rays proceeding from the wheel and at the side of the device introduce spangles, which are always largely used about ancient embroidery, but never laid upon it; they either form separate rays or small devices, as in this design, or are used upon each side of rays, as shown in Fig. 131. Always catch them down to the foundation material, and never Appliqué them, and fasten them down with bright-coloured silk. The devices used in ancient work from the thirteenth to the sixteenth centuries are noticeable for their constant repetition; and, considering the very large amount of embroidery that was then executed, and the ingenuity and care expended upon it, this fact indicates that variety in those days was not looked upon as essential, the aim of the worker being excellence in execution. Thus,

the reign of Henry VIII. ; and, although it continued for another century on the Continent, it gradually became confined to the nunneries, and was no longer the universal labour of the ladies of the land ; whilst, even among the nuns, the embroidery produced was much inferior to that of earlier times. The taste for it has during the last twenty years revived, old specimens are eagerly sought for, and the stitches carefully copied; and the productions of the present age can vie in minuteness and beauty with the most elaborate old work, for, with the exception of a few alterations, it is identically the same. In modern work, even the sprays and minor parts are Appliqué, and laid upon the material when worked; while in old embroideries, although the chief parts were worked upon double flax linen that had been boiled to take out its stiffness, the lighter were frequently embroidered directly on to the foundation, and the lines laid over to conceal the junction were stitched on after the two were together. Now these cords are worked on the Appliqué, and a small second cord laid to conceal the edges, as by this means the larger cord is more likely to be evenly stretched and laid down. The linen foundations are no longer doubled, it being evident that a double foundation is more troublesome to work through than a single; and the linens now used, being expressly woven for the work, are made of the right thickness. In old work, gold lace is often cut into the shape required for a small filling and inserted instead of needlework, but this practice has not been revived. Requiring great attention and much labour to bring to perfection, Church Embroidery should not be attempted by anyone who cannot devote a large portion of her time to it; but its difficulties are soon overcome by an earnest worker.

The materials necessary are: Embroidery frames of various sizes and shapes; good strong unbleached linen, boiled to take out the stiffness and used single (bleached and cotton materials are injurious to the gold work, and have a nap on them, so should be avoided); best English made Genoa velvet, 13s. the yard; rep silk, 22s. the yard, or broadcloth, 21s., for foundations, which are always of the best; piercer, for helping to lay on floss or pick up gold bullion; stiletto, for puncturing holes; two thimbles, one for each hand; nail scissors; round-eyed needles of many sizes; carpet needles, Nos. 2, 9, 10, for gold and silk cord; packing-needles to pull twist with; the various floss silks, Dacca, sewings, purse, Mitorse, gold and silver threads, pearl purl, coloured cords, spangles, bullion, &c. Floss is the most used of all; the thick floss is split and subdivided into many pieces, or a finer floss used that needs no splitting; both are laid on or worked in LONG STITCH over all the various powderings and chief parts of the embroidery. Dacca silk is used in the same parts of the work; sewings for tacking edges down; purse silk for all parts requiring strength, and frequently for Couchings; Mitorse for leaves when floss is not employed; twist, purse silk, gold and silver thread, for Couchings and for ornamental sprays; spangles for ornaments, and bullion of five kinds for raised work. Cloth of gold and silver is inserted into the devices instead of the embroidery, and sometimes brocades, the "bawdkin" of the ancient chroniclers. All materials must be of the best, and bought at the best shops, it being worse than folly to execute such laborious work with materials that quickly deteriorate; cheap gold and silver thread, or inferior floss, quickly betraying themselves. The hands of the worker must also be smooth, and should be rubbed daily with pumice stone. Plain needlework, or anything that causes the flesh to grate or peel, should be put on one side for the time, as the floss silk catches in everything, and soon spoils. The hands also should be dry; people who have moist hands cannot work with silk and gold, as they quickly tarnish; and the left hand must be as ready and expert as the right, as it is constantly employed under the frame where the needle, without the help of eyesight, has to be put accurately up to the front in perfect lines of stitchery.

Before commencing the embroidery, draw a full-size design of it upon paper, and tint it as the colours are to come. The design when representing a large piece of needlework, such as an altar cloth, curtain, or pall, is too large and too heavy to be worked in one frame; portions of it are therefore selected and worked separately, and afterwards united, and Appliqué upon the velvet or silk background; but the full-size design gives a just idea of the whole, and enables the worker to fit the various pieces correctly together. Stretch the linen foundation in a frame, and pounce the outline of the part to be worked upon it with charcoal, and set or paint this outline with Indian ink. Carefully

FIG. 128. CHURCH EMBROIDERY.— WORKING DETAIL.

tack in any pieces of enrichments, such as gold tissue or brocade, and commence the work with raised Couchings or with the laying down of gold threads. Work these lines of gold thread so as to follow the wave of the part they are ornamenting. Thus, the flower shown in Fig. 128 is entirely executed with lines of gold or silver, placed as the shading of the pattern indicates. Fig. 128 is much reduced from natural size; an ornament so small as it is represented rarely has threads laid down. Use wavy lines of gold more than straight ones; they are shown in working detail in Fig. 129, and are managed in two ways,

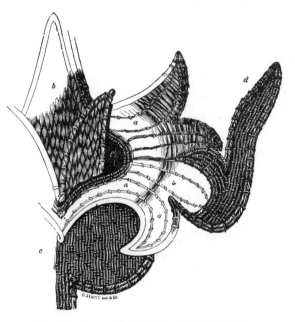

FIG. 129. CHURCH EMBROIDERY.—WORKING DETAIL.

thus: For the first, through a hole made by the stiletto in the foundation linen, bring to the front of the work from the back two pieces of gold twist of equal size and thickness, and make a bend or curve in them by curling them once round the stiletto, and then lay

L

them on the foundation with the curve still in them, and catch them down with the holding thread thrown across both at once. For the second, use very fine gold twist, and, instead of putting the ends through to the back of the work, stitch them securely down on the front part. Lay the gold twist so curved between each securing stitch (*see* Fig. 129, *c*) on the space it is to cover in an upright direction, then turn and bring it down, turn again and bring it up, and so on until the space is quite filled. These lines need not be laid close together, but with a space between them equal to one line in width, and this space may be filled in with a line laid afterwards; the gold twist lying flatter on the surface when so arranged than when laid down in consecutive lines. Turn the twist wherever possible, but in many places this cannot be done, and it must be cut and fastened, and again commenced. When angles and curves are being laid, it is a task of dexterity and patience to lay the lines and turn them so as to fill the paces with the fewest breaks. The fastening threads are of bright-coloured purse silk.

In Fig. 129 these fastening threads are shown worked in two ways. To work: Arrange them in the space marked *c* so as to form open diamonds, while in the long narrow space marked *d* make every other fastening thread form part of a straight line arranged across the work. An illustration of the two ways of using floss silk is also given in this working detail. In *a* lay it in flat lines across the surface of the foundation, and catch it down with lines of purse silk of a contrasting colour to the floss, and laid in a contrary direction. Fasten these above the floss silk by catching stitches of silk brought from the back of the work and returned there. Lay the lines of purse silk over the floss silk at nearly equal distances from each other, to imitate the veinings of a leaf, and make the threads that catch them down of a silk matching them in colour, or a contrasting shade. The space marked *b* shows the manner of working the floss silk when it is passed through the foundation and not laid upon the surface. It is LONG STITCH; but work it so that each stitch is placed in a slanting direction, and does not follow the preceding one with the regularity

FIG. 130. CHURCH EMBROIDERY.—STITCH IN FLOSS SILK.

of a straight line. The Long Stitch is more fully illustrated in Fig. 130, where it is considerably enlarged.

Fill the small space with black silk lines, which catch down by three lines, two of gold tambour, and one of silk. Make the border to the detail of two lines of thick silk cord of·harmonising colours, and catch both down with the same stitch. The single cord that surrounds the piece of work between *e* and *b* is a silk cord, round which

twist a fine gold thread, and COUCH this down with a silk thread. This working detail is an extremely useful piece for a beginner to try her hand upon, as it combines several of the stitches that must be known.

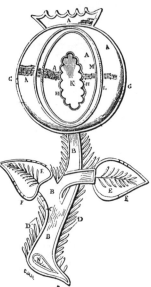

FIG. 131. CHURCH EMBROIDERY.— WORKING DETAIL.

The powdering, from an ancient chasuble, given in Fig. 131, is another suitable working detail, and should be carried out as follows: Lay gold tambour in waved lines, as at A A A A, and catch these down with even rows of purse silk. Lay down the head of the seed pod with gold tambour, as at A, but make the lines straight. Fill the stalk B B B with green floss silk of three distinct shades, work in LONG STITCH; the leaves are of the same, except the veins E E, which make of yellow floss silk; D D represent the soft hairs on stalk, and are in green floss silk; K, the centre of the seed pod, which work

FIG. 132. CHURCH EMBROIDERY.—POWDERING FROM HARDWICKE HALL.

with two shades of pinky red floss in upright lines, and surround with a silk cord; work H H with silver thread twisted round it and caught down with pale blue silk; in the inside of the cord place a narrow black cord, and catch it down with black thread. The two succeeding oval cords laid upon the gold tambour are of yellow silk, one thick, L, and one thin, M, but both with a silver twist round them. The outside cord, G, is also of yellow, but thicker than either of the others, and caught down with black. Fig. 132, p. 74, is a powdering, taken from some ancient work at Hardwicke Hall. To work: Fill the centre with lines of gold thread laid horizontally, catch them down with stitches arranged as broad diagonal bands, and surround with a line of black crochet twist. Lay gold thread down, to form the calyx, in perpendicular lines, and catch it with stitches arranged in a reverse direction to those worked in the centre part of the powdering. Make the leaves surrounding the centre in LONG STITCH, of floss silk, in three distinct shades of green, and edge them with crimson cord. Fill the pine-shaped head,

FIG. 133. CHURCH EMBROIDERY.—CURTAIN OR FRONTAL.

as to its centre, with dark crimson floss silk, and secure this with lines of silver twist, forming diamonds; as to the half leaves on each side, in their upper parts work Long Stitch in pink, shading to crimson floss, and their lower with light blue floss, shading to dark, also in Long Stitch; divide the crimson stitches from the light blue ones with a line of black crochet twist; outline the whole powdering with a gold cord caught down with crimson silk. Work the sprays, proceeding from the powdering, with gold thread, and ornament the upper ones on each side with spangles caught down with crimson silk.

The next illustrations are for more advanced work, and therefore are shown in smaller sizes, so as to give some idea of a whole design. Fig. 133 is a border and powderings suitable either for altar frontals or for altar

curtains. Work the large fleur-de-lys in LONG STITCH, with green floss of three distinct shades, and edge it with blue purse silk. Fill the band in the centre of the fleur-de-lys with crimson floss laid in perpendicular lines, and secure these lines either with gold passing or with gold tambour, and edge them with black crochet silk. The various tendrils or sprays springing from the fleur-de-lys should be made of gold thread, laid in lines, and caught down with crimson silk. These lines of gold thread require a line of floss silk laid close to them, and following their outline; this is not shown in the illustration, but is always worked when gold thread is laid over an unornamented spray. Work the smaller powderings in Long Stitch with floss silk; their colours are alternately crimson and green, the crimson shading to pink, the green from dark to light. Surround them with black crochet silk, and with branching fibres of gold thread and floss silk. The rounds are spangles, four to each round, caught down with red or green silk. Work the border upon a band of silk of a darker shade of colour to that used for the large surface; work the wheels or stars upon it in gold thread or yellow purse silk, caught down with black; work the leaves in shades of blue in Long Stitch, with stems and tendrils of gold cord, and add small spangles where shown. The three shades of blue, green, and rose colour used should be perfectly distinct from each other, not chosen, as in ordinary embroidery, so that one shade

FIG. 134. CHURCH EMBROIDERY.—BORDER FOR SUPER FRONTAL.

blends imperceptibly into the other; but, although harmonising, every one must be distinct from the shade above and below it. Fig. 134 is another border for an altar frontal or super altar. This is worked upon the same coloured velvet as the rest of the embroidery. Form the chief stem with several lines of gold tambour, caught at intervals across with coloured purse silks. Work the flowers with shaded silks, and further enrich them with lines of gold bullion laid over them, and tiny spangles; while the little buds should be made of yellow purse silk, surrounded with black cords, ornamented with sprays of red cord, and crossed with the same. Straight and battlemented lines of various coloured cords finish the work. Work these on the material, the set centre only being APPLIQUÉ. The colouring of the flowers in this pattern will depend upon the colour of the foundation, which should always be introduced to a certain extent in the embroidery, but not forming the prevailing tint. Work the flowers alternately in colours that harmonise and introduce the shade of the foundation, and in those that contrast with it.

ss for altar frontal, Fig. 135, is more
y previously shown, and requires very
ship. The difference in this design to those
y given, is that some of the parts forming it are
ked directly on to silk, and others Appliqué on to velvet,
of a different colour to either the foundation or to those
used in other parts of the same design. The stitches on
the cross work are upon white silk; the round enclosing
the four arms upon deep crimson silk, on to which the
floriated ornaments are Appliqué; and the boss forming
the centre of the cross, and containing the centre jewel,
first work on to a linen foundation, and then Appliqué on

Couching in yellow silk or gold thread. Partially cover
the ends of the cross that appear beyond the round with
embroidery, leaving visible the foundation of blue velvet
of the same colour as used round the centre boss; make
the crowns finishing these ends of gold thread, laid upon
the velvet, also the thick line from which they proceed.
Work the leaves in crimson silk, shading to pink. The
round inclosing the cross is of crimson silk, on to which
the floriated ornaments that proceed from the cross are
Appliqué after having been worked upon a linen foundation; work the outside leaves of these ornaments in Long
Stitch in three shades of green floss, the space they

Fig. 135. CHURCH EMBROIDERY—CENTRE FOR ALTAR FRONTAL.

to deep blue velvet, which lay over the white silk foundation. The cross is shown as it would be worked in the
embroidery frame. When removed and applied to the
foundation, rays of gold thread or yellow silk surround its
outside circle, and branching fibres proceed from the four
limbs, with spangles carried up each side of them. Make
the five bosses of jewels; surround each with gold thread
and with rays of green floss silk, shading to light green.
Form the body of the cross with white silk, which ornament with lines of gold thread laid in diamond patterns
caught down with spangles and red silk, and with straight
lines in floss silk; arrange the outside lines in BRICK

inclose fill in—the lower part with crimson silk, worked in
Long Stitch, and ornament with Bobs or knots formed of
gold-coloured silk; above this lay lines of gold thread,
and catch them down with crimson silk; the points which
finish the ornament work in Long Stitch with pale blue
silk. Carry pale blue cords round the edges of the ornaments, to hide the stitches connecting them to the silk
foundation. The scrolls that fill in the rounds, form of
lines of gold threads, terminating with spangles, and
catch them down with blue silk.

The designs given illustrate all the various ways of
using floss silk in flat Church Embroidery. Thus, it is

either laid down in even lines of one shade of colour and kept in position with gold or silk cords placed in devices over it, or it is worked in Long Stitch with three shades of colour. These shades are distinct from each other, and are worked with the lightest uppermost; they never blend together, but they match in tint. If contrasts are used, such as pink and blue upon the same leaf, they are divided either by a line of black crochet twist, or gold thread. In Church Embroidery no regard is paid to copying any device in its natural colours; the designs are never intended as realistic, but as conventional ornaments, and blue, lilac, crimson, and yellow are used about leaves and other floral ornaments as well as green; though, in examining old work, it will be seen that green and gold are more used about the powderings and borderings than brighter hues, which are found in all their glory in the picture centres. The faces of figures are worked in Satin Stitch, in one or two shades of flesh colour, or in SPLIT STITCH; the shade and contour of the features are managed by the direction given to the stitches, which follow the lines that would indicate them in an engraving. The manner of embroidering the various raised and flat COUCHINGS is described under that heading. The raised are as diversified as the flat, and were particularly popular as backgrounds during the fourteenth and fifteenth centuries; the cords that raise them are laid under floss silk, or Dacca silk, as well as under gold and silver threads, with binding threads worked in almost endless varieties. A very rich and favourite raised Couching for backgrounds is the Spider or Wheel pattern. In this fine whipcord is laid upon the foundation in rays like the spokes of a wheel, only curved (each wheel being about an inch in size); the gold floss silk is laid over them, and the catching threads put in on each side of every cord, so that when finished the appearance is like raised spiders' webs. Upon rich materials open Couchings are frequently laid for borders. These are made of diagonal lines of gold caught down with crosses of coloured silk, and the centre of the diamonds formed by lines filled in with spangles, beads, or French Knots; in fact, the variety that can be made by laying down one colour and attaching it to the material with stitches of a different shade is almost endless.

Having worked the various parts of the design upon frames and on linen foundations, it now remains to attach them to their proper backgrounds. This, when the article is an altar frontal or curtain, and large and heavy, is better done for the lady worker at a shop where they possess the necessary large sized frames to stretch the foundation in when applying the embroidery, as, unless that is perfectly tight, no work can be properly laid upon it. First stretch the background, and then transfer the various outlines of the traced pattern to it by dusting pouncing powder through pricked holes. Upon these lines lay the various detached worked pieces after they have been carefully cut out from their frames with very sharp scissors, leaving a small edging of about the sixteenth of an inch of linen round them. Stretch and hold down these pieces in their proper positions with a number of fine pins, and then secure them all round with fine stitching of

waxed silk or sewings. The large cord that always finishes these detached pieces, sew on to them before they are cut out: it will nearly cover the stitches, and is caught down over them; but, when in their right positions, a fine outline cord is run round them, and entirely conceals any joins. After the Appliqué work is arranged, sew spangles and other ornaments on the foundation; also sprays made of lines of gold thread. When not otherwise enriched, these gold thread sprays require the finish of a line of floss silk following their outline. Lay the floss silk as a line close to the gold thread, but not touching it, and catch it down with a silk matching it in colour. A fringe is generally added to an altar cloth; it is made of silk, the colours used in the embroidery, as well as the background colour, being represented. It is always knotted together in a cross pattern at the top, and should be exceedingly rich and good.

A less laborious kind of Church Needlework, useful for pede mats, altar cushions, and other inferior Church uses, is made upon canvas, and the threads either drawn away and the embroidery left upon velvet or cloth foundations, or the whole filled in with needlework. Brown canvas is generally used. To work: Stretch the materials in a frame, and select geometrical designs of ecclesiastical symbols; work these in TAPESTRY or CROSS STITCH, partly in Berlin wool and partly in coloured filoselles. Cross Stitch makes the embroidery coarse, unless worked entirely with silk; therefore Tapestry Stitch is the best to use. Damask and diaper patterns are suitable, while the Church rose, lily, and passion flower, treated conventionally, are good. Attempt no design that does not fit easily and with a good margin into the space intended for it, nothing looking so bad as work that is evidently too big for its surroundings. Work church carpets, &c., in squares, so as to fit into the embroidery frames, and afterwards join them together with a pattern edge placed round them. This work, being similar to Berlin Work, requires no further explanation. Crewel Work is also used for Church Embroidery, and adapts itself admirably for many purposes; but it can never vie with the true Church work of gold threads and floss silks.

Church Work over Cardboard.—This is a kind of Church Needlework which was not known in olden times, and has only been introduced since the revival of interest in church decoration. All ancient needlework was in flat embroidery, and was raised from the ground, when necessary, by means of twine and cord; but the cardboard foundations forming this variety are used for sacred monograms and emblems, and are found invaluable when clear, distinct, and slightly raised work is required. This work over cardboard is only employed in church furniture for such minor details as the emblems on stoles, burses, alms bags, mats, book markers, sermon cases, &c.; it being considered too severe in outline, and too mechanical of execution, for altar frontals and the vestments of the Church. Being worked with silk of one shade of colour throughout, and over rigid outlines, it requires no artistic taste in execution, but it must be arranged with precision, and the stitches laid down with great neatness, or it will entirely fail of effect; therefore patience and knowledge should be bestowed upon it. The designs are simple, nd correct as to ecclesiastical forms. .e the Latin cross, the initials of our patron saints, triangles, circles, and other ..ed devices. Some of these are shown in Figs. , 137, 138, and 139, in their plain cardboard foundation. Fig. 136, the double triangle, is an emblem of the Trinity, as is also Fig. 137, the circle. Fig. 138, the Latin cross, combined with the anchor and the circle, an emblem of atonement and patience; and Fig. 139, the Greek cross, surrounded by triangle and trefoil combined, a symbol of the Godhead. The manner of working is as follows: Select the design, and trace it out upon paper; prick this outline thoroughly, and transfer it to thin Bristol board by pouncing charcoal through it. Colour the design yellow, and cut it out carefully, leaving little supports, that are called "stays," to any part of the letter or emblem that is too fine to support itself before it is caught down in its position. The stays in the designs given would only be required to keep the extremities of the Greek cross (Fig. 139) in position. Tightly frame a piece of

great nicety; the thread or purse silk is kept evenly twisted, and each line laid down with great regularity, as the whole work is spoilt with one irregular stitch. When the cardboard is covered, outline the letters or emblems with a Couched line of gold, blue or red cord, or gold thread, as shown in Fig. 140. This Couched line will take away any unevenness of outline that may have been made in the working. Cut the material away from the frame, and the holland from round the edge of the embroidery at the back, and the work is finished. Fig. 141 is an illustration of a single letter worked in this manner. Cut out the exact shape and size required in cardboard, and lay the cardboard on the foundation, and carefully sew it down; the arm of the "r" requires very delicate adjustment. Then lay a line of carpet thread down the centre of the letter and fasten it, and cover all the cardboard over with lines of yellow purse silk. Fig. 140 shows the manner of working interlaced letters and adding the Couched line round them. Cut these out in one piece, lay them on the foundation, and cover with lines of yellow

FIG. 136. CHURCH WORK OVER CARDBOARD.—DOUBLE TRIANGLE.

FIG. 137. CHURCH WORK OVER CARDBOARD.—CIRCLE.

FIG. 138. CHURCH WORK OVER CARDBOARD.—LATIN CROSS, ANCHOR, AND CIRCLE.

FIG. 139. CHURCH WORK OVER CARDBOARD.—GREEK CROSS TRIANGLE, AND TREFOIL.

grey holland, sold expressly for the purpose, and secure the material to be embroidered to it. If velvet, or a large piece of plush, paste it down; if silk, sew on with great care, and sew round the centre when the emblem is arranged. Then lay the pricked outline of paper on to the velvet or silk, and pounce it through over with pipeclay; this will show where the cardboard is to come, which put on and then carefully tack down into position, and as soon as every part is secure, cut away the stays. Fix a strand of yellow twine or carpet thread down the middle of all the straight lines or the middle of rounds of cardboard, to give the work the appearance of relief; this adds to the effect, but is not absolutely necessary. Now commence the embroidery. Do this either with yellow purse silk or with gold twist of short lengths, and follow the manner of working shown in Fig. 140. Bring the needle up from the back of the frame on the left-hand side, and pass the thread over the cardboard. Use the point of the piercer to lay it flat, and insert the needle on the right side in a line parallel to where it came up. This operation, though seemingly an easy one, requires

purse silk; put on no centre cord of carpet thread to raise them, their forms being too intricate, and no stays,

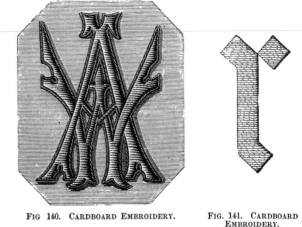

FIG 140. CARDBOARD EMBROIDERY.

FIG. 141. CARDBOARD EMBROIDERY.

as the cardboard foundation is not disjointed. Add the Couched line, and the work is complete. A variation in colouring devices is allowable, but there is no shading necessary. Thus, in Fig. 142, "I.H.C." placed upon a cross, and which can be used for a sermon case, bookmarker, or alms bag, is worked as follows: Work the cross in gold purse silk or gold thread, and COUCH it round

FIG. 142. CARDBOARD EMBROIDERY.

with a line of black silk; work the "I.H.C." in crimson silk, and Couch it round with pale blue silk, and place the device upon green or blue velvet. The large "I.H.S." of Fig. 143 is arranged for a banner. Work the "I" in gold silk, the "S" in blue, and the "H" in red;

FIG. 143. CARDBOARD EMBROIDERY.

outline all the letters in black, and make the foundation of white silk; work the wreath in SATIN STITCH and in flat embroidery.

The chief use of this embroidery being for such furniture as ladies can make without the assistance of shops,

the lengths and widths of these various ornaments will be welcome. For book-markers a very thick ribbed ribbon is required, from one to three inches in width, according to the size of the book, and a yard and a quarter in length if a double marker, which should then have an ivory barrel dividing it in the middle to keep the ends even. These barrels cost 3s. 9d. to 4s. 6d., according to their make, some being covered with a network of silk, others with gold twist. Tack the ribbon to be embroidered down to the framed holland, and put on the device at its lowest part six inches from its end, so as to allow of five inches or more turning up at the back to hide the lining. The length of the book-marker is regulated by the size of the book; a yard and a quarter being the longest required. The opposite sides of the ribbon are embroidered, or the work will not fall properly when used. The fringe, which requires to be very handsome, is either of gold thread or knotted silk, double the width of the marker and an inch over, so as to turn in. Sew one side on and then turn the work, and fix the other side so that both may be neat; hem the ends of the ribbon that turn up, and tack down with frays from the ribbon to render the stitches invisible. For alms bags there are two shapes: one, a regular bag hung upon a ring or hoop of brass, and made of a straight piece of velvet eleven inches wide and nine inches deep, joined, gathered, and sewn into a circular velvet bottom, stiffened with cardboard; and the other, the ordinary handbag, nine inches in length, six in width, with a front flap of six inches long upon which the motto or emblem is embroidered. Line the bag with white silk, but cover any part that shows with coloured velvet surrounded with an ornamental cord of gold and silk. The upper part of the alms bag is shaped, and is either curved or pointed. Make the alms mats to fit the plate, and work the monogram ornamenting them so as to be contained in a square. The ornament upon a stole consists of Greek crosses in gold silk. The length of the stole is to the knees of the wearer, and it is a narrow piece of silk that slightly widens at the ends where the cross is placed, and is finished with a handsome fringe or lace. Work a small cross at the back of the stole in the centre. Make sermon cases of velvet, lined with silk; strengthen with a cardboard foundation. The burse is used to keep the corporal and smaller eucharistic linen in. It is a kind of pocket made of silk, strengthened with cardboard and ornamented with needlework, and is in the shape of a portemonnaie without the flap, being a square of from ten to eleven inches. The colours of these ornaments vary with those used upon the altar, which are as follows: White for festivals of our Lord, the Virgin, and saints (not martyrs), and for Easter; blue for week days after Trinity, and indifferently used with green on ordinary Sundays; red, all Feasts of Martyrs, Evensong of Vigil, and of Pentecost, to the following Saturday; violet for Advent, Lent, Rogation Days, Ember week, and vigils; black for Good Friday.

Church Lace.—An Italian Needle Lace made in the seventeenth century expressly for trimmings to altar cloths and priests' vestments. It was a thick coarse Lace, the ground of which was first made and the pattern added afterwards, and worked entirely of thick Buttonhole

Stitches. The patterns were chiefly figure subjects illustrating passages in the Old and New Testaments, or the chief events in the history of the Church.

Cinq Trous, ou Mariage.—A lace made at Puy and in other parts of France, with five-sided mesh, similar to the Réseau grounds of some of the old Dieppe Lace.

Circles.—When working Pillow Lace it is often necessary to form Circles and curves with the threads for the proper delineation of the design. In the inner part of a Circle there will be fewer pinholes than on the outer, so that it is necessary to work back in this part without setting up a pin. To work: Upon reaching the end of the pins, make a CLOTH STITCH and a half with the RUNNERS that will be waiting; give a TWIST to the outside pair, and return to the pins on the outside. If pins are put up on both sides, the worker will have to miss every other on the inside; and, if that does not give room enough, two stitches are worked into the same pin on the inner side. This is called making a FALSE PINHOLE. Take the runners across to the inside, Twist three times, put up a pin; do not take up the pair that will be waiting behind the pin, but return with the same pair, and put up the pin on the outer edge; finish the stitch, and return with the pair behind the pin. When they arrive at the inner pin, take it out and stick it in again, so that it holds the row just worked, putting it in the same hole as before; work the PLAIN EDGE with the pair left behind. By this plan there are two outer pins to one inner. In a very sharp curve it is better to only Twist twice, as otherwise it would give the lace a heavy and puckered appearance. To keep the lace firm while it is being curved, occasionally drive a pin down to its head.

Clavi.—These are bands of embroidery that were worn by Roman senators, and, at a later period, by knights, on their robes of state. These bands were embroidered with thick silk or gold, and frequently ornamented with jewels. The orphrey of the priests' robes were similar in make.

Cleaning Woolwork.—If the Woolwork is not much soiled, stretch it in a frame and wash it over with a quart of water, into which a tablespoonful of ox-gall has been dropped. If much soiled, wash with gin and soft soap, in the proportions of a quarter of a pound of soap to half a pint of gin. When carefully washed, stretch the work out to dry, and iron on the wrong side while it is still damp. If the Woolwork is only faded, and not dirty, stretch it in a frame, and sponge with a pint of warm water, into which a piece of soap the size of a walnut, and a tablespoonful of ox-gall, have been dropped. Wash out the mixture by sponging the work over with clean warm water, and leave in the frame until it is perfectly dry.

Clear Point.—A lace made at Puy, in Haut Loire, after Valenciennes pattern. The lace is of durable make, but coarse, and of low price.

Clew (Anglo-Saxon *Cleow*).—A ball of thread.

Clocks.—These are ornamental embroidered finishes to the leg and instep of knitted stockings and socks, and are worked with filoselle or washing silk of a colour that either matches or contrasts with the stocking they adorn, or with two shades of one colour. They are embroidered before the foot is Knitted and after the heel is finished.

The name given to this decoration is considered to have originated in the resemblance to the pendulum of a clock.

To work: No tracing is required, but run a guiding line up the foot from the point where the heel joins the foot; the height of this line for a stocking is seven inches, for a gentleman's sock three inches. The Clock consists of a plain line and an ornamental finish. Work the plain line as follows: OVERCAST the two stitches in the stocking that run up the leg from the point where the heel joins the foot to a height of four inches, then Overcast two more inches, but only over one stitch of the stocking. The plain line thus made will be six inches in height. The ornamental finish to this is varied to suit the worker's taste, the simplest being the fleur-de-lys and the arrowhead. Make the fleur-de-lys by thickly Overcasting the three leaves that form the well-known conventionalised copy of that flower; for the arrow-head, take the plain line already formed up another inch of the stocking and add to it on each side six diagonal lines graduating in length; those nearest the end of the line, or the tip of the arrow, make the shortest, and the last, half-an-inch in length, the longest.

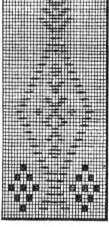

FIG. 144. CLOCK.

Fig. 144 is an illustration of a much more elaborate final to a Clock than the two described above; it is worked in two shades of one colour, the darker forming the centre, and the diamonds on each side. Make these diamonds of raised dots formed with OVERCAST; the rest of the design is simply Overcast. Overcast a line along the side of the foot of the stocking or sock three inches in length, after the foot is nearly knitted and before commencing to narrow.

Close Cord.—The thick lines in Macramé are called Close Cords.

Close Knitting. *See* KNITTING.

Close Leaf.—In Honiton Lace the Close Leaves of the sprigs are worked in Cloth Stitch, which is illustrated in Figs. 145 and 146, as a leaf with a Plain Edge half finished and completed. To work: Commence by first running the lace pin down to its head to hold firm the twelve pairs of bobbins required to make the leaf; TWIST the outside pair on each side 3 times to the left, put the left-hand pair aside, and take the next two pairs, numbering them 1 and 2, and 3 and 4. 1 and 2 are the RUNNERS, and will work across, taking the other bobbins as they come. First stitch—put 2 over 3 with the left hand, then with both hands put 4 over 2, and 3 over 1, 1 over 4 with left hand, push away 3 and 4 with left hand, and bring forward 5 and 6 with the right. Second stitch—2 over 5 with the left hand, 6 over 2 with the right, 5 over 1 with the left, 1 over 6 with the left, push away 5 and 6 with the left hand, bring forward 7 and 8 with the right. Third stitch

CREWEL WORK.

—2 over 7 with left hand, 8 over 2 with right, 7 over 1 with left, 1 over 8 with left, push away 7 and 8 with left hand, bring forward 9 and 10 with right. Fourth stitch—2 over 9, 10 over 2, 9 over 1, 1 over 10. Fifth stitch—2 over 11, 12 over 2, 11 over 1, 1 over 12. Sixth stitch—2 over 13, 14 over 2, 13 over 1. 1 over 14. Seventh stitch— 2 over 15, 16 over 2, 15 over 1, 1 over 16. Eighth stitch —2 over 17, 18 over 2, 17 over 1, 1 over 18. Ninth stitch—2 over 19, 20 over 2, 19 over 1, 1 over 20. Having now worked across the leaf to within one pair of bob-bins, do the plain edge. Twist 1 and 2 three times to the left with the left hand, while the right is taking a lace pin from cushion; then holding both bobbins in the left hand, stick the pin in front of the twisted thread into the first pin hole on the right hand, give a small pull to draw the twist up; this had better be done after the twist. Two pairs are now outside the pin. The right-hand pair will be found twisted as it was done in commencement. Make the stitch about the pin 2 over 21, 22 over 2, 21 over 1, 1 over 22. Twist both pairs three times to the left, using both hands at once; pull the Twist up gently. The first

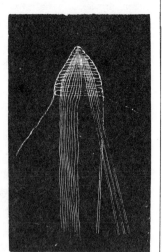

FIG. 145. CLOSE LEAF—HALF FINISHED.

FIG. 146. CLOSE LEAF—FINISHED.

pair have now worked across, and are put away, the last pair becoming 1 and 2 in their turn. In the first row the bobbins were taken as they came; in arranging them so as to make the knots belong to the Hanging bobbins they were, of necessity, twisted over each other. This is imma-terial at the commencement, but each bobbin must now have its own place, and every twist will be a defect. In putting down a pillow the bobbins run together, and become twisted, and half a beginner's time is taken up in dis-entangling them. It is a tiresome process, but it has its uses, as it gives facility in handling, and accustoms the eye to detect wrongful twists. In the 2nd row the bobbins must be numbered from right to left, 4 and 3, 2 and 1, the latter being the active pair. The stitch is apparently reversed, but the theory is the same. There are two pairs of bobbins used, a right and a left-hand pair; the middle left-hand bobbin is always put over the middle right-hand one; each of the latter pair is put over the one nearest to it, and the middle left-hand again over the middle right-hand one. In working from left to right the Runners begin and end the stitch, in returning, the Hangers begin and end it.

First stitch—3 over 2 left hand, 2 over 4 left hand, 1 over 3 right hand, 4 over 1 left hand, put away 3 and 4 with the right hand, bring forward 5 and 6 with the left. Second stitch—5 over 2, 2 over 6, 1 over 5, 6 over 1. Third stitch—7 over 2, 2 over 8, 1 over 7, 8 over 1. Fourth stitch—9 over 2, 2 over 10, 1 over 9, 10 over 1. Fifth stitch—11 over 2, 2 over 12, 1 over 11, 12 over 1. Sixth stitch—13 over 2, 2 over 14, 1 over 13, 14 over 1. Seventh stitch—15 over 2, 2 over 16, 1 over 15, 16 over 1. Eighth stitch—17 over 2, 2 over 18, 1 over 17, 18 over 1. Ninth stitch—19 over 2, 2 over 20, 1 over 19, 20 over 1. Having now reached the edge where the pair of bobbins were put aside at commencement of row, twist 1 and 2 thrice to the left, stick a pin in the first left-hand pinhole in front of the Twist; make the stitch about the pin 21 over 2, 2 over 22, 1 over 21, 22 over 1, Twist both pair thrice, and pull Twist up. Repeat these two rows until three rows near the end are reached, then cut off a passive pair in each row close up to the work, and when the three rows are finished, plait the threads into a beginner's stem. *See* Finished Leaf Fig. 146.

Close Stitch.—In Needle-point Lace the Close Stitch is a simple Buttonhole worked without any openings.

Close Trefoil.—A Honiton Lace sprig, as in Fig. 147,

FIG. 147. CLOSE TREFOIL.

the leaf being worked in LACE STITCH, and the petals in CLOTH STITCH. Commence at the end of stem, and hang on six pairs of bobbins; work straight up the stem and round the inner circle of flower, make a SEWING when the circle is crossed. In the petals, which are next worked, there are more pinholes round the outside edge than there are on the inside, therefore false pinholes will here be required; and as the petals require a greater number of bobbins to form them than the inner circle and stem, they will have to be added. Work the first two rows of petal in Cloth Stitch with the six pairs, and, before putting in the second pin on the outside, hang on a new pair of bobbins, winding the knot well out of the way; pass the new thread well underneath the two workers, and run it close up to the hanging bobbins; stick a pin, and complete a PLAIN edge. The pair just added will count as the seventh pair, and will hang on to the threads which come across; work two rows in Cloth

M

Stitch, and hang on an eighth pair in the same manner. When the eighth pair is added it will be necessary to make a false pinhole, in order to keep the outer and inner edges level with each other. This is done as follows: Work across to the inside in Cloth Stitch, TWIST the bobbins thrice, and stick a pin in; but instead of completing the edge, come back with the same pair, and again to the outer edge; then return to the inside edge, take out the pin, re-stick it in the same hole, and finish the Plain Edge with the idle pair left. Two pins, by this arrangement, are stuck in the outer edge to one in the inner, and a curve is thus smoothly made. When the pins are put up close together, Twist the bobbins twice instead of thrice at the edges to prevent any puckering. The false pinholes must be repeated until the petal is rounded and the thinner part arrived at, when a single pair of bobbins is cut away. When turning the corner of the first petal and commencing the second, SEW twice to the circle, and hang on two pairs of bobbins in two following rows, and cut them off when the petal is rounded and the thinner part of it reached; the middle petal being wider than the others requires an extra pair of bobbins; the last petal will only require one additional pair of bobbins, hung on where it widens; the first and third petals require eight pairs of bobbins to work them, and the middle nine. When working, turn the pillow as the work turns, so as to keep the hanging bobbins straight in the front; and when the third petal is finished, Sew at each side; tie all the threads up inside one of the working pairs, tie these working pairs separately, and cut quite close. The leaf requires eight pairs of bobbins, and two gimp bobbins; the latter will take the place of the STREAK STITCH, the gimp being passed through the working pair on each side, but in all other respects the leaf is worked in HALF STITCH. When the leaf is nearly finished, tie up two pairs of bobbins in successive rows, and cut off, Sew to the stem on each side, cut the gimp close, tie the remaining bobbins inside the working pair, tie these separately, and cut off.

Cloth.—(Derived from the Saxon *Clath*, signifying any woven textile, whether of silk, wool, flax, hemp, cotton, arras, or hair.) A woollen material of several descriptions, as also a generic term applied equally to linen and cotton. Broadcloths are the best and stoutest, and are seven quarters wide. They vary in fineness; there is the superfine, second, and inferior. Narrow Cloths are half the width of the last, or three-quarters, or seven-eighths. Habit cloths are a thinner and lighter description of material, generally seven quarters wide. Royal cashmere is used for summer coating, being a fine narrow cloth, made of Saxon wool, in worsted weft. The best superfine is made of Saxon or Spanish wool; the inferior superfine of the English, as also the seconds, which is used for liveries, beside coarser sorts. The excellence of the cloth depends on the quality of the wool, the permanence of the dye, and the degree of perfection attained in the processes of manufacture. In judging the quality of broadcloth, the fineness of fibre and closeness of texture have to be observed; and the hand should be passed along the surface against the lie of the nap, when the fineness of the wool will be made evident by the silkiness of the

feeling. A portion being taken up loosely in both hands, a fold pressed strongly between the fingers of one hand, and a sudden sharp pull given by the other, the peculiar vibrating clearness of the sound produced by the sudden escape of the fold indicates, to the experienced ear, the goodness of the cloth. The gloss on cloth should not look very satiny.

Cloth Appliqué.—A modern imitation of the Cloth embroidery so largely worked by Eastern nations. It consists of cutting out and arranging upon a coloured cloth foundation variously coloured and shaped pieces of the same material, and securing these by fancy stitches worked in silk or wool.

To work: Select a dark coloured cloth as a foundation, trace upon it a geometrical design, and then stitch it in an embroidery frame. Prepare pieces of cartridge paper by

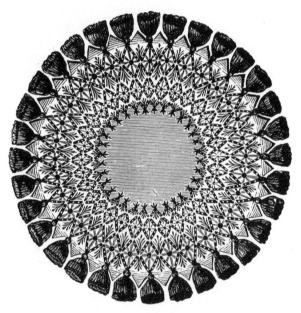

FIG. 148. CLOTH EMBROIDERY

cutting them into the shapes that fit the various parts of this design, and lay these upon the coloured cloths selected to form the pattern. Cut out these shapes accurately in the coloured cloths, pin them on to the cloth foundation in their right positions, and secure them by working round their edges either with HERRINGBONE or POINT LANCÉ stitches. Use fine Pyrenean wool or filoselle for these fancy stitches, and further enrich the work by others, such as FRENCH KNOTS, TÊTE DE BŒUF, and SATIN STITCH, worked over the pieces of coloured cloth, or made to form tendrils, bosses, and other ornaments to the pattern.

Cloth Embroidery.—A kind of needlework extensively practised by the natives of India and Persia, and other Asiatic nations, who excel in joining together coloured pieces of cloth in handsome designs, and covering them with various fancy stitches made in floss silk or gold and silver thread. The work is a species of Inlaid Appliqué, the pieces of cloth not being laid on any foundation, but sewed together continuously.

Fig. 148 is a mat of this description. To work: Make the centre of crimson or deep blue cloth, and the outside edge of cream white, pale blue, or grey. Hide the parts where these two pieces join with a row of POINT LANCÉ stitches worked over the overcasting. Make the embroidery upon the light cloth with WHEELS and Point Lancé, cut and turn down the outside edge to form vandykes, and ornament with a coloured silk tassel in every hollow. The beauty of the embroidery depends

paper, and go over the lines so made with water colour mixed with gum to render them permanent. Work the whole pattern in SATIN STITCH, with the exception of the centres to the flowers, which either fill in with FRENCH KNOTS or with LEVIATHAN STITCH. Work the large flower in three distinct shades of one colour, using the lightest as the outside colour and for the innermost circle, and fill the centre of the flower with French Knots made of the medium shade of colour. Work the small flowers

FIG. 149. CLOTH EMBROIDERY.

upon the judicious colouring of the floss silk fancy stitches, which should be bright and distinct, like all Eastern colouring, but not of hues that become gaudy by reason of their violent contrasts.

Fig. 149 is of another description of Cloth Embroidery, worked upon a dark-coloured cloth, such as maroon, peacock blue, or invisible green, and is useful for valances, tablecloth borders, and other purposes. Trace the outline of the design upon cloth with white carbonised

in two shades of colour, place the darkest shade inside, and finish the centres with a Leviathan Stitch made in the lightest shade used. Work the buds and leaves in two shades of colour, also the small forget-me-not shaped flowers; but in these last, keep each individual flower to one shade of the two colours employed. In the small pattern that forms the border of this design, use two shades of one colour, and work all the under stitches (*see* Fig. 149) in the light shade, and the stitches that fill in the centres, and that are worked so as partly to cover the first made ones, in the dark. A handsome design is produced when the whole pattern is worked with a red brown filoselle as the darkest colour, and orange gold as the lightest, upon a cloth of a medium brown shade. Shades of blue upon peacock blue foundation, and cinnamon upon russet red, are good, as the embroidery worked

ing cushions and footstools. Materials required: a frame, skeins of various coloured filoselles, No. 2 gold braid, and Berlin canvas. To work: Stretch the canvas in a frame, and stitch the gold down upon it, line by line, until the canvas is completely covered. Select an easy geometrical pattern of those printed for Berlin wool work, and work out the design in GOBELIN STITCH over the gold braid

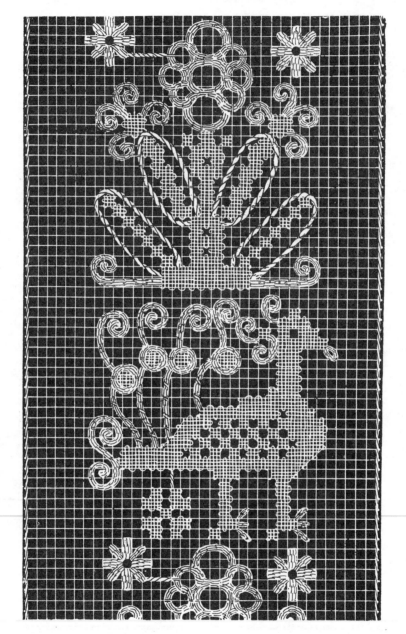

FIG. 150. CLUNY GUIPURE LACE.

out in shades of one colour is more artistic than when many bright colours are used. The border in the illustration is of chenille gimp, but a soft ball fringe of the colours used in the work would look equally well.

Cloth of Gold Embroidery.—A modern work, formed with gold braid and filoselle silks, and useful for cover-

with coloured filoselle, take each thread over one strand of the gold braid foundation, and count it as one stitch. No shading need be attempted, and two colours, such as red and grey, are sufficient to work the whole design, the foundation of braid being already bright enough for effect.

Cloth Patchwork.—This is Patchwork of the ordinary kind, but made with pieces of bright cloth instead of scraps of silk. *See* PATCHWORK.

Cloth Stitch.—The close stitch used in most Pillow Laces, and consisting of simply weaving the threads like those of a piece of cloth. It is fully described in BRAIDWORK (*Cloth or Whole Braid*) and in CLOSE LEAF.

Cluny Guipure Lace.—One of the Darned Net Laces whose origin is lost in antiquity, and which were known as "Opus Filatorium" in early times, "Opus Aranum," or Spider Work, in the Middle Ages, and "Filet Brodé," or Guipure d'Art, in more modern times. Numerous patterns of these laces are to be seen in the pattern books of Vinciola, sixteenth centuries, and much mention is made of them in the inventories of lace from the fourteenth to the seventeenth centuries. The groundwork is plain Netting, commenced with one stitch, and increased and decreased like ordinary Netting, and upon this is worked the pattern with counted stitches, darned in and out like the modern Guipure. The name "Point Conté," generally given to Guipure, is derived from this counting of stitches. Cluny was only a variety of this Darned Netting, but into it were introduced raised stitches, wheels, circles, and triangles, which distinguished it from the plain darned Guipure. A shiny glazed thread was also introduced about parts of the lace as a contrast to the unglazed thread forming the rest of the pattern.

Fig. 150 is a reproduction of a piece of Cluny Guipure formerly ornamenting a bed quilt belonging to Louis XIII., and is a good example of the quaint kind of patterns that were anciently worked, and that have been lately revived in French and Irish lace manufactories. In this the glazed thread forms the raised feathers of the bird, the stars and the circles, and also surrounds what is intended for a tree in the design. In many designs the glazed thread is worked as an outline round every part of the pattern, and Buttonhole Stitch used; but here Point Passé, Point de Toile, and Point Feston are employed, and there is no Buttonhole. This lace requires its foundation to be stretched in a frame while the pattern is worked upon it. Its stitches and manner of working them are similar to those used in GUIPURE D'ART.

Coatings.—Black or blue cloths, in checks, stripes, or diagonals, manufactured for men's wear. The widths comprise both the narrow and wide, and their several prices vary according to quality and width.

Cobble. — (Danish *Cobbler*, to mend coarsely; the Welsh *Cob* being a round stone, making a rough street pavement; descriptive of the puckering of work; old French *Cobler*, to knit or join together.) A term employed in needlework to denote coarse and unevenly drawn work or mending.

Coburgs.—These stuffs are composed of wool and cotton, and in their make resemble a twilled Orleans or French merino. Some of the varieties have a silk warp and woollen weft. They can be had in all colours, and measure from 30 to 36 inches in width, varying in price according to their quality and width. They are chiefly used for coat linings and for dresses by the lower orders, who always employ them for mourning.

Cockscombs.—A name given by laceworkers to the uniting threads known in Needle Laces as Bars and Brides. *See* BAR.

Cocoa Bindings.—These are to be had of 2½ inches and 3 inches width, and are sold by the gross. The lengths run from 18 to 24 yards. They are employed for sewing round cocoa-nut mattings as bindings.

Coins.—A French term signifying the clocks of a stocking; that is to say, the decorative embroidery, consisting of a mere line made with floss silk, with a finish more or less ornamental, running from the foot to about half way up the leg of the stocking, on both sides of the ankle and calf. These are sometimes of a uniform colour with the stocking and sometimes contrast with it. *See* CLOCKS.

Coive.—A French term to designate the lining of a bonnet, of whatever material it may be made.

Colberteen Lace.—A lace made in France in the seventeenth century, and named after Colbert, the King's Minister, the founder of the French lace manufactories. There is no accurate record of its make, but it is considered to have been a coarse network lace of an open square mesh, and to have been used for ordinary occasions. It is frequently mentioned by English and French authors and poets of the seventeenth century, as a common and gaudy lace.

Coloured Handkerchief Embroidery.—A modern embroidery that imitates Indian embroidery. The materials required are all shades of filoselle silks, gold thread, and a large cotton handkerchief, such as worn by peasants in France and Switzerland round the shoulders. The handkerchief is selected for its oriental design and colouring, and for its good border. To work Back the handkerchief with a piece of ticking, and RUN lining and material together. Work round the chief outlines of the pattern with CREWEL or ROPE STITCH, then COUCH down a line of gold thread outside the outlines. Fill up the centres of the pattern and the groundwork with CREWEL and SATIN STITCH worked in filoselles that match the colouring; in fact, reproduce the whole design in rich materials. Finish with a border of plain velvet or plush, and use for a banner screen or a table cover.

Coloured Twill.—A stout cotton material, made in all the principal colours, and employed for linings of curtains and embroidery; it will not bear washing. It is 1¾ yard in width.

Combed Out Work.—This is of two kinds: The first consists of inserting loops of wool an inch and a half in length into alternate rows of plain Knitting during the process of making, and, after a sufficient length has been knitted, cutting these loops and combing them out with first a large toothed comb, and then a small one, until the wool assumes the texture of hair, and entirely conceals the knitted foundation. This is fully explained in BIRD NEST MATS. In the second, detached flowers are formed of combed out wool and bits of velvet. This latter kind is illustrated in Fig. 151, which shows two different coloured and shaped pansies, and the manner of finishing them at the back.

The materials necessary for this Combed Out Work are different shades of single Berlin wool, pieces of good velvet, fine green wire, and gum. Each petal is made separately, thus: Wind single wool of a light colour six times round two fingers of the left hand, then take the wool off the fingers without disturbing it, and run a piece of fine wire through the loops at one end, and fasten the wire firmly by twisting it so that it secures all the wool at that end. Cut the loops at the end where they are not secured with the wire, and proceed to comb out the wool; use a coarse comb to commence with, and then change to a smaller toothed one until the wool is as fine as floss silk, then snip the edges of the wool to the shape of a pansy petal. Carefully drop a little pure gum in and about the wool forming the petal, to keep the combings from getting out of place, and also use gum to fix on to the petal the

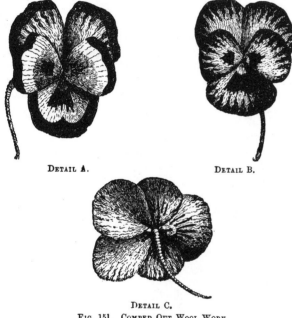

DETAIL A.   DETAIL B.

DETAIL C.
FIG. 151. COMBED OUT WOOL WORK.

light fibres of different coloured wool that form the markings in Details A and B. Comb these out before they are laid on the petal, and fix them to their places with the points of scissors, not with the hands. Make the eye of the pansy and the dark outside lines of Detail A with pieces of velvet cut to shape and caught down with long stitches of coloured silk, but gum the edges of the velvet into position. As each petal is made, crook the end of the wire supporting it, and hang it up by this crook to dry; when all are finished, combine the separate wires, cover them with green wool, and finish off the back of the flower quite neatly, to present the appearance of Detail C. The colours of Detail A are a foundation of white wool with dark ruby velvet forming centre spots and edges, and light bits of combed out ruby wool put on the petals, to shade the velvet into the white in the centre of flower and at the edge. The silks used are yellow purse silk. Detail B has an amber ground, with violet markings, with a deeper violet velvet used for the eye of the flower, and violet

purse silk used for the lines. Pansy leaves are generally formed like those used in WOOL WORK FLOWERS, or they can be made of various shades of green wool combed out and fastened as the pansy petals.

Commence a Loop.—A term used in TATTING.

Common Heel.—*See* STOCKING KNITTING.

Cone.—A term sometimes used in Guipure d'Art for POINT PYRAMID.

Confection.—A French term applied to any kind of ready-made article of dress.

Connaught.—A species of cotton cloth, otherwise known as BASKET CLOTH, made after the manner of AIDA CANVAS or TOILE COLBERT, the French name by which it was first known. It is employed as a foundation for embroidery. JAVA CANVAS and FANCY OATMEAL are names applied to the same cloth.

Connaught Yarns.—An Irish yarn recently produced by the peasants of Valencia Island. The fibre of the wool employed is fine, soft, and elastic; and the staple being longer than that usually spun for the purpose of knitting or weaving, it is durable in wear. CONNAUGHT YARNS are thinner than the BLARNEYS produced in the same island, and are more loosely twisted. The Fingerings are to be had in 3 ply and 4 ply. They may all be had in black, white, grey, heather, ruby, navy-blue fancy mixtures, &c. *See* BLARNEYS.

Continuous Inner Pearl.—Used in Honiton and other braid laces as an ornament to the inner side of any leaf that is not filled in with stitches. It is shown in the left-hand leaf of Fig. 152. To work: Hang on ten pairs of

FIG. 152. CONTINUOUS INNER PEARL.

bobbins and two gimps at the tip of the hollow leaf and do CLOTH STITCH to the place where the opening begins; work to the centre, stick a pin in the top hole, hang on a pair of gimps round it, TWIST the two pairs of working bobbins twice, make a stitch about the pin and work first down one side of the opening and then down the other. The stitch at the inside edge is the Inner Pearl, made thus: Work to the inner gimp, pass it through the pair, Twist the workers six times, stick a pin, pass the gimp through the pair, and work back, Twist the workers six times, stick a pin, pass the gimp through again and work back. When both sides are finished all but the lowest hole the two working pairs of bobbins will meet in the middle; make a stitch, stick a pin, tie the gimps and cut them off, and let one of the working pairs merge into the passive bobbins; finish the leaf, cut off all but six pairs of bobbins, work the circle, and then work the other leaf in LACE STITCH.

Contract an Edge.—A term used in CROCHET.

Coques.—A French term to denote bows of ribbon arranged in loops as a decorative trimming.

Corah Silk.—A light Indian washing textile, of a cream white, lighter in shade than any of the other undyed silks, either Indian or Chinese. It is much used by young ladies for evening dress, and is very economical in wear. Sold in pieces of 7 yards or 10 yards each, and running from 30 inches to 34 inches in width. Corah silk is one of the class called "cultivated," in contradistinction to the Tussore, or "wild silk," produced in India.

FIG. 153. DOUBLE CORAL STITCH.

Coral Stitch.— *See* EM-BROIDERY STITCHES.

Cord.—In Needle-made Laces the fancy and thick stitches that form the centres of the flowers and sprays are surrounded with a raised rim closely Buttonholed, and called either a Cord or Cordonnet. This rim varies as to thickness and size in almost all the laces, a peculiarity particularly noticeable in the old Spanish and Venetian Rose points. It never, however, varies as to being finished with close lines of Buttonhole, the difference in its shape and size being attained by the larger or smaller amount of padding (made of coarse thread) that is run in under the Buttonhole. For manner of working, *see* CRESCENTS.

Cord.—Part of MACRAMÉ.

Cord, and Fancy Check Muslins.—These are cambric muslins, with stripes and cords placed across each other, in plaid fashion; thick threads being introduced into the warp and weft. They are a yard wide, and are employed for children's dresses and servants' aprons.

Corded Muslin.—This muslin is also known as "Hair-cords," having a thick hair cord running one way only. It is made a yard wide, and is employed for infants' dresses, and otherwise.

Cording.—*See* CORD STITCH.

Cordonette.—The French term to signify an edging, or small cord or piping to form an edging. It is also the name given to French netting silk, which is finer than our crochet or purse silk, and is sold wound on reels.

Cordonnet.—The raised rim in Needle Laces, identical with CORD.

Cordova Lace.—This is the name of a stitch or filling used in ancient Needle Point Lace and in modern Point. There are two ways of working it, one like the Point de Reprise of Guipure d'Art, and the other as follows: Commence by throwing three threads across the space to be filled in a horizontal direction, putting them in as near together as they can be worked. Twist the needle and thread round the third or under thread twice, so as to carry the thread along the third line for a short distance from the commencement of the stitch, and DARN a flat spot over the three lines by working up and down them twice. Twist the thread again round the third line twice and darn another spot, and continue in the same manner to the end of the row. For the next row leave an interval the width of three threads between it and the first, and work like the first. Continue to work the second row to the end of the space, and then throw three threads perpendicularly across the space to form a square with the horizontal threads, passing them one over and one under the horizontal threads and between the spots already worked. Darn spots on these as upon the others, and continue the perpendicular lines to the end of the space requiring to be filled.

Cordovan Embroidery.—A modern Embroidery founded upon Appliqué. The materials used are gold or silver American cloth, Serge and Filoselles. To work: Trace a bold but conventional pattern, either of flowers and leaves, or a flowing arabesque that is continuous, upon the back or under side of a piece of gold-coloured American cloth. Cut this out, and lay it upon thick brown holland or coarse canvas, and paste the two materials together. Cut out the canvas to the pattern shape when the paste is dry. Stretch a piece of dark blue, green, or crimson serge, tack the gold American cloth to that with long stitches taken over, not through the cloth. With gold-coloured filoselle BUTTONHOLE the cloth to the serge round the outer edges, and with crimson and green filoselle work on the cloth in SATIN STITCH, the centre of the flowers, veins of the leaves, or any detail that will mark out the design. On the serge background work detached sprays, tendrils, and stems in CREWEL STITCH.

Cords.—These are of various kinds. Black silk Cords, employed for watch guards, and for button loops and coat edging, sold in knots of 35 yards and by the gross. The numbers run from 2 to 10; 3, 5, and 7 being the most useful. Black mohair Cords, formerly employed for coat edgings, are now much used for looping up dresses; the numbers run up to 8; 2, 4, and 7 being the most useful. They are sold by the gross—four pieces, 36 yards in each. Blind Cords are of cotton thread, linen thread, and flax covered with worsted, and can be had in various colours—scarlet, crimson, amber, blue, green, &c.—sold in lengths of 72 yards, two pieces to the gross. Cotton Cords, in black and white, are extensively used by dressmakers for pipings, and in upholstery; they are sold in bundles of 5lb., mixed sizes or otherwise, and in single skeins. Picture Cords, a heavy-made article, are sold in lengths of 36 yards, and may be had in scarlet, crimson, green, amber, and other colours, so as to correspond with the walls. There are, besides, silk mantle Cords, also heavy-made, and much in use, having four pieces of 36 yards to the gross; the numbers run from 1, 1½, 2, 2½, 3 and 4: Nos. 1, 2, and 3 being most employed in black or colours.

Cords, Cloth.—A fancy woollen material, ribbed after the manner of a rep, only in vertical lines instead of horizontal ones. It measures 28 inches in width.

Cord Stitch.—A decorative needle stitch, sometimes called Cording, formed by interlacing two lines of silk or

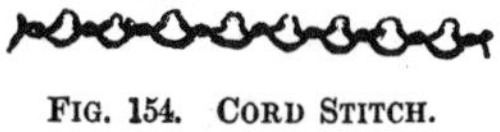

FIG. 154. CORD STITCH.

thread in the manner shown in Fig. 154. Cord Stitch is

also used in working Bars in Modern Point lace and Damascene lace, when the Bars are not finished with Buttonholes.

To work: Throw a line of thread across the space to be filled, and secure it tightly to the braid. Return the thread to the spot it started from by winding it round and round the tight line made as described.

Corduasoy.—A thick silk, woven over a foundation of coarse thread.

Corduroy.—(From the French, *Cord du Roi*.) A description of fustian. It is made of cotton, having a pile, but has a cut, ribbed, or corded surface. The best kinds are twilled, and they may be had in grey or slate colour, and in drabs. There is likewise a very superior make of Corduroy, especially made for ladies' jackets and for the trimmings of warm cloth dresses, which has a very broad rib and high pile, is soft and pliable, and has no smell. It is three-quarters of a yard in width.

Cord Work.—This is made with a needle, and is a kind of coarse Needle Lace executed with black or coloured purse silks, fine bobbin cord, or strong linen thread. It loses its character unless worked with thick materials, but it is immaterial whether silk or linen threads are used. It is made in the form of rosettes (see Fig. 155),

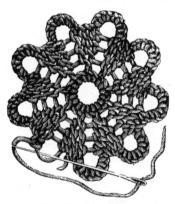

Fig. 155. Cord Work.

or in squares, and the patterns are taken from Crochet designs. Mark out the patterns upon tracing linen, and back with Toile Ciré. The only stitch is the ordinary Buttonhole, the varieties in the patterns being attained by either working these Buttonholes close together in compact masses, or separating them by carrying the working thread plainly along the pattern over a certain fixed space.

The rosette shown in the illustration is worked as follows: First row—work into a small loop eighteen Buttonholes. Second row—work a Buttonhole, miss the space of one and work another, continue to the end of the row, making nine Buttonholes and nine spaces. Third row—work two Buttonholes, one on each side of the one in the previous row, and carry the thread plainly along in the spaces. Fourth row—as second, but working three instead of two Buttonholes. Fifth row—as third, but working five Buttonholes instead of three. Sixth row—make nine loops, commencing each loop from the final Buttonhole of the pattern and fastening it to the first Buttonhole on the next pattern, so that the loop is situated over the spaces in the rosette, and not over the Button-

holes; run the thread across the thick parts of the rosette between the loops. Seventh row—work nine Buttonholes into each loop, and two over the thick part of the pattern. Rosettes, of whatever design, are commenced from the centre with a circle made of cord, and Buttonholed round. They are increased by two to four extra stitches being worked in every round of Buttonhole. In working squares, commence at the top with a line of close Buttonhole worked upon a cord foundation, and from this work either a plain square Crochet pattern or a simple modern point stitch, such as Cadiz or Escalier; if the latter, see that it is enclosed on every side with a line of close Buttonhole·

Another Variety of work with the same name is formed over bodkins, and is suitable for quilts and couvre-pieds, but not for flat articles, as when finished it has the appearance of raised stars or wheels formed into round or diamond-shaped patterns. It can be worked with worsted, single Berlin or fleecy wool, or coarse, but soft, knitting cotton, and each wheel is made separately and joined together.

To work: Commence by taking three equal sized large steel bodkins, and tie them firmly together in the middle with the wool, opening them out to form a six-pointed wheel with equal distances between each spoke, and with their eyes following each other, as shown in Fig. 156. Pick up the wool that tied the bodkins together and loop it round the nearest bodkin, pass it on to the next, and loop it round that, and so on round all six spokes, as shown

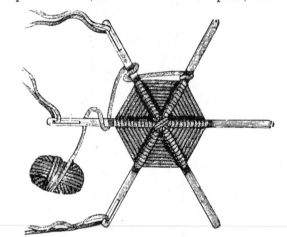

Fig. 156. Cord Work.—Detail A.

in Fig. 156, detail A. Work twelve rows in this way; the space between the spokes will be wider in each row, and the wool will have to be kept at even lengths, and untwisted; fasten off by running the wool into the wheel. Thread the bodkins with a long double piece of wool, and pull them through and out of the wheel, filling in their places with the doubled wool. Work other wheels in the same way and thread them together. It will require some practice to place these wheels together into designs of diamonds and squares, so as to secure them firmly, but the principle of all will be the same. Pass a diagonal thread in one wheel horizontally through the next wheel, and *vice versâ*, and when no spoke of the next wheel touches a thread, run it underneath the work until it can be drawn through another wheel. The manner of doing this is shown in the illustration, in which the doubled thread is drawn through the top wheel, and then taken under the part of the work where the side wheels join. The manner of connecting these wheels

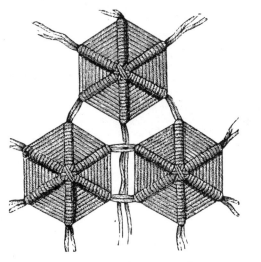

FIG. 157. CORD WORK—DETAIL B.

together is shown in Fig. 157, detail B. When all are firmly drawn together into a solid body, work a row of DOUBLE CROCHET round their outer edge, and draw and work into this line all ends of threads, so as to secure them without knots.

Corfu Lace.—A coarse Greek lace or Reticella, still made by the natives of that place, but of no commercial value.

Cork Lace.—*See* IRISH LACE.

Cornet.—A French term used in dressmaking to signify the open, trumpet shape of a sleeve at the wrist.

Coromandels.—A description of Manchester made cotton stuffs, chiefly made for the African export trade.

Corsage.—A French term to signify a bodice.

Corset.—The French term to signify a pair of stays.

Corset Cord.—This cord is made both of linen and of cotton. It is sold either by the dozen yards or by the yound.

Costume.—A French term to signify a complete dress.

Côteline, or Côtelaines.—A kind of white hair cord muslin, printed in all kinds of patterns and colours. It is of French manufacture and designed for a dress material. The width measures 31 inches. The printing and shading of these goods are considered remarkably good.

Cotton.—(Latin *Coctona*, Welsh *Cottwn*, French *Coton.*) The soft white downy pods of the *Gossypium*, or cotton plant, which is spun and woven into a great variety of textiles, and also employed for sewing thread. This plant is a native of India and America, &c., and grows best near the sea.

Cottonade.—A description of cotton cloth, in black and white, of very inferior quality for wear, made for women's skirts and suits for boys. It is 27 inches in width.

Cotton-backed Satin.—This material is comparatively a new manufacture in England, but is inferior in one respect to those Indian-made, under the name of *Mushroo*, as the latter, in every variety of coarse and fine, wash well, while our home-made examples and the French do not. Our cotton-backed satins vary in width from half a yard to three-quarters.

Cotton Bullion Fringes.—These are heavily made, the widths running from 3 inches to 12. The lengths run from 24 to 36 yards.

Cotton Canvas.—This textile is both home-made, and also manufactured in France and Germany; the French, or patent, being the best in its firmness, regularity, and clearness of each thread, the meshes being remarkably square. German cotton canvas is inferior, but may be had both limp and stiffened. The French and German are made in all sizes and widths; the latter will not bear much tension. That made in imitation of silk soon soils. They have produced a kind especially for tapestry-stitch. The German cotton canvas is generally made with every tenth thread dyed yellow, for the assistance of the embroiderer in counting. It is made both limp and stiffened.

Cotton Cords.—These are made in white and black, and are extensively used in dressmaking, as well as in upholstery. They are made up in half-bundles of 5lb., in mixed sizes, or otherwise; they may also be had in skeins, in single pounds. The numbers run from 1 to 0, 00, 000, 0,000, and 00,000.

Cotton Crape Cloth.—An imitation of the woollen Crape Cloth; it is employed for children's wear.

Cotton Damasks.—Made in imitation of the linen; cheaper, less durable, requiring frequent bleaching, and not much in request. Cotton damasks having a linen face have been, and are, in use for table linen; these being decorated with coloured borders in ingrain red and blue designs. Table cloths may be obtained in a variety of lengths. Cotton damask is also the name given to a beautiful material woven in different colours for curtains, and the other purposes of upholstery. It is 54 inches in width, and varies in price; is most durable, and bears almost endless cleaning. It has, however, been much superseded by CRETONNE.

Cotton Ferrets.—A description of binding resembling unsized tape. They are chiefly employed in black and drab colours, and are made up in rolls of nine pieces, containing 16 yards; numbers 8-18, or 6-24.

Cotton Prints, or Calico Prints.—Calico cloths printed in various colours and patterns to serve for dresses. Specimens of cotton fabrics sent out of the country, from Manchester alone, have shown upwards of 1,500 different kinds, varying in strength and pattern, from coarse cloths to the finest muslins, and from the richest chintz to the plain white.

Cotton Quilting.—A material made for waistcoat pieces, resembling diaper, strong and thick in quality.

Cotton Reps.—Handsome cloths dyed in all colours, 35 inches wide, and at 11d. a yard. They are chiefly employed for the linings of cretonne curtains.

N

Cottons for Sewing.—These are of several kinds—the white ball, distinguished by letters or numbers; and balls in every colour. Reel cotton is superior in make, and to free it from the projecting fibres, it is passed rapidly through the flames of coal gas. Darning cotton, used for repairing stockings, is composed of two threads but little twisted, and can be had in black, white, and colours. Embroidery cotton, a loose soft make, which can be bought in skeins, by the pound or gross; the numbers run from 4 to 100. It is used for decorating all kinds of white cotton or muslin, wearing apparel, and for handkerchiefs. Trafalgar, or Moravian cotton, is quite soft, and is employed for working nets, muslins, and cambrics. Knitting cotton is twisted less hard than sewing cotton, and is used for gloves, mittens, &c. Bonnet cotton, a coarse thread, consisting of eight or sixteen strands twisted together, employed for the making of seaside, and countrywomen's calico bonnets, and also in upholstery. Crape cotton is unsized, of quite a dull black, and only made in five numbers; it is used for sewing crape. Crochet cottons may be had in reels, skeins, or balls, the numbers running from 8 to 50. Marking cotton is dyed before being twisted, and is sold both in balls and on reels. Lace thread is made expressly for repairing lace or bobbinette. Gimp thread is soft in quality and make, and is used for embroidery on muslin; and glazed cotton, otherwise called *glacé* thread.

Cotton Sheetings.—The best make in cotton sheetings varies from two yards upwards to three in width. There are also intermediate widths, and prices vary accordingly. They can be had twilled, double warped, and plain made.

Cotton Ticking.—This material is made in stripes of white and blue, ingrain colours, both in twill and plain made. It is employed both for bedding and other purposes of upholstery, and also for embroidery. The price varies, and the ticking measures from 30 to 36 inches. *See* BELGIAN TICKING.

Cotton Velvet.—A material made in exact imitation of silk velvet, both in plain colours, and printed in patterns. It was employed for a dress material, but has been for some years almost entirely superseded by a better description of fabric, composed of silk and cotton, called Velveteen. Ribbon is also made of cotton velvet, an article inferior in quality, being cut in strips from piece velvets, and thus having raw edges. The fraying of the edges is to some extent prevented by sizing. They may be had in various colours, and in rather short lengths of 12 yards each. The numbers run from 1 to 40, and the widths from 1 and 1½ to 10 inclusive, consecutively, and every even number to 24, inclusive; then passing over those intervening, to numbers 30 and 40. There are also fancy velvet ribbons partially of plain silk, as well as of velvet, produced in various colours and patterns, and very commonly in plaid designs.

Cotton Wool.—The raw cotton, after having been passed through the "willow," "blowing," and "scutching" machines, is spread out into broad, soft, fleece-like wadding, when it is wound on a roller. It is employed for lining garments, quilts, &c., being placed between the material and its lining, and then sewn and kept in position by diagonal runnings at even distances, called "quilting." We obtain cotton wool from Cyprus.

Couching.—A term signifying the various ways, in Church Embroidery, that materials too thick to pass through the linen foundations as stitches are formed into patterns. All ancient Church needlework was profusely decorated with Couchings, which although of endless variety of names and designs, are of two descriptions only, the Flat and the Raised. They are formed with gold or silver thread, passing, gold braid, pearl purl, tambour, purse silk, three corded silk, Crochet twist, floss silk, mitorse, and Berlin silk. Gold twist and gold thread are costly, as is also passing (which is partly silk and partly gold); therefore gold silk frequently takes their place when expense is an object of consideration. The silk is also less likely to suffer from damp and gas than the gold threads, which are not now manufactured as pure as in the olden times, and are therefore liable to many changes, some kinds of silks acting deleteriously upon them, while the vapour of incense and the touch of a warm hand affect them. Flat Couchings are formed of threads of silk or gold laid smoothly down upon the linen foundation, and caught to it with small stitches brought up from the back of the work, and returned to it. Raised Couchings are the same threads laid upon the linen, but over whipcord that has been previously arranged upon it in a set design, the laid lines of thread being secured in the Raised in the same manner as in Flat. The names given to Couchings are taken from the direction of these securing stitches; they are called Basket, Battlemented, Brick, Broad, Diagonal, Diamond, Diaper, Plain, Shell, Spider, Vandyke, Wavy, Wheel. The manner of working them all only differs in the patterns formed by the securing threads, and the direction of the whipcord in the raised designs.

To work the plain Flat Couchings: Take threads of floss, mitorse, or purse silk, and lay them smoothly down from side to side in the space to be filled, either in horizontal, diagonal, or perpendicular lines; then thread an embroidery needle with fine purse silk or sewings, and catch the laid threads down; bring the needle up from the back of frame, put the silk in it over two or more laid lines, and the needle again through the foundation to the back; work over the laid lines until all are secured, and form the stitches into a pattern by altering the distances between them.

There are two ways to work more elaborate Flat Couchings. The first: Lay the floss silk down as before mentioned, then lay over it, one at a time, lines of purse silk or gold thread, and catch these down upon the floss with a stitch brought from the back of the work, and returned to it as before described. Each line of purse silk must be laid with reference to the pattern that it is helping to form over the floss foundation. The second manner of arranging the stitches is as follows: Lay two or more threads of floss or gold upon the foundation linen, and at once secure them with a stitch. Bring this stitch from the back of the work, and work it at equal distance down the two laid threads; then lay two more threads and secure them in the same manner.

Work Raised Couchings as follows : Sew securely down to the linen foundation a number of strands of whipcord as straight or waved lines, or form them into a set pattern ; over these lay floss silk or gold thread, and secure this with a stitch brought from the back and returned there as already described. On each side of the raised part formed by the whipcord that is underneath the floss, work a continuous line of these securing stitches so as to distinctly outline the whipcord ; in the intervals between these raised parts work the securing stitches up and down as in Flat Couchings, and make them into any pattern that may be required without reference to the raised design. When Couching in various devices, hold the laid threads in one hand and regulate them with that or with the piercer, and bring up the securing threads with the other, and do not change the position of the hands until the work is finished. Outline the Couching with a cord of silk or gold, and sometimes with more than one, according to the design. Use the Raised Couchings for backgrounds, the Flat for the centres of the various devices used as Powderings (*see* CHURCH EMBROIDERY) and for the centres of altar frontals and embroidered vestments.

Basket Stitch.—(Fig. 158). This is a Raised Couching. To work : Lay down perpendicular lines of whipcord upon the foundation, and SEW them firmly into position. Take four threads of purse silk, gold thread, or floss silk, and STITCH them down with purse silk of the same colour brought through from the back of the material and

FIG. 158. BASKET RAISED COUCHING.

returned to it. Place these securing stitches between every second strand of the cord. Form the next line with four threads laid over the whipcord and stitched down ; but, in order to prevent the lines of stitches all coming directly beneath each other, the first line must secure the

FIG. 159. BASKET RAISED COUCHING.

floss silk over one cord only, the rest over two cords as before. Repeat these two lines until the space is filled in.

Fig. 159, also of Basket Couching, is worked as follows : The whipcord and the floss silk lay down as before described, but over them lay short lines of fine gold thread or purse silk. Bring these from the back by

making a hole with the stiletto for them to pass through, and return them in the same way.

Fig. 160 is a Flat Couching with securing threads, arranged as *Battlemented* lines. Lay the floss silk in

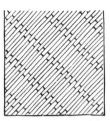

FIG. 160. CHURCH EMBROIDERY – BATTLEMENTED FLAT COUCHING.

diagonal lines across the foundation, and then work the securing stitches to imitate the design.

Brick Stitch, illustrated in Figs. 161 and 162, is worked in two ways. For the design shown in Fig. 161 : Lay down lines of floss silk in a diagonal direction, and secure them with stitches from the back, pass each stitch over two lines of floss, and work it in at an even distance from the stitch preceding it to the end of the pattern. Work the next line of securing stitches over

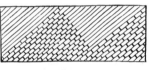

FIG. 161. BRICK FLAT COUCHING.

two laid lines of floss, not directly under the stitches in the preceding row, but between them. It will be seen on reference to the illustration that these securing stitches are not taken over the whole of the foundation, but are arranged to form vandykes. Fig. 162 is Brick

FIG. 162. BRICK FLAT COUCHING.

stitch differently worked : Lay down two threads of purse silk, and catch these down with a stitch from the back also of purse silk, and placed at regular distances along the line ; work the second line as the first, but place the fastening stitches in it between those of the previous row,

Broad Couching, Fig. 163 : Work like the Brick Couching last described, but with the securing stitches slightly

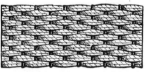

FIG. 163. BROAD FLAT COUCHING.

draw the foundation floss together where they stitch it down.

Diagonal Couching is a Flat Diagonal Couching. Make with lines of securing stitches worked through the material in a diagonal direction, or lay threads over the floss silk in a slanting direction.

Diamond Couching.—A Flat Couching (shewn in Fig. 164) worked as follows: Lay down lines of floss silk, and above them lay lines of purse silk or gold thread singly, but in a diagonal direction, and at equal distances apart.

FIG. 164. DIAMOND FLAT COUCHING.

Secure each single line with a stitch brought from the back. Lay all the lines in one direction first and secure them, then lay the lines that cross them, and wherever the two meet and form one of the points of a diamond, work a pearl or a spangle in at the junction.

Diaper Couching is the same as Plain Couching, the securing stitches in it being worked so as to form zigzag lines, diamonds, and crosses.

Plain Flat Couching.—Lay down floss silk evenly over the foundation, and secure, it with stitches brought from the back. Take these over two threads of silk and return to the back again. Arrange these securing stitches

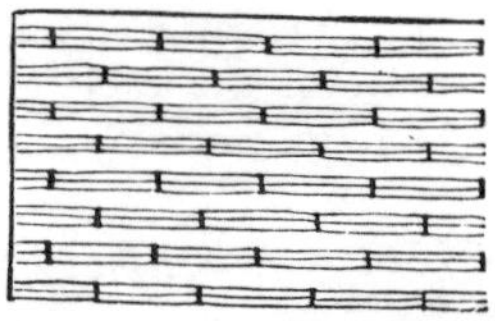

FIG. 165. PLAIN FLAT COUCHING.

to form straight or curved lines or diamonds across the space covered. The Couched lines (shown in Fig. 165) are

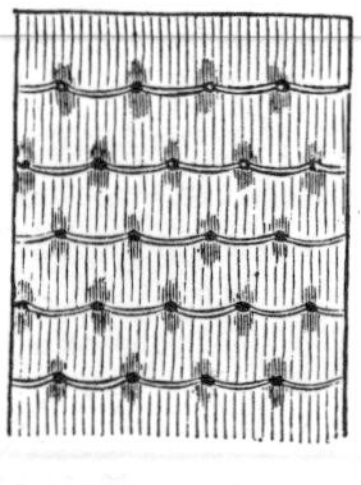

FIG. 166. PLAIN FLAT COUCHING.

not placed close together, but allow the material upon which they are laid to show between them when so arranged; the foundation must be of silk, not linen. Fig. 166 is a variety of plain Couching. It is worked thus: Lay down perpendicular lines of floss silk close together, then horizontal and wide apart single lines of

purse silk or gold thread, and secure these at even distances by a stitch from the back; wherever the stitch from the back is made, work in a spangle or a bead.

Shell Couching.—A Flat Couching, in which the securing stitches are arranged in half curves, and bear some resemblance to the shape of a scallop shell.

Spider Couching.—A Raised Couching. Upon a linen foundation fasten down short pieces of whipcord. Cut these of equal length, and arrange them like the spokes of a wheel or the chief threads of a spider's web. Fill in the whole of the foundation with threads so arranged, place the wheels they make as near together as they can be. Then lay lines of floss silk over the whipcord and secure it by stitches from the back of the work. Work these stitches in lines on each side of every raised cord, so that the shape of each wheel or spider's web is clearly indicated.

Vandyke Couching.—A Raised Couching. Form with lines of whipcord laid on the linen foundation in the shape of vandykes; lay floss silk over them, and secure it, and outline the whipcord with securing stitches from the back.

Wavy Couching.—This is a Raised Couching, and is illustrated in Fig. 167. To work: Arrange upon the linen foundation curved lines of whipcord; lay a medium sized purse silk over them and the foundation, two strands at a time, and secure the silk as in Broad Couching, omitting

FIG. 167. WAVY RAISED COUCHING.

the stitches wherever the raised part formed by the cord underneath is approached. When the Broad Couching is finished, lay a thread of gold or silk cord on each side of the waved line, and catch it down with securing stitches from the back, or work the line on each side of the raised part with a continuous line of stitches brought from the back.

Wheel Couching.—Similar to Spider.

Coudre.—The French term signifying to sew.

Coulant Nattée.—*See* MACRAMÉ LACE.

Coulisse.—(French.) A small slip-stitched pleating, sewn upon a dress by means of slip stitches.

Coulissé.—A French term denoting the gathering, by fine runnings and drawing, so as to pucker up any material, and to form irregular wrinkles, yet so as to preserve a general uniformity of hollows and puffings. *See* SHIRRED.

Counter-Hemming.—To execute this description of plain sewing, place two edges of material together, one overlying the other, so as to form a flat joining. The wrong side of one piece should overlap the right side of the other to the depth of an ordinary seam. If the pieces so united have selvedges, nothing should be turned in; but if either piece have a raw edge, it must be once folded.

The flat seam should then be tacked down throughout its entire length, and afterwards felled (or hemmed), and as soon as one side has been finished, the second, or "counter-hem," is made in the same way. This is an untidy method of working, inferior to the ordinary plan of simply "running and felling."

Couronnes.—An ornament to the CORDONNET, used in Needle Point laces, and identical with Crowns. To make: Work tiny loops of thread along the outer edge of the CORDONNET, and BUTTON-HOLE these over with a close line of buttonholes, and finish with small Bobs placed, at equal distances along the outer edge of the loops. The Couronnes are either worked as a decoration to the Cordonnet that forms the edge of the lace, or round any raised Cordonnets in the body of the pattern; when in the latter position they, with Spines and Thorns, are known as Fleurs Volantes.

Coutille.—A French word to denote a description of jean used for stays. It has a small kind of *armure* pattern all over it, woven in the material, like a succession of small *chevrons* or zigzags. It is of a lighter make than English jean, is usually employed without a lining, and measures 27 inches in width.

Coutrai Lace.—In Belgium, at a town of this name, Valenciennes is made. It is known as Coutrai Lace, and commands a ready sale in England, being worked in wider widths than the Valenciennes produced in other Belgian cities. *See* VALENCIENNES.

Cover Cloths.—All pillows used for the purpose of lacemaking require three Cover Cloths. Make the largest, known as the under cloth, the size of the pillow, of washing silk or fine linen, and use to cover the pillow entirely. Place it on the pillow before the PASSEMENT pattern is adjusted, it cannot be removed until that is detached; but as the lace is worked upon it, it must be taken off and washed whenever it looks at all soiled The other cloths are detached from the pillow and altered at will as to their positions. They are made of silk or linen, in size 18 inches by 12 inches. Pin one over the top of the pillow to protect the finished lace, which is there rolled up out of the way, and pin the other down over the lower part of the Passement and under the bobbins, to prevent the lace threads becoming entangled with the pricked holes in the design. When the lace is not being made, throw this cloth over the pillow to keep it clean.

Cradle, or Shuttle.—An appliance (otherwise called an attachment) belonging to a SEWING MACHINE (which *see*).

Crankey.—A bend or turn, significant of the description of ticking employed for beds, composed of linen and cotton, the patterns on which are irregular or zigzag. It measures 54 inches in width.

Crape.—A delicate transparent crimped gauze, made of raw silk, sized with gum, twisted in the mill, and woven without dressing. It may also be had both crisped and smooth, with or without a twill, the former being of double width, and generally ranging from 23 inches to 42 inches in width. White crape is manufactured for a dress material, and for trimmings. The production of coloured varieties originated at Bologna, thence introduced at Lyons, where those of Areophane and Crêpe Lisse are largely made. Our own manufactures at Norwich and Yarmouth are likewise of superior make. The best sorts are entirely of silk, but a new kind, called Albert Crape, is composed of silk and cotton, and another, called Victoria Crape, is made of cotton only. There is an improved variety, of recent manufacture, having a small indented pattern, which resists the influence of rain and a damp atmosphere. The dyeing and dressing of crape are performed after it has been woven. *See* CHINA CRAPE and YOKOHAMA CRAPE.

Crape Cloth.—A woollen material, woven in imitation of crape, dyed black, and employed for mourning in the place of real crape. It is made of double width, in different qualities, and varies in price accordingly. It bears washing, and wears well, and is known in the various shops by several different names.

Crape Cotton.—An unsized cotton of a dull black, employed for sewing crape, and made only in five numbers.

Crash.—Called also Russia Crash, and round towelling, the width running from 16 to 22 inches. This material was utilised in the early days of crewel work for embroidery, on which account that species of work was called Crash Work. In process of time various makes of unbleached linen, copied from ancient examples of crewel work textiles, have been misnamed Crash. These are to be had in various degrees of fineness, width, and make. *See* BARNSLEY LINENS. A description of linen misnamed Crash is a closely woven cloth, even in grain, rather fine, and unbleached, which is employed as canvas for the purposes of embroidery. It is 37 inches in width. Another description of Crash, also used in embroidery, is known as Buckingham's hand-made Crash, having a chessboard pattern, and made after the style of Huckaback. It is of double width. The real Crashes are only two in number, Russian and Barnsley. Russia Crash, which is not used for embroidery, is unbleached and unpressed, and varies from 16 to 18 inches in width; Barnsley Crash may be had at 16, 18, 20, and 22 inches in width, and it is this material that is employed for embroidery. It is beautifully bleached and pressed.

Crazy Patchwork.—This method of forming Patchwork is otherwise, and more correctly, called APPLIQUÉ PATCHWORK. (*See* PATCHWORK.)

Cream-twilled Linen.—A description of linen cloth employed for purposes of embroidery, of 2 yards in width.

Crénelé. — (French). Battlemented, or cut in square scallops, producing that effect, as a bordering of a dress.

Crêpe.—The French for CRAPE (which *see*).

Crêpé.—A French term to signify crimped, after the style of crape.

Crêpe de Dante.—A combination of silk and wool, and silk and Lisle thread and wool, woven together.

Crêpe de Lahor.—A washing material designed for women's dresses, and made in various colours. Its width is much narrower than that of Crêpe Lisse, measuring only 26 inches.

Crêpeline.—Crêpon, or Crape Cloth. A dress material,

having a silken surface, much resembling crape, but considerably thicker. It is 24 inches in width; and is to be had in wool and in silk unmixed with wool. Those of mixed materials have the warp twisted much harder than the weft. Crêpon made at Naples is of silk only. It is chiefly manufactured in black, but is also to be had in colours. Norwich is the chief seat of the manufacture in England, and Zurich and Naples abroad.

Crêpe Lisse.—A thin description of crape, like gauze, chiefly employed for making frills and ruffles. It may be had in white, cream, and other colours, and is 36 inches in width.

Crêpe Work.—This work consists of forming imitation flowers or leaves of crêpe, and either sewing them to the silk or satin backgrounds, or making them up upon wire foundations as detached sprays. When attached to wire, they are used for wreaths and dress or bonnet trimmings; when sewn to backgrounds, for ornamenting sachet cases and necktie ends. They are formed for the last-mentioned as follows: Select crêpe of a colour matching the satin background; cut out the size of the flower petal to be made upon paper, and cut to it a piece of doubled crêpe; turn in the raw edges, and draw the crêpe together at one end to form the narrow part of the petal; then sew this end to the foundation, and allow the other to stand

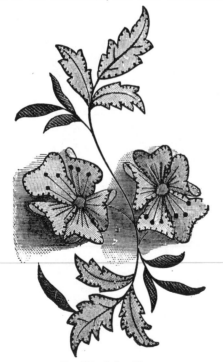

FIG 168. CRÊPE WORK.

up. To form the flower, five petals are made as described, and sewn down as a round, their raw edges being well tacked down and concealed by FRENCH KNOTS made either of gold and silver thread or floss silk. The shape of the flowers made of crêpe cannot be much varied; their centres may, however, be filled up with three or four small petals made like the outside ones instead of French knots; the number of flowers will depend upon the space available.

Make the leaves of pieces of doubled crêpe cut and notched to the shape of leaves, APPLIQUÉ these to the backgrounds, and surround them with wide apart BUTTONHOLE STITCHES of filoselle that matches the crêpe in colour.

The detached crêpe flowers can be made of fine muslin instead of crêpe, and, this latter material being the stiffest, they last in shape better when formed of it. The materials required for them are muslin or crêpe, green wire, beads or spangles, and embroidery silk. Fig. 168 is of this kind of Crêpe Work; the flowers in it are formed of gold coloured muslin or crêpe. To work: Cut the petals out to shape upon a flat but doubled piece of crêpe, and then Buttonhole them round with a line of wide apart stitches (this may be done before cutting out). When all are shaped, sew them round a gold coloured pad, which should be wadded and attached to the top of a piece of wire ready to receive them. Form the stamen lines of yellow purse silk, and lay them over the petals after the latter are attached to the pad, and finish them with a bead. Make the back of the flower neat by winding green purse silk round the wire to conceal the ends of the crêpe. Form the leaves like the petals, with veins marked out in SATIN STITCH. When a large bunch of flowers is being formed, and not a single spray, so much care need not be taken over each individual part, the flower petals not requiring Buttonholed edges, but being made of double crêpe turned in at the sides, and the leaves of a straight piece of material, 2 inches wide, and a quarter of a yard long, with edges cut to vandykes. This piece of crêpe is box pleated, and doubled, so that both edges turn to the front, and is then sewn close to single flowers and in and about groups, forming bouquets. These leaves should be darker in tint than the flowers, but of the same colour.

Crescents.—These crescents are raised Cordonnets that enclose the flat stitches of needle point laces or join the separate pieces of work together. Their use adds immensely to the effect of the lace, and gives it strength and beauty at the same time. They are of various shapes, lengths, and thickness, according to the pattern of the lace, but are all worked alike.

To work: Prick the shape of the Crescent out upon a leather foundation, being careful to prick two holes close together, and to make the same number of holes on the

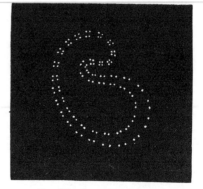

FIG. 169. CRESCENT—PRICKED.

inside as upon the outer edge (*see* Fig. 169). With a needle threaded with No. 12 Mecklenburg thread, outline the crescent thus bring up the needle from the back of the leather through the first of the two holes close together and put it back through the second, thus making a short stitch upon the surface and a long one underneath. Continue in this way all round the crescent, then fasten off by tying the two ends of the thread together at the back of the pattern. Fill the needle with No. 7 Mecklenburg thread and commence to work by making a foundation for the padding that raises the Cordonnet. Bring the needle up from the back and slip the thread under the small stitch already made between the two holes, then take the thread across the

FIG. 170. CRESCENT—MANNER OF WORKING.

crescent and slip it under the two holes opposite, and continue to pass it backwards and forwards under the holes opposite each other, never pulling the thread up fully until it has been run through all the stitches. Upon these crossed threads DARN in soft Moravian thread until a handsome raised foundation is formed (*see* Fig. 170), the centre of which is thicker and higher than the pine shaped end. Now work an even close line of BUTTON-HOLE STITCHES over the padding.

Fig. 171 is a piece of Spanish rose point that illustrates the use of a raised crescent. The stitch in the centre of the crescent is worked before the outline, and is a close Buttonhole, with open spaces left systematically

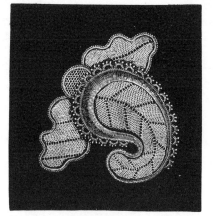

FIG. 171. CRESCENT, WITH FLEURS VOLANTES.

unworked to give the appearance of veins or tracery. Make these open stitches by missing three Buttonholes wherever they occur. The pieces of lace shaped like wings work separately and tack on to the leather

foundation and the outer edge of the Crescent in such a manner that they join together in the process of Buttonholing the padding over. The trimming to the outer edge of the Crescent work last; make it of COURONNES edged with Thorns or Spines, which, when arranged round the edge of a Cordonnet, are called Fleurs Volantes. Unpick the work from the leather foundation by cutting the outline thread that was tied at the back, and join the piece of lace on in its place in the pattern.

Crete Lace.—An ancient pillow lace, of the Torchon description, made in the island of Crete. The grounds were either formed of coloured silks or flax, and the distinctive feature of the manufacture consisted in embroidery being worked upon the lace after it was made. This embroidery was executed with coloured filoselle in Chain Stitch, which was made to outline the pattern, like Fil de Trace. The designs of Crete laces were chiefly geometrical, and the colours used in ornamenting them so varied and bright as to give an Oriental appearance to the handiwork.

A modern imitation of the ancient Crete laces, with their coloured silk embroideries, and made by working a pattern in coloured filoselles and gold cord over thick lace, is easily produced. It is a kind of embroidery that most ladies find easy and effective, and is adapted for furniture lace, if executed in coarse lace, and suitable for chimney-board covers, and for small round tea tables. For dress trimmings, the lace used is fine, and of a colour to match the dress it is placed on. The lace used is either black or white Yak or Torchon machine lace, a crochet imitation of these, or blonde or Breton lace. The design selected is distinct and rather open, and, when selecting, especial attention is given to the ground, as a light open ground is more effective than a close, thick one.

To work: Commence by cutting a strip of coloured cloth or serge to the exact width of the lace, and lay it under that as a background. Tack the two together, and proceed to work EMBROIDERY STITCHES on the lace, taking them through the cloth background. Work these stitches in two or more coloured filoselles, and make SATIN, FEATHER, or CHAIN STITCH. Work them upon the thick parts of the lace, leaving the open parts bare, so that the coloured cloth background is seen through. The following arrangement of the stitches produces a good pattern: Make a number of festoons, either of Feather or Satin Stitch, along the whole length of the lace, commence a festoon at the top of the lace, and carry it down to the edge, each festoon taking up the width of 4 inches; then fill in the spaces left by the curves with stars, rosettes, or rounds, worked in variously coloured filoselles, and in Satin Stitch. Any shades of colour are used in one pattern, provided they are not violent contrasts; the ancient Crete laces, of which this work is the imitation, being embroidered with many colours. The colour of the background cloth should be rich and dark, such as deep plum, Indigo blue, sap green, or maroon; the filoselles amber, sky blue, sea green, and crimson.

Cretonne.—A French name for a cotton fabric which has latterly superseded, to a considerable extent, the use of chintz for upholstery work. It is to be had in every colour, both of ground and floral design; is twilled, but unglazed (or calendered), and is made from 30 inches to a yard wide. It is manufactured in England as well as in France. The original material, called Cretonne, or Cretonne chintz, was originated by the Normans two centuries ago, and was made at Lisieux, being woven with flax and hemp, and in different qualities, for the purpose of body linen.

Cretonne Appliqué. — *See* APPLIQUÉ, BRODERIE PERSE.

Creva Drawn Work.—This is a lace made in Brazil by the negroes. It is a drawn lace, and evidently copied from the Italian drawn work. Some of it was exhibited in England at the late Exhibition.

Crewel.—In early times known as *Caddis, Caddas,* or *Crule.* Derived from the Anglo-Saxon *Cleow,* afterwards changed to *Clew* (a ball of thread), and subsequently called *Cruell,* or *Krewel,* old German *Kleuel.* Worsted yarn loosely twisted, employed in the sixteenth century for embroidery on linen textiles, curtains, and household furniture, and also for decorating the dresses of the lower orders; but now extensively for embroidery. It is to be had in every colour, and is made in three sizes, and known as tapestry crewel, very soft and even, sold in cuts of about 1s. 4d. the oz., or by the hank; medium crewel, sold in upwards of 300 art shades; and the fine crewel, by the cut, or the hank.

Crewel Stitch.—One of the old embroidery stitches, and well known in earlier times as Stem stitch; but since the revival of Crewel work, of which it is the most important stitch, its original name has become superseded by that of the embroidery now associated with it.

To work: Put the needle into the material in a slanting direction, as shown in Fig. 172, and keep the crewel upon

FIG. 172. CREWEL STITCH.

the right hand side of the needle. Work to the end of the line, every stitch being made in the same manner; then turn the material and place a line of stitches close to the one already made, keeping the wool always to the right of the needle. If the crewel wool is allowed to slip to the left of the needle the stitch is not properly made, although it appears so to the inexperienced. When using this stitch, except for stems and outlines, the regularity of each succeeding stitch is not kept so perfectly as shown in the illus-

tration, but is more carelessly done, although the stitch is not otherwise altered. This is particularly the case when forming the edges of serrated leaves; the irregular Crewel Stitch will give them the notched appearance of the natural leaf, while the regular one makes the edges straight and formal. Leaves and flowers of various kinds are worked in Crewel Stitch with regard to their broad natural outlines. A small narrow leaf, such as that of a carnation or jasmine, requires no veining, and is worked up and down. Put the needle in at the base of the leaf, take a line of stitches up the right hand side to the point, then turn the work, and take the same line down the left side (now the right) to the base of the leaf. Then work the centre up and fill in the two sides afterwards in the same manner, turning the work at every line. To save this constant turning of material, good workers put their needle backwards down the line, but this is not so easy for a beginner to accomplish. With a large leaf, such as an orange, or a smaller leaf with deeply indented veins, a different plan is necessary. In such a case take the stitches, instead of upwards and downwards, in a slanting direction downwards from the outside to the centre of the leaf, all the stitches tending from both sides to the middle. By this means a deeper indented line is given to the centre vein; afterwards work up the centre as a finish, and work the side veins over the other Crewel Stitches, but in a different shade of colour, and in the direction the natural veins would follow. A rose leaf requires another modification: Work from side to centre like the last-named, but with a long stitch and a short one alternately at the outside edge, so that the deeply indented sides may be properly rendered. Work rounded flower petals as shown in Fig. 173, the stitches following each other, but decreasing in

FIG. 173. CREWEL STITCH—PETAL.

length as they approach the end of the petal, while in pointed petals, like the jasmine, simply take the stitch up and down, or cross the whole length with a SATIN STITCH. Work in Satin stitch any flower petal that is small enough

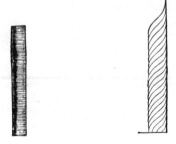

FIGS. 174 AND 175. CREWEL STITCHES—IMPROPERLY MADE STEMS.

to allow of a Satin stitch carried across it; large ones require Crewel Stitch. Use FRENCH KNOTS or BULLION

BACK-STITCH EMBROIDERY   Copied from a priests stole of the 17th century

GLASS CLOTH EMBROIDERY

KNOTS for the centre of flowers, as they add to their beauty. When the centre of a flower is as large as that seen in a sunflower, either work the whole with French Knots, or lay down a piece of velvet of the right shade and work sparingly over it French Knots or lines of Crewel Stitch. A Marguerite daisy is sometimes so treated, but after that size French Knots alone are worked, and no velvet foundation added.

Always work stems in Crewel Stitch and in upright lines; Figs. 174, 175 illustrate two ways of making stems that should be avoided, but which are constantly seen in badly worked embroidery. The rounded appearance given to them by the direction of the stitches serves to raise them from their backgrounds, and gives, instead of the decorative flat design that is desired, one in relief. Stems should be simply worked up and down in Crewel Stitch in the manner shown in Fig. 172.

Crewel Work.—This is work that claims to be raised from the level of ordinary fancy to an art work. The name is but a modern one for embroidery with worsteds or "Krewels" upon plain materials. Ancient Crewel Work was indifferently classed with embroideries of silk and gold or work upon canvas, as "wrought needlework" in old chronicles, therefore it is difficult to separate one particular kind by hard and fast lines of demarcation from other embroideries. The proper definition of Crewel Work is embroidery upon linen, twilled cotton or stuffs, the foundation material being in most cases left as an unworked background, or, when covered, only partially concealed with open Diaper or Darned Fillings. The employment of crewels in needlework was the first form of embroidery known, and worsteds mingled with thin plates of gold, or the latter pulled into fine wire, ornamented all the fine needlework of the earlier times before silk was used. The art came from the East, thence spread into Egypt, acquired there by the Hebrews, Greeks, and Romans, and taken by the latter wherever they carried their conquests; and though by their time embroidery with silk had become prevalent and superseded the plainer worsteds, still working with crewels in various forms never entirely died out until the present century, when the introduction of the new Berlin wools, in 1835, with their softer texture and more varied dyes, supplanted it for a time; but in 1875 it was reinstated by artists who found it the best vehicle for the expression, through embroidery, of design and colour. Amongst the earliest examples of this needlework are the curtains of the Tabernacle, the coloured sails of the Egyptian galleys, and the embroidered robes of Aaron and his priests. These are worked with gold and worsted, and though the stitch used on them is believed to be CROSS STITCH, yet from the foundation material of fine linen, and the workmen forming their own designs, they undoubtedly rank among art as Crewel Work. In latter times the Bayeux tapestry and the productions of Amy Robsart and Mary Stuart are witnesses to the industry of the sixteenth and seventeenth centuries, while most of the hand-made tapestry of that time consisted simply of crewel stitches entirely covering coarse linen backgrounds. In the eighteenth century large quantities of Crewel Work were done, much of which is still extant, and gives evidence of the individual energy

and taste of that period. The great merit of the work and the reason of its revival lies in the capability it has of expressing the thought of the worker, and its power of breaking through the trammels of that mechanical copying and counting which lowers most embroidery to mere fancy work. Lifted by this power into a higher grade, it ranks with laces and ancient gold and silver embroideries that are in themselves works of art, and which were done in times when the best part of a life was spent in the effort to give to the world one new type of beauty. Crewel Work has also the inestimable advantage of being adapted to homely decoration, the cheapness of its material, the ease with which it is cleaned, and its strength to resist rough usage, justly making it the chosen vehicle in the decoration of all common home objects of beauty. Partaking, as Crewel Work does, of the general nature of ancient embroideries, it will be sufficient under this heading to point out its characteristics and manner of working. In it good work is known by the design and colouring being treated as a decorative, and not as a realistic, copy of nature. It is well ascertained that the materials capable of producing embroideries are not of a kind that can imitate nature in her glories of form and colour, and that any copy will be a failure; therefore all work claiming to be good must be conventionally treated, the design being represented flat upon a flat background, and no attempt made, by means of shadows and minute shadings, to raise and round it from its surface as in painting, and in correct Crewel Work this rule is followed. Many unthinking persons object to this, proud of the idea of only copying from nature; but let the effect be tried of flowers worked as they see them, and the same treated decoratively, and a short experience will soon convince them that one group can be looked upon for ever with rest and repose, while the other offends by the badness of its copy, and the harshness of its colouring.

Crewel Work is a difficult embroidery, because it depends for its success not upon the exact putting in of stitches, and their regularity, or upon the time and labour bestowed upon reproducing a pattern, but upon the absolute necessity there is for the mind of the worker being more than a copying machine, possessing the power of grasping and working out an idea of its own, and of being able to distinguish between a good or bad design or system of colouring. The technical difficulties of the work are so few and so simple that when described they seem to be trifles, for after the broad rules of what to do and avoid are stated, a written instruction is of little help, as it cannot give the subtleties of form and colour upon which the work depends for its perfection, nor can it convey to an inartistic mind the power of right selection between conflicting colouring. What can be learnt from instruction, is the manner of forming the various stitches used in the work, while practice will give a free use of the needle, and the power of setting the stitches so that each is put in with regard to its place in the whole design, and is neither worked too close to its neighbour nor too far from it, but by its direction expresses the contour of a line or the form of a leaf. Just as in painting no master can inspire his pupil with his own gift of colouring unless the power of seeing

o

and delineating is already possessed, and only requires to be brought out and strengthened by instruction, so in Crewel Work the learner must have an innate taste for what is true in form and colour to profit by the rules that are exemplified in the best examples of needlework.

One of the great advantages of this work over other descriptions of embroidery is its usefulness for everyday needs, as, from the nature of its materials, it is adapted to almost all kinds of household decoration, and is not out of keeping with either homely or handsome furniture, provided the stuffs it is worked upon are selected with regard to the ornaments and purposes of the room. The selection of such suitable materials must be particularly borne in mind when the work is employed to decorate such permanent articles as wall hangings, friezes, portières, and window curtains. In a handsomely furnished sitting room for winter use, these should be either of plush, Utrecht velvet, velveteen, waste silk, velvet cloth, diagonal cloth, or serge, according to the richness or simplicity of the accompanying furniture, and the ground colour in all cases dark and rich, with the embroidery upon it in lighter shades of the same, or in a light shade of a colour that harmonises with the background. Plush is the handsomest of all these materials, as it dyes in such beautiful tones of colour; its disadvantages lie in its expense, and that the pattern traced upon it is not permanent, and, unless worked over, at once wears off; it also requires a lining, and is therefore more used to work upon as a bordering to curtains of velvet cloth or diagonal cloth than as whole curtains, but if the above defects are not objected to, there is no doubt about the softness and beauty of a portière or chimney curtain worked in plush. Utrecht velvet is harder to work through than plush, and is more used for curtain dados than for a whole curtain or curtain borders. Velveteen of the best quality works well, but is more suitable for screens and chimney curtains than large hangings; it looks best when embroidered with coarse filoselles. Velvet cloth is a soft, handsome material, warm looking, and falling in easy folds; it is a good texture to work upon, and takes the tracing lines perfectly. Diagonal cloth, felt cloth, and serges are soft materials, easy to work upon, and artistic in colouring, their only defects being that they do not take the tracing lines well, and require to be worked at once, or the pattern lines run with fine white cotton as soon as marked out.

Summer curtains, &c., for sitting rooms, are either made of waste silks, silk sheeting, China silk, Kirriemeer Twill, real Russian Crash, and the superior makes of Bolton Sheeting. The cheap sheetings and crash are not recommended for large surfaces of embroidery; they are too harsh in texture and too coarse altogether to be used when so much time and labour is expended over their decoration. Waste silks and China silks are either worked with filoselles or crewels, but the crashes and twills being washing materials, should only be worked with crewels.

In such articles as chair tidies, bed valances, toilet covers, aprons, &c., cleanliness has to be the first object, and for these the washing materials known as Flax, Smock Linen, Oatcake and Oatmeal Linens, Kirriemeer Twill, Crash, and

Bolton Sheetings are used, while the work upon them is limited to one or two shades of colour.

The embroidery upon all large objects is worked upon the material, and not applied to it, it being always better, in an art point of view, to distribute the work in such cases over the whole surface than to confine it to certain limited spaces, such as a line of bordering, or a strip placed across the background. The material is cumbersome to hold, but the heaviness is much mitigated when curtains, &c., are made with dados of a different colour, but of the same material, the embroidery being done before the two are sewn together. Embroidered hangings of any kind are never made either long or full; and wall panels and friezes are laid flat against the wall. Portières and curtains are allowed sufficient stuff in them to admit of a little fulness when drawn across, and they should not do more than just touch the floor to exclude draughts. All large pieces of needlework require patterns that convey the feeling of breadth without the work being too fine to be appreciated upon such objects. The best designs for these articles are rather large flowers in outline, with long upright stems and leaves starting from the bottom of the hanging, and branching stiffly over the surface of the material, or decorative or geometrical designs, such as are familiar in Italian wall paintings or outline figure subjects. The colours chosen for the embroidery when upon dark handsome backgrounds are lighter in shade than the backgrounds, and of little variety; but when the embroidery is upon light backgrounds, greater variety of tint and contrasts of colour are allowable in the decoration.

The patterns known as Outlines will be found sufficient for most decorative work, but where the design is to be filled in, select flowers that are large and bold in outline and that are single, and discard small and double ones. Employ but few shades of colour to work together, and do not include more than two primary colours in one piece, filling in the rest of the design with those that harmonise with the primaries, and with half tints of the two chief colours. Avoid those that contrast with each other, and choose harmonies—it is one of the chief faults of Berlin work that violent contrasts of bright primary colours are introduced together—be careful that the same fault does not creep into crewels. Avoid all aniline dyes, firstly, because they never blend with other colours, and always make the object they are attached to harsh and garish, and, secondly, because they fade sooner than the other hues, and, instead of fading with the quiet tones of softer dyes, look utterly dead and worn out.

The question of the colour of backgrounds to work upon is most important. Avoid pure white or black, as both are crude; cream or lemon white are good, but not blue white. Most colours will look well upon a cream background, but the brightest shade of any colour is not worked upon white. Reds and crimsons of a yellow tinge harmonise together better than blue shades of red; yellow and sage greens agree with other colours better than vivid blue greens; yellow blues better than sky blues; citrons and lemon yellows better than orange coloured yellows. In working upon coloured backgrounds the same attention to harmonious colouring must be exercised. It will be generally correct that the background colour is repeated for the work if lighter and deeper tones of the colour are selected for the chief parts of the needlework than for the background, with a few needlefuls of the exact tint of the background used in the embroidery. Thus, upon a blue green ground, work a pale pure blue shade of crewels; yellow green backgrounds allow of yellow crewels, and brown, gold colours; while maroon backgrounds allow of scarlet crewels. The great thing to remember is that the eye to be pleased must be contented by harmonious colouring; therefore the tints selected, although they can be bright, must never be vivid, and must assimilate with their surroundings, and not oppose them.

The materials, as already said, upon which crewels are worked, are plush, velvet, satin, silk cloth, serge, unbleached linens, cheese cloths, crash, oatmeal cloths, and the numerous varieties of these; in fact, there is hardly any limit to the stuffs that are capable of being so ornamented. Upon the crewels used much of the durability of the work depends. Those known as "Appleton's," and used at the School of Art, are smooth and fine, without much twist, and work in without roughness; they are dyed in fast colours and of correct shades. Unfortunately these crewels are not generally used, their place being taken by those that are fluffy in texture, harsh to the feel, tightly twisted, and dyed in brilliant aniline shades, and it is owing to the use of these and printed designs that the Crewel Work generally seen does not come up to the true standard of art needlework, the patterns being defective in drawing and the colouring too bright. There are three kinds of crewels made—the coarse, used for large pieces of embroidery; the medium, the one generally required; and the very fine, used for the faces and hair of figures and for fine outlines upon d'oyleys and other small work. This fine crewel is giving place to undressed silks, but it is still used. Silk embroidery in Crewel Stitch is so similar to other flat silk embroideries that it is described under that heading.

None of the stitches used in Crewel Work are exclusively crewel work stitches; they are all used in embroidery or church needlework. They comprise CREWEL STITCH, which is really STEM STITCH; FEATHER STITCH, the *Opus Plumarium* of the ancients; SATIN or LONG STITCH, CHAIN STITCH, BULLION and FRENCH KNOT, besides fancy embroidery stitches used to ornament parts of the work, where the foundation is left exposed, and for borders, which, being only accessories, are not counted as belonging to Crewel Work proper. Stem Stitch is the chief crewel stitch, although the others are all used, and Satin Stitch employed when the design is executed with silks. The manner of working these stitches is given under their own headings. Crewel stitch is used for leaves and stems; Feather and Satin mainly for the petals of flowers; French and Bullion knots for centres to flowers and to imitate shrubs and trees in landscape designs. Flowers worked in silk are done in Satin stitch. Chain Stitch in silk is used equally with Satin stitch to fill in the faces, &c., of figure designs, while draperies are executed with crewels in Crewel stitch. Faces are worked like those already described in church embroideries, the lines of stitches being made to follow the contour of the features, and an appearance of shade thus imparted to a flat surface. Ancient Crewel Work was either done in this manner, or in the style of the celebrated *Opus Anglicanum*. Chain Stitch was more used in outline embroideries in olden days than it is now, the introduction of it into machine work having led to its being discarded by hand workers. During the last century nearly all Crewel Work was done upon light linen or cotton surfaces, and was used for much larger kinds of ornament than the shortness of time enables ladies of the present day to accomplish. The hangings for four-post bedsteads, with heavy curtains, valances, and other appendages, are some of the most frequent specimens of old work met with, also portières, room hangings, and bed quilts. These large embroideries are not spread over all the foundation material, much being left plain; and their designs are necessarily bolder than are those in use now. Vine trees with large stems, with each leaf separately formed, birds, animals, rocks, water, flowers, and fruit, are the finest specimens. These large patterns are worked in double or coarse crewels, with rather long stitches, and the colours used are of little variety and of subdued tint. The main parts are filled with close Crewel Stitch, but a great variety of fancy stitches, such as HERRINGBONE, FEATHER, and POINT LANCÉ, are allowed in the minor details. Birds are always worked in Feather Stitch, so arranged that a few individual feathers are completely defined. Leaves have one side in Crewel Stitch, the other filled with French knots or with open fancy stitches. Bushes and other groundwork are entirely of Bullion knots.

Crewel Work includes, besides working a filled-in pattern upon an unornamented background, another variety, which is filling in the background with a fancy stitch, and only outlining the real design and its principal parts. The effect of this depends upon the stitch which fills in the ground being chosen so as to give an appearance of relief to the outlined pattern.

The simplest background is the plain darned lines, formed with silk or worsted, darned in and out as in ordinary darning in perpendicular lines about the sixteenth of an inch apart over the whole background, missing, of course, any part of the design. Again, these darned lines are taken diagonally or horizontally, or are made so as to form diamonds.

Another background stitch is given in Fig. 176, and

FIG. 176. CREWEL WORK—BACKGROUND.

is worked thus: Fig. 176—Trace the background design

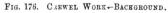

O 2

upon the material, being careful not to mark it out upon any part of the pattern; take fine crewels or raw silk of one colour and darn the long lines of the crosses, but work the

FIG. 177. CREWEL WORK—BACKGROUND.

small lines in SATIN STITCH. In Fig. 177, darn the long lines forming the broad arrow part of design, and work the short lines in SATIN STITCH. In Fig. 178—Trace the

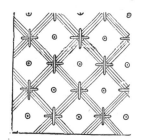

FIG. 178. CREWEL WORK—BACKGROUND.

long diagonal lines that form diamonds where they intersect, and darn them down with three rows of fine crewels or raw silk. Then cross the lines where they meet with a CROSS STITCH worked in a different coloured crewel or silk to that used in the darned lines, and work a BULLION or FRENCH KNOT in the centre of the diamond.

Background stitches are numerous, those used in DARNED EMBROIDERY all being available, the most effective are those containing continuous lines, such as the following: A straight darned line, followed by a laid line caught down with a fastening thread concealed with a FRENCH KNOT; Vandyke lines laid and fastened with knots; two perpendicular straight lines caught across at intervals with three short horizontal

FIG. 179. CREWEL WORK—CURTAIN BORDER.

ones; lines intersecting each other and forming stars; lines like waves and BASKET COUCHINGS, &c. Filled-in backgrounds with outlined designs all require foundations of coarse linen, silk, or cloth, the coarse linen being the most used, as the threads in that assist in forming the darned lines at right distances from each other. An ornamental border should finish these various stitches.

The example shown in Fig. 179 is worked as follows: Draw threads out of the material as a guide for the two horizontal lines, and work one line over with three rows of CREWEL STITCH and the other with one row; then make half circles at equal distances apart with lines of SATIN STITCH arranged to form that device, and fill in the spaces between them by lines of SATIN STITCH arranged like the mark known as the broad arrow.

Fig. 180 is a finished style of Crewel Work. It is intended for a curtain border, and is a design of lilies and their buds worked upon claret coloured plush. Work the lilies in cream white silk, shading to grey and yellow, with stamens and pistils of deep orange, buds with grey and white crewels, leaves and stems with olive green crewels of four shades.

The illustration (Fig. 181) of sweet peas is intended as a working design in Crewel Stitch for a beginner, and is therefore given the right size. To work: Trace the outline upon fine linen or oatmeal cloth with tracing cloth and carbonised paper, and commence by working all the stems of the design. The colours used for the flowers are either a yellow pink and cream white or shades of red

FIG. 180. CREWEL WORK—CURTAIN BORDER.

purple and soft blue; for the leaves and stems, three shades of yellow green; for the seed pods, one of the greens and a russet yellow. Work in CREWEL STITCH in the directions depicted in the illustration, and be careful to follow the lines indicated, as much of the effect of the pattern depends upon so doing. For one blossom and the buds, use the pink and white crewels, the upright petals are pink, the drooping white; work the other flowers red purple for upright petals, soft blue for the drooping. Make the stems in the darkest green, the leaves in the two other shades, and mix green with the russet yellow of the seed pod. Work loosely, and do not draw up the material more than can be helped ; a little does not matter, as it will come straight when the work is damped and ironed. Make each stitch with regard to its proper place in the formation of the design, and hold the work over the fingers rather tightly, so that the stitches are looser than the ground. Work with a needle with a large eye, and use short pieces

any parts drawn up by the stitches. Crewel Work upon satin, silk, velvet, or plush is smoothed out as follows: Make ready a basin of cold clean water, a soft linen rag, and a hot iron. Have the iron firmly held by a second person, its flat part uppermost, then take the linen rag, dip it in the water, and lay it smoothly over the flat surface of the iron. While the steam is rising, quickly draw the embroidery, right side uppermost, over the iron, and, as

FIG. 181. CREWEL WORK—SWEET PEAS—WORKING DETAIL.

of crewel, as the wool becomes thin if frayed by the eye of the needle, or pulled frequently through the material.

When a crewel work pattern is finished, slightly damp it at the back, and pin it, fully stretched out, upon a flat board, or iron it on the wrong side with a warm, but not hot, iron. All Crewel Work upon washing materials that is not worked in a frame requires this damping and straightening to restore the fresh look to the material lost in the process of embroidery, and also for flattening out

soon as the steam ceases, take the work away, wet the rag again, and draw the work again over the iron; use both hands to hold the work, and be careful that no lines or wrinkles are made.

Crewels upon satin or silk backgrounds are finished with a wide hem of the material, or with a ball fringe made of the same colours that are used in the embroidery; crewels worked upon linen textures have the threads, one way of the material, drawn out to a depth of from two to three inches, and where the drawn threads finish a line, wide apart, of Buttonhole stitches made with crewels. The threads are also drawn out above this line, to form open squares and other fancy patterns. These are described in DRAWN WORK.

Washing Crewel Work.—Crewel work done upon cotton and linen materials, and in constant use, requires to be occasionally washed or sent to a cleaner's. The process is one that requires care, as if the work is sent in the ordinary way to the laundress, or washed hastily at home, the colours will run and the work be spoilt; while if extra care is given, the embroidery can be washed over and over again without losing its colour. The great matters to avoid are hard boiling water, rubbing with soap, exposure to the sun while wet, and a hot iron. To wash: Buy a pennyworth of bran, sew it up in a muslin bag, and put it into a saucepan with a gallon of soft rain water; boil, and pour out into an earthenware pan; take the bran out, and leave until the water is tepid. Put the material in and rub with the hands, using as little friction as is consistent with cleaning the background, and rubbing the Crewel Work itself very little. Rinse out twice in clean cold rain water, and expel the water, not with hard wringing and twisting, but by passing the hands down the material; then roll the work up in a towel so that it does not touch itself, and leave in a warm room until nearly dry. When ready, pin it out upon a board until it is dry, or iron it on the wrong side with a warm (not hot) iron. The pinning out is the safest plan, as the heat of the iron will sometimes cause the colours to run. Should they do so, rinse out again in clean rain water several times. The bran is only required at the first washing to set the colours of the crewels; warm rain water is sufficient afterwards. If the article is very dirty, a little hard white toilet soap is required.

Cricketings.—A superior quality of flannel, twilled, and resembling cloth. It is of the same colour as the Yorkshire flannels, and is employed for cricketing and boating costumes. The widths run from 32 to 36 inches. *See* FLANNEL.

Crimp.—To make very fine plaitings with a knife, or machine designed for the purpose, called a crimping machine, in the borders of a cap, or frill, or in ruffles. The machine for that purpose consists of two fluted rollers.

Crimped Plaitings.—*See* PLAITINGS.

Crinoline.—A plainly woven textile, composed of haircloth, and employed for expanding certain portions of women's dress, as well as for other purposes. It is made in two widths, one of 18 inches, and the other of 22.

Crinoline Steels.—Flat narrow bands of steel covered with a web woven upon them. They are manufactured in widths ranging between Nos. 1 and 16, and are made up in lengths of 36 yards, and sold by the gross.

Crochet.—The word crochet is derived from the French *croches*, or *croc*, and old Danish *krooke*, a hook. This art was known upon the Continent in the sixteenth century, but was then chiefly practised in nunneries, and was in-

differently classed as Nuns' work with lace and embroidery. It was brought into Ireland at an early date, and there, under the name of Irish Point, attained to great perfection, the patterns from which it was worked being evidently taken from those of needle lace. It was known in England and Scotland, but never attracted much attention until about 1838, when it became fashionable, and numerous patterns were printed and cottons manufactured. Since that date it has taken a prominent position among fancy works, which it is likely to sustain. Simple crochet is well adapted to the wants of everyday life, as it requires little skill in execution, will resist wear and tear, and costs a comparative trifle for materials. The finer kinds, known as Irish Point, Raised Rose crochet, and Honiton crochet, though costing little for material, require greater skill and patience, and are chiefly made for trade purposes by the peasantry of England and Ireland.

Crochet is done with almost any thread materials. Thus, all kinds of fleecy and Berlin wool, worsteds, netting silks, and cottons are used; also gold and silver cords, chenilles, and ornamental fine braids. According to the requirements of the article so is the material selected. Warm heavy couvrepieds require double Berlin wool or thick worsted; light shawls, Shetland and Pyrenean wool; comforters, &c., fleecy or single Berlin; antimacassars, purses, &c., and other fine work, netting silks; washing trimmings, &c., Arden's crochet cotton or Faudal and Phillips', or Brooks' Goat's head.

The chief stitches in crochet are CHAIN, SLIP, SINGLE, DOUBLE, TREBLE, CROSS TREBLE, HOLLOW and OPEN SPOTS, and PICOT, with fancy stitches founded upon these plain ones, and made by passing the thread round the hook several times, crossing it, and manipulating it in various ways. The method of working these various stitches will be found under their respective names.

The foundation of all crochet work is the CHAIN, or TAMBOUR stitch, and the various combinations that form crochet are simply caused by either taking cotton over the hook before making the loop of the Chain stitch, or inserting the hook into the foundation by drawing the made loop of the Chain stitch through two or more chains, or leaving it on the hook unworked, or by missing a certain number of chains; therefore, there is nothing in the work that cannot easily be understood from written instructions.

The work, being a series of small stitches worked over and over again, requires the names of the stitches to be abbreviated, and certain marks made to show where the lines and stitches can be repeated, or the explanations of the patterns would be both long and tedious. The principal mark used in crochet is the asterisk (*), two of which are placed in the explanation of the pattern at particular parts; this means that the stitches placed between the two are to be repeated from where they end at the second asterisk, by commencing them again from the first asterisk and working them to the second as many times as are directed. The following is an example—work 5 treble, 3 chain, * miss 3 on foundation, work 3 double, and repeat * three times, would, if not abbreviated, be written thus: work 5 treble, 3 chain, miss 3 on foundation, work 3 double miss 3 on foundation, work three double, miss three on foundation, work 3 double, miss 3 on foundation, work 3 double. Occasionally letters are used, as, for instance, when a row is worked to a certain stitch and is then repeated backwards. The letter B is then put at the commencement of the row, and A where the stitches are to commence being worked backwards. Repetitions will sometimes occur within each other, and when this is so, the piece of work to be repeated within the other part is marked off between two asterisks, and the second repetition placed within plain crosses.

Before commencing, be careful to select a hook suitable in size to the cotton or wool, and one that is firmly made and smooth. Hooks that have been used are much preferable to new ones, and only those fitted to their handles should be employed. Wool crochet is done with bone hooks, and cotton and silk crochet with steel hooks. Make a certain number of CHAIN stitches for the foundation, holding the work in the left hand between finger and thumb, with the thread over the first and second fingers of that hand. Take the hook up between thumb and first finger of the right hand, throw the thread round it with a jerk of the wrist of the left hand, and commence to make the stitch required. Good crochet is known by the work being loose, even, and firm, while every stitch corresponds in size, and takes its proper space in the pattern. From one end of the foundation chain to another is called *a row*, and the work is done backwards and forwards, so as to form no right side, unless it is especially intimated that the crochet must all commence from one end. For shawls and other large pieces of square work, commence in the centre, work all round, and increase at the corners; this is done in order that they should have a right and a wrong side; but work ordinary crochet in lines backwards and forwards.

To add fresh cotton during the progress of the work, make a Reef Knot, and work into the crochet one end of the two on one side of the knot, and the other on the other, so that there is no thick part in one place. When different colours are used on the same line of crochet, work in the threads not in use along the line, as in joining cottons, the old colour commencing a stitch, and the new finishing it.

Leaves, stars, and points are often required to be joined to the main work in Honiton and other fancy crochet patterns. They are managed thus: Slip the hook with the loop last made on it through the extreme point of the piece of work to be joined to the one in progress, and make the next stitch without considering this extra loop. Passing from one point to another in Rose and Honiton crochet is often advisable, without breaking the thread or leaving off the work; therefore, when one part of the pattern is complete, make a CHAIN corresponding to the stitch that commences the next point, draw this up by putting the needle into the first chain, and it will form the first stitch of the new pattern. Make a chain at the back of the work with SLIP STITCH to where the second point commences, should it not be opposite the point of the finished piece.

Contract edges in crochet work by working two stitches as one, thus: Put the cotton round the hook, insert it into the foundation work, and draw it through one loop; put the cotton round again and the hook through the next foundation stitch, draw through, and work up all the loops on the hook; continue until the part is sufficiently contracted.

Increase crochet by working two stitches into one hole, or by working two or four stitches on the regular foundation line, with Chain stitches between them.

When working from the centre of a piece of crochet and forming a number of close rounds, it is often difficult to trace where the last round ends and the next begins, and the errors caused by this uncertainty will throw the work out. To prevent this, tie a needleful of a bright and different coloured thread in the last stitch of the second row made, and draw it through every row into the stitch above it while working, until it arrives as a perfect line at the end of the work.

When using beads in crochet work thread them before the work is commenced and run them singly down at each stitch. The bead will fall on the reverse side of the work, so that when crochet with beads is being done, take the reverse side as the right side.

As examples of crochet work we give details of a few good patterns:—

Baby's Boot.—Worked in single Berlin wool of two shades, either blue and white or pink and white. Make Foundation Chain of coloured wool of 36 stitches, and work backwards and forwards in Ribbed Stitch for ten rows, increasing a stitch every row at one end, and keeping the other edge straight. Cast off 20 stitches, commencing from the straight end, and work backwards and forwards with the 16 stitches left for seven rows; at the end of the last row make a chain of 20 stitches, and work all stitches for ten rows, decreasing at the same end that was increased before, and keeping the other straight, and cast off. This forms the foot of the boot. Take white wool and tie it in the centre where the rows are short, and pick up nine stitches which rib backwards and forwards, increasing once on each side; then carry the white wool along the coloured to the back and round again, and rib backwards and forwards until a sufficient length is made to form the leg of the boot, decreasing twice on each side for the instep. Make a heading of an Open Chain, 1 Single and 3 Chain into every other stitch, fasten off, and sew up the coloured or foot part of the boot.

Ball Pattern.—Work with double Berlin wool and a good sized bone crochet hook. Make a CHAIN the length required, wool over the hook, and insert the hook in the fifth Chain from the hook, draw the wool through and raise a loop, wool over the hook, and raise another loop in the same stitch, wool over the hook and raise another loop, wool over the hook and draw it through all the loops which thus form a kind of ball, as shown in the illustration, Fig. 182, in which the hook is about to be drawn through the loops, then draw the wool through the two stitches on the hook; * 1 Chain, wool over the hook, miss one Chain, and raise another ball in the next stitch. Repeat from * to the end of the row; fasten off at the end. Second row—beginning again at the right hand side, wool over the hook, and raise a ball as described above under the Chain at the commencement of the preceding row, 1 Chain, then a ball into the space formed by the 1 Chain of last row. Continue working in the same way all along, to keep the work straight. This row will end with 1 Treble after the Chain stitch, the Treble to be worked over the ball of last row, fasten off. Third row—commence with a SINGLE CROCHET over the ball at the beginning of the last row, then 4 Chain, and make a ball

FIG. 182. CROCHET—BALL PATTERN.

under the first space in the preceding row, * 1 Chain, 1 ball in the next space, repeat from *. Repeat the second and third rows alternately, taking care to keep the same number of balls in every row.

Border.—Useful for trimming shawls and hoods, and looks well when worked in wool if formed with two shades of one colour. First row—make a foundation Chain the length required for trimming, and on that work one long

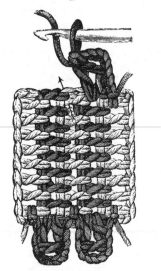

FIG. 183. CROCHET BORDER.

Treble Crochet and one Chain into every alternate stitch. Second row—take up the second colour and work 1 long Treble and 1 Chain into every Chain of preceding row; five of these rows make the width of the border, three of one shade and two of the other. To form the ornamental

edging, hold the work side uppermost (*see* Fig. 183), join the wool into first loop, make a Chain, and work a long Treble into same place, * 6 Chain, 1 long Treble, put into the first Chain of the 6 and worked up to where 2 loops are left on the hook, then put the hook into the same space, and work another long Treble with all the stitches on the hook worked into it (*see* Fig. 183). Put the hook into the next space, repeat from * to end of border; work the other side the same.

Cable Pattern.—To be worked in double Berlin wool in stripes of constrasting colours, four shades of each. Commence with the darkest wool with 16 Chain, in which work 15 Double Crochet. Fasten off at the end of this, at every row, beginning again at the right hand side. Second row—Double Crochet. Third row—3 Double Crochet, * wool over the hook and insert the hook in the fourth Double Crochet of the first row, bringing it out in the next stitch (the fifth stitch of the first row), draw the wool through very loosely, wool over the hook, and raise another loop in the same place, wool over the hook again and raise another loop, draw through all the loops together, then through the two stitches that are on the hook, miss 1 Double Crochet of last row, and work 3 Double Crochet in the three next consecutive stitches. Repeat from *. Fourth row—Double Crochet with the next lightest shade of wool. Fifth row—3 Double Crochet, * wool over the hook and insert the hook under the bunch of raised loops that were formed in the third row, raise 3 loops in the same manner as there directed, miss 1 Double Crochet of last row, and work 3 Double Crochet in the three next consecutive stitches: repeat from *. Sixth row —Double Crochet with the next lightest shade of wool. Seventh row—the same as the fifth row. Eighth row—Double Crochet with the lightest shade of wool. Ninth row—3 Double Crochet *, wool over the hook and insert the hook under the bunch of raised loops that were formed in the seventh row, raise 3 loops and draw through all the loops together, wool over the hook, raise another bunch of 3 loops in the same place, draw the wool through them, and then through the 3 stitches that are on the hook, miss 1 Double Crochet of last row, and work 3 Double Crochet in the three next consecutive stitches; repeat from *. Tenth row—with the same shade of wool, 3 Double Crochet * wool over the hook, and insert the hook so as to take up the first bunch of loops formed in the last row, and also the thread of wool that lies across between the two bunches, raise 3 loops and draw through all the loops together, wool over the hook and insert the hook under the second bunch of loops formed in the last row, raise 3 loops here, and draw the wool through all the loops together, and then draw through the 3 stitches that are on the needle, miss 1 Double Crochet of last row, and work 3 Double Crochet in the three next consecutive stitches; repeat from *. Eleventh row—plain Double Crochet, the same shade as the sixth row. Twelfth row—the same as the fifth row, only inserting the hook under the double bunch of the cable. Thirteenth row — plain Double Crochet with the next darkest shade of wool. Fourteenth row—the same as the fifth row. Fifteenth row—plain Double Crochet with

OLD ALENCON LACE — RARE.

OLD BRUSSELS LACE — RARE.

COLOURED LACES MADE IN FRANCE DURING THE 18TH CENTURY ON THE PILLOW

the darkest shade of wool. Sixteenth row—the same as the fourteenth row. Seventeenth row—the same as the fifteenth row. Repeat from the third row for the length required.

Couvrepied (1).—This design, which is worked in Tricot Ecossais and in Tricot, the centre strip in Tricot, and the sides in Ecossais, is shown in Fig. 184. Wool required, 8 ply Berlin, with No. 7 Tricot hook. Colours according to taste. Work the centre of the strip in the lightest colour, the Vandykes next to it in a middle shade, the outside in the darkest, and the little crosses and stars in filoselle after the Crochet is finished. The Couvrepied looks well made in three shades of crimson wool with yellow-green filoselle for the crosses and stars. To work:

same way for four rows. Work the green filoselle in CROSS STITCH over the junction of the colours, and form the stars with 8 Chain Stitches for each loop, catch them together in the centre with a wool needle, and also at each of the eight points. The outside strips are in Tricot Ecossais, and require a foundation of 11 stitches. The centre and outside strips are joined together with rows of Slip Crochet; five rows on each side are worked up the selvedges, in alternate rows of black and sea green wool.

Couvrepied (2).—The Couvrepied shown in Fig. 185 is worked in wide and narrow strips of Cross Tricot, and consists of eight broad and nine narrow strips, which are joined by being crocheted together with Slip Stitch,

FIG. 184. CROCHET COUVREPIED.

Make a Foundation Chain of 22 stitches with medium shade. First row—miss the first stitch and work 7 stitches in Tricot, then tie the lightest shade on, and leave the medium shade at the back of the work, and raise 8 stitches, put on another ball of medium wool, leave the lightest at the back, and work the remaining stitches. Work back with the medium shade of wool first through the first stitch, and then through 10 loops, which will leave 2 loops of its colour unworked; take up the light colour, pass it through them and through 16 loops, then drop it, pick up the medium colour that was left at the back at the commencement, and finish with it. Work the whole strip in this style, the only alteration being in making a Vandyke with the light wool by increasing it a stitch at a time for five rows, and decreasing it in the

the outer corresponding stitches in each strip being thus drawn together. The wool used is of three shades—crimson, green, and grey, and is either Berlin Tricot or 4 thread fleecy; hook No. 13. For the broad stripes make a CHAIN of 12 stitches in grey wool, and work a row of common Tricot and a row of Cross Tricot (*see* Fig. 185). Third row—work with the crimson wool in Cross Tricot reverse the cross stitches by working and crossing the loops that are separated, and not those close together. In this row pass over the first perpendicular stitch, or the crosses will not fall right. Fourth row as second, continue working second and third row to the end of eight rows, counting from the commencement of the crimson; then work two rows in grey wool, eight in green, two in grey, and return to the eight crimson rows, and so on until the pattern and strip is complete. Always finish with the two grey lines, and be careful to keep twelve stitches on the hook, and neither to increase nor decrease in working. The narrow strips are in grey wool: Make a chain of 4 stitches,

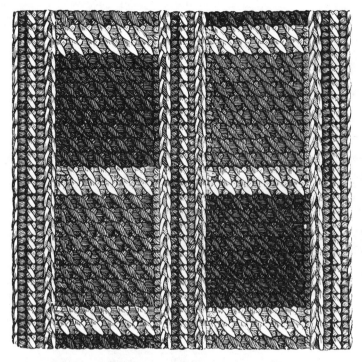

FIG. 185. CROCHET PATTERN FOR COUVREPIED.

the 2 outside being left unworked at commencement of rows; in this strip there will be only one Cross Tricot, which always cross in the way shown in the illustration. A knotted fringe of the three colours completes the Couvrepied.

Darning. — An imitation of Netting and Darning. The designs used are those printed for Cross Stitch Berlin work, or for plain square Crochet. The foundation is of square Crochet formed with 2 Chain and a Double. Work the double of the second row over the double of the first row, and so on throughout the work. The edge is formed thus: First row—work 6 Chain, and loop into the middle stitch of the outer line or every second line on foundation. Second row—work 8 Slip Stitches over the 6 Chains of the last row. Third row— work 8 Chain and a Double into the middle of the loops of the last row. Fourth row—2 Double, 8 Treble, 2 Double, into every 8 Chain of the last row. When the foundation and edging are complete, form the pattern on the work by darning soft knitting cotton in and out the squares to make a design. Fig. 186 illustrates Crochet Darning when used as a furniture lace.

Edging. (1).—This pattern is useful for trimmings to pinafores and underlinen. Work with a fine hook and Evans's Crochet cotton No. 30. Commence with a 7 Chain, work 1 Treble into 4 Chain from the hook, 5 Chain and loop into the last stitch on the Foundation Row, turn the work, 2 Chain, 3 Treble, and 5 Double into the 5 Chain of the last row, 3 Chain and loop into the last stitch of the last row*,

turn the work, 1 Treble into the last stitch, 3 Chain looped into the last Double on preceding row, 5 Chain looped into the Treble of the preceding row next the Doubles, turn work, 2 Chain, 3 Treble, and 5 Double into the 5 Chain loop, 3 Chain and loop into last stitch of preceding row. Repeat from * until the edging is complete as to length, then turn the plain side uppermost, and work 1 Treble and 1 Chain into every other side stitch of the edging, so as to create a straight foundation. Fig. 187 illustrates the edging when finished, and will assist workers in following the instructions.

Edging. (2).—A useful pattern for trimmings. The work is commenced from the centre, the Foundation Chain forming the waved line. To work: Make a Foundation Chain a third longer than the required length. First row— miss first Chain, and work 18 Double Crochet along chain, then make 5 Chain, and, turning this back to the right, join it with a Single to the eleventh stitch of the 18 Double Crochet on this chain, work 4 Single Crochet, repeat the 18 Double Crochet to the end and fasten off. Second row—commence at the fourth stitch of the Double Crochet on last row, work 2 Double *, then 3 Chain and 1 treble in the centre of the 4 Single of last row—2 Chain and 1 Treble in the same stitch as last Treble, 3 Chain and 2 Single in the centre of the 10 Double Crochet of last row, repeat from * to the end. Third row—*, work 5 Double Crochet into 5 consecutive stitches of last row, make 3 Chain, and form a PICOT or loop upon the fifth Double Crochet, and repeat from * to end of row. Fourth row—*, work 5 Chain, looping the fifth into the third to form a Picot, and then

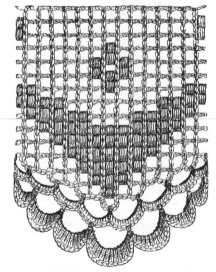

FIG. 186. CROCHET DARNING.

3 Chain, miss 5 stitches of last row, counting the one with the loop upon it as the centre stitch, and fasten the Chain to work with a Single, and repeat from *. To form the edge: First row—turn the work so as to Crochet on the

Foundation Chain made at the beginning of the pattern, and commence at the first of the 9 stitches, which form a half circle, and on it work 1 Chain and 1 Treble alternately

FIG. 187. CROCHET EDGING.

9 times, then 1 Chain, and missing 9 stitches between the half circles, repeat the Chain and Treble stitches. Second row—commence on the third Treble stitch of the last row, * make 5 Chain and loop back to third to form a Picot, then 2 Chain, then miss 1 Chain on the foundation row, and work 1 Treble on the next Treble stitch of last row, repeat from * until 5 Treble stitches are made; then miss between

FIG. 188. CROCHET EDGING.

the scallops and work 1 Treble on the third Treble of next scallop; repeat until the edging is completed. The effect of this edging is shown in Fig. 188.

Fringe. — Work a Chain the length required, take up the first stitch, * draw the cotton through to double the distance the width the fringe is to be, keep the cotton on the hook, and twist the cotton round (*see* Fig. 189); when twisted give a turn upwards in the middle of its length, take up the stitch on the hook again,

FIG. 189. CROCHET FRINGE.

and work a Double Crochet, working in the end of the cotton on the hook; repeat from * to end of Foundation Chain.

Hairpin Crochet.—So called as the work is made between the prongs of an ordinary large hairpin, though bone imitations of the same are used. The crochet can be done with fine black purse silk, coloured silk, and Arden's crochet cotton No. 26. When worked with silks it makes pretty mats, gimp headings, and lacey looking trimmings; when worked with white crochet cotton, capital washing edgings, as it is strong. To commence: Hold the hairpin in the left hand, the round part upwards, twist the cotton round the left prong, pass it over the right prong to the back of the hair pin, and lay it over the left forefinger. Take up a crochet hook and draw this back thread to the front under the first crossed one, and make a Chain by taking up fresh cotton and pulling it through. Take the hook out and turn the hairpin; * the cotton will now be

in front; put it over the right hand pin to the back, hook into loop, and make a Chain by drawing the cotton through; then put the hook through the twist on the left hand prong, and make a Chain

FIG. 190. HAIRPIN CROCHET.

having two stitches on the hook, make a stitch drawing cotton through these two loops, so that only one loop is left. Take out the hook, turn the work, and repeat from *. When the hairpin is filled with work slip it off; to steady the prong ends put them through some of the last loops, and continue to work as before (*see* Fig. 190).

Work that is well done has all the large open loops at the sides of a uniform length. The example shown is an edging. To form rosettes fasten off after sixteen or eighteen loops on each side are made, tying one side of them together to form a centre, and when several are thus prepared make a crochet Foundation with two rows of Double Square Crochet, and catch four or six of the loops in each rosette to it. When the first set of rosettes are thus secured, another set beyond them is added by sewing the loops together where they touch, or form Vandykes by sewing rosettes above and between every second one of the first set. Scalloped and Vandyked braid is often used for foundations to these ornamental trimmings instead of Square crochet.

Honeycomb Crochet.— White single Berlin wool; medium size bone crochet hook. Make a Chain the length required for the shawl. First row—1 Treble in the sixth Chain from the needle, * 1 Chain, miss 3, 1 Treble, 3 Chain, 1 Treble in the same loop as the other Treble, repeat from *, turn. Second row—1 Double Crochet, 5 Treble, 1 Double Crochet under every loop of 3 Chain of last row, turn. Third row—4 Chain, * 1 Treble between the two Double Crochet stitches of last row, 3 Chain, another Treble in the same stitch as the last, 1 Chain, repeat from *, 1 Chain, 1 Treble at the end of row. Fourth row—1 Double Crochet, 5 Treble, 1 Double Crochet, under every loop of 3 Chain of last row; at the end of the row work 1 extra Double Crochet in the corner loop. Fifth row—6 Chain, 1 Treble between the 2 Double Crochet at the corner of last row, * 1 Chain, 1 Treble between the next two Double Crochet stitches of last row, 3 Chain, another Treble in the same place as the last, repeat from *. Repeat from the second row according to the size required for the shawl.

Honiton or Point Crochet.—An imitation of Guipure

P 2

Lace, in the making of which the Irish peasantry excel. It should only be attempted by skilled workwomen, as it is difficult and troublesome. It requires Brooks' Goatshead, No. 48, crochet cotton, and a fine crochet hook. To simplify the directions for working Fig. 191, the various sprigs (which are all made separately and joined together) are named as follows: The sprig in the top left hand corner of the pattern is called a Rose, the one beneath it a Feather, the one by its side a Curve, the five Sprigs with five loops Daisies, the two of the same make, but with 3 loops, Trefoils, and the one with a trefoil centre a Bud.

For the Daisies, work three with stems, and join them to the fourth, which is without a stem; work 1 with a stem ready to be worked into position; work one Trefoil with a stem, and two without; work the Feather without a stem, and the Rose with a stem, joining it to the Feather in working. The illustration shows how the Curves and Trefoils are joined.

Daisy.—Take a coarse knitting needle, No. 1, and wind the crochet cotton thickly round it ten times, slip it off and crochet 40 Single (this forms the raised centres of

work 8 Chain for the stem from curve and 8 Single upon it, connect it to the centre round and work back upon its other side with 8 Single, and fasten the stem into a trefoil and fasten off. Second row—return to the centre round and commence on one side of stem 1 Chain, 1 Double into 2 stitch on foundation, * 1 Chain and 1 Treble into fourth, repeat from * twelve times, then 1 Chain, 1 Double into stitch close to stem. Third row—work a chain underneath stem and 3 Single into every space in the last row, ornament every third Single with a Picot made of 3 Chain. Upon reference to the pattern it will be seen that one curve has a thick stem and one an open; for the last the 8 Chain forming it cover with 8 Single, and the open work in 2 row continue down it, also the thick work and Picots of third row.

Bud.—Make 3 loops of 8 Chain each, and cover these with 20 single, make a chain of 15 to form the stem, and cover on each side with Singles and fasten off. Second row—commence on the point of first loop, work 8 Chain and slip into the centre of next point, 8 Chain and slip into the centre of 3 point, then work Singles, all along the

FIG. 191. CROCHET HONITON OR POINT.

most of the sprigs). First row—10 Chain, miss 6 single, and slip into seventh, repeat four times, then make 15 Chain and a Single into every Chain; for the stem turn the work and work a Single into the other side of the 15 Chain until the end is reached, when fasten off or join to another sprig. Second row—return to the centre round and work 18 Single into the 10 Chain; repeat four times. This completes the daisy; for the ones without the stem, leave out the 15 Chain.

Trefoil.—Make a centre round over the knitting needle as before, and work 40 Single. First row—* 10 Chain, miss 7 Single and slip into eighth stitch, slip 5 Single, and repeat twice. Second row—crochet 15 Single into every 10 Chain, Slip Stitch the 5 single on first row. Third row—crochet 15 single over the Singles in last row, and work Singles over the Slip stitches of last row. This completes the trefoil with a round centre; the others make with 3 loops of 8 Chain each, cover with 20 Singles for the first row, and with 26 Singles for the last row.

Curve.—First row—8 Chain, join and work 24 Single, but do not close up the round when 24 Single are made,

side of last loop. Third row—turn the work, and work a Single into every stitch. Fourth row—turn the work, work a Single into every stitch, and occasionally 2 Single into the same stitch, and make a Picot with 3 Chain into every fourth stitch, and also upon the outer edge of stem.

Feather.—Make the centre round over the knitting needle, as before described, and work 40 Single into it. First row—* 10 Chain and a Single into every Chain, connect the last with the centre round and repeat from * twice. Cover 8 stitches on the round with these three points; Slip stitch 4 and repeat; Slip stitch 4 and again repeat; Slip stitch 10 and commence. Second row—work Singles up the first point of 8 Stitches, and work down from the point to the centre round with a Chain caught in at the back of the work; * join the point finished to the one next it by slipping the hook first into a stitch upon the edge of the finished point, and then into the edge of the next point, and make a loop by drawing both together; work in this way up three-quarters of the length, and then Slip stitch round the point of the unfinished feather, and work Singles down it to the centre round; repeat from * for the third feather. Commence the next three feathers from *, and work two sets.

Rose.—Make the centre round over the knitting needle, and work 40 Single into it; make each petal at once. First row—*, 8 Chain, 2 Chain, 1 Double into last Chain but one; 1 Treble, 1 Chain into every other Chain of the last row three times; turn the work, and work 1 Chain, 1 Treble three times, and 1 Chain, 1 Double once upon the other side of 8 Chain. Second row—work Singles into every stitch. This completes a petal—repeat from * four times. Each petal takes up the space of seven stitches on the centre round, the five remaining form the foundation for the stem. To work the stem: Slip stitch along the foundation 2 stitches, make a Chain of 24, join this to the feather sprig in the middle of the place left to receive it, work 24 Singles back to the Rose fasten, into the Rose and work back upon other side of Chain 24 Single, and fasten into the feather.

Join each sprig to the others where shown in the illustration with bars made with Chain Stitch, work back in Slip stitch where necessary with occasional Picots, made by working 3 Chain and joining them by slipping the hook back into the first of the three Chain, and drawing the Chain stitch that continues the bar through that. Ornament the square straight crochet lines enclosing and joining the flowers at top and bottom of lace with the same description of Picots, making the last line on both sides in Double Crochet. The point edging is not crochet work, but is made with an ordinary needle and crochet cotton in thick Buttonhole. Form loops of cotton, Buttonhole them over, and ornament them with Picots. Make the three loops connected together in the pattern at one time, the two on the line first, and add the third on the top of the others when they are completed.

Insertion.—This pattern is worked with Boar's head cotton No. 18, and hook No. 4. It commences in the centre, and half the circle, half the diamond, and one oval is formed first, and the work is then turned and the other halves and the headings added. The first side: First circle—make 13 Chain, turn, miss the last 8 Chain, and work 1 Single in the ninth stitch, so as to form a round loop, and leave 4 Chain, turn, and in the round loop work 8 Single, which should cover half of it. To work the oval at the side and half the centre diamond, make 10 Chain, miss the last 4 Chain, and work 1 Slip stitch in the fifth stitch, leaving 5 Chain; this forms the first Picot; and for the second Picot make 5 Chain and work 1 Slip stitch in the first stitch of these 5 Chain. Then for the third Picot, make 5 Chain and 1 Slip stitch in the first stitch; and for the fourth Picot, 5 Chain and 1 Slip stitch in the first stitch. To join the Picots, work 1 Single in the last stitch of the 5 Chain left before the first Picot; repeat the circle and oval until the length required is made, ending with the 8 Single in the circle (see Fig. 192). The second side: To finish the circle—work 8 Single in the half left plain, then on the next stitch of the 4 Chain left between the circle and Picots work Slip stitch; and for the first Picot make 9 Chain, and missing the last 4 Chain, work 1 Single, leaving 4 Chain; and for the second, third, and fourth Picots make

5 Chain, and work a single stitch in the first stitch of the 5 Chain three times. To join the Picots—work 1 Single on the last stitch of the 4 Chain left before the first Picot; make 3 Chain and work 1 Single on the first Chain stitch before the next circle; repeat from the commencement of the second side. The heading: First row—commence on the centre of the 8 Single of the first circle, and work

FIG. 192. CROCHET INSERTION.

1 Long Treble, then 5 Chain and 1 Single between the second and third Picots, 5 Chain and 1 Long Treble on the centre of the next circle, repeat to the end, fasten off. Second row—commence on the first stitch of the last row, make 2 Chain, miss 2, and 1 Treble, repeat to the end; work the heading on the other side to correspond.

Knitting.—By working strips of Knitting and joining them together with bands of Crochet, a greater variety is given to large pieces of work, such as counterpanes and couvrepieds, than when the whole is made of one description of fancy work. The knitted strips can be in any raised fancy knitting stitches, the crochet strips in open square Crochet or in Treble Crochet. The Knitting should be twice as wide as crochet.

Lace Crochet. (1).—This is a light and graceful trimming, formed of a combination of Crochet and Point lace stitches, and makes a pleasing variety to ordinary crochet.

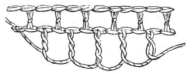

FIG. 193. CROCHET LACE.

In Fig. 193 the edging is given when completed. It is commenced as follows: Make a foundation Chain of the length required (say a yard), and work an open row of one Treble into every other Chain on foundation

FIG. 194. CROCHET LACE—DETAIL A.

row, and one Chain between (*see* Fig. 194, Detail A); thread a sewing needle with the crochet cotton, fasten, and make a loose twisted stitch into every open space of last row. Arrange these stitches as scallops, six to a scallop, the centre loop being the longest. Commence from same place as last row, and work close

Buttonholes into the spaces between the loops (*see* Fig. 195, Detail B). The next two rows are a repetition of the looped and the Buttonhole row, but the loops are shorter

FIG. 195. CROCHET LACE—DETAIL B.

than on the scallops, and worked between every third Buttonhole (*see* Fig. 196, Detail C). The next row after

FIG. 196. CROCHET LACE—DETAIL C.

the Buttonhole is formed of three twisted loops close together, the space that three more would have filled being missed, and another three then worked, and so on to end of row. The last row consists of Buttonholes, with Vandykes made at equal distances, thus—work four Buttonholes, return the thread to first one, and work four more, the first four being the foundation; return the thread and work three Buttonholes above the four, and lastly work one as a point, run the thread down through the Vandyke, and continue the Buttonhole row until another Vandyke has to be formed (*see* Fig. 197, Detail D).

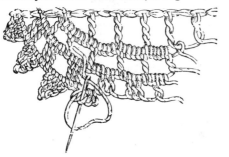

FIG. 197. CROCHET LACE—DETAIL D.

Place these Vandykes above the open spaces in the last row, and not above the stitches. The cotton used is Brooks' Goat's head No. 48, hook No. 5.

Lace Crochet. (2).—Make a Foundation Chain of length required, into which work 1 Chain and 1 Double Crochet into every 2 stitch. Second row—5 Chain and 2 Treble, missing 3 Chain on foundation for the whole row. Third row—1 Chain, 1 Double into every other stitch, and fasten off. Make half stars separately, work a 14 Chain, form a round, and surround it with Slip Stitch; into the upper half of round work 7 loops, putting them into the stitches one after the other. The first loop requires 24 Chain, second and third 16 each, middle loop 24, repeat the first three loops, reversing their order; unite the plain part of the round to the border, crocheting them together, and fasten the stars in at a distance of 48 stitches from each other. Fourth row—commence at the 22nd stitch from centre of star,* work 3 Chain, and pick up first loop,

6 Chain, pick up second loop, 6 Chain, pick up third loop, 8 Chain, pick up middle loop, repeat backwards for three loops, and fasten into the twenty-second stitch from the middle of the star, slip the cotton along four stitches, and repeat from*. Fifth row—work a Double into every Chain except the one in the centre loop: in this one the increase is managed, and requires 1 Double, 2 Chain, 1 Double. For the open lattice part (*see* Fig. 197), work 4 Chain, catch it into three row, and then 4 Chain. Repeat fifth row eleven times, always increasing at the pointed stitch; and for the lattice part work a plain 8 Chain alternately with 4 Chain caught into third stitch of the previous row and 4 Chain. Work the border without the straight lines which are put in by mistake in the pattern close to the thick Vandykes, and make it of a number of Picot Chains interlaced, as shown in the illustration, which is easier to follow than complicated written directions.

Mignardise.—This is a variety of Crochet, formed by inserting narrow fine braids into the design as the heavy part of the pattern, that would otherwise be formed by continuous stitches of Treble or Double Crochet. The braid is woven into various sizes and forms, and with an edging of fine loops, and the crochet stitches connect it by passing the hook and the crochet cotton through these loops. Mignardise is used almost entirely to form narrow edgings for underlinen and children's dresses. The cotton used is sometimes white and blue, sometimes white and pink, the colour working one row of the centre, and one of the extreme edge of a pattern.

Simple edging.—Take the braid, hold it in the left hand and work an outside edge to it thus—join the braid to the cotton with a Double Crochet through the first loop * six Chain, put the hook into the second Chain and make a Picot of the rest, 1 Chain, and a Double Crochet; repeat five times from *, 3 Chain, and miss one loop on the braid, gather together the four next loops, and work a Single Crochet, 3 Chain and miss a loop, and work a Double Crochet. This forms a pattern which is to be repeated until the length required is worked. Second row — the edge being finished, turn the other side of the braid uppermost, and fasten the cotton into the braid in the centre above the four loops fastened together in last row *; work 1 Chain and a Single into next loop, and then 12 Chain, miss the loop on the opposite side of the loop missed in first row, and pick up the seven loops that are opposite the five ornamented with Picots, make a Chain between each loop, and draw them all together to form a circle, and connect them to the last twelve Chain; work 3 Chain, and draw that through the seventh Chain to form two lines above the circle; work 6 Chain, and miss the loop opposite the one missed upon last row; work a Single, 1 Chain, 1 Single, repeat from the third row 1 Treble and one Chain into every other stitch upon last row.

Scalloped edging.—Formed of two rows of Mignardise braid. Each scallop requires eleven loops of braid upon the inside, and twelve upon the outer. Pick up the braid, and hold it in the left hand, and commence by making the crochet upon the inside of the scallop; this consists of four Vandykes radiating from a half circle, the points of the Vandykes being the loops upon the braid. First row—1 Single Crochet into first loop of braid, * 10 Chain, miss one loop, work Single into next loop, turn the work, and make the Vandyke, work 2 Single into the first, 2 Chains, then 2 Double, and 1 Treble into the next three Chains, making 5 stitches, then 5 Chain and 1 Single in the third loop on braid, missing one loop; turn the work, 2 Single, 2 Double, and 1 Treble upon the 5 Chain, 5 Chain 1 Single into the second loop from one last worked (missing one);

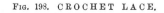

FIG. 198. CROCHET LACE.

turn work, 2 Single, 2 Double, and 1 Treble on the 5 Chain, 5 Chain 1 Single into the second loop on the braid from last worked loop; turn work, 2 Single, 2 Double, 1 Treble on the 5 Chain; turn the work, 5 Chain 1 Single on the second loop from the one last worked, 4 Chain 1 Single into next loop. Repeat from * to length required and fasten off. Second row—1 Single upon first Single of last row *; upon the 5 Chain, 2 Single, 2 Double, 1 Treble, 9 Chain, miss out all the 4 Vandykes, and work 1 Treble 2 Double and 3 Single upon the chains in last row. Repeat from * and fasten off. In the next row the second piece of braid (which is worked as a straight line) is inserted. Third row—1 Double Crochet upon last stitch of last row *, 2 Chain, insert

the hook into loop of braid and make a stitch, 2 Chain, miss two stitches on foundation and work 1 Double Crochet, repeat from * to end of the row and fasten off. Fourth row—Turn the work, and form the edge to the scallop upon the unfastened side of braid * 2 Chain, 1 Single into first loop, repeat from * and fasten off. Fifth row—commence by drawing the 3 loops together that are over the 4 Chain of first row, and work a Double Crochet, then 3 Chain and 1 Double Crochet in the loop following, repeat to end of the row. Sixth row—over every 3 Chain of last row work 1 Double Crochet, 5 Treble, and 1 Double.

Crochet Netting.—A variety of Crochet founded upon Hair-pin Crochet. The Netting is worked with a Crochet hook, and large wooden shuttles terminating in four or two prongs resembling the large teeth of a comb. The prongs are of different sizes, the lower one of a shuttle with four prongs being either twice or three times the width of the other three, but all are placed at equal distances from each other. A shuttle fitted with two prongs resembles the old wooden lyres used for making chains, and its two prongs are set at a considerable distance from each other. The different widths of the prongs are intended for the making of looped fringes to the work, the double prongs for a narrow strip of Netting, with loops at each side of equal sizes, and the four-pronged shuttle for making broader and thicker centre lines of work between the loops, the stitches being placed on each side of the second prong and over it, instead of only as a centre line. The work consists of long narrow strips finished at both edges with loops. These loops give the appearance of open Netting, and are used to join the various strips made by being fastened together with lines of Crochet. Varieties of Crochet Netting are made by the Crochet-work designs that join them together, or by passing the stitches over the centre prongs of the shuttle, or by simply working them in one of the spaces between the prongs. The shuttles are to be obtained at 131, Edgware-road.

To work a narrow strip of Crochet Netting.—Take a shuttle of four prongs; hold it in the left hand by the widest prongs with the three small prongs uppermost. Take a skein of single Berlin wool, or of fine Arrasene; make a loop near the end; pass a medium-sized Crochet hook through the loop, and hold the hook in the space between the top and second prong, and the waste piece of wool in the left hand. Throw the working end of the wool over the top prong and commence. Draw the wool from the back of the prong through the loop on the hook, and make a stitch thus*; turn the shuttle in the left hand until the broad prong is uppermost; throw the wool round the two small prongs from the front of the shuttle to the back, and make a stitch as before by drawing it through the one on the hook, which still hold in the space where the first stitch was made; put the hook with the stitch still on it over the top and through the loop made by the first stitch on the first prong (which is now the one held in the left hand). Put wool on the hook and draw it through this loop; wool on again, and draw it through two of the stitches on the hook; wool round, and draw it through the remaining two stitches; turn the shuttle round, throw the wool over the top prong, make a stitch, put the hook across the top thread of the loop on the second and third prongs, through that loop, wool on hook, draw through the loop, wool on hook, draw through two loops, wool on hook, draw through two loops, repeat from *. When the shuttle is filled with the Netting, take off the loops, re-adjust the last two on the prongs, and continue the work. The strip made with the above will have loops at one edge longer than the loops at the other; if even size edges are needed, work over but one prong on both sides. Fringes are made as above, one set of loops being made on the broad prong of the shuttle.

To work a thick broad centre line of Netting.—Hold the shuttle in the left hand by the broad prong; loop and hook in the space between the top and second prong waste wool held down with the left thumb, and working wool over the top prong. Make a stitch by drawing the wool from the back of the shuttle through the stitch on the hook. Pull this stitch out with the hook until it stretches over the second prong, and is in the space below it; draw the wool from the back of the shuttle through this stitch*; turn the shuttle in the left hand until the wide prong is uppermost, and turn the hook in the stitch at the same time; throw the thread over the prong next the wide one from the front to the back, bring it through the last stitch, lengthen out the loop so obtained until it reaches below the second prong; make a stitch with the thread from the back of the shuttle; put the hook into the already made loop on the bottom prong, not over the top thread of it as in the last pattern, but through the loop and out under the left or under thread of it; take up wool on the hook, draw it back through the loop on the prong and to the front; take up wool, and draw it through the two stitches on the hook, turn the shuttle, throw the wool over the top prong, make a stitch as before, draw this out over the second prong, make a stitch with the wool at the back, put the hook into the loop on the bottom prong, bringing it out under the under thread, wool on the hook, drawn through the loop, wool on the hook, and through the two stitches on the hook. Repeat from *.

Attention to the holding of the shuttle and the right manipulation of the Crochet-hook is important, otherwise the Netting comes apart when removed from the shuttle.

On Net.—This work is an imitation of Honiton and Brussels lace. It is made with Raised Rose Crochet sprays or simple Crochet edging, fastened down upon net.

There are two ways of working on the net: in one, over-cast detached sprigs of crochet upon Brussels net, and connect them together with Brides. In the second, work a simple flower pattern edging, and connect this to the net with Chain stitch worked to form tendrils and sprays. As these Chains are worked take up portions of the net on the crochet hook so that they are incorporated into it.

Over Brass Rings.—For a Mat.—Thirty-seven curtain rings, and four shades of one colour, either of wool or silk, are necessary. Cover one ring for the centre with the lightest shade of wool, work fifty Double Crochet over the ring, making the edges of the stitches on the outer edge of the ring. Cover six rings with the next shade, twelve with the third shade, and eighteen with the last. Place the light ring in the centre, the six rings round it and sew them to the centre ring. Arrange the twelve rings round the six, and the eighteen round the twelve. The side of the mat where the rings are sewn together will be the wrong side; keep it still upon that side, and finish the rings with working an eight-pointed star in filoselle in the centre of each. Make a fringe of beads round the mat, and ornament the rings with a cross of white beads in their centres.

To form a Bag.—One hundred and one rings are required, covered with Double Crochet in colours according to taste. Sew the rings together in the shape of a cup. First row or centre—1 ring; second row—6 rings; third row—12; fourth row—16; fifth row—20; sixth row—22; seventh row—24. Above the last row of rings work a row of Crochet, 3 Trebles into the top of a ring, 5 Chain and 3 Trebles into next ring; repeat 5 Chain and three Trebles to the end of the row. Second row—1 Treble and 2 Chain into every third stitch on the foundation. Repeat second row eleven times. Fourteenth row—2 Long Trebles and 3 Chain, missing 3 foundation stitches for the 3 Chain. Line the bag with soft silk, run a ribbon in and out of the last crochet row to draw it up, and finish the lower part with a silk tassel.

Point de Chantilly.—To be worked with double Berlin wool and a rather large bone Tricot hook. Commence with 16 Chain, insert the hook in the second Chain from the hook, raise a loop, and work a Chain stitch in it, then raise another loop and work a Chain stitch in that, and so on to the end of the row, keeping all the Chain stitches on the hook, work back as in ordinary Tricot. Second row—1 Chain, insert the hook in the first perpendicular loop and also through the Chain stitch belonging to it, raise a loop, and work a Chain stitch in it, * insert the hook in the next perpendicular loop and through the chain belonging to it, raise a loop and work a Chain stitch in that, repeat from *, keeping all the Chain stitches on the hook, and work back as in ordinary Tricot. Every succeeding row is the same as the second row.

Raised Marcella Cherries and White Narcissus Flower.—Materials required: Single Berlin wool, red, grey, green, yellow, black, and white; a fine bone crochet hook. For the red strip work 23 Chain, 1 Double Crochet in

BULGARIAN NEEDLEWORK.

BULGARIAN NEEDLEWORK.

the third from the hook, and Double Crochet all along, 21 Double Crochet in all; two more rows of plain Double Crochet, viz., 1 Chain to turn and 21 Double Crochet along, take up both front and back loops. Fourth row—1 Double Crochet, insert the hook through at the bottom of the third Double Crochet in the last row, draw the wool through and raise five loops, draw the wool through the five loops, and then through the 2 stitches on the needle, * 3 Double Crochet on the three succeeding Double Crochet of last row, then insert the hook at the distance of four stitches from the place where the preceding cherry was raised, draw the wool through, and raise five more loops to form another cherry, repeat from *, and end the row with three Double Crochet. Fifth row—plain Double Crochet. Sixth row—3 Double Crochet, insert the hook through at the bottom of the fifth Double Crochet of the last row; and raise a cherry as directed above, 3 Double Crochet, another cherry at the distance of four stitches, 3 Double Crochet, a cherry, 3 Double Crochet, a cherry, 5 Double Crochet at the end of the row. Seventh row—plain Double Crochet. Repeat from the fourth to the seventh rows twice more, then leave a space where the narcissus flower is to be placed, omit the middle cherry in the sixteenth row, the two middle cherries in the eighteenth row, and three in the twentieth row, working instead plain Double Crochet; in the twenty-second, twenty-fourth, and twenty-sixth rows bring these cherries gradually back again, and then repeat from the fourth row for the length required for the antimacassar. For the narcissus flower, white wool, work 7 Chain, 1 Double Crochet in the first from the needle, 4 Treble along, 6 Treble in the top stitch, 4 Treble and a Double Crochet along the other side, and a Single Crochet to fasten off; secure the ends firmly. Work six of these white leaves, then a dot of yellow for the centre of the flower, 4 Chain, join round, work 2 Double Crochet in each chain, and a Double Crochet on each of these, tack the six leaves together in the shape of a flower, the wrong side of the Crochet uppermost, and place the yellow dot in the centre, arrange it by means of a few stitches in the middle of the flat space that is left among the cherries. For the grey stripe, work 15 Chain, 1 Double Crochet in the third from the needle, and Double Crochet all along, 13 Double Crochet in all. Two more rows of plain Double Crochet, viz., 1 Chain to turn, and 13 Double Crochet along. Fourth row—1 Double Crochet, a cherry, 3 Double Crochet, a cherry, 3 Double Crochet, a cherry, 3 Double Crochet. Fifth row—plain Double Crochet. Sixth row—3 Double Crochet, a cherry, 3 Double Crochet, a cherry, 5 Double Crochet. Seventh row—plain Double Crochet. Eighth row—1 Double Crochet, a cherry, 3 Double Crochet; a green cherry, 3 Double Crochet, a cherry, 3 Double Crochet; compose the green cherry of 5 loops of green wool worked in without breaking off the grey wool, which draw through the two stitches (1 green and one grey) on the needle, leaving the green wool at the back. Ninth row—plain Double Crochet. Tenth row—the same as the sixth row, both the cherries to be green ones. Eleventh row—plain Double Crochet. Twelfth row—the same as the eighth row. Thirteenth row—plain Double Crochet. Fourteenth row—the same

as the sixth row, and the same colour. Fifteenth row—plain Double Crochet. Sixteenth row—same as the fourth row. Seventeenth row—plain Double Crochet. Eighteenth row—the same as the sixth row. Nineteenth row—plain Double Crochet. Repeat from the fourth row until the stripe is the same length as the red one, work a double Cross Stitch with yellow wool in the centre of every group of four green cherries. It will take three of the red and two of the grey stripes to make a good sized antimacassar. With black wool work a row of Double Crochet round all the stripes, and join them together with a row of white Double Crochet. For the border: First row—white wool, 1 Double Crochet, 6 Chain, miss 4, repeat the whole way round, but do not miss any stitches between the Double Crochet at the corners. Second row—black, 1 Double Crochet over the Double Crochet of last row, 6 Chain, repeat. Third row—black, 1 Double Crochet, 4 Chain, 2 Double Crochet, 4 Chain, 2 Double Crochet, 4 Chain, 1 Double Crochet, under every scallop of six Chain.

Raised Rose in Crochet Cotton.—For the mat shown in Fig. 199, and consisting of a large Raised centre rose, surrounded by eight smaller Raised roses, use Evans' crochet cotton No. 10. For the large centre rose—Commence with 8 Chain, join round, and work 16 Double Crochet in the circle. Second round—1 Double Crochet, 3 Chain, miss 1, repeat (there should be eight loops of three Chain). Third round—1 Double Crochet, 4 Treble, 1 Double Crochet under every loop of three Chain. Fourth round—1 Double Crochet at the back above the Double Crochet in the second round, 4 Chain. Fifth round—1 Double Crochet, 5 Treble, 1 Double Crochet, under every loop of four Chain. Sixth round—1 Double Crochet at the back above the Double Crochet in the fourth round, 5 Chain. Seventh round—1 Double Crochet, 7 Treble, 1 Double Crochet under every loop of five Chain. Eighth round—1 Double Crochet at the back above the Double Crochet in the sixth round, 6 Chain. Ninth round—1 Double Crochet, 9 Treble, 1 Double Crochet under every loop of six Chain. Tenth round—1 Double Crochet at the back, above the Double Crochet in the eighth round, 7 Chain. Eleventh round—1 Double Crochet, 11 Treble, 1 Double Crochet under every loop of seven Chain. Twelfth round—Double Crochet between the two Double Crochet of last round, * 7 Chain, 1 Double Crochet upon the sixth Treble, 7 Chain, 1 Double Crochet between the next two Double Crochet of last round, repeat from *; fasten off at the end of the round. This completes the large rose.

For the small roses—Begin with 6 Chain, join round, and work 12 Double Crochet in the circle. Second round—1 Double Crochet, 3 Chain, miss 1, repeat (there should be six loops of three Chain). Third round—1 Double Crochet, 4 Treble, 1 Double Crochet under every loop of three Chain. Fourth round—1 Double Crochet at the back above the Double Crochet in the second round, 4 Chain. Fifth round—1 Double Crochet, 5 Treble, 1 Double Crochet under every loop of four Chain. Sixth round—1 Double Crochet at the back above the Double Crochet in the fourth round, 5 Chain. Seventh round—1 Double Crochet, 7 Treble, 1 Double Crochet under every loop of five Chain. Eighth round—1 Double Crochet between the two Double Crochet stitches of last round, * 3 Chain, 1 Double Crochet on the second Treble, 3 Chain, 1 Double Crochet on the fourth Treble, 3 Chain, 1 Double Crochet on the sixth Treble, 3 Chain, 1 Double Crochet between the two next Double Crochet stitches, repeat from *; fasten off at the end of the round.

It requires eight small roses to complete the circle, and they are to be joined to the large rose by a Single Crochet taken from the first stitch of the second group of Chain of the fourth leaf, into the third Chain from the centre of one of the leaves of the large rose, and again by a Single Crochet taken from the first stitch of the next group of Chain into the corresponding third Chain on the other side of the same leaf of the large rose, and they are also to be joined to each other by a Single Crochet on each side, as shown in the illustration (Fig. 199).

For the outside edge—1 Double Crochet over the Single Crochet between the roses, * 8 Chain, 1 Single in

FIG. 199. CROCHET—RAISED ROSE IN COTTON.

the fourth from the hook, 8 Chain, 1 Single again in the fourth from the hook, 3 Chain, 1 Double Crochet above the Double Crochet in the middle of the next leaf, 12 Chain, 1 Double Crochet above the Double Crochet in the middle of the next leaf, 8 Chain, 1 Single in the fourth from the hook, 8 Chain, 1 Single in the fourth from the hook, 3 Chain, 1 Double Crochet above the Single Crochet at the joining of the roses; repeat from *, and fasten off at the end of the round. Last round—1 Double Crochet between the two Picots, * 4 Chain, 1 Double Crochet in the next Picot, 7 Chain, 4 Double Crochet under the 12 Chain of last round, 7 Chain, 1 single into the last of the four Double Crochet, and 4 more Double Crochet under the 12 Chain, 7 Chain, 1 Double Crochet in the next Picot, 4 Chain, 1 Double Crochet between the two Picots, 7 Chain, 1 Double Crochet between the two Picots in the next rose, repeat from *, and fasten off at·the end of the round.

Raised Rose in Wools.—These raised roses are much used for wool antimacassars. They are made separately,

and joined together. For a wool rose use single Berlin wool, work a 6 Chain, and form into a round. First row— 8 Chain, * 1 Treble under nearest stitch of round, 5 Chain. Repeat from * three times, then 5 Chain, and loop on the third of the first 8 Chain. Second row—* 1 Double, 8 Treble, 1 Double, under all the succeeding 5 Chain scallops. Third row—* 6 Chain, 1 Double, putting hook in between the two next leaves; the stitches of the next 6 Chain place behind the next leaf in the same way, and all the rest in following rows. Repeat from * 4 times. Fourth row—1 Double, 10 Treble, under next 6 Chain, repeat four times. Fifth row—7 Chain, 1 Double behind leaves of preceding row. Repeat four times. Sixth row —1 Double, 12 Treble, and 1 Double in the next 7 Chain. Repeat four times. Seventh row—8 Chain, 1 Double, worked in from behind between two next leaves. Repeat four times. Eighth row—1 Double, 14 Treble, and 1 Double in the next 8 Chain. Repeat four times. Ninth row—9

FIG. 200. CROCHET—RAISED ROSE IN WOOL.

Chain, 1 Double, hook from behind as before. Repeat four times. Tenth row—1 Double, 16 Treble, and 1 Double in the next 9 Chain. Repeat four times. Eleventh row—10 Chain, 1 Double, hook from behind. Repeat four times. Twelfth row—1 Double, 18 Treble, and 1 Double in the next 10 Chain. Repeat four times. Thirteenth row—Double stitches over Doubles and Trebles of preceding row. Fourteenth row—commence at fourth Treble of leaf, work 2 double Trebles and 7 Chain all round, making three of these stitches into every rose leaf (*see* Fig. 200). Fifteenth row—work a Double into every Chain of preceding row. Sixteenth row (not shown in illustration) is 1 Double, 1 Chain into every other stitch of last row. Seventeenth row—1 Treble and 2 Double into every alternate stitch. Eighteenth, and last row, is a looped chain ornamented with Picots to form an edge, 2 Chain, 12 Chain divided into 3 Picots, and 2 Chain, into every other space between Trebles of last row. For an antimacassar make the roses separately, and join when all are finished, as then they will be fresh and clean.

Sequin Lace.—A modern name given to a work formed with coloured braid and coloured crochet cotton, formed into various easy patterns, and worked like Mignardise waved braid and crochet. It is suitable for furniture lace and dress trimmings.

Shawl.—There are two ways of commencing to work a large crochet shawl. One, to commence from the centre, and work round and round until the right size is attained; the other, to make a Foundation Chain of the full length of the completed shawl, and to work backwards and forwards, as in a large quilt, until the width is the same as the length. For a square shawl worked in most crochet stitches, the number of rows worked will be one half more than the number of crochet stitches cast on for the first row. Thus, if 300 stitches are cast on, 450 rows will make a square, with perhaps the addition of three or four rows, if the crochet is tightly worked. Fig. 201 represents the commencement of a shawl begun from the centre, the first part of which is the only difficulty, and with that explained the rest is easily accomplished. Square shawls should be made of fine Shetland or Pyrenean wool, which are both extremely light in texture and yet warm. The needle should be of bone, medium size. Make a Foundation Chain of nine stitches, join it up, and work for first row 3 Treble and 3 Chain four times. Second row

3 Chain, and 3 Treble into the first corner stitch, * 3 Chain and 3 Treble into every space until the next corner is reached, repeat *, and work in this manner until the shawl is a yard and a quarter square. Different

FIG. 201. SHAWL IN SQUARE CROCHET.

coloured wools can be used near the end as border, and a closer shawl made by working 2 Chain and 2 Double, instead of the 3 Chain and 3 Treble, into every space.

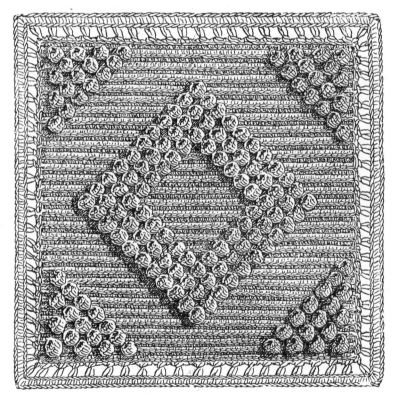

FIG. 202. CROCHET SQUARE.

—into the space of every 3 Chain work 3 Treble, 3 Chain, and 3 Treble. This second row turns the round loop of that foundation into a small square, and commences the increasing at the four corners of the square, which continues throughout the work. Third row—work 3 Treble,

Square for Quilt.—Use for this pattern Strutt's knitting cotton, No. 6. Commence with 43 Chain, 1 Double Crochet in the third from the work, and work Double Crochet all along, making 40 Double Crochet in all; turn, 1 Chain, miss the first Double Crochet of preceding row, and work 40 Double Crochet along, working upon the back of the stitches so as to form a ridge. Third row—1 Chain to turn, 3 Double Crochet, pass the cotton twice round the hook, insert the hook to take up the fourth Double Crochet of the first row, and work a Double Treble, but leave the stitch belonging to the Double Crochet stitch on the needle, work 2 more Double Treble in the same place, and, having finished them, draw the cotton through the last and through the Double Crochet stitch; this forms a ball; 3 Double Crochet, and another ball, 3 Double Crochet, a ball, 3 Double Crochet, a ball, then 9 Double Crochet, a ball, 3 Double Crochet, a ball, 3 Double Crochet, a ball, 3 Double Crochet, a ball, 3 Double Crochet; 1 Chain to turn, and work back in plain Double Crochet, having 40 Double Crochet in the row. Fifth row—1 Chain to turn, 5 Double Crochet, 3 balls with 3 Double Crochet between each, plain Double Crochet across the centre, and corresponding balls at the other side, ending with 5 Double Crochet; 1 Chain to turn, and work back in plain Double Crochet. The centre diamond begins in the ninth row, and the 3 Double Treble are to be worked into the twenty-first stitch of the seventh row; increase the diamond until there are 11 balls along the side, then decrease, gradually bringing it again to 1 ball. The corners begin in the row where there are four balls in the centre diamond. Having completed the square, work a row of 1 Treble, 1 Chain all round it, putting 3 Chain at each corner; then a round of plain Double Crochet. (*See* Fig. 202.)

Stitches.—The various Stitches used in Crochet are described at length, in their Alphabetical order, after the article upon Crochet.

Tatting Crochet.—This is a variety of Crochet used to ornament ordinary Crochet with rosettes, and worked with any materials suitable for Crochet. The stitch has the appearance of Tatting, and is a double loop connected together at the base with a cross thread, and is made by forming two different loops or knots on the hook. The chief art in making these loops is the manipulation of the left hand, the thread being held firmly between the thumb and second finger while the twists to it are being given. To commence: Work 2 or 3 Chain, then make a loop round the left hand forefinger as shown in Detail A (Fig. 203), insert the hook over the front thread and under the back, and draw up the thread on to the hook as a knot, change the arrangement of the loop with a twist of the left hand, and insert the hook this time under the first thread and over the second and draw up the loop on to the hook (*see* Detail B, Fig. 204) as another knot; this completes the stitch. Work 9 Double Knots and then thread round the hook, and draw it right through every loop on the hook, casting them off in this manner (*see* Detail C, Fig. 205). Thread again round the hook, and draw it through the loop left (*see* Detail D, Fig. 206), thus completing the rosette shown in Detail E (Fig. 207), which represents three of these tatted rosettes connected by 3 Chain. These rosettes can be formed into a pretty border, like Detail F (Fig. 208), by working the rows alternately in different colours. Work the first row as already shown, and reverse the rosettes in the second; begin this row with a Long Treble, as shown, which

takes through the middle of first rosette; work for rosette 4 Double Knots *, and the first half of the fifth, and with the second half join the rosette to first stitch in the 3

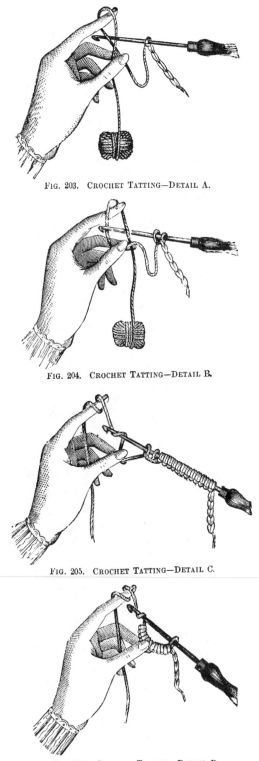

FIG. 203. CROCHET TATTING—DETAIL A.

FIG. 204. CROCHET TATTING—DETAIL B.

FIG. 205. CROCHET TATTING—DETAIL C.

FIG. 206. CROCHET TATTING—DETAIL D.

Chain, placing the hook as shown by arrow in Detail F (Fig. 208); carry the thread down in front of the hook, pass it back under the hook, and then through the stitch just taken upon the hook; this forms the second half of fifth Double Knot. Pass over 1 Chain and repeat *,

FIG. 207. CROCHET TATTING—DETAIL E.

working into the third, instead of 1 stitch of Chain, 4 Double Knots, draw up loop, 3 Chain, repeat to the end of the row. All the rows are made like the second row, except that the Long Treble commencement is only made in every alternate one.

cotton No. 20 is used instead of crochet cotton. Commence with a Chain of 4, join and work 2 Double Crochet into each stitch. Second row—3 Double Crochet in first stitch, 1 Double Crochet, 3 Double Crochet in third stitch, 1 Double Crochet in fourth, 3 Double Crochet in fifth stitch, 1 Double Crochet in sixth, 3 Double Crochet in seventh, 1 Double Crochet in eighth stitch, 1 more Double Crochet; the last side of the square will always have an extra stitch on the side, which mark, as all the rows commence from it. Third row—3 Double Crochet in corner stitch *, 3 Double Crochet on side, 3 Double Crochet in corner, repeat from *. Fourth row

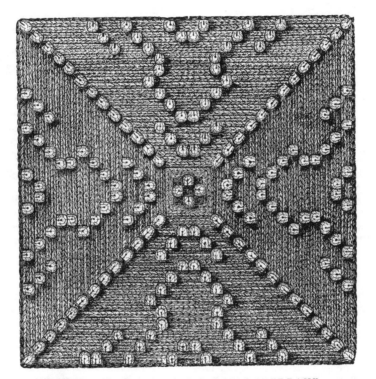

FIG. 209. CROCHET TATTING—COUNTERPANE.

Fig. 209 is a square of Crochet, being part of a counterpane ornamented with Crochet Tatting as tiny rosettes. Fig. 210, Detail A, gives the commencement of the square

FIG. 208. CROCHET TATTING—DETAIL F.

and manner of working the rosettes into the plain Crochet. The foundation is in Double Crochet, and knitting

—3 Double Crochet into every corner, and 5 Double Crochet on every side. Fifth row—3 Double Crochet in corner stitch *, 3 Double Crochet on side, and work rosette, making 4 Double Knots, and then secure the loop by passing the hook and thread through the loop in

FIG. 210. CROCHET TATTING—DETAIL A OF COUNTERPANE.

the second row, finish and draw up the rosette; 1 Double Crochet in next stitch, working the stitch on the hook from the rosette as a Double Crochet, 3 Double Crochet on the side, 3 Double Crochet in the corner, repeat. Sixth row—plain Double Crochet, work 3 into each corner, and miss the stitch made by the rosettes. Seventh and eighth rows—3 Double Crochet in every corner, an increase of 2 on each side in each row. Ninth row—* 1 Double Crochet in the corner, then a rosette in the same corner, and 1 Double Crochet, 15 Double Crochet at the side, repeat from *. Tenth row—plain Double Crochet 3 in each corner stitch.

Having thus commenced the corners, and shown how the increase is managed and the rosettes are secured, the worker will follow the rest of the square from the illustration, being careful always to work 3 Double Crochet in every corner, with a rosette in every alternate row, and to count and work that stitch as a Double Crochet next time, while the rosettes that ornament the other part of the design are treated like those on the fifth row and the stitch they make passed over in the plain line that follows them. The square is completed in thirty-four rows.

Tatting and Crochet Edging.—This edging is composed of Tatting and Crochet, and is used to slide ribbon through, as shown in Fig. 211. It is worked with cotton No. 20, a fine steel crochet hook, and a tatting shuttle. The little diamonds in the centre work first; these are

FIG. 211. CROCHET AND TATTING EDGING.

Tatted. First diamond: First oval—6 Double Crochet, 1 Purl, 3 Double, 1 Purl, 3 Double, 1 Purl, 6 Double, draw close. Repeat this oval 3 more times, then join the two ends of the cotton neatly together. Work as many diamonds as are required for the length, join them to one another by the centre Purl in the last oval of the first diamond and the centre Purl in the first oval of the second diamond. When all are worked, join the thread to the centre Purl of the first oval at the side; work in it 1 Double Crochet *, 6 Chain, 1 Single Crochet in the next Purl of the same oval, 3 Chain, 1 Single in the Purl connecting the two diamonds together, 3 Chain, 1 Single in the first Purl of the next oval, 8 Chain, 1 Single in the fourth Chain of the first six Chain worked, 3 Chain, 1 Single on the 7 Chain of eight Chain just worked, 1 Single on the sixth Chain, 3 Chain, 1 Single on the fifth Chain, 1 single on the fourth Chain, 3 Chain, 1 single on the third Chain, 1 Single on the second Chain, 3 Chain, 1 Double Crochet in the next Purl, repeat from *; work each side in the same manner, then work loops of Crochet Chain at the back of each point to connect the top and bottom point together, and in these loops run a coloured ribbon the width of the work.

Watch Guard in Crochet.—This is made with the finest purse silk and a small steel crochet hook. Work a round of 6 Chain, and work round and round in Single or Double Ribbed crochet until the right length is formed. The guard is ornamented, if wished, with a bead

dropped into every stitch. Thread these beads on the skein of purse silk before the work is commenced.

Waved Braid Crochet.—A variety of Crochet in which waved tape braid is used instead of Mignardise braid to take the place of the thick stitches in a Crochet pattern. The use of this braid saves much time, and it can be introduced into either Crochet edgings or into rosettes for antimacassars. The braid is woven in various widths, but the medium size, with Evans's crochet cotton, No. 14, is the best to use. To work an edging for linen or children's frocks: First row—work 1 Treble into the first point of the braid, 3 Chain, and a Treble into the next point of the braid, repeat until of sufficient length, and fasten off; this forms the plain edge which is sewn to the material. Second row—turn the work and commence upon the other side of the braid, 2 row, * work 1 Single into first point, 1 Chain 1 Treble into next point, 3 Chain 1 Treble into the same, 1 Chain, and repeat from * to end of row, and fasten off. Third row—Slip Stitch into the one Single on last row, * cotton over the hook, 4 treble into the 3 Chain between the 2 Trebles of the last row, 6 Chain slip the hook through the second, so as to make a Picot with the 5 Chain, 1 Chain, 4 Treble into same, loop Slip Stitch into next Single, and repeat from * to end of row and fasten off.

To Form a Rosette.—8 Chain, join and work 16 Double into it. First row—4 Chain, * miss 1 stitch on foundation and work 1 Treble into the next stitch, 2 Chain, repeat from * to end of row. Second row—4 Chain, * 1 Treble, 2 Chain, 1 Treble first loop on last row, 2 Chain, repeat from * to end of the row. Third row—5 Chain, then take the waved braid in the left hand and pass the hook through a point while making the next Chain, then 1 Chain, 1 Treble into the loop of the last row, * 2 Chain, pick up the next point of the braid, 1 Chain, 1 Treble into the next loop on the foundation, repeat from * to the end of the row; when finished, sew the ends of the braid together neatly, so as not to interfere with the round. Fourth row—3 Chain up to point of the braid and fasten into it, 6 Chain 1 Treble into the same point, * 2 Chain, 1 Treble into the same, repeat from * end of the row. Fifth row—take up the braid again, work 4 Chain, put the hook through the point of the braid, 1 Chain, and make a Double into the first loop, * 2 Chain, hook through the next point, 2 Chain, 1 Double into the next loop, repeat from * to the end of the row, sew the points of braid together as before. Sixth row—same as the fourth. Seventh row—* 1 Treble into Chain between the 2 Trebles on the last row, 6 Chain, put the hook into the second Chain to form a Picot, 1 Chain, 1 Treble into the same loop, 3 Chain, and repeat from * to end of row, and fasten off.

Wool Aster in Crochet.—Materials required: Yellow, black, and three shades of crimson double Berlin wool, and medium-sized bone crochet needle. Commence with the yellow wool, with 5 Chain, join round, and work 12 Double Crochet in the ring. Second round — yellow, 1 Double Crochet, 1 Chain, twelve times. Third round—darkest shade of red, 1 Double Crochet, 2 Chain, 1 Treble, a Picot (viz., 4 Chain, 1 Double Crochet in the first of the chain), 1 Treble Chain, 1 Double Crochet, all in the front loop of every Chain stitch of the last round, thus making twelve petals. Fourth round—next lightest shade of red, 1 Double Crochet in the back loop of every Double Crochet stitch of the second round, and 1 Chain between each Double Crochet. Fifth round—same colour, 1 Double Crochet, 2 Chain, 1 Double Treble, Picot, 1 Double Treble, 2 Chain, 1 Double Crochet, all in the front loop of every Chain stitch of the last round, again making twelve petals. Sixth round—lightest shade of red—1 Double Crochet in the back loop of every Double Crochet stitch of the fourth round, twenty-four Double Crochet in all. Seventh round—same colour, 1 Double Crochet, 2 Chain, miss 1, repeat. There should be twelve loops of 2 Chain. Eighth round—Same colour, * 1 Double Crochet on the Double Crochet of last round, 2 Chain, 1 Double Treble, Picot, 1 Double Treble, 2 Chain, all under the 2 Chain of last round; repeat from *. This will again make twelve petals. Ninth round—black, 1 Double Crochet in any Picot, 2 Chain, 1 Double Treble

next Treble, and another Picot, as just described; repeat. There should be 10 Double Crochet stitches and 10 Picots in the round. Third round—next lightest shade of red, 1 Double Crochet over the Double Crochet of last round, insert the hook in the next Chain stitch, draw the wool through and work 5 Chain, draw the wool through the chain and through the stitch on the hook; repeat, increasing 1 Double Crochet and 1 Picot in the course of the round. Fourth round—lightest shade of red, the same as the third round, making 12 Double Crochet and 12 Picots. Fifth round—the same colour, and to be worked the same as the fourth round. Sixth round—brown, 1 Double Crochet, 4 Chain, miss 2, repeat. There should be 8 loops of 4 Chain. Seventh round—work 5 Double Crochet under every 4 Chain. Eighth round—brown, 1 Double Crochet on the first of the 5 Double Crochet of last round, 1 Treble on the next, 1 Double Treble on the next, four Chain, 1 Double Crochet in the first of the Chain, 1 Double Treble on the same Double

FIG. 212. CROCHET—YAK LACE.

on the Double Crochet stitch of last round, 2 Chain, repeat. Tenth round—same colour as the fifth round, 1 Double Crochet on the Double Crochet stitch of last round, 3 successive Picots, repeat. Twelve of these asters will make a good sized antimacassar, and to fill up the spaces between each aster, work the two rounds as directed for the yellow wool, and a third round in black of 1 Double Crochet, 3 Chain.

Wool Dahlia in Crochet.—Materials required: double Berlin wool, brown, black, and three shades of crimson, and medium-sized bone crochet hook. Commence with the brown wool, with 3 Chain, join round, and work 10 Treble in the ring. Throughout the dahlia take up both the top loops of preceding row. Second round—darkest shade of red, 1 Double Crochet, insert the hook in the same stitch as the Double Crochet is already worked in, draw the wool through, and work 5 Chain, draw the wool through the last of the Chain and through the stitch on the hook to form a Picot, 1 Double Crochet on the

Crochet as the other Double Treble, 1 Treble on the next Double Crochet, and 1 Double Crochet on the last of the five Double Crochet of last round; repeat. There should be eight leaves in the round. Ninth round—black, 1 Double Crochet under the four Chain, 3 Chain, 1 Double Treble in between the 2 Double Crochet of last round, 3 Chain, repeat. Tenth round—darkest shade of red, 1 Double Crochet on the Double Crochet of last round, 1 Treble, 1 Double Treble, 4 Chain, 1 Double Crochet in the first of the Chain, 1 Double Treble, 1 Treble, all under the next three Chain of last round; repeat. There should be sixteen leaves in this last round.

Yak Lace, Crochet.—This is a description of crochet that is a copy of real Yak and Maltese lace, and is worked in either fawn-coloured or black Maltese thread, with a medium-sized hook. It is illustrated in Fig. 212. Make a Chain the length required. First row—work 1 Long Stitch, make 1 Chain, miss 1 loop, work 1 Long Stitch, make 3 Chain, work a stitch of Single Crochet into the first of 3 Chain, miss 1 loop. Second row—work 3 extra Long Stitches into the first Chain *, make 6 Chain, work 1 stitch of Single Crochet into the third from hook, repeat from * once, make 2 Chain, miss 4 loops of first row, work 1 stitch of Double Crochet into the next Chain, make 10 Chain, work a stitch of Single Crochet into the third from the hook, making the loop of Chain, turn under the third Chain, work 1 stitch of Single Crochet into the first, making the loop of 3 Chain over the 3 Chain, work a stitch of Double Crochet in Chain- after the next 4 Long of first row, make 6 Chain, work a stitch of Single Crochet into the third from hook, make 3 Chain, work 1 stitch of Single into the first stitch, make 7 Chain, work 1 Single stitch into the third from the hook, make 3 Chain, work a stitch of Single into first, make 3 Chain, work a stitch of Double Crochet into same loop as last, make 6 Chain, work a stitch of Single Crochet into third loop, the loop of three Chain over, make 3 Chain, miss 4 loops of first row and repeat third row, make 1 Chain, work a stitch of extra Long Crochet into first Chain after three extra Long stitches, make 8 Chain, work a stitch of Single into the third, the loop of 3 to be under, make 3 Chain, take up the third, and fasten the loop of three Chain over, make 3 Chain, work a stitch of Single Crochet in the third Chain under, 1 stitch of Double Crochet into fourth loop of ten Chain in last row, make 7 Chain, turn, miss the first from the hook, work 1 Double Crochet into each, make 1 Chain, work 1 Double Crochet into each loop on the other side of 6 Chain, 1 single at point, make 2 Chain, work 2 Double Crochet into central loops of four Chain, between the loops of three Chain in first row. This forms the centre of festoon; work the remainder to correspond. Fourth row —work 5 stitches Double Crochet into successive loops, beginning on the first Chain in last row, make 9 Chain, work 2 Double Crochet, beginning on the Single at the point of leaf, make 4 Chain, continue the row to corre- spond. Fifth row—work 1 Double Crochet over the first in the last row, make 1 Chain, miss 1 loop, work 10 of Double Crochet into the next, make 1 Chain, miss 1 loop, work 1 Double Crochet, make 3 Chain, miss 3 loops, work 1 Double Crochet, make 3 Chain, miss 3 loops, work 1 Double Crochet, make 4 Chain, miss 4 loops, work 2 stitches of Double Crochet, and continue the row to correspond. Sixth row—work 5 stitches of Double Crochet into successive loops, beginning on the first loop of the last row, make 13 Chain, work a leaf the same as in third row, work 2 stitches of Double Crochet, beginning on the second of 4 Chain, make 6 Chain, work a stitch of Single Crochet into the third from the hook, make 3 Chain, work 1 stitch of Single Crochet into the first, make 12 Chain, work a stitch of Single Crochet into third from the hook, make 3 Chain, work a stitch of Single Crochet into first, make 1 Chain, work a stitch of Double Crochet into second loop of 6 Chain, make 1 Chain, continue the row to correspond. Seventh row— work a stitch of Single Crochet over the Double in the last row, work 5 stitches of Single, beginning on the first of 13 Chain, 1 stitch of Single Crochet in the point of the leaf, make 12 Chain, work a Double Crochet into

fifth loop of 9 left between the loops of 3 Chain in last row. Eighth row—work 3 stitches of Single Crochet, beginning on the first of last row, miss 3 loops, *, work 1 Long stitch into the next loop, make 1 Chain, miss 1 loop, repeat from * five times, * work 1 Long stitch into the next loop, make 1 Chain, repeat from * eight times, continue the row to correspond. Ninth row — make 4 Chain, work an extra Long stitch single, miss 1 loop, work 1 Long stitch, miss 3 loops, work 1 Long stitch, make 3 Chain, work 1 Long stitch into the same loop as last, * make 3 Chain, miss 3 loops, work 1 Long stitch, make 1 Chain, miss 1 loop, work 1 Long stitch, repeat from * once, make 5 Chain, continue the row to correspond. Tenth row—work 4 extra Long stitches in the fourth Chain at the beginning of the last row, miss 4 loops, work 3 stitches of single Crochet, * make 4 Chain, work a stitch of Single Crochet into the third from the hook, repeat from * twice, make 1 Chain, miss 3 loops, work 3 stitches of Single Crochet, work another loop of 3 loops of Chain, join the crochet, miss 3 loops, work 3 stitches of Single Crochet, work a loop of 5 loops for the centre, each made of 3 loops as before.

Chain Stitch.—All the stitches of Crochet are formed of varieties of Chain Stitch. It is a loop drawn through an already formed loop, a single loop counting as one Chain. To work: Hold the crochet hook in the right hand,

FIG. 213. CROCHET—CHAIN STITCH.

the work in the left, with the cotton thrown over the forefinger of that hand. Hitch the cotton round the hook by a movement of the right hand and draw it through the loop already upon the hook (see Fig. 213). A given

FIG. 214. CROCHET—CROSS STITCH.

number of these Chains form the foundation of Crochet patterns, and open spaces in the work are always passed over with a given number of these loops. The abbreviation is "chn" in Crochet Instruction. *See* FOUNDATION CHAIN,

Cross Stitch.—Commence with a DOUBLE FOUNDA-TION, and then work as in SLANTING STITCH, except that the hook is put through both loops of the Foundation. To work: Put the hook through both the loops on the line beneath and round the cotton, as shown by the arrow in Fig. 214, draw the cotton through as a loop, put the cotton round the hook, and draw it through the two loops.

Cross Stitch, Open.—A useful stitch for light shawls or petticoats. Make a FOUNDATION CHAIN of width required. Put the wool twice round at the back of the hook, exactly contrary to the usual manner of putting it round, and pass the hook downwards through the next stitch (as shown in Fig. 215 by the left-hand arrow)

FIG. 215. CROCHET—OPEN CROSS STITCH.

at the back. Bring the wool in front, take it up with the hook, and draw it through the three loops that are already on the hook. This stitch is shown by the right-hand arrow. Continue to the end of the row, and in the return row work in the same way.

Cross Stitch, Raised.—This stitch is used for couvre-pieds and other large pieces of Crochet. The wool used is four-thread fleecy or double Berlin, and the work is formed in stripes of various colours. The ground is

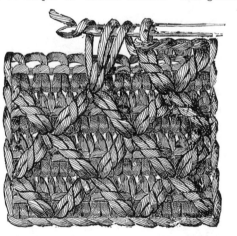

FIG. 216. CROCHET—RAISED CROSS STITCH.

in DOUBLE CROCHET, the crosses in TREBLE CROCHET. To work: Make a FOUNDATION CHAIN with any number of stitches that will divide into five, and work back to the right-hand corner of strip. Second row—2 Double

Crochet and 1 Treble put into the lowest part of the first stitch in first row, * 1 Treble into the fourth stitch in first row, put in as the first Treble, 3 Double Crochet, 1 Treble worked into the stitch on the first row next to the last-made Treble, repeat from *. Third row—all stitches in Double Crochet. Fourth row—commence with Treble, put one into the top part of the Trebles in second row, 3 Double Crochet, * a Treble taken back to the last one, and looped into the same stitch, then a Treble into the top part of the Treble in the second row (as shown in Fig. 216), 3 Double Crochet, repeat from *. Fifth row—like the third. Sixth row—like the second row; and so on to the end of the pattern. The Trebles should be worked loose.

Cross Treble.—See *Treble Crochet.*

Cross Tricot Stitch.—See *Tricot Stitch, Cross.*

Double Crochet.—To work: Twist the cotton round the hook, and draw it through the FOUNDATION, take

FIG. 217. CROCHET—DOUBLE STITCH.

the cotton on the hook again, and draw it through these two loops, as shown in Fig. 217. Abbreviation in Crochet Instructions, " D. C."

Double Crochet, Long.—A variety of Double Crochet Stitch. To work: Take the cotton round the hook, and

FIG. 218. CROCHET—LONG DOUBLE STITCH.

insert the hook into FOUNDATION, draw the cotton through this as a loop, which will make three loops upon the hook (*see* Fig. 218); take the cotton round the hook again, and draw it through the three loops on the hook at once.

FIG. 219. CROCHET—RAISED DOUBLE STITCH.

Double Crochet, Raised.—A variety of Double Crochet.

R

Work the first row with DOUBLE CROCHET, and for the rest of the pattern work Double Crochet, but instead of putting the hook through the top part of the loop of the preceding row, as in ordinary Crochet, put it over the whole of the loop and into the middle part of the stitch under it in the preceding row, as shown in Fig. 219.

Double Knot.—Used when imitating Tatting with Crochet. Work 3 CHAIN, then make a loop of cotton round the left forefinger, insert the hook over the front thread and under the back, and draw up the thread on to the hook as a knot, change the arrangement of the loop with a twist of the left hand, insert the hook under the first thread of the loop and over the second, and draw up the loop on the hook as another knot.

Edge Stitch.—The first stitch of a row. Work as the other stitches in the pattern, unless attention is especially drawn to the Edge Stitch by a direction to work it plain. To work plain: Retain the loop of the last stitch of the previous row on the hook; do not work it, but count that loop as the first stitch on the new row.

except the last one, which only requires 1 Double Crochet into it; work back as follows: Work the first stitch, shown in pattern as *a* and *b*, draw the wool through the three stitches on preceding row, and then through the loop that has run through them. This is illustrated in Fig. 220. Draw the stitch thus made through the next three loops on preceding row, make as before, and so on to end of row. Long loops will be formed with the wool, and these must be loosely worked and pushed to front of work. The next row consists in working 3 Double Crochet into the three stitches drawn through. Work these behind the loops that are shown by the figures 1, 2, 3 in design. The made stitch in last row is not worked; only the ones the work was drawn through. These last two rows form the pattern, and are worked alternately to end of strip. Be careful, in working this pattern, to count the stitches every second row, so that none are left unworked.

(2).—A suitable stitch for couvrepieds when made in thick fleecy wool and with a large No. 8 bone hook, but

FIG. 221. CROCHET—FANCY STITCH.

Fancy Stitch (1).—A pretty stitch, used for making the strips of couvrepieds or antimacassars when worked with fine fleecy or single Berlin wool, and with a small bone

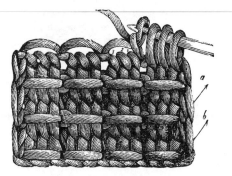

FIG. 220. CROCHET—FANCY STITCH.

hook. Make a FOUNDATION CHAIN of an uneven number of stitches. Work 2 DOUBLE CROCHET into second stitch of Chain, and continue working 2 Double into every Chain

which does not look well worked with fine cotton. Make a FOUNDATION CHAIN of an even number of stitches, work a row of TRICOT, and work back. Second row—Work the first stitch plain, and then put wool round the hook, bring it out at front, push the hook through the next two long loops, still keeping the wool before the work, put wool round hook, as shown in Fig. 221, and draw it through the two loops. Put wool again round hook, thus making a stitch for the one lost in the work, and continue to end of row; work last stitch plain. Draw the wool back through the EDGE STITCH, and then through two stitches, as in Tricot. The second row is repeated throughout.

Fool's Crochet.—See *Tricot Stitch.*

Foundation Chain.—There are three ways of making a Foundation to Crochet, all of which are varieties of Chain. The simplest and most used is the plain Chain Foundation illustrated in *Chain Stitch;* the others are *Double* and *Purl* Foundations. The *Double Foundation* is made with two Chain stitches instead of one, and is illustrated in Fig. 222. It is worked thus: Make 2 Chain, put the hook into first Chain, draw the cotton through it, take up more cotton, and draw it through both loops on the hook, put the hook into left loop of the work, draw cotton through so as to have two stitches on the hook, then draw the cotton through both to have but one, put the hook through the left loop of the work,

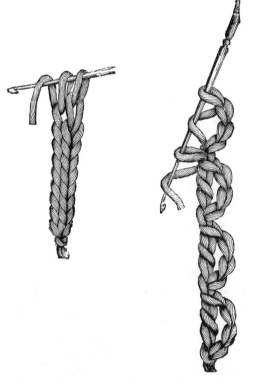

FIG. 222. CROCHET—DOUBLE
FOUNDATION.

FIG 223. CROCHET—PURL
FOUNDATION.

and continue until the length of Foundation is made.
Purl Foundation (Fig. 223): Commence with making a 4 Chain, make a TREBLE into the first of the 4 Chain, make another 4 Chain, and another Treble into its first Chain, and repeat to end of length required. The line just worked in any part of Crochet is known as Foundation, and into it place the stitches of next row.

Half Stitch.—When two stitches are worked as one in contracting an edge they are called Half Stitch. To work: Put the hook with cotton round through FOUNDATION and draw through as a loop, and then put the cotton round the hook again, insert into next stitch on Foundation row, and this time the stitch is completed by all the loops that are upon the hook being worked up.

Hollow Spot Stitch.—See *Spot Stitch, Hollow.*
Idiot Stitch.—See *Tricot Stitch.*
Josephine Tricot Stitch.—See *Tricot Stitch, Josephine.*
Long Double Stitch.—See *Double Crochet, Long.*
Long Treble Stitch.—See *Treble Crochet, Long.*
Loops Stitch, Raised.—See *Raised Loop Stitch.*
Open Crochet Stitch.—The name given to either DOUBLE or TREBLE CROCHET, or their varieties when worked in squares with spaces missed to correspond with

the height and number of stitches worked. Thus, to form two Double Crochet stitches into a square of Open Crochet, follow them by 2 CHAIN, which pass over 2 stitches on FOUNDATION CHAIN, or if three or four Treble Crochets are to be made as a square, work four or five Chain, and pass four or five Foundation stitches over.

Open Cross Stitch.—See *Cross Stitch, Open.*
Open Stitches Tricot.—See *Tricot Stitches, Open.*
Picot.—This is a Crochet stitch similar in appearance to the PICOT formed in needle-made laces. In fine Crochet, such as Irish and Honiton, it is used to finish the Bars that connect the detached sprigs together, as well as to ornament the edge of the sprigs and design. In coarse or ordinary Crochet it is used to give an appearance of a lace finish to the edge of the design. To make: Form a CHAIN of 6 or 4 stitches according to the thickness of the cotton, and put the hook back and through the first Chain, and draw the cotton through that and through the loop upon the hook at once, so that the stitches between them are formed into a round or knob. It is sometimes called *Purl.*

Point de Tricot Stitch.—See *Tricot Stitch, Point de.*
Point Neige Stitch.—An extremely effective stitch, suitable for children's jackets or petticoats, also for couvrepieds and quilts. When worked in a round the thread can remain unbroken, but for straight work it must be fastened off at the end of each row and commenced from the starting point. To start with: Calculate that the first stitch will take five of the FOUNDATION CHAIN to make, and the rest only two, so make Foundation Chain accordingly. First row—Make a Foundation Chain the length required, put the hook into the Chain next the last one, and draw the wool through, then into the next three Foundation Chain in succession, draw the wool through each and leave all on the hook; five loops will be now on the hook; draw the wool through them all at once and make 2 Chain; this completes the first stitch. Second stitch—* put the hook through the first of the last two Chains just made, and draw the wool through, then push the hook through the loop on the last stitch on to which the five loops were cast off, and draw the wool through it, and then return to Foundation, and draw the wool successively through the two next Chain on it, to again have five loops on the hook, make 2 Chain, and repeat from * to the end of the row, work the last stitch plain, fasten off, and return to the other end. When the last mentioned row is finished, each stitch will have a point rising up above the line of work. Second row—Fasten the wool into the side of the work, make 3 Chain, draw the loops through the second and first of these singly, then through the stitch that makes the point mentioned above, and lastly through the first or farthest away loop of the five cast off together in the last row. The five necessary loops being now on the hook, cast them off together by drawing the wool through them, and then make 2 Chain. Second stitch—put the hook through the 1 Chain, take up the loop at the back upon which the five last loops have been cast off, then the loop that forms the point in the previous row, and the stitch farthest away of the five loops in the last row, and draw these five loops through as one; continue this last stitch to the end of the row, and

make all the previous lines as the second. (*See* Fig. 224.) When using Point Neige as an edging, make a border of

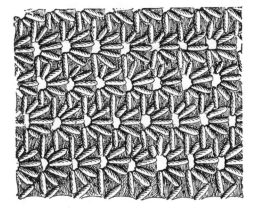

FIG. 224.   CROCHET—POINT NEIGE STITCH.

a SINGLE CROCHET on each side before commencing the regular stitch.

Purl Stitch.—A useful stitch for edgings to Crochet, and worked in three ways. The first, and the one that most imitates Tatting or lace edgings, is shown in Fig. 225, and is formed thus : * Work a DOUBLE CROCHET, and pull up the loop, as shown, take out the hook, and put it

FIG. 225.   CROCHET—PURL STITCH.

through that part of the Double Crochet through which the loop comes out, take the cotton round the hook and make a loop, work one Double, and repeat from *. The second Purl edging, which is shown in Fig. 226, work as follows; One TREBLE, * 7 CHAIN, pass the hook downwards into the second stitch of 7 Chain, put the cotton put round it in that position and draw it through,

FIG. 226.   CROCHET—PURL STITCH.

so that the Purl thus formed with the 5 Chain is turned upwards and forms an edging; work 1 Chain, and make a TREBLE into the fourth stitch on the FOUNDATION from the last stitch, and continue from *. The other variety of Purl is to turn this loop downwards, so that a straight, and not a Purled, edge is formed. It is

worked like Fig. 226; but when the 7 Chain is made, take the hook out and put it into the top part of the second Chain, and the loop of the seventh Chain and the fresh cotton draw through upwards. This brings the purl below, and not above the row that is being made. Also *see* PICOT.

Railway Stitch. — Another name for *Tricot Stitch* (which *see*).

Raised Cross Stitch.—See *Cross Stitch.*

Raised Double Stitch.—See *Double Crochet.*

Raised Loop Stitch.—A pretty stitch for making Crochet borders and edgings that are executed with wool. It should be done separately from the main work, and sewn to it when finished. To form the design shown in Fig. 227, make a FOUNDATION CHAIN of eight, and work two TRICOT rows ; the third row will be a return row, and upon this the loops are formed. Make a five CHAIN at every alternate stitch, and loop it in to the next plain stitch. Leave the EDGE STITCH plain. The next row is Tricot; pick up the loops as usual, taking care to take up those close behind the loops, keep the latter to the front, and count the stitches before working back ; in this return row the loops will be taken alternately to those of the third row. In the design shown in Fig. 227 two

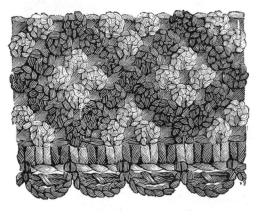

FIG. 227.   CROCHET—RAISED LOOP STITCH.

colours are used in the border, and the loops are arranged to form a diamond shape pattern. The colours are red and white. The Foundation is all in red, and when any white loops are made, bring the white wool from the back of the work, instead of the red through the stitch preceding it. Make the 5 Chain with it, and draw it through the next loop, but draw the red through with it ; then drop the white wool until again required. A reference to the pattern will show where it is inserted. The scalloped edging is added when the border is finished. First row—DOUBLE CROCHET with red wool. Second row—a white and red Double Crochet alternately, finish each stitch with the colour to be used in the next one. Third row—like first. Fourth row—with red wool, 1 Double Crochet * 5 Chain, 1 LONG TREBLE in the first of 5 Chain, and fasten with 1 Double Crochet, put into the fourth stitch of Foundation row; repeat from *.

Raised Open Tricot Stitch.—See *Tricot Stitch, Open Raised.*

Raised Spot Stitch.—See *Spot Stitch, Raised.*

Ribbed Stitch.—This stitch is also called Russian stitch. It is much used for babies' socks and muffatees, and is also a good stitch for crochet counterpanes when worked in various coloured wools. It is ordinary Double Crochet, to which the appearance of ribbing is given by the hook being put into the back part of the Foundation every time a stitch is worked instead of into the front part. Provided the rows are worked backwards and forwards,

FIG. 228. CROCHET—RIBBED STITCH.

by always leaving the front loop and taking up the back one, a rib is formed; but if they are worked as a continuous round, a loop line only is the result. To work: Put the cotton round the hook, put the hook through the back loop of the FOUNDATION CHAIN as shown in Fig. 228, put the cotton round the hook and draw it through the two loops, continue to the end of the row, turn the work, and repeat.

Russian Stitch.—Another name for *Ribbed Stitch* (which *see*).

Single Crochet.—A stitch used in close Crochet. To work: Push the hook through the FOUNDATION CHAIN, draw the cotton through as a loop, place cotton round hook and through both loops upon the hook. Abbreviation in crochet instructions "S. C."

Slanting Stitch.—A variety of Double Crochet. Commence by putting the hook into the FOUNDATION as shown by the arrow in Fig. 229; do not take any cotton upon it, but pass it over the cotton after it is through the

FIG. 229. CROCHET—SLANTING STITCH.

Foundation, and then draw the cotton through the Foundation as a loop; then put the cotton round and draw the two Foundation loops through into one. By this arrangement a slanting appearance is given to the stitch.

Slip Stitch.—A stitch much used in Raised Crochet, both in joining together detached sprays, and in passing from one part of a pattern to another at the back of the work. Put the hook through the FOUNDATION at the back part, and draw the cotton back with it through the loop

already on the hook, as shown on Fig. 230, where the Foundation is slightly turned up to show where the hook

FIG. 230. CROCHET—SLIP STITCH.

should go through, the arrow marking the direction. Abbreviation in crochet instructions "S."

Spot Stitch, Hollow.—A stitch made with a Foundation of Double Crochet with spots upon it in Treble Crochet. A useful stitch for counterpanes, couvrepieds, and antimacassars, and worked with fleecy or double Berlin wool. Commence with a FOUNDATION CHAIN of length required, upon which work a straight row of DOUBLE CROCHET. First row—work five Double Crochet stitches, insert the hook into the bottom front part of the stitch of the preceding row, and work four TREBLES without touching the loop on the hook left from the Double Crochet,

FIG. 231. CROCHET—HOLLOW SPOT STITCH.

always putting the hook into the same stitch in preceding row. For the fifth Treble put it into the same stitch as preceding four, then take up the cotton and work off the three loops on hook, as in Treble Crochet. (*See* Fig. 231, which illustrates this last stage of the Hollow Spot.) Work five Doubles, missing the stitch of preceding row under the spot. The second row will have the spots worked as above in it, but they will be placed so as to come alternately with the ones first worked. Must be worked all on right side, each row being fastened off, the next commenced at the opposite end.

Spot Stitch, Raised.—This stitch is useful for large pieces of work, such as counterpanes, couvrepieds, &c., and is generally worked in strips of various colours, and sewn together when finished, as the return Double Crochet row allows of this. Berlin or fleecy wool required. It is formed with a FOUNDATION of DOUBLE CROCHET, upon which dots made with TREBLE CROCHET are worked, and so raised. Work two rows of Double Crochet, and for third row commence with 2 Double Crochet, * put the cotton round the hook and insert into the third stitch of the first row, passing over the second row; take up the cotton and work a Treble up to where two loops are left on the hook, work 2 more Treble into the same stitch up to the same length (*see* Fig. 232, which shows the stitch at this stage); take the cotton on to the hook, and draw it through the four loops, leave the stitch of the preceding row under

FIG. 232. CROCHET—RAISED SPOT STITCH.

the spot unworked, work five Double Crochet; and repeat from *. Fourth row—a row of Double Crochet. Fifth row—work seven Double Crochet, and then commence the Raised Spot so that it may not come under that last worked.

Square Stitch.—This is made either *Close* or *Open.* A Close Square contains 2 Double Crochet and 2 Chain, or 3 Double Crochet and 3 Chain; an Open Square requires 2 Chain and 1 Double Crochet, or 3 Chain and 1 Treble, missing the same number of stitches on the Foundation Chain as the Chains worked. Example: To form a *Close Square* in Double Crochet, * work 2 DOUBLE CROCHET into the 2 following CHAINS on FOUNDATION, 2 Chain, miss 2 stitches on Foundation, and repeat from *. To form a Close Square with Treble Crochet, work as in Double Crochet, but work three TREBLES into the three following stitches on Foundation, 3 Chain, and miss 3 Foundation stitches. To form an *Open Square* in Double Crochet, * work 1 Double Crochet, 2 Chain, and miss 2 stitches on Foundation; repeat from *. To form an Open Square in Treble Crochet, * work 1 Treble, 3 Chain, and miss 3 Foundation stitches; repeat from *. In Close Squares the Doubles or Trebles forming them are worked in the second row, upon the Chain stitches, and not above the Doubles or Trebles of first row; in Open Squares they are worked above those made in preceding row.

Tambour Stitch.—For straight Crochet this stitch requires the wool to be fastened off at the end of each row, but for round articles it will work correctly without the wool being fastened off. In Fig. 233 two shades of fleecy wool, one for Foundation and one for Tambour, are used. To work: * Make 1 DOUBLE CROCHET, 1 CHAIN, miss one stitch on FOUNDATION row, and repeat from * to end of row. In the return row work Double Crochet put into each Double Crochet of the preceding row, shown by arrow in Fig. 233. When a sufficient length of Foundation has been worked, fasten off and commence the Tambour with another coloured wool. To make the Tambour stitch over the Foundation, join the new wool with 1 Chain on to the first Chain in the last row of Foundation, keep the wool at the back of the work, and turn the work so that the

first part made is the uppermost; put the hook into the first hole formed with the Chain stitches, draw the wool through and make a Chain stitch as an outer rib, continue up the line of holes left with the Chain stitches, draw the wool through every hole, and make the Chain or Tambour

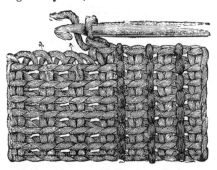

FIG. 233. CROCHET—TAMBOUR STITCH.

above each one at the end of the line, and work SLIP stitch to the next hole; turn, and work up, and continue these lines of Tambour (three of which are shown in Fig. 233), until the entire set of holes are ornamented with the raised Chain. The work can be diversified by using several colours instead of one in the Tambour lines, but the Foundation should be all of one shade of wool.

Fig. 234 is a variety of the same stitch. In this the Foundation is all worked in Double Crochet, and the raised lines worked at the same time as the Foundation. The design of this pattern is to imitate square tiles. To work: Commence with a row of DOUBLE CROCHET in dark wool,

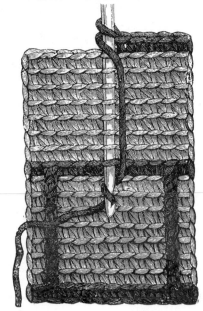

FIG. 234. CROCHET—TAMBOUR STITCH.

then work 7 rows of light wool and commence the eighth with the dark, work 5 Double Crochet and then *, run the hook downwards through the loops on the sixth stitch of the seven preceding rows (*see* Fig. 234); put the wool round the hook, draw it through the last loop on the hook and make a CHAIN, put the wool round the hook and draw through the next loop and make a Chain, and continue until all the loops are worked off and a raised Chain is made, then continue the row of Double Crochet with the dark wool, work 7 Double Crochet, and repeat from *, work 7 plain light rows of Double Crochet and repeat the eighth row, but in this make the lines of Chain Stitch not above the previous ones, but in the centre stitch of the 7 of last line.

Treble Crochet.—Put the cotton once round the hook, which insert into FOUNDATION, put cotton again round, and draw it through, having now three loops on the hook

FIG. 235. CROCHET—TREBLE STITCH.

(*see* Fig. 235), place cotton again round hook and pull it through two of the loops, leaving two on the hook, place cotton again round and pass it through the two left on the hook. Abbreviation in Crochet Instructions, " T. C."

Treble Stitch, Cross.—Take the cotton twice round hook, and put it into the FOUNDATION next to stitch last worked, take cotton once round hook and draw it through as a loop, take on more cotton and draw it through two loops on the hook, which will leave three still there, wind cotton once round the hook and put the hook into

FIG. 236. CROCHET—CROSS TREBLE STITCH.

Foundation, 2 stitches from last insertion (*see* Fig. 236) and draw it through, forming a loop, thus having five loops on hook; take up cotton and work off two loops at a time until only one remains, make 2 CHAIN and make 1 TREBLE into the upper cross part of stitch, and repeat for the next Cross Treble.

Treble Stitch, Double Long.—A variety of Treble Crochet, but where the cotton in Treble the first time is wound once round the hook, in Double Long Treble it is wound three times, and cast off with the worked stitches one by one. It is but little used in Crochet, as the stitch formed by so many castings off is too long for anything but coarse work. Abbreviation in Crochet Instructions, " d. l. t."

Treble Stitch, Long.—A variety of Treble, in which the cotton is wound twice round the hook, and cast off with the worked stitches one by one, thus making a longer stitch than ordinary Treble. To work: Wind cotton twice round hook and insert into FOUNDATION CROCHET, draw through, wind cotton once round and draw through two loops, wind cotton once round and draw through two loops, wind cotton once round and draw through two loops, wind cotton once round and draw through last two loops. Abbreviation in Crochet Instructions, "L. T." See *Treble*.

Treble Stitch, Raised.—Work three rows of RIBBED STITCH. Fourth row—work 2 Ribbed Stitches, and make a TREBLE for next, putting the hook into the stitch underneath it of the first row, work 2 Trebles in this way, then 2

FIG. 237. CROCHET—RAISED TREBLE STITCH.

Ribbed Stitches, then 2 Trebles, and continue to the end of the row. Fifth row—turn the work and work a row of Ribbed Stitch. Sixth row—commence with the 2 Trebles,

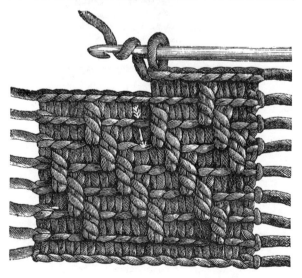

FIG. 238. CROCHET—RAISED TREBLE STITCH.

putting them into the third row beneath the stitch, and continue to work 2 Ribbed and 2 Trebles to end of row, as shown in Fig. 237. Seventh row—like fifth. Eighth—like sixth; and so on to end of the pattern. By working the

RIBBED between the Treble row the raised part of the work is always kept on the right side.

A variation of this stitch is shown in Fig. 238, in which one Raised Treble is taken up the work in diagonal lines. As this arrangement does not allow of the work being turned, commence each row on the right-hand side, or work the whole round. Commence with FOUNDATION CHAIN and two rows of DOUBLE CROCHET. Third row— work TREBLE CROCHET between every third Double Crochet; take it over the lines already made, as described in the first pattern, and put it in, as shown in Fig. 238, by the arrow; in the next row work as before, only putting the first Treble in the stitch beyond the one worked in the previous row. Always work 3 Double Crochet between each Raised Treble.

Tricot Stitch. — Also known as *Tunisian Crochet, Railway, Fool's,* and *Idiot Stitch.* The easiest of Crochet stitches, but only suitable for straight work; it is usually worked with Berlin or fleecy wool, and a wooden hook, No. 4, and is suitable for couvrepieds, counterpanes, muffatees, mufflers, and other warm articles. The hook must be sufficiently long to take the length of the work upon it at one time, and when large pieces are required work them in strips and sew together, to render them less cumbersome while in progress. To work: Make a FOUNDATION CHAIN of the required length, with 1 Chain over for second row, put the hook through the second Foundation Chain, and make a stitch, leave it on the hook, pick up the third Foundation Chain, make a stitch, and leave on the hook; continue until all the Foundation stitches are picked up,

FIG. 239. CROCHET—TRICOT STITCH.

made, and on the hook. Third row—wool over the hook, which draw through 2 loops, wool over and draw through the next 2, and so on to the end of the row. Fourth row— upon the work will now be visible a number of long upright loops, put the hook through the first of these and make a stitch, leave it on the hook, and continue to pick up loops, make them and keep them on the hook to the end of the row. The rest of the work is third and fourth row alternately. Be careful to count the number of stitches on the hook from time to time, as the end loops are frequently overlooked. The work is increased in any place by a stitch made at the end, and narrowed by two stitches being looped together. The stitch is shown in Fig. 239, which

is a Tricot of 14 Chain as Foundation, and worked with shaded wools.

Tricot Stitch, Cross.—This stitch, worked with a fine bone hook and in single wool, is a close, useful one for comforters and muffatees, and with a large hook and fleecy wool makes good couvrepieds or crossover shawls. It is a variation of ordinary Tricot, in which the second stitch is crossed under the first and worked before it. To work: Make a FOUNDATION CHAIN of width required, and work a row of TRICOT, which take back in the usual manner. Second row—work the EDGE STITCH plain, then take out hook and draw the second loop through the first, as shown in Fig. 240, by the direction of the arrow and

FIG. 240. CROCHET—CROSS TRICOT STITCH.

the figures 2 and 1, work the loop number 2, and retain it on hook and then the loop number 1, which also retain (*see* illustration); continue to the end of the row, working the last stitch like the Edge stitch plain, return back as in Tricot. In the next row the Cross stitches will not come under the ones below them, but will be altered in position. Work the first loop on the row without crossing it, and turn the loop next to it over the first loop of the second cross, thus working together the two stitches away from each other instead of the two close together; these two lines constitute the whole of the work.

Tricot Stitch, Ecossais. — Commence by making a FOUNDATION CHAIN of eleven stitches, keep the loop on the hook, the wool being at the back of it, bring the wool over the hook to the front and leave it at the back, put the hook into the last Chain stitch but one, and bring the wool through in a loop. There will now be three loops on the hook, put the hook into the next Chain stitch, bring the wool through in a loop, put the hook into the next Chain, and bring the wool through. There will now be five loops on the hook. Hold the second of these five loops with the finger and thumb of the left hand, turn it over the other three loops at the back, and raise three loops from the three upright stitches of those which appear tied together. These three stitches are marked in Fig. 241 by an arrow and the figures 1 and 2. Then turn the loop made on the hook over these three loops, repeat from the commencement of the row twice more, and at

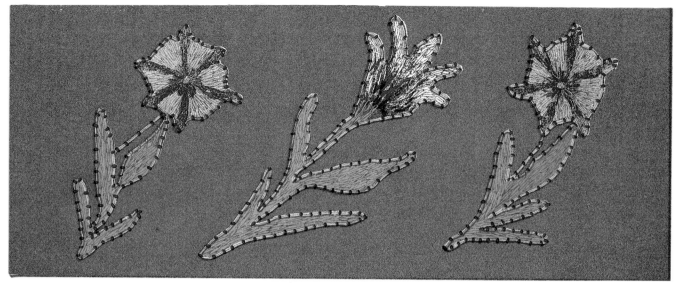

EMBROIDERY UPON ROMAN SHEETING.

EMBROIDERY UPON PLUSH.

the end put the hook into the last stitch and raise one loop; work back as in the first row. Repeat the second row until the length is made.

FIG. 241. CROCHET—ÉCOSSAIS STITCH.

Tricot Stitch, Fancy (1).—An arrangement of Tricot by which perpendicular loops are formed. It is worked with the usual Tricot wooden hook and with fleecy or Berlin wool, and is useful for comforters and petticoats, as it makes a warm, close stitch. Make a FOUNDATION CHAIN of the width required, and work a line of TRICOT, which take back, first stitch through one loop and the

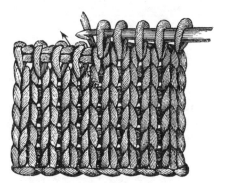

FIG. 242. CROCHET—FANCY TRICOT STITCH (No. 1).

rest through two. Second row—instead of picking up the loops, as in Tricot, push the hook through the stitch below the horizontal line and out at the back, as shown by the arrow in Fig. 242; take up the wool, draw it through to the front, and leave it on the hook. Repeat to the end of the row, and work back as described before.

(2).—This is a pretty stitch for handkerchiefs, shawls, &c., or as a stripe for a blanket. Cast on a FOUNDATION CHAIN the length required. First row—raise all the loops as in TRICOT, and work back very loosely. Second, or pattern row—keep the wool to the front of the work, take up the little stitch at the top of the long loop without drawing the wool through, put the hook from the back of the work between the next two loops, draw the wool through to the back across the long loop, pass the stitch thus formed into the one above the long loop

without taking the wool on the hook again, take up the next small stitch above a long loop (the wool should be still in front), insert the hook from the back between the next two long loops, draw the wool to the back, and pass

FIG. 243. CROCHET—FANCY TRICOT STITCH (No. 2).

this stitch into the last raised, continue to the end, work back in the usual way very loosely, and repeat the second row. The arrow in Fig. 243 shows how the wool should cross the loop, not where the hook is to be inserted.

(3).—This stitch is useful for petticoats and muffa-tees, as it is thick and close. It requires a bone hook and single Berlin or fleecy wool. (*See* Fig. 244.) To work: Make a FOUNDATION CHAIN 8 inches long, take up all the loops as in TRICOT, and work back. Second row—take up the Chain between the first and second perpendicular loops, draw the wool through, put the hook through the second long loop (see the arrow in Fig. 244) into the

FIG. 244. CROCHET—FANCY TRICOT STITCH (No. 3).

third loop (see dot), and draw the third loop through the second which crosses them; then draw the wool through the third loop, which is now on the hook, * take up the next Chain after the third loop; then cross the two next long loops, and draw the wool through the last; repeat to the end of the row; work back in Tricot. Third row— Tricot. Fourth—like the second. Continue these two rows to the end of the work.

(4).—A variety of Tricot, and worked thus: Make a FOUNDATION CHAIN the width required, and take up all the stitches, and work them off one by one for first row, as in Tricot. Second row—* thread round hook, pick up two stitches together, repeat to end of row from * until the last stitch, which pick up singly; this is the row shown in

S

Fig. 245; work back, making a separate stitch of each one in last row. Third row—thread round hook, do not work the first loop of last row, so as to keep the edge of the work smooth, * pick up next two long loops, thread round

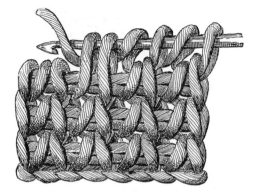

FIG. 245. CROCHET—FANCY STITCH.

hook, and repeat from *, work the last loop by itself, and making a loop before it, return back as before. The work when seen on the wrong side looks like Treble Crochet.

Tricot Stitch, Josephine.—This stitch, which is shown in Fig. 246, is used for shawls or antimacassars. Commence by making a CHAIN of the full length as a foundation. First row—insert the hook in the fourth Chain stitch, draw a loop through it, draw another loop through the newly formed stitch, which loop must be retained on the hook, repeat this once more in the same stitch, insert the hook again in the same stitch, and draw a loop through. There will now be three loops on the hook as well as the loop,

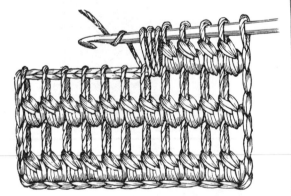

FIG. 246. CROCHET—JOSEPHINE TRICOT STITCH.

which was there at the beginning. Draw a loop through the three loops, and let that loop remain on the hook; repeat in every stitch of the row. Second row—work off as in ordinary TRICOT. Third row—make 2 Chain stitches, work in the same way as for the first row, with the exception of working under instead of into the stitches. Work off as the second row, continue to repeat the third row and second row until the work is the length required. Only work the two Chain stitches at the commencement of the rows to make them even.

Tricot Stitch, Open.—A fancy arrangement of Tricot so that an open stitch is formed. Work with fine Shetland wool and with a wooden Tricot hook as large as can be used with the wool. First row—make a FOUNDATION CHAIN, and work the second and third rows as in TRICOT. Fourth row—put the hook in between the two perpendicular threads that look like a plain knitting stitch, and push it through to the back of the work under the straight Chain (*see* Fig. 247 and arrow), draw the wool

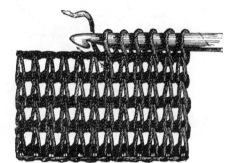

FIG. 247. CROCHET—TRICOT OPEN STITCH.

through and make a loop, which keep on the hook, and repeat to the end of the row. Fifth row—like the return row of Tricot. Sixth row—as the fourth. The work should look, as shown in the illustration, like a number of open loops with a horizontal chain as a Foundation. If the wool used is very fine, stretch the work out when finished on a board, wet it, and press it with a warm iron, protecting it from the iron with a handkerchief. This will draw the work into its right position.

Tricot Stitch, Open Raised.—A handsome raised stitch used for crossovers, petticoats, and comforters. It should be worked in double Berlin or four thread fleecy wool. Make a FOUNDATION CHAIN of the width required, and work a row of TRICOT, and then back. Second row—work the first stitch plain, then bring the wool in front of the work and put the hook into the hollow between the first

FIG. 248. CROCHET—OPEN RAISED TRICOT STITCH.

and second loop, allow this to catch hold of the wool at the back, the wool passing from the front to the back over the work, bring the hook back again to the front with the wool on it, put it into the hole between the second and third loops, and let it catch the wool, returning with it on the hook, where there will now be three loops for the one stitch, draw the last made loop through the other two (*see* Fig. 248), and retain it on the hook. For the next stitch put the wool forward, and the hook into the same space as before, between the second and third loops, and repeat from *. Work the last stitch as the first stitch, and work back in Tricot.

Tricot Stitch, Point de.—A pretty stitch, suitable for children's quilts and couvrepieds, worked with double or single Berlin wool, according to taste and the size of the article to be made. It should be worked in strips for large couvrepieds of various colours, or in shaded wools in one piece for children's quilts. Make a FOUNDATION CHAIN of the width required. First row—wool round the hook, pass the hook through the third Chain and draw the wool through, leave it on the hook, wool round the hook and again into the same third Chain, draw the wool through, wool round the hook and pass through the first two loops on the hook, then round and through three loops on the hook; (there will now be two loops left on the hook); * wool round the hook and pass it through the second Chain from last on the Foundation, draw the wool through, and leave it on the hook, wool round, and again pass the hook through the second Chain and draw the wool through, wool round and through the first two loops on the hook, wool round

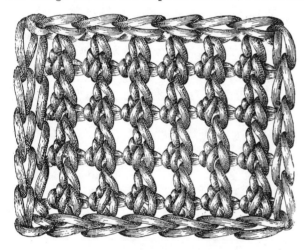

FIG. 249. CROCHET—POINT DE TRICOT STITCH.

and through the next three, leave three loops on the hook; repeat from * to the end of the row, always increasing the stitches left on the hook; work the last stitch by putting the wool through and drawing it up to the length of the rest. Second row — work back, wool through the first loop, * 1 Chain, wool round and through the loop of Chain and one on the hook; repeat from * to end of the row. Third row—1 Chain, * wool round the hook, put the hook through the long loop and through a horizontal thread that will be seen between the stitches of the last row beneath the line made in working back, draw the wool at once through these two loops, wool round the hook, and this time put into the horizontal thread, only putting the hook under and through it, not over it; draw the wool through, then wool round the hook and through the two first loops on the hook, wool round the hook and through the next three loops, and leave two on the hook; repeat from * to the end of the row, always leaving after each stitch a fresh loop on the hook. Repeat second and third rows

throughout the work. Fig. 249 shows the stitch fully worked.

Tunisian Crochet.—See *Tricot Stitch.*

Crochet Braid, or Cordon Braid.—A description of cotton braid, very fully waved. It is heavy-made, and is employed both for braiding and as a foundation for crochet work; hence its name.

Crochet Cottons.—So called because manufactured expressly for crochet work. They can be had on reels, in balls, or in skeins. The numbers run from 8 to 50.

Crochet Needle, or Hook.—A name derived from the French *Crochet*, a small hook. It consists of a long round bone or gutta percha needle, having a hook at one end, or a steel one fixed into a handle.

Crochet Silk.—(*Soie Mi-serré*). This silk is so called by the French because only half tightened in the twisting. It is a coarse description of Cordonnet, varying only from that material in the mode of twisting, but more brilliant and flexible than the usual purse and netting silks, and thus distinguished from them by the name of the work for which it is intended. A finer twist in black for Russian stitch is to be had. There is also the ombré crochet or purse silk.

Crochet Twist.—Otherwise called NETTING SILK and PURSE TWIST. A more tightly twisted cord than that called *Soie Mi-serré.* It is sold in large skeins of eight to the ounce, by the single skein, or by the dozen.

Cross Bar, Open.—A stitch used in pillow laces for Braids, or to form an open side to a leaf where the thick side has been made in Cloth Stitch. The manner of working is described in BRAID WORK. (See *Open Cross Braid.*)

Cross-Barred, or Checked Muslin.—Also called Scotch Checks. These muslins are all white and semi-clear, having stripes of thicker texture and cords to form the pattern, either in checks or stripes. The widths run from 32 inches to a yard, and the prices vary much. They are employed for curtains and covers of furniture, as well as for dresses, aprons, and pinafores. There are also Hair Cord and Fancy Muslins of the same description of material.

Crossing.—*See* KNITTING.

Cross Stitch.—The manner of making CROSS STITCH in Berlin Work and Crochet is described under those headings, but the stitch is also largely used in various fancy

FIG. 250. CROSS STITCH.

embroideries upon silk, cloth, and linen materials, and is formed with all kinds of purse and other embroidery silks, and coloured linen threads. The stitch is made as shown in Fig. 250. Its beauty consists of its points being enclosed in a perfect square. To work: Take the first part of the stitch from the left-hand bottom side of the square across to the right-hand top side, and the second from the right-hand bottom side to the left-hand top side, crossing over the first stitch.

Cross Tracing.—Cross Tracing is used in Honiton Pillow Lace as a variation to Vandyke tracery and Cloth and Shadow Stitches for leaves. It requires to be executed with extreme attention and care, as it is not marked out with pins, and, as two arms of the cross are in progress together, two twists have to be attended to. The two arms are commenced at different sides, brought down to meet in the middle, and carried again to the sides. In making a Cross Tracing it is advisable to put a pin into the middle hole, to mark it. The directions given are for working a Cross Tracing over ten pairs of BOBBINS, and in a small space; in a large space the twist can be thrice instead of twice, and the work taken over a greater number of Bobbins. The workers are twisted twice as they pass to and fro, and the passive Bobbins on each of the strands thus formed only once; the pattern is made by varying the place of the twist. First row—work 1, twist, work 8, twist, work 1. Second row—work 2, twist, work 6, twist, work 2. Third row—work 3, twist, work 4, twist, work 3. Fourth row—work 4, twist, work 2, twist, work 4. Fifth row—work 5, twist, stick a pin, work 5. Sixth row—work 4, twist, work 2, twist, work 4. Seventh row—work 3, twist, work 4, twist, work 3. Eighth row—work 2, twist, work 6, twist, work 2. Ninth row—work 1, twist, work 8, twist, work 1.

Crowns.—These are used in needle-point laces to ornament the Brides and Cordonnet, and are identical with COURONNES.

Croydons.—A description of cotton sheeting, from two to three yards wide; also a make of calico varying from 27 to 36 inches in width. They are stout, and have a slightly glazed finish.

Crumb Cloths.—A heavy Damask, made in grey and slate colour, of all sizes, in squares and widths, the latter varying from 14 to 36 inches. The designs on these Cloths are adopted for the purposes of embroidery, being worked over in outline with coloured wools, silks, and crewels. For stair coverings they can be had in grey and slate colour, and also with borders, varying from 18 inches to two yards in width.

Crystal Silk Wool.—A knitting yarn, composed of a mixture of wool and silk, of fine texture, and very durable. When knitted it shows more silk than wool, and has a brilliant lustre. It may be had in twenty distinct varieties of colour, as well as in plain black, in 8oz. packets.

Cubica.—A very fine kind of Shalloon, used for lining coats and dresses. It is made of worsted, and varies in width from 32 to 36 inches. *See* SHALLOON.

Cucumber Braid.—*See* BRAIDS.

Cucumber Plaitings.—*See* PLAITINGS.

Cuir.—The French word to signify LEATHER (which *see*).

Curragh Point.—*See* IRISH LACE.

Curtain Serge.—This is a new material, produced in several "art colours." It is a stout all-wool stuff, employed for portières and other hangings. It is 54 inches in width, and is a handsome-looking fabric.

Curves.—These are made in pillow laces, with the false pinholes, in the same manner as CIRCLES (which *see*).

Cushion.—A term sometimes given to the pillow upon which pillow laces are made. *See* PILLOW.

Cushion Stitch.—Cross Stitch has become confounded with Cushion Stitch, in consequence of its having been so called when used in ancient Church embroidery to ornament kneeling mats and cushions; but the real Cushion Stitch is of almost as ancient an origin, and is a flat Embroidery stitch largely employed to fill in backgrounds in old needlework. It was sometimes worked very minutely, to fill in the faces and hands of figures, before the introduction of the peculiar Chain Stitch in Opus Anglicanum work. As a background stitch it is well known, and is to be found in many pieces of needlework executed in the fourteenth and fifteenth centuries. After Church embroidery fell into disuse, Cushion Stitch was formed with worsteds upon canvas that was slightly open, but woven with the same distance between each thread; it then formed both pattern and background. It is now worked in a frame upon an evenly woven, close, coarse canvas, the threads of which serve as guiding lines. It is a variety of Satin Stitch; its peculiarities are its forming regular vandykes, curves, and half-circles, one above the other, on the background, instead of being taken from end to end of the space without variation. To work: Keep the embroidery silk entirely on the surface of material, bring the needle up from the back at one end of vandyke or curve, and put it down at the other in a straight line from where it came out. Bring it up close to where it went down, a thread of the material being sufficient to hold it, pass it back across the space to the side it first came from, and put it through the material, to form another straight line. Continue until the space is covered, and lay the lines of stitches with the evenness and precision of weaving.

Cut Canvas Work.—This is similar to BRITISH RAISED WORK.

Cut Cloth Flower Embroidery.—A fancy Embroidery that is now out of date. It consists of producing upon a flat surface garlands and groups of raised flowers in their natural colours. Cut out of fine cloth that matches them in tint, the petals of the flowers and the various leaves. To work: Lay these upon the foundation, and either fasten them to it with BUTTONHOLE STITCH in filoselles, as in Broderie Perse, or with long SATIN stitches. Fill in the centres of the flowers with FRENCH KNOTS and various fancy Embroidery stitches, and ornament the leaves and form tendrils and sprays that are too fine to be cut from the coloured cloth with CORAL and FEATHER STITCH worked upon the background.

Cutting off Bobbins.—Lift the pair to be tied and cut in the left hand, and place the scissors, closed, under the threads, which bring round over them; then turn the scissors, the points facing the pillow, open the blades wide, and draw the upper threads in between them as high as the hinge; close the scissors gently, and the threads will not be cut. Now draw the scissors down out of the encircling threads, and a loop will come through on one point of the scissors; snip this, and the bobbins will be cut off and yet tied together for future use.

Cutting Out.—Cutting-out is the art of dividing a piece of material into such forms, and agreeably to such measurements, as that, when sewn together according to a due arrangement of the several pieces, they shall form the garment or other article desired. To do this correctly and without waste of the material, lay the patterns upon it, in various positions, so as to utilise every spare corner, taking care to lay each piece the right way of the grain, and to leave the " turnings-in " sufficiently deep not only to allow for the stitching, but also for enlarging the article if found to need alteration. The various pieces of the pattern having been fitted to the stuff, tack them down and then cut out. If the material be carefully doubled, the two sides may be cut out simultaneously; but take care to make no mistake as to the right and wrong sides, if there be any difference, or both may be found cut for the same side. The following are a few general and essential rules applicable to the cutting out of every article of wear or use, more or less.

All *linings* should be cut out first. If about to prepare a *Bodice*, for example, lay the rolled lining on the table in front of you, the cut end towards you, having first pinned a smooth cloth tightly across the table, on which to fasten the work when necessary. Along the selvedge of the lining on the left side place the right front of the bodice pattern (the side with the buttonholes or eyes), and pin along the edge of the pattern parallel with the selvedge, allowing an inch and a half for turning in. The whole pattern must be smoothed out well, and pinned down. Then place the left hand side (where the buttons are placed) on the front, on the opposite side of the lining, and pin it down likewise at the selvedge, running or tacking down the whole model upon the lining, following the outline throughout. Then the two backs should be laid upon the lining, the centres being laid parallel with the selvedges, one inch being allowed from them; pin them down and tack the outlines. Then follow the sleeves, which must be so turned that the upper part in front is placed straight with the material, which will throw the under portion a little on the bias. This done, cut out each outlined piece half an inch beyond the outline, to allow for turning in; but the fronts must be left uncut to preserve the selvedge edges. You should then chalk, or run in cotton, the letters "R." and "L." on the right and left sides of the bodice, and also on the two sleeves, adding a "T." to distinguish the top of each of the latter. After cutting out the lining, the material itself is to be tacked to it, and cut out likewise, having previously been laid smoothly on the table and pinned down. Supposing the article to be a bodice, as soon as prepared, and the material and lining are tacked together, try it on inside out, tightening it in at the "darts" by means of pins run in successively along them.

In cutting out side-gores, side-pieces, and back-pieces of a polonaise or bodice, be careful to lay the grain of the material in an exact line parallel with the line of the waist. The bodice will be drawn aside if the cutting out be at all

on the bias. Cut the fronts the long way of the stuff, If the material be striped, or a plaid, the matching of the several parts of the pattern should be carefully attended to. There should be a perfect stripe down both the front and back of the bodice.

Silk materials are sometimes too narrow for a large sleeve to be procured from a breadth of it. In this case the joining of two selvedges would be advisable, making the union underneath the sleeve. A little of the latter should be sloped out in front at the top, to make it less deep there than at the back, where room is required, remembering always that the sleeve must be cut on the straight in front, the crosswise part of the same falling behind. Make no mistake as to cutting them in pairs. The length of the sleeve on the upper part of the arm should be about 2 inches longer than that of the underneath portion, where it has been cut out. In shaping out the shoulder-pieces and arm pieces, which stand in lieu of sleeves on mantles such as dolmans, remember to cut them with the bias down the middle. When cutting any piece of stuff on the bias, such as trimmings, flouncings, &c., it should be correctly and completely so done, otherwise the work will be drawn awry.

In cutting out a *Skirt*, the front sides of the gores must always be straight, and the bias sides towards the back. The same rule applies to overskirts and trains. Seams in the middle of either the front or back of a skirt should be avoided. Figured materials and those having a nap or pile need careful attention, so that the several portions of the cloth should be cut to lie in the same direction, the flowered designs running upwards, the ordinary nap of the cloth running downwards, and the pile of velvet or plush whichever way may be preferred, provided that uniformity be observed; but as sealskin— which supplied the original idea of plush—is always laid with the fur lying upwards, so it is usually thought that velvet looks more rich when laid thus, than downwards. No incision in the material should be made until every portion of the pattern has been laid in its proper place.

The method of cutting out a *Bodice* has been given, because a more complicated undertaking than that of a skirt, while the general rules of tacking on the pattern, and then cutting out the lining, and then the material, applies equally to all parts of a garment. It is usual, however, to cut out the skirt first, then the polonaise or bodice and overskirt if there be one. The sleeves might be made up underneath by means of joinings, were there a scarcity of material, and the trimmings should be left to the last, as scraps might be utilised for them. When there is any deficiency in stuff it may be economised by facing the fronts, or adding a false hem, instead of turning down the hems, also by adding small pieces under the arms, as well as piecing the sleeves, and often both fronts of a bodice may thus be obtained out of one breadth.

When cutting from a *pattern*, take the right side of the bodice, and when you have cut another right side from it, turn it on the other side, the reverse side now being uppermost.

Should there be a floral design on the material, take care not to cut it double, without first taking note of the position of such design, that the flowers, pines, or other such pattern may not be turned upside down on one of the two pieces.

Frills, to be sufficiently full, should be cut twice the length of the piece of stuff (cap front or collar) on which they are to be sewn when whipped, and

Linings of hats, bonnet fronts, tippets, and other round forms should be cut on the cross, and so should strips for pipings and linings for broad hems.

To cut cloth of any kind on the *cross* or *bias*, that is, diagonally with the grain, fold the end of the stuff corner over, like a half handkerchief, so as to lay the raw edge along the selvedge. Then cut off the half square, and from this obliquely cut piece take the strips for piping if required. To take off a yard crosswise, measure a yard along each of the selvedges, after the half square has been removed, crease the material carefully across obliquely, let someone hold it in place, and cut it in the fold. Satins, velvets, and silks may be purchased cut either on the bias or straight. In order to save the trouble of measuring each bias length to be taken off, it is a bad habit of some workers to place the first-cut piece on the material, and cut by it. This causes the bias to be untrue throughout, and the flounces to hang badly. Experienced workers begin by cutting the edge of the material very straight, and then folding it cornerwise, so as to lie on the selvedge. A perfect bias line is thus formed. The required widths of the fabric should be marked at each side of the selvedge with chalk when measured; they can then be kept to the bias line. It must be remembered that a flounce of 4 inches wide must be measured on the selvedge 6 inches and so on. In cutting twilled fabrics and crape, the right side of both materials must be laid down on the table, and the left-hand corner turned over. This brings the twilled lines to the perpendicular, keeping the right side always uppermost.

So various are the patterns of underclothing, and so different the sizes required, that it would be impossible to supply hard and fast directions for the cutting out of special articles for infants, children, and adults. Thus a few general rules respecting them alone can be given, but these will be found sufficient to guide the needlewoman, and enable her to avail herself of the paper patterns in every style, and of any dimensions which she can procure.

All linens and calicoes should be washed prior to being cut out. All linens, including lawn, cambric, and Holland, should be cut by the thread, one or two strands being drawn to guide the scissors. All calicoes, muslins, and flannels may be torn, but to do so the material should be rolled over on each side at each tear that is given. All the several portions of underclothing which are liable to be stretched in wearing, such as skirts, sleeves, wristbands, shoulder straps, collars, and waistbands, should be cut with the selvedge, or straight way of the stuff. Frills and pieces gathered or fulled between bands and flounces should be cut across the material, from selvedge to selvedge.

For the cutting out of ordinary *Underlinen* for adults the following are the average quantities that will be required. For a *Chemise* of longcloth, from 2½ yards to

3¼ yards, and from 2½ to 3½ yards of embroidery edging. For a *Combination Garment* about 3 yards of longcloth, 2¾ of embroidery for the neck and arms, and 1 yard 4 or 6 inches of ditto for the legs. For *Drawers* 2½ yards of longcloth and 2½ yards of frillings. For flannel *Knicker-bockers* 2¾ yards. For a square-cut *Petticoat Bodice,* cut the same behind as in front, 1¼ yard of longcloth, and 2¼ yards of trimming for the neck and armholes. For a *High Petticoat Bodice* cut down V shape in front, 1¼ yards of longcloth, and 1¾ yards of trimming.

To cut out a *Nightdress* of ordinary length and proportions 4 yards of longcloth will be required, and the quantity of trimming depends on the pattern and the fancy of the wearer. Those intended to be made with a yoke at front and back, should be cut 5 inches shorter; or if with a yoke at the back only, the back alone should be cut shorter, because the yoke drops it off the shoulders at that part. The yoke must always be cut double, and on the straight way of the stuff, to allow the gatherings of the skirt depending from it to be inserted between the sides of the double yoke, and to be stitched down.

A *White Petticoat* of longcloth, of walking length, will require about 4½ yards, supposing that the front breadth be slightly gored, one gore on each side, and one plain breadth at the back.

Having given the quantities required for several under garments, the order of cutting out the same follows; but the rules in reference to certain amongst them will be given *in extenso,* such as—for adults, a *shirt, chemise, nightdress,* and *drawers;* and an infant's *barrow, shirt, stays, petticoat,* and *nightgown.*

Shirt.—To cut out an ordinary medium sized shirt, like the annexed pattern at Fig. 251, allow 37 inches in length for the back and 36 in front, cutting from a piece of linen or calico 33 or 34 inches in width. About three yards of this width would suffice for one shirt. Were half a dozen required, an economical and experienced cutter could procure them out of 17 yards of material.

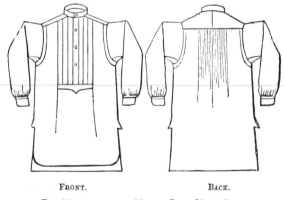

FRONT.   BACK.

FIG. 251. DIAGRAM OF MEDIUM-SIZED MAN'S SHIRT.

So place the back and front pieces of the body together as to leave the difference in their length or "tail" at the lower end. Mark off at the side, from the top, the 9 inches in depth for the armhole, and divide the remainder below it into two equal parts. At the upper half the back and front pieces must be sewn together; the lower must be left open and the front corner rounded. Next slope out the armhole. Mark off 2 inches at the top, and cut down to within 2 inches of the bottom, which is to be curved out to a point. From the armhole, along the shoulder, mark 6 inches, taking off a slope of 1 inch in depth, cutting from the armhole, gradually decreasing in depth towards the 6 inch mark, finishing in a point, and preserving a straight line.

The neck piece is measured and cut as follows: Draw the line A 9½ inches long, and dot at 3½ inches from the bottom. Draw with a square the lines C, D, and B. Mark 2 inches on B, 4¼ on D, and 2½ on C, and draw line E, as indicated in the diagram, then, with a piece of chalk in the right hand, draw a half circle, or small arc from D to

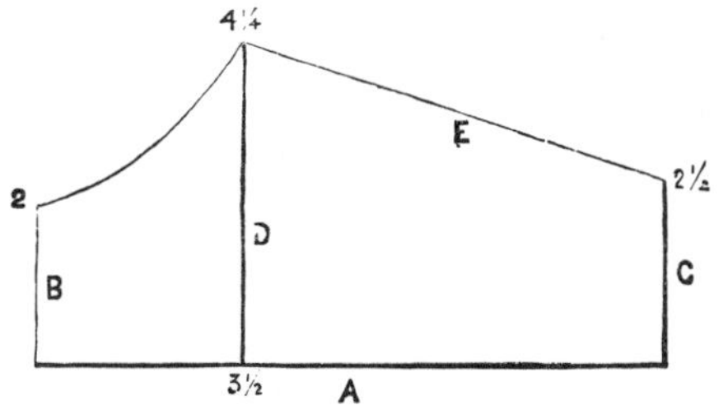

FIG. 252. NECK PIECE OF SHIRT.

B to give the proper curve for the neck. The pattern for half of the neck piece being completed, it should be arranged on the material so that the neck piece may be cut on the bias, from shoulder to shoulder, the seam uniting the two halves being in the centre of the back. The neck pieces must always be double. (*See* Fig. 252.)

The breast of the shirt has now to be made. Mark the centre of the front at the top of the body, and cut out of it a piece 6 inches on each side of the point marked to the extent of 14½ inches. The piece to replace this should be cut 15 inches long, that when inserted it may be 8 inches in width. If it be desired to make the breast quite plain on each side of the centre plait, the linen must be doubled; otherwise, the fulness allowed for the plaiting must depend on the current fashion or individual fancy. The neck band must be 17 inches long and 1¼ inches in depth at the centre of the back, gradually sloping to ¾ of an inch in front, and should likewise be of double linen. For the sleeves take 22½ inches of the material, cut it on the bias, 14 inches, broad at the wrist, and 20 inches broad at the shoulder. One width of 34 inch linen or calico will be sufficient. But should the material be narrower, a small gore placed at the top of the sleeve on the straight side will give the necessary width. The wrist should be 8½ inches in length, and may be 3½ inches or more in depth, according to the fashion of the time or personal fancy. If intended to turn over, and lie back on the wrist, a single lining will be sufficient, as the thickness should be reduced.

For a man's night shirts a greater length must be allowed than for day shirts, and the collars and wristbands wider. Strong calico should be employed instead of linen or calico shirting. Otherwise there is little difference between the two garments. To make half a dozen of full size about 21 yards of yard wide linen or calico will be required. Lay aside 15 yards for the bodies of the shirts, dividing the piece into six. Each will then be 2½ yards long. Then cut from the remainder of the piece 3⅜ yards for the sleeves, which subdivide again into six parts. Each will then be about 20 inches long, which, when cut lengthwise into two parts each, will make a pair of sleeves. For the collars cut off 1 yard and 4 inches from the original piece of calico, subdividing the width of the collar piece into three parts, and each piece into two in the length. This division of the 1 yard and 4 inches will give six collars of 20 inches in length; 20 inches more will be wanted for wristbands, subdividing it so as to allow 10 inches in length for each. The sleeve gussets will require 12 inches of the calico, the shoulder straps 10½ inches, and the neck and side gussets 9 inches.

For cutting out an ordinary *Chemise* in the old fashioned, and but slightly gored style, suitable for poor persons, the following are the leading rules: Take 2¾ yards of calico of ordinary width, and cut off a strip 7 inches in depth for the sleeves. Double the remaining length. On the centre crease, or fold, measure off from the selvedge 3½ inches for the width of the side gores, and from this point measure 4 inches for the length of the shoulder, marking at the corresponding points for the opposite selvedge. Cut each gore down, sloping gradually from the point, 3½ inches from the selvedge, to a point at half the length of the chemise. The straight side or selvedge of each gore is to be joined to that of the chemise, the selvedges being sewn on the right side. Oversew and fell the sides, leaving 11 inches open for each of the armholes. Cut out a piece 4 inches in depth for the neck at back and front, and from the point marking the length of shoulder, to the corresponding point on the opposite shoulder, rounding out the corners. The half of this piece which has been cut out will serve to make the neck band, which latter may be about 36 inches in length and 2 in depth. Into this band the neck of the chemise must be gathered, stroked, and stitched. Cut the sleeves 14 inches in width, and each gusset 4 inches square. These latter can be obtained from the remainder of the piece cut out of the neck part of the material. Unite the gussets to the sleeves, run or stitch and fell the latter, stitch the ends of the sleeves, stitch and fell them into the armholes, stitch or hem the skirt, and trim the neck, sleeves, and skirt according to taste.

The rules for cutting out a *Night Dress* resemble in many respects those for a shirt. The alterations requisite will be too obvious to the needlewoman to require any notice here, and the same diagram supplied for the neck piece of the shirt will suffice for a night gown or night shirt. *See* GORED UNDERLINEN.

To cut out women's ordinary *Drawers* the following are good general rules, always remembering that differences in size, both width and length, and certain variations in cut, may be made from this pattern to suit individual convenience. From a piece of calico 2⅝ yards in length cut off one-eighth for a waist band. Then fold over half of the remaining length from the centre of the width, so that the two selvedges shall be even, one lying exactly over the other. At the lower end mark a point 12 inches from the centre crease, and on the selvedge another at 21 inches from the lower end of the leg, or ankle. At the top make a mark on the crease at a point 2½ inches from the waist, and on the selvedge likewise one at the same distance from the waist. Below this point mark one at 5½ inches from the selvedge, and on the waist at 3 inches from the latter. Cut from point 12 inches at the extremity of the leg to point 21 inches on the selvedge, forming a well-curved line, and from thence to 5½ on the waist line. Then turn back the upper fold, and cut the single mate-

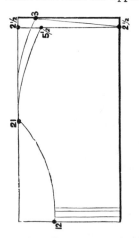

rial from point 21 to that at 3 inches at the waist, and proceed to cut along the under fold from this point, 3 inches, on the waist, to the point on the crease marked 2½ inches in a straight line, crossing the material obliquely. From this point cut straight along the upper fold to the point marked at 5½ inches, and thence on to the 2½ inch point, making a cutting parallel with that of the waist; this completes the half of the drawers. If many tucks be desired, the length given must be augmented, and insertion, or edgings of white embroidery may be added at pleasure. *See* Fig. 253.

FIG. 253. WOMAN'S DRAWERS.

The making of infants' clothing is usually learnt at an early age, and is almost too simple to need description, but two or three garments may be made an exception, and general rules given.

To make an infant's *Barrow* a yard of flannel will be required. Make three box pleats in the centre, down the

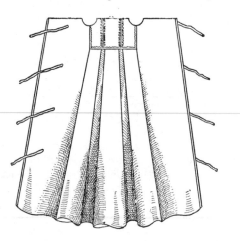

FIG. 254. INFANT'S BARROW.

length-way of the stuff, tack or pin them securely, and then HERRINGBONE them down on each side to a depth of about six inches. The pleats should be so regulated in width as to make the Herringboned back of the same width as each of the fronts, which are to fold across

each other, so dividing the bodice portion of the barrow into three equal widths, the armholes being sloped out so as to bring the centre of each to the outer line of Herringboning. The whole barrow should be bound round with flannel binding, and four strings attached on either side, placed on the edge on one side, and further inwards on the other, so as to make the fronts overlap. There should be a crossbar of double stitching where the box pleating opens free from the herringboning. *See* Fig. 254.

To cut out an *Infant's Shirt*, about 22½ inches of cambric or lawn will be required. Fold it so as to overlap across the chest, and then fold it back again straight down the centre of the piece at the back. Allow for the width of the shoulder-strap, and cut through the four folds of the cambric to a suitable depth—say 2¼ inches for the front and back flaps, which are to be turned over the stays. Then cut down from the top of the shoulder on each side to a depth of from 2¾ to 3 inches for the armhole. The depth of the shirt, cut down the selvedge, should be 11¼ inches. If sleeves be not worn, frills round the armholes supply their place.

For an *Infant's Stays*, about a quarter of a yard of a corded cotton material will be required; or, if not made of this, stitchings should be worked at even distances, in doubled *piqué* from the top downwards. A band of linen, doubled, should be stitched down at each side for the

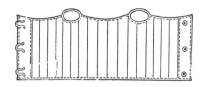

FIG. 255. INFANT'S STAYS.

buttons and buttonholes, and a cutting made for the arms (*see* Fig. 255), the shoulder-straps to which may be of white or pink elastic. The stays should measure about 18 inches in width, and be bound round.

For an *Infant's Petticoat*, two yards of fine flannel and a quarter of a yard of longcloth will be required. The latter will be needed round the body; it should be doubled, and left about 20 inches in length at the waist. The flannel should be cut in two and joined, so as to leave two breadths in width for the petticoat. It should then be gathered into the deep bodice band, and bound all round. The former should be stitched and bound, and tapes sewn to it, two on each side, but one pair within the edge, that it may lap slightly over the other side.

The Bronze Medal was awarded by the National Health Society, at their Exhibition, 1883, for a new design in the cutting-out of infants' clothing, each article of which is fastened in front. The clothes are shorter, the skirts fastened to the bodice by buttons, so as to be quickly removed, without denuding the child completely; an elastic knitted "body-belt" being substituted for the old flannel binder, and flannel shirts for lawn or linen ones.

Cut Work.—The name given by English writers to one of the earliest known laces that shared with Drawn Work and Darned Netting in the general term of Laces, and one by which all laces was designated by ancient writers: but known individually as Point Coupé, Opus Seissum, and Punto Tagliato.

The first mention of the lace occurs in chronicles dating from the twelfth century. The manufacture was then confined to the nunneries, and kept a secret from the general public. The work was used to adorn priests' sacramental robes and the grave clothes of saints. From the fifteenth to the seventeenth centuries it was universally made, and formed the chief occupation of high-born ladies, who ornamented all their fine linen with it, and made costly gifts of palls and altar cloths ornamented with the lace to the Church, while in the pictures of those centuries it is often represented as borders and trimmings to dresses. The pattern books of those times, particularly those of Vinciola, published in 1587, are full of numerous

the frame close together, in others leave open spaces between them, and cross and interlace them where necessary. After these threads are arranged take a piece of fine lawn (that used in olden time was called Quintain, from the town in Brittany where it was made), gum it on at the back of the fastened threads, and tack them to it. Wherever the pattern is to be left thick, shape the fine lawn to form the design, and BUTTONHOLE round the edge of that part, and where the pattern is left open interlace and draw the threads together, and, when the work is finished, cut away the fine lawn from underneath these parts. Form an edge to the lace with Buttonhole, and ornament the Buttonhole with PICOTS and COURONNES. Ornament the parts of this lace where large portions of lawn are left with embroidery in coloured silks and gold and silver threads.

The lighter kind of Cut Work is made thus: Fasten into the frame a number of unbleached threads and tack underneath them a parchment pattern. Where the pattern

FIG. 256. CUT WORK.

geometrical designs for this work. Two kinds of Cut Work were made—the most ancient, a thick kind in which the threads were backed with linen; and a light sort, where the threads were embroidered without a foundation. This was the commencement of needle made lace, and was elaborated in Venice into the celebrated Venetian Point, while in other parts of Italy it gradually merged into Reticella, and in the Ionian isles into Greek Lace. The making of Cut Work has gradually been superseded by the finer and more complicated lace making, but in Sweden it is still to be met with, and in England and along the coast of France during the last century it was occasionally worked. The stamped open work decorations used inside coffins, and known in the trade as "pinking," owe their origin to the trimming of grave clothes in olden times with this lace.

The thick Cut Work is made as follows: Fasten a number of fine and unbleached threads in a frame, and arrange them to form a geometrical pattern by their crossing and interlacing. Fasten them in some parts of

is to be thick, Buttonhole these threads together to form a device. Buttonhole together a larger or smaller number of threads, according to the width of the part to be made solid. Ornament the edge of the lace with fine Buttonhole and with Picots and Couronnes. Fig. 256 is one of Vinciola's patterns, and is intended to be worked in both kinds. Back the cross forming the centre of the right hand scallop with lawn, and Buttonhole its edges round; make the star surrounded with a circle, in the left hand scallop, entirely of threads Buttonholed together. Form the light edgings with Buttonholed threads ornamented with Picots.

Cyprus Embroidery.—In the twelfth and thirteenth centuries the Island of Cyprus was celebrated for its embroideries with gold and silver thread, an art the natives had probably acquired from the Phrygians and Egyptians. The work was of Oriental design, but has long ceased to be manufactured in the place.

Cyprus Lace.—The lace known under this name was

T

identical with some kinds of Cut Work, and was of very ancient manufacture. It formed a great article of commerce during the twelfth and thirteenth centuries, and is mentioned both by English and French writers as having been used in their countries. It was made of gold and silver threads. A coarse lace is still made by the peasants, but it is not valuable.

Cyprus, or Cyprus Lawn, or Cyprus Crape Cloth.—A thin, transparent, elastic stuff, somewhat resembling crape, and exclusively designed for mourning attire. It is known by the three names given above. It is 26 inches in width, and was formerly manufactured in both white and black, the latter being the most common:—

> Lawn as white as driven snow,
> Cyprus black as any crow.
> —*Winter's Tale.*

Cyprus used to be worn wound round the hat as a hat-band in the time of Elizabeth and James I. In " Gull's Hornbook " (1609) Dekker speaks of " him that wears a trebled Cyprus about his hat."

D.

Dacca Muslin.—In Sanscrit the word *Dacca* appears as *Daakka*, signifying the "hidden goddess," the town in Bengal being so named because a statue of Durga was found there. Dacca muslin is an exceedingly filmy and fragile textile, manufactured at Dacca, in Bengal, and much used by women for dresses and by men for neckerchiefs in England about 100 years ago. The Dacca Muslin now employed resembles the modern MADRAS MUSLIN, and is used for curtains. The figured is made 2 yards in width, and the plain 1¼ yards.

Dacca Silk.—Dacca silk is called by the French *soie ovale*. It is employed for embroidery, and is sold in knotted skeins. That which is now in ordinary use is not Indian made, although it is so-called from having had its origin at Dacca.

Dacca Twist.—A description of calico cloth, produced at the so-called "Dacca Twist Mills" in Manchester. It is made both twilled and plain, but woven after a peculiar method, by which the threads of the warp are " drawn " or " twisted " in—that is to say, threaded through the " healds "—or, where it is possible, twisted on to the remnants of the old threads. As many as a hundred varieties of calicoes are produced at these Mills, and amongst them the finer qualities of sheeting, twills, and shirtings, and much of the work is so fine that a square yard of calico will require 6000 yards of yarn. Dacca Twist Calico is suitable for underlinen, and measures 36 inches in width.

Daisy Mat.—A wool mat, made in a wooden frame, and called Daisy from the likeness the round, fluffy balls of which it is composed are supposed to bear to the buds of daisies. The frames used are of various sizes, ranging from a square of 8in. to 6in., and are grooved at intervals on their outer edges. The number of skeins of wool required to make the mat is regulated by the number of

grooves in the frames. Thus, for a frame with ten grooves upon each side twenty skeins of wool are required, and for one with twelve grooves twenty-four skeins. Choose single Berlin wool, either of two shades of one colour, or of five or six ; the most effective colours are deep shades of crimson, blue, or green. When more than two shades are selected, four skeins of each shade will be required, except for the lightest, when only two skeins will be necessary. Provide also purse silk, matching the wool in colour, and a netting mesh. Commence with the darkest shade of wool, and wind each skein of it on the frame into the four outside grooves, then pick up the next shade of colour and wind that upon the grooves, next the outside ones, and continue until all the grooves on the frame are filled. Each skein must keep to its own groove, and cross with the others in the centre of the frame. Wind the purse silk upon the netting mesh, and commence to secure the wool, wherever it crosses in the centre of the frame, by cross loops or knots, made thus: Fasten the silk on to the wool in the centre of the mat, put the mesh through the frame at the place where two skeins cross at the left-hand side at the bottom, bring it up in a diagonal direction on the right-hand side, loop it through the silk in the front, put it again down on the left-hand side this time at the top, bring it out on the right-hand lower side at the bottom, loop it through the silk, and thus make a knot which forms a cross at the back of the frame. Pull these knots very tight, and never make a straight stitch, always a cross one. Enclose the whole of the two skeins of wool that cross each other at that particular place, but not a strand of any other. Work from the centre stitch in squares, carrying the silk from one knot to the next along the wool. When all the wool is secured, turn the frame back to front, and cut the wool in the spaces left between the knots, but not entirely through, only that part wound upon the upper side of the frame, the wool wound upon the lower being left as a foundation. In cutting the wool be careful never to cut the knots or cross threads of silks, as these are the chief supports of the fluffy balls, while on the outside row of balls only cut the two sides, or the fringe will be destroyed. As each space is cut round the knots, little square fluffy-looking balls or Daisies will rise up. Hold the mat over steam, when the wool will rise round the knots and conceal them, then fluff the balls so made with scissors, and cut them round, should they not form good shapes. The last operation is to take the mat out of the frame by cutting the wool in the grooves ; it should be cut quite straight, as it forms the fringe.

Dalecarlian Lace.—A lace still made by the peasants of Dalecarlia (a province of Sweden) for their own use, and not as an article of commerce. It is a kind of coarse GUIPURE lace, and is made of unbleached thread. Its peculiarity lies in its patterns, which have remained unchanged for two centuries. A specimen of the lace can be seen at South Kensington.

D'Alençon Bar.—Identical with ALENÇON BAR and used as a connecting Bar in Modern Point lace. It is shown in Fig. 257. To work: Pass a thread as a HERRINGBONE backwards and forwards across the space to be covered, and either strengthen the thread by covering it with Buttonhole Stitches or by Cording it. The thread is covered with Buttonholes in the illustration.

FIG. 257. D'ALENÇON BAR.

Damascene Lace.—An imitation of Honiton lace, and made with lace braid and lace sprigs joined together with Corded bars. The difference between Damascene and Modern Point lace (which it closely resembles) consists in the introduction into the former of real Honiton sprigs, and the absence of any needleworked Fillings. The worker can make real HONITON LACE braid and sprigs upon the pillow, and is referred to the instructions on Honiton Lace for them, or can purchase the sprigs and the braid at good embroidery shops. The cotton used is a fine Mecklenburgh thread (No. 7). The method of uniting together the sprigs and the braid is as follows: Trace the design upon pink calico, tack the braid and then the sprigs into position, keeping the tacking threads well in the centre of the braid and in the middle of the sprigs. OVERCAST all the edges of the braid, and wherever it crosses or in any way touches another piece, or is turned under, firmly stitch the parts down and together. No fancy stitches or Fillings being required, it only remains to join the braid to the sprigs by a variety of Corded Bars (see CORD STITCH), HEXAGONS, and variously shaped WHEELS. Commence a Bar by joining the lace thread with a loop instead of a knot, as in

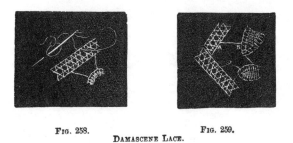

FIG. 258.　　　FIG. 259.
DAMASCENE LACE.

Fig. 258, as the edge of the braid is too open to hold a knot. Form the connecting bars with a treble thickness of thread, as illustrated in Fig. 259, thus: Commence the bar at A, fasten it to B, return the thread to A, and back again to B, fasten the Bar firmly in position with a BUTTONHOLE STITCH, shown in Fig. 260, and then Cord it back to where it commenced. The Bars need not all be straight, but they can be Corded part of the way and then divided into two lines, as shown in Fig. 261. Throw a loose thread across, as shown by the dotted line in Fig. 261, from D to C, and tie with a Buttonhole Stitch, Cord to X, tighten the thread and draw it up, and begin the arm by throwing a third thread from X to E, tie, and draw the Bar up to its proper position at F; Cord up from

E to F, and throw the thread across to D; Cord back again to the centre and return to D, or Cord every line again should they look thin.

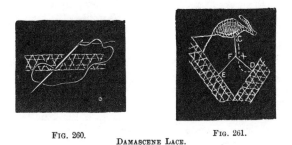

FIG. 260.　　　FIG. 261.
DAMASCENE LACE.

Hexagons are composed of a number of Bars arranged as in Fig. 262, and worked as follows: Commence with a loose thread thrown from G to H, tie the cord to T, and throw the thread across to J, and Cord up to K; throw the thread to L, tie, and Cord to M; thread to N, tie, and Cord to O; thread to P, tie, and Cord to Q; thread to R, and Cord over all the Bars. The Bar X is not part of the hexagon, being added afterwards.

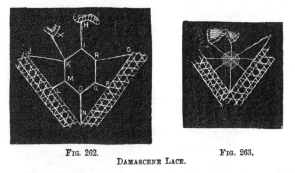

FIG. 262.　　　FIG. 263.
DAMASCENE LACE.

Wheels are made in various ways, and can be worked with any number of bars. To work Fig. 263: Throw threads across the space to be covered, tie them to the braid, and Cord back to the centre, taking care that all meet there; unite them in the centre with a backward Buttonhole Stitch, and run the needle round under one thread and over the other until the Wheel is of the desired size. To

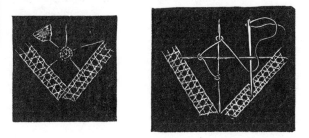

FIG. 264.　　　FIG. 265.
DAMASCENE LACE.

work Fig. 264: Throw five threads across the space, tie, and Cord back to the centre as before; run three threads loosely round the centre, and Buttonhole these tightly over, taking care that the circle thus formed is an open one, and that the centre of the Wheel is not closed up.

To work Fig. 265: Throw four lines across the space, tie

T 2

and Cord back to the centre, secure with a backward Buttonhole Stitch, then Cord a little way down one of the bars, make a Buttonhole Stitch, and throw the thread across the space to the next Bar at the same distance from the centre as the first Bar, make a Buttonhole Stitch, and repeat until a transparent Wheel is formed.

Having secured all the sprigs to the braids with the various Bars and Wheels, untack the lace from the pattern, by cutting the tacking threads at the back of the pattern and unpicking, and then slightly damp and stretch the lace if at all drawn in any part.

To work design for necktie end, shown in Fig. 266: Tack on the lace and braid, and make the Hexagons, Wheels, and divided Bars as indicated. Work the six Bars con-

century it flourished in the City of Abbeville. The designs were Oriental in character, and usually represented birds, quadrupeds, and trees. Royal and noble personages much affected the material. Its introduction into England was due to the French weavers, who took refuge here in the time of Queen Elizabeth. Damask is now made of silk, intermingled with flax, wool, or cotton, the warp being of the first named. These mixed Damasks are chiefly employed for furniture. Some of the patterns require upwards of 1200 changes of the draw-looms for their completion. There is also a species of Damask solely made of worsted, employed in upholstery. Damask Linen is a fine twilled fabric, manufactured for table-linen, which is chiefly made at Belfast and Lisburne, and also at Dun-

FIG. 266. DAMASCENE LACE.

nected together with a centre line upon the right hand side of the pattern, thus: Always Cord back the Bars to the centre, there make firm with a Buttonhole and a few turns of the thread to form a spot, and take the thread straight down the centre for a little distance between every divided line.

Damask.—A twilled stuff, decorated with ornamental devices in relief, woven in the loom, and deriving its name from Damascus, where the manufacture had its origin. The ancient textile so manufactured was of rich silk, the threads being coarse, and the figure designs executed in various colours. The Normans found this industry already established at Palermo in the twelfth century, and carried it on there, while in the following

fermline. It is made both single and double. The Cotton damasks, made in crimson and maroon, for curtains, measure from 30 inches to 54 inches in width; the Union Damasks for the same purpose 54 inches, and the Worsted, in all wool, in blue, crimson, and green, the same width. *See* LINEN DAMASK.

Damask Stitch.—A name given to SATIN STITCH when worked upon a linen foundation. To work: Bring the thread from the back of the material, and pass it in a slanting direction over the space to be covered; put the needle in, in this slanting direction, and bring it out close to where the thread was brought up from the back. Continue these slanting stitches, keeping them all in the same direction.

Berlin Wool Work.—To make: Take the wool over four horizontal threads of canvas in a slanting direction, and over two upright threads. *See* BERLIN WORK.

Damassé.—A French term, applied to all cloths manufactured after the manner of damask, in every kind of material.

Dame Joan Ground.—This is a Filling used in Needlepoint lace, and also in Pillow lace, where sprigs and patterns are made upon the Pillow and connected together with a ground worked by hand. It is of hexagonal shape, with a double thread everywhere, and must be begun in a corner of the design, otherwise the pattern will work out in straight lines, and not in honeycombs. To work: Fasten No. 9 lace thread to the side of the lace, in a corner, and make a loose stitch nearly a quarter of an inch off. Examine Fig. 267 carefully, and two threads will be seen in it, one that runs up and one that comes down; the thread that is working is the latter. Insert the needle between these threads, and make a tight POINT DE BRUSSELS stitch on the first—that is, on the thread

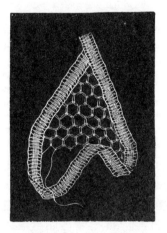

FIG. 267. DAME JOAN GROUND.

belonging to the loop just made; this makes the double thread on one side of the stitch. Fasten the thread firmly, and work back for this row. Continue the loops and the Point de Brussels stitch, until the space is filled in succeeding rows. For the return row: Make a DOUBLE POINT DE BRUSSELS stitch into the centre of each loop, and also over the tight stitches in the centre of each loop. Dame Joan Ground requires to be worked with great care and exactitude; every loop in it must be of the same length, and the Filling, when finished, lie flat upon the pattern, as the effect is spoilt if perfect uniformity is not maintained throughout.

Danish Embroidery.—This is an embroidery upon cambric, muslin, or batiste, and is suitable for handkerchief borders, necktie ends, and cap lappets. To work: Trace the design upon the material, then tack it to a brown paper foundation, and commence the stitches. These are partly Lace and partly Embroidery stitches. Work all the parts of the design that appear solid in Fig. 268 in thick SATIN STITCH, with a very fine line of

BUTTONHOLE round their edges, and thick OVERCAST lines to mark their various divisions, and make the WHEELS, STARS, and BARS, that fill open parts of the work as in MODERN POINT LACE. Surround the embroidery with a fine lace edging, and connect it with Bars.

FIG. 263. DANISH EMBROIDERY.

Another Kind.—A variety of the work only useful for filling in spaces left in Crochet, Tatting, and Embroidery. It consists of a variety of Lace stitches, worked upon Crochet or Tatting foundations, and is made as follows:

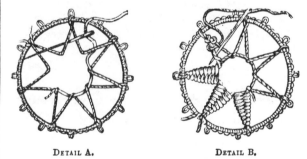

DETAIL A.   DETAIL B.

FIG. 269. DANISH EMBROIDERY.

Make a round of TATTING or of DOUBLE CROCHET, size of the space to be filled, and ornament its edge with PICOTS, tack this round upon Toile cirée, and fill it in with various lace stitches. These are shown in Fig. 269.

To work Fig. 269, Detail A: Fill a round of Tatting with seven long loops, which draw together at their base, to form an inner circle. Take the thread through them in the manner shown. Then run the thread up to where one of the loops commences, and darn it backwards and forwards, as in POINT DE REPRISE, to fill in the loop in the form of the Vandyke, shown in Detail B.

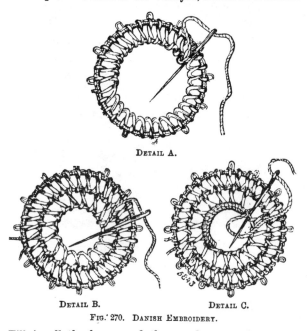

DETAIL A.

DETAIL B.   DETAIL C.

FIG. 270. DANISH EMBROIDERY.

Fill in all the loops, and then work seven short loops in the centre of the circle, and draw them together with a line looped in and out at their base, as shown in Fig. 269.

For Fig. 270, Detail A: Fill a Tatted round with thirty-two small interlaced loops, and draw together with a thread run through them at their base. Work sixteen

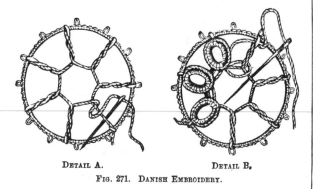

DETAIL A.   DETAIL B.

FIG. 271. DANISH EMBROIDERY.

interlaced loops into this thread (*see* Detail B), and draw the lower part of the sixteen loops together with a thread through their base. Finish the round by working a line of thick BUTTONHOLE stitches into the last thread (*see* Detail C).

To work Fig. 271, Detail A: Into a Tatted round make a WHEEL; form it of seven long loops interlaced as worked, thus: Fasten the thread into the Tatted round, and carry it as a loose thread to the seventh part of the round. Fasten it into the Tatting and return down

it, twist the cotton round the straight thread for three-quarters of the distance down. Then carry the thread to the next division of the round, and repeat until the Wheel is formed, twisting the thread round the first stitch made as a finish (*see* Detail A). To finish: Make an oval of each arm of the Wheel, and work it over with Button-hole stitch. Form the foundation of the oval with a thread, which pass through the top and bottom part of twisted thread (*see* Detail B), and work in the twisted thread as one side of the oval.

Darn.—A term generally used to signify the method employed for the reparation of any textile, whether of loom or hand manufacture, by substituting a web by means of a needle. This reparation is effected in various ways, viz., by the common Web darning, by Fine drawing, Cashmere twill, Damask darning, Grafting, Ladder filling, and Swiss darning. For the repairing of all linen textiles "Flourishing thread" should be used.

In the ordinary *Web darning* every alternate thread is taken up by the needle, and these runnings, when made in a sufficient number, crossed at right angles by similar runnings, thus producing a plain web or network. By this method a hole in the material may be refilled. The thread should not be drawn closely at any of the turnings, when running backwards and forwards, because it may shrink in the washing. The darn should be commenced and finished at all four sides at some distance from the beginning of the hole, a little beyond the worn or thin portion requiring to be strengthened. The toes and heels of socks and stockings, if not of extra thickness, should be darned one way, but not across the grain, when new; and the knees of children's stockings strengthened in the same way.

Cashmere Darning.—The method of replacing the web of any twilled material, such as Cashmere, is to employ the

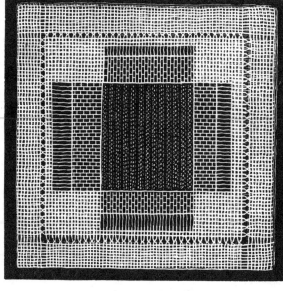

FIG. 272. CASHMERE DARN.

ravellings of the cloth itself; and having tacked the latter closely to the hole, on a piece of Toile cirée, begin as in ordinary darning, by running threads across the hole to form a warp. Then take up two threads and miss two; and in every succeeding row raise two together, one of the threads being taken up in the preceding row, and the other missed. This will produce the diagonal lines of the twill. The foundation must now be crossed on the same principle as the border darning, working from right to left. Our illustration, Fig. 272, is taken, like many others, from worked specimens produced in the Irish schools of needlework.

Corner-tear Darn.—The darning of a corner-shaped or triangular tear in any textile must be effected as illustrated, thus: Draw the edges together, having tacked the material all round the torn square to a piece of Toile cirée. Then darn backwards and forwards, the runnings extending double the length and width of the rent; and afterwards turn the work and repeat the process, until, as represented

fourth row—leave 3, take 3, leave 5, take 1 three times, leave 5, take 3, leave 3. Fifth row—leave 4, take 3, leave 3, take 1 three times, leave 3, take 3, leave 4. Sixth row—leave 5, take 3, leave 1, take 1, leave 5, take 1 twice, leave 5, take 3, leave 5. Seventh row—take 1, leave 5, take 3, leave 5, take 1 twice, leave 5, take 3, leave 5, take 1. Eighth row—leave 1, take 1, leave 5, take 3, leave 3, take 1, leave 5, take 1, leave 5, take 3, leave 5, take 1, leave 1. Ninth row — leave 2, take 1, leave 5, take 3, leave 5, take 1 twice, leave 1, take 3, leave 5, take 1, leave 2. Tenth row—leave 3, take 1, leave 5, take 3, leave 5, take 1, leave 5, take 3, leave 5, take 1, leave 3. Eleventh row—leave 4, take 1, leave 5, take 3, leave 5, take 1, leave 3, take 3, leave 5, take 1, leave 4. Twelfth row—take 1, leave 5 twice, take 3, leave 1, take 5, leave 3, take 1, leave 5 twice. Thirteenth row—take 1, leave 5 twice, take 3, leave

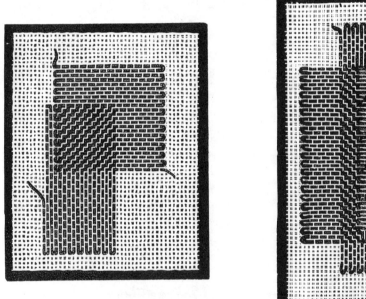

FIG. 273. CORNER-TEAR DARN.

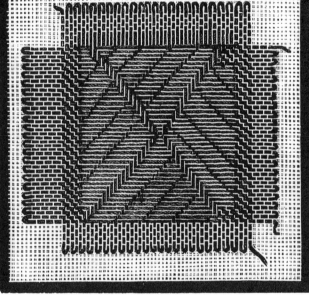

FIG. 274. DAMASK DARN.

in the wood-cut (Fig. 273), taken from a worked specimen, the former opening shall form two sides of a square of crossed darning.

Damask Darning needs close examination of the woven design to be restored by means of the needle and "Flourishing thread," and to supply directions for the reproduction of one design will be sufficient as a guide to the needlewoman to enable her to copy others, after the same method of darning. The pattern (Fig. 274), showing a St. Andrew's Cross, of which we have given an illustration, taken from a specimen of the work, may be reproduced in the following way: For the first row take 3, leave 5, take 1 four times successively, leave 5, take 3. Second row—leave 1, take 3, leave 3, take 1, leave 5 four times, take 3, leave 1. Third row—leave 2, take 3, leave 5, take 1 four times, leave 1, take 3, leave 2. For the

5, take 3, leave 5, take 1 twice. Fourteenth row—leave 1, take 1, leave 5, take 1, leave 5, take 3, leave 3, take 3, leave 5, take 1 twice, leave 1. Fifteenth row—leave 2, take 1, leave 5, take 1, leave 5, take 2, leave 1, take 1, leave 1, take 1, leave 1, take 2, leave 5, take 1 twice, leave 2. Sixteenth row—leave 3, take 1, leave 5, take 1 twice, leave 3, take 1, leave 5 twice, leave 3. Seventeenth row —leave 4, take 1, leave 5, take 1 twice, leave 1, take 1, leave 5, take 1 twice, leave 4. Eighteenth row—leave 5, take 1 five times, leave 5. The nineteenth row is a repetition of the seventeenth, and the twentieth of the sixteenth.

Filling a "Ladder," formed by a stitch being dropped in the stocking-web, should be effected thus: Insert in the stocking the DARNING BALL employed in darning, pass the eye of the needle from you upwards through the loop, which has slipped from its place, and run up; thus leaving a "ladder" or line of bars, as in Fig. 275. Insert

FIG. 275. LADDER IN STOCKING-WEB.

the needle between the first and second bars of the ladder, bringing it out through the loop, and under the first bar. The needle will thus have brought the first bar through

FIG. 276. SQUARE FOR INSERTION.

FIG. 277. GRAFTING KNITTING.

the loop, which is to be pulled sufficiently far through it to form a new one, through which the second bar is to be drawn after the same method. Be careful to avoid splitting any of the threads, and when you have filled the ladder, fasten off the end of the thread, as in grafting. A crochet needle or hook may prove a more convenient appliance than an ordinary needle for the purpose of filling a "ladder."

Fine Drawing is a method of darning cloth or stuff materials of a thick substance. A long fine needle, perhaps a straw needle, will be required, and the ravellings of the stuff employed when available. In the event of there being none, as in the case of cloth or baize, very fine sewing silk may be used to repair the latter, and the ravellings of Mohair braid for the former, the exact colour of the material being carefully matched. The runnings should not be taken quite through the cloth, but the needle should be run straight through the nap, so as to be quite concealed from view in the thickness of the stuff. Some

authorities in plain needlework direct that the loops made at each turn of the thread, at the ends of the runnings, should be cut; but it might be more secure to draw the needle out at the back, and to pass it through to the front again, for every fresh running, leaving the loops out of sight at the back. This style of darning is called in French a *Reprise perdue.* In former times the art of fine drawing was much cultivated, and brought to such extraordinary perfection in this country, that extensive frauds were practised on the Government, by sewing thus a heading of English cloth on a piece of foreign importation, and *vice versâ*, in such a dexterous manner that the union of the two edges and the threads that united them were not to be discerned. Thus the whole piece was nefariously passed off as being either home made, or foreign, so as to escape paying the duties imposed or the penalties due for infringement of the law. All fine drawings are supposed to

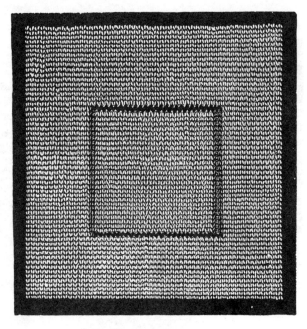

FIG. 278. GRAFT COMPLETED.

be indicated by the manufacturer by a piece of packthread tied to the selvedge, that the draper may allow for that blemish when he sells to the tailor.

Grafting.—This term signifies the insertion of a sound piece of stocking-web into a space from which an unsound piece has been cut out, and is illustrated in Figs. 276 and 277. Cut the unsound portion exactly with the thread, on either side, the long way of the web; and rip, by drawing the thread, which will at once run out, at top and bottom of the square to be filled. The piece for insertion should be prepared in a similar way. The square formed should correspond with the dimensions of the hole cut, only rather wider across, to allow for turning in the sides (Fig. 276). Hold the two parts to be joined in juxtaposition very firmly between the left hand thumb and forefinger, so that the rows of loops left in unravelling may stand out clearly, running from right to left, the thread having been secured on the wrong side, at the right hand

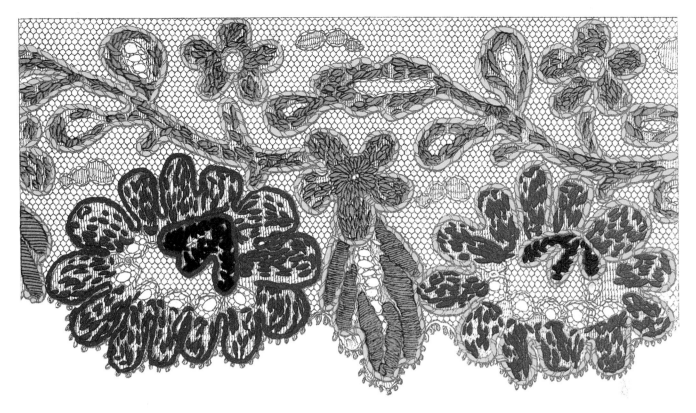

CRETE LACE.—IMITATION.

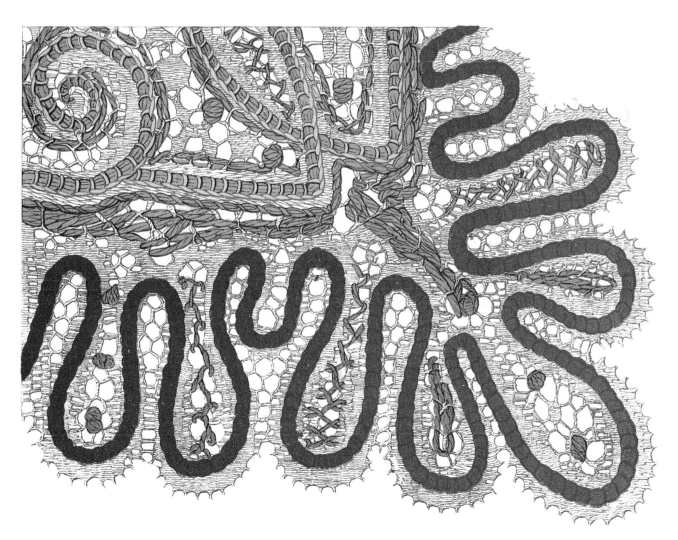

CYPRUS LACE.—IMITATION.

corner. Bring the needle through, and pass it through the first loop of the stocking, pointing the needle to the left, then through the first and second loops of the patch of web, drawing the thread gently so as not to disarrange the two rows of loops, then insert the needle again through the first loop of the stocking, only taking with it the second loop also; draw the thread gently again, then pass the needle through the second loop of the patch last taken up, take with it the loop next to it, and thus continue, so that, by this process, the separate pieces may be completely joined, as in Fig. 278.

Machine Darning must also be named, as a perfectly new idea, carried out by means of a "mending attachment," employed on a sewing machine. Rips, tears and holes in table linen, underclothing, or silk and cotton goods, men's clothing, and every description of article, may be effectually repaired, the rents, &c., at the same time being scarcely discernible, by an arrangement attached to the middle of the machine, while no skill is required in the needlewoman for its attachment or use. The repairs thus executed are not patchings, but *bonâ fide* darns.

Swiss Darning is the method of reproducing "stocking-web" by means of a darning needle and thread of yarn worked double. The warp must first be made with a single thread, as in plain darning, and, when formed, place a darning ball inside the stocking, and begin with the double thread at the left-hand side, securing it in the unbroken part of the stocking, at about four stitches from the hole

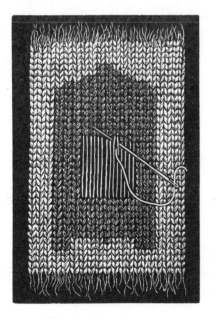

FIG. 279 SWISS DARNING.

to be filled. Run the needle through these stitches, as in plain darning, until the first thread of the warp is reached. Then insert it between the first and second threads of the warp, bringing it out under the first thread, then pass it between the second and third threads, bringing it out under the second, that is, between the first and second, and proceed to insert it between the third and fourth, bringing it out under the third. Continue thus until the

last thread of the warp is crossed, always pointing the needle towards the left hand. As soon as the last thread is crossed, plain darn a few stitches into the stocking, then turn the needle, and darn back again to the hole, the threads being kept as closely together as possible, and a loop left at each turning, to allow for contraction in washing. Cross the threads of the warp from right to left in the same way as at first. *See* Fig. 279.

Darned Crochet.—Make the foundation of this work of SQUARE CROCHET, upon which work a pattern in soft netting cotton. DARN the netting cotton in and out of the Crochet so as to form a design. The patterns are the same as used for Crochet. *See* CROCHET DARNING.

Darned Embroidery.—An art needlework, practised in Europe during the sixteenth and two following centuries, but originally of Oriental origin, and still worked in India, the natives of that country executing, without a pattern, upon almost any material, elaborate designs formed of Darned lines. The Darned Embroidery most practised in Europe has been chiefly worked upon cotton, linen, and other washing materials, and is well fitted for the wear and tear such articles are exposed to. The patterns used in the earlier centuries are diaper arrangements as backgrounds to more important work, and these diaper patterns are much the same as the designs found in the missal painting of the same period; but in the seventeenth century Darned Embroidery received a greater impetus from the East, and was made in intricate designs and carried over the whole material. Some elaborate specimens of English, Italian, and Indo-Portuguese work of this date are still extant, and should be objects of study to anyone seeking to bring the work again to perfection. In one, upon a curtain of white linen, a pattern of yellow silk is executed in Darned lines, representing in compartments a fleet in full sail; while upon another, on a red cotton ground, darned with red silk, are hunting groups, in which elephants, lions, and various wild animals are chased by Indian officers, who are mounted upon horses and elephants. The Darned lines in these designs partially filling in the figures are run so as to take the direction of the limbs and clothes of the object, and are so beautifully curved and arranged as to give all the appearance of shading. Small portions of the design, such as saddlecloths, are enriched with very minute diaper patterns, while the manes of lions are arranged as curls, made with a number of Knots, and the bodies of leopards and stags spotted with the same. During the reign of Queen Anne, Darned Embroidery returned to its earlier patterns, and it is this kind that is now attracting attention. The eighteenth century patterns are all of large conventional flowers, worked in outlines, with their backgrounds run with horizontal lines, as shown in Fig. 280, p. 146. The effect of this partially filled in groundwork is most artistic, softening, as it does, the embroidery into the material, and throwing up the pattern with a boldness hardly conceivable from such simple means. The Darned lines are generally run parallel to each other, in one given direction; but this rule is not absolute, and much variety is gained by altering the direction of lines and introducing fancy stitches. The following are the best known Darned Backgrounds;

U

Point minuscule a darned line, one thread taken and one left, and both sides of the material alike; *Point sans evers*, a Cross Stitch surrounded with four stitches inclosing it in a square, or a number of Cross Stitches—in both varieties the back and front of the stitch alike; *Point de Carreau* and *Point Droit*, lines forming a design, both sides being alike; *Point de Rosette*, or *Point d'Etoile*, isolated stars, worked so that both sides are alike.

To imitate Indian work, the lines are curved, either making complete circles or flowing along in rising and falling waves.

It will be understood that a clearly woven background is a great assistance to Darned Embroidery, but other materials can be made to conform to the design.

The colours for this Embroidery are few and harmonious. They are selected to contrast without being

FIG. 280. DARNED EMBROIDERY.

Combinations of stitches make good background designs. Thus, a number of waved and run lines filling the space and crossed by horizontal run lines; stitches dividing the background into a number of small squares, with stars worked in the alternate square; Vandyke lines, made with Chain Stitch, alternating with Holbein Stitch.

To work these fancy stitches, *see* EMBROIDERY STITCHES.

in violent opposition—that is to say, if Yellow and Blue are chosen for the same embroidery, the tint of the Yellow should be what is called a Blue Yellow, and the tint of the Blue a Yellow Blue. Pink, if selected, choose of a Yellow shade, and not a Blue Pink; and when using Crimson or Green, the Crimson should shade to Yellow, not to Blue, and the Green to Yellow, not to Blue. The best combinations are dull Yellow with dull

Pink and Green. Blues are better used by themselves than with other colours. Yellows, when used alone, should shade into chestnut.

The materials now used for Darned Embroidery are unbleached cottons and linens, Huckaback towellings, Java canvas, and twilled and diaper linens. The old work was done upon Indian cloth; but, as long as the material chosen is woven with distinct and straight threads, any kind is suitable. The work is executed with Vegetable and Raw silks and fine Crewels. Vegetable silk is the best for small pieces of work, but large curtain borders, &c., require Crewels, the time and labour

flowers with a double line of CREWEL STITCH, using dull crimson silk. Fill the centres of the flowers with SATIN STITCH, worked in a medium shade of crimson. The same pattern can be used with a different ground, thus: Darn lines at even distances in a parallel direction, and intersect them with similar lines that cross them, and so form open diamonds. Fill the centre of each diamond with a FRENCH KNOT. Another ground: Make similar lines upon the foundation, and, wherever they cross each other, work thick pointed stars. Another ground: Run a diagonal, but straight line, then a line of French Knots only, and repeat these lines alternately over the whole of

FIG. 281. DARNED MUSLIN.

spent over a pattern being doubled when silk is used instead of worsted. To work: Trace the design upon the material with tracing paper and tracing cloth, and then embroider the background lines. Work up and down the pattern; take up only a small portion of the material in the needle, and make the design evenly.

When the ground is finished, outline the pattern in Crewel Stitch, and work two rows of Crewel Stitch, if the pattern is bold and requires to be outlined with a broad line.

The pattern of Darned Embroidery shown in Fig. 280 is worked thus: Trace out the design, DARN in the background lines with yellow pink silk, and work the outline of the

the background. Another ground: Work a series of parallel Vandykes across the material, and work seven lines of one shade of colour, and seven of another, alternately. Another ground: Form circles upon the background, all of an equal size, and fill these either with lines arranged as lessening circles, or with curved lines radiating from the centre like the spokes of a wheel.

Darned Laces.—The Darned Laces are amongst the oldest of all lacework, and the term is a general one to denote Embroidery upon a Netted ground. The various laces so made are described under FILET BRODÉ, GUIPURE D'ART, and SPIDER WORK.

Darned Muslin.—An easy and effective kind of fancy

work, used for ornamenting white muslin dresses, aprons, or for antimacassars. It consists of working with fine darning cotton in floral patterns upon good, clear white muslin, and is illustrated in Fig. 281. To work that design: Draw out the pattern upon pink or white calico, back this with brown paper to stiffen it, and tack the muslin on to it. Commence with the stems, branching sprays, and tendrils. Work them up and down as in ordinary DARNING until of sufficient thickness, then work the leaves. Begin each leaf close to the stem, and work a series of HERRINGBONE; take up but little of the muslin, and increase and decrease the length of the stitches according to pattern. The point of the leaf being reached, HEM STITCH back to the stem, work up the centre of leaf, and secure the loops made with the Herringbone. Work the berries in SATIN STITCH, and Darn the little points and connecting lines. The work should be very neat; some people turn it when finished, in order that the herringbone stitches may show through the muslin; but this is entirely a matter of taste. When soiled, have the work cleaned, not washed.

Darned Net.—A very effective and fashionable imitation of lace, and used for all kinds of dress trimmings, and for table and cushion borders. It can be worked with fine lace thread, with coloured purse silks, or with floss and filoselles, either upon white, coloured, or black nets. Darned net is carried to great perfection in the lace that is known as Imitation Brussels Lace, and a very great variety of

FIG. 282. DARNED NET.

stitches can be formed if GUIPURE D'ART and MODERN POINT LACE STITCHES are taken as guides. When used as trimmings to ball dresses, black net is usually selected for the foundation, and the embroidery worked in bright-coloured floss or filoselle. The designs for Darning upon net are extremely varied, those that are suitable for embroidery in SATIN STITCH being the best; but simple

geometrical designs, such as a series of vandykes, crosses, diamonds, or spots, are also used. The embroidery is done in Satin Stitch or in plain Darning. To work Fig. 282: Trace the design upon pink calico, tack the net down with the honeycombs in straight lines, with its wrong side uppermost upon the calico, and thread a long lace needle with the Embroidery cotton or silk. Fill in all the centres of the leaves or flowers, by Darning the silk in and out of the honeycombs in the various directions shown in illustration, and work the spots over the net. Thread the needle with another coloured silk, and double it, and Darn this doubled silk as an outline all round the outer edge of the leaves and flowers, and form the stems and sprays with it. The double thread is run in and out of the net as in plain Darning. Join and fasten off the silk on the upper side of the net, the right side of the work being underneath. Unpick and turn the work, and finish the edge of the lace with a series of scallops made in BUTTONHOLE STITCH.

Fig. 283 is intended for a border. The net is laid upon a background, but a traced pattern is not necessary. Work the design with six slanting upward and downward SATIN STITCHES, the commencement and end of the stitches forming straight lines up the net. Pass each stitch over

FIG. 283. BORDER IN DARNED NET.

three honeycombs, and put the silk into the first and fifth honeycomb. Commence the next line of stitches in the honeycombs the first line finished in, and work this line either upward or downward, but slanting in a contrary direction to the last.

Fig. 284 is formed with a series of Diamond-shaped Satin stitches. To form a diamond: Loop the silk through two honeycombs for the first stitch, over three, five, and seven honeycombs for the three next, and then decrease by

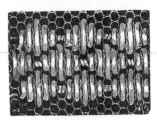

FIG. 284. BORDER IN DARNED NET.

reversing the stitches thus—five, three, and two. Continue to work in this way down the net for its length, and then commence another row. Work the centre stitch over seven honeycombs of these Diamonds beneath the first stitch of the previous row. Work to the end of the net, and work a third row of Diamonds like the first.

Figs. 285 and 286 are fillings for the centre of any designs that are not worked in Satin or Darning stitch. Fig. 285 is given in its natural size, and upon net the size it should be placed upon. In Fig. 286 the stitch and net are enlarged to more plainly show the manner of working. Run a fine lace thread in curves over three lines of honeycomb, pass entirely over the centre line, and loop the curves at

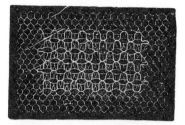

FIG. 285. FILLINGS IN DARNED NET.

even distances into the first and third lines. In the second line, run the thread through the same honeycomb as the top curve of the first line, and continue running these curved

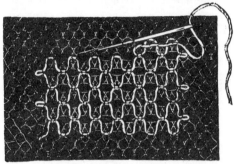

FIG. 286. FILLINGS IN DARNED NET.

lines backward and forward, until the space is filled. The little loop upon the ends of the lines shows how the thread is carried from one line to the other in an ornamental manner, without any join. This loop corresponds to the curve on the lines.

Fig. 287 is a pattern for embroidering coarse nets in imitation of Darned Netting or Filet Brodé. To work: DARN the thick lines up and down in POINT DE REPRISE

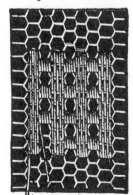

FIG. 287. PATTERN IN DARNED NET.

or plain Darning stitch, and leave every alternate honeycomb plain: work in OVERCAST STITCH, and run the thread into the thick line to carry it down, without showing, to the next honeycomb that is to be Overcast.

Fig. 288 is another pattern to be worked upon coarse net. The Embroidery for this design is worked with purse silks of different shades of colour. To work: Leave the centre honeycomb line unworked; upon each side of it work in

OVERCAST one honeycomb, miss two honeycombs, pass the silk over these, and work the third in Overcast, continue to the end of the row, pass the silk alternately over the

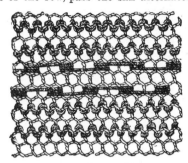

FIG. 288. DARNED NET.

upper and lower part of the honeycomb line. (*See* Fig. 287.) The lines upon each sides of these two centre lines work as DARNED lines, and catch the silk alternately over and through every honeycomb upon the line.

Darned Netting.—This work is an imitation of the ancient Point Conté, Spider Work, or Darned Laces, and consists of a plain netted foundation, upon which a pattern is worked in a stitch known as POINT DE REPRISE in GUIPURE D'ART, but which is simply plain DARNING. It is much used for making summer curtains, window blinds, and other washing articles, as it is very durable, and, when a suitable pattern is selected, extremely handsome. It is worked either with ingrain cottons, raw silk, or plain darning cotton. The netted foundation is either coloured or plain. To work: Commence the Netted foundation with one loop or mesh, and increase one stitch in every row until the desired width is obtained. To form a square article, decrease a stitch every row until one loop only is left, but for a pattern that is longer than its width, such as are required for curtains or window blinds, NET a certain number of plain rows and then decrease. Slightly starch the Netted foundation, and pull it out to its proper shape, pinning it upon a board until dry. Upon this foundation work the pattern. Take this either from a Cross stitch Berlin Work pattern or a square and open Crochet design. Thread a coarse darning needle with soft knitting cotton, and fill in the meshes, counting each mesh as a square in the Crochet or a stitch in the Berlin pattern. Work from left to right, and Darn in and out of the meshes four threads of cotton, two going one way and two the other. Work the stitches as continuous lines where possible, pass the cotton up and down until the meshes are filled, and then commence the next line. Always commence on the line that contains the smallest number of stitches, and work the lines with the greatest number of stitches second, as, unless this rule is attended to, the cotton passing from one line to another will be visible. Work detached stitches by themselves, fasten off, and commence them in the stitch. Make a WEAVER'S KNOT, and Darn the ends in when fresh cotton is required, fasten off, and commence by running the cotton at back of work, and not with a knot.

Darners.—Long needles, with considerably elongated eyes, somewhat like the long eye in a bodkin, intended to receive the coarse, loosely-twisted strands of darning yarn, either of wool or cotton. They are to be had in various sizes. They are sold, like all other needles, in papers containing a quarter, half, or a hundred needles. They may also be purchased separately.

Darning Balls.—Egg-shaped balls, made of hard wood, ivory, cocoanut shells, and glass, and employed as a substitute for the hand in the darning of stockings. Instead of inserting the hand into the foot of the stocking, and drawing the latter up the arm, one of these balls is dropped into the foot, and the worn part of the web is drawn closely over it; and, being firm, smooth, and rounded, it forms a better foundation than the hand to work upon. Sometimes these balls are hollow, and can be unscrewed in the middle, the darning cotton being kept inside.

Dart.—A term employed in needlework, denoting the two short seams made on each side of the front of a bodice, whence small gores have been cut, making the slope requisite to cause the dress to sit in closely under the bust. These should be firmly stitched on the inside, sufficient edge being left to allow for letting out the waist part of the bodice if required. If the bodice be turned inside out, during the fitting upon the figure, the darts will be the better adjusted.

Dé.—The French word for a thimble.

Decorative Darning.—A general term, including DARNED CROCHET, DARNED EMBROIDERY, DARNED NET, and DARNED NETTING.

Decorative Needlework.—This name includes, under one head, all needlework that is intended as an ornament, and is not a necessity upon the article that is being made.

Decrease.—A word used in Crochet, Knitting, Netting, Tatting, and Pillow Lace, to intimate where parts of the pattern are to be diminished. To decrease in Crochet: Work two stitches as one, or pass over one foundation stitch without counting it. To decrease in Knitting: Knit two stitches together as one. To decrease in Netting: Net two stitches together as one. To decrease in Tatting: Work a fewer number of stitches in a given space. To decrease in Lace: Plait the threads closer together for narrow parts, but, where a marked difference in the widths is required, tie the Bobbins together in pairs and cut them off.

De Laine.—A common abbreviation for Mousseline de Laine, a thin woollen fabric, but sometimes of a mixed material. *See* MOUSSELINE DE LAINE.

Delhi Work.—An Indian Embroidery, so named from the work being done chiefly in the neighbourhood of Delhi. It is an embroidery in CHAIN and SATIN STITCH, worked in silks and gold and silver threads, upon satin and other materials. The patterns are extremely rich, the ground being in many places entirely concealed with various coloured silks, while gold and silver thread are profusely worked into the material. *See* INDIAN EMBROIDERY.

Demyostage.—A description of Taminy, or woollen cloth, formerly used in Scotland, but now superseded, or known under a different name. (*See* TAMINY.) The name Demyostage appears to indicate that the textile was only partially stiffened with dressing.

Denmark Satin.—A kind of worsted stuff employed in the making of women's shoes, measuring 27 inches in width.

Dentelé.—The French term denoting that a border is scalloped.

Dentelle.—The French word for lace. Laces were known by this name in the latter part of the sixteenth century; before that time they were known as PASSEMENT.

Dentelle à la Reine.—The name given to a Needlepoint lace manufactured for a short period in Amsterdam, by French refugees, after the revocation of the Edict of Nantes, 1685. The lace was not peculiar to this particular band of workers, having been made in France before that time, but it gained a certain popularity during the short time it was made in Holland.

Dentelle à la Vierge.—A double-grounded Normandy lace, made at Dieppe, and so named by the peasants. *See* DIEPPE POINT.

Dentelle au fuseau.—One of the ancient names for Pillow lace.

Dentelle de fil.—A name by which simple patterned Thread laces are known.

Dentelle de Moresse.—A coarse, geometrical pattern lace, made in the sixteenth century in Morocco, the art of making which was acquired either from the Spaniards or the Maltese. It is no longer manufactured, but may still be bought at Tetuan.

Dentelle des Indes.—A name sometimes applied to Drawn Work. A machine-made Yak lace, made in the Jacquard looms at Lyons, is also called Dentelle des Indes.

Dentelle Irlandaise.—The name by which Modern Point lace is known in France. *See* MODERN POINT LACE.

Dentelle Nette.—A coarse net having a lace pattern, employed for window blinds, and for walls at the back of washstands. It may be had both in écru or coffee colour, as well as in white; both descriptions are made from 1½ yards to 2 yards in width.

Dentelle Volants.—A term for lace in relief, whether made upon the pillow or by hand.

Dents.—A French term employed to denote either pointed or square scallops, cut as a decorative bordering to a flounce or frill of a dress.

Derries.—A description of coloured woven cotton cloths, manufactured in blue and brown, and employed for women's dresses. It measures 34 inches in width.

Design.—Since the revival of taste in the matter of Embroidery, great attention has been paid to the pattern or Design of the work, and various rules have been laid down as to what constitutes a good Design; the following are the most important: Patterns of needlework should be drawn with reference to the articles they will ornament, and neither in form nor colour attract attention from the main harmony of the room they help to decorate. Simplicity of pattern, breadth of tone, and harmonious colouring, are all essentials to a good pattern, while great contrasts between light and shade, loudness of colour, and marked peculiarity, are to be deprecated. Natural objects, when imitated, except in very fine Church Ecclesiastical embroidery, or fine silk work, are not shaded to throw those objects up in relief from their ground, as in picture painting, but are conventionalised, and depicted as lying flat upon a flat ground, as in wall painting.

Devonia Ground.—A ground used in Duchesse lace, and as a variety when making Honiton lace. It is worked as follows: Hang on four pairs of Bobbins at the place

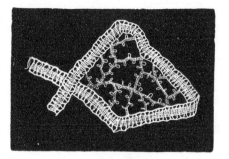

FIG. 289. DEVONIA GROUND.

where a line is to be commenced (*See* Fig. 289), and, to avoid pulling the lace while working, stick a pin on each side of the hole to be sewn to, and several in the lace already formed. First row—work STEM STITCH thus: Give three twists to the outside pair of bobbins, and put them aside, and with the next pair work across until the last pair are reached, then make a stitch and a half, or TURN STITCH, on the left side, thus: Work a CLOTH or WHOLE STITCH, give each pair of bobbins one twist to the left, put the middle left-hand bobbin over the middle right bobbin, lift the two pairs with each hand, and give a pull to make the inner edge firm, and put aside the inner pair of bobbins. Second row—work back with the other, making a PURL on the right side, thus: Twist the worker bobbins seven times to the left, lift one of them in the left hand, take a pin in the right hand, and place it under the thread, give a twist to bring the thread round the pin, stick it, lay down the bobbin, and pass the other one round the pin from the lower or nearest side, twist once, and make a Cloth stitch. Third row—work to the Turn stitch, left side. Fourth row—make a Turn stitch

to the right. Fifth row—make a Purl to the left, which differs from the right Purl, thus: In the right Purl the loop is formed by placing the pin under the thread, and carrying the other thread round the pin after it is stuck from the lower side, moving the thread first to the right. In the left Purl, place the pin upon the thread, and bring the bobbin over it with the left hand, then stick the pin, and bring the other bobbin round the pin from the lower side, moving first to the left. Sixth row—turn stitch to the right. Seventh row—turn stitch to the left. Eighth row—purl to the right. A Purl is made every third row on alternate sides. The more irregularly the lines are arranged the better, and when a fresh one is made to start from some part of the line being worked, hang on four pairs of Bobbins at that place before doing the Purl stitch, and leave them there until the original line is finished. Three or four sets of Bobbins may be left behind in this manner, and afterwards carried on in different directions. Where a line is crossed make a SEWING, and commence, where possible, with a ROPE Sewing. Fasten off with great care.

Devonshire Lace.—At one time the bulk of the female population of Devonshire was engaged in lace making, and many were the varieties produced in that county, all which, with the exception of the celebrated Honiton, were copies of Belgium, French, and Spanish laces. A

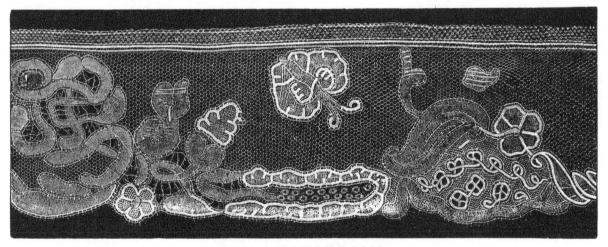

FIG. 290. DEVONSHIRE LACE.

coarse kind of Bone lace was made prior to the sixteenth century, at which period the immigration of the Flemish and French Protestant lace makers to England improved the manufacture, while in the seventeenth century a certain John Rodge, of Honiton, discovered the secret of working the fine stitches used in Brussels and Flemish Lace. Fine flax thread and Flemish patterns were introduced, and the lace made from these during the sixteenth and seventeenth centuries was so beautiful as to rival the far-famed Brussels lace. Fig. 290 is a specimen of this work, the pattern being decidedly Flemish, although the lace is Devonshire make. Besides this description of lace, Venetian and Spanish Needle-point, Maltese, Greek, and Genoese laces have been successfully imitated by these workers. For the last hundred years the lace makers

have chiefly turned their attention to the making of
Honiton lace, but during the French war the making of
Devonshire Trolly lace, copied from Normandy lace, was
successfully carried on. Honiton Lace is now the chief
lace made, but since the revival of interest in this
English manufacture, Spanish, Italian Guipure, and Venetian Point Laces are worked.

Diagonal Cloth.—A soft, woollen, twilled material,
made in various colours, without any pattern. It
measures 52 inches in width, and is much employed for
purposes of decorative embroidery.

Diagonal Couching.—A flat Couching, and one of
the numerous varieties of that stitch. It is chiefly employed in Church Work. To make: Lay lines of floss
silk flat upon the foundation, and close together, and to
secure them in position bring up a thread of silk through
the foundation, pass it over one or two strands of floss
silk, and return it to the back of the foundation material.
Arrange the direction of these securing stitches so that
they form diagonal lines across the floss silk. A variety
of Diagonal Couching is formed thus: Over the floss silk
foundation lay a line of purse silk or gold twist in a
diagonal direction, and catch this down with the securing
stitch, brought from the back of the material as before
described; continue to lay down diagonal lines of purse
silk, keeping them at an even distance from each other
until the floss silk is covered.

Diamond Couching.—One of the Flat Couchings used
in Church Work, illustrated in Fig. 291, and worked
as follows: Lay down lines of floss silk upon a flat foundation, and above them single threads of purse silk or gold
twist, at equal distances apart, and in a diagonal direction.
Lay each line singly, and secure it with a thread brought

FIG. 291. DIAMOND COUCHING.

from the back of the material and returned there. The
lines running in one direction first lay and secure, then
cross them with lines laid in an opposite direction, so as
to form, with the ones already secured, a number of
diamonds; catch these down to the material in the
manner already described, and ornament the points of
the diamonds with a bead, pearl, or spangle.

Diamond Holes.—The Fillings in the centre of
Honiton lace sprigs are made in various fancy stitches,
the various arrangements of open squares or holes which
form Diamond Holes, Straight Rows, Chequer stitch,
being some of the most used. To form Diamond Holes:
Hang on twelve pairs of Bobbins, and work across from
left to right in CLOTH STITCH six times, putting up the
pins on each side. in holes pricked for them, then divide
the bobbins into two equal numbers, and put a pin in the

centre. Take up left-hand bobbins, and work Cloth stitch
with six pairs up to pin in the centre, work back to the
left without twisting or putting up pin with the same six
pairs, twist and put up a pin, and leave bobbins hanging,
take up those on right hand; put up a pin and work right
across the whole twelve bobbins to the left hand, and so
enclose the centre pin. Work a couple of Cloth stitch
rows, and then make a hole upon each side, dividing the
bobbins into fours, and working the two sides as mentioned above. Plait the four bobbins under the upper
hole in Cloth stitch, work two Cloth stitch rows with the
twelve bobbins, and make a hole in the centre under the
one first made.

Diamond Lace.—A stitch either worked as open or
close Diamonds, and used in Modern Point and in Ancient
Needle-points. In the first row, for making the open
diamond, work 6 thick BUTTONHOLE stitches, leave the
space of two open, work 14 Buttonhole, leave the space of
two open, work 6 Buttonhole. Second row—work 4
Buttonhole, leave the space of two open, work 2 Buttonhole, leave the space of two open, work 10 Buttonhole,
leave the space of two open, work 2 Buttonhole, leave the
space of two open, and work 4 Buttonhole. Third row—
work 2 Buttonhole, leave the space of two open, work 2
Buttonhole, leave the space of two open, work 2 Buttonhole,
leave the space of two open, work 8 Buttonhole, leave the
space of two open, work 2 Buttonhole, leave the
space of two open, work 2 Buttonhole. Fourth row—
work 4 Buttonhole, leave the space of two open, work 2
Buttonhole, leave the space of two open, work 10 Buttonhole, leave the space of two open, work 2 Buttonhole,
leave the space of two open, work 4 Buttonhole. Fifth
row—work 6 Buttonhole, leave the space of two open,
work 14 Buttonhole, leave the space of two open, and
work 6 Buttonhole. Sixth row—work 19 Buttonhole,
leave the space of two open, and work 19 Buttonhole.
Seventh row—work 17 Buttonhole, leave the space of
two open, work 2 Buttonhole, leave the space of two
open, and work 17 Buttonhole. Eighth row — work
15 Buttonhole, leave the space of two open, work 2
Buttonhole, leave the space of two open, work 2 Buttonhole, leave the space of two open, and work 15 Buttonhole. Ninth row—work 17 Buttonhole, leave the space of
two open, work 2 Buttonhole, leave the space of two open,
and work 17 Buttonhole. Tenth row—work 19 Buttonhole, leave the space of two open, and work 19 Buttonhole. Repeat, and work the ten rows in the same order
to end of the space.

Diamond Linen.—This is also known as Diaper, and
the name includes several varieties of the latter, such as
Bird's-eye, Fish-eye, and Russian Diaper. *See* DIAPER.

Diamond Netting.—*See* NETTING.

Diamonds.—A stitch used in Macramé lace to vary
the design. It consists of MACRAMÉ KNOTS made over
slanted threads, that are called LEADERS. There are three
ways of making Diamonds: The *Single*, which is composed
of a single Leader from right and left hand, slanting outwards to a certain distance, and then returning to the
centre to form a Diamond. The *Double*, made with
a greater number of threads, and with two Leaders on

each side; and the *Treble*, with more threads, and with three Leaders on each side. *To Work a Single Diamond*: Take twelve threads and divide them, make the seventh thread into a Leader, and slant it down from left to right in an angle; make a Macramé Knot upon it with the eighth thread, then with the ninth, and so on to the twelfth. Pin it down to the PILLOW, and pick up the sixth thread. Turn this over the first threads from left to right, in a reverse direction to the other Leader, and make Macramé Knots upon it; commence with the fifth thread, and work all up. Pin it to the Pillow, and slant it back in a diamond shape to the centre. Use the same thread as Leader, and work Macramé Knots upon it with the others in their order; then take the Leader left at the right hand, slant it to the centre, and work it over with Macramé Knots; when the two Leaders meet tie them together. *To Work a Double Diamond*: Double the amount of threads, so that there are twelve upon each side, and make two Leaders on each side. With twelve threads on each side, the two right-hand Leaders will be the first and second threads of the second set of twelve; commence by knotting the threads round the second thread first, and then knot them round the first. The two threads for Leaders on the left hand are the eleventh and twelfth of the first twelve threads, counting from left to right. Work the eleventh as a Leader first, and knot upon it all the other threads, then knot them all upon the twelfth. *To Work a Treble Diamond*, sixteen threads and three Leaders upon each side are necessary. The Leaders are the first three on the right hand and the last three on the left hand, and the work is similar to that in the other Diamonds.

Diaper.—A term originally denoting a rich material decorated with raised embroidery. It is now generally employed to denote figured linen cloth, the design being very small, and generally diamond-shaped. It is also used to signify a towel:

> Let one attend him with a silver basin,
> Another bear the ewer, the third a diaper.
> —*Shakespeare.*

Diaper is a damask linen, manufactured in Ireland and Scotland; there is a kind called Union, composed of linen and cotton. There are also cotton ones, including Russia Diaper. The finest linen Diapers, with the smallest Diamond, Fish, or Bird's-eye patterns, are chiefly used for infants' pinafores, and other articles of their dress. The name of this material is derived from that of the city in Flanders where the manufacture originated being formerly called *d'ipre*—or, Ypres. The Birds'-eye may be had in either linen or cotton, the former measuring from 34 inches to 44 inches in width, the latter 34 inches; Pheasant-eye or Fish-eye measures from 36 inches to 44 inches in width. Russia linen Diaper may be had in four varieties — the cream-coloured at 21 inches, the half-bleached Irish at 24 inches, the Basket-pattern (Barnsley) at 26 inches, and the Fancy Barnsley (which is an extra heavy cloth) at 32 inches in width.

Diaper Couching.—A variety of Couching used in Church work, and made as follows: Lay down upon a flat foundation, even and close together lines of floss silk.

Secure these by bringing a thread of purse silk from the back of the material, pass it over two, three, or four strands of floss silk to form a succession of CROSSES, Diamonds, or other Diaper patterns, and return to back of material.

Diaphane.—A woven silk stuff, having transparent coloured figures, and for some years past out of use, and scarcely to be procured.

Dice Holes.—This is a stitch, shown in Fig. 292, used in Honiton and other Pillow-made lace, as a Filling

FIG. 292. DICE HOLES.

or a straight BRAID. The manner of working it is fully explained in Braids, as it is easier to learn to make it as a Braid than a Filling. *See* BRAIDS.

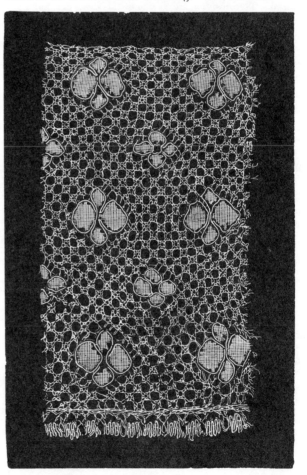

FIG. 293. DIEPPE POINT—DENTELLE À LA VIERGE.

Dieppe Point.—The two centres of the Normandy lace trade are Dieppe and Havre, and the manufacture in both towns is very ancient, dating back to before the introduction into France of Alençon. Normandy laces are among those enumerated in the "Revolt des Passemens," a poem written upon a protest made to Colbert by the original lace workers against the manufacture of Alençon. Brussels, Mechlin, Point de Paris, and Valenciennes were all made during the seventeenth and eighteenth centuries in Normandy, but the true Dieppe Point was a kind of Valenciennes, made with three instead of four threads, which received many local names, the narrow make being known as Ave Maria and Poussin, the wider and double-grounded as Dentelle à la Vierge, of which Fig. 293, p. 153, is a specimen. The laces of Havre were considered superior to those of Dieppe, but the manufacture of both was nearly destroyed at the time of the Revolution; and though the Dieppe lace manufactures were restored in 1820, and afterwards encouraged by Napoleon III., the trade has almost disappeared, owing to the cheap machine laces.

Dimity.—A cotton fabric, originally imported from Damietta, the Dimyat of the Arabs. It is made both striped and cross-barred, plain and twilled, and is stout in texture, being made of double thread, with the pattern raised. The designs are various, and some are not only embossed, but printed. This fabric is employed for bedroom hangings and furniture, for other articles, and was in old times utilised for women's petticoats. It is made in two widths, 27 inches and 32 inches.

Dimity Binding.—This is also called Bed Lace, and is a kind of Galloon, having plain edges, and a pattern raised in the weaving down the centre of the braid. It may also be had twilled and in diamond patterns. It is sold by the gross, in two pieces, of 72 yards each.

Distaff.—An implement formerly employed in spinning flax, tow, or wool. It consisted of a staff, round which the yarn was wound; in early times it was held under the arm of the spinster, and subsequently placed upright in a stand before her. The distaff was introduced into England, by the Italians, in the fifteenth century.

Doeskin Cloth.—This cloth is distinguished by having a smooth dressing on the upper surface. It is made of different qualities in thickness and colour, and employed for clerical garments and riding trousers. The single-milled doeskins measure from 27 inches to 29 inches in width.

Doeskin Leather.—This leather, being softer and more pliant than buckskin, is employed for riding and driving gloves. It is thick, durable, and, being dressed in a particular manner, washes well. The seat of the manufacture of doeskin gloves is at Woodstock, Oxon.

Doeskins.—These woollen stuffs are classed among NARROW CLOTHS, and so distinguished from BROAD CLOTHS (which see).

Domett.—A plain cloth, of open make, of which the warp is of cotton and the weft of wool. It is a description of Baize, and resembles a kind of white flannel made in Germany. It is manufactured both in white and black, the former of 28 inches in width, the latter of 36 inches, and there are 46 yards in the piece. Both kinds are used as lining materials in articles of dress, and in America to line coffin caskets.

Dornick.—This is also written *Darnex* and *Dornek*. A stout Damask linen, made at Tournay, or Doornik, or Dorneck, in Flanders, for hangings, as well as for table linen.

Dornock.—Also known as *Dorrock*. A coarse linen cloth, closely resembling Diaper, decorated with a pattern of checkers in the weaving. It is made for household purposes, and chiefly for table cloths. It takes its name from the town, in Sutherlandshire, on the Firth of Dornock, where it is manufactured. It is also made at Norwich; the weaving of "Dornick" was a pageant paraded before Queen Elizabeth on her visit to that city.

Dorsetshire Lace.—From the time of Charles II. to the middle of the eighteenth century Dorsetshire was celebrated both for its Bone and Point laces, which were considered the best productions of the English market, and were not inferior to the laces of Flanders. Blandford, Sherborne, and Lyme Regis were the towns that produced the best kinds. No specimens of the lace seem to have been preserved, but it is believed to have been a kind of Point d'Argentan. After the trade declined, no lace seems to have been made in Dorsetshire, but at the present time, along the coast, and at Lyme Regis, Honiton lace sprigs are manufactured.

Dorsour.—A species of cloth, made in Scotland, expressly for the wall-hangings of halls or chapels, to supply the place of Tapestry. The name is probably a corruption of Dorsal, derived from the Latin *Dorsum*, the back. These hangings were probably placed behind the altar or the seats, or employed as *portières*, to preserve the people from draughts behind them at the entrance doors.

Dot.—An Embroidery stitch used in all kinds of fancy work, and known as Point de Pois, and Point d'Or. To make: OUTLINE a small round, and OVERCAST it. Work in the stitches all one way, and fill up the round space with them.

Dotted Stitch.—DOT is the right term.

Double Bar.—A stitch used in the making of Macramé lace. To work: Work with three or four strands of thread, according to the thickness of the BAR required, and tie these together with a succession of MACRAMÉ KNOTS.

Double Coral Stitch.—An Embroidery stitch much used in Ticking Work and for ornamenting linen. It is composed of a straight centre line, with long BUTTONHOLE stitches branching from it on each side, in a slanting direction, and at even distances. To work: Bring the thread up in the line, hold it down in a straight line, and at a short distance from where it came up, put the needle in on the right side of this line, in a slanting direction, bring it out in the straight line and over the thread held down, and draw up thread; repeat the stitch on the left side, then on the right, and continue working stitches on the left and right of the centre line. *See* EMBROIDERY STITCHES.

Double Crochet.—A stitch used in Crochet, and made as follows: Put the cotton round the hook, and draw it through the foundation; cotton again round hook, and draw it through the two loops. *See* CROCHET.

Double Cross Stitch.—An Embroidery Stitch used in Cross Stitch Embroidery when both sides of the work are required alike. *See* POINT SANS EVERS, EMBROIDERY STITCHES.

Double Diamonds.—A stitch in Macramé Lace, made with a slanting thread covered with MACRAME KNOTS, worked like SINGLE DIAMONDS, but with twelve threads upon each side and two Leaders. *See* DIAMONDS.

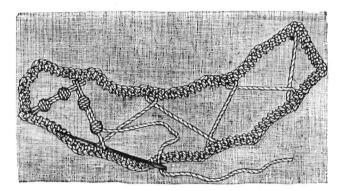

FIG. 294. DOUBLE CROSS STITCH.—DETAIL A.

Another Kind.—A fancy Embroidery Stitch used to ornament cloth, linen, and silk materials, and worked with fine No. 100 embroidery cotton or purse silk. To work: Make a series of evenly-placed HERRINGBONE stitches across the space to be filled, and as wide apart as shown in Fig. 294, Detail A. To finish the stitch as a plain Double Cross, make a return line of Herringbone in between the points of the Herringbone already worked. To finish the stitch as a Double Cross Stitch ornamented with Knots, as shown in Fig. 294, Detail A, which is the stitch usually made, return the thread at the side of the line already made, so as to make a double line, and cross it twice with ornamental KNOTS. Hold the fixed and working threads together, and cross them with a foundation of BUTTONHOLE stitches, over which work OVERCAST STITCH until a Knot is formed. Secure the second line close to the first with a Herringbone (*see* Fig. 295, Detail B), and continue the double line to end of space.

Double Feather.—A variety of FEATHER STITCH, and

FIG. 296. DOUBLE FEATHER STITCH.

worked thus: Hold the material in the left hand, bring up the cotton, and hold it under the left thumb; put the needle into the material on the left side, on a level with the place where the cotton was brought up, but one-eighth of an inch away from it; make a stitch, slightly slant the needle in doing so from left to right (see Fig. 296), and draw the cotton up, keeping the thumb upon it and the needle over it. Again insert the needle to the left on a level with the lower part of the last stitch, but one-eighth of an inch from it, and in a

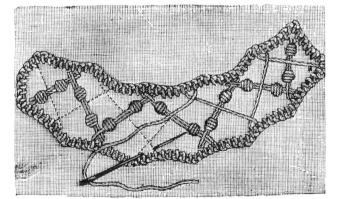

FIG. 295. DOUBLE CROSS STITCH.—DETAIL B.

Then make a single line of Herringbone between the points, as in plain Double Cross (Fig. 295, Detail B), and ornament the plain line with a double thread and Knots.

slightly slanting direction. Draw up as before. To return: Put the needle in to the right of the last stitch, as shown by the figures 1 and 2 on Fig. 296, hold the cotton with the thumb, and draw it up as before, and repeat the stitch to the right. Continue to work two stitches to the right and two to the left until the space is filled, The beauty of Double Feather consists in the perfect Vandyke line it makes down the material when worked with regular and even stitches.

Double Knitting.—A stitch in Knitting, which, producing a double instead of a single web, is especially useful when light and yet warm articles are to be knitted, or stocking heels are to be strengthened. The double web is formed by every other stitch of a row being a SLIP stitch and the intermediate one a Plain stitch; the Slip stitch is worked in the next row, while the Plain stitch, worked in the first row, is slipped in the second. To knit: Cast on an even number of stitches, miss the first stitch, knit one, wool forward, slip the next stitch, pass the wool back, knit the next stitch, and continue slipping and knitting for the whole of the row; work last stitch plain. Second row—knit the slip stitch and slip the knitted. To make loose Double Knitting, put the wool twice round the needle instead of once when knitting. *See* KNITTING.

Double Knot.—A knot used in Tatted Crochet, and made as follows: Commence with 3 CHAIN, make a loop with the cotton round the left forefinger, and nold it

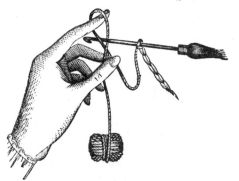

FIG. 297.　DOUBLE KNOT.

down with the thumb (*see* Fig. 297). Insert the hook over the front thread and under back, and draw up the thread on to the hook. Now change the arrangement of the loop on the left hand with a twist of that hand (*see*

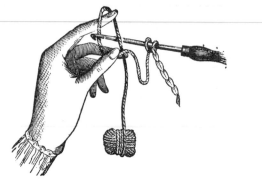

FIG. 298.　DOUBLE KNOT—DETAIL A.

Fig. 298, Detail A), and insert the hook, this time under the first thread and over the second, then draw the loop on to the hook. *See* CROCHET, p. 116.

Double Long Treble.—A stitch used in Crochet as a variety to TREBLE CROCHET. To work: Wind the cotton three times round the hook, put the hook through the Foundation, and draw the cotton through as a loop, * take cotton on the hook and draw through 2 loops, and repeat from * 3 times. The stitch is a long one, and one not often required. *See* CROCHET.

Double Overcast Stitch.—This is Buttonhole Stitch worked in a straight line. To work: Trace the outline, and run along it a straight line of embroidery cotton. Over this work an even and continuous series of BUTTONHOLES, using the run line as a guide to keep the Buttonholes perfectly even. *See* BUTTONHOLE STITCH.

Double Point de Brussels.—A stitch used in needlepoint laces as a Filling. To work: Make a BUTTONHOLE stitch at a distance of one-eighth of an inch from the commencement of the space to be filled, then a second close to it; miss one-eighth of an inch, carry the thread along it as a loop, and work 2 Buttonholes, and continue to miss a space and work 2 Buttonholes to the end of the row. To work back: In the loops made in the last row work 2 Buttonholes, and make loops under the Buttonholes of the first row. Repeat the second row to the end of the space, and work loosely.

Doubles.—Thick, narrow, black ribbons, made for shoestrings. They are supposed to be entirely of silk, but are mixed with cotton, and are done up in rolls of 36 yards each, four to the gross. The widths are known as twopenny, threepenny, sixpenny, and eightpenny. Watered Doubles are called Pads. *See* BINDINGS.

Double Satin Stitch.—A Satin Stitch worked over a prepared foundation, and similar to Raised Satin Stitch.

Double Square.—An Embroidery stitch, also known as Queen Stitch. It is formed of LONG or SATIN Stitches, arranged as squares, one within the other. To work: Make the outside square first, with four Satin stitches, then work a smaller square inside it, with four shorter Satin stitches.

Double Stitch.—Used in Berlin Work and in Tatting. In Berlin work it is a variety of Tent stitch, and made thus: Cross a square of four threads of canvas in the centre with a TENT STITCH, and fill up the square with a small Tent stitch placed on each side of the first made and long Tent stitch. *See* BERLIN WORK.

In Tatting, pass the thread to the back of the hand, push the shuttle upwards between first and second finger, and draw up, then work the usual TATTING STITCH. *See* TATTING.

Double Warp.—A cotton cloth in which the warp and weft are of a uniform size. This kind of calico, being stout and heavy, is in much request for sheetings. The width varies from 2 to 3 yards.

Doublures.—A French term to signify Linings.

Dowlas.—A strong, coarse, half unbleached, linen cloth, made for sheeting, chiefly manufactured in Yorkshire, Dundee, and Forfarshire. It is now almost superseded by calico. It is also made and used by the peasantry in Brittany for common shirts, aprons, and towels. It varies in width from 25 inches to 35 inches, and is to be had of various qualities. The threads are round, like Russian Crash. *See* LINEN.

> MISTRESS QUICKLY.—I bought you a dozen of shirts.
> FALSTAFF.—Dowlas, filthy dowlas; I have given them away, &c.
> —*Merry Wives of Windsor.*

Down.—The soft and almost stemless feathers of birds, such as swans, geese, eider ducks, &c., and employed in needlework for quilting into skirts, quilts, tea coseys, dressing-gowns, &c. Before using, the feathers undergo a process of washing and purification, so as not only to cleanse, but to free them from any unpleasant odour. Down is sold by the pound, the white being regarded as superior to the grey. That of the eider duck is the best to be procured for ruffs for the neck, muffs, linings of hoods, and trimmings for infants' cloaks. Opera cloaks are also made of the white swan's down.

D'Oyley.—This was once the name of a woollen stuff, but is now that of a small article of NAPERY (which *see*). It is usually produced with fringed edges, for use at dessert, or for the toilet. D'Oyleys are woven in both cotton and linen; in white and in ingrain colours. The name appears to be derived from the Dutch *dwaele*, signifying a towel.

Drabbet.—A description of coarse linen material or duck, made at Barnsley. It is heavy in quality, and twilled, and is made both undyed and in colours. It may be had in widths of 27 inches and 30 inches respectively.

Drab Cloth.—A dun-coloured woollen cloth, woven thick, and double-milled; it is employed for overcoats, and is manufactured in Yorkshire.

Drafting—The drawing or delineating a pattern or diagram; it is a technical term employed in reference to the execution of outline plans for needlework, and the cutting out of materials employed for the same.

Drap.—The French term signifying Cloth.

Drape.—A term employed in dressmaking and upholstery, signifying the decorative arrangement of folds

Drapery.—A comprehensive term denoting cloth of every description. It seems to be derived from the French word *drap.*

Drap Sanglier.—A loosely made, all-wool French stuff, 44 inches in width. It is of a rather coarse grain, plainly woven, and has a good deal of nap or roughness on the face. It is more especially designed for the purposes of mourning, and will be found lighter in wear, as a spring or summer travelling dress material, than its appearance promises.

Drawbays.—A description of Lasting, being a double warp worsted material, employed for making shoes and boots, chiefly for women; it is 18 inches in width. *See* LASTING.

Drawing.—A term employed in reference to the making of Gathers, by means of RUNNING or WHIPPING, when the thread used for the purpose must, of course, be drawn through the material, in and out of the stitches taken, leaving a number of small folds or gathers compressed together. This thread is called a Drawing Thread. Ribbons and tapes employed within casings, for the same purpose, are called Drawing Strings.

Drawn Work.—One of the earliest and most ancient forms of open work Embroidery, and the foundation of Lace. It was known in the twelfth century as Opus Tiratum, and Punto Tirato, and later as Hamburg Point, Indian Work, Broderie de Nancy, Dresden Point, Tonder Lace, and Drawn Work, and seems at one time to have been known and worked all over Europe, being used largely for ecclesiastical purposes and for the ornamentation of shrouds. The ancient specimens of Drawn Work still to be seen are of such fine material as to require a magnifying glass. They were formed of fine linen, the threads being retained in the parts where the pattern was

FIG. 299. DRAWN WORK.

thick, and, where it was open, cut, or drawn away, so that only a sufficient number of warp and woof threads were left to keep the work together, and these were BUTTONHOLED together (three to each stitch) so as to form a groundwork of squares like Netting. The edges of the pattern were also Buttonholed over. Fig. 299 is of a later description of Drawn Work, and would be known as Indian Work, as its foundation is muslin. It is two hundred years old, and, as it is unfinished, shows how the threads were drawn away and those retained for the thick parts of the pattern and Buttonholed round. The ground of Fig. 299 is not worked in Buttonhole squares, but is made in the HONEYCOMB RÉSEAU ground of lace. The leaves and sprays forming the pattern are outlined round with a thread, and then Buttonholed before any threads are drawn away. The threads going one way of the stuff are then carefully cut for a short distance and pulled away, and the Honeycomb ground, made with the threads that are left, OVERCAST together in that shape. This kind of Drawn Work is now quite obsolete, as is likewise the geometrical, which succeeded these grounded flower patterns. In the geometrical the threads that were retained were Overcast together, and formed patterns without grounds.

In Fig. 300 is given a pattern of Drawn Work in the Reticella style, which has been revived. It is worked as follows : Take a piece of coarse linen, and draw warp and woof threads away, to form a succession of squares (this process has to be very carefully done, or the squares will not be perfect). Leave six threads each way between the squares to form a support, and commence the work by covering these threads. Divide the six threads in the centre, and work POINT DE REPRISE thickly over them; first throw the thread over the three to the right and bring

Drawn Work was frequently enriched with Embroidery and Lace stitches made with coloured silks. Broderie de Nancy, Dresden Point, and Hamburg Point were of this description of Drawn Work. Fig. 301 (p. 159) is a modern adaptation of this kind, and is made thus : Draw the squares out as in the last pattern, leaving sixteen to twenty threads between each. BUTTONHOLE round the outer edge of the drawn part of the work with coloured silk, and then work the Lace stitch. Thread the needle with coloured silk, fasten it firmly to the edge, and loop it twice into the side of one square; when it comes to where the threads are left, divide them in half, and loop it through one half of them; cross the thread over the thick undrawn parts, and continue to loop it twice in every side of the square until all the squares are worked round and all the left threads

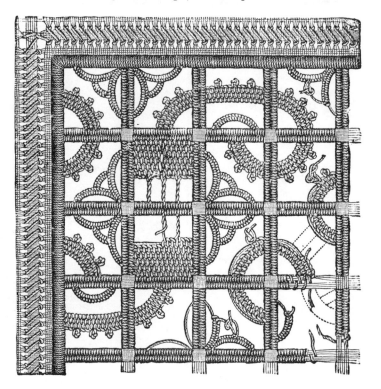

FIG. 300. DRAWN WORK—RETICELLA.

it back to the centre, and then over the three to the left and bring it back to the centre, as shown in the illustration. Work until the threads are quite covered. Fill the open squares with BUTTONHOLE stitches. Throw a thread across the space as a loop, and cover it thickly with Buttonholes; leave it as one line, or continue to throw threads and Buttonhole them over and down to the first line until the pattern is formed. Where this is done is amply shown in the illustration, in many parts of which the Buttonholed lines are given half-finished, in others completed and ornamented with PICOTS, while dotted lines indicate where other fillings, formed of Buttonholed lines, are to come. For the bordering, draw out threads, leave an undrawn space between, and work HEM STITCH first on one drawn-out line, and then upon the other. Take up four threads in every Hem stitch.

secured. Then work the ornamental WHEEL in the centre of the open squares upon the loops. Make the Wheels of three Buttonholes close together, with a space left between the ones made and the next to be worked. Three Buttonholes are worked in every loop, eight forming a Wheel.

When Drawn Work is done upon fine linen, muslin, or cambric foundations, it is tedious pulling out the threads before any design is commenced; but upon such materials as cheese cloth and open linen canvas the whole of the material can be drawn without trouble and embroidered. The pattern shown (Fig. 302) is intended to be worked upon coarse linen, and is made as follows : Draw out a succession of squares, leaving sixteen threads between each open square. Take coarse knitting cotton or coloured silk, and work down each square, twisting the left threads thus: Pick up the fifth, sixth, seventh, and eighth threads upon the needle, and twist them over the first four threads; draw the needle and silk through them, and pick up the thirteenth, fourteenth, fifteenth, and sixteenth threads

coarse cheese cloth. It is ornamented with fine chenille or wool instead of silk, and is worked thus: Draw out squares on the material, leaving eight threads between

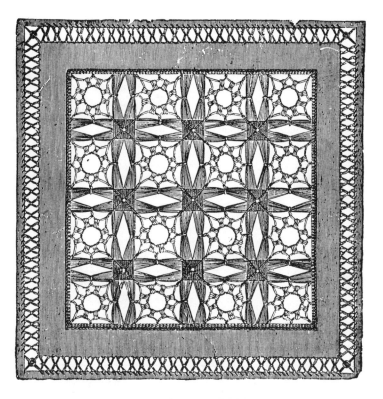

FIG. 301. DRAWN WORK.

and draw them over the tenth, eleventh, twelfth, and thirteenth threads; work in this way all down the left threads, then turn the work, and work from the side in

each square. Make LONG CROSS stitches as in Berlin Work, with various coloured chenilles or wools, to secure the threads that are left. Work the under or dark line of stitches first, fasten the dark coloured chenille into one of the open squares, miss the open square upon the

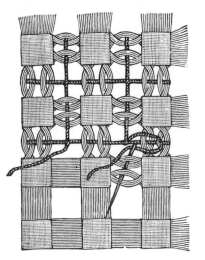

FIG. 302. DRAWN WORK.

the same manner, knotting the silk together where it meets, as shown in the illustration.

Fig. 303 is a pattern intended to be worked upon

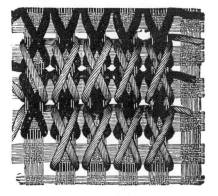

FIG. 303. DRAWN WORK.

next row, and loop into the square on the right in the third row, making the first half of a Cross Stitch. Bring the needle out to the left through the open space on that side and finish the Cross stitch by returning it back to the first row into the space on the right hand to where it first began. Continue to make this Cross stitch until all the spaces are filled or covered over. Then take light Chenille, and work with it over the dark Chenille in the same stitch, looping it into the squares that were only covered in the first row.

The borders that can be made with Drawn Work are very numerous, and are much used as ornamental finishes to Embroideries upon linen and other washing materials, not only in needlework coming from India, Turkey, and Arabia, but by English ladies for Ecclesiastical linen and Crewel Work. The first of the stitches used is HEM Stitch, to secure the threads, but after that Fancy Stitches are worked to embellish them. Fig. 304 shows

FIG. 304. DRAWN WORK.

two stitches much employed for borders. To work the one on the left hand: Draw out the thread one way of the stuffs to the width of three-quarters of an inch, and commence the work on the wrong side of the material, holding it so that the left threads are in a horizontal position, and work in a straight line down them and close to the undrawn material. Secure the thread, and make the Hem stitch, thus: Take up eight threads on the needle, and loop them with the thread, as if making a Buttonhole Stitch: Draw up tight, make a short stitch into the material to secure the thread, and make another Hem stitch; then take up eight more threads on the needle and repeat. Work down one side and then down the other, at the top and bottom of the drawn-out space. Insert a centre line made of crochet cotton, twist the threads round it; take four threads from the first Hem stitch and four from the next for each twist, to give the plaited look to the threads shown in the illustration. For the stitch upon the right-hand side of Fig. 304, Draw out threads to the width required, and work at the back of the material, holding it as before-mentioned; Hem stitch as before at the top and bottom of the space, but inclose four threads instead of eight in every Hem stitch. Cover with a line of BUTTONHOLE the threads composing every seventh Hem stitch, and make a narrow slanting line running across the six Hem stitches between the ones Buttonholed, with four Buttonholes worked across every two stitches.

Fig. 305 is worked thus: Draw out the threads lengthways of the material. First draw out six, then leave three, draw out another six, leave three, draw out twelve, leave three, draw out twelve, leave three, draw out six, leave three, draw out six, and leave three. Then BUTTONHOLE the top and bottom edges of the drawn space (use fine lace cotton for so doing), and secure the left threads together in loops at the same time, making six threads into one loop. Make a loop by twisting the cotton twice round the six threads and drawing it up. Turn the work, and hold it as before mentioned. Work the second

line in HEM STITCH as before described, and for the third line make a CHAIN STITCH line with cotton down the centre, drawing up twelve threads in every Chain stitch. Repeat the Chain and Hem Stitch lines for the remaining spaces.

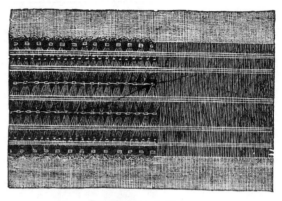

FIG. 305. DRAWN WORK.

To work Fig. 306: Draw out threads of the material one-eighth of an inch deep, leave three threads, draw out threads for a space of half an inch, then leave three threads and draw out for one-eighth of an inch. Work at the back of the material from left to right. Take up six threads on the needle, and make them into a loop by twisting the thread twice round them, run the needle slantwise through the three threads left undrawn, then take three of the threads just secured, and three in front

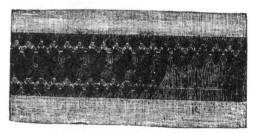

FIG. 306. DRAWN WORK.

of them, and make a loop of them, upon the side of the three undrawn threads nearest the centre of the work. Continue to work these two loops, one upon each side of the left three threads, until the line is finished. Work the line similar to this, and opposite it before the centre line. For the centre line: Take one cluster of six threads and three threads from the cluster upon each side, and OVER-CAST them together, keeping the Knot thus made in the centre of the line. Finish each Knot off, and do not carry the cotton from one to the other.

To work Fig. 307: Draw out an inch of lengthways threads on the material, and leave at equal distances apart in this space. Work at back of the material with lines of HEM STITCH at the top and bottom of the space, and along lines made with the centre lines; the threads that are left use as a groundwork for the three centre lines of Hem Stitch. Secure six threads with every Hem stitch, take three from one stitch and three from the next in the second line. Work the original

ARRASENE UPON PLUSH.

GOLD THREAD UPON PLUSH.

six together for the third line, and repeat the second and third line for the fourth and fifth. The Hem stitching being finished, ornament it by Overcasting two stitches

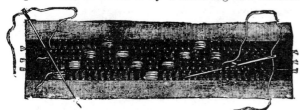

FIG. 307. DRAWN WORK.

together with coloured silk, and work these Overcast stitches in a Vandyke line over the whole of the inch of Drawn threads, as shown in Fig. 307.

To work Fig. 308 : Draw out six threads of the material, and leave three threads, then draw out threads to an inch in depth of the material, then leave three threads, and draw out six threads. Work lines of BUTTONHOLE down the upright threads in the centre space upon the right

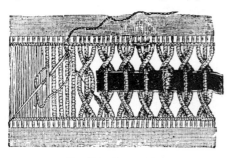

FIG. 308. DRAWN WORK.

side of the material, and take in four threads into each line. When all the threads are Buttonholed over, take a narrow piece of ribbon, and run it through the lines thus : Take up the third line and twist it over the first, put the ribbon over it, and pass the ribbon through the second line, twist the first line over the second and third, and pass the ribbon over it. Treat all the Buttonholed lines in this way.

Dresden Point.—The exact date of the introduction of lace making into Germany is still a matter of dispute, but there is no doubt that the movement owed much of its success to the labours of Barbara Uttmann (born 1514, died 1575), who, with the hope of lessening the poverty of her countrywomen, founded a lace school at Annaberg, and, with assistance from Flanders, taught Pillow lace-making to 30,000 persons. To her labours may be added the help given to the manufactory by the constant passing over into Germany of French and Spanish refugees, many of whom brought with them the secrets of their various trades. For some time the laces of Germany were simply copies of the common peasant laces made in France and Spain, and were only known to, and bought by, the non-wealthy classes, but gradually copies of better kinds of laces were attempted, and Silk Blondes, Plaited Gold and Silver Laces, Point d'Espagne, Brussels and Mechlin laces produced. Dresden became celebrated during the last part of the seventeenth century, and for the whole

of the eighteenth, not for a Pillow lace, but for a Drawn lace, an imitation of the Italian Punto Tirato, in which a piece of linen was converted into lace by some of its threads being drawn away, some retained to form a pattern, and others worked together to form square meshes. This Dresden Point was likewise embroidered with fine stitchery, and was largely bought by the wealthy during the time of its excellence. Its manufacture has now died out, and Dresden only produces either coarse Pillow lace or imitations of old Brussels.

Dressed Pillow.—A term used by lace makers to intimate that all the accessories necessary for the art are in their proper positions. These are : A Pillow (for Honiton lace this is flat, for Brussels round, for Saxony long), (see PILLOW), three covers for the same (see COVER CLOTHS), a hank of lace thread, a hank of shiny thread known as a Gimp, four dozen pairs of bobbins, lace pins and common pins, a small soft pincushion, a needle pin or darning needle with a sealing wax head, a fine crochet

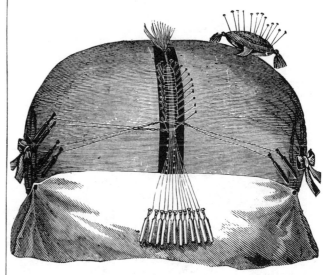

FIG. 309. DRESSED PILLOW, WITH LACE IN PROCESS OF MAKING.

hook, a bobbin bag, a pair of sharp scissors in sheath, and a passement pattern. The bobbin bag is made shorter than the bobbins, and stitched up in compartments, so that each division holds twelve pairs of bobbins; it is finished with a little tongue by which to pin it to the Pillow, as are also the pincushion and the scissor sheath. The fine crochet hook is required to make the Sewings, and is stuck into the pincushion, with the pins and the darning needle, the latter being required to prick patterns and wind up thread.

The Pillow is dressed as follows: Lay the under Cover Cloth on the Pillow before the passement is adjusted, then the passement, over whose lower end pin a second cover cloth, to lie under the bobbins and protect them from getting entangled in the pricked pattern. The pincushion, the scissor sheath, and bobbin bag, pin on to the right-hand side of the pillow, to be out of the way of the work; the Pillow is then ready to receive the bobbins and commence the lace. Fig. 309 illustrates a

Y

Dressed Pillow, with a piece of Lace Braid in making upon it. The first Cover Cloth is tied on with ribbons; the second at the lower end of the Pillow is shown white. The passement is covered with the lace already made, which is secured to it by the pins pushed through its pricked holes in the process of working. The tuft of threads at the top of the Pillow show where the bobbin threads are tied together and pinned on to the pattern, the Passive Bobbins are laid down over the second Cover Cloth, while the

Dressing Frame.—A frame shaped like the trunk of a human body to the waist, and thence extending outwards like the skirt of a dress. It is made of steel wires, and upon it dresses and skirts are placed for the purpose of draping, and otherwise arranging the costume in making it.

Dressmaking.—The first step to be taken in Dressmaking is to cut out the material. For all rules of general application, as well as for certain notes having especial reference to Dressmaking, see CUTTING-OUT.

FIG. 310. DIAGRAMS FOR TAKING MEASUREMENTS WITH A TAPE.

Workers are pinned up on each side of the passement, not to become entangled.

Dressing.—The stiffening, or glaze, applied to silk, linen, or cotton fabrics, to give an artificial substance and firmness. It is made of china clay, starch, or gum. In the selection of Calico and Longcloth for underlinen, it is expedient to rub the end of the piece to remove the Dressing, so as the better to ascertain the real quality and substance of the cloth, which is sometimes much disguised by it, and thus given a fictitious excellence.

The above diagrams (Fig. 310) will indicate to the dressmaker the exact method of taking measurements by means of a measuring-tape, thus obviating the necessity for supplying further directions. The tape marks show the manner in which the measurements are to be taken from point to point.

Commencing with the *skirt*, the following may be regarded as the order in which the work is to be carried out: Always run the *seams* down from top to bottom, so that if any unevenness should occur it may be pared off from the latter edge, but if cut out accurately there will be nothing to spare. When a gored edge is put next a selvedge, take great care that it be not stretched, nor too loosely fixed to the other piece. Begin by uniting the gores on either side nearest the front width, then the next gores to those right and left, and so on to the back. The stitching should be ½ inch from the edges, the placket hole opening left unjoined in the seam of the back width on the left hand side, which is the usual place for it, if the skirt or tunic be separate from the bodice. If the dress be unlined, sew over each edge of the seams separately, using fine cotton, and neither work too closely, nor pull the thread tightly. When all are over-sewn, press open the joins with an iron, by laying a wooden roller longwise up the joins underneath them, on the right side of the dress, and ironing up the centre of the separated edges on the wrong side. Very stout or springing materials need a damp cloth laid over the seam to be pressed. A broom handle is the best roller, and it is well worth while for one to be kept for the purpose, covered with two or three layers of ironing cloth sewn round it. By using a roller the heater only presses on the actual stitching of the seam, and not on the turnings, the marks of which always show through on the right side, if the seams be pressed open on a table. With silk it is better to lay a dry cloth over the seam to be ironed on, instead of rubbing the heater immediately upon the silk. The very delicately tinted, such as French grey, dove, and lavender, must not have a very hot iron applied; and it is better not to rest the seam on a roller, but to get two persons to hold the seams, at the top and bottom, pulling firmly, while a third shall pass the iron up and down the parted edges of the join. Cotton and other washing skirts do not need the turnings quite so wide as ½ inch, and the two edges are sewn over together instead of being opened. Gauze, thin barège, or any yielding, flimsy material, is usually joined by a MANTUA MAKER'S HEM, and, whenever possible, the selvedge of it is used for the turning which is hemmed down, thus saving an extra fold of the stuff.

If the dress be gored, but not lined, and a shaped facing used, tack it smoothly round the bottom after the seams have been pressed, and then HEM the cover and lining up to the 1½ inches allowed in the length when it was cut, of course only putting the needle into the hem and the lining, not taking it through to the face. The top edge must be hemmed with small stitches taken very far apart, and with fine silk or cotton.

With *petticoats*, or *round skirts* that are little gored, it is quicker not to stitch up the hem after the facing is tacked in, but to place the right side of the facing against the right side of the skirt, and projecting beyond it as much as the hem of stuff which has been accounted for; then run the dress stuff against the facing, ¼ inch within the edge, and afterwards turn the facing over on to the inside of the skirt, and hem down the upper edge. Pull the lining up a little higher than the actual depth of the hem, so as to make the extreme edge of the dress of double material.

Whatever *trimming*, in the way of flounces, &c., has been prepared, is now put on the skirt. Begin with the bottom row in horizontal trimming, and fix it by having

the hem, and not the waist, of the skirt over the left arm while the running is executed; the trimming being first fixed in its place with pins. Work diagonal and longitudinal puffs, quillings, or ruches from the waist to the feet, and be careful that the fulness of puffs decrease towards the top. These trimmings, however, mostly apply to ball dresses, and in making transparent skirts, it is more convenient to leave a join (one of those next the train) open, until after the trimmings have all been put on, and join it up subsequently; for if they be of net, tarlatan, grenadine, tulle, or gauze, the running on of such flounces or puffs should be done from the inside of the skirt, as the drawing threads and pins are as plainly visible from that as the right side, and there being then nothing in which the sewing cotton can be caught, the work is more rapid, and becomes less tumbled. Always use a long straw needle, No. 5 or 6, and avoid coarse cotton.

After the trimming, make the *placket hole*, which needs a facing on the right-hand side, and a false hem on the left, when the placket fastens behind. Cut the facing and false hem on the bias or the straight, according to the breadth to which they are attached, and the false hem ought to be quite 1½ inches wide.

Next sew on the *waistband*, and let it be as much longer than the waist, as the placket hole's False Hem is wide. Turn down the waist edge for the ½ inch allowed in the cutting, and sew the top of the False Hem for its width to the left end of the band, and stitch two eyes on in a line with the sewing of the false hem. Pin the band with its right side to that of the skirt, and hold it with the band towards you, while sewing the two together strongly. The fulness, which is either pleated, or gathered at the back of the waist, must also be kept from you while being sewn to the belt. The size of the gathers depends on the quantity of the skirt to be gathered into a certain space, but the stitches are usually made an inch long on the wrong side, and very small on the right, so that when the gathering thread is drawn up, the inch is folded in half, and makes GATHERS ½ inch deep. Sew these to the band at their threaded edge, and then sew them over at the opposite one, so as to keep all the corners regular, and make the Gathers set in uniform folds. Sew the hooks a little way in from the right hand end of the band, and a third one, with eye corresponding, to keep up the lapped piece which holds the false hem. Sixes are the best sized hooks for waistbands.

Make the *pocket* from the same stuff as the body lining, the sides sloped off to a point at the top. Face the opening for the hand with dress material, and put a strip of the same on the inside of the pocket opposite the opening, so as not to show the white lining when the pocket-hole bulges. Dot the edge of the pocket either with a Mantua Maker's Hem, or stitch it on the inside close to the edges, turn it inside out, and stitch it round again, so as to inclose the raw turnings. The top of the pocket should be about 9 inches from the waist.

Put the *braid* on last of all, and it looks and wears better if folded in half, width way, and so used double. Hem it on, and slightly ease it if coloured, as it shrinks from damp. Black, and some dark shades will bear shrinking prior to use, and whenever the shade will stand the process, it is better to plunge the braid in boiling water, that the scalding and subsequent drying may prevent the necessity of easing it in hemming.

In making the *bodice*, TACK the lining, which has been cut and fitted on, to the covering material near the edge all round, including both sides of the darts, but the hem tacking should be further in than the others. When every part of the lining is BASTED to the material, and cut out by it (leaving no margin beyond the lining, unless it be of a stuff that frays greatly), turn down the fronts, and RUN them near the folded edge, to keep them in shape until the buttons and buttonholes be added, which will then fix the front Hems, the turnings of which are not actually hemmed down. After Tacking down the fronts, stitch the seams, doing so closely, and being cautious to hold both edges with equal firmness. Join down the centre of the back next, then attach the side pieces to it, by stitching the edges together on the inside, if there be two or more side pieces; but when there is only one on each side, they are sometimes stitched on from the outside, the edge of the side piece being tacked down and Basted in place on the back, and then stitched very near the folded edge; but this is not an unalterable rule, and depends on whether the taste of the day be to make seams conspicuous, or as little observable as possible. The under arm seams follow, after the side pieces are done, and then the shoulders. Always begin the stitching of joins and darts at the top, and so work downwards. Shave off any ravellings, and then oversew the cover and lining together, on either side of each seam, and press them open. The seam from neck to arm is not opened, but the four layers are oversewn together, and the piece turned towards the back, when the sleeve and neckband are added, which then confines the ends of this shoulder seam. With a clear bodice, such as Swiss, book, or organdie muslin, join the shoulders by a Mantua Maker's Hem, if both fronts and back be plain; but if the fronts be full and the back plain, tack a piping cord, laid in a crossway casing, on the back parts, and stitch the fronts to it. When a very thick cord is laid up all the bodice seams, to act as a trimming, cut away the ends of the cord, when it reaches the seam into which it has to be stitched, like a pencil point, until only enough of its centre remains to be held securely in the stitching. If this thick cording be used for the backs of bodices in which there are side pieces, which run into the shoulder seam, that seam is then turned forwards, instead of backwards, when the collar and sleeves are put in.

Now make the *buttonholes* on the right front hem, and mark their relative positions, each being sewn over with fine cotton before it is worked with the twist. BUTTONHOLES with "bar" ends are nicest for silk, washing, and thin stuff dresses; but real cloth ought to have proper tailors' buttonholes. If silk, velvet, or other buttons without shanks be used, in sewing them on take up so much of their base through the dress at the back that the buttonhole, when extended over it, will not spread, causing a looseness between each buttonhole. Thus, in order to leave room for the shank of the button, a little of the hole should be cut away. A buttonhole, thus wider one end than the other, must be worked round both ends radiatingly, instead of with bars. "Medium" twist (there are three sizes) is best for most dress materials, but "coarse" is best for extra thick serge or cloth.

If there should be any trimming over the shoulder, or down the fronts, ending at the basque edge, waistband, or throat, it must now be put on, so that the ends may be enclosed. When those parts are finished off, put on the bodice, and button it up, and place a tacking thread where the trimming is to go, as it is almost impossible to obtain a correct square, or equidistant Brételles, &c., by sight alone, when the bodice is in the hand. It is quite easy for the worker to do this for herself by standing before a mirror, placing pins where the trimming is to be, and winding a cotton from one to another of those pins. The back, being a flat surface, can be marked for the trimming when the bodice is taken off. While it is on, see that the neck is of a right height, particularly where the shoulder seams end, and quite at the back, for if at all too high there it will drag into creases. Put the neck band on next. If a straight one of even height, cut it from the straight of the material, and used it double, stitch one edge on at the right side, and FELL the other down on the wrong, but if very stout or rough, it must be of one thickness for the outside, and a strip of silk run to its top edge, and Felled down for the inside, over the stitching made by the exterior of the band. Should the neck band be one of those that stand out from the throat, and are deeper at the back than the front, cut it of that shape in book muslin, and cut the muslin (used as a stiffener), the material, and its inner lining, with the direct cross of the stuff at the centre. In sewing on neck bands or collars, do not draw them in the least degree.

Cord the *armholes* now, if desired. Lay the cord in the centre of a ¾ inch bias casing and tack it there, so as to use the cording ready made round the armhole, instead of embedding the cord at the same time as tacking it on the dress. Commence it immediately under the arm, not at the seam, and cross the beginning and ending of the cord.

The lower edge of the *bodice* has next to be seen to. If one with a waistband, first run the tapes for whalebones down the opened and pressed seams, at the darts and under the arms, leaving the tops of the tapes (which should not reach the armhole by 2½ inches) open for the insertion of the bones, when everything else has been done, for when stitching in the sleeves it is easier to handle if it be limp. Cut the bodice the right length, and ⅓ inch additional in the first place, and then tack up the ⅓ inch, and put a wide (1 inch) twilled tape on the inside, stitching it from the outside close to the edge, and afterwards hemming up the top of the tape.

A *basque* should be corded or faced on the inside, but must never be itself hemmed up. Cut the facing on the cross, 1½ inches wide, and run it with its right side on that of the basque about ⅓ inch from the edge, and afterwards turn it over to the inside and hem it up. Before running on the facing, pull its edge so as to stretch it, to make it take a better curve for the first running; by doing so the inner edge can be hemmed up flatly, without having to make any pleats, unless the basque describes a point, or be deeper in the middle than the sides, or *vice versâ*.

The *sleeves* are put in last. If of a plain coat shape, lay the right sides of the linings together, and place this on the top of the exterior stuff, which is also put face to face; then stitch all four through together, the hand inserted between the two linings, so as to draw the sleeve through, and thus turn the top layer of lining over to the under side of the stuff, when the sleeve, though inside out, will be completely lined, and the raw edges hidden by being under the lining. If the coat sleeve be so tight as to require pleats at the elbow, to give the arm play, the joining ought not to be done in the foregoing way, but the linings should be tacked to the stuff, and the halves stitched together and OVERSEWN. With sleeves so fitting the arm as to need pleats, care must be taken not to leave the lining in the least degree loose, or the strain then put on its cover will make it ravel out at the seams. The margin beyond the joining should not be more than ⅓ inch. Transparent materials, such as gauze or grenadine, are sometimes lined, and then the stuff and lining should be all closed together in the way first mentioned. While the sleeve is inside out, run a band 2 inches wide on the edge of the sleeve, by putting the band against its right side, and so farthest from you. Begin it at the inner seam of the arm, and on reaching the outer one, ease in the band a little, and when again arrived at the inner seam, fasten off, and then turn the wrist facing down on the sleeve lining, and FELL it there, before closing the opening at the seam with blind or SLIP stitches. These are made by inserting the needle under the fold of the hem, and running it in and out between the two inner sides, out of sight, so as to form an invisible connection between them. When a sleeve is to be trimmed by straight rows of braid at the cuff, leave the inner seam undone till the last, so as to lay the sleeve out flat for the trimming, and when the seam is closed, stitch in the ends of the braid. The cuff should be made up separately, and applied to the sleeve by Slip-stitching the two at the wrist, letting the cuff project the smallest possible degree beyond the edge. All cuffs should be made on book muslin, whether deep and plain, ornamental, or only a band dividing two frills. Sleeves that are in puffs downwards, take the same extra length as do puffs that go round—viz., about half as much again for opaque materials, but net or tulle requires rather more, and these filmy tissues are made on a foundation of the same, to keep the puffs in place. Begin the runnings at the shoulder end, commencing at the middle first (that where the elbow seam is), and bring the rest nearer together towards the wrist, so that the puffs may not be as large there as at the top, then secure all with pins to regulate the fulness, and run down with fine cotton. For puffs that go round the arm run a cord at the required distances, for a thread alone does not give sufficient support. The same rule applies to muslin, gauze, or grenadine, when puffed longitudinally without a foundation. To prevent their falling to the wrist when the sleeves are gathered across, and are unlined, sew a cord, the length of the arm, from running to running, at the seam, and put a second cord in more immediately under the arm. With net or tulle, whether the puffs go up or round makes no difference to the lay of the material; they must be laid in the direction of the selvedge from shoulder to hand. For short sleeves for ball dresses cut the deepest part directly on the cross of the lining, and when covered by a little puff, make this by a bias strip, and pleat fully as long again as the lining. Single puff it rather than gather, doing the top edge first in small single pleats all turned one way, and then the lower edge, but turn the pleats there in the opposite direction to those at the top. The mouth of the sleeve may be faced with a narrow ribbon, or corded. For long hanging sleeves cut the longest part on the straight way of the material. Transparent bodices with low linings, have long transparent sleeves over short thick ones, the edge is piped, and short and long sleeves are tacked together, that they may be attached to the armhole by one stitching. The stitching must be very firm, and with stout thread, and the raw edges should be sewn over. When no cording is put round the armholes, take care not to pull it on the sleeve, and in addition to firm stitching, Hem a silk ribbon over the turnings, the ribbon being of the precise width to allow of hemming each edge on the line of stitches made by putting in the sleeve.

Low bodices may be finished at the neck in two ways. Sometimes the edge is turned down, and a ½ inch wide sarsenet ribbon hemmed over it on the inside, the ribbon being used as a runner for a string (silk lace) to draw the top to the figure; the other plan is to cord the edge with a fine piping cord, as the neck can be drawn in a little when this is being done. If a low body be fastened behind and have a seam up the front, place a bone up the join, from its extreme end to within 2 inches of the top, and put a bone in every gore seam, but do not carry it high, for if so the tops of the bones will press outwards and push through. In most cases the seams of low bodices are so shallow, that they do not need opening, but will in themselves act as bone cases. If the lower edge of a low body be peaked or basqued, cord it either single or double, and take great care to turn the peak point well, by taking two or three secure stitches, when the centre is reached, after going down one side, before turning the piping to go up the other, and do not allow any easiness in the piping at the bend, or it will not be a sharp turn.

For double cording, lay a cord under each edge of a crossway strip, then fold it so as to inclose the raw edges in the middle of the casing, allowing one cord to lie below the other, and run them together close to the lower. Then place this face downwards on the edge to be piped, and fix it to that part with an occasional BACK STITCH, using the last row of running as a guide to sew by. The folded edge of the piping is then ready to be hemmed to the lining without making a turning. This is a quick method, and answers for straight lines, but it will not do for curves, as the outer cord would have to describe a wider circle than the inner one, and so would be strained. For proper double or treble cording, tack each into its own casing, and run on separately by first putting on the one nearest to the dress, then run the second cord over the first, so as to project beyond it, and the third beyond the second, in the same way, finally laying a crossway piece over the last cording, and turning it over to be Felled up on the inside, and so hiding the numerous raw edges.

Square necks should be piped, and sharp turning at the corners is essential; but while in turning a peak there will be a piece to fold over there, when felling up in the corners of a hollow square it will be reversed, and the casing of the piping must be snipped in a precise line with the corner, quite up to the cord itself, that the angle may be acute.

Polonaises, dressing gowns, mantles, and such like long garments are frequently made to meet, but not lap at the front, and, when so, use hooks and eyes to connect them, placing a hook and an eye alternately on either side, so as to prevent their coming undone. After they are sewn on, lay a sarsenet ribbon over the shanks, leaving only the ends of the hooks, and two-thirds of the eyes exposed.

In reference to the many varieties of form, and of trimming, which the fashion of each season may prescribe, the dressmaker must be guided by the illustrations provided in the periodicals of the current time, and by the paper patterns of the same. The method of making various descriptions of trimmings, and the signification of the terms employed in the construction of dresses, such as Box Pleating, Flouncing, Fringing, Gathering, Gauging, Honeycombing, Pleating, Puffing, Quilling, Quilting, Reeving, Ruching, Slashing, &c., will be found described under their respective headings.

Drills.—A very stout linen twilled cloth, having a treble cord; it may be had unbleached, white, and in colours, and is used for summer trousers. It is less thick and heavy than Duck, and somewhat resembles thick twilled Holland, and is suitable for men's wear in India and other hot countries. It is much used in the navy and army, and is also useful for boys.

Droguet.—A French term for a worsted Rep-made dress material, not much known at present, or else under a different name.

Dropped Stitch.—In Knitting, a stitch is frequently slipped off the needle without the knitter being aware of the mistake, and speedily runs down through the rows, and, unless picked up, destroys the whole work. This is called a Dropped stitch, and is detected by the loop heading the line which a stitch forms in the Knitting becoming disconnected from the rest of the work. The number of stitches should be constantly counted during the progress of Knitting, and when a stitch is found short, the work if fine and complicated, unpicked until the loop is reached, or if in plain Knitting the stitch picked up thus: Take a medium sized Crochet hook, put it through the Dropped loop, stretch the Knitting out straight and Chain Stitch the loop up the line of threads above it until the last row of Knitting is reached, when slide it on to the Knitting needle in its proper place in the work.

Drugget.—A coarse cloth made of Felt, and printed in various patterns and colours, not only employed as a carpet and to underlie carpets—to preserve them from being cut and worn, and to render them softer to the tread—but also employed as linings for rugs made of skins. They should measure 1½ yards in width, but are rarely found to exceed 1¼ yards.

Duchesse Lace.—A beautiful Pillow lace, a variety of Point de Flandre or Brussels lace made in Belgium, and similar in workmanship and design to Honiton Guipure Lace, the patterns of which originally came from abroad. Duchesse Lace is worked with a finer and different thread to that of Honiton, and the leaves, flowers, and sprays formed are larger and of bolder design, the Primrose flower and leaf of Brussels Lace being the design chiefly worked. It contains a greater amount of the Raised or Relief work, that distinguishes the best Honiton, but the stitches and manner of working in both are the same, and

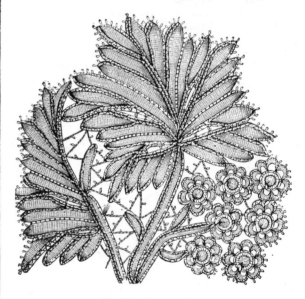

FIG. 311. DUCHESSE LACE.

a reference to the instructions for Honiton Lace will teach the worker how to form the sprays of Duchesse Lace.

When working Duchesse Lace unite the large sprigs together with the ground described as Devonia Ground, and fill in other open places with the same ground. Work nearly all the leaves and Flowers in Cloth Stitch (*See* Braid Work, *Close or Whole Braid* and Close Leaf), and make Rope Sewings for veins and stems when they are in Relief, and Cross Tracings and Cucumber Plaitings when they are open work. Work a few leaves and sprays in Half or Lace Stitch, but generally use this stitch for the foundation to Relief work, working leaves, tendrils, and stems in Cloth stitch in Relief over the parts in the body of Lace filled with Half or Lace stitch. Make a Plain Edge round the sprays with a Gimp, except on the outside edge of the design, when make a Pearl Edge with a Gimp.

The illustration of Duchesse Lace given in Fig. 311 has no complicated Raised work in it. It is of a flower and leaf frequently met with in Duchesse patterns, and shows a peculiar manner of working a Rope Sewing, and one often met with in the Lace. Fig. 312, Detail A, illustrates the leaf part of the design, and is worked as follows : Hang on six pairs of bobbins at *a*, and work in Cloth Stitch with Plain Edge on both sides and without a Gimp to *b*; here make a Pearl Edge on the outer side, but continue Plain Edge on

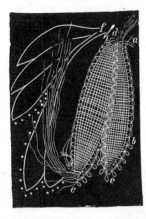

FIG. 312. DUCHESSE LACE—DETAIL A.

the inner. At *c* collect the bobbins together, and with the exception of the two used for the edge, and shown detached at *e*, return all the bobbins to *d* over the Plain Edge on the inner side of the leaf, making a Rope Sewing over them with the two threads and two Pearls close to *c*. From *d* work down to *e* in Cloth Stitch with a Plain Edge on the inner side; make a Pearl Edge on the other, hanging on the

FIG. 313. DUCHESSE LACE—DETAIL B.

bobbins where the leaf parts. Work back to *f*, as before described, and continue until all the divisions of the leaf are filled. The flower in Fig. 313, Detail B, is an enlargement of the pattern to show Devonia Ground and the working of the flower. The stitch used is similar to the one described in *Plain Braid* (see BRAID WORK.) Work in Cloth Stitch with a Gimp and Plain Edge on the outer side, and a Plain Edge, without Gimp, on the inner, for piece of braid. For

the flower, work a plain Braid with Plain Edge on both sides from *a* to *b*, then continue the Plain Edge, and Cloth Stitch round the outer circle of the flower, but detach the threads forming the inner edge and carry them from *b* to *c*, fasten them there into the Lace, and then carry them to the next curve, and so on until the outer part of the flower is made. Then finish the centre with Cloth Stitch.

Duchesse Satin.—A thick, plain satin, exceedingly durable, and made of extra width. It is to be had in all colours, the white and cream being much used for wedding dresses.

Duck.—A white fabric made of flax, finer and lighter than canvas, and used for trousering, and small sails. Irish Ducks are made in white, or unbleached, and in black, brown, blue, grey, and olive colours. They are used for labourers' blouses. The cloth is strong, plain, and very thick, having a glazed surface. It varies in width from 27 inches to 36 inches.

Duffels, or Duffields. — A species of stout, coarse, woollen cloth, having a thick nap or frieze, resembling small knots, on the face. It is 52 inches in width, and is in much use for the cloaks of poor persons and children, and employed for charitable purposes. Reference is made to " Good Duffel gray, and flannel fine," by Wordsworth.

Dunkirk Lace.—In the districts round Dunkirk during the seventeenth century a Pillow lace with a flat thread was manufactured, which, with the laces produced at Bruges and Ypres, was indifferently classed as Mechlin Lace.

Dunster. —The old name for Kerseymere, for the manufacture of which the ancient town of Dunster, in Somersetshire, was once famous. The industry, with which the wooden market-house is associated, is mentioned in an Act of James I., where the stuff is called "Dunsters" (*see* CASIMIR).

Durants, or Durance. — A stout, worsted cloth, formerly made to imitate buff leather, and employed for dress. It is now made in various colours, and in three widths, 27 inches, 36 inches, and 40 inches, and is employed for covering coloured stays, and also for window blinds. This stuff is a description of Tammy, or Everlasting.

Is not a buff jerkin a most sweet robe of Durance ?
—*Shakespeare.*

Duratee, or Durety.—This cloth is more generally known under the name DURANTS (which *see*).

Dusters.—These are made in squares, each bordered; in various sizes, checked or twilled, and are made of linen and cotton combined. They can be bought by the yard, the material being ½ yard in width. Those sold separately measure 20 inches by 24 inches; 24 inches by 24 inches; 24 inches by 27 inches, or 27 inches by 36 inches square.

Dutch.—A kind of tape made of fine linen, the numbers running as in the IMPERIAL, from 11 to 151. See TAPE.

Dutch Corn Knitting. *See* KNITTING.

Dutch Heel. *See* KNITTING.

Dutch Lace.—Although for many years the finest and best flax thread for lace making was supplied to France and England from Holland, being grown in Brabant and steeped in the rivers near Haarlem, the inhabitants of the country have never become celebrated for their lace manufactories. At various epochs lace schools have been established in Holland, particularly one about 1685, by French refugees, for making a Needlepoint known as Dentelle à la Reine, and another for plaited Point d'Espagne, while the native manufactories were protected by the Government and foreign laces forbidden to be imported in the eighteenth century, still the industry has never really flourished. Home manufactured lace was largely worn at the Dutch Court, and was also used to trim house linen, &c., but it was not of a fine description or make. Fig. 314 is an example of real Dutch lace. It is a kind of coarse Valenciennes, made with a thick ground,

throughout the world. Climate has much influence on the success of certain dyes, and the scarlet produced on cloth in this country is considered the finest in the world. Wool has generally the strongest affinity to colour. Next to wool, silk and other animal substances receive it best; cotton is the third, and hemp and flax follow successively. As a rule, pigments and dye-stuffs do not produce permanent colours, and some substance is required to produce an affinity between the cloth and the colouring matter. The substances that are employed to act as this bond of union are called "Mordants," the principle being known to the Egyptians and other nations of remote antiquity. The use of aniline dyes is one of recent date, and a great variety of colours have been introduced into the "dry goods" trade. More recently still the Oriental shades of colour have superseded them in favour, and are known by the name of "Art Colours."

FIG. 314. DUTCH PILLOW LACE.

and of a heavy design, and though substantial and good, it is not equal to the laces of France and Belgium.

Dyeing.—Anglo-Saxon *Deagan* and *Deagian*, to dye, tinge, or stain. The art of dyeing is one of great antiquity. Moses speaks of stuffs dyed blue, purple, and scarlet, and of sheepskins dyed red; and the Israelites derived their acquaintance with it from the Egyptians, but doubtless the art was of much earlier date. The Greeks preferred their woollen stuffs to remain in their natural colour, but the external dresses of the wealthy were dyed, scarlet being in great favour, and Tyrian purple the colour reserved for princes, which dye was procured from a shellfish (a species of the Murex) found on the shores of the Mediterranean, and very costly, owing to its scarcity. Amongst the Romans, also, purple was restricted to the use of persons of the highest rank. A great advance has latterly been made in the art, both in England and

E.

Ecaille.—A French term, which, as applied to needlework, signifies pieces of flattened quill cut into the form of fish scales. This is effected by means of a punch, whilst the quill is in a soft condition, and which, at the same time, pierces little holes, through which it is sewn to the material to be thus decorated.

Ecaille Work.—This is an imitation of NACRE, or mother-of-pearl work, and consists of sewing quills upon a velvet or silk foundation and forming with them patterns in relief. To work: Take small pieces of soft and flattened quills, and with a punch or pair of scissors cut these so that they fit into and make some device. When the usual punch is used to cut the quills into shape, it will at the same time pierce a small hole large enough for a needle to

INDIAN BRAIDING.

ENGLISH BRAIDING.

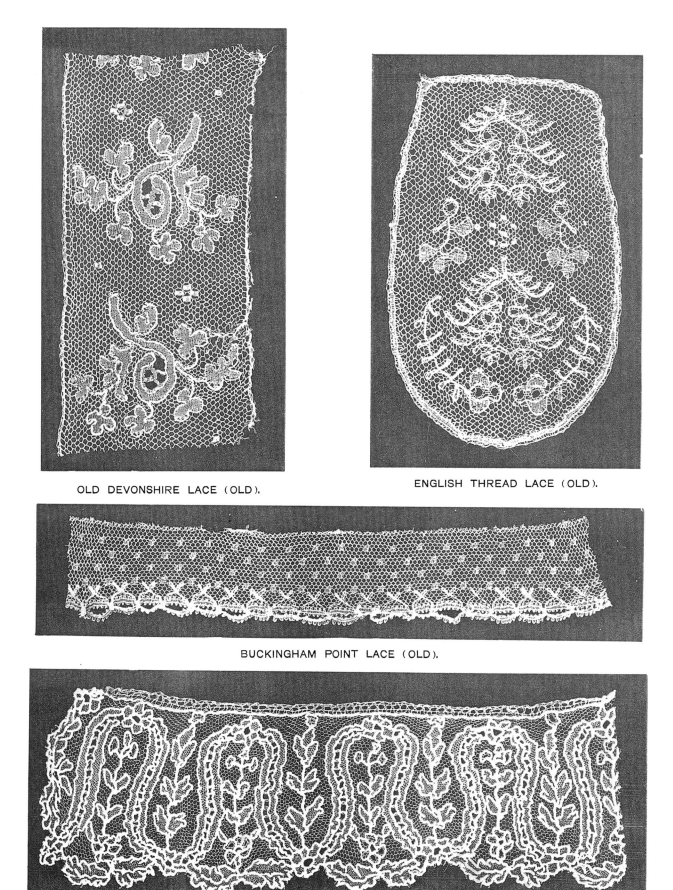

OLD DEVONSHIRE LACE (OLD).

ENGLISH THREAD LACE (OLD).

BUCKINGHAM POINT LACE (OLD).

BRUSSELS APPLIQUÉ LACE (MODERN).

pass through. Make this hole with the point of the scissors, when they are used. When the pieces of quill are ready, arrange them upon the foundation, and sew them down to it, passing the needle through the pierced holes. Having fixed the quills, take gold thread or cord and outline them with it; lay the cord upon the surface of the work, and Couch it down with a securing stitch, brought from the back of the work, as in COUCHING.

Ecclesiastical Embroidery.—A term used for needlework dedicated to the service of the Church, better known as CHURCH WORK.

Echevau.—A French term, denoting a SKEIN (which *see*).

Ecru.—A French term, denoting the colour of raw silk or unbleached linen and cotton. Much lace is sold of this colour, a hue which may be more fully described as *Café au lait.*

FIG. 315. ÉCRU LACE.

Écru Lace.—A modern lace made with two kinds of braid, connected together with various WHEELS and BARS. To work Fig. 315: Procure a plain braid coarsely plaited, and of écru colour; also a crinkled or Honiton braid of the same colour. Trace the design upon pink calico, back it with brown paper, and tack the braid to the calico. The crinkled braid will not require to be cut in the upper part of the pattern; where it forms the medallions, make the narrow connecting lines between the centre parts by turning the braid over itself, sewing it firmly together, with one of the outside edges uppermost. CORD the Bars that connect the upper Braids together, BUTTONHOLE the ones between the medallions, ornament these with PICOTS, and work the pyramid-shaped Bars in POINT DE REPRISE. Fill the centres of the medallions with an open Wheel, and finish off the scalloped edge of the lace with a narrow bought edging.

Edge.—There are two edges to lace: the outer rim,

which is either scalloped or plain, and is ornamented with Picots, and called the Cordonnet in needle-made laces, and the Engrêlure, or Footing, which is used to sew the lace to the material. *See* CORDONNET and ENGRÊLURE.

Edge Stitch.—In Crochet, Knitting, and Netting, the first stitch upon a row is sometimes called by this name. Treat it as the rest of the pattern, unless special notice is drawn to it, when either do not work it at all, or work it according to the instructions set forth. When it is not worked, keep the loop of the last stitch in the last row upon the needle, and, without working it, count it as the first stitch in the new row (this is known as Slipping a Stitch in Knitting or Netting). By not working this first stitch when making straight lines of Crochet, Knitting, and Netting, a uniform edge is attained, and the strip kept more even than it is when the first stitch is worked.

Edgings.—Narrow lace or embroidery, used to trim cambric and muslin frills, or to sew as a finish on net insertions. Those of real lace are made chiefly in Buckinghamshire, those of imitation Valenciennes at Nottingham. Coventry is famous for its machine-made and cheap embroidery edging. Edgings are sold by the yard and by the piece.

Effilé.—A French term signifying Fringed, usually with reference to a narrow width of fringe.

Egyptian Cloth.—A basket-woven cotton cloth, employed for crewel embroidery. It is otherwise called "Momie Cloth," being made in imitation of that in which Egyptian mummies are found enwrapped. It is from 32 inches to 34 inches in width.

Egyptian Needlework.—The Egyptians (800 B.C.) were distinguished for their beautiful Bead work, of which head dresses and other handsome ornaments were made, besides its being used for fringes and borders to garments. Their embroidery in coloured silks was used to elaborately ornament their garments. The designs, as gathered from the mural paintings still perfect, are chiefly borders. Some of these are of distinctly coloured and wide apart horizontal lines, finished as a heading with diagonal lines. Conventional flowers and plants, placed in separate compartments, and finished with wide borders, are amongst the specimens, the flowers being arranged without any set pattern, but with great spirit. Mythological figures and subjects are worked on the robes used in a royal enthronement. Amongst these are visible eagle-headed figures, winged divinities, the sacred tree, and gryphons. The stitches used resemble SATIN, CHAIN, and OVERCAST, but as no actual piece of embroidery of the date when Egyptian art most flourished is preserved, the nature of the stitches can only be surmised.

Eiderdown.—The fine down taken from the nests of the Eider ducks of Iceland and Greenland, which nests are so lined by the female bird from her own breast. The down is light, warm, and soft, and is sold by the pound weight, and likewise by the skein. The down plucked from the living bird possesses much elasticity, but taken from it when dead is deprived of this characteristic to a considerable extent. It is much employed as wadding for quilts and petticoats, being both lighter and warmer than any

z

other material so used. The Eider is twice the size of the ordinary duck, and frequents the shores of solitary islands.

Eider, or Eyder Yarn.—This yarn is made of the wool of Merino sheep, and is employed for knitting shawls and other articles of wear. It may be had in black and white, in scarlet, blue, and violet, and other colours, and is sold by the pound, ounce, and half ounce.

Eis Wool (sometimes written "Ice Wool").—A very fine glossy description of worsted wool, made of two-thread thickness, and employed double for making shawls. It may be had in all colours, and also shaded, and is sold by the one ounce ball.

Elastic Belting.—This material is stout and firm in texture, made as the ELASTIC WEBBING (which *see*). It has a plain edge, and is to be had in black, drab, white, and fancy-coloured stripes, of half an inch, three-quarters of an inch, one inch, and upwards in width, and is sold in pieces of 12 yards and 16 yards. It is employed for chest expanders, belts, garters, &c.

Elastic Flannel.—This description of flannel is woven in the stocking loom, and has a pile on one face, on which account it is styled *Veleurs de Laine*, and by other names, according to the fancy of the several manufacturers. The chief seat of the industry is in Wales. These flannels measure from 32 inches to 36 inches in width, and are principally employed for women's dressing-gowns and jackets. They are usually made either in coloured stripes on a white ground, or else in plain rose or blue colour.

Elastic Textiles.—These consist of bands, garters, braces, elastic stockings, kneecaps, ribbons employed for articles of women's dress, surgical bandages, &c. The warp of this material is made of indiarubber, and the woof of silk, cotton, mohair, or worsted thread. It was first made at Vienna, having been invented by a major in the Austrian service, who afterwards removed to Paris, and erected a large factory at St. Denis. It is now manufactured in this country. *Boot elastics* are made from 3 inches to 5 inches wide, and may be had in silk, mohair, and thread. Methods of weaving are adapted to produce the quality of elasticity, as in the various kinds of LAINE ELASTIQUE (which *see*), as also in knitting, a rib being made in stockings and vests, enabling them to cling closely, and yet to expand in proportion to the size to be fitted.

Elastic Webbing.—This material consists of india-rubber covered with cotton, mohair, or silk. The india-rubber is spread out into very thin, flat sheets, and cut with a knife, by means of machinery, into square threads no thicker than a fine pin, if so desired. The width is decided by the number of these cords—1 to 16, or upwards. These narrow and single cords are turned out in two lengths of 72 yards to the gross; and the wider, in four pieces, of 36 yards each.

Elephant Towelling.—Although primarily designed for towelling, this cloth has latterly been much used for crewel embroidery. It is a variety of the HUCKABACK and HONEYCOMB (which *see*).

Elephant Towelling Embroidery.—This is a combination of DRAWN WORK and EMBROIDERY, and takes its name from the material upon which it is executed. It is suitable for making antimacassars and mats. To work: Take a piece of Elephant Towelling the size required, allowing for a fringe all round. Trace out in its centre a sixteen pointed star, or a Vandyke, or Cross, and work over this in flat SATIN STITCH with coloured Pyrenean wool. Make a wide border round this centre ornament thus: 3 inches from the edge of the material draw out inch squares of threads, leaving a plain square between each drawn out square. BUTTONHOLE round the drawn out squares and fill them with WHEELS, and fill in the plain squares with an eight-pointed star, worked with fine Pyrenean wool of the same colour, but of a different shade to the wool used in the centre star. To make the Fringe: Draw out the threads round the edge of the material for the depth of 1½ inches, and ornament with a line of wide apart Buttonhole in Pyrenean wool of the same shade as that used in the centre star.

Eliottine Silk.—A description of knitting silk which is the especial manufacture of a particular firm, and so called after a popular writer on the subject of Needle-work. This knitting material is a composition of silk and wool.

Ell.—A standard measure of length, employed for textiles. It measures 45 inches, or 3 feet 9 inches, or 1¼ yards. It was fixed at 45 inches by Henry I., A.D. 1101. A French *ell* is 1½ yards, or 54 inches; a Flemish *ell* is only equal to 27 inches. The English *ell* to the Flemish is in proportion as 5 to 3. The Scotch *ell* comprises $37\frac{2}{10}$ English inches. The term is one which also is used proverbially to denote an indefinitely long measure.

Elysée Work.—An arrangement of two coloured cotton materials after the manner of APPLIQUÉ, and an easy and inexpensive kind of Embroidery. The designs are floral, and are cut out of light coloured sateen cloth, laid upon dark sateen cloth, and ornamented with EMBROIDERY STITCHES in coloured filoselles. To work: Select a continuous running pattern, chiefly composed of sprays of leaves and tendrils. Trace this upon pale green sateen cloth, and cut it out with a sharp pair of scissors. Frame a piece of olive green or ruby coloured sateen cloth, in an EMBROIDERY FRAME, paste the sea-green leaves, &c., on to it, and leave it to dry. Then unite the leaves together with stems of CHAIN STITCH, made of various shades of green filoselles. Vein the leaves with green and ruby coloured filoselles in STEM STITCH, work the centres of flowers with FRENCH KNOTS, and fill in any open or bare spaces with tendrils in Stem Stitch, made with ruby filoselles.

Emboss.—A term employed in Embroidery to signify the execution of a design in relief, either by stuffing with layers of thread or succession of stitches underneath the Embroidery, or else by working over a pad made with thick materials.

The formation of ornamental figures in relief entered largely into all ancient Embroideries, and was considered as a distinguishing mark of good workmanship. The taste for it has not been encouraged with the revival of needlework, it not now being considered true art to detach from the surface of a material a representation of natural objects which should, when copied in needlework, never be treated save in a flat and conventional manner. Figures were slightly raised from their grounds and padded out in the earlier centuries, but it was during the seventeenth century that this padding attained its greatest relief, and became known as EMBROIDERY IN THE STAMP, as well as Emboss, as the latter term includes all raised parts, whether made by Paddings or Raised Couchings, or by sewing to various parts of the design, hammered up plates of gold and silver, or bullion, tinsel, spangles, paillons, mother-of-pearl, beads, precious stones, and other materials. To Emboss: Pad out the surface of the material with wool or hair, and confine this padding to its right place by sewing white or coloured silk tightly down upon it. Lay the bullion over it, as described in BULLION EMBROIDERY, or fasten the other materials to the work by sewing them on through holes expressly drilled in them for that purpose.

Embossed Plush, or Velvet Embroidery.—A handsome work, very fashionable at the present date. The materials used are stamped plush or velvet, Japanese gold thread, filoselles or floss silks, and very narrow silk cords. To work: Select a bold conventional flower design, clearly stamped out on its material. COUCH down on to the flat parts either the narrow silk cords or the gold thread, outline with these the chief parts of the pattern, cut off the cord or gold thread where each outline finishes with care, and SEW it down on the right side of the material until it is quite secure. The outline finished, take the floss silks and work in SATIN stitch with them, fill up the small parts of the pattern, and make the veins of leaves, and the centres of flowers or buds, with the silks, using several shades and varieties of colour over the various parts.

Embroidery.—An art which consists of enriching a flat foundation, by working into it with a needle coloured silks, gold or silver thread, and other extraneous materials, in floral, geometrical, or figure designs. The origin of embroidery is lost in antiquity, but it is known to have existed before painting, and to have been the first medium of reproducing natural objects in their natural colours. The work came from the East, and was first called Phrygium, or Phrygian work, while an embroiderer was called Phrygio, and designs worked entirely in gold or silver thread, Auriphrygium; and these names seem to indicate that it was first brought to excellence by the Babylonians, although Sir J. G. Wilkinson has discovered upon Egyptian monuments painted in the Eighteenth Dynasty, before the time of Babylon, designs in arabesque Embroidery upon the garments and furniture of the Egyptians. There is no doubt that both the Assyrians and the Egyptians were particularly lavish in their needlework decorations, not only in their temples, houses, and garments, but even for the sails of their boats; and it was from them that the Jews learnt the art, and considered it worthy of express mention in Exodus as part of the adornment of the Tabernacle, and of the sacred robes of their priests. From the Egyptians and the Hebrews, and also from Eastern nations, the Romans and the Greeks became acquainted

with its higher branches, and the latter appropriated the honour of its invention to their goddess Minerva, while Homer introduced into his writings descriptions of the Embroidery executed by Helen, Andromache, and Penelope. The Romans, after their conquests, became possessed of much spoil in the way of Embroidery, and the needlework of Babylon, which retained its reputation until the first century of the Christian era, was highly prized by them. The veils given by Herod to the Temple came from Babylon, and Cicero describes the magnificence of the embroidered robes of Babylonian work worn by Tarquin the Elder. Gradually the Romans learnt to Embroider, and after the introduction of Christianity into Europe and the founding of religious houses, the art became of great importance and almost a science, the designs being contributed by artists and a lavish expenditure of time and money bestowed to bring it to a high state of perfection. At one time only the borders of garments were worked, and as the name of Phrygium gradually died out, the Latin words *Brustus, Brudatus, Aurobrus,* were substituted to denote needlework, and from these the French *Broderie* and the English Embroidery are derived. From the first to the end of the sixteenth century, Italy was looked upon as the centre of Embroidery, the Popes of Rome collecting from all countries the most beautiful specimens, and ordering that costly presents of needlework should be made by the faithful to the churches and religious houses. As the knowledge of needlework increased, its varieties were no longer classed under one name, but were each distinguished with separate titles: Thus, Opus Consutum meant two materials applied to each other, like our modern Appliqué; and also Cut Work, Opus Plumarium, Embroidery in Satin or Long stitch, in which the stitches are laid over each other, like the plumage of a bird; Opus Pulvinarium, or work upon canvas in Cross, Cushion, or Tent Stitch, like our modern Woolwork; and Opus Anglicum, a name given to an English needlework that attained great celebrity both at home and abroad, from the thirteenth to the sixteenth century, from the peculiarity of a stitch used in its manufacture. Up to the time of the Wars of the Roses English Embroidery was justly famous, but it then languished, and when the taste for it revived, it was never again executed with the same amount of gorgeous simplicity, the patterns becoming too overloaded with ornament for true taste. On the Continent during this period the work flourished with increased vigour, and in Paris the Embroiderers formed themselves into a guild, and were in esteem, grants of land being frequently given for their handiwork. The Reformation may be said to have given the death blow to Church work in England, and, through it, to the finer sorts of Embroidery. Churches were no longer allowed to be decorated with altar cloths, priests' robes were almost abolished, and the convents (the great schools of the art) were destroyed. During the reigns of James I. and Charles I., besides work with crewels, very fine Embroidery was done upon silk and satin foundations for secular purposes, but this never attained the dignity and costliness of the Church work. The chief patterns were heraldic devices, portraits, and flower scenes. During the wars between Charles I. and his Parliament, Royalist ladies were fond of embroidering miniatures of the King, and working into them the real hair of that monarch; and mention is made in old chronicles of the granting of hair for that purpose. After the King's execution these miniatures were treasured as sacred relics, and many of them can still be seen in a good state of preservation. A peculiar kind of Raised Embroidery, known as Embroidery on the Stamp, was much in vogue at this period, and for a century afterwards. During the reign of Queen Anne the patterns for Embroidery were extremely good and well considered, and the work, chiefly in flat Satin Stitch upon flat grounds, was essentially artistic, both in design and in colouring. This fine Embroidery flourished during the reign of that queen and that of the Georges, the patterns becoming gradually more refined, and consisting of light garlands of flowers, or delicate sprays, and groups or figures in the Watteau style, all shaded and worked in imitation of the most minute of paintings. In the earlier part of the present century fine Embroidery was succeeded by a coarser kind, into which large figures were introduced, whose hands and faces were not worked, but painted, while their dresses and surroundings were either worked in silks or crewels. Etching Embroidery, or Print work, was then also much the fashion. To this period the works of Miss Linwood belong, which are full-size copies from Guido, Carlo Dolci, Opie, and Gainsborough. Embroidery then sank to its lowest ebb, Church work had entirely disappeared, the fine silk work became out of date, and the only work that at all flourished was the mechanical copying of Berlin patterns, first in Tent, and finally in Cross stitch; but the revival of the taste for design fostered by the Exhibition of 1851 produced a favourable change in needlework, and from that date old work has been hunted up and copied, and artists have emulated each other in pointing out the differences between bad and good designing, and in fresh patterns; and at present both Church work and Embroidery for home uses are carried to as great a perfection as, if not actually surpassing, the needlework of the Middle Ages.

During all these changes in the history of European needlework, the art of Embroidery in the East may be said to have remained in its original state. True to their Oriental character, the Eastern nations have continued steadily to reproduce the ancient patterns without inventing new ones; and, as they possess in a high degree the most magnificent conceptions of colouring, they execute needlework of the most gorgeous tints, yet of such harmonies as to be in perfect good taste. The Chinese, Persians, Indians, and Japanese are all remarkable for their skill, and the modern Egyptians, Bulgarians, and Algerians are not far behind them, embroidering head veils and towels with gold and coloured silks, and frequently enriching these with precious stones, and executing the whole with great taste; in fact, until the introduction into the East during the last few years of our meretricious aniline dyes, and the inharmonious colouring produced by them, Eastern needlework continued to be as beautiful as it was in the time of Moses.

Embroidery is divided into two chief heads: that worked upon white with washing materials, and that worked with coloured materials upon a coloured foundation. The latter of these is the original Embroidery, and embraces most of the finest kinds of work, and it is again subdivided under three heads—*Guimped Embroidery, Embroidery on the Stamp,* and *Low,* or *Plain Embroidery.*

Guimped Embroidery consists in cutting out shapes in vellum and laying them upon the surface of the material, or raising the groundwork with cords and then covering these parts with gold or silk threads. It also includes the hammering out of very thin plates of metal and attaching these to the surface of the material. It survives in our modern Church work.

Embroidery on the Stamp is formed by raising in high relief from the groundwork figures, animals, and other objects. It is done by outlining the figure upon the groundwork, and then padding it up with horsehair and wool to a great height, and covering this with thick white or coloured silk and satin. Above and upon this most elaborate Embroidery stitches are worked; sometimes the figures are entirely clothed with the most delicate of needle-made laces, at others with the finest of Embroidery, and with real jewels, such as pearls and garnets, interwoven into the pattern. This work flourished in the seventeenth century; it has no counterpart in modern times.

Low, or *Plain Embroidery,* includes all the Embroidery in Satin and other stitches upon a plain foundation, whether worked alike upon both sides or slightly raised from the surface by run lines (not by padding), or worked as the usual Embroidery with coloured silks upon satin, velvet, cloth, or linen foundations.

White Embroidery, so called from its being worked upon white or other light materials with cotton or ingrain silks, was imported from the East, particularly from India, whose natives still excel in it, as do the Chinese in Tambour work, one of its varieties. It gave the first idea of lace, and may be looked upon as one of the foundations of lace work. The Guipure Carrickmacross lace is a fine white embroidery on cambric connected with Lace Stitches. For a very long period in Europe it was only worked in nunneries, and used for sacerdotal purposes, but it at length became more universally practised, and the natives of Saxony were the first who were particularly expert in making it. It does not seem to have been introduced into France until the middle of the eighteenth century, into Scotland and Ireland at the end of that time, and into Switzerland at the beginning of the present century. Wherever it becomes established, it adds considerably to the comfort of the poorer classes, as it forms the staple occupation of the women and children in those districts. It is of two descriptions, the *Open* and the *Close.* In the *Open,* the pattern is produced by the disposition of the holes cut and Overcast, and includes Broderie Anglaise, Madeira, and Irish work, besides other kinds differing but little from these; in the *Close,* the stitches are worked upon the cambric or muslin foundation in the same manner as in flat Embroidery, and the stitches are described alphabetically under the heading of STITCHES, which will be found after the EMBROIDERIES.

EMBROIDERIES.—*Embroidery alike upon both sides of*

material.—This Embroidery requires to be worked in a frame. The patterns are the same as used for flat Embroideries, and the work is executed in Satin Stitch, with filoselles on floss silk. To work: Trace a design consisting of small flowers and leaves upon a material, and place in a frame. Bring the needle up upon one side of a traced flower or leaf, and put it down again on the opposite side, and in a slightly slanting direction; return it along the back of the material to the place it first came up at, and bring it out there, close to the last stitch and on the right-hand side. Put it down close to where it went in in the last stitch and on the right-hand side, and continue this manner of working for the whole design. Shade by working leaves or petals in different colours, not by blending colours in one leaf, and fasten off, and commence threads by running them in, so as to show neither at back nor front of work.

Embroidery, au Passé.—See EMBROIDERY IN SATIN STITCH.

Embroidery, Beau Ideal.—This is a machine-made, imitation of Broderie Anglaise, and consists of strong and well made strips for trimmings, varying in width from three-quarters of an inch to 1½ inches. It is an extremely clever imitation of hand made Embroidery, the edges being finished with plain and scalloped lines of Double Overcast, and the holes forming the design worked over in Overcast. A thread is run in readiness to draw the trimming up into gathers, so that it can be sown on to a foundation with little trouble.

Embroidery in Satin Stitch.—This work was anciently termed Low or Plain Embroidery, to distinguish it from the Guimped Embroidery or Embroidery on the Stamp, and it is now sometimes called Embroidery au Passé. The work, though named after one particular stitch, includes all flat Embroideries done with coloured silks, filoselles, or wools upon coloured satin, silk, velvet or linen foundations, and these materials may either be worked into the foundation as shaded embroideries or as needlework executed in one colour. Satin Stitch Embroidery, when the designs are shaded, is capable of producing the most beautiful results, and is equal in effect to painting. It was this branch of the art that was brought to such perfection in the time of Queen Anne and the Georges, when sprays and garlands of flowers were worked upon light silk or satin grounds in tints that matched their natural colours to the minutest detail. The Satin Stitch Embroidery in one colour is much easier and more quickly executed than the shaded, and is adapted for many purposes that the shaded is too good for, such as mats, table-borders, bags, sachets, slippers, and other articles of daily use. To work a shaded pattern: Draw upon light silk or satin a delicate pattern consisting of flower sprays, and tint this design in natural shades with water-colours. Then frame it in an EMBROIDERY FRAME and commence to work. Let the right hand be always above the frame, ready to receive the needle when pushed through, and the left beneath the frame; bring the needle out to the right hand and put it in to the left. Do not handle the silk at all, and make the stitches rather long and of unequal lengths, as in FEATHER STITCH, and be careful that the outlines of all the filled-in design shall be clear and distinct, and blend the various shades of one colour into each other by running the stitches one into the other. Arrange that the lightest shades of silk shall be worked in so as to show where the light falls most prominently, and see that these lights all fall from one side of the work to the other. Use eight shades of silk in a medium sized flower, and work flowers of the same kind in

FIG. 316. EMBROIDERY IN SATIN STITCH.

the same shades, but make some darker and some lighter than the others, by leaving out the lightest or the darkest shades in these, and so altering their appearance, and make the stitches of different lengths in the petal of a flower, as in Feather Stitch. Fill in the centres with FRENCH KNOTS, and also work these as finishes to the stamens. Work the leaves in eight or ten shades of green, using greens shading to yellow and brown, and green shading to blue, upon different leaves. Make the edges

FIG. 317. EMBROIDERY IN SATIN STITCH.

of the leaves lighter than the centres, but preserve the fall of light; shade one side of the leaf differently to the other, and vein with light or dark veins, according to the position of the leaf. Work the veins in SPLIT STITCH; work the stems and tendrils of the design in ROPE STITCH. Make no knots in the embroidery silk, but run the ends in on the right side of the work, both when commencing and fastening off a thread.

Embroidery in Satin Stitch in one shade need not be worked in a frame. The design is traced upon the foundation, and then worked in various Embroidery Stitches. Several distinct tints of colour can be used upon the same patterns, but there must be no shading or blending of shades of one tint into the other. The appearance of the work is dependent upon the judicious selection of primary colours and the amount and precision of the Embroidery stitches. Fig. 316 is intended for a border of this kind of Embroidery, and is worked as follows: Trace the design upon olive green satin or silk, work the petals of the flowers in Satin Stitch in orange gold silk, and fill in their centres with French Knots of a deeper shade of orange silk. Work one side of the leaves in Satin Stitch of an olive green shade of filoselle, Overcast round the outer edge of the other side of the leaves, and fill in with Point de Pois worked in a light olive green shade; work the small leaves in the same shade, and the stems in a brown filoselle and in Crewel Stitch.

To work Fig. 317: Select a light-coloured silk foundation, and work the Embroidery in three contrasting tints; outline the battledores in Double Overcast, and raise them with a padding of run lines; work their centres in Point Russe, and surround with a line of Chain Stitch. Work the shuttlecocks in two shades, and in Satin Stitch, their feathers in Point Russe. Work the rose with Satin Stitch, petals and centre in French Knots, the leaves in Point de Plume and Satin Stitch, the grapes in Point de Pois, the ribbon outlines with Chain Stitch in a light colour, and fill in with Satin Stitch in a dark colour.

Embroidery on Canvas.—The chief ancient Embroidery upon coarsely woven canvas or unbleached materials is known as Tapestry, and when this became out of date it was superseded by Crewel Work, and then by patterns drawn and painted by hand upon an open-meshed yet fine canvas, and executed in Tent Stitch with English worsted or crewels. This fine canvas allowed of every stitch being worked of the same size and length, but as it was a tedious operation to fill in large pieces of work with such fine stitches, a coarse canvas with wide apart meshes was introduced, and Berlin patterns executed upon it, first in Tent and then in Cross Stitch. The old-fashioned Canvas Work allowed of some display of the worker's taste and ingenuity in drawing the design and shading it, and patterns so drawn could be shaded without the tedious attention to counting stitches necessary when executing Berlin patterns, but since the introduction of the last named it has almost entirely fallen into disuse. *See* Berlin Work, Canvas Work, and Tapestry.

Embroidery on Chip.—The material upon which this work is executed is manufactured abroad, and is made either of fine plaited chips or wood shavings. Rushes dried

and plaited together would form the same kind of foundation, and would have the same appearance of coarse Java canvas, and are as suitable as the chips to form the mats and other articles for keeping heat and wet from furniture for which this work is used. The Embroidery is executed in bright coloured silks, and the designs and stitches are extremely simple. The design given of this work in Fig. 318 is a mat with its four corners filled in with sprays of flowers, and the centre ornamented with a star. To work: Make the centre a star of twenty-four points and of three shades of a bright-coloured silk, and where the points meet in the centre of the star, work one Cross Stitch in the medium shade of silk. Work the cornflower spray in blue and green silks, the cornflowers in Picot, the leaves in Satin, and the stems in Crewel Stitch. Work

FIG. 318. EMBROIDERY ON CHIP.

the rosebuds in rose colour and green silk, the buds in Picot and Satin Stitch, the leaves in Satin, and the stems in Crewel stitch. Work the pansies in shades of purple silk with amber centres, leaves and flowers in Satin Stitch. Work the ragged robin in white and green silks, the flowers in Picots of white silk with a French Knot as centre, the principal leaves in Picot, the stems in Crewel Stitch. Edge the mat with a double Vandyke line in Point Russe worked with the darkest shade of colour used in the centre star.

Embroidery on Lace.—A modern work made with a foundation of machine-made laces, selected for their bold designs, and worked with coloured filoselles, tinsel, and gold cord. The lace, when ornamented, is used for dress trimmings, and curtain or table cloth borders.

Coloured, white, or black laces are used. To work: Select a coarse lace with an effective pattern, outline the chief parts of the design with gold cord or tinsel; sew this down on the material, as in Couching, with a coloured silk. Work over the centre parts of the pattern with variously coloured silks, using colours that contrast but yet blend together. Work in the silks with Crewel, Herringbone, or Satin Stitch. Use Japanese gold

lin, and rub powdered blue through the holes, and then back the muslin with brown paper. Outline the pattern with a run thread of Embroidery cotton. Work the stems in Rope Stitch, the leaves, with the veins left unworked, in Point de Plume, the rest in flat Satin Stitch, the flower by itself in Satin Stitch, with a centre of French Knots, the two flowers together in French Knot centres, surrounded by Satin Stitch, with outer leaves made with

Fig. 319. EMBROIDERY ON MUSLIN

thread and raw silks for mantel borders; tinsel, filoselle, or crewel wools for less permanent work. Leave the lace background untouched.

Embroidery on Leather.—The patterns for this Embroidery are the same that are used for Embroidery in Satin Stitch, and the foundation is either of kid or very fine leather. To work: Trace the design upon thin leather, and prick holes for the needle to pass through, or buy a pattern already traced and pricked. Work the design in Satin Stitch, with various coloured filoselles,

Point de Pois, and finished with Overcast, and work the large balls as raised Dots.

Embroidery on Net.—This work is a combination of Lace stitches, Embroidery stitches, gold thread, and Braid, and is suitable either for Insertion or Edgings in Dress Trimmings. To work as an Insertion, and as shown in Fig. 320: Draw out the Design upon pink calico, and tack fine black or white net upon it. Take the black or white lace braid that is made in loops, cut it, and tack each loop separately in its place on to the pattern.

Fig. 320. EMBROIDERY ON NET.

and when the work is finished, paste the back of the leather upon thin linen to keep it from splitting.

Embroidery on Muslin.—This is a fine kind of close white Embroidery, and is also known as Irish, Saxony, or Madeira work, from the skill exhibited in its manufacture by the peasants of those countries. The work is illustrated in Fig. 319, and is done upon fine cambric or muslin, with Embroidery cotton, Walter and Evans' No. 40. Trace the design upon thin cartridge paper, prick it round with a number of pin pricks, lay this pattern on the mus-

Where the design shows large stitches in the centre of these loops, Back Stitch them to the net with coloured filoselles, and where they are left plain, Overcast their edges on to the net with the same coloured filoselles. Fill the centres of the flower with Wheels, and work the stems by darning coloured filoselles in and out, or by couching gold thread down on them.

Embroidery on Net with Silks.—Worked without braid, with écru or coloured net, filoselles of various shades, and gold and silver threads. To work: Trace a group of flowers, or a bold Arabesque pattern, upon pink calico, tack the net to it, and outline all the design with lines of gold thread, COUCHED down, or with BUTTON-HOLE worked with filoselle. Finish by DARNING the silks in and out of the net, to fill in the leaves, or thick part of the design. Work the centres of flowers, and other light parts, with open Point Lace stitches, using the net foundations as a background, or cut them away and secure with BUTTONHOLES.

To work the Edging shown in Fig. 321: Trace the design, and lay the net over; tack the Braid down, and make the BARS. BUTTONHOLE the net where left as an edging, and OVERCAST the braid to the net where it is to be cut away. Work the sprays in SATIN STITCH,

FIG. 321. EMBROIDERY ON NET.

untack the pattern, run the net on the wrong side to the braid, close to where it is to be cut, and cut it away from underneath the Bars.

Embroidery on Netting.—A name given to DARNED NETTING.

Embroidery on Silk.—This Embroidery is executed in any of the usual Embroidery stitches, but Satin, Feather, Crewel, and French Knots are most selected. To work Fig. 322: Trace the design upon olive green silk, and frame it in an Embroidery Frame. BACK STITCH down gold braid, and work with Pearsall's silks, the cornflowers and poppies in their natural shades, and in SATIN STITCH, except the centres of the poppies, which work in FRENCH KNOT, and the diamond crossings over the calyx of the cornflowers. Work the leaves in shades of olive green, and in Satin Stitch, the stems in CREWEL STITCH, and the barley in Satin Stitch.

Embroidery on the Stamp.—Also called Raised Embroidery. The figures in this work were raised in high relief from their backgrounds by means of pads formed of wool or hair being placed under the needlework, as already described in the general introduction to this article (see p. 172).

Embroidery on Velvet.—There are two descriptions of this work. The first, or true Embroidery upon Velvet, is an imitation of the celebrated Benares work, and is made as follows: Frame the velvet, and back it with a thin holland foundation (*see* EMBROIDERY FRAME), and

then trace the design upon it with white chalk. Work this over with SATIN STITCH, FRENCH KNOTS, and other

FIG. 322. EMBROIDERY ON SILK.

EMBROIDERY STITCHES, using bright coloured floss silk, and a large quantity of gold and silver thread. Should

ANGLO SAXON EMBROIDERY.

CHAIN STITCH EMBROIDERY.

the velvet foundation be of light gold colour, work the pattern with dark and brilliant shades of floss silk only; but should it be cream or white, work with gold and silver thread only; should it be of rich and dark velvet, use both gold and silver thread and bright floss silks. Use the primary colours, and carefully avoid all colours obtained by aniline dyes.

The second description of Embroidery upon velvet is an APPLIQUÉ. To work: Cut the pattern out upon velvet, which must be previously framed and backed with holland, and paste it upon a silk foundation. Lay two lines of gold thread or purse silk round the velvet outlines, secure them as in Couching, work the stems and tendrils of the design with gold bullion, ornament the centres of the flowers with FRENCH KNOTS made with embroidery silk or filoselle, and mark out the veins of leaves and other parts of design with long SATIN STITCH, in filoselle or floss silk.

Embroidery with Gold and Silver. — When gold and silver threads are used for Embroidery, they are generally associated with coloured silks and filoselles, and

raised over vellum, or laid flat and COUCHED, and fill in the border with spangles and long shaped beads crossed with coloured silks.

STITCHES.—The stitches used in Embroideries are distinguished by names selected, as far as possible, to indicate their appearance when worked. They are as follows:

Arrow Stitch.—A name sometimes given to Stem Stitch, because of its slanting direction. See *Stem Stitch.*

Au Passé Stitch.—Also known as Point Passé, Passé, and Long. It is a name given to Satin Stitch when worked across the material and without any padding. See *Satin Stitch.*

Back Stitch.—A stitch also known as HEM STITCH, and used in fancy Embroideries, and in plain needlework. To work: Bring the needle up upon a traced line, and insert it into the material, a little behind where it came up, and bring it out a little beyond, both putting it in and bringing it out upon the straight line. Put the

FIG. 323. EMBROIDERY WITH GOLD AND SILVER.

when used with these materials for Ecclesiastical purposes the work is called Church Work. The same kind of work is, however, notwithstanding its expense, occasionally used for secular purposes, such as table borders, cushions, and chimney vallances. To work: Stretch the material in a frame, and draw the design; cut out little pieces of parchment to fill in any raised parts, such as the flowers and leaves, shown in Fig. 323, and tack these down into their position. Make small holes through the material with a stiletto, run the gold or silver thread into a large-eyed needle, and bring it up from the back of the material, cross it over the parchment, and return it to the back through one of the holes. Fill in the centres of the flowers, the lower part of the buds, and the points of the stamens, with spangles crossed with coloured silks, and ornament the centres of the leaves with laid rows of these spangles. Make the open net pattern, the small spray-shaped leaves, the stamens, and the stems, with gold purse silk. Work the two lines of the border with gold thread,

needle down again in the same hole made when it first came up, and bring it out again on the line a few threads forward. Continue to make small even stitches in this way along the line. The beauty of the work consists in every stitch being made of the same size, and kept in an even line.

Barred Witch Stitch.—See *Herringbone Stitch.*

Basket Stitch.—A Raised Couching Stitch chiefly used in Church Work, but occasionally in silk Embroideries. To work: Lay down perpendicular lines of fine whipcord upon the material, at even distances apart, and secure them with tacking threads. Upon this foundation lay down three or four strands of purse silk or gold cord. Pass these threads over two lines of whipcord, in a horizontal direction, and secure them with a stitch brought from the back, pass it over them, and return it to the back, and repeat this stitch until the four strands of silk or gold cord are stitched down between every two pieces of whipcord. For second row—Lay down the four threads

A A

of silk or gold over the whipcord, and close to those first laid, and secure them with stitches brought from the back of the material, and returned there. Make the first securing stitch over one strand of whipcord, so as to prevent the securing threads forming a line down the work, then secure the threads over two strands of whipcord as before. Repeat these two rows to the end of the space.

Battlemented Stitch.—An arrangement of Overcast, Holbein, or Point de Russe, to imitate in Embroidery the indented line of battlements upon castles, &c. The stitch is used in Ticking and other ornamental Embroidery, and is shown in the centre line of Fig. 324. To work in Holbein stitch with both sides alike : Run the thread first over, then under, and then over the traced line, so that every alternate stitch fills up a marked space. In the second running, work over the plain spaces and under the ones already filled in. To work in Overcast : Trace a battlemented line on the material. Bring the needle up from the back, and cover the line with fine and even OVERCAST stitches, working from left to right. To work in

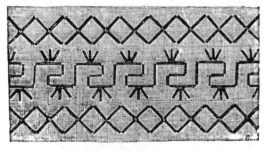

FIG. 324. BATTLEMENTED STITCH.

Point de Russe : Trace a battlemented line. Bring the needle up from the back of the material, at one end of the short line forming the top of one Battlement, put the needle back at the end of this line, only take up a few threads of material, and bring the needle out, at the top of the short upright line, put it down at the end of the line, take up a few threads of material, and bring it up ready to make the next line in the same manner. Work from right to left, and continue to the end of the traced line. The three diverging lines at the top and bottom of each battlement (See Fig. 324) work in LONG STITCH, as also the diamond border above and below the Battlemented; they are inserted as an ornamental finish to the work, and have no connection with the stitch.

Blanket Stitch.—This stitch is employed to form an ornamental finish to cloth, serge, and other thick materials, when they are used as the foundation for embroidered counterpanes, tablecloths, &c., whose substance is too thick to allow of their edges being turned in and hemmed over. The stitch derives its name from its having originally been used as an edging to blankets, but its foundation is Buttonhole worked in various patterns, all of which can be used upon one edging if desired, the only essential to Blanket Stitch being that it is formed of wide-apart Buttonhole, and is worked with coarse crewels or filoselles. To work : Make a BUTTONHOLE upon the edge of the material, take up a quarter of an inch of the

material in the length of the stitch, and slant it from right to left; make another Buttonhole of the same length, but an upright stitch, and close to the first one, then a third, slant this from left to right; miss the space of half an inch, carrying the filoselle along the edge of the work, and repeat the three stitches.

Another kind : Make an upright BUTTONHOLE one-eighth of an inch long, miss the space of one-eighth of an inch, and make a Buttonhole a quarter of an inch long, miss the same space, and make a Buttonhole half an inch long, miss the same space, and make a Buttonhole a quarter of an inch long, miss the same space, and make a Buttonhole one-eighth of an inch long, miss the space of half an inch, and repeat these five stitches.

Another kind : Make a BUTTONHOLE a quarter of an inch long, then four half an inch long, and one a quarter of an inch long, miss one-eighth of an inch between each Buttonhole, and half an inch between every group of six stitches.

Brick Stitch.—A Flat Couching, and used in silk Embroideries. To work : Lay down two strands of floss silk or filoselle upon the material, and to secure these bring a stitch up from the back of the material, pass it over them, and return it again to the back. Secure the whole length of the strands with these stitches, at even distances apart; then lay down two more strands, and secure them in the same manner, but arrange that the stitch that secures them shall come exactly between two in the last row, and not opposite to them. Fill in all the space with second row.

Broad Couching Stitch.—A Flat Couching, and made as follows : Lay down three or four strands of filoselle or floss silk on to the material, and secure them with a fastening stitch brought up from the back, pass it over them, and return it to the back. Make these stitches at set intervals down the laid threads, then lay down more threads and secure them, also at set intervals, but so that they come between, not opposite, the ones already made.

Bullion Knot Stitch.—Used in silk Embroideries, Crewel Work, and Church Work, forming a raised roll

FIG. 325. BULLION KNOT.

laid along the surface of the work. To make : Secure the thread at the back of the work, and bring it through to the front. Put the needle into the material, and bring it out so that the point is close to the thread, and take up from a quarter to half an inch of material on the needle, according to the length desired for the Knot. Wind the thread round the point of the needle from ten to twelve times (*see* Fig. 325); hold the needle down with the left thumb, and wind with the right hand. Still holding the needle down, pull it through the material, pull up the thread to where the needle was inserted, and let the Knots lie evenly along the surface; then put the thread through to the back at this place, and repeat for a second Bullion Knot. In the illustration two Bullion Knots are arranged as an oval, but they can be laid down upon the material as single Knots, or in any other device.

Burden Stitch.—A Flat Couching, and used in silk Embroideries. To work: Lay down a line of floss silk or filoselle, and, to secure it, bring up a thread from the back of the material, on one side of the filoselle, and put it back again on the other. Arrange these securing stitches at even distances along the line of filoselle.

Buttonhole Stitch.—In Broderie Anglaise and other ornamental Embroideries this stitch is chiefly used to form an edging to the work, and is then known as Feston, or Double Overcast. When used in Point Lace work, of which it is the chief stitch, or as a filling to the various parts of Fancy Embroidery, it is called Close Stitch, Point de Brussels, or Point Noné. To work as a Feston or Double Overcast: Run a straight or scalloped line at the edge of the material, and commence to work from left to right. Bring the needle up from the back of the material, put it down into the material over the run line, and bring it up under that line, and draw up with the needle over the working thread, so that a loop is formed on the material. Continue to make these loops along the line, put the needle down above the run line, and close to the stitch last made,

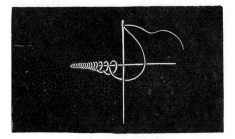

FIG. 326. BUTTONHOLE STITCH.

bring it up under the run line, and take up the same amount of material at each stitch. To work as Point Noné, &c., and without a foundation (*see* Fig. 326): Throw a thread across the space to be filled, from right to left, and secure it firmly upon each side. Commence to work from left to right, put the needle into the piece of lace or material above the thread thrown across, and then downwards behind the foundation thread. Bring it up on the other side of the foundation thread and over the working thread, so that it forms a loop. Continue to make these loops to the end of the row. Then throw another foundation thread across, and cover this with BUTTONHOLE; put the needle into the first line of Buttonhole instead of into the material. Continue to throw threads across, and cover them with Buttonholes until the space is filled.

Chain Stitch.—This stitch is also called Point de Chainette and Tambour Stitch. It is largely used in all Fancy Embroideries, particularly in Indian and other Oriental work. Upon fine cambric or muslin Chain or Tambour Stitch is worked with a Crochet hook thus:

Thread in the front of the work, put the hook through the material, and bring it out to the front, thread round the needle, and draw it up as a loop through the piece of material on the hook *; hook through the material, thread round the hook, and draw through the

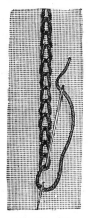

FIG. 327. CHAIN STITCH.

material and loop upon the hook; repeat from * to make every Chain. To work Chain Stitch with a Needle: Bring the needle from the back of the material up in the line to be embroidered, put the needle down close to the place it came out, but on the right side *; hold the thread down with the left thumb, and bring the needle out upon the line, one-eighth of an inch below where it was inserted, and over the thread held down. Draw up, and the stitch will be formed. Put the needle down on the right side, close to where it came up, and in the Chain already made (*see* Fig. 327), and repeat from * for the whole of the pattern.

Close Stitch.—See *Buttonhole Stitch.*

Chain Twisted Stitch.—See *Twisted Chain Stitch.*

Coral Stitch.—A stitch worked either Double or Single. It is much used in Ticking and other fancy Embroideries, and also to decorate plain linen. To

FIG. 328. CORAL STITCH.

work Single Coral: Bring the needle up in the centre line, hold the thread down with the left thumb one-eighth of an inch beneath where the needle came out. Insert the needle on left side of the line (*see* Fig. 328), even to where it came up, but a short distance away, and bring it out in a slanting direction, so that it comes up in the centre line, and over the held down thread. Draw up, and repeat this stitch to the right of the line, and work on the left and right of the line until the space is covered.

FIG. 329. DOUBLE CORAL STITCH.

To work Double Coral: The beauty of Double Coral consists in the perfect Vandyke line it makes down the material when properly worked. The stitch is the same as Coral, but is worked twice to the left and twice to the right, as in Fig. 329, where the needle is inserted in the second left-hand stitch, and the numbers 1 and 2 indicate the place the needle is put through to make the stitch on the right hand.

Cord Stitch.—A stitch used in Embroidery to cover straight threads thrown across spaces, and not run into the material; also known as Twist Stitch. To work: Throw a line of thread across a space and fasten it firmly. Return the thread to where it first started from, by twisting it over and over the straight and tight line first made.

Couching Stitch.—The stitches that are classed under the head of Couching are more used in Church work than in other kinds of Embroidery. They rank amongst the best and most difficult of Embroidery stitches, and require to be worked in frames. Couchings are used to embroider with materials that are too thick to thread upon needles and pass backwards and forwards as stitches, or that are of a texture that such constant friction would fray and destroy. They are divided into two kinds, *Flat* and *Raised*. The chief varieties of Flat Couching are Brick, Broad, Burden, Diagonal, and Diamond; of Raised, Basket, Vandyke, and Wavy. The Flat Couchings are laid straight down upon the foundation material; the Raised have paddings of various cords put between them, and the foundations are laid over these raised surfaces. The principle of all Couching stitches is as follows: Lay down two or more threads of floss silk or gold cord upon the foundation as horizontal or perpendicular lines, and close together, and to secure these bring up a needle threaded with silk from the back of the material on one side of the laid threads, pass it over them to the other, and return it to the back from there. Make a series of these securing stitches at even distances along the laid threads, and then lay down more threads and secure them in the same manner. The varieties in Couching are

formed by the designs made by these securing stitches being arranged in patterns, the *Raised* as well as the *Flat*.

Crewel Stitch (also known as Rope and Stem Stitch). —This stitch is much used in Crewel Work, being the chief one in that Embroidery, and is also used in Broderie Anglaise, and other kinds of Embroidery, to form thick stems to flowers, tendrils, and branching sprays. To work: Bring the needle up from the back of the material, and insert it above where it came out in a straight line, but slightly slanting from right to left (*see* Fig. 330). Keep the thread upon the right side of the needle, and draw up. Insert the needle in the same way above the last made stitch in an upright, but slightly slanting, direction, and so work until the line is finished. Work in this manner backwards and forwards for a thick stem, always turning the material at the end of a line. In curved sprays and tendrils follow their traced outlines and make the same stitch. *See* CREWEL STITCH for CREWEL WORK. CREWEL REVERSED, *see* TWISTED CHAIN.

FIG. 330.
CREWEL STITCH.

Cross Stitch.—This stitch is also known as Point de Marque, and is used for fancy Embroideries, and particularly in work known as Kreuzstickeri, and for marking. Its beauty consists of the two lines of which it is formed crossing each other, so that their points form a perfect square. To work: Take the first part of the stitch from

FIG. 331. CROSS STITCH.

the left-hand bottom side of the square across to the right-hand top side, and the second half of the stitch from the right-hand bottom side to the left-hand top side, crossing over the first half, as shown in Fig. 331. To work both sides alike *see* POINT DE CROIX SANS EVERS. To work a cross inside a square *see* SPANISH STITCH.

Cushion Stitch.—The name given to Satin Stitch when that stitch is arranged in a series of geometrical Vandykes or half circles across a material as a background. The stitch is more used in BERLIN WORK and Church Work than in fancy Embroidery, but is occasionally required in the latter. To work: Trace out on the material two parallel vandyke or curved lines, an inch apart from each other. Bring the needle from the back of the work up in the lower line, and put it down in the upper line exactly above where it came out. Bring it out on the upper line, with but a thread of the material separating it from the first stitch, and put it down in the lower line. Continue to work the stitch with the precision and evenness of weaving until the lines are filled in. To work Cushion stitch alike on both sides: When the needle is put down to the back of the work, bring it up again close to where it was first brought out, instead of close to where it was put down. This will fill the back of the flower or leaf with the same straight stitches that it fills the front part with.

Crumb Stitch.—Similar to *Dot Stitch*.

Damask Stitch.—A name given to Satin stitch when worked upon linen for household purposes. To work: Bring the needle from the back of the material to the front, and make a slanting stitch over the part to be embroidered. Bring out the needle close to where it first came out, but on the right side, put it down close to where it was put back, and continue to make these slanting stitches across the material until the space is filled in.

Diagonal Stitch.—A Flat Couching. To work: Lay down two threads of floss silk or gold cord upon a linen foundation. To secure these into position bring a stitch from the back of the material, pass it over the threads, and return it to the back. Lay down repeated lines of silk and secure them, and arrange the securing stitches so that they form diagonal lines upon the work.

FIG. 332. DOT STITCH.

Diamond Stitch.—A Flat Couching. To work: Lay down lines of floss silk over the whole of the foundation to be covered, and, to secure these, take a single thread of purse silk and gold cord, lay it in a diagonal direction over the floss silk, and secure it with a stitch from the back at set intervals. Continue to lay down diagonal lines over the silk, at equal distances apart, and all in one direction, and to secure them until the space is filled. Then cross these lines with other diagonal ones, so as to form a diamond-shaped pattern upon the surface of the floss silk. Secure these last lines at the points of the diamonds, and ornament the stitch by introducing a pearl or bead at the junction.

Dot Stitch.—A stitch also called Point de Pois, Point d'Or, Point de Poste, and Dotted, and used in all kinds of Embroidery, either to fill in the centres of leaves and flowers, or to trace out a pattern with a number of single lines made with a series of small Dots. To work: Bring the needle up from the back of the work, outline a tiny round, and work OVERCAST over it until a small

raised knob is formed. Fig. 332 is an illustration of a piece of Embroidery intended for the corner of a handkerchief, in which the name is worked in the centre of a leaf. The name, the outline of the leaf, the fibres, and the stem are worked in SATIN STITCH, the tendrils in Overcast, and the body of the leaf filled with Dots. These Dots are too small to outline with a run thread, and are made of two Overcast stitches.

Dotted Stitch.—See *Dot Stitch*.

Double Cross Stitch.—A fancy stitch used in Ticking Work and other Embroideries upon materials where the foundation is allowed to show. To work a plain Double

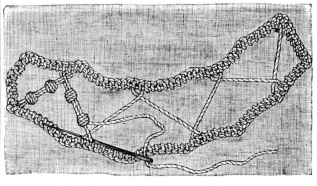

FIG. 333. DOUBLE CROSS STITCH—DETAIL A.

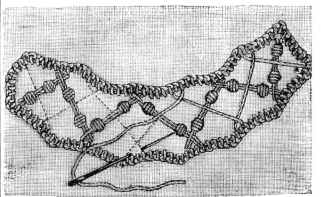

FIG. 334. DOUBLE CROSS STITCH—DETAIL B.

Cross: Fill the space to be worked with a line of wide apart HERRINGBONE stitches (*see* Fig. 333), and make a return line of Herringbone between the wide apart first line.

To work an Ornamented Double Cross: Make a line of wide apart HERRINGBONE, return the thread close to the stitches just made, so as to make a double line, and cross this while in progress with ornamental knots. Hold the fixed and working thread together, and cross them where a knot is to be made with a BUTTONHOLE to secure them together. Then make a knot or knob with OVERCAST. Work two knots upon every Herringbone, and continue to make the double line to the end of space. Then make a single line of Herringbone between the stitches, as in plain Double Cross, and as shown in Fig. 334 (Detail B) on p. 181.

Double Cross Stitch (a variety).—A name sometimes

given to Point de Croix Sans Evers, and described under that heading.

Double Overcast Stitch.—See *Buttonhole Stitch.*

Double Square Stitch.—See *Queen Stitch.*

En Couchure Stitch.—The French name for *Couching* (which *see*).

En Ronde Bosse Stitch.—A term occasionally met with in descriptions of old needlework, and intended to denote that the Embroidery Stitches are raised from the foundation, either in low or high relief.

Eyelet-hole.—This is used in Broderie Anglaise, and in all kinds of Embroidery where the material is cut away and the edges of those places sewn over. Eyelet-holes are generally round, but they are also formed as ovals and Vandykes, their shape depending upon the pattern they are to make. To work: Trace the design upon cambric or other thin material, and tack this to Toile Ciré. Outline each hole by running a thread of embroidery cotton round it, and then, if it is an oval, cut it with a sharp pair of small scissors down the centre; or if a round, push a stiletto through it, turn the material under until the outline thread is reached, and then work round the hole in OVERCAST from left to right. Put the needle in on the hole side of the running, and bring it out on the other, so that the Overcast Stitch is worked over the run line. Work close, and make each stitch of the same size. Eyelet-holes are sometimes worked with BUTTONHOLE instead of Overcast. To work: Trace a double line round the hole, and fill in between the two lines with runnings of embroidery cotton. Cut out the centre, turn under the material until the inner traced line is reached, and then work a succession of evenly-made Buttonholes round the Eyelet-hole.

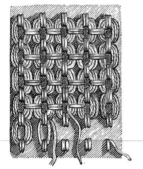

FIG. 335. FANCY STITCH.

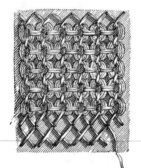

FIG. 336. FANCY STITCH.

Fancy Stitch.—These stitches are used in Embroidery to fill in and enrich parts of the design. To work Fig. 335: First make a line of DOTS, formed of two loops at equal distances apart, and then make a second line of Dots in a similar manner a quarter of an inch from first line. Loop through a Dot upon each line with a thread carried three times through, and when all the Dots have been filled, work a third line of Dots, and loop these through, taking the threads through the second line of Dots to form part of the stitch. When all the space is thus filled in, work Dots upon each side of the stitches to correspond with the ones already made.

To work Fig. 336: Arrange lines in Diamonds across the space, and catch these down at the points of the Diamonds. Then make flat loops over them with three coils of thread, and when all are filled in finish by catching these flat loops in four places.

Fancy Hem Stitch.—The varieties of Fancy Hem Stitch are used in Open Work Embroideries of all kinds, but more particularly in Drawn Work, where they are employed either to catch together and secure the threads left in the material after the others are drawn away, or to fill up spaces that the drawn away threads have left quite bare. To work Fancy Hem to secure threads: Having drawn out the threads necessary, turn the work to the wrong side, hold the material so that the threads are horizontal, and work in a straight line down them and close to the solid material. Take up six or eight threads on the needle, and hold the working thread down, the point of the needle over it. Then draw up, making a BUTTONHOLE STITCH. Pull up tightly the six or eight threads well together, and then secure them by taking a short stitch underneath them into the material. Repeat until all the threads are drawn together.

To fill in open spaces: Make a series of loops upon each side of the space, opposite to each other (*see* Fig. 337), and join them together thus: Fasten the thread to the first bottom loop, and run it into the middle; put the needle into the loop opposite on the top line, and back again

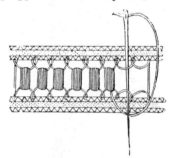

FIG. 337. FANCY HEM STITCH.

into the bottom loop, and make a Buttonhole of this stitch. Then pass the thread backwards and forwards between the two loops several times, but do not make any more Buttonholes. Pass on to the next two loops, and make the first stitch a Buttonhole, and fill in the rest with the plain backwards and forwards thread. Work all the loops together in this manner.

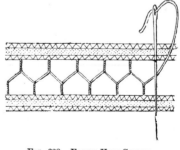

FIG. 338. FANCY HEM STITCH.

To work Fig. 338: Commence by making a BACK STITCH in the upper part of the space, taking up only sufficient material to hold the stitch. Cross the thread to the other side of the space, and make another small Back Stitch there. CORD up the thread for a short distance, and make a Back Stitch into the upper part of the space; Cord this up a short distance, and make a Back Stitch into the lower part of the space, and continue to the end, being careful to make every stitch the same distance apart.

Feather Stitch (1).—The Opus Plumarium of the ancients, and so called from the likeness this stitch has, when arranged as long stitches, radiating from a centre or from a straight line, to the feathers of a bird. It is largely used in Ancient Embroideries and in Crewel Work, and is either worked in a frame or on the hand. The stitch consists of a number of SATIN STITCHES of irregular length and size, worked in between each other in rows, some long and some short, but so arranged as to fit into each other without showing any foundation, and so that the outline and contour of the design are followed. To work in a frame: Bring the needle up from the back of the material, and put it down again in a slanting direction, make a stitch a quarter of an inch long, bring it out again close to the first stitch, and put it down to the back in a slanting direction, making the stitch one-eighth of an inch long. Make this long and short stitch alternately for the first row; for the next, fill in the spaces with the same kind of stitches, work them long and short where the design will allow, but arrange so that they follow the line of the outline. To work on the hand: Make the same irregular SATIN STITCH, but bring the needle up in the commencement of the second stitch when put down at the end of the first stitch.

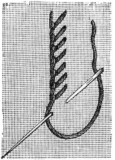

FIG. 339. FEATHER STITCH.

(2).—A stitch also known as Point d'Epine, used in Ticking work, and to ornament children's dresses and underlinen. It is worked either as a *Single* or *Double Feather*. To work Single Feather: Trace a straight line down the material, bring the needle up in this line, and hold the thread down under the left thumb on the line, but a quarter of an inch below where it came out. Put the needle in in a slanting direction on the right side, and bring it out in the traced line, over the thread that is held down, as shown in Fig. 339. Draw up, and commence another stitch, keeping all the slanting lines on the right side of traced line.

To work Double Feather (the variety of the stitch most in use): Bring the needle up in the traced line as before, make the slanting stitch described on the right side, and

then make a similar stitch on the left-hand side into the same spot on the traced line, or hold the thread down on the traced line for a quarter of an inch, and then make a slanting stitch to the left. Again hold the thread down, and make a slanting stitch to the right, hold the thread down, and make a slanting stitch to the left, and continue to form stitches on each side of the line to the end of the work.

Feston Stitch.—See *Buttonhole Stitch.*

French Knot Stitch.—A stitch much used in Embroidery of all kinds for filling in with raised Knots the centres of Flowers, Stars, or Circles. French Knot requires to be worked with a thick and not a thin thread, purse silk, filoselle, or crewel being the materials with which it is usually made. To work: Bring the needle up from the back of the material, hold the thread between the left thumb and forefinger, twist it once round the needle, turn the needle round, and put it back into the material a little behind where it came out.

French Plumetis Stitch.—A name given to Raised Satin Stitch. See *Satin Stitch.*

Gobelin Stitch.—A short upright stitch, also called Tapestry. It was largely used in ancient Tapestry work, from which it derived its modern name, and it is now employed only for very fine Embroideries executed with silks, or work upon canvas. It requires to be made in a frame, as its beauty consists in every stitch being made of the same length and height. To work: Bring up the thread from the back of the work, and put it down again at a short distance from where it came out, and

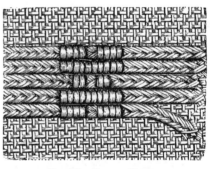

FIG. 340. GOBELIN STITCH.

quite upright. The length of the stitch should be twice its width. Bring the needle up again close to where it was first brought out, and put it down again close to where it was put down, and continue to make even rows of these stitches, one row above the other, until the space is filled. Begin to work from the left-hand side at the bottom of the material. Gobelin stitch is sometimes worked as a raised stitch in Ticking and other ornamental Embroideries; it is then padded with braid (*see* Fig. 340), and the upright stitches taken over every line of braid, either concealing the padding, or allowing it to show in places according to the braid used.

Hem Stitch.—The ordinary Hem Stitch is identical with Back Stitch (which *see*), but the Hem Stitch used in Drawn Work, and for other fancy purposes, is made as shown in *Fancy Hem Stitch.*

Herringbone Stitch.—A stitch used in plain needle-

work to join flannel stuffs together, and also as an ornamental stitch in Embroidery. It is sometimes called
Witch Stitch. The beauty of Herringbone depends
entirely upon the execution. Every stitch requires to be
put in at an exact distance from the last made, and the
amount of material taken up upon the needle should

FIG. 341. HERRINGBONE STITCH.

always be the same; without this uniformity of execution
the work is spoilt. To work: If the worker's eye is not
straight enough to judge the distances without a guide,
make two parallel lines, a quarter of an inch apart, upon
the material, with a succession of dots, hold the material
in the left hand, with the part to be worked along the
first finger, bring the needle up from the wrong side in
the top line, put it into the bottom line in a slanting
direction, take up only a small quantity of material,
and put the needle in with the point to the left hand
(*see* Fig. 341). Draw up the cotton, and put the needle
in the top line in a slanting direction, the point of the
needle towards the left. Draw up, and the cotton of the
last stitch will cross over the cotton of the first. Continue to cross the cotton in this manner until the lines
are filled.

Herringbone (Fancy) Stitch.—A Fancy Herringbone
stitch, also known as BARRED WITCH stitch. To work:
Commence with a line of Herringbone, and work the
Herringbone more upright and less slanting than in
ordinary Herringbone. Then take a new thread, bring it

FIG. 342. HERRINGBONE FANCY STITCH.

from the back, and twist it over the cross of the Herringbone, run it down under the slanting line to the next
cross, twist it over that, and continue running the
thread up and down the slanting lines and over the
crosses until a barred appearance is given to each cross.
See Fig. 342.

Holbein Stitch.—This stitch is also called Italian,
and derives its name of Holbein from being the stitch

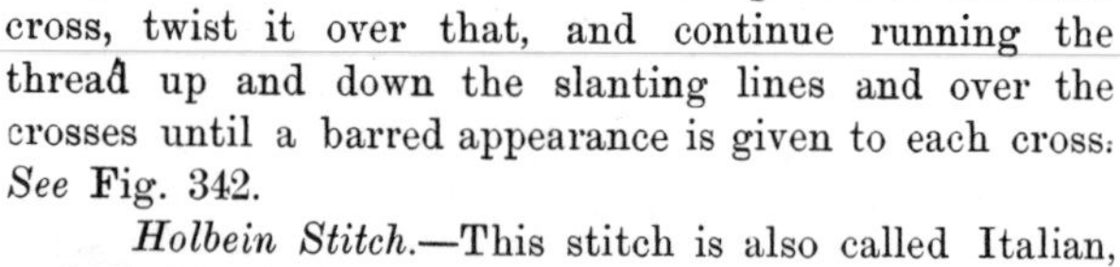

FIG. 343. HOLBEIN STITCH.

employed in that work. Upon open canvas materials it
can be worked as squares or vandyke lines, both sides
alike. When this effect is not required, it is either a
Satin Stitch or Back Stitch, worked as an outline stitch.

To work as shown in Fig. 343: Trace the outline of
the design, and then cover every line with a long or
short SATIN STITCH, according to the length of the
traced line. If the work is to look the same upon both
sides, for this pattern cover the outline with BACK
STITCHES.

To make Holbein Squares with Both Sides of the Work
Alike: Bring the thread out on the right side of the
material, pass it over four perpendicular threads of the
canvas, and under four horizontal right-hand threads,
over four perpendicular threads below the horizontal
ones, and under four left horizontal ones, bringing out
the thread on the same line as the first stitch made,
but four threads below it. Continue these stitches if a
long line of squares is required; if only two are wanted,
turn back, and fill in the squares thus: Make a stitch
upwards over the four perpendicular threads, under the
first made stitch, and out where it commenced, over the
four horizontal threads on a line with it, under four
perpendicular threads, over four horizontal threads on the
left, under four perpendicular threads concealed with an
already made stitch, across the horizontal threads, under
four perpendicular threads in an upward direction, and
over the four last threads that require covering. Two
perfect squares on both sides of the material are now
made.

To make a Vandyke Line Both Sides Alike: Take the
thread over four perpendicular threads, under four horizontal threads to the right, over four perpendicular
threads, and under four horizontal threads to the right
for the length; return by running up this line over the
horizontal threads and under the perpendicular. A waved
line is made in the same manner.

Honeycomb Stitch.—This stitch is used to draw
together in an ornamental pattern the gathers upon the
neck and sleeves of smock frocks, and also for all kinds
of decorative gathering. It requires to be executed with
great care and exactness, so as to form the cell-shaped
cavities that give it its name, and should be worked upon
materials that are fine in texture, and yet sufficiently
stiff to form even and straight folds. The best materials are cambrics, hollands, and stiff muslins. To work:
Take a piece of holland, and draw out horizontal threads
the distance from each other the honeycombs are to be;
set it in gathers that are perfectly even. Draw these
up, and stroke them down with a knitting needle in
straight lines the length of material to be ornamented.
Thread a needle with black or dark coloured purse silk.
Commence at the right-hand side of the work, bring it up
from the wrong side of the material, and catch the
first two gathers together with a BACK STITCH, about
a quarter of an inch from the line of gathers, and on
one of the drawn-out threads (*see* Fig. 344). Put the
needle down at the back of the material a quarter
of an inch, bring it up at the third gather, and
catch the third and second gathers together with a
Back Stitch. Return the needle to the back, and to
the height of the first made stitch, and catch the
fourth and third gathers together with a Back Stitch;
put it back in a line with the second stitch, and catch

the fifth and fourth gathers together, and continue working in this way, first in one line and then in the other, catching a new gather and an old gather together with a Back Stitch every time, until all are secured. Work the third line as the first (commencing at the right-hand side of work), and the fourth as the second line, catching the gathers together in these lines in the same order as the ones already worked, and keeping them straight with the drawn out threads. The illustration (Fig. 344) shows Honeycomb Stitch commenced, with the run thread, two lines of Honeycomb finished, and two lines in progress,

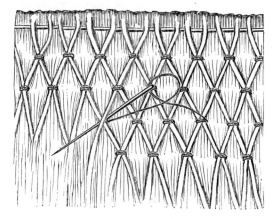

FIG. 344. HONEYCOMB STITCH.

with the gathers stroked, ready to fasten together. A variety of Honeycomb is formed by treating each gather as a laid thread, and forming a pattern over it, as in COUCHING, with a thread brought from the back of the material. The material is gathered very evenly, put into an Embroidery Frame, and stroked down. Each gather is then caught down singly with a Back Stitch, and these securing stitches are arranged in parallel diagonal lines, or as open diamonds. When forming open diamonds the number of gathers must be counted, and a tiny pencil line drawn over the work, so that each diamond is made of the same size.

Indots Stitch.—This is similar to Dot Stitch. Outline a small circle and OVERCAST it, working the stitches all one way.

Italian Stitch.—See *Holbein Stitch.*

Jacob's Ladder Stitch.—See *Ladder Stitch.*

Japanese Stitch.—Used in Crewel work and in Embroideries upon silk to represent water, and made with long Satin Stitches. To work: Bring the needle from the back of the material, carry the thread along in a straight line the distance of two inches, and then return it to the back. Bring it up again underneath where it first started, one-eighth of an inch to the right, and make a long two-inch stitch, and continue to make these long stitches in parallel lines one-eighth of an inch shorter on the left hand, and one-eighth of an inch longer on the right, until the space is filled in.

Knot Stitch.—This stitch is also called Knotted, and is used in ornamental Embroideries to form lines decorated at set distances with Knots, and in Drawn Work to tie threads together in variously arranged

patterns. Lines ornamented with Knots are made in several ways; the simplest is worked as follows: Work along the line to be covered, and at even distances, a succession of raised dots (*see* Fig. 345). Make each dot by working two BACK STITCHES over each other, and run the working thread at the back of the material between each Knot.

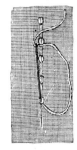

FIG. 345.
KNOT STITCH.

To work Fig. 346: Bring the needle from the back of the material into the spot where the stitch is to be formed, put it down to the back, and bring it out again, only taking up a few threads of the material. Wind the cotton twice round the point of the needle, and keep the cotton tight. Draw out the needle, and then put it back into the material at the

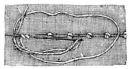

FIG. 346. KNOT STITCH.

spot where it was first inserted, drawing the two threads wound round the working thread up tight, so that they stand up upon the work. Bring the needle up where the next Knot is to be made, and repeat.

Fig. 347 is made as follows: Carry the thread along the surface of the work for a short distance, and hold it down with the left thumb, then twist it once round the needle, insert the needle into the material, and bring it up again. Twist the cotton twice round the point of the needle, and draw up until the thread is quite over the

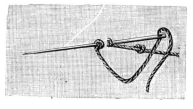

FIG. 347. KNOT STITCH.

first twist, put the needle down into the material at this place, and bring it out again at the other side of the Knot. Then take a long stitch, commence to twist the thread round the needle, and make another Knot.

To make a Knot upon the surface of the work, *i.e.*, the Knot that is called a *French Knot*: Bring the needle up from the back of the material, hold the thread between the left thumb and finger, twist the thread once round the needle, and put it back into the material a little behind where it came out. Work this Knot with coarse thread or silk.

To make a Knot with drawn threads: HEM STITCH a dozen drawn threads together for the first row. For the second, take 6 threads from one Hem stitch, and 6 from the next, and OVERCAST them together at the distance of an eighth of an inch from the first row (*see* Fig. 348). Fasten off or run the thread along the drawn threads and commence another Knot, take 6 threads from one stitch and 6 from the other, and work until all the stitches are divided and knotted. For the third row, divide the first stitch, and make a Knot with 6 of its threads. Then

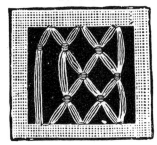

FIG. 348. KNOT STITCH WITH DRAWN THREAD.

make a Knot with the 6 threads left from the first stitch and 6 taken from the second stitch, and take 6 stitches from one stitch, and 6 from the other, and Overcast them together for all the row. Work the fourth row like the second, and the fifth row like the third.

Knotted Stitch.—See *Knot Stitch.*

Ladder Stitch.—There are two kinds of this stitch, the open, called Ladder Point, or Point d'Echelle, in which the bars forming the stitch are taken across an open space; and the closed, known as Jacob's, and Ship Ladder, in which the bars are worked on to the material itself.

To work Fig. 349, an Open Ladder: Trace out upon the material two parallel lines an inch apart. Take a thread and run it down the top line for a quarter of an inch, then carry it across to the bottom line as a bar (*see b*), loop it into the material, and run it along the bottom line for a quarter of an inch, loop it in at *c*, and carry it across as

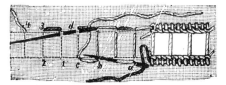

FIG. 349. OPEN LADDER STITCH.

a bar to top line to *d*, loop it in, carry it across to 1, run it along to 2, cross it to 3, and run it along to 4. When the bars are thus made, run a plain line over each parallel tracing, and work over in DOUBLE OVERCAST, turning the edges of the stitches to the inside. Cut away the material between these two Overcast lines, and leave the bars crossing it.

To work Fig. 350, an Open Ladder: Trace out two parallel lines, with an inch and a half space between them, HERRINGBONE from one to the other with a wide apart line. Then return a line of Herringbone in between the one first made. Run a line of thread down each parallel line, and work over in Double Overcast, turning the edges of the stitches to the inside, and cut away the material between these lines. Then take a thread down the centre of the space and Knot the two lines of Herringbone

together with it in the centre, thus: Put the thread under the two lines where they cross, and bring it out, make a loop with it, put the needle in under the

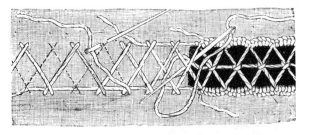

FIG. 350. OPEN LADDER STITCH.

two lines, and bring it out over the loop and draw up, then pass on to where the two next lines cross, and Knot together in the same way.

Fig. 351 is an Open Ladder stitch, surrounded with padded lines of Overcast. To work: Trace the outline and run the bars of the ladder as shown in Fig. 351, then

FIG. 351. LADDER STITCH AND OVERCAST.

pad the outside and inside circle, and work them thickly over in OVERCAST. Work the centre star in flat SATIN STITCH.

To work Fig. 352, an Open Ladder: Make a number of stiletto holes as a curved line across the space. Work

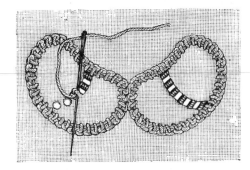

FIG. 352. OPEN LADDER STITCH.

over the material left between the holes with OVERCAST. The stiletto holes will form the open part of the stitch, the Overcast the bars of the Ladder.

To work Jacob, or Ship Ladder: For this close Ladder, trace a straight line down the centre of the material, take a stitch down it, a quarter of an inch in length, put the needle in, and bring it out on the right-hand side, a little above where it went in, and a quarter of an inch off. Then make a slant stitch from left to right, turning the needle so that the point comes out on the traced line (*see* Fig. 353); draw up thread, and put the needle in where marked 1 on illustration, bring it out at 2, put it in at 3, and bring it out at 1; repeat to the end of the traced line.

FIG. 353.
SHIP LADDER STITCH.

Lancé Stitch.—Identical with *Point Lancé Stitch* (which *see*).

Lattice Stitch.—A stitch used in Ticking work and other ornamental Embroideries for borders, and formed of straight interlaced lines. To work: Trace along the edge of the border two straight lines, half an inch apart, and in between these lines work the LATTICE STITCH. Carry five straight but slanting lines of silk across the space and close together. Cross these in a contrary direction with five other lines, interlacing these with the first laid by passing each thread over

FIG. 354. LATTICE STITCH.

one line and under one line as they cross (*see* Fig. 354). Miss the one-eighth of an inch, and commence to throw the five lines again across the space, and interlace these as before mentioned.

Leaf Stitch.—An ornamental stitch resembling an ear of barley when complete. It is a combination of Chain and Picot Stitch. To work: Work a CHAIN in the centre line, a RAILWAY STITCH slanting to the right of the Chain, and a PICOT STITCH to the left, then return to the centre line, and repeat the three stitches.

Long Stitch.—Also known as Point Passé, Passé, and Au Passé. It is a name given to Satin Stitch when worked across the material without any padding. See *Satin Stitch.*

Loop Stitch.—See *Picot.*

Opus Plumarium Stitch.—See *Feather Stitch.*

Outline Stitch.—This stitch can be made of Back, Holbein, Overcast, Crewel, or Point Russe. It merely consists in covering the traced outline of a design with a line of single and narrow stitches made of one of these varieties.

Overcast Stitch.—A stitch used in Broderie Anglaise and in all kinds of Embroidery. It is used to work round parts of the material that have been cut away to form an open pattern, as in Eyelet-hole, or to form outlines to stems, flowers, or leaves worked in Satin and other stitches when they are to be raised from the surface of the Embroidery, or to work the entire design in. There are several varieties of Overcast. *The Plain,* which is worked over a run line and called Overcast; *Slanting Overcast,* similar to Rope and Stem Stitch; *Raised Overcast,* better known as Point de Tigre; and *Double Overcast,* which is a plain Buttonhole Stitch.

To work Plain Overcast: Run a foundation line along the part to be embroidered, from right to left. Bring the needle out in the work just beyond the end of the line, put the needle into the material over this line, bring it out under it, and in an upright position, and keep the working

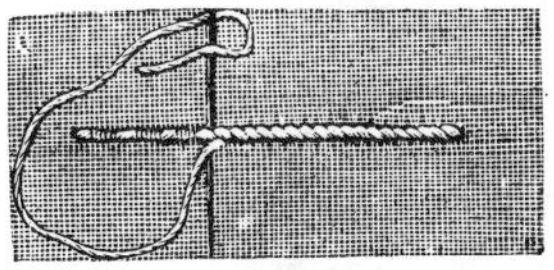

FIG. 355. OVERCAST STITCH.

thread away from the stitch (*see* Fig. 355). Cover the foundation thread with a series of small close-together stitches so made, and put the needle in each time at the same distance from the stitch last made, and quite straight down.

To work Slanting Overcast: Trace a line on the material, but do not run a foundation thread. Cover this traced line with small evenly made slanting stitches. Put the needle in over the traced line and bring it out under the line, letting the needle slant from left to right to give a slanting direction to the stitch.

To work Point de Tigre, or Raised Overcast: Over the traced outline of the design tack a fine cord. Work

FIG. 356. RAISED OVERCAST, OR POINT DE TIGRE.

a series of close OVERCAST stitches over this cord (*see* Fig. 356, which is a design entirely worked in Point de Tigre, or Raised Overcast).

To work in Overcast for Stems: Trace the design, and run one or two lines of embroidery cotton over it, according to the thickness of the design. Fasten the thread to the back of the work, bring it out beneath, and put it down over the lines, so that it takes up the material covered by them, and no more. Work stitches close together, until the whole outline is filled in.

To make Eylet-hole in Overcast. See *Eyelet-hole.*

To work double Overcast. See *Buttonhole.*

Passé Stitch.—See *Satin Stitch.*

Persian Cross Stitch.—A stitch used in Ticking and other fancy Embroideries, and largely employed in Persian and other Oriental embroideries; it is also called Vienna Cross. It consists of a long slanting stitch, crossed with one half its size, and used irregularly about the work to fill in spaces, and not formed into rows. It can, however, be worked in rows, and then forms a line resembling Herringbone, with one of the vandyked lines longer than the other.

To work as a separate stitch: Take a slanting stitch across the material, a quarter of an inch long, and cross it in the centre with a stitch one-eighth of an inch long.

To work in rows: Take a long stitch across four perpendicular threads, and cross it with a stitch taken over the two last of these threads. Commence the next stitch thus: Cross over the two last threads of the first stitch and over two new ones, and cross back over the last two threads. Work this last made stitch until the line is filled in.

Petit Point Stitch.—The French name for *Tent Stitch.*

Picot Stitch.—Also known as Loop Stitch, and used in Ticking work and other fancy Embroideries, and to ornament plain linen. It is formed of a loop made like a Chain, and secured with a short stitch holding down the loop at its broad end. To work: Bring up the thread from the back of the material, hold it down with the left thumb, put the needle in to the right, and close to where it came

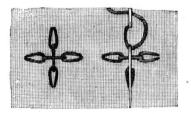

FIG. 357. PICOT STITCH.

up, and bring it out one-eighth of an inch below, in a straight line over the held down thread (*see* Fig. 357). Draw the thread up, and put the needle down through the material a short distance below the chain. Fig. 357 illustrates a cross formed with four Picot Stitches. The Chains form the arms of the cross, and the short stitches the body.

Fig. 358 is an arrangement of Picot Stitch in a pattern.

FIG. 358. PICOT STITCH.

The straight centre line of Picot is worked first, and the branching Picots on each side afterwards.

Fig. 359 is composed of a centre line of CORAL STITCH,

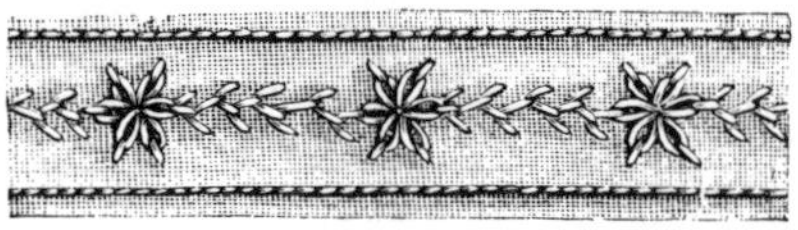

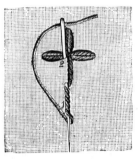

FIG. 359. PICOT AND CORAL STITCHES.

broken at set intervals with stars formed with six Picot Stitches.

Point à la Minute Stitch.—An Embroidery stitch worked like Bullion Knot, and used to fill in small stars,

FIG. 360. POINT À LA MINUTE.

leaves, and other devices. To work Fig. 360; Trace an outline of the star, put the needle in at 2, where one of the arms is commenced, bring it out at 1 (the end of that

FIG. 361. POINT À LA MINUTE STITCH.

arm), wind the cotton several times round the point of the needle, and hold that down with the left thumb; draw up the thread, and put the needle down at 2 again, where it

FIG. 362. POINT À LA MINUTE STITCH.

first came out. Cover the other side of the arm with a similar stitch, and work all the arms of the cross in the same way. Fig. 361 gives an arrangement of Point à la

Minute as an eight-pointed star, with the centre left unworked; and Fig. 362 is a pattern composed of a star surrounded by triangles, all made in this stitch.

Point Anglaise Stitch.—One of the French terms for *Feather Stitch.*

Point Chemin de Fer Stitch.—See *Railway Stitch.*

Point Croisé Stitch.—A variety of Back Stitch that forms an interlaced pattern at the back of the material and two straight rows of Back Stitches at the front. To work: Trace two straight lines on the right side of the work, and

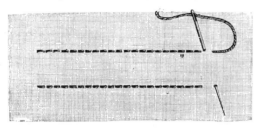

FIG. 363. POINT CROISÉ STITCH.

at even distances from each other. Insert the needle as if to make an ordinary Back Stitch in the top line, and put down into the bottom line in a slanting direction (*see* Fig. 363). Turn the needle and make a BACK STITCH, and bring the needle out upon the top line a short distance from where it first appeared (*see* Fig. 363). Put it down again to the bottom line and repeat. The interlaced

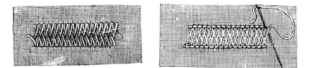

FIGS. 364 and 365. POINT CROISÉ STITCH, BACK AND FRONT.

threads at the back of the work are shown in Fig. 364, while Fig. 365 gives the appearance of the stitch in the front, when the back threads are seen through muslin, and Fig. 363 when the material is thick, and only the lines worked in the front are visible.

Fig. 366 is an illustration of this same stitch, formed with two threads. The only difference is: Work a row of BACK STITCH from one line to the other, as before, but leave

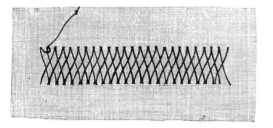

FIG. 366. POINT CROISÉ STITCHES.

the space that one stitch would take between each stitch. Then work another row of Back Stitch with a differently coloured thread to fill in the spaces left in the first row.

Point d'Armes Stitch.—A stitch also known as Point de Sable, and used in Embroidery upon muslin or fine Cambric, to fill the centres of leaves and flowers, and to

make a variety with SATIN STITCH. It has all the appearance of Back Stitch, but it is worked differently, and forms a series of interlaced lines at the back, which show through to the front of the work in transparent materials. To work: Run round the outline of the design upon the back of the material, and fasten the thread at the back. Commence by taking a short slanting stitch through to the front of the work and out again at the back, and then cross over the piece of work with a slanting

FIG. 367. POINT D'ARMES STITCH, SHOWING RIGHT SIDE.

thread, taking two small stitches through to the front in each line (*see* Fig. 367); then cross these lines in a contrary direction with the same kind of stitches, and interlace the threads in the working. The appearance of

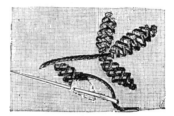

FIG. 368. POINT D'ARMES STITCH, SHOWING WRONG SIDE.

this stitch at the back, and manner of working, are shown in Fig. 368, while in Fig. 367 it is illustrated as it looks upon the right side of the material.

Point d'Attache Stitch.—A term given to the stitch that secures fancy materials, such as braid or cord, to the main work. Point d'Attache can be worked as BACK STITCH, or as plain RUNNING, or as in COUCHING, thus: Bring the needle up from the back of the foundation, pass it over the material to be secured, and put down again to the back of the foundation stuff.

Point de Biais Stitch.—A fancy Embroidery stitch, used in Ticking work, and consisting in filling in a square piece of material with five slanting SATIN STITCHES of unequal length. To work: Trace out a square, and to commence, make a long Satin Stitch from the left-hand bottom corner of square to the right-hand top corner. Make a shorter stitch on each side of this, to fill in the sides of the square, and then two short stitches, one on each side of the two last made, to cover over the left-hand top point and the right-hand bottom point of square.

Point de Cable Stitch.—See *Rope Stitch.*

Point de Carreau.—A name given to Holbein Stitch when worked both sides alike, and used to form tendrils, sprays, or waved lines in flower designs. To work: Take the silk or crewel up the traced line as a running, make each stitch and each reverse of the same size. Finish by running another thread of silk over the first, and with it fill in the spaces left on the last line on both sides of the material.

Point de Chainette Stitch,—See *Chain Stitch.*

Point d'Echelle Stitch.—The French term for *Ladder Stitch* (which *see*).

Point de Coté Stitch.—See *Rope Stitch.*

Point de Croix Stitch.—See *Cross Stitch.*

Point de Croix Sans Evers.—A stitch made in two ways : In one, a cross appears on both sides of the material ; in the other, a cross is made on one side, and a square of stitches, enclosing an unworked space, on the other.

To work a Cross on both sides : Take a square of canvas with four threads each way. Make a half-stitch over two horizontal and two perpendicular threads from the bottom left-hand corner to the middle, bring the needle back to the left-hand corner, and make a TENT STITCH from there to the right-hand top corner. Return the needle to the middle of the stitch, and work a half-stitch to the top of the left-hand corner, bring it out at the bottom of the right-hand corner, and make a Tent Stitch crossing the first one.

To work a Cross and a Square : Make a TENT STITCH from the right bottom to the left top corner of a square of eight or four threads. Pass the needle at the back of the material from the left to the right top corner, and make a Tent Stitch across the first ; pass the thread at the back of the material into the top left-hand corner. Make a Tent Stitch into the bottom right-hand corner, over the one already there, and work the thread at the back up into the right-hand top corner, ready for another cross to be made above the one finished.

Point de Diable Stitch.—This is a stitch that is formed with eight lines meeting in the centre of a square. To work : Make a St. Andrew's Cross from corner to corner of the square, and overlay these lines with a Greek or even-armed cross, the arms coming from the centre of each side of the square.

Point de Jours Stitch.—The French name by which those parts of Embroidery are indicated where the material is cut away, the sides BUTTONHOLE or OVERCAST, and the centres filled in with WHEEL, Star, LADDER, or Point de Reprise stitch.

Point de Marque Stitch.—See *Cross Stitch.*

Point d'Epine Stitch.—One of the French terms for *Feather Stitch.*

Point de Plume Stitch.—A variety of Raised Satin Stitch, in which the veins of leaves and flowers are left unworked, and the rest of the leaves padded. *See Satin Stitch.*

Point de Pois Stitch.—See *Dot Stitch.*

Point de Poste Stitch.—See *Dot Stitch.*

Point de Reprise Stitch.—A stitch resembling the one bearing the same name used in Guipure d'Art. It is employed in Embroideries upon linen, to ornament open spaces in the work from which the threads have been drawn or cut away. Fig. 369 shows Point de Reprise arranged as bars ; Fig 370, the same stitch formed into Pyramids.

To work Fig. 369 : Work a row of thick BUTTONHOLE round the open space, and then a second row of open Buttonhole. Throw a horizontal thread across the space to be filled, a quarter of an inch from the top, and secure it into the open Buttonhole line. CORD this thread back for a short distance, then take the cotton in an upright direction, secure it into the material, and bring it back to the horizontal thread with a distance of an eighth of an inch between the lines. Secure it to the horizontal thread with a knot, and throw it up again to

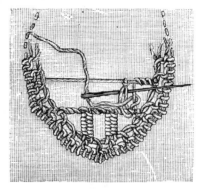

FIG. 369. POINT DE REPRISE STITCH.

the top of the two lines. Work it down to the horizontal thread with an interlaced stitch, working in the last thrown up thread as one line with the knotted one (*see* Fig. 369). To Interlace : Put the needle over one thread and bring it out between the two and draw up, then put it over the opposite thread, bring it out between the two, and work in this way until both lines are covered. Cord the horizontal line for a short distance, and then commence another bar, made of Point de Reprise.

To work Fig. 370 : Loop a thread from side to side of the open space, and then fasten off. Take a fresh thread, and commence at the first loop. Work the new thread in and out of the loop, first from the right thread into centre, then over the left thread into the centre. Allow

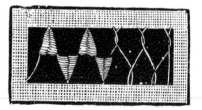

FIG. 370. POINT DE REPRISE STITCH.

the interlacings to widen at each twist, and when the centre of the open space is reached, pass the thread on to the loop opposite the one just worked over, and work over this in the same way, but commence with the widest stitch, and narrow to a point as a finish. Work over all the loops in this manner.

Point de Riz Stitch.—This stitch should be worked so as to resemble grains of rice loosely scattered over a flat surface. To work : Bring the thread from the back of the material, and put the needle down again, so that it makes a stitch one-eighth of an inch long, in a slanting direction, upon the surface of the work. Continue to make these short slanting stitches until the space is covered, and arrange them so as to be carelessly thrown over the work, and not in any design. Fig. 371 is a flower with its centre filled with Point de Riz, surrounded by Point de Cable,

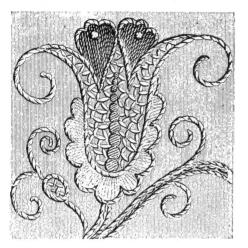

FIG. 371. POINT DE RIZ STITCH.

or Stem Stitch. The thick parts of the flower are worked in Au Passé, and the sprays form part of the Au Passé design, shown in Fig. 371.

Point de Rose Stitch.—A variety of Feston or Buttonhole, and used to fill in the petals of flowers, particularly of roses, hence its name. The difference between this stitch and ordinary Feston consists in the stitches being worked over a padded surface, and being broader. To work for ordinary edgings: Commence by running a plain curved line to mark the inside of a wide scallop edging, then run another line, at the distance of an eighth of an inch from the first. Make this line of a number of small curves, allowing four or five of these curves in the space of the one wide scallop. Pad the space between the two lines with lines of embroidery cotton, and BUTTONHOLE over them, scalloping the outer edge of the line of Buttonholes to suit the curves made in the second line. When using Point de Rose for flower petals, commence by tracing the outlines of the petals with a double line, and fill in the spaces between these traced lines with a pad of embroidery cotton, run or darned in between them. Then, for the petals that fill in the centre of the flower, Buttonhole over the pad and work the outer edge of the line of Buttonhole stitches towards the centre of the flower, and not towards its edge. Work the outer petals with the Buttonhole edge to the outside, as in ordinary Feston.

Point de Rosette.—Made like Point de Smyrne (which *see*).

Point de Sable Stitch.—A name given to *Point d'Armes Stitch* (which *see*).

Point d'Escalier Stitch.—See *Ladder Stitch.*

Point de Smyrne.—A name given to Point Lancé when the stitches are arranged as a star, and are alike upon both sides of the material. To work as shown in Fig. 372: Bring the needle up from the back, on the extreme edge of one of the star rays, put it down in the centre of the star, and bring it out at the edge of the next point. Continue the work until all the rays are covered.

Point de Tigre Stitch.—A name given to *Overcast Stitch* (which *see*).

Point d'Etoile.—A stitch similar to *Point de Smyrne.*

Point d'Or Stitch.—The French term for *Dot Stitch* (which *see*).

Point Lancé Stitch.—A simple stitch, also known as Lancé, much used in Ticking and other fancy Embroidery work. It consists of short straight lines, arranged in various designs upon the surface of a material, and can be made with purse silk, coloured fisolelle, and white or ingrain cotton. To make: Trace an outline of the pattern to be worked upon the material, bring the needle, threaded with silk, up from the back, at one of the points of the design, and insert it again into the material at the finish of the line at whose point it came out, then bring it out

FIG. 372. POINT DE SMYRNE.

again at the point of a fresh line, and draw the thread up. Continue to cover the drawn lines with lines of silk thus made until all are worked over.

Point Mexico Stitch.—A name given to Buttonhole Stitch when used as an outline stitch in Mexican Embroidery. To work: Trace an outline of the design, and then, with fine black or coloured silk, work over this outline with an even row of BUTTONHOLE, placed one-eighth of an inch apart.

Point Minuscule.—A fine stitch, used in Background or Darned Embroidery. To work: Darn the cotton or silk as a line into the material, taking up one thread and leaving one thread alternately. The new American Tapestry, known as the Wheeler Tapestry, is worked with this stitch.

Point Natté Stitch.—A Satin Stitch arranged to form branching lines. To work: Trace the lines upon cloth

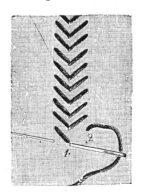

FIG. 373. POINT NATTÉ STITCH.

materials, or if for linen materials, draw out a centre and two outside threads for guiding lines. Bring the needle up from the back of the material on the right-hand side line, insert it in a downward slanting direction in the centre line (see Fig. 373), and bring it out in a straight line to where it was put in, but upon the left-hand side line. Return it to the centre line at the spot marked 1, and bring it out on the right-hand outside line at the spot marked 2. Work in this manner down the centre line, make the stitches one-eighth of an inch apart, and let their points be always exactly opposite each other.

Point Noné Stitch.—See *Buttonhole Stitch.*

Point Noué Stitch.—See *French Knot Stitch.*

Point Passé Stitch.—See *Satin Stitch.*

Point Perlé Stitch.—One of the names given to *Satin Stitch.*

Point Plumetis Stitch.—A name given to Raised Satin Stitch. See *Satin Stitch.*

Point Russe Stitch.—This stitch is much used in all kinds of fancy Embroideries upon linen, cloth, or silk materials. It is very quickly worked, and is easy of execution, consisting of covering a traced outline with lines of long straight stitches. The patterns intended to be worked in Point Russe should be arranged with reference to the manner of working, and should contain no lines of any great length, but short straight lines, vandykes, angles, sprays, diamonds, and crosses, and not rounds and curves. To work: Trace the design upon the material, bring the needle up from the back of the work, at the end of one of the traced lines, and put it through to the back of

the work at the other, covering the straight line with the cotton or silk. Bring the needle up again at the end of next line, return it to the

FIG. 374. POINT RUSSE STITCH.

same spot that the first stitch ended at, and put it through to the back of the material there. Continue to work lines in this way until all the outline is worked over, taking care that no part of it is left uncovered. Should a traced line be too long to look well covered with only one stitch, divide it into two or three equal parts, and make that number of stitches upon it. To work Fig. 374: Trace the outline of the vandykes and crosses, and commence in the centre of the cross. Work one bar of the cross, and put the needle down into the vandyke at the spot marked 1, and bring it out at 2. Draw it up, and put it down into 1, then bring it out again at 2, and make another stitch in the vandyke, and then one in the cross. Continue to the end of the pattern.

Point Turc Stitch.—See *Ladder Stitch.*

Queen Stitch.—Also known as Double Square. To work: Trace upon the material two squares, one within the other; work over the outside square first with four SATIN STITCHES. Commence and finish them at the points of the square; then work the inside square with four smaller Satin Stitches, arranged in the same way.

Railway Stitch.—Also known as Point Chemin de Fer, and given these names because of the rapidity with which Embroidery patterns can be executed when worked with it. The designs for the Embroidery should always be of small flowers and leaves, such as forget-me-nots, and arranged in detached sprays dotted about the surface of the material, and the stitch executed in coarse white embroidery cotton, Pyrenean wool, or filoselle. To work: Trace a small spray of forget-me-not flowers and leaves, but do not outline the design with a run thread. Commence to work from the centre of the flower, and make

each petal with one stitch. Bring the needle up from the back, hold the thread down with the left thumb, put the needle in close to where it came out, and bring it out at the point of the petal, and over the thread held down by the left thumb. Draw up, making a kind of long loop, held down in the centre with the drawn up thread. Put the needle down again just outside the loop, making a very small stitch at the end of the petal, run the needle out again in the middle of the flower, and commence to work another petal. Finish off the centre of the flower with FRENCH KNOTS, or BUTTONHOLE it round, or pierce it with a stiletto, and OVERCAST round the hole so made. Each leaf will only require one Railway stitch to fill it. Overcast the stems of the sprays.

Rice Stitch.—See *Point de Riz* stitch.

Rope Stitch.—This stitch is similar to Crewel and Stem Stitch in appearance, and only differs from those stitches in being worked from the top of the material

downwards, instead of from the bottom upwards. It is also known as Point de Cable and Point de Coté. To work: Trace an outline of the line to be covered, bring the needle from the back of material at the top of the line on the left side, put it in slightly slanting on the right-hand side, and bring it out on the left-hand side a little below the last stitch made (*see* Fig. 375);

FIG. 375. ROPE STITCH.

slightly slant it to the right, and continue to cover the traced line with these slanting stitches. Rope Stitch is worked as a perfectly even and regular line of slanting stitches, and closer together. than Crewel Stitch.

Satin Stitch.—The needlework executed with Satin Stitch, in combination with other stitches, ranks amongst the most beautiful and the most difficult of Embroideries, and, upon white materials, great proficiency has been attained in its execution in China, Japan, Ireland, Madeira, and Saxony, while upon dark silk or cloth foundations the work is almost universal. It is executed upon silk, satin, fine cambric, and muslin, and is largely used to embroider handkerchiefs, or to work designs upon satin with fine embroidery silks. It should be worked in a frame, and requires great knowledge of the art, as well as patience. Satin Stitch is of two kinds, the *Flat* and the *Raised.* The Flat Satin stitch is also called *Damask, Long, Au Passé, Point Perlé, Point Passé,* and *Passé,* and is an easy stitch, worked, without any padding, straight upon the material. To work: Trace the design upon the material, and arrange so that none of the petals of flowers or parts of the work are of any size. Bring the needle up from the back of the material on one side of the traced petal, and put it down exactly opposite where it came out upon the other side, leaving the thread lying flat across the intermediate space. Work a number of stitches in this way perfectly flat and even, until the traced petal is filled in. The stitches may be slanted instead of straight, but must always follow each other in the same direction, and with perfect regularity. Flat Satin is used by itself, or to fill in parts of Raised Satin designs,

CHANTILLY BLONDE LACE — FLOWERS "EN GRILLE."

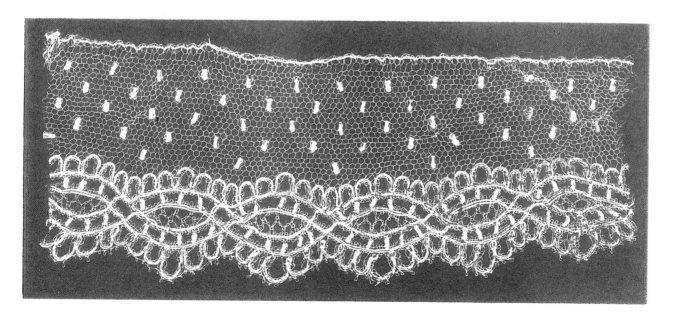

CHANTILLY BLONDE LACE — DOT PATTERN.

and it is sometimes varied in the manner illustrated in Fig. 376, where it fills in with interlaced stitches one side of the leaf, of which the other is worked in Back Stitch, the outline is Overcast, and the centre vein in a series of Eyelet-holes. To work: Work a row of SATIN STITCH, and miss the space one stitch would fill between every stitch. For the next row, fill in these spaces with a Satin Stitch, and carry each stitch beyond the ones made in the first row. Fill in the spaces left in the second row with a third row of stitches, carried beyond as before, and work in this manner until the leaf is filled in.

FIG. 376. FLAT SATIN, OVERCAST, EYELET, AND BACK STITCHES.

Another variety of Satin Stitch is made by working a long and a short Satin Stitch alternately. This is used for working small rose leaves, or any leaves that are slightly irregular in outline.

Raised Satin Stitch, also known as Point Plumetis and French Plumetis, is more difficult of execution than flat Satin Stitch. It is worked over a padded foundation, thus: Trace the outline of the design, run it round with a thread, and fill in the parts to be raised with a padding of run threads. Run these so that they are thick and solid in the centre of the Embroidery, and graduate down on both sides; or run them so that they are raised on one side and graduated down upon the other, according to the design, and work in these lines in an opposite direction to the

FIG. 377. RAISED SATIN STITCH.

stitch that is to cover them. Fig. 377 shows a Raised Satin petal with the padding raised on one side and sloped down to the other, and with horizontal runnings worked over

FIG. 378. RAISED SATIN STITCH.

with a slanting stitch taken from left to right; while Fig. 378 illustrates a padded petal raised in the centre and graduated to the sides, the runnings put in horizontally, and the covering stitches in an upright direction. Raised Satin Stitch is rarely used to fill in the whole of a design, but is combined with other Embroidery stitches.

Fig. 379 gives a leaf executed in three stitches: Back, Overcast, and Raised Satin. To work: Outline the leaf in OVERCAST, run a cord as a pad under the veins of the leaf, and Overcast this cord; then work the right-hand side

of the leaf in rows of large BACK STITCHES, and pad the left hand with perpendicular runnings, giving the greatest height near the centre veins. Work horizontal lines of SATIN STITCH over this padding.

FIG. 379. RAISED SATIN, BACK, AND OVERCAST STITCHES.

The handsomest manner of using Raised Satin Stitch is in Relief Embroidery executed with it in combination with other Embroidery Stitches. This consists in Embroidering detached pieces of material, and attaching these to the main part of the work, so that they stand out and above the flat Embroidery. Fig. 380 is a design of a Bluebell so worked, when finished, and the Details A and B (Figs. 381, 382) show the manner of execution, which consists of embroidering the material, and sewing over that an extra piece of work. To work: Trace the out-

FIG. 380. RAISED SATIN STITCH —BLUEBELL.

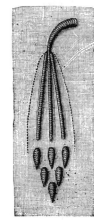

FIG. 381. RAISED SATIN STITCH —BLUEBELL—DETAIL A.

line of Detail A upon the main work, and OVERCAST the petals and their points, as shown in that illustration. Trace upon a detached piece of material the outline of Detail B,

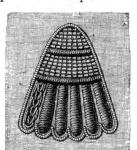

FIG. 382. RAISED SATIN STITCH— BLUEBELL—DETAIL B.

and BUTTONHOLE all the outline in very fine stitches; work the petals and the two horizontal lines in Raised Satin, and pad them so that they are most raised in the centre. In the detail one petal is left unfinished, to show the lines of padding; the rest are covered with Overcast. Fill in the body of the Bluebell with large BACK STITCHES worked in even rows. Cut out the piece of Embroidery, and stitch it on to the main part of work where the dotted lines are shown in Detail A. The piece of detached Embroidery is larger than the flat part of the flower, and will stand up from the rest of the work where not attached to the main body of it.

A variety of Raised Satin is known as Point de Plume. It is used in combination with Satin and other stitches, and consists of leaving unworked upon the petals of flowers and leaves the parts intended to indicate the veins; it is illustrated in Fig.
383. To work: Trace the design, but leave out the markings of the veins. Fill in the petals with run lines, leave the veins quite clear, and run the padding in so that the parts nearest the veins and centre of flower are the most raised. Work straight lines of SATIN STITCH over this padding, and vary their direction to follow the contour of the petals. Fig. 383 represents a flower worked in POINT

FIG. 383. POINT DE PLUME STITCH.

DE PLUME, with the veins marked with a black line; the centre of the flower is filled with three EYELET-HOLES for stamens, and the calyx is enclosed with fine OVERCAST, and filled in with BACK STITCH.

Ship Ladder Stitch.—See *Ladder Stitch.*

Spanish Stitch.—This stitch is of two kinds, one where a Cross Stitch is worked on the face of the material and a square on the back; and the other, where a cross enclosed in a square is at the front, and a square at the back. They are only worked when both sides of the material are required to be neat. To work the Cross Stitch: Make an ordinary CROSS STITCH, making the back stitches the top and bottom lines of a square. Recross the first stitch, and bring the needle out in front, ready to begin the next stitch; three lines of the square at the back are made with each Cross, but they fit into each other, so as to form squares as the work proceeds. To work the second kind: Make a square of stitches in the front of the material, and work a CROSS STITCH in the open space, passing the thread in horizontal lines from one point to the other at the back of the material.

Split Stitch.—A stitch much used in ancient Church Embroidery, and in silk Embroideries, to work the faces and hands of figures. It has the appearance of Chain Stitch, but lies flatter on the surface, and is more capable of forming the small half-curves, rounds, or lines that follow the contour of the figure, and give the appearance of shading to Embroidery only executed in one colour. It requires to be worked in a frame, and is made as follows: Bring the silk up from the back of the frame, and make a short stitch on the surface, and return the needle to the back. Then bring it up again to the surface through the middle of the first stitch, dividing or splitting the strands of silk of which it is formed by the passage of the needle. Put the needle down again to the back of the work, a short distance above where it came out, and bring it out again to the front in the centre of the second stitch, splitting the strands as before.

St. Andrew's Stitch.—An Embroidery Stitch made of four SATIN STITCHES arranged in the form of a St. Andrew's cross. To work: Mark out a square of the material, and commence the first stitch from the top left-hand corner of the square, and finish it in the centre of the square; work the next stitch from the top right-hand corner of the square into the centre, and take the two remaining stitches from the two bottom corners of the square into the centre in the same manner.

Stem Stitch.—See *Crewel Stitch.*

Tambour Stitch.—See *Chain Stitch.*

Tapestry Stitch.—See *Gobelin Stitch.*

Tassel Stitch.—A stitch used to make a looped fringe as an edging to Embroideries. To work: Double the thread and bring the needle up from the back, hold the thread down with the left thumb to the length of an inch, put the needle in on the right-hand side of where it came out, but on the same line, make a horizontal stitch from right to left at the back, bring it out under where it first came up, and draw up, keeping the left thumb on the thread, so as not to draw it up beyond the inch held down. Make a CROSS STITCH over the top of the loop. When the edge is covered with a line of loops cut their ends.

Tent Stitch.—Also known as Petit Point, and used in Berlin Work, and in Embroidery upon solid materials, such as silk and cloth. It is a succession of small SATIN STITCHES worked in even lines, and in a slanting direction, from left to right. To work: Trace a horizontal line upon the material, bring the needle up from the back upon this line, and put it down again to the back, slightly above the line, and in a slant from left to right. Continue to make these small slanting stitches close together, and all of the same height, until the line is filled; then draw a line underneath the first one, a short distance from it, and fill this line in the same way; work the top of the new line of stitches on the bottom of the first line, and in between those first made.

Tête de Bœuf Stitch.—The name of this stitch is derived from its shape, the two upper stitches having the appearance of horns, and the lower ones of an animal's head. It is a useful stitch in Ticking and other Ornamental work. To make: Draw a line

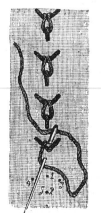

FIG. 384. TÊTE DE BŒUF STITCH.

that can be rubbed out down the centre of the space. Commence by making two slanting stitches apart at the top and meeting in the line at the bottom. Bring the thread out in the line a little above the bottom of the slanting stitches, insert the needle close to it, and bring it out a quarter of an inch below and upon the line, making a Loop or BUTTONHOLE. Draw the thread up, and put the needle through the material to the back on the line, and a little below the loop. Fig. 384 shows the working of Tête de Bœuf. In this illustration the two slanting stitches are already formed, and the loop is in progress. When drawn up, after the loop is made, the needle is inserted into the hole marked 1 for the last stitch, while 2, 3, 4, and 5 mark the places where the needle is inserted and brought out for the two slanting stitches that commence the next Tête de Bœuf.

Thorn Stitch.—A line of interlaced loops resembling Single CORAL Stitch, and made in the same way, except that the loops are closer together, not so large, and the needle is put in on a parallel line to where it came out. To work: Bring the needle to the front of the material, hold the thread under the left-hand thumb, make a loop with it, put the needle down on the right side of where it came up, and exactly on a line, and bring it out lower down over the loop of thread, and quite in its centre. Repeat the stitch, putting the needle in on the left-hand instead of the right, and continue working these two stitches to the end.

Twisted Chain Stitch.—Bring the thread out on the right side of the material, and hold it down with the left-hand thumb; put the needle in to cross this held down thread from left to right, draw up the thread, letting the held down piece go in the final pull.

Twist Stitch.—Identical with *Cord Stitch.*

Vandyke Stitch.—A raised Couching. To work: Lay down whipcord upon a linen foundation, in the shape of vandykes, and tack this firmly down. Over this lay down lines of floss silk or gold cord, and to secure, bring a stitch from the back of the material, pass it over the threads, and return it to the back, and with a number of these stitches mark out the vandyked outline of the cords upon each side.

Vandyke Stitch.—Used in Ticking work and embroidery upon thick materials. It forms a vandyked line, with its points at even distances apart. To work: Make a slanting Chain Stitch from left to right of the material, then a slanting Chain from right to left, bringing this one back under the commencement of the first stitch; continue these two stitches for the length, taking care that they are all of the same size, and that their points come under each other.

Vienna Cross Stitch—See *Persian Cross Stitch.*

Warp Stitch.—An Embroidery Stitch used when threads are drawn away from the material to form the pattern. Warp stitch consists of drawing away the threads that form the weft, or cross the material, and leaving the warp, or lengthways threads. These are secured together with ornamental HEM STITCH.

Wavy Stitch.—A raised Couching. To work: Lay down upon a linen foundation lines of whipcord arranged in curves, and tack these into position. Over these lay down floss or purse silk, or gold cord, and to fasten them down, bring a stitch from the back of the material, pass it over two strands of silk, return it to the back, and outline the curved and raised lines on both sides with these securing stitches.

Wheatear Stitch.—This stitch is a combination of Point Natté and Chain Stitch. It is used in Ticking and other fancy Embroideries, and also instead of Coral and Feather stitch, for ornamenting children's dresses and underlinen. It

FIG. 385. WHEATEAR STITCH.

can be worked in two ways:—First way: Make a series of POINT NATTÉ down the space to be covered, and then work over their centres a line of CHAIN STITCHES, taking care that the loop of each Chain Stitch begins at the spot where the Point Natté met in the centre of the work. The second way is to complete the stitch in one line (*see* Fig. 385), thus: Make a Chain Stitch down the centre, and then a slanting stitch to the right and a slanting stitch to the left, both finishing in the Chain Stitch.

Wheel Stitch.—A stitch resembling a spider's web, and worked into the material, and not over an open space, like English wheel and other lace Wheels. To work: Trace out a perfect circle upon the material, and divide it into four quarters. Make three long stitches in each quarter, at equal distances apart, and all ending in the centre of the circle. Bring a thread up from the back of the material in the centre of the circles, and interlace it; work it under and over each thread in succession (*see* Fig. 386). Run this thread in circles nearly to the

FIG. 386. WHEEL STITCH.

top of the long stitches, but not quite, and then fasten it off. Fig. 386 is a pattern formed with Wheels and diamonds; the centres of the diamonds are crossed with diagonal lines, forming a LATTICE STITCH.

Whipcord Couching.—See *Couching Stitch.*

Witch Stitch.—The name given to Herringbone when used in Fancy Embroidery. See *Herringbone Stitch.*

Embroidery Frame.—All the best kinds of Embroidery, such as Church Embroidery, Crewel Work, Embroidery with silk, Tambour Work, and Berlin Work, require that their foundations shall be stretched in frames, as the stitches are apt to draw the material together when the work is embroidered in the hand, whereas the frame keeps the foundation evenly and tightly stretched in every part, and renders it almost impossible to pucker it, unless the Embroiderer is very unskilful. Frames are of two makes: the best are those upon stands, as their use prevents habits of stooping being acquired by the worker, leaves her hands free, and gives unimpeded access to the back part of the work, without the artificial aid of slanting the frame from the corner of some piece of furniture to her hands, or the holding that is necessary with the other kind. But as these stand Frames are cumbersome and expensive, the second kind is most used; these are Frames made of four equal sized pieces of wood (*see* Fig. 387), or with the two horizontal pieces longer than the two upright, held together with nuts or pegs. They vary in size from 4 inches to 3 yards in length. The oblong Frames are used for long and narrow pieces, and the square for large pieces of work; and the same Frame is used indifferently for Church, Satin, and Crewel Embroideries, and for Berlin Work. The frame for Tambour Work differs from the others; it is made of two circular wooden hoops, one smaller than the other.

c c 2

Both the hoops are covered with velvet cut on the cross, and exactly fit one into the other. The material to be embroidered is fastened to the smaller hoop, and kept tight by the large hoop being passed over it. The ordinary frames are made of four pieces of wood. The two upright pieces are called Bars; on these are nailed stout pieces of narrow webbing, to which the material

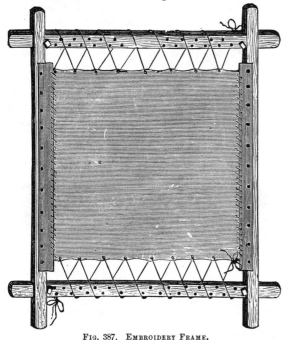

FIG. 387. EMBROIDERY FRAME.

is attached. The two horizontal pieces are called Stretchers; these are bored through with holes placed at equal distances, through which metal or wooden pegs are run to fasten the pieces of wood together. In the stand Frames these holes and pegs are not used, the wooden supports being lengthened or shortened by the aid of screws.

The fastening of the material into the frame is called "dressing a frame," and requires to be done with great nicety, as, if it is rucked, or unevenly pulled in any part, the advantage of the stretching is entirely destroyed. Slight variations in the manner of framing are necessary according to the materials worked upon; they are as follows :

For Canvas and Cloth and Serge Materials.—Select a frame long enough to take in the work in one direction, turn down the canvas or cloth about half an inch all round, and sew it down. If the length of the material will not allow of all of it being placed in the frame at once, roll it round one of the bars of the frame, with silver paper put between each roll to prevent it from getting lined. Sew the sides of the canvas to the webbing with strong linen thread, and put the frame together, stretching the material to its fullest, and fastening the pieces of wood together through the holes with the pegs. Then take a piece of twine, thread it through a packing needle, and brace the material with it to the stretchers. At each stitch pass it over the stretcher and into the material, and make the stitches close together. Brace both sides of the material, and then draw the twine up upon each side evenly and quite tight. Commence the Embroidery from the bottom of the material for canvas, and count the stitches and regulate the position of the pattern by them ; and for cloth, see that the design is laid evenly upon it before tracing.

To Stretch Canvas and Cloth Together.—This is required when a Berlin pattern is to be worked with cloth, for the ground. If the cloth foundation does not require to be bigger than the frame, cut it half an inch smaller every way than the canvas, as it stretches more. Turn the cloth down, and tack it to the canvas, right side uppermost, then tack them both together, and hem them where the raw edges of canvas are. If the cloth has to be rolled over the frame, put soft paper in between the rolls of cloth, and as the edges of the cloth are turned under, and are therefore thicker than the centre parts, lay more silver paper in the centre of the rolls than at the outside, or a line will appear upon the cloth on each side of the frame. Having sewn the two pieces of material together, attach them to the frame in the ordinary manner, and put them in, with the canvas uppermost. When the pattern is embroidered, cut the canvas from the cloth, and draw the threads away before the cloth is taken out of the frame.

To Stretch Velvet.—When the size of the velvet to be embroidered does not exceed that of the frame, and the work is not for Church Embroidery, hem it round, and sew it to the webbing of the bars by its selvedge. When it is larger than the frame, stretch holland, as in canvas framing, and tack to this holland with tacking threads just the parts of velvet that are to be embroidered. Work the Embroidery through the holland, and when finished, cut the refuse holland away from the back of the material, only leaving that part that is covered by the stitches. Velvet that is used as a background in Church Embroidery requires to be entirely backed with holland, in order to sustain the weight of the Embroidery laid upon it. Frame the holland (it should be of a fine description) as in canvas framing, and then paste it all over its surface with EMBROIDERY PASTE; over this, by the aid of three persons, lay the velvet. Take the velvet up, fully stretched out, and held by two people, and lay it down without a wrinkle upon the holland ; keep it fully stretched out, and hold it firmly. Then let the third person, with hands underneath the frame, press the holland up to the velvet, so that the two materials may adhere together without the velvet pile being injured.

To Stretch Satin or Silk.—Stretch a piece of fine holland in the frame, and paste the silk down to it with Embroidery Paste, but only tack the satin to it.

To Stretch Leather or Kid.—Stretch a piece of unbleached cotton in the frame, and paste the leather to it with Embroidery Paste, or tack the leather firmly down at the parts it is to be worked ; cut the calico from underneath when the Embroidery is finished. Do not stretch the leather or kid in the frame ; merely see that it lies flat, and without wrinkles.

To Stretch Crêpe.—Sew it to Book muslin, and frame that in the usual way.

Embroidery Needles.—There are two or three descriptions of Needles for Embroidery. For canvas work they are short, thick, and blunt, and the eyes wide and long. For Chenille embroidery they are wider still in the eye, and sharp at the point. For use on cambric and muslin, as in the Irish close and cut-work, and that called "Madeira" embroidery, a "between" is employed. For Art work on close materials, such as cloth, the needle has a long eye and sharp point, and resembles a darning needle, but is neither as long nor as thin. For Tambour and Crochet work they are thick, and have a hook at the end instead of an eye.

Embroidery Paste.—Embroidery paste is used for two purposes in needlework; first, to effect the adhesion of two materials; secondly, to strengthen and stiffen Embroidery at the back.

For Pasting Materials Together: Take 1oz. of the best gum, 1oz. of sugar candy, and a small piece of alum; reduce this to fine powder, lay in a shallow vessel, just cover it with cold water, and leave it to dissolve for four hours. Then take 1oz. of flour, and mix it smoothly in water. Put the mixed flour into an earthen vessel, add the mixture above-mentioned, place the vessel in a saucepan, and surround it with water. Put the saucepan on the fire, and let the mixture simmer (not boil); stir it, to prevent its getting lumpy, keeping the saucepan on the fire until the mixture is as thick as cream; then take it off the fire, but continue to stir until it is cold. Put the paste in a bottle, as it will keep for some time. Should it thicken after keeping, add a little cold water. Another recipe: Take three tablespoonfuls of flour, and as much powdered resin as will lie on a shilling; place these ingredients in half a pint of water, and boil for five minutes; stir until it boils, and afterwards, and use when cold. To this a teaspoonful of essence of cloves can be added as a preservative, while the paste is boiling; but this is not necessary.

For Strengthening Embroidery: Use size instead of the gum or resin of the above recipes.

Emery.—This is a variety of *Corundum*, and, with the exception of the diamond, is the hardest substance known. It is produced in the island of Naxos, in the Grecian Archipelago. It is imported in lumps, and has to be reduced to powder for use by means of stamping mills; it is then sifted into different degrees of fineness, and rendered available for grinding down surfaces by moistening with oil or water. It is also made to adhere, by the use of size, as a coating on paper or thin calico, and thus rendered available for polishing steel. For the purpose of needlework, the powder is placed in very small, closely-compressed cushions, into which needles are rapidly inserted and pulled out several times, for the removal of damp and rust. For children learning plain sewing these emery cushions are very essential, especially if the material be thick and stiff.

En bias.—The French term for "On the *bias*"—that is to say, folded or cut diagonally across the web of any textile in a slanting manner.

En Châle.—A French term to denote trimmings laid upon dresses, and formed with a corner point at the back, an angle being made at the junction of two sides of a square. Small capes, so shaped at the back, and just reaching to the waist, but with long ends in front, worn crossing each other, have been much in vogue at different times, usually at periods when belts have been in fashion.

En Cœur.—The French term to denote heart, or "V-shaped," and employed by dressmakers to describe the style of the opening in front of a bodice, which is otherwise "square cut."

Encolure.—A French term to signify the opening at the neck of a dress, and that at the arm-hole, to receive the top of the sleeve.

En Coquille.—The French term to denote "shell-shaped." The ribbon or lace is laid like a succession of scallop-shells, one above or over the other, in groups of threes, having been previously lined and plaited, and then drawn closely together at the top of each scallop, leaving the lower portion of the "coquille" to spread out in a half-circle. When employed as a trimming for crape or gauze, the strips of material of which they are to be made should be cut double the width of what is required, and folded over on each side, so that the edges may overlap where it is tacked down the middle, while the double material is being pleated. The space between the edge of the top pleat of one group and the lower one of the group succeeding it must never exceed the width of the strip which is worked upon.

En Couchure.—*See* EMBROIDERY STITCHES.

En Echelle.—*See* EMBROIDERY STITCHES. A French term to signify in ladder form; also a word applied to trimmings consisting of a succession of narrow plaitings laid on horizontally between two upright side folds or bands, forming, as it were, a kind of insertion with a ladder-like appearance. Folds of this description were at one time extended across the front of a bodice, wide at the shoulder, and gradually reduced towards the waist.

En Evantail.—A French term to signify "designed after the form of a fan," and employed to describe methods of trimming in dressmaking and millinery. Flounces at the end of a skirt are sometimes thus made, openings being cut at regularly recurring distances, and a piece of material of a different shade of colour, or a different piece of material, inserted into each opening, which is plaited, closely confined together at the top, and allowed to flare open like a fan at the bottom, giving much freedom, as well as a more ornamental character, to the flounce.

English Embroidery.—A simple kind of white Embroidery, also known as Broderie Anglaise. The patterns are generally worked open—that is to say, composed of holes from which the interior has been cut, and the holes run round and OVERCAST; but the finest and best sorts of English Embroidery are ornamented with Embroidery Stitches as well as with open work. *See* BRODERIE ANGLAISE.

English Laces.—For three centuries the making of Pillow Lace was carried on in England to a very considerable extent, and, until the manufacture of machine-made lace, was looked upon as one of the great industries of the poor in the Midland and Western counties. At the present time, with the exception of Honiton lace, made in Devonshire, and Maltese Guipures, made in Buckinghamshire, Bedfordshire, and around London, the art is not practised to anything like its former extent, the work being extremely laborious, and the remuneration most inadequate. Messrs. Marshall and Snelgrove are encouraging the making of Flemish, Italian, and Spanish laces in the West of England.

A coarse description of Bone Lace was made in England before the sixteenth century, but never attained any celebrity; and it was not until the arrival of Flemish refugees, and an interest had been taken in its manufacture by Katherine of Aragon, that English lace became of any value. Owing to that Queen's exertions, and the impulse given to its manufacture by religious refugees from Holland and France, English lace began to be of good make and design, and mention is made of presents of it to Queen Elizabeth by her courtiers. It continued to improve, and was until very recently protected from foreign competition by Acts of Parliament, the result being that vast quantities of Belgian lace were smuggled into England and sold as Point d'Angleterre. The laces made in England are all copies of foreign laces, and some are considered to equal in beauty of design and workmanship the originals, Old Devonshire rivalling Brussels lace, Honiton, and Point Duchesse, and the Valenciennes made at Northampton, that produced in Belgium and the Low Countries. Although no kind of lace-making, with the exception of Honiton, has been confined to a particular locality, consequent upon the various settlements of foreign workers, Bedfordshire, Buckinghamshire, and Northampton are considered the centres for the production of Run Laces, English Lille, Valenciennes, Regency Point, Plaited Laces, Old Brussels, Maltese Guipures, and Black laces; and around London, for black and white Blonde laces. Wiltshire and Dorsetshire were at one time celebrated for a lace made at Blandford and Lyme Regis, but the manufacture became extinct in the eighteenth century. The laces made in Devonshire and on the borders of Cornwall were formerly of considerable variety, but at present Honiton application and Honiton Guipure are chiefly made. The manufacture of these is, however, in a flourishing condition; new patterns and stitches are constantly worked, and that exhibited at the Exhibition of 1862 was so good as to obtain very high commendation from the judges. For a description of the Laces, see their various headings.

English Lace Stitch.—This stitch is used in Needle Point and in modern Point Lace. It requires to be worked with the finest thread. To work: Cross the space in one direction with a number of closely twisted BARS, a little way apart, but equal in distance*. Then, under these Bars, pass a thread in the opposite direction, and secure it to the braid, twist it to the first place where the threads cross, and work the needle round it until a fair sized spot is made, thus: Carry the needle over one thread and under the other alternately. Twist to the next place

where threads cross, work in the same manner, and repeat from *, as shown in Fig. 388. Another way of working this stitch is: Place the lines diagonally across the space, and radiate them, by making them farther from each other at one side than the other; work the spots over

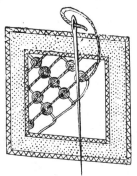

FIG. 388. ENGLISH LACE.

the lines large to commence with, and at the end very small. For a second variation, known as Open English Lace, make four lines of thread cross each other diagonally, horizontally, and perpendicularly, and work a spot on the last line.

English Lille.—This is a name given to some of the Pillow laces manufactured in Bedfordshire and Buckinghamshire during the eighteenth century, because the patterns originally came from the districts around Lille and Arras.

English Netting.—*See* NETTING.

English Point.—The English Point made during the last century seems to have been entirely the production of the wealthier classes, and never to have been universal. It was Spanish Point or Rose Point, and was taught to the daughters of people wealthy enough to send their children abroad to be educated in foreign convents; and though worked as an article of commerce, and mentioned in various official reports, its manufacture never became so popular as that of Bone or Pillow Lace. The lace worked in England at the present time, and known as Modern Point, is formed with braids of various sizes arranged as patterns, and filled in with most of the original stitches used in ancient Needle-points. *See* MODERN POINT LACE.

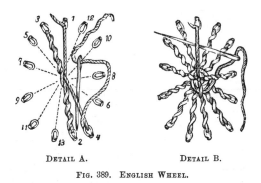

DETAIL A.   DETAIL B.

FIG. 389. ENGLISH WHEEL.

English Wheel.—Used in Modern Point Lace, and also called Point à l'Aiguille. To work as shown in

Fig. 389—Fill up the space with thirteen BARS, made as follows : Pass the thread from 1 to 2, and CORD the thread back to the centre of the space round 2, then pass the thread to 3, and Cord back to the centre, and continue to pass the thread into the points marked with the figures, and Cord them back to the centre, until all are made and Corded with the exception of the first Bar, which leave uncorded. To make the spot in the centre : Insert the needle over and under each Bar, and work round them in this manner until a handsome spot is formed, then cord the thread up Bar 1, and fasten off (*see* Fig. 389, Detail

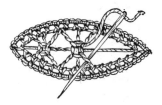

FIG. 390. ENGLISH WHEEL.

A and B). Fig. 390 is an illustration of an English Wheel made with six Bars. Three of these Wheels are required to fill in the design. They are worked as already described.

Engrêlure.—A lace term used to distinguish the upper part of a lace edging, and the one that is fastened to the dress, from the lower and scalloped edging. It is also called Footing. The Engrêlure is sometimes made with the rest of the lace, and at others separately, as a narrow piece, and afterwards sewn on to the main part.

En Ronde Bosse.—*See* EMBROIDERY STITCHES.

En Tablier.—The French term to signify "in the style of an apron," in reference to the form or trimming of the front of a skirt, which is made to appear as if an apron covered it.

Entoilage.—The French term for the ground of lace, on to which the Toile, or flower part of design, is worked.

Entre deux.—The French term for Insertion, Embroidery, or Lace—literally translated, "between two," that is to say, sewn between two other pieces of material as a decorative trimming ; a style which obtains extensively in the making of infants' robes and other clothing, in white cambric, lawn, or muslin.

Envers.—A French word, signifying the wrong side of any textile or garment. If a garment be put on inside out, it would be said that it was "*mis à l'envers.*"

Epaise.—The French term to express thick in substance, and applied frequently to describe textiles.

Epaulette.—A word borrowed from the French *Epaul*, meaning the shoulder, and the diminutive which follows, combined with it, forms the word into a term meaning an ornament for the shoulder, both in dressmaking, and in reference to uniforms and liveries.

Epingles.—The French for pins.

Ermine (*Mustela Erminea*).—This animal is of the Weasel tribe, in common with the Fitch, or Polecat, and the Kolinski. The skins are imported from Russia, Siberia, Norway, and Sweden, of which countries the Ermine is a native. It measures about 10 inches in length, and nearly resembles the Marten in form, but the common Weasel of this country in habits and feeding. During the winter the fur becomes snow-white, but throughout the summer it is a dingy brownish hue. The tail is jet black at the end, while the other half, towards the body, is yellow. This fur was so highly esteemed in the reign of Edward III. that its use was restricted to the Royal family. But while free to all now, it continues to be employed for the linings and trimmings of the State robes of England, Russia, Spain, Germany, &c. The black spots which decorate the white fur in every square inch of these robes, are made with the feet of the black Astrachan Lamb. The tails of the Ermine are used on cloaks, tippets, muffs, boas, and other articles of women's dress. The skins measure about 4 inches by 9 inches, and their small size adds necessarily to the costliness of the articles made from them.

Escalier Lace.—A stitch used in Modern Point Lace, and also called Cadiz Lace. It is shown in Fig. 391. To work : Make POINT DE BRUXELLES stitches close together in straight rows, and only miss the space that two Point de Bruxelles stitches would fill where the open diamond is formed in the illustration.

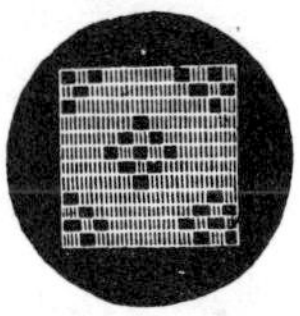

FIG. 391. ESCALIER LACE.

Estamene.—A French made all-wool cloth, somewhat like a serge, twilled, but having a rough face. Being made in different qualities, it varies in price, but uniformly measures 25 inches in width. It is employed for women's dresses. In weather suitable for the wearing of Serge, Estamene might be a fitting substitute, but, at the same time, as a superior kind of dress material to the former.

Estrich (or *Estridge*).—The fine soft down beneath the feathers of the ostrich, which is employed as a substitute for beaver in making hats, and in the manufacture of a stuff resembling fine linen cloth. It was imported free of duty to this country as far back as the reign of Charles II., as "Estridge," or "Bever Wooll."

Etamine.—A coarse description of Woollen Bunting or Canvas, more or less transparent. It is employed as a dress material, and intended to be worn over a contrasting colour. The threads are of a fluffy character, and the material is to be had in a bright but dark blue, navy blue, russet and other shades of brown, in black, cream colour, maroon, and sage green. Etamine is also woven with stripes of velvet, embroidered, and in plaited woven stripes ; and it is also produced in cotton.

Etching Embroidery.—This variety of needlework was originally called Print Work, and was much in vogue during the first part of the present century ; many specimens of it are still to be met with as framed pictures. It was intended to reproduce, by the aid of Embroidery coupled with Painting, fac-similes of line engravings, and was worked with fine black silk over a sepia tinted ground. To work : Stretch in an EM-

BROIDERY FRAME some good white or cream-coloured silk, and pencil upon this the chief outlines of a landscape engraving with prominent objects or figures.

silk a short distance apart, and work the darkest shades in flat SATIN STITCH close together. Graduate between the medium and the deepest tints with separate Satin

FIG. 392. ETCHING EMBROIDERY.

Take a sable brush, and form the sky by washing in sepia for the darker parts, leaving the surface of the silk untouched for the white clouds; and then colour the rest of the picture with washes of sepia, in shades corresponding to those of the engraving. Thread

Stitches; commence them close together, and end them more apart. Work the foliage of trees in fine FRENCH KNOTS.

Etching Embroidery is at present worked more in outline than in filled-in Embroidery, and is used for

FIG. 393. ETCHING EMBROIDERY.

FIG. 394. ETCHING EMBROIDERY

a needle with fine black silk, and commence to cover the painting. Leave unworked all light parts, such as the sky; work the medium tint with run lines of black

d'oyleys and small pictures. Fig. 392 is an illustration of a pattern intended for a picture, and is worked as follows: Draw the design in pencil upon jean, and tint it with washes of sepia, then outline all the chief parts with fine black silk run lines. Fill in the boat, the oars, and part of the frogs and lobster, with run lines close together, and mark out the lily flowers and the veins of the leaves in the same way. If the work is intended to wash, leave out the sepia, and only work in the black silk lines.

The two medallions (Figs. 393 and 394) are intended to be framed, and are entirely worked with black silk, without any painting. To work: Trace the outlines upon cream-coloured silk, and work them over in CREWEL STITCH with fine black silk, filling in those parts of the picture that are represented black. Work the whole of the background with a number of FRENCH KNOTS.

Eternelle Lace.—Another name for SAXONY LACE.

Etoiles.—These are required in Guipure d'Art, and are made with Slip Stitch, Point de Toile, Point de Venise, or Point de Reprise, arranged to fill in the meshes of the netted Foundation with star patterns. Fig. 395 is an Etoile worked in Slip Stitch and Point de Reprise, and is made as follows: Commence with SLIP STITCH, take a square of four meshes, and wind the thread four times round the right-hand top corner and the left-hand bottom corner, then reverse the winding, and wind the threads

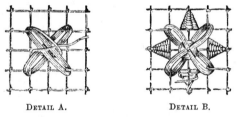

DETAIL A.   DETAIL B.

FIG. 395. ETOILE IN SLIP STITCH AND POINT DE REPRISE.

round the other corners (*see* Fig. 395, Detail A). Bring the thread out in the middle of the square, and wind it round and round the centre, passing it over and under the Slip Stitches in that place. Complete the Etoile by working POINT DE REPRISE as four points, in the manner shown in Detail B. Make a VANDYKE with two threads on each side of the centre mesh, and then interlace the thread in and out of these Vandyke lines and the mesh foundation, first over the right-hand thread, under the middle thread, and over the left-hand, and then over the middle thread and under the right-hand.

FIG. 396. ETOILE IN SLIP STITCH AND POINT DE TOILE.

Fig. 396 is an Etoile worked in SLIP STITCH and POINT DE TOILE thus: Take a square of nine meshes, and work Slip Stitch in each outside corner. Then cross the centre square with four straight threads laid in one direction, and darn these together with four threads in a contrary direction, working the cone-like finishes to the centre square in the same way.

Everlasting.—A description of woollen JEAN, employed for the tops of boots. It is another name for PRUNELLA (which *see*).

Eyelet-hole.—The word eye is derived from the French *œil*; "et" is merely a diminutive, suitably applied in reference to the small opening made in any material, which

the compound word is used to designate. EYELET-HOLES are made to receive a lace, cord, or ribbon in an article of dress or furniture, and are either finished with BUTTON-HOLE STITCH, or with a metal binding affixed by means of machinery.

F.

Fabric.—A term derived from the Latin *Fabrica*, rendered in French *Fabrique*, and not only employed to signify the structure or frame of any building, but of general application to manufactures of the loom—otherwise, and more correctly, designated TEXTILES. Thus, it is very usual to speak of fabricating tissues of silk and wool, to avoid a repetition of the word manufacture.

Facing.—A term employed by dressmakers and tailors to signify the lining applied to the extreme edge of a dress or other garment; when used in reference to uniforms and liveries it denotes the differently coloured breast, cuffs, and collars, the colours being selected so as to accord with those of the regiment, guild, city, or family represented.

Façon.—A French term, signifying the make or external form of anything—the shape, style, appearance, or pattern.

Fag.—The idea attached to the term is that of imperfection, inferiority, and consequent rejection or destruction. Thus, FAG is employed to signify a knot or blemish in the web of cloth, an imperfect or coarse part of it.

Fag-end.—The rough, unfinished end of a web of any textile, where it is secured to the loom. It is usually imperfectly or wholly undyed, and is disfigured with holes. Sometimes it is of a poorer or coarser quality than the rest of the cloth, and purchasers are allowed to exclude it from the calculation of the length for which they pay.

Faille.—This is a French term, denoting the ribbed or corded make in the weaving of ribbon or of piece silk; but there is likewise a silk stuff especially known by the name of FAILLE, employed for evening dresses, and trimmings of hats and bonnets. It is soft in quality, and has more substance than a FOULARD, has but little gloss, and is expensive. Faille looks better in light than in dark colours.

Fall.—A term much employed in dressmaking and millinery, in reference to trimmings of lace, when applied after the fashion of a fringe, depending from an edge or border. For example, a trimming of deep lace, depending from the neck part, and round the shoulders of a low bodice, would be called a FALL of lace. In millinery, lace sewn to the brim of a bonnet, to serve as a veil, is called a Fall.

False Buttonholes.—These are sometimes adopted as decorations for dresses and jackets. They are made by sewing a cord, or small roll of the material cut crosswise, of the same size and shape as a buttonhole, the button being sewn on the two ends of the roll or cord, at their junction. The deception can be made more complete by cutting an opening in the stuff, running a narrow binding round it on the right side, and turning the other edge through the hole, and hemming it on the wrong side. They may also be simulated thus: Insert the needle at one end of the supposed length of the opening at the top, then twist the silk round the end of the needle on its appearance up through the material, at the opposite end of the opening, until the length of twisting shall equal that of

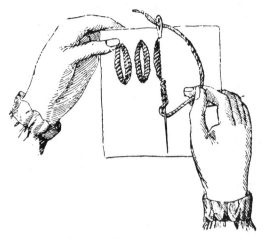

FIG. 397. FALSE BUTTONHOLES.

the hole. Then place the thumb of the left hand on the roll so made, to keep it in place while the needle and silk are drawn through it (see Fig. 397).

False Hem.—This is applied to a fold-over at the extreme edge of any portion of dress or other article, made of whatever kind of textile; it has the appearance of a hem, and serves its purpose, but is not one in reality. Making a FALSE HEM is a method of lengthening a skirt or sleeves, or widening a bodice or jacket. It is effected thus: Open out the material of the dress or jacket to its extreme proportions, run a piece of lining on to the edge of the material, and turn in the strip of lining employed to form the False Hem, hemming it down on the inside. Thus, instead of turning in a comparatively wide strip of an inch in depth, a very narrow edge only is turned in with the lining, and the whole of the material is made available to enlarge the dress.

False Pin Holes.—These are required in Pillow Lace making, in the inner part of curves or circles, to keep the outer and inner edges level with one another, and are also called False Stitches. As the outer edge of the curve or circle is necessarily larger than the inner, a greater number of pinholes are required at that edge than at the other, and as the working threads must pass backwards and forwards across the passive threads as usual, the only way of arranging them so as to lie flat is to stick one inner pin to two outer, and to work twice over the inner pinhole instead of only once, the usual way. To work: Take the working BOBBINS across to the inside, twist three times, put up a pin, and, instead of completing the edge, return with the same pair, and put up the pin on the outer edge; finish the stitch, and return with the pair from behind that pin. Work with these to the inner pin, take it out, and stick it in again, so that it holds the row just worked, putting it in the same hole as before; work the edge with the pair of Bobbins waiting at the inner edge. Repeat until the circle or curve is rounded. By this process two outer pins are stuck to one inner, and the curves rounded without puckering. Occasionally drive a pin down to its head to keep the lace firm, and, should

the curve required be a small sharp one, only twist the threads twice instead of three times.

False Stitches.—Used in Pillow Lace for rounding the inner edges of curves and circles, and identical with FALSE PINHOLES.

Fancy Checks.—These are varieties, produced in every description of stuff, more or less after the models of the original Scotch Tartans, but in no degree distinctive of any Clan. See TARTANS.

Fancy Cotton Ribbon.—This Ribbon is made like a species of Tape, and employed for strings of nightdresses and caps, and for use on articles made of white cotton. One variety is ornamented with open work, after the style of lace, and is about an inch in width. Some FANCY COTTON RIBBONS are made with a velvet pile, cut in strips from the piece, and having a raw edge, which is sized to prevent a fraying out. See COTTON RIBBON VELVETS.

Fancy Materials.—Under this name an indefinite number of fabrics must be classed, some of ephemeral character, many appearing under Trade names, differing respectively in the various shops. Collectively they are called "Fancies" by the Trade, and consist of varieties—produced in the weaving, the patterns, and the combinations of colour, together with newly-produced dyes, according to the fashion of the time—in Stuffs of every description, of permanent use. For example, in Woollen cloths for dress, there are "Moorish" and "Bouclé, canvas," "Canvas Raye," "Sanglier Raye," striped "Moorish Crape Lawn," "Meguet Broché," "Beige Brodé," "Foulé Brodé," &c. In Silk stuffs, the "Theodora," "Faille Française," and "Black Satin Damas"—both the latter in geometrical, or small floral, designs, and corded. In Velvets, also, there are "Fancy" makes—such as those woven in stripes with Grosgrain, and produced in two shades of colour, as well as in black, or any single colour. As so many of these varieties are continually appearing and disappearing, and are each frequently known by different names, they must be classed under the general name of "Fancy Materials." A war, a victory, a hero, a diplomatist, an author, or an actress, very usually give a name to these novelties of the season.

Fancy Silk Sheeting.—This material has a small diaper pattern thrown up in the weaving. It is to be had in all colours, and is employed for embroidery. It is 22 inches in width.

Fancy Tambour.—See TAMBOUR WORK.

Fancy Tricot.—These are various arrangements of TRICOT, and are described in CROCHET.

Fancy Work.—A term applied to Needlework that is intended for decorative, and not for useful, purposes.

Fan Lace.—Used in Ancient Needle Lace and in Modern Point. To work: First row—Make six close POINT DE BRUXELLES STITCHES, leave the space of six; repeat to end of the line. Second row—work six Point de Bruxelles Stitches into the six in first row, carry the thread to the next six Point de Bruxelles, and work over those; repeat to end of the row. Third row—work six Point de Bruxelles Stitches into each of the loops of the last row, and make loops between. Fourth row—work six Point de Bruxelles Stitches into every six of the last row, and six into each loop. Fifth row—work six Point de Bruxelles Stitches into the six in the loop, and leave the space between them. Repeat from the third row.

Fashion.—A term employed in reference to the style, cut, pattern, colours, or prevailing usage with regard to dress, or other matters.

> Fashion wears out more apparel than the man.
> —*Shakespeare.*

Fast Pile Velveteen.—This is a velveteen made after a new and superior method, ensuring the fixity and firm adhesion of the pile, which used to wear out of the web when manufactured according to the original plan. The names given to it vary according to the fancy of the several manufacturers who produce it, and amongst them it is known as " Imperial," " Louis," " Mancunium," " Brunswick Finish," the " Peacock Velveteen," &c., by which names it may be inquired for.

Feather Cloth.—A mixture of cloth and feathers woven together, the cloth being undyed, and produced in drabs and greys. This curious material measures 1½ yards in width. It has a very unfinished appearance, as the feather ends protrude from the face here and there throughout, yet are woven into the web sufficiently well to preclude their falling out. The cloth is naturally a warm one, comparatively light, and probably waterproof, without being rendered so by artificial means. It is a specialty of a large firm.

Feather, or Fringed Ruche.—This description of RUCHE is made by cutting a piece of silk parallel with the selvedges, at distances of about 2 inches apart, throughout the whole width of the material, and then drawing out the threads of the warp. Being cut on the straight, this Ruche needs to be fuller than those made crosswise, and three times its own length will be necessary in calculating the amount required for the space to be trimmed.

Feathers.—Almost every description of bird, from the small humming bird to the ostrich, supplies plumage that is employed for dress decoration; and not only so, but for actual clothing. Feathers are worn both in their natural hues and dyed, and employed in upholstery for the stuffing of beds, pillows, &c. The word is derived from the Dutch *veder.*

Feather Stitch.—The two varieties of this stitch are the Opus Plumarium of ancient writers, used at that period and at the present time for filling in Embroideries worked in silk and crewels upon silk, cloth, and serge materials, and Feather and Double Feather Stitch, used to make the ornamental lines that decorate underlinen and children's dresses. *See* EMBROIDERY STITCHES.

Feather Work.—This consists of covering buckram or other stiff foundations with birds' feathers, arranged in designs, and sewn entirely over the foundation. The work is very handsome, and is used for vallances, picture frames, chairs, brackets, fire screens, muffs, bonnets, and for dress trimmings. Large articles are covered with Aylesbury duck or white poultry feathers, dyed in various colours, and small with peacock, pheasant, parrot, ostrich, marabout, pigeon, Guinea fowl, and black-cock feathers used in their natural shades.

The feathers are prepared as follows, if white, and obtained from domestic poultry : First, gently wash the bird in soapsuds and lukewarm water to which a little whisky has been added, and let it dry in a clean, warm place ; after it has been killed, pick off the feathers, enclose them in a strong bag, and bake in a moderate oven. Shake each feather separately, cut off the fluff and the little hard piece at the top of the quill, and keep them where they are not likely to be crushed. To dye: Pour into two quarts of boiling water a table or teaspoonful of Judson's dye, according to the depth of shade required, and steep the feathers in this for five minutes; take them out one by one with a pair of pincers, so as not to touch them, then add more dye to the water, and thoroughly stir the mixture ; throw the feathers in, stir all up together, and take out the feathers separately, without touching them, when they are sufficiently coloured. Crawshaw's dyes may also be used.

To Work for Dress Trimmings, a large quantity of these dyed feathers, and strips of webbing, or Petersham, are required. Fasten the foundation of webbing to a weight cushion, and sew the feathers, one by one, on in lines across the width; slope their ends inwards and to the centre, and conceal the edge of the foundation by making the feathers overlap, laying the second line of feathers over the first, to thoroughly hide the securing stitches. Stitch each feather four times with a waxed thread. Put these stitches close to the end of the quill, two upon each side of it, and crossing each other.

To Work for Bonnets.—Procure a black bonnet shape, bind the edges, and sew the feathers on singly, on the brim as straight lines, on the crown as circles.

To Work for Muffs.—Make the shape in buckram, and sew the feathers on singly, and in upward lines.

To Work Vallances and Brackets.—Cut a buckram foundation the size of the article, rub it over with a little carbolic acid, and arrange well-marked natural feathers in straight lines along the foundation, taking care that they thoroughly overlap each other. Begin at the lower end of the material, graduate the colours, put in all one colour birds' feathers in a line, and follow by a contrasting line; sew each feather on separately with a waxed thread.

To Make a Screen.—These are usually made with peacocks' feathers. Cut out an oval or round shape, and sew on as the first round the largest eyed peacocks' feathers ; for the second round, the smaller size ; for the third round, the dark blue neck feathers ; for the fourth, the breast feathers ; and finish with the head feathers and crest. Should the screen be a large one, sew on two lines of each kind of feathers, but keep to the same order.

To work Fig. 398 : Cut out the shape on buckram, and sew round it, so that the edge is thoroughly concealed, the fine filaments of peacocks' feathers ; make the next round with parrots or pheasants' feathers, then fill in the centre with white poultry feathers, and over them arrange a large tuft of peacocks' filaments as a finish. Conceal the back of the buckram with a cardboard foundation, covered with fluted silk, which gum on to the buckram ; or simply cover the buckram with black paper.

To work Fig. 399.—This Butterfly is intended as an ornament to be worn in the bonnet or in the hair, and is made as follows : Cut out the shape in buckram, allow for each wing 1½ inches in depth, and 1⅛ inches in width, and for the body 1⅛ inches in length, and ¼ inch in width. Shape the wings like the pattern, and round the lower extremity of the body. To cover the two upper wings, sew on large and strong pheasant feathers; shape these by cutting them with scissors, so

FIG. 398. SCREEN IN FEATHER WORK.

that they slope to meet the underwings, and notch their edges. Make the under wings of the neck feathers of the peacock, and let these slightly overlap the upper wings, and notch their edges. Paint the edge of all the wings with lampblack in oil colour, and make the white spots with Chinese white. Upon the upper end of the body sew

FIG. 399. BUTTERFLY IN FEATHER WORK.

down two fine peacocks' filaments, 1¾ inches in length, to form the antennæ, and then cover over the foundation with black velvet; shape the head, and make the eyes with two black beads; bar the velvet body across with gold thread, and finish it off with a line of gold thread, where it joins the wings. Cover the back of the buckram with black velvet, and sew a loop of wire into the velvet, through which to pass a hairpin.

Felling.—A term used in sewing. Two pieces of material being first RUN together, turn the raw edges

over, and HEM them double, placing them flat down upon the stuff. The turn-over edge should be deeper than that underneath, so that the HEM may be less bulky, and that the needle employed for HEMMING may pass through two folds only, instead of four. This difference in the depth of the two edges of material should be made before they are Run together. A FELL has a second signification, and means the end of a web (textile).

Felt.—This is made of matted wool, hair, rabbits' fur, or other substances, first carded, then fulled, rolled, and pressed, and converted into a stout nap by a process that interlaces the several fibres. It is employed for hats, and heavy cloths used as carpets, but does not wear well, as the dye is liable to be rubbed off the surface. French-made FELT, being softer and more pliable, is considered superior to our own, and preferred for hats. It is stiffened and made waterproof by the application of shellac, on both sides, with a brush. Felt is of ancient and Eastern origin. The Tartars employ it for their tents and clothing. Hats made of Felt were in use in this country in the Middle Ages, and were superseded by beaver ones, as well as by those of velvet in the reign of Elizabeth. The article is much used still for other purposes, the waste wool from weaving mills, and the hair of rabbits' fur, when cleaned, damped, rolled, beaten, and pressed together, being much employed for druggets.

Fendu.—A French term to denote cut open or slashed, after the manner of dress decoration in the time of Henry VIII., Elizabeth, and for some time subsequently. The style was derived from the Swiss. *See* SLASHING.

Fents.—A technical term denoting the ends of calicoes, of various descriptions, tacked together. The name is likewise given to ends of imperfectly printed cambrics, which are sold by weight, and used for patchwork quilts.

Ferret.—A kind of tape, narrower than ordinary bindings, and made of silk, cotton, or worsted. The Cotton FERRETS have the appearance of unsized tape. Those in drab colour and black are mostly employed. They are made up in rolls of nine pieces, containing 16 yards, Numbers 8-18, or else 6-24. The manufacture has lately deteriorated. Cotton Ferrets should be stouter than tapes, but are now usually of a flimsy quality Italian Ferrets are made of silk only, and all of one width, although of various colours, besides black and white. There are four pieces, of 36 yards each, in the gross.

Feston.—The French term for BUTTONHOLE, or Double Overcast, when used as a scalloped or plain edging to Broderie Anglaise and other Embroideries. *See* EMBROIDERY STITCHES.

Fibre.—There are three descriptions of FIBRE employed in the manufacture of textiles: The animal, which is represented in alpaca, mohair, silk, wool, and catgut; the vegetable, represented by cotton, flax, grass, hemp, leaf fibres, bark, and jute; and the mineral, which is only represented by asbestos, gold and silver thread, and glass. Some 360 species of plants produce fibre capable of utilisation for cloth or cordage, but the friability of most of them renders their use of comparatively small value, and only five amongst them are in general request.

Fibre Stitch.—A stitch used in Honiton and other

Pillow Laces to make open leaves, with a fibre running down their centres, as shown in the leaves with holes in them in the Honiton spray illustrating Flemish Stitch (Fig. 404). To work: Hang on eight pairs of BOBBINS, and a GIMP upon each side of the Bobbins. Work the leaf in WHOLE or CLOTH STITCH, with a fibre running down the centre; make the fibre by twisting the workers both before and after the centre stitch is made. For the first four rows, twist the workers at this place once, then twist them twice in all the rows until the widest part of the leaf is reached, when, for two rows, twist them three times. Then return to twisting them twice until the narrow part of the leaf is reached, when twist only once. In the last three rows, cut off a pair of Bobbins in the first and second rows, and two pairs in the third row. Tie up the Gimps and cut them off. Take the four pairs of Bobbins remaining, stick the end pin in, make a stitch about it, and twist the outside pair, but not the second; in this pair tie up all the others very neatly. Take out all the pins except three upon each side (running these down to their heads), turn the Pillow round, first slanting the two end pins outwards (be sure to do this), bring the threads in between these end pins, and lay them down over the leaf. Lift the pair in which they are tied up, and pass it round the other threads; take out one of the end pins, but not the one put in last; make a SEWING, re-stick the pin, pass the same pair round, make another Sewing in next pinhole, tie up, and cut the Bobbins off. The leaf is thus finished on the wrong side, and the right side made tidy.

Fichu.—A French term signifying a half-square of any material cut diagonally, or from corner to corner. This name also denotes a small covering of silk, muslin, lace, or tulle, for the neck or shoulders.

Figured Muslin.—This name is usually applied to clear BOOK MUSLINS decorated at regular intervals by a small raised spot or trefoil leaf. The width of such muslins ranges from 32 inches to 36 inches.

Figure of Eight Knot.—Take a piece of thread, make a loop with it turning to the left, and put the top end of the loop under the lower end, and hold them tight in the left hand. Curl the under thread round and under the upper thread, and pass it into the loop and out on the left hand. Draw the two ends tight, and a knot resembling the numeral eight will be made.

Fil.—The French for thread of any description.

Fil de Trace.—The name by which the outlines of Needle-made laces are distinguished. The various pieces forming the design are made separately, and, when completed, sewn into their proper position in the main part of the work. They therefore require a separate thread or foundation before they can be commenced, which is made as follows: Take a piece of parchment, and tack it on to paper, and with a needle prick the outline of the lace to be worked through the parchment; prick two holes close together, leave a space, then prick two more, and so on, until the pattern is outlined. Rub into the holes a little white paint, to render them clear to the sight. Then, with a coarse needle and No. 12 Mecklenburgh thread, proceed to fill in this pricked outline. Begin with the thread at

the back, and bring it up to the front through the first of the two holes close together, and put it down in the second. Bring it up again in the next group of two holes, in the first, and put it down in the second hole, so that a long stitch is made at the back and a short stitch at the front of the

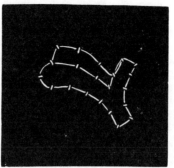

FIG. 400. FIL DE TRACE.

work. . Fasten off by tying the ends of the thread together at the back of the work. Then take another thread (No. 7 Mecklenburgh), and begin at the back of the pattern; pass the needle up through the first hole, and slip the thread under the small stitch between the two holes, and so on all round the pattern, as shown in Fig. 400, where the two lines of stitches are given; so that a thread caught with small stitches outlines the piece of lace to be worked, and forms its foundation. When that piece of lace is finished, the small stitches of the first line are cut at the back of the parchment, and the outline thread, with the lace attached to it, will then come away from the pattern, without the lace being pulled or dragged.

Fil de Trace is also the name of the thread of a different texture to that forming the design, with which the outline of the pattern in laces is sometimes traced, as in Cluny Guipure and Blonde Laces.

Filet Brodé.—Also known as Darned Laces, Guipure d'Art, and Spiderwork. *See* GUIPURE D'ART.

Filet de Canasier.—The French name for MACRAME.

Filet Guipure.—*See* GUIPURE D'ART.

Filière.—The French term signifying a GAUGE for the measurement of knitting needles. Some are round, and others spade-shaped. They are made of steel. *See* GAUGE.

Filigree Point.—This work is an imitation of the old gold laces, and is made with lines of gold thread, arranged in patterns, and held together with Buttonhole Stitches of coloured silks. To work: Select a simple star or Vandyke pattern, and trace this upon linen, which back with stiff paper. Tack along the traced lines three to four rows of gold thread; connect these gold threads together with wide apart BUTTONHOLE, made with white silk, only putting in sufficient stitches to keep the thread in position. Make loops of gold thread as an edging to the outside of the work. Make each loop separately, and secure it with an OVERCAST STITCH to the work, then make another loop close to the first, and secure that with an Overcast Stitch. Fill in the ground of the pattern with BARS, ornamented with PICOTS, and work WHEELS, STARS, or LACE STITCHES as FILLINGS to the pattern. When finished, untack the lace from the linen foundation.

Fill Bobbins.—*See* BOBBINS.

Filletings.—An unbleached and very heavy description of HOLLAND TAPE, cut into various lengths, and numbered 3¼ to 10. There is another striped variety called Stay Tape, employed by tailors to protect selvedges and buttonholes.

Fillings.—These are the various stitches in Needle-made and Pillow Laces that occupy the centres of the sprays and other devices that form the Toile, or design, of the lace. In Needle-made laces these stitches are always surrounded by a raised or flat Cordonnet, which serves as their foundation, and which is made of a series of Buttonhole. With the exception of the Wheels, the Fillings in Needle laces are formed either of close Buttonhole, varied with open spaces, or with varieties of Knots and Corded lines ornamented with circles. The varieties of Buttonhole Stitches used as Fillings are ones taken from old Spanish and Venetian Points, with other stitches taken from Darned laces or Filet Brodé. Most of the Fillings in Needle laces are now worked in modern Point, and have received names, under which headings they are described, with the exception of Figs. 401, 402, 403, which are given as examples. The illustrations give the Buttonhole as dark lines, the open spaces as white squares.

To work Fig. 401: First row—work 15 BUTTONHOLE, * miss the space of 3, work 21, repeat from * to the end of the row, but finish with 15 Buttonhole. Second row—work the whole row in Buttonhole, carefully counting the stitches. Third row—* miss the space of 3 Buttonhole, work 3, miss 3, work 15, repeat from *. Fourth row—work 3 Button-hole, * miss the space

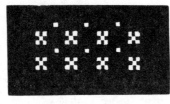

FIG. 401. FILLINGS.

of 3, work 21, repeat from *. Fifth row—like the third. Sixth row—like the second. Seventh row—like the first, and repeat all the rows from the first row.

To work Fig. 402: First row—work 9 Buttonhole, * miss the space of 3, work 15, repeat from *. Second row—work 6 Buttonhole, * miss the space of 3, work 3, miss the space of 3, work 9 Buttonhole, repeat from *. Third row—* work 3 Buttonhole, miss the space of 3, work 9, miss 3, repeat from *. Fourth row—* miss the space of 3

FIGS. 402 AND 403. FILLINGS.

Buttonhole, work 15 Buttonhole, repeat from *. Fifth row—* work 3 Buttonhole, miss the space of 3, work 9, miss the space of 3, repeat from *. Sixth row—work like the second row. Seventh row—work like the first row, and repeat from the first row.

To work Fig. 403: Begin with two plain rows. First row—* miss the space of 3, work 3, miss the space of 3, work 3, miss the space of 3, work 9, repeat from *. Second row—work 3 Buttonhole, * miss the space of 3, work 3, miss 3, work 15, repeat from *. Third row—* work 6 Buttonhole, miss the space of 3, repeat from *. Fourth row—* work 15 Buttonhole, miss the space of

3, work 3, miss 3, repeat from *. Fifth row—work 12 Buttonhole, * miss the space of 3, work 3, miss 3, work 3, miss 3, work 9 Buttonhole, repeat from *. Sixth row—work like fourth row. Seventh row—work like the third row. Eighth row—work like the second row. Ninth row—work like the first row, and repeat all the rows from the first row.

The Fillings in Pillow Laces are composed of Plaitings, Stitches, and Braid, and are all described under their own headings.

Filoselle (French, *Bourre de Soie*).—A silk thread used in embroidery, composed of the refuse of silk covering the exterior of the cocoon, and other kinds of inferior quality. It has been introduced for decorative needlework within the last fifty years, and has greatly superseded *floss* silk for general purposes, being less expensive and more easily kept smooth in the working; but it lacks the great gloss of the latter, which is spun from the finest portion of the silk. FILOSELLE is that portion of the ravelled silk thrown on one side in the filature of the cocoons, which is then carded, spun like cotton or wool, and formed into spun silk. This silk is not only used as thread, but is formed into a textile for dresses, scarves, and shawls.

Fil Tiré.—The French term for DRAWN WORK (which *see*).

Fine Drawing.—The method of DARNING adopted by tailors to mend broadcloth and such like stuffs. Pare the edges perfectly even, and hold the severed parts lengthwise on the finger of the left hand. Then pass the needle (directed from you) through the edge of one piece, and back again (pointed towards you) through the edge of the other. Let in the needle at half the thickness of the cloth, and draw the stitches closely together, so that the edges may meet, yet neither overlap the other, and carefully avoid ravelling out the threads of the stuff. When the work is finished, press it with a hot iron on the wrong side. *See* DARN.

Finger.—A measure of length, employed for every description of textile for wearing apparel or upholstery, &c. It comprises 4½ inches, and is much in use by needlewomen.

Fingering.—Worsted employed for stockings, sent out by the manufacturers in half pounds, consisting of eight skeins, each weighing an ounce; the weight, however, is usually short. Various descriptions are to be had—the SCOTCH in three or four qualities and many colours, including the ingrain shades. There is also GERMAN FINGER-ING in many colours, including that known as HEATHER; WELSH YARD FINGERING, PEACOCK FINGERING, and other kinds, the names varying according to the fancy of the several manufacturers or shopkeepers. FLEECY wools may be had in many colours; they are supplied in 3lb., 6lb., and 12lb. bundles. The SCOTCH FINGERING is a loosely spun worsted yarn, and is sold by the spindle of 6lb., and also by the pound and the ounce. The price varies with the quality, of which there are the Middle, Super, Ex. Super, and Ex. Ex. Super qualities. Each skein of the original Scotch Fingering contains sixty rounds, or 120 yards. It may be had in very bright colours for articles of children's wear.

Finger Shield.—A silver appliance made to fit the first finger of the left hand, on which materials are laid and held by the thumb, in Plain Sewing. It resembles a ring, one side being an inch wide, and the other quite as narrow as an ordinary finger ring. It is employed to protect the finger from the needle when much hard sewing has to be done, or the finger has been accidentally hurt.

Finishing.—This word, so far as Plain Sewing is concerned, refers to the securing of the thread employed. As in beginning the work—whether HEMMING or OVERSEWING—so in finishing, no knot should be made, but take two stitches in the same place, one over the other, and then finish by running the needle backwards through the material, so as to be invisible for about half an inch or more. In the same way joinings should be accomplished, so as to avoid the bad habit of making knots. In flannel work, make the back runnings of still greater length, on account of the looseness of the material. DARN in the last thread very carefully, and take a BACK STITCH where the last HERRINGBONE STITCH ended, before recommencing the work with the new thread. In FINISHING the runnings in darning, leave the thread in loops at each end of every running.

The term, as applied to materials, might denote the turning-in, and sewing, or hemming, or buttonholing of all raw edges, or the fringing out of ribbon, linen, or silk, by drawing out the ravelling threads (running across the web), and lightly sewing in the last few strands over and over through the fringing, three or four strands in depth.

In reference to dressmaking and Mantua makers' work, FINISHING denotes the binding of raw-edged seams with narrow sarcenet ribbon, and the removal of tacking threads. In fact, all the last work, not essential to the sewing together of any garment or other article, so as to complete its form, and render it capable of wear and use, but designed only to render it neat, and to prevent ravelling, may properly be designated Finishing.

Fisher Fur.—The Fisher is of the genus Weasel, and is a native of America, whence upwards of 11,000 of these skins are annually imported to this country. They are larger than those of the SABLE, and the fur is deeper and fuller, and very beautiful. The tail is long, round, and gradually tapering to a point, and is employed for hats, as well as to form a decoration in the national cap worn by the Polish Jews. One skin of the FISHER will suffice to make a muff, for which three MARTEN skins would be required. The ground of the fur is dun-coloured. Those of the darkest shade are the best; but the darkness of the colour and the depth of the fur depend on the season when the animals are trapped.

Fisherman's Knot.—Used in Square Netting. *See* NETTING.

Fish Scale Embroidery.—This kind of work is extremely effective as an ornament where it is not liable to friction, and is a variety from ordinary Embroideries. It is worked upon silk, satin, or velvet foundations, from flower patterns, such as are used in Crewel Work or Silk Embroidery. The principal parts of the design, such as flower, leaves, butterflies, birds, are covered over with brightly tinted Fish Scales, sewn to the foundation with coloured silks; the stems, veins, tendrils, and other fine traceries, are worked in SATIN STITCH with fine chenille, gold thread, or filoselle; and the centres to flowers, &c., filled in with FRENCH KNOTS, beads, pearls, or spangles.

The Fish Scales have to be prepared before they are used. Select the iridescent scales of the carp, perch, or goldfish, and, while quite fresh, detach from the fish by scraping with a knife from the tail to the head; steep them in cold water until they are soft, then lay them upon a cushion, and puncture each with two holes, close together, near their base. Make these holes with a needle. Should the scales be all of one tint, colour them in places by mixing Damar varnish with powdered colours of various tints. Draw out a design upon cartridge paper, containing a spray of not very large flowers, and a bird or a butterfly, and prick out the outlines with a needle. Frame a piece of good velvet, satin, or silk, lay the pattern upon it, and pounce French Chalk through the holes, and go over the dots thus made with lines of white paint. Then commence to work the flowers. For yellow daisies, and other flowers formed with large open centres, commence the work from their outside edge. Draw a circle, and sew the Fish scales round this circle; leave between each scale a little less space than one scale will cover; sew the scale to the foundation with coloured silk, bring the needle up from the back, through one of the punctured holes, and put it down through the other. Sew on a second circle of Fish scales, so that they lay over the first line, and fill in the spaces there left. Fill in the centre of the daisy with FRENCH KNOTS, made of maroon silk or with fine chenille. Small sunflowers are worked in the same manner as daisies, but have four to six circles of scales sewn round them before their centres are begun. Chrysanthemums and half-opened flowers, with a calyx of green arrasene or chenille, are effective to work; they are made with the largest Fish scales. Arrange the Fish scales so that they open out from the calyx all in one direction, and form an irregular half circle; let the scales forming the petals overlap each other in the middle of the half circle, so as to conceal the stitches that sew the first laid scales to the foundation; lay new scales over them, and conceal their uniting stitches with stitches of chenille. Roses are formed as moss rosebuds, with the moss imitated in chenille, or as full flowers, with the centre petals of Fish scales turning inwards, and the others turning outwards. Rose petals are rounded and shaped by placing large Fish scales in the middle of the petal, and small ones on each side.

Leaves for the Embroidery are formed in two ways. To make the large ones: Arrange Fish scales so that they radiate on each side from a centre vein, with their securing stitches upon the centre vein. Conceal these with a line of gold thread or chenille, laid above them, and secured from the back as in COUCHING. Small leaves are made with a Fish scale cut and shaped and caught down with lines of silk passing over them, and into the two holes at their base. Arrange these lines as side and centre veins over the whole leaf. Butterflies have the wings made of overlapping Fish scales secured with gold thread. Arrange the scales so that they radiate from the body of the butterfly. Work the body in gold thread and coloured floss silks, over a pad of silk, and sew in two beads for eyes. For Birds: Work the breast, head, and body with coloured silks, and glue in glass eyes; then make the wings and the tail feathers with the Fish scales

Fitch, Fitchet, or Polecat Fur (*Mustela putorius*).—The Fitchet is a native of Europe, including Great Britain. The fur is soft and black, having a rich yellow ground; but the odour from it is unpleasant. This can, however, be much overcome, and the fur made available for use.

Flags.—There are three descriptions of FLAGS, those used at sea, on the river, and at school feasts. Sea flags include national, yachting, and ship flags, the colours of which are given in yachting and ship lists. They are made of various coloured buntings, joined together with Mantua makers' hems, and upon this foundation such distinguishing marks as coats of arms, crowns, &c., after having been painted in their proper shades upon white materials, are attached. River flags, not being exposed to salt water, are made of silk, serge, or flannel, the different colours forming them being sewn together, and the distinguishing small marks embroidered in silk upon the coloured foundation. School and festival flags are made of coloured calicoes, and have mottoes or emblems, cut out of gilt paper, gummed on. All flags are made with a wide hem, to admit the pole or cord that keeps them in position. This hem is made at the side for large flags, at the top for long, narrow flags, and on both sides for school flags.

As it is impossible to allow the space necessary for a description of all flags, the Union Jack is selected as an example. It consists of the crosses of St. George, St. Patrick, and St. Andrew united. The ground is blue, with an upright and diagonal red cross surrounded by white lines. The usual size is 3 yards long and 1 yard and 25 inches wide. The flag is made in two ways. Either the various strips of colour are cut out and joined together; or the pieces are laid upon red bunting, and sewn down to it, when double sets of pieces are necessary, that both sides of the flag may show the quarterings. To make: Cut a strip of red bunting 3 yards long and 10 inches wide, and lay it down as a centre. Join on to it, so as to form an upright cross, two strips of red bunting, 10 inches wide and 25 inches long, and then join four diagonal strips of red bunting, 3 inches wide, into the spaces left above and below the arms of the upright cross. Surround both the crosses in the inside of the flag with an edging of white bunting, 4 inches wide, but do not carry this white edging along the outer edges. Fill in the spaces between the diagonal and straight cross with wedge-shaped pieces of blue bunting. RUN together the edges of these various strips of bunting with coarse worsted, and FELL them down, cutting away the red bunting from underneath; or cut the same pieces out, and join them on to the back of the red bunting. HEM round the outside of the flag, and add the wide hem or rings of rope on the side where it is to be attached to the pole or rope.

Flanders Lace.—Flanders claims to be one of the first countries in Europe where Needle and pillow Laces attained celebrity and became articles of commerce. She disputes with Italy the invention of Pillow Lace, and old Flemish writers assert that Flanders Lace was used even in the fourteenth century, and certainly in the first part of the fifteenth century. However remote the commencement of lacemaking in that country, no other can show such a continuous and successful manufacture, not confined to the making of one lace, but embracing many beautiful kinds that flourish in the present day, after having supported their workers during the disastrous wars of the sixteenth century, and, through religious and political refugees, having introduced the art into many neighbouring States. The principal laces of Flanders are as follows: Old Flemish Lace, known as Trolle Kant, an early Pillow Lace distinguished by its grounds, and after which the English Trolly Laces have been named, though they are of much inferior make: Brussels, or Point de Flandre, or Point d'Angleterre, and Point Gaze, both of Needle and Pillow, made in the villages round Brussels, first made in the fifteenth century, and still in existence in a flourishing condition; Mechlin, or Point de Malines, made at Antwerps; Lierre, Turnhout; Lille, made in French Flanders; Valenciennes, made at Ypres, Menin, Alost, Courtrai, and Bruges; and Black Blonde Lace, made at Grammont. For the descriptions of these laces and their varieties, see their own headings.

Flannel.—A woollen stuff, loosely woven. To be had in various makes—both heavy and light, twilled and plain, white and coloured. Lancashire Flannels have a plain selvedge, a blue tint, and the surface on one side slightly raised. Welsh Flannels have also a bluish shade, and a broad grey selvedge on both sides, and run from 30 inches to 36 inches in width. A similar article is made in Lancashire, equal in quality, and superior in finish. Yorkshire Flannels have a plain selvedge, and are superior to the Lancashire manufactures. Both sides are alike, and they are in the natural colour of the wool, and improve in appearance when washed, without being in other respects deteriorated. Patent Welsh and Saxony Flannels are of a very fine and superior texture, but are not durable. They are said not to shrink in washing. These are principally used for infants' clothing, and have a long pile on one side only. Bath coating is thick-made, with a long nap The widths run from 4-4, 7-4, to 8-4. GAUZE FLANNEL is of a very loose, porous texture, and ZEPHYR very fine and delicate, being a union of wool and silk. There are likewise striped Flannels in various colours, of a cloth-like texture. Cricketing Flannel is of the nature of cloth, and of the natural colour of the wool. It has a plain surface, alike on both sides. Blanketing can be had of every variety of quality and size. Some FLANNELS are milled, some are coloured or checked. Upwards of fifty-four million yards are annually made in this country. In Ireland, a coarse description of flannel is manufactured, called GALWAY, and used by the Irish peasant women for cloaks, &c.; this is probably identical with the stuff called Faldynge, of ancient Saxon manufacture, resembling FRIEZE. Faldynge was designed for external wear, and was employed in

CROCHET MANTEL BORDER
ILLUSTRATING THE VARIOUS STITCHES.

the Middle Ages for bed-covering and cloths for sideboards. Chaucer makes two allusions to this material. His "Ship-manne" is said to have been clad

All in a gown of Falding to the knee—(*Canterbury Tales*);

and in his "Miller's Tale," the clerk is said to have

His presse icovered with a Faldyng red.

In France and Belgium a superior make of fine twilled Flannel is made, much patronised in this country.

eight or nine MACRAMÉ KNOTS, worked by knotting alternately the two threads forming the Bar to the right or left. *See* MACRAMÉ.

Flat Point.—A general term distinguishing laces made without any Raised work, or work in relief, from Raised Points.

Flattened Canvas.—This textile can be had both of thread and cotton, and is much used in France.

FIG. 404. HONITON SPRAY, ILLUSTRATING FLEMISH AND FIBRE STITCH. (*See next page.*)

Flannellette. — A description of very soft warm Flannel, measuring 28 inches in width.

Flap.—In reference to needlework, this term signifies a portion of any material affixed to the dress, or other article, at one side, and left to hang loosely from it at the other. It may be employed either for a useful or a decorative purpose. Sometimes a Flap is sewn on a garment to conceal hooks or buttons.

Flat Bar.—These are parts of the pattern of Macramé, and are made, according to the length required, with

It differs from other descriptions of canvas in having been passed through the cylinders of a flattening machine, for the purpose of rendering it the more suitable for the drawing of designs upon it. These devices are afterwards traced with fine silk or cotton, in the colours to be used in the after working.

Flax.—This is composed of the filaments of the bark, or fibrous covering of the stem, of a plant of the *Linum* genus, or *Linum usitatissimum*, an annual, and a native of Europe. From these filaments linen thread is

E E

spun. The thread is prepared as follows: The flax is "Rippled," then "Retted," "Scutched," and "Hackled." The coarse, entangled fibres, when separated by the Hackle, are called tow, and the hackled Flax called Line; the latter, when sorted according to its degrees of fineness, is ready to be spun, and made into cloths called linen, cambric, lawn, and thread. For lace-making, Flax is cultivated in most European countries, but the Flemish is the best.

Flax Canvas.—This description of canvas may be procured in various degrees of fineness and make, one of them being of very fine thread. That known as Flattened Canvas is of flax combined with cotton. All descriptions of Canvas are distinguished by numbers denoting their several degrees of fineness, the finest being generally known as Mosaic, irrespective of its being woven of silk, flax, or cotton, the woollen and hemp-made kinds not included.

Fleece.—The curly hair, or woollen coat of a sheep, before it is dressed for manufacture into yarn and cloth.

Fleecy.—Sheep's wool prepared in loose threads for Darning and Knitting. Being loosely twisted, it has the advantage of not becoming hard and stiff when washed. Its thickness is counted by the threads. The two-thread fleecy is the finest, and is of the same size as the "double Berlin wool." The other numbers are, respectively, the four, six, eight, and twelve-thread fleecy. It is less expensive than Berlin wool, and, being rough in quality, is rendered unsuitable for embroidery work. It may be had in black, white, partridge, various self or uni-colours, and ingrain colours.

Flemish Diamonds.—These are used as Fillings to Honiton Lace, and consist of the holes made in Flemish Stitch being arranged as diamonds of four, instead of being scattered about the pattern. *See* FLEMISH STITCH.

Flemish Point.—A Guipure Lace, also known as Point de Brabant, and described under GUIPURE LACES (which *see*).

Flemish Stitch.—One of the Fillings in Honiton Lace, and illustrated in Fig. 404 (page 209) in the leaves dotted with holes. To work: Work the open fibre down to the tip of the leaf (*see* FIBRE STITCH) with six pairs of BOBBINS, then hang on four more pairs, and add two extra pairs where the leaf widens. Work each side of the leaf separately in WHOLE or CLOTH STITCH (*see* Cloth Braid, in BRAIDS), and, when a hole is reached, twist the worker Bobbins twice, stick a pin below them, work to the end, and, when the hole is reached in the return row, twist the passive Bobbins on each side of it at once, and twist the working Bobbins twice as they pass below the pin. Make the holes close together, or at a distance from each other according to the pattern. To work the rest of Fig. 404: Work the large stems in BUCKLE STITCH, the open flower in HALF or SHADOW STITCH, and the half open flowers as follows: For the flower covered with tendrils, work in Half Stitch, and first work the tendril that touches the leaf, and then the one running up to the stem. In the next sized half flower, work down the stem and round the circle in PLAIN FRAID (*see* BRAIDS),

then do ROPE SEWING to the flowers, carry them down one side, making a double TURN STITCH occasionally as the pinholes are on the inner curve. At the end of the stem hang on four more pairs of Bobbins, and work Whole Stitch across the flower; turn and work a few rows of Half Stitch, sewing one side to the Whole Stitch; then, with five pairs of Bobbins, work STEM STITCH round the triangle, then finish the flower with Half Stitch. To work the smallest half flower: Work the stem as in last flower, hang on three pairs of Bobbins, work four rows of Half Stitch, leave those Bobbins; hang on five pairs, at the further end of triangle, work round it, then continue Half Stitch, taking up all the Bobbins, and finish the flower with it. Work the tendril in Plain Braid or Stem Stitch, with one edge only Pearled. The leaves worked with BRANCHING FIBRES (*see* BRANCHING FIBRES) and in Whole Stitch have two holes made in each side with INNER PEARL. These leaves require ten pairs of Bobbins.

Fleurette Stitch.—*See* POINT DE VENISE.

Fleurs de Tulle Nette.—This is a French descriptive phrase applied to figured Tulle or Net.

Fleurs Volants.—The general term given to the Pinwork that ornaments the raised Cordonnet in Rose, Spanish, and other Needle-point laces, and which is one of the peculiar beauties of the work. The Fleurs Volants are distinguished by the names of Couronnes, Loops, and Crowns, for one description; and Spines, Thorns, Picots, and Knots for the other. Their varieties are shown in Fig. 405, and they are worked as follows:

FIG. 405. LACE ILLUSTRATING FLEURS VOLANTS.

The round in the centre of design is trimmed with Couronnes ornamented with Spines. To work: Fill the needle with fine lace thread, fasten it on at the left side of round, and make a small loop into the COR-DONNET, run the needle back underneath to the place from which the thread starts, and BUTTONHOLE about one-third of the loop. Take a pin, and put it in at a short distance from the thread, the length the Spine is to be, pass the thread round the pin, and make three Buttonholes into the main loop; repeat this PIN-

WORK twice, to make the three Spines seen on the Couronnes, then Buttonhole over the rest of the loop. The single Spines that trim the three centre scallops are worked before the pattern is joined together. Work them either with a single loop of thread fastened into the Cordonnet, and the working thread put back into the loop and drawn up, or wind the cotton several times round the needle, push the needle through the Cordonnet, and draw up tightly. The Couronnes trimming the outer edge of the design are larger than those ornamenting the round, and are made thus: Make the loop into the Cordonnet as before, but pass it over a small knitting pin, and run the thread back round the knitting pin instead of underneath the work, so that the foundation for the Couronne is rather thicker; then Buttonhole the loop, and ornament it with three Spines. For the Fleurs Volants or the rest of the work: Make Couronnes unornamented with Spines, but with two Spines between each Couronne. In all these stitches the Buttonhole must be both tight and even, as, unless this is done, the stitches become loose the first time the lace is cleaned, and the appearance of the work is destroyed.

Flock.—This word is radically the same as Flake, and is applied to hair, the "f" being dropped, and the tuft or curl termed a "lock." Hence, a bed stuffed with pieces or tufts of wool is designated a Flock bed.

Florence.—This dress stuff is also known as Florentine, and is a description of Corded Barége or Grenadine. It is to be had both in black and colours, and is 26 inches in width. There is also a thin description of Taffeta, fabricated at Lyons, Avignon, and Zurich, which had its origin at Florence, and thence derived its name.

Florentine.—A material made for gentlemen's waistcoats, but when in plain colours it is sometimes fashionable for ladies' dresses. It is to be had for the former purpose both figured and striped, as well as plain. It is a twilled silk, thicker than Florence, which latter is, however, sometimes called by the same name.

Florentine Lace.—The manufacture of Raised Needle Points in Florence flourished during the earlier part of the sixteenth century, mention being made of Florentine lace having been brought into France by the sister of Francis I.; and of Henry VIII. granting privileges of importation into England to two Florentine merchants; but since these early chronicles, Florentine lace has become merged into Italian lace, and no particular account taken of it.

Floret.—A French term, synonymous with the descriptive word *Broché* when applied to silk and satin stuffs, and signifying flowered. The original term denoted the small blossoms clustered together in compound flowers and grasses, such as those that compose laurestina and heliotrope blooms.

Floss Embroidery.—The most beautiful description of this work is made in India, the natives of that country being celebrated for their skill in Embroidery with white or coloured floss upon richly tinted cloths and silks. In England, because of the delicacy of floss silk, it is chiefly used in large quantities in Church Embroidery, and there laid upon a flat foundation, and fastened down with securing stitches of silk brought from the back of the material, passed over the floss, and returned to the back. Floss silk is also used for the high lights in Crewel and Silk Embroideries, but its place is frequently taken by Filoselle, or ravelled silk, which is stronger in fibre than floss. To work: Select for a pattern a floral design of Satin Stitch Embroidery; trace this upon a thin silk or thin merino or net foundation, and frame the material in an EMBROIDERY FRAME. Carefully wind small portions of Floss silk upon separate cards, take a short length of one of these, smooth it down with the fingers, thread it through a large-eyed needle, and fill in the pattern with flat SATIN STITCH. Bring the stitch up at one side of an outline leaf or petal, and put it down at the other, to cover the ground with as few stitches as possible. Make holes with a large needle to bring the Floss through, should it at all fray in its backward and forward movement, and use very short strands of floss. Embroidery with Floss upon net and thin materials can be worked over the hand, but it has a much better effect when worked in a frame.

Floss laid with Passing.—A term used in Church Embroidery to denote that floss silk is laid down upon some part of the design, and kept into place with a gold cord or Passing Couched down upon it. *See* COUCHING.

Floss Silk.—Anciently called Sleine, or Sleided silk. It is the soft external covering of the silkworm's cocoon, ravelled and downy in quality, and is carded, spun, and made into hanks. The English is superior to the French. This silk is made of the finest part of the cocoon, and does not undergo the process of twisting, and must not be confounded with Filoselle. Allusion is made to Floss silk by Shakespeare:

> Thou idle, immaterial skein of sleided silk.
> —*Troilus and Cressida.*

Flôts.—A French term, used to signify successive loops of ribbon or lace, arranged to lie over-lapping one another in rows, so as to resemble the flow of small waves, following closely on the decadence of their predecessors. What is called a Flôt-bow is made after the same style. A good idea may be gathered from our illustration (Fig. 406).

FIG. 406. FLÔTS.

Flounce. — A term used to signify a strip, more or less wide, of any kind of material sufficiently slight to be gathered or plaited along one side, and left loose on the other. It should be attached to the dress, or other article which it is designed to decorate, on the gathered side, and may be cut either on the straight or the bias way of the stuff. In the fourteenth century it was called a Frounce, and in the reigns of William and Mary a puckered flounce or plaited border of a dress used to be called a Furbelow. This term was a corruption of *Falbala*, the Spanish for Flounce.

Flourishing Thread.—A flat, silky, linen thread, specially adapted for mending Damask, Linen, and most flax-made textures. It is sold by the skein and the ounce, in qualities varying from Nos. 4 to 20, but the most useful sizes are 4, 5, and 6. One golden brown variety, known as Luxembourg Thread, is employed in Netted Guipure; others, in different colours, are very effective in embroidery, imparting almost the sheen of silk when used in combination with wools. It is also called Flax Thread.

Flowers (Artificial).—These are manufactured of ribbon, velvet, feathers, wax, paper, the pith of plants, dyed grasses, satin, mother-o'-pearl, wings of beetles and other insects, glass, hair, muslin, beads, porcelain, shells, and thin sheets of whalebone, &c. Most of these materials are employed in the flowers manufactured for wear in millinery and dress, dyes of all kinds being utilised to supplement the natural colours. The Chinese, Romans, and South American Indians excelled in the art from very remote times; the French have for some years past been pre-eminent in it; but our own manufacturers can now produce very superior descriptions, as likewise can those of Austria, Portugal, Sweden, Mexico, and other parts. Artificial flowers composed of *Seal-skin Fur*, in beautifully variegated tints, and designed for use in millinery, have been recently produced at Zurich. In Auvergne, delicate glass flowers are manufactured for articles of wear, such as brooches, pins, and other decorations for the hair. In the great Exhibition of 1851, a great variety of flowers was contributed from Sweden, Madeira, Hamburgh, the Channel Islands, and our Colonies, besides those places already named.

Fluted Ruche.—Otherwise called by the French name of *Ruche à la Vielle.* It is composed of single Box-pleats stitched to a certain depth inwards, so as to leave the edges of the pleats loose. About half-an-inch is the usual width of each pleat, if the material be muslin or tarlatan, and such thin fabrics, and from half-an-inch to one inch for silk. In the first-named materials, the raw edges may be snipped into small points, to resemble " Pinking," by tacking several strips together, and cutting through all simultaneously. In reference to silk, it is necessary to put in a book muslin lining of the same width as the Ruche when finished (including the headings), and the silk must be folded over the edges of the muslin to the depth of the width of the fluting.

Flutings. — Piping or frill ornaments, shaped as a flute, applied to dress, the latter being gathered at both ends with great evenness and regularity. A collection of Flutings resemble the pipes of an organ, as will be seen on reference to our illustration (Fig. 407).

FIG. 407. FLUTINGS.

Fly.—The term used to denote a strip of material which is sewn under the edge of a dress, or coat, at the button side of the opening, extending sufficiently far beyond it as to underlie the buttonholes at their extreme ends. The Fly thus serves the purpose of concealing the dress underneath the coat or bodice. It is called a Fly because, like a Flag, or Pennon, it is attached on one side only, and is allowed to fly loose on the other.

Fly Fringe.—A kind of fringe composed of tufts of floss silk attached to a cord of gimp, which passes along the centre of the edging. It was a fashionable trimming for ladies' dresses in the reign of George III.

Folds. — The draping produced by Pleating or Gathering at the waist of a skirt; or the flat plaits on any part of a skirt, bodice, or sleeve, secured at each end to the dress to keep them in place; or the doubling of any cloth so that one part shall lie over another.

Fond.—Identical with Champ, Entoilage, and Treille, terms by which the groundwork of lace, whether of Needle or Pillow, is distinguished from the Toilé, or pattern, which it surrounds and supports. These grounds are divided into Fonds Claire, Brides Claire, and Brides Ornées. The *Fonds claire* include the Réseau, or net-patterned grounds, and varieties of the same, such as Dame Joan, Honeycomb, and Star grounds; the *Brides claire* are the simple Buttonhole Bars that connect the various parts of a detached pattern together; and the *Brides Ornées*, the same Bars, profusely ornamented with Picots and Spines, and shown in Devonia Ground.

Fond Clair.—*See* Fond.

Fondeuse. — The term by which lacemakers distinguish the workers who attach the Toilé, or pattern, to the Fond, or Ground.

Fool's Crochet.—A name sometimes given to Tricot. *See* Crochet.

Foot.—*See* Stocking Knitting.

Footing.—A term employed in the Knitting of stockings, when the feet of the latter, having been worn out, have to be replaced by others knitted on to the original legs. The word is also known as Engrêlure, and is used by laceworkers to distinguish the edge of the Lace that is sewn to the dress from the scalloped and unattached edge. The Footing is sometimes worked with the rest of the design, and at others as a separate narrow lace, being then sewn on to the main part.

Forfars.—A coarse, heavy description of linen cloth, made of unbleached flax, and varying in width from 32 inches to 75 inches.

Foulard.—A washing silk, originally made in India, of which there is a fair imitation manufactured at Lyons and Avignon. It is a very light material, and is printed in colours on black and white grounds. Although the Indian is the superior article in make and consistency, a combination of yellow and red being the favourite design, the French designs and colours are the most elegant. The width varies from 27 inches to 30 inches.

Foulardine.—An imitation of Foulard produced in cotton, of a very soft make, for women's dresses. Foulardine is now little to be seen, and is almost out of date, Sateen (which *see*) having superseded it.

Foulé Cashmere or Cloth.—An all-wool twill textile, of a coarse description, called Cashmere, but only an imitation. It measures from 24 inches to 26 inches in width, and is used as a dress material. It is softer than the Foulé Serge (which *see*).

Foulé Serge. — This material is sometimes called Estamine. It is of a heavier and much rougher make of all-wool twill than the Foulé Cashmere, and is from 25½ inches to 27 inches in width. It is used as a dress material.

Foundation Chain.—Used in Crochet as the commencement to all patterns. *See* CROCHET.

Foundation Muslin.—A very coarse description of Muslin, of very open make, stiffened with gum. It is employed for stiffening dresses, and may be had in black and white.

Foundation Net.—A coarse quality of Net, made with large meshes, gummed, and employed for stiff foundations in millinery and dressmaking. It is to be had in black and white, and measures from 27 inches to 30 inches in width.

Foundation Stitch.—Used in ancient Needle Lace and Modern Point. To work: First row—work a number of POINT DE BRUXELLES stitches close together.* Second row—take the thread back from right to left, to form a Bar, and fasten. Third row—work close Point de Bruxelles stitches over the thread, and put the needle in between each of the stitches in the first row. Repeat from * until the space is filled in.

Fox Fur.—Besides the common animal preserved for sport, several other varieties are valuable for their skins. The most costly skins are obtained from the Arctic, or silver, and the black fox (*C. Lagopus* and *C. Argentatus*). The "crossed" fox (*C. decussatus*) and the red fox (*C. Fulvus*) supply linings for cloaks and collars; Silver and blue fox furs are employed for women's dress, as well as for rugs and robes for sleighs. Red fox skins measure 14 inches by 28 inches, and all other varieties will be found of much the same size. To give an idea of the value of some of these skins, it may be observed that as much as £100 has been given, in London, for one of exceptional beauty; and that the Imperial pelisse of the Czar, exhibited in 1851, and made of the black necks of the Silver Fox, was valued at £3500.

Frame Knitting.—A description of Frame Work which, when finished, has the appearance of Knitting. It is made upon a frame of the shape shown in Fig. 408. The length of the frame regulates the width of the work;

FIG. 408. KNITTING FRAME.

frames of various sizes can be procured. The most useful one is made of two pieces of wood, 14 inches long by 4 inches high and 1 inch thick, and two short pieces, 4 inches long, 4 inches wide, and 1 inch thick. These pieces are spliced together at their corners, so that a hollow space is left inside the frame, and pegs are fastened upon three sides, round the upper part of the frame. Twenty-four pegs, each 2 inches in height, are required for each long side, and one or two for one of the short sides, the other (not visible in the illustration) being left without any pegs.

The work has the appearance of very loose stocking knitting. The hollow space in the centre of the frame receives the work as it is formed, and thus keeps it out of the way of the new rows. To work: Wind up into balls several large skeins of white or coloured fleecy wool, and tie its end round the first peg on the left-hand side of the long side of the frame, with the short side of the frame without a peg behind it. Take the wool, and twist it once round the next peg, pass the wool on the inside of the frame to the third peg, and twist it once round that. Twist the wool once round all the pegs on the three sides, always passing it from peg to peg on the inside. For the next row, twist the wool once round the last peg worked, then, with the thumb and first finger, pick up the loop on that peg made in the first row, and draw it over the loop just made, and off the peg, leaving the last loop on the peg, and the first hanging down inside the frame. Work the second and all following rows in this way until the length of scarf or petticoat is made. For the last row, make the loop on the peg, and draw the loop on it over the new loop as before for the first peg; for the second, make the loop on the peg, draw the loop already there over it as before, and then put the loop from the first peg on to the second (thus leaving the first empty), drawing the loop on that peg over it. Work this second stitch until all the stitches are secured, then make a knot in the wool, and CROCHET the end into the work. Work loosely, and be careful to have a long piece of wool for the last row. A ¼lb. of thick fleecy wool, or ½lb. of thin fleecy, makes a scarf, leaving sufficient wool for a tassel at each end.

Frame Tape.—This is a stout, half-bleached linen tape; but there is one called by the same name, consisting of a union of linen and cotton, which is much in request. The distinguishing prefix, "Frame," refers to the loom on which it is woven. *See* TAPE.

Frame Work.—This work, also called *Travail au Métier*, is formed with wools and silk upon a flat, solid wooden Frame cut to the size required. Mats and their borders can be made upon it without joins, but larger articles require to be worked in squares, and sewn together when finished. The materials necessary are, the wooden frame, brass-headed small nails or stout pins, Saxony or Shetland wool in ½ ounce skeins, filoselles, and a rug needle. To work: Draw upon a sheet of thin paper, the size of the frame, a number of horizontal lines a quarter of an inch apart, and cross these with upright lines the same distance apart, so arranged that the middle line will come in the exact centre of the frame. Paste this paper round its edges on to the frame, and knock the brass nails in, so that they head every line. Take two of the ½ ounce skeins of wool, and wind the two ends together as a double thread upon one ball, and be careful that the skeins are free from joins. Tie the end of this doubled wool round the top nail, at the left-hand corner, then pass it without twisting to the nail below it on the left-hand side of the frame (*see* Fig. 409, p. 214); then cross the frame with it to the peg at the top of the frame next to the one it was tied to, run it along to the third peg, then cross the frame with it to the third peg on the side, run it along to the fourth, and cross the frame again with it to the fourth peg on the top line. Continue in this way, guided by the illustration, until the first set of diagonal lines is made, and crossed by the second. When finished, do not cut off the wool, but make the edge shown in Fig. 410 with it. Twist the

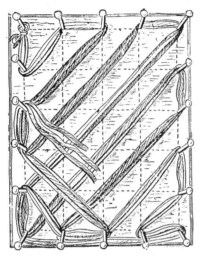

FIG. 409. FRAME WORK.

wool over the front part of one nail, and then round the back of the next nail, and so carry it along the edge of the frame and back again, putting it inside in the second row where it was outside in the first row. To secure these lines, and also the ones across the frame, thread the wool into the rug needle, and make a loose BUTTON-HOLE at every peg, taking all the wool at that place into the stitch. Then return to the centre, and make

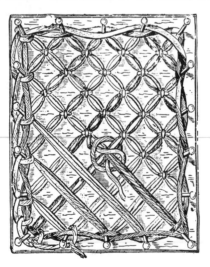

FIG. 410. FRAME WORK.

the diamond pattern. Thread a rug needle with a con-trasting shade of wool to the one already used, and secure the horizontal and upright lines where they cross on the paper pattern with a CROSS STITCH, thus forming the diamond pattern shown in Fig. 410. The effect of the work depends upon the regularity of these diamonds, so

the Cross Stitches must be placed exactly over the junction of the traced lines. Carry the wool from one stitch to the other, and cover the wool Cross Stitch with one made of filoselle when all the diamonds are secured.

Fig. 411 is another pattern made in the same frame. The squares are traced as before on paper, and fastened

FIG. 411. FRAME WORK.

into the frame, and the wool is doubled; two colours, one light and one dark, are used in the groundwork, the light colour to form the stars, the dark the diamonds and squares. The light wool is put diagonally round the pegs, and fills in the centre outside squares; the dark wool fills in the middle square, and the four corner outside squares; the straight lines of dark wool are arranged last. Make the edge as before, and secure the diamonds and the straight lines with a CROSS STITCH, as in the first pattern; leave the squares holding the light wool untouched, then draw all the wool in one of these squares up into its centre, and make a Cross Stitch there, thus forming a Star. Work all the stars in the same way. The border of fringe for both these mats is the same, and is shown in Fig. 412. It requires to be made upon a long narrow frame, but a straight strip of wood will answer all the requirements. Draw the squares upon the paper, make the lines half an inch, and not a quarter of an inch, apart; paste the paper on, and fasten the nails in at the end of these lines, round the bottom and two sides of the frame, and then round the top $1\frac{1}{2}$ inches from the edge. Fasten a second row of nails, a quarter of an inch apart, at the edge of the frame, and two nails the same distance apart upon each side. Take four skeins of thick wool, or eight of thin, and wind them together, and then lay them over the frame in diagonal lines, as before, round the inner line of pegs at the top, and round the other three edges at the sides. Be careful that the wool wound round the edge at the bottom of the frame, and that will form the end of the fringe, is put round a peg and run up into the next diagonal line at once, and not carried on from peg to peg; and do not let the wool on the right-hand side of the frame, where the fringe will be continued, be cut off, but wound up out of the way. Secure the diagonal lines where they cross in diamonds, with a Cross Stitch made with fine twine, and commence the upper edge. Lay three horizontal lines of filoselle, fasten them into the side pegs, and take the fine wool and twist it round the upper and lower row of the pegs, putting in extra pegs in the lower row to match those in the upper. Secure these and the horizontal lines with a Cross Stitch of filoselle. Make the fluffy balls

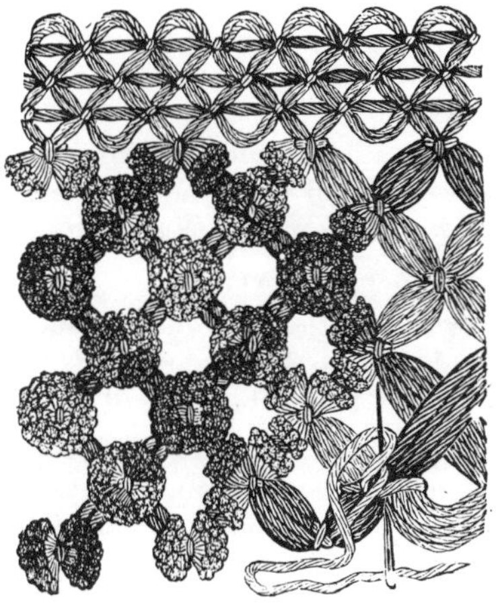

Fig. 412. Frame Work Fringe.

shown in Fig. 412, by cutting the wool round the crosses made of twine, cut the upper four threads, and leave the under four as a support to the balls.

Frame Work.—This second kind of Frame Work is known as Frame Knitting, and is described under that heading.

Frange Grillée.—The latter word (Grillée) is descriptive of the fringe, being the French for broiled or baked, and thus may be applied to a crimped Silk Fringe, probably so waved by means of heat as well as of pressure. The widths in which it is made are various, and likewise the degrees of fineness. It is worn in mourning as well as out of it, because the crimping has somewhat of the appearance of crape; but it may also be had in colours, and is likewise known as Crimping Fringe. There is another description of fringe, so called from having an open heading like network, Grill signifying a grating, made like a lattice.

Fray.—To ravel out a piece of stuff, so as to produce a kind of fringe, by drawing out threads of the warp from the weft. Also, to rub or scrape the face or border of any textile, so as to injure it by removing the nap.

French Cambric.—A very superior make of cambric, fine in quality, and very silky in appearance. It is imported in boxes of twenty-five pieces, each containing 7½ yards, in widths of ⅝ inch or ⅞ inch. It is a comparatively costly material. French cambric handkerchiefs may be had in three different widths, and may be bought by the yard, from the piece of 24 inches in width.

French Canvas.—The material so named is a description of Grenadine, of a stout, wiry character, varying in pattern, and measuring from 24 inches to 26 inches in width. It is a dress material, and of excellent wearing quality.

French Chalk.—A variety of indurated Talc, in masses composed of small scales, of a pearly white or grey colour. It much resembles Soapstone and Jade, and is employed for removing spots of grease from cloth of all kinds, and light coloured silks. It should be scraped, and the fine powder rubbed into the spot with the finger, left there for some hours, and then shaken or brushed off. When applied to silk, it should be rubbed on the wrong side.

French Chalk is also employed for pouncing through the holes made in pricked Embroidery patterns, for the purpose of transferring their outlines to velvet, cloth, and serge materials. To use: Select white French chalk, grind it to a fine powder, and enclose in a coarse muslin bag. Firmly press it through the holes in the pattern, and remove the pattern, when a number of fine dots will be left upon the material. Take a sable brush, filled with Chinese white mixed with size, and make lines of paint over these dots, so as to connect them together, and so mark the outlines of the pattern. Coloured chalks may also be had.

French Façon Flannel.—A very fine make of Basket-woven twilled Flannel, to be had in various colours. It is 31 inches in width, and is designed for children's dress, such as pelisses and hoods.

French Foulé.—A felted cloth, being twilled dress-material, all wool, measuring 24 inches in width, and produced in all plain colours.

French Heel.—*See* Stocking Knitting.

French Hem.—A description of Hem employed for the finishing of Flounces, in lieu of employing a silk binding, and especially suitable for such materials as Mohair and Alpaca. It is made thus: Hold the right side of the flounce towards you, and turn the top edge down, also towards you, so that its inside shows. The piece so turned down must measure ¾ inch for silk, and 1 inch for stuffs that fray. Then make a close Running, using an inappreciable quantity of the turned-down doubled edge that is over the left hand, and when the whole has been Run, turn the flounce wrong side towards you, and Fell down the False Hem on the line of Running just made. The raw edge of the Hem must be turned in nearly half way, that it may make the Hem of double stuff, so as not to lose the appearance of a hollow roll.

To make a double French Hem: Cut the Flounce as wide as it is to be when finished, with the addition of 1 inch for turnings used in the Hem, and also the depth that the Hem is to be. Then cut off this Hem and its 1 inch for turnings; line it with leno, and run the piping or silk fold upside down on the right side of the Hem, so that all four raw edges may be laid together; then Run the other edge of the hem to the edge of the flounce, placing the right side of the former to the wrong side of the latter, so that the joining is enclosed inside the Hem, when it is turned over on the face of the flounce, pinned in place, and sewn to it by Running along on the ridge made by the cording. This is done on the inside of the flounce, by feeling the ridge. The Hem must not be pulled up to its whole extent, as the actual edge of it must be of double material, and betray no signs of the join, which is ½ inch up on the inside. It is this ½ inch, and ¼ inch used for joining the silk to it, and ¼ inch for the join of the Hem to the flounce, which uses the 1 inch extra which was allotted to the Hem, in detaching from the flounce. The Hem now really projecting ½ inch beyond the depth which the flounce was given, will be accounted for by ¼ inch of it having been used at the join below, and the other ¼ inch for the turning at the top.

French Knot.—A stitch largely used in all kinds of Embroidery to fill in the centres of flowers, and in old Crewel Work to represent the foliage of trees. *See* EMBROIDERY STITCHES.

French Lace.—France, like Flanders, has for centuries directed much attention to Lace, the manufacture of which has been the support of many thousands of its inhabitants. Before Colbert, in 1665, established his celebrated Alençon, or Point de France, at Alençon, there existed a large and flourishing community of laceworkers in various districts, who made Bisette, Gueuse, Mignonette, Point Coupé and Point de Paris laces, besides imitating the Italian and Spanish Needle-points. These workers rebelled against the power granted to the Royal manufacturers, of appropriating the best lacemakers of any district, and obtained, as a compromise, the concession that, after 200 workers had been selected, the others might keep to their own trades. From the time of Colbert the laces made in France have been as follows: Alençon, the chief of all, a Needle-point considered to rival the Needle-points of Brussels, which has flourished from the time of its establishment until the present day, being still made at Bayeux, but no longer at Alençon; Argentan, coeval with Alençon, a different lace, but often confounded with the latter, and of very great beauty; this is no longer manufactured, the art having died out during the Revolution; black and white Blonde silk laces, made, during the eighteenth century, at Bayeux, Caen, and Chantilly; the black is still made at Bayeux, but the making of the white ceased about thirty years ago. Lille lace, made in French Flanders in the sixteenth century, and a variety of Lille, made at Arras and Mirecourt, in which latter city it still flourishes; a Guipure resembling Brussels and Honiton Guipures; Point de Paris and Point d'Espagne, made round Paris in the eighteenth century; while in Normandy, from Arras to St. Malo, laces in imitation of Point de Paris, Mechlin, Brussels, and Valenciennes, were largely made from the beginning of the sixteenth century until some thirty years ago, when the demand for them failed, with the exception of Valenciennes, which is still manufactured. Dieppe and Havre are known for their narrow Petit Poussin, Ave Maria, and Point de Dieppe laces, also for the Dentelle à la Vierge, or old Normandy lace; but none of these are now made in sufficient quantities to constitute a manufacture, and the art is gradually becoming extinct. For a description of these laces see their various headings.

French Merino.—This cloth is manufactured of very superior wool from the Merino sheep, and has the same appearance on both sides. The twill is exceedingly fine; it is to be had in all colours, and of double width. Some years ago French Merinos greatly excelled our own manufactures, but at the present time we produce them of equal quality, and many are sent to France, reshipped to this country, and sold to the public as French. Those of the best quality may easily be mistaken for genuine cashmeres.

French Plumetis.—The French term for Raised Satin Stitch. *See* SATIN STITCH.

French Point.—A name by which Alençon lace is sometimes called. *See* ALENÇON.

French Quilting.—A variety of QUILTING (which *see*). It is also a variety of Piqué of a fine and superior description, measuring 28 inches in width. It may be had in different patterns, the price varying according to the quality, and is employed for children's dress, pelisses, &c. It is also known as Marcella. *See* PIQUÉ.

French Stitch.—*See* TATTING.

French Twill.—Although called French, this is an English-made dress material, a variety of French Merino, to be had in various qualities and in all colours. It is of double width, and is suitable for servants' dresses.

Frieze.—A napped coating, of which the right side is covered with little tufts, or burrs, produced by a machine. A kind of woollen cloth, or baise, which we find mentioned by writers of the sixteenth century. It is much employed for men's clothing, especially in Ireland. In allusion to his marriage with the sister of Henry VIII. (Queen Dowager of France), Charles Brandon applied it to the well-known verse:

> Cloth of gold do not despise
> To match thyself with cloth of frize;
> Cloth of frize be not too bold
> That thou art matched to cloth of gold.

Frieze was originally a woollen cloth or stuff, introduced from Friesland; at the same time, the name is a descriptive one, the Welsh *Ffris*, signifying "the nap of cloth," and the Old English, and Irish *Frise*, and the French *Friser*, signifying "to curl."

Frilled Elastics.—These articles are made of India-rubber encased in cotton, from ½ inch and ¾ inch to 1 inch in width, and have a small frilled edge on one or both sides. They may be had in black and coloured silks, and are employed, amongst other uses, as garters or suspenders for stockings. They may be had in lengths containing 12 yards or 24 yards.

Frills and Frilling.—Ornamental borderings, formed like very small flounces, which may be made of the same

FIG. 413. A WHIPPED FRILLING.

material as the dress to be trimmed, or the furniture covering. They may also be made of a different material. Those sold ready-made are of cambric, muslin, lace, and ribbon, and are usually of machine manufacture. Formerly shirt fronts and sleeves were ornamented with cambric and deep lace ruffles or frills, and the underclothing of women likewise. Frills of great depth, and three or four-fold, edged with narrow lace, were worn round the throat, both by men and women, separately from the shirt or chemise, as frequently represented in Dutch and Flemish pictures. Frilling is also sold for the latter purpose, as well as for collars and cuffs, with an embroidery pattern and edge, machine or hand-made. In making a frilling for any under garment, it should be WHIPPED, as in the illustration (Fig. 413). The amount of fulness to be allowed is half as much again as the space on which it is to be sewn —that is, for example, 1½ yards of material to be GATHERED up as Frilling for 1 yard of space to be supplied with it. A metaphorical significance was once given to Frilling by Sydney Smith, who used it as implying a florid style of speech : " Mr. —— has good sense, but I never knew a man so entirely without frill."

Fringe.—Fringe is a decorative bordering, consisting of loose or twisted threads, single or many, and composed of silk, cotton, wool, gold or silver twist, fastened on one side into a braid or heading, by which it is attached to dress or furniture. Those descriptions which are in general use for the latter purpose vary from 2½ inches deep to 4 inches, and are of three kinds, viz., plain head, plain head and bullion, and gimp head; those for dresses are called fancy fringes, and are made of silk or worsted, from ½ inch to 2 inches or 3 inches in width. Common fringes are classified by the trade as follows : Cotton bullion fringes are of a heavy make, and sold in widths from 3 inches to 12 inches, and chiefly used for bedroom furniture; the lengths run to 24 yards or 36 yards. German fringe, of white cotton, made in various fancy patterns; their widths run from 1½ inches to 3 inches, and they are sold in lengths of 36 yards; they are used for blinds and bed furniture. Toilet fringes are likewise of white cotton, their widths being from ¾ inch to 2 inches, and are sold in pieces of 36 yards : they consist of various kinds — bullion, loop, star, plain, and open. FRANGE GRILLÉE is another description (which see).

Detached borders are added to most pieces of Fancy work when the main part is completed. Ancient fringes were formed by unravelling the material, drawing away the threads one way of the stuff, and knotting the left threads into various patterns. These fringed ends to garments were the earliest description of knotted lace, and are frequently mentioned by old chroniclers; and as civilisation advanced, gold and coloured silk threads were introduced into the threads of the material, and these were most elaborately tied together, and enriched with fancy stitches. At the present time, the material, where it will allow of it, is still drawn away, and the threads that are left secured with a line of Buttonhole or Fancy Hem for a simple fringe, or Knotted as described below for an elaborate border. Where the material will not allow the threads to be drawn away, Ball Fringes, Tassel Fringes, and Knotted Fringes are made upon it as an edging, or Fringes are Crocheted, Knitted, or Netted, and sewn round the work. Knitting and Netting fringes are so rarely disconnected

from their own work, that they are described under their own headings; the other descriptions are used indifferently in Embroidery, Crochet, and Wool work, and are as follows:

Ball Fringe.—Take a skein of single Berlin wool or filoselle, double it, and cut it in half; fasten it with a knot to one end of a long thread of gold cord, purse silk, or coloured wool, which bring it down three-quarters of an inch along the skein; loop it over the skein, and knot it into the loop, then carry the thread down three-quarters of an inch, and loop it again over the skein and knot the loop; make these loops at even distances apart until the skein is used up. Take a sharp pair of scissors, and cut the wool between the loops, cutting all the skein of wool, and only leaving the looped single thread; fluff these cut pieces over the loop into little round balls. Sew the fringe to the material, allowing it to hang down to the length of three or four balls.

Crochet Fringe.—This is made with two large bone Tricot needles, and with coarse wool. Make a six or twelve FOUNDATION CHAIN, according to the depth of Fringe required. First row—put the wool round the hook to make a stitch, and then work the next two stitches; when finished, cross the last worked stitch over the first, and let the first down, retaining only the last worked stitch on the hook; wool round the hook, work the two next stitches, cross them over each other, and drop one as before, and so on until the row is finished. Second row— turn the work, hold it in the left hand, and pick up the second hook. Work back with the second hook, making the same stitches, but using the made stitch of last row as one of the crossed stitches of this row. Third row like the first, using the first hook to work with. Fourth row like the second row, using the second hook; work until the proper length of fringe is made, then unravel half the stitches to form a series of loops at one side.

Fringe Made Over a Mesh.—Take a large wide mesh, or a strip of wood, according to the size required, and single Berlin wool or Crochet cotton. With a crochet hook make a CHAIN, then pass the wool round the mesh, and draw it through the loop of the Chain on the hook, pass it again round the mesh, and draw it through the Chain on the hook, make 1 Chain, and pass the hook through the first Chain made. Repeat the stitch from the commencement. The single Chains are necessary to prevent the long loops formed on the mesh becoming irregular when the mesh is withdrawn. A variety of this fringe is made by having the loops twice the length, and knotting them together as Knotted fringe.

Knotted Fringe.—Fix along the edge of material, at even distances apart, four to six doubled strands of filoselle or purse silk. Make a hole in the material with a stiletto, and knot them into this hole, or knot them on as in the last Fringe. Fasten the material to a lead cushion, and take half the threads from one knot and half from the next, and, with a needle threaded with the same silk, fasten them together as a knot with OVERCAST STITCH, run the needle up and down the threads to the place where the next knot is to be formed, and repeat. The knots can be tied instead of Overcast. In the second row of Knots, knot the threads together that are together at the edge of the material. For the third row, repeat first row.

Knotted Fringe like Fig. 414.—Wind over a thin flat book, or piece of wood, a good quantity of wool or thread, cut it at one place, and lay it straight. Pick up three threads, place them evenly together, and fold them in half. Push a crochet hook through the foundation material, take up the bent end of the threads, and draw them through the material for a short distance, then put the crochet hook round the end of the threads, and draw them all bodily through the loop, and well tighten the knot thus made. Continue to fasten these strands of thread into the material until a thick fringe is made.

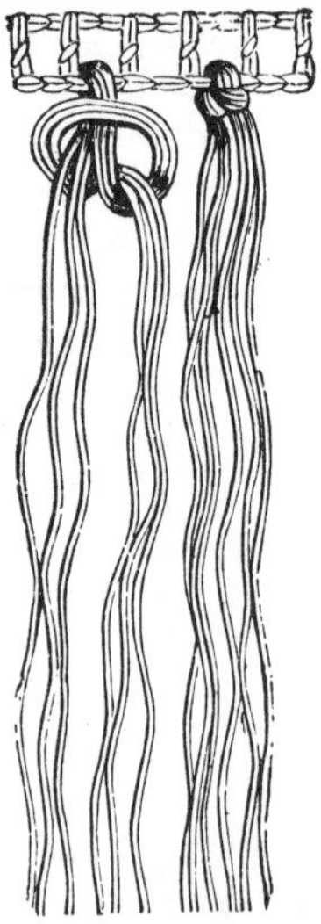

FIG. 414. FRINGE.

Tassel Fringe.—This can be made with wool, crewels, cotton, or silk. Cut a number of even threads, take up enough to form a good bunch, and fold them in half; wind thread or silk round them, near their upper end, push a crochet hook through the knot thus formed, and draw the end of the wound thread up with it, making a loop; make another loop over the top of the tassel thus formed, and knot it into the edge of the material.

Fringing Machine.—Fringing machines may be procured for making what is required at home. The small appliance so called is incorrectly described as a machine. It consists of a flat piece of wood, divided into a broad and a very narrow mesh, upon which the fringe is made by means of a crochet needle or hook (*see* Fig. 415). The

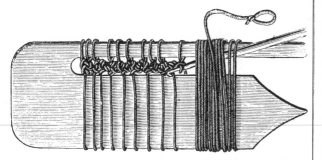

FIG. 415. FRINGING MACHINE.

method of working is as follows: Wind the wool in four or six strands, and tie the ends in a knot. Then fasten the ends of the wool to the small mesh, hook the wool up in the centre between the two meshes, and make a CHAIN STITCH, enclosing the small mesh in the Chain. Make another chain, withdraw the hook from the loop, turn the small mesh to the left side, and the last Chain Stitch will now be in the space between the two meshes, while the wool will be in front *. Insert the hook, and bring the wool round the back of the mesh to the space, and draw it with the hook through the loop which is already on it, and make a DOUBLE CROCHET in the loop which is round the

opposite or left mesh, then withdraw the hook from the loop, turn the mesh on the reverse side, and repeat from the *. Observe that the mesh must be always turned over from the right side to the left. Two Double Crochet Stitches, instead of one, give a variety to the pattern, but will not prove suitable when the wool is thick. The wide portion of the pattern must be cut to form the fringe, but if made in crochet cotton may be left uncut.

Frivolité.—The French term for Tatting. *See* TATTING.

Fronces.—A French word derived from *Froncer*, the verb to gather, now in use for Gathers. There is an old English word exactly similar—Frounce, to gather the edge of cloth into plaits, to wrinkle any textile, or to curl or frizzle the hair.

> Nor tricked and *frounced* as she was wont.
> —*Milton.*

Furs.—The skins of animals coated with Fur suitable for purposes of clothing, trimmings, and wraps, are for the most part included in the following list, and information may be found relating to them under their several headings: The Angora Goat, Astrachan, Bear, Beaver, Chinchilla, Ermine, Fitch, Fox, Hamster, Genet, Kolinski, Lamb skin, Marten, Mink, Musquash, Russian Musquash, Opossum, Perewiaska, Polecat, Rabbit or Coney, Squirrel, Sable, Sealskin, Rabbit skins, and Persian Lamb. In addition to these skins of animals, we have those of birds, supplying the place of Furs, viz., Eiderdown, Grebe, Penguin, Pheasant, Ptarmigan, and Swanskin or Down.

Although some believe that the "Gris" of the olden times was the Fur of the Grey Squirrel, it is more generally believed to have been that of the Marten (which *see*).

Fur Trimming, Imitation.—Made with Smyrna, Double Berlin, or Fleecy Wool, and used as an ornamental fringe to work baskets, mantel borders, &c. To work: Cast on to a large wooden knitting needle as many stitches as it will hold, using together three strands of Smyrna wool, or six of a finer kind. Thread a needle with strong cotton, and secure each knitted stitch by passing the cotton first through the loop on the needle, and then through the loop made at the side of the stitch, when casting on, and the cotton loop. Work in this way until all the loops are secured, then take off the knitting needle, cut them, and comb out until a long thick line is the result; this forms the heading. To make the tassels: Wind the wool twelve times round the hand, knot the strands together near the end cut, comb out, and sew to the heading.

Fustian.—A coarse, stout, twilled cotton fabric, including many varieties — corduroy, jean, barragon, cantoon, velveret, velveteen, thickset, and thickset cord. Plain fustian is called "pillow;" the strong twilled, cropped before dyeing, is called "moleskin;" and when cropped after dyeing, "beaverteen." From their strength and cheapness they are much employed for the dress of labouring men. They had their origin at Barcelona, the name being derived from *fuste*, the Spanish word for strong; but they were imported here from Flanders, used for jackets and doublets in the fifteenth century, and were first manufactured in this country at Norwich, in the time of Edward VI. It was then a mixed material, composed of linen and cotton; but since Arkwright furnished water-twist for the warp, it has been made entirely of cotton. The common plain, or pillow fustian, is very narrow, seldom exceeding 17 inches or 18 inches in width. Cut from the loom in half-pieces, or "ends," of about 35 yards long, it is then dyed, dressed, and folded ready for the market. Cantoon has a fine cord on one side, and a satiny surface of yarns, running at right angles to the cords, on the other. The satiny side is sometimes smoothed by singeing. It is a strong and handsome stuff. Corduroy is ribbed, the projecting part having a pile; it is strong in wear, and the best kinds are twilled. Velveteen, velvet, and thickset, are imitations of silk velvet in cotton, and are cheap, and to be had in various colours. Camelote is another and coarse variety of fustian.

G.

Gadroon. — A term employed in dressmaking and millinery, borrowed from architecture, denoting a kind of inverted fluting or beading. Plaits of a similar form are made on caps and cuffs, as composing a decorative style of trimming.

Gala. — A Scotch cotton fabric, employed for servants' dresses. Gala is said to be only a local name.

Galatea. — A cotton material striped in blue on a white ground. It is made for women's dresses, and washes well. It measures 27 inches in width.

Galloon. — There are two descriptions of this article. One is a strong, thick, gold lace, with an even selvedge at each side. It is woven with a pattern in threads of gold or silver, on silk or worsted, both plain and watered, and is employed in uniforms and on servants' livery hats. The other kind is of wool, silk, or cotton, combined with silk or worsted, and is used for trimming and binding articles of dress, hats, shoes, and furniture. This sort is only a narrow ribbon, done up in rolls of 36 yards each, four to the gross. The widths are called "two-penny," "four-penny," "six-penny," and "eight-penny." Galloon is employed for the bands and bindings of men's hats, for the trimmings of women's dresses, and for curtains. The finest qualities are produced at Amiens and Lyons, where it is chiefly made of wool. Swift mentions "a hat edged with silver Galloon" in his "Memoirs of P. P., Clerk of the Parish;" and in D'Urfey's "Wit and Mirth" (*temp.* Queen Anne), a country girl is said to wear "a jacket edged with blue Galloon."

Galway Cloth. — A closely woven cloth, of a coarse quality, suitable for cloaks, dyed scarlet, and worn by the Irish peasantry.

Galway Flannel. — A coarse make of flannel, of a dark red colour; thick, warm, and waterproofed. It is 33 inches in width. A fine quality is also produced under the same name.

Gambroon. — A kind of twilled linen cloth, made for linings.

Gammadion. — An ornament frequently met with in ancient Church Embroideries, and given the name by which it is known because formed with the Greek letter Gamma, drawn four times, so as to make the shape of a cross. It was employed by the early church workers as an emblem of Christ's crucifixion, but was borrowed by them from the East, having been used in India and China, before the time of Buddha, to express the Deity.

Gants, or Gands. — The French name for GLOVES (which *see*).

Garniture. — A French term signifying any description of decorative trimming and ornamentation, whether employed on dress or any other article.

Garnitures of Art.—*Addison.*

Gathering. — A term used in plain sewing. To effect it, fold a piece of stuff in half, and then into quarters, placing pins at the measurements so made; do the same with the piece of stuff on which the gathered portion of material is to be sewn, and place them together, pin to pin. Begin with the gathering thread at about twelve or fourteen threads from the top; take up three threads of the needle and miss four, more or less, according to the fulness desired. When a quarter is completed, draw the gatherings rather closely, securing the thread by twisting it round the pin. Stroke down each gather with a large needle, to make them lie evenly together. Then release the drawing

FIG. 416. GATHERING.

thread from the pin, and loosen the gathers, so as to make the length of space they occupy correspond with that on the plain piece of material upon which they are to be sewn. Fasten the thread again securely to the pin, and

FIG. 417. SEWING IN GATHERS.

sew on the gathers, sloping the needle to make the thread slant and slip between the gathers. When gathering flounces, the character of the dress material should be considered. If one intended for washing, the gathers should be cut the straight way of the stuff; otherwise it should be on the bias; in either case, whether cut straight with the threads of the web or diagonally, gather half as much again of the flounce as the space on the skirt to be occupied, if the material be thick in substance. Care should be taken to conceal the gathering thread.

Gauge for Knitting Needles. — These are bell-shaped or circular in form, and made of steel or bright wire metal, the outer edge having graduated circular cuts through to the extreme rim. Each hole has a number, to distinguish it from its fellows, and there are larger circular holes in the centre. Some gauges have the holes within the outer rim, only occupying the central portion. As there are upwards of two dozen varieties, one only is here illustrated. These appliances are employed by wire-drawers, and are essential to the Knitter as well as to the seller of Knitting Needles. They can be obtained at cutlers', and at wholesale establishments where other materials and articles necessary for the work-table are to be procured.

FIG. 418, GAUGE FOR KNITTING NEEDLES.

Gauging and Gathering Machine.—This machine is said to produce Gauging at one-twentieth the cost necessary to produce it by the hand when unassisted. The speed is estimated at 2500 stitches a minute, and as two needles can be employed simultaneously, double that number can as easily be produced, so accomplishing as

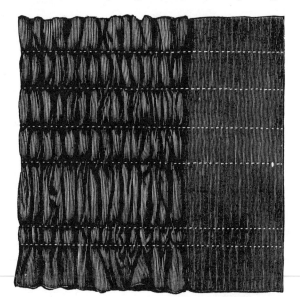

FIG. 419. GAUGING.

much work, in a given time, as could be performed by twenty persons. It is an American invention, is smaller than an ordinary sewing machine, and is available for purposes of dressmaking, millinery, and the plain sewing of underlinen. It is known as the "Heberling Running-stitch Gauging Machine."

Fig. 419 shows a specimen of Gauging executed by a hand machine, a portion being left undrawn to show the runnings.

Gauging, or Gaging.—A term applied to a series of close parallel runnings, which are all drawn up so as to make the material between them set full by gatherings; but the runnings are not brought together on a narrower space than they are themselves apart, as would be the plan if the same directions were followed and "puffings" desired. Gauging, which is also known as "shirring" (an objectionable Americanism), is pulled nearly tight from row to row of the runnings, but not so much as to make the line of the gathering threads take an uncertain course, the beauty of this trimming depending on the lines being of extreme accuracy. It may be made in groups at even distances; the runnings, separated by wider spaces, either longitudinally or latitudinally, to trim the bodice or sleeves of a dress, the head of a flounce, or for a bonnet, those of young children especially. A guide for running the lines at correct distances must be made as in quilting, by holding a paper strip under the thumb of the left hand, the further edge of the strip placed against the running last made, and the nearer one to serve as a guide to the needle for the next running.

Gauze.—A delicate, transparent textile, of a gossamer-like appearance, woven of silk, or silk and thread, as well as in other varieties, deriving its name from Gaza, in Palestine, where the tissue was first manufactured. The threads of silk and hemp are woven either singly or together, and the several kinds are plain made, brocaded or spotted, the designs being composed of silk, or else striped with satin or velvet. There is an inferior description of Gauze, on which the designs are of "Maquesia," merely gummed upon the Gauze. Those fabrics imported from China or India are sometimes decorated with flowers in gold. Gossamer is a variety of GAUZE (which *see*); so is Crêpe Lisse, which is crimped. China Crape, Mousseline de Soie Crêpe, and Indian Net—a strong variety, made of silk and worsted, and employed for women's gowns—are all of the same description of textile. The best kinds are made in France. The Italian is another variety, bearing a resemblance to *Taffetas*. Gauze was highly prized by the Romans, and was introduced into Ireland in 1698. Its manufacture in this country was carried on for a long period at Spitalfields, where the beautiful Chinese Gauzes were successfully imitated, with flowers in gold and silver thread. It has been woven at Paisley, in Scotland, ever since 1759.

Brocades and damasks, and tabbies and gauzes, have been lately brought over (to Ireland).

—*Dean Swift.*

Gauze Broché (otherwise known as Empress Gauze and Lace-patterned Grenadine).—This stuff, although bearing a resemblance to Grenadine, is not always a wholly silk, nor wholly linen textile, but may be a mixture of both, or of one or other exclusively. It has a foundation woven transparently, as Gauze, but is decorated with a floral design of satin make. The width varies from 30 inches to 32 inches.

Gauze Flannel.—This stuff is otherwise known as Zephyr Shirting, a very fine description of flannel, having a silk warp, striped with black or pink, on a grey ground. It is 32 inches in width, and is employed for a superior kind of shirting made for men's use in hot climates.

Gauze Ribbons.—These ribbons are a description of silk muslin, produced in fancy patterns and plain, and in all colours. They are employed for old ladies' caps, but are no longer fashionable. *See* RIBBON.

Gaze au Fuseau.—*See* GRILLÉ.

Gaze Point.—*See* POINT GAZE.

Genet Fur.—The Genet is a species of the Polecat, and is a native of Africa, Asia, and the South of Europe. Its fur is of a grey colour, spotted with either black or brown, the long tail being ringed with black and white. The skin is comparatively inexpensive, and is employed for muffs, collarettes, and cuffs.

Geneva Embroidery.—This is a modern work resembling Ticking Work. The foundation material is chessboard canvas, or Java canvas, and upon this broad lines of velvet are laid, and attached with Cross, Tent, Herringbone, and other stitches, worked in coloured silks, chenille, or wool. To work: Upon the chessboard canvas lay down velvet bands 1 inch in width and 2 inches apart. Cross these, to form squares with similar bands of velvet, and HERRINGBONE them at their sides to the canvas. Fill in the squares of canvas with Rosettes or Stars made with a bright-coloured chenille. The embroidery is sometimes worked

Genoese Embroidery.—This is a modern Embroidery, named after the celebrated Genoese Lace, to which it bears but little resemblance. It is worked upon fine linen or muslin, and the designs surrounded with narrow cord closely Buttonholed over. The work is suitable for dress and underlinen trimmings. To work as shown in Fig. 420: If the muslin or linen is clear, trace the design upon calico, and tack the material to that; if thick, trace the design directly on to it with the aid of the tracing paper and cloth, and tack that to brown paper. Outline the whole of the pattern with the fine cord, and make the loops with the cord at the same time. Cover the cord with a close and fine line of BUTTONHOLE, and work plain BARS to connect the various parts of the design together; fill in the centre pattern with a plain WHEEL, and the open parts branching from the Wheel with LADDER STITCH. Untack the work from the brown paper, and cut away the linen from between the Buttonhole lines of cord.

FIG. 420. GENOESE EMBROIDERY.

without the velvet bands, entirely in chenille or Arrasene, and the canvas foundation left exposed.

Genoa Lace.—The manufacture of lace in the city of Genoa and the surrounding country flourished during the seventeenth century, and both the Pillow and Needle Laces produced there were then held in high estimation. The earliest Needle Laces were made of gold and silver thread, or of gold wire, and the method practised of drawing out the wire was similar to that used in the time of the early Greeks. The Genoese Laces include a Pillow Lace resembling in pattern the Greek Points, Tape Guipures, Lace made from the fibre of the aloe, and Knotted laces, known in modern times as Macramé. The manufacture of the three first has died out, but the making of Macramé has been revived, and flourishes in Genoa and along the coast.

Genoa Lace.—A Modern Point Lace Stitch, similar to SORRENTO STITCH (which *see*).

Genoese Velvet.—The velvets manufactured at Genoa are considered to be very superior, and are, perhaps, the best quality produced. The pile is thick, close, and of fine silk, and the web on which it is placed is likewise of silk, and closely woven. At the time of the coronation of Charles I., the red and purple robes for such occasions were usually made of Genoese velvet; but, according to De Quincey, "by some oversight, all the store in London was insufficient to furnish the purple velvet necessary for the robes of the king, and for the furniture of the throne. It was too late to send to Genoa for a supply, and through this accidental deficiency it happened that the king was attired in white velvet at the solemnity of his coronation, and not in red nor purple robes, as consistent with the proper usage." De Quincey further observes, that the forebodings of the misfortunes of this "white King," according to the prophecy of Merlin, were supposed to have had their fulfilment in his case, white being the ancient colour for a victim, a curious coincidence being notice-able in the fact that his pall was white with snow, which fell on it as a sheet when he was carried to the grave.

German Cross Stitch.—Identical with KREUZSTICH.

German Fingering.—A fine soft yarn, said to be of a more durable character than any other wool of an equally fine quality. It may be had in white, black, drabs, and greys, in ingrain colours, mixtures, and navy blue, and is sold by the pound and ounce.

German Fleecy.—This description of woollen yarn is likewise known as Berlin Fleecy; but there is much deception as to the sheep from which the wool is taken, as bales of the best description are now imported from Australia. *See* FLEECY.

German Fringes.—These are made of white cotton in various fancy patterns. The width is from 1½ inches to 3 inches, and the fringe is used for bed furniture, blinds and curtains. It is sold in lengths of 36 yards.

German Heel.—*See* KNITTING.

German Hemming.—A term used in describing plain needlework—a kind of substitute for what is called Sewing —a method employed when desirable that the seam made should lie very flat. It looks better than Felling, and is as strong. The raw edges of two pieces of cloth are turned down once—the fold turned towards the sempstress—so that the smooth top of the lower one should not touch the edge of the upper, but is just below it. The lower one is then felled (or hemmed) to the cloth against which it is laid—like hemming it upside down. When completed, the material—sleeve or other article—being opened, the upper fold should be laid over the lower edge, and felled down.

German Lace.—Germany owes its best manufactory of Lace to the exertions of Barbara Uttmann, who estab-lished, in Saxony, in 1561, the making of a Pillow Lace resembling Brussels Lace; while in 1685, owing to the Revocation of the Edict of Nantes, religious refugees from France settled themselves in Germany, and manufactured so much and such good lace that they were enabled to export it, not only into Russia and Italy, but into France. Dresden, Nurnburg, and Saxony were the places most celebrated for their laces during the eighteenth century, and large quantities of the lace known as Torchon is still made in Saxony, but of a make and pattern inferior to that formerly manufactured there.

German Linen Thread Embroidery. — An em-broidery upon thick white linen, with blue, white, or red linen thread. The patterns used are hunting scenes, surrounded with conventional foliage, and are all taken from old German designs. To work: Outline all the pattern with REVERSED CHAIN, or ROPE STITCH, made in blue linen thread. Work a row of CREWEL STITCH inside this line with white thread. Fill in leaves and flowers with SATIN STITCH in white linen thread. Work the clothes of figures, feathers of birds, and fur of animals with white thread, and with MODERN POINT Lace Stitches, or DARNED BACKGROUND Stitches.

German Stitch.—*See* BERLIN WORK.

German Wool (termed in French *Zephyr Menoir*).— This is another name for BERLIN WOOL (which *see*). It is

very evenly twisted, smooth and soft, excelling Fleecy in these respects, and all other kinds of wool in its capability of receiving the most brilliant dyes. The wool so-called was obtained from German sheep, although chiefly spun at Keighley, in Yorkshire; but much of our best wool has latterly been imported from our own colonies in Australia. There are two sizes sold, the double and the single.

Ghent.—Valenciennes Lace of good quality is made in this town, and is sold in Holland, France, and England. The school in Ghent for lacemaking was founded by the Beguins about the year 1756, and the lace was then termed Fausse Valenciennes. It is less solid than true Valen-ciennes, and is made in narrow and medium widths only. The network ground is more quickly made than the true Valenciennes, not so many turns in the Bobbins being given when forming the Honeycombs, and for this reason the lace is cheaper.

Gilet.—A French term signifying a waistcoat. It is employed by dressmakers. Gilets are sometimes made separately from the bodice, but are as often merely simu-lated, the central portion of the front of the bodice being so bordered as to appear like a separate article of dress.

Gimp.—This is the shiny, or coarse glazed thread used in Honiton and other Pillow Laces, to mark out and slightly raise certain edges of the design, as a substitute for Raised Work. It is also used in Needle-made Darned laces, as a run edging, to emphasise the chief parts of a pattern.

To work for Honiton Lace, as shown in Fig. 421: Fill two Bobbins with GIMP, and make the Half Hitch to keep the thread tight to the bobbins; tie them together and wind away the Knot. Hang eleven pairs of bobbins

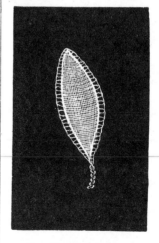

and the gimps to the point of the leaf, which arrange so that the gimps fall out-side the other bobbins on each side. Work the leaf in CLOTH STITCH with PLAIN EDGE, but pass the gimp through the Runners each row, thus: In the first row, working from left to right, pass the gimp over No. 2 and under No. 1 to begin, and under No. 2 and over No. 1 to end the row. In returning from right to left, pass the gimp under No. 2 and over No. 1 at the beginning, and over No. 2 and under No. 1 at the end. Work down the leaf

FIG. 421. LEAF WORKED WITH GIMP.

in Cloth Stitch and Plain Edge, working in the gimp as described, and when the leaf is finished, tie up and cut off the gimps, and then make BEGINNERS' PLAIT with the other bobbins for the stem.

Gimp, or Gymp.—An open work trimming, used on both dress and furniture, and in coach lace making. It is made of silk, worsted, or cotton twist, having a cord or a wire running through it. The strands are plaited or twisted, so as to form a pattern. The French word Passementerie has much superseded that of Gimp in reference to the finer sorts used for dress.

Gingham.—A thin chequered cloth, made of linen, the threads being dyed in the yarn, and measuring 32 inches in width. It was imported from India, and is extensively manufactured in England, and employed for dresses. There are several varieties, known respectively as Earlston Ginghams, Power Loom, Seer-Suckers, Coloured Diapers, Muslin Grounds (stripes and checks), Umbrella Ginghams, Crossover Stripes, Jean Stripes, Derries, plain common light and ditto dark grounds; besides Gingham handkerchiefs, which are made of linen or cotton, much used in the North of England as market handkerchiefs, for tying bundles, and carried on the end of a stick over the shoulder. When recently re-introduced as a fashionable dress material, Gingham was given a new designation, and is now known by the unsuitable name of Zephyr. A superior kind is made of linen only, the other sort being made of cotton.

Glacé Silk.—A slight and peculiarly lustrous quality of silk, of plain make—i.e., without rib or twill, or brocaded design. Glacé silk is to be had in single colours, and also in fine stripes, shot, or chiné, and is comparatively inexpensive. It is peculiarly well adapted for summer dresses.

Glass Cloth.—This is a beautiful material, which has appeared in various exhibitions. Manufactories for the production of ecclesiastical decorative fabrics composed of glass fibre are in operation in Austria, France, and Italy, and it is also made at Pittsburg, in Pennsylvania. When toughened it will be rendered more satisfactory as trimmings for articles of dress and upholstery. With reference to the method pursued in its manufacture, the thread is drawn out of a molten bar of glass, by means of a rapidly revolving wheel, at the rate of 200 yards a minute; the weaving is done by looms, as with silk. The colouring is applied with minerals, while the glass is in a state of fusion, before spinning, and the most beautiful shades are easily produced. A glass tablecloth shines with a satiny opalescent lustre by day, and under gaslight shows remarkable beauty. Imitation plumes in opal, ruby, pale green, and other hues, are also wonderfully pretty. The chief difficulty in the manufacture seems to lie in the "manipulation of these threads, which are so fine, that a bunch containing 250 is not so thick as an average knitting needle." The introducers of this new industry declare that "garments of pure glass, glistening and imperishable, are among the possibilities of the near future."

Glass Cloths.—These cloths are made of linen, and have a large Cross-bar check of red or blue thread. They have been diverted from their primary use, and much adopted for the purpose of embroidery, as well as for aprons and chair covers, small designs being worked within the several squares with crewels or ingrain cotton. They vary in price in England, from 6d. to 1s. a yard, and measure from about 27 inches to 30 inches in width.

Glazed Calico.—A thin calico of a loose texture, having a high glaze on one side, produced by a process of damping and extreme pressure, known as "calendering." It is made for linings only, and can be procured in every colour.

Gloves.—A covering for the hand, or hand and wrist, having a separate sheath for each finger. The earliest kinds worn in England had no divisions for the fingers, but were supplied with a separate sheath for the thumb only. They are mentioned in the records of dress in the most remote times, Homer alluding to them in the Twenty-fourth Book of the "Odyssey," where Laertes is described as wearing them when found by Ulysses tending his garden:

His buskins old, in former service torn,
But well repaired; and Gloves, against the thorn.

Xenophon speaks of their use by the ancient Persians, and Pliny of the two descriptions, with fingers and with a thumb only divided, made of either wool or felt. In England, the ceremonies connected with gloves are curious. Two bishops were put in possession of their Sees, A.D. 1002, by each receiving a glove. In the time of Edward II. deprivation of gloves was a ceremony of degradation. The Glovers' Company of London was incorporated in 1556. The importation of foreign manufactures of the article was not permitted in England until the year 1825. At our coronations, the Champion of England (a hereditary office and distinction belonging to the Dymoke family) rides up to Westminster Hall, on the day appointed for the ceremony, to challenge anyone who disputes the right of succession. The office was established by William the Conqueror to Marmion and his male descendants, and thence came in the female line to De Ludlow, and from his family, again in the female line, to Sir John Dymoke, in the reign of Richard II. It was, and still is, a part of the ceremony to throw down a glove as the token of a challenge, and to wait for a time to see whether any opposer of the succession would take it up:

These Lincoln lands the Conqueror gave,
That England's glove they might convey
To Knight renowned amongst the brave—
The Baron bold of Fontenoy.
—*Anglo-Norman Ballad.*

Another old custom in reference to gloves, which is still observed in England, is the practice obtaining at a maiden assize, when the sheriff presents a pair of white gloves to the judge; also the fashion of presenting white ones to wedding guests, and black to those at funerals. In the Northern counties, amongst other customs connected with gloves, white paper ones are hung up, with chaplets, in churches, in memory of persons deceased, as being emblematic of their purity, and having "clean hands." This obtains in Yorkshire and Lancashire. It is not etiquette to wear gloves in the presence of Royalty, a rule having its origin in the emblematic use of gloves in giving a challenge, which inferiority in rank, as well as the loyalty due to them, would preclude. On the same grounds, the habit obtains of removing one or both gloves in church, being a mark of respect which, if due to an earthly potentate, is thought more incumbent still on those engaged in the acts of Divine worship. Following out the same idea of showing respect by removing the gloves, until quite recently the custom obtained amongst men to take off, not only the hat, but the right glove, when offering the hand to a lady, and on entering a room as a visitor.

Gloves with long tops extending up the arm from the wrist were much worn in the fourteenth century in this country. Some were jewelled on the back, and were worn with regal robes, forming part of the costume; and others were mailed, like the defensive armour they were intended to match, or had one or more metal plates on their backs, while inside the glove was soft and flexible. Embroidered ones were introduced into England in 1580. There is much historical interest attached to gloves. Knights of the Middle Ages used to wear their lady-loves' gloves as badges in their helmets, and threw down their own as a challenge to private combat. In the last century, chicken skin gloves were much in vogue, for the especial preservation of ladies' hands, as was imagined; and rat skin gloves have been, and still are, to be had. Those now in ordinary use are of various descriptions. The kid gloves of home manufacture are principally made at Worcester, Yeovil, Ludlow, Leominster, Leicester, Nottingham, and London. Buckskins, strong, close-grained, stiff and durable, will bear cleaning better than those of any other kind of leather. Doeskins are very durable and thick, but soft and flexible. Woodstock is a superior kind of beaver glove, well-shaped and sewn, and warm for winter wear. Those of Woodstock and Worcester are of ancient celebrity.

Besides the leather gloves before named, there are woven ones of thread, silk, cotton, and wool. Berlin gloves, so called because originally made there, are composed of cotton, made to resemble kid. The Berlin silk gloves are superior to others of that material, and are made in all colours. Aberdeens are made of worsted, or of cotton yarns. They are machine-knitted, and wear well. Worsted gloves, and those of lambs' wool, are much used in agricultural districts. Gants de Suède are made of thin skins, turned inside out. Thick white cotton gloves are used in servants' liveries, or plain dress, for waiting, or driving, and outdoor attendance. Thick white "wash leather" gloves, with gauntlets, are worn by the Life Guards.

Goats' Hair Cloth.—*See* CASHMERE.

Gobelin Stitch.—*See* BERLIN WORK and *Embroidery Stitches.*

Gobelin Tapestry.—This is a revival, on a small scale, of ancient Tapestry work, and is named after the celebrated Gobelin manufactory in Paris. Like the true Gobelin, the work is executed from the back, and can be made either of purse silk, filoselle, or single Berlin wool. Silk work in Gobelin is very beautiful, the variety of shades and the number of stitches used contributing to give it a soft and pleasing appearance; it is useful for hand-screens, bags, pincushions, where part of the background can be shown, and for squares in chair backs alternately with heavy lace; but the wool Gobelin, with bold patterns, should be selected by all beginners until the *minutiæ* of the work is understood, as it will form a change to Cross Stitch work, will be as durable, and is executed from counted patterns. It forms excellent cushions, fender-stools, mantel and table borders. A strong wooden embroidery frame, with webbing up the sides, is necessary for the wool work, while small ones, also with webbing at the sides, are sufficient for the silk. The frames used for Guipure d'Art, and covered with silk, are large enough for many pieces of

Tapestry. The frame being ready, strings are carried backwards and forwards from one piece of webbing to the other. These strings are made of fine whipcord, and are laced closely together and perfectly parallel. They take the place of canvas, and bear the stitches; therefore, it is of vital importance to the work that they should be arranged at even distances, and be close together and tightly stretched. Their number must be the same as the number of lines required in the pattern, therefore they are counted. Whipcord is used for the wool, very fine twine for the silk, tapestry. The patterns chosen are the same as are used for Cross Stitch on linen or Berlin wool work, detached flower sprays or landscape patterns, the first-named being the easiest.

In copying patterns with a good deal of ground, one shade of colour is carried straight up the work, but designs of various colours have to be more carefully treated. It is then necessary to thread a number of needles with the shades of colour, to secure them, and work them in their places, carrying the wool along the work where not required, putting it in and making a stitch, and then carrying it on again until the top of the frame is reached. When silk Gobelin is worked, the silk need not be threaded, but sufficient for one line should be wound upon a thin fine card, and that passed through the cords and the loop so made.

To work: Set up the frame and lace the cords across it, counting them, and putting them in at even distances apart. Commence to work from the bottom of the frame, at the left-hand side. Thread a wool needle with a shade of grounding colour, and tie it on to the first cord, and, bringing the wool up over the cord, put the needle in over and under the second cord, and bring it out, forming a loop on that cord with the wool, and so that the returning wool crosses over the wool coming from the bottom cord; then make another stitch on the right of the one just formed, and on the same cord. These two loops count as one stitch; they must be always drawn up evenly and close together. The next stitch is made on the third line in the same way, and so on until every line of cord has a stitch upon it, and the top of the frame is reached. The wool is then fastened off, and another line commenced from the bottom, and close to the one first made. The appearance on the right side (the work being executed on the wrong) is like the tight loops seen in carpets. The work is executed for silk Gobelin as for wool, the difference being in the fineness of the pattern produced.

Another Variety.—Another manner of imitating Gobelin tapestry with silk is only practicable for small articles, such as necktie ends, bags, and hand screens. It is done on the right side, and the stitches are taken over fine knitting needles. The needles should not be large, as they are withdrawn, and, if big, leave loops too long for beauty. The patterns are the same as before described, the pins taking the place of cords. A silk or satin foundation stretched on a frame is necessary, and the pins are attached to this, close together, with strong tacking threads. To work: Bring the embroidery silk from the back of the material, pass it over the knitting needle and return it to the back, and pass it over the needle again

RUSSIAN CROSS STITCH PATTERN.

GERMAN CROSS STITCH PATTERN.

ITALIAN CROSS STITCH PATTERN.

close to the first place to complete the stitch. Work two or three stitches of the same colour if close together on the same line at once, but the tendency of the work should be always upward, from the bottom line to the top, and but little deviation from this rule allowed. The material being the ground, only the pattern is worked. When the pattern is finished, paste over the back with EMBROIDERY PASTE, and leave the needles in position until this is thoroughly dry, then pull them out. If the design is an Arabesque, the work can be enriched with a line of gold thread COUCHED round every portion of the outline. If both sides are shown, as in a necktie, a piece of silk should be laid over the back part, but this is not otherwise necessary.

Another variety is worked upon Java Canvas, or Woollen Canvas. Select bold Kreuzstich design, and work in GOBELIN STITCH instead of Cross.

Gold and Silver Lace.—The twisting of gold and silver, or gold wire, into various patterns, was the first method of making lace, and though its origin is lost in obscurity, the authentic records still remaining of its use carry the making of Gold Lace back to the time of the Egyptians and Romans. The origin of all lace came from the desire to ornament the edges of garments, and at first, in order to do this, the material itself was ravelled out and fringed; then, into these ravellings coloured silk and gold threads were introduced and worked up together; and, finally, the ornament was detached from the garment and worked separately, and elaborate needle-made stitches introduced.

Cyprus produced Gold and Silver Lace in 1390, while Venetian and Italian claim to be the originals of all the Gold and Silver Laces, and the rest to be but copies. Point d'Espagne at one time signified Gold and Silver Lace into which coloured silks were introduced, and this description of Lacemaking flourished in Spain during the fourteenth century, declining in beauty after the expulsion of the Jews from that country, they being the best workers. In Sweden, Gold Lace was made in the fifteenth century; in Russia it was the first description of lace which was manufactured. In France, Gold Lace was made before the time of Colbert, at Aurillac, while at Arras it flourished up to the end of the eighteenth century. The gold used in its manufacture was of considerable value, and a work called Parfilage, or Ravellings, which consisted of unpicking the lace to obtain the gold, was at one time very fashionable. Gold Lace is now made by machinery, and is only used for uniforms, theatrical purposes, and servants' liveries.

The Gold and Silver Laces of the present day consist of warp threads of silk, or silk and cotton combined; the weft being of silk thread, covered with silver or silver gilt. The metal is drawn into a wire, and then flattened between steel rollers. Although the gold alone be visible, ninetenths of the lace is of silk. Several strands of the flattened gold wire pass round the silk simultaneously, by means of a complex machine, having a wheel and iron Bobbins. Though called Lace, the manufacture would be more correctly described as Braid. It varies in width, and is employed for uniforms, ecclesiastical, Court, and civic dress, liveries, furniture, and church decorations. Gold Fringes and Gold Passing, employed for Embroidery work, are made in the same way.

Gold Beaten Out.—Also known as Batuz Work and Hammered-up Gold. Much used in the Embroideries executed between the eleventh and sixteenth centuries. It consists of fine gold or silver gilt, beaten out with hammers into extremely thin plates, which are shaped to fit into certain parts of the work. These plates are attached with silk to the material, or glued to it. *See* BATUZ WORK.

Gold Bullion Embroidery.—*See* BULLION EMBROIDERY.

Gold Embroidery.—*See* EMBROIDERY WITH GOLD.

Gold Fringe.—*See* GOLD AND SILVER LACE.

Gold Passing.—A silk thread encased in flattened gold wire, employed in embroidery work. *See* GOLD AND SILVER LACE.

Gold Twist or Thread.—*See* GOLD PASSING and GOLD AND SILVER LACE.

Gold Wrought Work.—Used largely, during the eleventh to the sixteenth centuries, as ornaments to ladies' embroidered dresses, and for the crests and other insignia upon embroidered banners, or as adornments to coronation and funeral garments, and consisting of thin plates of gold, beaten out flat, and then worked up with silks into patterns in relief.

Gore.—A term used in Needlework to signify a piece of any material, cut somewhat wedge-shaped, wider at one end than the other, which, being let into a skirt, or any part of a garment, increases the width at one end, while it lessens it at the other. As a rule, the sloping side of the Gore is always joined to the straight side of the next breadth in a skirt; and when hand-made, the sloping side is held next to the sewer. In a machine the straight side should be uppermost. One breadth of material will make two Gores, it being first measured, and then cut obliquely. These dress-skirt Gores are not cut to a point at the small ends, as in the Gore for under-garment sleeves. In the skirts of underclothing the Selvedges are SEAMED together.

Gorget.—This term denotes an article of dress, copied from the throat portion of a military uniform, and worn by women in the sixteenth century, which is now creeping into fashion again. As the term applies to any wide and stiff covering for the throat or gorge, it signifies not whether made of silk, satin, or velvet, decorated with lace or fringe, and worn plain, beaded or embroidered.

> And gorgets brave, with drawn work wrought,
> A tempting wear they are, &c.
> —*Pleasant Quippes for Gentlewomen*, 1596.

Gossamer.—A rich silk gauze, so called from its resemblance to the finely woven silken thread spun by spiders, and which seems to derive its name from the fact of its being chiefly found in the Gorse, or Goss, this film being anciently called Samyt. According to an ancient legend, Gossamers were said to be the ravellings of the Blessed Virgin Mary's shroud on her Assumption, which fell from her. The term *Gossamer* was formerly applied to cotton threads, or the fine filaments on the seeds of certain plants, such as the dandelion and thistle,

G G

being derived from *Gossypium*. The textile now called "Gossamer" is strong in quality, and is made in black and colours. It is much employed for veils, and worn by both sexes, being four times as thick and strong as ordinary gauze, although nearly as open in texture. It may be procured either at a yard or a yard and a quarter in width.

Gown.—The outer garment worn by women, combining a bodice and skirt, and, till recently, for many years designated by the less distinctive term "Dress." (*See* DRESSMAKING.) In the Middle Ages men wore what were called "Gowns"—

> The lord shall shift his *gowne* by night.
> —*The Boke of Courtasye* (Fourteenth Cent.)

Later on we find that Shakespeare speaks of being

> Dressed in the *gown* of humility,

and, in the "Taming of the Shrew" the tailor says

> Imprimis, a loose-bodied *gown*,
> With a small cape,

and

> With a trunk sleeve. . . . .
> The sleeves curiously cut.

Tennyson likewise alludes to the garment thus:

> *Gowned* in pure white that fitted to the shape.

Ecclesiastical, collegiate, civic, and legal so-called "gowns" are worn by men, cut and made up in different styles and of different materials; but all characterised by the union of a skirt, with a covering of the body to the throat. A very early name employed to signify a gown is "Gite," as may be seen in several old works, such as Chaucer's "Wife of Bath," viz.:

> Gay scarlet *Gites*.

Grafting.—A term employed in DARNING, to signify the insertion of a sound piece of stocking web into a space from which an unsound piece has been cut out. The original English word "graff" for "graft," is employed in the Authorised Version of the New Testament. Pope also alludes to it thus:

> And *graft* my love immortal on thy fame.

An illustration is given under DARNING (which *see*).

Grammont.—A cheap kind of white thread Pillow lace was first made in the town of Grammont, but lately a black silk lace, resembling the Chantilly Blondes, has been manufactured. The Grammont laces are made in large pieces for flounces and shawls, and are used more in America than in Europe. The ground of the lace is coarser, and the patterns not so clear as the true Chantilly, also the black silk is not so pure in colour; but the quality of the lace is good, and it is cheaper than the French lace.

Grandrills.—A dark grey material, made of cotton, usually of about 27 inches wide, and employed for the making of stays; a description of coarse Jean.

Grass Cloth, or Lawn.—A fine, light quality of cloth, resembling linen, made from the *Urtica nivea* and other plants. As imported from the East for the home retail market, it is sold in pieces of 40 yards, of 16 inches in width.

Grass Embroidery.—This Embroidery consists in using grass instead of silk or wool to form ornamental needlework patterns. It is practised by the West Indian tribes, who adorn their mocassins, head ornaments, and belts with this material. The designs are worked in flat SATIN STITCH, and the grass is dyed in various shades of colour.

Grebe (*Podicipinæ iristatus*).—The bird so called is a waterfowl, a native of England, inhabiting the fens of Shropshire, Cheshire, and Lincolnshire, where it is called a "Gaunt." It is, however, to be found all over the old and new world. It is remarkable for the thickness and beauty of its plumage, and the breast is employed for making articles of dress—such as hats, pelerines, cuffs, and muffs, as a substitute for fur. There are five different species known in the British Islands, viz., the common Dabchick, the Eared Grebe, Horned Grebe, Red-necked Grebe, and the great Tippet Grebe. The skin measures 8 inches by 9 inches. The bird is peculiar in appearance, possessing no tail, short wings, and a long conical beak. One species of Grebe has a crest, and thence the derivation of the Welsh name *Criebe*, or crest, by which it is known in Wales.

Grebe Cloth.—A cotton cloth, made very much in the style of *Swanskin*.

Grecian Netting.—*See* NETTING.

Greek Embroidery.—This is a modern work, and is used for small mats, banner screens, and other fancy articles. It is a description of Appliqué, and consists in arranging upon a flat foundation pieces of coloured cloth

FIG. 422. GREEK EMBROIDERY.

or silk, in arabasque designs, and attaching these to the material with Chain, Herringbone, and other Embroidery stitches, and these stitches are also repeated upon the plain foundation. To work as shown in Fig. 422, which is a section of a round mat: Draw out the design upon dark

Turkey red cloth, cut out the diamond-shaped piece of the pattern and the design in the centre of the oval from a dark art blue shade of cloth, and the oval from a blue cloth, paler, but of the same shade as that used for the diamond. Lay these upon the Turkey red foundation, and to attach them to the material lay a silk cord round their edges, of their own shade, and catch this down with red

Guipure. This needle-made lace, one of the earliest, was worked in the Ionian Isles and at Venice during the fifteenth century; but its greatest celebrity was obtained during the sixteenth century, as, though manufactured in the seventeenth, its character was then altered, and it was superseded in popularity by the Renaissance Points. The Lace worked in the Ionian Isles is the real

FIG. 423. GREEK POINT.

silk, as in COUCHING. Work the star in the centre of the diamond in TÊTE DE BŒUF STITCH with red silk, and HERRINGBONE over the oval with blue silk. Finish the pattern by working CHAIN STITCH round the oval in old gold silk, and make the Feathers, Dots, and Lines with the same old gold coloured silk.

Greek Point.—Also known as Roman Lace, Italian Reticella, Reticella, and erroneously called Venetian

Greek Point; that worked in Italy, although of the same kind, is of a finer make, and is known more frequently as Reticella and Italian Reticella. The principal places of manufacture of Greek Point were the Ionian Isles, Zante, Corfu, Venice, Naples, Rome, Florence, and Milan. In Spain, France, England, and Germany, Greek Point was made, but it was not original, being copied from the Italian laces, many patterns of which were published in Vinciola's collection in 1587. The designs of the early laces are all geometrical, and the oldest are the simple outlines, worked over laid and arranged cords, or over threads left after others have been withdrawn. These geometrical outlines were succeeded by laces made with the same style of pattern, but with the plain outline filled in with half circles, triangles, and wheels, and this description finally merged into open work with thick stitches, made like other needle laces. The stitches used in old Greek Points are the ones now worked either in Guipure d'Art or in Modern Point Lace. The materials were silk of various colours, gold and silver thread, or linen thread. The modern Greek Point is only made with linen thread.

To work Fig. 423, p. 227, an illustration of the manner of

To work Fig. 424: This pattern is partially worked with cords, but most of the lines are formed with Genoa Two-Thread Stitch. The cord used is Calt's linen cord of two widths. Trace the pattern upon parchment or Toile ciré, and tack down on to it the outside straight lines, using the wider cord for the outside line, the finer for the inner line. Then make the horizontal lines. Throw a thread across from the inner outside line to the inner line on the opposite side, secure it, and return it to where it came from, leaving a small space between. Work over the two lines by darning in and out in GENOA STITCH. Work all the straight lines of the lace in this way, and then BUTTONHOLE over the outside cords. Work the ovals and stars in Buttonhole, ornament them with PICOTS, and work the

FIG. 424. GREEK POINT.

working with drawn threads: Take a piece of fine cambric and draw the threads out so as to leave a number of open squares surrounded with fine lines, and tack this upon a piece of parchment upon which the design of the lace has been traced. Commence to work by OVERCASTING all the fine lines with fine Mecklenburgh thread, and then fill in the open squares with the pattern; throw a thread across a space and BUTTONHOLE it over, and Buttonhole backwards and forwards until the width of that piece of the pattern is obtained; ornament its edge with PICOTS. Finish the edge of the lace with a line of Buttonhole, and work a fancy stitch beyond on the cambric with a line of slanting SATIN STITCHES, outlined with BACK STITCHES.

cones in POINT DE FESTON. To form the edge, tack an ornamental braid in scallops, and secure it to the Buttonhole cord with BARS made of Buttonhole, or simply ornament the Buttonhole line with Picots.

To work Fig. 425: This design is of a similar make to the last, but it is intended as the border to a fine linen tablecloth, and is worked on to the edge of the linen, which is cut away from underneath when the work is finished, the lace being thus made part of the cloth. To work: Trace the pattern on the linen with blue carbonised paper and tracing cloth, and back with brown paper, run a cord to form the outer lines of the pattern, and cover with BUTTONHOLE. Work the thick parts of the lace as shown in Detail A (Fig. 426) thus: The thick lines make with two-thread

GENOA STITCH, the cones in POINT DE FESTON, and the looped edge in Buttonhole finished with PICOTS. When

ways: Either trace the pattern, and outline every part

FIG. 425. GREEK POINT.

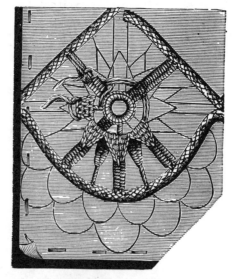

FIG. 426. GREEK POINT — DETAIL A.

the lace is completed, cut away the linen from beneath it, when it will appear as in Fig. 425.

with a fine cord, and fill in all thick parts with BUTTON-

FIG. 427. GREEK POINT OR RETICELLA.

To work Fig. 427: This pattern which is a specimen of the latest kind of Greek Point, and is a copy of a piece of lace found in a convent at Milan, can be worked in two

HOLE STITCH, and open parts with LADDER STITCH: or, Trace the design upon fine cambric, and tack that to parchment; work over all the lines of the outline in fine

Buttonhole, connect these together with corded BARS, and finish by cutting away the superfluous cambric outside the Buttonhole.

Greek Point can be imitated with the aid of braids, as shown in the design below (Fig. 428). To work: Trace the design upon pink calico, and tack a braid with an open edge round the outlines of the pattern. OVERCAST the edge of the braid, and secure it in its place with BUTTONHOLE BARS ornamented with PICOTS, carried across the open parts of the lace, and then sew on a fine cord into the centre of the braid, and fill in the spaces with SORRENTO STITCH or POINT DE BRUXELLES, where the lace is to be thick, and where open with ornamental WHEELS and STARS. Sew a lace edging to the scalloped edge of the work.

Grenadine.—An open silk, or silk and wool textile, much resembling a *barège*, made both plain and figured.

Grillé.—A lace term used with Gaze au Fuseau and Toile to distinguish the ornamental flower or pattern of lace from the ground surrounding it. Grillé, Grillage, or Gaze au Fuseau, are terms especially applied to ornaments that have open spaces barred or grated across them, while Toilé is used to describe those ornaments that are worked quite thick and without open spaces.

Gris, or Grey.—The Fur thus named as having been so much worn in the Middle Ages, although mentioned by Chaucer as denoting any description of valuable fur, has likewise been affirmed by others to have been that of the grey squirrel, and was more probably that of the MARTEN (which *see*).

Grogram.—A mixed material, composed of silk and mohair or stuff, manufactured in Scotland. The texture

FIG. 428. GREEK POINT—IMITATION.

There are a great many varieties of this description of dress material, employed for summer or evening wear. The widths vary, running generally from three-quarters of a yard to 1 yard.

Grenadine Crépon.—A new description of black dress material, suitable for summer or evening wear. It is made entirely of wool, and has a transparent check pattern composed of rows of coarse cords, each stripe of the same width as the thin squares enclosed by their crossings. It is 24 inches in width.

Grey Calicoes.—Those classed as Domestic run from 29 to 33 inches in width; the Mexican (fine double work), Victoria, and Wigan, 33 inches; and the Wigan Twills (heavy extra) and Bolton are all of the same width.

is loose, and the surface rough, being woven with a large woof and rough pile; and the name is a corruption of the French *gros grain*. It is a kind of coarse Taffety, stiffened with gum, and is an inferior article to the more modern and fashionable material, which it somewhat resembles, known as GROS GRAIN (which *see*). The threads of the warp in both the above-named materials pass over two of the shoots at once, taking up one only, a method often adopted in finishing the edge of a ribbon.

'Twas madam in her *grogram* gown.
—*Swift.*

And scorned the charmful village maid,
With innocence and *grogram* blest.
—*Thomson.*

Gros de Messine.—A variety of Gros de Naples, having a raised narrow pin-rib. It is 18 inches in width.

Gros de Naples.—The term " Gros " being the French for thick, the name signifies a thick Naples Silk. It is a material somewhat similar to lutestring, but less stout, and made both plain and figured, in various qualities, and coloured. It is much used for dresses, and is manufactured in this country as well as in France, whence it was formerly imported. The chief seat of the manufacture in England is at Spitalfields.

Gros de Naples Ribbon.—This is a handsome make of ribbon, sufficiently described by its name, being called after a kind of Rep-made Italian silk, much in vogue.

Gros des Indes.—A French name for a silk textile, produced by the use of different shuttles with threads of various substances for the weft, by which means a stripe is formed transversely across the web.

Gros de Suez.—A description of silk stuff employed by milliners for lining bonnets. It is slight in substance, of narrow width, has a very small rib, and is known also as " Turquoise Silk."

Gros Grain.—A stout black silk, having a fine cord like that of Rep. The colour is dull, and therefore very suitable for mourning. It wears well, and the width varies according to the price. *See* GROGRAM.

Gros Point.—The French name for CROSS STITCH (which *see*).

Gross.—A term employed in commerce in reference to certain materials or appliances used in Needlework. It signifies twelve dozen.

Ground Downs.—A description of sewing Needle, so designated because they are cut shorter than the ordinary sewing needles called " Sharps," and formerly ground shorter, instead of being cut to the desired length.

Grounding—The background, or supposed foundation of any decorative design in tapestry, wool work, or other description of embroidery. In Berlin or German wool work, English wool is preferable to any other for grounding, as it is less quickly soiled, less deteriorated by brushing, and altogether more durable. The colour of a background or the " grounding " of a piece of embroidery should be selected with a view to showing off the colours of the design.

> L'ke bright metal on a sullen *ground.*
> —*Shakespeare.*

Grounds.—The grounds of Laces are divided into two kinds—one being called the Bride and the other the Réseau. The Bride grounds are formed with plain or ornamented Bars, taken across the open spaces left in the design in such a manner as to connect the ornaments forming the pattern together ; they are worked by the needle in Needle Laces, and on the Pillow in Pillow Laces.

To work Bride Grounds with the needle : Throw several threads across the space left between two parts of a design, and cover these with a thick line of BUTTONHOLE STITCHES ; ornament the BAR thus made with PICOTS while working, or leave it plain according to the pattern. To work Pillow Bride Ground : Hang on four pairs of

BOBBINS to a Pin hole by drawing up a loop of one pair through the edge and passing the other Bobbins through it, and work in CLOTH STITCH or in BEGINNERS' STEM to another edge in the pattern, to which attach the Bar by drawing up a pair of Bobbins as a loop through the edge, and passing the other pairs through it tail foremost ; draw this loop tightly, twist the Bobbins, and carry them on to the next Bar required. To work a Bride Ground ornamented with a Pearled Edge upon one side : Hang on the Bobbins as before, work across and back in Cloth Stitch, twist six times, take the last Bobbin on the right hand in the left hand, raise it, take a pin in the right hand, twist it once under the thread, so as to make a loop round the pin, put it in the Pinhole, take up the Bobbin next to it, and twist it once round the pin ; work back in Cloth Stitch to the left hand, and return again to the right, and repeat. When the required length is obtained, attach the Bar to the pattern as before described. To work a number of Bars so as to form a complicated Bride Ground *see* DEVONIA GROUND and HONITON GROUND.

The Réseau Grounds in Needle and Pillow Laces are much more difficult to make than the Bride Grounds, and from the time they take to execute, and the cost of the flax threads required for working them, they double the worth of the lace upon which they are executed. The foundation of all Réseau Grounds is a net pattern, and in Needle and Pillow Lace Ground is usually worked in the Brussels Net Ground, shown in Fig. 430 for the Needle made, and in Fig. 429 for the Pillow made. To work

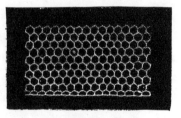

FIG. 429. GROUND PILLOW RÉSEAU.

Fig. 430 : Begin the ground at a corner, as the holes will not otherwise pull into shape ; fasten the thread to the lace or FIL DE TRACE, insert the needle at about the distance of one-sixteenth of an inch, bring it out as for a BUTTONHOLE, but twist the thread once round it, so as to make a twisted strand ; work to end of space, and at the end of each row fasten the thread to the lace with a strong stitch, and sew over and over the threads back to the commencement, putting two twists into each loop ; OVERCAST down the edge of the lace for 1-16 of an inch, and recommence making the row, putting the stitches this time into the loops made by the first row. The varieties of Needle made grounds, DAME JOAN, STAR, and STRAND, are described under their own headings. The Pillow Réseau Honeycomb ground (illustrated in Fig. 429) is worked but little at the present time, it having given place to the Pillow made Bride and the machine made net grounds. It is worked thus : Put up ten pairs of BOBBINS, make a whole CLOTH STITCH behind the pin on the right hand side, take up the pair nearest the left hand, and make a HALF STITCH with the pair next to it; twist each pair twice, and put up a pin between them; take the pair on the left hand side of the pin, and make a Half Stitch with the pair next to the left hand; twist each pair twice, and put up a pin between them; continue this with each pair to the end of the row; make a whole Cloth Stitch behind the left hand pin, and work back to the right with the same stitch. The varieties of Réseau grounds are ITALIAN and MECHLIN,

Guimpe.—The French word for GIMP (which *see*), while it also stands for a wimple.

Guimped Embroidery.—A description of Raised Embroidery largely used in ancient church embroideries. To work: Cut out from parchment the portions of the work to be guimped, and tack these pieces on to the foundation material. To cover this padding over: Bring gold, silver, or silk thread up from the back of the material and pass it over the parchment and put it down again to the back,

FIG. 430. GROUND NEEDLE RESEAU.

POINT DE PARIS, TORCHON, TROLLY, and VALENCIENNES, and they are mentioned under their own headings.

Gueuse Lace.—This lace was manufactured in France before the time of Colbert, and also during the seventeenth century, and is better known as Beggars' Lace. Gueuse lace is a thread lace made upon the Pillow, the ground is Réseau, and the Toilé worked with a thicker thread than the ground. The lace that is now made resembling it is called Torchon, and is not so good.

opposite to where it came up. Work in this manner until the padding is quite concealed.

Guipure.—A lace term which has gradually become so widely diffused as no longer to bear a definite designation. The word comes from Guipé, a thick cord or thread, round which gold, silver, or silk threads were twisted, and became a lace term, when it was applied to the cord introduced into lace that was covered over with thread, and used to raise into relief the chief parts of a design.

Guipure gradually came to be applied to all laces of large patterns that were connected with the Bride Ground or required no groundings, but as lately the word has also been applied to large flowing pattern laces worked with coarse net grounds, it is impossible to lay down any hard and fast rules about it, but no fine patterned laces or delicately grounded laces are ever known as Guipures. *See* GUIPURE LACE.

Guipure à Bride.—A term applied to Guipure laces whose grounds are made with BRIDES, to distinguish them from Guipures having no spaces left between the patterns.

Guipure Bar.—For the manner of working needle-made Guipure Bar *see* GUIPURE D'ART. To work a Pillow Guipure Bar: Throw out, while the pattern of the lace is in progress, four pair of BOBBINS, and work in CLOTH STITCH to the opposite side, and work the Bobbins into

Conté, but the patterns were also cut out of fine linen, and Appliqué to the ground. The work was then known as Lacis, although we find that term often used by old writers for the darned as well as the appliqué pattern. The Cluny Guipures of modern times are another revival of Opus Filatorium, and closely resemble Guipure d'Art. In ancient times the netted foundation and the pattern embroidered upon it were executed with gold and silver threads, or with coloured silk or flax, but the lace is now worked with the finest of linen thread when used for dress trimmings, and with a coarse thread if for furniture. A glazed thread or gimp can be run into the design as in Cluny Guipure.

The materials necessary for the work are wire frames of various sizes, with their wire foundation covered with flannel or ribbon, a wooden netting mesh, an ivory netting needle, long embroidery needles without points and with

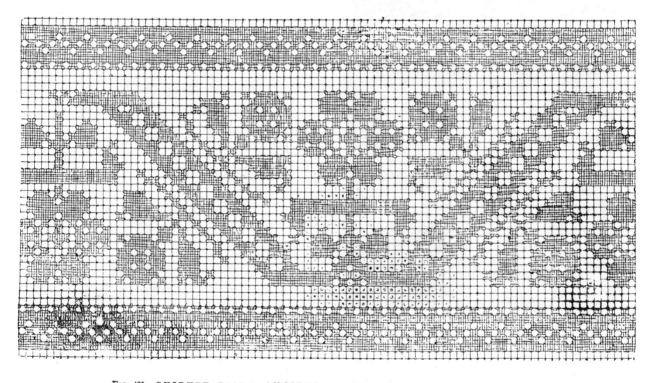

FIG. 431. GUIPURE D'ART—ANCIENTLY KNOWN AS OPUS FILATORIUM.

the lace at that point. Work the Bars alternately from side to side of the different parts of the patterns, so that the Bobbins taken away to form one Bar are returned by another if they are required.

Guipure d'Art.—In this lace, also known as Filet Brodé and Filet Guipure, we have the modern revival of the Opus Filatorium, or Darned Netting, or Spiderwork, so much used in the fourteenth century. During the Middle Ages this Network was called Opus Araneum, Ouvrages Masches, Punto a Maglia, Lacis, and Point Conté, and its patterns are found in Vinciola's book, published in 1588. The network ground at that time was called Rezel and Réseau, and is identical with Netting. When this ground was darned with a counted pattern the lace was known as Point

large eyes, and fine and coarse linen threads. To commence, the foundation has to be netted. The stitch used is the same as plain NETTING. For a square of lace, commence from one NETTING STITCH, and increase a stitch every row, until the width is formed. Then decrease a stitch every row, until only one stitch remains. For a long piece of lace, commence with one stitch, increase a stitch each row until the width is obtained, then net without increasing or decreasing until the length of the strip is worked, and then decrease every row until only one stitch remains. To make a circle foundation, net it as a square, and when in the frame mark out the circle with a thick row of BUTTONHOLE STITCHES, and cut away the foundation beyond the Buttonhole circle when the

H H

lace is completed. After the foundation is netted, attach it, by lashing each outer stitch separately to the frame. The foundation must fit exactly into the frame, and each mesh must be square and drawn out to its fullest extent. If this is not properly done, the stitches worked upon the squares will be irregular, and the lace spoilt.

The stitches are now commenced. In ancient designs only one stitch, Point de Toile or the plain darning stitch, was used for the Guipure, not raised from the surface, and this description of lace is illustrated in Fig. 431, p. 233, where the darned meshes form a conventional rose and leaf pattern connected together with diagonal lines. In the Guipure en Relief, or raised patterns of the same period, two or three stitches were introduced. These are illustrated in Fig. 432, where the netted foundation is covered over

FIG. 432. GUIPURE D'ART—GUIPURE EN RELIEF.

with Point d'Esprit, the thick parts of the pattern in Point de Toile, and the relief parts in Point de Reprise. The varieties of stitches that are now used in Guipure d'Art are of modern origin : they are, however, chiefly copied from old Needle Point laces, and their use serves to increase the value of the work and to enhance its beauty ; but not more than from four to six varieties should be worked in one design, or its uniformity and solidity will be destroyed. The different stitches are described under their various names. They are all worked on to the netted foundation as follows : Be careful that the netted foundation squares are perfectly true before commencing the stitches ; begin in one corner of a square by attaching the thread firmly to the knot, and work from side to side until that square is finished ; then run the thread over the line of the netted foundation to the next square, and work in that. Should the next stitch to be worked not commence

in the square immediately joining the last worked, CORD the thread over the lines of the intermediate squares, to conceal it until the place is reached. Solitary squares must be begun and fastened off in the square, but do not fasten off the thread unnecessarily, and take great care that the commencement and fastening off is perfectly secure. Fig. 433 is a working detail showing an unfinished square of lace, so as to give the manner of working. The centre is a POINT CROISÉ WHEEL surrounded with POINT DE FESTON in cone shape, and finished with long ovals, taken over one or two meshes, according to the size. These are surrounded with a line of POINT DE TOILE, worked to form a diamond and enclose the other stitches. The dots on the pattern indicate where the Point de Toile is to be worked to complete the diamond. The letters a, a, a, a, mark where POINT VENISE is worked

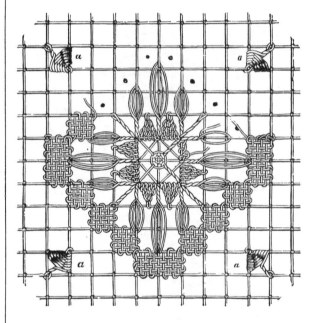

FIG. 433. GUIPURE D'ART—WORKING DETAIL.

on the four corners of the square. For manner of working the various stitches see their headings. When the netted foundation has been sufficiently covered, unpick it from the frame, and either surround it with an edging formed of BUTTONHOLES, or tack a narrow lace to it as a finish, or make it up in alternate squares with coloured silk or satin. In some Guipure d'Art designs the netted foundation is cut away, so as to leave quite open squares between the thick pattern parts. When this is done four or sixteen meshes are cut away, and the edges firmly Buttonholed round, PICOTS being formed over the knot of the netted foundation wherever it appears, thus securing the cut edges more firmly, and ornamenting the sides of the open space.

Cone.—This stitch is also known as Point Pyramide ; and is made of Point de Toile worked in a cone shape over the centre of four squares. To work : Take four meshes arranged as a square, and from the centre line at the top carry four threads down to the bottom line, fastening two at the outer knots on each side, and the other two at an even distance between these knots and the centre. These lines all meeting at the top in the centre and diverging over the whole space at the bottom, form the Cone or Pyramid. Interlace them with POINT DE TOILE, darning over and under each line, and take in the middle line of the mesh in the working. Fill in from the point to the bottom of the Cone, and keep the lines in their pyramid form and without dragging the stitch. Cone can be made with only three lines if required. It is then worked over three meshes upon one line, and a centre mesh above, instead of over a perfect square. Add the two outer lines and one as a centre, and form the two side lines of the Pyramid by the two sides of the middle mesh of the three on one line.

Cord Stitch.—This is a thick stitch worked round three sides of a square with a number of corded threads, and taking up six square meshes. To work: Carry a thread across the outer right hand square (*see* Fig. 434), and CORD

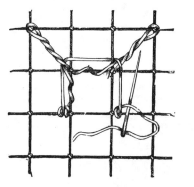

FIG. 434. GUIPURE D'ART—CORD STITCH—DETAIL A.

it back by twisting round it; then Cord it along the centre mesh and carry it across the left hand outer mesh, and Cord that back; Cord down the left side of the centre mesh, and pass the thread round three sides of it (as shown in Fig. 435), and return back by twisting the cotton

FIG. 435. GUIPURE D'ART—CORD STITCH.

round the thread; pass another thread round the three sides of the centre mesh, and Cord that back; work four lines until the stitch is finished, as shown in Fig. 435.

Etoile Stitch.—Also known as Star, and made to fill in nine or sixteen squares of a netted foundation, with combinations of Slip Stitch, Point de Toile, Point de Venise, or Point de Reprise, arranged to form stars. To

make an Etoile over sixteen squares (as shown in Fig. 437): Make SLIP STITCH over the four corners of the square of four meshes, crossing in the centre, as shown in Detail A (Fig. 436). Bring the thread out in the centre of the square, and wind it round and round, over and under the Slip Stitch, to form a close WHEEL: Work POINT

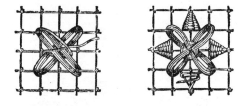

FIG. 436. ETOILE—DETAIL A.　　FIG. 437. ETOILE.

DE REPRISE as a CONE, so as to form the four points that complete the Etoile. To make an Etoile over four squares: Make a plain cross, and then a St. Andrew's Cross over the four squares, and form a Wheel centre by darning over and under the threads forming the crosses.

To make an Etoile over nine squares (as shown in Fig. 438): Work SLIP STITCH in each outside corner, and POINT DE TOILE to fill in the centre square, and the Cones that fill in the other squares and form the star. To make an Etoile over sixteen squares: Make a cross from the four corners of the outer squares, and knot the cross to the netted foundation in

FIG. 438. ETOILE.

the centre. Then Slip Stitch round every outer knot of the square, and take the stitch to the centre each time. Treat the cross just made as a knot, and Slip Stitch round it, so that sixteen rays are formed. Each ray is formed with three threads passed round the knot and into the centre. Complete the Star with a close WHEEL centre. Fancy Etoiles can be made so as to entirely fill in a whole square of lace with a star-shape pattern like Fig. 439 and 440, or so as to fill in the four corners of a square, like Fig. 441 (page 236).

To work Fig. 439: Work a POINT CROISÉ as a

FIG. 439. GUIPURE D'ART—ETOILE, FORMED OF MALTESE POINT.　　FIG. 440. GUIPURE D'ART—ETOILE, FORMED OF POINT DE TOILE.

centre, and fill in the four squares round it with MALTESE POINT. Leave the four squares beyond the Maltese Point ones plain, and fill the ones at the side with WHEELS, and work POINT DE TOILE over the rest of the netted foundation.

To work Fig. 440: Make an eight-armed WHEEL over the four centre squares, with a BUTTONHOLE square as a finish. Work POINT DE TOILE in pyramid shape in the four squares on each side surrounding the Wheel, and outline the lace with a Buttonhole edge. Fig. 441

· FIG. 441. GUIPURE D'ART—ETOILES, FORMED WITH POINT DE VENISE.

illustrates Etoiles used at the four corners of a square. The Etoiles make with POINT DE VENISE, the thick part of the design with Point de Toile, and the open part with POINT D'ESPRIT and Wheels.

Genoa Stitch.—Used in the making of Greek Lace as well as in Guipure d'Art, and resembling the Point de Reprise used in Guipure en Relief. Genoa Stitch is worked over two or three foundation threads, according to the thickness of the Bar it is to form. To work over two foundation threads, as shown in Fig. 442: Pass two threads across the space to be filled, secure them

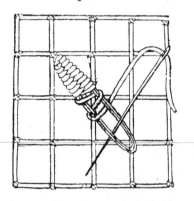

FIG. 442. GUIPURE D'ART—GENOA STITCH.

tightly, and leave one-eighth of an inch between them, then darn over and under the two threads until a solid compact line is made, with a plait in the centre. To work over three foundation threads: Cross the space to be filled with three threads, putting them not quite an eighth of an inch apart, and darn in and out of them as before; the third thread will make the thick close line wider than the one formed with only two foundation threads.

Guipure Bar.—Only occasionally used in Guipure en Relief as part of the design. To work: Either throw a

thread across a square mesh and cover it with a thick line of BUTTONHOLE, or use the netted foundation for the Bar, and work over that a close, thick row of Buttonhole.

Guipure en Relief.—The most effective ornament to Guipure is the Raised Work that is made as part of the design, and that is worked over the flat stitches that fill in the netted foundation. This Raised Work is principally formed of Genoa Stitch or in Point de Reprise, arranged as sprays of leaves and flowers, quite separate from the work beneath; but large raised crosses and stars and long lines

FIG. 443. GUIPURE EN RELIEF—FLOWER SPRAY.

can be formed with it. The foundation beneath the raised work is sometimes left plain, but is generally filled in with either POINT DE TOILE or POINT D'ESPRIT. To work Guipure en Relief: Fasten the thread across two or more squares, according to the length of the leaf, and make an oval with it, then darn the thread thickly in and out of this oval.

To work the spray shown in Fig. 443: For the petals of the flower, throw the thread across two squares and form an oval, and then bring a thread up the centre of the oval, darn in and out between these three threads, the additional thread giving the veined look to the petals. Work all the

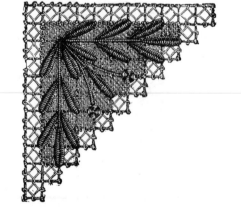

FIG. 444. GUIPURE EN RELIEF—CORNER.

petals in this manner, and fill the centre of the flower with a WHEEL. Work the leaves in the same way and form the stems with a thread thickly OVERCAST. Connect the stems to the netted foundation by occasionally including that in the Overcast.

To work the corner shown in Fig. 444: Commence

the netted foundation with one stitch, work ten rows, and increase a stitch each row. Fill in the outside line of stitches with POINT D'ESPRIT and the whole of the interior with POINT DE TOILE. Over the last work the Guipure en Relief; the leaves in GENOA STITCH, as shown in Fig. 442, the stems in OVERCAST, and the buds as close WHEELS.

To work the lappet shown in Fig. 445: NET the foundation and BUTTONHOLE round the edge. Work the stars in POINT DE TOILE, the loops proceeding from them as OVALS, and the twelve-armed star in GENOA STITCH, with three foundation threads, distinct from foundation,

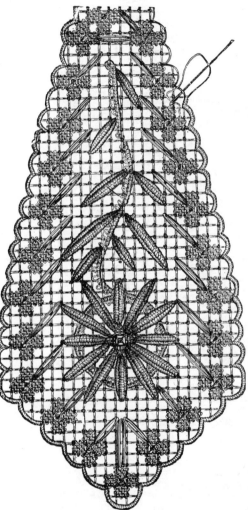

FIG. 445. GUIPURE EN RELIEF—LAPPET.

as shown in Fig. 446, and the leaves in the same stitch; for the stem and the circle Buttonhole a thread laid over the foundation, and ornament it with loops as PICOTS. Cut away those parts of the foundation that are not required when the work is finished.

To work the corner shown in Fig. 446: NET the foundation as before mentioned, fill in the outside line of stitches with POINT DE TOILE and the rest of the netting with POINT CROISÉ. Work the sprays of leaves in GENOA STITCH, as shown in Fig. 442, and the stems in OVERCAST. For the seed vessel, work the centre in Point de Toile,

and fill in four squares of the foundation with that stitch. Darn over the outside of these squares in the oval shape shown in the illustration, so as to raise that part above the centre. Work three small Genoa Stitch leaves at

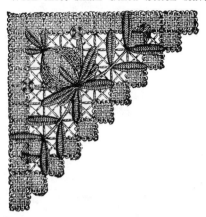

FIG. 446. GUIPURE EN RELIEF—CORNER.

the point of the seed vessel, and four large and three small leaves at the base. Make the buds of close WHEELS, and with Point de Toile and SLIP STITCH.

Jours.—These are the open stitches in Guipure, and are so called to distinguish them from the thick stitches. The term includes Point d'Esprit, Point Croisé, Ovales, Point de Gerbe, and Wheels formed with Point d'Esprit.

Maltese Point.—A variety of Cone or Pyramid, and deriving its name from its stitches being arranged so that four of them form a Maltese Cross. To work: Twist the thread for a short distance round the lower line of a square mesh, then loop it round the upper line and return it to the lower, so that the two lines form a pyramid; twist the thread up one of these to the top, and interlace these two threads together with POINT DE

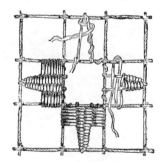

FIG. 447. GUIPURE D'ART—MALTESE POINT.

VENISE for half the length of the square (*see* Fig. 447); then carry the thread so as to take in the netted outer lines of square, and work in Point de Venise down to the bottom of the square, passing the thread over and under the four lines each time.

Ovals.—These are long loops of an oval shape worked in the centre of a square mesh, or in the centre of four meshes. To work: Twist the thread round the netted foundation until it reaches the centre of a square, then carry it down from the top to the bottom line of the mesh, loop it through and bring it back to where it started from;

loop it through at that place, and form the Oval with three loops, then twist the thread round the netted foundation

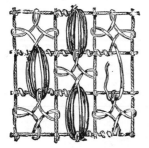

FIG. 443. GUIPURE D'ART—OVALS AND POINT D'ESPRIT STITCH.

to the next square.   Fig. 448 is an illustration of a piece of

Picot.—These ornaments to the edge of Wheels, Bars, and the outer edge of Guipure, are made in various ways. To finish a Bar or an Edge with a fringe of loops: Work a BUTTONHOLE upon the Bar, and insert the needle into the lower part of it, to make a loop at its edge, then continue the row of Buttonholes, and work a loop into every third Buttonhole.

To ornament a Wheel or a Bar with a thick Picot: Make a BUTTONHOLE into the edge of the foundation, leave the working thread plain for the eighth of an inch, then make a tight Buttonhole upon it, two upon the space left plain, and one into the foundation close to the first made Buttonhole. Picots are also made round a knot of the netted foundation in the shape of a cross or star; they then form part of the design of the lace in the manner illustrated in Fig. 449.

FIG. 449. GUIPURE D'ART—SHOWING STAR, PICOTS, GUIPURE EN RELIEF, AND POINT DE TOILE.

Guipure where four Ovals form an open cross, with corners and centre filled in with POINT D'ESPRIT.

Overcast.—Used to form the fine stems to the leaves in Guipure en Relief. To make: Either cover a line of the netted foundation with close OVERCAST STITCHES, or throw a thread across the lace, secure it with a knot, and Overcast over that.

To work as a cross: Fasten the thread securely and push the needle half through the knot, so that the point comes out in one of the angles of the mesh; wind the thread round the needle from right to left ten times, place the left thumb upon it to keep it steady, and pull the needle through, leaving the wound threads forming a thick loop between the meshes. Secure this with an OVERCAST, and push the needle again half through the knot and bring it out in another angle and repeat. Fill in the four angles surrounding the knot so as to make a cross in this manner.

To make the eight pointed star in Fig. 449 (page 238): Work a POINT CROISÉ over a square of four meshes, knot it to the foundation in the centre, then fill in each angle as described in the Star. The remainder of the design work as follows: The centre work in POINT DE TOILE, BUTTONHOLE round its edge, and ornament it with GUIPURE EN RELIEF in a Star pattern. Surround this centre with a diamond in Point de Toile, and form the thick outer edge with the same stitch, where ornament it with HERRINGBONE worked over it; run lines of thick Glacé thread upon each side of the thick edges, and connect the last to the Buttonhole surrounding the inner square with a line of Herringbone.

Point Croisé.—This stitch is either used for grounding a design in the same manner as Point d'Esprit, or to fill in single meshes, and it is varied by being made with either a plain or twisted thread. The stitch consists of two lines of Point Serré, forming a cross in a mesh, which is finished with a single Buttonhole on a rosette in the centre, where the four threads meet. To work simple Point Croisé: Work a line of POINT SERRÉ across a certain number of square meshes, from left to right of the lace, and return back over the same meshes with another line of Point Serré, but where the second line crosses the

FIG. 450. GUIPURE D'ART TWISTED POINT CROISÉ.

first in the centre of the square, make a single BUTTONHOLE with it over the diagonal line there, then take it down to the lower left knot of the mesh, twist it round, and pass it into the next mesh. Buttonhole it over the diagonal line there, and take it up to the top left hand knot of that mesh, and repeat until all are filled with the cross.

To work a twisted Point Croisé: Make a loose loop from the left hand top knot to the right hand top knot of a mesh, and twist the thread back to the centre, then loop

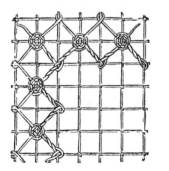

FIG. 451. GUIPURE D'ART—POINT CROISÉ.

it into the right hand lower knot, and twist it back to the centre, then into the left hand lower knot, and twist back into the centre, unite the threads with a Buttonhole or form a close WHEEL (as shown in Fig. 450), and

finally twist the thread up the first loop to the place it started from.

To work Fig. 451, which is a combination of the twisted and simple Point Croisé, over four meshes: Take a diagonal line across two meshes from left to right, and twist this up to the centre; take the thread down to the left hand lower knot, twist it up to the centre; here make a close WHEEL round the three threads, and then pass the thread, without twisting it, up to the top right hand knot, and commence another stitch over the next four meshes.

Point de Bruxelles, also called *Point de Feston* (which *see*).

Point d'Esprit.—This is a light open stitch, most used in Guipure, as it fills in the netted squares with many varieties of design, the foundation of all being a simple loop. It can be worked as a single loop in each square, as shown in Fig. 452, or as four loops in a square, also shown in Fig. 452, or as an interlaced thread, as

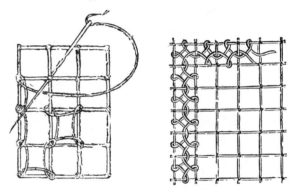

FIG. 452. POINT D'ESPRIT.   FIG. 453. POINT D'ESPRIT.

shown in Fig. 453, or as filling in the entire ground of the netting, except where a thick pattern is worked in Guipure en Relief (*see* Fig. 432), or as a Wheel or Star; in fact, the combinations that can be made with it are numerous. To work for a single line: Fasten the thread close to a knot in the square, put the needle under the next knot, and draw up loosely so as to make a loose BUTTONHOLE (*see* Fig. 452), and work a row of these loose Buttonholes one into every square. To fill in a square: Work a loose Buttonhole over every knot of the netted foundation. To interlace: Work a loose Buttonhole into every mesh, not round the knot, but in the centre, and return by a similar row of Buttonholes on the line beneath those just made, interlacing the second loops with the first made ones over the side lines of each mesh (*see* Fig. 453).

To make Diamonds with Point d'Esprit: Fasten the thread at the right hand top knot of the square, put it under the bottom line of the square without looping it, and then over the left hand top knot without looping it; work the whole line so, and then return back with the same stitch, only varied, by taking in the old thread with the new. Where they meet in the centre of a square, a diamond is formed by the points of the stitches in the two rows.

For interlaced Point d'Esprit with an open round in the centre: This requires four square meshes, two each way; work a single BUTTONHOLE line round the outside of all the squares, and then run the thread into the loose part of every loop, and draw it up as a circle, and finish by OVERCASTING this circle. For WHEELS in Point d'Esprit *see* WHEELS.

Point de Feston.—This consists of a Buttonhole Stitch worked from side to side of the mesh, either as a single line to form a border to a pattern, or as a number of lines to fill in a mesh with a pyramid-shaped design. To work as a Border: Fasten the working thread to a knot, and OVERCAST round each side of the various meshes that are to form the border to the lace, or to that piece of the pattern. Work close rows of BUTTONHOLE over this Overcast, and ornament the thick line thus formed with PICOTS, or leave it quite plain.

To work to fill in successive meshes, and as shown in Fig. 454: Begin at the left side of a mesh and work six loose BUTTONHOLES to the opposite end, making each stitch loose enough to allow of a needle being put into it. Work back from right to left, and make four loose Buttonholes, fastening them into the four centre Buttonholes of the last row. Work again from left to right with three

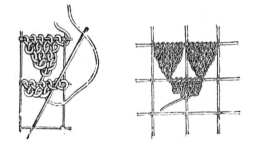

FIG. 454. GUIPURE D'ART—POINT DE FESTON.　　FIG. 455. GUIPURE D'ART—POINT DE FESTON.

Buttonholes fastened into the centre stitches of the last row; return with two stitches, and finish with only one Buttonhole quite in the centre, and forming a point. Pull this stitch down to the square beneath, and fasten it there in the centre of the line, then OVERCAST to the left of that mesh, and commence another stitch.

To work Fig. 455: Fill in a square mesh as described above, but with eight BUTTONHOLES, and when the last stitch is reached, instead of Overcasting along the square beneath it to the left and filling that mesh, commence at once to work Buttonholes to the right, and work four Buttonholes upon half that mesh, and four upon the mesh on the right hand next to it; work the stitch as before, but upon each side of two meshes, and not in the centre of one. Point de Feston is sometimes used instead of POINT DE TOILE or POINT DE REPRISE to fill in a mesh; it is then made with straight rows of eight Buttonholes worked backwards and forwards without diminution until the entire square is filled in.

Point de Gerbe.—So called from the resemblance the stitch bears when completed to a sheaf of corn. It is a variety of Point Faisceau. To work: Loop the thread

over the top line of the mesh, and secure it after looping with a BUTTONHOLE, then simply loop it over the lower line of mesh without securing it; repeat the stitch in the same square five times, and then draw the threads together in the centre by enclosing them all in a Buttonhole.

Point de Repasse.—See *Point de Toile.*

Point de Reprise.—This is a thick stitch, and will be found in nearly all patterns, either filling in one separate netted square or a number together with thick lines of thread. To work for one square: Pass the needle under the top line of the square and over the bottom, and work upwards and downwards until the square is filled (*see* Fig. 456).

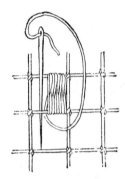

FIG. 456. GUIPURE D'ART—POINT DE REPRISE.

To work several squares together: Pass the needle over and under each thread of a mesh until the last is reached, then return with a similar line back, only reversing the over and under so that the threads interlace.

To work large netted meshes quite thick: Make a foundation of four diagonal lines to fill in the square, and then darn these in and out and backwards and forwards, including the outer lines of foundation in the darning, and forming the ribbed appearance shown in Fig. 457.

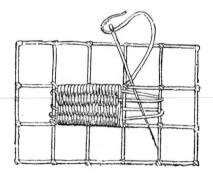

FIG. 457. GUIPURE D'ART—POINT DE REPRISE.

Point de Toile.—Also known as Point de Repasse, and one of the stitches most used in Guipure, as either it or Point de Reprise are worked to form the thick parts of most designs. It is a simple darn, worked with great care and exactitude in and out the meshes, and so filling in their centres. Each mesh can be separately darned over, or a whole row darned over at once, the important part of the stitch being that the same number of threads are used

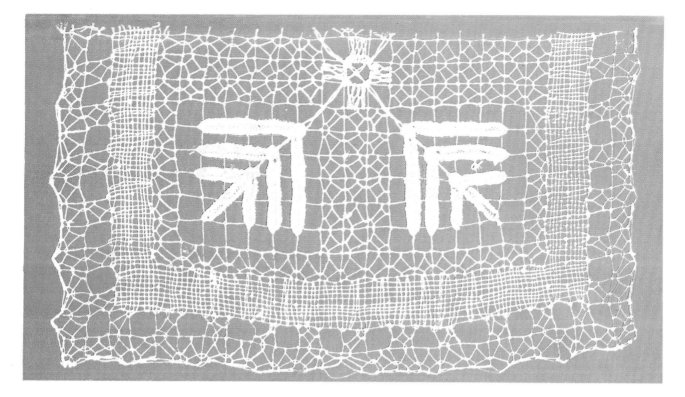

GUIPURE D'ART.

MACRAMÉ   MODERN POINT.

in every square, any departure from this rule entailing a loss of regularity in the work. To work Point de Toile as one square: Fasten the thread firmly in one corner of the mesh to be filled, then pass the needle round the thread of the mesh nearest it, cross to the opposite side, pass it over that thread, bring it back to where it started from, and repeat, so that four or six threads, according to the size of the mesh, are laid across the square; then slip the thread round the corner, and darn in and out of these threads, by taking and leaving each alternate thread. Darn in four or six threads corresponding with the number laid across.

To work Point de Toile as shown in Fig. 458, and over several squares: Take the longest line of squares, and pass the four or six threads from end to end of them, over and under each mesh as they reach it; then slip the thread round the last corner, and darn as before if the stitch is to cover one long single line of meshes; but when it is required to form several thick squares in different directions, place the threads across in position both for their length and width before they

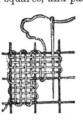

FIG. 458. GUIPURE D'ART —POINT DE TOILE.

are darned together, and darn straight down their width at once without reference to the number of squares to be filled in.

Point de Venise.—A stitch largely used in Guipure to fill in the angles of meshes, and also in Guipure en Relief to form raised masses. Different designs can be made by the various arrangements of Point de Venise in angles, but the stitch is the same in all of them. To work single Point de Venise: This consists of filling in only one angle of a square, and is shown in Fig. 459. Carry a thread diagonally across a mesh, twist it round the upper knot, and loop it backwards and forwards over the two sides of the mesh, so as to interlace the diagonal thread each time,

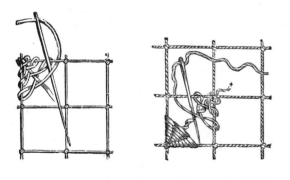

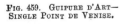

FIG. 459. GUIPURE D'ART—
SINGLE POINT DE VENISE.

FIG. 460. GUIPURE D'ART—DOUBLE
POINT DE VENISE.

and cover over the three threads and form a triangle. Work until the mesh is half filled; then CORD up the diagonal thread, and commence in another square.

To work Double Point de Venise, as shown in Fig. 460: Work as before, but before the centre of the mesh is quite reached CORD up the diagonal line, and make another Point de Venise into the corner opposite the one first filled.

Single Point de Venise is frequently worked as shown in Fig. 461, in the corner angles of nine meshes, the other meshes being filled in with WHEELS made with POINT CROISÉ, and with a centre of POINT DE TOILE.

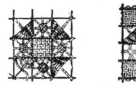 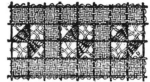

FIG. 461. GUIPURE D'ART—POINT
DE VENISE, POINT CROISÉ,
POINT DE TOILE, & WHEEL.

FIG. 462. GUIPURE D'ART—BORDER
OF POINT DE VENISE, POINT
D'ESPRIT, AND POINT DE TOILE.

A good border pattern is made as shown in Fig. 462, with Point de Toile, POINT D'ESPRIT, and Single Point de Venise.

Point Eventail.—A variety of POINT DE VENISE, and a stitch formed by filling up with a three-quarter Wheel three of the centre corners of four meshes. Point Eventail is made in two ways; the simplest, illustrated in Fig. 463, is worked as follows: Fasten the working thread

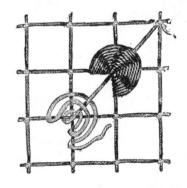

FIG. 463. GUIPURE D'ART—POINT EVENTAIL.

diagonally across a mesh and wind it round the lower knot, and then over and under as in darning the four threads of the meshes and the one thread across the mesh just added. Do not darn the thread as a continuous

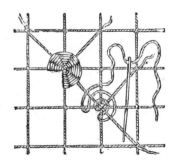

FIG. 464. GUIPURE D'ART—POINT EVENTAIL.

round, but loop it back each time it reaches the two outer threads of the mesh, so that it forms a three-quarter WHEEL and leaves one side of the knot unenclosed. When a large enough Wheel is formed, run the thread

I I

close up to the knot and pass it diagonally across the mesh on that side at the part not filled in and commence another stitch.

To work Fig. 464: Before commencing the stitch, carry a separate thread in a diagonal direction across three or four meshes; then fasten the working thread in a contrary diagonal direction across a mesh, so as to meet the first thread at a knot, and darn in and out the six lines that there meet in the same way as already described, leaving one side of the knot free.

Point Faisceau.—A stitch not much used in Guipure, but forming a variety of Point de Toile and Point de Feston for filling in thick parts of the lace. When worked it presents the appearance of a number of Herringbone Stitches united together with a loop in the centre. To work: Fasten the thread securely to the left hand top knot of a square mesh, take it down to the bottom, and loop it there round the bottom thread and secure it with two turns round that thread, take it up to the top, loop round, and secure it as before; take it down again to the bottom, cross it over the last thread in so doing, and secure it. Continue to pass up and down the mesh in this way until it is filled with ten threads, then fill in the next square with the same stitch and any others in the pattern. Finish by fastening a fresh thread where the first was fastened, carry this down to the centre of the first square, and make a BUTTONHOLE, taking in all the ten threads in it; run the thread up to the right-hand top knot of the mesh and fasten there, and then down into the middle of the second mesh, where repeat the Buttonhole, and continue to repeat the Buttonhole in every square.

Point Lâche.—A stitch worked diagonally across a mesh to form a filled-in triangle. To work: Fasten the thread to the top left-hand knot of the mesh, secure it with a BUTTONHOLE round the top line, then pass the thread to the left-hand line of the mesh, and there secure it with a Buttonhole, and continue to pass the thread between the two lines, and Buttonhole it to them until it fills in the mesh to the centre with a number of diagonal lines.

Point Pyramide.—See Cone.

Point Serré.—A variety of Point de Feston worked as a single line or as a filled-in diamond in the centre of four square meshes. It consists of a POINT DE FESTON drawn tight at each stitch instead of being left as a loop. To work as a singe line: Loop the thread round the bottom left-hand knot of a square, and then round the top right-hand knot, draw it up tight, and continue to the end of the space. (This is shown in the top line of Fig. 465.) For the rest of the design, work

FIG. 465. GUIPURE D'ART—
POINT SERRÉ.

a close diamond as a centre, surrounded by SLIP STITCH.

To work as a diamond: Loop the thread round the centre knot of four squares, and then round every thread of the foundation that holds that knot in succession. Work round the knot seven times with these loops,

until the close diamond, shown in Fig. 466, is made. To finish Fig. 466, work three more of the close diamonds, and surround them with interlaced POINT D'ESPRIT and a line of BUTTONHOLE scallops.

FIG. 466. GUIPURE D'ART—POINT SERRÉ.

Point Tiellage.—An open stitch formed of crossed threads, and worked as follows: Carry the thread diagonally across a mesh, and twist it round the knot so that it comes out at the back of the next mesh. Run up the netted foundation across the squares with this

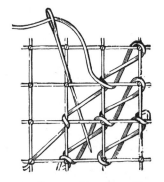

FIG. 467. GUIPURE D'ART—POINT TIELLAGE.

stitch (see Fig. 467), and to return make the same stitch back, but reverse the direction of the diagonal line, so that it crosses the first one in the centre of every square.

Rayleigh Bar.—Worked like Guipure Bar, but instead of straight Bars along a design, work irregularly shaped Bars.

Rone.—Also called Wheel and Spider Stitch, and made either with Point Croisé and Point de Toile, or of Point d'Esprit. To work as shown in Fig. 468, with POINT CROISÉ: Pass the thread across into the four corners of the square and into the centre of the four sides, and twist it up each thread in returning to the centre. Then pass it over and under each thread as in POINT DE TOILE until a large rosette is formed in the centre. The outer edge of this rosette can be ornamented with PICOTS. The size of the Rones made in this manner are varied by the number of the squares of the netted foundation they are worked over, one square being the smallest, sixteen the largest, and four squares the usual size. Rones of Point d'Esprit are made

FIG. 468. GUIPURE
D'ART—RONE.

thus: Work upon a square made of four meshes, and fill in with an open Rone made in two ways. For one, work a POINT D'ESPRIT in every square, and connect the loops together with a thread run into them to draw them

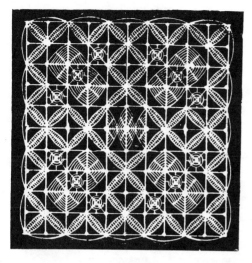

FIG. 469. GUIPURE D'ART—ARRANGEMENTS OF RONES.

together, and make an open round; for the other, make a POINT CROISÉ from the four corners of the square and

half way between the centre knot and the Point d'Esprit edging.

Fig. 469 illustrates various arrangements of Rones. The thick parts of the pattern are made of GENOA STITCH as worked in GUIPURE EN RELIEF, the Rones filling in one square of POINT CROISÉ, while the Spider web Rones are made as follows: Take a foundation thread across the square from corner to corner, and CORD it back up to the centre, run the thread from this to the knot and Cord it back to the foundation thread and along to where it first commenced. Then fill in the angle with lines of thread at even distances apart, and loop each line round the thread taken to the knot when they come to it. To make a perfect Rone fill in the angles of four squares with this stitch, but in the illustration, with the exception of the centre, only three angles are thus filled, and the fourth is filled with a Point Croisé Wheel.

Slip Stitch.—Worked as Point Lâche to fill in half a mesh with a thick triangle, but as a series of loops from corner to corner without the securing Buttonhole (see *Point Lâche*).

Spider.—See *Rone*.

Wheel.—See *Rone*.

Guipure de Flandre.—The name given generally to old Flemish Laces made on the pillow, to distinguish them from the Flemish Laces made with the needle.

Guipure en Relief.—*See* GUIPURE D'ART.

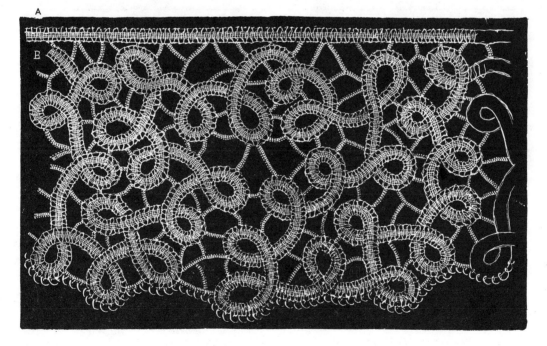

FIG. 470. GUIPURE LACE.

knot it together in the centre, work a loose Point d'Esprit in every square, counting the threads as a square so that eight Point d'Esprit are made. Draw these loops together with a thread run round them, to form an open circle

Guipure Laces.—The making both of Braid and Tape Guipures and the more elaborate kinds, such as Flemish Point or Point de Brabant, differs but slightly from that used in Honiton Lace, which is a Guipure worked with very fine thread, a variety of stitches, and with Raised Work, while the ordinary Braid Guipures are worked with coarse thread and with Cloth Stitch, joined by Bars, and with plain patterns; and the Flemish Points without Work in Relief. The method of dressing the Pillow, pricking the patterns, winding the Bobbins, and making the stitches are the same in all, and are described under their own headings; therefore it will not be necessary to recapitulate them for these coarser laces. To work the pattern, Fig. 470, which is entirely formed with Braid and Bars, and is a copy of a lace made in the seventeenth century: Prick the pattern upon parchment, and mount it upon the PILLOW, with the straight tape edge to the right. Dress the Pillow, and hang on seven pairs of BOBBINS, filled with fine thread, and a pair

Plain Edge until the first curve is reached; round the curve with FALSE PINHOLES on the inside until the place where the braid crosses is reached; make a SEWING by drawing up a thread with the crochet hook and passing the next Bobbin through the loop tail foremost; make this Sewing upon each side of the Braid, working over the Braid to prevent it from moving when taken off the Pillow; drive the pins in at the places where the Sewings are made, so that they do not catch in the lace, and as the work proceeds remove these pins, leaving only a sufficient number to keep the lace in its place. Work with Cloth Stitch and Plain Edge all the rest of the pattern, making the curves with False Pinholes in the inside, and attaching the pattern wherever it touches either the curves or the

Fig. 471. FLEMISH POINT GUIPURE LACE.

filled with GIMP. Tie the pairs together, wind the knots out of the way, and then knot them all together and pin them to the pillow where the letter A is shown in pattern, pushing in the pin to its head. Arrange the Bobbins as three working pairs or Runners, four Hangers or Passive pairs, and the Gimps to strengthen the edge, and work the straight piece of Braid that borders the work for the length of the pattern in CLOTH STITCH and PLAIN EDGE; leave the Bobbins hanging so as to continue this edge when the pattern is shifted, and tie up eight new pairs, filled with fine thread, into the pinhole marked B in the illustration. Divide these new Bobbins into three pairs of Runners and five pairs of Hangers, and commence to work the looped part of the braid with them. Work in Cloth Stitch with

straight braid edge with Sewings. Having finished the pattern, work the BARS with PURL EDGE that connect it together thus: Take eight pair of Bobbins, wind the knots out of the way, attach them to the Plain Edge at a Bar by drawing up a loop of one pair through the edge, and passing the others through it, draw up tight, and work Cloth Stitch across, and without setting up a pin, work back, twist six times, take the last Bobbin on the right hand in the left hand, raise it, take a pin in the right hand, twist it once under the thread in a loop round the pin, put it in the Pinhole, take up the Bobbin next it, twist it once round the pin, work back in Cloth Stitch to the left hand, return again to the right without putting up a pin on the right, put up a Purl pin, and work in this manner until the Bar is completed and the place it is to be joined to is reached, then draw up a loop with the hook, and pass two of the Bobbins through it tail foremost; draw the loop tightly up, cut off two pairs of Bobbins, being careful that they are not the ones used in making the loop or those that passed through it; twist the remaining four very tightly, and carry them on to the next Bar if close to the last made, if not, cut off and plait up all the Bobbins, and hang them on where required. The Bars can be made like the BRIDES in Needle laces with BUTTONHOLE, and ornamented with PICOTS instead of being made on the Pillow. When the pattern is completed as far as shown in illustration, and it is wished to continue it, take up all the pins, leaving those at the last

open work between the leaves, by either working with the whole forty-four Bobbins from side to side, making one LADDER STITCH and steadying it with a pin, or by twisting a pair of Bobbins first from A into B and then from B into A until the end of the leaf is reached. Work the BARS in this pattern, when the tracing of them is reached, with four pairs of Bobbins thrown out upon each side, and make them alternately from side to side, so as not to decrease the number of Bobbins, make them either by rolling the top Bobbins round and round, drawing one up through the Pinhole, passing a Bobbin through the loop tail foremost, and drawing up the loop; or by working them in Cloth Stitch, and adding Purl Pin Work. The working the Bars at the same time as the lace makes it

FIG. 472. GUIPURE LACES.

part of the work still in the lace; roll up the lace finished in a small bag, and re-arrange its end over the commencement of the pattern, take up the Bobbins laid aside with the straight edge, and work that part first, and then pick up those that formed the curved braid and continue as before.

To work the Flemish Point Guipure, as shown in Figs. 471 and 472: Prick off the pattern, and trace the outlines of the Bars with a fine pen. Dress the PILLOW, and put the pattern on to it with the Purl pins on the left hand side; put up twenty pairs of BOBBINS at A, and twenty-four pairs at B, and work down with both sets in CLOTH STITCH as far as the division, making the small holes in the curved piece, as shown in HOLE STITCH and BRAID and the

necessary to put up all the Bobbins at the same time, and is a little confusing, but the Bobbins not in immediate use can be rolled up out of the way, and where the pattern narrows they can be tied off gradually and again added at the side pins where it widens. Put up for the Purl Edge and for the FOOTING when commencing the lace, six pairs of Bobbins for the Purl, and four pairs for the Footing. The small wheel in leaf A, work in WHEEL STITCH. Work leaf C in Cloth Stitch with Wheels, form the centre with two rows of PINHOLES, and the knots between them make with a Cloth Stitch with a pair of Bobbins taken from each side, put in the pin, give the Bobbins three twists both before and after making the stitch. To work leaf D: Put up Bobbins at D, and work round the curve with FALSE

PINHOLES, work in Cloth Stitch and Ladder Stitch. To work leaf E: Work in Cloth Stitch on its left side, and in Hole Stitch on its right. The leaf F work with Cloth Stitch, Hole Stitch, and a Wheel. Work leaf G in Cloth Stitch and in SLANTING HOLE STITCH thus: Work with twelve Bobbins, take the four on the right hand and work to the pin, leave them hanging, and take the two first pairs after the pin, twist them twice and leave them hanging; take the second pair, twist them twice, and leave them hanging, and continue this up to the last pair on the left hand side; return to the right hand four behind the pin, work them over to the left side, give the Runners a twist twice between each stitch until the work is carried across and the pin worked in, then twist the pair in front of the pin twice, and leave them hanging; twist each pair twice, and take up the left hand Bobbin behind the pin; work in the pin and twist the Runners twice between each pair of Bobbins, work back to the right hand. The curved leaves near G work in Cloth Stitch, with Hole Stitch and Wheel where drawn. The leaf H work in Cloth Stitch down the outer side, Ladder in the centre, and Wheel on the left side. Where the Bars form a triangle at the point of H unite the two sets of Bobbins that work the two Bars, and make with them the third Bar. To work the Cone marked I set up three sets of Bobbins at the three points of the cone, work the centre point in Cloth Stitch, with Knots between each Pinhole, as described for leaf C. In the right hand point make a hole decorated with PURL PIN, and all the lower leaves with one or two holes decorated in the same manner. Work the stem in Cloth Stitch, and make the open work between the leaves by twisting the Bobbins and putting in a pin. Work leaves J, K, L in Cloth Stitch with Hole Stitch on the under side and Ladder Stitch to divide them. Commence the flower, M, in the centre with a Wheel, and bring the Bobbins down for the under part and stem. Work the right hand part of the leaf underneath the letter M in LATTICE STITCH, the left hand part of the same leaf in Cloth Stitch, with the divisions made by twisting the Bobbins and putting up pins, and be careful to add Bobbins for any wider part. Commence the leaf N at the under part of the curve, work in Cloth Stitch with Holes, adding Bobbins at O and P, and decorate this leaf with Purl Pin. Commence leaf Q at the curved point, work in Cloth Stitch and OPEN CROSS STITCH. Work the under part in Cloth Stitch, with additional Bobbins put up at the points, and work down and tie off, and when R is reached leave enough threads to work up round R, S, T, and U, and then tie them off. Work round all these leaves with Purl Pin. Having worked the pattern, remove the lace from the pillow and roll it up in a piece of clean linen, pin it flatly again on the pillow at the upper part of the pattern, and recommence the work. The illustration, Fig. 472, is the same pattern as Fig. 471, but without the letters.

Figs. 473 and 474 illustrate an insertion and edging made of coarse lace thread (No. 40), or with black silk or écru coloured mohair. The pricked pattern and the lace are both given to show the manner of working, which is extremely easy. To work Fig. 473 prick the pattern, put up twenty-four BOBBINS for the edging, ten Bobbins for each border, and four for the lozenges in the centre. Work in CLOTH STITCH, detach two of the centre Bobbins and

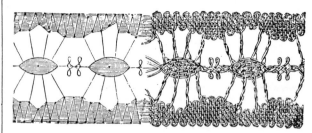

FIG. 473. GUIPURE INSERTION.

twist to form the Bars, and make the loops in the centre with PURL PIN. Work the edging, Fig. 474, in Cloth Stitch, twist the threads for the Bars, plait them together

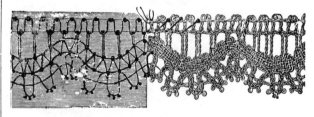

FIG. 474. GUIPURE EDGING.

to form the plaited edge, and ornament the scallops with Purl Pin in the same way.

Guipure Renaissance.—An embroidery worked in imitation of the Tape Guipure Laces, and made with coarse cheese cloth, écru coloured cords of various sizes, and écru sewing silk. The work is used for mats, antimacassars, and furniture lace. To work as shown in Fig. 475: Select the kind of cheese cloth that is used to strain cream through, three sizes of ordinary cord, and a fine cord made of écru silk. Commence by making the largest centre round of the largest sized cord, then fold pieces of the cheese cloth into eight wedge-shaped pieces, and secure their turned-in edges at the back; stitch these on to the round of cord, make a smaller round with the second sized cord, and stitch the points of the wedges to this. Sew inside the second cord a round made with the third sized cord, and to that sew the fine écru silk cord, twisting it in the manner shown in the pattern. Form the smallest circle with the largest sized cord, secure that to the points of the twisted écru cord, and fill in the centre with a WHEEL made of écru silk, with a well padded centre covered with BUTTONHOLE in écru silk. Return to the larger circle, and shape the cheese cloth to form the half circles and the straight lines that proceed from them. Connect the straight pieces together with a half circle, made of the largest sized cord, sewn to the large circle, and finish that with a twisted half circle of écru cord. Bend the large cord round the outside of the lace, in the shape shown in the pattern. Finish the lace by covering all the cords, except the écru silk one, with close Buttonhole made with écru silk, and OVERCAST the edges of the half circle and straight pieces of cheese cloth with the same silk; also work the Wheels between the wedges in the same material.

Guipure Richelieu.—*See* RICHELIEU GUIPURE.

Gunny, or Gunnies.—A coarse description of sacking, made from the fibres of two plants of the genus *Corchorus*, a native of India. The fibre is employed to make cord-

end of a sleeve, by which it is connected with the body of the garment under the arm, for the purpose of giving more play to the latter. Small ones are also inserted at the openings above the wristbands of a shirt, to prevent the tearing of the seam. Gussets should be cut the straight way of the material, and a selvedge procured for one side, if possible. Half gussets are sometimes employed for the shoulders of nightshirts, towards the neck They should

FIG. 475. GUIPURE RENAISSANCE.

age, and also a kind of coarse linen, called *Tat*. The manufacture of Gunny or Bagging Cloth is one of the principal occupations of the lower orders in Bengal, Bombay, and Madras; and, owing to its great strength and cheapness, it is in extensive demand in all countries. In Europe, China, Australia, and America this cloth is employed in the packing of their several products. Rice, spices, and cotton are packed in it.

Gusset.—A square piece of material let into the upper

be folded over on the bias, one corner laid against that opposite; two sides should be sewn into the body of the garment under the arm, and the other two sides into the sleeve underneath the arm. Thus, when the shirt or chemise is laid flat on the table, with the sleeves spread out horizontally, the gusset presents a triangular form in its half section. . It should be sewn into the sleeve before it is attached to the body.

Gusset.—*See* KNITTING.

Gutta Percha.—So called from *Palo Percha*, the island whence was first obtained the gum, which is produced by a forest tree—the *Isonandra Gutta*—which grows in the great woods of the Malayan Peninsula, Borneo, and other islands of the Indian Archipelago. The material produced is sent to this country in large blocks of 3lb. or 4lb. in weight, and it then goes through a process of purification, and is cut into long strips for purposes of wear or otherwise, such as in the making of boots and shoes. It is a rival to indiarubber in its uses for all articles demanding elasticity or to be rendered waterproof. *See* INDIARUBBER.

Gymp-head.—A description of narrow open-worked braid, made as a binding or finish for the purposes of upholstery work. It is applied to chairs, sofas, &c., and nailed on to conceal the turnings-in of the cloth or velvet, and sewn over the seams round cushions. It varies in width, and may be had in every colour and of mixed colours.

H.

Haberdashery. — In the Danish, *Tuischer*, and in German, *Tauscher*, means a seller of trifling wares, such as Tapes, Buttons, Needles, Ribbons, Hooks and Eyes, &c., to which articles—all employed in Needlework—the term Haberdashery applies in English. The fraternity in ancient times was called "Hurrers," and also "Milliners." They were incorporated by Letters Patent in the reign of Henry VI., 1407, by the style of the "Fraternity of St. Catherine the Virgin, of the Haberdashers of the City of London." Their modern and present denomination is "The Master and four Wardens of the Fraternity of the Art, or Mystery, of Haberdashers, in the City of London."

> A walking haberdashery
> Of feathers, lace, and fur.
> —*The Bridal of Triermain.*

Habit Cloths.—These cloths are of a thin, light make, usually of seven quarters in width, and suitable for women's wear.

Hainault.—In Binche, a town of Hainault, Brussels Lace was made during the seventeenth and eighteenth centuries; also a heavy patterned Dutch Lace. *See* BINCHE LACE.

Hair-cloth, or Hair-seating. — Woven fabrics of various descriptions made from the hair of animals. That of the camel, being long and as fine as silk, forms a beautiful material for the weaving of dress and mantle stuffs, of which there are three kinds employed—the red, white, and grey; that of the Angora goat, from which a light and expensive cloth is made of the description of plush called angola cloth, which, from its repelling heat, is employed for paletots, overcoats, &c.; and that from the Cashmere goat, from which is manufactured fine and costly shawls, and of which material there are three kinds, the Rizargee being of the finest texture. A very rough, coarse description of hair cloth is woven in bands, and for gloves used for the purpose of friction, and by the monastic orders for shirts, worn as an act of penance. This kind of cloth is made of horse-hair. There is likewise a cloth made of horse-hair which is dyed, the white receiving permanent colours—crimson, claret, green, and scarlet; the warp of the cloth being either of worsted or cotton, and used in Upholstery, especially for steam ships, railway carriages, &c. It is largely manufactured at Sheffield and Worcester, and is partially hand-made in a loom, owing to there being no continuous thread of hair to render machinery available. The hair is chiefly procured from Russia and South America for our home manufacture. The cloth is likewise made in Paris.

Hair-cord Muslin.—A very fine kind of cotton cloth, the threads running the long way, and presenting the appearance of fine cords. It is 38 inches in width, and is employed for infants' robes and frocks. *See* MUSLIN.

Hairpin Crochet.—*See* CROCHET, page 107.

Hair Work.—Also called Point Tresse. In the time of Charles I. it was much the custom of embroiderers to work miniatures, and to form the hair with the real hair of the person represented. To this fashion we owe several likenesses of that monarch containing portions of his hair, as ladies loyal to the Royalist cause generally obtained from the King hair for this purpose; but the true Point Tresse is of much older date than this kind of Embroidery. It is mentioned in old writings that the Countess of Lennox worked it during her captivity in the Tower and presented it to Queen Elizabeth, and there are notices of it in the Middle Ages. The true Point Tresse resembles extremely fine Knitting, in which the human hair twisted round fine silver thread or plain linen thread is knitted and so worked in. The peculiarity of the work is, that it will not burn, but only smoulders, when subject to the action of fire. The Indians plait or weave the tail hair of elephants in a similar manner, and the Americans are accustomed to plait up hair into detached flowers, leaves, and sprays. The only remnant remaining in England of this Hair Work consists in the almost obsolete brooches formed with bows of plaited or knitted hair, the true Point Tresse being no longer made.

Half Hitch.—A term used by Pillow Lace makers to denote the loop given to tighten the thread after it has been wound upon the Bobbins. To make: After the thread has been wound upon it, hold the BOBBIN in the left hand, with the palm upwards, take the end of the thread in the right hand, and pull it tight; place the middle finger of the left hand upon it, and give a turn of the wrist, to bring the thread round that finger; then put the loop over the head of the bobbin with the middle finger, gently pulling the thread all the time with the right hand. This loop, sometimes called rolling as well as Half Hitch, keeps the thread from coming off the Bobbin, and the amount of thread left free can be lengthened by tightening this loop, or shortened by lifting up the loop with the needle pin and winding the bobbin up.

Half Stitch.—Also called Lace and Shadow Stitch, and used in Pillow Lace making to form the shadow of a pattern, to fill in the inside of curves, flowers, and circles, and to make lighter leaves and parts of a design than those formed with Cloth or Whole Stitch. The principle of the stitch is, that only one Bobbin works across the leaf each time. The Bobbins are treated as pairs, but as the working pair is continually changing, one thread runs straight across, and the others slant crosswise down the work. Half Stitch, when worked as a Braid, is illustrated and described in BRAID WORK. To work the leaf shown in Fig. 476: Stick a pin at the tip of the leaf, and hang on eleven pairs of BOBBINS, run the pin down to its head, and work a row of CLOTH STITCH to bind all the threads together. The three working pairs having been twisted three times, give the rest of the Bobbins a twist to the left, except the two pairs immediately inside the pins upon each side of the leaf. These two pairs are never twisted, but a WHOLE or Cloth Stitch is made as the working Bobbins pass them at the beginning and end of each row. The effect of this is to form the streak upon each side of the leaf in Fig. 476, which gives the appearance of a GIMP. Second row—make the Cloth Stitch, put the pair of Bobbins that made it on one side, and give the Working Bobbins a twist to the left; bring forward the next pair,

Commence at the tail, and hang on seven pairs of BOBBINS and two GIMPS, work in CLOTH STITCH to the place where the pattern narrows, then cross the Gimps underneath the Bobbins, and continue the upper part of the body. When the head is reached, cut off two pairs of Bobbins, and tie up and cut off the Gimps. Work STEM round the head, and sew and tie up to finish. Make a ROPE SEWING to where the right-hand wing begins, and hang on another pair of Bobbins. Work Stem along the upper part of the wing, and for the PEARL EDGE twist twice before the last stitch and after the first in the return row. Continue Stem round the circle at the end of the wing, changing to PLAIN EDGE where it turns inside; make a SEWING where it joins, and tie and cut off all but two pairs; make a stitch with these, twist twice, and stick a pin between them in the nearest single hole. Fill the circle with PLAITINGS. Return to the body of the Butterfly, and to work the HALF STITCH, hang on five pairs of Bobbins and two Gimps. Sew each outside pair to the body, and increase the width of the lace by hanging on a pair of Bobbins at the slanting side for six rows. When the point of junction with the

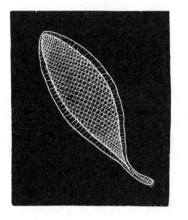

FIG. 476. LEAF IN HALF STITCH.

FIG. 477. BUTTERFLY IN HALF STITCH AND PLAITINGS.

which is already twisted, put the middle left-hand Bobbin over the middle right, twist both pairs once to the left; bring the next pair forward, and put the middle left-hand Bobbin over the middle right hand, and twist both pairs once; continue to bring forward a pair of Bobbins, put the centre ones over each other, and twist both pairs once, until the end pair is again reached; make a Cloth Stitch without twisting, then twist thrice and work a PLAIN EDGE. Return in the same manner, not forgetting the twist after the Cloth Stitch. When within a few rows of the end, tie up and cut off a pair of Bobbins, work another row, tie up and cut off another pair, and finish the leaf by plaiting the rest for the stem. This stitch does not require to be drawn together tightly, but a firm pull at the Hanging Bobbins is given from time to time to keep it straight, as, unless the threads are kept even, the lace will be thick in some places and open in others. The threads must not be broken, as knots cannot be made while the stitch is in progress, except at the edge in the Cloth Stitch.

To work Fig. 477: Work the body and head first.

lower wing is passed, commence the Pearl Edge, which will be LEFT PEARL. When the Half Stitch is nearly finished, cut off a pair of Bobbins in each of the two rows before the last one, and three pairs in the last row; join one side to the circle by Sewing where they touch when working the Half Stitch. Make a final Sewing at the end, and tie and cut off the Bobbins. For the lower wing, commence at the body, hang on six pairs of Bobbins, and work the band in Cloth Stitch round the wing; begin with making a Plain Edge, and turn to Pearl Edge below the tail. From the place where the wings join, sew each row to the upper wing, not working the Edge on that side. The left side of the Butterfly is worked similar to the right side, and the Plaitings are filled in last. Fill the lower wings with LONG PLAITINGS, with six pairs of Bobbins; the upper with CUCUMBER PLAITINGS; and to finish the Butterfly, make the antennæ with five pairs of Bobbins in Cloth Stitch, commencing at the head.

Hamburg Point. — A lace made at Hamburg by Protestant French refugees, after the revocation of the

Edict of Nantes. The lace is now obsolete, but was a description of Drawn Work, like that described in DRESDEN POINT.

Hamburg Wool.—This is one of the varieties of German wool prepared for the purposes of embroidery, and is composed of from four to twelve strands of the yarn. It is glossy and brilliant in colour, and is suitable for working on coarse canvas. An imitation is made, of inferior quality, called Hamburg Worsted.

Hammered-up Gold.—Gold hammered out into very thin plates, and sewn upon Embroidery. The gold plates were either formed into plain heraldic shields and other devices, or a pattern raised in relief upon them. The work decorated in this manner is generally called BATUZ WORK (which *see*).

Hamster (*Cricetus Vulgaris*).—A native of Germany, from whence upwards of 100,000 skins are annually collected. The fur being poor, coarse, and rough, is exclusively employed for cloak linings, more especially by the Greeks. The back is of a reddish brown, and the rest black, with a few light spots. The skin measures 5 inches by 12 inches.

Handkerchiefs.—A handkerchief was the square of fine linen formerly employed by women to cover the head, and more recently also used in the hand. The term Handkerchief is not met with earlier than in the fifteenth century, when, in the "Wardrobe Accounts of Edward IV.," we find "V. dozen handcouverchieffes" are named as having been made and washed by one Alice Shapster, to whom a payment had been made. Modern handkerchiefs are to be had of different dimensions, those for women being smaller than those for men. They are produced in silk, both Chinese and Indian, as well as English; of cambric, cotton, and muslin; some designed for the pocket, and others for the neck. Some of the Indian silk ones are in self colours, others have patterns upon them, and are necessarily in two colours; these are known as BANDANA HANDKERCHIEFS (which *see*). Cambric, muslin, cotton and gingham handkerchiefs are to be had, with hem-stitched or ribbon borders, and some are more or less embroidered; others have black or coloured borders in various designs. Bales of coloured cotton Handkerchiefs are manufactured in this country in Oriental colours and designs, so prepared to suit the native taste, for the Indian export trade. Trimmings of lace applied to Handkerchiefs came first into fashion in the reign of Queen Elizabeth.

> Handkerchiefs were wrought
> With names and true-love knots.
> —*Friar Bacon's Prophesie*, A.D. 1604.

> Have you not sometimes seen a handkerchief
> Spotted with strawberries in your wife's hand?
> —*Othello.*

Hangers.—This term, with that of Passive Bobbins, is used by Pillow lacemakers to distinguish those Bobbins that lie straight down the cushion, from the Worker Bobbins, that pass backwards and forwards, from side to side, and interlace the Hangers.

Hangings.—Tapestry, or such-like woollen fabrics, used as ornamental or useful drapery of the household.

> No purple hangings clothe the palace walls.
> —*Dryden.*

Hank.—This term denotes a certain measure of yarn, coil, skein, or head of silk, thread, or cotton, prepared for sale. When not required for weaving in a factory, the yarn is reeled, and wound off in lengths of 840 yards each, twisted together and secured. For worsted the hanks are longer than for cotton. However fine the yarn may be the same length is given; and the quality or fineness of the material is indicated by the number of hanks which make a pound weight. Water twist means a coarse yarn of twenty hanks to the pound, and is used for the warp, or the longitudinal threads, of the cloth. Mule twist is used for the weft, or cross threads. In some places the words hank and skein have different meanings—the former including two or more skeins, and consisting of two or more threads twisted or tied together.

Hank, Worsted.—A description of yarn for knitting hose, which is done up in ¼lb. skeins, and sold by the single, dozen, or half-dozen pounds. It may be had in various colours — plain, white, speckled, grey, scarlet, Spanish brown, black, &c.

Hard and Soft Silk.—The former kind is that in which the natural gum is left, the latter in which it has been removed by scouring.

Harden.—This cloth is otherwise known as *Hurden*. It is made from Tow (which *see*), or of the coarsest description of flax or hemp. Under garments, tablecloths, sheets, and towels, were made of Harden in the olden times. In the will of Johan Wiclif, dated 1562, ten pairs of Harden sheets are named, valued at 20s.; nine tablecloths of Harden at 10s.; and hand towels made of the same cloth. Six years later, Walter Strykland made a bequest of 40 yards of Harden cloth, the whole piece being valued at 13s. 4d. (See FLAX and HEMP.)

Hare-skin Fur.—This is an inferior and cheap description of Fur, but is thick and soft. If taken from the animal in the winter, when the coat is thick, it will bear a close resemblance to sealskin, when well dyed and dressed. It is in much request.

Harrateen.—A kind of cloth made of combing wool.

Havenese Embroidery. — A modern Embroidery formed of Buttonhole Stitch, worked with coloured silks or crewels upon crash, cloth, or any thick material. The patterns used for this work are the conventional flower-shaped designs, or the geometrical designs used in Crewel Work; and where the design would be too heavy if entirely covered over with Buttonhole, the open darning stitches used in Crewel work backgrounds (see page 99) are inserted into the centres to lighten the effect. To work: Trace out a design upon oatmeal cloth or crash, and, should it contain large leaves, cover them entirely with BUTTONHOLE. Graduate the length of the Buttonhole from the stem to the point of the leaf, and fill in one side of the leaf with a row of Buttonholes, turning the raised edge to the centre of the leaf to form the middle vein.

Work all the stems in CREWEL STITCH, work the flowers in single distinct petals; fill each petal with Buttonholes. and turn the edge to the centre of flower. Cover detached parts of the design, and leaves too small to require a centre vein, with rows of Buttonhole, and turn the edge of the Buttonhole to the interior of the design.

FIG. 478. HAVENESE EMBROIDERY.

To work a geometrical design, as shown in Fig. 478: Two shades of gold are required for this pattern. Work all the sprays and thick parts with lines of BUTTONHOLE in the darkest shade, and turn the edge to the inside. Make the CONES in the lightest shade, with an open LATTICE STITCH, and fill in with this stitch the other open parts of the design; work the seed vessels in the corner with SATIN STITCH.

Head-dress. — This is a comprehensive term, under which a very large number of coverings and adornments for the head may be classified; but for those Head-dresses which belong to women's costumes of the present day, and to the Art of Needlework, including Hats and Bonnets, &c., see MILLINERY.

Heading. — A term sometimes used instead of Footing, to distinguish the edge of the lace that is upon the side of lace sewn to the dress from the edge that is left free. Headings are either made of Braids worked separate from the pattern, and attached to it, or they are worked as part of the design.

Health Crape (*Crêpe de Santé*). — This is a new material, designed for underclothing, manufacturered at Zofingen, Switzerland. It is composed of pure silk and pure wool, which are woven into ridges, and a fabric is thus produced that resembles white crape. Though close in texture, it is porous, and possesses great elasticity. It is likewise light, yet exceedingly warm, and, being undyed, bears washing very well, and without shrinking. Its width is about 24 inches.

Heather Wool. — This name does not denote any special kind of wool or yarn, but has reference only to the mixed and speckled colour which produces a hue like Heather in yarn of any description. There is much German wool manufactured for the knitting of stockings, each strand of which is parti-coloured.

Heel. — *See* STOCKING KNITTING.

Hemmer. — The name of an "attachment" employed to execute the stitch called HEMMING by means of its use in a sewing machine.

Hemming. — This is a term used in plain sewing, and the stitch, and method of its application, is to produce a firm, neat border to any article of clothing, upholstery, or of household use, instead of leaving a raw edge, which would ravel out. To make a Hemming, turn in the raw edge of the stuff with a double fold-over, insert the needle, and secure the thread under the edge of the fold, and, directing the needle in a slanting position leftwards, take up a couple or three strands of the stuff of single portion, below the fold, bringing the needle through the edge of

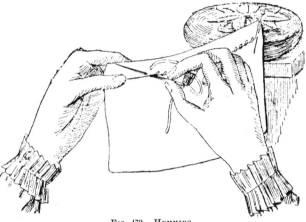

FIG. 479. HEMMING.

the fold likewise. Make a continuous succession of fine regular stitches thus, resembling teeth, which will confine the fold closely to the rest of the material (Fig. 479).

> All the skirt about
> Was hemmed with golden fringe.—*Spenser.*

There are various other styles of hemming besides the ordinary hem described above, such as Counter Hemming, German Hemming, and Mantua Makers' Hemming. The latter is employed where the ridge formed will be of no consequence, while speed in finishing is an object. Lay two pieces of stuff together, the raw edge of the nearest to you a little below that of the other piece. Turn the upper edge over the lower, and then fold both together over as in ordinary Hemming, and Fell through the double stuff, so as to leave a projecting hem, forming a ridge, instead of a flat one, such as would be suitable for a border. In the seams of sleeves, pockets, bags, or skirts, it may be suitably used.

German Hemming is a substitute for top-sewing. Turn down the raw edges of both pieces of cloth to be united once, and lay them one below the other, so that the smooth top of the lower should not touch the edge of the upper one, but lie just beneath it. Then Hem and FELL the lower one to the cloth against which it is laid, like hemming upside down.

The Counter Hem, although adopted in the teaching of very young children, is not a style to be recommended, while it cannot be omitted in the list. The working of this method is as follows: Mark one side of the material A, the other side B; turn one edge down on side A, turn the opposite edge down on side B, lay the fold B under the fold A, Hem the edge A, then turn the work over and Hem the side B, and by this means never have a wrong or a right side. If the edge A were neatly BACK STITCHED, instead of Hemmed, there could be no objection to the Counter Hem. The needle should be inserted in a sloping direction—not straight upwards.

Hemp.—This plant is supposed to have been originally a native of Persia. The inner fibrous bark is detached from the wood by immersion in pools of water, and made into coarse cloths, cordage, and canvas. It is naturalised in Europe and in England, as well as elsewhere. The hemp grown in this country supplies material for Towelling—such as Huckaback, Buckram, Canvas, and cordage. Russian and Polish Hemp is converted into sails and cordage, and the Manilla into ropes. The hemp plant grows to a height of about 3 feet to 4 feet, the stems branching with alternate leaves on long foot stalks, the flowers growing in clusters. Hemp is of the Nettle tribe. Herodotus writes of it thus: "Hemp grows in the country of the Scythians, which, except in the thickness and height of the stalk, very much resembles Flax; in the qualities mentioned, however, the Hemp is much superior. The Thracians make clothing of it very like Linen; nor could any person, without being very well acquainted with the substance, say whether this clothing be made of Hemp or Flax."

Hem-Stitch.—A term in needlework designating the mode of producing a delicate kind of open-work, by drawing together certain threads in the material of the stuff, to be sewn in small successive clusters. Draw out a few parallel threads in the cloth—whether linen, cambric, or muslin—at the head of a hem, and fasten up the upper and last cross-thread to the folded hem above it, so as to prevent its ravelling downwards; thus leaving small open spaces between each of the clusters of strands.

Hem Stitch, Fancy.—See EMBROIDERY STITCHES.

Henrietta Cloth.—A material employed for mourning, the warp composed of spun silk, and the weft of fine Saxony wool. It is stouter than Parramatta in the warp, measures 40 inches in width, and varies in price.

Henriquez Lace.—Used in Ancient Needle Lace and in Modern Point. The finest thread is required to work this stitch. To work: Take a twisted thread across a space from one finished piece of work to another, and a single one back very near to it. Twist a thread twice round the second line, and DARN a spot on both; twist again on the single thread five or six times, and repeat the spot. Do this to the end of line.* Then take the two single threads across at a small distance from the others, and keep the two apart by working a twisted stitch between. Repeat the twisted threads and Darned spots as before, and make the spots fall underneath the others. Continue from * until the space is filled. Then work the two single lines in exactly the opposite direction, and make them go under and over in returning. The Darned spots must be worked in the spaces between where the four lines meet.

Hercules Braid.—A thick, corded, worsted braid, employed for trimmings. It varies in width from half an inch to about 4 inches.

Herringbone Stitch.—A stitch used in plain sewing, and also in Embroidery, being a kind of Cross Stitch, worked backwards, from left to right. It is chiefly used in the making of seams in flannel, when, a running having been made, the two raw edges are turned back the one from the other, and the two either separately Herringboned, or else the stitches are taken across the running into the material beyond the raw edges, exactly parallel with them, and so confining the loose strands of the flannel. Direct the point of the needle to the left hand, and take up two vertical strands, leaving four strands between the top row of stitches and the lower one; then re-insert the needle at the fourth thread from the spot where it entered the previous time on that row, so working backwards, from left to right, that the threads successively drawn through, above, and below, may cross each other diagonally, and form a series, resembling the letter X, in regular order. The material should be held across the first two fingers of the left hand. The stitch is employed in embroidery, and with coloured silk, cotton, or wool.

Herringbone Stitch, Fancy. — See EMBROIDERY STITCHES.

Herringbone Twill.—A name by which a soft slight dress material is known. It is one of the varieties in the Rampoor Chudda all-wool textiles, woven to resemble Herringbone Masonry, and measuring 42 inches in width.

Hessians.—A strong coarse cloth, made of a mixture of Hemp and Jute, and is employed for the packing of bales.

Hibernian Embroidery.—An Embroidery with Satin and Buttonhole Stitches upon velvet, silk, or net foundations, with coloured silks or filoselles. It is used for banner screens, cushions, and dress trimmings, and is but little distinguishable from Satin Embroidery. To work: Trace the design upon the material, and select a flower Satin Stitch pattern. Fill in the stems of the flowers with SATIN STITCH, and work the leaves in Satin Stitch, shading them with various colours. Work small flowers, such as Forget-me-nots, with Satin Stitch petals, and finish them with FRENCH KNOT centres. Work larger flowers in BUTTONHOLE laid over a padded surface, and fill in their centres with beads, or work them in RAISED SATIN STITCH. Form fern sprays with a number of POINT LANCÉ STITCHES, and wheat and barley with irregular Satin Stitches worked over a padded foundation.

Hodden Grey.—The word Hodden is evidently derived from *Hoiden*, or rustic and clownish, and thus descriptive of a material worn by the peasantry. Hodden grey is a cloth peculiar to Scotland, and made from the natural undyed fleece. A black lamb is usually kept for the manufacture of this cloth in farming districts, as its wool is very suitable.

Holbein Stitch.—Also known as Italian Stitch, and used in Holbein Embroidery to cover the outline patterns forming that work. The beauty of the stitch entirely depends upon its exact regularity. The idea of the stitch is that both sides are alike, therefore every stitch must be either perfectly upright or horizontal, and accord in length with its complement. To work: Follow the exact outlines of the Embroidery with single RUNNINGS, worked with great precision, and return back along the same line to complete it upon both sides, thus: To work a straight line, thread a coarse wool needle, and RUN the line with a series of stitches exactly the same upon both sides; this produces upon the right side of the work a series of short stitches, with gaps of the same length between them; return along the line with another Running, so that these gaps are filled in, and a straight line upon both sides of the stuff is made. To make a Vandyke line: Make with a SATIN STITCH every left-hand line of the Vandyke upon the right side of the work; the under side will have the right-hand lines of the Vandyke formed with the under thread. In returning along the pattern, make all the right-hand lines of the Vandyke with a Satin Stitch upon the right side of the material; the under side will thus be completed with the under thread forming the left-hand Vandyke lines. To work a Battlemented line: On the right side work in Satin Stitch all the upright lines; form on the under side with the under thread all the horizontal lines. Return and finish the pattern by making all the horizontal lines on the right side, the under threads of which will form the upright lines of the Battlement upon the wrong side of the material.

Holbein Work.—This is a modern revival of work executed in the time of Holbein, and frequently to be seen in his paintings. It consists of an outline Embroidery, executed with great care and exactitude, so that the right and wrong side of the work are alike. The designs are carefully drawn to scale, and each stitch worked so that it fills its exact place, and the one next it arranged so as to be capable of meeting it. The work, which is durable, and quickly done, is chiefly executed in flax and linen materials, and used to ornament tablecloths, towels, and other washing articles, and is then worked with ingrain silks and cottons: but it can also be

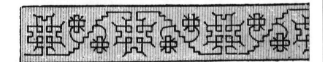

FIG. 480. BORDER IN HOLBEIN WORK.

used upon cloth or silk foundations, and worked with filoselles and fine crewels; it then makes tea cosies, mats and cushions. To work as shown in Fig. 480 (a design intended for a border to a tablecloth, and considerably reduced from its right size), upon coarse écru coloured linen, with crimson ingrain silk: Trace the pattern on to the linen with tracing cloth and blue tracing paper. Work the short stitches with HOLBEIN STITCH. Work the Battlemented lines thus: First all the upright lines, and then return back and form the horizontal, RUN the long lines, and fill in the gaps by returning. Work all the squares by Runnings, returning back until they are filled. Work the single stitches with a double Satin Stitch. Be careful to give

the pointed square look to each stitch, as that is the characteristic of this work.

Hole Stitch.—A stitch used in Pillow Lace making to form holes or small round spots in the centre of the thick parts of a pattern. Numerous designs can be made by the different arrangements of these holes, of which one is called Flemish Stitch; a single hole is described in BRAIDS. But whatever the pattern, the hole is always made in the same way, although the number of the Bobbins used to make it can be increased or decreased. To work: Hang on twelve pairs of BOBBINS, and work across from left to right in WHOLE or CLOTH STITCH six times; put up the pins each side into their pricked holes, then divide the Bobbins into two equal numbers, and put a pin in the centre. Take up the left-hand Bobbin, and work Cloth Stitch with six pairs up to the centre pin; work back to the left with the same six pairs, without twisting or putting up a pin at the edge, twist, and put up a pin, and leave the Bobbins hanging. Take up the right-hand Bobbins, and work with them to the centre pin in Cloth Stitch, and return with them without twist or pin to the right hand; put up a pin, and work right across the whole twelve Bobbins to the left hand, and enclose the centre pin, which makes the hole. Keep the Hanging Bobbins while the stitch is in progress drawn towards the centre pin, and when dividing the Bobbins do not draw them away too much from the centre, or a stretchy, wide hole will be the result.

Holland.—A kind of linen originally imported from the Low Countries (whence its name), but now British made, and chiefly in Scotland. It is unbleached, and is made in two descriptions—the glazed and unglazed. The former is employed for carriage or chair covers and trunk linings; the latter for articles of dress—men's blouses, women's and children's dresses, and many other purposes. Hollands may be had from 30 inches to 36 inches in width, including the rough, dressed, and undressed descriptions, brown lawns, and Drills for boys' suits. A description of Holland is employed for window roller blinds, made in cotton as well as linen. They are highly glazed and sized, so as to be less influenced by dust, and are made in white, blue, buff, green, and in stripes of different colours. The widths begin at 28 inches, and increase by 2 inches up to 100.

Hollie Point.—A needle lace much worked in the Middle Ages. The word is a corruption of Holy Point, and was used to denote Church Laces, whether formed of Drawn or Cut Work, or with Darned Netting or Needle Point when the pattern of the lace was a Scriptural subject or contained sacred emblems. Italy, Spain, Flanders, and England, all produced Hollie Points, the designs of which were either figures illustrating the fall of Adam and Eve, and other Old Testament events, or the Tree of Knowledge, the Holy Dove, and the Annunciation Lily, with or without its flower pot. It was not until the beginning of the seventeenth century that Hollie Point was used for anything else but church purposes, and the fashion of wearing it was first adopted by the Puritans in the reign of James I. The designs shown in Figs. 481 and 482 are of great antiquity, and are executed in Needle Point, and have been used to adorn a child during its christening, the round pattern to form the centre of the baby's cap, and the long, to ornament the "bearing" cloth or long garment of fine linen that in ancient days was used when carrying the child to the font, and which was always handsomely decorated with lace. The stitch for this description of Hollie Point is described in HOLLIE STITCH; it is a Button-hole with an extra twist. To work the Border shown in Fig. 481: Take a piece of green linen or green leather cloth, and tack it on something stiff, then lay upon it three threads the length of the piece of insertion; fasten them firmly from the underneath, leave the three threads on the green surface, then thread a needle with fine thread and bring it up from underneath with a very small stitch, so as to hold the three threads firmly together. Begin at the left hand corner. First row—work 78 HOLLIE STITCHES with space enough between each for two stitches to come on the next row under; take the thread back to the left hand, and in every row take up this thread with the lower part of the stitch of the row above. Second row—work 4 and miss 2, work 6, miss 2, work 6 and miss 2 alternately to the end of the row; take the thread back to the left hand. Third

FIG. 481. EDGING IN HOLLIE POINT.

row—work 2 and miss 2 to the end of the row. Fourth row—miss 2 and work 6 alternately to the end of the row. Fifth row—work 4, miss 2, and work 2 alternately to the end of the row; the four worked at the beginning must not be repeated. Sixth row—work 6 and miss 2 alternately to the end of the row. Seventh row—work 8, miss 2, work 2, miss 2, work 2, miss 2, work 2, miss 2, work 2, miss 2, work 2, miss 2, work 2, miss 2, work 2, miss 2, work 21, miss 2, work 14, miss 2, work 12, miss 2, work 2, miss 1, work 1, miss 1, work 1, miss 2, work 1, miss 2, work 22, miss 2, work 1, miss 2, work 1, miss 2, work 1, miss 2, work 1, miss 2, work 1, miss 2, work 30, miss 2, work 2, miss 2, work 2, miss 2, work 2, miss 2, work 2, miss 2, work 2, miss 2, work 2, miss 2, work 2, miss 2, work 10. Eighth row—work 10, miss 2, work 6, miss 2, work 6, miss 2, work 6, miss 2, work 15, miss 2, work 1, miss 2, work 1, miss 2, work 10, miss 2, work 1, miss 2, work 1, miss 2, work 10, miss 2, work 4, miss 2, work 2, miss 2, work 4, miss 2, work 20, miss 2, work 16, miss 2, work 28, miss 2, work 6, miss 2, work 6, miss 2, work 6, miss 2, work 12. Ninth row—work 12, miss 2, work 2,

miss 2, work 2, miss 2, work 2, miss 2, work 2, miss 2, work 2, miss 2, work 17, miss 2, work 1, miss 2, work 1, miss 2, work 10, miss 2, work 1, miss 2, work 1, miss 2, work 10, miss 2, work 4, miss 2, work 6, miss 2, work 4, miss 2, work 22, miss 2, work 20, miss 2, work 29, miss 2, work 2, miss 2, work 2, miss 2, work 2, miss 2, work 2, miss 2, work 2, miss 2, work 14. Tenth row—work 14, miss 2, work 6, miss 2,

FIG. 482. CIRCLE IN HOLLIE POINT.

work 6, miss 2, work 16, miss 2, work 1, miss 2, work 10, miss 2, work 1, miss 2, work 1, miss 2, work 10, miss 2, work 4, miss 2, work 8, miss 2, work 4, miss 2, work 18, miss 2, work 24, miss 2, work 30, miss 2, work 6, miss 2, work 6, miss 2, work 16. Eleventh row—work 16, miss 2, work 2, miss 2, work 2, miss 2, work 2, miss 2, work 16, miss 2, work 14, miss 2, work 1, miss 2, work 12, miss

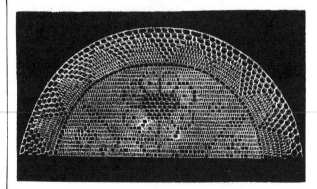

FIG. 483. CIRCLE IN HOLLIE POINT (ENLARGED).

2, work 4, miss 2, work 8, miss 2, work 4, miss 2, work 16, miss 2, work 10, miss 2, work 1, miss 2, work 1, miss 2, work 10, miss 2, work 12, miss 2, work 1, miss 2, work 1, miss 2, work 14, miss 2, work 2, miss 2, work 2, miss 2, work 2, miss 2, work 18. Twelfth row—work 18, miss 2, work 6, miss 2, work 16, miss 2, work 14, miss 2, work 1, miss 2, work 16, miss 2, work 4, miss 2, work 8, miss

2, work 4, miss 2, work 14, miss 2, work 10, miss 2, work 6, miss 2, work 8, miss 2, work 10, miss 2, work 7, miss 2, work 14, miss 2, work 6, miss 2, work 20. Thirteenth row—work 20, miss 2, work 2, miss 2, work 6, miss 2, work 8. miss 2, work 14, miss 2, work 22, miss 2, work 4, miss 2, work 6, miss 2, work 4, miss 2, work 14, miss 2, work 10, miss 2, work 6, miss 2, work 8, miss 2, work 14, miss 2, work 2, miss 2, work 22. Fourteenth row—work 22, miss 2, work 6, miss 2, work 10, miss 2, work 1, miss 2, work 1, miss 2, work 1, miss 2, work 1, miss 2, work 1, miss 2, work 1, miss 2, work 1, miss 2, work 1, miss 2, work 1, miss 2, work 1, miss 2, work 1, miss 2, work 12, miss 2, work 4, miss 2, work 2, miss 2, work 4, miss 2, work 14, miss 2, work 12, miss 2, work 4, miss 2, work 6, miss 2, work 1, miss 2, work 1, miss 2, work 1, miss 2, work 1, miss 2, work 1, miss 2, work 5, miss 2, work 4, miss 2, work 14, miss 2, work 24. Fifteenth row—work 20, miss 2, work 2, miss 2, work 6, miss 2, work 6, miss 2, work 33, miss 2, work 12, miss 2, work 4, miss 2, work 2, miss 2, work 5, miss 2, work 14, miss 2, work 12, miss 2, work 11, miss 2, work 1, miss 2, work 1, miss 2, work 1, miss 2, work 1, miss 2, work 1, miss 2, work 1, miss 2, work 1, miss 2, work 10, miss 2, work 14, miss 2, work 2, miss 2, work 22. Sixteenth row—work 22, miss 2, work 10, miss 2, work 2, miss 2, work 1, miss 2, work 1, miss 2, work 1, miss 2, work 1, miss 2, work 1, miss 2, work 1, miss 2, work 1, miss 2, work 1, miss 2, work 1, miss 2, work 1, miss 2, work 11, miss 2, work 16, miss 2, work 14, miss 2, work 2, miss 2, work 18, miss 2, work 7, miss 2, work 1, miss 2, work 1, miss 2, work 1, miss 2, work 1, miss 2, work 1, miss 2, work 1, miss 2, work 10, miss 2, work 16, miss 2, work 24. Seventeenth row—work 20, miss 2, work 2, miss 2, work 10, miss 2, work 27, miss 2, work 2, miss 2, work 6, miss 2, work 16, miss 2, work 10, miss 2, work 2, miss 2, work 19, miss 2, work 1, miss 2, work 1, miss 2, work 1, miss 2, work 1, miss 2, work 1, miss 2, work 1, miss 2, work 1, miss 2, work 1, miss 2, work 1, miss 2, work 1, miss 2, work 1, miss 2, work 1, miss 2, work 1, miss 2, work 1, miss 2, work 18, miss 2, work 2, miss 2, work 22. Eighteenth row—work 18, miss 2, work 6, miss 2, work 38, miss 2, work 10, miss 2, work 16, miss 2, work 10, miss 4, work 20, miss 2, work 7, miss 2, work 1 miss 2, work 1, miss 2, work 1, miss 2, work 1, miss 2, work 1, miss 2, work 1, miss 2, work 1, miss 2, work 1, miss 2, work 7, miss 2, work 15, miss 2, work 6, miss 2, work 20. Nineteenth row—work 16, miss 2, work 2, miss 2, work 2, miss 2, work 2, miss 2, work 34, miss 4, work 2, miss 2, work 2, miss 4, work 2, miss 2, work 1, miss 1, work 1, miss 1, work 1, miss 1, work 1, miss 1, work 1, miss 1, work 1, miss 1, work 1, miss 1, work 1, miss 1, work 1, miss 1, work 1, miss 1, work 1, miss 1, work 1, miss 1, work 1, miss 1, work 1, miss 1, work 22, miss 2, work 10, miss 2, work 1, miss 2, work 1, miss 2, work 1, miss 2, work 1, miss 2, work 1, miss 2, work 1, miss 2, work 10, miss 2, work 11, miss 2, work 2, miss 2, work 2, miss 2, work 2, miss 2, work 18. Twentieth row—work 14, miss 2, work 6, miss 2, work 6, miss 2, work 30, miss 2, work 4, miss 2, work 2, miss 2, work 4, miss 2, work 4, miss 2, work 14, miss 2, work 30, miss 2, work 4, miss 2, work 6, miss 2, work 1, miss 2, work 1, miss 2, work 1, miss 2, work 1, miss 2, work 1, miss 2, work 6, miss 2, work 4, miss 2, work 8, miss 2, work 6, miss 2, work 6, miss 2, work 16. Twenty-first row—work 12, miss 2, work 2, miss 2, work 2, miss 2, work 2,

miss 2, work 2, miss 2, work 2, miss 2, work 28, miss 2, work 4, miss 3, work 7, miss 3, work 4, miss 2, work 4, miss 2, work 14, miss 2, work 28, miss 2, work 10, miss 2, work 8, miss 2, work 6, miss 2, work 9, miss 2, work 7, miss 2, work 2, miss 2, work 2, miss 2, work 2, miss 2, work 2, miss 2, work 2, miss 2, work 14. Twenty-second row—work 10, miss 2, work 6, miss 2, work 6, miss 2, work 6, miss 2, work 26, miss 2, work 4, miss 2, work 11, miss 2, work 4, miss 2, work 3, miss 2, work 1, miss 1, work 1, miss 1, work 10, miss 2, work 1, miss 2, work 1, miss 1, work 24, miss 2, work 6, miss 2, work 10, miss 2, work 8, miss 2, work 7, miss 2, work 5, miss 2, work 6, miss 2, work 6, miss 2, work 6, miss 2, work 12. Twenty-third row—work 8, miss 2, work 2, miss 2, work 2, miss 2, work 2, miss 2, work 2, miss 2, work 2, miss 2, work 2, miss 2, work 2, miss 2, work 24, miss 2, work 4, miss 2, work 11, miss 2, work 4, miss 2, work 6, miss 2, work 1, miss 1, work 1, miss 1, work 9, miss 2, work 1, miss 1, work 1, miss 1, work 24, miss 2, work 1, miss 2, work 6, miss 2, work 4, miss 2, work 4, miss 2, work 1, miss 1, work 1, miss 1, work 4, miss 2, work 2, miss 2, work 2, miss 2, work 2, miss 2 work 2, miss 2, work 2, miss 2, work 2, miss 2, work 2, miss 2, work 10. Twenty-fourth row—work 6, miss 2, work 6, miss 2, work 6, miss 2, work 6, miss 2, work 6, miss 2, work 21, miss 2, work 4, miss 2, work 11, miss 2, work 4, miss 2, work 8, miss 2, work 1, miss 1, work 1, miss 1, work 10, miss 2, work 1, miss 1, work 1, miss 1, work 26, miss 2, work 10, miss 2, work 10, miss 2, work 8, miss 2, work 6, miss 2, work 6, miss 2, work 6, miss 2, work 6, miss 2, work 8. Twenty-fifth row—work 4, miss 2, work 2, miss 2, work 2, miss 2, work 2, miss 2, work 2, miss 2, work 2, miss 2, work 2, miss 2, work 2, miss 2, work 2, miss 2, work 2, miss 2, work 18, miss 2, work 6, miss 2, work 7, miss 2, work 4, miss 2, work 12, miss 2, work 1, miss 1, work 1, miss 1, work 10, miss 2, work 1, miss 1, work 1, miss 1, work 26, miss 2, work 6, miss 2, work 2, miss 2, work 6, miss 2, work 6, miss 2, work 2 to the end of the line. Twenty-sixth row—work 2, miss 2, work 6, miss 2, work 6, miss 2, work 6, miss 2, work 6, miss 2, work 6, miss 2, work 14, miss 2, work 6, miss 2, work 2, miss 2, work 4, miss 2, work 20, miss 2, work 14, miss 2, work 26, miss 2, work 1, miss 2, work 1, miss 2, work 6, miss 2, work 1, miss 2, work 1, miss 2, work 8, miss 2, work 6, to the end of the line. Twenty-seventh row—work 2, miss 2, work 6, miss 2, work 6, miss 2, work 6, miss 2, work 6, miss 2, work 6, miss 2, work 14, miss 2, work 3, miss 2, work 2, miss 2, work 3, miss 4, work 25, miss 2, work 14, miss 2, work 48, miss 2, and work 2 to the end of the line. Twenty-eighth row—work 6 and miss 2 the whole row. Twenty-ninth row—work 2 and miss 2 to the end of the line. Thirtieth row—work 6 and miss 2 to the end of the line. Thirty-first row—work 2 and miss 2 the whole line. Thirty-second row—miss 2 and work 6 the whole line. Thirty-third row—miss 2 and work 1 the whole line.

The circle shown in Fig. 482, and given in an enlarged scale in Fig. 483, is worked in the same manner as the edging with regard to the formation of the stitches, and as they can be counted from the illustration, it is needless to enumerate every line. Work the centre round of the pattern first, and commence with thirty-six HOLLIE STITCHES, which increase in every line until the centre of the circle is reached, and then decrease the stitches in the same proportion. After the centre is finished, work a row of open Hollie Stitches quite round it, and increase to widen this circle by working two stitches into one in the centre of every thick point. The line of thread is put round every line as before. Should there not be sufficient increase by working two stitches into one at every thick part, also increase at every open space in the same manner; but as this depends upon the thickness of the Honiton thread used, it can only be regulated by the worker.

Hollie Stitch.—The Stitch used in making Hollie Point is a description of Buttonhole, and is worked as follows: Fasten a thread across from right to left of the work, and place the needle in and draw up as if commencing a BUTTONHOLE; put the left-hand thumb firmly on the thread, and twist it round, then thread, pass the needle into the loop on the right of the thumb, and draw up. Commence each line of stitches from the left-hand side of the lace and work to the right, then throw the thread back to the left, and commence another line there, working each stitch into the lower part of the stitch above it in the first line, and enclosing the thrown thread.

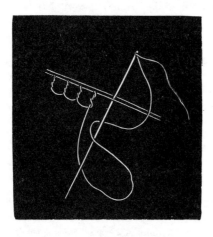

FIG. 484. HOLLIE STITCH.

The stitch, as shown in Fig. 484, is worked wide apart, and forms a line of open work between the thick pattern in the lace, but the thick and the open parts of HOLLIE POINT are worked in the same stitch; in the thick these are placed close together; in the open, the space of two or more stitches are missed.

Hollow Spots.—See CROCHET.

Homespun.—A coarse and rather loosely woven woollen material, employed for men's and women's dresses. The origin of the name is derived from the circumstance that, in former times, women used to spin the wool at home, and send it to country manufacturers to be woven into cloth. It has within the last few years been brought into fashion by some members of the Scottish nobility, who probably procured it from their own tenants for country wear; and it has been successfully imitated by the manufacturers, in both fine and coarse qualities.

Honeycombing.—A term used to describe a pattern formed in silk, or any material equally thin. There are two methods of producing the effect of a Honeycomb. That in Plain Sewing is as follows: Make RUNNINGS diagonally across the material, the distances between each depending on the proportions of the piece of textile to be covered. Then cross all these Runnings again diagonally from corner to corner, and draw up each thread so as to produce diamond-shaped cells of loose and partially puffed appearance. For the second method, *see* EMBROIDERY STITCHES.

The effect of Honeycombing is produced in certain kinds of canvas, used for Embroidery, and in towelling.

Honeycomb Knitting.—See KNITTING.

Honeycomb Stitch.—See EMBROIDERY STITCHES.

Honiton Application.—This form of Honiton Lace was at one time popular, and the lace thus made and applied to a hand-made ground is most valuable. At the present date, the Honiton Guipure is more worked than the Honiton Application. This latter is formed by working the lace sprays on the Pillow, and then adding to them a Brussels net ground, formed either with the needle or on the Pillow. The lace so finished is very valuable, but, from the length of time the ground takes to form, and from the fineness, and consequent dearness of the Antwerp thread used, hand-made net grounds are rarely worked, except for Royal trousseaux. The principal Honiton Application now made consists of working the Honiton Sprays on the Pillow, laying them upon machine-made net, and sewing them down to it in the following manner: Cut out upon blue paper the exact size of the lace to be made, whether it is a flounce or only a small piece. Tack down upon this in their right positions the various Honiton sprays; lay them right side downwards upon the paper, and secure them just sufficiently to prevent them curling over, but not tightly. Over them lay the net, cut the wrong way of material. The net selected should be of delicate thread, of a cream, and not blue white, slightly stiff, and with holes sexagon in shape. Pin down this net to the paper without stretching it, and then sew it to the sprigs. Use Lund's No. 12 needles, and 175 lace thread, and sew down the sprig to the net by passing the needle through every other outer pinhole of the sprigs. Cut away the net from under the sprigs where there are open parts in the lace that have been ornamented with open FILLINGS, and OVERCAST round the edges of the net at these places to prevent the net fraying, and turn in and sew firmly down the net at the outer edge of the lace. When the net has been joined to the lace, cut the tacking threads at the back of the blue paper, pull them carefully out, take off the lace, and slightly iron the net side over. To work the ground, *see* NET GROUND.

Honiton Crochet.—See CROCHET.

Honiton Ground.—This is used in Honiton Lace, and consists of filling in with a number of Bars, that cross each other and form diamonds, the groundwork of the lace. To work: Rule blue paper into a number of diamond lines, ¼ inch apart. Tack the sprays of lace, face

CROCHET LACE — IRISH.

DARNED LACE — OLD.

downwards, to this paper; pin the paper on to the pillow, and work along the lines. Work all the lines first that go in one direction. Hang on to a line four pairs of Bobbins, and work in STEM STITCH with a PEARL EDGE down to the end of that line, and for the others going in the same direction. Then work the cross lines in the same manner, but make a SEWING as each line is crossed, by drawing the loop underneath the line to be sewn to, and passing the other through it. When the lace is reached in any part make a ROPE SEWING, or plait BEGINNERS' STEM to the next line, if at all possible; otherwise, tie up and cut off the Bobbins, after having fastened them with two Sewings to the lace.

Honiton Guipure.—The form of Honiton Lace now worked and described under HONITON LACE.

Honiton Lace.—The first laces made in England were the Cutworks and Darned Laces, and to these succeeded Bone Laces, a manufacture brought from the Continent by early emigrants. The record of the first making of Bone Lace in Devonshire is obscure, but Honiton was the centre of the trade in the time of Queen Elizabeth; and it is believed that Bone Lace was made there in the very early part of her reign. The laces then made were a coarse thread lace, and plaited laces of gold and silver thread, after the Italian and Greek Reticellas. The making of English Lace was from an early date protected by Royal enactments, which forbade the importation of foreign laces, particularly excluding Flemish. The Honiton Lace workers attempted to imitate Brussels Lace, that made by them being largely worn at the Court of Charles II.; but it was very inferior to the true Brussels Lace, the delicate Fillings and openwork stitches so profusely scattered over that lace being omitted, and heavy Guipure Bars substituted. The patterns also were not true copies of the originals, but rendered unmeaning by the alterations made in them, and by the coarseness of the thread used. Queen Anne repealed the lace edicts, but George II. and George III. re-enacted them; and as by this time the Guipure Bar Ground in Honiton Lace had been succeeded by the working of true Brussels Ground, or Vrai Réseau, and the patterns formed of detached flower sprays, English lace improved, and gradually became perfect. The workers executed the Vrai Réseau with the finest of Antwerp thread, and with great delicacy; and as the sprays used could be made over and over again by the same worker, great precision and beauty were attained in the manufacture; and during the forty years preceding 1820, the Honiton Lace produced stands unrivalled by its contemporaries. After that date, when machine-made net was first introduced, the trade fell into obscurity, the patterns being designed by the workers themselves, and debased in composition; and although attempts were made by the Royal family to raise the standard of manufacture, the lace produced was rejected by the foreign markets, and it was not till International Exhibitions opened the eyes of traders to the importance of good designs that they were again sought out, and the lace reinstated into its old position. The present manufacture of Honiton Lace is almost exclusively confined to Honiton Guipure, in which detached sprigs, after being worked, are attached to each other with fine Buttonhole Bars, or else joined with stitches. Honiton Application, or the detached sprigs sewn to machine net, is also made, but not so. frequently as Honiton Guipure. Nearly all Honiton lace is made of white thread; but when black Honiton is required, it is made of fine ingrain black silk—the only material that takes a sufficiently rich black colour. White thread will not dye black, but a rusty brown, so lace worked with it should never be altered to black. Working with silk is more troublesome than working with thread, as the silk loosens after the stitches are made, unless carefully manipulated. In the present stage of Honiton Lace making, there is every reason for the lace continuing to form a valuable article of commerce; the work produced is extremely white and delicate, is

FIG. 485. HONITON LACE SPRIG.

executed with great care, and from good designs, and is remarkable for its Raised Work, or Work in Relief, of the finest description. The making of it can be acquired by all who possess a good sight and touch, and a certain amount of patience.

The materials for making Honiton Lace are as follows: The pattern traced as a whole, and portions of it separately pricked, known as Passements, upon which the lace is worked; a Pillow, with Covering cloths, Lace and common Pins, Pincushion, fine Crochet Hook, Needlepin, six dozen Bobbins, Honiton Lace Thread (Nos. 195 and 175), and the shiny lace thread called Gimp.

The chief stitches used in the Lace are described under their own headings, as they are used in other Pillow Laces. The two most important are Whole or Cloth Stitch, an imitation of close weaving, and used for all the thick outlines of flowers or thick leaves, &c., and Half, or Lace Stitch, used for lighter parts of the outlines, or lighter leaves. After these come the Fillings, or open stitches, used to lighten the centres of the patterns. These include Diamond Holes, Chequer, Dame Joan, Flemish, Fibre, Lace, Net, Open Dots, Star, Vandyke and Cross Tracing; Wheel, Cucumber, Long, Crinkle and Square Plaitings; Devonia, Honiton, Italian, and Net Grounds; Plain, Pearl, and Inner Edges; False Pinholes; Buckle, Beginners', and Ordinary Stems; Branching and Centre Fibres; Headings; Footings; Twists; Tracings; Vandyke Tracings; Gimps; Knots; Rope and Return Rope; Curves; Circles; Turns.

Besides these recognised stitches, there are certain manipulations, with the Bobbins and other implements, to be learnt before the lace can be properly made.

more, are called the Workers, or Runners, and really form the lace as they work backwards and forwards, from side to side, over the Hangers, or Passive Bobbins, which simply hang down the pillow, and should be spread out in a fan shape there, and not allowed to lie together in a heap. The increasing and decreasing the width of the lace is managed by adding or cutting off Bobbins in pairs at the pinholes, or by spreading out the threads over a wider surface, or drawing them closer together; the latter plan can only be pursued at small increases or decreases, or when rounding curves. The Bobbins change their positions so continually that it is useless to put a distinguishing mark upon them, but an expert lacemaker understands the order they should be used

FIG. 486. HONITON LACE—POPPY AND BRYONY DESIGN. (FIRST PART.)

They are as follows: When holding the Pillow on the knee, let it rest against something that will resist it, and arrange so that the worker does not stoop. Always treat the Bobbins as pairs, with the exception of the Gimps, which hang on with the other Bobbins, so as to lie on each side, immediately inside the pin. Hang the number of Bobbins required for a leaf or other part of a pattern at the tip or base of the part as directed, tie them up first in pairs, with the knot that secures them placed on the passive Bobbin, and then knot all the ends together in one big knot, through which stick a pin, and put it into the pinhole. The length of the thread from the Bobbin to the knot is 4 inches, and when it is used in the lace and more is required, unwind from the Bobbin by lifting the Half Hitch. Divide the Bobbins into two sets; one set, consisting of three pairs or

in, and mentally numbers them. The threads twist and tangle themselves together as they lie, and when the pillow is put down—this roughens the thread and renders it brittle, and is one of the chief difficulties that a beginner has to encounter, as every twist must be patiently undone, an extra one causing a hole in the work. Knots and brittle places in the thread require to be wound out of the way, the thread cut off, and a fresh Bobbin put in, or the lace is rendered coarse and uneven. The Bobbins, when working, should not be looked at; the pins should be stuck in rather slanting, and only far enough to hold the lace, and the hands used together simultaneously to pass the Bobbins over and under each other mechanically, without following them with the eye, which should be fixed on the lace, ready to detect an error in the making. Take out any false stitches and rough or untidy looking holes, by patiently untwisting the Bobbins until that part is reached. The lace is executed upon the wrong side, so that all irregularities and Knots should be upon the upper surface. Ornamental Fillings are worked upon the wrong side, unless directions to turn the work are given. Good lace will present a firm and compact surface; the pinholes in it will be close together, the open stitches and holes of uniform shape and size, and the edge firmly twisted; while bad lace will fail in all these particulars, and present an untidy, dragged appearance. Before commencing any Lace pattern, learn the stitches by working them as braids. *See* BRAIDS.

near the end, and, when the flower, is reached Sew two pairs to each Pinhole, Tie and cut off. Return to the tip, pick up the four pairs of Bobbins left there, and work down in Half Stitch, adding a pair at the widest part of the leaf; make a ROPE SEWING to next leaf, work half of this in Cloth Stitch, as far as the reverse fold, there turn and work the other half, finishing in the flower as before. To complete the leaf hang on seven pairs of Bobbins at the tip, and work the reverse fold. Commence the third leaf at the flower, Sewing to each pinhole two pairs of Bobbins for four holes; work the leaf in halves in Cloth Stitch with an open Fibre. The centre of the flower is now filled in with SQUARE PLAITINGS, which have to be carefully worked, as there is no securing stitch between

FIG. 487. HONITON LACE—POPPY AND BRYONY DESIGN. (SECOND PART.)

To work the Honiton Sprig shown in Fig. 485 (page 257): Prick out the pattern upon parchment, DRESS THE PILLOW, and commence with the middle round of the flower, where the Half Stitch is drawn. Hang on six pairs of BOBBINS and a GIMP, work round the inside petal in HALF STITCH, then hang on another pair of Bobbins, and work round again, SEWING to one edge; then work round the last time, half the way in Half Stitch, and the remainder in CLOTH or WHOLE STITCH, cut off the Gimp and two pairs of Bobbins, and work FIBRE STITCH down the stem of the front leaf; at the tip hang on four pairs of Bobbins, which fasten down on the pillow and leave. Turn the pillow, and work down the side of the leaf where the Cloth Stitch is shown with the six pairs worked with before, hanging on another pair

them; twist the threads twice instead of four times, and, to keep the Bobbin worked second from pulling, lay it with its pair back on the pillow, so that the threads are slack, while the next Square Plaiting is made with pairs three and four, and the pairs nearest them. The flower being finished, the stalk is next worked. Commence at the tip of the tiny leaf near the bottom, hang on eight pairs of Bobbins at the tip, and work in Cloth Stitch; cut off a pair of Bobbins as the corner is turned, and work up to the reversed leaf; here hang on five pairs, and leave six behind with which to work the stalk, and work STEM along the upper part of the right-hand side of the leaf and the lower of the reverse fold; return with eight pairs (adding a pair), and work first in Half Stitch, then in Cloth Stitch, and cut off the Bobbins at the end. Pick up the Bobbins left on the stalk, and work with them to the top bud as before; work Stem round one side and across the top of the calyx; add a pair of Bobbins, and work the bud in halves, connecting the first row to the middle row of stem. Cut off the Bobbins when the calyx is finished, and hang on at the main stalk for the other bud. Work according to pattern, but at the turn of the stem, where the bud springs from the calyx, make a pinhole at the INSIDE EDGE instead of a TURNING STITCH, which will bring the inner edge into a peak. Work the three small leaves, two in Cloth Stitch and one in Half Stitch, with six pairs of Bobbins. For the largest half-opened flower: Begin at the bottom of the lowest petal, and work the three middle ones in RAISED WORK and Half Stitch with eight pairs each. Hang on eight pairs of Bobbins at the tip of each back petal, and work them in Cloth Stitch. For the calyx: Begin at the tip of the lowest leaf with six pairs, work that and the middle one, then up the outside petal of the flower in Cloth Stitch, and do the open back petals; pass the thread across the one closed petal in à PLAIT. Finally, work the third calyx leaf with nine pairs of Bobbins, as it is worked over the middle leaf, and Sew to the Raised Work strands. Cut off three pairs, and work Stem to the main stalk; cross this, and work the hollow leaf. Commence the other flower at the tip of the middle calyx leaf with six pairs of Bobbins in Cloth Stitch, then work the two middle petals in Half Stitch; work one over the calyx leaf, which connect at the tip as it crosses, then the calyx in Half Stitch, and Stem to the main stalk. Return to the flower: Work the upper calyx leaf and up the side petal in Half Stitch, then the open back petals and down the lower side petal in Cloth Stitch, and finish with the lower side calyx leaf in Cloth Stitch. Work the stalk of the flower and the two leaves on the main stalk in BRANCHING FIBRE, Cloth and Half Stitch.

The Poppy and Bryony pattern given in Figs. 486 and 487 (pp. 258 and 259) is a Honiton Lace pattern, into which Raised Work is introduced, and should be worked by good lacemakers. The specialties of the pattern are the inner petals of the flower, the butterflies' wings, and all parts that stand up in the bold relief which is the most difficult and effective part of Honiton Lace. The long leaves which form the framework of the pattern are done first, then the inner leaves, flowers, and buds. The border is then formed, the ground filled in, the lace unpicked, and the same pattern worked over the Passement until a flounce length is completed. When the length is made, the lace is taken off the Pillow, and the Relief work arranged with a needle. Commence with the long leaf that has VANDYKE PLAITINGS as a centre. Work with eight pairs of Bobbins from the base of it, and carry Stem along the inner side to the tip of leaf, turn, and work back. The first two jags are made by spreading the Bobbins, adding more if required; and, following the course of the pinholes, as the indentures become deeper, leave the three inside pairs of Bobbins, and carry Stem to the tip with the others, hang on a fresh pair at each Pinhole and leave it behind; when the tip is reached, turn and work straight back across these new pairs. Pursue this plan always when indentations stand out clear and square from a leaf; the number of Bobbins left behind vary according to circumstances;

the Raised Work usually requires five pairs, but four are enough for a small indentation. When, however, the points of the jags run upwards, treat the indentations as small leaves, add extra Bobbins at the tip, and work back down the point, making SEWINGS on one side to prevent the hole showing where the stem first turns upwards, and add an extra pair there to be left behind and worked in at the base. Work FIBRE up the centre stem, the open dots with INNER PEARL, the small dots as FLEMISH STITCH, the zig-zag device on some of the leaves in VANDYKE TRACING and CROSS TRACING.

The lace in relief has now to be worked. Begin with the flower shown in Fig. 488, Detail A. This is worked flat upon the Pillow, the centre petals first. Work round the inner ring with five pairs, join the circle, add another pair, and work up one side of petal, add three more pairs, then work CLOTH STITCH, SEWING first to the stem and then to the inner circle, add by degrees four pairs, and Sew twice into each pinhole of the centre ring, to bring the Bobbins round; as each petal finishes, gradually cut off the Bobbins down to six pairs, then work the next petal. These petals are not joined where they touch, but, when the last is finished, and the Bobbins are cut off to six pairs, the back petals in HALF STITCH are worked over them. Each of

these takes sixteen pairs of Bobbins; add them gradually as the stem is worked. Work this stem one-third of the way round; work over the part already done without minding it, take the pieces out, and leave it to be held

FIG. 488. HONITON LACE—RAISED FLOWER.
DETAIL A.

down with the covering petal. The difficult part of the work is in the Sewings, which are attached to the inner circle like the first made ones. To make these: Sew the small petals to the outer strands of the circle, and the large ones to the cross strands. Make three Sewings in the same place when doing the final leaves; when these are finished, put a SQUARE PLAITING in the centre of the flower, and cut off the Bobbins. Finish the flower by working leaf, stem, and seed pod in Half and Cloth Stitch and OPEN BRAID. The flower opposite the one just worked is done in the same manner, the difference in the effect being produced when the lace is taken off the Pillow by the needle, one flower being made to fold up its petals, the other to open them out. CRINKLE PLAITINGS are worked in the centre of this last flower, on the right side, after the lace is taken off the Pillow.

The centre flower, shown in Fig. 489, Detail B, is next made. It consists of three tiers of petals. Work the two inside tiers in CLOTH STITCH, the outside tier in HALF STITCH, and these last finish with PEARL where they form the edge of the scallop. Work these petals in the same manner as those described for the first flower, the SEWINGS being the most difficult part, which are made in the same place three times over.

Next work the centre leaves and seed pods. Begin with the stem of the drooping one, and carry it round the curve until it reaches the seed pod; here upon the pattern are two sets of pinholes in the form of ovals, one inside the other. Work the large oval first, and carry STEM all round it at the base; hang on eight more pairs of Bobbins, and work CLOTH STITCH to the tip, then cut off the middle Bobbins, and leave five pairs on each side, with which make the two points, carry Stem to their tips, and return to the oval, where SEW securely; tie up the Bobbins and cut them off. Thus, having finished the upper part of the seed pod, take the pins out, and turn the pod back on the Pillow, with a pin to fasten it; hang on six pairs of Bobbins at the base of the inside oval, Sew to the stem of the upper one; work Stem to the tip, hang on seven more pairs and a GIMP, and work back in Cloth Stitch; this being the foundation oval, the work requires to be close and firm; fasten once more to the upper stem, tie up and cut off the Bobbins. Take out the pins, bring the first oval down into its place, and pin the small one over it; when the GROUND is put in it must be sewn to the small oval. Fasten six pairs of Bobbins to the stem where it intersects the drooping leaf, work Stem to the large poppy, return with eight pairs of Bobbins, and add gradually four more pairs where the leaf widens, fasten to the flower where leaf and flower touch, and work the second half of the leaf in the same way, then tie up and cut off the Bobbins. Work

FIG. 489. HONITON LACE—CENTRE FLOWER. DETAIL B.

the other leaf, and then the stem of the upright seed pod. This is made like the first one, except the finish, which is Stem worked round the small scallops, and fastened off and filled in afterwards with CRINKLE or PLAIN PLAITINGS.

Work the raised Butterfly as follows: Commence with the body, and work it with seven pairs of Bobbins, then with five pairs work the tracery inside the foundation wings, and carry STEM all round the foremost wing; do the outside edge first, and as it is worked hang on a pair of Bobbins at each pinhole, except at the three corners, to which hang on two pairs; leave these extra Bobbins behind for filling in the wing in HALF STITCH, which commence when the base is reached, and fasten the tracery with a SEWING as it is passed. PEARL the wing of Butterfly where it forms the outer edge. In working the first foundation wing, leave off at the further corner: cut off five pairs of Bobbins and work Stem round the other wing to the base, hang on two extra pairs at the three corner holes, and one at the remaining holes, leave these, and work with them the inside of the wing in Half Stitch, then tie up the Bobbins and cut off. Now turn the wing completely back, fold a piece of thin paper, and pin it down over it. Hang on five pairs of Bobbins to the body

of the Butterfly, and work the wings as before, but fasten them to the framework leaves on each side. These wings cannot be worked over the foundation wings on account of the tracery.

The half open Bryony leaf needs a description, but the Bryony leaf and bud in HALF STITCH, the tendrils, the half opened flower, and the drooping bud càn be worked from the illustration. For the Bryony leaf: Begin at the end of the tendril, follow it to the leaf, then continue the STEM up the back. Hang on two pairs at the tip, and work back in CLOTH STITCH, SEW to the outside strands of the stem. When the first division of the leaf is reached, carry RAISED WORK to the tip, hang on two extra pairs of Bobbins at the first hole, and one at each succeeding hole, work straight back from the tip to the centre fibre, Sew twice or thrice into each hole, as there are more outside than inside holes. Spread out the Bobbins to form the next point of the leaf, and follow the course of the outside holes; when that tip is reached, and the work is being carried down the last edge, gather the five pairs next to the pins in a cluster, which pass between the working Bobbins in one row, and under them in the next like a Gimp. Arrange the Sewings so as to finish this side of the leaf neatly at the base. Turn the pillow without cutting off any of the Bobbins, and work back the reverse way over the same ground in Half Stitch. The Sewings to the stem must be made to the cross strands, and two or three in one hole; the outside edge work in the same holes as before, but not in Raised Work, for fear of joining the two sides together in drawing the Sewings: compress or expand the work according to the holes, and leave one unworked wherever the holes are close together, so as to keep the outside and inside level. Bring a cluster of five pairs of Bobbins down the side of the last point, cut off eight pairs, work to the tip, tie up the Bobbins, and leave them there to work the ground with, which, when sewn to this in any part, must be attached to the lace worked last, and not to the lace below it. Fill in all the flower part of the design with DEVONIA GROUND, and then commence the border and the ITALIAN GROUND.

The border is worked in WHEEL STITCH, and with DIAMOND HOLES. The latter is worked first, and resembles CHEQUER STITCH worked slantwise: Hang on eleven pairs of Bobbins at the tip of one of the border leaves, thus—three Working pairs, and one Passive or Hanging pair on each side next the pins, and six other pairs in sets of three. Work from the outside across the Hangers next the pins (called the side pair), twist the Workers thrice, work three stitches, the last a TURNING STITCH, return to the edge, and twist the Workers before doing the side pair. In the third row, work the side pair, twist, work two, the last a Turning Stitch, and return to the edge. Fifth row—work the side pair, twist, make a Turning Stitch, and return, then work the side pair only and back again; this will bring the Workers down another hole, and is the same as doing two SEWINGS together. Twist all the Hangers, except the two side ones, four or five times, and the preliminary diamond is made, and the work slanted. For the rest of the Diamonds, work 1, twist, work 3, twist, work 3, twist, work 1; repeat this row three times, then, whichever side the row is finished, work over the side pair and back again, twist the six middle pairs, and work three rows, again twisting after the 1st, 4th, and 7th stitches; one side will finish before the other, because of the slant in the stitch; wind up as commenced, working across four pairs and back, then across three, and finally across two pairs. When the Diamond leaf is finished, cut off six pairs of Bobbins, and work the circle and the companion leaf—the circle in Raised Work, the leaf in HALF STITCH, and the wheel as given in Wheel Stitch; this completes the border.

The grounding to this part of the lace is composed of ITALIAN GROUND (which *see*).

The completion of this design is given in Fig. 486; it is almost similar to the first portion, the difference being, that the Bryony buds are worked in CHEQUER STITCH, and the butterfly with expanded wings in HALF STITCH; work it separately, and sew on after the Italian Ground is made.

The lace being finished and taken off the pillow, work the CRINKLE PLAITING centres to the poppies, and then adjust the Relief Work. Lay the lace on tissue paper, and thread the finest possible needle with lace thread, and with them adjust the petals, sewing them to their proper places. Make a little knot on the thread to begin with, and to fasten off make a stitch, pass the needle once through the loop, and draw it up and cut the thread off close. For the first poppy, which folds over towards the middle, run a thread along the edge of the inner petals, and draw them close, or leave them partially open. The opposite poppy, that curves its leaves back, arrange by attaching the curved petals to the back petals, run the thread at the back of the lace, and give two stitches to one petal and one to another; do not sew them regularly down, but vary their effect. The middle poppy requires the inner petals to stand up, and the outer to lie down; treat them as described above. For the long flower, sew both sides together; the other flower, which is more open, sew only partially, and catch the middle petal to the side ones. For the seed pods, sew the large oval to the small one on both sides, but not at the tip, as this should stand up. Fasten down the calyx of the opening flower with a stitch at the tip, and sew on the loose butterflies.

To stiffen the lace: Boil a quarter of an ounce of rice in a pint of water, strain when cold, and brush this over the inside of the parts that are in Relief; but only damp, not thoroughly wet them. Brush over the ordinary Relief parts with a camel hair brush, but where a bold curve or round is to be given to a petal, mould that piece over an ivory knitting needle that has been dipped into the rice water. The knitting needle is more effective than the brush for stiffening the inside of buds or seed pods, and, in fact, wherever a rounded appearance to the lace in Relief is required it will be found useful.

Honiton Trolly.—This is Honiton Lace with a Trolly Ground, and was worked before Honiton lace became celebrated.

Hood.—One of the various descriptions of head-dress, equally adopted by the two sexes. In some countries ladies use them instead of Hats and Bonnets, making them of cloth of a light scarlet colour, and braided. They are also attached to burnouses, opera cloaks, jackets, and ulsters. When employed for evening wear they used to be called Caleches. The Hood forms part of the Bedouin's national dress, and of the costume of the monastic orders. They are also worn attached to thick coats or ulsters, by sailors on Arctic expeditions, and by soldiers engaged in campaigning and sentry work.

Hoohoo.—A check cotton stuff exclusively manufactured for the African trade.

Hooks.—An appliance made of white metal wire bent in the centre, and pressed closely together, then bent across so as to form a tongue, which may be passed through an eye of the same metal wire, so as to make a movable connection between them. The remaining portions of the wire are each curled outwards—below the end of the tongue formed—and rounded into a pair of small rings, by means of which the hook is sewn to any material. They may be had both in black and white, and of various sizes and thickness, to suit the textile and the dress of either men or women. They are sold on cards, and also loose in bags of ½ cwt., by the lb., or the oz.; likewise in papers of from 3lb. to 6lb. The numbers run from 4 to 8 inclusive.

Hoops.—A graduated collection of steel bands, either enclosed in casings in a petticoat, or fastened together with a succession of tapes, at regular distances, preserving the form of a hooped petticoat; common kinds are composed of whalebone, cane, or even of coarse hemp cord. This form of dress extender has been fitly described as a "pyramidal bell hoop." There were also "circular bell hoops" and "pocket hoops," besides other even more extravagant and grotesque varieties, which for more than 200 years were successively in fashion, and, since the time of Queen Elizabeth, have had fitful extinction and revivals down to the present day. Hoops extending only halfway round have also been in vogue, and small extenders of the petticoats, called "bustles," worn just at the back from the waist, reaching halfway down the skirt, made of crinoline, as well as whole petticoats of the latter material, frequently supersede the use of the most ungraceful and inconvenient Hoop. *See* CRINOLINE.

Hopsacking.—These are very coarse cloths, made of a combination of Hemp and Jute. *See* SACKING.

Horrocks' Calico.—A superior make of calico, so called from the name of the manufacturer. These are sold "A 1" and "B 1," both 36 inches in width, and are suitable for underlinen.

Hose.—Another and more ancient name for stockings. Sometimes called "Hosen," as in the Book of Daniel, chap. iii., v. 21, and in Robert of Gloucester's *Chronicle*: "Hosyn enclosyd of the most costyous cloth of cremsyn." The "Trunk-hose" of the reigns of Elizabeth and James I. were very wide breeches.

Hosiery.—In olden times this term—now altogether restricted to stockings—used to denote men's breeches.

His youthful hose, well saved, a world too wide
For his shrunk shanks.
                —*Shakespeare.*

Hosiery signifies every description of stockings and socks. Amongst the former there are white cotton, unbleached, striped, white merino, coloured merino, ribbed merino, lambs' wool, cashmere, black worsted, both plain and knitted. Each has its sizes, which are numbered from No. 1 to No. 9 in stocks and stockings. The size is known by a corresponding number of small holes to be found manufactured in the feet. Hose and half hose, for men, youths, and boys, are of the following description: Men's lambs' wool, merino, worsted (both plain and knitted), fancy stripes, and brown cotton (plain and knitted). Women's stockings are also to be had in Lisle thread, silk (both plain and ribbed) with clocks only or open work, and in various colours, as well as in black. The best cotton stockings are the fine unbleached Balbriggan. The several sizes of women's stockings are known as full size, medium, slenders, and small women's. Under the same term, Hosiery, other articles besides stockings and socks are included, viz., all descriptions of underclothing worn by men, and their ties, handkerchiefs, belts, and braces.

Hosiery-fleecy.—A textile of the common stocking make, woven of fine fleeces of wool, the webs, when woven, being cut up into waistcoats and other articles of dress.

Huccatoons.—A description of cotton cloth, manufactured in Manchester expressly for the African export trade.

Huckaback.—A coarse kind of linen cloth, manufactured in small knots at close and regular intervals, making a rough face. It is employed for towels, and is very durable. Huckabacks may also be had in cotton, and likewise of a mixture of both. The towels may be purchased ready made in towel lengths, or cut from pieces.

Huguenot Lace.—An imitation lace worked some fifty years ago, but now obsolete. It is made of a net foundation, on to which aster or rosette shaped flowers of mulled muslin are sewn. To work: Draw out upon pink calico a simple pattern formed with rosette-shaped flowers, with buds and single leaves connected together by a flowing and entwined stalk. Back this pattern with brown paper and tack the net to it. Prepare several strips of mull muslin 1 inch in width, 6 inches in length, double the muslin, and place the edges so that they

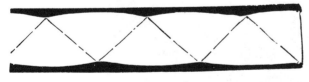

FIG. 490. HUGUENOT LACE. DETAIL SHOWING THE MANNER OF MAKING THE FLOWERS.

meet in the centre at the back of the strip; then fold it into points, thus: turn the corner of the strip down to the back where the first broken line is shown in Fig. 490, and make the second line, by folding the strip over the first, turn also to the back, make the third line by folding the closed strip over to the front, and the fourth by folding the closed strip over to the back, the number of points or folds required will depend upon the size of a flower, every alternate point forming a petal. Thread a needle with fine lace thread, and run it along the muslin, so that it follows the lines made by the folds, and as

shown in Fig. 490. Join the muslin together, and draw the run thread tightly up so as to form a rosette composed of points like the rosettes formed with Tape in TAPE WORK. Sew this rosette to the net, attach every point or fold securely to the net, and, carrying the thread quite round the petal, make another rosette of muslin with a smaller number of points, which sew inside the first so that the two form a raised flower. Leave in the centre flower enough of the net foundation visible so as to have an eight-armed WHEEL worked over it. Buds are formed with nine points of muslin. Prepare the muslin as before, but do not connect it together; draw it up as a half circle, and sew it in this shape to the net foundation. Form leaves like buds, but with only four or three points, and make stalks and tendrils by DARNING in three threads of lace in the lines over the pattern. A glazy thread, such as is used for GIMP, is the best for these lines. Edge the lace with a number of leaves tacked close together with their points turning outward. Numerous varieties of patterns can be formed by altering the number of petals to a flower, working Wheels surrounded by OVERCAST holes, and by using fancy Darning Stitches about the net; but the manner of making the muslin petals does not vary.

Hungarian Embroidery.—A description of Appliqué, with linen and twill materials, used for chair backs and table borders. To work: Trace out a bold flower design upon écru coloured holland, and back the holland with scarlet or blue twill, of the same length and width. BUTTONHOLE round the outlines of the pattern, and fasten with the stitches the two materials together. Cut away all the holland outside the Buttonhole lines, and expose in these places the twill background. Work TÊTE DE BŒUF, CORAL, SATIN, and fancy embroidery stitches on the écru holland design. Use the same colour thread for these as for the Buttonhole lines—either white, scarlet, or blue.

I.

Idiot Stitch.—One of the names given to Tricot Stitch (*see* CROCHET, page 128).

Illusion.—A French term, denoting a description of silk tulle, made in widths of 54 inches and 72 inches.

Illusion Wool Work.—An easy Berlin Wool Work, intended for young children. To work: Make in single Berlin scarlet wool a number of scarlet rounds in CROSS STITCH. Ground in between them in Cross Stitch with dark blue wool. The name is also given because, on shaking the work, the scarlet rounds appear to dance.

Imitation Lace.—Machine-made lace, made both of flax and cotton thread, woven to resemble different kinds of lace and small edgings. It may be had in many varieties of width and finish, and is comparatively inexpensive. It is chiefly made at Nottingham. In the years 1817-19 English workmen established themselves at Calais, taking with them a machine on the "straight bolt" principle, and the manufactory there established has prospered and kept pace with all the English improvements. There are four varieties of superior quality made at Calais, and St. Pierre-les-Calais, the Malines, and Valenciennes imitations amongst them. At Caen, Lille, St. Quintin, Cambray, Chantilly, and Lyons, the machine-made imitations

FIG. 491. IMITATION HONITON LACE.

of lace, both in black and white, are very beautiful, and scarcely to be detected as imitations.

formed with thick Pillow-made braid, or with thick Needle-made Buttonhole lines. These can be so easily imitated by the machine braids formed into patterns and joined together with needle-made Bars and Fillings that hardly any kind of braid or tape lace has escaped copying. One of the simplest arrangements of these machine braids is shown in Fig. 491, which is an imitation of Honiton lace, carried out with the assistance of three kinds of braid. These consist of the open straight braid used for the straight lines, the thick braid resembling Cloth Stitch, and the open braid resembling Half, or Lace Stitch. The two last named are manufactured in a series of ovals, and not as straight pieces. To work: Trace the design upon pink calico, and tack down the plain straight lines of braid to it. Take the Half Stitch Braid, and, without cutting it, arrange it in a succession of Vandykes along the upper part of the pattern, so as to fill in where shown, and arrange the Cloth Stitch Braid in a similar manner. After the Cloth Stitch Braid is arranged, sew the alternate ovals composing it thickly over to form the stem of the leaf, and then tack on the Half Stitch Braid at the bottom of the pattern in two Vandyke lines. Having thus tacked all the braids in position, secure them together. Take fine lace cotton.

FIG. 492. IMITATION VENETIAN LACE

Since the manufacture by machinery of ornamental braids made of fine linen thread, numerous laces have been imitated with their help, particularly those laces

and OVERCAST all the edges of the ovals to the straight braid wherever they touch each other, Overcast all the edges of the three descriptions of braid, and make CORDED

Bars and plain Wheels while Overcasting; and, as a finish, sew an ornamental lace edging to the lower edge of the pattern.

Fig. 492 is an imitation of hand-made Venetian Lace, and is worked with a thick braid, with a cord sewn round its edge to imitate the raised Cordonnet of the old Spanish and Venetian Point. To work: Trace the design upon pink calico, and tack down to it a plain, thick linen braid half an inch in width, and tack down and neatly turn in this braid wherever the pattern by its sharp curves and twists requires the braid to be doubled; round all the edges of this broad braid run a fine cord. Fill in the open parts of the pattern with Wheels, Escalier, and Point d'Espagne, and connect the various parts together with Buttonhole

lace stitches, and finally stitch down in the centre of the braid a fine line cord, which forms the raised Cordonnet. The outer edge of the lace ornament with a bought lace edging.

Fig. 495 (p. 266) is a lace worked in imitation of the Tape Laces of Italy and Greece. To work: Trace the pattern, outline it entirely with a plain thick linen braid, and connect the various parts together with Buttonhole Bars, ornamented with Picots. Fill in all the spaces left between the outline braids with a single Point de Bruxelles.

Imitation Breton Laces and Imitation Brussels Laces being already described, can be referred to. These differ from the imitation Braid Laces, as they are worked upon net, to which a braid is sewn, and the

Fig. 493. IMITATION GREEK LACE.

Bars ornamented with Picots. As a finish, go over the cord forming the Cordonnet. Leave this uncovered where plain in the design, but stitch it down to the braid, and work it over with fine cotton and with close Buttonholes in some parts and in others with thick cotton and in Rope Stitch to form the difference in the edging. Where the Cordonnet is ornamented, work Point de Venise as an edging.

Fig. 493 is an imitation lace resembling some of the Greek Laces. It is worked with a braid made with an open edge upon each side, and thick in the centre. To work: Tack the braid upon the pattern, Overcast round all its edges, taking care to keep the open lace-like look of the edging untouched, and make the Buttonholed Bars, which ornament with Picots. Fill in the centres of the pattern with various fancy

fancy stitches ornamenting them are formed with the needle, the net being used as their foundation. Haythorne's linen braid and Mecklenburgh linen thread are the best to use for all Imitation Laces.

Another imitation lace is a modern Embroidery, intended as an imitation of Spanish Lace. It is worked upon fine linen or cambric, with Mecklenburgh lace thread and fine cord. To work as shown in Fig. 494 (page 266): Trace the design upon cambric and tack it to a piece of Toile Ciré, outline all thick parts of the design with a fine cord, which stitch down securely, and Buttonhole round the outer edge of lace. Work the ground as follows: Arrange upright and horizontal lines of fine cord across the spaces to be filled, and wherever they cross, work over and under the four meeting lines, drawing them together in the

M M

shape of a small WHEEL, or STAR, or work simple Buttonhole or BARS ornamented with PICOTS as a ground. When the ground is finished, cover the out-

FIG. 494. IMITATION SPANISH LACE.

line cords with lines of fine Buttonhole, and then cut away the linen from underneath the ground.

Imitation Smyrna Work.—Made with canvas, thick wool, Berlin wool-work patterns, and a crochet hook,

will show the number of stitches, the front will resemble COMBED-OUT WORK. Having finished the pattern, comb out the ends of wool.

Imperial Tape.—A superior description of Tape, firmly made, and sold in numbers running from 11 to 151. *See* TAPE.

Impermeable. — The term Impermeable is more especially used in reference to the passage of fluids. It is, therefore, employed in commerce to signify waterproof, in reference to articles of wear, or for other uses.

Inch.—A measure of length, being equal to three barleycorns in its extent, or $\frac{1}{12}$th of a foot. It is employed in commerce for the measurement of textiles, especially those of which short lengths are required, such as lace, or other trimmings.

Increase.—A term used in Crochet, Knitting, and Netting, when the number of the stitches forming the pattern are to be enlarged. *See* CROCHET, KNITTING, and NETTING.

Increase Widths. — In working Pillow Lace it is continually necessary to enlarge the pattern. When this enlargement is but small and quite temporary, it

FIG. 495. IMITATION TAPE LACE.

as an imitation of SMYRNA RUG KNITTING. To work: Use canvas of a large size, cut the various shades of wool into three-inch lengths, take up a piece matching a square of the pattern, double it, and hold it at the back of the canvas with the left hand. Pass the crochet hook through the canvas to the back, and let it draw the loop to the front, but keep the ends of the wool held by the left hand, and still at the back. Pass the crochet hook over two upward strands of canvas, and through to the back again; here pick up the ends of wool and draw them through to the front and through the loop on the hook. The back of the work

is sufficient to spread out the Bobbins already in use, so that the lace while working fills in the space between the pinholes at its edge, but when the increase is of some length and width, fresh Bobbins have to be added, thus: Work the lace until near the part, and just before the last row is completed and the outside pin is added, take a pair of BOBBINS, tie them together, wind the knot away from the middle, pass the thread under the two working Bobbins, run it up close to the passive Bobbins, stick a pin and complete the edge, and work these new Bobbins in in the next row with the old ones. Directions are often given in lace patterns to hang on

Bobbins; either as a single or double pairs they are both managed in the same way.

Indian Cloths.—A large number of cotton and woollen cloths are comprised in the term India Cloths, which are subdivided into many distinct varieties. The muslins are produced in many parts of the country, but chiefly at Dacca (*see* DACCA MUSLIN), some of the beautiful productions of which manufactory are very significantly described by their native names, which, being translated, are Evening Dew, Running Water, and Woven Air. One piece of muslin, 4 yards long and 1 yard in width, weighed 566 grains; and another, 12 yards in length, and of the same width as the former piece, weighed 1565 grains. The loom-figured muslins, called Jamdanee, are exquisitely delicate; the designs are complicated, and, being regarded as a *chef d'œuvre* of Indian weaving, are the most costly of the Dacca productions. The common unbleached calicoes bear names varying with the localities where they are made. Some of the Indian cotton cloths are woven with coloured thread in imitation of English designs, such as "shepherds'" tartans. Indian cotton sail-cloth is remarkable for its lightness and strength. Chintz and other printed fabrics are produced in many places here and there over the country, the former being chiefly manufactured at Musulipatam, Arnee, and Sydaput, in the Madras Presidency, where the cloth is known as Kheetee. Those of Musulipatam show great variety, both in quality and in style. These manufactures are distinguished by the native name of Calum Kouree. Besides, some of the chintzes made for women's clothing show a dazzling variety of colour—crimson, puce, pink, and green, all blended together. The common bleached cotton for turbans is chiefly produced in the handlooms of Bharlpore, and those of the finest texture from Cashmere. Those made in Sinde are rich and various in quality, and the dyed cottons produced for the same purpose are some of them very fine, and of great richness of colour, which latter is in some cases laid on with a stamp. Gold stripes decorate certain examples, and others have an admixture of silk, and are fringed with gold thread, or have deep gold borders. Besides these cotton textiles, the woollen and hair fabrics present many beautiful varieties, such as the Cashmere Cloths and those of camels' hair. The Puttoo is composed of the inferior kinds of wool used for their shawls, which latter are made of a substance like swans' down, growing nearest to the skin, underneath the thick hair of the Tibetian goat, and which is called Pushum. The Indian Kersemeres are unlike the Puttoos, being of rather a hard quality like our own. Striped woollen cloths are made in Nepaul, Thibet, and Sikkim, the Cumblee being employed in cold weather as a covering for the head and shoulders. Felts are also made for cloaks, leggings, blankets, cushions, &c. The Cashmere Cloths manufactured into shawls form the most important loom industry of the Punjaub, which about thirty or forty years ago was almost entirely confined to Cashmere; but, while the best kinds produced in the Punjaub are those of Umritsur, none of them can compete with the original manufactures of Cashmere. One of the best specimens of a Cashmere woven shawl, and weighing 7lb., will cost as much as £300 in the country. Of cloths for carpets and rugs there are five descriptions. One is entirely of cotton, close and stiff in texture, and having a smooth surface. They are known by the name of Suttringee, are made all over the country, and are in almost universal use, being very durable. Another cloth made for the same purpose is of a mixed material, as the woof is of wool. A third kind, made of cotton only, has a short thickset pile of cotton worked into it, while a fourth has a pile of wool. Piece goods of cotton cloth are extensively made in India for home use, and likewise for export, including pocket handkerchiefs, d'oyleys, and table napkins, large quantities being produced in imitation of European made examples. Calico cloths, made in scarf patterns, are some of them very bright in colour. They are woven in half widths, and have a border on one side; and two of these scarfs being sewn together, an entire scarf, bordered on both sides, is intended to be produced. These have silk borders and ends, and show an endless variety of both colours and quality. They are also made with a union of silk, and likewise of silk only. Cotton rep is a coarse cloth used as a dress material and covering for horses by the natives. Cotton Palempore for bed covering is produced in Bengal.

Silk textiles, not being classed under the name of "Cloths," do not enter into the present list of Indian manufactures (for which *see* INDIAN SILKS, and INDIAN MUSLIN). India was the cradle of cotton manufactures and of cotton printing; and she supplied Great Britain with yarn and cotton textiles long previously to furnishing the raw material. Dorcas, Jaconets, and Mulmuls all originated there; and for hundreds of years Arabia, Persia, and the eastern parts of Africa were mainly supplied thence with their cotton cloths, muslins, and chintzes.

Indian Anglo Embroidery.—A modern embroidery worked in imitation of the coloured Indian embroideries. The foundation of the work is a large cotton neck handkerchief, such as is worn by peasants in France or Switzerland. These handkerchiefs are selected for their patterns, which are oriental and bright coloured; and these patterns are reproduced by the embroidery executed over them in silks and gold or silver thread. To work: Back the cotton handkerchief with a Ticking lining, outline each distinct portion of the design with REVERSED CHAIN STITCH worked with a thick strand of filoselle, SEW round this outline lines of gold or silver thread. Fill up the pattern and the ground work with coloured silks that match their colouring, and work with CREWEL and SATIN STITCH chiefly, but occasionally introduce CORAL, HERRINGBONE, and other close embroidery stitches. No part of the original grounding is left visible. Finish with a broad band of plush as a border, and sew a silk fringe to that. The work makes handsome table covers, cushions, and fire screens, and is now very fashionable.

India Muslin.—An exquisitely fine description of Muslin, the most beautiful and delicate kinds of which are produced at Dacca, in Bengal, especially the loom-figured ones, called Jamdanee. The weavers work under sheds by the banks of the Ganges, and size the warp with rice starch. Some of these muslins are chequered, and three persons are then employed in the manufacture—one pulls the thread to form the design, another twists it, and the third weaves it. Spinning and weaving are occupations which may be followed without loss of caste. Indian Muslins were first introduced into this country about the year 1870. Simple and primitive, as they still continue to be, in the method of their weaving, they are superior to our own productions in their durability, and the retention of their whiteness. There are different varieties of Indian Muslin made; some are figured in colours, others spotted with gold or silver, or else are plain white cloths. Amongst them is the Mulmul, or a description of Jaconet, which name is a corruption of Jaghernout, only slighter in quality than ours; others resemble a soft, undressed, plain Buke. *See* INDIAN CLOTHS.

Indian Dhurrie.—A coarse description of thick cotton cloth, imported to this country from India. It is made for hangings, curtains, and other articles of furniture. It has

hangings that are still in existence, and which must be seen before any conception of the untiring patience and skill required in the working out of the elaborate designs, in stitches arranged in every conceivable form and colour, can be appreciated. Under the title of Indian Embroidery are included many varieties of needlework, of which the principal are Cashmere work, Embroidery in Chain Stitch, in Braiding; Embroidery upon Cloth, Muslin, or Net; Embroidery in Floss Silk, and Quilting. These various kinds of work are done in many parts of India, but take their name from the district in which they are especially worked. All Indian work, with the exception of Floss Silk upon Net, and Muslin work, is better for study than for imitation, as it is impossible to give the time necessary for an exact copy, and a partial one frequently perpetuates all the faults and none of the beauty of the originals; but an European worker will do well to study the

FIG. 496. CLOTH EMBROIDERY.

a pattern consisting of very broad stripes, of equal width, in blue and red, or two shades of blue, running across the cloth, and has a deep striped border. It somewhat resembles a Rep in its style of manufacture, and measures about 1½ yards in width.

Indian Embroidery.—Eastern Embroideries have for many centuries excited the admiration of the world for the magnificence displayed both in their material and workmanship. Four centuries before the birth of Christ, when the art in Europe was hardly commenced, the needlework that was displayed upon State occasions by Indian princes was as gorgeous and as well worked as it is at the present day, and full details of it were given by the Europeans who travelled in those times. No Western nation has ever attained to the profound knowledge and management of colour that the Indian workmen displayed before their taste was corrupted by the introduction of European dyes, and in no article is this knowledge better shown than in the numerous State counterpanes and

polychrome effects produced, and the elaborate and yet pure designs.

Cashmere Work is one of the principal Indian Embroideries, and the shawls imported to England of this Embroidery are highly prized; in them the needlework almost covers the material, and the work is carried out in every conceivable shade. The prices these shawls command vary from £50 to £300, according to the needlework upon them, and their value is generally decided by the height of their borders, an inferior shawl being only worked to a certain depth, and a rich shawl having a border nearly filling up its centre. Cashmere work is generally done upon silk or woollen fabrics, the colours of which are red, black, green, and white, all of which are frequently used in one piece of needlework. They are joined together as in Inlaid Appliqué, so as to appear one piece, and form in themselves masses of colour, but they are covered either with SATIN STITCH Embroidery in shaded floss silks, or with a number of stitches, such as CROSS

STITCH, POINT LANCÉ, HERRINGBONE, BACK STITCH, POINT DE RIZ, and KNOTS, worked with twisted purse silks. These stitches are not worked in the European fashion, in straight lines, or all in one direction; on the contrary, an Indian worker rarely fills in two spaces of the pattern alike, using continually the same stitch, but altering the direction to suit the flow of the pattern, and arranging it over the place indiscriminately, and filling in with any other stitch or variety of the same that may strike his fancy. The effect of the pattern is much increased by this manner of Embroidery, but it renders it almost impossible of imitation.

Cloth Embroidery is worked much in the same manner as Cashmere Work, but upon various coloured cloths, such as black, red, and green. These are joined together as in Inlaid Appliqué, and are either braided with gold braid, or worked with gold thread and gold silk in CHAIN STITCH, or covered with conventional flowers, worked in flat SATIN STITCH, with brightly shaded floss silks. Much of the Cloth Work in gold and silver, upon black and red grounds, comes from Delhi, and is known as DELHI WORK; but Embroidery with coloured floss upon cloth is also called by that name. Embroidery upon Cloth with gold or silver thread is more easily copied than Cashmere work, as it contains no elaborate stitches, and much of it is simple BRAIDING, either with fine gold braid, BACK-STITCHED to the material, or with gold thread COUCHED down upon the surface. Of this description is Fig. 496, which is the half of an Indian cloth. To work: Join together, as in INLAID APPLIQUÉ, different coloured cloths; make the outside rim of black cloth; also the centre scalloped line; the rest make of scarlet cloth, except the centres of the pine-shaped ornaments; make these alternately of green and blue cloth. Form the fine curled lines round the chief parts of the design with Japanese gold thread sewn to the outside of the material, making the thicker lines with fine silver braid, back-stitched down, and work the round bosses and other ornaments in OVERCAST and with blue and green floss silk.

Indian Chain Stitch.—This Embroidery is one of the most ancient of all needleworks; for a long time it was known as Tambour Work, and then as Indian Work upon muslin. It is executed in many forms, either upon Turkey red twill, with white cotton, or upon muslin and net for dress materials, or upon coloured cloth embroidered in silk for articles that do not require washing. The stitches used are CHAIN STITCH and a simple KNOT; most of the patterns consist of outlines worked over with Chain Stitch lines, and such places as the veins of leaves, the stamens of flowers, &c., indicated by short Chain Stitch lines, or by a succession of DOTS. The work when executed upon net is not always in Chain Stitch, but is formed with a shiny thread RUN along all the outlines and in and out the net. Indian Work upon fine muslin or cambric is the same as the fine Embroidery executed in Ireland upon the same materials, except that it is almost entirely worked with flat SATIN STITCH and without open stitches.

Indian Floss Silk Work is of two kinds, one where it is worked upon coloured cloth or cashmere in elaborate patterns of many shades of floss silk, and the other where

it is embroidered upon plain net. The first named is the handsomest, and large quantities of it are exported to England. The patterns are generally geometrical designs or conventionalised flowers and leaves, and the Embroidery is executed to entirely conceal the material. The stitch used is flat SATIN STITCH for all the chief parts, and ROPE or STEM STITCH for the dividing lines of a pattern and the stems of flowers. CHAIN STITCH is also introduced, but not to any extent. Some of the handsomest Floss Embroideries are those worked with white floss upon scarlet grounds, and used as scarfs or sashes.

Indian Quilting Work was carried to great perfection during the Middle Ages, and many specimens executed in those early times are still preserved. The art in India is still carried on, and though nothing is now produced there equalling the old elaborate designs, still, the least skilled Indian worker will quilt up anything given him to wad, in radiating circles and geometrical designs, without any pattern and with perfect accuracy. Much of the old Quilting is done upon silk foundations, but some is executed upon cotton tissue, and so arranged that in places the material is puffed up, and in others left plain, and these last parts embroidered with designs in many colours; or the pattern is entirely formed with quilted lines arranged as figures, animals, or foliage. These shapes are not simply indicated in outline, but are filled in with lines that follow the right contours of the object they delineate, and the smallest spot upon a leopard, or the curl of a horse's mane, is as faithfully rendered as the more important parts of the work. Indian Quilting Work was brought to Europe by the Portuguese, and from that country it spread over all the Continent, and became a favourite needlework during the fifteenth and sixteenth centuries. *See* QUILTING.

Indian Floss Silk Embroidery.—This work is executed upon black or white net with white or coloured floss silks, and is an imitation of the floss Silk Embroidery made by the natives of India. From the nature of the materials used, the Embroidery should not be subject to much wear and tear, but it is not difficult of execution, is extremely Oriental in appearance, and is suitable for brackets and mantelboards and evening dress trimmings. To work: Trace out upon pink calico an Oriental design, composed of conventional leaves and flowers, and work out the design as in ordinary SATIN STITCH Embroidery. Tack down to the calico black or white net, and cover the pattern over with a series of long Satin Stitches worked in floss silk. Insert the needle in the lower part of a leaf, and carry the stitch up to the top of the leaf, here twist the needle round one mesh of the net just to hold the silk, and carry the silk back to the lower part of the leaf on the upper side of the net, so that none of the silk is wasted at the back of the work. Work long Satin Stitches in this manner over all the pattern, slanting them outwards when forming the petals of flowers, and curving and sloping them, when by so doing the lines of the designs are more fully indicated. Work large leaves, not from the top to the bottom, as before mentioned, but with two lines of stitches radiating from the centre vein, and stems with a number of short slanting stitches. Designs in cream white floss silk are more Oriental in appearance than those into which colours are introduced.

Indian Hemp, or Sunn.—The fibre of the *Crotalaria juncea*, a totally different plant from the *Cannabis Sativa*, from which Hemp is obtained. *See* SUNN.

Indian Lace.—There is little trace of the art of lace-making to be found in any part of India, which is remarkable in a nation endowed with such wonderful patience and skill over the sister art of Embroidery. All the famous Indian collections of gorgeous textiles and needlework supply only a few specimens of a native lace, consisting of a simple open meshed gauze, embroidered with gold and silver, of the poorest design and execution. The only other work that at all resembles Needle-made lace is a description of Knot Work made with a continuous series of thick Buttonholes, every three stitches of which are drawn together with a loop passed across them. These rows of Buttonholes are only varied with lines of Chain Stitch, and the whole forms a compact, massive fabric, not partaking in any way of the lightness and elegance of lace.

Indian Point Lace.—One of the terms for DRAWN WORK (which *see*).

Indian Silks.—Amongst the many varieties manufactured in India, five may be more especially indicated as entering extensively into the English home market. Indian silks are classified as the "Cultivated" and the "Wild." Amongst the former we import the Corah, Mysore, Nagpore, and Rumchunder; and from the latter category, or Wild Silks, the Tusore, otherwise called Tusah, and Tusar. There is also that called the Moonga, a superior description of silk of the same class, but employed in the trade with Arabia. The Kincobs are Satin textiles, decorated with designs in gold flowers, and are employed for ladies' skirts; the Mushroos have a surface of silk, but a cotton back, and are decorated with loom-embroidered flowers; the silk brocades are very beautiful, and are chiefly manufactured at Trichinopoly. Those brocades with white silk flowers are from the Deccan, though to be purchased in Madras. The most costly examples of brocaded silks are massively embroidered with gold, and with silk stripes; the costliest of all, produced at Hyderabad, are very striking in appearance, having wavy stripes of rich yellow, pink, and white, combined with gold. Silk stuff, manufactured for trousering, is produced of the very slightest texture, 9 yards of which would scarcely weigh as many ounces.

India Rubber.—Otherwise known by the French term Caoutchouc, a gum obtained from a species of fig tree, or *Ficus elastica*, a native of the East Indies. Besides other uses to which it is applied, India rubber is introduced into articles of wear, which are thereby made waterproof; and into surgical bandages. When elastic materials are manufactured, such as bands, garters, and braces, and cloth from which "spring-sides" of boots are made, the warp only is composed of India rubber. Both silk and cotton cloth are now produced in all colours, and shot on each side, waterproofed with India rubber, and having a beautiful lustre. *See* ELASTIC TEXTILES and WEBBING.

India Tape.—This variety of tape was formerly known as Chinese tape. It is sold in large quantities, and is of superior strength, and is made both sized and soft. The numbers run from 00 to 12, and it may be had cut in any length desired.

Indots.—*See* EMBROIDERY STITCHES.

Ingrain.—A term used in connection with textiles dyed before being woven. The advantage of employing them is that they can be washed without thereby discharging their colours. The cotton cloth called Turkey red, and the red marking cotton, are what is called Ingrain. There are also double and treble-ply Ingrain carpets.

Inkle.—A kind of linen tape or braid, employed in the sixteenth century as a trimming, and worn on soldiers' uniforms. It was made in different colours—plain yellow, plain white, or striped in blue and pink, or blue and red. It was much worn by the peasantry as a trimming for dresses and hats. The term Inkle had likewise another signification in early times—viz., a particular kind of crewel or worsted with which flowers and other designs were embroidered.

> With her neeld (needle) composes
> Nature's own shape, of bud, bird, branch or berry,
> That even her art-sisters, the natural roses,
> Her inkle, silk, turn with the ruby cherry;
> That pupils lacks she none of noble race
> Who pour their bounty on her.
>
> *Pericles*, Act V.

Inkle used formerly to appear in the list of Customs duties described as "wrought" and "unwrought inkle," or the plain and embroidered varieties.

Inlaid Appliqué.—The description of Appliqué, which consists in cutting out various pieces of material so that they fit into each other, and joining them together without their overlaying. *See* APPLIQUÉ.

Inner Pearl.—The Pearls are the ornamental loops used in Honiton and other Pillow laces as a finish to the edge of the design; and the Inner Pearls are the same loops worked round an opening in the centre of the lace. There are two ways of making these: one with a Gimp, and one without. To work with a Gimp, as shown in the

FIG. 497.   INNER PEARL WITH A GIMP.

Hollow Leaf in Fig. 497: Hang on ten pairs of BOBBINS and two GIMPS at the tip of leaf, and work in CLOTH STITCH to the place where the opening begins. Work to the centre of the row, stick a pin in the top hole, hang on a pair of Gimps round it, twist the two pairs of RUNNERS twice, make a stitch about the pin, and work first down one side of the opening and then down the other. The inside stitch is the Inner Pearl, and is made thus: Work to the inner Gimp, pass it through the pair, twist the Runners six times, stick a pin, pass the Gimp through again, and work back. When both sides are finished all but the lowest hole, the two runner pairs will meet in the middle, make a stitch, stick a pin, tie the Gimps, cut them off, and let one of the Runner pair of Bobbins merge into the Hangers, or Passive Bobbins, and finish the leaf in Cloth Stitch. The remainder of the pattern is worked with the circle in RAISED WORK, with six pairs of Bobbins, and the closed leaf in HALF STITCH.

To work the Inner Pearl without a Gimp, as shown in Fig. 498 (page 271), in the Butterfly's Wing: Work the body, beginning at the tail, with five pairs of BOBBINS and two GIMPS. Cut off the Gimps at the head of the butterfly, hang on three more pairs of Bobbins, and work the antennæ with four pairs each, which tie up and cut off. Hang on six pairs of Bobbins at the body, work up the upper wing, there hang on four pairs, come back with CLOTH STITCH, and work the Inner Pearl as directed in the previous pattern. At the bottom cut off all but six pairs of Bobbins, work STEM from the lowest part of the

FIG. 498. INNER PEARL WITHOUT A GIMP.

other wing for seven holes, then hang on a pair of Bobbins at each hole for four holes, which are not worked in, but lie back by the pins. When the point of junction with the other leaf is reached make a SEWING, work straight across in Cloth Stitch, bringing in the added pairs left at the pins: twist each of these twelve times.

Insertion.—In reference to textiles, this term is employed to denote strips of lace, or embroidered muslin, or cambric, having the edges on each side alike, and a plain portion of the material outside the work, by which it can be sewn to a garment, collar, or cuff on one side, and to the plain part of the lace, or muslin edging, or border, on the other. It is also much employed for infants' bodices and robes, being inserted in parallel stripes between portions of the dress material, whence the name is derived. It is always worked on the straight way of the stuff, and is called in French *Entre-deux*. Insertions are likewise made in Crochet Work and Tatting, as also by means of Tape and Braid, and worked in silk and cotton, as an openwork decorative connection between two pieces of material.

Irish Cambric.—A linen cloth as fine as French Cambric. It is sold by the yard, and handkerchiefs of this material can be had with grass-pattern borders, broad tape hems, or hem stitched.

Irish Ducks.—A linen textile of stout make, in white, unbleached, and black, blue, brown, olive, and grey. It is used for labourers' blouses.

Irish Guipure.—*See* IRISH LACE.

Irish Lace.—Lacemaking in Ireland has only within the last fifty years become the industry of the people, and the laces produced are none of them national, but are all copies of those worked in other countries. Until the time of Charles I. the Irish clung to their national costume, in spite of the laws forbidding its adoption; and as this consisted of a large three-cornered cloak, thickly-plaited vest, knitted trousers, and plain skull cap for the men, and women's dresses of the same simple pattern, lace trim-

mings of any description were not required, and would have obtained no sale had they been produced. When Charles I. repealed the dress enactments, English fashions, with their profuse lace decorations, were assumed, and the want of a cheap native lace was felt by all to whom expensive foreign laces were unattainable; but no effort to establish a manufactory was made until 1731, when the Dublin Society founded a school, which was, however, dissolved when that society ceased in 1774. In 1820, Carrickmacross Lace was made from Italian patterns. In 1829, a school was opened at Limerick for Limerick Lace; but it was not until the great famine years (1846 to 1848) that any real attempt to make lace a general production was commenced. In those years, by the exertions of ladies and the Government, lace schools were opened in various parts of the country, and the fine Irish Point—an imitation of Brussels Appliqué—was commenced at the Curragh schools. Limerick Lace, Irish Point, and the fine Crochet imitations of old Points, are the laces that have attained the greatest celebrity as Irish productions; but, besides these, numerous imitations of other laces are worked, especially Irish Guipure, or Carrickmacross Point, Jesuit, Spanish, Venetian and Rose Point, Pearl Tatting, Knotted and Lifted Guipure, Black and White Maltese, silver, black, and white Blondes, and wire ground Valenciennes, all of which command a certain price.

Limerick Lace is of three descriptions—Tambour, Run, and Appliqué. To work the Tambour: Frame the Brussels net in a TAMBOUR frame, and work the pattern in lines of CHAIN STITCH made with a Tambour needle and floss thread. To work the Run Lace: Frame Brussels net, and work the pattern in RUN lines with a point needle and fine linen thread. To work the Appliqué: Lay Cambric over net, or net over net, work out the design by overcasting the lines of the pattern, cut away the background of the upper material, and allow the foundation material to show through as the background to the design.

Irish Point.—This lace is sometimes called Curragh Lace, but its chief manufacture is at Youghal, where it is taught in the schools attached to the convent, besides being made at New Ross, Kenmare, Killarney, Kinsale, Clonakilty, and Waterford. The best Youghal Irish Point is made with a needle, Réseau ground, and flower and Arabesque designs, copied from Brussels Point Lace, and filled with fine and well-arranged Point Lace stitches. Another kind consists of working with the needle detached flower sprays, joining these together with Corded Bars, attaching them to Brussels net, and cutting away that foundation where it is not required. To work: Trace out the design as a whole upon a piece of blue paper, and each leaf or spray separately upon patent cloth or parchment. Prick these small patterns round their outlines with two holes close together, a slight space left, and two more holes close together, with great regularity, and commence to work with 250 eight-fold lace thread. Over the outline of a flower or leaf lay several strands of fine thread or a thin cord, and attach this to the pattern by COUCHING it down. Bring up the needle through the first pinhole on the outside of the flower, pass it over the threads, and put it down in the second pinhole. Catch the whole of the outline down to the pattern, and then commence to fill in the stitches. The stitches employed are the same needle stitches used in old needle-made laces and in Modern Point lace. Work the light fillings with POINT DE BRUXELLES and its varieties, and with BARCELONA LACE and POINT DE VENISE; and the thicker with POINT NONÉ. Having worked the fillings, go over the outline with fine even rows of BUTTONHOLE, and ornament this CORDONNET with LOOPS and PICOTS, and work over all stalks, veins, and tendrils with fine Buttonhole lines. These Buttonhole lines require great care; the thread, while making them, must not take up any of the tacking threads or the parchment, and the stitches

the RÉSEAU ground with the needle. This real ground add after the separate sprays are worked and tacked together.

Carrickmacross Lace.—Of two descriptions, an Appliqué and a Guipure. The Appliqué is worked upon net like that made at Limerick, but the designs are better and more elaborate. The Guipure is illustrated in Fig. 499. This is really a description of Embroidery, and is worked as follows: Take the very finest mulled muslin or fine lawn, trace the design upon it, and lay it upon Toile Ciré. Run a thread round all the outlines, and OVERCAST this thread over very closely; cut away the centres of the flowers, BUTTONHOLE these round, and fill them with WHEELS and fine open stitches, the same as are used in MODERN POINT, or fill them in with a Honeycomb net,

FIG. 499. CARRICKMACROSS GUIPURE LACE.

must be worked with a uniform regularity. When the detached pieces are made, unpick them from their patterns by cutting the tacking threads at the back of the pattern, and pulling out every thread singly. Lay all the detached pieces, face downwards, upon the complete design, and tack them to it, then connect them together with CORDED or BUTTONHOLE BARS. If the Bars are only Corded, lay fine cream-coloured Brussels Net over the sprays, and attach this to them by OVERCASTING into every other pinhole in the outer edge of the sprays. Cut away the net, and Overcast the edges where the fancy fillings occur in the sprays, and finish the outer edge with a line of Buttonhole ornamented with Picots. Work the best Irish Point entirely as old Brussels needle point, and form

and DARN in and out of this, so as to form an open pattern. Connect the various detached parts of the pattern together with a number of BUTTONHOLE BARS, which freely ornament with PICOTS. Unpick the work from the Toile Ciré, and, with a very fine and sharp pair of scissors, cut the material away close to the Overcast, so as to leave an open ground. This lace will not stand hard wear, and should be cleaned, not washed, as the edges are only Overcast and not Buttonholed, as its lightness and beauty would be impaired by the thick edge a Buttonhole line would give. The patterns most worked are the Rose and Shamrock.

Irish Crochet.—This is an imitation of the Guipure points of Spain, Greece, and Venice. Its reputation as

HONITON LACE.

OLD BUCKINGHAM LACE — RARE.

BEDFORDSHIRE LACE.

an Irish Lace is universal. The Knotted, Jesuit, Lifted, and Greek Guipures are all imitated with fine crochet.

Irish Linen.—This linen, being so much superior to that manufactured elsewhere, is inquired for in the shops by the name of Irish. The evenness of the threads, the softness of the texture, and the gloss of the surface, are said to be partly attributable to the quality of the flax grown in Ireland. The principal seats of the industry are at Belfast, Carrickfergus, and Londonderry. *See* LINEN,

Irish Point Crochet.—This Crochet is worked in imitation of the early Spanish Guipures, and is also known as Honiton Crochet. *See* CROCHET.

Irish Stitch.—*See* BERLIN WORK.

Irish Work. — The beautiful white Embroidery executed in Ireland is illustrated in Fig. 500, but does not differ from the white Embroideries manufactured in Saxony, Madeira, and Scotland. The peasantry of Ireland have obtained a well-deserved reputation for the excellence of the work produced by them, which is as remarkable for the delicacy of its execution as for the beauty of its designs. Irish work is done upon fine cambric, linen, or muslin, and the stitches used are Flat and Raised Satin,

For Crewel Work upon Cloth or Serge: Make an open wooden frame with four pieces of wood, damp the material, stretch it into the frame, and, while damp, iron it carefully upon the wrong side. If ironed over a solid frame the work becomes flattened.

For Crewel Work upon Linen: Damp and pin out the work until dry upon a drawing-board.

For Woolwork: Damp the work upon the wrong side, stretch it, and firmly pin it down upon a drawing-board, with the wrong side uppermost. Pass a warm iron over the surface, then rub a little EMBROIDERY PASTE into the back of the work, and leave on the board until quite dry.

Isle of Man Lace.—The lace really made in the Isle of Man during the last century was a Pillow-made edging lace, resembling Valenciennes in design and ground; but much lace was conveyed from that island into England, under the name of Isle of Man lace, that was smuggled over from the Continent, as, during the time that foreign laces were forbidden importation into England, the Isle of Man was one of the chief smuggling depôts. The real Isle of Man Lace was of no value, and is no longer made.

FIG. 500. BORDER IN IRISH WORK.

French Knots, Overcast, and Dot. The work is principally made with flat and raised Satin Stitches, relieved by the others named; the open parts are formed with Eyelet-holes, but these are never large or numerous, thus distinguishing Irish Work from Broderie Anglaise, where they form the chief part of the design. To work Fig. 500: Trace the design upon fine cambric, and back it with Toile Ciré. Work the round balls in OVERCAST, the leaves in RAISED SATIN STITCH, the stems in ROPE STITCH, the flowers in Raised Satin Stitch, with FRENCH KNOTS for their centres; and DOTS, surrounded with fine Overcast, for the outside leaves.

Ironing.—Embroidery worked over the hand, and not in a Frame, requires to be stretched when completed, if at all puckered. The process of finishing differs according to the work.

Embroidery upon Silk or Satin requires two people to stretch the material. Take a hot iron, and hold it with the flat end uppermost; cover it with a damp handkerchief, and, as the steam rises, pass the Embroidery over the iron, with the wrong side downwards. Stretch it firmly while drawing it across the iron, and be careful not to make any creases.

Isle of Wight Lace.—During the last century a Pillow Lace was made in the island resembling that made in Wiltshire and along the South Coast; but it has now entirely disappeared, the lace now known as Isle of Wight Lace being made upon machine net. It is a Run lace, resembling some of the Northampton Run laces. It is of no particular value, but, being a native industry, some articles composed of it were worn by the Princess Royal at her first presentation. To work: RUN the chief part of the design with fine lace thread, until quite thick, then form the outline by doubling the thread and running it round the close portions of the pattern. Make Open Fillings, by DARNING the net in various designs, to imitate lace fillings, and ornament the net ground with single DOTS or Diamonds, made with four Dots together, and formed with OVERCAST and RUN lines.

The name of Isle of Wight Lace is sometimes given to Tatting worked in large pieces.

Italian Cloth.—Otherwise called Venetian Cloth. A description of linen jean, satin woven, and dyed black. It is employed for women's petticoats, and as linings for men's coats. It measures 1 yard in width.

N N

Italian Darned Netting.—This kind of lace is known as Punto Maglia and Lacis by the Italians, and was one of the first kinds of lace made. It was worked all over Italy during the sixteenth century, although some authorities declare that it was for some time only worked at Sienna, and was called Sienna Point for that reason. The lace is made like other Darned Laces, upon a Netted Foundation, and is revived in our modern Guipure d'Art. To work: NET a foundation of plain square meshes, which slightly starch and stretch in a FRAME, and work upon that a design formed by thickly DARNING in and out of the meshes, filling some in entirely, and others only partially. The stitches used are the same as those illustrated in GUIPURE D'ART; but to imitate the old Italian Laces do not work more than two or three different stitches in one design. *See* GUIPURE D'ART.

Italian Ferrets.—A kind of silk galloon, made in white, black, blue, scarlet, crimson, and other colours, of one width only. Four pieces, of 36 yards each, to the gross. It is used for binding dressing gowns and flannels.

Italian Ground. — This Pillow Lace ground was anciently used in Italian coarse laces, and is composed of hexagons, having all the sides equal. It is illustrated in the Poppy and Bryony design, as worked for HONITON LACE, the real stitch being slightly different, the alteration being made on account of the fine thread required for Honiton. To work for Honiton Lace: Begin at the left-hand side of the place to be filled, and fasten on four pairs of BOBBINS, and work a PLAIT right and left as far as the two holes below; stick a pin there temporarily to hold the Bobbins, fasten on four more at the tip of a leaf, and Plait right and left as before. The Plait first made will meet the left-hand one of the second set. The Bobbins are now dealt with in pairs, and not as single threads. Take out the pin put in temporarily, pass the middle left-hand pair over the middle right-hand pair, stick in the pin again between them; twist each pair to a fine strand, and, with these four strands, make a Plait down the straight side of the hexagon, stick a pin in the hole at the bottom, untwist the threads, and make a Plait right and left as before. Return to the border, fasten on four more pairs, and bring a fresh line of Plaits down in the same manner; there will be no difference in the size of the Plaits if the strands are firmly twisted. The stitch when made in coarse thread is as follows: Put the middle left-hand Bobbin over the middle right-hand one, give both pairs one twist to the left, and repeat. When the right and middle lines meet, twist the strands, put the middle left strand over the middle right, stick a pin to hold them, then work with the twisted strands in the same stitch as before. This manner of making Italian ground, when done with fine thread, makes the hexagons small and close.

Italian Lace.—Italy is as celebrated for its lace-making as Belgium, and good lace was produced in the former country at a much earlier period than in Flanders. The Italian needle-made laces, particularly those of Venice and Milan, are of great value and unrivalled beauty. Italy asserts her claim to the invention of Needle Points, although Greece and Spain also lay claim to its production; but which of these nations first invented Needle Point must remain a matter of conjecture; however, there is no doubt that Italy produced good needle laces in the fifteenth century, and in the sixteenth the art was almost universally practised in her convents. The great luxury of the Venetian and other Republican States, and the pomp and magnificence attending upon the Romish ritual, fostered the production of the most costly Needle Points, until they were superseded by the newer Belgian and French manufactures, when the art of making them gradually died out. The earliest laces made in Italy were the Cutwork, Darned Laces and Drawn Work, also the gold and silver laces, and, beside the fine Needle Points and the Raised Needle Points made at Venice, the Réseau grounded Needle laces made at Milan and Burano, and the Knotted and Pillow Laces of Genoa. The making of Pillow Lace spread all over Italy, and what are known as Guipure and Tape Laces are all classed under the heading of Italian Lace. This description of Italian Pillow Lace is illustrated in Fig. 501, where the pattern is formed with a thick Braid, ornamented with a Pearl Edge. The Braid is lightened with a number of devices formed upon it by various shaped holes, made by working PINHOLES, while CRINKLE PLAITINGS and DIAMOND FILLINGS fill in the centre of the thick outlines. The BRIDES uniting the various parts of the pattern together are formed with thickly plaited plain BARS. For description of Genoese Knotted Laces, *see* MACRAMÉ, and for Milan and Venetian Laces, their several headings.

Italian Punto.—The Italian name for Italian lace.

Italian Punto à Groppo.—The modern MACRAMÉ (which *see*).

Italian Stitch. — A name applied erroneously to COUCHING. HOLBEIN Stitch is sometimes so called.

J.

Jabôts.—A French term, originally employed to signify a description of frilling, or ruffles, decorating the front of a shirt. It is now applied by dressmakers and milliners to the full decorative frilling of lace worn on the front of a bodice, much in the same style as those originally so named, and first worn by men.

Jacob's Ladder.—*See* KNITTING.

Jacconet.—A thin, yet close, cotton textile, of a quality between muslin and cambric, being thicker than the former and slighter than the latter. The name is derived from Jaghernout, the district in India where the manufacture originated. It is the thickest of the soft muslins employed for making dresses and neck cloths, and other articles of infants' clothing, &c. Nainsook is a variety of Jacconet, of a thicker make. There are also glazed Jacconets, which are dyed in various colours, the thick glazed finish being on one side. Much of this description of cloth is made in France. The width ranges from about 30 inches to a yard.

Jamdanee. — The finest and most beautiful variety amongst the Indian loom figured muslins, produced in the Deccan. Their designs are so complicated, and their texture so delicate, that they are more costly than any others of Indian manufacture. *See* INDIAN MUSLINS.

FIG. 501. ITALIAN PILLOW LACE.

NN 2

Janus Cord.—The material so named is a description of Rep, composed of wool and cotton, made for women's dresses, and, being a black material, is peculiarly well suited for mourning. It is a specialty of a large house of business. The width is 30 inches; and the fine cord running through shows equally on both sides, so that there is no right or wrong side to the material.

Japanese Embroidery.—We are indebted to the opening up of the islands of Japan to Europeans for the introduction into this country of some of the most curious and elaborate achievements in the way of needlework ever produced. The cradle of Embroidery was in the East, and, in the earliest times, that wrought at Babylon excited the admiration of the Egyptians, Hebrews, and Greeks; but there are few people who have realised that, during the centuries succeeding Alexander's Eastern conquests, in a remote and seemingly barbarous kingdom, Embroidery was executed of the highest class, while the art in Europe was passing through the stage of its first acquirement, its period of excellence, and its final decay, for it is only within the last few years, and mainly from the stimulus again given to it from the East, that the craft has been rescued from oblivion. Because the work executed in Japan is in general good, it does not follow that all is; or that it should be copied by us until we understand the reason of its design. Like all Eastern work, much of it is symbolical, and should be reproduced only in its spirit, as many pieces that seem to us grotesque and unsightly are merely truthful enough representations of some old religious legend, quite out of place for English home use. It is the spirit in which the work is done, the originality and force of the designs, and the marvellous power attained in the management of colour, combined with the patience and care brought to the execution, that should excite our emulation. Japanese workers are able to compete with most nations in their figure, bird, and flower designs, and in the marvellous manner they produce, with a few lines, a distant landscape or foreground object, subordinate to the centre figures; but their geometrical and conventional designs are not so good as those produced in China and India.

Three descriptions of Embroidery are made in Japan. First, that upon silk and other grounds, worked with Flat Satin Stitch in coloured silks, and with gold and silver thread; second, Raised Embroidery, similar to our Embroidery on the stamp; and, thirdly, the Raised Work, composed of various coloured cottons and cloths. The Japanese silk embroidery commonly seen in England is done for the English market, and is much inferior to the work used in Japan to cover over wedding gifts when passing from one house to another, or for screens or dresses. These are all heirlooms, and their embellishment is of the best description. Black is rarely used as a ground in native Japanese work, pale blue, purple, scarlet, and brown being preferred, as giving a softer tone to the design. The stork is the sacred bird, and, as such, is constantly depicted; it is generally worked with white silk shading to grey and black silks, and with pink legs; but it is also made with gold thread. In a flight of storks across a screen, it will be found that, however great their number,

no two are alike, and that all are in attitudes of easy flight; while their distance from each other, and the space they are flying into, is admirably rendered by the foreshortening of the birds, and the few lines indicating the horizon and the clouds. Besides the storks, eagles and small gay-plumaged birds are constantly worked, and with such attention to plumage that almost every feather is indicated. This fine work is the result of using silk threads of so fine a texture that the worker makes them as required. The silk web is passed round a fixed pin, doubled, stretched, and the two ends twisted together by being rolled in the palms of the hands. The cherry blossom, hawthorn, acacia, and laburnum are the favourite small flowers, the double anemone, iris, and chrysanthemum the large ones of the worker; the colours they are worked in are true to Nature, and are all executed in Flat Satin Stitch, though occasionally the stem of a tree, reeds, or other foreground objects, are worked with gold thread laid down, two strands together, but separately Couched to the material. The ability of the Japanese to work figures in silk is shown in Fig. 502 (page 277), which represents a female sweeper, and is taken from a very ancient piece of embroidery. In this is found many curious stitches, and also the peculiarity of human hair being used for the hair of the figure, which, after being secured to the top of the head, is allowed to flow freely down the face and back, being looped under the head-dress, and the ends left free. To work: Make the face in flesh-coloured silk, and all the wrinkles and lines with slightly raised parts; indicate the features by black silk lines, the eyeballs white, and the hair white. Work the face in SATIN STITCH, arranging the lines, as the shading indicates, across the face. Form the head-dress with lines of laid gold thread, also the bow behind the ear, and the piece hanging down the back. Make the upper dress with lines of gold-coloured floss silk laid downwards, and then caught at stated intervals with three lines of silk of the same colour, which arrange to form the pattern; make the wavy lines down the garment in the same colour, and work collar and sleeves with gold thread; make the under dress with pale blue floss silk, with gold thread stitched round it with scarlet silk. Silver thread and small white silk KNOTS form the edging below the sleeve. Work the hands and feet like the face, and make the broom with gold threads, COUCHED down with yellow silk. Fasten the threads used, either in beginning or finishing, in the front.

The Embroidery upon the Stamp is chiefly used when large animals, such as dragons, tigers, and lions, are represented, and large fish and birds; but it is also employed when various Japanese deities, in all their grotesque fierceness, are delineated. All the leading muscles and contours of the object represented are padded to a great height with raw cotton, and glass eyes are inserted into the figure. All the padding is then covered with lines of gold thread Couched down, and these lines are so arranged that they follow the true natural lines of the figures, while the raised parts give the effect of light and shade. Flat parts are generally worked in brightly coloured floss silk, but sometimes the whole design is executed with gold or silver thread.

Raised figures covered with coloured cotton or cashmere are a peculiarity of Japanese art, and have an extremely curious effect. The subjects chosen are illustrations of the mythological fables of the country, or scenes from Japanese everyday life; a whole screen will be covered with these raised figures engaged in all the varieties of person in reality. The faces are painted and raised, and have much the same look as those of the best rag dolls; but the hair and moustaches are real, the hair of the women being ornamented with raised hairpins and combs. Every garment is distinct from the figure where it would be in real life, and any implements held in the hand

FIG. 502. JAPANESE EMBROIDERY.

Japanese labour, and with the surroundings and landscapes worked in Flat Satin Stitch in coloured silks. The raised figures are managed by filling out, until quite prominent, all the contours of the figure with waste cotton, and then covering this over with clothes made of white or coloured linen, or coloured materials, such as would be worn by the are almost detached from the surface. This kind of Japanese work cannot well be copied by Europeans, as it would lose all its quaintness in any other dress; but much can be learnt from their Silk Work, and from the spirited and elegant designs for which they are so justly celebrated.

Japanese Native Cloth.—A very narrow, and rather fine, plain made, and undressed cloth, 14 inches in width, originally designed for the embroidery of curtain borders, but sold for articles of fancy work of various kinds.

Japanese Silks.—These silk stuffs are produced in three descriptions of dress material, of more or less degrees of thickness respectively. There is the "double warp gros grain," which may be had in all colours, both dark and very delicate light tints. These are all 22 inches in width, and are softer in quality than those of a plain make. The Damassé Japanese, which has apparently as much substance in them, but is not so soft, has a rather small floral design, which covers the ground of the silk very closely. It may be had in many varieties of colour, both dark and light, and measures 19 inches in width. The plain made Japanese silks are slight in quality, but vary in thickness. They are, for the most part, 20 inches in width; but one kind, which is described as "leather made," is stouter than the rest, is 45 inches in width, and is produced in a silvery-grey colour, of which the black warp is soft, and the grey woof is stiff. The slighter kinds may be had in a great number of colours, both dark and light—the latter in very delicate tints—and are almost transparent in quality. The stiffness of the woof of this description of silk is such that it has the great disadvantage of creasing.

Japanese Stitch.—*See* Embroidery Stitches.

Java Canvas.—A close make of canvas, having the appearance of being plaited, and made in many sizes and degrees of fineness. Some kinds are white, some yellow, and some like fine Berlin canvas. Java Canvas is employed in the new Kreuzsticherie. *See* Canvas.

Java Canvas Work.—This Embroidery is named from the material upon which it is worked, and is used for mats, work cases, music cases, and for any description of article that requires a pliable, yet moderately stiff, foundation. The Embroidery upon the Canvas is worked either with wools, silks, or filoselles, and the stitches used are Flat

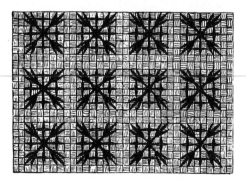

FIG. 503. JAVA CANVAS WORK.

Satin, French Knots, Point de Riz, Cross Stitch, and other Embroidery Stitches. The patterns executed are all simple geometrical designs, worked in large open stitches over the canvas, which is left visible in most places, as, from its stiff nature, it would be great trouble to fill it up with Embroidery, and, being in itself ornamental, it does not require concealment. To work Fig. 503: Select a well and

evenly woven Java Canvas, of as pale a colour as procurable, and have the design marked out upon Point Paper, such as is used for Berlin patterns. Count the squares used in the Point Paper for the design, see that the threads of the Java Canvas correspond, and then copy the pattern upon it, using deep rose colour, dark green, orange, and bright blue silk. Make the Cross Stitches of one figure of dark green, and the Satin Stitch rays of it of orange, and work the next figure in blue and crimson. Diversify the design by altering the colours. When the work is finished, edge it by sewing doubled ribbon round the edge of the canvas to keep it from fraying out.

Jean.—A twilled cotton cloth, or species of fustian, of thick and strong make, to be had both plain and in stripes, and in single colours. Satin Jeans, or sateens, are of a superior quality to ordinary Jean, having a smooth glossy surface, and being made after the manner of satin. These latter varieties are much employed for stays, belts, waistcoats, and for shoes and boots. The "Laces of Jeane," and "Lace of Jeane Silk," of which mention is made in Mediæval documents, denoted "Laces" of Genoa; although a common material, described as "Whitt Jeanes," and "Jeanes Fustian" (which seems to have been employed for stockings), was in use in the fourteenth and fifteenth centuries.

Jeanette.—A variety of jean, coarser in quality, yet not so closely woven. Some Jeanettes are twilled, and have a finished surface like sateen. These textiles are chiefly employed as linings.

Jennet Fur (Genet).—This designation is applied to cat skins, dyed, and carefully prepared so as not to betray their common origin. The best animals are the Dutch and the Bavarian. The former are reared for the sake of their fur, are treated with much consideration, and fed on fish, until the coat is in a state of the highest perfection. Large numbers are also collected in England and other countries. The wild cat (*Felis catus*) is much larger, is longer in its fur, and is chiefly met with in the extensive forests of Hungary. The colour is brownish-grey, mottled and spotted with black. The softness and durability of the fur renders it very suitable for cloak linings. It is also made into wrappers for open carriages and railway rugs. The real Jennet Fur is that of the Civet cat, and is very pretty. It has a dark ground, variegated with narrow stripes and spots of yellowish-white. The skin measures 12 inches by 4 inches.

Jersey.—The finest portion of wool separated from the rest is so designated; also fine woollen yarn and combed wool. Jersey and Guernsey are names likewise given to woven, close-fitting vests of coarse wool, worn by sailors and fishermen in lieu of jackets, or under their pea-jackets and waterproof blouses. The names of these vests have reference to their origin in the Channel Islands. As a boating costume, and one adapted for athletic and other sports, it has been long adopted by gentlemen, only the materials are of a finer quality, and woven in stripes of different colours—as white and blue, white and pink, &c. These vests have also been adopted by women—usually young ones—and were woven entire at first, and afterwards made of what is called Elastic Cloth, or

"Stockingette" (which *see*), and also in silk, cotton, and woollen yarn, of many degrees of fineness, and sold at varying prices. H.R.H. the Princess of Wales introduced the fashion as a yachting costume. These Jerseys were first manufactured by a firm in the Isle of Wight. What is commonly known as Jersey Cloth (or Elastic Cloth) is 30 inches in width.

Jesuit Lace.—A Guipure lace imitated in Ireland with Crochet.

Jetted Lace.—This work makes a useful trimming, and, though expensive to buy, can be made at a comparatively small cost. It is composed of black machine lace, bugles of an equal size, and black sewing silk, and can be worked in two ways, first, by entirely covering the pattern, and only leaving the ground visible; secondly, with lines of bugles marking out the principal lines of the lace. To work thickly, select a coarse lace, with a thick, prominent pattern. Cover this pattern with bugles, sewn on with the black silk, and arrange them so as to follow the curves and lines of the lace they cover up. To work leaving the lace visible: Select either a Chantilly Blonde or Maltese Silk Guipure Lace, of a bold and flowing design, and sew the bugles separately along the centre of every part of the design; work a BACK STITCH after every fourth bugle, to keep the bugles from getting out of place. Cover entirely over with bugles any rosette, or small flower parts of the pattern, and double the line of bugles where the design will be improved by so doing.

Joining.—*See* CROCHET, KNITTING, and TATTING.

Join Threads.—*See* MACRAMÉ.

Josephine Knot.—This knot is used to join two pieces of thread together, where both the ends are afterwards required for use. It is known to nautical men as a Carrick Bend, and is illustrated under the heading of KNOTS (which *see*).

Jours.—A term used by lacemakers to denote the open stitches that form the Fillings in Needle and Pillow Laces.

Jupe.—A French term signifying the skirt of a dress, a petticoat skirt being distinguished from it by the name of Jupon.

Jute.—The silky fibres growing underneath the bark of the two plants, *Chonch* and *Corchorus*, which are extensively cultivated in Bengal, but common, here and there, all over India, Ceylon, and China. Coarse cloths have been manufactured from it for centuries, as well as sacking and cordage. Indian Jute is first cleaned, and then pressed into bales, each containing 300lb., for exportation to Europe. It was introduced into this country rather more than forty years ago, the chief seat of home manufacture being at Dundee; it is also manufactured in London, Manchester, and Glasgow. It is likewise utilised in France and the United States. Our home manufactures consist of canvas, carpeting, cording, Ducks, Hessians, sacking, sailcloth, and sheetings. Besides the manufacture of these cloths—to make some of which, as in the carpet manufacture, it is used in conjunction with cocoa fibres—Jute is likewise extensively employed in the adulteration of silk stuffs, which, owing to its great lustre, it greatly resembles. Many other unions are formed in connection with Jute by its incorporation with

cotton, flax, tow, and wool. It is for the most part used in its natural state, but it is also bleached, dyed in various colours, and finished.

K.

Kangaroo Fur.—The Kangaroo is a ruminating marsupial animal, of the genus *Macropus*, and is a native of Australia and the adjacent islands. Kangaroo skins vary in size; those of the so-called "Foresters" are of considerable proportions, the animals being from 7 feet to 7½ feet in height. The fur is somewhat similar in colour and quality to that of the raccoon, though not so handsome nor valuable. It is much employed in Australia for articles of dress, and fetches a good price.

Kashgar Cloth.—Synonymous with CAMEL HAIR CLOTH (which *see*).

Kerchief.—*See* HANDKERCHIEF. According to Martin, the Highland women in ancient times wore nothing on their heads until after marriage, when they invariably put on a head-dress formed of a handkerchief of fine linen, which was tied under the chin, and was called a Curtch.

> Hir coverchiefs weren full fine of ground,
> I dorse sware they weyden a pound,
> That on the Sonday were upon hir hede.
> *Chaucer* (1328—1400).

Kersey.—According to Booth, Kersey is double-twilled Say, the name being a compound of Danish and Swedish *Kersing* and the Scotch *Kors*—cross; because Tweeling is woven so as to have the appearance of lines of plaited threads, running diagonally across the web. Kersey is a kind of coarse, narrow, woollen cloth, woven from long wool, and usually ribbed. Sometimes, however, it used to be made of a finer quality. In Stafford's "Briefe Conceipte of English Policye," 1518, he speaks of the vanity of servingmen, who would have their "hosen of the finest Kersey and that of some strange dye, as Flanders dye or French puce." According to Planché, many descriptions of Kerseys are mentioned in the reigns of Henry VIII. and Edward VI., "varying according to the texture in length, breadth, and weight of the piece, which was strictly regulated by Statutes." There were the "ordinary Kerseys, sorting Kerseys, Devonshire Kerseys (called 'washers,' or 'wash-whites'), Check Kerseys, Kerseys called 'dozens,' and Kerseys called 'straits.'"

Kerseymere.—A twilled, fine woollen cloth of a peculiar texture, one-third of the warp being always above, and two-thirds below each shoot of weft. It is of two thicknesses, single and double milled, being reduced in width by the process of milling from 34 inches or 36 inches to 27 inches. It is thin, light, and pliable. The name is derived from the locality of the original manufacture, on the "mere" or brook which runs through the village of Kersey in Suffolk. We learn from Stow that "about the year 1505 began the making of Devonshire kersies and corall clothes." Kerseymeres must be tested by their feeling in the hand, and by a close inspection. If of good quality, they are more durable than plain cloths.

Kid Skin (Leather).—The best kid skins employed in

the manufacture of gloves are collected from the south of France. They are also imported from Ireland, Germany, Switzerland, and Italy. Those exported from Ireland are much esteemed. As soon as the kid ceases to be nourished on milk only, the fineness and delicacy of the skin becomes deteriorated, and it is rendered unsuitable for the best gloves. The French dyers of kid gloves have produced between ninety and one hundred different shades of colour. *See* GLOVES.

Kilting.—A term employed in dressmaking to denote an arrangement of flat single plaits, or pleats, placed closely side by side, so that the double edge of the plait on the upper side shall lie half over the preceding one on the inside, each showing about 1 inch and hiding 1 inch. The arrangement is precisely that of the short petticoat worn by Scotchmen as a part of their national costume, and whence the term Kilting is derived. It must always be made on the straight way of the material.

Kilting Machine.—An appliance used for the purpose of both Kilting with more perfect regularity, and greater speed, than in working by hand. Under the name of "Accordian," whole skirts of fine machine-kilting may be had; as well as Trimmings, in Ruchings of Net Tulle, and dress stuffs.

Kincob or (Kincaub).—An Indian textile fabric of muslin, gauze, or silk, woven in various ways, and sometimes embroidered with gold or silver. It is used for both male and female dress, and is sometimes very costly. It is chiefly manufactured at Ahmedabad, Benares, and Trichinopoly, and is produced in several varieties. In some the silk predominates, and in others the silver or gold. Tunics for men's wear are made of this material, and it is much employed for women's skirts, for which latter purpose, were the petticoat of moderate length, the price would vary from £3 to £5 sterling.

Kirriemure Twill.—A fine twilled linen cloth, named after the town where it is manufactured, in Forfarshire. It is employed for purposes of Embroidery.

Knickerbocker.—A species of Linsey cloth, manufactured for women's dresses, having a rough surface on the right side, composed of what appear like small knots in the yarn. They are of variegated colours, speckled, yet without any design; and also to be had in grey, black, and white.

Knitting.—The art of Knitting was unknown in England until the sixteenth century, but before that time it was practised both in Italy and Spain. The tradition in the Shetland Isles is, that it was first introduced there when the Spanish Armada was dispersed, the ship belonging to the Duke of Medina Sidonia being wrecked at Fair Isle, and the rescued sailors teaching Knitting to the inhabitants; and that from those islands it was imported into Scotland and England. But before that date knitted silk stockings had been presented to Edward VI., from Spain, and some stockings had been made in England. The Scots claim the invention of Knitting, because the first Knitting Guild, founded in Paris, took for their patron saint, St. Fiacre, the son of a Scotch King. Knitting obtained an unenviable notoriety in the time of the great French Revolution, from the practice of the Parisian

women, when viewing the executions in the Place de la Concorde, of Knitting, and as each head fell from the guillotine, of counting the number as if they were counting their Knitting stitches. The best knitters on the Continent are undoubtedly the Germans and Poles, but the art is universally practised, and even in Turkey the scarlet fèzes are knitted, and then blocked, dyed, and made to resemble cloth. The Pyrenean Knitting executed in the Bas Pyrénées is justly celebrated for its lightness, and also for the diversity of colours used in it; but no Knitting exceeds in beauty of texture that made in Shetland, at Unst. The wool from which this is made is obtained from sheep which resemble those in the mountains of Thibet, and is of three kinds, that from the "Mourat," a brown coloured-sheep, being the most valued, that from the "Shulah," a grey sheep, ranking next, and the white and black varieties being the least esteemed. The finest wool is taken from the neck of the living animal, and is spun and prepared by the natives, and Knitted in warm shawls 2 yards square, and yet so light and fine that they are easily passed through a wedding ring. The Knitting from Fair Isle is closer in texture, and is dyed by the islanders with dyes procured from seaweeds or rag and madder wort, and the colours produced are delicate pinks, grey-blues, and soft browns. These colours, with white, are knitted upon patterns in the stockings and caps worn in Shetland, and in many cases the designs of these patterns are extremely good.

The word Knit is derived from the Anglo Saxon *Cnittan*, and means threads woven by the hand. It is executed by means of long needles or pins, formed of bone, steel, or wood; one thread only is worked, which is formed into loops, and passed from one pin to another. In Straight or Flat Knitting, two pins are used; in Round, four or five. The excellence of the work is judged by its evenness and regularity, and when stitches are carelessly dropped off the pins the effect of the Knitting is marred, as they cannot be raised without spoiling its appearance.

The materials used are silk, wool, worsted, and cotton; the silk used is generally Adams' or Faudell and Phillip's Knitting silk, but silk should not be employed until the worker is somewhat experienced, as the shiny look of the silk is destroyed if unpicked or split; a piece of silver paper put over the knitted parts prevents their getting spoilt by the hands while working the rest of the pattern. Pyrenean or Shetland wool is used for fine Knitting, such as light and warm shawls and babies' socks; Eider yarn, lamb's wool, four thread-fleecy, and Andalusian for medium sized Knitting; Scotch Yarn, worsted, and fleecy wool for strong and rough Knitting; and Strutt's and Arden's cotton for ordinary Knitting for toilet and breadcloths, and the finest Crochet cotton for d'oyleys and pincushion covers.

All Knitting should be worked loose enough for the pins to pass easily through the stitches, but not too loose. If really worked with intelligence, there is much scope in Knitting for individual art, as, after the preliminaries are once understood, new shapes and designs can be invented. When the learner has thoroughly taken in that a Knit stitch will make a Chain stitch, a Purled; a Raised rib, an Over; will Increase if Knitted, or, if Slipped the next time will make a hole or open stitch; and that all open spaces in Knitting are formed as to the size by the number of Overs put round the pin; and that open parts can be made in the work without increasing the number of stitches on the pins or spoiling the evenness of the work, by Knitting two stitches together instead of one, a great variety of forms and shapes will be within the power of the Knitter to attempt.

TERMS.—The various terms used in Knitting instructions are as follow:

About.—Similar to a *Round* (which *see*).

Back Stitch.—Similar to *Purl* (which *see*).

Binding.—See *Joining Together.*

Bring Forward, or Pass the Thread in Front.—Take the working thread and pass it between the needles to the front of the work.

Cast Off.—The manner of finishing. To work: Knit two stitches and pass the first over the second, and drop it, so that only one is left upon the needle; then Knit another stitch and pass the second made stitch over that and drop it, and continue knitting in this manner, never keeping more than one stitch upon the right-hand needle, until the whole of the stitches have been Knit and dropped. For the last stitch draw the wool through it, and sew the end down.

Cast On.—The manner of commencing the work, and done with either one or two pins. To Cast On with one pin, as shown in Fig. 504: Hold the knitting pin in the right hand (marked A), and allow a long end of cotton to hang down, holding it in the right hand, twist that

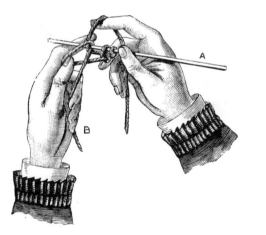

FIG. 504. KNITTING—CAST ON.

round the thumb of the left hand (marked B), and put the pin through the loop thus made, pass the end of the cotton that is on the ball of cotton round the needle tightly, and draw the needle back through the loop to make a stitch, and then slip the cotton off the left thumb, and draw that end tight.

Another way: This second plan is used chiefly in Stocking Knitting, where a raised edge strengthens the work. Put the two knitting pins together, leave an

end of about a yard, or more, according to the number of stitches required, and make a loop on the pins, hold them in the left hand, put the end over the third and fourth fingers, and the thread from the ball of cotton under the thumb, pass both the threads round the little finger of the right hand, leaving 3 inches of thread between the hands, and then put the thumb and first finger of the right hand, opened wide, in between the threads, twist the thread from the ball round the right thumb, and into the loop thus formed put the closed pins so as to bring the loop on to the pins, twist the other round the pins with a movement of the first finger of the right hand, and draw the loop on the thumb over it and drop it; a stitch will thus be formed upon the pins with a ribbed edge.

To Cast On with two pins, as shown in Fig. 505:

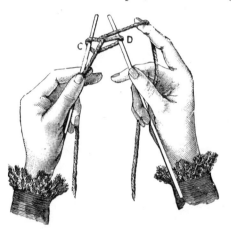

FIG. 505. KNITTING—CAST ON WITH TWO PINS.

Make a loop at the end of the thread, and put it on the left-hand pin (marked C), hold the other pin (marked D) in the right hand, and put it into the loop, pass the thread between the pins, and bring the point of the right-hand pin in front, pass the thread through the loop on the left pin; there will then be a loop upon each

FIG. 506. KNITTING—CAST ON WITH TWO PINS.

pin, finish by slipping the right-hand loop on to the left-hand pin. Work in the rest of the stitches as shown in Fig. 506, thus: Put the right-hand pin through the stitch last made, KNIT it, and SLIP the stitch from the right pin on to the left.

Cast Over.—Similar to *Over* (which *see*).

o o

Crossings.—These are formed as follows: When the part where a Crossing is to be made is reached, take off upon a spare pin three or four of the first stitches on the left pin, and keep it to the front of the work, then KNIT the next three or four stitches loosely, or PURL them; when these are knitted, Knit or Purl the stitches upon the spare needle, on the needle held in the right hand. By so doing, the stitches first knitted are laid under the last stitches, which are raised above the rest of the work.

Decrease.—There are several ways of Decreasing, and the methods are also known as Narrowing, or Taking in; but when the word Decrease is used in the instructions without other explanations, it is understood

FIG. 507. KNITTING—DECREASE.

to mean KNIT two stitches together. To Decrease see Fig. 507: Put the right-hand needle through two stitches on the left-hand needle, and KNIT them as if they were a single stitch.

Decrease when Purling.—Put the right-hand needle through the first stitch on the left-hand pin, and draw the stitch on to the pin without Knitting it; Knit the next stitch, and draw the unknit stitch over it, and let it drop.

Double Stitch.—One of the methods of Increasing, and consisting of making two stitches out of one. To work as shown in Fig. 508: KNIT a stitch, but leave it

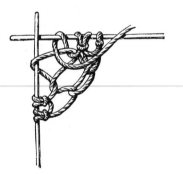

FIG. 508. KNITTING—DOUBLE STITCH.

on the left-hand needle, then bring the thread to the front of the work between the pins, then Knit the same stitch again, putting the right-hand pin through the back part of the stitch and the thread round it at the back; return the thread to the back of the work when the stitch is finished. The illustration shows the stitch Knitted once, and the thread brought to the front ready for the second part.

Another way: Put the right pin through a stitch, and pass the thread once round the pin (*see* Fig. 509), then pass it again round the pin, as shown in Fig. 510,

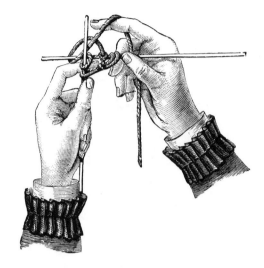

FIG. 509. KNITTING—DOUBLE STITCH.

and KNIT the stitch, bringing two threads through it and on to the right-hand pin instead of one.

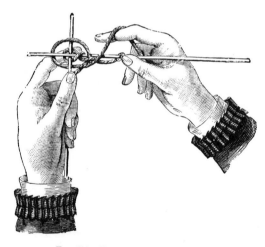

FIG. 510. KNITTING—DOUBLE STITCH.

Dropped Stitch.—Stitches are Dropped in Knitting for the purpose of making open spaces, or when Decreasing; but no stitch should be Dropped unless it has been caught, and will not unravel the work. There are two ways of Dropping a stitch: First way—When an Increase in the Knitting has been made in one row, put the cotton round the needle (termed an Over) in the next row, slip that Over off the needle without being Knitted, and allow it to amalgamate into the work without fear of unravelling. Second way—SLIP a stitch from left to right pin without working it, KNIT or PURL the next stitch, and pass the Slipped Stitch over the last made, and allow it to drop on to the work, it being secured by being held up by the second made stitch. Dropped Stitches that are slipped off the pins without the Knitter being aware of the mistake must be picked up at once, or the work will be spoilt; their loss is detected by the loop which forms the stitch running down the work. The Knitting is either undone until the line where the loop is is reached, or if simply Plain Knitting, the stitch is picked up thus: Put a crochet hook through the dropped loop, stretch the Knitting out until every line run through is visible, and CHAIN STITCH the loop up these lines until the last row of Knitting is reached, when slip it on to its pin.

Edge Stitch.—The stitches in straight Knitting that begin and end the work are known as the Edge Stitches. They are rarely mentioned in the instructions for Knitting patterns, but they are added as extra stitches in all cases, as they serve to keep the Knitting straight and to form a compact edge. Edge Stitches are Knitted and Slipped alternately.

Fasten On: When commencing the Knitting, tie a loop of the thread upon one of the needles.

Fasten Two Threads together: Lay the two threads together contrarywise, and KNIT a few stitches with them both, or fasten them together with a WEAVER'S KNOT, and Knit the ends in, one upon each side.

Form a Round.—Rounds are worked with either five or four pins, and are required in Stocking and other Round

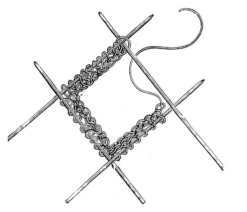

FIG. 511. FORM A ROUND.

Knitting. The Germans use five pins, and the English four pins in this kind of Knitting. To work, as shown in Fig. 511, with four pins: CAST ON the number of stitches

and Knit with it the first stitch upon the first pin, and draw the thread tight, and with it the third pin, up to the first. Work several Rounds, and then SLIP some of the stitches from one pin to another, so that in no place is the division of the stitches the same through all the work.

Gauge.—The instrument used for measuring the size of the Knitting pins. These are usually either circular, bell-shaped, or elongated, and are made of wire or steel. In the circular Gauges the outer edges have graduated circular cuts through to the extreme rim, to form what look like the cogs of a wheel; each hole has a number to distinguish it from its fellows, and there is a still larger circular hole in the middle of the instrument. Bell gauges are shaped like a bell, with the same arrangement of holes as the circular. In the elongated gauges the holes are within the outer rim, and occupying the central portion likewise. But as there are upwards of two dozen varieties, two only are illustrated in Figs. 512 and 513. These appliances are employed by wire-drawers, and are essential to the Knitter as well as to the seller of Knitting Needles.

Hang On.—Another term for *Cast on* (which *see*).

Hole.—These are formed in open fancy Knitting in the following manner: For a small hole—Make a stitch with an OVER in the previous row, and DROP that stitch without Knitting in the place where the open space is required. For a large hole: In the previous row pass the wool round the pin either two, three, or four times, according to the size of the hole required, and when these OVERS are reached in the next row, KNIT the first, PURL the second, and repeat the Knitting and Purling until they are all formed into stitches.

Increase or Make a Stitch.—Terms used when the number of stitches upon the pin have to be augmented. The ways of Increasing are as follows: The simplest is the Over or Bring Forward, used for open plain Knitting. It is worked as follows: Bring the wool from the back of the work to the front between the pins, and put it over the right-hand pin ready to KNIT the next stitch; form the same Increase when Purling, by passing the thread already at the front of the work quite round the right hand-pin, and bring it back to where it started from, ready to PURL the next stitch. DOUBLE STITCH is another form of

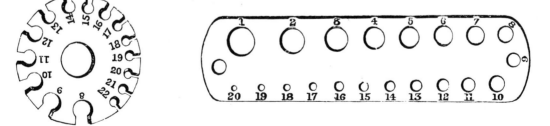

FIG. 512. CIRCULAR GAUGE.   FIG. 513. STRAIGHT GAUGE.

required upon one pin, and KNIT or PURL them off on to the three pins. Divide them so that the number of stitches upon each pin are nearly the same. Take the fourth pin

Increasing, and one chiefly used for close work. When stitches are to be Increased at the end of a row, Knit the last stitch but one, make an OVER, and Knit the last stitch. An Increase is also formed by picking up or raising a stitch, thus: Hold the work right side to the front, and put the pin into the work so as to pick up the loop nearest the last one, Knit, pull this up as a loop on the pin, and pass the working thread round the pin and through the picked up loop, to form a stitch, let the loop off the pin as in ordinary Knitting.

Join Together or Binding.—To work as shown in Fig. 514: Put the two pins containing the work together, the one holding the longer piece at the back. Take a spare

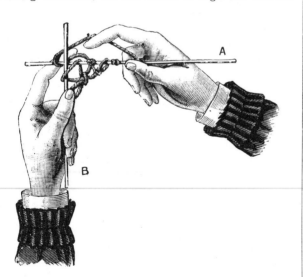

FIG. 514. KNITTING—JOIN TOGETHER.

pin and put it through the first stitch upon the front pin, and the first stitch upon the back, and KNIT the two together; continue to Knit the stitches together in this manner until all are absorbed.

Knit.—The first and chief stitch in Knitting, and sometimes called Plain Knitting. There are two ways of making the stitch, the one shown in Figs. 515 and 516

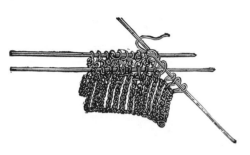

FIG. 515. KNIT—ENGLISH METHOD.

being the English method. To work: Hold the pin with the stitches on in the left hand (marked B), and the pin to which they are to be transferred in the right hand (marked A), and wind the thread round the little finger of that hand, bring it under the third and second finger, and over the first finger, and keep it tight; put the right pin into the front part of stitch, so that the front of the stitch lies across the pins, and slide the right pin behind

the left; then, with a movement of the right forefinger, pass the thread between the pins (*see* Fig. 516); draw it through the loop and up on to the right pin as a stitch, push the left pin down with the right forefinger, slide the KNIT Stitch off it, and let it drop.

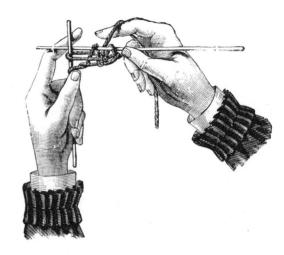

FIG. 516. KNIT—ENGLISH METHOD.

To work in the German method: Hold the hands over the pins, and these between the first finger and

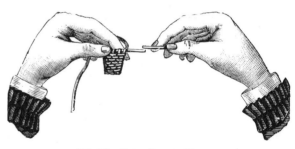

FIG. 517. KNIT—GERMAN METHOD.

thumb of each hand, as shown in Fig. 517, with the thread over the first, second, and third fingers of the left hand, and held tight between the little finger and third finger. Put the right pin through the stitch, but at the back, not front (*see* Fig. 518), open the stitch out, twist the pin round the thread stretched on the left fingers, draw it through the stitch, with a movement of the left wrist bring the right pin to the front, push the left pin down, and drop the stitch on it. The hands are held closer together than shown in the engraving; they are there divided in order that their position may be made clear. The German manner of Knitting is the quickest, and also, from the stitch being Knit from the back, it lies more smoothly upon the surface. Fig. 518 also gives the appearance of a piece of work with all the front part in the plain loops formed by Knitting. In Round Knitting, this is accomplished by Knitting every Round: In Straight Knitting, where the work has to be turned, the back row is Purled, so that the knots of the Knitting are all at the back, and the loops in front.

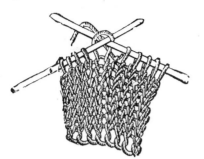

FIG. 518. KNIT.

Knit from the Back.—A term used when in English Knitting the Knit Stitch is to be taken at the back as in German Knitting: it is done for the purpose of making the work smoother in that place.

Knit Three Stitches Together.—Put the right pin through three stitches on the left-hand pin at the back, and KNIT them as one, or SLIP the first stitch of the three, Knit the two next together, and Slip the first stitch over them and drop it.

Knit Two Together.—One of the ways of diminishing, and also known as Decrease or Narrow; it is illustrated in Fig. 519, and worked thus: Put the right pin (marked A) through two stitches on the left pin (marked B), and KNIT them as one.

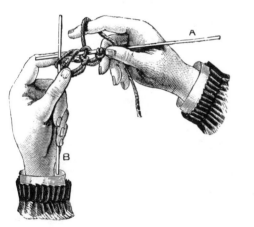

FIG. 519. KNIT TWO TOGETHER.

Loop.—A term used occasionally instead of Stitch.

Make a Stitch.—To INCREASE in the various ways described.

Marks.—These are used in Knitting patterns to save the trouble of recapitulation. When an asterisk (*) is twice put, it indicates that the instructions for Knitting between the two asterisks are to be repeated from where the first asterisk is placed to the last, thus: Knit 3, * Purl 1, Knit 6, Over, repeat from * twice, would, if written out at full length be, Knit 3, Purl 1, Knit 6, Over, Purl 1, Knit 6, Over, Purl 1, Knit 6, Over. When a row is worked to a certain stitch, and is then repeated backwards, either the place is marked by the letters A and B, or by a cross (+). For example: A, Purl 4, Over, Knit 6, B, means that after the stitches are once worked they are repeated thus: Knit 6, Over, Purl 4. Other marks beside the asterisk and the cross are occasionally used, but they are generally explained in the instructions given with the work.

Narrow.—To DECREASE either by ·Knitting two together or by a TAKE IN.

Over.—To INCREASE: In plain Knitting, pass the thread to the front of the work through the pins and back again over the pins; or in Purl Knitting, when the thread is already at the front of work, pass it over the needle and right round it, so that it again comes out at the front. The Over makes a new stitch when Knitted off on the next row, and the method of Increasing by Overs is the one commonly employed in open Knitting patterns.

Pass a Stitch.—See *Slip Stitch.*

Pass the Thread Back. — When changing Purling to Knitting, pass the thread which is at the front of the work for Purling to the back.

Pass the Thread Forward.—When changing Knitting to Purling, the thread that is at the back of the work for Knitting is passed between the stitches to bring it to the front for Purling. This movement of the thread is generally understood, but not expressed, although the term is sometimes used in old books.

Pick up a Stitch.—See *Raised Stitches.*

Plain Knitting.—See *Knit.*

Purl.—Also known as Back, Reversed, Ribbed, Seam, and Turned. It is the stitch next in importance to Knit, and produces the ribs or knots in the front of the work where they are required, or, when worked as the back row,

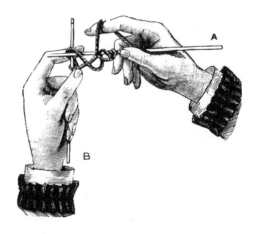

FIG. 520. KNITTING—PURL (ENGLISH METHOD).

gives the appearance of Round Knitting to a straight piece of work. To Purl as worked in England, and as shown in Fig. 520: Hold the thread in the right hand (marked A), and be careful that it is in the front of the work, put the right pin through the stitch in front of the left pin (marked B), lift the thread with the right forefinger, and pass it round the pin, keeping it quite tight, bring the right pin out behind the left, and draw the stitch off.

To work in the German method, as shown in Fig. 521: Hold the hands over both pins, and the pins between the thumb and forefinger of each hand. Bring the thread to the front of the work, pass it over both pins, and hold it tightly over the left hand. Put the right pin through the stitch and before the left pin, and, with a jerk of the left hand, bring the thread behind it, then draw the pin out

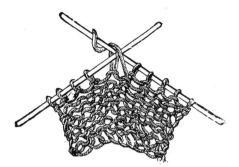

FIG. 521. KNITTING—PURL (GERMAN METHOD).

behind the left pin, and with the stitch on it. The German manner of Purling is the quickest and smoothest. Fig. 521, besides showing how to Purl, gives the appearance of a piece of Knitting which has been Knitted at every back row and Purled in every front row.

Purl Three Stitches Together.—PURL the first stitch, put it back on the left pin, draw the next two stitches on that pin over it and drop them, and put the first stitch on the right pin.

Purl Two Stitches Together.—Take two stitches on the pin at the same time, and PURL them as one stitch, or Purl the first stitch and put it back on the left pin, and then draw over it the stitch next it on that pin, which drop, then take the first stitch on to the right pin.

Quite Round.—To make an Over in Purl Knitting. See *Over.*

Raise Stitches.—Hold the work in the right hand, and with the right pin pick up a loop, then pass the thread through it, and so make a stitch.

Reversed.—To make an Over in Purl Knitting.

Rib.—Another name for Purl. Rows Ribbed the length of the Knitting are made by KNIT 2 stitches, PURL 2, and repeat to the end, and in the next row Purl the Knitted and Knit the Purled.

Round.—When Knitting with four or five pins, each time the stitches have once been Knitted is called a Round.

Row.—When Knitting in straight Knitting with two pins, when all the stitches have been Knitted off one pin on to the other it is called a Row.

Seam.—A name given to Purl Knitting, but usually indicating the one Purled Stitch down the leg of a stocking, to form the seam, and which aids in counting the stitches.

Slip.—To Slip a stitch, proceed thus: Take a stitch off the left pin, and slip it on to the right pin without securing it in any way. The Slipped Stitch in Fig. 522 is shown upon the right pin. To Slip a stitch the

reverse way: Pass the stitch from one pin to the other, taking that part of the loop that is towards you.

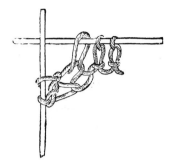

FIG. 522. KNITTING—SLIP.

Take In.—One of the ways of DECREASING. The term either means KNIT two or three stitches together, or

FIG. 523. KNITTING—TAKE IN.

as shown in Fig. 523. SLIP the first stitch, Knit the second, and pass the Slipped Stitch over the Knitted.

Take In Reversed.—PURL the first stitch, put it back on the left pin, and draw the second stitch over it.

Tucked.—Used when wide or narrow tucks are made as ornaments to the work. To make: When arrived at the spot, KNIT and PURL the rows until sufficient depth is made. Pick up on a spare pin the loops showing of the first row, and place this pin alongside of the one in the Knitting. Knit a loop from one pin and a loop from another together. Be careful to arrange the tuck to fall on the right side of the knitting.

Turned Row.—A Purled row, or a row at the back of Straight Knitting.

Turn Stitch.—Another name for PURL, which *see.*

Widen.—To Increase.

PATTERNS AND STITCHES. — Knitting Stitches, although so few in number, are capable of forming a great variety of patterns, of which the following are a selection :—

Boule de Neige.—This forms a raised knob between open parts. CAST ON any number of stitches that divide into six, for the pattern, and three extra stitches. First row—KNIT very loosely. Second row—Knit three, * Knit five together, make five stitches of one, thus: PURL and leave stitch on the needle, OVER, Purl, Over, Purl, and then take off, repeat from *. Third row—Knit. Fourth row—Purl. Fifth row—Knit. Sixth row—Purl. Seventh row—Knit loosely. Eighth row—repeat from second row. In every pattern row the five stitches made in the previous pattern row must be the ones knitted together, so that the raised knobs are formed at the side, and not over the last made ones.

Brioche Pattern.—This is also known as Patent Knitting, and is used for warm petticoats, waistcoats, and couvrepieds. The name Brioche originated in the stitch being used first to make cushions whose shape resembled a French cake of that name, but which are now obsolete. To work: CAST ON the number of stitches required, and that will divide by three. First row—PURL. Second row—Slip 1, * OVER, Slip 1, KNIT 2 together. Repeat the second row to the end of the work, always taking care that the Over of the last row is the second of the two stitches knitted together in the new row.

A variety of the stitch is made by Knitting the Over of the last row as the first of the two stitches Knitted together; this alteration turns the knitting from a close piece of work, with perpendicular lines running up it, to a stitch with raised knobs and open places.

Brioche Knitting in two colours is worked upon needles without knobs at the ends, securing the colours one at each end, and alternately working them backwards and forwards.

Cable Pattern.—This is also known as CHAIN STITCH. It can be worked either with coarse or fine wool or thread, and with any even number of stitches, and it forms a raised cable in the centre of the work, surrounded with Purled knitting. The raised cable is managed by slipping upon a spare needle 3 or 4 of the centre 12 stitches (according to the width of the strip), and Knitting the remaining number of centre stitches, and then Knitting the ones put on one side; by this means a twist is given to the cable. To work with No. 18 needles and fleecy wool: CAST ON 14 stitches, and KNIT first and second rows. Third row—Knit 3, PURL 8, Knit 3. Fourth row—Knit. Repeat third and fourth rows six times each. Seventeenth row—Knit 3, take off 4 stitches upon a spare pin, Knit the next 4, drawing the wool tight, and then Knit the 4 on the spare pin and the 3 still upon the needle. Commence the next cable by Knitting 3, Purling 8, and knitting 3 stitches, as in third row, and repeat from that row.

Another Cable Pattern is made by Knitting long strips of Knitting, and then Plaiting them together.

Close Pattern.—This simple stitch is useful for making gloves, knitting heels to stockings, or for anything that requires to be close and warm. CAST ON any number of stitches that divide into 2. First row—KNIT 1, SLIP 1, and repeat. Second row—Knit. Repeat these two rows to the end of the work, being careful that the Slipped Stitch of the new row should come always over the Slipped Stitch of the last row.

Cross Pattern.—The stitch shown in Fig. 524 is suitable for scarves, counterpanes, and antimacassars. It is worked in strips, and when used for the last mentioned articles the strips are made in contrasting colours and sewn together. It requires fleecy wool and bone needles. To work: CAST ON any number of stitches that divide into 6, with four extra for EDGE STITCHES. First and second row—Knit and PURL. Third row—Knit two,* OVER three times, Knit one, repeat from * until within two stitches of the end, which simply Knit. Fourth row—Knit two, * draw the next six stitches on to the right-hand needle as long loops, and then pass the left-hand needle

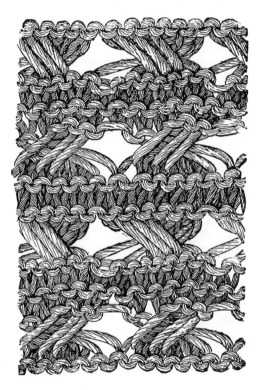

FIG. 524. KNITTING—CROSS PATTERN.

through the first three loops taken on the right-hand needle, and draw them over the other three, keeping them in regular order; put all six loops back on the left-hand needle, and knit them one after the other. Repeat from * to within two stitches at the end, which Knit. Fifth row—Purl. Sixth row—Knit. Seventh row—as fourth. Repeat fourth, fifth, and sixth rows to the end of the pattern.

Double Knitting Pattern.—There are two ways of Knitting this stitch so that the fabric, although only knitted with two needles and at one time, has the appearance of two pieces of knitting laid together. Double Knitting is suitable for all warm articles, such as comforters and petticoats. It is worked with fleecy and fine wools upon pins suitable to the thickness of the wool. To work: CAST ON an even number of stitches, and add EDGE STITCHES, which always KNIT. First row—Knit one, and put the wool twice round the pin; when doing so, bring the wool to the front between the pins, SLIP a stitch, and put the wool back; repeat. Second row—Knit the

Slipped Stitch, with the wool twice over the pin, and slip the Knitted Stitch, bring the wool to the front before Slipping, and pass it back afterwards. Repeat these two rows to the end of the work.

Another Way.—This is worked on the wrong side, and turned inside out when finished. To work: Cast on an even number of stitches, and two extra for Edge Stitches, which always Knit. First row—wool in front, Purl 1, Slip 1, continue to the end, always keeping the wool in front of the needle. Second row—slip the Purled Stitch and Purl the Slipped.

Dutch Corn Knitting Pattern.—Hold the work in the left hand, also the wool, and, instead of making a stitch in the ordinary manner, wind the wool round the little finger to keep it from slipping, insert the right-hand pin into the stitch, and let it draw the wool from the back of the work to the front through the stitch. The stitch on the left pin is then let go, and the wool on the right pin makes the new stitch. Repeat for every row.

Fancy Patterns (1).—The open pattern, shown in Fig. 525, is a useful one for working scarves and small shawls in. It should be worked with fleecy wool and ivory needles. To work: Cast on an even number of

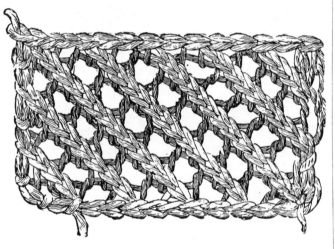

Fig. 525. Knitting—Fancy Patterns.

stitches, and two extra as an Edge Stitch upon each side, which Knit and Slip alternately. First row—* Over, Knit 2 together; repeat from * to the end of the row. Second row—Purl every stitch. Repeat the first and second row for all the pattern.

(2).—The pattern given in Fig. 526 is useful for counterpanes, and is worked in strips with No. 8 Strutt's cotton and No. 17 needles, or with fleecy wools and bone pins for couvrepieds. The stitches require careful counting, and attention should be frequently given to the direction of the slanting lines, that they diverge from and join each other as drawn. The lines slanting from left to right are formed by Knitting two stitches together, the ones slanting from right to left by Slipping 1, Knitting 1, and passing the Slipped Stitch over knitted; this is called Take In in the directions. When decreasing the diamonds in the pattern, and Knitting stitches together, always Knit them from the back of the stitch, as, by so doing, the

stitches that are dropped lie flatter. To work: Cast on twenty-nine stitches and Purl back. First row—Knit 1 *, Over, Knit 2 together, Over, Knit 2 together, Over, Knit 2 together, Over, Knit 1, Over, Take In, Over, Take In, Over, Take in, Over, Knit 1, repeat from *; there will be thirty-three stitches now upon the needle. Second and all even rows—Purl. Third row—Knit 1, *, Knit 2 together, Over, Knit 2 together, Over, Knit 2 together, Over, Knit 3, Over, Take In, Over, Take In, Over, Take In, Knit 1, repeat from *. Fifth row—Knit 2 together, Over, Knit 2 together, Over, Knit 2 together, Over, Knit 5, Over, Take In, Over, Take In, Over, Knit 3 together, Over, Knit 2 together, Over, Knit 2 together, Over, Knit 5, Over, Take In, Over, Take In, Over, Take In. Seventh row—Knit 1, Knit 2 together, Over, Knit 2 together, Over, Knit 7, Over, Take In, Over, Take In, Knit 1, Knit 2 together, Over, Knit 2 together, Over, Knit 7, Over, Take In, Over, Take In, Knit 1. Ninth row—Knit 2 together, Over, Knit 2 together, Over, Knit 1, Over, Knit 2, Knit 3 together, Knit 2, Over, Knit 1, Over, Take In, Over, Knit 3 together, Over, Take In, Over, Knit 1, Over, Knit 2, Knit 3 together, Knit 2, Over, Knit 1, Over, Take In, Over, Take In. Eleventh row—Knit 1, Knit 2 together, Over, Knit 3, Over, Knit 1, Knit 3 together, Knit 1, Over, Knit 3, Over, Take In, Knit 1, Knit 2 together, Over, Knit 3, Over, Knit 1, Knit 3 together, Knit 1, Over, Knit 3, Over, Take In, Knit 1. Thirteenth row—Knit 2 together, Over, Knit 5, Over, Knit 3 together, Over, Knit 5, Over, Knit 3 together, Over, Knit 5, Over, Knit 3 together, Over, Knit 5, Over, Knit 2 together. Fifteenth row—Knit 2 together, Over, Knit 1, Knit 3 together, Knit 1, Over, Knit 3, over, Knit 1, Knit 3 together, Knit 1, Over, Knit 3 together, Over, Knit 1, Knit 3 together, Knit 1, Over, Knit 3, Over, Knit 1, Knit 3 together, Knit 1, Over, Knit 2 together, Seventeenth row—Knit 1, Over, Take In, Over, Take In the three stitches at the top of the diamond, Over, Knit 5, Over, Knit 3 stitches together at top of diamond, Over, Knit 1, Over, Knit 1, Over, Knit 1, Over, Take In three stitches, Over, Knit 5, Over, Knit 3 together, Over, Knit 2 together, Over, Knit 1. Nineteenth row—Knit 2, *, Over, Take In, Over, Take In, Over, Knit 1, Knit 3 together, Knit 1, Over, Knit 2 together, Over, Knit 2 together, Over, Knit 3, repeat from * at end, Knit 2 instead of 3. Twenty-first row—* Knit 1, Over, Take In, Over, Take In, Over, Take In, Over, Knit 3 together, Over, Knit 2 together, Over, Knit 2 together, Over, Knit 2 together, Over, Knit 1, Over, repeat from *, end at Knit 1. Twenty-third row—Knit 2 together, * Over, Take In, Over, Take In, Over, Take In, Knit 1, Knit 2 together, Over, Knit 2 together, Over, Knit 2 together, Over, Knit 1, Over, Knit 1, Over, Knit 1, repeat from * at the end, Knit 2 together instead of the first Knit 1. Twenty-fifth row—Knit 1, Over, Knit 1, Over, * Take In, Over, Take In, Over, Knit 3 together, Over, Knit 2 together, Over, Knit 2 together, Over, Knit 2 together, Slip 1, Knit 1, Slip 1, repeat from * at the end instead of last, Knit 2 together, Knit 1, Over, Knit 1. Twenty-seventh row—Knit 2, * Over, Take In, Over, Take In, Over, Take In, Knit 1, Knit 2 together, Over, Knit 2 together, Over, Knit 2 together, Over, Knit 2 together, Over, Knit 3, repeat from * at the end, Knit 2 instead of 3,

OLD GREEK EMBROIDERY - RARE.

ORIENTAL EMBROIDERY.

Twenty-ninth row—Knit 3, * Over, Take In, Over, Take In, Over, Knit 3 together, Over, Knit 2 together, Over, Knit 2 together, Over, Knit 5, repeat from * at the end, Knit 3 instead of 5. Thirty-first row—Knit 4, * Over, Take In, Over, Take In, Knit 1, Knit 2 together, Over, Knit 2 together, Over, Knit 7, repeat from * at the end, Knit 4 instead of 7. Thirty-third row—Knit 1, Knit 2 together, Knit 1, Over, Knit 1, Over, Take In, Over, Knit 3 together, Over, Knit 1, Over, Knit 2 together, Over, Knit 2, Knit 3 together, Knit 2, Over, Knit 1, Over, Take In,

3 together, Knit 1, Over, repeat from * at the end, Knit 3. Forty-first row—Knit 4, * Over, Knit 3 together, Over, Knit 3, Over, Take In with 3 stitches, Over, Knit 5, repeat from * at the end, Knit 4 instead of 5. Forty-third row —Knit 1, Knit 2 together, Knit 1, Over, Knit 2 together, Over, Knit 2 together, Over, Knit 1, Over, Take In, Over, Take In, Over, Knit 1, Knit 3 together, Knit 1, Over, Knit 2 together, Over, Knit 2 together, Over, Knit 1, Over, Take In, Over, Take In, Over, Knit 1, Knit 2 together, Knit 1. Forty-fifth row—Knit 3 together, Over, Knit 2

FIG. 526. KNITTING—FANCY (No. 2).

Over, Knit 3 together, Over, Knit 2 together, Over, Knit 1, Over, Knit 1, Knit 2 together, Knit 1. Thirty-fifth row —Knit 2 together, Knit 1, Over, Knit 3, Over, Take In, Knit 1, Take In, Over, Knit 3, Over, Knit 1, Knit 3 together, Knit 1, Over, Knit 3, Over, Take In, Knit 1, Knit 2 together, Over, Knit 3, Over, Knit 1, Knit 2 together. Thirty-seventh row—Knit 2 together, * Over, Knit 5, Over, Knit 3 together, Over, Knit 5, Over, Knit 3 together, repeat from * at the end, Knit 2 together instead of 3. Thirty-ninth row—* Knit 3, Over, Knit 1, Knit 3 together, Knit 1, Over, Knit 3 together, Over, Knit 1, Knit

together, Over, Knit 2 together, Over, Knit 1, Over, Knit 1, Over, Take In, Over, Take In, Over, Knit 3 together, Over, Knit 2 together, Over, Knit 2 together, Over, Knit 1, Over, Knit 1, Over, Knit 2 together, Over, Knit 2 together, Over, Knit 3 together. Forty-seventh row— * Knit 3 together, Over, Knit 2 together, Over, Knit 2 together, Over, Knit 1, Over, Knit 1, Over, Knit 1, Over, Take In, Over, Take In, Over, Knit 5 together, Over, Knit 2 together, Over, repeat from * at the end, Knit 3 together instead of 5. Forty-ninth row—* Knit 1, Knit 2 together, Over, Knit 2 together, Over, Knit 2 together,

Over, Knit 3, Over, Take In, Over, Take In, Over, Take In, repeat from * at the end, Knit 1. Fifty-first row—like fifth row.

(3.)—The pattern shown in Fig. 527 is suitable for open work Stocking Knitting when worked as Round Knitting, or for breadcloths, &c., when worked as Straight Knitting, with No. 20 needles, and fine cotton. The TAKE IN means Slip 1, Knit 1, and pass Slipped Stitch over the Knitted. For Straight Knitting: CAST ON any number of stitches that divide by 11, and 2 or 4 extra stitches for EDGE STITCHES; these latter are not mentioned in the directions. KNIT a row and PURL a row, and then commence the pattern. First row—* Over, Knit 3, TAKE IN, Knit 2 together, Knit 3, Over, Knit 1, repeat from *. Second row, and every alternate row, Purl. Third and fifth rows, the same as the first row. Seventh row—Knit 1, * Over, Knit 2, Take In, Knit 2 together, Knit 2, Over, Knit 3, repeat from * at the end of the row, Knit 2 instead of 3. Ninth row—Knit 2,* Over, Knit 1, Take In, Knit 2 together, Knit 1, Over, Knit 5, repeat from * at the end of the row, Knit 3 instead of 5. Eleventh row—Knit 3, * Over, Take In, Knit 2 together, Over, Knit 7, repeat from * at the

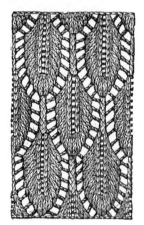

FIG. 527. KNITTING—FANCY (No. 3).

end of the row, Knit 4 instead of 7. Thirteenth row—Knit 4, Over, Take In, Over, Knit 3, Take In, repeat. Fifteenth row—Knit 2 together, Knit 3, Over, Knit 1, Over, Knit 3, Take In, repeat. Work seventeenth and nineteenth rows like the fifteenth row. Twenty-first row—Knit 2 together, Knit 2, Over, Knit 3, Over, Knit 2, Take In, repeat. Twenty-third row—Knit 2 together, Knit 1, Over, Knit 5, Over, Knit 1, Take In, repeat. Twenty-fifth row—Knit 2 together, Over, Knit 7, Over, Take In, repeat. Twenty-seventh row—Knit 1, * Over, Knit 3, Take In, Knit 4, Over, Take In, repeat from * after the last Over, Knit 1 instead of Take In. Commence again at the first row for the twenty-ninth row.

To Knit Round for stockings: CAST ON any number of stitches that divide into 11, and use four needles. KNIT the alternate rows instead of Purling them, and work the pattern as directed to the twenty-seventh row, there pass the first stitch without Knitting it to the right hand needle, and leave it there, Knitting

it at the end of the row in the Take In. Where Take Ins occur at the end of a needle, be careful to put both the stitches used on to one needle.

(4.)—The pattern given in Fig. 528 is suitable either for the open work of stockings or for the tops of stockings, worked upon four needles, or for breadcloths, &c., when worked as Straight Knitting. It looks well either worked with fine or coarse cotton. To work for the tops of stockings: CAST ON any number of stitches that divide by 12, and PURL 3 rounds, and KNIT 1 round. In the directions the TAKE IN will mean SLIP 1, Knit 2 together, and pass the Slipped Stitch over the two Knitted together. First round—Knit 4, Take In, Knit 4, Over, Knit 1, Over, repeat. Second round—Knit 3, Take In, Knit 3, Over, Knit 3, Over, repeat. Third round—Knit 2, Take In, Knit 2, Over, Knit 5, Over, repeat. Fourth round—Knit 1, Take In, Knit 1, Over, Knit 7, Over, repeat. Fifth round—Take In, Over, Knit 9, Over, repeat. Sixth round—In commencing the pattern again, the Knit 1 with Over upon each side of it, comes on the first stitch of the round formed by the three stitches knitted together in the last round, and as that round also ends with an Over a second one cannot be made; the Over of the last round is

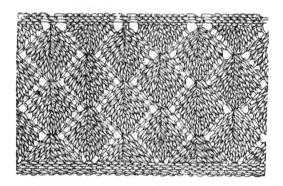

FIG. 528. KNITTING—FANCY (No. 4).

therefore put on to the right hand needle, then Knit 1, * Over, Knit 4, Take In, Knit 4, Over, Knit 1, repeat from *. Seventh round—Over, Knit 3, Over, Knit 3, Take In, Knit 3, repeat. Eighth round—Over, Knit 5, Over, Knit 2, Take In, Knit 2, repeat. Ninth round—Over, Knit 7, Over, Knit 1, Take In, Knit 1, repeat. Tenth round—Over, Knit 9, Over, Take In, repeat; commence again at the first round, which will now come right.

To work for Straight Knitting: CAST ON any number of stitches that divide into 10, and two extra as EDGE STITCHES; these latter are not included in the directions. First row—KNIT 3 together, Knit 2, * OVER, Knit 3, Over, Knit 2 together, Knit 2, repeat from *. Second row and all even rows—PURL. Third row—Knit 2 together, Knit 1, * Over, Knit 5, Over, Knit 1, Knit 3 together, Knit 1, repeat from *. Fifth row—Knit 2 together, * Over, Knit 7, Over, Knit 3 together, repeat from *. Seventh row—Knit 2, * Over, Knit 2, Knit 3 together, Knit 2, Over, Knit 3, repeat from *. Ninth row—Knit 3, * Over, Knit 1, Knit 3 together, Knit 1, Over, Knit 5, repeat from *. Eleventh row—Knit 4, * Over, Knit 3 together, Over, Knit 7, repeat from *. Thirteenth row—Knit 2 together, Knit 2, * Over, Knit 3, Over, Knit 2 together, Knit 2, repeat from *. Fifteenth row—like third row.

(5).—The stitch shown in Fig. 529 is used as an ornamental edging for the tops of stockings, and is worked

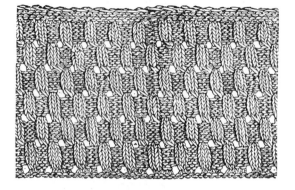

FIG. 529. KNITTING—FANCY (NO. 5).

as follows : CAST ON any number of stitches that divide by four, and work the first six rows in Ribs with KNIT 2, PURL 2 stitches alternately. First round (which is the pattern row)—OVER, Knit 2 together, Knit 2, repeat to the end. Second round—Purl the Over of the last row and the stitch next it, Knit 2, repeat to the end. Third, fourth, fifth, and sixth rounds—Purl 2, Knit 2, and repeat. Seventh round—Knit 2, Over, Knit 2 together, repeat to the end. Eighth round—Knit 2, Purl the Over of the last row and the next stitch, repeat to the end. Ninth, tenth, eleventh, and twelfth rounds—Knit 2, Purl 2, and repeat. Thirteenth round—same as the first round, repeat all the rounds to the thirteenth until the depth is sufficient. This stitch is easily worked as a Straight Stitch by Purling the Knitted stitches in the back row and Knitting the purled.

(6).—The design given in Fig. 530 is particularly suitable for coarse Knitting where the work is not required

FIG. 530. KNITTING—FANCY (NO. 6).

to be open. With coarse wool or cotton the branching parts of the pattern stand out with much effect. It also looks well worked with Strutt's cotton, No. 8, and No. 15 needles for counterpanes. To work: CAST ON for each pattern twenty stitches, and add one at each end for the

EDGE STITCH, and KNIT and SLIP these at each alternate row; they are not again referred to in the directions. First row—PURL 5, * KNIT 2 together, Knit 3, Over, Knit 1, Over, Knit 3, Slip 1, Knit 1, pass Slipped Stitch over, Purl 9, repeat from *, at the end of the row Purl 4 instead of 9. Second row—Knit 4, * Purl 11, Knit 9, repeat from *, Knit 5 instead of 9 at the end. Third row—Purl 4, * Knit 2 together, Knit 3, Over, Knit 3, Over, Knit 3, Slip 1, Knit 1, pass Slipped Stitch over, Purl 7, repeat from *, Purl 3 instead of 7 at the end. Fourth row—Knit 3, * Purl 13, Knit 7, repeat from *, Knit 4 instead of 7 at the end. Fifth row—Purl 3 *, Knit 2 together, Knit 3, Over, Knit 5, Over, Knit 3, Slip 1, Knit 1, pass Slipped Stitch over, Purl 5, repeat from *, Purl 2 instead of 5 at the end. Sixth row—Knit 2 *, Purl 15, Knit 5, repeat from *, Knit 3 instead of 5 at the end. Seventh row—Purl 2, * Knit 2 together, Knit 3, Over, Knit 7, Over, Knit 3, Slip 1, Knit 1, pass Slipped Stitch over, Purl 3, repeat from *, Purl 1 instead of 3 at the end. Eighth row—Knit 1, * Purl 17, Knit 3, repeat from *, Knit 2 instead of 3 at the end. Ninth row—Purl 1, * Knit 2 together, Knit 3, Over, Knit 9, Over, Knit 3, Slip 1, Knit 1, pass Slipped Stitch over, Purl 1, repeat from *, end with Slip 1, Knit 1, pass Slipped Stitch over. Tenth row—Purl 19 *, Knit 1, repeat from *. Commence again at the first row.

(7).—The pattern shown in Fig. 531 is more open when worked than it appears in the engraving, and it is very light and elegant, looking well when worked in coarse cotton for couvrepieds, and in fine cotton for toilet covers and bread cloths. As much of the instructions consist of various Take Ins, to avoid using unnecessary space in the directions the worker must understand them as follows : For TAKE IN: SLIP 1, KNIT 1, pass Slipped Stitch over Knitted and drop it. For REVERSED TAKE IN: Work 1, PURL, return it to left-hand needle, pass the

FIG. 531. KNITTING—FANCY (NO. 7).

next stitch on that needle over it, drop it, and return the Purled Stitch to the right hand needle. To work: CAST ON any number of stitches that divide into 10, with an extra stitch at each end for EDGE STITCHES—these will not be referred to again—they are Knitted and Slipped at each alternate row. First row—* OVER, TAKE IN, Knit 8, repeat from *. Second row—* Purl 7, Reversed Take In, Over, Purl 1, repeat from *. Third row—* Over, Take In, Over, Take In, Knit 6, repeat from *. Fourth row—* Purl 5, Reversed Take In, Over, Reversed Take In, Over,

Purl 1, repeat from *. Fifth row—* Over, Take In, Over, Take in, Over, Take In, Knit 4, repeat from *. Sixth row—* Purl 3, Reversed Take In, Over, Reversed Take In, Over, Reversed Take In, Over, Purl 1, repeat from *. Seventh row—* Over, Take in, repeat from * three times, then Knit 2, and repeat from beginning. Eighth row— Purl 1, * Reverse Take In, Over, repeat from * three times then Purl 1, and re-commence from the beginning of the row. Ninth row—* Over, Take in, repeat from *. Tenth row—Purl. Eleventh row—as first row.

(8).—The pattern shown in Fig. 532 is a useful and easy stitch, and is both light and durable. When worked with coarse wool or cotton it is suitable for couvrepieds and counterpanes, or with fine cotton and in Round Knitting, it is suitable for open work socks or stockings. When used for Round Knitting, one stitch is added to the directions as a Seam Stitch, and the return, or Purled rows, omitted. To work for Straight Knitting: CAST ON any number of stitches that divide by 9, and a stitch at each edge for an EDGE STITCH. These Edge Stitches are not mentioned in the directions—they are Knitted and Slipped each alternate row. First

FIG. 532. KNITTING—FANCY (No. 8).

row—PURL. Second row—SLIP 1, KNIT 1, * TAKE IN (or OVER, Slip 1, Knit 1, passed Slipped Stitch over, this Take In always includes an Over), Take In twice, Knit 3, repeat from *, after the last repeat Take In twice. Third and all alternate rows—Purl. Fourth row—Slip 1, Knit 2, * Take In 3 times, Knit 3, repeat from *, after last repeat, Take In, Knit 1. Sixth row—Slip 1, Knit 3, * Take In 3 times, Knit 3, repeat from *, after last repeat, Take In, Eighth row—Slip 1, Knit 4, * Take In 3 times, Knit 3, repeat from *, after last repeat, Knit 1. Tenth row— Slip 1, Take In, Knit 3, * Take In 3 times, Knit 3, repeat from *. Twelfth row—Slip 1, Knit 1, Take In, Knit 3, * Take In 3 times, Knit 3, repeat from *, at the end, Knit 2 instead of Knit 3. Fourteenth row—Knit 2 together, Knit 3, * Knit 2 together, Take In 3 times, Knit 3, repeat from *, after last repeat, Knit 1. Sixteenth row—Slip 1, Knit 3, * Knit 2 together, Take In 3 times, Knit 3, repeat from *, at the last, Knit 5 instead of Knit 3. Eighteenth row—Slip 1, Knit 2, Knit 2 together, Take In 3 times, Knit 3, repeat from *, after last repeat, Knit 2 together, Over, Knit 1. Twentieth row—Slip 1, Knit 1, * Knit 2 together, Take In three times, Knit 3, repeat from *, after

last repeat, Over, Knit 2. Twenty-second row—Slip 1, * Knit 2 together, Take In 3 times, Knit 3, repeat from *, after last repeat, Knit 2 together, Over, Knit 2 together, Over, Knit 1. Twenty-fourth row—Knit 2 together, Take In 3 times, Knit 3, repeat from beginning, after last repeat, Knit 2 together, Over, Knit 2 together, Over, Knit 2. Commence the pattern again.

(9).—The stitch illustrated in Fig. 533 is very suitable for counterpanes and couvrepieds, when worked with the ordinary sized needles and cottons, and will also be found effective in very fine knitting. To work: CAST ON any number of stitches that divide into 12, adding a stitch at each end for an EDGE STITCH, which is always worked plain, and is not referred to again in the instructions. First row—* PURL 1, thread back, SLIP 1, KNIT 1, pass Slipped Stitch over, Knit 3, OVER, Knit 1, Over, Knit 3, Knit 2 together, repeat from *. Second row—* Purl 11, Knit 1, repeat from *. Third row to eighth row like the

FIG. 533. KNITTING—FANCY (No. 9).

first and second rows. Ninth row—* Purl 1, Over, Knit 3, Knit 2 together, Purl 1, thread back, Slip 1, Knit 1, pass Slipped Stitch over, Knit 3, Over, repeat from *. Tenth row—* Purl 5, Knit 1, repeat from *. Eleventh row— * Purl 2, Over, Knit 2, Slip 1, Knit 1, pass Slipped Stitch over, Purl 1, Knit 2 together, Knit 2, Over, Purl 1, repeat from *. Twelfth row—Knit 1, Purl 4, Knit 1, Purl 4, Knit 2, repeat from *. Thirteenth row—Purl 3, OVER, Knit 1, Slip 1, Knit 1, pass Slipped Stitch over, Purl 1, Over, Knit 2 together, Knit 1, Over, Purl 2, repeat from *. Fourteenth row—* Knit 2, Purl 3, Knit 1, Purl 3, Knit 3, repeat from * Fifteenth row—* Purl 4, Over, Slip 1, Knit 1, pass Slipped over, Purl 1, Knit 2 together, Over, Purl 3, repeat from *. Sixteenth row—* Knit 3, Purl 2, Knit 1, Purl 2, Knit 4, repeat from *. Seventeenth row— * Knit 1, Over, Knit 3, Knit 2 together, Purl 1, thread back, Slip 1, Knit 1, pass Slipped Stitch over, Knit 3, Over, repeat from *. Eighteenth row—* Purl 5, Knit 1, Purl 6, repeat from *. Nineteenth row to twenty-fourth as seven teenth and eighteenth. Twenty-fifth row—* Purl 1, Knit 2 together, Knit 3, Over, Purl 1, Over, Knit 3, Slip 1, Knit 1, pass Slipped Stitch over, repeat from *. Twenty-sixth row —* Purl 5, Knit 1, repeat from *. Twenty-seventh row— * Purl 1, Knit 2 together, Knit 2, Over, Purl 3, Over, Knit 2, Slip 1, Knit 1, pass Slipped Stitch over, repeat from *. Twenty-eighth row—* Purl 4, Knit 3, Purl 4, Knit 1, repeat from *. Twenty-ninth row—* Purl 1, Knit 2 together, Knit 1, Over, Purl 5, Over, Knit 1, Slip 1, Knit 1, pass Slipped Stitch over, repeat from *. Thirtieth row—* Purl 3, Knit 5, Purl 3, Knit 1, repeat from *. Thirty-first row—* Purl 1, Knit 2 together, Over, Purl 7, Over, Slip 1, Knit 1, pass Slipped Stitch over, repeat from *. Thirty-second row—* Purl 2, Knit 7, Purl 2, Knit 1, repeat from *. Commence to work from the first row.

(10).—The stitch shown in Fig. 534 is useful for toilet covers and breadcloths if Knitted with Strutt's cotton, needles No. 17 or 18, or with needles No. 20, and crochet cotton for pincushions. To work: CAST ON any number of stitches that will divide into 12, adding 6 stitches at the beginning, four to be used in the pattern and two for EDGE STITCHES, one upon each side of the

FIG. 534. KNITTING—FANCY (No. 10).

work. These last are Slipped and Knitted alternately, and are not again mentioned in the working. The stitches are not increased or decreased, and every row takes the same number. First row and every alternate row, PURL. Second row—KNIT 4, * Knit 2 together, OVER, Knit 1, Over, TAKE IN (which means, SLIP the first stitch, Knit the second, pass the Slipped Stitch over the Knitted), Knit 7, repeat from *. Fourth row—Knit 3, * Knit 2 together, Over, Knit 3, Over, Take In, Knit 5, repeat from * at the end, Knit 6 instead of 5. Sixth row—Knit 2, * knit 2 together, Over, Knit 5, Over, Take In, Knit 3, repeat from * at the end of the row, Knit 2 together, Over, after the last, Knit 3. Eighth Row—* Knit 1, Knit 2 together, Over, Knit 1, Over, Take In, Knit 1, Knit 2 together, Over, Knit 1, Over, Take In, Knit 1, repeat from * at the end of the row, Knit 2 together, Over, Knit 1 after the last, Knit 1. Tenth row—Knit 2 together, * Over, Knit 3, Over, Slip 1, Knit 2 together, pass Slipped Stitch over, Over, Knit 3, Over, Slip 1, Knit 2 together, pass Slipped Stitch over, repeat from * at the end of the row, Over, Knit 2 after the last Take In. Twelfth row—* Knit 1, Over, Take In, Knit 7, Knit 2 together, Over, repeat

from * at the end, Knit 1, Over, Take In, Knit 1 after the last Over. Fourteenth row—Knit 2, * Over, Take In, Knit 5, Knit 2 together, Over, Knit 3, repeat from * at the end, Over, Take In after the last, Knit 3. Sixteenth row—Knit 3, * Over, Take In, Knit 3, Knit 2 together, Over, Knit 5, repeat from * at the end of the row, Over, Take In, using an Edge Stitch in the Take In. Eighteenth row—Knit 4, * Over, Take In, Knit 1, Knit 2 together, Over, Knit 1, Over, Take In, Knit 1, Knit 2 together, Over, Knit 1, repeat from *. Twentieth row—Knit 5, * Over, Slip 1, Knit 2 together, pass Slipped Stitch over, Over, Knit 3, Over, Slip 1, Knit 2 together, pass Slipped Stitch over, Over, Knit 3, repeat from * at the end of the row, Knit 2 instead of 3. Twenty-second row—commence again at the second row.

(11).—The stitch given in Fig. 535 is much reduced in the illustration, and when worked is somewhat thicker, but it is useful for Round Knitting, and as the bars cross each other and form raised lines above the rest of the Knitting, the effect is good. To work: CAST ON with the ordinary sized Knitting cotton any number of stitches that divide into 13. First round—* KNIT 3, PURL 7, Knit

FIG. 535. KNITTING—FANCY (No. 11).

3, OVER, repeat from *. Second round—* Knit 3, Purl 7, Knit 3, Purl 1, repeat from *. Third round—Knit 2, Knit 2 together reversed, Purl 6, Knit 3, Over, Purl 1, Over, repeat. Fourth round—Knit 3, Purl 6, Knit 3, Purl 3, repeat. Fifth round—Knit 2, Knit 2 together from the back, Purl 4, Knit 2 together, Knit 2, Over, Purl 3, Over, repeat. Sixth round—Knit 3, Purl 4, Knit 3, Purl 5, repeat. Seventh round—Knit 2, Knit 2 together from the back, Purl 2, Knit 2 together, Knit 2, Over, Purl 5, Over, repeat. Eighth round—Knit 3, Purl 2, Knit 3, Purl 7, repeat. Ninth round—Knit 2, Knit 2 together from the back, Knit 2 together, Knit 2, Over, Purl 1, Purl 2 together, Over, Purl 1, Over, Purl 2 together, Purl 1, Over, repeat. Tenth round—Put the first three stitches on a separate needle and keep it to the front, Knit 3 rather loosely, then Knit the 3 from the separate needle (these six stitches make the crossing), Purl 9, repeat. Eleventh round—Pass the first stitch of each needle on to the needle before it, Knit 2, Over, Knit 2, Knit 2 together from the back, Purl 3, Over, Purl 2 together, Purl 2, Knit 2 together, repeat. Twelfth round—Take off the last stitch of the eleventh round, and use it without Knitting it as the first of the twelfth round, Knit 3, Purl 1, Knit 3, Purl 7, repeat, passing the last stitch upon each needle to the next needle. Thirteenth round—Knit 3, Over, Purl 1, Knit 2, Knit 2 together from the back, Purl 6, repeat. Fourteenth round—Knit 3, Purl 3, Knit 3, Purl 6, repeat. Fifteenth round—Lift the first stitch from the left hand needle on to the right needle, keeping the thread behind it, and leave it there. Do this with all the needles, Knit 2, Over, Purl 3, Over, Knit 2, Knit 2 together from the back, Purl 4, knit 2 together, repeat. Sixteenth round—Take off the last stitch of the fifteenth round as in the twelfth round, Knit 3, Purl 5, Knit 3, Purl 4. Seventeenth round—Pass the first stitch to the right hand needle as in the fifteenth round, Knit 2, Over, Purl 5, Over, Knit 2, Knit 2 together from the back, purl 2, knit 2 together, repeat. Eighteenth round—pass the first stitch of each needle as in the twelfth round, Knit 3, Purl 7, Knit 3, Purl 2, repeat. Nineteenth round—Pass the first stitch to the right hand needle as in the fifteenth round, Knit 2, Over, Purl 1, Purl 2 together, Over, Purl 1, Over, Purl 2 together, Purl 1, Over, Knit 2, Knit 2 together from the back, Knit 2 together, repeat. Twentieth round—Slip the last stitch off the right hand needle on to the left hand, then place upon a separate needle the next 3 stitches, and work as in the tenth round. Re-commence the pattern at the eleventh round.

(12).—The pattern shown in Fig. 536 forms a series of raised scallops or leaves, and requires to be worked with very fine cotton and No. 20 needles, as, when worked with coarse needles and cotton, the dropped Overs are too large for beauty. The Purled side of the pattern is the most raised, but either side can be used as the right side of the work. To work: Cast on any number of stitches that

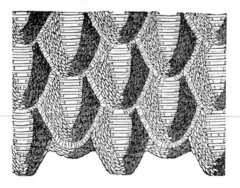

FIG. 536. KNITTING—FANCY (No. 12).

divide into 20, and four more for two EDGE STITCHES upon each side. PURL and KNIT the Edge Stitches every other row: they are not mentioned in the directions for Knitting. The Take In here means Slip 1, Knit 1, pass Slipped Stitch over the Take In reversed, Purl 1, return it to the left hand needle, pass the next stitch on that needle over it, drop it and return the Purled stitch to the right hand needle. First row—Purl. Second row—Over, * TAKE IN, Knit 8, Over, Knit 8, Knit 2 together, Over,

repeat from *. Third row—Over, drop the Over of the last row (in future explanations the word "drop" will indicate this movement), * Purl 2 together, Purl 7, Over, then upon the over of the last row Purl 1 and Knit 1, Over, Purl 7, Take In reversed, Over, drop, repeat from *. Fourth row—Over, drop, * Take In, Knit 6, Over, Knit 4, Over, Knit 6, Knit 2 together, Over, drop, repeat from *. Fifth row—Over, drop, * Purl 2 together, Purl 5, Over, Purl 6, Over, Purl 5, Take In reversed, Over, drop, repeat from *. Sixth row—Over, drop, * Take In, Knit 4, Over, Knit 8, Over, Knit 4, Knit 2 together, Over, drop, repeat from *. Seventh row—Over, drop, * Purl 2 together, Purl 3, Over, Purl 10, Over, Purl 3, Take In reversed, Over, drop, repeat from *. Eighth row—Over, drop, * Take In, Knit 2, Over, Knit 12, Over, Knit 2, Knit 2 together, Over, drop, repeat from *. Ninth row—Over, drop, * Purl 2 together, Purl 1, Over, Purl 14, Over, Purl 1, Take In reversed, Over, drop, repeat from *. Tenth row—Over, drop, * Take in, Knit 8, Over, Knit 8, Knit 2 together, Over, drop, repeat from *. Eleventh row—Purl the over of the last row, Over, * Purl 7, Take In reversed, Over, drop, Purl 2 together, Purl 7, Purl and Knit the Over of the last row, Over, repeat from * after the last, Purl 7, Over; only Purl the Over of the last row. Twelfth row—Knit 2, Over, * Knit 6, Knit 2 together, Over, drop, Take In, Knit 6, Over, Knit 4, Over, repeat from *, end with Knit 2 instead of Knit 4. Thirteenth row—Purl 3, Over, * Purl 5, Take In reversed, Over, drop, Purl 2 together, Purl 5, Over, Purl 6, Over, repeat from * after the last Purl 5, work Over, Purl 3. Fourteenth row—Knit 4, Over, * Knit 4, Knit 2 together, Over, drop, Take In, Knit 4, Over, Knit 8, Over, repeat from * after the last Knit 4, work over, Knit 4. Fifteenth row—Purl 5, Over, * Purl 3, Take In reversed, Over, drop, Purl 2 together, Purl 3, Over, Purl 10, Over, repeat from * after last purl 3, work Over, purl 5. Sixteenth row—knit 6, Over, * Knit 2, Knit 2 together, Over, drop, Take In, Knit 2, Over, Knit 12, Over, repeat from * after the last Knit 2, Over, work, Knit 6. Seventeenth row—Purl 7, Over, * Purl 1, Take In reversed, Over, drop, Purl 2 together, Purl 1, Over, Purl 14, Over, repeat from * after the last Purl 1, work Over, Purl 7. Eighteenth row—Knit 8, * Knit 2 together, Over, drop, Take In, Knit 16, repeat from * after the last Take In, work, Knit 8. Nineteenth row—Over, * Purl 2 together, Purl 7, Over, Purl and Knit the Over of the last row, Over, Purl 7, Take In reversed, Over, repeat from *. For the twentieth row commence again at the fourth row.

(13).—Fig. 537 is a light pattern, either used for Knitting square shawls, for open work socks, or for other open knitting. To work for a shawl: Cast on 242 stitches, use bone needles (No. 6), and Shetland wool. To work for socks: Calculate nine stitches for the making of each diamond. For open work straight knitting: Cast On nine stitches for each pattern and add a stitch at each end for an EDGE STITCH. To work: First row—Cast On number of stitches and KNIT a row. Second row—Knit 2, SLIP 1, * OVER, Slip 1, Knit 2 together, draw the Slipped Stitch over the last, Over, Knit 3, repeat from * to the end of the row, Knit the last 2. Third row—Knit 2, Purl to the end of the row, where Knit 2. Fourth row—Knit 2, Slip 1,

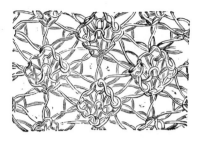

FIG. 537. KNITTING—FANCY (No. 13.)

Knit 3, * Over, Slip 1, Knit 2 together, draw the Slipped

eighteen of which are required for the middle and twenty for the stripes at the side. In repeating the pattern, repeat the middle and then the strip, in order that the latter should not be of double width. The TAKE IN in the directions stands for SLIP 1, KNIT 1, pass the Slipped Stitch over. In every round the Knitting that is required for the middle pattern is enclosed within a cross, thus, X. First round—Knit 2 together from the back, OVER Knit 1, Take In, Over, Knit 1, Take In, Over, Knit 2, X Over, PURL 7, Purl 2 together, Purl 2 together, Purl 7, Over, X Knit 2 together, Over, Knit 1, Take In, Over, Knit 1, Take In, Over, Knit 2. Second round—Knit 1 from the back, Knit 1, Over, Knit 2 together, Knit 1, Over, Knit 2 together, Knit 1, Over, Knit 2 together, X Knit 1, Over, Knit 6, Knit 2 together, Over, Knit 2 together,

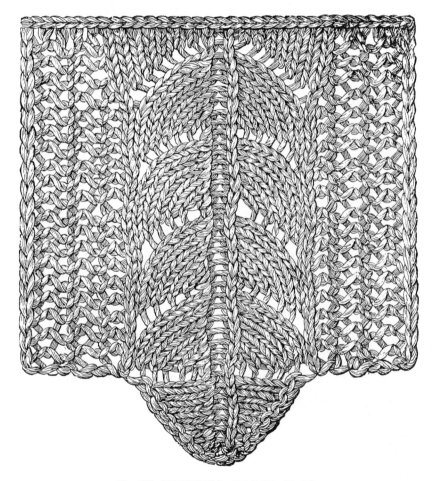

FIG. 538. KNITTING—FANCY (No. 14).

Stitch over the last, Over, Knit 3, repeat from * to the end of the row, Knit the last 2. Fifth row—Knit 2, Purl to the end of the row, where Knit 2. Sixth row—as the second row, repeat from the second row until the length is sufficient. When working the top of a sock, leave out the two edge stitches.

(14).—The pattern shown in Fig. 538 is worked as Round Knitting, and is repeated until the right width is obtained. For the pattern, CAST ON thirty-eight stitches,

Knit 6, Over, Knit 1, X Knit 2, Over, Knit 2 together, Knit 1, Over, Knit 2 together, Knit 1, Over, Knit 2 together. Third round—Knit 2 together from the back, Over, Knit 1, Take In, Over, Knit 1, Take In, Over, Knit 2, X Knit 2, Over, Knit 5, Knit 2 together, Over, let the Over of last row drop, Knit 2 together, Knit 5, Over, Knit 2, X Knit 2 together from the back, Over, Knit 1, Take In, Over, Knit 1, Take In, Over, Knit 2. Fourth round—Knit 1 from the back, Knit 1, Over, Knit 2 together,

Knit 1, Over, Knit 2 together, Knit 1, Over, Knit 2 together, X Knit 3, Over, Knit 4, Knit 2 together, Over, and let Over of last row drop, Knit 2 together, Knit 4, Over, Knit 3, X Knit 2, Over, Knit 2 together, Knit 1, Over, Knit 2 together, Knit 1, Over, Knit 2 together. Fifth round—like the first round to the X, then Knit 4, Over, Knit 3, Knit 2 together, Over, let drop the Over of last round, Knit 2 together, Knit 3, Over, Knit 4, work the end like the end of the first row. Sixth round—like the second round to the X, and for the middle Knit 5, Over, Knit 2, Knit 2 together, Over, let drop the Over of the last round, Knit 2 together, Knit 2, Over, Knit 5, X work the end like the end of the second round. Seventh round—like the first round to the X, then Knit 6, Over, Knit 1, Knit 2 together, Over, let drop the Over of the last round, Knit 2 together, Knit 1, Over, Knit 6, X end like the end of the first round. Eighth round—like the second round to the X, then Over, Knit 7, Knit 2 together, Over, let drop the Over of the last round, Knit 2 together, Knit 7, Over, X end like the second round. Ninth round—work the first and second part like the first round, the middle part like the middle of the second row. Tenth round—work the first and end part like the second round, the middle part like the middle of the third round. Eleventh round—first and end like the first part of the first round, and the middle part like the middle part of the fourth round. Repeat from the first round.

Gusset or Mitre.—See *Mitre.*

Honeycomb Pattern.—CAST ON any number of stitches that divide by six. First row—KNIT. Second row—PURL. Third row—Knit. Fourth row—Knit 4 and Slip 2 to the end of the row. Fifth row—Purl the Knit stitches of last row, but slip the stitches slipped in fourth row. Sixth row—like fourth row. Seventh row—like fifth. Eighth and ninth rows—like sixth and seventh. Tenth row—Purl every stitch. Eleventh row—Knit. Twelfth row—Purl. This completes one Honeycomb. Commence the next by Purling a row, Slipping the fifth and sixth stitches, taking

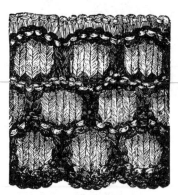

FIG. 539. HONEYCOMB STITCH—FANCY.

care that these two stitches come in the centre of the previous pattern. Continue alternately Knitting and Purling a row, Slipping 2 stitches until six rows are worked, then for the seventh row Knit all the stitches, and for the eighth Purl all the stitches.

Honeycomb Fancy Pattern (1).—The stitch shown in Fig. 539 is used for working muffatees in with coloured wools; two colours are necessary, half an ounce of the lightest and eight skeins of the darkest, and four needles, No. 12. To work: CAST ON with darkest wool 56 stitches, put 20 on one needle, and 18 each on the other two needles, and PURL 3 rounds. Pick up the light wool, and commence the first pattern round. KNIT 6, SLIP 2, keeping the wool behind them and repeat. Work to the seventh round the same as the first round. Seventh round—Knit all the stitches with the dark wool, including those slipped in the previous rounds. Eighth and ninth rounds—Purl with the dark wool. Tenth round—the same as the first round, except that the Slipped Stitches must be the centre ones of the six Knit before. Work the next five rounds as the tenth round, and then repeat the seventh, eighth, and ninth rounds. Twentieth round—work exactly as the first round. Sixty rounds will complete the muffatee; end with one Knit and three Purl rounds.

(2).—The pattern shown in Fig. 540 is another variety of Honeycomb, and is arranged for a couvrepied or baby's counterpane. The directions are given for a square, but they can be increased. To work: Two shades of four-thread fleecy wool and two bone needles, No. 4, are required. CAST ON, with the darkest wool, 29 stitches, and KNIT three rows. First pattern row—Take the lightest wool and Knit 7, SLIP 2, and repeat, at the end Knit 2 instead of 7. Second row—PURL 2, * Slip 2, these are the same stitches that were slipped before, Purl 7, repeat from *. Third and fifth rows—like the first. Fourth and sixth rows—like the second. Seventh row—take the darkest wool, Knit the whole row, including Slipped Stitches. Eighth and tenth rows—like the seventh. Ninth row—Purl. Eleventh row—with the light wool, Knit 2, * Slip 2, Knit 7, repeat from *. Twelfth row—* Purl 7, Slip 2, repeat from *, at the end Purl 2 instead of 7. Thirteenth and fifteenth rows—like the eleventh. Fourteenth and sixteenth rows—like the twelfth. Seventeenth row—Knit with dark wool. Eighteenth and twentieth rows—Knit. Nineteenth row—Purl. Twentieth—commence at the first row.

Huckaback Pattern.—CAST ON an uneven number of stitches, and KNIT and PURL alternately. Commence each row with a Knit Stitch.

Rib.—For a straight rib CAST ON any number of stitches that may be required. First row—KNIT. Second row—PURL. Third and fourth rows—Knit. Fifth row—Purl; Knit two rows and Purl one to the end.

To Rib sideways, Cast on any number of stitches that divide into four. First row—OVER, KNIT 2 together, PURL 2, repeat. Second row—Knit 2, Over, Purl 2 together, repeat.

Slip Pattern.—A pretty and easy close pattern, forming a raised knot, can be worked with coarse needle and fleecy wool for couvrepieds, or with fine No. 17 needles and Strutt's cotton for close knitting. To work: CAST ON an uneven number of stitches and KNIT a row. First row—Knit 1, * bring the wool to the front of the work, take off the next stitch as if about to PURL, but slip it on to right hand needle, pass the wool back, Knit 1, repeat from *, end with Knit 1. Second row—Purl 2, * pass the wool back,

Slip the next stitch, pass the wool to the front, Purl 1, repeat from *, finish the row with a Slipped Stitch. Repeat the first and second rows.

Spider Pattern.—Cast on any number of stitches that divide by six. First row—Over, Slip 1, Knit 2 together, pass Slipped Stitch over, Over, Knit 3. Second row—Knit. Third row—Over, Knit 2 together, Over, Knit 2 together, Knit 2. Fourth row—Knit. Fifth row—Over, Knit 3, Over, Slip 1, Knit 2 together, pass Slip Stitch over. Sixth row—Knit. Seventh row—like the first row.

Another Way.—Cast on any number of Stitches that divide into four, Purl 3 stitches together, then Knit 1, Purl 1, Knit 1, all in one stitch. Second row—

last two stitches, which Knit. Fifth row—Slip 1, Knit 1, * Purl 3 together on the fourth stitch, Knit 1, Purl 1, Knit 1, and repeat from *. Sixth row—Like fourth. Repeat from the third row.

Knitted Articles.—Knitting is used for a great variety of purposes, and the patterns previously given can be turned to many uses. The following articles, however, require distinct directions for working, and are described in detail as follows:

Bed Rest.—Use Strutt's No. 4 Knitting cotton, and pins No. 8. Cast on thirty stitches, Knit seventy rows, then Increase in the seventh stitch of every row until there are 110 stitches, Knit 160 rows, and Decrease at

Fig. 540. HONEYCOMB STITCH—FANCY.

Purl. Third row—Knit 1, Purl 1, Knit 1, all in one stitch, Purl 3 together. Fourth row—Purl. Fifth row—as the first.

Spotted Knitting.—A pretty open stitch, with a raised solid knob as pattern, and useful for comforters and shawls. Should be worked with bone needles (No. 10) and fleecy wool. To work: Cast on any number of stitches divisible by four, and two over as Edge Stitches (these Edge Stitches are not again mentioned); Knit two rows. Third row—Slip 1, Knit 1, * make three loops of the next Stitch by Knit 1, Purl 1, and Knit 1, all on the third stitch, Purl 3 together, repeat from * at the end, Knit 2. Fourth row—Slip 1, Knit 1, Purl the remainder, except the

the seventh stitch to thirty stitches, Knit seventy rows, and Cast off. Place the round or increased part over the patient's shoulder, and sew strong loops, 6 inches long, to each end of the strip of knitting, and tie to the bottom of the bed with unbleached tape.

Braces.—These should be worked with twisted crochet silk, in long skeins, and with No. 14 needles. Two and a half ounces to three ounces of silk are required for a pair of braces. The Knitting should be loose, as the stitch is troublesome to work tight. To work as shown in Fig. 541, on next page: Cast on twenty-one stitches. First row—Slip one, bring the thread to the front of the work, and take the second stitch off as if about to Purl, thread back, * insert the point of the needle from

Q Q

the back between the third and fourth stitches and put it into the fourth stitch, draw this out to the side behind and beyond the third stitch and KNIT it, then Knit the third stitch and Slip both stitches off the left hand needle, repeat from * to the end of the row, Knit the last stitch. Second row—Slip the first and second stitch and then bring the thread to the front of the work, * Purl the fourth stitch, and then Purl the third and Slip both off the needle, repeat from * to the end, Knit last stitch; repeat these two rows to the end of the brace. A buttonhole requires to be made in the brace after the first twelve rows, thus: Divide the stitches and begin on the right side of the work, Knit eleven stitches according to the first row, turn and work back like the directions for the second row, and continue Knitting backwards and forwards in this way for twelve rows. Leave the silk hanging, take up another piece, and work up the other half of the stitches. To make these equal with the ones on the other side, Knit the first from the back and do not drop it, bring the thread to the front of the work and take the first off on to the right hand needle, then work the other

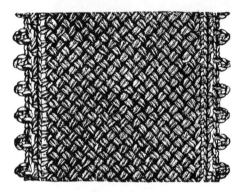

FIG. 541. KNITTING—BRACES.

stitches in the usual way, Knitting the last plain. Work twelve rows to correspond with the other half of the buttonhole, then Slip all the stitches on to the first needle and Knit the whole way across with the silk left at the outside edge of the first made side. To take in the extra stitch when the first stitch of the second made side is reached, insert the needle between the second and third stitches instead of the first and second, and bring out the third stitch beyond the others, Knit it, and then Knit the first and second stitches together. Fasten off securely the silk used for the second half of buttonhole. Crochet the edge of the braces, when the Knitting is finished, as follows: Begin at the buttonhole end, raise a loop in the three following EDGE STITCHES, keep them on the crochet hook, then take the thread through them all at once, and work four CHAIN and make a PICOT on the first Chain, * pass over an Edge Stitch, raise a loop in the second, so that three loops are on the hook; pass the thread through all three, work four Chain, and make a Picot on the first, repeat from·*, and work all round the edge of the brace. Work the narrow straps in plain Knitting, Cast on twelve stitches; make buttonholes as before described, and line the work when finished with white sarcenet.

Clouds.—These are Knitted either in Shetland or Pyrenean wool, with two shades of colour, and with No. 4 wooden pins. CAST ON 244 stitches very loosely, and commence with the darkest shade, thus: * KNIT 1, OVER, Knit 2 together, repeat from * to end of row, making a Knit stitch the last. Repeat for fifty rows, then fasten the light colour wool on, and work fifty rows with that. Three strips of each colour, or 300 rows, are sufficient for an ordinary length Cloud. CAST OFF very loosely, draw the ends together, and finish with a tassel. To make a thicker cloud, Knit every stitch. To make a Cloud with raised ridges, Knit one row with thick wool and one with fine wool alternately. Knit every stitch.

Coral.—Knitting to imitate coral is worked with fine scarlet silk or woollen braid, and with needles No. 17. It is used to ornament babies' sleeves. To work: CAST ON four stitches, SLIP the first and KNIT the other three; repeat to the end of the work.

Edging (1).—The edging illustrated in Fig. 542 is suitable for any of the purposes for which a Knitted Edging

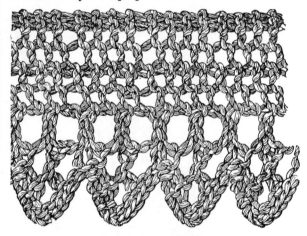

FIG. 542. EDGING (No. 1).

is required, as it looks well when worked either with the finest cotton and needles, for d'oyleys, or with coarser materials, for toilet covers and counterpanes. To work: CAST ON eighteen stitches. First row—SLIP 1, KNIT 1, * OVER, PURL 2 together, repeat from * 3 times, then Knit 10. Second row—Knit 2, Over twice, Knit 2 together, Over twice, Knit 2 together, Over 4 times, Knit 2 together, Knit 2 together, Knit 2 together, * Over, Knit 2 together, repeat from * 3 times. Third row—Slip 1, Knit 1, * Over, Purl 2 together, repeat from * 3 times, Knit 1, Knit and Purl, Knit and Purl the Over of last row, * Knit 1, Knit and Purl the Over of last row, repeat from *, at the end Knit 2. Fourth row—Knit 13, Knit 2 together, * Over, Knit 2 together, repeat from * 3 times Fifth row—Slip 1, Knit 1, * Over, Purl 2 together, repeat from * three times, Knit 12. Sixth row—Knit 2, CAST OFF 5 stitches, Over twice, Knit 2 together, Over 4 times, Knit 2 together, Knit 2 together, Knit 1, * over, Knit 2 together, repeat from * 3 times. Seventh row—Slip 1, Knit 1, * Over, Purl 2 together, repeat from * 3 times, Knit 1, Knit and Purl, Knit and Purl the Over of last row, Knit 1, Knit and Purl the Over of last row, Knit 2. Eighth row—Knit 12, * Over, Knit 2 together, repeat from * 3 times. Ninth row —like the first row.

(2).—This edging, when worked with very fine crochet cotton, is suitable for pincushions or d'oyley edgings and other fine work, and with coarser cotton for ordinary edgings. CAST ON 13 stitches. First row— OVER, KNIT 2 together, Knit 1, Over, Knit 7, Over, Knit 2 together, Knit 1. Second row—SLIP 1, Knit 2, Over, Knit 2 together, Knit the rest, but PURL the last stitch. Third row—Over, Knit 2 together, Knit 1, Over, Knit 2

together, Over, Knit 2 together, Over, Knit 2 together, Over, Knit 2 together, Knit 4, Over, Knit 2 together, Knit 1. Fifteenth row—Over, Knit 2 together, Knit 2 together, Over, Knit 2 together, Over, Knit 2 together, Knit 5, Over, Knit 2 together, Knit 1. Seventeenth row—Over, Knit 2 together, Knit 2 together, Over, Knit 2 together, Knit 6, Over, Knit 2 together, Knit 1. Nineteenth row—Over, Knit 2 together, Knit 7, Over, Knit 2 together, Knit 1. Twenty-first row—repeat from first row.

(3).—To work Fig. 543, a pattern useful as an edging to counterpanes and antimacassars. CAST ON 23 stitches.

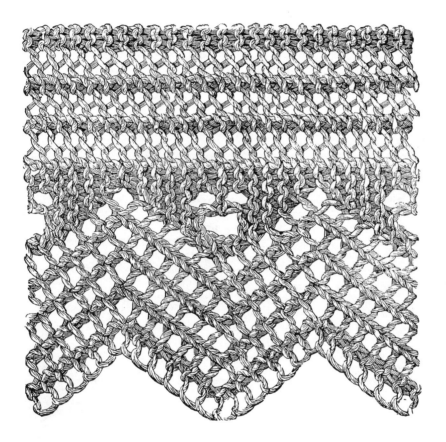

FIG. 543. KNITTING EDGING (No. 3).

together, Over, Knit 6, Over, Knit 2 together, Knit 1. Fourth row and all even rows like the second. Fifth row— Over, Knit 2 together, Knit 1, Over, Knit 2 together, Over, Knit 2 together, Over, Knit 5, Over, Knit 2 together, Knit 1. Seventh row—Over, Knit 2 together, Knit 1, Over, Knit 2 together, Over, Knit 2 together, Over, Knit 2 together, Over, Knit 4, Over, Knit 2 together, Knit 1. Ninth row—Over, Knit 2 together, Knit 1, Over, Knit 2 together, Over, Knit 2 together, Over, Knit 2 together, Over, Over, Knit 3, Over, Knit 2 together, Knit 1. Eleventh row— over, Knit 2 together, Knit 2 together, Over, Knit 2 together, Over, Knit 2 together, Over, Knit 2 together, Over, Knit 2 together, Knit 3, Over, Knit 2 together, Knit 1. Thirteenth row—Over, Knit 2 together, Knit 2

First row—thread OVER twice, PURL 2 together, Over, KNIT 2 together, Over, Knit 2 together, Over, Knit 2 together, Over, Purl 4, Knit 1, Over, Knit 2 together, Knit 1, Over, Knit 2 together, Knit 1, Over, Knit 2 together, Knit 2; twenty-four stitches will be on the needle at the end of the first row. Second row—SLIP 1, Knit 3, Over, Knit 2 together, Knit 1, Over, Knit 2 together, Knit 1, Over, Purl 2 together, Purl 12. Third row—thread Over twice, Purl 2 together, Over, Knit 2 together, Over, Knit 2 together, Over, Knit 2 together, Over, Purl 5, Knit 1, Over, Knit 2 together, Knit 1, Over, Knit 2 together, Knit 1, Over, Knit 2 together, Knit 2; there will be twenty-five stitches on the needle at the end of this row. Fourth row—Slip 1, Knit 3, Over, Knit 2 together, Knit 1,

Over, Knit 2 together, Knit 1, Over, Purl 2 together, Purl 13. Fifth row—thread Over twice, Purl 2 together, Over, Knit 2 together, Over, Knit 2 together, Over, Knit 2 together, Over, Purl 6, Knit 1, Over, Knit 2 together, Knit 1, Over, Knit 2 together, Knit 1, Over, Knit 2 together, Knit 2; twenty-six stitches now on the needle. Sixth row—Slip 1, Knit 3, Over, Knit 2 together, Knit 1, Over, Knit 2 together, Knit 1, Over, Knit 2 together, Knit 2 Purl 14. Seventh row—thread Over twice, Purl 2 together, Over, Knit 2 together, Over, Knit 2 together, Over, Knit 2 together, Over, Purl 7, Knit 1, Over, Knit 2 together, Knit 1, Over, Knit 2 together, Knit 1, Over, Knit 2 together, Knit 2; twenty-seven stitches now on the needle. Eighth row—Slip 1, Knit 3, Over, Knit 2 together, Knit 1, Over, Knit 2 together, Knit 1, Over, Purl 2 together, Purl 2, thread Over three times, Purl 13; twenty-eight stitches now on the needle. Ninth row—thread Over twice, Purl 2 together, Over, Knit 2 together, Over, Knit 2 together, Over, Knit 2 together, Over, Purl 5, Over, and Slip Over of the last row on to the right hand needle without Knitting it, Knit 1, pass Slipped Stitch Over, but back on the left hand needle, then Over twice, Purl 3, Knit 1, Over, Knit 2 together, Knit 1, Over, Knit 2 together, Knit 1, Over, Knit 2 together, Knit 2; twenty-nine stitches now upon needle. Tenth row—Slip 1, Knit 3, Over, Knit 2 together, Knit 1, Over, Knit 2 together, Knit 1, Over, Purl 2 together, Purl 2, Over, Slip Over of last row on to the right hand needle without knitting it; Purl 1, thread Over three times, Purl 13; thirty stitches now on the needle. Eleventh row—thread Over twice, Purl 2 together, Over, Knit 2 together, Over, Knit 2 together, Over, Knit 2 together, Over, Knit 1; put the needle in at the back of the work, which turn, and work the twelfth row, which forms the point, only as a half row, thus: Slip 1, and Purl to the end; thirty-one stitches on the needle. Thirteenth row — thread Over twice, Purl 2 together, Slip the first stitch of the left needle over the last made stitch on the right, Over, Knit 2 together, Over, Knit 2 together, Over, Knit 2 together, Over, Purl 2 together, Purl 1, Purl 2 together, Over, and Slip Over of last row on to the needle without Knitting it; then Slip it over the last stitch on left needle, Purl 4, Knit 1, Over, Knit 2 together, Knit 1, Over, Knit 2 together, Knit 1, over, Knit 2 together, Knit 2; twenty-nine stitches now upon the needle. Fourteenth row—Slip 1, Knit 3, Over, Knit 2 together, Knit 1, Over, Knit 2 together, Knit 1, Over, Purl 2 together, Purl 2, thread Over twice, Slip the next stitch over the second, and Purl that, Over, Slip the Over of last row on to the right needle without knitting it, Purl 11; twenty-nine stitches upon the needle. Fifteenth row—thread Over twice, Purl 2 together, Slip the first stitch on the left needle over the last one on the right needle, Over, Knit 2 together, Over, Knit 2 together, Over, Knit 2 together, Over, Purl 2 together, Purl 3, Over, Slip Over of last row on to the right needle without knitting it, Purl 3, Knit 1, Over, Knit 2 together, Knit 1, Over, Knit 2 together, Knit 1, Over, Knit 2 together, Knit 2; twenty-eight stitches now on the needle. Sixteenth row—Slip 1, Knit 3, Over, Knit 2 together, Knit 1, Over, Knit 2 together, Knit 1, Over, Purl 2 together, Purl 4, Purl 2 together, Purl 10; twenty-

seven stitches now on the needle. Seventeenth row—thread Over twice, Purl 2 together, Slip the first stitch on the left needle over the last one on the right needle, Over, Knit 2 together, Over, Knit 2 together, Over, Knit 2 together, Over, Purl 2 together, Purl 5, Knit 1, Over, Knit 2 together, Knit 1, Over, Knit 2 together, Knit 1, Over, Knit 2 together, Knit 2; twenty-six stitches now on the needle. Eighteenth row—Slip 1, Knit 3, Over, Knit 2 together, Knit 1, Over, Knit 2 together, Knit 1, Over, Purl 2 together, Purl 14. Nineteenth row—thread Over twice, Purl 2 together, Slip the first stitch on the left hand needle over those on the right needle, Over, Knit 2 together, Over, Knit 2 together, Over, Knit 2 together, Over, Purl 2 together, Purl 4, Knit 1, Over, Knit 2 together, Knit 1, Over, Knit 2 together, Knit 1, Over, Knit 2; twenty-five stitches on the needle. Twentieth row —Slip 1, Knit 3, Over, Knit 2 together, Knit 1, Over, Knit 2 together, Knit 1, Over, Purl 2 together, Purl 13. Twenty-first row—thread Over twice, Purl 2 together, Slip first stitch on left hand needle over the last made on the right hand, Over, Knit 2 together, Over, Knit 2 together, Over, Knit 2 together, Over, Purl 2 together, Purl 3, Knit 1, Over, Knit 2 together, Knit 1, Over, Knit 2 together, Knit 1, Over, Knit 2 together, Knit 2. Twenty-second row like twentieth row, only Purl 12 instead of 13 at the end. Twenty-third row like twenty-first row, only Purl 2 instead of 3. Twenty-fourth row like twentieth row, only Purl 11 instead of 12. Recommence the pattern from the first row.

(4).—The edging shown in Fig. 544 is extremely simple, and is a combination of Knitting and crochet. It is used for children's petticoats or knitted jackets. To work: Pick up the stitches round the article and KNIT six rows, then cast off, and with a crochet hook and two shades of wool finish thus: Commence with the light shade of wool; fasten on and work six CHAIN, miss the space of

FIG. 514. KNITTING EDGING (No. 4).

four stitches and loop the wool through the fifth with SINGLE CROCHET; repeat to the end of the stitches. Then take the dark wool, fasten it on, work six Chain, and loop it into the material between the loops formed with the light wool interlacing the dark chain with the light, as shown in the illustration. Repeat to the end of the material.

Fringe (1).—The Fringe shown in Fig. 545, on following page, is formed with loops, and is worked either with four-thread fleecy wool and bone Knitting needles for the edging of wool mats, or for toilet covers, &c., with the same sized cotton and needles used that the centre is worked in. CAST ON the number of stitches that make the length of the article. First row—KNIT. Second row —SLIP 1, put the needle into the next stitch, and put the cotton on the needle as if about to Knit, then place a mesh an inch in width behind the right hand needle, and pass the wool round it, being careful not to take it off the needle, then put it again on the needle and Knit; repeat to the end, Knit the last stitch without a loop. Third row—leave the mesh in, turn the work, and Knit the row and Knit the looped stitch as one stitch. Repeat the first and second rows three times.

FIG. 545. KNITTING—FRINGE.

(2.)—The following fringe is useful as a strong, thick ending for toilet covers. To work: Cut a number of lengths of cotton 8 inches in length, and double them twice. CAST ON seven stitches. First row—KNIT 2, pick up a length of cotton, and lay it between the second and third stitch; let part of the length be on both sides of the work, Knit 1, and pass the ends on the right side of the work to the back, Knit 1, and repeat between the fifth and sixth stitches, and Knit the last stitch. Second row—PURL. Repeat these two rows three times. Ninth row—like the first. Tenth row—Repeat the ninth and tenth rows three times, and then commence again at the first row.

Gloves, Men's Size.—Work with Heather mixture or single Berlin wool of a neutral tint. CAST ON eighty-four stitches on three needles, and use needles No. 17. KNIT two rounds, then RIB with two PURL and two Knit stitches alternately for twenty-four rounds. Knit one round and then commence the pattern. This takes four rounds, and is as follows: First round—Purl 1, Knit 3, and repeat. Second and Fourth rounds—Knit. Third round —Knit 2, * Purl 1, Knit 3, repeat from * to end, but Knit the last stitch. Repeat the pattern until twenty-four rounds are worked. Commence to INCREASE for the thumb at the twenty-first round by knitting twice into the first stitch on the first needle, and mark this stitch with a bit of coloured thread. Work the twenty-first round as the first pattern round. Twenty-second round—Knit. Twenty-third round—Increase on both of the stitches by working two stitches into one, then continue the round as the third pattern round. Twenty-fourth round—Knit. Continue to Increase two stitches in this manner in every alternate round, working the new stitches as pattern

stitches until there are thirty-six stitches or nine patterns extra on the needle. Take off these thumb stitches on a short spare needle for use after the hand part is finished, and work backwards and forwards with the rest of the stitches for twenty straight rows, Slip the first stitch of each row, Purl the Knit rows, and reverse the pattern in the alternate rows to make the right side of the work. Join by Knitting a round, and Increase one stitch for the stitch lost at the thumb, and Knit twenty rounds with the pattern. Then commence the fingers. First finger—Take off thirteen stitches on each side, and Cast on six stitches between them on the side away from the thumb, and Knit fifty-two rounds in the pattern with these thirty-two stitches, then DECREASE by Knitting 2 together at the commencement of each needle in one round. Knit three rounds without Decreasing. Decrease in the same way in the next round. Knit a round without Decreasing, and Decrease in every round until only eleven stitches are left; continue the pattern through the Decreasing. Draw these eleven stitches together with a needle, and fasten off. Second finger—Take off ten stitches upon each side, pick up and Knit the six that were Cast on for the first finger, and Cast on six more opposite to them. Knit sixty rounds, then Decrease as before. Third finger—Take off eight stitches on each side, take up and Knit the six Cast On before, and Cast on six stitches opposite them. Knit fifty-two rounds with these and Decrease as before, but to seven stitches. Fourth finger—Pick up and Knit the six stitches Cast on before, add them to the remaining sixteen stitches, and Knit for forty rounds, then Decrease as third finger. Now return to the thumb. Pick up the thirty-six stitches on to three needles, and pick up and Knit upon each side of them the stitches Slipped in the straight rows. First round— Decrease by Knitting 2 together at the first stitch of the first needle and last stitch of the last needle. Work a Knit round, and Decrease at every alternate round until thirty-six stitches are on the needles, working the pattern during the Decreasings. Continue the pattern without any De-creasings until there are seventy-six rounds, or nineteen patterns from the first Increase of the thumb, then Decrease as in first finger until eleven stitches are left, which fasten off as directed above.

Gloves, Women's Size.—Work in silk or fine wool in plain Knitting, and with No. 16 needles. CAST ON sixty-four stitches on to three needles and RIB, with 2 PURL, 2 KNIT, for twenty-four rounds. Then Knit two rounds in the last, place upon one needle five stitches for the thumb, Purl 1, Knit 3, Purl 1, Knit thirty rounds, and where the thumb stitches are, Purl the first and last stitch and INCREASE the three Knit stitches gradually to fifteen by Knitting twice into one stitch every alternate row. Take these seventeen stitches, place them on two needles, and Increase with six stitches where the inside of the thumb is; work three rounds with these twenty-three stitches, on the fourth, DECREASE by Knitting two together in the centre of the six Cast On stitches. Work thirty-three rounds, nar-rowing the thumb down to seven stitches by Decreasing in every alternate round. Sew these seven stitches together. Return to the hand. Work with the stitches left, and pick up twelve on the thumb, so as to connect it. Knit three rounds, and in the fourth Knit two together twice opposite the thumb, Knit three rounds, and in the fourth Knit two together opposite the thumb. Work in all twenty-four rounds; then take eighteen stitches on two needles on each side of the thumb, and put the rest on spare needles and work the first finger. Add six stitches on the side away from the thumb and Knit thirty-six rounds, Decreasing by Knitting two together three times at every fourth round. Sew together when eight stitches are reached. Second finger: Pick up six stitches from the side of the first finger and Knit them on to the needle, take fourteen stitches from each side of the spare needles (seven on each side), and Cast on six stitches on the side opposite the picked up stitches; narrow as on the first finger. Third finger: Pick up and Knit six stitches as before, Increase as before, and take fourteen stitches on each side (seven from each side), and Knit thirty-nine rounds, Decreasing as in the first finger. Fourth finger: Pick up and Knit six stitches as before, and take all the stitches from the spare needles. Knit thirty rounds, and only narrow after the joint of the finger is passed, then narrow every alternate round.

Marking.—The marking of the initials of the wearer should be done in the Knitting, as follows: PURL or RIB the first rounds of the work, then KNIT six rounds and in the seventh Purl those stitches that commence the letters of the initial desired, Knit the next round and Purl the stitches forming the letters in the ninth round, continue to work until the letters are formed like the seventh and eighth rounds. A small bead of a contrasting colour to the Knitting is introduced when the Marking is done upon articles that are not often washed.

Moss.—This is used to ornament the edges of mats, and is made as follows: Join together pieces of green single Berlin wool of any shade in one long skein. CAST ON forty stitches upon No. 15 needles, and Knit backwards and forwards until the wool is used up. Then damp the work and bake it in a slow oven for six hours, iron it over, and then unravel it, and place the unravelled threads round the mat so that they form a thick raised mass resembling moss. Sew to the mat here and there to keep the threads in their proper position.

Pincushion.—The following directions are for Knitting, with No. 20 needles and the finest Knitting cotton, a round pincushion cover. The Knitting is done with four needles, ninety stitches are Cast on and worked plain for the underside of the cushion, and the pattern part is worked from eight to ten times according to the size of the cushion. The plain Knitting is not alluded to in the directions. First round—CAST ON nine stitches for each pattern and three stitches between each pattern, PURL 1, KNIT 1, Purl 1 (these are for the three intermediate stitches between the patterns), * Knit 1, OVER, eight times, then Purl 1, Knit 1, Purl 1, and repeat from *, seventeen stitches will now be on the needles instead of the nine original pattern ones, not counting the intermediate stitches. Second round—Purl 1, Knit 1, Purl 1, * Knit 17, Purl 1, Knit 1, Purl 1 and repeat from *. Third round—* Purl 1, Knit 1, Purl 1, Slip 1, Knit 1, pass Slipped Stitch over Knitted, Knit 13, Knit 2 together and repeat from *. Work

the third round over again, reducing the pattern stitches by two each round until they have returned into their original nine, not counting the three intermediate stitches, and then commence again at first round. This pattern can be worked with coarse needles and cotton for open worked stockings.

Purse.—To Knit a purse upon two needles, use needles No. 17 and three skeins of fine purse silk: CAST ON 48 stitches. First row—OVER, KNIT 2 together, repeat to the end. Second row—Over, Purl 2 together, repeat. Repeat the first and second rows to the end.

To Knit a purse upon four needles, use needles No. 17 and three skeins of purse silk. CAST on fifty-four stitches, and KNIT two rounds. Third round—Knit 2 together. Fourth round—pick up a stitch and Purl it, Purl 1, repeat to the end of the round. Fifth and sixth round—Knit. Seventh and eighth round—like third and fourth round—Knit these eight rounds alternately for three inches, then make the slit, thus: First round—Knit, and turn back. Second round—Purl and turn back. Third round—Knit 2 together to end, then turn back. Fourth round—Over, Knit 1, * pick up a stitch and Knit it, Knit 1, repeat from * to the end of the round. Work these four rounds until the slit is three inches long, then Knit all round the purse in the pattern, commencing at the first round and working to the eighth; repeat for 3 inches. Purses should be made 11 inches long, and when finished, damped and stretched upon a cylinder before being drawn together at the ends.

Shawls.—(1).—Use German fleecy wool and two needles, size No. 19, and one needle, size No. 13. CAST ON 360 stitches for a shawl 1½yds. square, if made in one colour, or sixty stitches if worked in stripes of contrasting colours, six stripes being then required. First row—with the small needles—OVER, KNIT 2 together, repeat to the end. Second row—Knit with the large needle. Third row —Knit with the small needle. Fourth row—PURL with the small needle. Fifth row—As the first.

(2).—Work with fine Shetland wool and No. 14 needles. CAST ON any number of stitches that divide into six and two extra at each end for EDGE STITCHES, which are not mentioned in the instructions. First row —OVER, KNIT 1, Over, Knit 1, SLIP 1, Knit 2 together, and pass SLIPPED STITCH over Knitted, Knit 1, and repeat. Second row and all even rows—PURL. Third row—Over, Knit 3, Over, Slip 1, Knit 2 together and pass Slipped Stitch over Knitted, repeat. Fifth row—Knit 1, Slip 1, Knit 2 together, pass Slipped Stitch over Knitted, Knit 1, Over, Knit 1, Over, repeat. Seventh row—Slip 1, Knit 2 together, pass Slipped Stitch Over Knitted, Over, Knit 3, Over, repeat. Eighth row—commence again from first row. The fancy stitches already given in the Knitting instructions can be used for shawl Knitting if worked in strips.

Socks and Stockings.

Baby's Boot, Open Work Shell Pattern Sock.— White Pyrenean wool, white Shetland wool, and Knitting pins No. 16. CAST ON thirty-six stitches with the Berlin wool, and KNIT four rows. Fifth row—SLIP 1, Knit 2 together, Knit to within three stitches of the end, and there Knit 2 together, Knit 1. Sixth row—Knit, repeat these two rows three times more; twenty-eight stitches on the needle. Thirteenth row—Slip 1, pick up the thread that lies under the second stitch and Knit it, Knit to the end of the row, pick up six stitches along the slanting side, Knitting them as picked up. This is the heel. Fourteenth row—Knit. Fifteenth row—Slip 1, pick up the thread that lies under the second stitch and Knit it, Knit all the rest. Sixteenth row—Knit, repeat these two rows four more times; forty stitches on the needle. Twenty-fifth row—Knit 14, then, keeping the other stitches still on the needle, turn, and Knit these fourteen stitches backwards and forwards for twenty-three rows. Forty-ninth row—Knit 14, Cast on 26; forty stitches on the needle. Fiftieth row—Knit. Fifty-first row—Slip 1, Knit 2 together, Knit all the rest. Fifty-second row—Knit, repeat these two rows four more times. Sixty-first row—Slip 1, Knit 2 together, Knit all the rest; thirty-four stitches on the needle. Sixty-second row—CAST OFF 6, Knit the rest. Sixty-third row—Slip 1, pick up the thread that lies under the second stitch and Knit, Knit all the rest, pick up one of the Cast off stitches at the end of the row and Knit it. Sixty-fourth row—Knit, repeat these two rows three times more (thirty-six stitches on the needle), Knit two rows and Cast off; then, with the same needle on which there are twenty-six stitches, pick up twelve stitches across the instep, and twenty-six where the other twenty-six were Cast on, Knitting each as picked up, Knit one row and Cast off all.

For a sock, with Shetland wool: Pick up twenty-two stitches over the instep, holding the boot the right side towards you and Knitting the stitches as picked up. First row—PURL. Second row—Purl 2 together, taking one stitch from the side with it, Purl 2 together again, make 1 and KNIT 1 three times, make 2, Purl 2 together four times, make 1, Knit 1 three times, make 2, Purl 2 together twice, taking a stitch from the side with the last of these. Third row—Purl. Fourth row—Knit, Knitting one stitch from the side together with the first and last. Fifth row—Purl, repeat from the second row four more times, and then Knit the second and third rows once more. Twenty-fourth row—Knit 22, and pick up twenty-two stitches along the side, Knitting them as picked up. Twenty-fifth row—Purl all along and pick up twenty-two stitches on the other side, Purling them as picked up. Twenty-sixth row—Purl 2 together twice, * make and Knit 1 three times, make 2, Purl 2 together four times, repeat from *, end the row with Purl 2 together twice. Twenty-seventh row—Purl. Twenty-eighth row — Knit. Twenty-ninth row — Purl, repeat from the twenty-sixth row eleven times. For ribbing round the top of leg: Knit 3 and Purl 3 alternately for twelve rows, CAST OFF. Sew the boot up neatly, rounding the toe off to shape, and finish off with a white ribbon rosette in front and a white ribbon to tie round the ankle.

Child's Fancy Sock.—Work with Strutt's Knitting cotton No. 14, needles No. 17. CAST ON sixty stitches, and work twenty-six RIBBED rounds, KNIT 2, and PURL 2 alternately. After the Ribbing, work two strips of the fancy pattern down the leg, with no Take Ins, thus: First round—OVER, Knit 2 together, Knit 1, Purl 3, repeat. Second round—Knit 3, Purl 3, repeat. Third

round—Knit 1, Over, Knit 2 together, Purl 3, repeat. Fourth round—as second, repeat the four rounds twelve times more, then divide for the heel. Take thirty-one stitches on the heel needle, the raised stitch of a stripe make the centre of the heel, and fifteen stitches on each side, Knit and Purl alternate rows, SLIPPING a stitch each row until fifteen loops are counted on each side of the heel. Leave off with a Purled row. Then for next row—Knit to the fourth stitch past the SEAM STITCH, Slip 1, Knit 1, pass Slipped Stitch over Knitted, Knit 1 and turn, Slip the first stitch and Purl to the fourth stitch past the Seam Stitch, Slip the fourth stitch. Purl the next and pass Slipped Stitch over it, Purl 1 and turn, and repeat these. TAKE IN on the fourth stitch on each side of the Seam Stitch, until all the stitches are Knitted off on the sides. Then pick up the fifteen loops on the left side of the heel, Knitting them as picked up, and Knit to these the stitches on the next needle, continuing the fancy pattern round the front. Take a fresh needle and Knit the stitches of the next needle, and pick up and Knit the fifteen loops on the right side of the heel. Knit one round and DECREASE on each side pin, by knitting 2 together in the centre in every other round until fifty stitches are on the needles. Knit twenty rounds with the fancy pattern as before, then discontinue the pattern and Knit twelve rounds. For the toe—divide the stitches in half on a line with the Gussets, putting one half of the stitches on one needle, and the rest on two needles. Decrease, by Knitting together the second and third stitch of one of the needles with the small quantity of stitches, and the last third and second stitch at the end of the companion needle. Knit 2 together at both ends for the centre needle, Knitting one stitch at each end; Knit a round and repeat these two rounds four times. Put the stitches on the back needles on to one needle, place the needles together, and Knit together a stitch off each pin twice, and then slip the first of these stitches over the second. Repeat until all the stitches are CAST OFF.

Gentleman's Striped Sock. — Knitted with Scotch fingering wool, two skeins of a dark shade and four of a light shade, and to be worked in stripes, seven rounds with the dark shaded wool and nine rounds with the light wool. Needles, No. 17. If Knitted with silk—Adams' Knitting silk—the dimensions must be enlarged and finer pins used. With the darkest shade CAST ON ninety-five stitches, thirty-two on each of the two needles, and thirty-one on the other. Work in RIBBED Knitting, KNIT two and PURL two alternately for 3 inches, keeping for a SEAM STITCH the last stitch on the third needle with thirty-one stitches. Now Knit to the heel, commencing the stripes thus: Join on the light shade of wool and work nine rounds, then pass up the dark wool and work a stripe of the dark, doing seven rounds, thus carrying on the two balls of light and dark wool without breaking off. Knit on for five stripes of the dark and five stripes of the light. TAKE IN nine times for the calf of the leg, commencing from the thirty-fifth round of the plain Knitting, and Take In on each side of the Seam Stitch once in every stripe. For the ankle, Knit twenty-eight rounds after the last Take In. Then divide the stitches for the heel, placing twenty stitches on each side of the Seam Stitch on one needle for the heel, and leave the other stitches behind equally divided on two needles until the heel is done; or divide the sock in half, and put one half on to one needle for the heel, and leave the rest behind on two needles. Work the forty-one stitches backwards and forwards, Knit a row and Purl a row alternately, always SLIPPING the first stitch in each row until eighteen loops can be counted up each side of the heel, and leave off with a Purl row; these form the stitches to be lifted for the foot. In the next row the Seam Stitch is to be discontinued. * Knit to the fifth stitch past the Seam Stitch, Slip the fifth stitch, Knit the next stitch and pass the Slipped Stitch over it, Knit the next stitch, turn, Slip the first stitch and Purl to the fifth stitch past the Seam Stitch, Slip that, Purl the next stitch and pass the Slipped Stitch over it, Purl the next stitch, and turn again. Repeat from *, always Slipping the first stitch on the other side of the opening now formed until all the stitches are Knitted off from each side, leaving the heel finished. Pick up the eighteen loops on the left side of the heel, Knit each as picked up; Knit to these the stitches on the next needle, which is one of the needles left when the heel was commenced. Take another needle and Knit the stitches off the next needle, and then pick up the eighteen loops on the right side of the heel, also Knitting these. This makes two GUSSET or side needles, and the needle with the heel still remaining on it makes the third needle. There should be about forty-two stitches on each Gusset needle. Knit round. Commence the left hand side Gusset needle, Knit the eighteen stitches which were picked up from the side, then Knit the next two stitches together, and Knit the remainder. Next needle, Knit 22, Knit 2 together, and Knit eighteen stitches. * Knit the heel pin. Then a round of Knitting to this same place again. Knit, and Take In as before, keeping twenty-two stitches after the Take In. Next needle, Knit twenty-two, then take in, and knit the rest. Repeat from *. Take in eighteen times altogether. The heel is to be all one colour to where the Gusset commences, then continue the stripes again. Knit in stripes until it is time to DECREASE for the toe, which will be 7 inches from the heel. Divide the stitches exactly in half, putting one half on one needle, and the other half on two needles, taking care that the sock is divided in half on a line with the Gussets. At the beginning of the first of the two needles Knit 1, then Knit 2 together and at the end of the second needle Knit 2 together, Knit 1. Take in thus both at the beginning and end of the third needle (with the other half of the stitches on). Knit four rounds, then a round in which Take In as before, four rounds, Take In again three rounds, Take In, two rounds, then Take In for the next five consecutive rounds. There will be fifteen stitches left on the one needle, and fifteen stitches on the two back needles; put the latter all on one needle. Place the needles in a line with each other. Knit 1 stitch off each needle together, * another stitch off each needle together, then Slip the first of these over the last. Repeat from * till all the stitches are CAST OFF.

Stockings.—The art of Knitting stockings came from Spain, and the first mention of their introduction into England is when Edward VI. had a pair of silk ones presented to him. Queen Elizabeth, in 1561, had a pair presented to her, which were the handiwork of her waiting woman, but until then had only worn cloth or woollen materials shaped to the leg. The art once learnt in England soon became universal, and for a very long time was one of the chief industries and supports of the peasantry in both England and Scotland, although as early as 1589 William Lee invented a machine for weaving stockings. At the present time stocking Knitting is chiefly the work of the ladies of England and the peasants of the Shetland Isles and Scotland, as machine made stockings, though not wearing so well, are cheaper than hand made ones. The beauty of stocking knitting consists in the evenness of the stitches, and the skill and regularity with which the shaping of the leg, the putting in of the heel, and the rounding off of the toe are managed.

The pins used are short ones, and should have already been knitted with, as the ease with which they move is important. Their size is proportionate to the thickness of the material used. The number of stitches Cast on to commence with, depends so much upon the size of the person that no certain number can be given, but the following scale will be some guide: Gentleman's knicker-bockers in four ply fingering worsted, needles No. 16, stitches 156. Gentleman's socks, in the same wool, sixty-nine stitches. In fine wool or silk for socks, 120 stitches or more. Lady's stockings, needles No. 18, merino wool or silk, 148 stitches. Sock for boy of twelve, in worsted, eighty-four stitches; in lambs' wool, sixty-nine stitches. Boy's sock of eight years of age, in fingering wool, seventy-two stitches; in lambs' wool, fifty-two stitches. Stocking for a child of five years, in merino wool, needles No. 18, 118 stitches. For a child of eight years, same wool and needles, 132 stitches. For a girl of fourteen, lambs' wool, and needles No. 18, eighty-four stitches.

To commence the work: Divide the stitches, CAST these on equally between three or four needles, and into the stitch that is to be PURLED all down the leg to form the SEAM put a coloured thread, so that it may be easily detected. Work the top of the stocking, or Welt either in ribs, by Purling three stitches, and KNITTING three alternately, or by working some of the open fancy stitches illustrated on pages 290 and 291, and Knit the leg down to the heel, not drawing the stitches tightly, TAKING IN at the ankle according to the directions, and holding the work as shown in Fig. 546. The Take In, or Intakes in the leg, are all made on the third and fourth stitches on each side of the Seam Stitch, and the Rounds where this decreasing is managed are separated from each other by a fixed number of Rounds plainly Knitted. The number of Intakes must be regulated by the length of the stocking and the size of the wearer round the ankle; twenty are the usual number, with five Knit rounds between each Decreasing. When the leg is finished, put half the stitches, with the Seam Stitch as centre, upon one pin, and divide the others on to the two pins, as shown in Fig. 547, leaving the two pins with the lesser number of stitches unworked

CANADIAN OR LOGHOUSE PATCHWORK.

MOSAIC PATCHWORK WITH EMBROIDERY.

CRAZY PATCHWORK.

until the heel is finished, which work as straight Knitting; alternately Knit and Purl for forty rows for a man, and thirty-eight for a woman, or more if the stocking is a

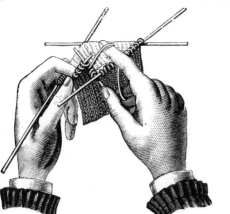

FIG. 546. STOCKING KNITTING—LEG.

large one, as upon the ease with which the heel fits the wearer much of the comfort of the stocking depends.

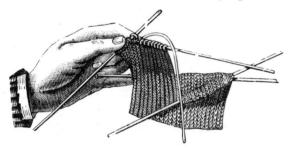

FIG. 547. STOCKING KNITTING—HEEL.

To strengthen *Heels*, they are often Knitted with double thread, or with a silk thread wound round the worsted one. In Knitting the straight part of the heel always SLIP the first stitch of every row on to the new pin without Knitting it, as this is the stitch that is afterwards picked up. The narrowing or finishing off of the heel is worked in various ways. For the Common heel only Knit and Purl eight rows, and then CAST OFF and sew up; for Dutch and French Heels, every alternate row is narrowed at a certain stitch from the Seam Stitch, thus: For a *Dutch Heel*, Knit to within six stitches of the Seam, SLIP 1, Knit 1, pass Slipped Stitch over Knitted, Knit to Seam Stitch, Purl that, Knit 4, then Knit 2 together, turn the work, leaving the unknit stitches on the pin and Purl back, when the fifth stitch is reached from the Seam, Purl it and the sixth stitch together and turn back, work to the fifth stitch on the other side of the Seam, and take one of the unknit stitches to make the Take In. Proceed until all the unknit stitches are absorbed, and only the plain stitches left between the Take Ins on the needle. *French Heel* is similar to Dutch Heel, except that the Take Ins are commenced on the third and fourth stitches from the Seam Stitch.

The heel finished, pick up the Slipped Stitches on the left side on the same pin, Knit them on and Knit round the stitches left on the spare needle; on reaching the other

side of the heel pin, pick up the Slipped Stitches there, and Knit them and work them to the Seam. Count the stitches, and INCREASE, if necessary, where the Slipped Stitches are.

In dividing the stitches to form the *Gusset* or *Mitre*, place double the number and four extra on to the pin that carries the front stitches than are on the side pins. Increase six stitches at the back of the foot before beginning the Gusset, if the foot is at all stout, and make the Gusset by Knitting two stitches together from the back where the pieces forming heel and instep meet. Make an Intake upon each side every third round eight times, and Knit two plain rounds between. There will be four more stitches after the gusset is finished upon the pins than there were when the heel commenced, and the appearance of the work will be the same as Fig. 548.

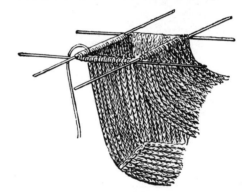

FIG. 548. STOCKING KNITTING—GUSSET.

Work up the foot in plain Knitting without any Seam Stitch until the *Toe* is reached—the length of foot must be measured from wearer's stocking—and when long enough, commence to Take In for the toe. The decreasing of the

FIG. 549. STOCKING KNITTING—STAR TOE.

toe is formed in several patterns; the one shown in Fig. 549 is called the Star Toe, and makes a four or three pointed star, according to the number of pins upon which the stocking is worked; it is obtained thus: Knit two stitches together from the back at the beginning of every pin, and Knit two plain rounds between each pattern round, continue until only four stitches are left, Knit 2 together twice, and

CAST OFF. To form the plain toe, shown in Fig. 550: Knit the first two stitches and Take In at the third and fourth, work to within four stitches of the end of the second pin and Take In there, work the third pin, which should hold the stitches belonging to the back of the foot without a

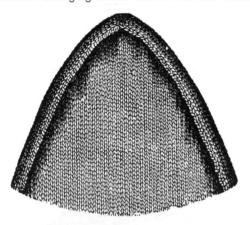

FIG. 550. STOCKING KNITTING—PLAIN TOE.

Decrease. Work three plain rounds and a Take In round, three times, putting fresh stitches on to the pins from the back pin, then two plain rounds and a Take In round twice, and then an alternate Take In round, and Knit round, until four stitches are left, which treat as before mentioned.

Re-Footing.—Unpick the foot until the bad places are taken out, then re-work from that place.

Re-Heeling or Grafting, as shown in Fig. 551. The heel of a stocking wears out before the other parts, but can be renewed as follows: Cut away the bad heel, and pick the stitches up where the heel was first commenced, upon fine short pins. Cut away the EDGE STITCHES and take up the Gusset Stitches upon two pins, re-KNIT the

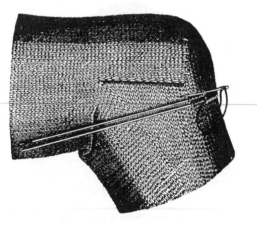

FIG. 551. STOCKING KNITTING—RE-HEEL.

heel and Cast off the last stitch of every row with one of the Gusset Stitches on the Knit side of the heel, Cast off by Slipping and Knitting the two stitches on the plain side, by PURLING the two together on the Purled side, and when all but three of the Gusset Stitches are used, close the heel to match the Knitting upon the other

stocking, or Knit back to the end of the pin, work the three Gusset Stitches there, return and work the three upon the other side. Now place together the pin holding the heel stitches and those holding the foot stitches, and Cast off on the wrong side as in JOINING KNITTING, or thread a darning needle and sew the stitches up.

Re-Kneeing.—Unpick the worn away Knitting by unravelling, cutting it down the centre of the bad part, and leaving the ravelled out wool in lines upon each side. Pick up the stitches at the top and bottom of the work, and place them on needles, join on some fresh wool at the top line, and KNIT and PURL rows alternately until the place is filled in, taking care to work in with each row the ravelled threads lying on each side of it. When the last row is reached, lay the needle with the new stitches on it and the needle with the old together, and Knit the two off as shown in JOINING KNITTING, or sew together the two opposite loops upon each part. Then sew neatly over the sides of the work, so as to completely join the new piece to the old.

Stocking, Lady's Striped.—That given is the size for a foot that takes small threes in boots, and is knitted with German fingering wool of two shades, three skeins of light wool and four of dark, and worked in stripes, seven rounds being Knitted with the dark shade and nine rounds with the light shade. Needles, No. 17. With the dark wool CAST ON 108 stitches, thirty-six stitches on each needle, and KNIT forty rounds of RIBBING, two Knit and two PURL stitches alternately. Begin with the lightest wool for the stripes, work nine rounds of plain Knitting, and keep the last stitch on the third needle for a SEAM STITCH; work seven rounds with the dark wool, also plain Knitting, and carry on the two balls of wool without breaking off. Continue Knitting nine rounds with light wool and seven rounds with dark wool until there are six light stripes and six dark stripes. The whole piece from the commencement should measure about 9½in. in the centre of the sixth light stripe. Now commence to TAKE IN by Knitting two together on each side of the Seam Stitch. Take In in every eighth round, always doing seven rounds between each Take In. The Taking In part alone should measure 7½in. Now Knit 3in. for the ankle. The whole length of the stocking should measure 20in., and consist of seventeen light and sixteen dark stripes, besides the Ribbing. For the heel, in dark wool, divide the stocking in two, place half the stitches with the Seam Stitch in the centre on one needle, and the other stitches equally divided on two needles, which are to be left behind. Knit the heel backwards and forwards, one Knit row and one Purl row alternately, continue the Seam Stitch, and always Slip the first stitch in every row. Knit until there are eighteen loops up each side of the heel; leave off with a Purl row. Next row—*Knit to the fifth stitch past the Seam Stitch (which now discontinue), slip the fifth stitch, Knit the next stitch and pass the Slipped Stitch over it, Knit the next stitch, turn, Slip the first stitch and Purl to the fifth stitch past the Seam Stitch, Slip that, Purl the next stitch and pass the Slipped Stitch over it, Purl the next stitch, and turn again, and repeat from *, always Slipping the first stitch on the other side of the opening formed, until all the stitches are Knitted off from each side. Pick up the eighteen loops on the left side of the heel, Knit each one as picked up, Knit to these the stitches on the next needle (which is one of the needles left behind when the heel was commenced), take another needle, Knit the stitches off the next needle, and then pick up the eighteen loops on the other side of the heel, also Knitting these. These make the two Gusset or side needles, and there should be about forty-two stitches on each, and the needle with the heel still remaining on it makes the third needle. Knit one round. The stripes now commence again. When the left hand side Gusset needle is reached Knit the eighteen stitches that were picked up from the side, then Knit two stitches together, and Knit the remainder, which should be twenty-two. Next neeedle, Knit 22, Knit 2 together, and Knit 18 stitches. *Knit the heel pin. Then a round of Knitting to this same place again. Knit and Take In as before, keeping twenty-two stitches after the Take In. Next needle, Knit 22, then Take In, and Knit the rest. Repeat from *. Take In twelve times altogether. Then Knit in stripes as before, until it is time to DECREASE for the toe, which will be about 6in. from the heel. Divide the stitches exactly in half, on a line with the Gussets, putting one half on one needle, and the other half, divided, on two needles. Knit 2 together at the beginning of the first of the two needles, and again at the end of the second needle, and Knit 2 together at both the beginning and end of the third needle. Then Knit four rounds; then a round, with a Take In as before, four rounds, Take In again. three rounds, Take In, three rounds. Then Take In for the next five consecutive rounds. Put the stitches that are on the two back needles on to one, and place the needles in a line with each other. Knit one stitch off each needle together, * Knit two more stitches off each needle together, and then Slip the first of these over the last ; repeat from * until all the stitches are CAST OFF.

Strengthening.—This is done by working doubled threads into the heels or toes of stockings, or by twisting a silk thread round the woollen one, and working that in.

Knitting Cotton, Silk, and Wool.—Knitting Cotton is to be had in all sizes, according to the name of the maker. Alexander's are in three and four threads, and white or unbleached. Kingsbury's in all sizes, in the best quality, and unbleached. Strutt's best marble, in blue and white, brown and white, navy blue; also Faudel's and Phillip's, and Manlove's Knitting Cotton. Strutt's and Evans's are very popular. The numbers run as follows, viz., 6, 8, 10, 12, 14, 16, 18, 20, 24, 30, in three and four threads. Amongst the best Knitting Silks are Pearsall's Imperial, which is warranted to bear washing. The Peacock Knitting Wool of Faudel and Phillips may be had in all colours.

Knitting Machine.—With this machine, socks and stockings of all sizes may be made from Scotch fingering yarns, whether ribbed, plain, or in fancy stitches. A sock may be produced in twenty minutes, and a stocking in half-an-hour. Re-footing or partial re-footing can be effected with it. A larger sized machine can be had for knitting jackets, under vests, petticoats, &c. The size of the cylinders required by any knitter depends on the

description of yarn to be employed. To make articles for ordinary family use, for both summer and winter wear, not more than two cylinders (with their needles and dials) are requisite. The 72 or 84 cylinder will knit Scotch yarns, and the 108 and 120 merino, cotton, cashmere, silk, &c. The other sizes of cylinders are used generally for special makes of hosiery.

There are various other Knitting Machines possessing improvements on the ordinary sort, just described; notably the "Rothwell" which has a "side-runner," taking the weight of the machine off the "beds," and which is suitable for stockings and small articles. For Jerseys, window-curtains, skirts, vests, and all open work, it has a double "bed" in the front bed, and two behind. It also has 6 "locks" for fancy patterns, and will produce stripes in two colours, without any tying of the wool. There is also a "Rothwell Power Machine," with sectional needle-beds ; this is self-regulating, and produces "Cardigan Work," one colour on one side and another colour on the other. This Machine can be worked either by hand or Steam.

Knitting Needles.—Some of these are made of steel of various degrees of fineness, and designed for fine and circular work. Formerly they were longer than those now in use. Knitting pins may be had in gutta percha, ivory, bone, and wood, having a button on one end. These are much thicker than those of steel, and considerably longer, being designed for shawl knitting, and for other articles of large dimensions and patterns. *See* GAUGE for KNITTING NEEDLES and KNITTING GAUGE.

Knot.—When working Pillow Lace the Bobbins are apt to twist and form knots upon the thread. These knots must never be worked in the lace, and if they cannot be undone must be removed thus : If the knot is on a Passive Bobbin, lift the BOBBIN, draw the thread back over the

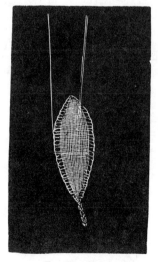

FIG. 552. KNOT.

work, and either twine it in and out among the pins until the knot is passed, or stick a pin in the Pillow behind the work and carry the thread round it, not pulling it very tight, and bring it down straight to its proper place, lengthen the thread, turn the Bobbin to the left, and continue the work. If the knot is on a Working Bobbin, the Working Bobbin must be changed into a Passive Bobbin by giving it one twist with either of the Bobbins inside the pins; there the change will not show, but in the middle of the work it would. The Bobbin thus made Passive should be worked for three or four rows, and the thread then taken out of the way as directed above. When a knot occurs while working in HALF STITCH, tie it up with its pair, cut the knotted thread off, fasten on a new thread round a pin, bring it down to its pair, and tie it up with it. The illustration (Fig 552) shows how the threads that have knots upon them are drawn up away from the work.

Knots.—A complication of threads, cords, or rope, either secured by interlacing the ends together, or entangled so as to render their separation difficult. Knots, or what may resemble them, are employed in fringe making and decorative needlework, and are simulated on various textiles, such as a certain make of woollen cloth for men's great coats, knickerbocker cloth, fringe, &c.

It is often necessary in Needlework to join two pieces of thread together, and there are also knots which, when made with thick braid or cord, are extremely useful for ornamenting dresses and jackets.

Bowline Knot.—This knot, shown in Fig. 553, is useful for joining threads or cords together, and is made as follows: Take a loop with one cord, and hold it in the

FIG. 553. BOWLINE.

left hand, pick up the other cord in the right hand, pass one end of it through the loop, then over and under both the ends held in the left hand, and over its own end.

Carrick Bend.—The knot shown in Fig. 554 is also called a Josephine knot, and is used as a trimming knot; the illustration shows it made with a double cord. To

FIG. 554. CARRICK BEND.

make: Make an upward loop with one cord, and fold the right end under the left. Take the second cord, pass one end into the loop over the curve at the right side, and out at the left side still over the loop, put it under the end of

that first cord in the left side, and over the end on the right, then into the loop under it and over its other end there, then under the loop and so out at the top of the knot. Before drawing tight, run the double cord in, and then draw up altogether.

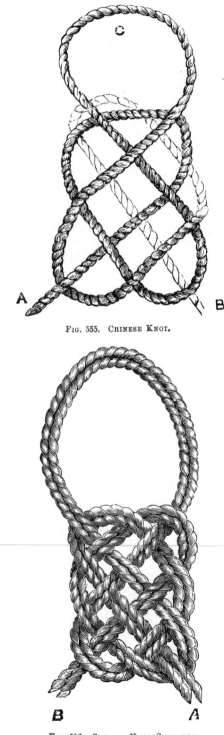

FIG. 555. CHINESE KNOT.

FIG. 556. CHINESE KNOT COMPLETE.

Chinese Knot (*see* Figs. 555 and 556).—This is the knot sailors use to ornament the lanyards they hang their knives from when they wear them round their necks, the loop C being made of sufficient size to go round the neck, and the knife tied at the ends, A B. The knot forms a very handsome ornament to a lady's jacket, particularly when it is made with double lines of silk cord; it is given in the illustration, Fig. 555, of the making with a single cord, in order to show the manipulation more clearly, but in the complete knot, Fig. 556, the double cord is introduced. To make : Lay the end of the cord A on the table, and arrange it as in the drawing, thus—form the loop in the centre, and the large loop marked C, and bring the cord down underneath A, and up to where the dotted line commences, there interlace it over and under the shaded lines, and bring it out at B. The last part of the Knot is not interlaced in the illustration, for fear of confusing the laying down of the cord A. Draw the knot tight, taking care not to pull it unevenly, and by so doing turn it over. When made with a double cord, form the knot as above described, and before drawing it tight run in the second cord.

Common Bend.—Make a loop with one cord, and twist the right end over the left. Pass one end of the second cord into the loops over the curve, then out and over the two ends, into the loop again under the right end, and out again over the curve. Pull the ends of the two cords simultaneously.

Figure of Eight Knot.—This knot is used to shorten a piece of cord or thread by means of a flat knot. Take a piece of thread, make a loop with it turning to the left, and put the top end of the loop under the lower end, and hold them tight in the left hand. Curl the under thread round and under the upper thread, and pass it into the loop and out on the left hand. Draw both ends tight.

Fisherman's Knot.—This knot is used in many kinds of needlework for fastening two ends tightly together, and is illustrated in Fig. 557. To form : Make a downward loop with one cord, passing the right end over the left.

FIG. 557. FISHERMAN'S KNOT.

Take the other cord, put one end through the loop, over it and out again under it, then let it cross the first cord where that crosses itself, and bring it round those ends, then under and over itself outside of the loop, and draw up tight.

French Knot.—A Knot made with a needle, and only used in Embroidery. See EMBROIDERY STITCHES.

Josephine Knot.—See *Carrick Bend.*

Ornamental Knots.—These are shown in Figs. 558 and 559, and are used to form ornamental knots down and front of a jacket or dress. To be made with stout silk cord. To make Fig. 558 : Form a loop by crossing the ends,

FIG. 558. ORNAMENTAL KNOT.

and turn both ends upward, make the longer of the loops the end that crosses to the right, and cross it over the left-hand cord. Hold the loop in the left hand, between finger and thumb, or press it down upon the table, take the right-hand end of the cord, round it, and bring it into the middle of the loop, simply crossing over it; then put it under the left-hand cord, outside the loop, and bring it out to the right side, pass it there over itself and under the right cord of the loop and into the loop, then over itself and out of the loop under the round at the bottom. Pull all the loops thus made evenly together, run in the second cord, and then pull up tightly. By making this knot at once with a piece of doubled cord, with the loop formed by doubling the cord used as the short left-hand end, a loop for a Buttonhole for a jacket, finished with an Ornamental Knot, is formed.

To make Fig. 559.—This knot must be made on a table. Take a piece of cord, divide it unequally, and make the short end the one upon the right hand; lay it down on

FIG. 559. ORNAMENTAL KNOT.

the table, take the long or left-hand end, round it to the left and pass it over the right cord at the bottom of the knot, round it to the right, and pass it across the centre of the knot and over both cords, round it towards the bottom, put it under the two middle cords and over the right hand and last cord, round it upwards and under the loop at the top of the knot and into it, then over and under the two cords, crossing horizontally the centre, and out at the bottom of the knot over the third horizontal line. Draw the loops together very evenly, hold them down on the table while so doing, then run in the second cord following the first, and draw the knot up tight.

Overhand Knot.—Used for making a knot in one cord where it requires shortening, or to connect two ends together. To make: Hold the thread in both hands, take the two ends, twist one over the other, and draw tight.

Reef Knot.—This knot is used to tie together when both the ends are afterwards required for use, or when it is important the knot does not slip. To make: Twist one end over the other, take the end not twisted, and turn it over the

FIG. 560. REEF KNOT.

otner; draw up both ends. To make as illustrated in Fig. 560: Make a loop with one cord, and lay its ends parallel with each other; take one end of the second cord, put it through the loop at the rounded part, then under both ends of the first cord, then into the upper part of the loop, coming out underneath and parallel to its other end.

Splice.—This knot, which is illustrated in Fig. 561, is used to join the cords together without the join altering

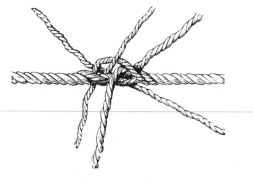

FIG. 561. SPLICE.

the thickness of the line or a knot being made. Unravel the two ends to be joined, and put the middle strand of one end through the middle strand of the other, then under the second strand and over a third strand, and put each strand from the two cords in and out its pair cord of the other end, and wind them in and out for some distance, gradually reducing the number of strands, by pulling them through to the outside of the cord and cutting them.

Square Knot.—Used for tying bandages, and in all cases where a flat and secure knot is required. To make:

Tie a tight OVERHAND KNOT with the left end, then take the right-hand end and pass it over and under the left-hand end, and pull both ends tight.

Weaver's Knot.—A knot mucn used in all kinds of needlework for joining two ends together. To make: Take the two ends to be joined, and cross the right end under the le°t, holding both in the left hand; pass the long thread of the right end as a loop over the left forefinger, and put it between the ends and under the left thumb, then cross the ends again, holding them under the left thumb, and draw the loop over the left thread again, and draw the rignt-hand long thread tight, which pulls the loop down upon the crossed threads, and makes the knot.

Knotted Bars.—*See* MACRAMÉ.

Knotted Laces.—These are Italian Laces, and known in Italy as PUNTO A GROPPO. The word Groppo signifies a tie or knot, and the laces are made of knotted threads. The modern Macramé is worked like the knotted laces. *See* MACRAMÉ.

Knotting.—This work is one of the varieties of the Ragusa and Reticella Guipures invented after those laces became obsolete. The first notice of Knotting in England occurs in the time of William III., when a poet, enumerating the domestic virtues of Queen Mary, wrote—

> Who when she rides in coach abroad,
> Is always knotting threads;

but it was probably known on the Continent before that date. The Knotting executed in Queen Mary's day, and

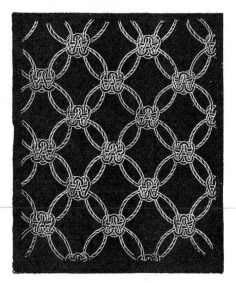

FIG. 562. KNOTTING.

for a century after, was worked upon a wooden support or pillow, and was entirely composed of the stitch illustrated in Fig. 562, which is one of the stitches used as a Filling in Macramé Lace. The work was used to make ornamental covers for hand bags and other articles that were afterwards lined with coloured silks. The stitch is illustrated in Fig. 562, and is one well known to workers of MACRAMÉ. It is a DOUBLE MACRAMÉ knot, made with the fingers, with equal spaces left between each knot. In fact, Macramé is in reality but an improved variety of the Knotting executed in Queen Mary's time worked on a cushion, and with better and more elaborate designs.

Another kind equally ancient is done with a tatting shuttle and coarse knitting cotton. To make: Hold the end of the cotton with the thumb and first finger of the left hand, wind it round the other fingers, and tie a simple knot with the shuttle, then withdraw the fingers, draw the knot close, and recommence the movements. For a large knot, put the shuttle twice through before drawing up.

The lines of Knotting so made are sown on to coloured grounds, as outlines to large flower patterns. If filled-in designs are done, the Knotted lines are made in various shades of coloured silk and sewn down, entirely filling in the pattern.

Another kind.—A description of Knotting formed with the needle and with bobbin cord is shown in Figs. 563, 565, and 566. These are patterns intended for dress trimmings and for medallions with which to ornament pincushions, and to use for antimacassars with satin backgrounds They are worked as follows. To work Fig. 563: Procure

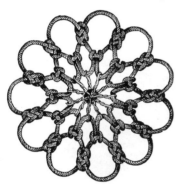

FIG. 563. KNOTTING.

white bobbin cord and good thread, or black or coloured silk cord of the same thickness as bobbin cord, large pins, and a soft large pincushion. Trace out the design upon a piece of note paper, and pin it to the cushion. Run pins through the pattern where the knots are to come, and put pins in round the centre of the medallion, in the centre of every loop, and also in the centre of the last round of loops. Commence from the outside, and fasten on two cords, which thread on large needles. Wind one cord round the pin in the centre of the first loop, and bring the second

FIG. 564. KNOTTING.

cord round the pin put in as a guide for the knot of the second or centre row. Bring the cords together where the pin indicates the big knot of the first row, and make an OVERHAND KNOT here. Make a loop of one thread, curl the other round and into this loop, and then draw both ends tight, taking care that the pin forms their centre. Work

in this way all round the outer circle of the medallion, and then commence the second or inner circle. One thread is sufficient for this. Work from right to left. Loop the thread through the inner thread of the first circle, where the pin marks its deepest part, and make a knot in that place thus: Loop twice round the thread, as shown in Fig. 564, and draw it up tightly, then pass it round one of the innermost pins, and loop it into the next inner thread of the outside circle, and work in this manner to the end. Fill in the centre with an eleven-armed WHEEL, made with white thread or sewing silk, matching the colour used for the medallion.

Fig. 565 represents a dress trimming, and is worked in the same manner as the medallion. Trace out the design upon paper, and pin it upon a flat cushion. Stick large pins in wherever a knot is to be made, and at the outer edges of the Knotting to keep the curves even. Work the outside knots first with two threads, as before described, and make the centre knots from a thread from each outer

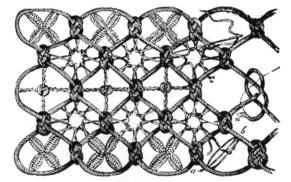

FIG. 565. KNOTTING.

line. The knots are all made like the outside knots in the medallion. When the knots are finished, keep the work still on the pins, and make the four-armed and eight-armed Wheels with silk, and make the crosses in GENOA THREE THREAD STITCH, as in GUIPURE D'ART. Commence these crosses at *a* for the laid threads, but commence to cover the threads at *b*, work to the centre of the cross, then throw the side arms out and work them over, and finish off at *a*.

The pattern shown in Fig. 566 is intended to be worked with the material it is to ornament as a founda-

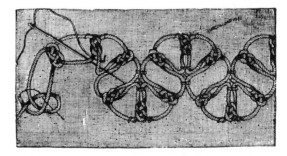

FIG. 566. KNOTTING.

tion, and it is worked as follows: Mark out with pins upon a cushion the exact distance required between the knots, measuring from the first two knots on the left hand of the illustration, and work one long row of these knots with the two threads. Calculate the length of this row as double that of the length of the material to be ornamented, and work a little more than is required. Then upon the material mark out faintly the pattern, and arrange the line of knots just worked upon it. Take a needle and thread, and sew this line down with strong stitches to the foundation wherever the curves have to be drawn together that form the design.

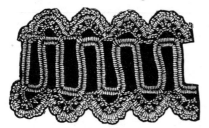

FIG. 567. KNOT WORK—GRECIAN PATTERN.

Knot Work.—This is an old work recently introduced from the Continent into England, where it was much

netting needle and crochet hook. To work: Select fine linen thread, crochet cotton, a fine netting needle, and a crochet hook. Commence by joining together two threads of stout crochet cotton to form the foundation lines. Then proceed to cover these lines with the linen threads, connecting the lines together, or working them over separately, according to the design. The stitch is called a WHOLE LOOP when both foundation threads are covered, while when only one foundation thread is covered the stitch called a HALF LOOP. To make a Half Loop on the right thread, as shown in Fig. 568: The netting thread being between the foundation threads, bring it out to the right under the right thread, and put the netting needle in between the two foundation threads, and over the right one. To make a Half Loop on the left thread, as shown in Fig. 569: The netting thread being in the centre, between the foundation threads, bring it out to the left, and put it over the left foundation thread and back into the centre. The combination of these two stitches make the Whole Loop, which work thus: Lay the end of the thread wound on the netting needle on the foundation, hold it with the left hand thumb, pass the netting needle

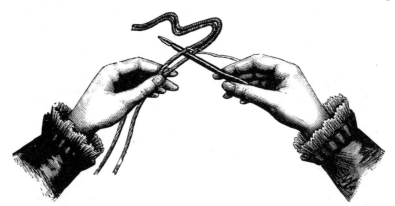

FIG. 568. KNOT WORK—HALF LOOP ON RIGHT THREAD.

worked during the sixteenth century as Ragusa or Mediæval Guipure. The old Ragusa Guipure was executed with gold and silver threads, silk or flax; the modern Knot

between the two threads, over the left thread, then under it, over the right thread, under it, and into the centre. When pieces of Knot Work are joined together in the

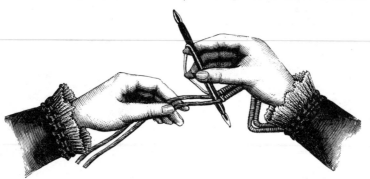

FIG. 569. KNOT WORK—HALF LOOP ON LEFT THREAD.

Work is made with fine silk or thread, knotted over crochet cotton or cord, with its edging made with crochet. The old work was either done upon the Pillow, or worked with a needle or hooked instrument; the new is worked with a

working, the process is as follows, and is illustrated in Fig. 570: Entirely work one foundation piece, then work the second until the part is reached where it is to be joined; here take a crochet hook and pull the working thread through a loop on the finished line as a loop, and pass the netting needle through that loop, and draw it up tightly.

The stitches having been learnt, proceed to work the Grecian pattern, as shown in Fig. 567. Cover the foundation threads with WHOLE LOOPS for the straight lines of the pattern, but where the turns are made work in Half Loops upon the outer foundation line when the curve is outwards, and upon the inner foundation line when it is inwards. Make a length of the pattern to correspond with the length of the lace required, and then take the thread off the netting needle, and proceed to CROCHET the border. First row—Commence at an outer point of pattern, fasten on, work 4 CHAIN, 1 DOUBLE CROCHET, twice, then 4 Chain, and fasten into the end of the point, work 3 Chain to connect the next point, and fasten in; repeat to the end. Second row—1 Chain, 1 TREBLE into every alternate chain of the last row. Third

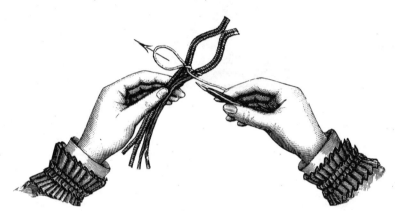

FIG. 570. KNOT WORK—JOIN TWO PARTS TOGETHER.

row—2 Chain, 1 Double Crochet into every space of the last row.

To work the Edging shown in Fig. 571 : Work a straight foundation length entirely in Whole Loops, and join the vandyke edge to it. Knot two threads together and pin to a lead cushion. Work twelve Whole Loops * and six

FIG. 571. KNOT WORK—EDGING.

Half Loops over the left thread, twelve Whole Loops, and two half on the right thread, then join the foundation line to the vandyke at the eighteenth Whole Loop there, work two half loops on the right thread of vandyke, twelve whole loops, and repeat from *.

Kolinsky Fur (*Mustela Siberica*).—This animal is the Tartar sable, which has a fur of a bright yellow colour. It may be had of the natural hue, or dyed to resemble Sable. The whole of the fur, when in a natural condition, is of a remarkably uniform colour, having no difference of shade in any part nor spot of any description, the tail being included in this uniformity. This latter is much used for artists' painting brushes.

Kolrosk Fur.—The Kolrosk is an animal of the Ermine or Weasel tribe, a native of Russia and the northern lati-

tudes. Its fur is much used for lining cashmere cloaks, and is of a brownish colour.

Kreuzstich Stickerei. — The work known by this name is Cross Stitch upon thick materials. It has always kept its place among needlework on the Continent, particularly in Germany, Italy, Hungary, and Spain, and is well known in Morocco, though but little practised in England, and we owe its present revival in this country to the exertions of Mr. Julius Lessing, who has collected together and published a selection of the quaint old-world patterns found by him in German country houses. Kreuzstich Stickerei presents no difficulty to the worker beyond the counting of the stitches upon a pattern, and its quaintness and adaptability to the decorations of articles in daily use will recommend itself to all. The work is of two kinds, one where the pattern is filled in with stitches, and the other where the pattern is left plain and the background filled in. The Germans generally work the pattern, the Spaniards and Italians the ground. It is particularly useful for decorating white articles, as when worked with ingrain cottons or silks it can be washed without detriment and the stitches worked both sides alike. The materials best suited to it for washing purposes are the various kinds of German canvases, which are woven so that each thread is distinct and perfectly regular, and Java and honeycomb canvas, coarse linens, and linens divided into squares. For articles not intended to wash, silk sheetings, plain cloths or serges, and fine white silk canvases are used. Strips of the work done upon satin sheeting look well placed between velvet or plush, and form handsome chair backs or mantel borders, and good dress trimmings are made by working it in yellow or blue floss silks upon black satin. When heavy materials are used as the backgrounds, and not stuffs in which the threads can be counted, the work has to be done over ordinary Wool Work canvas, the threads of which are drawn away when the stitches are all made. The materials used are either embroidery silks or cottons. The peasants of Spain and Italy use the coloured cottons, but the Arabs use a kind of coarse knitting silk. The cottons known as Brodera la Croix come from abroad, and only three shades of blue, four of red, one of amber, one brown, two chocolate, and one green can be relied upon as really ingrain. The embroidery silks can be had in a much greater variety of shades.

The stitches used are CROSS STITCH, or POINT CROISÉ SANS EVERS, if both sides of the material are to show. By the Germans this stitch is worked as a double cross, thus : Bring the wool out at the left-hand bottom corner of a square, put the needle down in the centre of the square, and out where it first came up. Cross to right-hand top corner, and back to the centre, cross to left-hand top corner, and up at right-hand bottom corner, cross to left-hand top corner, and out at right-hand bottom corner, ready to commence a second stitch. Worked by the Italians, the stitch is a cross inclosed in a square, both sides alike. To make: Secure the wool and cross at the back, from left-hand top corner, to right-hand bottom corner, cross in the front to left-hand top corner, and bring the needle out at left-hand bottom corner, cross to right-hand top corner, and out at left-hand bottom corner, straight stitch to right-hand bottom corner, and back to left bottom corner, over to left top, under right-hand top side, over to right-hand bottom corner and back to the top

geometrical patterns. The one illustrated in Fig. 573 is of this class, and is easier to work out than those formed of mythological animals. To work: Work in CROSS STITCH with black silk all the stitches filled in with black in the illustration, in green silk all the stitches filled in with a black cross, in crimson all filled in with a diamond, in blue all those with a line across them, and in violet all that are dotted.

FIG. 572. KREUZSTICH STICKEREI.

corner, over to left-hand top corner, and needle out where next stitch begins.

To work as shown in Fig. 572: Work the dragons in CROSS STITCH in deep crimson silk or ingrain cotton for their bodies, heads, and claws; their tails in two shades of olive green, the lighter being indicated by the square crosses in the stitches in the illustration, the darker by the black stitches. Work the ribbons hanging from the

L.

Lace.—The origin of lacemaking is lost in antiquity, and no certain date can be ascribed to it, because of the practice of ancient writers of mentioning fringed garments, cauls of network, veils of gold network, embroidery upon fine linen, and woven networks together indifferently as needlework. We know, however, that the art was un-

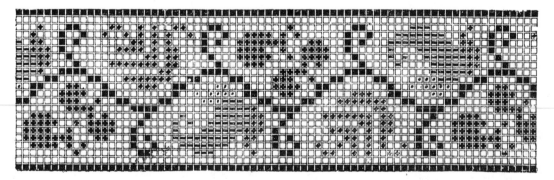

FIG. 573. KREUZSTICH STICKEREI.

dragons' mouths in pale blue, the border lines in dark olive green, with the centre stitches in alternate blue and crimson colours. The pattern can be repeated, as the tails of the animals join, and it is used either for a table border, mantel border, or apron. If the design is used for an apron, work one pattern on the bib, three on the bottom of the skirt, and two on the large pocket.

The designs for this work are not all executed in three colours, and can be formed of conventional flowers or from

known to the Asiatics, but was practised in Egypt, and that amongst the early frescoes upon the tombs of that nation, plaited gold, silver, and coloured fringes are depicted as adorning the edges of the robes of kings. From the Egyptians, lacemaking became known to the Jews, Greeks, and Romans, but the art was quite in its infancy, and no specimens of it before the time of the early Christians have been handed down to us. Lace by them was regarded as too valuable for anything but church purposes or as trimmings to the grave clothes of saints, and although a rude description of gold lace was used by the Scandinavian kings for secular purposes, the real lace was made entirely in convents, and devoted to the adorning of churches, the patterns being either Scriptural subjects or emblems used in the church. It was not until the time of the Renaissance that lace became part of the dress of the laity, and for some years was even then too costly for any but kings, but gradually its adoption became universal amongst the nobility, and it was used with so much profusion and extravagance, that not only every article of underclothing became trimmed with it, but it was let in between the seams of garments (hence the origin of the term Seaming Lace), and all toilet accessories, even to the coverings of baths and bed furniture, were made with it. Noblemen frequently ruined themselves with the enormous sums they gave for their lace collars, ruffles, and knee and boot trimmings. The amount of lace worn at the end of the sixteenth, and during the seventeenth and eighteenth centuries, caused its frequent mention in the wardrobe accounts of great people, and it is from these inventories that our knowledge of the introduction of different laces, their decline, and the substitution of other descriptions, according to the dictates of fashion, is derived, joined to the enactments forbidding their exportation to foreign lands, and the Sumptuary Laws, as little mention of any particulars about this costly article of commerce is to be found in history. The fashion of wearing large quantities of lace with every costume gradually passed away, until finally it was no longer recognised as an article of gentlemen's attire (only lingering as ruffles upon Court suits), and ladies became content to keep it for outward adornment. This decline in the demand for so costly an article, added to the very small remuneration each lace worker could hope to receive for almost unremitting toil, the loss of eyesight entailed, the troubles in France and Holland (the principal places of its production), and the invention of the Bobbin net machine, and, finally, of the lacemaking machine, have all contributed to the decay of this art, and now only such laces as Brussels, Lille, Mechlin, Valenciennes, and Honiton are made to any amount, these, by their beauty, intrinsic value, and merit, being still able to contend against all disadvantages, and obtain high prices; but for how long they can stand against the cheap and good machine imitations is a matter of doubt, and much fear is entertained that the delicate art of lacemaking will become extinct.

The word Lace is either derived from "Lacinia," the hem or fringe of a garment, or from "Lacez," a braid, but it was not used to distinguish this fabric until the end of the seventeenth century. The Italians used the general term of Puntos, and the more universal appellation was Passement au fuseau, for Pillow laces, and Passement à l'aiguille, for the needle made, while lacemakers were called Passementiers, deriving their own name and that of the lace they made from the pattern upon which the lace was worked being traced upon parchment. "Dentelle" is only once applied to lace in the inventories belonging to Mary, Queen of Scotland, and

not before her time, and it is not until 1660 that it is met with, or that it superseded Passement in common usage.

Laces are divided into those made with the Needle, and those made upon a Pillow with Pins and Bobbins, and from these two great divisions spring the numerous varieties of the handicraft. The earliest lace of any note (if we except the fringed and knotted edges of material, and the few rude gold and silver woven threads) are the Cutworks, or Point Coupé. These are founded upon open work Embroidery, and are generally met with upon the same piece of linen as white Embroidery; coeval with the Cutworks are the Drawn thread work, from one branch of which spring the Reticellas, or earliest Needle laces, in which the drawn threads are placed in a frame and Buttonholed together in a pattern; next come the Lacis, or Darned Netting or Spider Work, and the Knotted Laces, or Punto Groppo. The Reticellas speedily gave way to the beautiful Spanish and Venetian Points, made entirely with the needle, and the early Tape Pillow laces of Flanders and Italy. In the same century were produced the Thread Pillow laces of Bisette and Mignonette in France, and the celebrated laces of Brussels, Mechlin, and Valenciennes in Flanders, while Colbert established, in 1665, at Alençon, in France, a lace manufactory, intending to rival the Points of Spain and Flanders, and ended in producing a lace unlike its prototypes, but one that ranks amongst the best Points. Since the seventeenth century, with the exception of the white and black silk blondes of Spain and Chantilly, no entirely new lace has been invented, but varieties of the above kinds have been produced, and the industry has spread from its parent countries over the whole continent. In England, although the lace made has been produced from copies of other laces, the manufacture has been known from the fifteenth century, edicts having been passed in 1483 to prohibit the importation of foreign laces, and to protect the home trade; but, except old Devonshire and Honiton lace, English laces have not ranked very highly. At present the Honiton lace trade is good, but that of the fine thread laces of Buckingham and Bedfordshire is nearly extinct. In Scotland, lace is rarely made, while in Ireland, lace was not introduced until the present century.

Needle-made laces, claimed by the Italians and Spanish equally as their inventions, are all made with the Buttonhole Stitch as a foundation. The lace pattern is cut into segments, a ground thread is run on to one of these sections, to which a row of open Buttonholes is attached, and from this the pattern is built up, open fillings being formed by working and missing the space occupied by Buttonhole stitches at stated intervals, and close parts by covering the places with thick lines of the same stitch. These fillings are then surrounded with a raised Cordonnet of Buttonhole worked over a pad, and the piece of lace is transferred to its position in the pattern, and connected together either with Buttonhole Bars, Réseau Ground, or another section worked in a similar manner. The first Needle-made laces were of thick pattern designs, surrounded by thick raised Cordonnets, heavily ornamented with Picots, and with grounds almost entirely omitted, the pattern covering all the spaces, or a Bar ground. To this heavy description of lace succeeded the lighter Caterpillar Points, also made with the needle and with Bar ground, but of so delicate a design, and so ornamented with airy Picots, as to resemble the finest fibres of seaweed. The net-patterned grounds were invented after the Bar grounds, and were made with light twisted threads, but still in Buttonhole or Overcast Stitches. As the ground so made required to be formed with the very finest thread, and took much longer to make than the pattern, the value of the lace was determined by the fineness and amount of labour bestowed upon the ground; and this standard remaining in force until the introduction of machine net grounds, in the place of hand-made, is the reason why old laces made before the time of machinery are so much more valuable than modern. The chief Needle Laces are the Cutwork, Drawn Work, Reticella, Spanish, Venetian, and Burano Points, Brussels, or Point d'Angleterre, Point Gaze, Alençon, Argentan, Point de Dieppe, and old Devonshire. The word "Point" should indicate a needle-made lace, but is often erroneously applied to Pillow Laces.

The materials and terms used for Needle-made laces are as follows: For Cutwork (Punto Tagliato, Opus Scissum), and Drawn Work (Punto Tirato), and the Reticellas (Punto d'Arie), are required the peculiar strong linen that is almost indestructible, and known as Quintain, very fine flax thread, and long, narrow, upright frames, into which the threads are arranged. For Darned Netting (Opus Filatorium, Punto a Maglia, Ouvrage Masches), the usual Netting materials, and either flax thread or gold, silver, silk, or fibre, to darn the design upon the netted meshes.

For the Needle-made Laces (Passement à l'aiguille, Dentelle à l'aiguille), including Venetian and Spanish Points, Alençon, Brussels, and Honiton Points, parchment patterns, and the very best flax thread, known as Lille, Brabant, and Flanders threads, are used, and the different parts of the lace are distinguished by the following terms: The groundwork, worked after the various parts of the pattern are made, is called Brides Claires when formed with plain Buttonhole Bars, Brides Ornées when these Bars are ornamented with Picots, or Réseau ground when made with meshes of net work. The flat part of the pattern is known as Flat Point, the Raised as Raised Point; the flat part is either filled in with close lines of Buttonhole, or with Band Work, Fillings, Jours, Lerd Works, or Modes, made with fancy stitches. These are all enclosed in thick lines of Buttonhole, known as the Cordonnet, which is ornamented with Picots or Pearls, Crowns, Thorns, Spines, or Dentelles Volants, which are little loops, knobs, or raised points that trim round the Cordonnet in all important parts of the design, and give lightness to an otherwise heavy pattern. Lastly, there is the Engrelure, or footing, to the straight edge of the lace, which is made more coarsely than the rest, and used to tack the lace to the dress; this is sometimes made with the lace, and sometimes attached to it afterwards.

Pillow lace is considered to have originated in Flanders, although Italy also claims its invention. It is made upon the principle of plaiting together or weaving various threads. A perforated parchment pattern is pinned to a hard round or oval pillow. The thread is wound on Bobbins having grooves at their upper ends to retain it, and the lace is formed by placing pins into the perforated pattern, and working between them for the thick parts, interweaving the Bobbins together, and for the lighter parts twisting the Bobbins round the pins, and leaving open spaces between them. Pillow lace is valued for its ground when it is of delicate Réseau pattern, and as, since the introduction of machine nets, this ground, by reason of its extreme costliness, is rarely worked, old Pillow laces made before the time of machinery are more valuable than those made at the present day. The chief Pillow laces are the Flemish and Italian Guipures, Genoa plaited laces, Brussels, bright Mechlin, Valenciennes, Lille, and Maltese, beside the blonde silk laces of Caen, Chantilly, and Calvados.

Knotted laces—the description of lace most answering to the ancient Egyptian borders to garments, first produced at Genoa for ecclesiastical purposes, and lately revived under the name of Macramé—are not made with Bobbins and parchment patterns, although they are regarded as Pillow laces. These laces are made upon a pillow, with twine cut into short lengths, and formed into designs by being tied by the fingers into knots. After the width of the lace is thus formed, the ends of the twine hang down and form the fringe, and as the length of the twine used is limited, for fear of entanglements, only edgings or borders can be worked.

For Pillow lace making (Passement au fuseau, Dentelle au fuseau) the following materials are required: A large dressed Pillow, Pattern, Bobbins, Thread, Pins, and Needle Pin. The Bobbins are filled with thread, and half of them, when attached to the Pillow, hang downwards, and are called Hangers, or Passive Bobbins, as they take no active part in the making of the fabric. The other half are called Workers, or Active Bobbins, and these work from side to side of the pattern, over and under the passive Bobbins, and make the lace. The chief stitch is the Cloth Stitch, resembling weaving, and answering to the close Buttonhole of Needle-made lace; while the lighter stitches, answering to the Band Works and Fillings, are formed with Half Stitch and the varieties of Plaitings and Braid Works. The Gimp threads woven in at the side of the pattern form the raised portions, the Pearls make the open edgings to the same, the False Pinholes adjust the lace at curves and rounds, and the Sewings connect various pieces of the design together. The groundwork is either the Bar ground, formed by plaiting together four threads from one part of the design to another, and ornamenting it with Pearls, answering to the Brides Ornées of Needle laces, or the Réseau, or net-patterned ground, made by sticking pins in to form hexagons, and twisting and plaiting the threads round them.

Lace, which has contributed so much to the beauty and elegance of dress, by its unrivalled lightness of make and texture, is, from its very nature, a purely ornamental fabric, and in its manufacture these characteristics should never be forgotten. The border or edge of lace is the part where the pattern should be most fully developed, and from it should spring a light, graceful design, thick at the bottom, and filling up the ground either with diapers of sprigs, or arabesque or conventional, not natural, flower sprays. All straight lines about a pattern should be avoided, and the distribution of the ornaments or heavy parts should be so managed that they accentuate and draw attention to the light ground and the thinner parts of the fabric, rather than themselves, the pattern being so designed as not to prominently bring forward the amount of labour bestowed upon it, but rather to keep that in the background, and show an appreciation of the right distribution of masses and of delicacy and refinement in its ornament. The earlier laces did not come up to the proper standard of lacemaking; they were, by the material used, of a heavy description, and being designed chiefly for church furniture or vestments, partook of the solid nature of the articles they were to adorn; but the light Venetian Points, known as Caterpillar and Venetian Points in Relief, answer all the requirements of lace, as do the Alençon, Argentan, Brussels, Lille, Mechlin, and Valenciennes makes of the seventeenth and eighteenth centuries. But modern laces frequently are made with too much ground and too weak a pattern. Foreign laces have been superior to English makes, because of the fine appreciation of the workers of the relative proportions of ground and design; but since the Exhibition of 1851, English lace has made great advances in its design, and, the workmanship and thread used being excellent, it bids fair to equal, if not rival, its foreign contemporaries.

Lace Grounds.—Laces made either upon the Pillow or with the Needle, however diversified their pattern, are filled in with grounds of two kinds only. These are the Bar or Bride ground, and the net pattern, or Réseau ground. The Bride grounds are formed with the needle in Needle-made laces, by throwing strands of thread from one part of a design to the other, and covering these strands with a line of Buttonhole, either ornamented with Picots or left plain. In the Pillow lace, they are made by plaiting together in Cloth Stitch four threads, and carrying this plait from one part of the pattern to another, and securing it with a Sewing, cutting off the Bobbins there, or using them in the formation of the lace at that part. *See* GROUNDS.

The net-patterned, or Réseau ground, in Needle laces are formed by loose Buttonholes arranged across the space, in a net pattern, and their manner of working is explained in GROUNDS, and their varieties, DAME JOAN, STAR, and STRAND, under their own headings. The Pillow Réseau grounds, although all of net patterns, are made by various plaitings and crossings of the threads round pins stuck into the pattern, at the corners of the meshes. They are known as BRUSSELS, DEVONIA, ITALIAN, MECHLIN, POINT DE PARIS, SAXONY, TORCHON, TROLLY, and VALENCIENNES grounds, and are described with the laces they are used with, and under their own headings.

To Clean Laces.—Valuable Laces should never be washed, in the common acceptation of the term; but if worn with any regularity, they require to be occasionally cleaned by experienced and patient hands, as the delicate Needle and Pillow Laces lose their beauty if subject to rough treatment. The following methods are employed:

To Clean Black Lace.—Take off upon a piece of stiff paper the most prominent outlines of the Lace, and be careful that the exact width and length is obtained. Make a mixture of a teaspoonful of Eau de Cologne to four of cold water, and leave the Lace in this for thirty minutes; take it out and rinse it in cold water. Make another mixture of two teaspoonfuls of cold water, two of beer, and half a teaspoonful of Eau de Cologne, and put the Lace into this for five minutes; take it out, and roll it evenly up in a cloth, and keep it there until it is only damp, not wet; and when in this condition, lay it on the paper outline, and stretch and pin it so that it is quite flat, and covering its right parts on the paper. Let it remain on the paper until perfectly dry, when unpin it, and place it on an ironing board, with stout tissue paper over it; iron it gently with a warm iron, and see that the edges of the Lace are quite smooth.

To Clean Inferior White Lace.—Tack the Lace between two pieces of flannel, soak in cold water all night, and make a lather of curd soap and hot water, and pour this upon the Lace until it is clean; then rub it over with the palm of the hand, rinse it with cold water until clean, add a little blue to colour; let it nearly dry, pin it out upon a board, and iron it, upon the wrong side, with a piece of tissue paper between the iron and the lace.

To Clean White and Tinted Laces.—Take an outline of the Lace on stiff paper, as mentioned before. Procure either a perfectly clean, smooth, sherry bottle, or one of the white earthenware slabs made for the purpose. These slabs range from 8 inches to 14 inches square, are 1 inch in depth, and are perforated with small holes for drainage; make a book muslin or strong white net cover, to fit either the bottle or slab perfectly. Take the Lace, and roll it evenly round the bottle or slab, tacking it at the end to prevent its coming undone, and put the cover of muslin over it. Measure out a gallon of cold water and three ounces of Sapoline (or Hudson's Extract of Soap, if the Lace is very soiled), and mix in an earthen vessel; put the Lace into this, and leave it to soak for twelve hours. Rub it with the palm of the hand for five minutes before taking it out, then put it into a clean mixture, rub it gently, and put it into some clean cold water. The number of times that the mixture should be changed will depend upon the look of the Lace; it should be put in three mixtures if very dirty. Put the Lace into a copper vessel, in which mix a gallon of water with four ounces of soap, and boil for two hours: or, if the Lace is not very dirty, let it simmer instead of boil. Return the Lace to the earthen vessel, and pour over it a gallon of warm (not boiling) water, and rub it with the hand to get the soap out. Then take the muslin cover off, turn the Lace, replace the cover, and put the Lace back into the mixture for five minutes, rubbing it over; then pour warm water over it, put it into cold water, and rub it to get the soap out. Take it out of the vessel, let the water drain away thoroughly, and then stiffen the lace. Dissolve three lumps of sugar in half a pint of warm water, and rinse the Lace in it, or make a starch thus: Put one ounce of Glenfield starch into two tablespoonfuls of cold water, and mix, and to that add gradually one pint of boiling water, stirring with a spoon the whole time. Put the Lace in a slanting position, and dash this mixture over it; leave it to drain off, and then dry the Lace by rolling it up with a thick roll of linen until the moisture is absorbed. Finish the Lace by placing it upon a smooth board that has been covered with Bath coating and a firmly nailed down piece of linen, on to which the paper outline has been marked out, as to its chief lines, with pins stuck thickly in. Take the lace off the bottle or slab, lay it on this board, right side downwards, and pin it with small pins down to the lines indicated with the rows of pins, which remove, and let it thoroughly dry. Then take out the small pins, and, if necessary, iron it over with a warm iron, but leave out the ironing if possible. When quite finished, raise up any parts in relief by lifting them with a stiletto, and put the point of the stiletto through any loops at the edge, or other parts, that would be the better for it. When the Lace is cleaned in the country, and in summer time, it can be exposed to the sun's rays, instead of boiling it. This process will require several days, and the Lace will have to be turned and re-wetted several times; but it has the advantage of not hurting the material, and of making it a good colour. It must not be attempted near a town.

To Colour the Lace.—The right colour for old Lace is that of pure unbleached thread; and should that tint be desired, after the Lace has been cleaned and stiffened, throw some water over it, or lay it in the water in which coffee has been boiled. Take a quarter of a pound of the very best coffee, grind it at home, and pour six pints of boiling water upon it; let it remain for thirty minutes, and strain it through muslin.

To Mend and Restore Lace.—Ascertain what lace it is, and particularly what the ground is made of and with, before commencing any operations. Decide whether the whole of the Lace is made by hand or on the Pillow, or whether the pattern is only so made, and the ground of machine net; and also see if it is a Lace made on a pillow as to pattern, and filled in with a needle-made ground. Laces in which the design is laid upon machine net are easily repaired by the substitution of a new ground for an old one, and are not deteriorated by so doing; but Laces whose grounds are made by the needle, or on the Pillow, lose the greater part of their value if that ground is destroyed (unless it can be exactly imitated, which is almost impossible, as the very fine thread of which old Laces are composed is not procurable), and the ground should be mended to the very last. Of these are Old Brussels, Burano, Point Gaze, Alençon, Argentan, Mechlin, Old Devonshire, and Lille.

To Mend Cut Work, neatly DARN the holes and BUTTONHOLE the edges over.

To Mend Darned Netting.—Cut out the broken meshes, and NET new ones in their place; unpick the darned design beyond the junction of new and old mesh, and then DARN the pattern again in.

To Mend Drawn Work.—Pick up the old threads, and strengthen them by inserting new threads, and work over the pattern in BUTTONHOLE STITCH, or GENOA THREE-THREAD STITCH.

To Mend Needle-made Laces with Bar Grounds.—

Mend the broken parts of the pattern by cutting out the FILLINGS in the centre, and working in new Fillings that match the old in design. BUTTONHOLE round the COR-DONNET, cut out the ragged Bar Ground where necessary, and work new BARS in.

To Mend Needle-made Laces with Machine Net Grounds.—Clean the Lace, unpick the pattern from the net, and mend the pattern with needle and thread, putting in the FILLINGS, &c. Tack it on to blue paper, right side downwards, lay a new piece of net that matches the old over the sprays, and tack it to the edge of the paper; then, with a fine needle and thread, sew it round each spray, taking up the edge, and not the centre of the work. Remove the tacking threads, and sew round it a PEARL edge, either made on the pillow, or formed with a number of PICOTS. Lay the Lace, with the flowers upwards, on a board covered with flannel, which has been nailed to the board, and, with the round end of a crochet hook, or with an AFICOT, or a lobster claw, rub each little leaf, spot, or flower, and along each spray, to make all the Raised work stand up.

To Mend Needle-made Laces with Réseau on Net Grounds.—Mend the pattern as above, and then make the needle ground, as shown in GROUNDS, in the parts where it is worn away, but join it to the old, and retain the old whenever possible.

To Mend Pillow Lace Appliqué on a Machine Net Ground.—Repair this in the same way as Needle Lace upon a similar ground.

To Mend Pillow Laces.—These are repaired on the Pillow. The Bobbins must be passed into the meshes beyond the holes, and the new work will then resemble the old part. Pin the lace on to the pillow in the old Pinholes. Put up as many BOBBINS as were used for the original pattern, and arrange them in pairs, wind all the knots out of the way, draw the loop up through the Pinhole, pass one of the Bobbins through the loop, and then draw up the loop and work in the vacant part of the Lace, attaching the thread right and left when arriving at the sides. When tying off at the bottom of the mended place, fasten some of the Bobbins on one line, some on another, so as not to make a straight ridge, and so show the join. More care is necessary when mending than when making Pillow Lace, as a great deal of it is very rotten, and has often been badly repaired, with wrong kinds of thread. When mending *Tape Guipure*, it is often advisable to cut away the whole of the BAR GROUNDS, and to DARN in the pattern before restoring the Bars. A fine cord is then to be sewn round each spray, and the whole arranged upon blue paper, face downwards, and the Bars worked in with the needle, and ornamented with PICOTS. If the Lace is not so very bad, repair it entirely upon the Pillow, and make new Bars by plaiting together in CLOTH STITCH four strands of threads, and secure these to the lace through the Pinholes in the usual way.

Laces (Haberdashery).—A description of tape, or else of cord, designed for the purpose of drawing together two sides of a garment, boot, or shoe, or surgical appliance. For boots and shoes there are seven varieties, viz., Ordinary black cotton, oval ditto, flat silk, and round ditto, whip-cord and worsted, both flat and round. Of Stay Laces there are six varieties, viz., the Bath Cotton, a fine kind, made of unbleached cotton, sold by the gross, the lengths running from 8-4 to 12-4, inclusive; the Bath Worsted, likewise called Alpaca Laces, fine in quality, sold by the gross, the lengths generally running 8-4, 10-4, and 12-4; Corset or Stay Cord is made both in cotton and in linen, and is sold by the gross yards. The Paris Silk Stay Laces consist of a flat silk braid, the lengths 6-4, 8-4, 10-4, 12-4, 14-4, 16-4, and 20-4, and the numbers are 1, 2, and 3. Round

Lace Stitch.—Another term for HALF STITCH.

Lacet Work.—This work is made with a braid known as Lacet Braid, which is either of silk or cotton, and woven of various widths and descriptions. The narrow Lacet Braids have generally a looped edge to them, and are used to form edgings and narrow trimmings, being made into patterns either with the help of Crochet or Tatting. The broader Lacet braids are used for forming designs in the manner illustrated in Fig. 574, and these designs are used either for church decorations or secular purposes, according to the words selected. To work Fig. 574: This

FIG. 574. LACET WORK.

Cotton Laces consist of a bleached cotton cord, and are neatly tagged; the lengths are 8-4, 10-4, and 12-4, and the numbers 0, 1, and 2. The Swiss Laces are made of bleached cotton, and are of a finer quality than the Bath Cotton; they are sold by the gross, and their ordinary lengths are 8-4, 10-4, and 12-4. For dresses—more especially for evening ones—the Laces consist of a narrow Silk Braid. These may be had in every colour, and are sold by the gross; but, like every other description of Lace before named, they may be purchased singly. Silk Dress Laces are generally made in lengths of 5-4 and 6-4.

pattern is much reduced in size, and must be enlarged by the following process: The size of the illustration is a square of 5 inches; to enlarge that to a 25 inch square, take a piece of paper 25 inches square, and draw upon it five horizontal and five upright lines, at a distance of 5 inches apart. Draw the same number of lines upon the pattern at a distance of 1 inch apart, and whatever part of the design is inclosed within the small square draw upon the corresponding large square, so as to fill it up. To work: Transfer this outline on to red twill, cover the lines made with Lacet Braid, and sew it securely down upon the twill. Make the BARS that connect the letters together and to the edging with white Bobbin cord; take the cord across once, and work the loops round the letters with the same cord.

Lacis.—One of the ancient names for DARNED NETTING LACES.

Ladder Braid.—See BRAID.

Ladders.—See DROPPED STITCH.

Ladder Stitch.—See EMBROIDERY STITCHES.

Lady Betty Wool.—This kind of yarn may be had in white only, two and four-fold, and is sold by the ounce and the pound. It is employed for knitting shawls, scarves, and fancy articles, being soft and even in quality, and is described by Miss Lambert, in her "Handbook of Needlework" (p. 58), as a very fine description of FLEECY.

Lagetta.—There is a tree grown in Jamaica of this name, the inner bark of which resembles lace thread, and which is used to make a kind of lace. The bark is very fibrous, and is first separated into a number of thin layers of fibre, which are then arranged to resemble meshes. The manufacture of this lace was known to the people of Jamaica as far back as the time of Charles II., to whom specimens of it were presented, as they have been, in latter times, to Queen Victoria.

Laid Embroidery.—Another name for Guimped Embroidery, now better known as CHURCH EMBROIDERY.

Laine.—A French term, signifying Woollen Fleece. The several descriptions are indicated in commerce by the addition of other terms in conjunction with the word LAINE.

Laine de Ternaux.—The French name for Merino Wool of native growth. It is sometimes employed in France for needlework, but is more expensive than the genuine German Wool. See MERINO.

Laine Elastique.—This is an all-wool material, known in France as *Armure Victoria*, and to be had in several varieties of make and design. Amongst these, one description has the appearance of a Crape cloth; another has a corded check, 1 inch square, is semi-transparent, and of the character of a Grenadine; a third is woven with a very much smaller check, not larger than the smallest size of Shepherd's Plaid, and, as the material is of a closer make than the corded check before-named, it is scarcely perceptible, unless closely inspected. These cloths are all of so dull a black, that they form admirable dress materials for mourning, in the summer season, worn over a slight black silk skirt. They measure 45 inches, or double width.

Lambskin Fur.—This is made from the woolly coat of lambs, and employed as a fur, and not sheared from the skin, as is generally the custom, for the purpose of spinning and weaving. As a fur it has long been known as BUDGE. Those of foreign origin so employed in the manufacture of articles of dress are the grey Russian, Crimean, black Ukraine, black Astrachan, Persian grey, Persian black, and the Hungarian and the Spanish lambs. Lambskin furs measure 14 inches by 24 inches.

Lambskin Leather.—In France, Italy, and Spain, lambs are killed at an earlier age than in England, and as

the skin is fine and thin, it is used as a substitute for kid, but is less strong and glossy than the latter. The skins of the highest value are brought from the Vale of the Arno; they are imported in other qualities from Turkey, Austria, France, and Spain. They are largely manufactured into gloves in the counties of Somerset and Worcester. Small English skins, taken from young lambs that die shortly after their birth, are frequently dressed with the wool, and used for lining gloves and shoes, and also for coloured leather gloves.

Lambswool.—The curly hair or fur of lambs is to be had in two varieties—viz., the fleece, which is shorn from the living animal, and the pelt, which is taken from the skin by the fellmonger, after it has been slaughtered. The former is superior to the latter, which is both harsher and weaker, and incapable of taking as good a dye. It is, also, very frequently too short to be worked without an admixture of longer wool. Short skin wools are seldom used for the manufacture of cloths, as the process of separating it from the skin tends to harden it, and to injure its felting or milling property. It is, therefore, made into Flannels and Serges, and such textiles as require but little milling. On this account, as well as others, Pelt is less valuable than Fleece. The longer kinds of the former are used for Hosiery yarns, or for hand yarn, for the warps of Serges and certain other cloths having a warp of combed, and a woof of carded, wool. Lambswool is softer than that of the SHEEP, has the Felting quality in a high degree, and is much used in the hat manufacture. In the northern parts of Europe the lambs of certain breeds of sheep have a fleece so delicate and soft, that they are dressed on the skin, and used as costly fur for articles of dress, and especially for morning gowns, by Russians of wealth.

Lambswool Yarn.—A woollen yarn very little twisted, dyed in every colour and shade, and employed in various kinds of fancy work. The numbers run from $0\frac{1}{2}$ to 4, and are sold in 3lb., 6lb., and 12lb. parcels, as well as by the skein. A larger quantity of Lambswool Yarn is to be had in drab, grey, and white, than in other colours.

Lancashire Flannels.—The chief characteristic of these Flannels is that the surface is slightly raised on one side of the cloth. The selvedge is plain, and the colour is of a bluish hue. See FLANNEL.

Lancé Stitch.—Also known as POINT LANCÉ. See EMBROIDERY STITCHES.

Landscape Picture Embroidery.—A kind of Embroidery much worked during the last century, and revived in this, first in the Berlin Patterns, and now in the Crewel and Silk designs. The work originated in the desire to imitate Tapestry and Church Embroidery without bestowing the labour required in those elaborate needleworks. The patterns of Landscape Embroidery were principally procured from abroad, and were chiefly Scriptural; the landscapes contained figures whose flesh parts, such as faces, hands and feet, were painted in colours upon silk, and laid on to the material, which was a close, well-woven canvas. Distant objects in the landscape and the sky were also painted. The pattern thus prepared was framed in an Embroidery Frame, and the

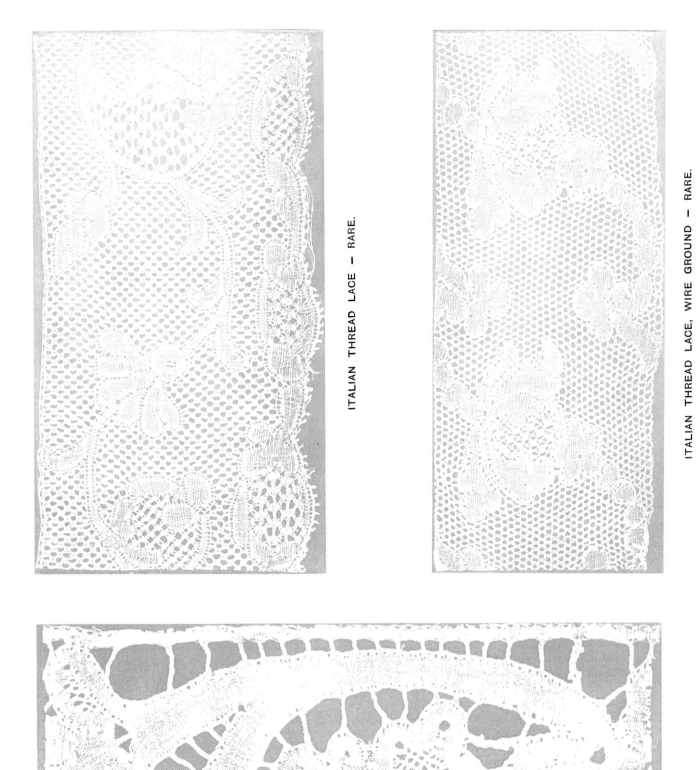

ITALIAN THREAD LACE — RARE.

ITALIAN THREAD LACE, WIRE GROUND — RARE.

ITALIAN PILLOW BRAID LACE.

work commenced. This was either worked in coloured silks, like ordinary Satin Stitch embroideries, in English wool in Satin Stitch, or in black silk like the Etching Embroideries. To work: Draw upon close canvas a landscape with figures, paint upon silk, in water colours, face, hands, and feet of figures, and APPLIQUÉ that to the canvas. Work the drapery and chief parts of the landscape in SATIN STITCH, the leaves of trees in FRENCH KNOTS, and shrubs and bushes in BULLION KNOTS.

Lapel, or Lappell.—A term signifying the lapped, or turned-over corner of the breast of a coat or bodice, so cut and folded back when an open front is desired.

Lappa.—A silk brocade manufactured in India.

Lappet, or Tab.—The lace pendants of a woman's head-dress, as worn in the eighteenth century. The same term is now used to denote the lace cap ends, or strings, of elderly ladies' caps. In Walpole's "Anecdotes of Painting" we find the following allusion to Lappets: "The habits of the times were shrunk into awkward coats and waistcoats for the men, and for the women to tight-laced Gowns, round Hoops, and half-a-dozen squeezed plaits of Linen, to which dangle behind two unmeaning pendants, called Lappets, not half covering their straight-drawn hair."

Lasting.—This is one of those woollen cloths distinguished from others as "stuffs," such as Linseys and Rateens. The name is a contraction of the word "Everlasting," which was the original name of a woollen textile, made of "Combing Wool," during the last century. It was a stout textile, of double or treble warp and single weft, made with a five-heald Nottinghamshire twill and the best Lincolnshire wool. There are, however, varieties in Lasting bearing different names; those woven with a satin twill are known as DENMARK SATINS; others had a double twill. Prunellas were worked with three healds, and Serge de Berry, a heavier article, with seven. Amens, or Draft, is, comparatively, a very fine kind, and much exported to the Continent for church furniture. Another description is figured. Lasting, as employed for women's shoes, is a strong material, and, owing to its unyielding consistency, being made of hard-twisted yarn, is as disagreeable in wear for shoes as satin is. In addition to Prunella and Amens, there are varieties known as FLORENTINA and DRAWBAYS. The width of Lasting is 18 inches; though usually dyed black, it may be obtained in colours.

Lattice Braid.—*See* BRAIDS.

Lattice Stitch.—*See* EMBROIDERY STITCHES.

Lawn.—This name designates a delicate linen, originally of French manufacture, which was first introduced into England in the reign of Queen Elizabeth, when it was employed for the making of shirts, handkerchiefs, ruffles, and ruffs. Lawn closely resembles cambric, but is thinner and finer. The thread employed in the weaving is made so as to be as cylindrical as possible, and is not pressed so much as the cotton thread used for calicoes. The Irish and French Lawns are the best. Lawn is employed for certain portions of a bishop's canonicals; hence the allusion made by Pope:

A saint in crape is twice a saint in lawn.

It is also used for shirt fronts. There are various cloths called Lawns, which are really muslins made of cotton, such as FRENCH LAWN, above named, and VICTORIA LAWN, which is a thick make of book muslin, in black and white, used for dress linings. *See* MUSLIN.

Lawn Tennis Net.—*See* NETTING.

Lead Works.—Also known as Lerd Works and Fillings, Modes, and Jours. These terms are applied by lacemakers as general names to denote the various fancy stitches employed to fill in the centres of designs both in Pillow and Needle-made Laces. For a description of various Pillow Lead Works *see* BRAIDS and PLAITINGS, and for Needle Lead Works, *see* their own headings. Fig. 575 illustrates one of the Lead Works used in Needle-

FIG. 575. LEAD WORKS.

made Lace, and Fig. 576, Detail A, gives the detail by which it is worked. To work: The flower upon the right-hand

FIG. 576. LEAD WORKS—DETAIL A.

side of the stalk in Fig. 575 is worked separately, and attached to the stalk. Make the outer part of the seven scallops, filled in with close lines of BUTTONHOLE, thus: in the centre three of the scallops make an open diamond by not working Buttonhole Stitches in the four open spaces that form the diamond. For the fancy stitch in the centre, illustrated in Fig. 576, Detail A: First row—work 15 Buttonhole. Second row—work 3, miss 3, work 6, miss 3, work 15. Third row—work 6, miss 3, work 6, miss 3, work 15. Fourth row—work 9, miss 3, work 6, miss 3, work 3, miss 3, work 12. Fifth row—work 9, miss 3, work 6, miss 3, work 9, miss 3, work 12. Sixth row—work 6, miss 3, work 6, miss 3, work 6, miss 3, work 6, miss 3, work 9. Seventh row—work 6, miss 3, work 6, miss 3, work 6, miss 3, work 3, miss 3, work 6, miss 3, work 6. Eighth row—work 9, miss 3, work 6, miss 3, work 6, miss 3, work 6, miss 3, work 6, miss 3, work 3. Ninth row—work 12, miss 3, work 6, miss 3, work 9, miss 3, work 6, miss 3, work 6. Tenth row—work 12, miss 3, work 6, miss 3, work 3, miss 3, work 6, miss 3, work 9. Eleventh row—work 3, miss 3, work 9, miss 3, work 6, miss 3, work 9. Twelfth row—work 3, miss 3, work 9, miss 3, work 6, miss 3, work 9. Thirteenth row—work 6, miss 3, work 3, miss 3, work 6, miss 3, work 12. Fourteenth row—work 9, miss 3, work 6, miss 3, work 15. Fifteenth row—work 9, miss 3, work 3, miss 3, work 6, miss 3, work 9. Sixteenth row—work 15, miss 3, work 9, miss 3, work 6, miss 3, work 6. Seventeenth row—work 18, miss 3, work 6, miss 3, work 6, miss 3, work 6, miss 3, work 3. Eighteenth row—work 9, miss 3, work 6, miss 3, work 3, miss 3, work 6, miss 3, work 6. Nineteenth row—work 6, miss 3, work 6, miss 3, work 3, miss 3, work 3, miss 3, work 9. Fill in the rest of the space with rows of close Buttonhole, and work a thick, well-raised CORDONNET round the Fillings, which edge with PEN-WORK.

In the centre of the roses shown in Fig. 577 is illustrated a Lead Work in Pillow Lace. The whole of the lace is worked before the centre of the roses, and these are filled with Long Plaitings. To work these: Hang on two pairs of Bobbins where the Plaiting touches the rose,

FIG. 577. LEAD WORKS.

at the top, on the right-hand side, and two more pairs of Bobbins on the left side, at the distance of two Pinholes from the first set. Work these two sets of Bobbins separately, in Cloth Stitch, to the cluster of holes; here stick pins, and make the holes, and work the rest as described in PLAITING.

Leaf Netting.—See NETTING.

Leaf Stitch.—See EMBROIDERY STITCHES.

Leather.—The skins of animals, which have been subjected to certain processes, so as to cleanse, dry, and render them as supple as when in a living state, and prepare them for dyeing to suit the purpose for which each

respectively is designed. The art of preparing Leather is of the most remote antiquity, and is named by Homer. It was also known by the ancient Egyptians and the Greeks; and thongs of prepared hides were used for ropes and harness by all ancient nations. The famous Gordian Knot was made of Leather thongs (B.C. 330). There are three methods of producing Leather, but in this country two only are usually followed, viz., by Tanning and by Tawing; and both of these are sometimes combined, as in the case of sheep, goat, and deer skins. The skins employed for the manufacture of Gloves are kid, sheep, beaver, tan-leather, buck, doe, rat, and dog. These are subjected to the process of Tawing—a combination of tanning and aluming—and are thus rendered suitable for gloves and bookbinding. Morocco Leather is prepared from goat skin, and was originally imported from the north of Africa; but an inferior kind is made of sheep skin. Russia Leather derives its agreeable perfume from the empyreumatic oil of birch which is rubbed over it, and which preserves it from mould and the attacks of insects. Maroquin somewhat resembles Russia Leather, and is made at Astrachan and other parts of Asiatic Russia. Buff Leather is made of the skin of the buffalo, dressed after the manner of Chamois Leather. It is so strong that it will turn the edge of a sword, and is sometimes pistol proof, on which account it was employed in the time of Charles II. in lieu of armour. But most of the so-called Buff Leather of the present day is made of cow hides, and employed for soldiers' belts. Chamois Leather, and an inferior imitation, called "wash leather," are dressed with oil, without salt, alum, or tan. They are brought to a state of pelt by liming and washing. The grain is rubbed off with pumice stone or scraped with a knife; the skin is soaked in water, the oil forced through by beating in a fulling mill; it is then "stoved," scoured with water and alkali, dried, and smoothed with rollers. Inferior kinds of Chamois Leather are made of sheepskin. As linings for dress and underclothing, Chamois, or Washed Leather, is in much esteem. Ox hides are employed for the soles of boots and shoes, and Calfskin for the top leather; the latter is much employed for bookbinding and upholstery. Roan, which is an inferior description of Leather, made of sheepskin, prepared to look like Morocco, and tanned with sumach, is used for making slippers and women's shoes, and also for bookbinding and upholstery.

Leather Appliqué.—This is a variety of ordinary Appliqué, and used chiefly for ornamenting banner screens, brackets, and slippers. To work: Select some arabesque pattern, or conventional flower design, and trace this upon a piece of dark cloth, which stretch in an Embroidery Frame. Then take pieces of coloured kid, or thin Leather, and trace out on their under side the outline of the various parts of the design they are to cover. Cut these pieces out with a sharp pair of scissors, or lay the thin Leather upon a piece of glass, and cut it out with a knife and a glass ruler. All the pieces having been cut, lay them on to the stretched cloth, in their right positions, and slightly gum them to the cloth. Finish the work with different shades of purse silk and silk cord. Lay a cord matching the leather round its edges, catch the cord down, as in COUCHING, securing it to the leather and the material with the same stitch; work all stems, tendrils, and sprays in CREWEL STITCH, and all leaves too small to be cut out in leather in SATIN STITCH. Prepared pieces of work, with the leather already attached, can be bought. These only require to be finished off as to their tendrils and smaller parts, and do not require framing. A great improvement to the appearance of the work is given by painting the pieces of leather with water-colours mixed with gum, and shading them naturally.

Leather Patchwork.—*See* PATCHWORK.

Leaves.—The making of single leaves, or sprays of the same, forms an important part in Honiton Lace making, or of any Pillow Lace where the designs are sprigs, either attached to each other with Bar Grounds, or laid upon Net Foundations. The leaves most frequently worked are

FIG. 578. LEAF SPRAY IN CLOTH AND HALF STITCH.

the ones shown in Fig. 578, in which the leaf upon the right side is formed with CLOTH STITCH, the others in HALF STITCH, and all surrounded with a PEARLED EDGE. For the manner of working these leaves, *see* CLOSE LEAF and HALF STITCH.

Leaves with centres filled with Branching Fibres, as

FIG. 579. BRANCHING FIBRE.

FIG. 580. CENTRE FIBRE.

shown in Fig. 579, are worked with No. 9 thread, thus: Hang on eight pairs of BOBBINS, and work to the first fibre, there leave two pairs, and work the fibre with four pairs, coming back with RETURN ROPE; work the opposite fibre the same, then continue the main stem, taking up the Bobbins left. At the top of the leaf hang on a pair of

Bobbins, turn and work down over the fibres, connecting to the tip of each as it is passed, and twice to the main stem. Work the leaf in CLOTH STITCH, and then hang on a pair of Bobbins at every other row until there are sixteen pairs; or work in HALF STITCH, as shown in the illustration, and add Bobbins more slowly up to fourteen pairs. When the narrow part of the leaf is reached, make FALSE PINHOLES at first, and then gradually cut off the Bobbins.

Leaf with centre fibre, as shown in Fig. 580, is worked thus: Hang on five pairs of Bobbins at the stem, work up the middle of the first leaf, and, when the last pin is stuck, work TURNING STITCH and back with the pair of Bobbins at the pin; make a ROPE SEWING at the back of the stem. Work the two next fibres in the same manner, the middle one last, and then run a pin to its head in the centre hole, and take out the others. Carry RAISED WORK to the tip of middle leaf, hang on two pairs of Bobbins, work back in CLOTH STITCH, and when the fibre is reached take out the pin, stick it in lower down, insert the hook into the top hole, and make a SEWING with the centre stitch of the work to the cross strand to secure the fibre, and then work over it. Repeat for other leaves.

Leaves Serrated and in Relief are fully described and shown in HONITON LACE (Bryony pattern), and need not be recapitulated.

Hollow leaves are shown in Fig. 581, and are worked as follows: Hang on ten pairs of Bobbins at the tip of the hollow leaf, and two gimps, and work in CLOTH STITCH to the place where the opening begins; there work to the centre, and stick a pin in the top Pinhole. Hang a pair of gimps round it, twist the Worker Bobbin twice, make a stitch about the pin, and work first down one side of the

FIG. 581. HOLLOW LEAF.

opening, and then down the other, and make the INNER PEARL. Hollow leaves, with open branching fibres, are worked thus: Work the main fibre down the centre of the leaf first with five pairs of Bobbins and in STEM STITCH; when the bottom of the leaf is reached, hang on one or two pairs of Bobbins, according to the size of the leaf, and work an outside band round the leaf, in Cloth Stitch, with PEARL EDGE, joining the main fibre to the top of the leaf. For the open fibres branching from the centre, SEW a pair of Bobbins to the band round the outside of the leaf, but on the inside of it, and near the top, twist the threads, slant them downwards, and sew to the centre fibre; slant upwards again with a twisted strand, and sew to the band on the opposite side, and fix there; and repeat this, according to the size of the leaf, until four or six side fibres are formed.

Leaves worked in BUCKLE STITCH and in FLEMISH STITCH are described and illustrated under those headings.

Leaves in Raised Work, as shown in Fig. 582, are worked as follows: Commence at the end of the stem, and, when the middle leaf is reached, change the side for the pins, and continue the stem up the lower side of the leaf until the last pin but one is stuck. Take the Passive pair of

FIG. 582. RAISED WORK.

Bobbins that lie next the pins, lay them back over the work, and do a row of STEM without them. At the last pin hang on four pairs of Bobbins, letting them lie by the side of the pair put up, make the stitch about the pin, and do a row of Stem Stitch with the Bobbins worked with before; come back to the edge, turn the pillow quite round, so that the Bobbins lie down, the leaf facing the worker. Take out all the pins but the last three, and work straight across in CLOTH STITCH; make the last stitch with the pair put up, tie this pair once, and work back with it. Work in Cloth Stitch with PLAIN EDGE at one side, and SEWINGS to the cross strands of the stem at the other side of the leaf, until the leaf narrows, where cut off four pairs of Bobbins and make a ROPE SEWING down the Stem. When the leaf worked in HALF STITCH is reached, work

FIG. 583. LEAVES DIVIDED.

Stem up the upper side, hang on three pairs of Bobbins at the top, and work down in Half Stitch, making the Raised work as described in the previous leaf. Cut off three pairs where the leaf narrows, cross the Stem, carry Stem up the lower side of the third leaf, hang on three pairs, and work as in the second leaf; at the end tie the Bobbins up in the last Sewed pair, and cut off.

Leaves divided in the middle, and worked with a different stitch upon each side, as illustrated in Fig. 583, are worked as follows: Commence at the inner circle in the centre of leaf, and work round it; carry STEM down the middle of the first leaf, and return with CLOTH STITCH and RAISED WORK; hang on four pairs of Bobbins at the top of the leaf, and cut them off as it narrows; make a ROPE SEWING down the leaf at the back of the Stem, where the leaf divides work Stem, then hang on four pairs of Bobbins, and finish the leaf in HALF STITCH with PEARL EDGE. Work the two other double leaves in the same way; make a Rope Sewing on the circle to the place each starts from, and finish by tying and cutting off the Bobbins.

Leg.—*See* KNITTING STOCKINGS.

Leno.—A gauze-like textile, of open thread work of the nature of muslin, much employed for curtains and blinds, and as a covering for pictures. It is one of the varieties of MUSLIN, but is made of Linen, much stiffened, and is produced in a great variety of patterns.

Lerd Works.—*See* LEAD WORKS.

Levantine.—A very rich-faced, stout, twilled, black silk material, exceedingly soft, and of excellent wear. Its face and back show respectively different shades; if the former be a blue-black, the latter will be a jet, and *vice versâ*. The name it bears refers to its origin, it having been imported from the Levant.

Leviathan Canvas.—A very coarse and open description of canvas, employed for decorative embroidery. It is composed of cross bars of double strands, illustrations of which are given under BERLIN WORK.

Leviathan Stitch.—*See* BERLIN WORK.

Leviathan Wool.—A full, many-stranded, soft wool, for use on Leviathan canvas, for grounding or embroidery. There are special stitches produced by it, and, owing to the great thickness of the wool, and the character of the work for which it is employed, a piece of embroidery executed by its use is very quickly accomplished. It may be had in white and in all colours.

Liège Lace.—A manufactory of Lace was carried on at Liège from the seventeenth century to the end of the eighteenth. The Lace resembled that made at Binche, was known as Dentelle de Liège, and was made both in fine and coarse thread.

Lille Lace.—The precise date of the introduction of Lace making into Lille is unknown, but it was probably during the first part of the sixteenth century, as in 1582 the makers of Lace in that city were distinguished by their costume from other artisans, and their productions were well known in Flanders, and described by contemporary writers as a coarse Pillow Lace with a clear ground. After the treaty of Aix-la-Chapelle, 1668, when Lille (or Lisle, as it was then called) became the property of France, many of the Lacemakers went to Ghent and England; but enough workers remained to carry on their trade with great success, notwithstanding all the troubles that afflicted the country, for two centuries. Some Lace is still made at Lille, though, since 1848, other and more remunerative trades have gradually absorbed the younger workers. The Laces made at Arras, Mirecourt, Bedfordshire, and Buckinghamshire, are similar in pattern to that of Lille, but are inferior as to workmanship, no other town having attained to the beauty and lightness of the Fond Clair, or single Réseau Ground, that distinguishes the Lille Lace, and to which it owes its popularity. The design of the Lace is very simple. It consists of a thick run thread, enclosing CLOTH STITCH for thick parts, and PLAITING for open parts. The old Lille Laces, of which Fig. 584 is an illustration, is always made

FIG. 584. LILLE LACE.

with a thick, straight edge, and with a stiff, formal, small pattern as a design, with square instead of the usual round dots worked over the ground. The ground is made by twisting two threads together for two sides of the mesh, and crossing the threads over each other for the other sides, by which means the thicker look, given by Plaiting the threads together, as is the usual manner, is avoided. The old conventional patterns have lately been superseded by more open and scalloped edges and designs, similar to those of Mechlin, but the square dots and the clear ground are the same in new and old Lille.

Limerick Lace.—The Lace made at Limerick is Appliqué, Tambour, and Run Lace, upon machine-made net of a make peculiar to Ireland. *See* IRISH LACE.

Limoge Lace.—A Guipure Lace similar to Flemish Guipure. *See* GUIPURE LACE.

Line.—The hackled Flax prepared for spinning, before which it is sorted according to the various degrees of fineness.

Linen.—Cloth made of Flax, the manufacture of which dates back to the remotest antiquity. Some produced in

ancient Egyptian looms has been preserved, and is already 4000 years old. A piece of Linen Cloth found at Memphis is said to have had 540 threads in one inch of warp. Linen was not made to any great extent in England before the reign of Charles II., yet, in ancient British barrows, Linen Cloth has been found wrapped round the burnt and charred bones of the natives. Before the end of the seventh century the art of Weaving seems to have attained remarkable perfection, for it is named by Bishop Aldhelm, about A.D. 680, when speaking of the work executed by ladies of rank and piety in "Webs, woven with shuttles, filled with threads of purple, and many other colours, flying from side to side." After the Conquest, a new impulse was given to the weaving of Linen by the importation of weavers by William I. Flemish weavers were established in England under the protection of Henry III., A.D. 1253, and a company of English weavers inaugurated the industry in London in 1368; but the first Guild of the craft consisted of Flemings, established here by Richard III. (1386). Linen was woven in Ireland in the eleventh century, and in the reign of Henry III. (1272) Irish Linen is mentioned as being used at Winchester, where a Roman Linen Factory was established; and it was exported to foreign countries also about the middle of the fifteenth century. Mill Spinning began in Belfast in 1830. In the United Kingdom, Ireland long held the pre-eminence in her Linens, Cambrics, and Damasks; but Dundee and Glasgow have latterly attained an almost equal celebrity. For a long period Scotland produced only coarse kinds of Linen Cloth, but the immigration of French refugee weavers, at the beginning of the seventeenth century, gave a great impetus to the manufacture and improved its style; and in 1822, Dundee supplanted Lanarkshire as the chief seat of the industry. The art of Staining Linen was known in this country about the year 1579.

Amongst European countries, Italy took the lead in the manufacture of Linen; but it had its origin in the East, from whence it was at first exported in several varieties. At the beginning of the last century Linens were everywhere made at home in Scotland; the spinning done by the servants during the winter evenings, and the weaving by the village "webster." Every woman made her web and bleached it herself; the price never rose higher than 2s. a yard, and with this cloth everyone was clothed; but the young men procured Linen from Holland for their shirts. Our exports at the present time are very great. The varieties produced are very numerous, and all of them are known under distinctive names, amongst which we may enumerate Hollands; Cambrics (handkerchiefs); Cranky, a kind of bed-tick, a compound of Linen and Cotton, with an irregular pattern; Crumb Cloths, a heavy sort of Damask, made in many sizes, and in grey and slate colour; Stair Damask, to preserve the carpet, from 14 inches to 36 inches wide; Diapers, with bird and fish-eye designs; Dowlas Towelling, a half-bleached material, with round threads, from 25 inches to 30 inches in width; Drabbets, Drills, and Dusters, a mixture of linen and cotton, of various patterns and sizes, in pink and in blue, which can be bought by the yard in squares; Forfars, a coarse, heavy stuff, of unbleached flax, from 32 inches to 75 inches wide; Hessians and Hop Sackings, a mixture of hemp and jute; Osnaburghs, a narrow make of linen, used in mangling; French Cambrics, a very fine make, bright and silky; Glass Cloths, made of superior flax, loose in texture, and pliable, from 27 inches to 30 inches in width; Cheese Cloths, from 18 inches to 26 inches; Tea Cloths, from 25 inches to 34 inches; Huckabacks; Irish Ducks; Lawns, Linen, Damasks, and Linen sheetings; Russia Crash, a very durable cloth, used for jack-towels, from 16 inches to 32 inches in width, the threads of which are coarse and rough. Ecclesiastical Linen Cloths, for altar use, are generally manufactured in fine Double Damask, from 27 inches to 2 yards in width, or else they are made of a plain satiny Linen, measuring 27 inches broad.

Linen Damask.—A fine-twilled textile, made of flax, in which every description of design is woven. Those made at Belfast, Ardoyne, and Lisburn (Ireland) are remarkably fine; and the manufacture at Dunfermline (Scotland) is celebrated, and said to turn out upwards of 10,000 yards

both of the nature of Drawn Work and Embroidery, and is in extremely good taste, besides wearing well, and being of handsome appearance. It is made by tracing upon good hand-made Linen a bold conventional outline, drawing away the Linen Threads at stated intervals, and Overcasting those left, so as to form a ground composed of open squares, while the plain Linen within the traced outline is Buttonholed round and forms the design.

To work as shown in Fig. 585: This pattern is taken from an old German piece of work, and is executed upon good, but not too fine, Linen, with red washing silk, or Turkey red ingrain cotton. Transfer the pattern to the Linen by means of tracing paper and carbonised paper, and back the Linen with parchment or toile ciré. Then BUTTONHOLE all round the outline with the red silk, and make the Buttonhole lines very narrow. Draw out the upright threads of the material in sections, pull out six or eight threads, and leave two, and repeat to the end of the linen, but cut the drawn threads where they touch

FIG. 585. LINEN EMBROIDERY.

daily. At Barnsley, Yorkshire, there is also a Linen Damask manufactory. There is a double, as well as single, Linen Damask, the former being the more expensive; but the price is likewise influenced by the design, the artist providing the latter frequently obtaining as much as £50 for an effective or elaborate pattern. Those with sprigs or spots are comparatively cheap. Linen Damask may be had unbleached.

Linen Diaper.—A description of Damask, but having a simpler and smaller design—of a diamond pattern, or somewhat similar. Some varieties are called "Fish-eye," some "Birds'-eye" Diaper; they are made for children's pinafores, articles of infants' clothing, and for towels. Inferior kinds are made with cotton and linen, called "Unions," and others of cotton only,

Linen Embroidery.—This description of Embroidery was well known on the Continent during the last century, particularly in Germany, where it was used to decorate the borders of towels, tablecloths, and counterpanes, it having the merit of looking well upon both sides. It partakes

the thick parts of the pattern. Having finished the upright lines, draw out the horizontal ones in the same manner, so that a network of squares is formed upon the ground. Thread a needle with silk, and OVERCAST over all the left threads. The difficulty in the work will be in the even Overcasting of these lines; they should be steadied by being held down by the left thumb, and the silk used in the Overcasting should be selected without blemishes or rough places.

Another kind.—In this, the work and background are quite solid, lines of Drawn threads being used only to form ornamental borders. To work: Trace a bold conventional flower pattern upon Russian Crash, or coarse white linen. Work the outlines of the same in CREWEL STITCH, with blue linen thread, and work the fillings with SATIN, FEATHER, CORAL, CROSS STITCH, and FRENCH KNOTS. Alter the direction of the stitches, and the stitches in various parts of the work, and thus produce a variety of effects from the same design.

An imitation of this Linen Embroidery is made upon

Java canvas, and is used for cushions, mats, and other articles; the threads of the Java canvas not being drawn away, the ground of the Embroidery is solid. To work: Trace the design as before mentioned, then take coarse silk, and RUN it along the squares of the canvas, making one stitch answer to one side of a square. Run all the upright and horizontal lines in this manner, and so form a groundwork of squares. Then take fine silk, of the same colour as used on the ground, and OVERCAST all the lines of the design.

Another variation is to cut out the pattern upon linen, lay that upon the Java canvas, OVERCAST it down, and then RUN the lines upon the groundwork. Neither of these imitation Linen Embroideries can be used upon the wrong side like the real Linen Embroidery.

Linen Sheetings.—A heavy-made cloth, of flax thread, manufactured expressly for bed linen. Belfast, Armagh, and Leeds are famous for the best cloths, and common sheetings are chiefly made in Scotland, more especially at Arbroath, Dundee, Forfar, and Kirkcaldy. They are named the Scotch and the Barnsley bleached, the Loom Dowlas, and Loom Scotch. They may be had unbleached. Loom Dowlas is a particular description of sheeting (*see* DOWLAS). The widths of sheetings are known distinctively by the number of inches.

Linen Thread.—The fibres of flax reduced to thin threads of uniform size, employed both for the weaving of cloths and for sewing. The latter consists of two or more yarns or spun threads, twisted firmly together. To produce linen thread, a spindle and distaff were first employed, then a spinning wheel, and, later, the inventions of Arkwright and Hargreaves. The English centre of the manufacture is at Leeds. There are foreign ones in Bohemia, Moravia, and Lombardy.

Linge.—The French term for LINEN.

Lingerie.—A French term, more especially employed to denote Collars and Cuffs of Linen, Muslin, Cambric, or Lace.

Linings.—These are of various descriptions, depending on the materials they are respectively designed to stiffen or strengthen. Glazed Cambrics are used for chintz, Sarcenet for silks, and Persian silk, which is an inferior, slighter, and cheaper kind. Victoria lawn, starched black Mull, and Alpaca, are used for skirts, and either a thin silk, Silesia, white, grey, or black Holland for men's clothing; a strong cotton coloured twill is often used, and several other materials, for the linings of coats and cloaks; for bodices, calico, black on one side, figured grey the other. The French term for Lining is *doublure*.

Linsey.—A coarse, mixed material, of wool and flax, named after the town of Linsey, in Suffolk, where first manufactured. This is a strong and durable material, comparatively inexpensive, and much employed by the labouring classes for dresses and skirts. The warp is of thread, and the woof of worsted. Linseys are made in plain blue, plain white, striped blue and white, and other colours.

Woolsey is a mixture of cotton and wool, and, like Linsey, is made in various colours to suit certain locali-

ties. The two names are sometimes associated together when a combination of the two materials before named is woven into a cloth.

> To weve all in one loon
> A web of Lylse wulse.
> —SKELTON'S *Why Come Ye not to Court?*

Lisère.—A French term, signifying a narrow edging or binding. It also denotes a SELVEDGE. The coloured edge which furnishes the selvedges of Silk, Satin, and Velvet textiles is so named.

Lisle Thread.—A very fine description of Linen Thread, made originally at the Flemish town of that name, but now imitated closely, if not even surpassed, by our own manufactures. Lisle Thread is employed for sewing Cambric, and is also used in the weaving of a superior kind of stockings. *See* THREAD.

Lisse.—A description of silk gauze, uncrimped, and employed for dresses and frillings.

List.—The grey, violet, or pink-coloured bordering of flannel, or the strips of a darker colour that are woven at the selvedge of cloth, which are used for various purposes, such as tippets, muffs, and petticoats for children.

List Work.—This work is used for charitable purposes, as many children's warm garments can be made by its aid at a nominal cost. To make babies' hoods: Cut the shape of the hood out of a piece of coloured calico, then take the list and sew it on to the calico in rows, tacking down the edges of each row that it may overlap the one before it. Ornament each row of list with CROSS STITCH, HERRINGBONE, or SATIN STITCH, worked in single Berlin wool of a bright colour, and use odds and ends of wool so as to make each line different in colour. Edge the hood with two rows of ruching made of list, cut into narrow strips, and make a rosette at the side of the same.

For petticoats, stays, and bodices: Cut out the size of the articles upon unbleached calico, and sew the strips of list to this lining, overlapping them as before. Bind the edges of the garments with scarlet braid, and work a row of CORAL STITCH round the articles, as an ornamental border, in single scarlet Berlin wool.

Little Folks' Work.—The work shown in our illus-

FIG. 536. LITTLE FOLKS' WORK.

tration (Fig. 586) is extremely easy, and is suitable fancy work for children from eight to ten years of age. It is worked upon white cotton canvas, of the pattern shown in the illustration, with scarlet or blue Pyrenean, or single Berlin wool. To work: Cut the canvas into a square to form a mat, and RUN a straight line round the four sides of the square, 2 inches from the edge. Run the wool that forms this line underneath the top and raised thread that divides the cotton canvas into numerous small squares, and return over this Run line with a line of OVERCAST (*see* Fig. 586). Simply Overcast over the wool, and do not secure it into the material. The outer line finished, work the Vandyke line inside it in the same way, Overcasting as shown in Fig. 586, and work a second Vandyke line, to form a series of diamonds beneath the

Longcloth.—A kind of Calico of a fine texture, so called on account of the length of the pieces in which it is made, those intended for exportation being shorter. The surface is smooth, all the short filaments being removed in the peculiar mode of dressing applied to it, called "gassing," which obviates any necessity for glazing, the cloth being passed rapidly through, and singed in a jet of gas. It is naturally more expensive than ordinary calico, owing to this process of smoothing, and is not so quickly soiled; some are more dressed than others. Shirting, skirts, infants' dress, and body linen, are generally made from it.

Long Plaitings.—*See* PLAITINGS.

FIG. 587. LOUIS QUINZE LACE.

first one. Finish the work by ravelling out the edges of the canvas, to the depth of 1 inch, to form a fringe, and, where fringe and solid material meet, place a line of wide apart BUTTONHOLES, to prevent more of the canvas coming unravelled than is required.

Llama Wool.—The fleece of the goat of Peru and Chili, otherwise known as the Vicuna, or Guanaco. It is superior in its silky quality to all the varieties produced from the European breeds of sheep or goats, and is employed in the weaving of very fine and warm textiles. The fleece of the animal, in its domesticated state, is smoother and closer than that produced from the wild animal. The skin is made into leather.

Loghouse Quilting.—*See* PATCHWORK.

Long Stitch.—*See* EMBROIDERY STITCHES.

Long Stitch Embroidery.—Similar to SATIN EMBROIDERY.

Long Treble Stitch.—*See* CROCHET.

Loom Sheeting.—*See* LINEN SHEETINGS.

Loonghie.—A mixed fabric, composed of richly coloured silk and cotton. It is manufactured in Scinde, and is about 4 yards in length by 2 feet in width.

Loop.—A term used instead of stitch in Crochet, Knitting, Netting, and Tatting. In Lacemaking the word Loop is sometimes employed instead of Picot. It is also a term employed both in Dressmaking and Plain Sewing. Loops may be composed of Ribbon as a trimming, after the manner of FLÔTS; or they may be manufactured by the seamstress, by means of three or four threads, forming an attachment to hold a small button. To produce a Loop of this description, secure the thread to a spot a little within the edge of the side opposite to that of the Button, then take up a stitch, far enough from where the thread was drawn through to suit the size of the Button, as if going to Stitch. Leave a loop of thread long enough to be passed freely over the button, and take up another stitch at the spot where the thread was first drawn out. Continue to multiply the loops of thread, until sufficiently strong for the purpose of a Loop, and then proceed to form a covering over it, which will connect all the strands together into one cord. This is done by

the making of Pillow Laces, from the necessity there is, when using the machine braid that forms the imitation, of turning under and sewing down this braid when curves, vandykes, or rounds have to be formed. In the true Lace made upon the pillow, these curves and rounds come in the natural formation of the design, and are made by the contraction or expansion of the threads forming the pattern at that particular part; therefore, no sewing together and under is required in the real, while it is impossible to dispense with them in the imitation.

Louis Quinze Lace is formed of a braid known as Louis Treize. This is a coarse linen braid, of various widths, woven with a straight plain edge, but with great exact-

FIG. 583. LOUIS QUINZE LACE.

passing the needle round them, and through the thread below it, in BUTTONHOLE STITCH, securing the thread well at the other end of the Loop, on the wrong side of the material on which it has been formed. Woven Loops may be obtained for sewing upon Dresses, Mantles, household Linen, &c.

Louisine.—A very thin plain silk material, suitable for children's wear, and for slight summer costumes. It is a kind of Surah silk, or Sicilienne, and is to be had in all colours, and also woven in small checks and stripes.

Louis Quinze Lace.—This is an Imitation Lace, and a copy of Roman Tape Lace, of which it is so good an imitation as to be sometimes taken for the real article. It is, however, easily detected by anyone who understands

ness and regularity. The same braid is frequently used in Modern Point. The Lace is made as follows: Mark out the design upon pink calico, which back with brown paper. Tack the braid to the calico, putting the stitches down the centre of the braid; when this is in position, OVERCAST the edges with fine lace cotton, draw the straight parts a little together, sew down any turned pieces, and draw in and round curves and sharp points, so that every part of the braid lies flat upon the pattern. Then take a lace cotton rather coarser than the one last used, and make the BARS that connect the braid together. These are CORDED, and not Buttonhole Bars. Take the lace off the pattern by cutting the tacking threads at the back.

U U

Fig. 587 (page 328) is an illustration of Louis Quinze Lace, and is made as follows: Prepare the pattern as before described, and then take two widths of Louis Treize Braid, one half an inch, and the other a quarter of an inch in width. First TACK the broad braid lightly on, and then the narrow, and be careful that, where the braid has to be cut off, the ends are well turned under and secured. Then take fine lace cotton, and sew down every curve or vandyke where the braid turns over, and draw in with a running thread all Rounds and other parts where the edge of the braid is wider than the centre. Having by these means well-flattened the braid, connect it together by CORDED BARS, which work in regular distances apart, as shown in the illustration, and finish the pattern by working eight-armed WHEELS in the centre of the small ovals, and Wheels with BUTTONHOLE centres in the large ones.

Fig. 588 (page 329) is formed with but one braid, which is half an inch in width, and is woven with a looped edge like Mignardise Braid. To work: TACK the braid upon the pattern, and sew down and run curves and rounds as described in Fig. 587. Then take the looped edges of the braid, and tie the opposite loops together, to form the BARS that connect the various parts of the braid. Tie these loops together with a strong KNOT, which make of Lace Thread. Form the generality of the Bars by simply tying the opposite loops together, but vary this where shown in the illustration by tying three or four loops together with one common knot. Fill in the grounded part of the lace with POINT DE SORRENTO, and form the edge of the pattern with lace cotton, which arrange as a series of loops, connecting these loops to the loops at the edge of the braid; or run a narrow cord through the loops at the edge, and BUTTONHOLE that cord closely over.

Love-Ribbon.—A narrow gauze ribbon, having satin stripes, varying in size, but always narrow. It may be had both in black and white. It was employed to tie on Crape Hat-bands when worn at funerals, and is now occasionally worn by ladies in their caps.

Low Embroidery.—This term includes all the needlework formed with Satin or other fancy stitches upon solid foundations, whether worked upon both sides alike, or slightly raised (not padded) by run lines from the foundation. *See* EMBROIDERY.

Luneville Lace.—Lacemaking was commenced, in the department of Lorraine, early in the seventeenth century, and is still continued. The Lace at first was coarse, but speedily became good and fine, and was made with a double ground. Mirecourt is the principal place where it is manufactured, but that produced at Luneville is also well known. The Lace now made is principally Brussels Application, and, the thread used being whiter, and kept cleaner than that used in Belgium, the Lace does not require to go through the deleterious process of bleaching with white lead, which is employed over some of the Brussels Lace. Luneville is also celebrated for its Embroidery upon Tulle, which is very fine, and consists of Satin Stitch upon Tulle backgrounds, worked either with coloured silks or white cotton,

Lustres.—A species of Poplin, composed of silk and worsted, of a slight quality, but of which there are many varieties, both in consistency and colour.

Lutestring.—A term corrupted from "Lustring," derived from the French word, *lustre*—shining. According to other authorities, the name was derived from the cords running through the web forming some resemblance to an instrument much in vogue in the last century. The name is given to a very fine, corded, glossy silk fabric, which was much esteemed for ladies' dresses in the last century. Of this material there are many varieties in colours and quality. An Act was passed, *temp.* Queen Mary I., for the encouragement of the home manufacture of silk; and another, *temp.* William and Mary, in reference to "Alamode and Lutestring silks." Lutestring is made in various widths, with corded, pearled, and four edges,

Lutestring Ribbon.—This is a kind of Gros de Naples ribbon, made in a variety of widths, with corded, pearl, and four edges, the pearl edge being formed by the projection of some of the threads of the weft beyond the rest. It has no design, and can be obtained in any colour.

Lynx Fur.—This fur is obtained from an animal of the genus *Felis*, of which there are several species. Though resembling the cat, the tail of the Lynx is shorter, and the ears longer, the tips hanging over like tassels. The fur is long and soft, generally of a greyish colour, but in Norway is covered with brown spots. The belly of the Lynx is white, the fur silky, and not unfrequently spotted with black. The skins are dyed, prepared, and exported in large quantities for the American market, where they are much admired and valued, and employed for cloaks, muffs, tippets, linings, and facings; and, being soft, they are very suitable for such purposes. By the Greeks, Persians, and Chinese, the fur is employed in its natural state, undyed. The Canadian Lynx is, perhaps, the finest specimen of the *Felis* tribe. The fur of those animals that are found in the neighbourhood of Hudson's Bay is nearly white, on which account it is highly valued. Lynx fur is sometimes of a light reddish brown colour, variegated with dark long hair, tipped with white.

Lyons Satin.—A fine quality of Satin, produced at Lyons, having a silk back. Another description of Satin, which is sold as "Satin de Lyons," has recently been produced, having less lustre than ordinary fine Satins, and is of a thinner quality. The back is twilled or woven with a double warp. It is much used for trimmings, is suitable for mourning, and may be regarded as a description of Taffeta. No kind of silk textile of the variety called Satin was known in England until about the fourteenth century. Satin did not become a common—though costly—article of trade until the fifteenth century. In the year 1685, French refugees established the manufacture of this texile at Spitalfields; and, by means of the Jacquard loom, our Satins, produced by naturalised French weavers, became, and have continued to be of a quality equal to those produced in the manufactories of Lyons. *See* SATIN.

M.

Machine Work.—The several varieties of ordinary stitching which may be accomplished by means of small machines, hand-worked by the needlewoman, for Buttonholing, Darning, Fringing, Gauging, Kilting, and Knitting, and by the several kinds of ordinary Plain Sewing Machines, for all of which see their various headings. (*See* PLAITER and KILTER.)

Macramé Lace (also called FILET DE CARNASIÈRE). —This useful and easily made lace is a revival, under the name of Macramé, of the Italian Knotted Points (Punto a Groppo), which were much used in Spain and Italy for ecclesiastical linen, church vestments, and other trimmings, from the end of the fifteenth to the seventeenth century. This lace is first mentioned in the Sporza Inventory (1493); and in a painting by Paul Veronese, of the Supper of Simon the Canaanite, now in the Louvre, it adorns the tablecloth there depicted. The word Macramé is Arabic, and is used in the East to denote an ornamental fringe to any material; at Genoa, where Macramé Lace is chiefly made, the name was at first given to homespun huckaback towelling with plain fringed edges, and only gradually became the designation of the lace worked in likeness of these plain knotted fringes. The art of making Macramé has been taught during the whole of the present century in the schools and convents along the Riviera, but it was not until 1843 that any but the most simple designs were manufactured; at that date, a piece of old Knotted Point coming into the possession of one of the workers, she managed to unpick it, and learn from it the complicated knots.

The basis of all Macramé Lace is Knots, which are made by the fingers tying tightly together short ends of thread, either in horizontal or perpendicular lines, and interweaving the knots so made so as to form a design, sometimes slightly raised, but generally flat. From the nature of the work, the patterns thus made are simple, and are geometrical in form, it being almost impossible to form figures or flowers by such a process. Macramé is celebrated for its durability and excellence; the finer kinds, made with black and white silk threads, can be used as insertions or edgings to ladies' garments; the coarser, formed of écru coloured or black Maltese thread and twine, make mantel and table borders, and other furniture trimmings.

The materials required are as follows: A cushion, large black-headed pins, a crochet hook, or fine knitting needle, and a pattern; Italian twine, or Adams' silks, or Walter and Evans' flax, and Maltese thread of three sizes—coarse, medium, and fine. The coarse thread is used for large furniture pieces of lace, the medium for that required for ordinary uses, and the fine for dress trimmings. Make the Cushion as an oblong, flat-shaped pillow, 12in. long by 8in. wide; stuff it with sand to render it heavy, cover it with good Ticking, and arrange the lines woven in the Ticking evenly along the length of the Cushion, as they can then be used as guides for the horizontal lines of the work. An ornamental cover of scarlet ingrain twill, or blue silk, can be arranged over the Ticking cover,

if the latter is not considered ornamental enough, but it is not necessary. Prepare a piece of fine linen or silk, similar in shape to the Covers used in other Pillow Lace-making, and use this to pin over the lace while in progress, so as to keep it clean. The pins should be strong and good; they are required to pin the lace to the cushion. The crochet hook and knitting needle are very useful, especially to a beginner, in forming the knots, as they can be insinuated under the threads, without disarranging them, in places where the figures cannot go. Within the last year, a Tension Frame and Loom, known as Anyon's Patent, have been invented. These are used instead of the Cushions, and are made as long wooden frames, fitted with levers and screws that hold the horizontal threads, or foundation bars, in position, and keep them stretched. A clip is fitted to the Loom to work the Solomon Knot; it is used to draw the centre strands over the top of it, and hold them firmly while the knot is completed. The use of either Frame or Loom expedites the making of the lace, and renders the work much more firm.

The patterns used in Macramé are not, as in other laces, traced upon parchment, and pinned on to the pillow beneath the threads, as the lace is so simple that it is easily worked from a paper pattern, placed at the side of the worker, or from written directions. The difficulties to be mastered are these: To pin the cords which run along the length of the lace at even distances upon the Cushion, to work each Knot of the same tightness, to draw each Knot close up to the last, to preserve the same distance apart, when repeating the pattern, as kept at first, and to keep every thread lying straight down the cushion, in the order in which it was first arranged.

KNOTS OR STITCHES.—The stitches are all formed either of Knots or Loops, arranged as Bars, Cords Fillings, or Knots. They should be mastered before any design is attempted, as the whole beauty of the lace depends upon their being made close and tight, and placed apart at set intervals; and a beginner will have quite enough to do to keep them even, while forming a pattern, without having to trouble over how they are made. The stitches are known as Bars, Cords, Diamonds, Fillings, Knots, Open Knottings, Leaders, Rows, and Stars, and are made as follows:

Bars.—The Bar is used to form the lighter portions of the design. It is made with two, three, or four threads, according to the thickness required, and in the following varieties:

To make a *Chain Boulée*, or *Single Bar*: Pick up two threads lying close together, hold one in each hand, and keep the left-hand thread tight; pass the right-hand thread round the left as a loop, in making which bring the end of the thread out over the first part of the loop, push the loop up to the top of the thread, then hold the right-hand thread tight in the right hand, and loop the left-hand thread round it, and run the loop up to the top of the thread. Repeat these two loops until the length required for the Bar is obtained; the usual number of loops are nine, but these are increased or decreased according to the thickness of the thread used. The Chain Bar is illustrated in the Macramé pattern, Fig. 597.

To make a *Double,* or *Knotted Bar*: Take four threads lying close together, hold two in the left hand and two in the right, and loop the right over the left, and then the left over the right, as in Chain Bar.

To make a *Flat Solomon Bar*: Take four threads close together, and pin down to the lower part of the cushion the two centre ones; then take the left-hand thread (*see* Fig. 589), and pass it over the two pinned down threads and under the fourth, or last thread (*see* Fig. 590), take the fourth thread, twist it round the one put underneath it, put it under the two secured threads, and bring it out over the first, or left-hand thread (*see* Fig. 590); then hold the fourth and first threads, one in each hand, and run them up the secured threads to the top. Now reverse the movement; take the thread now on the right hand, and put it over the two secured threads and under the left-hand thread, which loop round it, and put under the secured threads and out over the right-hand

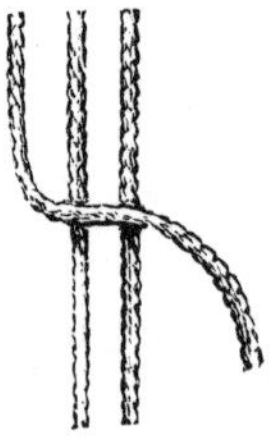

FIG. 589. MA-CRAMÉ—FLAT SOLOMON BAR.

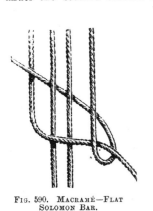

FIG. 590. MACRAMÉ—FLAT
SOLOMON BAR.

FIG. 591. MACRAMÉ—FLAT
SOLOMON BAR.

thread, draw the knot so made up close to the first knot. Repeat these two movements for the length of the Bar. A finished Solomon Bar is shown in Fig. 595.

To make a *Ridge,* or *Twisted Bar*: Take four threads, and work like the first part of a Solomon Bar, and go on repeating this movement until the right length of Bar is made. The Ridge, or Twist, will come after two knots have been made. This Bar is much used in the Raised Macramé. The Twisted Bar is shown in Fig. 595.

Cord.—The cord is the horizontal line that runs the whole length of the lace, and which is used in many patterns two or three times. To work: Before commencing the pattern, count the number of the straight horizontal lines running the entire length that are required, and for each, wind upon a separate flat card a doubled thread that is rather longer than the length the lace is to be made. Where the design requires a Cord, take one of these cards, Knot the ends of the doubled thread, and pin down to the left-hand side of the Cushion, laying the cord as close as possible to the last Row worked, and straight across the Cushion from left to right; there stick a big pin into the cushion, and wind the doubled thread tightly round it, so as to make the line across the thread quite taut, and then firmly

pin the card to the Cushion. The Cord being placed, cover it with the lace threads. Take the first thread lying on the left side of the work, loop it over the Cord (*see* Fig. 592), and pull it through again to the front with the help of the Crochet hook; pull it up quite tight, and close to the last line of work, and then

loop it over the Cord again in the same manner. Take up the next thread and repeat, and continue to the end of the lace. The beauty of the Cord depends upon the evenness with which the loops are made upon it, and the perfect regu-larity of the line it forms, and this de-pends upon the tightness of the laid thread and the firmness of every loop made. Short, slanting lines in the lace, made without the introduction of the double thread, are formed by using one of the lace threads as a Cord, for which see *Leaders.*

FIG. 592. MACRAMÉ
—CORD.

Diamonds.—These are made with the short threads, and of Macramé Knots; they are formed in the working of the lace by taking one thread, slanting it to the right or left, and covering it with Knots made with the rest of the threads looped over it. The slanted thread is known as the LEADER, and when a set number of Macramé Knots have been made over it, it forms one side of a diamond, which figure is completed by three other threads being slanted and covered in the same manner. Diamonds are made with 6, 8, 12, or 16 threads, and with Single, Double, and Treble Leaders.

To make a *Single Diamond*: Take eight threads, number them from left to right, and pick up thread No. 4 in the left hand and hold it tight, slanting it from right to left, to form the LEADER on the top side of Diamond that slopes from the centre outwards. Hold thread No. 3 in the right hand, get it under the Leader, and make with it two loops or the MACRAMÉ KNOT on the Leader; push these loops well up to the top of the Leader. Pick up No. 2 thread, and make a Macramé Knot, and do the same with No. 1 thread; push all the Knots up to the top of the Leader, and then pin the Leader down to the Cushion. Now pick up No. 5 thread, hold it in the right hand, and slant it to the right to form the top of the Diamond on the right side, and slant outwards, pass thread No. 6 under it, and make the Macramé Knot on the Leader, and repeat to thread No. 8. Form the other two angles of the Diamond by reversing the slanting of the Leaders, sloping them inwards instead of outwards, and make the Macramé Knots upon them as before, using thread 8 before thread 7, and thread 1 before thread 2. Single Diamonds can be made with any even number of threads, but 8 or 6 are the usual number.

To make *Double Diamonds*: Take sixteen threads, divide them in the middle, and wind the last eight out of the way. Make thread 8 into the LEADER, cover it with the other threads, as described in Single Diamond, and pin it down; then take thread 7 (the first one used upon the Leader) and form that into a Leader by slanting it, and covering it with MACRAMÉ KNOTS in the same way; keep it close up to the first Leader, and, when that is reached, unpin it, and form a Macramé Knot with it upon the second Leader; pin this Leader down to the cushion, and take the eight threads numbered from 9 to 16: Make No. 9 thread the Leader, and slant it outwards and cover it as before; pin it down and take thread No. 10, slant it and make it a Leader, and cover it as before, not forgetting to work the first Leader on to it at the last with a Macramé Knot. Finish the Diamond by reversing the slant of the Leaders, using the same threads for Leaders, and reversing the order of the Macramé Knots. Tie the Leaders together where they meet in the centre of the Diamond.

To make *Treble Diamonds*: Take sixteen or more threads, and work exactly like Double Diamonds, but make three LEADERS instead of two, by using threads 6 and 11 as Leaders, and reverse them in the same way as for Double Diamonds. In working Diamonds, the centre threads, before being used to cover the reversed Leaders, are frequently knotted together; these are either made in *Open Knotting* or in *Ornamental Knot*.

Edging.—The usual finish to Macramé is made as follows: Having worked all the lace, comb out and straighten the ends of the threads that hang down, and cut them to an equal length, so as to form a Fringe. Should a thick Edging, and not a Fringe, be required, bend the threads to the right, and BUTTONHOLE over them, so as to form a thick cord that follows the outline of the lace. Cut out, after every second Buttonhole, two ends of thread, so as to absorb all gradually, and yet keep the cord even throughout its length. Ornament the edge thus made with PICOTS.

Fillings.—These are made in the centres of Diamonds, either with Macramé, Ornamental, or Solomon Knots, or with Open Knotting. *See* these headings.

Genoese Groppo.—See *Ornamental Knot.*

Heading.—The part to which the lace threads are first fixed is known as the Heading, and there are two ways of attaching them. The one most used is formed with the cord as follows: Prepare a doubled thread, rather longer than the length required for the lace, and wind it upon a Card. Knot the ends together, and pin the Knot to the upper part of the Cushion, on the left side. Unwind the doubled thread until it reaches the right side of the Cushion, and stick a big pin in there, on a line with the first pin, wind the thread tightly round it, and then pin the card to the Cushion. Take a skein of thread, cut it across at each end, or only in one place, according to the width of the lace required, draw out one of the threads, double it in half, put the loop thus formed under the stretched Cord or Doubled Thread (*see* Fig. 593), draw it through with the crochet hook, slip the two ends through the loop, and draw up tight, so that a Knot is formed upon the horizontal Cord; pin this Knot down. Continue to loop the threads on to the Cord until there are sufficient for a pattern (it is a mistake to put on a greater number), and loop them on slightly apart, so that they lie flat upon the Cushion, and can be worked without interfering with each other. When the whole of the lace is made, the

FIG. 593. MACRAMÉ —HEADING.

doubled thread supporting the threads can be drawn out; the loops then form an open Heading.

The second manner of forming a Heading is as follows: Fix a line of black-headed pins along the upper part of the Cushion, from left to right, and a quarter of an inch apart. On to each of these pins fasten two doubled threads taken from the cut skein, and with their four ends work a SOLOMON KNOT. After the Solomon Knot has fastened the threads together, lay a CORD and work over it. This last Heading gives rather a better edging than the first.

Join Threads.—If a thread is to be inserted on a Leader or Cord, fasten it on as for the heading; if a thread requires renewing, make, with a new thread, a MACRAMÉ KNOT on a LEADER, and absorb the short end of the thread in the work. In other parts of the lace, tie the thread on with an Ordinary Knot.

Knot.—These are of three kinds—Macramé, Ornamental, and Solomon, and are described under those headings.

Leaders.—These are the threads that are slanted, either to form Diamonds or Stars. Take these threads from the ones forming the width of the lace, and when they have been covered with MACRAMÉ KNOTS to the length required, work them again into the pattern without distinguishing them in any way.

Macramé Knot.—This is the Knot from which the lace takes its name, and is worked with two, three, or four

threads. To make as shown in Fig. 594: Take three threads, and hold the third one in the right hand, pass it over the two, behind the third thread, and round underneath them, and bring it out over itself, repeat, and draw the knot thus made up to the top of the two threads. When worked with two threads, only one is enclosed; when worked with four threads, three are enclosed, but the knot in all cases is made with two loopings of the last thread.

FIG. 594. MACRAMÉ —KNOT.

Varieties of the Knot are formed by looping the thread three or four times instead of twice, and by working a whole row of these knots, and then commencing a second row as follows: Leave the first threads hanging, and take in the left hand the thread that formed the loops in the last row; make a Macramé Knot with this round the two threads in front of it, and draw up tight as before; continue to the end of the Row, always making the new Knots with the thread that made the knots on the first row, but that inclosed the strands behind the ones now looped together.

Open Knotting.—These stitches are used to fill up the centres of Diamonds, or are worked in rows along the lace. These Knots were used in the KNOTTING worked in the eighteenth century. To make as shown in Fig 596, on page 334: Take four threads, and number them from the left to the right; take the first, and pass it over the second and third and under the fourth; take the fourth, loop it round the first, under the third and second, and over the first, and draw up; then take the first thread (which is now on the right hand), and put it under the third and second and over the fourth (now on the left hand), then take the fourth thread, loop it round the first, and put it over the second and third and under the loop made by the first thread, and draw it up. While making the knot, keep the centre threads tight, and rather loosen the outer ones. Put a pin through this knot, take the four next threads,

make a Knot with them on a line with the last, and pin that down, and continue to the end of the row. For the second row — miss two threads, and make a Knot with two threads from the first, and two threads from the second Knot of the first row, pin down and repeat. For the third row—take on the two threads left

FIG. 595. MACRAMÉ—OPEN KNOTTING.

in the second row, and make the first knot with them, and with two threads from the first Knot on the second row. The difficulty in making Open Knotting, when working it in rows, lies in the necessity of making the Knots in even lines; this is obviated when one of the blue lines on the Ticking can be used as a guide. In Fig. 595 the Open Knotting is finished off with a RIDGE, or TWISTED BAR, and with two SOLOMON BARS.

To make Fig. 596: This Open Knotting is made like the one shown in Fig. 595, but with two Knots instead

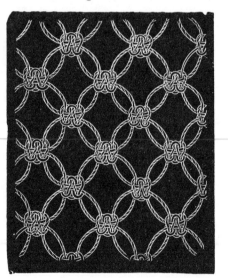

FIG. 596. MACRAMÉ—OPEN KNOTTING.

of one to each thick part. Work as in Fig. 595, and then repeat the Knot there made.

Ornamental Knot.—Used as a Filling in the centre of Diamonds, or to join Stars together, and worked as follows: Take four threads, and number them from the left

to the right; pin down two and three on to the cushion, at some distance from where the knot is being made; then take the four in the right hand, pass it over the two and three, under and over the one, then slip it under the two and three, and bring it out over itself, and draw it up tight. Repeat this until seven to nine knots are made, according to the thickness of the thread used. Take a Knitting needle (No. 10), place it upon the Ornamental Knot, and turn the ends of the knot over the pin, so as to inclose the pin in the Knot, and bring them out underneath the Knot in the place they started from, and there tie two ends on to the thread nearest them on the right side, and two ends on the left side. Smooth them down, and proceed to work the second half of DIAMOND or STAR with the threads used in the Knot. This Ornamental Knot is shown in Figs. 597 and 598.

Rows. — These are made either with horizontal CORDS or with MACRAMÉ KNOTS, worked over two or more perpendicular threads, or with OPEN KNOTTING.

Solomon Knot.—This Knot is much used in the lace to form Bars or centre fillings; the manner of working is fully described in SOLOMON BARS.

Stars.—These are used in the lace, and made with the working threads covered with MACRAMÉ KNOTS like Diamonds, but the first two Leaders, instead of slanting outwards, slant inwards to the centre, in order to form the right shape, and the two Leaders forming the bottom part of the star slant outwards from the centre. The Stars are made as Single, Double, and Treble Stars.

To work a *Single Star*: Take eight threads, number them from the left to the right, take the first as a LEADER, and slant it from left to right, and cover it with MACRAMÉ KNOTS, made with two, three, and four threads; pin it down, and take thread No. 8, slant it from right to left, and cover it with Knots made with seven, six, and five threads, and bring it to the centre, and tie the two Leaders together; then slant the right-hand Leader to the right, and the left-hand Leader to the left, and proceed to cover them in the same manner.

To work *Double Stars*: Take twelve threads, and use the first and the twelfth for LEADERS, work them to the centre as before, here pin them down, and make the second and the eleventh the next Leaders, and work them to the centre; make the last knots upon them with the first Leaders. Make an ORNAMENTAL KNOT with the four centre threads, and secure it, then divide the threads again, and work the second half of the Star, slanting the Leaders from the centre outwards. This Star is shown in the pattern given in Fig. 599.

To work *Treble Stars*: Take twelve threads, and repeat the instructions given for Double Stars, but make a LEADER of third and tenth threads, as well as of first and second, and eleventh and twelfth. Make the ORNAMENTAL KNOT in the centre, and then slant the Leaders outwards. This star is shown in the pattern given in Fig. 598.

PATTERNS.—The following Designs, illustrating the various stitches used in Macramé, will be within the scope of the worker who has learned the Knots. These designs are intended for Furniture Lace, and should be worked with either medium or coarse écru thread; they can be altered into trimming laces by being worked with fine black or white silk.

To work Fig. 597: In this pattern the threads are not Knotted on to a Cord as a Heading, but are arranged upon large-headed pins as follows. Place a row of pins, along a blue line of the Cushion, a quarter of an inch apart; cut a skein of threads at each end, take two threads, and double them over each pin. First row—work a SOLO-

knots in each Bar. Fifth row—Knot six Knots on the first Chain, then take the next two Chain Bars, and pass the fourth thread forming them round the others, as in the first part of MACRAMÉ KNOT; divide the threads again into pairs, and work the Chain Bar six knots to each Bar. Sixth row—make a Solomon Knot on every four threads, and pin it down. Seventh row—work a Cord as in the second row. Eighth row—take eight threads, divide them, and make the top half of a TREBLE STAR;

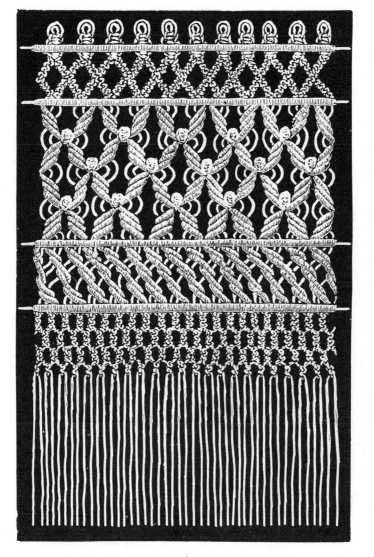

FIG. 597. MACRAMÉ PATTERN (No. 1).

MON KNOT below each pin with the threads on it. Second row—wind a double thread, long enough to work the length of the lace, upon a card. Pin the end of this to the left side of the Cushion, and lay it close along beneath the Solomon Knots as a CORD, and pin the card and the Cord firmly down on the right hand of the Cushion. Then work over the Cord with every thread, as explained in Cord. Third row—work a Solomon Knot with every four threads, and pin each down. Fourth row—work a CHAIN BAR with every two threads, tying six

repeat to the end of the row. Ninth row—make an ORNAMENTAL KNOT in the centre of each Treble Star, using the two centre threads of each half Star. Draw the Ornamental Knot over a knitting needle, bring the ends between the two corners of the Star, and turn them under; tie them in a common knot to the other ends, divide the threads again, and work the lower half of Treble Star; repeat to the end of the row. Tenth row—take the right-hand bottom quarter of the first Treble Star, and the left-hand bottom of the second Star, make an

Ornamental Knot between them, and work the lower half of Treble Star with these threads. Continue to make Ornamental Knots and lower halves of Treble Stars to the end of the row, then take the left-hand bottom quarter of the first Star, and make three slanting lines with it. Eleventh row—make an Ornamental Knot between the two first parts of the Star, and finish by working the lower half to it; repeat to the end of the row. Twelfth row—work a Cord like the second row. Thirteenth row—take the first three threads, and use the first as a LEADER, and slope it from left to right; cover it with a Macramé Knot from each of the other two threads; repeat to the end

FIG. 598. MACRAMÉ PATTERN (No. 2).

of the row. Fourteenth row—take the first thread as a Leader, slope to the right, and cover with Macramé Knots from four threads. Take the fifth thread, make it a Leader, and cover it with Knots made with the one thread left from the line above it, and two from the next; repeat this last slanting line to the end of the row, always taking the Leader from one slanted line in the previous Knot, and the covering threads from the slanted line before it; repeat this row from the commencement three times. Eighteenth row—work a Cord like the second row. Nineteenth row—make Chain Bars with every two threads of six Knots to each Chain Bar. Twentieth row—miss the

first thread, and make Chain Bars of all the rest, six Knots to each Bar. Twenty-first row like the nineteenth. Twenty-second row like the twentieth, but work four Knots instead of six to each Bar.

To work Fig. 598: Wind a double thread, the length of the lace, upon a card, pin it to the Cushion, and fasten the threads to it, as described in HEADING. First row—fasten a second double thread down, and work the CORD. Second row—take four threads, number them from left to right, and make a MACRAMÉ KNOT with the fourth thread over the other three. Work the Knot until there are four loops upon the thread. Repeat to the end of the row. Third row—take two threads from the first Macramé Knot and two from the second, and make the Macramé Knot with the fourth thread the same number of times as in the previous row; repeat to end. Fourth row—work the Cord. Fifth row—work the upper part of a DOUBLE STAR, using sixteen threads. Sixth row—work the Cord, but instead of making it a horizontal line, arrange it as a diagonal one, and pin it firmly in this shape to the Cushion before covering it with the double loops. Make the first slant of the Cord right across the first Star and upwards, the second into the centre of the second Star and downwards, the third from the centre of the Star upwards to the top, the fourth across the third Star downwards, and repeat from the commencement when carrying on the pattern. Seventh row—take the first eight threads, and work with them the two upper halves of a TREBLE STAR, then take the next sixteen threads, and work with them the two upper halves of a Treble Star, work another Treble Star with sixteen threads, and another Treble Star with eight threads, and repeat from the commencement of the row. Eighth row—work the second or bottom half of a Treble Star with the first eight threads, then take the four centre threads of the sixteen that worked the large Star, and make with them an ORNAMENTAL KNOT; divide these four threads, and work with the sixteen the second, or bottom half, of the Treble Star, repeat the Ornamental Knot and the lower halves of the large Treble Stars with the next sixteen threads, work the small eight-thread Star without a Knot, and repeat the whole pattern from the commencement. Ninth row—make an Ornamental Knot with the threads 23, 24, 25, and 26, and before commencing the pattern, then miss the first eight threads, and, with the next sixteen, make the upper half of a Treble Star and an Ornamental Knot with its four centre threads, then take the next sixteen threads and repeat the upper half of a Treble Star with them, miss the next eight threads, and repeat from the commencement. Tenth row—miss the first sixteen threads, and make the lower half of a Treble Star with the next sixteen, and an Ornamental Knot on each side of them; miss the next twenty-four threads, and repeat the lower half of the Treble Star. Eleventh row—take a double thread, and pin it down to make a Cord; arrange it as follows: lay it horizontally along the ends of the two small Stars, and close to them, then bring it down to the lowest point of the Treble Star worked in the last row, and up again to the commencement of the small Star, and pin it down carefully before covering it with the double loops.

MODERN ITALIAN LACES (PILLOW), CHIEFLY MADE ON THE "CAMPAGNA."

To work Fig. 599: Place along a line in the Ticking of the Cushion large pins a quarter of an inch apart; cut a skein of thread in one place, and hang two threads doubled on to each of the pins. First row—work with every four threads a SOLOMON KNOT. Second row—lay down a double thread and work over it as in CORD. Third

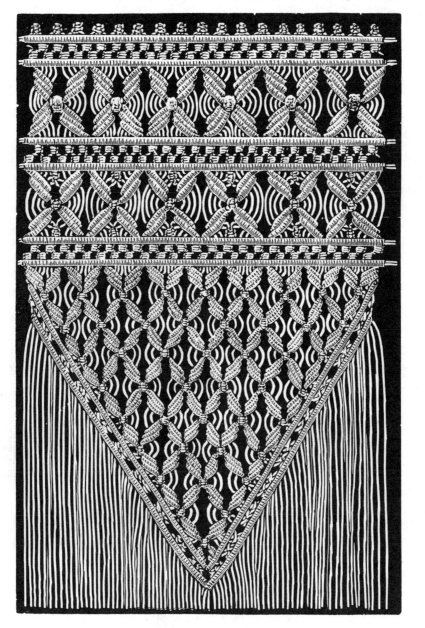

FIG. 599. MACRAMÉ PATTERN (No. 3).

row—take the first three threads, and make the MACRAMÉ KNOT over the first two with the third thread; loop the thread three times over the others; repeat to the end of the row. Fourth row—leave the first two threads, and take the one that was looped over the others, and with it make the three loops over the fourth and fifth threads; repeat these loops to the end of the row, always using the

last thread of one group to loop over the first two threads of the next group. Fifth row—lay down the doubled thread and work the Cord. Sixth row — take twelve threads, divide them, and work with them the upper halves of a TREBLE STAR, pinning each Star firmly to the Cushion as worked; repeat to the end of the row, and make six Stars. Seventh row — take the four centre threads of each group of twelve threads, and work an ORNAMENTAL KNOT with them, tie it it tight, re-divide the threads, and work the lower half of the Treble Star with them. Eighth, ninth, tenth, and eleventh rows—as the second, third, fourth, and fifth rows. Twelfth row—make a flat Solomon Knot with the four centre threads of

X X

each group of twelve threads, then commence with the first thread and work the upper halves of a DOUBLE STAR with the group of twelve threads six times, and in the centre of every Star work with the four centre threads another flat Solomon Knot. Thirteenth row—work the lower half of the Double Star, and then with the four centre threads of each group of twelve work a flat Solomon's Knot. Fourteenth, fifteenth, sixteenth, and seventeenth rows—as the second, third, fourth, and fifth rows. Eighteenth row—take the first eight threads, divide them, and work with them the upper halves of a Treble Star; repeat to the end of the row with eight threads to each Star, and make nine Stars, and then take the four centre threads of each group of eight, and work a Solomon's Knot with them, which pin down to the cushion as made. Nineteenth row—leave the first four threads alone, and then work exactly as the eighteenth row, leaving the last four threads of the ninth Star alone. Twentieth to twenty-sixth rows—repeat the nineteenth row, always leaving the first and last four threads unworked, so that the pattern is reduced finally to the upper half of one Star, which forms a point in the centre, as shown in the illustration. Twenty-seventh row —take the first thread and slant it down to the bottom of the last Star, pin it down there, and work over it as a Cord; then take the last thread of the ninth Star and slant that to meet the first, pin it down, and work over it as a Cord. Twenty-eighth row—make a Solomon Knot with every four threads of the pattern. Twenty-ninth row—repeat the twenty-seventh row, tying the two laid threads together where they meet in the centre of the pattern.

To work Fig. 600 : Fasten a row of pins into the Cushion a quarter of an inch apart, cut a skein of thread twice, and hang two doubled threads on to each of the pins. First row — work a MACRAMÉ KNOT on each four threads, reversing the Knot at every other group of threads. Second row—lay down a double thread as a CORD, and cover it with two loops from each thread. Third row—take the first twelve threads, and with the centre four work the OPEN KNOTTING with two knots, illustrated in Fig. 596 ; then divide the threads in half, and with the first six work the left hand top half of a DOUBLE STAR, and with the last six work the right hand half of the same Star, but cross the second LEADER of that half over the Leader of the first half, and keep it pinned down in that position ready for the next row; repeat to the end. Fourth row—take the threads Nos. 11, 12, 13, and 14, and make the Open Knotting with two Knots, and pin down firmly; repeat to the end of the row, using the last two threads of one group of twelve threads and the first two of another for the Knot, then finish the lower half of the Star; on the Leader crossed over from right hand to left work all the left hand threads except thread No. 6, which make the first Leader on the right hand side, putting it under the crossed Leader; having completed the Star, work with the four centre threads of each group of twelve an Open Knotting Knot, as worked in the third row. Fifth row — lay down a double thread and work a Cord. Sixth row — work an Open Knotting Knot with every four threads. Seventh row — work a Cord. Eighth row — take twenty threads

and make an Open Knotting Knot with the middle four, then with the four on each side of the Knot work a short Cord slanting towards the Knot, pin all down, take No. 1 thread, make it a Leader, and work the left hand top side of a TREBLE STAR, bringing in all the threads as far as No. 10; then, with No. 20 as first Leader, work the right hand top side of Treble Star, bringing in all the threads from No. 20 to No. 11; repeat to the end of the row. Ninth row—work a CHAIN BAR with six Knots with every two threads. Tenth row—knot two Chain Bars together, redivide them, and work two Chain Bars with eight Knots

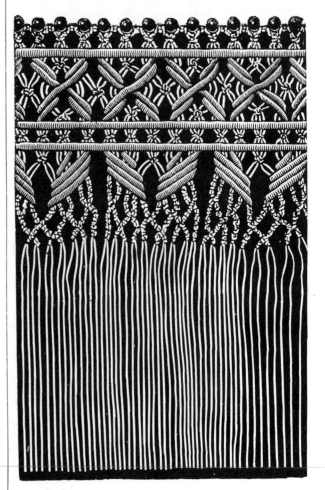

FIG. 600. MACRAMÉ PATTERN (NO. 4).

each; repeat to the end of the row. Eleventh row—repeat the tenth row, but only work four Knots to the Chain Bars.

The following pattern, from a piece of Macramé Lace worked in the eighteenth century, can be worked from instructions without a design. It is formed with flat Solomon and Twisted Solomon Bars, and with Open Knotting, and is very easily worked, and extremely elegant. To work : Lay a double thread as a HEADING, cut a skein of thread once, and loop on any number of threads that divide into four, and pin each down just enough apart to lie flat. First row—lay down a doubled thread and work it as a CORD. Second row—make with every four threads flat SOLOMON BARS, six knots to each Bar. Third row—leave the first two threads, and with the four next make a Solomon Bar with four knots; repeat to the end of the row, always taking two threads from one Bar of the last row and two threads from the next Bar. Fourth row—with the first four threads make a Solomon's Bar with four knots, and repeat to the end of the row. Fifth row—leave the first two threads, and make with the next four threads a Twisted Solomon Bar of eight knots; repeat to the end of the row, always making the Twisted Bar with two threads from one Bar and two threads from another Bar of the preceding row. Sixth row—commence with the first threads and make a Twisted Bar, as in the last row. Seventh row—leave the first two threads, and make Solomon Bars of five knots each. Eighth row—take the first threads and make Twisted Solomon Bars of twelve knots. Ninth row—leave the first two threads, and with the next four make the SINGLE OPEN KNOTTING, illustrated in Fig. 595. Tenth row—take the first two threads, and two from the first Knot, and with them work the Open Knotting, as in the ninth row. Eleventh row—work like the ninth. Twelfth row—Knot every four threads together and cut the ends of the threads straight, allowing two inches for fringe.

Madagascar Lace.—A native production of the island from which it takes its name, and of the neighbouring coasts of Africa. The lace resembles gimp more than lace, and is made of a number of loose threads twisted together, so as to form scallops and loops, and secured in those positions. It possesses no value beyond the fact of its being unlike any lace of European manufacture.

Madapolams.—A coarse description of calico cloth, of a stiff heavy make, originally of Indian manufacture, where it was employed for Quilts. It can be had either dressed or undressed, for underclothing, and measures from 29 to 33 inches in width, or in the double widths it is from 1¼ yards to 33 inches wide. These latter varieties are much employed for Curtains, Quilts, servants' Aprons, &c.

Madeira Lace.—The lace made by the natives of Madeira is not a native production, and the manufactory has only existed for fifty years. The laces made are Maltese, Torchon, and a coarse description of Mechlin.

Madeira Work.—This is white Embroidery upon fine linen or cambric, not differing from Irish Work or Broderie Anglaise in any material degree, but made by the nuns in Madeira, and eagerly sought by all admirers of fine needlework because of the excellence of its workmanship. To make as shown in Fig. 601: Trace the design upon fine cambric, work the outline in BUTTONHOLE STITCH, OVERCAST the EYELETHOLES, and fill in their centres with eight-armed WHEELS. Make the dots in POINT DE POIS, and the leaves in POINT LANCÉ, join the insertion to the edging, and hide the seam thus made by working over it in DOUBLE CORAL STITCH.

Madeira Work Trimmings.—These are hand-sewn Embroideries, executed by nuns in the Island which gives its name to the industry. Edgings, Insertions, Flounces, and children's Dresses, of very excellent quality, are worked on muslin, and imported to this country. It is to be had both in close and open work. Our own Scotch and Irish White Embroidery, especially the latter, is equally good.

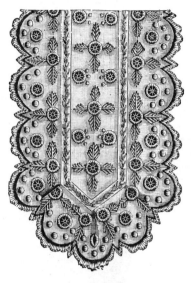

FIG. 601. MADEIRA WORK.

Madras Lace.—A school for lace making has lately been founded in Madras. The lace made is the black and white silk Maltese Guipure.

Madras-net Muslin.—This is a handsome, but coarse make of Muslin, produced in several varieties, some in cream colour, others with coloured designs of a bold character, and others again in uni-colour. They are all 72 inches wide. Those with coloured designs rise, from the price of the cream-coloured Muslins, to more than double their value.

Madras Work.—This work is so called from its being executed upon the brightly coloured silk handkerchiefs that are known as Madras handkerchiefs. When embroidered these handkerchiefs are used either for caps, mats, or workbasket covers, or are made into Chair Backs, by lace being sewn round them. To work: Select a brightly coloured handkerchief, with a deep border, composed of lines of various widths and of contrasting colours, and line it with calico. Work in Embroidery silks over these lines in DOUBLE CORAL STITCH, POINT CROISÉ, TÊTE DE BŒUF, and LATTICE STITCH, selecting silks that contrast in colour with the lines of the handkerchief. Having filled in with these open stitches all the lines that compose the border, select either a dark blue, green, or brown silk, and RUN it along both sides of each line, so as to enclose the fancy stitch decorating the centre.

Make One.—One of the ways in Knitting of enlarging the pattern. *See* KNITTING.

Making Crossings.—*See* CROSS TRACING.

Making up Lace Sprigs. — *See* HONITON APPLICATION.

Malabars.—Cotton Handkerchiefs, printed in imitation of Indian Handkerchiefs, the patterns of which are of a peculiar and distinctive type, and the contrasts of colour brilliant and striking. *See* Monteiths.

Malins Lace.—Another name for Mechlin Lace.

Maltese Lace.—Lace making was carried on in Malta during the sixteenth century, but the lace then produced was of a coarse description, and resembled Mechlin and Valenciennes without their fine grounds. But during the present century the manufacture of Greek Guipures was commenced in the island, and the first black silk plaited laces made of these designs came from Malta. The Lace is a handsome and heavy lace, made both in white silk and thread, and also in the black silk known as Barcelona silk, such as is used in Spain and France for the Spanish Chantilly Blonde Laces. The patterns are all simple, and either arabesque or geometric; they are worked upon the Pillow, are connected together with a Pearled Bar ground made at the same time as the designs, and are

Manteau.—The French name for a cloak, or loose external covering, worn out of doors.

Mantle.—An outer covering somewhat resembling a short cloak, from which it differs in being slightly fitted to the figure, and having either a loose frilling over the elbows, where the arms protrude from under it, or, sometimes, a very short sleeve commencing from the elbow. The size, form, and material of mantles vary with the season, the fashion, or the figure and taste of the wearer. They may be had in silk, velvet, cashmere, lace, and fur. After the Conquest, the cloaks so designated were introduced by the Normans, who wore them—at all seasons of the year—embroidered, lined with costly furs, fringed, and jewelled. The Mantle presented to Henry I. by Robert Bloet, Bishop of Lincoln, was valued at a sum equal to about £1,500 of our present currency. That of Cœur de Lion was of much greater value, and the inventories of our various sovereigns contain entries of their mantles. Those represented in Anglo-Saxon MSS. as worn by the ladies of

FIG. 602. MALTESE LACE.

formed of Plaiting and Cloth Stitch. The best are decorated with a little raised work, but the usual make is shown in Fig. 602, which consists of a simple Pearled Bar ground, with a pattern formed of Cloth Stitch, and Plaitings. The edge of the lace is distinguished by its lightness. The manufacture of Maltese Lace is not confined to Malta, but is largely carried on in Auvergne, Le Puy, Ireland, Buckinghamshire, and Bedfordshire, while the lace made in Ceylon and Madras resembles Maltese. Handsome shawls and veils, worth £30, were at one time made of this lace, but latterly the manufacture has been limited to narrow trimmings, costing from 1s. 6d. to 10s. a yard.

Manchette.—A French term denoting a cuff; the word *Manche* meaning a sleeve, and the fragmentary character of the sleeve represented by the final diminutive "*ette.*"

Manilla Hemp.—A fibrous material obtained from a plant allied to the Banana, and a native of the Philippine Islands. Mats, cables, and rigging in general are made of it. *See* Hemp.

that time were of the Poncho order, being a square with a hole in the centre, sufficiently large to admit the head of the wearer. Perhaps the earliest mention of them is to be found in the Book of Ruth; and, doubtless, such a form of garment dates back to the period immediately subsequent to the Fall. Amongst the Greeks it was called the *Pallium*, and the Romans the *Toga*. Our own old English name "pall" was a corruption of the Greek *Pallium*.

To make a Crape Mantle needs especial care. When making a small cape, or rotonde, without a lining, cut the piece so that the straight way of the material shall be preserved for the centre of the back. Fold the Crape together in equal halves, and then cut out the Cape upon the desired pattern, and thus avoid a seam down the back. If, however, a join be unavoidable, cut off the thick part of the extreme edge of the Crape at the selvedges, and unite them down the back by means of a Mantua-makers' Hem, which should be left unpressed. To make a Seam on the shoulders a method is adopted that has no name to distinguish it, as follows: Make a Running on the right side of the Crape, leaving the two raw edges standing up on the shoulders. Then fold back the two sides, laying them together, and make a second Running, sufficiently deep from the first as to enclose the raw edges (which may be seen perfectly well through so transparent a material), and to enable the needlewoman to take in the edges, and leave a joining free of loose ends of thread when placed back into position. It is less liable to stretch, and lies flatter for that part than a Mantua Makers' Hem. The extreme edge of the mantle is sometimes finished by a narrow sarsenet ribbon being run on, and then turned up on the inside, so as to give a firm foundation for a mourning fringe, and Crêpe rouleau Heading, as a trimming. If a double Crêpe tuck be used instead of fringe, it is easiest to place the raw edge of the Crape between the two of the Tuck, and TACK through all three sufficiently far in, to allow of afterwards turning the raw edge of the Tuck on the wrong side of the mantle, and SLIP STITCHING it down to make all neat. A fancy fold may then be laid over the cut edge of the Tuck on the mantle's right side.

Mantle Cloths.—A term employed in trade to denote every description of cloth suitable for mantles, cloaks, and all other purposes of exterior clothing for men, and, in many cases, also adapted for women's wear.

Marabout Feathers.—These are procured from a species of Stork, Adjutant, and Paddy or Rice Bird, and may be had in white, grey, or dyed. They are employed as plumes for Head dresses, Bonnets, and Trimmings for Dresses, Fans, Muffs, and Tippets, and are used with gold, silver, and pearls. White Marabout Feathers are more expensive than the grey, and have sometimes been sold for their weight in gold. The best Feathers are taken from the tail and underneath the wings.

Maracaybo Lace.—Better known as Venezuelan Lace, and consisting of Drawn Threads united with Darned Stitches. *See* VENEZUELAN LACE.

Marbled Cloth.—A new material, manufactured in two shades, composed of silk and wool, and interwoven so that the surface is mottled or "dappled." In the sixteenth century "marble-silk" was manufactured, the weft of which was of a variety of coloured threads, so woven as to give the appearance of marble to the web, stained with many hues. Many ecclesiastical vestments made of this description of silk were in use in old St. Paul's; and we read that the Lord Treasurer rode to meet "the old gwyne of Schottes" when she "rod thrught London," "with a C. gret horsse, and their cotes of marbull" on the 6th of November, 1551.

Marcella, or Marsella. — A description of cotton

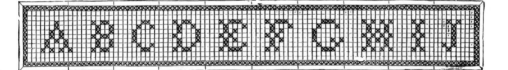

FIG. 603. MARKING IN CROSS STITCH.

Mantua Cushion Point.—A name sometimes given to GENOESE BRAID LACES.

Mantua-makers' Hem.—This is a quick method of Hemming, practised by dressmakers only, by which the Running together of two pieces of material, previous to their being Felled, is rendered unnecessary. The term Mantua-maker owes its origin to the rich silks produced at Mantua, in black and in colours, which were imported into this country in 1685 by the French immigrants, and which appear to have borne the first reputation for excellence. To work: Place the two raw edges together, fold both of them over, and HEM through the double fold of stuff, leaving the Hem so formed as a ridge, instead of a flat one, as it would have been had it been Felled. *See* FELLING.

Marabout.—A peculiar kind of "thrown" silk, frequently made of three threads of raw silk, which, being nearly white as it comes from the cocoon, is capable of receiving the most delicate shades of colour at once, without the discharge of its natural gum. A thin textile, very fine in quality, is produced from it, of which fancy scarves are made, having a white centre and coloured borders. The great delicacy of the strands of this tissue was the origin of such a name being applied to it, as the feathers of the bird so called are notable for their extreme delicacy.

Quilting or coarse Piqué, having a pattern resembling that of diaper in relief. The name is derived from the Marseilles Quilts, of which it is a lighter and cheaper variety. Marcella is sold by the yard for making toilet covers, dressing table mats, and other articles. The width measures from 30 inches to 36 inches.

Marking.—The art of Marking was carried to great perfection before the invention of the numerous modern marking inks, and during the years succeeding home-weaving of linen, when the name was woven into the material as part of the design. To be able to embroider the name of the owner, and the numerals standing for the number of articles possessed, was an accomplishment that no lady of the eighteenth and earlier part of the nineteenth century was without, and the work executed then was frequently of a very beautiful description, and always conspicuous for its neatness and finish. At the present date Marking in England is almost exclusively confined to pockethandkerchiefs, bed linen, and woollen materials; but upon the continent, Initials beautifully worked often form the sole ornamentation of silk cushions, table covers, and work-basket covers.

The marking of linen may be effected in a variety of stitches: in Cross Stitch, Embroidery Stitches, and Chain Stitch; but the orthodox style is after the first-named method. Fig. 603 is a sample of the easiest kind of

Marking. To work: Procure ingrain red cotton, and work upon Linen of a coarse texture, so as to be guided by the threads that are woven in it. Form the letters with CROSS STITCH, and place the stitches at the distance apart shown in the illustration, counting the linen threads as squares.

Fig. 604 shows the numerals used in marking To work: Trace their outlines upon the material, and RUN them with fine Embroidery cotton, then fill the centres with a padding of soft cotton, and work them entirely over in RAISED SATIN STITCH.

of this species is of a pure white, distinguishing it from the Baum, which has a yellow hue. It is a superior description of Fur, and is employed for women's dress. There is also the English Marten.

Maskel Lace.—An old lace, now obsolete.

Mastic Cloth.—A new variety of canvas, designed for embroidery purposes. It is woven in alternate stripes, from four to five inches in width; consisting of Basket woven Canvas, and a species of SATIN SHEETING. Mastic cloth measures 56 inches in width.

FIG. 604. MARKING IN SATIN STITCH.

To work the letters shown in Fig. 605: Trace the outline upon the material, and place the letter across a corner and not straight upon the article. RUN the outlines round with fine Embroidery cotton, and work the dark centres in RAISED SATIN STITCH, HERRINGBONING a light thread over the Satin stitch when complete. Work all the dots in POINT DE POIS, and the flower spray, the leaves, and flower petals in Satin Stitch, the centre of each flower as an EYELETHOLE, and the stems in OVERCAST.

Mat.—A lace maker's term for the close part of a design. In Pillow Laces this is worked in CLOTH STITCH, in Needle made laces with close and even rows of BUTTONHOLE.

Mat Braid.—A thick worsted Braid, woven after the manner of plaiting, of from half an inch to three inches in width. It is to be had in other colours besides black, and is employed as a trimming for coats, dresses, outdoor cloaks, &c.

FIG. 605. MARKING IN EMBROIDERY.

Marking Cotton.—An ingrain coloured sewing cotton, to be had in Turkey-red and blue, and sold in small balls and reels; the numbers running from 40 to 120, by tens.

Marten Fur.—This animal is of the Weasel tribe. There are two kinds of Marten, the Baum, or Pine Marten (*Mustela abietum*), and the Stone Marten (*Mustela saxorum*). This animal is a native of most European countries, and found in mountainous districts, while the manufactured skin is sometimes known as the French Sable. The Fur is of a dark brown at the extremity of the hair, while nearest the skin it is of a bluish white. The throat

Matelassé.—A French term applied to a silk or woollen textile, to denote the peculiar style of its manufacture. Such materials have a raised figured or flowered design on the surface, having a quilted or wadded appearance. This is indicated by the adaptation of the past participle of the verb *Matelasser*, to quilt or wad. Matelassé silk is employed for dresses and mantles, very fine descriptions having been recently produced. Those of wool are employed for a cheaper class of mantles and jackets, but not for dresses. Those of silk are made in white and in colours, and are much used for opera cloaks, as well as real hand-quilted silk and satin.

Mechlin Embroidery.—A term applied to Mechlin Lace, as the thread that was inserted round the outlines of that lace gave it somewhat the look of Embroidery.

Mechlin Grounds.—These are of two kinds, the Circular and the Hexagonal, but both are known as the "Vrai Réseau" by laceworkers, and used in Brussels and other laces as well as in Mechlin. The manner of making these grounds is shown in Figs. 606 and 607, in which they are purposely enlarged, to render them more easily understood.

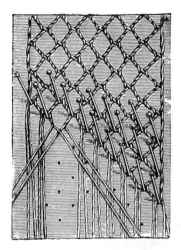

FIG. 606. MECHLIN GROUND—CIRCULAR MESH.

To work the *Circular Mesh* shown in Fig. 606 : For each twist two BOBBINS are required, so commence by

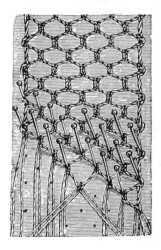

FIG. 607. MECHLIN GROUND—HEXAGONAL MESH.

hanging on four Bobbins at each Pinhole at the top of the pattern; take the two Bobbins at the outside of the left hand Pinhole, twist these three times, and pin them down straight so as to form the edge of the insertion; twist the other two three times, and pin them down in the Pinhole to the right; take up the next four Bobbins, divide them, twist two three times, and pin them down with the pin last stuck, twist the other two in the same way and put up a fresh pin to the right of them; repeat

with the four Bobbins until the first line is formed across the lace. In working the next line, twist and pin down the Bobbins as before, but take one of the Bobbins from one twist and one from the other to twist together, instead of using the same pair together always; the way to do this is shown in the illustration, as is also the line across the lace in which the meshes are made.

To work the *Hexagonal Mesh*, as shown in Fig. 607. This is both a plaited and a twisted ground : Put up two pairs of BOBBINS (four) at each Pinhole at the top of the lace, and work the two side Bobbins as before mentioned to form the outside edge, and twist the others down to the first row of Pinholes, as in Circular Mesh. Then with the four Bobbins work CLOTH STITCH twice or three times backwards and forwards without putting in pins, and forming a close plait. Work the whole row, and then divide the Bobbins that have been plaited together, putting up a pin between each pair; twist each pair twice, the right hand pair to the right, the left hand pair to the left, then take a pair of Bobbins from each side of the mesh and form a plait as before with Cloth Stitch. Work the ground entirely in this way, twisting the threads to form the sides, and plaiting them in Cloth Stitch where the pins are stuck. The manner of working the meshes across the lace is shown in the illustration.

Mechlin Lace.—Before the middle of the seventeenth century all Flemish Pillow Laces were indifferently classed as Mechlin or Malins Laces, and it is only by distinguishing the fabrics made at Antwerp, Mechlin, Lierre, and Turnhout by the flat shiny thread that surrounds their outlines that we know these old Mechlin Laces from the productions of Ypres, Bruges, Dunkirk, and Courtrai. These old Mechlin Laces are shown in Fig. 608, and generally have no grounds, and are frequently called Broderie de Malins by old writers, or "lace without ground." Mechlin Lace was worn by Anne of Austria, but the period of its greatest popularity was during the eighteenth century; it was then the only Lace used for ruffles and cravat ends, and for all purposes except full dress occasions. It was the favourite Lace of Queen Charlotte and Princess Amelia, and was exceedingly popular in England until superseded by Spanish Blondes. The Lace is made in one piece upon the Pillow, the ground being formed with the pattern, and, as both are made of the very finest thread, and require much skill to execute, the fabric is extremely costly. It is an extremely delicate lace and very transparent, and retains its original feature of a shiny plait thread surrounding the outlines of the sprigs and dots that form the design. The stitches are chiefly Cloth Stitch, but occasionally some of the light open Fillings are introduced. Mechlin Lace is always made with a Réseau ground, either of circular or hexagonal-shaped meshes, the old Malines à Bride occasionally met with being productions of neighbouring towns, and not true Mechlin.

Fig. 609, on the following page, is a modern Mechlin Lace design, showing the traced parchment pattern upon which it is worked. To work: Secure the pattern to the Pillow in the ordinary manner, and hang on sixty BOBBINS filled with thread (No. 250), and six filled with double thread (No 60). Use these last to form the plait outlines to the flowers. Work the ground as the Circular Mechlin Ground, the pattern in CLOTH STITCH. Pin the outline plait threads round the outside of the design, and secure them by working over them the threads that form the ground.

Mechlin Lace Wheel.—Used in ancient Needle Point and in Modern Point, and formed with a number of Bars

FIG. 603. MECHLIN LACE—OLD.

crossing each other, with a circle or wheel ornamented with Picots in the centre of the space. To work: Work on a single thread in BUTTONHOLE STITCH a number of Horizontal BARS at equal distances apart. Work the same Bars perpendicularly, but after having worked five or six Buttonhole Stitches past where the horizontal and perpendicular lines meet, commence to form a small circle or wheel in the centre; work half a quarter of the circle in Buttonhole, make a small loop with a pin, and into this three Buttonhole Stitches; then proceed as at the beginning of the circle, and work each quarter the same

design, such as pomegranates and their leaves and flowers, passion flowers with their fruit, &c. For Russian canvas: This material is sold, arranged for borderings, with a design already woven into it of a colour contrasting with the ground, therefore it will be sufficient to work over that as a pattern. To work the flowers: Fill them in with shaded floss silk in SATIN STITCH, make FRENCH KNOTS with purse silk for their centres, and secure round them as an outline a thread of purse silk, as in COUCHING. For the fruit, Couch down in BASKET STITCH or with plain laid threads, the gold thread to fill in their centres, and secure purse silk round them as an outline. For the leaves and stems, work in Embroidery silks of various shades in CREWEL STITCH, and edge them with a gold cord. Pieces of silk velvet can be introduced into this Embroidery, and APPLIQUÉ on to the ground instead of the elaborate stitches, and the ground can be worked over in TENT STITCH, or left plain, according to the fancy of the worker.

FIG. 609. MECHLIN LACE—MODERN.

as the first one. The loop or Picot is left out in some patterns.

Mediæval Embroidery.—This is a modern Embroidery worked in the same stitches as are used in Church Embroidery, and with Floss and Purse silks and Gold thread, but with less elaborate patterns and upon French or Russian canvas, with the material left exposed as a ground. To work, for French canvas: Select a grey or écru coloured canvas, and trace upon it a conventional flower and fruit

Mediæval Guipure.—A name given to the Knotted Laces now known as MACRAMÉ.

Melton Cloth.—A stout make of cloth suitable for men's wear, which is "pared," but neither pressed nor "finished." It is called after the name of the original manufacturer.

Mending Cottons.—These cottons may be had both white and unbleached, in small skeins of four, six, or eight to the ounce; in bundles of 10lb. or 5lb., or wound upon reels and cards. The numbers run from 8 to 40. Mending cottons may be had in a variety of colours.

Mendings.—These yarns are composed of a mixture of cotton and wool, and designed for the darning of Merino stockings. They are produced in a variety of colours, and medleys of colours, and are sold on small cards or reels.

Menin Lace.—This is a Valenciennes Lace. The variety made at Menin is considered both cheap and good. *See* VALENCIENNES.

Meraline Rayé.—An all-wool material, designed for women's dress for spring and summer wear. It is of about the thickness and weight of cashmere, is 42 inches in width, has a right side with an *armure* design and narrow stripe, and will bear washing.

Mercery.—A term denoting silk merchandise, the vendors of which latter are called Mercers. In former times a dealer in small wares was described as a " Mercer."

Merino.—A thin, woollen, twilled cloth, made of the wool of the Spanish Merino sheep, and employed for ladies' dresses, and for woven underclothing for both sexes. Merino is sometimes a mixture of silk and wool. French Merinos are of superior make and wool, are equally good on both sides, and may be obtained in all colours. This description of cloth was first made in England early in the present century. The seat of the manufacture is at Bradford, Yorkshire, socks and vests of white and grey Merino being chiefly produced in Leicestershire. The stuffs made in Saxony and at Rheims are superior to ours.

Mermaids Lace.—A name sometimes given to fine Venetian Points, from the legend of a lacemaker having copied the seaweed known as Mermaid when making one of the patterns in Venetian Point.

Merveilleux Satin.—A very thick and superior description of Satin. *See* SATIN.

Meshes.—A term used in Netting to denote the completed loops, and in Pillow Lace making, the threads that form a net pattern ground. Also, implements made of ivory, bone, or boxwood, and employed in Embroidery and Netting, are known as Meshes. Those for Raised work in Embroidery vary in width from $\frac{1}{16}$ inch to 2 or 3 inches and upwards. They are to be had with a groove on one side, as a guide for the scissors when cutting the loops. They are employed for the regulation of the looped stitches, and for the formation of the Knots in Netting. There is also a Cutting Mesh, used for highly finished kinds of Raised Work.

Metallic Embroidery.—An ornamental work suitable for cushions, footstools, and table borders. The materials used are velvet for the foundation, stiff gold, silver or bronze gauze, for the design, tulle to cover the gold gauze, and coloured silks and gold cord to embroider the pattern. To work: Stretch the velvet in the EMBROIDERY FRAME, cut out the design in gold gauze, and OVERCAST this to the velvet, SEW tulle upon the gauze, use that to count the stitches, and make ornamental fillings, by RUN LINES, HERRINGBONE, CROSS STITCH, &c., carried down through tulle, gauze and velvet; cut away the tulle beyond the gauze pattern, and COUCH, as outline lines, a line of gold,

and a line of coloured cord, round every part of the pattern.

Métre.—The French name of a measure of length employed in commerce in France. It is equal to 1¼ English yards.

Mexican Embroidery.—This is a variety of Embroidery suitable for ornamenting washing materials, such as linens, muslins, and cambrics. It is worked with ingrain silks or cottons, or Pyrenean wools, is easily and quickly executed, and will stand a good deal of rough usage. It is used for children's dresses and undercloth-

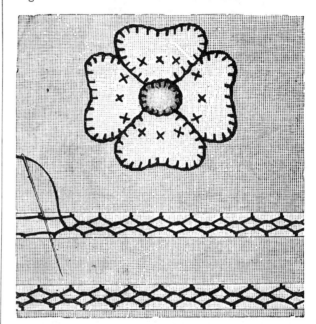

FIG. 610. MEXICAN EMBROIDERY.

ing, corners to d'oyleys, and borders for towels and tablecloths. To work as shown in Fig. 610 : Trace the outline upon a cambric material with a very faint line, and place under all the parts to be embroidered a lining cut out of the same material, which simply TACK down. Then outline the design with a line of BUTTONHOLE

FIG. 611. MEXICAN EMBROIDERY.

STITCHES, and work in the lining with every stitch. Use bright coloured silks or Pyrenean wool for the Buttonhole. Work POINT DE CROIX to fill up the outline design, and fill in the centre of the pattern with a thick, close round of Buttonhole. Finish the design by working over the two bottom rows. These are intended for tucks, and are made by folding the material, and tacking the lining between the folds. The stitch ornamenting the tucks need not be traced; it is made thus: Work a line of loops, at even distances, along the top of the tuck, and then a line along the bottom, taking care that the stitches in each line are between, and not opposite, each other. Then take a fresh thread, and with it draw the two lines together down the centre, and the stitch will be complete. Finish the work by cutting away the lining round the outline of the flower.

Fig. 611 represents Mexican Embroidery with a Raised instead of a Buttonhole outline, used for small figures, grotesque animals, and geometrical designs. To work: Trace the outline upon a thick material, such as well-woven linen or German canvas, which will not require lining, then cover it with a coloured cord. OVERCAST this cord down to the material with coloured cotton of the same tint, and, to finish, fill in the centres of the design with a number of RUN lines. Work the border inclosing the pattern with a line of CHAIN STITCH.

Mezzo Punto.—The Italian name for BEGGARS' LACE and LACET.

Mignardise Crochet.—*See* CROCHET.

Mignonette Lace.—One of the first Pillow Laces made, and a flourishing manufacture during the sixteenth seventeenth, and eighteenth centuries. The lace was light and fine, and often known as Point de Tulle, from the fine texture and beauty of its ground. It was made of Lille thread, and always of narrow widths. The chief places of its manufacture were Lille, Normandy, Paris, and Switzerland. It is mentioned in the celebrated poem known as "La Révolte des Passemens."

Mignonette Netting.—*See* NETTING.

Milanese Lace.—This is made in the Philippine Isles, with Manilla grass. The work is a combination of Drawn Work and open Embroidery, and has not much the appearance of lace. A specimen of it can be seen in the South Kensington collection.

Milan Point.—Lace was made at Milan as early as 1493, and in several varieties. The earliest kinds were the gold and silver thread laces, and the Reticellas; to these succeeded the Milan Points, which were fine laces similar to the Spanish and Venetian Points. The lace made at the present time by the peasantry is Torchon.

Mille-rayé.—A variety of Percale, so named as being descriptive of the pattern, which consists of minute threadlike stripes, alternately black and white. The width of this light printed cotton cloth is 32 inches; it is a washing material, and is suitable for children's frocks, pinafores, &c.

Millinery.—A term denoting the composition of any description of head-dress, whether bonnet, cap, veil, or other decorative or useful head covering. These articles, notably the bonnet and cap, are generally made up with a foundation of a stiff character, such as Buckram, Straw and Ribbon wire; but some consist entirely of lace, ribbons, flowers, feathers, silk, velvet, fur, or a mixture of two or three of these materials. Good taste, an eye for colour, and a light hand, are essential characteristics of a successful milliner. In former times, Millinery was a term

of much wider scope than at present, as the worker had to make up the foundations, or bonnet shapes, on which to arrange the materials employed, as well as to work in straw, and produce both Beaver and Felt Bonnets and Hats. In Paris, this additional branch of Millinery is still carried on in those great houses where fashions in this department are originated. Old-fashioned bonnets used to consist of three parts—the front, or shape; the back, or crown; and the curtain at the back. At present the whole is usually comprised in one, or else in two parts—the crown, and, possibly, a narrow brim attached to the foundation, merely sufficient to admit of some forms of trimming by which that brim is concealed.

When a bonnet is formed of two parts—the Front and the Crown—the method of making it is as follows: Cut a paper pattern, and lay it on the Willow, or Buckram, cutting it by the outline supplied: SEW wired chip round the outer edge of the Front, the wire being inclosed between it and the Front; and then BIND all with a strip of soft silk or muslin, cut on the bias, to cover all unevennesses. Proceed to wire the inside of the Front next to the head—the chip inside, the wire outside, and the Willow foundation between them. The Willow will project beyond the chip and wire, and must then be snipped at regular intervals, to make it expand at the edge, and turned up to fit better to the head, or Crown, which will afterwards be attached to it. Lay a piece of thin muslin smoothly over the Willow Front, upon which place the silk or satin material of the Bonnet, so as to lie the straight way of the web, and pin it on carefully, that it may not be drawn on the bias. Then TACK down the silk on the inside to the chip; in the same way line the Front, finishing the edge by SLIP STITCHING, or else with a plain binding or a cord edge.

The Crown of the Bonnet must be made next, either plain or full. Cut it out of the Willow, or Buckram, from a paper pattern, and join the extreme ends, so as to fit the Front made for it. The upper edge (if a plain Crown) must be stiffened with a wire chip. Crowns with plain round tops may be procured ready-made from a manufacturer. Cover the top with a flat piece of wadding or muslin, then lay the silk covering over it, and Tack it down to the sides. Then cover the sides, and take care so to place the join as that it shall be concealed under some trimming; otherwise, finish it with a Cord, and let the joining at the top, as well as of the side, be finished precisely at the edge of the Front.

The next business is to sew the Crown and Front together, which constitutes one of the chief arts of the trade, all depending on the degree of slant given—either forwards or backwards—to the Crown.

Full or fancy Crowns require to be made on a "dummy," having been first cut out of Buckram to a pattern, and then plaited upon the "dummy" head.

The old-fashioned Drawn Bonnets are no longer seen, excepting for children's wear, although the backs of fancy ones are sometimes Gauged. The Front, when drawn, was made of a length of material, cut the straight way, the selvedge going round the outer rim of the Front. Then a wide Hem was made, in which from three to five runnings were made, to form casings for the wires or canes to be introduced into them; a stiff wire was run into the outermost, the better to maintain the shape desired. Then the wires, canes, or whalebones, were secured at one end, the Gatherings evenly drawn, and then the other ends of the stiffeners were sewn down. The Crown was drawn in the same way, and the circular form obtained, by fixing it to a wired chip. We give these details on the chance of a return to such a style.

To make any description of light, transparent, summer Bonnet, such as Crape, Gauze, Muslin, or Net, the following rules may suffice: Employ a foundation of Paris net (this material is thin and brittle, and needs careful handling), sew a narrow, white, wired chip round the edge of the Front; lay on the transparent covering (cut on the straight), TACK it in position, and BIND the edge with satin, as likewise the chips and joinings of the Crown. These may be equally well concealed by folds of satin instead of bindings.

Bonnets worn in mourning must be made of Crape, or of silk trimmed with it. If of Crape only, cover the Willow foundation with thin black silk, to conceal it, as black Willow is not to be recommended, on account of its brittleness. Make a broad HEM on the Crape bow and strings; the double Hem being about an inch in width.

Caps of Lace must be made on a foundation of stiff, coarse muslin, or of wired chip; but all depends on its shape and size, and the fashion changes so much and so frequently in such articles of dress, that it should be studied in the show rooms and windows of the best houses in the trade, at the opening of each season, as no rules given at the present time might hold good for a year hence in reference to Millinery.

Miltons.—Hard thick cloths, produced in scarlet, blue, and brown, and originally introduced for use in hunting.

Miniver (otherwise *Minever*, or, according to the old spelling, *Mineveer* and *Minevair*).—The name is derived from *menu vair*, the latter word denoting the variety shown by this fur in its colouring. It was a valuable fur, and was much worn as linings to robes and hoods by nobles in the Middle Ages. It was composed of the skin of a species of Squirrel of the genus *Sciurus*, supposed to have been a native of Hungary, grey on the back, and white underneath and on the neck. The extreme end of the tail was black, and it was sewn on the white portion of the fur at equal distances apart, so as to produce small spots all over it. In heraldry this Fur is called *vair*, being one of the eight furs used.

Mink (*Mustela vison*).—This fur resembles Sable in colour, though considerably shorter and more glossy, as well as durable. It is exported in large quantities by the Hudson's Bay Company, and also from the United States, and is employed for tippets, muffs, and cuffs.

Mirecourt Lace.—The lace made at Mirecourt is a description of Lille Lace, but it is only within the last twenty years that it has been in any way better than other manufactures of Lille Lace; since that period it has steadily improved both in workmanship and design. The lace is made upon the Pillow in detached sprigs, and Appliqué upon a ground of fine machine net.

Mitorse Silk.—This is a half-twisted silk, employed for various descriptions of needlework. If skilfully handled, it proves superior to the floss silks, being less liable to become rough and fluffy after a little wear. Thus, for the embroidery of any article of dress it is the best for the purpose, and is very suitable for the working of slippers, stools, &c., in conjunction with wool. Mitorse resembles the silk employed by the Chinese for their double Embroidery.

Mitre.—A word sometimes used in old instruction books upon Stocking Knitting, instead of Gusset, when describing the part of a stocking that is worked after the heel and instep are made. To work: Divide the stitches on to three needles, putting double the amount and four extra on to the needle carrying the front stitches than on the two side needles. KNIT two stitches together upon each side where the pieces forming heel and instep meet, and TAKE IN, in this manner, every third round eight times.

Mitreing.—A term used by Stocking Knitters to denote a gusset. *See* KNITTING, *Socks and Stockings.*

It is also a term used in dressmaking, and is borrowed from architecture, in which it denotes the form given by following the line drawn by two sides of a square, producing an angle of 45 degrees, for the "striking" of which masons employ what is called "a mitre square." The border produced by cutting according to this pattern is employed for flounces and fillings in dress materials and underlinen.

Mittens.—Gloves without fingers, having either an opening for the thumb, or else a partial sheath for it, the rest of the glove ending with the palm of the hand. They are made for Arctic regions with a complete covering for thumb and fingers, but the latter have no separate sheaths, with which the thumbs are supplied. Mittens are to be had in kid leather, Beaver, Chamois, woven Stockingette cloth, also in silk, and knitted by hand. Some mittens in kid leather or woven silk extend up the arm to the elbow, when the sleeve of an evening dress is either short or very open.

Mixtures.—A term applied to any cloths of variegated colouring, such as Knickerbockers and Tweeds.

Mocassin Grass Embroidery.—*See* GRASS EMBROIDERY.

Modern Point Lace.—This lace is an imitation of the old Renaissance Lace, both Pillow and Needle made, and was first attempted about the year 1855. It has been brought to great perfection in France, where it is called Dentelle Renaissance, and it is also known in that country as Dentelle Irlandaise, from the beauty of Irish imitations of real lace.

The materials for this beautiful and useful lace are neither numerous nor expensive, and consist of a lace pattern, tracing cloth on which to copy the design, Toile Ciré, to give firmness to the lace while in progress, needles, linen braids, and linen thread. The braids, with which the outlines of all the designs, and the thick parts of the lace are made, are of various widths and thicknesses, and have sometimes an open edge resembling the pearled edge of Pillow Lace patterns, and at others a perfectly plain edge in imitation of the Tape Guipure Laces. They are sold in many varieties of design, or are made upon the Pillow; when made on the Pillow, the lace becomes a real, and not an imitation lace. The linen thread used is fine, and resembles the Mecklenburgh thread used in real lace; that known as Haythorne's is the thread most in use. The stitches known as Modern Point Stitches are all copies from the stitches used in making Point Lace, Spanish and Venetian Points, Rose Points, Hollie Points, and other Needle-made laces. They are all named and described under their own headings, as not exclusively belonging to this lace in particular. They are as follows: ANTWERP EDGE, ALENÇON BAR, ANGLETERRE BAR, BARCELONA STITCH, BRABANT EDGE, BRUXELLES EDGE, CADIZ, CORDOVA, DIAMOND, ENGLISH and ESCALIER LACE, FAN LACE, FLEURETTE STITCH, HENRIQUE LACE,

the thumb, without turning the braid over, and draw in the inner edge with an Overcast thread. Connect the braid in different parts where no stitches are worked with a BAR. To make a Bar: Pass a thread across the space three times, and BUTTONHOLE to the middle, then work a PICOT, and finish with a Buttonhole as before. Fill in the centre of the braid with POINT DE BRUXELLES STITCH.

To work Fig. 613: Trace the outline as before, tack the braid on, and OVERCAST the edges, make the BARS that connect the lace together, and fill in the thick parts with POINT DE BRUXELLES STITCH, POINT DE VENISE, SORRENTO LACE, POINT D'ESPAGNE, POINT DE BRABANÇON, ENGLISH WHEELS, and varieties of the same. Then work all round the braid forming the pattern, and at its outer edge, as a finish, with Point de Venise.

FIG. 612. MODERN POINT LACE.

MECHLIN LACE and WHEELS, OPEN ENGLISH LACE, POINT D'ALENÇON, POINT D'ANGLETERRE, POINT D'ANVERS, POINT DE FILLET, POINT DE FLANDRE, POINT DE REPRISE, POINT DE VALENCIENNES, POINT DE VENISE, POINT D'ESPAGNE, POINT DE GREQUE, POINT DE TURQUE, RAYLEIGH BARS, SORRENTO LACE, BARS, and WHEELS.

To work Modern Point as shown in Fig. 612: Draw the outline of the lace, and TACK the braid over it to the tracing cloth rather loosely, and without any stretching. Form the angles and curves, turn over the braid to prevent any lumpiness, and sew down each edge firmly, without taking the thread through to the tracing cloth. Then OVERCAST the braid round all its edges, and draw in the thread slightly at the inner edge where the corners or curves are formed. To make circles, form them first with

Modes.—A term used in Lacemaking to denote the open work FILLINGS between the thick parts of the design. It is also the French term to signify fashions in dress.

Mohair.—Fabrics are so called which are composed of the hair of the Angora goat, mixed with silk or cotton warps. These fabrics have a peculiar lustre, equal to that of silk, are remarkably regular in texture, and are both soft and fine. Mohair cloth is of very ancient origin, and was much worn in the Middle Ages. The yarn is sold in retail shops, and is chiefly spun and manufactured at Bradford and Norwich. The French purchase it in England for the purpose of lacemaking, and a species of Utrecht velvet is made of it at Coventry. There are many varieties of cloth made of Mohair, the dress materials being watered, striped, and checked.

The Angora goat, according to Mr. Hayes, secretary of

FIG. 613. MODERN POINT LACE.

the National Association of Wool Manufacturers, is the most valuable wool-bearing animal, not even excepting the Cashmere goat, which produces only two or three ounces of the *pushm* used for making Indian shawls. Mohair, the fleece of the Angora, is worth, on an average, 3s. a pound —more than double the price of the best Lincoln wool. It is used for making Utrecht velvets, or "furniture plush," the piles of imitation sealskin, the best carriage and lap robes, braids for binding, black dress goods, as before stated, laces, and for many other purposes, the number of which is only limited by the limited supply —the entire production of the world being only about 4,750,000lb. The English have obtained the highest success in spinning mohair, and it is owing to the stiffness of the fibre that it is rarely woven alone, either the warp or woof being usually of cotton, silk, or wool. A pure mohair fabric is considered nearly indestructible. The whitest variety of hair is imported from Smyrna and Constantinople, but quantities of an inferior description are sent out from other parts of Asia Minor. *See* ANGORA GOATS' HAIR.

Mohair, or Russian Braids.—These braids consist of two cords woven together. They are cut into short lengths, and sold by the gross pieces. The wider braids are in 36 yard lengths, four pieces to the gross, and the numbers run from 0 to 8. The various sizes may be had both in black and in colours.

Mohair Poplin Yarn.—A beautifully even yarn, having a fine lustre, produced for the manufacture of Poplin fabrics. The seat of manufacture of this particular description of yarn is near Bingley, in Yorkshire.

Moire Antique.—A description of silk of a superior quality. It is of double width, and of ordinary make, but stouter. To produce a "watered" effect, this silk is folded in such a manner as that, when heavily pressed, the air contained between the folds should not easily escape; and, when forced out, it drives the moisture employed for the watering before it, the pressure required to effect the purpose amounting to from 60 to 100 tons. Some inferior kinds of Moiré Antique are made having cotton backs. *See* SILKS.

Moleskin.—A description of Fustian, its peculiarity, as compared with others, consisting in the cutting short of the pile before the material is dyed. This material is very strong, and is, therefore, especially suited to the dress of labouring men.

Moleskin Fur.—The Mole, or Mould-warp, is a small insect-eating Mammal, belonging to the genera *Talpa*, *Scalops*, and *Condylura Cristata*. The Fur is exceedingly soft, thick, and fine in quality; and very warm for wear.

Momie Cloth.—This has a cotton warp and woollen weft, or else a silk warp and woollen weft, and has the appearance of very fine Crape. It is made 44 inches in width, and, being dyed black, is very suitable for mourning.

Monteiths.—A description of Cotton Handkerchiefs, which are dyed of one uniform colour, but have a pattern of white spots occurring at regular distances, produced by the discharge of the colour, effected by a particular process. These goods are known by the name of the manufacturers, at Glasgow. Cotton Bandanas are subjected to the same process. A large quantity of Handkerchiefs, dyed Turkey-red, are laid one on the other, and pressed under a perforated plate, when a liquid is poured through the openings, which discharges the colour at those places. This method is so rapid in its operation that, by the hands of four workmen only, 1600 pieces—representing 19,200 yards—of cotton may be thus figured with spots or other devices within a period of ten hours. *See* MALABARS.

Moorish Lace.—This lace is of very ancient origin, and is frequently called "Dentelle de Moresse" in old inventories when described by European writers, and under that name it figures in the poem known as the "Révolte des Passemens," published in 1661. The lace is really Drawn Work, and the art was probably taught to the Moors by the Italian or Greek peasants they captured and made slaves of. The lace is still made in Morocco, and forms an edging to the towels and dresses of the ladies in the harems.

Moreen.—A coarse and stout description of Tammie, only less stiffened, and watered or plain. It is employed for women's petticoats and for upholstery, chiefly for window curtains. There are some of very rich quality, resembling silk damask. The width runs from 26 inches to 27 inches.

Morees.—Manchester-made Muslins, much employed for the African export trade.

Morocco Leather.—This leather is known in France as *Maroquin*, and is made of goat skins tanned with sumach. There is an inferior sort, called Roan, made from sheep skins, which is much thinner, and neither so handsome nor so durable.

Mosaic Art Embroidery.—A modern name given to a species of Braiding combined with Embroidery stitches. To work: Trace a geometrical or conventional design upon black cloth, and stitch down on to all the outlines silk braids of various colours. Then take Embroidery silks matching the braids in tints, and fill in parts of the design with CREWEL and SATIN STITCH, and work over small leaves or flowers in the design in Satin Stitch and in shaded colours.

Mosaic Canvas.—The finest descriptions of canvas employed for Embroidery, whether of silk, thread, or cotton, have acquired the popular appellation of Mosaic.

Mosaic Woolwork.—This is a handwork made in imitation of woven goods and of Tapestry. The work is chiefly done in Yorkshire for trade purposes, and with large bold designs. To make: Prepare a large piece of paper, by ruling upon it a number of perfect squares; upon this draw the design to be executed in its full size, and colour it. Then, if the pattern is large, divide it into lengths ready for use, and lay it by the side of the worker. Have ready two steel bars, the length of the pattern, and fasten them so that they run parallel to each other, and are quite firm. Then take coarse Berlin wool of the shades matching the pattern, carefully match the colours on the pattern with it, tying two colours together where required on one line, and fasten it on to the bars. Stretch it tightly from one bar to another, and arrange it in the proper shades. Having stretched the wool, cover its surface with a strong solution of indiarubber, and cover a piece of stout canvas with the same mixture; lay the canvas upon the wool while both are wet, and press the two together; the wool and the canvas when once glued together will never come apart.

Moskowa Canvas.—This variety of canvas has the appearance of straw. It is woven in fancy patterns, and lines of gold and silver, black and blue thread being introduced in the groundwork. It is made for purposes of embroidery, but is sufficiently handsome to obviate the necessity of grounding.

Mosquito Net.—A coarse cotton net, employed for bed curtains in warm countries where Mosquitos abound. It is likewise employed for purposes of embroidery. It is made in double width.

Mossoul Embroidery.—This work is founded upon Eastern Embroidery, and is a pleasing variety to CREWEL WORK, as it possesses all the artistic attributes of that work. It is useful for table and mantel borders, for chair backs, toilet covers and towels, and is worked with either crewels or silks, upon linen and woollen materials. The patterns are the same as those so familiar to us in Persian and Turkish needlework, and consist of geometrical figures or much conventionalised flower and foliage designs. Any Eastern design can be used, as the distinctive feature of the work consists in its colouring and manner of filling in, not upon its pattern. The colours selected for the embroidery are all artistic, the greens shading to yellow, the reds to pink and yellow, and the browns to red and cinnamon; while magenta, scarlet, and bright blue are excluded. No shading is used, each isolated spray, leaf, or flower being filled in with one tint, and the variety of colour produced by blending together in harmony these various detached shades.

To work: Trace out upon the material a design, which select as much as possible of small detached pieces, forming conventionalised leaves and stems; fill in all these sprays with HERRINGBONE STITCH. Work the Herringbone Stitch so closely together that no part of the material shows between the stitches, and commence working across the part to be filled at its widest end, and work down to its narrowest, carrying the stitches across from side to side without a break. The stitch so worked will produce a plait down the centre of the part filled in, and this plait is the chief feature of the work. Fill in all the design with Herringbone Stitch, and then work round the outlines with ROPE STITCH. This stitch is really Crewel Stitch worked more closely together than usual. The colour used for all the outlines should be of one uniform tint, which should slightly contrast with the colours used in the design. Thus, if yellow-greens and brown-reds form the centres, dark peacock blue should be used for outlining them; or if the centres are formed of orange shades, green or russet brown tints should outline them. Finish off the embroidery with a bordering of DRAWN WORK, which work over with silks matching in tint those used in the design.

Motifs.—A French term, used to distinguish the pattern of a piece of Embroidery from the groundwork or material.

Mother-of-Pearl Work.—*See* NACRE WORK.

Mount Needlework.—*See* EMBROIDERY FRAME.

Mourning Stuffs.—These consist chiefly of Crape, Crape Cloth, Widows' Silk, Barathea, Paramatta, black Cashmere, Merino, Serge, Grenadine, Cotton, and any lustreless woollen stuffs, such as the new serge-like dress material called "Drap-Sanglier."

Mousseline de Laine.—A very fine light woollen cloth, of a muslin-like texture, introduced from France, and subsequently manufactured here, and at a much cheaper cost. An imitation of this fabric has been made, which is a union of cotton with the wool. Mousseline de Laine may be had for dress materials in every colour, with all kinds of designs printed on it, as well as plain; and it is frequently sold under some different name.

Mousseline de Soie.—A very delicate soft silk textile, of a make as open as that of muslin, and having a fringe. It is employed for women's neckerchiefs. It may also be had in the piece, which measures from 28 to 30 inches in width.

Mousseline de Soie Crépée.—A silk muslin, crimped after the manner of crape. At one time it was manufactured as a dress material and trimmings for the purposes of dressmaking and millinery. It measures about 28 inches in width, and is to be had in white and cream colour.

Muff.—A circular oblong covering for the hands, hollow in the middle, to admit both, and dating from the time of Louis XIV., in France, from whence it was introduced into this country. According to Fairholt, two examples are given in a piece of tapestry of that date, formerly in the possession of Crofton Croker, Esq., one being of yellow silk edged with black fur; the other of white fur, decorated with small black tails, probably ermine, and with a blue bow in front. The same author states that they used to be worn by gentlemen as well as women in the seventeenth century, and remained in fashion as an article of men's clothing for nearly a hundred years. In the eighteenth century they were covered with feathers, as many now are, and were also richly decorated with embroidery. They may be worn of every description of fur, or two strips of fur combined with one in the centre of velvet, and of grebe or other feathers. Cheap kinds are to be had of wool in Crochet Work. There are also varieties containing a pocket outside. The size changes with the current fashion.

Mule Twist.—Cotton thread, manufactured by the aid of steam engines, for the weaving of muslins, and the finest cotton goods, and which is rather softer than "water twist." It is so called because made by a machine called a "Mule-jenny," or Mill-jenny, *Mühle* being the German for a Mill, of which our word is a corruption.

Mull Muslin.—A very thin and soft variety of Muslin, employed for morning dresses, and for trimmings. It is undressed, whereas the Swiss Mull is dressed. It runs from 30 to 36 inches in width, the best varieties being of the latter dimensions. Mull Muslin is finer than NAIN-SOOK, is of a pure white colour, and has a perfectly soft finish.

Mummy Cloth.—An imitation of the ancient Egyptian make of flaxen cloth, which was employed for wrapping round mummies. It is now manufactured for purposes of embroidery; and the same make is also used for waist-coating. It is 30 inches in width.

Mungo (otherwise called **Shoddy**).— Wool obtained from disintegrated woollen cloths—old worn-out garments, or clippings left by tailors after cutting out. When thus reduced, cleaned, and prepared, Mungo, or Shoddy, is manufactured into cloth again.

Mushroo.—A costly satin cloth, manufactured in the Deccan, and sent for sale to Madras. It has a silk surface and a cotton back, and is decorated with loom-embroidered flowers in white silk. It is priced at about £2 for a piece of 5 yards, of about 30 inches in width, and weighing 1⅓lb. There are costlier examples, extensively flowered in gold, with stripes in silk. The productions from Hyderabad are remarkable for the brilliant tones and arrangements of the colours, which are composed in wavy stripes of rich yellow and gold, with pink and white Mushroos, and are superior to our English-made textiles of this description, as the fine kinds bear washing very well, an advantage which they possess equally over French satins. _See_ INDIAN SILKS.

Muslin.—A thin, and more or less transparent, cotton textile, of Eastern origin, deriving its name from Mosul, or Moosul, a large town in Turkey in Asia. There are many varieties of Muslin, such as Mull Muslin; a dressed and stiffened variety, called Swiss Mull; another, Foundation Muslin, which is very open in texture, and made both in white and black, for the stiffening of dresses and bonnets; Buke (commonly corrupted into "Book") Muslin, which is sold in a plain, clear, soft, and unstiffened state, or hard and dressed—this kind is used for Tambour Embroidery. There are also Figured Muslins, wrought in the loom, of various widths. Cambric Muslin is an imitation of linen of that make; it is sold coloured for linings, glazed white and black, plain and twilled, figured, striped, and corded. Seerhand Muslin is a kind between Nainsook and Mull, and valued for dresses on account of its retaining its clearness after having been washed. Tamboured Muslins are chiefly made in Scotland. Muslinette is a thick description of Muslin. Leno is a clearer, thinner, and softer material than the Buke, slight and gauze-like in quality, and much employed for window curtains; the threads of the warp and woof differ in size, and the material cannot be as easily starched as other kinds of muslins. There are also Cord and Fancy Checks, having stripes and cords crossing each other, forming squares, thick threads being introduced into the warp or weft. Nainsook is a thick sort of jacconet, made plain in stripes, the latter running the same way as the warp. India Muslins were introduced into this country about the year 1670, and the manufacture of Muslin was commenced at Paisley in 1700. It is now extensively made at Bolton and Glasgow. At Zurich and St. Gall their manufacture preceded ours, and there are now many factories for it in Germany.

Muslin Appliqué.—_See_ APPLIQUÉ UPON NET.

Muslin Embroidery.—_See_ EMBROIDERY ON MUSLIN.

Muslinette.—A thick variety of muslin, resembling a Brilliant; employed for infants' clothing, and for dressing gowns. It measures from 30 inches to 36 inches in width.

Muslin Grounds.—This is a description of GINGHAM.

Muslin Trimmings.—These consist of Edgings, Insertions, Scallops, and Flouncings of variegated needle-work. They are made in short lengths, and in pieces of from 24 yards to 36 yards.

Musquash, or Musk Rat (_Tiber zibethicus_).—The fur of this animal resembles that of the Beaver, and used to be employed for hats and bonnets. It is dyed for articles of dress, and other use, and is inexpensive. These animals are found in great numbers in America, inhabiting swamps and rivers. They have a peculiar odour, like that of musk. The fur is used by hat manufacturers, and is dyed by furriers for a variety of articles, such as muffs and boas. It is much used as an imitation Seal skin.

Mysore Silks.—These are fine, soft, undressed silk stuffs, both plain and printed, dyed and undyed. They may be had in all colours, of an Indian character, the designs being chiefly a close running all-over floral ones, although some printed in gold or in silver are a little bolder in pattern, and are printed in black, and in the natural colour of the silk. They all measure 34 inches in width, and are sold at 35s. per piece of about 7 yards. The Mysore silks are of the class termed "cultivated."

N.

Nacre.—The French word for mother-o'-pearl, employed in a certain kind of embroidery.

Nacre Work.—A peculiar kind of work, and one that is little practised in the present day. It was at one time used for embroidering borders to ecclesiastical vestments, and consisted in cutting out pieces of mother-of-pearl, and sewing them on to velvet or silk. To work: Trace out a flower and leaf design upon velvet, and back and frame this in an EMBROIDERY FRAME. Prepare a quantity of small pieces of mother-of-pearl cut into petal and leaf shapes, and bore holes in these. Attach these to the pattern with silk or gold thread, and lay them on flat, but arrange them to imitate the natural curves and lines of the objects they are intended to represent. Form the centres of the flower stems and sprays that are too small to lay the mother-of-pearl over with gold thread, and COUCH this to the velvet.

Napgore Silks.—These are all soft, slight, and un-dressed, and are to be had in every variety of essentially Indian colours. The pieces vary but little from 7 yards in quantity, and run about 37 inches in width. They belong to that class of Indian silk called the "cultivated."

Nail.—A measure of length employed for textiles, describing a length of 2¼ inches; four nails make 1 quarter, and four quarters 1 yard.

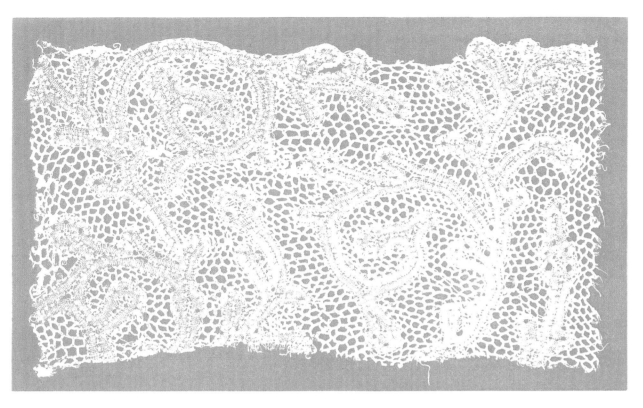

ITALIAN TAPE LACE, WITH PLAITED GROUND (OLD).

TAPE GUIPURE — GENOA (OLD).

Nainsook.—A description of Muslin made both plain and striped, the stripe running the way of the warp. It is a kind of Jacconet, or Bengal Muslin. *See* Muslin.

Nankeen.—A Chinese cotton cloth, of a natural buff colour, deriving its name from the city of Nankin, where it is chiefly manufactured. An imitation is made in this country, at Manchester and elsewhere; but this, though more even in texture, and equally fine in colour, is found to be inferior when washed, as the colour is obtained by dyeing; whereas the original Chinese Nankeen is made of the natural colour of the raw cotton grown in China, which is buff; in other countries white is common. The broad pieces, called the "Company's Nankeen," are of a superior quality to the narrow ones. Varieties of Nankeen, dyed blue, white, and pink, have been made, but are not often to be seen. On the banks of the Ganges, and in the Southern States of America, a Nankeen-coloured cotton grows, something peculiar in the soil being supposed to produce the buff hue by which it is distinguished. Nankeen was formerly much employed for both men's and women's dress, but is now almost limited to that of children.

Nap.—The pile, woolly substance, or knots which are produced, in the process of weaving, on the surface of certain textiles. All cloths have an uneven roughness unless they are shorn, but all have not a pile, which is expressly made. Women employed for this purpose are called Nopsters.

Napery.—A term employed to designate house linen, but more especially applied to table linen; the French term is *Nappe*, a tablecloth. Hollinshed, in his "Description of England" (1577), says:

Our innes are also verie well furnished with Naperie, bedding, and tapisserie, especiallie with naperie.

Narrow Cloths.—These cloths are so designated in contradistinction to those known as Broad Cloths. Narrow Cloths are made in both single and double milled Cassimere, and run from 27 inches to 29 inches in width; also in double and treble milled Doeskins, measuring the same number of inches wide as the Cassimere.

Narrowing.—In Crochet, Knitting, and Netting, the size of an article being worked can be Decreased by working two or more of the stitches or loops as one. *See* Decrease.

Natté Silk.—A French material, having a check pattern, overlaid by a plait, which in the superior qualities is coarse, and in the inferior fine. The name is derived from the French *Natter*, to plait or twist.

Needle.—A pointed instrument, sharp at one end, and perforated at the blunt extremity to receive the thread which it is designed to draw through any description of textile, whether in Plain Sewing or Embroidery. Mention of this implement, and of sewing, may be found in the *Sanhita* of the *Rig Veda* (Wilson's "Rig Veda," II., p. 288; IV., p. 60), and the Vedic word, " s' *úchi*," is identical with that now used to indicate a Needle (see "Indo-Aryans," by Rájendralála Mitra, LL.D. and C.I.E.). This notice of Needles dates back as far as six centuries before Christ— "Clothes, and the like, wrought with a Needle, last a

long time" ("Rig Veda," II., 288). In ancient times Needles were made of wood, bone, ivory, bronze, and iron, and were very coarse in quality and dimensions. Of these there are a variety of examples in our museums, some dating back to pre-historic times. Some Needles found in Herculaneum and Pompeii were of bronze. The Needles of modern times appear to have had their origin in Spain, and were thence introduced into this country in the reign of Queen Elizabeth. England was famous for the work of the Needle previous to the introduction or the manufacture of the appliance such as it now is, and the embroideries accomplished, and still preserved, compare well with modern art under better auspices. Rough as Needles were in the days of Edgitha wife of Edward the Confessor, she was pronounced by her historian to be "perfectly mistress of the Needle;" and English work was held in esteem above all other in Europe, even in her day. In the reign of Mary I., steel wire Needles were first made in England, and then by a Spanish negro, who kept his secret during his lifetime; they were afterwards made in the reign of Elizabeth, by one Elias Krause, a German. The great secret was lost after his death, and recovered again about a hundred years after. In the year 1656, Cromwell incorporated the Company of Needlemakers. Needles of English manufacture are now regarded as the best in the world, those of Germany coming next. The chief seat of our manufacture is at Redditch, Worcestershire. Needles pass through 126 hands before they are ready for sale.

Those in general use for hand work are as follows: Darners, Straws, Sharps, Long-eyed Sharps, Ground-downs, Betweens, Blunts, Tapestry, Whitechapel, Chenille, Rug, and Harness. Darners vary much in length and thickness, to suit the quality of the material to be repaired. The eye is long, and is easily threaded by turning back the loose ends of the yarn employed, and retaining them between the finger and thumb, passing them, flatly looped, through the long eye. Straws are used by milliners, for straw bonnets and braids. Long-eyed Sharps are employed for Embroidery in silk and wool, the numbers running from 1 to 10. Another variety of these is the Whitechapel, which are preferable for that purpose to the Long-eyed Sharps. Sharps are in general use for personal and household plain sewing; they may be had in a great variety of sizes, distinguished by numbers, and are sold in papers, either of mixed sizes, or each paper containing one size only. Some of them are gold-eyed, and are considered to be of superior quality, and warranted not to cut the thread. Ground-downs are shorter than the ordinary Sharps. Betweens are shorter than Ground-downs, and Blunts than Betweens. Blunts are thick and strong, and are employed by staymakers, tailors, glovers, shoe-binders, and others who work in leather; the sizes run from 1 to 15. Tapestry Needles are blunt at the point, and have a long and rather oval eye; the numbers in common use run from 14 to 25, but they may be had in other sizes. For use in hot and tropical climates they may be had in gold or silver. Rug Needles are thick, with large eyes and blunt points. Chenille Needles differ from the Tapestry only in having a sharp point, as they are employed for working on canvas, cloth, or silk. Harness Needles are used by Saddlers.

To this list others may be added, such as Machine Needles, made for the especial use of the sewing machines of various makers, such as those respectively of Howe, Grover and Baker, Wheeler and Wilson, Willcox and Gibbs, Thomas, Weir, the Wanzer, the Singer, &c. Besides these, Netting, Knitting, and Crochet Needles should be included in the list. The Knitting Needle is sometimes called a Pin.

Needle Etching.—Synonymous with ETCHING EM-BROIDERY.

Needle Point.—A title given indifferently to all kinds of real lace worked with a Needle, and not with Bobbins.

Needle-threader.—A small appliance, made for the use of persons of imperfect sight. It is usually made of ivory. The top portion above the handle is flat, on which a small metal plate is fixed, through which a hole is pierced; a corresponding hole being in the ivory, of larger size, the needle is passed through it, the eye fitting exactly over that in the plate, so that the thread passes through the three holes at once. Other kinds may be had; such, for

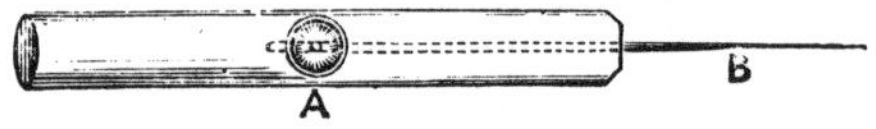

FIG. 614. NEEDLE-THREADER.

instance, as that illustrated at Fig. 614. A is the hole through which the thread is to be passed, and so through the eye of the Needle, which is to be placed with the eye exactly even with it; B is the pointed end of the Needle. The central hole is cup-shaped, sloping towards the middle, and so directing the thread into the small opening, which would be unseen to failing sight.

Needlework.—A generic and comprehensive term, including every species of work, whether plain or decorative, that can be executed by means of the Needle, and of whatever description the Needle may be. From the most remote ages the employment of the Needle has formed a source of recreation, of remunerative work, and no less of economy, the useful occupation of time and charity, amongst all classes of women, in all parts of the world.

The rise and progress of the ornamental part of the art, and the different modifications it underwent, down to the time of its final decay, have already been described in the article upon Embroidery; it, therefore, now only remains to enumerate some of the most celebrated Embroiderers and their productions, which have become matters of history. The high honour bestowed upon Needlework in ancient days, when it was considered one of the chief spoils of the conqueror, and a fitting gift to be presented to kings, is fully shown by its frequent mention by the sacred writers, and by Homer, Pliny, Herodotus, and others. The corselet presented by Amasis to Minerva, the spoils of Sisera, the curtains of the Tabernacle, the Peplus of Minerva at Athens, the Needlework sails of Cleopatra's vessels, the web of Penelope, and the works of Helen and Andromache, by the very fact that they were considered worthy of record by such writers, prove how much they were valued. Coming nearer to our times, we

find Needlework of the most beautiful description worked in England, and presented to Pope Adrian IV.; while the Banner of Strasbourg, the Stole of St. Cuthbert, the Glastonbury Cope, the Syon Cope, and many other ecclesiastical garments still in existence (with the exception of the Strasbourg Banner, burnt in 1870), all testify to the labour and art spent in their manufacture. The well-known Bayeux Tapestry is another of these historical pieces, and though its execution does not allow of its ranking with the more elaborate articles first mentioned, it is a remarkable production, both for its antiquity and the number of figures of great size that it contains. Following upon these ancient specimens come the hand-made tapestries, worked during the Middle Ages, as wall hangings, and the numerous altar-cloths and church vestments that embellished the gorgeous ritual of the Romish Church, of which many fragments remain in museums and private collections, and which, but for the mistaken zeal of the Reformers, who expended upon these inanimate objects some of their religious fervour, would be still as perfect as when first made.

The Anglo-Saxon ladies were celebrated, not only in their own country, but on the Continent, for their skill in Needlework, particularly in the Opus Anglicanum, or Opus Anglicum—a stitch in Embroidery that they invented. The four sisters of Athelstan, daughters of Edward the Elder, and Edgitha the Queen of Edward the Confessor, were particularly famed. After them came Matilda, the wife of William the Conqueror, and Adelais, the wife of Henry the First; but the most famous of all English queens is Katherine of Aragon, who came from a land celebrated for its Embroideries and Lace, and who enlivened the many sad hours of her life by instructing her maids of honour, and the poor people living near her palace, in the art of making Lace and Embroidery. We are told by Taylor, the Water Poet, who wrote a poem upon the "Needle's Excellency," in reference to this queen—

That her days did pass
In working with the needle curiously.

Her daughter Mary also excelled with her needle, and her works are mentioned by the same poet, who also devotes a couplet to the praise of the Embroidery produced by Queen Elizabeth; but other chroniclers are more inclined to consider that the shirt presented by this Queen to her brother, upon his sixth birthday, worked by herself, was almost her only achievement. Mary II. was the next queen who paid attention to Embroidery, and the beautiful work executed under her supervision still remains at Hampton Court. Queen Charlotte devoted much time to Needlework, frequently embroidering the Court dresses of her daughters, and constantly bestowing articles knitted by herself upon the poor; and at Oatlands, some of the woolwork executed by the Duchess of York is still preserved. Although not belonging to England, we cannot omit to mention two celebrated Embroiderers, whose works are to be found in almost every collection—Mary Queen of Scots, and Marie Antoinette, the wife of Louis XVI. To both these ill-fated ladies the Needle afforded a solace, both before and during their misfortunes, as it has done throughout all ages to women who, though of not so exalted a rank, have yet had as many sorrows. And upon both these queens' tombstones could have been written the epitaph that is inscribed upon a tablet in the Cloisters of Westminster Abbey: "She was excellent with her needle."

Net.—This was at one time made by ladies with the needle, as a foundation to Lace; it was then called Réseau Lace Ground, and will be found described under GROUNDS. Besides this true lace ground, another was made from fine Scotch gauze, which was drawn together by the needle until it assumed a honeycomb shape. The Scotch gauze necessary to this art is no longer manufactured; it consisted of very fine silk threads, woven as clear, but minute, open squares. The thread was taken diagonally across these squares with a kind of Back Stitch, and was twisted round each mesh as it was made.

Net may be had woven as well as hand-made. Machinery for its production was introduced early in the present century, the textile having been previously restricted to pillow work. Regular meshes are formed by the use of four threads of flax or silk, twisted together so as to form hexagonal, octagonal, or diamond-shaped forms. Net is usually rather more than a yard wide, or double width. Of all the varieties produced, the Brussels is the most highly esteemed, and may be obtained 2 yards in width for dressmaking. Three threads are employed in all descriptions of Net, one passing from right to left, another from left to right, and a third twining round the two former threads, so as to form a honeycomb-patterned tissue. The French Net made by machinery consists of single Press Points, when not ornamented called Tulle, and when ornamented called Dentelle. It is made of silk, and is pretty, but inferior. There is also the Trico-Berlin, in which the stitch is removed three needles from its place of looping; Fleur de Tulle, having a mesh of two descriptions; and Tulle Anglois, a double pressed point. The English kinds include a Silk Net in imitation of Blonde, 1 yard 3 inches wide, and machine made; Quilting Silk Net, slightly stiffened with gum; Pillow-thread Net, hand made; and Piece Bobbin Net, machine made, of various widths, from 3—8 and 8—4; the threads are so entwined as to form regular six-sided meshes. The material known as Italian Net is really not a Net in the style of its manufacture, but is a strong gauze, composed of silk and worsted, and produced in various colours for women's dresses. Cotton Net is the cheapest kind of woven Net, and is employed for stiff linings and foundations.

Net Embroidery.—An effective way of ornamenting

FIGS. 615 AND 616. NET EMBROIDERY.

White or Black Net for dress trimmings, caps, and other small articles of dress. To work as shown in Figs. 615,

616, and 617: Trace the design upon calico, and strengthen the calico with a brown paper backing. TACK the Net

FIG. 617. NET EMBROIDERY.

down upon the pattern, and work the various stars over in SATIN STITCH, with filoselles of bright colours, and shades that bear candle light.

To work Fig. 618: This design is for a Necktie end, and is worked with silk cord and filoselle upon Brussels Net.

FIG. 618. NET EMBROIDERY.

Trace the design as before-mentioned, lay the Net over it, and then loop the Cord over the lines so as to follow the pattern outlines. KNOT the cord together, and secure with a BUTTONHOLE STITCH taken through the Net where indicated, and make the centre Wheel and the small Pyramids with filoselle; also work the small Stars and the Buttonhole Edging with the same material.

Netted Lace.—*See* NETWORK.

Netting.—This art is so ancient that no date can be fixed for its invention. That it was practised for fishing and birdcatching purposes by the earliest inhabitants of the earth is without doubt, and there are still to be seen, in the Museum at Berlin, Egyptian Nets, and the implements by which they were made, that are 3000 years old. Besides these commoner specimens of work belonging to the Egyptians, it is evident, from the accounts still extant, and from ancient frescoes, that that nation from the very earliest period produced Netting—or, as it was then called, Caul Work and Network—of a much higher kind than modern workers have ever attained to. The figures painted upon Egyptian monuments are frequently clothed in tunics made of Netting, the loops being formed with gaily coloured silks, or gold and silver threads. Amasis, King of Egypt, presented a corselet to the Temple of Minerva, in the island of Rhodes, composed of the finest Netting, each thread containing 360 distinct threads, and yet the texture was so light and fine that the whole could easily pass through a man's ring. A netted corselet, matching this one in delicacy, was given by the same monarch to Mutianus, the third Roman Consul; but this was embroidered with animals and figures worked with gold thread into the Netting. In the writings of Pliny and Herodotus, the fine flax used by the Egyptians is spoken of with admiration; and Homer, in the "Iliad," mentions the Cauls and Networks of gold worn by the Trojan ladies. In the Bible there is frequent allusion to the art; some of the curtains adorning Solomon's Temple were made of Checker Work, or Netting; and Isaiah enumerates the Cauls of Network and Veils worn by the Jewish women; and when summing up the calamities that were to fall upon Egypt, includes in the general curse those who "weave Networks." We have little mention of Netting during the Roman Empire, and it is not until the thirteenth century that the art was practised in Europe so as to draw attention; Netting was then worked for ecclesiastical purposes, and looked upon as lace. St. Paul's Cathedral, in 1295, possessed a kneeling cushion of Network; and Exeter Cathedral, a few years later, several altar cloths. In the thirteenth and fourteenth centuries Netting was known as Opus Filatorium and Opus Araneum, or Spider Work; the ground only was Netted, the design being Darned or Embroidered upon it. But the plain, unembroidered Netting was frequently made either in silk or flax, and used as Curtains and Bed Hangings. At a later date, Darned Netting was known as Lacis, and was worked more with flax than gold or silk threads; and, in the sixteenth century, this Lacis is frequently mentioned in Wardrobe Accounts, and finds a place in the articles enumerated in the will made by Mary, Queen of Scots, before the birth of her son. Lacis, when not Embroidered or Darned, was called Réseau, or Rezeuil, and differed in no way from Plain Netting; nor do Lacis in any way differ from the modern Guipure d'Art, in which, upon a groundwork of Netting, a pattern is Darned and Embroidered. After the universal adoption of Pillow and fine Needle-made Laces, the Netted and Darned Lace was little used; but occasionally a specimen appears among the relics of palaces and old families, and a coverlet used by Louis XIV., still in existence, is made of a Netted Foundation with Darned Embroidery.

In England, Netting has always been practised for useful purposes, and sixty years ago was much worked for Curtains, Window Blinds, and Drawing-room Covers, either in Darned or Plain Netting. Crochet has lately superseded Netting, on account of its greater portability, but there is no doubt that the ancient art will again revive, and that its light and artistic productions are much superior to the work to which it has given place.

Netting is very easy to do, and likewise possesses the advantage of being extremely strong, each loop that is made being independent, and, if properly knotted, remaining firm, whatever accident happens, either to the ones before or behind it; for the same reason, nothing is more difficult than to undo a piece of Netting when once made, every loop requiring to be separately unpicked and undone with a sharp-pointed knitting needle or stiletto. The beauty of Netting consists in the regular size of the loops made, and the tightness of each individual knot, and this result cannot be obtained unless good materials are used, and the art has been well practised. Bad thread and silk are liable to break when under the strain of being pulled into a knot, and a break in the material necessitates the thread being joined in the working of a row, which is to be avoided, not only for the knot produced by the join always showing, but also by reason of the loop that contains it rarely being made the same size as the ones surrounding it. All joins in the working thread should be made at the first loop in a row, and with a WEAVER'S KNOT. Every loop or knot in Netting counts as a stitch in other work; but it takes four knots to make what is called a complete loop, or mesh, in Netting. These meshes are generally of a diamond shape, and are made with Plain Netting; but Round and Square Meshes are also worked, in order to give a certain variety and relief to the ordinary loop, which, however, is not capable of very much alteration; and varieties in Netting are more often made by working several loops into a loop, or by missing loops and crossing one over the other, than by changing the form of the loop worked. Netting is always made the contrary way to what it will hang when in use, and in some articles, such as curtains and purses, the loops forming the length are all put on the Foundation Loop at once; while in others, such as lawn-tennis nets, one loop is only put upon the Foundation Loop, and the right length made by Increasing in every row. When the article is finished, it should be slightly damped, and then well stretched, and pinned out upon a board, so that every mesh may assume its right position.

The implements used in Netting are few; they consist of a Netting Needle, which is a long piece of ivory, wood,

FIG. 619. NETTING NEEDLE.

or steel (*see* Fig. 619), split at each end to admit of the thread being wound upon it; Mesh or Spool, of various sizes, also made of ivory, steel, or wood (*see* Fig. 620), and

FIG. 620. ROUND MESH.

numbered as to sizes in the same way as the needles; Twine, fine Knitting Cotton, or Silk, for making the Netting; and a Stirrup, or Lead Cushion, to which to attach the Netting while working, so as to resist the pressure each Knot in making throws upon the work.

The manner of Netting is as follows: Wind upon the Needle sufficient cotton for one row of Netting, and be careful to use a mesh that will allow the needle to pass easily through the loops as they are made; then attach it to the FOUNDATION LOOP on the

Stirrup and place the latter round the left foot, so regulated as to length that the row to be Netted is about on a level with the waist of the worker. Take the Mesh in the left hand, and place that thumb over it, and the fingers underneath it; hold the needle in the right hand, with about twice its length in cotton between it and the work; hold the Mesh up to the Foundation loop, put the cotton over the Mesh, round the first three fingers, and back on to the Mesh, and over it, so that it is held down with the left thumb: throw the thread outwards round the work from left to right, and place the right hand holding the needle in the palm of the left hand. Push the needle through the under part of the loop on the Mesh, and into the Foundation Loop, the thread held from being drawn up by being round the little finger of the left hand. Draw this Foundation Loop up to the Mesh, release the thread under the thumb, and draw it up as a knot over the Foundation Loop; drop the thread on the third finger and draw up, and drop the thread on the little finger and draw up. The knot that is made with these movements should be close to the mesh, and so firm and strong as not to reply to any attempts to alter its position; it is repeated throughout the work, the loops on the previous row answering to the Foundation Loop. Form each row of Netting with a succession of these knots, and work them always from left to right. When the end of a row is reached, turn the Netting over, and commence to make the next row by working on the Loop last made.

TERMS AND MATERIALS.—The following Terms and Materials are used in Netting:

Cushion.—When the Stirrup is not used to keep the Netting taut, it is necessary to pin the work to a Cushion. The Cushion required is shown with the Foundation Loop in Fig. 621. It is a large Cushion, heavily weighted with lead, covered with cloth, and made so as to resist without yielding when each loop is pulled and knotted in the progress of the work.

Decrease.—This is managed by Netting two or more loops together of the preceding row. To Net two loops together: Work the LOOP as far as putting the netting needle into the loop formed on the preceding row; pass it through two loops instead of one on this row, and finish the loop in the ordinary way.

Foundation Loop.—All Netting, whether worked upon the Stirrup or the Cushion, requires a foundation, on to which the first row is Netted. The Foundation Loop, when the work is finished, is carefully cut, and the first row drawn out and straightened. To make a Foundation Loop for work pinned to a Cushion, as illustrated in Fig. 621: Take a piece of twine the size of the knitting cotton to be used in the Netting, make a loop in it, small or large, according to the length of the work and the consequent number of netted loops that will be required, and then make a very small loop; pin the Foundation Loop down by attaching the small loop to the cushion, and then fasten an end of the knitting cotton to it, and work the first row of loops on to it, as shown in the illustration.

To make a Foundation Loop upon a Stirrup: Pass a loop of strong, fine twine, through the upper end of the

Stirrup, and work the first row of Netting on to it in the same way as before described. Some workers Net a number of rows upon the Foundation before they commence their real pattern; these netted rows are retained

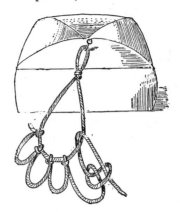

FIG. 621. FOUNDATION LOOP AND CUSHION.

upon the Foundation Loop, and serve as a starting point for many pieces of Netting. It is not necessary to do this, but the loops of the first row are of a more equal size when worked upon such a support.

Increase.—In Netting this is accomplished by making two or more Loops into the one Loop of preceding row. To work: Net a Loop into the Loop on the preceding row in the ordinary way, and then Net another Loop into the same Loop before proceeding to the next one.

Knot.—The Knot made by twisting the cotton round the Mesh and fingers is made with every Netted Loop, and is essential to its security. The manner of making it is described in PLAIN NETTING and FISHERMAN'S KNOT.

Long Loop.—Loops in Plain Netting are sometimes made of two different sizes in the same row. This is managed as follows: Net in the ordinary way until the place is reached where a Long Loop has to be Netted, then put the cotton twice round the Mesh instead of once, and make the KNOT as in PLAIN NETTING.

Loop.—A loop in Netting takes the place of a stitch; it is formed over the Mesh, and is secured by a KNOT, as described in PLAIN NETTING, or in FISHERMAN'S KNOT.

Mesh.—The instrument used in Netting to work the Loops upon, and made of bone, steel, or wood, of various sizes, either round or flat, according to the size of the loops to be made. A Mesh was at one time called a Spool, on account of the title Mesh being also given to the loops of Netting when quite completed as Squares, Rounds, or Diamonds.

Needle.—Used to hold the cotton, and made of sizes matching the Meshes.

Round.—When Netting is worked as a continuous looping, without any turning of the work, a Round has been made when each Loop upon a level has been worked. To net a Round: Join the Netting as in CIRCLE, and indicate the last Loop by marking it with a piece of coloured wool; Net until that loop has again to be worked.

Row.—In Netting this term indicates the Loops from one side of the work to the other. To make a Row: Commence on the left-hand side of the Foundation, and Net in every Loop until the last upon the right-hand side is reached. In working curtains, and other large articles, a Row is frequently a yard in length. As the loops forming this yard could not be contained upon one Mesh, slide the first-made ones off on the left side as the new ones are formed on the right, but always leave enough made Loops upon the Mesh to be a guide as to size to the ones being made. Draw the Mesh entirely out when the Row is completed, and commence a new Row. Turn the Netting over in the hand, place the Mesh close to the loop last made, make a new Loop upon it, and work from the left to the right to end of row.

Spool.—See MESH.

Stirrup.—Netting, which is really a succession of Loops secured in position by knots, requires to be kept stretched while in progress, or the Loops made are unequal in size, and the knots are not drawn up tight. This stretching is accomplished by either pinning the Foundation Loop of the Netting to a lead Cushion, or attaching it to the foot with the help of a Stirrup, the last plan being the one usually adopted, and the best. To make a Stirrup: Take a piece of oak or elm, 4 to 5 inches in length, and 1½ inches in width, and bore a hole in the centre through each of its ends. Take 2 yards of ribbon, 1 inch wide, of a strong make, pass each end through a hole, and sew the two ends together, or tie them underneath the piece of wood; put the piece of wood under the left foot, and bring the ribbon up as a loop. Regulate the Long Loop thus formed by the height of the worker, as it should always reach to the knee. If the ends of the ribbon are only tied together, the Stirrup can be shortened during the progress of the work, which is often an advantage. A more ornamental Stirrup can be made by Embroidering a narrow band, to pass over the instep, and attaching that to the ends of wood, and making the loop of ribbon rise from the centre of the embroidery; but for ordinary Netting the plain Stirrup is the best, as the whole of the weight of the foot is upon it.

NETTING PATTERNS.—Although the Loop, or, rather, Knot in Netting appears not to admit of much variety, it can be worked in the various ways here given.

Caroline Netting.—This can either be worked in single fleecy wool and round wooden Meshes, for scarves and shawls, or with fine crochet cotton of a medium size, and with a flat Mesh, 1 inch in width, for curtains and window blinds. To work: First row—Net in PLAIN NETTING, upon the Foundation Loop, enough Loops to make the length of the article required. Second row—work as for Plain Netting, but take up the second Loop upon the needle, and then push the first Loop over it, and net these two Loops as one, Net another and a Plain Loop into the same Loop, a Plain Loop upon the third Loop, and repeat from the commencement for the rest of the row. Third row—Plain Netting. Fourth row—as the second row. Repeat the second and third rows three times; then take a

rather wider Mesh, and Net a plain row with that, and repeat from first row.

Circle.—A Circle in Netting is formed upon the Foundation Loop, which makes the centre of the circle. To work as shown in Fig. 622: Make a very small Foundation Loop, and Net, in PLAIN NETTING, ten Loops into it, and, instead of reversing the work and commencing a new row as in ordinary Netting, Net the next Loop into the first Loop

FIG. 622. NETTING—CIRCLE.

of the ten just made, and draw these together as the first round and commence the second round. After this first drawing together, the Netting will form a Circle by simply working every Loop as reached, but as each Circle is larger in circumference than the preceding one, the Loops must be increased. The Increase is shown in Fig.

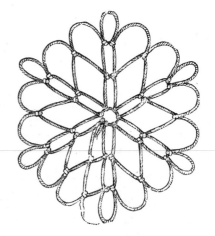

FIG. 623. NETTING—INCREASED CIRCLE.

622, and is thus worked: After the first round, which in Fig. 623 contains six Loops, work two Loops into every Loop for the second round. Third round —Work two Loops into the first Loop, one Loop into the second, and repeat to the end of the round. Fourth round—the Increase, by the time that the fourth round is reached, will have assumed the shape shown in Fig. 623; work into the Loop that is drawn longways in the illustration two Loops wherever it occurs, one Loop into all the other Loops; continue to Increase six times in this manner in every round until the Circle is complete.

Cross Netting.—This is used either for the centres of scarves, shawls, or curtains, or as a border to plain netted articles. Medium sized knitting cotton, and two flat Meshes, one half the size of the other, are required. To work as shown in Fig. 624: First row—take the smallest Mesh, and Net in PLAIN NETTING the length required. Second row—Net in Plain Netting with the largest Mesh. Third row—take the narrow Mesh, Net a Loop, taking the

FIG. 624. CROSS NETTING.

second Loop of the last row, then Net the first Loop of the last row, then the fourth, and then the third; continue to the end of the row, always Netting the second Loop on the last row before the one next the Mesh. Fourth row —use the largest Mesh, and Net a plain row. Fifth row —as the third row; this row is not completed in the illustration, so that the crossing of the two Loops in it should be fully indicated.

Diamond Netting.—This is a term applied to Plain Netting, and is worked as such when the loops are made of an uniform size, and following each other in regular succession. Fancy Diamond Netting is worked in three different ways, as follows:—*Single Diamond Netting.*— Work with fine silk or cotton, and Mesh and Needle No. 10. Net the first Loop in ordinary PLAIN NETTING, and the second in the same way, but pass the cotton twice round the Mesh, so as to make this Loop twice the size of the other. Repeat these two Loops to the end of the row. In the next row make the short Loop over the Long Loop of the last row, and work as in the first row. *Treble Diamond Netting.*—Use the same cotton, Mesh, and Needle, as for Single Diamond Netting. First row —make a Plain Netting Loop, but put the cotton twice round the Mesh. Then Net three Plain Netting Loops, and repeat these four Loops to the end of the row. Second row—a plain Loop over the Long Loop in the last row, then a Long Loop and two plain Loops; repeat to the end of the row, and withdraw the Mesh before a long Loop is Netted as a plain Loop. Third row—Net a Plain and a Long Loop alternately, commencing with two plain Loops, should the pattern require it. Fourth row—Net three plain Loops and one Long Loop; repeat to the end of the row. Fifth row—as the second row. *Diamond Netting made*

with Five Loops.—Use the same cotton, Mesh, and Needle as in Single Diamond Netting, and work the Long and the Plain Loop in Plain Netting; take the Mesh out of the work when a Long Loop has to be netted as a Plain Loop, and after this has been done, the pattern forms a diamond of small loops surrounded by an open space formed by the Long Loops; commence by Netting upon the Founda-tion Loop a number of loops that divide into six, and one over. First row—make a Long Loop with the cotton twice round the Mesh, and five Plain Loops; repeat to the end of the row; finish with a Long Loop. Second row—Plain Loop over the Long Loop, a Long Loop, 4 Plain Loops; repeat to the end of the row. Third row—a Plain Loop, a Long Loop, 4 Plain, the last over the Long Loop; repeat to the end of the row. Fourth row—a Plain Loop, a Plain Loop over the Long Loop, a Long Loop, 3 Plain, the last over a Long Loop; repeat to the end of the row. Fifth row—a Plain Loop, a Plain Loop over a Long Loop,* a Long Loop, 5 Plain, the last over a Long Loop; repeat from * to the end of the row. Sixth row —2 Plain, 1 Plain over a Long Loop, a Long Loop, 2 Plain, the first over a Long Loop; repeat to the end of the row. Seventh row—3 Plain, the last over a Long Loop, a Long Loop, 2 Plain; repeat to the end of the row. Eighth row—4 Plain, the last over a Long Loop, a Long Loop, a Plain Loop; repeat to the end of the row. Ninth row—3 Plain, the last over a Long Loop, 1 Plain; repeat to the end of the row. Tenth row—3 Plain, the last over a Long Loop, 2 Plain, the last over a Long Loop, a Long Loop; repeat to the end of the row. Eleventh row—2 Plain, the last over a Long Loop, 3 Plain, the last over a Long Loop, a Long Loop; repeat to the end of the row. Twelfth row—2 Plain, the last over a Long Loop, 4 Plain, the last over a Long Loop; repeat to the end of the row, but end with a Long Loop instead of a Plain one. Thirteenth row—work as the first, and repeat from there.

English Netting, also called Honeycomb.—Work with any sized Mesh and cotton, according to the article to be made. First row—PLAIN NETTING. Second row—also Plain Netting, but Net the second Loop before the first, the fourth before the third, and so on to the end of the row. Third row—Plain Netting. Fourth row—as the second, but commence with a Plain Loop before beginning the crossing. Fifth row—Plain Netting. Sixth row—as the second row, and repeat from that row.

Fisherman's Knot.—This Knot differs from the one ordinarily used in Plain Netting, and is considered to be stronger. It is used by fishermen for their nets, hence its name; and is also used for hammocks, lawn-tennis nets, and other articles subject to rough treatment and rain. The process of making is shown in Fig. 625, and the Knot when made is thicker than other Knots. To work: Hold the Mesh and the netting needle in the ordinary way, the thumb over the Mesh and the fingers sup-porting it; pass the thread round the Mesh, but not over the fingers, and put the needle upwards through the Loop that is to be worked, and then draw the Loop up to the Mesh, and keep the thread tight by holding it down with the thumb. Allow the loose thread to fall to the left of the work, and put the needle upward, behind the Loop being worked, and out on the left (*see* Fig. 625), so as to inclose it with the thread, and draw the thread tight. The illustration gives the Knot nearly completed; the

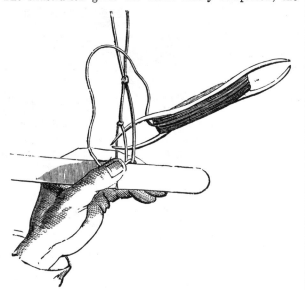

FIG. 625. NETTING—FISHERMAN'S KNOT.

thread in it is passed round the Mesh, through the Loop, and secured with the thumb, and the movement shown is that of the needle being passed at the back of the Loop, and to the left, before the final drawing tight of the Knot.

Fly Netting.—A very pretty and easy kind of Netting, suitable for scarves, shawls, and neckties, and made with wool and silk, or wool and cotton. To work: Wind upon the needle together a strand of wool and silk, so that they unwind as one. Net upon the Foundation Loop enough Loops to form the width required, and work these loops, and all others, in PLAIN NETTING. Continue to net rows of this Plain Netting over an inch sized flat Mesh until the width desired for the article is obtained, then cut the woollen thread round every Knot, and fluff it up, so that it conceals the Knot and makes a little ball; but be careful to leave the silk or cotton strand untouched. Make a Fringe or Edging to the work with some of the patterns given under EDGING and FRINGE.

Grecian Netting.—Used for purses when worked with fine silks, and for curtains and toilet cloths when worked with knitting cotton. The Loop is troublesome at first, and should not be tried by a beginner. Two flat Meshes, one half the size of the other, are required. To work: First row—Net in PLAIN NETTING, and with the largest Mesh. Second row—take the small Mesh, and make the usual Loop over the Mesh which commences a Plain Netting Loop, then pass the netting needle through the under part of the Loop, and bring it out clear of the Mesh; put it through the first Loop on the last row, and into the second, draw the cotton and Needle back through the first Loop, and then twist the second Loop round the first, and Net the first Loop, finishing it as in the ordinary Plain Netting. For the next Loop, Net the little Loop that is formed by twisting the first and the second Loop

together. Repeat these two movements to the end of the row. Third row—as the first. Fourth row—as the second. Repeat the first and second rows to the end of the work.

Hollow Square Netting.—A square of Netting with the centre left hollow is sometimes required as a groundwork for a piece of Guipure d'Art Lace, or for a pincushion cover or cheese cloth, in ordinary Netting. The hollow square is formed in the Netting, as it proceeds, in the following manner: Commence with one Loop upon the Foundation Loop as in SQUARE NETTING, and Net in PLAIN NETTING. INCREASE a Loop at the end of every row, as in Square Netting, until half the length of one side of the outside square is obtained; then divide the Loops, and leave those at the end of the row unworked, and Net the other half as if making OBLONG NETTING on the inside of the square; DECREASE by Netting two Loops together at the inside end, and Increase by Netting two Loops into the end Loop in every row upon the outside of the square. Work in this way until the whole length of one side of the outside square is made, turn the corner as it were, and commence another side by Netting the two outside Loops together, and Increasing in the inside by making two Loops in the outer Loop there in every row. Continue until half the outside line of the square is formed, and then drop the Loops, and pick up those left when the oblong was commenced. Work these in the same manner, Increasing at the outside, Decreasing at the inside, until the length of that side of the outside square is obtained, and then turn the corner, and Decrease on the outside and Increase on the inside, until these Loops are brought down to the level of the others. Work right across the whole number, and Decrease in every row until only one Loop is left on the row. The following example will make the working of this Hollow Square quite clear. To form a Hollow Square with fifteen Loops along the outer side: Commence with one Loop, and Increase in every row until there are twelve Loops in the row; drop the last six, and work six rows, Increasing at the outside of the square, and Decreasing at the inside; turn the corner, and work six rows, Increasing at the inside, and Decreasing at the outside of the square; leave those Loops, and pick up the ones first dropped, which Net down to the others in the same way. For the thirteenth row, work right across the twelve Loops, and Decrease until only one Loop is left in the row.

Honeycomb Netting.—See *English Netting.*

Leaf Netting.—Also known as Puff Netting, and worked so as to raise some of the loops of a row above the others. It is simply Plain Netting worked with different sized meshes, and can be adapted to any of the purposes for which Netting is employed. It looks particularly well worked as a border to netted curtains, or when made for window blinds. To work: Use medium sized crochet cotton and two flat Meshes (one twice the width of the other); a quarter of an inch and a half inch Mesh are good sizes, but all depends upon the destination of the work. First, Second, and Third rows—PLAIN NETTING. With the small Mesh make into the FOUNDATION LOOP as the first row, the number of Loops required for the length, and Net a Loop into each of these for the second and third rows. Fourth row—use the same Mesh, and Work one Loop in Plain Netting in the first Loop, and six Loops in the second Loop, the cotton to be put twice round the Mesh before making any of these six Loops; repeat from the commencement to the end of the row. Fifth and Sixth rows—use the small Mesh and work a Loop into every Loop on the previous row. Seventh row—use the large Mesh, work a Loop into every Loop on the previous row, work the first Loop in Plain Netting, the next six with the cotton twice round the Mesh, and repeat to the end of the row from the commencement. Eighth row—work a Loop into the first Loop, still using the large Mesh, take up the next six Loops, and work them as one Loop into the Second Loop; repeat these two Loops to the end of the row. Ninth and Tenth rows—Plain Netting with the large Mesh into every Loop. Eleventh row—use the large Mesh, and work two Loops in every Loop on the row. Twelfth row—use the large Mesh, and take up two Loops in every Loop on the row. Thirteenth row—as the tenth. Fourteenth and Fifteenth rows—as the eleventh and twelfth. Sixteenth row—repeat from the first row. The leaf, or raised part of this pattern, is contained in rows four to eight; the rest can be altered in any way, so long as the number of Loops, when once arranged, is kept to, and that part of the Netting left flat.

Long Twisted Netting.—This requires working with two Meshes of unequal widths; the larger one should be exactly double the size of the smaller. To work: First row—take the smaller Mesh, and work with it a row of Loops in ROUND NETTING. Second row—take the large Mesh, and work with it a row of PLAIN NETTING Loops. Repeat these two rows alternately to the end of the pattern.

Looped Netting.—This is used for either edgings or to form the whole of shawls, curtains, fire screens, window blinds, and drawing-room covers. The design shown in Fig. 626 is the width of work it is necessary to make for a border, but any width can be made. To work: Use a half-inch or quarter-inch flat Mesh, and knitting cotton

FIG. 626. LOOPED NETTING.

or wool, according to the article to be Netted. First row—Net in PLAIN NETTING the length required. Second row—make four Loops into every Loop of the preceding row. Third row—run the needle through the four Loops worked together in the last row, and work them together in Plain Netting; the illustration shows this third row uncompleted,

with the manner of passing the cotton through the four loops. Fourth row—repeat from the first row.

Mignonette Netting.—This is used for curtains and window blinds, it being extremely easy, and worked with one Mesh. To work: Use medium-sized crochet cotton, and a flat Mesh half an inch in width, or one smaller. First, second, and third rows—PLAIN NETTING. Fourth row—Net into the first Loop one Plain Loop, then put the cotton twice round the Mesh, and Net a LONG LOOP into the same Loop on the last row, and finally Net a Plain Loop into the same Loop; repeat to the end of the row, Netting three Loops into one Loop. Fifth row—Net in Plain Netting all the Long Loops, but leave the Plain Loops. Sixth row—repeat from the second row.

Netting with Beads.—When making ornamental articles with Netting, beads are often worked into the Netting, and are used particularly in Purse Netting and to ornament bags. The beads used are steel, gold, and coloured, the last two kinds wearing the best, steel being apt to tarnish. The beads should be German, selected so as to match each other perfectly as to shape and size, as any unevenness in the make of the beads is instantly detected when they are in position, and destroys the look of the work. Unless perfectly secured, beads will move upon the loop when netted. To work: Use a long Darning Needle instead of a Netting Needle, threaded with silk enough for the row that is to be beaded; thread each bead as required, bring it up in front of the Mesh, and keep it there with the left thumb upon it until the knot of the Loop is made; then pass the needle through the bead again from underneath, and pull the bead close up to the knot just made. Thread another bead, and repeat until the number of beads required are secured.

Oblong Netting.—This shape is much used for making lawn tennis nets, hammocks, and garden nets. It is shown in Fig. 627, and is worked either with Fisherman's Knot or Plain Netting. To work: Commence as for SQUARE NETTING, with a single Loop in the FOUNDATION LOOP; INCREASE by working two Loops into the last

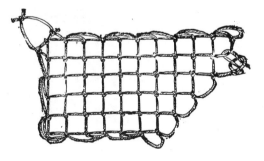

FIG. 627. OBLONG NETTING.

Loop in every row until the depth required for the article is obtained (in the illustration five rows make the necessary depth); tie a piece of bright-coloured wool into the last Loop, and, whenever the side is reached where the wool is, DECREASE by working two Loops as one (see lower part of the illustration); Increase at the other end of the row, whenever it is reached, by working two Loops into the last Loop. If attention is paid to keep the Increase and Decrease regular, a long straight piece of Netting is made. When this is sufficiently long, proceed to form the second short side of the oblong. To do this, Decrease by Netting two Loops together at the end of every row until only one Loop remains.

Open Netting.—A very simple manner of making an alteration in Plain Netting. Work with crochet cotton or silk, and with two flat Meshes, the larger an inch in width, the smaller half an inch in width. First, second, and third rows—PLAIN NETTING, with the small Mesh. Fourth row—Plain Netting, with the large Mesh. Fifth row—repeat from the first row.

Plain, or Diamond Netting.—This loop is the elementary one in Netting, and upon it all the more complicated loops are formed. It is used in all Netting as a foundation for Darning upon Net, or for Guipure d'Art, and its various stages are shown in Figs. 628, 629, and 630, in which the Netting is given without the hands that hold it, in order that the making of the Loop may be fully

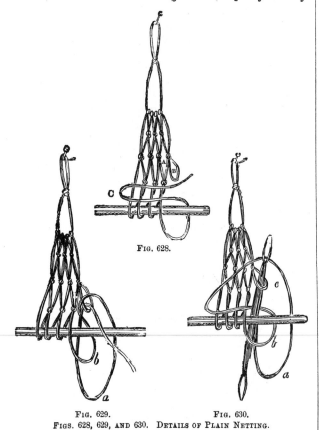

FIG. 628.

FIG. 629.   FIG. 630.
FIGS. 628, 629, AND 630. DETAILS OF PLAIN NETTING.

shown. To work: Having secured the FOUNDATION LOOP to the Stirrup, put the latter over the foot, fill the needle with cotton, and attach the cotton to the Foundation Loop; take the Mesh in the left hand, and the needle in the right hand, holding the Mesh with the thumb over it, and the fingers beneath. Pass the cotton over the Mesh, and round the first three fingers, and hold the Mesh close to the Foundation Loop. Bring the cotton round under the Mesh to the top, and put it under the left thumb and to

the left (shown in Fig. 628 by the letter C); then bring it round to the right, past the letter B in Fig. 628, and round the hand, as shown in Figs. 629 and 630, then by the letter *a* (this last Loop is held by the little finger of the left hand). The needle, by this action, is brought in front of the Mesh, and into the palm of the hand; it is then passed under the first Loop, between the Mesh and the fingers holding it, and into the Foundation Loop (see Fig. 630, letter C), and over that piece of cotton which is turned back from the left thumb, and then forms Loop *a* of Figs. 629 and 630. Before pulling the Mesh out of the Foundation Loop, it is necessary to change the position of the right hand; this, while pushing the needle through the cotton and Foundation Loop, is at the lower part of the needle, and must be transferred to the upper, so that it can grasp the needle firmly; make the change, and keep all the turns of the cotton on the left hand steady while doing so, then draw the Foundation Loop up to the Mesh; release the Loop of cotton held down by the left thumb, and pull it tight over the Foundation Loop with a pull upon the needle; let go the Loop over the three fingers, and pull that tight by opening the third and little fingers of the left hand, and enlarging the Loop upon them; and finally let this Loop go, and pull the cotton firmly up with the right hand. The Knot that is formed by these movements should be close up to the Mesh, but not upon it, and should be made by a strand of cotton firmly inclosing a piece of the Foundation Loop, and no true knot is formed unless this is the result. A repetition of these knots make a row in Netting, and the beauty and value of the work depends upon their being made with Loops of an equal size, which can only be accomplished when every knot is made close to the Mesh. It takes two rows to complete the diamond-shaped Loop from which this knot derives its name, the first Loop being shown by the letter B in Fig. 628, and the completed diamond by the letter A in the same illustration.

Puff Netting.—See *Leaf Netting.*

Rose Netting.—The meshes formed by this Netting are shaped like honeycombs, and are surrounded with a double line of thread. This variety is generally used for making fine silk veils, or mittens; but, if worked with Crochet cotton, it will make very lacy-looking curtains, To work in silks, use flat Meshes, sizes No. 9 and 18; if with cotton, a flat Mesh three quarters of an inch wide, and one half that size. First row—use the finer Mesh, and make upon the FOUNDATION LOOP in PLAIN NETTING the number of Loops necessary for the length of the article to be worked. Second row—with the larger Mesh, Net into every Loop in Plain Netting. Third row—draw the first Loop of the last row through the second Loop, and well up it, Net the first Loop in Plain Netting with the smaller Mesh, run the needle into the second Loop where it crosses the first Loop, and pull it out there and Net it as the first Loop. Continue to work in this way for the whole row. The only difficulty is the taking up correctly of the second Loop in the right place inside the first Loop, and not outside it. Fourth row—Plain Netting into every Loop, using the large Mesh. Fifth row—work like the third row with the small Mesh, but miss the first

Loop and draw the second through the third, to diversify the crossing of the Loops. Sixth row—Plain Netting, with the large Mesh. Seventh row—repeat from the third row.

Round Netting.—A Loop considered strong. It is used for purses, mittens, and other articles subject to wear. Round Netting has the appearance of a four-sided honeycomb. To work: Commence by making the Loop over the Mesh, as in the ordinary PLAIN NETTING, put the needle through the under part of the thread on the Mesh, then draw it well out, turn it, and pass its point from above the work into the Loop of the Netting that is to be completed; draw this up to the Mesh, and finish the stitch as in ordinary Plain Netting. As the manner of working Round Netting causes the work to contract, place one-fifth more Loops upon the FOUNDATION Loop than would be required for the same length when made in the ordinary way.

Square Netting.—The Loop in Square Netting is the same as that used in Plain Netting, but the work, having to form an exact square, is commenced with only one Loop upon the Foundation Loop, instead of the number of Loops corresponding to the length; it is then Increased until two sides of the square are formed, and then Decreased to the one Loop to form the two remaining sides. To work: Work one Loop into the FOUNDATION LOOP in PLAIN NETTING. Into this Loop work two Loops in the next row. In the third row, work two Loops into the last Loop, and continue to INCREASE by always working two Loops into the last Loop of each row until the length required for the square is formed. The Loops of the row across the square will be the same in number as those upon the outside edges. As soon as the length of the square is thus formed, commence to DECREASE by Netting two Loops together at the end of every row. The squares required as foundations to Guipure d'Art are Netted in this manner.

Star Netting.—This Loop can be made either as a finish to, or centre of, a curtain. It presents, when finished, the appearance shown in the small stars of Fig. 632, and its manner of working is considerably en-

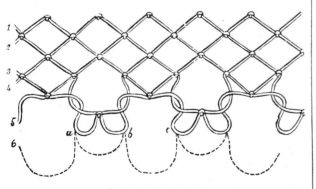

FIG. 631. STAR NETTING.

larged in Fig. 631, so that the complicated part of the Loop may be fully understood. To work as a border: Use Strutt's cotton No. 8, a round Mesh half an inch in circumference, and a steel Netting needle. Net in

PLAIN NETTING the first three rows. Fourth row—Net the first Loop in Plain Netting, the second in the same, but pass the cotton twice round the Mesh, to make a Loop twice the length of the first (this long and short Loop

FIG. 632. STAR NETTING.

is shown in Fig. 631, in row marked 4); repeat the two Loops alternately to the end of the row. Fifth row—pass the cotton round the Mesh, and the needle over and under the long Loop on the preceding row, and Net a Loop, pass the cotton again over the Mesh, and the needle over and under the same long stitch on the preceding row, and Net into the short Loop; repeat throughout the row (the letters a, b, and c, in Fig. 631 show the Loops formed in this row). Sixth row—repeat the fourth row, make the

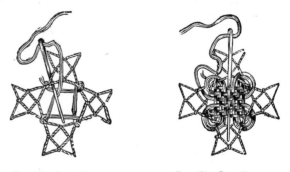

FIG. 633. STAR NETTING. FIG. 633. STAR NETTING (DETAIL A).

short Loop between the letters a and b in Fig. 631, and the long between the letters b and c in the same illustration; therefore, commence the row with a long Loop. Seventh row—as the fifth row. Eighth row—as the fourth.

Figs. 632, 633, and 634 are illustrations of the various devices with which this Star Netting can be ornamented when worked for curtains. The cotton to use for these decorations should be linen thread, No. 80. Fig. 632 shows a large Darned Star carried across four of the open spaces left in the Star Netting. It is worked thus: Thread a needle with the cotton, and carry it backwards and forwards across one of the large spaces four times, always ending in one of the small stars; repeat this filling up so that the four arms of the Star are formed. Fig. 633, Detail A, shows how one of these large spaces can be filled with a thick stitch, which resembles Point de Toile in Guipure d'Art. To work: Loop the needle into the four corners of the square, and continue these Loops, DARNING each thread in and out, as shown in Detail A, until the open space is quite filled up.

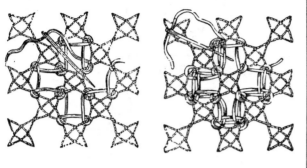

FIG. 634. STAR NETTING.   FIG. 634. STAR NETTING (DETAIL A).

Fig. 634 and Detail A show the same stitch worked so as to form a Maltese cross in a lighter way than in Fig. 633. To work: Loop the thread all round the outside line of the Maltese cross, so as to mark it well out, then repeat the outside line, working the second line over the first, and DARNING the two together, as shown in Fig. 634, Detail A. All these various stitches can be worked, if required, upon the same curtain.

Straight Netting.—In this Netting there is neither Increasing nor Decreasing; the number of loops that are required for the width of the work are Netted on to the Foundation Loop, and are then worked until the length required is obtained. To work: On the FOUNDATION LOOP (see Fig. 635), Net in PLAIN NETTING the number of loops required, and continue to Net

FIG. 635. STRAIGHT NETTING.

these, simply turning the work over in the hand, to work the next row from left to right without breaking off the thread, or Increasing or Decreasing a loop. Straight Netting, if required to be very even, should have two rows worked on the Foundation Loop before the real piece is commenced, as then every loop made will be of equal size, which is not always the case when the work is immediately begun from the Foundation Loop.

NETTED ARTICLES.—The patterns previously given can be used to work the following articles, but, as distinct directions as to number of loops and length of work is necessary, the manner of working is described in detail:—

Antimacassar.—The prettiest kind of Netted Antimacassar is formed with Netted rosettes of two different sizes; these rosettes are worked separately, and are then sewn together. One of the large rosettes forms the centre of the Antimacassar, and is surrounded by six rosettes of the same size; six small rosettes are placed to fill up the space outside these, and twelve large rosettes are sewn above, the six large ones forming the first circle; twelve small rosettes fill in the spaces between these last, and the Antimacassar is finished with twenty-four large rosettes forming the third circle. Thirty-one large rosettes and twelve small ones are required. Boar's-head cotton No. 12; two flat Meshes, $\frac{3}{8}$ and $\frac{3}{16}$ of an inch; and a round Mesh No. 12, are required. The Netting is easier worked attached to a Lead Cushion than to a Stirrup. To work the large rosette: First row—upon a small FOUNDATION LOOP, Net in PLAIN NETTING, on No. 12 Mesh, seven Loops, and join these together as a CIRCLE. Second and Third rounds—as the first round. Fourth round—use the smaller flat Mesh, and Net four loops into each loop upon the third round. Fifth and Sixth rounds—use No. 12 Mesh, and Net a Loop in every Loop upon the last round. Seventh round —use the largest Mesh, and Net two Loops into every Loop of the last round. Eighth and Ninth rounds—as the fifth round. For the small rosette, make a very small Foundation Loop over a pencil, and Net five Loops into it, using No. 12 Mesh; join these as a Circle, and net two more rounds upon them with the same Mesh. Fourth round— use the same Mesh, and Net two Loops into every Loop in the last round. Fifth round—Net with the smaller flat Mesh two Loops into every Loop upon the last round. Sixth and Seventh rounds—use No. 12 Mesh, and Net a Loop into every Loop. The centre of all the rosettes, after they are joined together, should be finished with an ORNAMENTAL WHEEL, such as worked in Modern Point Lace.

Bag.—Use Mesh No. 16, and coarse Netting silk, and Net sixty Loops on to the FOUNDATION LOOP; work the desired length, and draw one end up, and finish with a tassel, and running a ribbon through the other end.

Bag, Pence.—Use fine crimson silk, and Meshes Nos. 15 and 11. Net in PLAIN NETTING nine Loops upon the FOUNDATION LOOP, and join up. First and Second rounds—Net with the small Mesh in Plain Netting. Third round—with the small Mesh, Net two Loops into every Loop. Fourth round—small Mesh, a Loop into every Loop. Fifth round—small Mesh, Net two Loops into the first Loop, and one into the second Loop; repeat to the end of the round. Sixth round—small Mesh, a Loop into every Loop. Seventh round—small Mesh, INCREASE in this round by working two Loops into one eight times; these Increases should not be placed above the ones in the fifth round, but should be worked in the Loops before those. Eighth round—small Mesh, a Loop into every Loop. Ninth round—like the seventh round. Repeat eighth and ninth round seven times. Work forty-six rounds in Plain Netting with the small Mesh. Work a round with the large Mesh. For the next round, use the small Mesh, Net the second Loop before the first, and the fourth before the third; repeat to the end of the round. Work four rounds with the small Mesh in Plain Netting, and finish off with a SCALLOPED EDGING. Run a ribbon through the round worked with the large Mesh.

Cloud.—For a Cloud, single Berlin or Fleecy wool of two colours is required, and three flat Meshes, an inch, half an inch, and a quarter of an inch in width. To commence: Work 400 loops upon the FOUNDATION LOOP, with the half-inch Mesh. First and Second rows—PLAIN NETTING into every Loop with the half-inch Mesh and the darkest wool. Third row—use the lightest wool and the largest Mesh, and Net three Loops into every Loop upon the last row. Fourth and Fifth rows—use the smaller Mesh and the darkest wool, and Net into every Loop upon the last row. Sixth row—use the widest Mesh and the lightest wool, and work a Loop into every Loop upon the last row. Seventh row—use the half-inch Mesh and the darkest wool, and Net three Loops of the last row together. Eighth row—use the half-inch Mesh and the darkest wool, and work a Loop into every Loop upon the last row. Ninth row—as the third row. Tenth and Eleventh rows—as the fourth and fifth rows.

Curtains.—These are generally Netted in Plain Netting, and then ornamented with a pattern Darned upon them; but they can also be worked in any of the fancy Loops given under their own headings, and in that case will not require any Darned Pattern. The number of Loops that form the length of the Curtain will have to be put upon the FOUNDATION LOOP to start with; these, if Netted with a No. 9 Mesh, will measure four Loops to an inch, which will be a guide to the number required. In Netting such large articles as Curtains, the worker, from time to time, will have to tie up the work out of her way, so as to allow of room to move her hands when making the Knots. To do this without interfering with the shape of the Loops, run a tape into a row of the Netting, taking up every Loop, and being very careful to keep in the one row. Tie this tape to the foot as a Stirrup, and work until the length has again to be altered.

Edging.—(1). The Edging shown in Fig. 636 is worked with two Meshes, one a large flat Mesh, and the other a

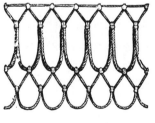

FIG. 636. NETTING—EDGING.

round Mesh; the flat Mesh should be an inch in width, the round, an inch in circumference. Two sizes of cotton are also used, one a coarse Knitting cotton, and the other a fine Crochet cotton. The Edging is worked in Plain

Netting, and the pattern can be repeated to any length, and, therefore, used for the centre of curtains or window blinds, as well as for Edgings. To work: First row—Net in PLAIN NETTING, with the fine cotton and the round Mesh, the length required for the work. Second row—Net in Plain Netting, with the Large Mesh and the coarse cotton, into every Loop in the last row. Third and fourth rows—as the first row. Should the width of the Edging be increased, repeat from the first row.

(2.) This border is worked with a round Mesh of a medium size, and with two different sizes of cotton, one coarse and one fine, Walker and Evans' Knitting cotton Nos. 12 and 30 being the required thicknesses. To work as shown in Fig. 637: First row—work in PLAIN NETTING, and with the fine cotton, the length required for the border. Second and third rows—as the first row.

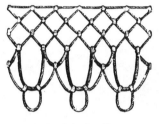

FIG. 637. NETTING—EDGING.

Fourth row—take the coarse cotton, and work the first Loop in Plain Netting; for the next Loop, work it in Plain Netting, but pass the thread twice round the Netting needle; repeat these two loops to the end of the row. Fifth row—Knot the fine cotton into the first Loop on the last row (a small Loop), and work two Loops in Plain Netting into the long Loop in the last row, then one Loop into the small Loop on the last row, and two into the next large Loop. Continue to the end of the row.

FIG. 638. NETTING—EDGING.

(3.) The Edging shown in Fig. 638 is an extremely light and pretty finish to curtains, or other articles that require borders. It is worked with a flat Mesh an inch and a quarter in width, and a round Mesh an inch in circumference, and with Strutt's knitting cotton No. 12. To work: Make a FOUNDATION with single cotton the length required for the Edging. First row—fill the Netting needle with doubled cotton, take the flat Mesh, and Net in PLAIN NETTING into every Loop of the Foundation. Second row—fill the Netting needle with single cotton, and use the round Mesh; Net the first two Loops together, and continue to Net two Loops together to the end of the row. Third row—use the round Mesh and the single cotton, and Net in Plain Netting into every Loop. Fourth row—take the flat Mesh and the doubled cotton, and Net two Loops into every Loop of the preceding row. Fifth row—use the round Mesh and the single cotton, and Net every Loop of the last row separately.

(4.) The Edging given in Fig. 639 is used for curtains and other articles that require borders; but, as it is a pattern that can be repeated indefinitely, it can also be

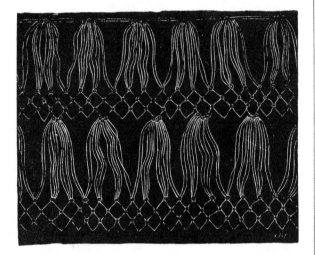

FIG. 639. NETTING—EDGING.

used to make curtains, centres, and other Netting patterns. The Edging should be worked with Strutt's Knitting cotton No. 12, and with two Meshes of unequal size, a flat Mesh an inch in width, and a round Mesh half an inch in circumference. To work: NET the FOUNDATION in single cotton, and with the round Mesh, and make Loops enough to form the length required for the Edging. First row—take the flat Mesh, and fill the needle with doubled cotton; work in PLAIN NETTING, and make three Loops into the first Loop on the Foundation row; then miss the second and third Loops, and Net three Loops into the fourth; repeat to the end of the row, missing two Loops, and making three Loops into every third Loop. Second row—take the round Mesh, and a needle filled with single cotton; Net in Plain Netting every Loop upon the preceding row. Third and Fourth rows—repeat the second row. Fifth row—commence again at the first row.

(5.) *Scalloped.*—A Scalloped Edging is a better border to a shawl or curtain than one made of vandykes, as the half-circles composing the scallops keep their stiffness and shape better than the points of the vandykes. Scallops are all formed in Plain Netting, and can be made either of silk, cotton, or wool, and with any size Mesh or number of Loops to a scallop, the usual number of Loops to each scallop being eight, twelve, or sixteen. The varieties in the scallops are formed by the size of the Meshes used (all requiring two Meshes, and some three) and the number of rows worked. To work for a medium sized scallop: Use the same cotton as the centre of the curtain or shawl is worked in, and three flat Meshes of different sizes, the middle size being the same as used in the centre part of the article. First row—with the largest Mesh work twelve or sixteen Loops into the first Loop of the edge, then miss eight or twelve Loops on the border, and work twelve or sixteen Loops into the ninth or thirteenth Loop; continue to the end of the row, missing a fixed number of Loops between each worked Loop. Second and Third rows—work into every Loop, using the medium-sized Mesh. Fourth and Fifth rows— work into every Loop, using the smallest sized Mesh. This scallop can be enlarged by a greater number of rows worked upon the two last-used Meshes, or made smaller by one row only being worked upon each Mesh.

(6.) *Vandyke.*—A pointed Edging, as shown in Fig. 640, particularly useful for making ornamental borders to d'oyleys, chair backs, and toilet cloths. After the plain Vandyke Edging has been Netted, a pattern should be Darned upon it in DARNED NETTING. To work as shown in Fig. 640: Make one loop upon the FOUNDATION LOOP, Net in PLAIN NETTING two Loops into this first loop, and INCREASE one Loop in each row until there are five Loops in a row. Then Increase at the end of every alternate row, until there are nine Loops in the row, taking particular care that the Increase is always made upon the same side of the work. In the next row, leave unworked four Loops on the side which has not been Increased, and thus form the Vandyke; work the other five (the dotted line in the illustration shows this row), continue the work, and Increase in every alternate row until there are nine Loops again, and then miss the four upon the Vandyked edge as before.

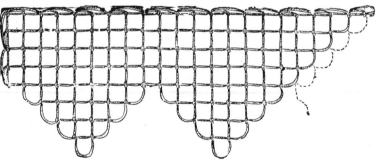

FIG. 640. NETTING—VANDYKE EDGING.

Fichu.—This can be worked either in bright-coloured silks or fine wools, and with a flat Mesh half an inch in width. The Loop is used in Plain Netting; but this can be varied and rendered more ornamental if worked as explained in Fly Netting. To work: Commence with one Loop upon the FOUNDATION LOOP, and INCREASE every row by working two Loops into the last Loop. Continue to do this until the widest part of the Netting is as long as the widest part of the Fichu, and then commence to work a border. For this, two different sized Meshes are required, one round, ½in. in diameter, and one flat, ½in. wide. Net the first and second rows round the sides of the Fichu, but not across the widest part, in PLAIN NETTING. Third row—take a different coloured wool or silk to that used in the Fichu, and the large Mesh; double the wool or silk, and Net it into every Loop of the second row. Fourth and Fifth rows—like the first row. Sixth row—use the large Mesh and the doubled wool, and Net two Loops into every alternate Loop upon the last row. Seventh and eighth rows—like the first row. Ninth row—like the sixth, but work the first double Loop into the second Loop, and not into the first on the row. Tenth and Eleventh rows—as the first row. Twelfth row—carry this row all round the Fichu; use the large flat Mesh and the coloured wool, but single, not double. Net eight Loops into the first Loop on the row, miss two Loops, Net eight Loops into the next Loop, miss two Loops, and repeat to the end of the row. Thirteenth and Fourteenth rows—Plain Netting into every Loop with the wool or silk used in the body of Fichu. Fifteenth row—use the round Mesh and the coloured wool, but single, not double; put the wool twice round the Mesh, miss a Loop, Net six Loops into the corresponding six on the row, put the wool again twice round the Mesh, miss a Loop, and Net six Loops as before into the corresponding Loops upon the row. Sixteenth row—work as in the fifteenth row, but Net the four centre Loops of that, and miss the outside ones, and pass the wool three times round the Mesh. Seventeenth row—as the fifteenth row, but Net the two centre Loops and miss the outside ones, and pass the wool four times round the Mesh.

Fringe (1).—This fringe is all worked in Plain Netting, and can be worked with single Berlin wool and flat Meshes an inch and half an inch in width, or with Crochet cotton of a medium size, and flat Meshes half an inch and a quarter of an inch in width. First, second, and third rows—PLAIN NETTING with the small Mesh into every Loop on the edge of the article. Fourth row—use the large Mesh, and work four Loops into the first Loop of the last row, miss two Loops on the last row, and work four Loops into the fourth Loop; repeat to the end, working four Loops into every third Loop, and miss the ones between. Fifth row—use the small Mesh, and Net into every Loop. Sixth row—use the large Mesh, and work four Loops into the second Loop on the last row, and miss the next two Loops, repeat to the end, work four Loops into every third Loop on the last row. Seventh row—as the fifth. Eighth row—as the sixth.

(2). Work with two Meshes, one half the size of the other, and use the same cotton as that with which the body of the article has been netted. First row—Net in PLAIN NETTING with the small Mesh into every Loop at the edge. Second, Third, and Fourth rows—Plain Netting, with the small Mesh. Fifth row—Plain Netting, with the large Mesh. Sixth row—draw the first Loop through the second, Net the second Loop, first using the small Mesh, and then Net the first; draw the third Loop through the fourth, and Net the fourth and then the third; repeat to the end of the row. Seventh row—use the small Mesh, and Net in Plain Netting. Eighth row—cut a number of 4-inch lengths of cotton, double them, and knot three into every Loop.

Hair-nets.—Net with fine Netting silk and a small round Mesh, work in PLAIN NETTING, and place upon the FOUNDATION LOOP twelve Loops, and Net in Plain Netting backwards and forwards for twelve rows to form a perfect square. Fasten off and pass a Loop through the middle of the square, so that all the edge Loops can be easily worked into, and Net all round the square. IN-CREASE at every corner by working two Loops into the corner Loop. Work round and round, Increasing in the corner Loops in every second round until the size required for the Hair-net is obtained; then work a round with a quarter-inch Mesh, and into this pass a piece of elastic with which to draw the net together. A circular Hair-net is Netted after the instructions given in CIRCLE.

Hammocks.—These should be very strong, and should, therefore, be made with mattress twine, and with a round Mesh, 3 inches in circumference, and a long, thin, wooden needle, made for Netting up twine, and with notched, and not scalloped, ends. Net thirty Loops, and then work sixty rows. Run a stout cord through the FOUNDATION ROW, and through the last row, and attach hooks to these with which to suspend the Hammock, and draw the edges of each side slightly together, by running a coloured cord up them, and fasten them with that to the top and bottom of the Hammock. Slip a notched bar, 27 inches long, and 1 inch in width, across the upper and lower ends of the Hammock when it is in use. A more ornamental Hammock can be formed by working with a double thread in Fly Netting. To do this, make one thread of twine, and the other of a bright-coloured, coarse worsted; and when the Netting is finished, cut the worsted thread, and fluff it up into a ball round the Knot.

Lawn Tennis Ball Bag.—This is useful for carrying balls about in, and for keeping them together when not in use. To make: Take some fine twine, and a three-quarter inch flat Mesh, and make a small FOUNDATION LOOP, into which work six Loops in PLAIN NETTING; unite them together, as in the directions for a CIRCLE, and continue to INCREASE as there directed for eight to twelve rounds, according to the size required for the bag; then work round after round without any Increase until a bag a foot and a half in length is obtained; cut away the spare twine, and run a piece of strong tape through the top round of the meshes, with which to draw the mouth of the bag together.

Lawn Tennis Net.—The Nets for lawn tennis are made of various dimensions, but all on the same plan, the alteration being in the width and length, which is done by working as in Oblong Netting. Nets are varied in size according to Tennis rules; they are mostly made 2½ feet in width, and 8 or 9 yards in length, and with a 2in.

Loop. To make: Procure good mattress twine, a flat Mesh of an inch in width, and a wooden needle. Commence with one Loop on the FOUNDATION LOOP, and work as directed in OBLONG NETTING; make the Loops with FISHERMAN'S KNOTS, and not in Plain Netting. INCREASE in each row until thirty-two Loops (for a 3-feet net) are in a row, and then Increase upon one end of the row, and DECREASE upon the other to form the straight piece of the net. Measure the length from time to time, and when 8 or 9 yards can be measured from the first Loop to the last Increase, commence to Decrease in every row without any Increase until only one Loop remains. Soak the Net, when finished, in indiarubber solution, or in boiled linseed oil, to render it waterproof.

Mittens.—Work with Meshes No. 3 and No. 6, and fine black or coloured Netting silk. Six or seven skeins of this are required, according to the length of the Mitten. The size given is for a Mitten 12 inches long. Commence by putting upon the FOUNDATION LOOP forty-eight Loops, and work with No. 6 Mesh eight rows, either in PLAIN NETTING or in CROSS NETTING; then, with the smaller Mesh, Net twelve rows in Plain Netting. Continue this Plain Netting with the same mesh for forty-eight rows, or make the same number of rows with two coloured silks in FLY NETTING, cutting one of the silks when the Mitten is finished and fluffing it as a ball round the knots. Work six rows in Plain Netting with the large Mesh, which completes the part of the Mitten up the arm. Unite the ends of the netting, and Net with small Mesh one round, INCREASE on the twelfth Loop and on the fourteenth, but not upon the other Loops (the Increase on these Loops is for the thumb). Net sixteen rounds, Increasing two Loops, to form the thumb, in the two Loops already mentioned every other round; finish off the thumb by Netting, upon the Loops that have been formed by the Increasing, seven to nine rows, according to the length required, Decreasing two Loops in every row, and working the last few rows like Edging No. 636 upon a very fine Mesh. Continue to Net the hand of the Mitten for sixteen plain rows with the small Mesh, and then finish with a SCALLOPED EDGING. Ornament the back part of the hand with tufts of silk matching the silk used in the Fly Netting upon the arm of the Mitten.

Netted or Darned Insertions.—These insertions look very well as stripes between coloured satin for antimacassars or sofa covers. Fig. 641 is worked with Evans' Crochet cotton No 40, and a flat Mesh three-quarters of an inch in width. To work: Net six rows of PLAIN NETTING of the length required for the antimacassar, and starch the Netting slightly. CROCHET the edges of the Netting as follows: One DOUBLE CROCHET into the first Loop, one CHAIN, one Double Crochet into the next Loop, continue to the end, and work both edges in this manner. Then TACK the Netting on to stiff paper, and Crochet along each side of each row of Knots, except the middle row, with one Double Crochet into the first Loop, one Chain and one Double Crochet into the next. Then DARN with fine Knitting cotton the pattern shown in Fig. 641 upon the meshes. Darn in and out five threads for the outside piece of the pattern, Knot two threads

together for the next piece, Knot four threads together for the next piece, and for the middle Knot the two centre

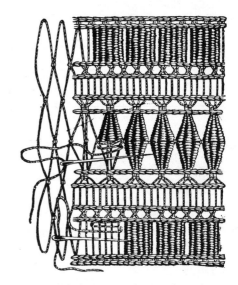

FIG. 641. NETTED AND DARNED INSERTION.

threads of four threads together, and then Darn them draw the ends together in the Darning, and expand the middle to form the cone shape in the pattern.

To work Fig. 642: This insertion differs but little from the one above, but is not so wide nor so much Darned. Use a half-inch Mesh and Walter and Evans' Crochet cotton No. 40, and Net five rows of PLAIN NETTING the

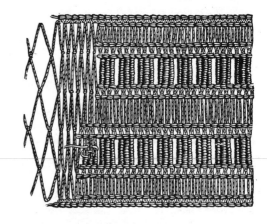

FIG. 642. NETTED AND DARNED INSERTION.

length required. CROCHET the edges of the insertion and in rows upon each side of every row of Knots, in the manner described above. For the Darned part of this pattern, DARN together six threads of the FOUNDATION, and draw these close, to have a clear space between the thick lines so formed. To Darn these six threads together, Darn over and under two threads at a time.

Purses.—Long netted purses for gentlemen's and ladies' use are either made all of one colour of Netting

LINEN EMBROIDERY.—HUNGARIAN.

LINEN EMBROIDERY.—GERMAN.

silk, or with contrasting shades. The purses are generally netted in Plain Netting, but single and treble Diamond Netting, or Cross Netting, can be used upon them if wished.

To net a *Gentleman's Purse*, 10 inches in length: Use Mesh No. 13, and five skeins of coarse Netting silk. Work eighty Loops into the FOUNDATION LOOP, and net rows of PLAIN NETTING until the 10 inches required are made. The same purse, if made with fine Netting silk, will require one hundred Loops to commence with. Sew up the sides of the purse, leaving a space for the opening; BUTTONHOLE round this opening with the Netting silk, then TACK it up, and place the purse upon a piece of wood, of a barrel shape, to stretch it; damp the Netting, and leave it on the wood until dry, when take it off, untack the opening, sew up the ends, and add the tassels and the rings. If a piece of wood of the proper size and shape is not procurable, damp and stretch the Netting, and then pass a warm iron over it.

To net a *Lady's Long Purse*, 9 inches in length: Use Mesh No. 10, and five skeins of fine Netting silk, of two different shades. Put ninety Loops upon the FOUNDATION LOOP, and Net in PLAIN NETTING, with the two colours, seven rows of the colour of which there are three skeins, and five rows of the colour of which there are two skeins. Repeat until the length required is obtained. Finish the purse in the same manner as described in the Gentleman's Purse.

To net a *Purse with Beads*: Use Mesh No. 3, and four to five skeins of fine Netting Silk, and the smallest beads procurable. Put ninety Loops upon the FOUNDATION LOOP, and close them up so as to have no seam. Work three rounds in PLAIN NETTING without any beads; in the fourth round put a bead into every third Loop; in the fifth round, a bead upon the loop upon each side of the bead in the last round; and work the sixth round like the first round. Repeat these three rounds for 3½ inches, then make the opening of the purse, by working as rows, and not as rounds, for 2 inches, and continue to put the beads in as before; then return to the rounds, and work 3½ inches as before, and end with three plain, unbeaded rows. Elaborate patterns for beading purses can be made by using the small diaper and sprig patterns that are printed for Berlin wool designs.

Stove Ornaments.—These netted ornaments are extremely light and pretty, and as they wash, will remain good for many years. The centre part is Netted with medium-sized Crochet cotton, the border with Strutt's Knitting cotton No. 12, and the Meshes used are flat, and half an inch and a quarter of an inch in width. To work: Commence the work at the side, and Net in PLAIN NETTING seventy-four Loops upon the FOUNDATION LOOP. First row—work a row of Plain Netting with the small Mesh. Second and following ten rows—Plain Netting with the small Mesh. Thirteenth row—in Plain Netting with the large Mesh. Fourteenth row—Net in Plain Netting with the same Mesh, but net the second Loop before the first, the fourth before the third. Fifteenth row—repeat the fourteenth row, but Net with the small Mesh. Sixteenth to Twenty-seventh rows — work with

the small Mesh in Plain Netting. Twenty-eighth row—repeat from the thirteenth row. Repeat the pattern twelve times, and at the end work twelve plain rows with the small Mesh, and then one plain row with the large Mesh. Commence the border on the Foundation side, and work round three sides of the Stove Ornament as follows: First row—use the small Mesh and the knitting cotton, work a plain Loop into the first six Loops, five LONG LOOPS into the seventh Loop, five Long Loops into the eighth Loop, and repeat from the commencement. Second and third row—use the small Mesh, and Net into every Loop. Fourth row—use the large Mesh, and Net a Loop into every Loop, but Net the second Loop before the first, and the fourth before the third. Fifth row—use the small Mesh, Net twelve Loops into the corresponding twelve Loops on the last row, three Long Loops into the thirteenth Loop, three Long Loops into the fourteenth, and three Long Loops into the fifteenth Loop, and repeat from the commencement. Sixth and seventh rows—use the small Mesh, and Net into every Loop. Eighth row—Net into every Loop with the large Mesh. Ninth row—Net into every Loop with the small Mesh. Having completed the border, starch and pull out the netting, run a tape through the side that has no border, and tie the Ornament with the tape to the register, fill the grate with muslin threads, arrange the netting over them, and finish by laying a few fern leaves upon the netting.

Netting Crochet.—*See* CROCHET NETTING.

Netting Needles.—These Needles are employed in conjunction with MESHES, and vary in length, according to the coarseness and width of the work on which they are used. They are divided at each end, the two points converging together, and the yarn or silk is wound round through these forks, from one end to the other, lengthwise along the Needle. There is a small hole through the latter, below the fork at one end, through which the yarn or silk is threaded to secure it. Netting Needles may be had in steel, wood, ivory, and bone.

Network.—In olden days, Netting, when ornamented with Darning, or when worked quite plainly, was known as Filatorium and Network, and ranked as a Lace. The Network produced by the Egyptians was worked with silk or gold threads, or with extremely fine flax thread, and further ornamented with beautiful patterns darned upon it with many colours, and was far superior to the productions of modern times. From the twelfth to the sixteenth century, Network was largely worked in Europe, and was used for ecclesiastical purposes.

New Lace Appliqué.—A modern work intended to give the appearance of lace laid upon satin. To work: Trace out a bold design of leaves and flowers upon a gaily coloured piece of satin. Lay some open meshed Brussels Net upon this foundation, and attach it to the design by lines of BUTTONHOLES. Work these lines round the design, and use various coloured filoselles, so as to diversify the colouring. When the outline is finished, cut away the Brussels Net where not secured, and finish the leaves and flowers by working veins and centres to them with bright silks. Connect the pattern together with stems and tendrils worked with dark filoselles.

Nœuds.—A French term, signifying bows of ribbon, or other materials, employed in Millinery and Dressmaking.

Noils.—The short wool taken, by combing, from the long staple wool, and employed to give thickness and solidity to wool stuffs, in the weaving.

Normandy Lace.—The Laces made in Normandy are of various descriptions. Of the narrow thread Pillow Laces, the Petit Poussin, Ave Maria, Point de Dieppe and Havre, and Dentelle à la Vierge are well known, as well as the imitation Brussels and Valenciennes; but besides these, there are the Silk Blondes, both black and white, which are manufactured at Caen and Bayeux, and which are similar to the Silk Blondes made at Chantilly and in Spain.

Norman Embroidery.—This is a modern work, founded upon Crewel Work, and consists of working a conventional design in the Crewel Stitch, and then covering over certain parts of that stitch with open and fancy Embroidery Stitches. To work: Select a Crewel Work design of a stiff and regular pattern, and trace this upon Oatmeal Cloth or a coloured material. Fill in all the design with CREWEL STITCH, and work with Crewel wools and with shades that are appropriate. Select various light shades of filoselle silk that harmonise with the colours used in the Crewels, and cover over the latter with light BARS made with the filoselles and with WHEELS, DOTS, HERRINGBONE, TRELLIS, and other Embroidery Stitches. Fill in the centres of the flowers with stamens and knots made with the filoselle, and cross all the stems and sprays supporting the foliage and flowers with Bars, also made with filoselle.

Northampton Lace.—Many descriptions of Pillow Lace are made in Northamptonshire, but none of them are of English invention, they all being copies of Brussels, Lille, and Valenciennes Laces. They are all good imitations, but the two best are the one shown in Fig. 643, of Lille Lace, with a ground that vies, as to its clearness and regularity, with that of foreign manufacture, and the narrow Valenciennes Lace. Much of the lace made in Northamptonshire is called Baby

FIG. 643. NORTHAMPTON LACE.

Lace, as it was at one time made in the narrow widths that were used for children's caps. Baby Lace is now obsolete, but the lace shown in Fig. 643 is still manu-factured, and is frequently called English Lille, as it possesses the beauty of Lille Lace, and imitates its clear ground and small running pattern.

Norwegian Yarn.—This yarn is made of the undyed hair of the Scandinavian lamb, which is very soft, and is especially suitable for the knitting of shawls and other wraps. It is to be had in both white and grey—the natural colours—and is sold by the skein.

Norwich Crape.—A textile composed of a silk warp and a worsted woof, generally of two different colours, or at least, of two shades of one colour. It somewhat resembles Bombazine, but is not twilled, and may be had in all colours.

Noué.—A French term to signify knotted, employed by dressmakers with reference to certain styles of trimming.

Nuns' Cloth.—This material is otherwise called Toille de Nonne, and by Americans, Bunting. It is a woollen dress material, superior to Grenadine in appearance and durability, yet light, is plainly woven, and to be had of every colour, as well as in white, but is chiefly worn in black. It is made in various widths, from 30 inches to 1 yard, and is, with Beige, Carmelite, and the comparatively new dress material, produced especially for mourning wear, called DRAP SANGLIER, a variety of the same description of cloth which is known as "Bunting"; but the latter is of so loose and coarse a texture, that its use is almost entirely restricted to the making of Flags. The name originated in Somersetshire, where the word Bunting was used for Sifting; and this worsted cloth, being of very open make, was employed for the sieves for sifting meal. There are few makes of woollen stuff which can be had in more extensive varieties of quality; the fine and delicately tinted light and white kinds being suitable for evening dresses; the dark, thick, and rough sorts equally satisfactory for ordinary wear, and, being durable, and not liable to creasing, are especially suited for travelling costumes. The Monks of Mount Carmel, being dressed in habits made of undyed wool, and woven after the manner of Nuns' Cloth, Beige, &c., originated the name of Carmelite, in France, for the stuff so called.

Nuns' Work.—Crochet, Knitting, Netting, Cut Work, Drawn Work, Pillow and Hand-made Laces, Satin Embroidery, and Church Embroidery, were at one time all known by this name. From the eleventh to the fifteenth century the best needlework of every kind was produced by the Nuns, who imparted their knowledge to the high born ladies who were educated in their convents, and from this circumstance each variety, besides being distinguished by a particular name, was classed under the general one of Nuns' Work.

Nutria, or Coypou Fur (*Myopotamus Coypus*).—An animal of the genus Rodent, somewhat resembling both the Musquash and the Beaver; it is smaller than the latter, but larger than the former, and inhabits the banks of rivers in Buenos Ayres and Chili, being a kind of water rat. Nutria skins are dressed and dyed as a substitute for sealskin, and are also used, in the manufacture of hats, as a substitute for beaver.

O.

Oatmeal Cloths.—Under this descriptive name there are textiles of Cotton, Linen, and Wool, deriving their designation from having a corrugated face, woven to represent Bannock Cakes. These cloths are thick, soft, and pliant, may be had in all colours, and are 54 inches in width. There are also Fancy Oatmeal Cotton Cloths, woven in diamond designs and stripes, but uncoloured, and measuring only 18 inches wide. Some amongst these varieties are employed as a foundation for Embroidery in Crewels and Silks, a thin quality being used for dress, and a thicker one for upholstery.

Octagon Loop.—A name applied to the loop made in Pillow Lace in BRUSSELS GROUND.

Œillet.—The French term for an Eyelet-hole.

Oilcloth.—A coarse hempen fabric, the fibres of which are saturated with oil; when dry and hard, it is painted with devices in various colours, by means of stencil plates, or blocks cut for the purpose, as in engraving. These cloths are employed for the covering of floors, stairs, &c.

Oiled Leather.—This description of Leather is sometimes called Washed Leather, being only an imitation of CHAMOIS LEATHER. The Leather is dressed with fish oil, and, when partially dried, is washed in a strong alkali, to render it very soft and pliable. It is employed as a lining, particularly for waistcoats and women's petticoats, perforated with small round holes, to obviate its air-tight character; it is also used for riding breeches and trousers, and for gloves.

Oiled Silk.—Silk so prepared by saturation in oil as to be made waterproof. It is used for linings, and likewise for medical and surgical covering of bandages and compresses. It is semi-transparent, and may be had in green and in gold colour.

Oiled Tracing Paper.—This substance is used in Embroidery, and many kinds of variegated needlework, for the purpose of obtaining a correct outline of the design to be worked, without the trouble of drawing the same.

Old English Embroidery.—A modern imitation of Anglo-Saxon embroidery. In this work, Crewels are used instead of gold and silver threads, and fancy Embroidery stitches fill in the design. To work: Use CREWEL STITCH to cover all the outlines of the design, and fill all centres with LACE or COUCHING STITCHES. Work stems and sprays with HERRINGBONE and FEATHER STITCHES.

Old Lace.—A term indifferently used either for Pillow or Needle-point Laces worked before the introduction of machine-made net grounds to Laces.

Oleograph Work.—A modern Embroidery, and a combination of Watteau figures printed in colours on to the material and embroidery. The colours are fast, and the work can be washed. To work: Procure the material, upon which a Medallion with coloured figures is printed Make a frame for the same with lines of CREWEL STITCH, and work a garland of small flowers in SATIN STITCH. and round the frame.

Ombré.—The French term for shaded. Braid Ombré is so called because it is shaded with graduated tints, from light to dark, of one colour.

Onlaid Appliqué.—*See* APPLIQUÉ.

Open Braid.—One of the stitches used in Pillow Lace making, and described under BRAID WORK.

Open Crochet Stitch.—*See* CROCHET.

Open Cross Bar.—The Bars that connect the various parts of Modern Point and Point Lace together are called Open Cross Bars when they cross each other to form that figure. To make: Throw two strands of thread from one edge of lace to the opposite piece, and cover the lines thus made with close BUTTONHOLE until the centre of it is reached. Throw from this place a thread to cross the first at right angles, and cover this with Buttonhole to the centre of the first line; throw a thread from there, so as to be exactly opposite the last one, cover that with Buttonhole to the centre of the first line, and then finish by covering the unworked part of the first line with Buttonhole.

Open Cross Braid.—One of the stitches used in Pillow Lace making, and described under BRAID WORK.

Open Cross Stitch.—*See* CROCHET.

Open Diamonds Stitch.—This is a general term applied to stitches used as Fillings in Modern Point and Point Lace that are worked with close rows of Buttonhole, except where an open space is left, which takes the shape of a die or diamond. Cadiz, Escalier, and Point d'Espagne are all varieties of Open Diamonds, as are the patterns of

FIG. 644. OPEN DIAMONDS.

Fillings shown in Figs. 402 and 403 (see page 206). To work in the Open Diamond shown in Fig. 644: Commence with twenty-one close BUTTONHOLES worked across the space to be filled, and work three plain rows. Fourth row—work 9 Buttonhole, miss the space of three, work 9, miss 3, work 15. Fifth row—work 18 Buttonhole, miss 3, work 3, miss 3, work 15, miss 3, work 3, miss 3, work 12. Sixth row—work 15 Buttonhole, miss 3, work 9, miss 3, work 9, miss 3, work 9, miss 3, work 9. Seventh row—work 12 Buttonhole, miss 3, work 15, miss 3, work 3, miss 3, work 24. Eighth row—work 9 Buttonhole, miss 3, repeat three times, and then work 15. Ninth row—work 18 Buttonhole, miss 3, work 3, miss 3, work 15, miss 3, work 3, miss 3, work 12. Tenth row—work 15 Buttonhole *, miss 3, work 9, repeat from * three times. Eleventh row—work 12 Buttonhole, miss 3, work 15, miss 3, work 3, miss 3, work 24. Twelfth row—work 9 Buttonhole *, miss 3, work 9, repeat from * twice, miss 3, work 15. Thirteenth row—work 12 Buttonhole, miss 3, work 15, miss 3, work 3, miss 3, work 24. Fourteenth row—work 15 Buttonhole *, miss 3, work 9, repeat from * three times. Fifteenth row—work 18 Buttonhole, miss 3, work 3, miss 3, work 15, miss 3, work 3, miss 3, work 12. Repeat from the fourth row until the space is filled in.

Open Dice Stitch.—Similar to OPEN DIAMONDS STITCH.

Open Dots.—These are holes made in Pillow Lace, in order to lighten any part of the design that might look too thick and close. To work: Continue to work in CLOTH STITCH until the centre of the lace is reached, there make a TURNING STITCH, and return to the same edge; take up the BOBBINS upon the other side, work to the opposite edge and back again to the hole, the last stitch being a Turning Stitch; now return to the first worked Bobbins, and work right across the lace with them, and continue to work in Cloth Stitch with the whole number of the Bobbins until the place is reached where another open Dot has to be made.

Open English Lace.—A stitch used in Point Lace and Modern Point Lace, similar to POINT D'ANGLETERRE.

middle, slant upwards again with the twisted threads, and sew to the opposite side, and to the band there, and repeat this twisting and sewing to the opposite sides, and to the middle, until the right number of Fibres is obtained. Work the other small leaves in the same way, and with the same number of Bobbins, but hang on seven pairs of Bobbins for the large leaf. To finish the spray: Work the flower in STEM STITCH for the outside petals, and in RAISED WORK for the inside. Work the Shamrock edge in CLOTH and HALF STITCH, the rosettes in STEM STITCH with CUCUMBER PLAITINGS, and the band with OPEN BRAID and CROSS PLAITINGS. For the ground, rule some blue paper in squares, and stitch the various pieces of lace on to this with their right side downwards;

FIG. 645. OPEN FIBRE IN HONITON LACE.

Open Fibre.—These are used in Honiton Lace making to form open centres to various parts of the pattern, and are illustrated in the open work in the centre leaves of Fig. 645. To work the leaves shown in centre spray: Commence at the lowest leaf, hang on five pairs of BOBBINS at the top of the main fibre, and work STEM down it; at the bottom of the leaf, hang on another pair of Bobbins, and work the band round the leaf in CLOTH STITCH, joining the middle fibre to this at the top. Carry the band in Cloth Stitch round one of the adjoining leaves, cut off a pair of Bobbins when the bottom of that leaf is reached, work the Fibre stem upon it, join to the band, and cut off the Bobbins. Work the open inside of the leaf thus: Sew a pair of Bobbins to the band near the top of the leaf, TWIST the threads, slant them downwards, and sew to the

then pin the paper on the Pillow and work along the lines. Hang on four pairs of Bobbins, and work over these lines in Stem Stitch and with a PEARL EDGE, and work in squares. Make all the lines one way first, and at the cross lines make a SEWING, thus: Drop the loop underneath the line to be sewn to, and pass the other through it. When, in the process of making the ground, the lace is reached, plait BEGINNERS' STEM with the Bobbins, after sewing to the lace, down to the next line, in preference to cutting off the Bobbins and re-tying them.

Open Knotting.—*See* MACRAME.

Open Lace.—A name sometimes applied to Netting when ornamented with a Darned Pattern. *See* DARNING ON NETTING.

Open Ladder Stitch.—See *Ladder Stitch* in EMBROIDERY STITCHES.

Open Stitches, Tricot.—*See* CROCHET.

Open Work.—A term employed in Embroidery, Lacemaking, and Fancy Work of all kinds, such as Knitting, Netting, Tatting, Cut Work, Crochet, &c. It simply means that the work is made with interstices between the several portions of close work, or of cut or open material. Much of the Irish White Muslin Embroidery and Madeira Work is called Open Work, and is fully described under BRODERIE ANGLAISE, IRISH WORK, and MADEIRA WORK.

Open Work Stitches.—These are all EMBROIDERY STITCHES, and will be found under that heading.

Opossum Fur.—The Opossum is of the genus *Dydelphys*, and is a marsupial quadruped, of which there are several species. One of these abounds in the United States, another in Texas, and others in California, South America, and Australia. The skins measure 8 inches by 16 inches, some being of a reddish-brown colour on the back, and of a buff colour on the stomach; some grey, but called "blue Opossum," the hair being rather short, thick, and soft. The Opossum of Australia is of this description, but of a particularly rich and warm shade of red-brown and buff. There is also, in America, a longhaired species, the skins of which look handsome when made into capes, tippets, muffs, and trimmings. It is more glossy than the other varieties, although dyed black, but is not so soft to the touch. The skins of all varieties of the Opossum are employed for articles of dress, and for sofa and carriage rugs.

Opus Anglicum, or Opus Anglicanum.—A name given to English needlework produced in the time of the Anglo-Saxons, which was celebrated for its extreme beauty and delicacy of execution, and also for the introduction of a peculiar stitch, said to be invented by the workers. This stitch resembles CHAIN STITCH, but is SPLIT STITCH, and was then, and is now, used to work the faces and hands of figures in CHURCH EMBROIDERY, and in the best kind of Embroidery.

Opus Araneum. — One of the ancient names for SPIDERWORK or DARNED NETTING.

Opus Consutum.—The ancient name for APPLIQUÉ.

Opus Filatorium.—The ancient name for NETTING and DARNED NETTING.

Opus Pectineum.—This was a fabric woven in a handloom so as to imitate Embroidery; it was manufactured with the help of an instrument resembling a comb, and from this received its name.

Opus Plumarium.—The old designation for FEATHER STITCH, and for Embroidery chiefly executed in that stitch, and upon thick, and not open, foundations.

Opus Pulvinarium. — The ancient name for Embroidery worked upon open canvas materials with silks and worsted, and with CROSS and TENT STITCH. This kind of Embroidery was also called Cushion Style, from its being used for kneeling mats and cushions. Our modern BERLIN WORK answers to the old Opus Pulvinarium.

Opus Saracenicum.—The ancient name for TAPESTRY.

Opus Seissum.—One of the names given in the olden times to CUT WORK, or lace of that description.

Opus Tiratum.—See DRAWN WORK.

Organzine.—This name is applied to the silk of which the warp of the best silk textiles is made, which has been cleaned, spun, doubled, thrown, and considerably twisted, so as to resemble the strand of a rope. It is composed of from two to four strands of raw silk, each thread being separately twisted in a mill, and then two twisted together in an opposite direction to that of each separate strand, which is accomplished by reversing the motion of the machinery, thus forming a thread like a rope. When finished, Organzine is wound on reels, instead of Bobbins, from which it is made into skeins, and sorted for sale. In former times we imported this article from Italy, as the Italians kept the art of "throwing silk" a profound secret; but Mr. John Lombe (of the firm of Thomas and Lombe) privately took a plan of one of their complicated machines, at the risk of his life, and, being a wonderfully ingenious mechanic, mastered all difficulties, and so procured the desired model in the King of Sardinia's dominions, which, on his return home, resulted in the establishment of a similar set of mills in Derby; and "throwing" was commenced in England in the year 1719. Since then, great improvements have been made in the mills, on the cotton "throstle" plan, driven by steam engines; but the old, hand-turned, small machines continue to be employed on the Continent. Thus, we scarcely import any Organzine, but supply ourselves. The name Organzine is French. The material is also known as THROWN SILK.

Oriental Embroidery.—Under this title is classed all the various kinds of Embroidery produced in the East, and which are described under their own headings. The Embroideries that are the most famous are Chinese, Indian, Japanese, Persian, Bulgarian, and Turkish. Oriental Embroideries are all celebrated for the amount of labour bestowed on their execution, the costliness of the materials used about them, and the vigour and boldness of conception and colouring displayed in their design. The East has always been looked upon as the cradle of fine needlework, and the Phrygians and Babylonians as the founders of the art; and for many centuries, during which nothing of any importance in Embroidery was produced in Europe, Africa and Asia continued to manufacture most beautiful articles; but since the introduction in the East of the bright-hued dyes of Europe, and the greater demand for the work, that which has been produced has not displayed either the same good taste or minuteness of execution that distinguishes the needlework of former days.

Oriental Rug Work.—See SMYRNA RUG WORK.

Orleans Cloth.—This cloth is composed of a mixture of wool and cotton, and designed for a dress material. It is plain made, the warp being of thin cotton, and the weft of worsted, which are alternately brought to the surface in the weaving. There are some varieties which are made with a silk warp; others are figured, and they may be had both with single and double warps. They are durable in wear, are dyed in all colours, as well as in black, and measure a yard in width. The name is derived from the town in France where the Cloth was first made. The only difference between this Cloth and a Coburg is, that the latter is twilled. The chief seats of the manufacture are at Bradford and Keighley, it having been introduced there in the year 1837.

Ornamental Knot.—*See* KNOTS and MACRAMÉ.

Orphrey.—The broad band, or clavi that adorns the priest's alb, and that was also used in olden days to border the robes of knights. These were always made of the very finest needlework, and the name given to them is considered to be derived from Auriphrygium and Phrygium, by which Embroidery worked with gold and silver thread and wire was called by the Romans, from the fact of the Phrygians being celebrated makers of this kind of needlework, and most of it being imported from Phrygia. Authorities, however, differ as to the origin of the word, and some consider that it is derived from a gold fringe. The word Orphrey, in some early chronicles, is found as distinguishing this band of needlework when entirely worked with gold and silver threads, and the word Orfrey when silk threads only were used; but in all later works, Orphrey stands for both descriptions of work when placed in the particular position indicated. The bands placed vertically on an altar cloth, reredos, ecclesiastical vestment, or hangings, are all called Orphreys. They may be of gold lace, or cloth of gold, embroidery, lace, velvet, satin, silk, or stuff, and sometimes are decorated with jewels and enamels. They vary in width, as well as in material, colour, and character of their adornment. The term Orphrey is in common use with all engaged in ecclesiastical needlework. In olden times it used to be written Orfrais.

> For it full wele,
> With Orfrais laid, was everie dele,
> And purtraid in the rebaninges,
> Of dukes' storeis, and of kings.
> —CHAUCER's *Romaunt of the Rose.*

Orris.—A comprehensive term, employed in trade to signify almost every kind of Galloon used in upholstery. In the early part of the last century, it had a more restricted application, and denoted certain Laces woven in fancy designs in gold and silver. The name is a corruption of Arras. *See* GALLOONS.

Osnaburg.—A coarse linen textile, made of flax and tow, which originated in the German town in Hanover after which it is called.

Ostrich Feathers.—The Ostrich has exceedingly long and soft plumage, of which there are several varieties in texture and quality, influenced by the climate and food to which the bird has been habituated. Ostrich Feathers are imported from Mogador, Aleppo, Alexandria, and the Cape of Good Hope. The Feathers on the upper part and extremities of the back, wings, and tails are valuable in commerce, being superior in quality and colour to the others; those of the wings being employed for head-dresses. The greyish Feathers of the female are less valuable than those of the male, which are better in colour. They may be obtained dyed in every hue, the art of dyeing having been brought to great perfection,

both in this country and in France. The Feathers of the Rhea, or American Ostrich, are imported from Buenos Ayres. They are dyed by the natives, and employed for coverings of the body, as well as the head. The flossy kinds are used in South America and in Europe for military plumes; and the long brown Feathers of the wings are made into brooms and dusting-brushes.

Otter Fur.—The Otter is a native of Europe and America. Its Fur is thick, soft, and glossy, of a grey colour at the base, but tipped with brown. The Otters found in Europe are rather smaller than those of America, which latter are of a dark reddish-brown in winter, and nearly black in summer. The Indian species has a fur of a deep chestnut colour. About 500 skins are annually collected for home use. Those employed by the Russians and the Chinese are obtained from North America. The Sea Otter is a larger and more valuable animal. In China, a fine skin of the Sea Otter is valued at about £40; and older and less beautiful specimens at from £18 to £20 each.

Ouate.—The French name for Wadding, and in common use amongst French dressmakers.

Ourlet.—The French word signifying a HEM.

Outline Embroidery.—An adaptation of Indian and Oriental quilting to modern uses, and a work particularly suitable to the present desire to ornament articles in daily use with needlework. Outline Embroidery is worked upon linen or other washing materials, either with ingrain silks or cottons, or in crewels; but upon cloth and silk materials the work is executed in filoselles. The real Outline Stitches are a double RUN line and CREWEL or STEM STITCH, which is sometimes called POINT DE CABLE and ROPE STITCH, when used for this Embroidery. To Crewel Stitch, such fancy Embroidery Stitches as POINT DE RIZ, POINT DE MARQUE, and POINT LANCÉS can be added at the pleasure of the worker; but these are not real Outline Stitches, and are only introduced with caution, the motive of the work being to produce effect by the contour of an outlined, and not by a filled-in, pattern.

Fig. 646 is intended for a square for counterpane or chair back. To work: Trace a number of these squares all over one large piece of linen, and then surround each square with a border of DRAWN WORK; or work each square on a separate piece of material, and join them together with lace insertions. Draw out the design with the help of tracing paper and cloth, and work in all the outlines with CREWEL STITCH. Put the needle in across the outline line, in a slightly slanting direction; keep the cotton to the right, and draw it up. Put in these slanting stitches up the outline, and work them close together to make a line closely covered with slanting stitches.

The variety is given to the pattern by the number of colours used, by Running some lines and working others in Crewel Stitch, or by using thicker cotton to mark out the bolder lines of the design. Three shades of red are used in Fig. 646, the darkest shade being used to form the centre ornament, the four outside circles, and the two lines at the outside of the square; the second shade to form the conventional sprays that fill in the four circles;

and the lightest shade for the rest of the design. The position of these colours is shown in the illustration by the different shading of the lines. Form the fancy stitch that fills in the curves left by the rounds with a series of square lines covered with POINT DE MARQUE, and work them in the darkest shade of red.

Outline Stitch.—*See* EMBROIDERY STITCHES.

Ouvrage.—The French term for Work.

the dress material, and two of the lining—are stitched together on the inside, leaving a projecting edge. The darts of the bodice, and the seams of the sleeves, from the shoulder to the wrist, are OVER-CAST. Insert the Needle about halfway between the Running and the raw edge, from the far side of the ridge, pointing inwards; and, beginning from the left, work to the right, taking the stitches rather widely apart.

FIG. 646. OUTLINE EMBROIDERY.

Ouvroir Musselman.—*See* ARABIAN EMBROIDERY.

Ovals.—*See* GUIPURE D'ART.

Over-casting.—A method of plain sewing of as slight a character as TACKING. It is employed for the purpose of preventing the ravelling-out of raw edges of material, which have been either Stitched or Run together, such as the seams of skirts and the edges of the sleeves and armholes of a bodice, when the four edges—two of

Over-cast Stitch.—*See* EMBROIDERY STITCHES.

Over-hand Knot.—*See* KNOTS.

Over-sewing.—A method of Plain-sewing, otherwise known as Seaming, or Top-sewing, and executed somewhat after the manner of OVER-CASTING. But the great difference between Over-sewing and Over-casting is that the former is closely and finely executed for the uniting of two selvedges or folds of material, and the latter is very loosely done, and only for the purpose of keeping raw edges from ravelling out. Place the two selvedges side by side, insert the needle at the far side of the seam on the extreme right, and, having drawn it through, re-insert it close to the stitch already made, working from right to left. Extreme regularity in the length and disposition of the stitches should be carefully maintained. If the two pieces to be united have not selvedges, fold each inwards; and when the Over-sewing has been done, make a small double HEM on the wrong side, to conceal and secure the raw edges. In olden times, this stitch was known by the name of Over-hand.

Oyah Lace.—A lace made in the harems in Turkey, Smyrna, and Rhodes, and sometimes called Point de Turque. It is formed with a Crochet hook and with coloured silks, and is a description of Guipure Lace; but, as it is made by ladies for their own use, it rarely becomes an article of commerce.

P.

Pad.—A Pad of soft cotton is used in making Raised Needlepoints, such as Rose or Spanish Point. To make: Having outlined the part to be raised, fill in the space between the outline with a number of stitches made with Soft Moravian thread. Be careful to carry these from point to point of the outline at first, and then gradually INCREASE them, and lay them over each other at the part where the Raised Work is to be the highest.

Padding.—Sheets of cotton wadding inserted between other materials and their lining, sewed lightly, sometimes after the manner of quilting, so as to keep it in its right place. It is much employed in uniforms and in riding habits, as likewise to supply deficiencies in the figure, in cases of deformity, or extreme spareness.

Padlettes.—A French term, signifying spangles, or small discs of metal, of gold, silver, or steel, pierced in their centres, by which means they can be attached to dress materials. The name refers to the thin plates or scales, easily separated, in the case of some mineral substances, such as mica.

Pads.—Watered Doubles, or silk ribbons, of extra thickness, made in various colours, plain or striped, in mixed colours, expressly manufactured for use instead of watch-chains. Narrow widths in black are made as guards for eye-glasses.

Paduasoy.—Also known as Poddissoy, Pou-de-soie, and Silk Farandine. A smooth, strong, rich silk, originally manufactured at Padua, and much worn in the eighteenth century.

Paillons.—A French term for tinsel, or small copper plates or leaves, beaten till very thin, and coloured. They are employed in the ornamentation of embroidery and the stuffs for fancy or theatrical costumes. They are also used as foil by jewellers, to improve the colour and brightness of precious stones.

Painted Baden Embroidery.—A modern Embroidery and a combination of water-colour painting and embroidery. The work is executed on canvas materials or upon satin, with Crewels, Berlin wool, or Filoselles. To work: Trace the outline of a group or spray of flowers upon the material, and paint the body of the leaves, and the centres and petals of the flowers, with powdered colours mixed with Chinese white and gum-water. Grind the powdered colour in a muller until quite fine before mixing with the white and gum-water. Work the outlines of leaves and petals in CREWEL STITCH, selecting shades that contrast with the painted parts; vein the leaves, and outline stems and stalks, with the same stitch. Finish the centres of the flowers with a few FRENCH KNOTS or CROSS STITCHES.

Painters' Canvas.—This is a closely woven material, also called TICKING, to be obtained both in grey and drab colour.

Pall.—This term has two significations—viz., the covering cloth of a coffin, and the mantle or robe worn by the Knights of the Garter when in full costume. It originated in name and in construction as a mantle from the Roman *Pallium*, which was shorter than the trailing *Toga*; and our Anglo-Saxon ancestors adopted it under the name *Pœll*, when it was made of costly materials and work. The name Pall was subsequently adopted to denote a particular description of cloth, of most valuable character, worn by the nobles; this has become a manufacture of the past, to which we find many references made by distinguished authors:

> Sometime let gorgeous Tragedy
> In sceptred Pall come sweeping by.
> *Milton.*

In an old Christmas carol, quoted by Hone, in his "Ancient Mysteries," it is mentioned in reference to our Saviour, in His infancy, viz.:

> Neither shall be clothed in purple or in Pall,
> But in fine linen, as are babies all.

Pan.—A French term employed in dressmaking, synonymous with Lappet, or Tab, in English. A flat ribbon-like end of material, or flap, which is sewn to the dress at one end, but is otherwise detached from it, and hangs as a decoration, like the end of a sash.

Panache.—An old French term, still in use, signifying a decorative arrangement of feathers in a helmet, hat, bonnet, or cap. The term is adapted from the French, to the exclusion of any English word, and was sometimes written Pennache.

Panama Canvas.—The old name for Java canvas. A kind of straw material, woven coarsely, after the style of ancient Egyptian cloth. It may be had in yellow, black, and drab, and is stiff and thick in quality. Another kind of this canvas is to be had in all colours of cotton; and a third, of linen thread, in white only. All these will allow of washing.

Panels.—A term employed in dressmaking to denote certain side trimmings to a skirt, which extend down its whole length, and are attached to it at the side next to the train.

Panes, or Slashings.—Straight vertical cuts made in dresses, designed to open out, and show some under garment of contrasting colour; or designed for the insertion of a piece of rich material sewn into the Panes, to simulate the exposure to view of an under-dress. When the Panes were real, the material inside was drawn through these openings like puffings. This fashion was of very ancient date. "Tissued Panes" are mentioned by Bishop Hall in his "*Satires*," A.D. 1598, as being then in vogue; and hose, "paned with yellow, drawn out with blue," are mentioned in "*Kind Hart's Dream*," A.D. 1582. The fashion had its origin a the battle of Nancy, 1477, when the Swiss overthrew the Duke of Burgundy, and recovered their liberty. The Duke's tents were of silk of various colours, as well as of curious Tapestry, and the Swiss soldiers, tearing them to pieces, made themselves doublets of one colour, and caps, breeches, and hose of others, in which gay apparel they returned home. This signal and decisive victory has been more or less extensively commemorated ever since by the wearing of parti-coloured dress. Henry Peacham—who wrote in 1638—says, in his "*Truth of our Times*," that their dress then consisted of "doublets and breeches, drawn out with huge puffs of taffatee or linen, and their stockings (like the knaves of our cards) particoloured, of red, yellow, and other colours." These Panes, or Slashings, were subsequently adopted by the Court of France, and from thence came over to our own. Even up to the present time, the Swiss Guards of the Papal Court at Rome may be seen in this quaint style of uniform.

Pannier.—A term used in Dressmaking to signify a description of puffed overskirt, which was the chief feature in the Watteau costumes. The large balloon-like puffings at the back, and on each hip, sprang from the waist, and were trimmed all round at the extremity with a flounce, or frill, or edging of lace. The petticoat-skirt appearing beneath was always of a different material or colour.

Paper Patterns.—These Patterns are employed in Dressmaking, Millinery, Plain Sewing, and Embroidery, and are all, with the exception of the latter, made of tissue paper, in white and in colours. Whole costumes, of which the several parts and trimmings are gummed in their respective places, may be procured, demonstrating the current fashions, for the use of dressmakers and sempstresses, or for private individuals who perform their own needlework, plain or decorated. Patterns for Berlin woolwork, coloured for the assistance of the amateur embroiderer, are executed on thick paper, called Point Paper, and in Germany have long formed an article of extensive commerce with other countries. Not only arabesques and floral designs, but copies of celebrated pictures, in landscape and figures, are comprised in the trade. Good artists are engaged in the designing, and subsequent engraving or etching on copper plates, previously ruled in parallel lines, crossing each other at right angles, in imitation of the threads of an open canvas webbing; the decorative design is executed over this. Then, one colour at a time is laid upon a number of these patterns at once, with great rapidity—one sweep or touch of the square-cut brush sufficing. Thus, every separate colour is laid on. These paper patterns are available for Embroidery on satin, cloth, or any other material, in either Cross or Tent Stitch, by attaching a piece of canvas securely to them, and working on the canvas, withdrawing each thread of the same singly when the Embroidery is finished.

Designs are now very frequently executed in outline upon the canvas, or other material to be worked—at least, a single "repeat," or a specimen of a portion of the same—some part being also completed in needlework.

Paramatta.—A kind of Bombazine, the weft of which is of worsted, and the warp of cotton. It is employed as a dress material for the purpose of mourning (*see* MOURNING MATERIALS). Being of a light quality, and as crape is worn with it, a lining is indispensable for its preservation. For this, black Mull Muslin is to be recommended as the most suitable. Were a lining dispensed with, Paramatta would be found to split wherever the weight of the crape trimmings caused a strain upon it. When it was first introduced, it was composed of a silk warp and worsted weft, on which account it resembled Coburg. The cloth had its origin at Bradford, but the name it bears was derived from a town in New South Wales, on account, in all probability, of the wool of which it was composed, being imported thence. Paramatta measures 42 inches in width.

Parament, Parement. — A cuff sewn upon the outside of a sleeve, as in the coats of the eighteenth, and beginning of the nineteenth, century. The literal meaning of the term is "ornament," and it is applied to decorative additions to certain textiles, or ornamental hangings and furniture of State apartments.

Parchment Lace. — In old wardrobe accounts, this term is often applied to Pillow Laces, irrespective of their make, to distinguish them from the Laces made with the needle. The name is derived from the pattern upon which Pillow Laces are worked.

Parchment, or Vellum.—The skin of the sheep, which has been subjected to a process rendering it suitable for use as a writing material, or for bookbinding. The description known as Vellum is made of the skin of kids, calves, and stillborn lambs. It is much employed for illuminated addresses and mottoes, being further qualified for the reception of water colours, and gilding, by means of a little prepared ox-gall. The ancient and beautifully illuminated Missals were all of Vellum. Drumheads are made of Parchment procured from the skins of goats and wolves. The process by which skins are converted into Parchment is simple, and consists of steeping them in lime and water, stretching them on a frame, working well with hot water, and then applying whiting, drying each application—of which there should be several—in the sun. All grease will thus be removed from the skin. By scraping with a round, sharp knife, which needs skilful use, a fine surface is procured; and when the skin is dry, it is ready for use. Should it be desired to write upon Parchment or Vellum, rub it lightly with a damp sponge, and, when dry, the ink will hold.

Parfilage.—This work is also called Ravellings, and consists in unpicking materials into which gold and silver threads or wire have been woven. It was an extremely fashionable employment with ladies in England and France during the latter part of the eighteenth century, and was pursued to such an extent in the Court of Marie Antoinette as to have led to many comments upon it by writers of that period. The original object of the work was to obtain from old and tarnished articles the valuable threads woven into them, and to sell such threads to the gold-beaters; but when the ladies who worked at it had used up all the old materials they could obtain, they did not scruple to demand from their gentleman friends the sword-knots, gold braids, gold laces, and bands, that were often worn as part of the fashionable dress of the day; and it was said that a courtier who had a reputation to maintain for gallantry and courtesy, was likely to go to an assembly fully dressed, and to return from it as if he had fallen among thieves and had by them been deprived of all his braveries. The work is now obsolete.

Paris Cord. — A rich thick silk, with small fine ribs running across the width, from selvedge to selvedge, and deriving its name from Paris, the place of its first manufacture. There are various close imitations of it made in England, but adulterated with cotton to form the Cord, which should be of silk. Paris Cord is chiefly employed for scarves, men's neckties, and waistcoats.

Paris Embroidery. — This is a simple variety of Satin Stitch, worked upon piqué with fine white cord for washing articles, and upon coloured rep, silk, or fine cloth, with filoselles for other materials. The designs are the same as those used for Crewel Work, but are selected with small leaves shaped, like those of the olive or jessamine flowers, with distinct and pointed petals, and circular or oval-shaped fruit or berries. To work: Trace the outline of the design upon silk or piqué, use fine white cord for the piqué, and filoselle of various colours for the silk; split the filoselle in half before using it. Thread a needle with the silk, and commence the work at the extreme point of a leaf or petal. Bring the needle up at the point of the leaf, and put it into the material in the middle of the outline, at the right side of the leaf, thus making a slanting SATIN STITCH; pass it underneath the leaf, and bring it out in the outline on the left side, exactly opposite the spot it went in at. To cross the Satin Stitch just formed, put the needle in at the top of the leaf on the right side, close to the point of the leaf, and bring it out on the left side of the point. Make another slanting Satin Stitch, by putting the needle into the material directly underneath the first-made one, on the right side of the leaf, bringing it out on the left, below the stitch there, and crossing it to the top of the leaf, next the stitch there on the right side, and out again at the left. Continue making these slanting Satin Stitches and crossing them until the leaf is filled in. Work the petals in the same manner, and make FRENCH KNOTS for the stamens of the flowers. Work the berries and fruit in OVERCAST, and the connecting stalks, stems, and sprays in ROPE STITCH.

Paris Net. — A description of Net employed in Millinery.

Paris Silk Stay Laces. — These consist of a flat silk Braid, the numbers running 1, 2, and 3; the lengths, 6-4, 8-4, 10-4, 12-4, 14-4, 18-4, and 20-4.

Parure. — A French term denoting a set of collar and cuffs, as well as one of ornaments.

Passant. — The French term denoting a piping without a cord running through it.

Passé. — The French term signifying the front of a bonnet or cap. It is likewise applied to gold and silver Passing.

Passement. — This term is one by which Lace was known, in conjunction with Braids or Gimps, until the seventeenth century. The common use of the word is considered by some to have arisen from the fact that the first Pillow Laces were little more than Open Braids, and by others, that the Lace trade was much in the hands of the makers of Braids and Gimps, who were called Passementiers. These men did not for many years distinguish the one work from the other, and they then termed Needle Laces, Passements à l'Aiguille; Pillow Laces, Passements au Fuseaux; and Laces with indented edges, Passement à Dentelle. The present use of the word Passement is to denote the pricked pattern, made either of Parchment or Toile Ciré, upon which both descriptions of Lace are worked.

Passement à l'Aiguille. — A term applied to Laces made with the Needle, and not with Bobbins.

Passement au Fuseau. — A term applied to Laces made upon the Pillow, and not with the Needle.

Passementerie. — The old name for lace-workers, derived from Passement, the term used to denote Lace, whether made upon the Pillow or by the Needle. Also a French term, employed in a collective manner to denote all kinds of Lace and ribbons, but especially to signify the lace or gimp trimmings of dresses.

Passe-Passante. — This is merely an old term, signifying the securing of laid gold or other thread with PASSING, employed in reference to embroidery.

Passé Stitch. — *See* EMBROIDERY STITCHES.

Passing. — A smooth, flattened thread, of either gold or silver, of uniform size throughout, twisted spirally round a thread of silk, and used in the same way as silk for Flat Embroidery, by means of a needle which should be round, and large in the eye. It can also be used in Knitting, Netting, and Crochet Work. In the early and Middle Ages, Passing was much used in the gorgeous dresses then worn.

Passing Braid. — A description of Braid employed in Embroidery, made with gold or silver thread, such as used on military uniforms. It is a description of Bullion Braid. In Ecclesiastical Embroidery, this Braid is often substituted for stitches to fill in certain parts of the pattern.

Pasting Lace. — A narrow kind of Coach Lace, used to conceal rows of tacks.

Patching. — Replacing the worn-out portion of any garment, or piece of stuff, by another piece of material. To do this: Cut the new portion exactly even, to a thread, and place it on the worn spot, also to a thread, and upon the right side, taking care to arrange the pattern, if there be any, so that the patch and the original material shall exactly correspond. Then TACK it on, to keep it in its place, and HEM all along the four sides to the original stuff, having turned in the raw edges. Then turn the work, cut out the square, and, turning in the edges of the original material, Hem them round, snipping the patch at the corners, to make the Hem lie flat and smoothly. The Patch should be nearly an inch larger each way than the worn part which it has to cover.

If the material be calico or linen, SEW—otherwise called Top-sewing — instead of Hemming it, and well flatten the work afterwards; but it should be Hemmed on the wrong side. Flannel Patches must be HERRINGBONED. Cloth should be finely BUTTONHOLED at the raw edges. In Knitting, to re-heel or re-toe a stocking is sometimes called Patching. *See* KNITTING STOCKINGS.

Patchwork.—This needlework, which consists in sewing pieces of material together to form a flat, unbroken surface, possesses many advantages, as it is not only useful and ornamental, but forms out of odds and ends of silk, satin, or chintz, which would otherwise be thrown away, a handsome piece of work. Its manipulation requires both patience and neatness, and also calls into play both the reasoning and artistic faculties, as the designs chiefly depend for their beauty upon the taste displayed in the arrangement and selection of the shades of colour used to produce them. Patchwork originally only aimed at joining together any kinds of materials in the shapes they happened to have retained, so that, when arranged, a flat surface was produced; but, at the present time, much more is required from the worker, and the pieces used are selected from the same make of material, though of varied colours, and are cut into one or several set shapes and sizes, and put together so as to make a design by fitting into each other, both as to shape and shade, and this design is reproduced over the whole area of the work. The designs so worked out are necessarily geometrical, as it is essential that they should reply to fixed and accurate measurements, and the figures selected are the angles formed by squares, diamonds, and hexagons, in preference to the curved lines formed by circles and ovals, as the joining together of ovals and rounds in perfectly correct patterns is much more difficult to accomplish than when points are fitted into angles, as is done with the first-named figures.

Patchwork, when completed, is used for many purposes, and is made of velvet, satin, silk, leather, cloth, cretonne, twill, and chintz; in fact, of any material sufficiently soft to be cut into set shapes, and to bear a needle through it. Velvet and satin form the handsomest kind of work, and brocaded silks mixed with plain silks the next. Satin and silk are not used together, but velvet can be used with either. Cloth should be used by itself; cretonne, twill, and chintz, together or alone. It is not judicious to use a material that requires washing with one that will keep clean, but this is often done. Satin, silk, and velvet Patchwork is used for cushions, hand-screens, fire-screens, glove and handkerchief cases, and pincushions; cloth Patchwork for carriage rugs, couvrepieds, and poor people's quilts; cretonne, twill, and chintz for couvrepieds, curtains, quilts, and blinds. These larger articles require a greater amount of material than can be collected from private sources, but large silk mercers and linen drapers sell bundles of pieces by the pound. The working out of the design, and the manner of making up the patches, are the same, whatever the material or size of the article, the difference being made in the size of the patches used, they being increased or decreased for the occasion. The great essential is that every piece should be cut with perfect uniformity, and the use of a thin plate of tin, cut to the size required, is therefore recommended; the other requisites are old envelopes and letters, or other stiff pieces of writing paper, the patches, and sewing silk or cotton matching the patches in colour, with which to sew them together.

The manner of working is as follows: Select the design to be copied and the shades of material, have a piece of tin cut out to correspond with each shape to be used, and lay this upon the silks or satins, and outline round with a pencil. Cut out the shapes larger than the outline, to allow of turning in the raw edges, and divide off the various pieces, keeping together all of one shade and all of one form. Then cut out upon the paper the exact outline of the tin plate, leaving nothing for turnings. TACK the paper and the silk piece together, turning the raw edge of the silk over the paper, and Tacking it down so as to keep it from fraying out while working. Arrange the patches thus made on a table, according to

FIG. 647. APPLIQUÉ PATCHWORK, OTHERWISE CALLED "PUZZLE."

the design and the position each is to occupy as to colour; take up two that are to be close together, turn the silk sides inwards, so as to stitch them together on the wrong side, and then carefully stitch them together so that they accurately join point to point, angle to angle. Continue to sew the pieces together until the size required is obtained, then tear the paper away from the silk, and iron the work upon the wrong side. Line it with twill or some soft, smooth material, and if it is required for a counterpane or couvrepied, wad and quilt the lining; if for a mat, handkerchief case, &c., put a ball fringe round it.

Patchwork Patterns can be made from geometrical figures, and are chiefly copied from old Mosaic or Parqueterie designs; however, the designs can be made as elaborate as the worker likes, and they have been carried to the extent of working coats of arms in their natural colours, and pictures containing large-sized figures. One of these works of art was exhibited lately, and was remarkable, both for the patience and skill displayed in its execution; and the beauty of the colours employed. The following Patchwork Patterns are amongst the best, and can be enlarged or decreased in size as required:

Appliqué, or Puzzle.—The pattern shown in Fig. 647 (page 379) is a useful one for using up odds and ends of material, but a difficult one to adjust. To work: Prepare a number of pieces of cretonne or silk, 4 inches long and 3 inches wide, and slope off one corner of some of these, to form a curve, leaving the rest perfectly square. Cut a few larger pieces, 5 inches long by 3 inches wide, and out of scraps cut some odd-shaped pieces, either of the right length or width. Arrange these various pieces upon a lining, to form the design shown in the illustration; but, instead of stitching two pieces together, as in ordinary Patchwork, lay one over the other, and turn under the edges of the top piece, and RUN it to the bottom. When all are in position, and RUN to each other and the lining, work round the edge of every patch with HERRINGBONE STITCHES made with bright-coloured filoselle. The whole beauty of this design depends upon the judicious selection of the colours and patterns of the patches used.

Block.—See *Box.*

Box.—This design is sometimes known as Block Pattern. It is made by arranging diamonds so that three of them form a solid raised block, of which two sides and the top are shown; and this look is given to the flat surface entirely by the arrangement of the diamonds as to colour. To form: Procure a number of pieces of silk of three shades of one colour, such as yellow, deep gold, and chestnut, or pale blue, peacock blue, and indigo blue, and cut out from each shade an equal number of diamonds. These must be made 3 inches in length, 2 inches in width, and 2 inches from corner to corner. Join a chestnut-coloured silk to a deep gold silk, so as to make a straight line between them, the slant of the diamond in each going upward; put the dark colour on the right hand, the lighter upon the left hand. These two diamonds form the sides of the Block. Take the light yellow diamond, and make with it the top of the Block, fit it into the angle formed by the upward slant of the sides, so that it lies across them, the points of its width being upwards, and those of its length horizontal. Make a number of these blocks, shading them all in the same way, and then join them together, thus: On the left side left unattached of the light yellow top, join the under side of a chestnut piece, and to the right side of the yellow top the under side of a deep golden piece. This will produce the effect of a number of successive blocks of wood arranged diagonally across the work. The dark side of these blocks is often made with velvet, and by this arrangement the sections stand out with great boldness.

Canadian.—This particular pattern in Patchwork is one that in Canada is known as Loghouse Quilting. It is a variety made of several coloured ribbons instead of pieces of silk or cretonne, and these ribbons are arranged to give the appearance of different kinds of wood formed into a succession of squares. To work as shown in Fig. 648: Cut out in lining a square of 12 inches, and TACK to it, in its centre, a small square of

a plain colour, 1½ inches in size. Procure ribbon three-quarters of an inch wide, and of two shades of every colour used; take the two shades of one colour, and TACK the darkest shade right down one side of the small square, and overlapping three-quarters of an inch beyond at both ends; sew to this, and to the square, a dark piece at the bottom and a light piece at the top, and allow both to overlap beyond the square on the left side for three-quarters of an inch; completely surround the square by filling it in with the light colour for the side not already filled up. Change the ribbons, and again surround the square with two shades of the same colour, putting the darkest underneath the dark part and the lightest against the light part, and arrange their manner of overlapping

FIG. 648. CANADIAN PATCHWORK.

(always allowing three-quarters of an inch extra for the same) according to the design. Seven rows of ribbon are needed to fill the 12-inch square; diversify these as to colour and design, but always make two shades of one colour form a square, and place the darkest of such shades underneath each other. Prepare a large number of these 12-inch squares, and then sew them together as ordinary patches, but so that the light side of one square is next the light side of another, and the dark against the dark, thus giving the look of alternate squares of light and dark colours. Large pieces of work, like counterpanes, should be made with the 12-inch square and the three-quarter inch ribbon; but small pieces, such as cushions, with narrow ribbon and 5-inch squares.

Check.—This design is worked to imitate a chess or draught board, and is one of the easiest patterns, being formed of squares sewn together. To work: Cut out a number of 2-inch squares in pale yellow, and a number of the same size in brown. Sew the brown square to the yellow square, and underneath and above the brown sew a yellow, and underneath and above the yellow square sew a brown one. Continue to join the pieces together in this manner, so that no squares of the same hue are next to each other. Any two colours can be used, or varieties of two colours, but it is advisable not to employ more.

Cloth.—Cloth Patchwork is used for carriage rugs and tablecloths, and can be made extremely effective, either as a bordering to these articles, or as entirely forming them. As cloth is of too thick a substance to allow of turning under the raw edges, each patch has to be bound with either a narrow ribbon or braid before it is sewn into its right position in the work, and as the material is only made plain, or with patterns that would not look well if inserted, bright self-coloured foundations are selected, which are embroidered with designs worked out with silks or narrow braids. To work: Select a large-sized pattern, either of a *Hexagon* or *Mosaic* shape, cut the pieces out in the ordinary way, and Embroider them in SATIN STITCH; bind each round with a braid matching it in colour, and then stitch it into its proper position. No lining is required.

Crazy.—Made with pieces of silk, brocade, and satin, of any shape or size. The colours are selected to contrast with each other; their joins are hidden by lines of Herringbone, Coral, and Feather Stitch, worked in bright-coloured filoselles, and in the centres of pieces of plain satin, or silk, flower sprays in Satin Stitch are embroidered. To work: Cut a piece of Ticking the size of the work, and BASTE down on it all descriptions of three-cornered jagged, and oblong pieces of material. Show no ticking between these pieces, and let the last-laid piece overlap the one preceding it. Secure the pieces to the Ticking, by HERRINGBONE, BUTTONHOLE, and FEATHER STITCH lines worked over their raw edges, and concealing them. Ornament them with CROSS STITCH, TÊTE DE BŒUF, POINT DE RIZ, and ROSETTES, if the patches are small; upon large, plain patches work flower sprays, or single flowers, in coloured silk Embroidery.

Diamonds.—The Diamond (next to the Hexagon) is the most used design in Patchwork, and looks well when made of two materials, such as silk and velvet, or silk and chintz. It is the easiest of all the figures. To work: Cut out a number of Diamonds, 3 inches in length and 2¼ inches in width. Make half of them in dark materials, and half in light; join them together so that they form alternate rows of light and dark colours across the width of the article, or join four pieces of one shade together, so as to make a large Diamond, and sew this to another large Diamond made of four pieces of a contrasting colour to the one placed next it.

Embroidered.—This kind of work is only suitable for small articles, such as cushions, handkerchief cases, and glove cases. It is formed by sewing together squares of different colours, after they have been ornamented with fancy stitches. To work: Cut a number of 3-inch squares in dark velvet and silk or satin, and upon each satin or silk square, work a spray of flowers, or a small wreath, in SATIN STITCH, and in filoselles matching the colours of the flowers; make each spray or wreath of a different kind of flower, and upon a different coloured satin, but care must be taken that the colours of the satins used will blend together. Take the dark velvet squares (these should

be all of one shade), and work a pattern upon each of their sides in lines of CORAL, HERRINGBONE, or CHAIN STITCH, and then join the velvet and satin squares together—a satin and a velvet patch alternately. A simpler pattern in Embroidery is made as follows: Cut out, either in silk or satin, small 2-inch squares of various colours, sew these together, and, when all are secured, work a RAILWAY STITCH in coloured filoselles from each corner of the square to the centre, and a Satin Stitch on each side of it; this, when repeated in every square, will make a pretty design. Another manner of embroidering squares is to make them of Holland and Plush alternately, and to work a line of Herringbone or Coral on two sides of the Holland square, but to leave the velvet plain.

Honeycomb, or Hexagon.—(1). The pattern known by these names is the one commonly used in Patchwork, as it is easily executed, produces many varieties of devices, according to the arrangement of the colours, and is a shape into which most remnants of silk or cretonne may be cut. To make as shown in Fig. 649: Cut out a number of Hexagons

FIG. 649. HONEYCOMB, OR HEXAGON, PATCHWORK.

and make each of their six sides three-quarters of an inch in length. Take a dark-coloured patch, and sew round it six light patches. These should agree in their shade of colour, but need not as to pattern. Into the angles formed on the outside of these light Hexagons sew dark-coloured patches, and continue to work so as to give the appearance of a dark patch surrounded by a set of light patches.

(2). Another variety of the same pattern is made with Hexagons, and arranged to form light-coloured stars upon a dark velvet ground. It is useful when only a few, but good, pieces of brocade or satin are available, and makes handsome sofa cushions or banner screens. The Hexagons are all of the same size, and should be three-quarters of an inch upon each side. To make: Cut out a number of Hexagons in deep maroon velvet or dark peacock-blue velvet, to form the ground; then take the satin scraps, and from them cut out the same sized Hexagons. Pick up one of these, and surround it with six other pieces, arranged as follows: Should the centre piece be pale blue, surround it with old gold; should it be crimson, with yellow-pink; should it be lavender, with purple; should it be yellow, with chestnut. Make a set of these stars, and then reverse the colours, putting the centre colour as the outside colour. Arrange as follows : Sew on two rows of the ground, and for the third row sew on the stars already made, and put one of the ground-coloured Hexagons between each star; for the next two rows, only use the ground-coloured patches, and then recommence the stars. Arrange these to contrast with those first placed, and to come between them, and not directly underneath.

(3). In this variety of the same pattern it is intended to produce the appearance of Raised Work without the stuffing. To work: All the pieces are made of equal-sided Hexagons, three-quarters of an inch to every side. Cut out a number of Hexagons, all in one light colour, and of the same material—these should be either of French grey, maize, or sky blue—then cut out a number of Hexagons in dark maroon velvet, and a few in brocaded silks, either pale blue, green, chocolate, flame colour, or peach. If brocade cannot be procured for these last pieces, work each with a small flower in silks, and in SATIN STITCH. Arrange as follows: Surround each brocaded Hexagon with six dark velvet ones, and make them all up in this way. Then stitch all round these a row of the light silk patches, so that every dark section is separated from its corresponding section with a border of light silk. Finish this pattern with a straight border worked with flowers, and a ball fringe.

Jewel.—The pattern shown in Fig. 650 is intended to give the appearance of large precious stones, set round with smaller ones, and a plain setting. Each of the large squares represents a cut stone with the light falling upon it, and to produce this effect is made either of two shades of blue satin brocade, two of ruby brocade, emerald, or yellow brocade. The small squares are made of any colours, and should be much varied; the long lines, of

FIG. 650. JEWEL PATCHWORK.

plain brown gold satin. To work: Cut out in paper a perfect square, measuring 2 inches each way, run a line across this from the left-hand top point to the right-hand bottom point, and horizontally across its centre. Cut down the diagonal line from the left-hand top corner to the centre of the square; cut across to the right on the horizontal line. The two pieces the square is thus divided into will be the two sizes required for the centres of the

pattern; have them copied in tin, and cut from the smallest piece half the light shades of satin and half the dark shades, and from the larger half the dark shades of satin and half the light shades required. For the straight pieces, cut out lengths of two inches, an inch wide; and for the small squares an inch every way. Join the light satin to the dark, so as to make a perfect square, and put the light colour on the right side of the dark colour for three patches on one line, two patches on the next line, and one patch on the third line of the work, and reverse it for the next three rows; surround a square thus made with the long brown pieces, and fill in the four corners with four little squares; then join on another large square, and surround that on the three sides left open with the straight pieces of brown satin and the small squares.

Kid.—This Patchwork is generally confined to the making of such small articles as pincushions, slippers, or mats, as the Kid generally used for the purpose is cut from old gloves, and, therefore, is not of a large size; but if the pieces can be obtained of sufficient size, cushions, footstools, and other larger articles may be attempted. To work: Select an easy geometric pattern, and cut out from a tin plate a number of Kid patches without allowing for any turnings, sew these together upon the wrong side, without turning any of the Kid under, and iron the work over when finished; then take a narrow cord of gold thread or silk braid, and COUCH this down to the Kid with a silk thread matching it in colour, so that it follows and conceals all the lines of stitches. Where it is not possible to turn the cord or braid, make a hole with a stiletto, and push it through this hole to the back and fasten it off there. If the Kid is stitched together with great neatness, and a very fine needle used, the outline cord will not be required; it is only used to hide the stitches where their size or irregularity would spoil the look of the work.

Leather.—Patchwork made with leather scraps differs in one essential from true Patchwork, as the pieces are glued to a foundation, instead of stitched together, as in the other kinds; but the patterns used, and the manner of cutting out the sections, are the same. The Leather used is morocco, and is procured of bookbinders and leather dressers, and the articles formed are chessboards, folding screens, flower mats, note cases, &c. To work: Having obtained scraps of Leather, fix upon some geometrical pattern that the scraps will most easily lend themselves to make; draw this pattern quite correctly out upon a sheet of millboard, and mark out what coloured scrap is to cover each space. Arrange the scraps on a table in their proper order, make hot some common glue (which is free from impurities and of equal consistency), spread it upon the backs of the Leather, and lay the Leather in its proper place upon the millboard. Work with despatch, but be careful that every point is glued down, and that all the pieces are accurately arranged; then press the millboard in a linen press, and keep it there until the glue has quite dried. The millboard can be covered, upon its wrong side, either with silk or watered paper, pasted down upon it; the edges at the sides should either have narrow ribbon pasted upon them before the

Leather is put on, or they should be gilded with shell-gold when the work is finished. A fringe, made by cutting strips of thin narrow leather into close, ⅛-inch lines, should be used for edging mats and any flat articles that would be improved by such a finish.

Loghouse Quilting.—See Canadian.

Lozenge, or Pointed Oblong.—A useful shape for using up small scraps of material, and one that is easily made. The Lozenge is a figure of six sides, and is an oblong with pointed instead of straight ends, the points being in the centre of the width, and formed with two angles. To work: Cut out a number of these figures, make them 3 inches from point to point, 1½ inches across, and 1½ inches for the side lines, and 1 inch for the lines from the point to the side. Sew these together in rows, placing a light Lozenge next a dark one. In the next row, arrange the Lozenges in the same way, so that, when all the patches are arranged, diagonal lines of alternate shades will cross the material.

Mosaic.—(1). The pattern shown in Fig. 651 is formed with squares and acute-angled triangles. It is a good pattern to use for cretonne patches, and for small pieces of silk and satin, the large square being made with pieces of cretonne of flower designs, and the small triangles of various coloured silks. Cut out the squares, and make them 6 inches each way; cut the triangles out, and make their base 6 inches, their height 3 inches. Take a cretonne square, and sew to each of its sides the base of a dark

FIG. 651. MOSAIC PATCHWORK (NO. 1).

triangle, and fill in the triangle with three other triangles; turn all their points inwards, and make a perfect square with their bases. Make this kind of square to the four sides of the centre, and fill in the sides of the cross thus made with four large cretonne squares. Join a number of pieces together in this manner, and then sew them to each other, and make a variegated pattern by using various patterned and coloured cretonnes and silks in different sections.

(2). Another variety of Mosaic is composed of three differently cut pieces, viz., squares, parallelograms, and unequal sided hexagons. To work: Cut out the squares in pale yellow silk, and make them 1½ inches in length. Make the parallelograms 2 inches long and 1 inch wide. The two side lines are upright, and of equal lengths, but the left-hand line commences before the right-hand one, and ends before it. The top and bottom lines join these

slants together; cut half the number required in dark brown silk brocade, and half in old gold silk brocade, and make the angles slope different ways in the two colours. Cut the unequal hexagons all from the same silk or brocade, which should either be dark blue, crimson, or black—their two sides are 2 inches long, their width 2 inches, and the four lines that form the angles 1½ inches each; join four parallelograms together at their long sides, the light colour to the left of the dark, and arrange their shades alternately; let their short lines slope upwards, and form angles; join a number of these together in this way before placing them. Take two squares, and fit them into the upper angles made by the parallelograms; and, into the angle made between the two squares, fix the pointed end of the hexagons. To the left of the hexagons sew the dark side of a set of four parallelograms; to the right, the left side of another set; and to the top, fit in the angle made by the second and third pieces of a set of four parallelograms. Repeat the pattern until the size required is made, then join a piece of silk to the top and bottom as a border, and make it straight at one side, and vandyked at the other, so as to fit into the angles of the pattern for the sides; cut some half hexagons, and fit them in, and finish with a plain straight border.

(3). The pattern shown in Fig. 652 is intended to be used in making counterpanes, and other large articles, and should be worked with cretonnes or gaily-coloured chintzes. It is made with squares of two different sizes, and of pointed oblongs. To work: Cut out in tin a square of 6 inches, and form a face 1¾ inches in length at each corner, by cutting away the point of the square.

FIG. 652. MOSAIC PATCHWORK (NO. 3).

Choose a flower-patterned chintz, with bunches of flowers, and from this cut the large squares, so that each has a bunch of flowers in the centre. Cut from various coloured chintzes a number of small squares, 1¼ inches in size, and from a coloured chintz of one shade, the pointed oblongs which make 6 inches from point to point, 2½ inches wide, and 3½ inches upon each side; join five of the small squares together, place the lightest-coloured square in the centre, surround it with four of a darker shade, and fit into the four angles that are thus made the points of four of the oblongs, and into the four corners of the outer squares, the angles of four of the large squares, which have been so cut as to join on to the small squares, while their straight sides correspond with the straight sides of the oblong; join the pieces together, so that every large square is surrounded with the ornamental border made by the oblong and small squares.

This pattern can be varied almost indefinitely by altering the colouring, and the material composing the patches; thus, all the large squares can be made of a ground colour, and differently coloured and shaped flowers APPLIQUÉ on to them, and the oblongs may be formed of different shades of one colour, instead of one shade only, while the small squares can be made of velvet or satin, instead of chintz, with the centre square of plain material, and the four outer squares of variegated, or *vice versâ*.

(4). A pretty set pattern, made with three different sized patches, and forming a combination of squares, crosses, and hexagons. To work as shown in Fig. 653: Cut out in black satin a number of perfect squares, 1½ inches in width and length, and some of the same size in yellow satin. Cut out in red silk, lozenge-shaped or pointed oblong patches, each measuring 3 inches from point to point, 1½ inches across, 1½ inches for the long lines, and ¾ inch for the short lines that form the right angle. Take some violet silk, and cut a number of larger Lozenges, 4 inches from point to point, 2 inches across,

FIG. 653. MOSAIC PATCHWORK (No. 4).

3 inches for the long lines, and 1½ inches for the short lines that form the right angle. Join together five squares as a square cross, one dark square being in the centre, and four light ones round it; take a black square, and join to it four red Lozenges, and sew the points of the Lozenges to each other. Sew the cube thus made to the outside of one of the arms of the cross, so that the centre square is on the same line as the centre of the cross, and fill in the spaces on the sides of the cubes and cross, with the violet Lozenges. Continue the pattern by connecting a cross to a cube, and a cube to a cross, always filling up with the violet Lozenges. The pattern measures across one cube

and a cross 9 inches, and as each design takes four light squares, two dark squares, four red Lozenges, and four violet Lozenges, a brief calculation will give the number of patches required for a given space, to which must be added a few extra of all the sizes, to fill in corners, &c.

Raised.—This is also known as Swiss Patchwork, and is made by stuffing the patches out with wadding, so that they are well puffed up. The shapes selected for the patches should be either good sized hexagons or diamonds, and only one shape should be used, as intricate patterns, made by combining various sized pieces, render the work troublesome. To work: Cut out the hexagons or diamonds, from a tin plate pattern, from pieces of silk or brocade; size of diamonds, 2½ inches upon each side; of hexagons, 1½ inches along each of the six sides; cut the same shapes out in old lining, and make a small slit in the centre of each; sew the lining patches to the silk patches, and join each lined patch together in the pattern selected. When finished, sew a piece of silk, 5 inches wide, all round the work, and ornament it with CORAL, HERRINGBONE, and other fancy Embroidery Stitches; this border need not be lined. Take soft wadding, and push it into every slit made in the lined patches, until they are well puffed out, and quite hard, fill them in thoroughly, and be careful that the corners are not neglected. TACK over the hole made in the lining, to prevent the wadding coming out, and then line the whole of the work, including the straight border, with a piece of old silk, or red or blue twill, or cretonne. A more difficult plan, but one that does not need the extra, or second lining, is as follows: Cut out the shapes, from the tin plate, in silk or brocade, and cut out cretonne or good twill linings to fit them, join these linings to the patches, but leave one side in all of them unsecured. Join the patches together as a row, leaving the open side of them exposed. Into this stuff the wadding, taking care to make each section quite hard and full. Sew the lining up, tack on another row of patches, and stuff them out as before, and continue to sew on row after row, and stuff them, until the size required is made.

Right Angles.—The principle of the pattern shown in Fig. 654 is much the same as that of the Box Pattern, but

FIG. 654. RIGHT ANGLES PATCHWORK.

in this case, the diamonds forming the design are cut away, so as to form a number of right angles. To work:

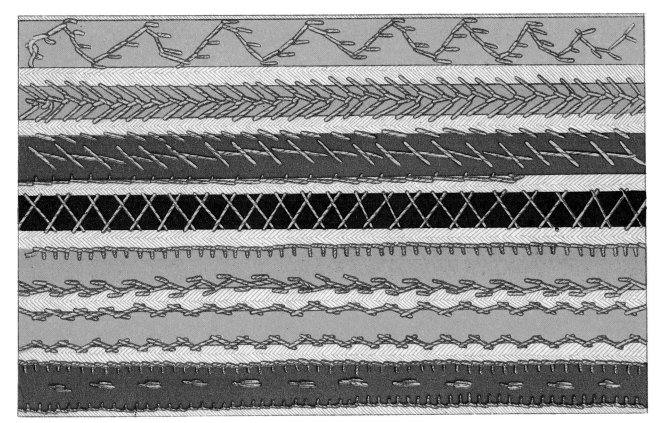

TICKING WORK.

RUG WORK OR SMYRNA KNITTING.

Procure a number of pieces of silk, three shades of one colour, such as pink, crimson, and maroon, of which the darker shade is brocaded. Cut out a diamond on paper, length 3 inches, width 2 inches, from point to point; out of one side of this cut out a right angle, leaving 1 inch upon each line, and cutting it to the depth of 1 inch, thus making the shape required for the design. Have this cut in tin, and from that cut out an equal number of sections from each coloured silk, and then join them together, according to the pattern; sew together the straight side of a ruby and crimson section with the cut-out edge to the right and left, and fit a pink section into the angle at the top of these two, with its cut-out edge upright. Make up all the pieces in this manner, and then join the figures together. The cut-out edge of the light pink of one figure will fit into the bottom angle of the crimson and maroon colours, and the angles at the sides of these sections will fit into the sides of a fresh row of figures. In making this pattern, care must be taken that the position of the colours is never altered.

Tinted.—A new variety, made with coloured muslin of a stiff description, and of four shades of one tint. The material is cut into hexagons, and embroidered with coloured filoselles and tailor's black twist. The hexagons are arranged to form stars, rosettes, and other devices, all the dark shades of colour being arranged in the centre of the device, and the light colours at the edge. To work: Cut out, on paper, a large eight-pointed star, or other device; then a number of hexagons, 2 inches in diameter. Use four shades of blue, crimson, purple, yellow, green, or other colours, arranging that each ray of the star is worked with a distinct colour. The hexagons cut, fill their centres with a star worked with yellow, white, or a shaded filoselle, and over this star, and across every point of the hexagons, bring a line of black twist, working the ends into the centre of the star. OVERCAST the hexagons together to make the pattern, laying them on it as a guide, and place one hexagon, made of white muslin, as the centre patch. Lay the star, when finished, upon a plain velvet or satin background. The work, when used for a footstool cover, is made with one large star, nearly covering the surface; for small tablecloths, cushions, &c., with a number of more minute devices fastened to a plain ground.

Twist.—This pattern is formed of eight-sided cubes and squares, which are separated from each other by long narrow patches, cut so as to appear to twist, or interlace each other, and twine round the squares and cubes. To work as shown in Fig. 655: Cut a number of squares measuring 1¼ inches each way, and eight-sided cubes measuring 1¼ inches at top, bottom, and side lines, but only three-quarters of an inch across the lines that form the four corners. Make these cubes and squares of pieces of dark-coloured satin and brocade. Cut out, in light silk or satin, the long, narrow stripes, make these half an inch in width, 2 inches in length on one side, and 2¾ inches in length on the other. Cut them so that one side of the width is quite straight, and the other pointed. Take one of the squares, stitch to it, on the left, a long, narrow piece, turn its short, or 2-inch, length to the square, make

it even on its straight width with the bottom line of square, and let the overlap and the point come at the top; to this end, but not to the point, join another long piece in the same way, fit it into the overlap where it is straight, and join its short 2-inch length to the top of the square, allowing the overlap and the point to be to the right hand. Come down the right side of the square, and put a piece

FIG. 655. TWIST PATCHWORK.

on at the bottom of the square; in the same manner join the long pieces to all the squares. Now arrange the cubes as to colour, and join them to the long pieces. The short corners of the cubes will fit into the points of the long pieces, four different cubes will join the four different points, and the straight parts will fit into the straight lines of the long pieces.

Patent Flannels (Welsh and Saxony).—A very fine quality of Flannel, said not to shrink when washed, but not durable. They are much used for infants' clothing.

Patent Knitting.—The old-fashioned name for Brioche Knitting. *See* KNITTING.

Patent Silk Sealskin.—This is a very beautiful textile, in every respect as perfect an imitation of sealskin as could be manufactured. The gloss is very fine, and the softness equally great, and it has the advantage of lightness, by comparison with the real skin. The pile is raised on a double warp of cotton. The material measures 52 inches in width; its wear is said to be very satisfactory, and the cost is estimated at about one-fourth of that of the real skins. Silk Sealskin has been patented by the inventors, and is produced at Newtown, North Wales.

Patterns.—These are required for every description of Ornamental Needlework, and are as diversified as the articles they help to form.

For Berlin Work, and in all Work with Wools upon Open Canvas: Trace the pattern upon point or ruled paper, with squares to represent each stitch, and colour the tracing as each stitch should be coloured when worked. Place this pattern upon the table, and work from it, counting the stitches upon it, and working the same number on the canvas.

For Church Embroidery: Draw out the pattern as a whole upon a large piece of paper, in proper scale, and colour this; then, upon separate pieces of paper, make sections of the pattern of those pieces that are worked in frames by themselves, and afterwards joined together. Trace these sections on linen stretched in Embroidery Frames, and colour them from the large pattern.

For Crewel Work, Satin Embroidery, Tapestry, and all Embroideries upon Thick Materials : Make a small coloured design, trace the outline of this, in its full size, upon oiled tracing linen, transfer this outline to the material with the aid of blue or white carbonised linen, and work out the colours from the small design. When the materials are rough and dark, it is extremely difficult for an amateur to trace a design upon them, but the following plan is the best : Trace the pattern upon oiled tracing linen (not paper), and place underneath it a cream-coloured piece of carbonised linen (not paper), lay the material and pattern upon a piece of glass, and trace the design through with a bone crochet hook. The traced lines will rub off some rough materials on contact, and for these the best plan is, immediately after tracing, to RUN round all the chief outlines with a fine white thread, or to paint them with Chinese white, with which water-colour size has been mixed. The carbonised linen is sold at Frances', in Hanway Street, Oxford Street, London, in several shades of colour.

For Crochet, Knitting, Netting, and Tatting : Make or obtain a small illustration of the article required, with directions of how to work it from row to row; the illustration is not necessary as long as the directions, either printed or written, are obtained, but it facilitates the work, and shows the effect.

For Holbein and Kreuzstich Sticherei Patterns: A want that has been widely felt by many workers in these Embroideries has been met by a French invention of a metal plate, which stamps small spots upon the material to be worked, and so does away with the constant and weari-some counting of thread, or the interposition, on dark and thick stuffs, of canvas, which has to be drawn away when the work is completed. With the help of these stamps, the tracing of patterns upon velvet, plush, or silk, need no longer present the difficulties, nor take the time, it has hitherto done. The French stamp is formed of a piece of thick wood, made of various sizes, from which a number of metal points protrude, these points being placed at even distances from each other. The colour they are to transport to the work is spread out upon a pad, and the stamp put face downwards upon that, and immediately afterwards on to the material, which it marks with even rows of tiny spots, over which Cross Stitch or Holbein Stitch is worked with ease. This stamp could be made less cumbersome if formed of a thin sheet of copper, and the holes punctured in it, and then the colour brushed over them as in Stencilling, or as the small name and figure plates for marking are manipulated. The colours for stamping are powder colours, just diluted with water, and strengthened with a small quantity of gum—but water-colours in cakes would do equally as well. For washing materials, blue is the best; for dark stuffs, Chinese white. The density and stiffness of the colour used for a washing material need not trouble the worker so much as that used over a non-washing; in the first case, the faint blue spots are removed at the first washing, but in the latter they are

brushed away with a soft velvet brush, and must, therefore, only contain sufficient gum to allow of their adhering temporarily. The mixture should be tried on a waste piece of stuff before using, and care taken that it is not very liquid.

For Pillow Lace Making : Prick the outlines of the sprig, or piece of lace, upon thin parchment or Toile Ciré, so that each pricking shall represent one of the holes required in the design, and into which a pin is stuck while the lace is in process of making, in order that a stitch can be formed round the pin, and kept in position by it.

For Point or Needle Laces : Trace the design upon parchment as a whole; take copies of portions of it upon small pieces of parchment, outline these with two prickings close together and a small space between each group, and work the portions of lace with the needle upon these scraps; then join all together.

For White Embroidery, including Work upon Muslin and Net, and Imitation Laces made with Braids : Trace an outline of the pattern upon pink calico, back this with brown paper, lay the white materials over it and work, guided by the lines of the pattern seen through them; or, in the case of the lace, tack the braid straight upon the pattern.

The word Pattern is likewise a term employed to denote a specimen of any material. Strips of these are fastened together, and are in universal use in trade, to show varieties in quality, make, design, and colour, in woven stuffs, braids, &c.; and cards of buttons, and other articles of Haberdashery, are likewise in use.

Pattes.—A term denoting the small straps securing the loose cuffs of an outdoor coat, jacket, or ulster; or designed to close the stand-up collar, by stretching across the opening which, only just meeting, could not be buttoned otherwise; also for drawing in an Ulster at the back, when there is no belt round the waist. It may consist of one piece with a button at each end, or of two short straps, each sewed on the article of dress at one end, and buttoned across its fellow by a single button.

Peacock Fingering.—This is also known as Peacock Knitting Wool.

Peacock Ice Silk.—This is a comparatively new description of silk, for the purpose of knitting. It is made in two sizes, twofold and fourfold. The former quality can be employed in the knitting of fine stockings, and is suitable also for Crochet Work. The fourfold quality is very suitable for gloves, shawls, stockings, socks, and scarves. Peacock Ice Silk bears the same relationship to other silks so employed as Eis, or Ice, Wool bears to ordinary wools. It is prepared in a particular manner, and is said not to become chafed in use. It can be had in ½oz. balls, and in almost every hue and shade; and the dyes in which it is produced are very beautiful.

Peacocks' Feathers.—The skin taken from the breast of the Peacock, of which the plumage is blue, with a peculiar shot appearance, is employed for the crowns of women's hats, as well as for collarettes and cuffs. The tips, also, of the beautiful tail feathers, some having an eye-like spot at their several extremities, and others a shining green fringe, extending just round the point on one side, and all the way down on the other, are employed as trimmings for dresses, as well as for hats, fans, screens, and mats. A Peacock's Crest was, in ancient times, employed as one of the decorations of our English Kings; and in China, at the present time, to be awarded the distinction of wearing three Peacocks' Feathers, is a point of ambition amongst all Mandarins.

Pearl.—The loops that decorate the edges of Pillow Lace are called Pearls, or Purls, and are made to any parts of the design that are disconnected in any way from the main body of the work, or upon the Bars forming the ground. These loops are called Right, Left, and Inner, according to the side of the Lace upon which they are made.

To Make a Left Pearl.—Work as in Right Pearl until the thread has to be placed on the pin. Place the pin upon, and not under, the thread, and bring the BOBBIN over it with the left hand; run this loop up to the pinhole, stick the pin, and bring the other Bobbin round the pin from the lower side, moving first to the left. The difference is slight, but, unless attended to, the edge of the left Pearl untwists.

To Make an Inner Pearl.—This Pearl, instead of being worked upon the outside edges of a lace design, is made so as to decorate any hollows left in the centre of lace patterns, such as a hole in the wings of a butterfly or hollow leaf. It is worked during the progress of the lace as follows: Work to the inside edge and TWIST the working pair of Bobbins six times, stick a pin into an inside hole, put the twist round it, and work the lace back with the same pair of Bobbins.

To Make a Right Pearl.—Continue working the Lace until the pinhole that is to form the loop is reached, then turn the Pillow until the edge that was on the left is on the right side. Bring the working pair of BOBBINS across the Lace, and TWIST once before the last stitch; then, without sticking a pin, make a CLOTH STITCH with the pair lying outside, pull this up, Twist the working pair seven times to the left, lift one of these Bobbins in the left hand, take a pin in the right hand, place the pin under the thread, give a twist of the wrist to bring the thread round the pin, run the pin up to the hole it is to be placed in, stick it in, lay down the Bobbin that was held, and pass the other one round from the lower side, Twist once, make a Cloth Stitch, again Twist once, and work back across the lace.

Pearl-edge.—Otherwise written Purl-edge. A narrow kind of thread edging, made to be sewn upon lace, as a finish to the edge; or projecting loops of silk at the sides of ribbons, formed by making some of the threads of the weft protrude beyond the selvedge.

Pearlin.—This is the old name in Scotland, for lace, and was there applied to all descriptions of it. During the seventeenth century it was used in Enactments against the importation of foreign laces into that country, and in all Scotch poems, legends, and histories written during that period. Pearlin and Pearling have the same meaning.

Pearling.—*See* PEARLIN.

Pearl-purl.—A gold cord of twisted wire, resembling a small row of beads strung closely together. It is used for the edging of Bullion Embroidery, is sold by the ounce, and is more costly than plain Bullion. It is too delicate to be drawn through the material to be embroidered, and must be laid on the surface, and stitched down with waxed yellow silk; it requires careful handling.

Pekin.—A French term employed to denote a silk stuff made in alternate stripes of satin and velvet, which vary in width in the different pieces manufactured. Pekin Silk goods may be had in black, and all colours, and are much used as portions of dresses and trimmings. There are also Pekin Gauzes, the Gauze being substituted for the satin stripe.

Pelerine.—This description of cape, or tippet, had its origin in that worn by pilgrims, and which had the addition of a hood—the French word *pélerin* meaning a pilgrim or palmer. As worn by English women, they only just reach the waist at the back, and have long, straight-cut ends in front, which are tied once, without a bow at the waist in front. They are made in silk, muslin, cashmere, and other materials.

Pelisse.—An over-dress for outdoor wear by women, formerly made of cloth, and often trimmed with fur, open all down the front, and fastened with closely-set buttons, the sleeves tight, like those of a coat. The Pelisse of former times resembled in style the modern "princesse polonaise." The form is still used for infants' and children's dress, in merino, cashmere, Nankeen, piqué, &c. The first mention of the Pelisse dates back in English history to the year 1185, when, in the reign of Edward the Confessor, the nobles wore dresses of fur, or skins called "Pelles," from the Latin *pellis*, a skin.

Pelisse Cloth.—A woollen textile, twilled, and made soft, of about seven quarters in width.

Pelote.—A French term, denoting a kind of Moss-fringe, employed for the trimming of dresses.

Pelts, or Peltry.—These terms denote the raw, unprepared, but dried fur-covered skins, which, subsequent to their "dressing," are called Furs.

Peluche.—The French name for PLUSH.

Penelope Canvas.—A description of cotton Canvas made for Berlin Woolwork, in which the strands run in couples, vertically and horizontally, thus forming squares containing four threads each. It is less trying to the eyes of the embroiderer than ordinary canvas, as there is little counting to do; and the squares are large compared with the single threads of the latter.

Penguin Skin.—The skin of the Penguin is used for purposes of women's out-of-door dress.

Peniche Lace.—On the little peninsula of Peniche, lying north of Lisbon, in the Estremadura Province, the lace industry of Portugal is chiefly carried on. In that place, the population being debarred from agricultural pursuits, the men become fishermen and the women are all engaged in the lace trade. The latter begin to acquire the art at four years of age, work all their lives, and, when too old to make elaborate designs, return to the first patterns they made in youth. For the last forty years this lace has become an article of commerce. The implements used are the same as in other kinds of Pillow Lace making, except that the Lace, being made in very wide widths without joins, necessitates a very long Pillow to work upon. The Pillows are made in the form of a cylinder; the women sit with this Pillow across their knees, and with its ends resting upon low stools or in baskets. It is made with a hole at each end to lift it by. The patterns are of card, and dyed saffron, to make them yellow, and look like parchment; they are designed and pricked by women whose trade it is. The Bobbins are of pine wood, Brazil wood, and ivory; a great number are needed, a large piece of lace often requiring eighty to a hundred dozen in use at one time.

The Lace is a coarse Pillow Lace, similar to the white

lace veil of a large size, reduced so that the pattern may be entirely shown. The ground is omitted, as the beauty of the design would not be visible in its present size if filled in. The flowers and leaves are worked thick in CLOTH STITCH, and are surrounded with a FIL DE TRACE or GIMP of a coarser and more shiny thread than they are filled in with. No open lace stitches are worked, the whole beauty of the design resting upon its boldness and the contrast between the fine filmy ground and the thickness of the pattern.

Percaline.—A fine cotton material, employed in ELYSÉE WORK.

Percals.—A fine calico cloth, bearing a French name, yet of Indian origin. It was manufactured in England in 1670, and in France in 1780. That home-made has a small

FIG. 656. PENICHE LACE.

Lace made near Lisbon, but at Peniche both black and white Lace are made, and a greater variety of designs worked than near Lisbon. Some of the patterns resemble Maltese designs, and are geometrical, having no grounds; others are similar to the large flower patterns so well known in Spanish Lace patterns, while another kind have hardly any pattern at all, and are made of a variety of grounds, with a few thick stitches intermixed with the grounds and a gimp thread run in and out, and forming a very simple design. In the thick Spanish Lace designs, the grounds are made of various kinds of Honeycomb and Star, two or three varieties being introduced into one pattern; the favourite varieties being either six or eight pointed Honeycombs of the usual size, or a number of large Honeycombs, each surrounded with a second or double line, filled in with a number of small holes. Fig. 656 is a

printed design, and measures 33 inches in width. It is stiffer, and has more glaze, than the original cloth made in Bengal.

Perewiaska Fur.—The animal producing this Fur is a small rodent mammal, of the genus *Mus*, and is otherwise known as the Russian Musquash. The Fur is employed for muffs, tippets, cuffs, and linings. The skin measures 6 inches by 6 inches.

Perforated Cardboard Work.—This fancy work is of so simple a description that it is generally only made by children, for whom it is peculiarly suitable; but it can be, and is, used for making church book-markers, and when the designs are worked out in many-coloured silks, and are shaded like Berlin Wool patterns, they are rather more difficult of execution. The materials required are perforated white cardboard, skeins of sewing silk, and patterns such as are used for samplers, or small Berlin Woolwork sprays of flowers. The silks, when used by children, are selected of bright colours, but all of one shade; for more difficult work, they are chosen so as to shade into each other. To work: Procure a sheet of cardboard, and count the lines of punctures upon it as rows, to find out how many rows are required for the pattern, one row counting for one stitch. Cut out the cardboard, and in its centre work the selected spray or the letters of a name. Work in CROSS STITCH, and for the letters form those illustrated in MARKING. Line the cardboard with a ribbon matching it in width, to hide the wrong side of the work, and secure this by working a Vandyke border round the edge of the cardboard and through the ribbon; three Cross Stitches to every slant will make a good Vandyke. If the edge of the work is required to be more highly ornamented, after the centre is worked, lay the cardboard upon a piece of glass, and, with a sharp penknife, cut it away to form open crosses round the edge, but leave two rows of board between the real edge and the open edge. Sew on the ribbon, and make the ornamental border inside the cutting, securing the edge with a plain, straight line of Cross Stitches along the rows left at the outside.

Perforated Cards.—These are Cards stamped for the purposes of Decorative Needlework, the designs being punched through them by machinery. At one time very beautiful floral designs used to be pricked in Card, so as to stand out in relief. These Cards were then bound with silk ribbon binding, and sewn together, to form small articles, such as pin-trays, pincushions, &c.

Permanents.—These are cotton cloths, of a light description, similar in texture to Turkey Cambrics; some of them have a slight glaze. They are dyed in a variety of colours, and are much employed for the trimming of dresses, especially Galatea stripes.

Persian.—An inferior description of silk stuff, thin, and designed for linings of women's cloaks, hoods, and articles of infants' dress. It is soft, fine, almost transparent, and not durable: it may be had in all colours, the width running to half a yard. It is extensively made in Persia—whence its name—and is exported to Turkey and Russia.

Persiana.—A silk stuff decorated with large flowers.

Persian Cord.—A slighter kind of dress material than Janus Cord. It is a mixture of cotton and wool, somewhat stiff, and unfinished on one side. It washes well, and is 27 inches in width.

Persian Cross Stitch.—See *Cross Stitch*, BERLIN WORK, and EMBROIDERY STITCHES.

Persian Embroidery.—Persia has given to Europe a large proportion of the art designs that are now so freely employed, not only in our embroideries, but in our textiles, gold, silver, and bronze works. That Embroidery came originally from the East is well known, but few are aware that, in the thirteenth century, Marco Polo, when describing Kerman, or Cashmere, mentions that "the ladies of that country produce such excellent embroidery of silks and stuffs, with figures of beasts, birds, trees, and flowers, that they are marvels to see." Persian Embroidery, from that date down to the present time, has been employed to decorate prayer and other carpets, curtains, shawls, quilts, housings, veils, and fine linen; and whatever has been produced has combined beauty and intricacy of design, variety in colour and workmanship, with skill in its execution. All the descriptions of Embroidery are executed in Persia, as Embroidery with gold and silver threads Couched upon the background, and answering to our Church Embroidery, Embroidery upon Silk or Cotton foundations in Satin Stitch or in Crewel Stitch, Embroidery upon Leather and Velvet, Inlaid Appliqué with coloured cloths combined with Embroidery, Embroidery covering the entire background, and worked in Tent and Cross Stitch, Darned, Netting, Drawn Work, and fine White Embroidery.

The materials used for the foundations to the Embroideries are various. Coarse cotton backgrounds are frequently used, also fine cotton fabrics, the soft silk known as Persian silk, velvet, leather, thin cloth, and wool obtained from goats. The last material is that used in the making of the celebrated Kerman shawls. These shawls are woven by hand, and are made from the under wool of a particular kind of white goat, whose wool attains a peculiar softness from the fine pasturage round Kerman. The pattern known as the Pine, which has been so extensively copied in our Paisley shawls, was used in Persia before the seventeenth century.

Darned Netting.—This is used for veils. The Netting is made with black and white silk threads, and with Diamond Treble Netting, and upon it is worked, with coloured silks, geometrical designs, stars, circles, &c.

Drawn Work.—This is carried, in Persia, to an extent and beauty that has rarely been attained by any European needlewoman. Not only are the borders to pieces of fine linen or muslin drawn out in the familiar squares of European work, but complicated designs are attempted, and the various parts of the material drawn away, so as to form regular patterns. On a piece of muslin in the South Kensington Museum, a Vandyke border is formed by alternately drawing away a section, and forming it into minute squares, each square being Buttonholed over with coloured silks, and leaving a section perfect, and covering that with silk embroidery, while the centre of the muslin is filled with a round of Drawn Work, edged with pots containing flowers, made with many coloured silks.

Embroidery in Tent and Cross Stitch was at one time used for the wide trousers worn by the ladies of the harems, and though no longer in request, many specimens of it are still to be met with. The foundation is a moderately coarse cotton, which is entirely concealed with patterns worked in Tent Stitch with fine wools and silks of many colours; one thread only of the foundation is covered each time a stitch is made, and the result of such work is so minute that, unless closely inspected, it looks like a finely woven material. The same background is employed when the needlework is done with Cross Stitch, but the appearance of this is slightly coarser, as coarser silks are used, and the stitch is not so minute.

Inlaid Appliqué, or Patchwork, is a most remarkable production. It is chiefly made at Resht, and is used for covers, carpets, and housings. It is Patchwork combined with Embroidery. The colours used are extremely brilliant, and the patches (which are of cloth) are cut so small, and into such intricate patterns, that it is marvellous how they can be joined together. Flowers, birds, and animals are freely used, besides geometric and conventional patterns; the pieces are stitched together, and every seam afterwards concealed with lines of Chain Stitch worked over them in coloured silks. Not content with a single line of Chain Stitch, two or three lines upon each petal of a flower, or feather of a bird, are embroidered, and each line is worked in a different coloured silk, while in many places the entire patch is concealed with embroidery, either of gold thread or silk, worked to

other designs, and then ornamented with wide borders of needlework, and with their centres covered with innumerable detached flower sprays. They are always known by the centre being shaped like the three sides of a square, and the other a protruding curve. In the centre of this elongated side a small round is formed with rich embroidery. This spot marks the place where the holy earth of Kerbela is placed, and which is touched by the forehead of the person who kneels in the marked out square while performing his devotions. No embroidery is too elaborate for these carpets, in which Satin, Crewel, Feather, and Herring-bone Stitches are worked in varied shades of many colours

FIG. 657. PERSIAN EMBROIDERY.

make a shaded design. Sometimes, instead of Chain Stitches, lines are made with fine gold thread; these are not laid on flat, but are twisted into very small circles, laid so close together as to form a broad, compact line. Gold and silver foil is used instead of gold or silk; it is cut very narrow, and folded over itself, so as to form zigzag lines, which are then sewn to the foundation, either as lines, or to fill up certain spaces.

Inlaid Appliqué Silk Embroideries.—These have been in use hundreds of years for prayer and other carpets, curtains, and for the covers thrown over State presents. The prayer carpets are generally of a pale coloured silk foundation, elaborately quilted in Vandykes, half circles, and

and gold and silver thread, Couched down in patterns like Basket, Wavy, Diamond, and Raised Couchings. The bath carpets are made of cotton fabrics, or of thin white silk. They are also quilted and embroidered, but are less ornamented than the prayer carpets. The covers used for State presents are worked like the prayer carpets, but are more thickly embroidered with gold and silver thread, after the manner of our Church Embroidery, and, being of a much greater size, have large, handsome borders of pomegranates, their leaves and flowers, birds in full plumage, carnations, tulips the size of life, and other bold designs. The pattern of one of the covers worked in the seventeenth century is shown in Fig. 657, and is selected for illustration as it is one that is handsome in itself and is yet capable of being copied without too much labour. It is made as follows: Trace out the design upon white Persian Silk, stitch the quilted lines, according to pattern, with salmon pink silk. Work the oval in the centre of the flower with pink silk in alternate squares, and leave the other part plain, the petals of the flowers in SATIN STITCH, and in crimson and orange silk. These two shades do not blend into each other, where one ends and the other commences being distinctly marked in the illustration. Use the same crimson and orange silk for the flower buds, put the crimson round the outside, and the orange in the centre, but add some pale yellow for quite the centre. Work the leaves in deep olive green and yellow silk, working the olive green all round the edges of the leaves, and the yellow in the centre. Use the same colours for the calyx of the flowers and buds. Edge every petal of the flowers with a line formed with fine gold thread and crimson silk doubled and run into one needle; stitch with this as an outline, and make the stems and stalks with gold thread and green silk threaded on one needle, and worked as close CREWEL STITCHES.

White Linen Embroidery.—This is worked upon fine linen, and in thick Satin Stitches, with a soft glazy thread. The patterns are remarkable for their extreme delicacy and finish.

Persian Lamb.—Of this animal there are two varieties, the black and the grey-furred. The skins are the most valuable of all Lamb Skins, are beautifully curly and glossy, and are employed for articles both of men's and women's wear. They measure 14 inches by 20 inches, and may be classed amongst the most costly of our furs.

Peruvian Embroidery.—A beautiful embroidery combined with Darned Work, executed in Peru, and used for curtain borders, quilts, towels, and other articles that require washing. The Embroidery, being executed on the linen or silk foundation, is lasting; and, as the patterns used are conventional flowers, or arabesques, the work is artistic, however coarse the material. To work: Trace out a bold flower pattern, like those used for the best Crewel Work, and carefully DARN all the background with POINT MINUSCULE. OUTLINE the pattern with CREWEL STITCH, but only work the veins of the leaves and the centres of the flowers. The materials used are China silks of the softest make, linen, or common towelling. The embroidery is done with raw silk, shiny linen thread, or crewels.

Perwitzky.—The fur of this animal, which is short, is chiefly employed for cloak linings, but it affords little warmth to the wearer.

Petersham Cloth.—This is a very thick, shaggy kind of woollen cloth, of a dark navy blue colour, employed for men's overcoats, and what are called "pilot coats," suitable for seafaring purposes, or for wear in very severe weather.

Petershams, or Belt Ribbons.—A similar description of article to Pads, being of double thickness, watered, of all colours, plain and in patterns. Skirts of dresses are sewn upon them; and they are likewise attached to the backs of bodices, on the inside, at the

waist; they are supplied with hooks and eyes, for the purpose of securing them in their right place upon the figure of the wearer.

Petit Coté.—A French term to signify the side piece of a bodice.

Petit Point.—The French name for Tent Stitch. *See* BERLIN WORK.

Petit Poussin.—*See* POUSSIN LACE.

Pheasant.—The plumage of this bird is sufficiently handsome to make it popular for the purposes of millinery, being employed for the crowns of hats, the skins being used entire; also for muffs and collarettes. The wings are likewise used as trimmings for hats.

Phrygian Needlework.—*See* EMBROIDERY.

Picôt.—The French term for a prick, as with a needle, being derived from the verb *picoter*. It is employed in lace-making.

Picots.—These are little Loops or Bobs that ornament Needle-made Laces of all kinds, and that are often introduced into Embroidery. To work: Make a tiny Loop upon the work, and cover it over with a number of BUTTONHOLE STITCHES worked into it, or put the needle into the work, and bring it out so as only to take up a very small piece of the material; wind the thread eight or nine times round the needle, place the left thumb upon it, and draw it out of the material, holding the thread down while doing so. The Loops made upon the needle will be transferred to the end of the thread, and will form a spiral raised Dot upon the work. *See* CROCHET, GUIPURE D'ART, and EMBROIDERY STITCHES.

Piece Goods.—The articles classed under this name include Grey Cotton, Mulls, Jacconets, Shirtings, Madapolams, Printers' Cambrics, Longcloths, Sheetings, Drills, Bobbin Net, &c.

Piecing.—Mending; joining two pieces of stuff together. A method adopted for the repair of sheets when worn in the middle, the thinnest portion being cut out, and the outer sides turned inwards, and sewed together up the middle.

Piercer, or Stiletto.—One of the useful appliances of a workbox, consisting of a small, sharply-pointed instrument of steel, ivory, or mother-of-pearl. It is employed for making holes for Embroidery, the shanks of buttons, eyelet-holes for lacings, and, in a somewhat different form, used by embroiderers in gold, who employ it for laying the Bullion in place, guiding the fine cord round the edges of the work, arranging the pattern, and making holes.

Pile.—The thick, short nap on the right side of velvet, cloth, or corduroy, formed in the first and last-named stuffs by the placing of part of the warp threads over a needle, more or less thick, according to the desired richness of the material. When the needle is withdrawn, it is replaced by a sharp instrument, which cuts through the loops formed. The Pile always lies in one direction.

Pillow.—This is an article required by all lace-makers who employ Bobbins, and from its use has given the name of Pillow Lace to the work manufactured upon it. To the Pillow the parchment pattern is secured, and the Bobbins holding the numerous threads attached while the other articles required in lace-making, such as pincushion, scissors, crochet hook, and pins, are all arranged upon it. The Pillows used are of several kinds; that known as the Round is chiefly used for Devonshire and Honiton Lace, the Flat for Brussels Lace making, the Oblong for Macramé, and the Long for Peniche Lace and other laces which are made in one piece, and whose width is great.

To Make a Flat Pillow: Take two circles of either Holland or twill material, 18 inches across, join them together, but leave a small opening, through which stuff the Pillow out with flock or horsehair; sew up the opening, and then, on the top, where the work is to be done, lay several folds of flannel; cover the Pillow over with a red twill or silk cover, made to take off and on as described in Round Pillow.

To Make a Long Pillow: Make this in the form of a cylinder, half a yard long, and 36 inches round. Make a cover of this size, and stuff it out with horsehair; but instead of filling the ends, make a hole like the entrance to a muff, into which the implements used in the lace-making can be put; sew the flock into the cover, so that these two cavities are kept from filling up, and then place a piece of flannel over the top of the Pillow, and finish with a red twill cover, made to take off and on. These Long Pillows are kept in baskets, or upon low stools, in order that, when transported from place to place, they can be carried without disturbing the work.

To Make an Oblong Pillow: Make a stout Holland bag, 12 inches long by 8 inches wide, and fill this with bran, so that it is perfectly hard; cover it over with a piece of strong blue ticking, of a kind woven for the purpose, with blue lines in it, placed at even distances from each other, and lengthways across the cushion. An oblong straw hassock will answer the purposes of this Cushion if covered with the blue ticking.

To Make a Round Pillow: This is made round like a ball, except on the top, where it is flat. Tie up into a round a quantity of horsehair or flock, and bind this over with list; make the Pillow 36 inches to 38 inches in diameter; over the part that is to form the top, lay a piece of flannel or Bath coating, and then cover over the whole with a Nankeen, or red twill, or silk covering. Make this to take off and on, the best way to manage it being to cut a circle the size of the top of the Pillow, run a straight piece of twill round the circle, of sufficient depth to cover the sides and meet underneath the Pillow, and finish this off with a broad hem, through which pass a string. Put the cover on the Pillow, and draw the string up tightly, to secure the folds of the material, and leave no rucks in which the lace threads might become entangled.

All these Pillows, before they are finished, are covered with three cloths, known as Cover Cloths, which are used to keep the lace clean while in progress; the largest Cover

Cloth, made of fine linen, the size of the Pillow, is laid over the Pillow before the pattern is pinned on, and upon this the lace is worked; it is removed and washed whenever it becomes dirty. The smaller cloths are made of fine linen, in size 18 inches by 12 inches. These are detached from the Pillow and removed at pleasure; one is doubled and laid over the pattern and under the Bobbins (see Fig. 658), and the other folded in the same way upon the opposite side of the Pillow, and so as to keep the finished lace clean. When the Pillow is laid by, take off the cover under the Bobbins, and lay it over the whole work. Fig. 658 shows a Round Pillow dressed with covers, with pattern, Bobbins, and pincushion attached, and the lace in the process of working. (*See* DRESSED PILLOW.) When working the lace, rest the Pillow upon the knees, arrange the Passive Bobbins so that they hang down straight in a fan shape, and keep them in this position, particularly when making curves and turns, as the Passive Bobbins are liable to run to the inner parts of the

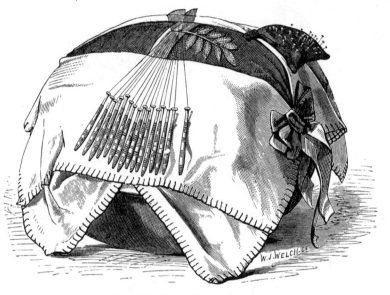

FIG. 658. ROUND PILLOW, DRESSED.

pattern, and leave the edge of the design open and bare. Keep the Working Bobbins at the side of the Pillow, and pin them out of the way of the lace until they are required. The Pillow is turned while the lace is making, if the pattern is more easily worked by so doing.

Pillow Bar.—This is used to connect various detached parts of Pillow Lace together that are made with Bar Grounds. The three kinds of Bar used are the Plain Bar, that forms a straight line from lace to lace; the Guipure Bar, that forms the same straight line, but is worked with threads proceeding from the lace, instead of attached for the purpose; and the Irregular, or Cross-bar, formed by Bars meeting together and starting off at angles to each other. All the Bars are ornamented with a Pearl Edge upon one or both sides.

To Make a Guipure Bar.—Throw out, when making the lace, four pairs of Bobbins from one piece of lace, and work these in CLOTH STITCH, without putting up pins until the lace upon the opposite side is reached. Work in the

Bobbins here as part of the pattern. The Bars must be worked from alternate sides, so that the Bobbins taken away to form one Bar are returned by another and used if required, if not, are secured by a loop and cut off.

To Make Irregular or Cross Bar. — Hang on four pairs of Bobbins and work as for Plain Bar with CLOTH STITCH until a place where the Bar is intersected is reached. Here hang on another set of four pairs of Bobbins and leave them alone until the first line is completed. Then work up these and carry the line thus made in a different direction to the first Bar. Several sets of Bobbins can be hung on to the first Bar at intervals, and completed and themselves intersected, if the ground to be filled in will admit of so many Bars being worked.

To Work a Plain Bar with Pearl Edge upon One Side: Take eight pairs of Bobbins and wind the Knots out of the way. Attach them to the lace where the Bar is to be made by drawing up a loop of one pair and passing the rest of the Bobbins through it; draw up tightly and work across in CLOTH STITCH, and back again without setting up a pin; twist six times, take the last Bobbin on the right hand in the left hand, raise it, take a pin in the right hand, twist it once under the thread, and make a loop round the pin; put it in the Pinhole, take up the Bobbin next it, and twist it once round the pin, and work back in Cloth Stitch (having made a PEARL). Return again to the right without putting up a pin on the right, make another Pearl, and repeat until the length of Bar is made and the lace is reached. Draw up a loop with the hook, pass two of these Bobbins through it, tail foremost, draw the loop tight, and cut off two pairs of Bobbins, but not those that made the loop; twist the remaining Bobbins tightly and carry them to the next Bar; make SEWINGS to keep them close where required. Hang on two more pairs of Bobbins at the new Bar, and work as before. A Pearl edge to both sides is made with Right and Left Pearl alternately.

Pillow Fustian. — The most common variety of Fustian. The cord is narrow, and the texture stout. It is chiefly made in Lancashire, and is manufactured in cotton after the manner of velvet. *See* FUSTIAN.

Pillow Lace Wheels. — These are used to fill in round spaces left in the centres of patterns in Honiton and other Pillow Laces. They are described under WHEELS.

Pillow Linens. — These cloths may be had in various qualities. The best Irish are made in widths of 40, 42, 45, and 54 inches. The medium sorts measure 40, 42, and 45 inches in width. *See* LINEN.

Pillow-made Braid Lace. — *See* BRAIDS.

Pilot Cloth. — An indigo blue woollen cloth, used for great coats, and for mariners' clothing. It is thick and twilled, having a nap on one side, and is very strong for wear. Pilot Cloth is sometimes incorrectly called Dreadnought, which should only be applied to the coat itself. Bearskin is a description of Pilot Cloth having a longer nap. It may be had of either 27 inches in width, or 54 inches, and of different descriptions, viz.: in wool-dyed woaded colours, and in unwoaded colours; also in piece-dyed woaded, and piece-dyed unwoaded colours.

Pin. — An appliance used for the temporary attachment of one piece of material to another, before it is basted; and likewise employed for purposes of the toilet. The original Pin was a thorn. Sharpened fish and other bones were also in use before the modern metal Pin was manufactured. The date of the latter in England is doubtful, possibly the thirteenth century. Bristol is credited with being the seat of the manufacture.

Pine, or Pina Cloth. — An expensive textile, made of the fibres of the pine-apple leaf, and manufactured into dress pieces, shawls, scarves, and handkerchiefs, by the natives of the Philippines. It is very delicate and soft in texture, transparent, and usually has a slight tinge of pale yellow. The threads of both warp and weft are each unspun fibres, and only small pieces of cloth can be produced. It is very strong, resembling horsehair cloth, but the best examples are finer than the finest Lawn. Some of the handkerchiefs are beautifully embroidered. This textile is only made at Manilla.

Pine Marten (or Baum) (*Mustela abietum*). — Distinguished from the Stone Marten by some admixture of yellow colour. The skin of this animal is dyed to imitate sable.

Pine Wool. — A description of wool produced from the fibres of the leaves, bark, and comb of the *Pinus Sylvestris*, or Scotch Fir; famous in Norway and Germany; employed for the manufacture of a kind of Stockingette Cloth resembling wool. It is of a light brown wood colour, with an agreeable odour, and is considered invaluable for the use of persons suffering from rheumatism, especially when a few drops of the essence of Pine Oil are applied, upon the wool, to any part especially affected. The Lairitz Pine wool manufactory at Remda, Thuringia, is one of great importance. Flannel, wadding, and woven underclothing of every description are produced there; and are in great repute for their hygienic properties.

Pinking Iron. — A small appliance having a sharp edge, shaped in after an ornamental outline. With this borders of silk, cloth, or leather may be cut, or stamped out with perfect regularity, in a decorative way; the material being laid on a thick block of lead, and the opposite end of the iron struck smartly with a hammer, so as to give a clear sharp cutting at the first application of the instrument.

Pinking, or Pouncing. — A method of decorating dresses, trimmings for furniture, rugs, and shrouds, by means of a sharp stamping instrument. Pieces of the material are cut out by it in scallops, at the edge, and other designs within the border. The stamping is of semicircular, or angular form, and the extreme edge is evenly jagged or notched. The use of the term Pouncing is now nearly, if not quite, obsolete.

Pink Tape, or Red Tape. — This Tape is made of cotton, and numbers 16, 24, 32. It is to be had in very long lengths on reels, and is chiefly employed in Law offices.

Pinna Silk. — This is a description of *byssus* secreted by a mussel of the Mediterranean, of the genus *Lamellibranchiate*. The beard of this mollusc is so abundant, that the Maltese and Sicilians weave stockings, gloves, and other articles of it. In the year 1754, Pope Benedict XV. was presented with a pair of stockings made of the silky material.　One species of this mussel—the *Pinna pectinata*—is found in our British Seas.

Pin-rib.—The very delicate lines, either printed or woven, in Muslin Textiles.

Pin Work. — Also known as Crowns, Spines, Thorns, and Fleur Volants.　These are stitches used in most Needle-points to lighten the effect of the Cordonnet edgings or of any part in the design that is Raised from the surrounding flat surface.　The stitch is formed of Buttonhole, and either shaped as half crescents or long points.　To work: Make a small loop into the Buttonhole Edging, run the needle back underneath the edging to where it started from, and BUTTONHOLE closely over the thread; this forms a plain crescent.　To form one ornamented with Spines or Thorns, lay the thread as before, and Buttonhole it over as far as the centre, then loop a piece of fine thread into the working thread, hold the two ends of this fine cotton firmly under the left thumb, and continue to Buttonhole with the working thread; then take up the thumb, draw out the fine thread, and leave the Buttonholes that were upon it as a lump or Spine by themselves.　Continue to fill up the loop with Buttonholes, until another Spine is desired, when make as before.　Spines and Thorns worked by themselves upon the Cordonnet make thus: Make a little loop of thread, and stick a pin in it to keep it tight, and then run the working thread up to the pin and cover the loop with Buttonholes until the CORDONNET is again reached.

Piping.—A border formed on any material of dress or furniture, by means of the introduction into it of a piece of Bobbin, for the purpose of giving an appearance of greater finish, or adding to its strength.　To make: Place a piece of Bobbin, or Cotton Cord, along a strip of material—cut on the bias—on the wrong side; leaving a depth of two-thirds of the width of the strip on the side which is to lie uppermost, when placed on the article to be bound.　TACK in the Cord lightly, and then lay it on the raw edge of the dress or other article to be thus finished; the Cord side inwards, that is, towards the working, and the raw edges all together outwards, and parallel with each other.　STITCH or BACK STITCH all together, keeping close to the Cord.　Then turn all the raw edges inwards, and turn in the one outside, over the others, so as to form a HEM, which should then be made.

Piqué.—A French material, made of two cotton threads, one thicker than the other, which are woven and united at certain points, and there make an extra thickness.　The pattern is usually of a lozenge shape; the material is strong and durable, and may be had with small printed designs, in white only.　It is suitable for children's clothing, and for men's waistcoats.　There are coloured and figured varieties, which are made from 30 inches to a yard wide.　They are to be had in many qualities, both thin and thick.

Placing.—The term commonly employed in reference to Needlework, meaning the adjustment of the several pieces of any article which have to be sewn together.

Placket.—The opening at the back of a skirt or petticoat, extending from the waist downwards, designed to enlarge the aperture made at the waistband, to allow for passing the skirt over the head and shoulders.　HEM the overlapping side, double *Stitch* that underneath, and *Face* the pleat at the extreme end of the Placket-hole, to prevent its being torn downwards.　In early times Placket was synonymous with Petticoat, as we find exemplified by a passage in Herrick's Poems:

> If the maides a spinning goe,
> Burn the flax, and fire the toe,
> Scorch their Plackets.

Plaids, or Tartans.—By this name certain textiles in silk, wool, and worsted are alike known.　The designs vary in colour, and in the breadths of the lines or bands, which cross each other at right angles, and form squares more or less large.　The colours are inserted in the warp, and then a further introduction made in the weft, kept respectively on separate shuttles, and thrown at regular intervals; the colours being woven into the material, and not printed upon it.　Tartan, correctly speaking, is the name of the coloured pattern, and Plaid that of the stuff, which is a coarse, strong worsted cloth, as made in Scotland, and worn in the national costume.　Plaids are made of finer quality, suitable for ladies' wear, both in dress-pieces and shawls, in England as well as in Scotland.　Shepherds' Plaid is a very small check, in black and white only.　Plaids can be had in both double and single widths.　Woollen and Worsted Tartans are very durable, and each distinct pattern supplies the badge of some clan.　Properly speaking, we should call silk stuffs, and Ribbons so checkered Tartan, not Plaid silks and Ribbons.

Plain Edge.—In Pillow Lace, when the outside edges of the parts of a pattern are not decorated with the loops that are known as Pearls, they are finished with what is called a Plain Edge, which is made by working as the last stitch a more open stitch than that used in the other part of the lace.　To work: Work across the lace to within one pair of Bobbins at the end.　Twist this pair three times to the left with the left hand, take a pin in the right hand, hold both Bobbins in the left hand, stick the pin in front of the twisted threads into a Pinhole on the right, give a pull to draw the twist up, make a stitch with the last pair of Bobbins, and the working pair, putting the second Bobbin over the last but one, the last over the second, and then the last but one over the first Bobbin, and the first over the last Bobbin.　Twist both pairs three times to the left, using both hands, pull the twists gently up, and then continue the thicker part of the pattern.

Plain Embroidery.—Also known as Low Embroidery.　This term includes all the Embroideries worked in Satin and other stitches upon a flat foundation, whether worked alike upon both sides or in the usual manner, so long as no Raised Work or padding is added.

Plain Flat Couching.—*See* COUCHING.

Plain Knitting.—*See* KNITTING.

Plain Netting.—*See* NETTING.

Plain Sewing.—A term denoting any description of Needlework which is of a merely useful character, in contradistinction to that which is purely decorative.　It comprises the following varieties: Hemming in two or three varieties, Sewing (or Seaming), Stitching, Hem-stitching, Running, Whipping, Tacking, Herringboning, Finedrawing, Darning, Overcasting, Buttonholing, Marking, Gathering, Gauging, Felling, Grafting, &c., Slashing, Fringing, Reeving, Quilling, Quilting, Ruching, Honeycombing, Slipstitching, &c.

Plaited Laces.—These are of two descriptions, one being made of silver or gold wire, and sometimes called Wire Lace; and the other being made of fine thread, and called Pillow Guipure. The Plaited Laces made of gold, silver, or silk threads, superseded the Knotted laces and the Reticellas towards the close of the sixteenth century. Italy claims the first invention of these, and much being made at Genoa, it was known as Genoese Lace, but as large quantities were also worked in Spain, and were largely exported thence to other countries, plaited laces also received the name of Point d'Espagne. France, Germany, and England made Plaited Laces, but never rivalled those produced at Genoa and in Spain, in which latter country the manufacture is still continued for ecclesiastical purposes. Plaited Laces are made upon a pillow and with Bobbins; the patterns are geometrical, and open, and have no grounds; for common purposes tinsel is used instead of real gold, and the lace is then used for theatrical purposes.

The thread Plaited Laces of the seventeenth century were first made in the geometrical designs used for the gold lace and for Reticellas, but soon became of much more elaborate design; they were largely employed to trim ruffs and falling collars in the seventeenth century, and only went out of fashion when flowing wigs came in, which hid the collar, and would not allow of a ruff being worn. At the present date the Plaited Laces have revived under the names of Maltese, Yak, or Cluny Laces, and are made at Auvergne, Malta, and in Bedfordshire and Buckinghamshire. These are made with either black or white threads, and with simple geometrical designs.

FIG. 659. PLAITED RIBBON WORK.

Plaited Ribbon Work.—A pretty work, of modern origin, made by plaiting ribbons together to form geometrical and open designs. It is used for sofa cushions,

mantel borders, handkerchief cases, and for any purpose that will admit of its being lined, as part of the effect depends upon the open spaces left between the plaits being filled with silk or satin of a contrasting colour to that of the ribbon. The materials required are wooden or millboard frames, fitting the work, a quantity of narrow silk

FIG. 660. PLAITED RIBBON WORK.

ribbon, rather less than half an inch wide, gold cord, gold coloured filoselle, and some pins.

To work as shown in Fig. 659: Procure a thin wooden frame, or make one with millboard, of the size required, and cut a good many lengths of ribbon an inch longer than the length from side to side of the frame. Pin two of these to the back of the frame close together (*see* Fig. 660), and fasten them to the opposite side; leave an inch space, and pin on two more lengths of ribbon, and

FIG. 661. PLAITED RIBBON WORK.

continue until one side of the frame is thus filled. Commence to fill the other side of the frame in the same manner, but interlace these second ribbons in and out the first ones whenever they cross them, as shown in the illustration. Finish the plait by interlacing into these straight ribbons some ribbons carried diagonally across the frame, as shown in Fig. 661. These cross ribbons are of various lengths, and should be cut as required; the shortest line will be across the corner of the frame, the longest across the centre of the work. Pin them to the back of the frame, and interlace them outside the square formed by the meeting of the straight ribbons, so that they surround it with a diamond. Weave

string is a suitable work for ladies with weak sight, or for anyone who, in the intervals of more engrossing employment, requires rest without being absolutely idle. The work makes good table mats on which to place hot dishes, and as such is shown in Fig. 662; it is also useful to put under ornaments that would otherwise injure the

FIG. 662. PLAITED STRINGWORK.

them over and under the straight ribbons. Run a gold cord down the centre of each plait between the two straight ribbons and over the ribbons forming the diamond, and under those forming the square. Tack the ends of these cords to the ribbon ends, and secure these latter together with a few stitches. Then take the work out of the frame and edge it with a straight line of ribbon. Procure ribbon an inch in width, double it, and sew into it every end of the ribbons forming the plaits, so that a tidy and straight edge is formed. Hide the stitches made in securing the ribbons by working a border of FEATHER STITCH along the edge, upon the right side of the work, which is the side undermost during the working. Make the work up on a coloured satin background, which cut larger than required, and pull up through the openings left by the plaits. Prevent these puffs moving by securing them to their places with a few stitches.

Plaited Stitch.—*See* BERLIN WORK.

Plaited Stringwork.—Amongst the numerous varieties of art needlework now so prevalent, all taxing to the utmost the attention and ingenuity of the worker, it is occasionally a relief to turn to work requiring little thought, and yet when completed of some use. Plaited

polish of the tables they were placed upon, and it is so inoffensive in colour and make when not embroidered, that the highest of high art ladies could not find fault with it in its pristine condition.

The materials are, a wooden frame, which can be of rough deal, size and shape depending upon the size mats to be made. Pegs are inserted into the wooden frame at the top and the bottom in the same manner as those used in daisy mat frames, and as shown in Fig. 663. Besides the frame,

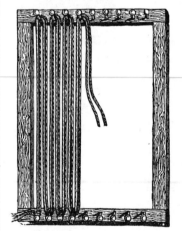

FIG. 663. PLAITED STRINGWORK

evenly made packing string, a packing needle, millboard, and silk ribbon, or linen tape are required.

To work: Double the string and wind it up and down the frame on the pegs (*See* Fig. 663), until the pegs are full, then thread the needle with double string, and DARN in and out the upright strands, under two and over two, as shown in Fig. 664. The darning must be done very evenly, and each horizontal line put in at any equal distance between the one above and the one below it; also, the string picked up and the string gone over must be varied in every other line, so as to produce a woven or plaited look in the work. Each line of string, as

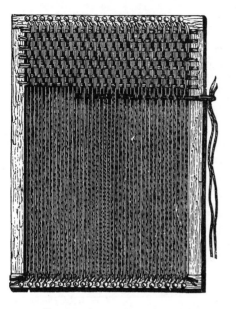

FIG. 664. PLAITED STRINGWORK.

it is Darned across, is not fastened at the commencement or the end, but cut. The whole of the Plaiting being done, paste the back side of the work while in the frame, and leave it to dry. Cut out the shape, whether square or round, in millboard, and cover this underneath with a piece of bright silk, so as to ornament that side. Then cut the plaited strings from the frame, and to the size of the millboard foundation, TACK the edges firmly to the

FIG. 665. PLAITED STRINGWORK.

millboard, and bind them over with silk ribbon or tape matching the lining. The looped edge shown in Fig. 665 is now formed with the double string, and sewn to the edge; it is merely a fine edging, and is enlarged in the design to clearly denote the method of twining the loops one within the other. To finish the mat, plait together in a three-plait nine strands of string, and sew this on so as to conceal the binding ribbon and the stitches round the edge. The plait is shown in Fig. 666.

This mat may be rendered much more attractive by being formed of different materials. Thus coloured braid is used instead of the string, and made to form dice patterns, or one colour used for the upright threads, and the other for the darned lines, which will give the appearance of Couching. Should the foundation be made with-

No. 666. PLAITED STRINGWORK.

out any colour, embroider simple Dots, Stars, or Sprays upon it, before it is pasted or withdrawn from the frame. Work these devices either with filoselle or with single Berlin wool, and introduce the same materials, with the string, in the Plait round the mat, or let them entirely take its place. The looped edge must always be of some stiff material, like string or braid, otherwise it would not retain its shape; but the materials forming all the other parts of the mat can be diversified according to the worker's fancy.

Plaiter and Kilter.—This is a small appliance by which the operation of Plaiting and Kilting may be accomplished with the greatest regularity and ease. The original invention was patented, under the name of the Centennial Plaiter, in 1876; and the little machine can be had in different sizes, so as to suit the finer as well as coarser kinds of Plaiting and Kilting. It has the appearance of a flat box, consisting of two parts, and containing a knife. The first part is a tray, having three compartments, formed by divisions like coarse wooden combs; the second part is a frame of wood, fitted with a number of very narrow flat steel bands, placed across it in close succession, but leaving spaces sufficient for the introduction of the material to be plaited. This frame is fitted into the tray when the work is to be executed. The knife, likewise, consists of two parts, a flat piece of wood and a similar piece of steel, which latter is laid upon it, and affixed by two screws or nuts. The holes in the steel being of some length, it can be made to project beyond the edge of the wood to any extent desired; and, as the knife has a blunt edge, it cannot cut the material to be plaited. The method of working is as follows: Lay the stuff across the steel bands in the frame, and press it in with the knife between them successively. This part of the work being accomplished, lay the flat piece of wood, which forms the cover of the box-like appliance, upon the material, as it remains pressed into the spaces, and turn the whole round, laying the side on which you have been operating downwards into the tray. Then press the folds, which protrude between the steel bars, with a hot iron, passing the latter lightly backwards and forwards, until the folds are rendered sufficiently well defined and permanent. Lastly, turn the frame round into its normal place again in the tray, removing the board (or cover of the box), and now hold the hot iron as near to the other side of the material as may be safe, without touching it. After having been thoroughly heated thus, the material may be removed from its confinement, and the work of plaiting or kilting will be found completed.

Plaitings.—These are Pillow Lace Stitches used as open Fillings for the centres of flowers, the wings of butterflies, or to finish off the centre of a geometrical design. They are used in many descriptions of Guipure Lace, particularly Honiton and Maltese. Plaitings are of various shapes and sizes, and are known as CUCUMBER, CRINKLE, DIAMOND or LONG, and SQUARE.

Crinkle Plaitings.—These Plaitings are used in the centre of flowers, and make Raised Loops in imitation of stamens. They are illustrated in Fig. 486, of Honiton Lace, where they form the centre of the fully-opened poppies. To work: Sew to the PEARL EDGE, two pairs of Bobbins, and PLAIT these together by laying Nos. 1 and 4 of the Bobbins on the outside, and No. 3 in the centre, and, working backwards and forwards across them with No 2, work twelve rows thus, then fasten this Plait back to the Pearl it started from, or to the one next it, with a SEWING. Repeat these Loops until the number of stamens required is complete.

Cucumber Plaitings.—These are illustrated in the upper wings of the Butterfly that forms Fig. 667. Having

FIG. 667 CUCUMBER PLAITINGS

worked the body, head, and the close wings in CLOTH STITCH, and the outlines of the open wings in Cloth Stitch, with a PEARL EDGE on the outside and a PLAIN EDGE upon the nside, proceed to fill in the lower wings and the Circles with DIAMOND PLAITINGS, and finally work the CUCUMBER PLAITINGS in the upper wings. These are attached to the Plain Edge on one side and the Pearl Edge on the other, as it is less difficult to make SEWINGS to the Plain Edge than to the Pearl Edge; they are all attached to the cross strands in the Cloth Stitch, and it is at first difficult to find out these strands. Prepare nine pairs of Bobbins, stick a pin into each Pearl upon the Pearled side, and hang on a pair of Bobbins at the second Pearl, and twist four times; hang on two pairs of Bobbins at the fifth Pearl, make a stitch with these last, twist twice, stick a pin, make a stitch about the pin, twist four times; then make a Plaiting with the first pair

hung on, and the pair nearest it, leaving the third pair idle. Make the Plaiting thus: Lay down Nos. 1 and 4 Bobbins on the outside of the plait, and well apart, and put No. 3 Bobbin down the centre, then take No. 2 Bobbin in the hand, and pass it backwards and forwards, under and over the other three, changing it from one hand to the other. For the first row, pass 2 over 3 and under 4; for the second row, pass 2 over 4, under 3, and over 1; for the third row, pass 2 under 1, over 3, and under 4. Repeat these last two rows until the Plait is long enough, but after the first two rows, draw 2 quite up, and pull out again with 1 and 4, so as to tighten the twist first made; do not repeat this pulling, and when the Plait is long enough (it requires about twelve rows), twist 2 and 1 together four times, so as to make 1 the outside Bobbin. SEW 1 to the thick wing side of the Butterfly, and pass 2 through it. Hang on two more pairs of Bobbins opposite the next hole, make a stitch, twist twice, stick a pin, make a stitch about it, and twist four times. Then make another Plaiting with the pair left idle in the first Plaiting, and the pair nearest it. For this and the succeeding Plaitings, pass the Bobbin that would be called 2, backwards and forwards, so as to make sixteen rows, then twist four times. Twist the Bobbins that made the last Plaiting four times, and take the third and fourth of those Bobbins, and the first and second of the one in working, and make a stitch with these four, and give 3 and 4 a gentle pull while so doing, but leave 1 and 2 as worked. Stick a pin, twist twice, make a stitch, twist four times. Hang on a pair of Bobbins upon the close wing side of Butterfly, and leave them. Hang on two pairs of Bobbins at the next hole, and make another Plaiting as described above. Hang on the two remaining pairs of Bobbins, make a Plaiting with one, twist the other four times, sew it to the Circle and the end of the wing, twist four times, and by this means bring this pair down, in readiness to make the securing stitch of the last Plaiting. Two more Plaitings will be required to finish the wing; when they are worked, and all the threads sewn to the close wing side of Butterfly, tie up the Bobbins and cut them off. The other wing is worked from its extreme end to the centre, in the same way. Great care is required when working Cucumber Plaitings, especially in handling Bobbin No. 2. A firm hand may be kept upon the other three, but if No. 2 is much pulled, it will throw the Plaiting out of place. The Bobbins must also be handled with great nicety while the securing stitch is made. After the pin is stuck and the stitch made about it, the Plaiting is secure, and may be left. The making of the rest of the Butterfly is described in HALF STITCH.

Diamond, or Long Plaitings.—These are illustrated in the centre of the Daisy shown in Fig. 668, and they are worked after the other parts of the spray have been made. Make the centre circle of the flower in STEM STITCH, round the outside edge, and in CLOTH STITCH, and the outer petals in STEM STITCH. When finished, tie up the Bobbins and cut them off, and commence the Diamond Plaiting. There are four holes in the centre of the four Plaits, and a hole at each commencement of a Plait in the Circle of the Daisy. Stick a pin into one of these last holes, and hang on two pairs of Bobbins, winding the knots out of the way. Connect to the flower by drawing a thread through the nearest hole, and pass one Bobbin from the other pair through it, take out the pin, and stick it into the sewed hole, make a CLOTH STITCH, twist each pair twice, stick a pin in the hole between them. Number the Bobbins 1, 2, 3, 4. Lay down Nos. 1 and 4 on the outside, and some distance apart, and No. 3 in the centre, and take No. 2 in the hand, and pass it backwards and forwards and under and over the other three, in the same way as in CUCUMBER PLAITINGS. Lift 2 with the left hand, 4 with the right, put 2 over 3 and under 4, pass it into the fingers of the right hand, drop 4, bring 2 back over it, lift 3 with the left hand, pass 2 under 3 and into the left hand, drop 3, take 2 over 1, lay it down, and turn 1 over it with the left hand, bring it over 3 and under 4. Every three turns pull 2 gently up to tighten the Plait, and if it is at all drawn in, pull 1 and 4 simultaneously, and this will restore the shape. When the Plait is long enough to reach nearly

FIG. 663. DIAMOND PLAITINGS.

to the centre of the flower, twist both pairs of Bobbins twice; stick a pin between them, and leave them. Hang on two pairs of Bobbins to the detached hole opposite the one first used, and work to the centre with these, as described above. Stick a pin between the two pairs of Bobbins last worked with, make a stitch with the two pairs that lie next one another between the pins, twist each thrice, and carry the respective twists in front of the pins, make a stitch with each outside pair, twist thrice, make a stitch with the two inner pairs, and thus complete the square of holes, twist, stick two pins, and work the two Plaitings that finish the centre. Bring the left-hand Plaiting down to the detached hole opposite it, and after sticking the pin and making the stitch, SEW to the flower, tie up and cut off the Bobbins; finish the other Plaiting in the same way. The spray is finished by working the leaves in CLOTH and HALF STITCH, with PEARL EDGE, and the stem in STEM STITCH, with Plain and Pearl Edge.

Square Plaitings.—The Square Plaiting, or Filling, is shown in the centre of the Camellia in Fig. 669. To work:

Having made the flower, with the exception of the centre, proceed to fill that in. Hang on at the top, and on the right side, a pair of Bobbins into the first Pinhole; miss the next Pinhole, and hang on another pair, and continue to hang on Bobbins in pairs, missing a Pinhole between each, until the space is filled up. Commence to work on the right side, twist the first and second pairs twice, and take these four Bobbins, and Plait them together until a square dot is formed, then twist the two pairs separately twice. Put away the first pair of Bobbins on the right side of the Pillow, and bring into the working the next pair on the left; work with the second pair as described, and continue to the end of the row. For the second row, hang on a fresh pair of Bobbins on the right side, and use them to make the square with the first pair. Work as before, adding another pair on the left side when reached. For the

FIG. 669. SQUARE PLAITINGS.

third row, hang on a fresh pair both at commencement and finish, and work as before. In the next three rows, SEW to the side, and gradually cut off the Bobbins as they were added, so that they are finally reduced to two pairs, which Sew to the bottom edge, tie up, and cut off. Work the rest of the pattern as described in HONITON LACE.

Plait, or Pleat.—A method of arranging frills, borders of lace or muslin, and trimmings of dresses. In ordinary Plaits the folds all lie in one direction; in Box-plaiting they are alternately reversed, two folds facing each other in pairs. When Plaits are sewn in a piece of Muslin or Net, the material should be cut on the straight.

Plaits are also made in Double Box, as well as in Triple and Quadruple form.

Double Box Plaits.—These resemble two single ones of different widths, the smaller set upon the wider, which thus shows at the sides of the upper. First PLAIT the top right-hand half, then the under right-hand half, and lastly, the under right-hand portion in the same way. Place the edges of the upper Plait so as to meet at the back, as for Single Box Plaits, but do not allow the lower one to meet in the centre by as much as it projects beyond the face of the upper one at the sides. Double Box Plaits are necessarily somewhat heavy, and, although they make a handsome trimming, it is not one suitable for all materials alike; nor does it look well for flounces of less than 7 inches in depth. For a skirt of 4 yards, take a strip of 16 yards for Plaiting. According to the thickness of the material and width of the folds, place the under ones farther apart at the back, to economise the quantity. Nothing under 1 inch for the top portion is heavy enough for this style.

Single Box Plaits are rarely more than 1 inch wide, and are never separated by more than their own width. Make them like two Kilt Plaits, turn one to the right, the other to the left, and let the heels of each half of the Plait touch at the back, but not overlap, or it would cause the Plait itself to set sideways. Single Box Plaits take twice the length to be trimmed—*i.e.*, for a skirt 4 yards round take a strip of 8 yards.

Triple and Quadruple Plaits are only occasionally employed, but, when desired, make the top fold 3 inches across, and the underlayers from ½ inch to 1 inch beyond. Place each group very near together—almost, or quite touching. Relieve the extreme heaviness of this trimming (which should be fully 15 inches deep) by cutting out large Vandykes at one edge of the strip, and then Plait them, that the point of each may be in the centre of the flat surface fold, and the narrowest part end at the last edge of that undermost. Arranged in this way, the deepening edge of the Vandyke of course hides the shallower part, which rises upwards inside with every succeeding fold; consequently, a muslin lining, RUN on the wrong side, and then turned over before the Plaiting is begun, will not show; but, if it be desirable to Plait the Vandykes in the reverse way, making the narrowest part of the flounce to come in the middle of each singly, and the long point in a line between each group, it follows that the inside of the material will be shown at every new bend of the folds; in that case, make a facing of its own material, or some of a different colour.

Plastron.—A term adapted from the French (for a breast-plate) to signify a trimming for the front of a dress, of a different material from itself, usually sewn about half-way down the seam on the shoulder, and narrowing as it descends across the chest to the waist. It may end at the waist, or extend to the edge of the skirt, gradually increasing again in width to its termination.

Plis.—The French for the term Folds, as applied to textiles.

Plissés.—The French term for flat plaits, or folds, in making up Crape. These are cut the selvedge-way of the material, lined with muslin, plaited at the top edge, and tacked at the bottom, that they may lie successively side by side, in regular order, while being pressed flat with a hot iron.

Plumes.—A term employed to denote the Ostrich Feathers worn as a head-dress by ladies at Court on special occasions. In the Middle Ages they were worn by men in caps and helmets, under this name; and those used to decorate hearses and catafalques are also thus described.

Plush.—A shaggy, hairy kind of silk, or cotton cloth, used for dress or upholstery. It is sometimes made of camels' or goats' hair. The pile, or nap, is softer and longer than that of velvet, and resembles fur. It is fabricated by means of a single weft of goats' or camels' hair, and double warp; one of the latter supplying the loose pile of woollen thread. Woollen plush made at Banbury is warm and serviceable for upholstery, and is known as Banbury Plush. A mixture of Cotton and Silk Plush, for the trimmings of infants' clothing, such as dresses, cloaks, and hoods, is made at Amiens and Lisle. Black Silk Plush for hats is made of a superior quality at Lyons. Plush is used for small frames and albums. There are also Plush Ribbons, satin backed; and others known as Pomponette Plush Ribbons. Plush Velveteen may likewise be had. Plush is much employed for liveries, and its manufacture dates back at least to the sixteenth century, as we find records of its use up to that time; but how much older it may be we have no data to determine. Counterpoints of Plush are named in the Wardrobe Accounts of James I.

Plush Stitch.—*See* BERLIN WORK.

Plush Velvet.—This is a variety of Plush having a shorter pile. It is made with both a silk and a cotton back. *See* PLUSH.

Ply.—A term signifying a fold, twist, or plait of thread, in any kind of material.

Poil de Chèvre.—This material, otherwise known as Vigogne, is made of the Angora goat's hair, and measures 48 inches in width. *See* VIGOGNE.

Point.—The French word for a Stitch in every description of Needlework, and also very largely used in the names of laces, and to denote the varieties of stitches employed in Guipure d'Art, Embroidery, and Needle Laces. The word Point, when prefixed to a lace, should mean that it is one made with the Needle, and not upon the Pillow; but as it has been applied to many laces that are only made on the Pillow, and to laces that are made either by the hand or on the Pillow, it cannot be looked upon as a perfectly correct indication of the nature of the lace.

Point à Carreaux.—One of the French names for lace made upon the Pillow.

Point à Aiguille.—This name is given to Brussels Lace sprigs that are made by the Needle, and not upon the Pillow. *See* also ENGLISH WHEEL.

Point à la Minute.—*See* EMBROIDERY STITCHES.

Point Alençon.—*See* ALENÇON POINT.

Point Anglaise.—*See* EMBROIDERY STITCHES.

Point Antwerp.—*See* ANTWERP LACE.

Point Appliqué.—A name sometimes applied to Appliqué, and sometimes used to denote lace, whether made upon the Pillow or with the Needle, that is worked in

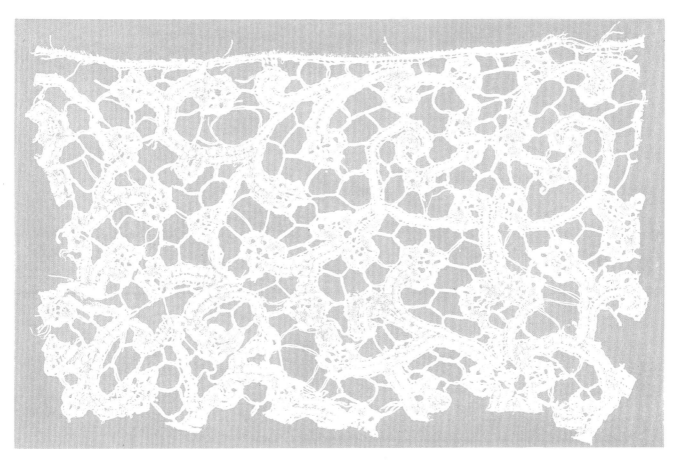

ITALIAN TAPE LACE WITH PLAIN BRIDE GROUND (OLD).

PILLOW LACE, MADE FROM THE FIBRE OF THE ALOE AT ALBISSOLA (OLD).

sprays, and then laid upon Machine Net for a ground, instead of the ground being made by the hand or on the Pillow.

Point Bisette.—*See* BISETTE LACE.

Point Brodé.—A term applied to sprigs of pillow Lace, in which the flowers are in relief, and made of Raised Work. Brussels, Honiton, and Duchesse Lace all contain this Raised Work.

Point Campan.—A narrow Pillow Lace, made in France in the early part of the seventeenth century. It was made with fine white thread, and as an edging, and was chiefly used as a border to wider laces.

Point Chemin de Fer.—*See* EMBROIDERY STITCHES.

Point Conté. — The French name for DARNED NETTING.

Point Coupé.—The French Term for CUTWORK LACES.

Point Croisé. — *See* EMBROIDERY STITCHES and GUIPURE D'ART.

Point d'Aiguille.—These are Needle-made Laces, such as Venetian and Spanish Point, Alençon and Argentan Points, and Old Brussels.

Point d'Angleterre. — A Pillow Lace made in Flanders, and smuggled into France by English ships, during the war between Louis XIV. and the Dutch.

Point d'Angleterre Edging. — *See* ANGLETERRE EDGING.

Point d'Argentan.—*See* ARGENTAN POINT.

Point d'Armes.—*See* EMBROIDERY STITCHES.

Point d'Attache.—*See* EMBROIDERY STITCHES.

Point de Biais.—*See* EMBROIDERY STITCHES.

Point de Bruges.—Lace is made at Bruges of two kinds, one being Valenciennes, and the other Point Duchesse, or Guipure de Bruges. The Valenciennes Lace is made on the Pillow, and with a round Net Ground, but as the Bobbins in making this ground are only twisted twice at every Pinhole, instead of four or five times, the lace does not possess the value of the best descriptions of Valenciennes. Point Duchesse is a beautiful lace, similar in workmanship to Honiton Lace, but made with bolder designs and a greater amount of Raised Work. For a full description of this lace *see* DUCHESSE LACE.

Point de Bruxelles.—The French name for BRUSSELS LACE. Also GUIPURE D'ART.

Point de Cable.—*See* EMBROIDERY STITCHES.

Point de Chainette.—*See* EMBROIDERY STITCHES.

Point de Champ.—A term applied to lace made with a Net Pattern or Réseau Ground.

Point de Chant.—A Pillow Lace Ground, also known as Point de Paris. *See* POINT DE PARIS.

Point de Chaudieu.—The French term for Chain Bar, used in Macramé. *See* CHAIN BAR, MACRAMÉ.

Point d'Echelle.—*See* EMBROIDERY STITCHES.

Point de Cone.—*See* CONE, GUIPURE D'ART.

Point de Coté.—*See* EMBROIDERY STITCHES.

Point de Croix.—The French term for CROSS STITCH. *See* BERLIN WORK and EMBROIDERY STITCHES.

Point d'Epine.—*See* EMBROIDERY STITCHES.

Point d'Escalier.—*See* EMBROIDERY STITCHES.

Point d'Espagne.—The French name for Spanish Point.

Point d'Esprit.—*See* GUIPURE D'ART.

Point de Diable.—*See* EMBROIDERY STITCHES.

Point de Dieppe.—*See* DIEPPE POINT.

Point de Feston.—*See* GUIPURE D'ART.

Point de Feuillage.—The French name for the Ridge or Twisted Bar used in Macramé Lace. *See* RIDGE BAR, MACRAMÉ.

Point de Flandre.—One of the names by which Brussels Lace is known. *See* BRUSSELS LACE.

Point de France.—One of the names given to Alençon Point when made in the style of Venetian Point and with the ground formed with Brides Ornées. *See* ALENÇON POINT.

Point de Genes.—*See* GENOA LACE.

Point de Gerbe.—*See* GUIPURE D'ART.

Point de Gibecière.—The French name for the Double or Knotted Bar used in Macramé Lace. *See* DOUBLE BAR, MACRAMÉ,

Point de Gobelin.—*See* GOBELIN STITCH, BERLIN WORK.

Point de Havre.—A narrow make of Valenciennes Lace, much in request during the seventeenth and eighteenth centuries, and resembling the laces made at Dieppe.

Point de Jours.—*See* EMBROIDERY STITCHES.

Point de Marli.—This was a species of tulle or gauze, made upon the Pillow during the seventeenth and eighteenth centuries, and used as a ground for Pillow Laces.

Point de Marque.—*See* EMBROIDERY STITCHES.

Point de Mechlin.—*See* MECHLIN LACE.

Point de Medicis.—The name given in France to the Italian Raised Points, because they were first rendered popular in that country on the arrival there of Catherine de Medicis.

Point de Milan.—*See* MILAN POINT.

Point de Paris.—Also known as POINT DOUBLE. It is a narrow lace made upon the Pillow, and resembles Brussels Lace. It flourished during the seventeenth century and until the great Revolution, and was made in Paris and the surrounding country, and in Normandy.

Point de Paris Ground.—Also known as POINT DE CHANT. A Pillow Lace Ground, and one that is still used when making Black Lace. The design of the ground is that of a hexagon and a triangle alternately, and the effect is extremely good, whether the stitch is used to fill up a large surface, or whether it is only used as a Filling for the centres of flowers and sprigs. To work the insertion shown in Fig. 670: Prick the pattern with two parallel rows of Pinholes, placing the rows the distance apart that is required for the width of the insertion. Hang on twenty-four BOBBINS, numbering them from 1 to 24, in order to distinguish them while working. Separate fourteen from the rest, numbered from 11 to 24, and lay them on the right side, and lay six Bobbins, numbered from 1 to 6 on the left hand, and leave Bobbins marked 7, 8, 9, 10 hanging down in the centre. Put up two pins close together at the edge on the left-hand side of the pattern, leave Bobbins 1 and 2 outside these pins, put up one pin at the top of the next line of stitches on the left side, and leave Bobbin No. 3 against it, put up a pin at the top of the next line of stitches and underneath the last pin, and leave Bobbin No. 4 against it. Put up a pin under the last and at the top of next line, and leave Bobbin No. 5 against it. Five pins are now in position, two stuck into the pattern close together, and three stuck in as headings to three lines. Make a CLOTH STITCH with Bobbins numbered 1, 2, 3, 4, pass 9 over 11 to the left hand, pass 5 over 9 to the left hand, pass 11 over 5 to the right hand, pass 9 over 11 to the left hand, 14 over 11 to left hand, 9 over 14 to the left hand, 11 over 15 to the left hand, 15 over 9 to the right hand, 14 over 15 to the left, 9 over 11 to the right hand, 3 over 9 to the left hand, 11 over 3 to the left hand, 9 over

FIG. 670. POINT DE PARIS GROUND.

11 to the left hand, 6 over 9 to the left hand, 11 over 6 to the left hand, 9 over 13 to the left hand, 13 over 11 to the right hand, 6 over 13 to the left hand, 11 over 9 to the left hand, 4 over 11 to the right hand, 9 over 4 to the left hand, 11 over 9 to the right hand; make Cloth Stitch with 1, 2, 9, 11; twist 1 and 2 twice to the left hand, and 9 and 11 twice to the left hand, set up a pin in the small hole at the left hand edge, pass 4 over 2 to the left hand, pass 1 over 2 to the right hand, pass 1 over 2 to the left hand. Leave the thirteen Bobbins on the left-hand side hanging, put up three more pins at the head of the three next lines, and place 12 and 17 at the first pin, 16, 18, and 19 at the next pin, 22 and 25 on the next pin, and 21 and 23 at the outside of the third pin : count these pins from the left hand of the centre; now pass 10 over 7 to the left hand, 8 over 10 to the right hand, 7 over 8 to the left hand, 8 over 17 to the right hand, 12 over 8 to the left hand, 17 over 7 to the left hand, 7 over 12 to the right hand, 8 over 7 to the left hand, 12 over 17 to the left hand, 24 over 8 to the left hand, 7 over 24 to the right hand, 8 over 7 to the left hand, 7 over 16 to the right hand, 16 over 8 to the left hand, 8 over 7

to the right hand, 8 over 16 to the right hand, 18 over 8 to the left hand, 16 over 8 to the left hand, 8 over 16 to the right hand, 7 over 8 to the left hand, 18 over 16 to the left hand, 19 over 7 to the left hand, 8 over 19 to the right hand, 7 over 8 to the left hand, pass 7 over 20 to the left hand, pass 22 over 7 to the left hand, pass 20 over 8 to the left hand, pass 8 over 22 to the right hand, pass 7 over 8 to the left hand, pass 20 over 22 to the left hand, pass 8 over 24 to the right hand, pass 24 over 8 to the left hand, pass 7 over 8 to the right hand, make a Cloth Stitch with 7, 8, 21, and 23. Twist 7 and 8 twice to the left hand, 21 and 23 twice to the left hand ; set up a pin in the border just under the former one, leaving the four Bobbins hanging on the right hand of the pin.

Pass 24 over 23 to the right hand, pass 21 over 24 to the left hand, pass 21 over 23 to the left hand. Leave fourteen Bobbins hanging on the right side, and pass 5 over 14 to the left hand, pass 15 over 19 to the right hand, pass 18 over 15 to the left hand, pass 19 over 14 to the left hand, pass 14 over 18 to the right hand, pass 15 over 14 to the left hand, pass 14 over 18 to the left hand, pass 14 over 19 to the right hand, pass 18 over 14 to the left hand, pass 19 over 14 to the left hand, pass 15 over 14 to the left hand, pass 14 over 12 to the right hand, pass 17 over 14 to the left hand, pass 12 over 15 to the left hand, pass 15 over 17 to the right hand, pass 14 over 15 to the left hand, pass 17 over 12 to the left hand, pass 24 over 15 to the left hand, pass 14 over 24 to the right hand, pass 15 over 14 to the right hand, pass 14 over 19 to the right hand, pass 16 over 14 to the left hand, pass 19 over 15 to the left hand, pass 15 over 16 to the right hand, pass 14 over 15 to the left hand, pass 16 over 19 to the left hand.

Having worked once across the pattern, take the numbers off the Bobbins and re-number them straight across from 1 to 24, and repeat the pattern as above. The stitch being worked across the pattern and not straight down, it is a difficult one to acquire, but the manner of working it renders it very suitable for a FILLING if not required for a GROUND. The illustration shows how the Pins are stuck, and how the Bobbins are placed that hang down from the top of the work and remain in that position throughout to form the straight lines, while the others are working across the lace and forming the triangles.

Point d'Or.—*See* EMBROIDERY STITCHES.

Point de Plume.—*See* EMBROIDERY STITCHES.

Point de Pois.—*See* EMBROIDERY STITCHES.

Point de Poste.—*See* EMBROIDERY STITCHES.

Point de Pyramid.—*See* CONE, GUIPURE D'ART.

Point de Ragusa.—*See* RAGUSA LACE.

Point de Repasse.—*See* GUIPURE D'ART.

Point de Reprise.—*See* EMBROIDERY STITCHES and GUIPURE D'ART.

Point de Riz.—*See* EMBROIDERY STITCHES.

Point de Rose.—*See* EMBROIDERY STITCHES.

Point de Sable.—*See* EMBROIDERY STITCHES.

Point de Smyrna.—*See* EMBROIDERY STITCHES.

Point de Tigre.—*See* EMBROIDERY STITCHES.

Point de Toile.—*See* GUIPURE D'ART.

Point de Tricot.—*See* CROCHET.

Point de Tulle. — A name sometimes given to Mignonette Lace.

Point de Valenciennes.—*See* VALENCIENNES LACE.

Point de Venise.—*See* GUIPURE D'ART and VENISE POINT.

in Fig. 672 is a variety, as the ground and the pattern of Hollie Point are worked together in close Buttonhole Stitches; and the other the laces worked in detached pieces and connected together with Bar or Bride Grounds. This division includes the Spanish and Venetian Raised and Flat Points, Caterpillar Point, and some of the early

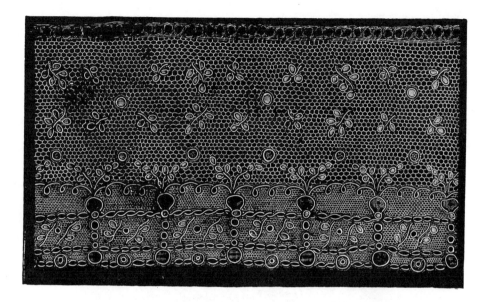

FIG. 671. ALENÇON POINT—RÉSEAU OR NET GROUND.

Point Devise.—This term, which is now only employed to signify perfection in dress or manner, was originally derived from stitches either in Embroidery or Lace, that excelled either for their beauty of arrangement or execution. Point is the French name for stitch, and Devise means well arranged.

Point Double.—*See* POINT DE PARIS.

Point Eventail.—*See* GUIPURE D'ART.

Point Faisceau.—*See* GUIPURE D'ART.

Point Gaze.—A variety of Brussels Lace. The Point Gaze contemporary with Alençon and Argentan lace was a Pillow Lace. The modern Point Gaze, the finest lace now manufactured, is a needle-made lace with Réseau ground.

Point Guipure à Bride.—A term applied generally to Guipure Laces, whose grounds are made with Brides or Bars.

Point Guipure à Réseau.—A term applied generally to Guipure Laces, whose grounds are formed with the Réseau or Net Pattern Ground.

Point Lace.—This name is applied generally to all Needle-made Laces except Cut and Drawn Works, that are made upon Parchment Patterns with varieties of Buttonhole Stitches. The Points are divided into two separate classes, one being for those laces made with the Réseau or Net Patterned Ground, as shown in Fig. 671 of Alençon Point, and including Alençon, Argentan, Old Brussels, and Burano, and of which Hollie Point, shown

Point de France, and is shown in Fig. 673 of Venetian Lace. These laces, though differing so essentially as to design have in common that all are worked with a needle and fine thread, in small sections upon Parchment Patterns, and that each part of the Pattern is surrounded by a line of Buttonholes, either thick and raised, or of

FIG. 672. HOLLIE POINT.

the finest make according to the lace, that the Fillings or centres which these lines surround are made with Buttonholes, formed into devices by working some parts close and others open, and that their grounds if Réseau are made with loose Buttonholes formed into hexagons, and if Bar, by thickly covering a line of thread with Buttonholes.

The art of making Point Lace fell into decay in the eighteenth century, mainly through the dictates of fashion which preferred the light and fine laces produced upon the Pillow to the heavier laces made by the Needle, but also because the Pillow Laces, being worked much more quickly than the Needle, were cheaper to buy; as the fine Points, such as Alençon, Argentan, and Brussels, from the time they took to make, were most expensive and only within the means of the wealthy. For many years Needle made Laces have not been worked for trade purposes, but

this in small sections upon separate pieces of parchment Prick the outline of each separate piece of lace, with two pinholes close together, and make the same number of pinholes upon the inside of the lace as upon the outside. With coarse Mecklenburgh thread, No. 12, outline this pricked pattern with a FIL DE TRACE, thus: Begin from the back of the pattern, bring the needle up in one of the pinholes that are close together, and put it down in its companion hole. Go all round the outline and then tie the two ends of the coarse thread together

FIG. 673. VENETIAN LACE WITH BAR OR BRIDE GROUND.

the art of making them has lately revived, and reproductions of old designs and stitches are now worked by ladies for their own adornment, although the peculiarly fine lace thread used in making old Points cannot any longer be procured.

The manner of working Needle Laces with Réseau Grounds is fully described in ALENÇON POINT and HOLLIE POINT, therefore it does not require recapitulation. For working Points with Bride Grounds, proceed as follows: Make a design of the lace upon Toile Ciré and then copy

at the back of the parchment; fill the needle with No. 7 Mecklenburgh thread and begin again underneath the pattern, pass the needle up through the first hole of two holes and go all round the outline, slipping the thread underneath the little stitches made with the coarse thread. These outline threads are required to keep the lace in position while it is working and to prevent its slipping about: when the piece is finished the coarse thread is cut stitch by stitch underneath the pattern and the work is thus released without its being pulled or disarranged.

Fig. 674 shows a piece of lace worked. Take No. 20 Mecklenburgh thread and commence by filling in one of the leaves of the design. Fasten the thread firmly to the left side of the leaf, pass the needle through the Fil de Trace, which use as a foundation, and work upon it a row of POINT NOUÉ or BUTTONHOLE STITCHES not too close together, and yet so as to fill in well. When one row is finished, fasten the last stitch firmly to the right side and pass the thread back again to the left side of the leaf and make another row of Buttonhole; work each stitch over the laid thread and into the Buttonhole above it. Continue to make rows of close Buttonhole until the open row in the pattern is reached, which work as a row

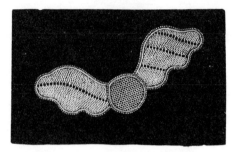

FIG. 674. POINT LACE.

of POINT D'ESPAGNE. Work the second leaf as the first, and the circle in the centre entirely in Point d'Espagne. Having finished the filling in of the design, run round the outside of the leaves and circle with a coarse thread, and Buttonhole this over so as to form a fine CORDONNET or Edge. Ornament the Cordonnet with PICOTS. All the various sections of the design are worked as described above, except that the Fillings are varied, and instead of close Buttonhole and Point d'Espagne, the stitches described below are introduced to give a variety, but not more than four or five different stitches are worked upon one pattern, and close Buttonhole Stitch is always used for thick parts, and in a larger proportion than the others.

The separate pieces of the lace having been taken off,

FIG. 675. ORNAMENTAL BARS.

their patterns are connected together as follows : TACK the various pieces of lace on to the full-sized pattern, and connect them together by working plain BUTTON-HOLE BARS from point to point, or by working the Ornamental Bars shown in Fig. 675, which are ornamented with Picots.

These Point Lace directions are given for the Flat Points; the Raised Points, which are a peculiarity of Spanish and Venetian Points, where they differ from Flat Points, are described under their own headings. They

differ from other Points, by being joined together with Cordonnets raised considerably above the rest of the lace, and which are ornamented with FLEURS VOLANTS. The stitches used in their Fillings are the same as are used in the Flat Points; these are as follows :

Picot or Dotted Bars.—To work : Prepare a foundation of loose threads as bars all over the space, work five close BUTTONHOLE STITCHES on to the first Bar, then a loose stitch, pass the needle under the loop and over the thread and draw up quickly. Work five Buttonhole Stitches, and repeat the dot. Another way to work—make four close Buttonhole Stitches, and one loose, put the needle through the loose stitch, wind the thread several times round the needle, hold tightly with the thumb, and draw the needle and twisted thread quickly through to form the Dot.

Point d'Alençon.—Used to fill up narrow spaces. To work : Make a number of HERRINGBONE STITCHES a quarter of an inch apart, and from left to right. To vary it, work a twisted thread over the plain Herringbone Stitches ; or, work a thick BUTTONHOLE STITCH on the plain Point d'Alençon.

Point d'Angleterre, or Open English Lace.—To work, as shown in Fig. 676: Fill up the space with single threads

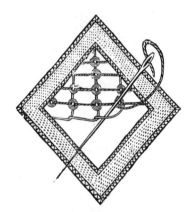

FIG. 676. POINT D'ANGLETERRE.

at an equal and short distance apart and in one direction. Then cross the threads in the opposite direction, and pass the needle over and under the lines alternately. Fasten the last thread well to the edge, and twist over with the needle to where the first lines cross. Work round the cross about six or eight times, and pass the needle over and under to make a spot. Twist again over the thread to the next cross, and repeat as before. Continue this until all the spots are made over the space.

Point d'Anvers.—This is not a real Point Lace Stitch, but is often used to fill up small spaces. To work : Take two single threads down the centre of the space, fasten to the edge of the lace, and DARN a Close Stitch over and under the two threads for a short distance ; then make a loop into the lace on either side, Darn again to the same distance, make a loop, and repeat to the end.

Point de Brabançon.—To work : Commence at the left side. First row—work one long and one small BUTTON-HOLE STITCH in succession to the end of the row, and fasten to the lace. Second row—work seven close Buttonhole Stitches into the long and two loose stitches into the small loops. Repeat the rows alternately. *See* Fig. 677.

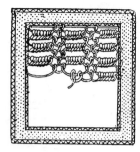

FIG. 677. POINT DE BRABANÇON.

Point de Bruxelles.—This is formed with successive rows of Buttonholes. To work: Commence on the right hand of the space in a corner, and make a loop across the work. Return by making a loose BUTTONHOLE into the

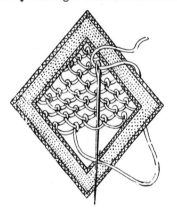

FIG. 678. POINT DE BRUXELLES.

first loop, and so form two loops. For each row, fill every loop of the previous row with a loose Buttonhole. Fig. 678 shows this stitch made as a row from left to right, and Fig. 679, the same stitch worked back from right to left.

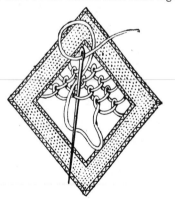

FIG. 679. POINT DE BRUXELLES.

Point de Cordova.—There are two ways of working this Stitch, one like the Point de Reprise of Guipure d'Art (which *see*), the other as follows: Commence by taking three threads across the space, place them nearly close together, then twist the needle twice round the third line, and DARN a spot across all three lines; twist the needle again over

the thread several times, and work a spot over the three lines. Continue to repeat to the end of the line, then fill in the rest of the space with three threads, over which work spots, putting the latter opposite the ones first made. When this is finished, work the three threads the opposite way to form a square, passing the threads one way over, and the other way under alternately, and between the spots already worked. Then Darn or work a spot on these as previously described.

Point d'Espagne and Point de Bruxelles.—Fig. 680 shows the manner of forming a fancy filling by working

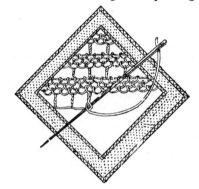

FIG. 680. POINT D'ESPAGNE AND POINT DE BRUXELLES.

these two stitches alternately. To work: Commence at the extreme point of a space, and work three rows of POINT DE BRUXELLES, and then one of POINT D'ESPAGNE. Continue these four rows until the space is filled up.

Point d'Espagne, or Spanish Point.—To work: Commence the first row from left to right, and keep the

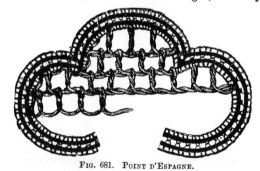

FIG. 681. POINT D'ESPAGNE.

thread turned to the right. Put the needle into the edge

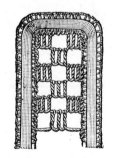

FIG. 682. TREBLE POINT D'ESPAGNE.

of the lace, and bring it out inside the loop made by the thread. Draw it up rather loosely, and pass the needle again under the stitch, fasten to the lace at the end of the row. Second row—return by OVERCASTING into each space, and put the needle once into every stitch to form a twist. Point d'Espagne is worked with the stitches close, or a little way apart (*see* Fig. 681). To work Treble Point d'Espagne : First row—work three close stitches and miss a space alternately. Second row—work three close stitches into the open space, and one long loop below the three close stitches. Repeat as before. *See* Fig. 682.

Point de Fillet.—This stitch makes a good effect as a groundwork. To work: Commence with a loose BUTTON-HOLE STITCH in one corner and fasten to the lace. OVER-CAST two stitches down the lace, and make a Buttonhole

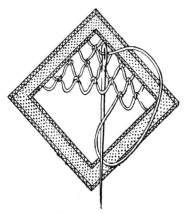

FIG. 683. POINT DE FILLET.

Stitch into the first one, and to make it firm, put the needle first under the knot, over the thread, and under it again. Then continue with the next stitch in the same way. Repeat the rows, and take two stitches down the lace each time. (*See* Fig. 683).

Point de Grecque.—To work: Commence from left

FIG. 684. POINT DE GRECQUE.

to right, and work one loose loop, then three POINT D'ESPAGNE near together ; continue the alternate stitches to the end of the space. Repeat the rows in the same way, and always work the three Point d'Espagne into the loose loop. (*See* Fig. 684).

Point de Reprise.—To work: Fill the space with a number of Vandyked lines, at an even distance from and intersecting each other, then into every alternate space formed by the single lines, work a DARNING Stitch over and under the opposite threads to form a triangle. *See* Fig. 685. Figs. 686, 687, 688, and 689, show this stitch

made in various angles, the first threads being arranged either as straight lines or double or single triangles, but

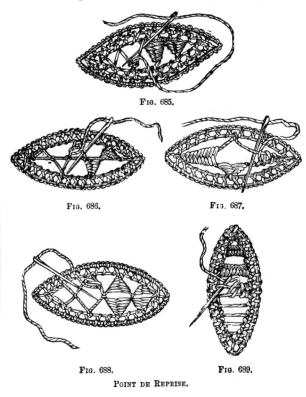

FIG. 685.

FIG. 686.   FIG. 687.

FIG. 688.   FIG. 689.

POINT DE REPRISE.

the varieties are all finished in the manner described above.

Point de Sorrento.—Also known as Sorrento Lace. To work : Make a loose stitch from right to left across the extreme point of a space, and in the return row work two BUTTONHOLE STITCHES into it, and fasten the thread on the right side of the space. Loop back again from left to

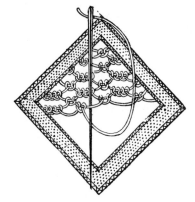

FIG. 690. POINT DE SORRENTO.

right with two loops, one before and one behind the two Buttonholes, and fasten the thread to the left side. Work two Buttonholes into the first space and four into the next, and fasten into the right side. Continue to work a row of loops, and a return row of alternately two and four Buttonholes (*see* Fig. 690) until the space is filled.

Point de Tulle.—A good stitch for the foundation of very fine work. To work: Commence with an open POINT D'ESPAGNE, which work all over the space, then go over a second time, thus—put the needle under the twisted bar in the first line, bring it out and go under the twisted bar in the second line, and alternate this backwards and forwards. When the two lines are finished, work the next two in the same manner, and continue until all the lines are completed.

Point de Valenciennes.—To work: First row—work one long and one short POINT DE BRUXELLES STITCH to the end of the row. Second row—into the long stitch work nine close BUTTONHOLE STITCHES, miss over the short stitch and work nine close Buttonhole Stitches into the next long stitch. Repeat to the end. Third row—work five Buttonhole Stitches in the nine of the last row, and two into the short Buttonhole Stitch. Continue to the end. Fourth row—work two Buttonholes into the five

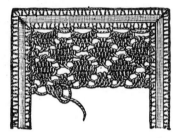

FIG. 691. POINT DE VALENCIENNES.

stitches, and five Buttonholes over the two Buttonhole Stitches, and repeat to the end of the row. Fifth row—work nine Buttonholes over the five stitches, miss over the two Buttonhole Stitches, and work nine Buttonhole over the next five stitches, and repeat. Sixth row—work five Buttonhole into the nine stitches, to the end of the row, two over the single stitch, and repeat. Seventh row—commence like the fourth row, and continue the rows until the space is filled in. *See* Fig. 691.

Point de Venise.—Commence to work from the left to the right, and work one loose BUTTONHOLE STITCH. Into this work four close Buttonhole Stitches, then make a loose stitch and work four close stitches into it. Repeat

FIG. 692. POINT DE VENISE.

to the end. Second row—work a Buttonhole Stitch into each loop, and fasten the thread at the end into the lace. Repeat these two rows alternately to the end of the space (*see* Fig 692.)

Point Feston.—This stitch is made with Point de Bruxelles Loops secured by being knotted at every loop. First row—make a POINT DE BRUXELLES loop across the

extreme point of the space. Second row—fasten the thread a little lower down than the first loop into the edge of the lace, and make a Point de Bruxelles loop into the first made one, draw it up and then across the Buttonhole that it forms (*see* Fig. 694—Detail A), make a tight Button-

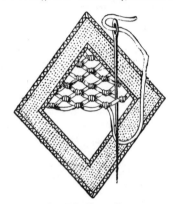

FIG. 693. POINT FESTON.

hole. Work all the rows like the second row. Fig. 693 shows the needle put into the loop of previous row.

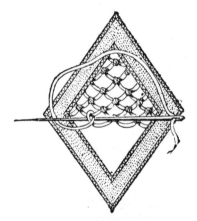

FIG. 694. POINT FESTON—DETAIL A.

Fig. 694—Detail A, the Loop being secured with a Buttonhole across it.

Point Mechlin.—This stitch can only be used to fill in small spaces that require an open stitch. To work as

FIG. 695. POINT MECHLIN.

shown in Fig. 695: HERRINGBONE across the space, twist the thread up one of the lines, and where the lines cross each other. Work a small round with BUTTONHOLE STITCHES over the two lines, twist the thread down the next thread and make another round where it crosses the third thread. Continue until rounds are formed over every cross of the Herringbone Stitches.

Point Noué.— This is the close Buttonhole Stitch, which is chiefly used in Point Lace. To work: Fasten the thread to the left of the Filling and work a row of BUTTON-HOLE STITCHES to the other side of the work, fasten the thread firmly to the right side, and then return it to the left

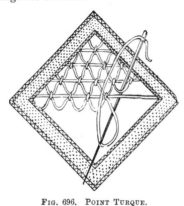

FIG. 696. POINT TURQUE.

and work the second row of Buttonhole over this thread and into every stitch on the last row. When Point Noué is worked with other stitches so as to form devices, the thread from right to left is omitted, and the stitches are worked across the row and back again without any foun-

loop formed by the twist, draw it close and repeat to the end of the row. Second row—take a single thread across from right to left, repeat the first and second row, and always pass the needle under the straight thread as well as into the loops. *See* Fig. 696.

Point Lache.—*See* GUIPURE D'ART.

Point Lancé.—*See* EMBROIDERY STITCHES.

Point Lancé Embroidery.—A modern Embroidery, deriving its name from the frequent use of a particular stitch. It is an extremely easy work, and one that is useful for working borders to tablecloths and curtains. It is made by ornamenting the foundation material with a band of a contrasting colour, and finishing off with Point Lancé and other Embroidery Stitches worked either with filoselles or Berlin wools. To work, as shown in Fig. 697: Select a pale blue or sea-green diagonal cloth, serge, or fine cloth material for the foundation, and a russet red for the band. This band should be 4 inches in width, and can be made either of satin or cloth or braid (ribbon could be used, but is more difficult to work through). Embroider the pattern, shown in the illustration, upon this band before placing it upon the foundation. Work the Star in the centre with a number of long RAILWAY STITCHES, in old gold-coloured filoselles or wool, and COUCH this star down to the material with

FIG. 697. POINT LANCÉ EMBROIDERY.

dation to them, supported by their connection with the preceding row as described above.

Point Turque, or Turkish Stitch.—An easy and useful stitch. To work: First row—make a loop on to the lace, and take the needle through the twist, then through the

a light yellow silk, and with stitches arranged to form two circles. For the long lines upon each side of the star, lay down double strands of filoselle or wool of the same colour as used on ·the star, Couch them down with yellow silk, and finish off with three small Railway Stitches at each of their ends. Having worked all the band, lay it down upon the foundation material, 4 inches from the edge, and tack it round all the sides. Fasten by RUNNING it upon each side, but do not turn any edge under. Take filoselles, or wool of two shades of russet red, one darker and one lighter than the strip, and lay these along the edge of the strip, the darker inside and the lighter outside. Couch these down with silk matching them in shade. Work the fan-shaped sprays upon the foundation with a pale blue or sea-green colour, and in POINT LANCÉ; the little stars beyond them in Point Lancé and in the two shades of yellow, and the Vandyke line in DOUBLE FEATHER STITCH.

Point Mexico.—*See* EMBROIDERY STITCHES.

Point Mignonette.—*See* MIGNONETTE LACE.

Point Minuscule.—*See* EMBROIDERY STITCHES.

Point Moscow.—*See* RUSSIAN LACE.

Point Natté.—*See* EMBROIDERY STITCHES.

Point Natté Embroidery.—This work is of modern origin, and is a kind of inlaid Appliqué, being formed with bright pieces of satin laid as a design upon a dark foundation, and their edges surrounded with braid, while their centres are covered over with Point Natté Stitches worked in filoselles of various colours. To work: Select a conventionalised flower design, such as is used in high art Crewel Work as a border to curtains or tablecloths, trace this out upon dark cloth or serge, cut out the various sections of the pattern that form the petals of the flowers, and the leaves, buds, or seed vessels in satin, choosing satin that matches the shade of the leaf or flower required; lay these pieces of satin down upon the foundation in their proper position, and TACK them on; then take a fine gold-coloured braid or cord, and lay it on the edge of the satin, to conceal the tacking threads. RUN or COUCH this to the foundation, thread a needle with filoselle slightly darker than the colour of the satin, and work over all the various pieces with POINT NATTÉ STITCHES, or with HERRINGBONE or LADDER STITCH where the first would not look well, make all the stems and tendrils with CREWEL STITCH, and with single SATIN STITCHES form rays upon the foundation where such ornaments would improve the edges of the Satin Flowers.

Point Neige.—*See* CROCHET.

Point Noné.—*See* EMBROIDERY STITCHES.

Point Noué. — *See* EMBROIDERY STITCHES, and POINT LACE.

Point Ondulé.—A French name for the Double Bar used in Macramé Lace. *See* MACRAMÉ, DOUBLE BAR.

Point Paper.—This kind of paper is employed for the purpose of forming and colouring designs for Berlin or Tapestry work. It is marked out in squares of minute size, and artists, engaged at high salaries, sketch outlines, and fill them in with colours. From these paintings on Point Paper, engravings and etchings on Copper are made. *See* PAPER PATTERNS.

Point Passé.—*See* EMBROIDERY STITCHES.

Point Perlé.—*See* EMBROIDERY STITCHES.

Point Plat.—A term applied to lace sprigs and flowers that are made upon a Pillow separately from their grounds.

Of these, Brussels Application Lace, Duchesse Lace, and Honiton Application are the best known.

Point Plumetis.—The French name for FEATHER STITCH. *See* EMBROIDERY STITCHES.

Point Rosette.—*See* EMBROIDERY STITCHES.

Point Raccroc.—*See* RACCROC STITCH.

Point Pusse.—*See* EMBROIDERY STITCHES.

Point Sans Evers.—*See* EMBROIDERY STITCHES.

Point Serré.—*See* GUIPURE D'ART.

Point Tiellage.—*See* GUIPURE D'ART.

Point Tiré.—The French name for DRAWN WORK.

Point Tresse.—Up to the sixteenth century a lace was occasionally made from human hair, and probably originated in the custom, during the barbarous ages, of forming the beards and hairs of the vanquished into fringes wherewith to adorn the mantles of the conquerors. That worked in the sixteenth century was made upon the Pillow, and woven simply for ornament, and was sometimes used to form a foundation, or pad, over which a lady's real hair was carried. Lace made with grey and white hair was valuable, not only for its rarity, but on account of the silvery gloss produced by using that coloured hair. A remnant of this lacemaking survived until our own times as a foundation for wigs, the hair which formed them being plaited together upon a Pillow, after the manner of making a Lace Ground. For work of a thicker description with hair, *see* HAIR WORK.

Point Turc.—*See* EMBROIDERY STITCHES.

Polecat, or Fitch Fur (*Mustela Putorius*).—The Polecat is of the Ermine or Weasel tribe, and its Fur is employed for general purposes of women's dress. The ground of the fur is a rich yellow, while the upper portion is a jet black. This fur has the advantage of being very durable; but the odour is disagreeable, and difficult of discharge. It is more in request in America than in this country. The skins measure 10 inches by 21 inches, and vary much in quality and price.

Polish Rabbit Fur (*Lepus Cuniculus*).—A white Fur, imported in large quantities into this country. It is much employed for the lining of women's cloaks, being one of the best and cheapest for that purpose.

Polygon Work.—Made with plaited ribbons, or braids, in the form of open-centred hexagons. The ribbons when plaited are laid upon velvet or satin foundations that show through the open work. The foundation should contrast with the colour of the ribbons. Thus, brown or grey ribbons are laid upon blue satin, rose-coloured ribbons upon black velvet, gold ribbons on brown velvet. To work: Trace a pattern of a number of hexagons side by side, and underneath each other, paste the pattern on to cardboard, cut long lengths of ribbon, and plait them, guided by the pattern; double the strips of ribbon, and pin the doubled pieces on to the top of a hexagon and down one of the sides, then interlace the side strips with the top ones, each going over and under alternately. The lengths of ribbon are not cut, but turned when they reach a side, or the open centre, and worked back.

Pompadour Patterns.—The distinctive characteristic of the small floral designs so named is the combination of pink with blue in the colouring. All the tints are of very delicate hues, and shades of the same. The style is named after the famous Madame de Pompadour, who appears to have been the first patroness of such a combination of colours in her costumes.

Pompon. — A French term used to signify a fluffy ball of silk or wool, worn in the front, at the top of a soldier's shako, and adopted as a trimming for bonnets and hats.

Poplin. — A kind of Rep made of silk and wool, or silk and worsted, having a fine cord on the surface, and produced in several varieties, brocaded, watered, and plain. There are three classes of Poplin—the single, the double, and the Terry. The difference between the first two kinds consists in the thickness respectively of their warps. The last-named, or third-class, is richly corded, and resembles a Terry velvet, excepting that it is alike on both sides. The single and double are alike figured, the design being thrown up in the brocade. Tartans are likewise produced in Poplins, of which the colours are durable, being woven of silks already dyed, and, like all other varieties of this material, are alike on both sides, rendering it a less expensive dress material than the comparative costliness would seem to promise. All these varieties are produced in every Poplin manufactory in Dublin, the seat of the industry, where upwards of six hundred looms are in constant work, yet each firm is distinguished by the special attention given to a particular characteristic of the stuff, the design, colouring, or material itself. The loom employed is the Jacquard. There are four large manufactories for producing Poplins in Dublin, two of which employ some 500 men and women. Magnificent Court dresses and hangings are produced in Poplin, the patterns being woven in gold and silver, on white, blue, and pink grounds, with flowers. Poplins of very good quality are manufactured at Norwich, for the most part plain and black. The French material known as such is inferior to both the British manufactures, the weft employed being of cotton, or partially so, instead of fine wool, and the silk of the warp very scanty by comparison. The material is, therefore, very sensitive to moisture, and liable to cockle, and receive stains, and is greatly inferior in this respect to the Irish, which never draws up in puckers from exposure to the rain or damp. The reason for this is easily explained. The wool employed is that fine kind of woollen thread known as "Jenappe," which is carefully selected, and dyed previously to its use, and having thus shrunk to the utmost degree of which it is capable, is rendered indifferent to moisture. Then the silk warp, which is of exceedingly fine quality, is so woven as to cover the woollen threads completely, both wrong and right side of the textile. The original invention of Poplin is claimed by Avignon, once a Papal See, on which account it was called "Papeline," in compliment to the reigning Pope, at which time (the fifteenth century) this rich material was produced to supply the gorgeous ecclesiastical vestments and hangings in use. The industry was introduced into Dublin by French immigrants, refugees, at the time of the Edict of Nantes, who settled in that part of the Irish capital called "The Liberties." The La Touche family established the first organised manufactory there, which commenced operations in 1693. The beautiful Terry Poplins that compose the draperies of Dublin Castle, Windsor Castle, Marlborough House, Osborne, and Blenheim, were produced by Dublin firms. Tabinet is a variety of the same description of textile as Poplin, and is employed for upholstery.

Portuguese Lace. — The laces made in Portugal are, with the exception of that made at Peniche, similar to those worked in Spain. In the olden days, Point Lace in no way differing from the Spanish Needle Points was worked, and at the present time the same kinds of Pillow Laces are made in both countries. *See* SPANISH LACE.

Pouce. — A French term for a measure of length, employed in trade. It is equivalent to an inch, or the first joint of the thumb. The literal meaning is thumb.

Pouf. — The French term denoting a Puffing of any material, as a style of trimming and ornamenting a dress, or other article of wear. *See* PUFFING.

Poult de Soie. — A description of corded silk dress material, measuring 26 inches in width. It is of a rich, thick quality, and may be had in every colour.

Pounce. — This is the gum of the juniper tree when reduced to a finely pulverised state. Besides other uses, it is employed to prepare material for embroidery when the tracing of outlines is requisite. A substitute is obtained in finely powdered pipeclay, which may be slightly darkened, if desired, by the addition of a little charcoal.

Pouncing. — The method of Pouncing is as follows: Rub the Pounce over a piece of paper on which the pattern has been drawn, secure it firmly on the cloth, silk, or velvet, to be embroidered, and prick the pattern through to the material beneath it, so as to deposit the Pounce upon it. Paint the outline with drawing liquid, which may be had in any colour. There are various preparations made; those of gum and white lead should be avoided, on account of the rough character of the surface, and the tendency to peel off, which injures the material employed in working the design. When tracing designs for Embroidery upon dark and raised materials, outline the design upon a piece of strong cartridge paper, then prick with a pin, or No. 6 needles, along every line of the outline, which for the purpose should be laid upon a roll of flannel, or other soft cushion, and make a number of clear round holes, an eighth of an inch, or less, apart. Lay the pricked pattern upon the material, flatten it well down, and keep it in position with heavy weights. Fill a small bag, made of coarse muslin, with white French chalk, or pipeclay, and rub the chalk through the pinholes until every one be filled with it. Raise up the cartridge paper very carefully, not to disturb the dots of chalk upon the material. Take a paint brush, and fill it with white paint (water colour) and gum or water size, and paint the lines upon the material that are indicated by the dots of chalk. When Pouncing through two light materials, use charcoal instead of white chalk, and brush this on with a drawing stump.

Poussin Lace. — Also known as Petit Poussin. This

is a narrow lace resembling Valenciennes, and is made at Dieppe, Havre, and other towns in Normandy. It was used to trim collars and caps, and, being easily made, was sold at a very cheap rate. The name Poussin, which means a chicken, is given to this lace to denote its delicacy.

Preserving Gold and Silver Lace.—This lace, when laid by for any length of time, will become dim and tarnished. If the gold be worn away, the whole surface must be re-gilt; but if not, restore in the following manner: Warm a small quantity of spirits of wine, and apply it to the lace with the help of a fine sable brush; be careful to omit no part of the gold, and to rub the spirit well into all the hollows and thick places.

Prickers.—These are used in Pillow Lace making to prick the holes in the Parchment Pattern that receive the pins, and keep the lace in position while in progress. The Prickers are simply fine needles, either put into a handle, or held in the hand.

Princettas.—This is an all-wool worsted material, which comes under the denomination of a Stuff. It is a description of Lasting, or Serge de Berry, and, like these, can be had of an inferior quality, composed of a union of wool and cotton.

Printed Blinds.—Similar to glazed Chintz, usually printed to look like Venetian blinds, but also to be had in various designs and colours. The widths run from 36 to 38 inches, 40 inches, 42 inches, and so on, by 2 inches, to 80 or 100 inches.

Prints.—Calico, Cambric, and Muslin stuffs, so called because printed with designs in colours. The art was commenced in England in 1676, but is of very ancient origin in India, and the Egyptians also practised it by the use of mordants. Lancashire is the chief seat of the manufacture in England. Lilac and pink are usually the fastest colours, but good washing prints can now be obtained in every colour. All the nap is singed off the surface of the calico before printing; it is then bleached and smoothed, and the designs, engraved on copper cylinders, are printed upon them. In cleansing them, chemical powders and dry soaps should be avoided. Vast quantities of Printed Cotton goods are exported yearly to all parts of the world. Amongst these there is a large proportion manufactured with colours and designs especially adapted to suit the taste of the native populations of certain parts of the African Continent, and also of India, which never appear in the English market. The printing of cotton or linen cloths is of very remote antiquity. Strabo (B.C. 327) mentions that finely-flowered Cottons or Chintzes were seen by the Greeks in India on the occasion of an expedition under Alexander. That the ancient Egyptians practised the art of dyeing is recorded by Pliny; Homer speaks of the variegated linen cloths of Sidon; and Herodotus of those produced in the Caucasus, which were dyed in durable colours. This last historical statement dates back beyond 400 B.C.

Pro Patria Tape.—A fine Linen Tape, of a similar make to Dutch Tape, the numbers running from 11 to 151.

Prunello (derived from the French *Prunelle*).—A thin woollen, or mixed Stuff, formerly used for scholastic black gowns, and now for shoes for elderly women. It is a kind of Lasting, a coarse variety of which is called, by the French, "Satin Laine."

Prussian Bindings.—These are designed for the binding of mantles, dressing-gowns, and waterproofs, and sometimes for flannels, in lieu of Italian Ferrets and Statute Galloons. They consist of a silk face and cotton back, having a diagonal twill, and are sold by the gross of four pieces, each containing 36 yards.

Ptarmigan (*Tetrao Mutus*).—A bird of the Grouse family. It is almost entirely white in the winter. The skin is employed for the making of women's hats, collarettes, and muffs.

Puckering.—A term used in reference to Needlework, both plain and decorative. It signifies the drawing-in of one side of two pieces of material tighter than the other, in reference to plain sewing; and in the execution of embroidery, it denotes a drawing of the surface of the material in and out, so as to make it uneven, by the irregularity with which the embroidery threads are drawn —some loose, some tight. It may also arise from using too coarse a thread for the closeness of the material to be embroidered.

Puffings.—Bands of any material, cut either straight or on the bias, and gathered on both sides; used as headings to flounces, round the sleeves, or down them. In olden times they were much in fashion for the dress of both men and women. The method of making these, like everything else, depends on the current fashion. At one time Puffs are made on the cross of materials, and at another, even those that are transparent, are invariably cut on the straight; and this from the length, not width, way of the stuff. The proportion, however, is the same, for both Tarlatan net and Tulle require as much again as the space they are to cover—*i.e.*, a skirt 4 yards needs a strip of 8 yards for the Puff. Grenadine and silk gauze, being slightly more substantial, do not need quite as much; and for thick, opaque fabrics, half as much again as the foundation is sufficient. When skirts are much gored it is impossible to make a group of Puffs; but you may divide every two with a ruche, or other device, to admit of cutting the Puffs asunder, so as to lessen the length for the upper ones. If all were made at once, by a series of Runnings on one width of stuff, the top Puffs on a gored skirt—which is, of course, narrower as it goes upwards— would be by so much the fuller than the Puffs nearer the Hem, and the effect would be very clumsy, as the trimming should be lighter above than below. Run crossway Puffs straight along a creased mark, and TACK the thread, when drawn up, lightly down to the foundation. Fold the skirt into four, and put a pin at each quarter; fold the strip into four, and do the same. Run a thread from pin to pin, fixing one on the Puff, to one on the skirt, at each division. Then, while spread over the corner of a table, far enough in to distend a quarter at a time, pull up the drawing thread, twist it round the pin, equalise the fulness with a needle, and secure it with pins every few inches. Every quarter being so arranged, turn the skirt inside out, and RUN along on the inside, to sew the Puff to the dress, which is seen through. This saves much fingering, as the left hand underneath need scarcely touch the dress. A long straw needle is the best for all trimmings made of clear tissues.

Puffs that seem to hang over at the bottom are called " falling *bouillionées*." Crease them down on the wrong side, and make a RUNNING a little way in, while still creased, so as to take up the material double. Sew each succeeding row, made on one piece, to the skirt by Running the inside of the Puff, to the right side of the dress, the creased edge lying upwards. The topmost Puff may have the edge turned down. Make a Running, so as to gather it up into a little frill heading. Puffs on the straight, not meant to hang downwards, as above, may not show the gathering thread; Crease them on the inside, and WHIP them scantily over.

Stout woollens and silks may be gathered up better, and are more durable, if a small cotton cord be run in the crease.

Upright Puffs are never much in use as skirt trimmings when gored dresses are in vogue, as the upper portions of them would project more than the lower. They do not look well unless fully as much again be gathered as the height they are to reach. Mark the portion of the skirt to be covered into spaces, by placing a pin at each division. Make the Runnings on the length of the material, secure the top of each Running to one of the pins, and draw the thread even with the skirt, twisting the loose end round a pin, opposite that of the top. As every two or three are so far arranged, distribute the fulness along the thread with tolerable equality, but more towards the lower part. Make a Running down the lines, and then continue the rest. Close the openings of the Puff at the bottom, by using the width in little plaits in the middle of the Puff; and draw the tops upwards, chiefly in the centre, and sew them there. Make a series of semicircles thus; presuming that no other trimming surmount them. If tiny Puffs be used for entire plastrons, from throat to feet, make them on one piece of material, and that on the selvedge-way; as widthway or crossway would show so many joins. When making them of such great length, cut off the quantity, and BASTE a line at every third or quarter, and also on the lining, or dress to be covered; then make the Runnings, ending them at every Basting, and fix them, division by division, beginning at the top one.

Puff Netting.—*See* NETTING.

Punto à Groppo.—Italian name for KNOTTED LACES.

Punto à Maglia.—Italian for DARNED NETTING.

Punto à Relievo.—The Italian name for VENICE RAISED POINT LACE.

Punto d'Aere.—Italian for RETICELLA LACES.

Punto di Milano.—Italian for MILAN POINT.

Punto di Venezia.—Italian for VENICE POINT.

Punto Gotico.—A lace made in Rome during the sixteenth century, and resembling the Italian, Venetian, and Spanish Points. The patterns are all geometrical, and resemble the designs used in Gothic Architecture. But few specimens of this lace are to be met with at the present time, as though not the oldest description of lace, Punto Gotico is nearly so. The specimens remaining are all of a coarse make, and are worked entirely in close

BUTTONHOLE over threads, and connected by BRIDES ORNÉES.

Punto in Aria.—Italian for flat VENETIAN POINT.

Punto Serrato.—The Italian name for the close Stitch used in Needle Points, and known as BUTTONHOLE or POINT NONÉ.

Punto Tagliato.—The Italian name for CUTWORK.

Punto Tirato.—The Italian name for DRAWN WORK.

Purdah.—An Indian cotton cloth, having blue and white stripes, used for curtains.

Purl.—For Pillow Lace making, *see* PEARL. For Knitting and Tatting, *see* KNITTING AND TATTING.

Purse Moulds.—There are two kinds of these moulds, which are made of ivory and wood; one is called a "Moule Turc," and has small brass pins fixed round the edges of the largest circumference; the other is formed for making a purse *en feston*, which is shaped like a thimble perforated with a double row of holes, like a band, round the open end, a little removed from the rim. Through these perforations the needle is passed, to secure the Purse to the Mould where the work is commenced.

Purse Silk or Twist.—A thick-twisted sewing silk, used with a needle in Embroidery, or with a Crochet needle in Purse making. It is also worked with an ordinary large needle, when the Purse is a short one, made on a thimble-shaped wooden frame, to be fitted with a clasp.

Purse Stretcher.—This small appliance is useful for drawing the several stitches made in Crochet, Knitting, and Netting long Purses, into their exact relative positions, and tightening each knot into a uniform rate of firmness. The Stretcher could easily be home-made, as it consists of two small pieces of wood round on the outside and flat inside, just like a split pencil. Long screws are introduced through apertures at either end of these pieces of wood, and the latter, being inserted into the Purse (before it is sewn up at the ends), it is stretched by means of the screws.

Pushmina Cloth.—A beautiful material made of Vicuna wool, produced in India. It is plain-made, exceedingly soft, and in grey and buff colours. It is to be had by the yard, and likewise in the dress, ready prepared for making up, and embroidered in silk.

Pushum.—The downy substance which grows only close to the skin of the Thibetan goat, below the long hair, of which the wool for shawls consists.

Putto.—The cloth made of camels' hair, which is inferior in quality to that called Pushum, or Shawl Wool (which *see*). It is employed by the natives for the making of their long coats called Chogas, which are decorated with braidings in silk. Putto is softer in quality than those resembling our Kerseymere cloths.

Puy.—The department of Haute Loire, and particularly the town of Le Puy, has been one of the most important lace centres since the fifteenth century, and the industry is still carried on, though it does not flourish as in the latter part of the eighteenth century, when the workers in the department numbered 70,000. The first laces made were a kind of coarse Darned Netting, to these succeeded an imitation of most of the Flanders Laces which obtained a large market both in England and Spain beside their own country. Latterly the manufacture has included Blonde Laces, Silk Guipures, and Brussels Application.

Pyrenean Wool.—A very fine description of woollen yarn, finer than the Shetland wool used for making crochet shawls. It does not wash well, and is sold by the pound weight.

Q.

Quadrille Paper.—This is paper marked out in squares, for the purpose of painting Embroidery Designs. It is also known as POINT PAPER.

Quality Binding, or Carpet Binding.—A kind of tape made of worsted, used in Scotland for binding the borders of carpets. This is the best description of Binding for carpets, but inferior kinds may be had of a union of cotton with worsted. *See* CARPET BINDINGS.

Queen Stitch.—*See* EMBROIDERY STITCH.

Quille Work.—An Embroidery executed by the Nuns in Canada, with split Porcupine quills, and fully described under CANADIAN EMBROIDERY.

Quillings.—Small round plaits made in lace, tulle, or ribbon, lightly sewn down, with an occasional back stitch, the edge of the trimming remaining in open flute-like folds. They are generally made for the frills at the neck and wrists of bodices, and the fronts of caps and bonnets. Quillings are distinguished from Kiltings by their roundness at the open or outer edge, the latter being ironed down in flat folds. Blond Quillings are sold highly sized and finished. There are also Mechlins made of silk, which are soft and unfinished; "Lisse Quillings" are also to be had. The Bobbin Quillings are a description of plain net lace, made of cotton of various widths. Ruffs and Frills are best made of Brussels Quillings, which have an extra twist round the mesh.

The name was probably given to this description of plaiting because of its round Goffer-like form, just sufficiently large to admit a goose or turkey quill. Plain Quilling is only used in the lightest materials, such as net, tulle, blond, &c., and principally for tuckers. It is made up either single or double, according to the thickness required. Make small single BOX PLAITS at one edge, each rather overlapping the next at the back, and wrapping over the whole width of the plait, if the Quilling be very thick. Hold the right side towards you, and the Quilling downwards, the plaiting being done at the upper edge. Use a long straw needle, and work it in and out as every plait is formed, but do not draw the needle and cotton out of the Quilling; as the needle fills, pass the plaits over the eye, on to the cotton, until the cotton itself be occupied by the plaits. It is bad Quilling which is done by withdrawing the needle, and giving a BACK STITCH to secure the plaits.

There is another description of Quilling, called SHELL QUILLING, which is one of the most effective of trimmings, when made of the same stuff as the dress; and which is specially useful in cases where a second colour is introduced; as the stuff to be Quilled is then lined with it, instead of being merely hemmed at the edges.

Shells are never pretty if made too large; 2 inches is the best width, but the make may be as narrow as desired. Shell Quilling is available also for crêpe or gauze, but the strips must then be cut double the width that is required, and be folded over on each side, so that the edges may overlap down the middle, where it is Tacked, while the (then double) material is being plaited. Stitch three little plaits in the middle of the strip, all one on the top of the other, and the edge of each barely showing beyond the one above it. Commence the next group of three, so that the edge of its first plait shall be as far from the edge of the last plait of the last group, as half the width is of the band which is being plaited. When the length is plaited up, catch the two corners of the top plait of each group together backwards, and sew them to the middle. Done thus, every shell touches, but the shells may be spaced, which takes less material, and marks the kind of trimming better than when close, if a contrasting lining be used to it. The spacing, however, between the edges of the top plait of the last group, and the bottom plait of the new group, must never exceed the width of the strip which is being worked upon.

Quillings, as sold in shops, may be had of two kinds, "Blond Quillings" and "Bobbin Quillings." Both are made up in a similar way, but the former are made of silk, and highly sized and finished; the Mechlins, however, though of silk, are perfectly soft and unfinished. They are equally designed for ruffles and frills for dresses, and may be had of various widths. The Bobbin Quillings are of a plain net lace, made of cotton; they may be had in various widths, and are employed for caps, dresses, and underclothing. Those of Brussels Net are of superior quality, having an additional twist round the Mesh.

Quilting.—This term is employed to denote Runnings made in any materials threefold in thickness, i.e., the outer and right side textile, a soft one next under it, and a lining; the Runnings being made diagonally, so as to form a pattern of diamonds, squares, or octagons, while serving to attach the three materials securely together. If a design of any description be made in tissue paper, and temporarily Tacked upon the right side of the coverlet, or other article to be Quilted, the Runnings may vary the design from the ordinary Plain Crossings. A piece of flannel is the best middle layer between the satin, silk, or piqué, and the lining. Quilting is usually employed for coverlets, silk slippers, linings of work boxes and baskets, and the hoods, bonnets, and bibs of infants. It may also be effected by sewing down, and covering with a button, the intersections of the tacking threads, previously made with long stitches, which form the connected points of the diamonds or squares. The tackings should, of course, be very lightly taken, and in the silk or satin only, not all through, and very carefully removed when the buttons are sewn on, or stars worked in their stead.

The diamond-shaped checkers produced in Quilting were anciently called "Gamboised." When Petticoats are to be Quilted, the Runnings should be well indented and the satin or silk set up puffily. To accomplish this, use the best and thickest wadding, split it open, lay the satin over the unglazed side, and stitch through the two, without having any lining behind the cotton wool. Common slips are generally Quilted through the lining of Silesia at the same time as the padding and outside; but, it must be remembered, that half the effect of thickness and lightness is thereby lost. The shiny side of the wadding is quite enough to protect the inner hairs from catching the feeding teeth of any machine, and no hand-quilting comes up to machine work. Mantles, opera cloaks, and babies' cloaks that are wadded for warmth, should not be so puffy as petticoats, or they would set clumsily; therefore thin muslin is put behind the wadding, and the sheets of this may be of the poorer unbleached quality. When Quilting is used more for appearance than warmth, as in lining Paramatta, Cashmere mantles, &c., it is done on Domett, without any cotton wool between it and the silken fabric. Sewing machines have their own Quilting gauges; but in hand-working, fold the material directly on the cross, at its longest part, iron it down, and then fold and iron—by the aid of a paper-strip cut the right width—each side of the centre, until all oblique lines from right to left, and left to right of it, be defined. Then cross them in a contrary direction with others made in the same way. Pressed lines can be more quickly followed than a strip of paper held under the thumb of the left hand, with one edge of it on the running last made, and the other serving as a needle guide.

(2). Ornamental Quilting, although practised in Europe, has never attained to the minuteness and beauty of design that distinguish Oriental Quilting. The patience and skill of an Asiatic worker are fully displayed upon the designs that are worked out with these stitched lines, scenes of the chase, battles, and ships in full sail being executed by them with the most marvellous minuteness. These pictorial scenes are worked by the natives of India, but the Persians are not behind that nation in this art, although they display it more by working elaborate geometrical designs or conventionalised flowers as backgrounds to their embroideries than as a separate needlework. A large amount of Quilting was executed in England and on the Continent during the seventeenth and following centuries, some specimens of which are still to be met with, and which are evidently copies of Oriental Quilting, but the art at present is now only practised for useful purposes, and has ceased to be considered an ornamental work, although anyone who is acquainted with good quilting would set such an idea on one side. The Run line backgrounds, so frequently seen in high art Crewel Work, are intended to imitate Oriental Quilting, and their designs are frequently taken from old Persian prayer carpets and covers of ceremony.

Quilts or Counterpanes.—These are made of cotton of various sizes, according to the dimensions of the bed to be covered, from 2¼, 2½, 2¾, to 3 yards in length. They are always of threefold thickness. Coloured Quilts and Fancy Linen Bed Coverlets are also to be had. Squares of embroidered linen still exist in old country houses, having emblems of the Four Evangelists worked at the corners, both large and small. In Dr. Daniel Rock's *Textile Fabrics*, we read that "At Durham, in 1446, in the dormitory of the Priory, was a Quilt *cum iiij. Or Evangelistes in corneriis.*" "Hospital" or "Scripture Quilts"

are made of Patchwork on certain squares, in which texts of Scripture are either written with marking ink or embroidered.

Quilts of Paper are much used for charitable purposes, as the material they are made of is very insusceptible to atmospheric influences, and promotes warmth by retaining heat. To make: Cut up a number of pieces of chintz, old silk, or any remnants, into four-inch squares, and join two of these together, as if making a bag. Join up three sides of this bag, then stuff it thickly with odds and ends of paper, shred into fine pieces, and sew the fourth side up. Having made a number of squares, sew them together, as in PATCHWORK, joining them, if possible, so as to form a design of contrasting colours and materials.

Quoifure.—A French term, denoting a head-dress. To be "*bien Coiffée*" means that a woman's head is becomingly and thoroughly well dressed. In former times, a Quoif was a plain and closely-fitting head-dress, worn alike by both sexes. The modern spelling is "Coiffure."

R.

Rabbit Fur (*Lepus cuniculus*).—The Fur of the common wild Rabbit is of a greyish-brown colour, and the tail is brown above and white underneath. There are also Fancy Rabbits, some of which are of a pure white, those having the handsomest skins being of a tortoise-shell colour—white, brown, and yellow. The chief use to which Rabbit Fur is applied is the making of felt hats; but the skins with the fur are dressed in many ways, so as to resemble various others of a more costly description. So-called Ermine, and Miniver, are made of the white rabbit skins, the tails being those of the real Ermine, and the spots of dark fur sewn upon the latter being of the Weasel or "Gris." In the reign of Henry VIII. Rabbit Fur was greatly esteemed, and worn by the nobility. Those dyed of a dark colour are "French lustred," and look well when employed for articles of women's dress and for trimmings. They measure about 10 inches by 18 inches.

Raccoon Fur (*Procyon tolor*).—The fur of this animal is grey, and diversified with gold colour and dark markings. The tails are bushy and variegated. They are employed both for dress and for rugs. The whole fur is thick and deep, and there is an under-growth of a soft woolly character, greyish in colour. In the year 1793 the fur was adopted as a distinctive decoration by the Jacobins. The skins measure about 10in. by 18in.

Raccroc Stitch.—Also known as Point de Raccroc and as Rucroc. This is a stitch used by the lace makers of Brussels and Calvados to join together Réseau lace grounds made upon the pillow in narrow stripes. This joining is made by using the very finest thread, and uniting the meshes together with it by Overcasting them in such a manner that the loops of two pieces fit into each other as if of one thread. It is done by experienced lace makers so cleverly that the join cannot be detected by the naked eye.

Radsimir, or Radzimir Silk.—This is a very rich description of silk textile, especially designed for Mourning, and otherwise known as "Queen's" Silk, her Majesty having always patronised it. It is a kind of silk serge, and the name is synonymous with the French "*Ras de St. Maur*," by which a silk dress material was designated in the last century, when it was much in fashion. Radsimir Silk measures about 32 inches in width.

Ragusa Guipure.—*See* Roman Work.

Ragusa Lace.—The lace made at Ragusa formed an important article of commerce during the latter part of the sixteenth and earlier part of the seventeenth century. It consisted of two kinds, one a Needle Point, and the other a Gimp Lace. The Needle Point was extremely costly, and was much appreciated both in Greece and Italy. It resembled Venice Point, and was frequently sold as Point de Venise. Its manufacture ceased when heavy needle points gave place to the lighter Alençon and Argentan makes and the cheaper Pillow Laces. Ragusa Gimp Lace seems of very early origin, patterns of it being published as far back as 1557; and the manufacture of it has not entirely died out, the peasants still making a Gimp Lace and using some of the sixteenth century designs. The Gimp Lace is made either with gold, silver, or silk threads; these are sewn together until they form a flat braid about a quarter of an inch in width, with the outer thread twisted into numerous loops to make an ornamental edging. The braid thus made is sewn down in designs and connected together with Corded Bars, but is rarely filled in with lace stitches.

Rag Work.—An easy and suitable employment for invalids and children, who, with little expense, can make rugs or bedroom strips by this means at a nominal cost. To work: Collect together all the pieces of cloth, serge, list, flannel, chintz, or cotton procurable, and sort the pieces as to colour; tear all of them into strips half an inch in width, and sew these together at their narrow ends; wind them into balls, and keep the different colours or shades of one colour apart. Take the largest pair of wooden knitting needles procurable, Cast on twenty-four stitches, and Knit in Plain Knitting with the rags a strip the length or width required for the carpet or rug, using the shades of one colour upon the same strip. Make a number of these strips, and join them together, so that the colours contrast, and then line them with a strong sacking or canvas, The rags, instead of being knitted together, can be woven; in that case the thick materials are cut half an inch in width, the thin three-quarters of an inch. Join, and make up into 1lb. balls, which send to a weaver with instructions to weave as strips of contrasting colours. Seven balls will make five yards of carpet of narrow width, and the cost of weaving will be from 10d. to 1s. the yard. No lining will be required for the woven articles. Silk pieces make good rugs. Ribbons and pieces of brocade can be mixed with the plain silks; they are cut into half-inch strips. They are knitted together with coarse knitting needles, lined with sacking, and bordered with imitation fur or stamped leather. With attention to the selection and disposal of the colours used, these silk rugs can be made very orna-

mental. They can be woven, like the thicker materials, it taking three 1lb. balls to make a good rug.

Another Kind.—Cut the cloth or silk rags into strips 3 inches long, and half an inch to an inch in width, according to their texture. Knit these together, using soft twine as a foundation, thus: Cast on 30 stitches with the twine, and Knit a row. For the next row, Knit 1, put the strip of cloth across the knitting between the first and second stitch, knit the second stitch, and put the end of cloth back to the side where its other half is; knit the third stitch, put the strip of cloth across the work, and repeat. Work to the end of the row and knit back without inserting any strips. Work these two rows to the end, always inserting the cloth in every other row, and leaving its ends on one side only of the knitting.

Railway Stitch.—*See* Berlin Work, Embroidery Stitches, and Crochet.

Raiment.—A generic and comprehensive term to denote Clothing of every description, both of men and women. It is a contraction of Arrayment.

Raised Crewel Work.—This work in no way resembles Crewel Work, except that the wools used in it are Crewel Wools. It consists in making flowers raised from the surface of the foundation with a number of loops, and forming buds and leaves for the same with raised Satin Stitches. As the work will not bear washing, it should be made upon cloth, satin, sheeting, or serge. To work: Trace the design upon the material, and select one in which the flowers are single petalled and round in shape. Take crewel wools matching the shades of the flower, and thread four strands of the same shade together. Work from the centre of the flower to the outside. Bring the needle up from the back of the work to the front, and put it down again quite close to the place it emerged from; leave about a quarter of an inch of crewel wool upon the front of the material, and fasten the work securely at the back to prevent the loop so formed from pulling out or becoming absorbed into the next stitch. Work loops in this manner until the design is filled in, altering the colour of the wools to suit the light and dark parts of the flower, For the stems, work them in ordinary Crewel Stitch; for the leaves and buds, lay down a foundation of lines in Satin Stitch until they are well raised from the background, and cover this padding with other Satin Stitches arranged as to the colour of the leaf or the bud, and following its shape.

Raised Cross Stitch.—*See* Crochet.

Raised Double Stitch.—*See* Crochet.

Raised Embroidery.—A handsome kind of Embroidery, but difficult to execute, consisting of working raised flowers upon a flat foundation. Two different methods are employed. In the first (the one shown in Fig. 698), the working is upon a thick material, such as cloth or rep silk, or with Satin Stitches laid over wadding to make the pattern. In the second, upon Penelope canvas, the design is formed with loops of Plush Stitch, which are afterwards cut and fluffed up, so as to imitate velvet, while the canvas is covered over with Cross or Tent Stitch, and forms the background. To work (as shown in Fig. 698): The materials required are

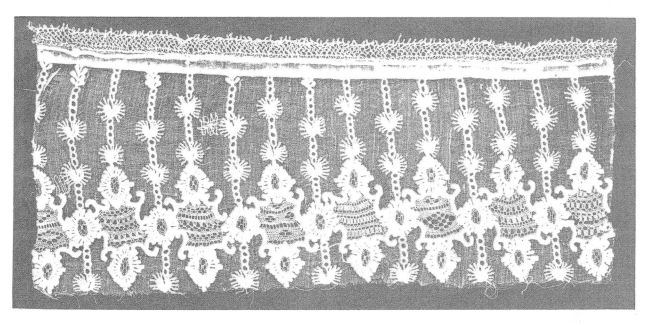

FINE ENGLISH EMBROIDERY, FINISHED WITH LACE STITCHES AND "BABY LACE."
WORKED IN THE 18th CENTURY.

RAISED EMBROIDERY ON MUSLIN.

DETAIL A.

DETAIL C.

DETAIL B.

DETAIL D.

FIG. 698. RAISED EMBROIDERY.

cotton wool, white embroidery cotton, filoselles, Zephyr wool, or Arrasene wool, the latter producing by far the best effect. The wools must be in shades of the natural colours of the flowers and leaves, and such as would be selected for Berlin wool work. To work: Trace the outline of the design upon cloth or rep silk, back this with brown holland, and frame it in an EMBROIDERY FRAME; work the raised parts of the pattern first. Take a piece of cotton wool the size of the Rose without its outer leaves, and half an inch thick, and fasten this lump to the canvas by a CROSS STITCH of embroidery cotton, as shown in Fig. 698, Detail A; then, with the same embroidery cotton, OVERCAST the whole with regular stitches, as shown in Detail B, where half the stitches are made; then re-cross the lump, as shown in Detail C, with long Cross Stitches, also made with embroidery cotton. Take the wool or Arrasene, and with that make the SATIN STITCHES that are shown in Detail D. In this Detail use the darkest-coloured wool, and work the Satin Stitches so that they overlap and culminate towards the centre; then proceed to make the petals that finish the centre of the Rose. Make them all with Satin Stitch; work the inner ones first, with wools shading gradually from dark to light, and make the Satin Stitches so that they take the shape of the petals. By commencing from the centre the outer leaves will be the parts most raised, and a kind of hollow will be formed in the centre. Work the turned back petals in flat Satin Stitches, and mix light-coloured filoselle with the wool used in making them. Having made the Rose, proceed to make the Aster, which is not so raised as the Rose: Take a piece of wadding, and fasten it down with a Cross Stitch to the material, and then work a number of Satin Stitches in embroidery cotton from the centre to the outside of the wadding; then with the wool or Arrasene form the petals. Make the outside ones first with the darkest shade, and work to the centre, making three rows of petals, each in a different shade of wool. Fill in the centre with a number of FRENCH KNOTS made with filoselle. To form the Rosebud: Tack down and Overcast a small ball of wadding; work the centre of the bud first, and the green calyx last. Form the rest of the flowers and all the leaves with long Satin Stitches, and with different shades of colour, but do not wad them. When working small sprays of Raised Embroidery for pincushions, handkerchief cases, &c., in which the design is small, make a padding with Satin Stitches of embroidery cotton, and then cover this padding with filoselles instead of wools, as wadding covered with wool would be too coarse for such fine Embroidery.

Raised Embroidery with Plush Stitch. — In this description of the work a number of flat Meshes, gauge 18 in breadth and gauge 11 in thickness, or steel Meshes with edges that will cut, are required; also wool or filoselle, and Berlin canvas, or white silk canvas. To work: Select a coloured Berlin pattern, and keep it by the side of the work for reference. Count the stitches on the pattern and canvas, and outline these upon the canvas, then place it in an EMBROIDERY FRAME. Work all the leaves of the design in TENT STITCH, shading them as in BERLIN WORK should the canvas be fine; if it is coarse, work the leaves in CROSS STITCH, and ground the work in Cross Stitch. When using silk canvas it is not necessary to ground the work, but when the embroidery is finished this description of canvas must be lined with coloured silk. The raised flowers are first worked. A number of Meshes are required for these, as when once covered with stitches they are not withdrawn until the flower is complete. Thread a number of wool needles with the colours required in the flower, take a MESH in the left hand, and lay it on the pattern at the bottom of a flower, so that its edge touches the line of canvas to be filled, and its length extends to the end of that line. Take up a needle filled with the colour used for the first stitch at the bottom of the flower, put it in at the back, and bring it out in the front of the work under the Mesh, cross it over the Mesh, and put it into the canvas two threads above, and on the right of where it came out, as if making a TENT STITCH; then cross this stitch as if making a CROSS STITCH, not over the Mesh this time, but slipped behind it. Work the next stitch in the same way, but should it be of a different shade of colour to the one last worked, do not fasten off the first thread, but keep it at the back of the work out of the way, but ready to make another stitch when required. Work a whole row of stitches over the Meshes, using the shades of wool as wanted, and when these require fastening off be careful that they are well secured. Take a fresh Mesh for the next row, and work all the rows that make the flower without removing any of the Meshes. Finish by gumming the back of the raised flower with gum arabic, and remove the Meshes when this is perfectly dry. The steel Meshes will cut the wool as they are withdrawn; when using the wooden ones, cut the loops with a sharp pair of scissors. Shape these loops with the scissors so as to form a hollow for the centre of the flower, when such a hollow is necessary, then comb out the wool with a fine tooth comb, until it resembles velvet pile. The French plan of working Raised Embroidery is to miss a thread of canvas between each stitch, and work over only one thread instead of working over two threads of canvas, and leaving no threads between the stitches. Also, see EMBROIDERY ON THE STAMP.

Raised Loop Stitch.—*See* CROCHET.

Raised Open Stitch.—*See* CROCHET.

Raised Patchwork.—*See* PATCHWORK.

Raised Point.—These are SPANISH and VENETIAN POINTS, and are described under those headings.

Raised Satin Stitch.—*See Satin Stitch*, EMBROIDERY STITCHES.

Raised Spot Stitch.—*See* CROCHET.

Raised Stitch.—*See* BERLIN WORK.

Raised Treble Crochet.—*See* CROCHET.

Raised Work.—This is the distinguishing mark of Honiton Lace and Point Duchesse, and consists of a Raised Edge worked down one side of the leaves, flowers, and stems of a spray or Honiton sprig. It is illustrated in Fig. 699, and worked as follows: Commence at the end of the stem, and wind the Knots out of the way; when the middle leaf is reached, change the side for the pins, and continue the STEM STITCH up the lower side of the leaf until the last pin but one is stuck. Take the Passive pair of Bobbins that lie next the pins, lay back over the work, and do a row of Stem Stitch without them. At the last pin hang on four pairs of Bobbins, letting them lie by the side of the pair put up; make the stitch about the pin, and do a row of Stem Stitch with the Bobbins worked with before; come back to the edge, turn the Pillow quite round, so that the Bobbins lie down the leaf facing the worker. Take out all the pins but the last three, and work straight across in Cloth Stitch. Do the last stitch with the pair put up, tie this pair once, and work back with it. Work in Cloth Stitch with Plain Edge at one side, and Sewings to the cross strands of the stem at the other side of the leaf, until the leaf narrows, where cut off four pairs of Bobbins in separate rows, and make a Rope Sewing down the stem. When the leaf worked in Half Stitch is reached, straighten the Bobbins, work

Fig. 699. Raised Work.

Stem Stitch up the upper side, hang on three pairs of Bobbins at the top, and work down in Half Stitch, making the Raised Work as described in the previous leaf. Cut off three pairs of Bobbins in separate rows where the leaf narrows, cross the stalk of the leaves, and carry Stem Stitch up the lower side of the third leaf; hang on three pairs, and work as in the second leaf; at the end tie the Bobbins up in the last Sewed pair, and cut off.

Raleigh Bars.—These are used in Modern Point. To work: Commence at the corner of the lace, and throw across a number of loose Loops, so as to fill up the space with irregular lines to make a foundation. Work four or five close Buttonhole Stitches to the centre of the first Loop. Make a Dot or Picot, and work the same number of close Buttonhole Stitches to finish the Loop. Cover every Loop in the same way until all are worked.

Rampoor-Chuddah. — This is the name of a fine twilled Indian woollen cloth, used as a shawl, as well as a dress material. The name Chuddah signifies a Shawl, being made of very fine wool, which is exceedingly warm and soft. Rampoor-Chuddah may be had in different shades of red and white, and in grey and dove colour. Rampoor is the name of a large State and town in Rohilkhand, North Western Provinces of India.

Ras de St. Maur.—A kind of serge silk textile. In the last century it was much used for mourning. It is known in the present day as Radsimir.

Rash.—This is an inferior description of silk stuff, or a combination of silk and cotton.

Ras Terre.—A French term in use amongst dressmakers, signifying that the skirt of a dress just touches the ground at the back, when fastened on by the wearer.

Rateen.—One of the class called Stuffs, chiefly employed

as a lining material. It is thick, quilled, and woven on a loom with four treadles—like serges. Some Rateens are dressed and prepared like cloths; others are left simply in the hair, while a third description has the hair or nap frizzed. Rateen was originally of Spanish manufacture. The name Rateen is likewise employed in commerce in a generic sense for a certain class of coarse woollen stuffs—such as Baize, Drugget, and Frieze, to which it bears a great resemblance—and which are classed as Rateens.

Rattinet.—A description of woollen cloth, of a thinner substance than Rateen. It is of French manufacture.

Ravel.—To draw, fray out, or untwist the weft threads of ribbon, silk, or linen, so as to produce a fringe from the threads of the woof. This method is much employed in trimmings, for the edges of d'oyleys, towels, &c., but it necessitates the Overcasting of the raw edge, where the threads of the fringe commence. Fine thread, or sewing silk should be used, and the stitches should be made very regularly, at a little distance from the edge, as accidental ravelling would spoil the article. The Ravelling of ribbon ends may be more or less prevented by cutting them on the bias, or rounding them. Flannels, and all woollen materials of a loose make, should be bound; but Broadcloth may be cut, and left with a raw edge. Buttonholes, in every description of textile—the latter included—need to be secured from Ravelling by means of Buttonhole Stitching.

The term is employed by Shakespeare, where Macbeth speaks of—

. . . Sleep, that knits up the ravelled sleeve of care.

Milton likewise adopts it—

Till, by their own perplexities involved,
They ravel more, still less resolved.

Ravellings.—*See* Parfilage.

Ravensduck.—A description of canvas or sail-cloth.

Raw-edge.—The edge of any textile which is not finished by a selvedge, and may, therefore, ravel out, if not either Bound, Hemmed, Overcast, or confined by Buttonhole Stitching.

Raw Silk.—Reeled silk before it is spun or woven, of which there are three kinds, the "Floss," "Organzine," and "Tram." The filaments of Floss are broken, and comparatively short; those of Organzine are fine, and twisted; those of Tram are inferior in quality, and are less twisted. The character of Raw Silk may be tested by its weight, although this appears to be a somewhat uncertain standard of merit; for as silk, when wound off the cocoons on reels, has to be detached by immersion in warm water, it absorbs a considerable quantity of moisture; and it is quite possible that an inferior kind may sometimes obtain a greater fictitious weight than that of a better quality. There is another method of deception in reference to Raw Silk—by means of the use of certain vegetable decoctions.

Rayure Bayadeur.—This is a French-named textile, manufactured for a dress material; it is made of silk and cotton, and striped horizontally. Its price varies according to the quality of the stuffs, and it measures 24 inches in width.

Reaving, or Reeving.—This term is synonymous with un-weaving, or dis-uniting the threads of any textile, such as unravelling knitting, or stockingette cloth, or drawing apart the threads of any kind of cloth.

Red Tape.—This is also known as Pink Tape, and is much employed in Law Offices for tying briefs and papers, and in the Haberdashery department in trade, for tying up sets of cambric handkerchiefs, &c. It is made of cotton, and can be had in different numbers, viz., 16, 24, and 32, cut in any length desired, or sold in long lengths, and on reels.

Reef Knot.—*See* KNOTS.

Reel.—A roller of wood, turning in a frame, for winding thread; also one of the appliances of a workbox, made of ivory or pearl, having metal stems, on which to wind silk; and, thirdly, the wooden article on which sewing cotton is sold, when not made up in balls. A manufacturing cotton

mechanics, and, more recently, for seaside costumes for women, for children's dresses, and for shirts. When employed for the latter it is more usually called Galatea, or Marine Stripes. The material is of a more durable quality than Prints, the pattern consisting of blue and white stripes of equal width.

Regency Point.—This is one of the Bedfordshire Laces. It was much made in that county during the first part of the present century, and therefore named after the Regent. The lace (*see* Fig. 700) is made upon the Pillow in narrow width, and is of a more complicated pattern than the ordinary Bedfordshire Laces, being made with Cloth Stitch and a Gimp for the thick parts of the designs, with Cucumber Plaitings and other open stitches for the Fillings, and with a Honeycomb or Net Pattern ground similar to Brussels ground. It is no longer manufactured in Bedfordshire.

Re-heel.—*See* KNITTING STOCKINGS.

Re-knee.—*See* KNITTING STOCKINGS.

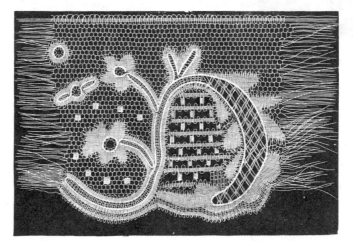

FIG. 700. REGENCY POINT.

or linen Reel is 54 inches in circuit, a worsted Reel 30 inches. "Reeling Yarn" of any description, means to make it into skeins by winding it round the appliance used in manufactories for that purpose, or thence on to "spools." In Ireland, all Reels are called "Spools," and in the North of England they are very commonly designated "Bobbins."

Reel Cotton.—Sewing cotton which is not made up in balls (otherwise called "sewing cotton"), and sold in lengths of from 25 to 1000 yards. In the best class, known as "six-cords," there is an extensive variety of makes, the most saleable lengths containing respectively 200, 300, and 400 yards. Reel Cotton in colours may be had in many shades. For sewing machines, a Reel has been recently brought out, for which it is especially adapted as to shape and size. The numbers run, almost without exception, from 1 to 100; but it is unnecessary to keep Nos. 14, 18, 22, 26, or 28. *See* COTTONS FOR SEWING.

Re-foot.—*See* KNITTING STOCKINGS.

Regatta Stripes.—By this designation a calico cloth is known, which is extensively employed by sailors and

Relief Satiné.—The French term for Raised Satin Stitch. See *Satin Stitch*, EMBROIDERY STITCHES.

Relief Work.—This is used in Honiton Lace, and is fully described under that heading.

Remnants.—A term applied in trade to odd lengths of dress stuffs, ribbons, linen, cotton, and woollen cloths, left unsold from the original pieces, and which are disposed of at a cheaper rate for children's clothing, patchwork, and other purposes. The uses to which the needlewoman may apply almost the smallest remains of material after making any article are very numerous. Strips of woollen stuff may be cut sufficiently narrow to be knitted with large needles (of wood, bone, or gutta-percha), and made into coarse rugs, suitable for the use of the poor.

Remnants of cloth may be used in Appliqué Work; cloth, flannel, and all woollen stuffs, every cotton, silk, satin, all descriptions of velvet, and of ribbon, can be used in Patchwork for cushions, quilts, and window blinds, the latter being of silk (as being semi-transparent), and the colours selected so as to represent diamond-shaped panes of stained glass.

Renaissance Braid Work.—This is also known as Renaissance Lace, and is really only Modern Point Lace, worked with a very Open Braid, and with only one stitch as a Filling, instead of several. To work as shown in Fig. 701: Trace out the design upon pink calico, and Tack the Braid to it, placing the Braid that forms the Vandykes over the one forming the curves; OVERCAST round all the edges of the Braid, and sew the curves and Vandyke points (where the Braid has to be turned in) securely down. Connect the two upper straight lines of Braid together,

FIG. 701. RENAISSANCE BRAID WORK.

either with a thick strand of lace cotton, passed alternately backwards and forwards between the two Braids, or with the stitch shown in Fig. 702, Detail A, which work thus: Take a line from one Braid to the other, and CORD this back to the Loop it started from on the outer edge of the lowest line of Braid; work three lines on one side of the first line and three on the other. Cord them all, and start them all from the same Loop; first fasten them into the top Braid and into separate Loops. Miss a space of a quarter of an inch on the lower Braid, and work the stitch

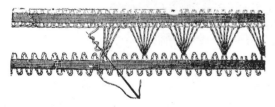

FIG. 702. RENAISSANCE BRAID WORK—DETAIL A.

as before. Work BUTTONHOLE BARS ornamented with PICOTS and eight-armed WHEELS between the Braids upon the lower part of the pattern, and in the thick parts of the lace work the following stitch: Make two BUTTONHOLES, miss the space of two, and work two more. Repeat to the end of the row. In the return row work two Buttonholes into every Loop, and a Loop under the Buttonholes of the previous row. Repeat these two rows to the end of the space; finish the edge of the lace with a bought lace edging.

Renaissance Embroidery.—This term is so general, that any descriptions of Lace or Embroidery worked from old designs are indifferently called by the name. The best known Renaissance Embroidery is an Appliqué. Designs formed with quaint figures of animals, hunters, &c., are traced upon coloured materials, cut out, transferred to a flat background of velvet or silk, and outlined with coloured silk cords, a process fully described under the heading of APPLIQUÉ.

Renaissance Guipure.—*See* GUIPURE RENAISSANCE.

Renaissance Lace. — *See* RENAISSANCE BRAID WORK.

Renaissance Work.—This work is formed with large, heavily-made braids, arranged in geometrical forms, and kept in those positions with plain or ornamental Buttonhole Bars. To work: Draw out, upon pink calico, a bold lace design, and back this with brown paper; take some of Haythorne's coarsely woven linen braid, three-quarters of an inch in width, made with a plain edge, and Tack this down upon the calico with ordinary cotton. Turn in all the edges and points of the braid where required to form the design, and sew them down with lace cotton; then connect the various parts of the braid together with BUTTONHOLE BARS and WHEELS. Make one or more PICOTS upon each Bar, and use the Wheels to fill in the centres of the design, instead of working any lace stitches. When the work is finished, cut the tacking threads at the back of the pattern, and pull them out, which will release the lace from the calico without stretching it.

Rent.—A term synonymous with tear, and applied to any textile that is accidentally torn.

Renter.—A technical term employed by Tapestry workers, derived from one of the French names applied to this class of artists. To *Renter* is to work new warp in a piece of damaged Tapestry, upon which to restore or supply again the original design.

Rep, Repp, or Reps.—Of this textile there are three descriptions, those composed of silk, those of silk and wool, and those of wool only, and which measure from 30 inches to 32 inches in width. It has a thick cord, and has much resemblance to Poplin. Silk Rep is chiefly made at Lyons; its width is 27 inches; but Curtain Rep averages 1½ yards in width. Silk Rep is used for dresses and waistcoats, and also for ecclesiastical vestments and hangings. The quality made for upholstery is composed of wool only. The ribs of all Reps run across the width. There are figured kinds, measuring 53 inches wide.

Reprises Perdue.—The French term for Fine Drawing, which is a description of Darning applied to Broadcloth, and other varieties of thick woollen stuffs. *See* FINE DRAWING.

Rep Stitch.—*See* BERLIN WORK.

Réseau.—Identical with Rezel, Rezeul. This is the Net-patterned or Honeycomb ground of lace, made either with the needle or with Bobbins, and called Réseau to distinguish it from the Bar or Bride Ground, made in irregular lines across the lace, and so joined together. The Réseau ground connects the lace pattern together by filling in every space with fine meshes, made with great exactness, either with the needle—first making a Buttonhole, and then, by successive stitches, forming that into a hexagon—or by the Bobbins being twisted round each other and round a pin a certain number of times. These grounds are extremely laborious to execute, and occupy so much time in making that the lace, when finished, can only be sold at very high prices; and since machine nets have been manufactured they have fallen into disuse, except for special orders, the lace being made and then APPLIQUÉ on to machine net, instead of the ground being also made. To make a Réseau Ground, *see* GROUND.

Réseau Malins.—*See* MECHLIN GROUND.

Réseau Rosacé.—The name given to the Réseau Lace ground worked in ARGENTAN LACE.

Genoa Stitch. In the first-made Reticellas the patterns are chiefly formed by these stiff lines, which are ornamented at set intervals with Picots; but later specimens of the work show more variety of execution and more solid patterns. Fig. 703 is one of this description, and is a copy from a piece of lace found in a convent at Milan. The making of Reticella has been revived, and will be found fully described under GREEK POINT.

Return Rope.—*See* SEWINGS.

Revers.—A French term, adopted by dressmakers in lieu of an English word, and signifying the turned back corner of the basque, or lappel of a bodice, or the robing of a dress skirt, so placed to show the lining, and producing

FIG. 703. RETICELLA, OR GREEK POINTS.

Restore Lace.—*See* LACE, *Mend* and *Restore.*

Retaper.—A French term, signifying to "make up" a bonnet or hat. It is chiefly employed by milliners.

Reticella.—The Reticellas, or Greek Points, are considered the first Needle-made Laces; they succeeded the Cutworks, and have somewhat the same appearance. They flourished from the end of the fifteenth century to the beginning of the seventeenth century, and were used for altar cloths, Church vestments, and the starched trimmings to ruffs, their stiff and geometrical patterns being peculiarly adapted for the purposes for which they were designed. This Lace is produced by lines of thread being thrown across a space, so as to form a pattern, and afterwards connected, either with Overcast, Buttonhole, or

thereby a decorative variety in colour and form. In such cases, the linings are of some suitably contrasting colour, and may be of silk, satin, velvet, plush, brocade, &c. The tails of uniform tunics and coats, and the facings, are sometimes thus turned back, and are, in these cases, of a differently coloured cloth.

Reversed.—*See* KNITTING.

Reversible Linings.—These Linings are of linen, having a white or a grey side, and decorated with a small pattern in black, the other side having a plain black face. They are especially made for lining black dresses, the black side being laid on the wrong side of the dress material, and the white, or grey figured side, outwards. They are made a yard wide.

Reversibles.—Cloths having the back of a different colour from the face, and sometimes having a check pattern, the right side, or face, being of some uni-colour. They are used for men's coats.

Révolte des Passemens.—This poem is so frequently quoted to fix the date of various laces, that a short glance at its theme will help our readers to understand why it is so universally referred to. When the Minister Colbert introduced the manufacture of Alençon Lace into France, he compelled the most skilful of the workers of other laces to labour at the Royal manufactory, and thus produced a revolt amongst them, which was terminated by a compromise. Shortly afterwards, in 1661, an Enactment against the luxury of dress was passed, and this was seized upon for the theme of a poem, in which the Laces, fearing that they would become extinct if no longer used as an article of dress, take example from their makers, and determine to revolt. They assemble in battle array, and all make speeches; but as soon as they are opposed they run away. Every lace that was of any importance in the year 1661 is mentioned in this poem, and its value and beauty shadowed forth in the speech it makes, thus enabling the lace collector to fix upon the date and worth of various laces; hence the value at the present time of a poem that was merely written to amuse the circle surrounding Madame de Sevigné.

Rezel.—*See* RÉSEAU.

Rhea Feathers.—The Rhea is the Ostrich of South America; its plumage is imported from Buenos Ayres, and is not only valuable for women's head-dresses, but the flossy kinds are used for military plumes in Europe, as well as in South America; while the long brown feathers of the wings are made into brooms and dusting brushes. The feathers of the Rhea, made up for wear by the *plumassiers*, are called by them "Vultures'" feathers. *See* OSTRICH.

Rhodes Lace.—The islands in the Grecian Sea have been celebrated for their laces since the art was known, Crete, Cyprus, and Rhodes, besides producing CUT WORK, RETICELLA, or GUIPURE, and GOLD NET WORKS, were celebrated for their coloured SILK LACES, or GIMPS. At the present date, two descriptions of lace are made at Rhodes: a fine white silk guipure Lace, of Oriental design, worked with a tambour needle, and a coloured silk lace, sometimes called RIBBON LACE. In this, upon a gauze foundation, floral and conventional flower designs are embroidered in coloured silks. The floral designs are varied with pyramidal and geometrical patterns, but the embroidery is alike on both. It consists of thick borders of silver thread, pattern outlined with raised cords, flowers shaded on every petal, silver thread round every petal, or part of pattern, and the design, by the labour and number of stitches lavished upon it, made to stand out in high relief from the ground.

Ribbed.—A term signifying woven or knitted so as to make the textile have a barred appearance, the surface presenting alternate ridges and hollows. Stockings so made have a double degree of elasticity, and fit more closely than others. *See* KNITTING.

Ribbed Stitch.—*See* CROCHET and KNITTING.

Ribbed Velveteen.—*See* VELVETEEN.

Ribbon, or Riband.—Strips of silk, satin, gauze, and velvet, sometimes having a selvedge edge on both sides, and designed as trimmings to dresses, caps, and bonnets, for the use of recruiting sergeants, and other purposes. They are to be had in a variety of widths and colours, and with or without patterns. Satin Ribbons may be obtained of stout quality, having a different colour on one side to the other, and equally perfect on both. Ribbons are woven much after the method of weaving cloth; and, in the "engine looms," from eight to twenty-eight may be woven simultaneously. The French Ribbons, chiefly made at Lyons, are of the best quality; but our own manufacturers, especially those at Coventry, have reached a high degree of excellence. Ribbons are classed as the Satin, Sarcenet, Lutestring, Gauze, Velvet, Fancy, Pads, and Chinas—the latter a common kind of Satin Ribbon, used for rosettes and book markers—and may be had in any colour. The Gauze are but little worn at present. Lutestrings are a kind of Gros de Naples, which may be had in various widths, with a corded pearl and four edges. The Sarcenets have plain edges. Velvet Ribbons of silk in the common kinds are cut in strips from the piece, and have no selvedge, the edges being only gummed; the superior kinds are woven in strips; their widths run in even numbers (no odd ones) up to 50, and then to 200, 250, and 300; the lengths ought to be 18 yards, but, always proving short in measure, have to be joined.

Ribbons are usually woven in pieces of 36 yards each, the best kinds being those made of Italian silk, and the inferior, of the Chinese and Bengal. There is often a considerable amount of cotton mixed with the silk used in the making of Ribbons, and a meretricious glaze is given to them to produce a silky appearance. Fancy Ribbons may be had in combinations of velvet, satin, and silk stripes, and likewise brocaded in all colours.

Pieces of Satin Ribbon contain 36 yards, those of Sarcenet, 18 yards only. French Ribbons generally have more substance in them than those of our own manufacture.

Cotton-made Ribbon Velvets are cut in strips from piece velvets, and the edges, having no selvedge, are sized, to prevent ravelling. They are made in lengths of 12 yards, the numbers running from 1 to 40. They are also produced in a variety of colours besides black, and the widths run from 1 inch, 1½ inches, and 2 inches, up to 10 inches, then in even numbers up to 20 inches, and then to 24 inches, 30 inches, and 40 inches. The lengths (of 12 yards nominally) run short in Cotton Ribbon Velvets, as in the inferior kinds of Silk Ribbon Velvets. Ribbons designed for waist-belts are called Petershams; and Watered Doubles, which are made in various colours and patterns, are called Pads. Some of the French Brocaded varieties, which are produced in several colours, and in floral designs, are as rich looking as hand embroideries. Coventry is the chief seat of the industry in England, and the art has been brought to such perfection, that landscapes, portraits, and pictorial representations are produced there rivalling those of the Lyons Ribbon Weavers. By a peculiar style of management in the process of dyeing, "clouding" is produced in Ribbons.

Doubles, Ferrets, and Galloons are all varieties of Ribbons. Ferrets are coarse and narrow in width, and are shot with cotton. According to Planché, "it is not until the sixteenth century that Ribbons, in the present sense, are seen and heard of; and only in the seventeenth that they acquired that hold on public favour which has lasted to the present day." As a trimming for a dress, Ribbon is mentioned by Chaucer in his *Romaunt of the Rose*:

> . . . . . . Full well
> With Orfraies laid everie dell,
> And purtraied, in the Ribaninges,
> Of dukes' stories, and of kings.

Ribbon Embroidery.—*See* China Ribbon Embroidery.

Ribbon Lace.—*See* Rhodes Lace.

Ribbon Wire.—A narrow cotton Ribbon, or Tape, into which three or four wires are woven, and which is sold in packets containing twelve pieces, of as many yards each, eighteen of 18 yards, or six of 24 yards. But, as in the case of other varieties, Ribbon Wire is usually deficient in measure. It is employed in the millinery trade.

Rice Embroidery.—This is a white Embroidery upon washing materials, in which the principal stitch used is Point de Riz, or Rice Stitch. The work need not be confined to washing materials or to embroidery cotton, but looks well when made upon silk, diagonal cloth, or serge foundations, and with filoselles or coloured crewels. To work as shown in Fig. 704: Trace the outline upon the

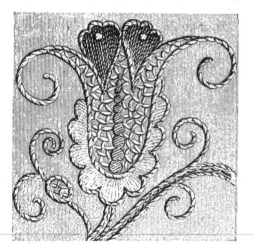

Fig. 704. Rice Embroidery.

design, and work the centre of the flower in Point de Riz Stitch, which scatter carelessly over the surface; fill in the calyx of the flower with Au Passé, or flat Satin Stitch, and in the same stitch work the two upright petals. Work round the flower in Point de Cable, so as to outline every part, and also work with it the stems and tendrils; make the dots in the centre of the flower in Overcast.

Rice Stitch.—This Stitch resembles Rice, or Crumbs, loosely scattered over a flat surface. To make: Bring the needle up from the back, and put it down in a slant, one-eighth of an inch from where it came up. Scatter these stitches over the surface to be covered. *See* Embroidery Stitches.

Richelieu Guipure.—This is work of a modern date, and differs but little from Roman, Strasbourg, and Venetian Embroidery. It is founded upon the ancient Point Coupé, or Cutwork, which was one of the first laces, and was extensively used in conjunction with Linen Embroidery, on the Continent and in England, from the fourteenth to the sixteenth centuries, when it was superseded by Reticella Lace. The modern Richelieu Guipure differs from the old Cutwork in being worked in more open patterns, and separated by Bars formed of threads Buttonholed over. In the old work, the linen foundations were cut, and Buttonholed over wherever bars were required, and the patterns were closer and more solid, almost entirely covered with needlework, and required greater patience and skill in their execution.

For many varieties of trimmings, and for washing materials Richelieu Guipure is well adapted, for, as long as the foundation is selected of good strong stuff, there is no reason why the Embroidery should not be as lasting as the old Point Coupé, specimens of which, worked in the fifteenth century, are still to be seen. To work as shown in Fig. 705: Select cream white, pure white, or écru coloured linen, or cotton foundation, upon which trace the outline of the pattern, and indicate the lines for the Bars. Back this foundation with brown paper should it not be stiff; but this is not generally necessary. Then Run all the outlines with a double line of thread or silk, using a colour matching the material; Run the second line of thread the sixteenth of an inch above the first, and work the Bars during the process of Running. These make thus: Throw two threads across the space the Bar is to cover, catch them well into the edges of the pattern, and then Buttonhole them thickly over, and make a Picot in the centre Bar. Then carefully Buttonhole over every outline with the same coloured silk or thread; always turn the edge of the Buttonhole to the side of the material that is to be afterwards cut away. Great nicety is required to keep so many lines of Buttonhole all of the same width and thickness, and the second running of each line will here prove very useful, as, if the needle be always put in just beyond it, the width of each line will be the same. The thickness will depend upon the perfect regularity of distance with which each stitch is taken after the preceding one. This Embroidery can be done with any coloured washing silks or washing threads. The usual practice is to match the colour of the foundation, but red, blue, and black silks make pretty borders to écru or drab-coloured linens.

If the work is intended for a trimming to a mantel board, as shown in Fig. 705, one edge of it will be made straight where it is sewn on, and the other scalloped. This scalloped edge must be ornamented with Picots, like those made upon the bars. Having finished all the Buttonholing, proceed to cut away the foundation material from under the Bars. Use sharp and small scissors, and cut very slowly from underneath the Bars, and not over them. The Bars are much stronger and neater when made during the progress of Running than if worked when the material is cut away (as is sometimes recommended), but the cutting out of the superfluous stuff is rendered much more troublesome by their presence.

This work requires a background to throw it in relief, although it can be worked as an edging to tablecloths, and will then not require one. A coloured cloth is the most suitable one for mantel borders, but satin or velvet look rich when Richelieu Guipure is used for cushions or banner screens.

Rick Rack Work.—Made with crinkled white and very narrow braid, and Point Lace stitches, worked with fine crochet cotton. Rick Rack Work is very strong, and will bear constant washing; it is used for trimming children's underlinen. To work: Buy a hank of narrow crinkled braid, and sew five rows of it together in the shape of a diamond; commence this diamond at the left-hand lower side, and bend the braid backwards and forwards in lines of 1½ inches in width. The fifth row of braid will form the top right-hand side of the diamond;

six shades of one coloured wool, and rings 1 inch in diameter. Cover the rings with the wool thus: Cut the skeins of wool, thread a wool needle, and BUTTONHOLE over a curtain ring with the wool until it is quite covered, and a wool ring formed. Prepare a number of curtain rings in this way; make them of the shades of wool, so that each shade will make a circle of rings; but as the circle will enlarge towards the outside, there must be more rings covered with the colours selected for the outside shades than for those that form the centre. Sew the rings together with silks for a mat. Commence with one ring, round this sew six rings, which sew to the centre ring and each other, and round the second circle sew twelve rings for a third circle, and eighteen rings for a fourth circle. For a basket: Make the base as for a mat, and for the sides turn the first row of rings so that they stand upright

FIG. 705. RICHELIEU GUIPURE.

carry this down to form the first and bottom row of the next diamond, and make a number of connected diamonds in this manner for the length required. SEW the bottom points of the diamonds on to tape, and fill in between them with POINT DE BRUXELLES, worked coarsely with the crochet cotton.

Ridge.—A term employed to denote a raised line, like that produced by Gathers when drawn together by means of a drawing thread. Also, the furrow produced by Over-sewing selvedges, or seams in linen or calico. It is likewise demonstrated in a certain style of knitting, and weaving, by which the article is rendered very elastic; and by the raised nap on corduroy, which is produced in parallel lines across the cloth. *See* also KNITTING.

Ring Work.—An easy work used for forming mats and baskets, and made with small brass curtain rings, single Berlin wools, and beads. To work: Select five or

upon the last circle of the base, and do not increase in that row, but increase in all the succeeding rows, and sew together, so that they rise upwards in circles. Having sewn the rings together, fill in their centres with WHEELS made with coloured beads. Thread enough beads to cross one ring, and fasten it to the ring on the wrong side. Cross it with a second line of beads, and interlace with the first in the centre; fill in the sides with diagonal lines of beads taken across the centre from side to side. Rings can be covered with CROCHET instead of BUTTONHOLE if preferred. The rest of the work is executed in the same way.

Ripon Lace.—A lace manufactory was at one time carried on at Ripon, and twenty years ago coarse lace was still made there; but the trade has completely died out, and only the tradition of it now remains.

Ripping.—A term used in needlework to signify the

cutting of the stitches made to connect two parts of a garment or other article together; or the drawing out of the Sewing Threads.

Robe.—The French term for a woman's gown or dress. *Robe de chambre* signifies a dressing gown, but at times the name *Saut de lit* is substituted for it. There are also Robes of State worn by sovereigns, peers, and peeresses, judges, sheriffs, and mayors; and the term Robing is used in reference to the putting on of their Vestments by the clergy. The Fur Rugs used in sleighs are called Buffalo Robes.

Robing.—A description of flounce-like trimming which is attached to the front of a dress, skirt, or infant's frock. In the latter the robings extend from the shoulders, and in skirts from the waist to the lower edge of the skirt, gradually diverging as they extend lower down, to represent a false outer skirt, like a polonaise over an inner petticoat. When Robings are made of crape, they must be taken from the selvedge; because, when dresses have long unbroken lines in length or circumference, the width across from the two selvedges would not be sufficient to enable the dressmaker to dispense with joinings, which would be unsightly, both in Plastrons and Robings. To make: Cut the Crape Robing, when it reaches its full length at the lower end of the skirt, diagonally; and cut the fresh piece which is to be joined to it in the same way—first laying it upon the part of the Robing already sewn on the skirt—to measure the slant in which the cuttings should be made, so as the better to match them; thus, a good mitred corner will be produced. A Crape Robing should be lined, turned in about half an inch in depth, and slightly Herringboned to the muslin lining. Then lay the trimming on the skirt, pin it in its place, and turn the skirt inside out, laying the Robing on your hand. With the points of the left-hand fingers you can feel the edge of the Crape, and you can then RUN the lining of the trimming and the skirt of the dress together, so as to show no stitches taken through the Crape.

Rococo Embroidery.—This is of two descriptions, one formed with China ribbons sewn to satin or velvet foundations, and which is fully described under CHINA RIBBON

FIG. 706. ROCOCO EMBROIDERY.

EMBROIDERY, and the other, a variety of Roman Work, and shown in Fig. 706. This latter description of Rococo Embroidery is used for table borders, fire screens, and cushion

covers, and is made with écru linen foundations, ornamented with filoselles. To work: Draw out the pattern upon écru batiste or linen; select a filoselle of a bright and contrasting shade to the batiste, and split a thread of it into four threads. Thread a needle with one of these, and BUTTONHOLE the outline of the pattern over with even and rather wide rows of close Buttonholes, taking care to turn all the outer edges of the rows so that they are always to the outside of any section of the pattern. When the whole design is thus worked, take a sharp-pointed pair of scissors and cut away the batiste not inclosed by the lines of Buttonhole, and consequently not required. The pattern, by this cutting away of the batiste, will assume the appearance of Open Work. Line the batiste with a coloured Persian Silk before using it.

Rolling.—Also known as HALF HITCH. A peculiar twist given to the thread when bound upon the Bobbins used in Pillow Lace, by which the thread, when the Bobbins are hanging downwards, is prevented from unwinding. It is done as follows: Wind the thread upon the Bobbins; hold the latter in the left hand, with the palm upwards, and the thread in the right hand, the middle finger of the left hand upon the tightened thread; with a turn of the wrist bring the thread round the finger; transfer the loop formed by this twist to the Bobbin thus: gently pull with the right hand while the loop is put by the left finger over the head of the Bobbin. The thread can be shortened at any time thus: lift up this loop, wind up the thread, and then put the loop back; or it can be lengthened by tightening the loop and turning the Bobbin round to the left at the same time.

Roll Towellings.—These are described under LINEN. They may be had in crash, crape, diaper, fancy stripe, Forfar, grey twill, huckaback, and loom twill, and vary in width from 14 inches to 18 inches.

FIG. 707. ROMAN WORK.

Roman Work.—Also known as Ragusa Guipure, Strasbourg Embroidery, and Venetian Embroidery, and differing but slightly from Richelieu Guipure. It is made with washing materials, and is very durable, as, from the nature of the materials used, it neither fades nor comes to pieces by wear. To work as shown in Fig. 707: Draw out the design upon écru-coloured linen or batiste, and RUN the outlines over with thread of écru colour. Take machine silk or Pearsall's washing silk matching the écru in colour, and work over the outlines of the pattern with close and even rows of BUTTONHOLE. Turn the outside edge of these Buttonhole rows so that they always outline the edge of the various parts of the pattern, and follow its curves, a result that, in a complicated one, will require care. Connect together the various outlines of the pattern with CORDED BARS, or BUTTONHOLE BARS, and work WHEELS in any large spaces left between these parts. Having finished the work, take a sharp-pointed pair of scissors, and cut away the écru linen wherever the outer edge of the Buttonhole lines are, so that the pattern only is left connected together by the Bars and Wheels, which must be carefully avoided in the cutting away. These Bars and Wheels can be made after the pattern is cut out, but they are made more easily, and fit their spaces better, when worked before that process. Line the work with a bright-coloured silk or velvet, and use for cushions or banner screens.

Rond Bosse.—A term applied, in old needlework accounts, to denote that the Embroidery is raised up from the background it is upon, either by a padding, or by a number of stitches placed one over the other.

Rond Point.—Sometimes applied to laces that are made with work in relief, like Spanish and Venetian Rose Point, Point Duchesse, and some of the most elaborate of Honiton Laces.

Rone.—*See* GUIPURE D'ART.

Rope Sewing.—*See* SEWINGS.

Rope Stitch.—*See* EMBROIDERY STITCHES.

Rose Point.—*See* SPANISH and VENETIAN LACES.

Rosette.—A collection of bows of narrow ribbon, so arranged as to form a circle, and to resemble, in some degree, the form of a rose or dahlia. These little loops of ribbon are attached to a foundation of stiff, coarse Muslin or Buckram, cut in circular form, which can be sewn upon a dress, an infant's hat or cap; or used as wedding favours, attached to the breast of a man's coat.

Rouleau.—A French term denoting a large Piping, or rolled trimming, sometimes used as a decorative covering for the heading round a Flounce, or any such kind of Hem. The common way of making one is as follows: Take a strip of material cut on the bias (or diagonally), of 2 inches or upwards in width, lay a strip, or even roll of lambswool or wadding along it, fold the former over it, and run it down at the back. To conceal the stitches it would be better still to adopt the following method: TACK a piece of cord, and a length of wadding or lambswool, to the end of the strip of bias covering. Fold the latter together, leaving the lambswool outside, and the cord lying inside the fold of material. When the running is done, pull the cord, and, as it draws the lambswool or wadding inwards, it will turn the covering fold of material inside out at the same time—that is to say, the right side

will be turned out, ready for laying on the dress. The raw edges and stitches will thus be neatly turned in.

Round.—This term is applied, in CROCHET, KNITTING, and NETTING, to the stitches in those works which complete one circle.

Round Cotton Laces.—These laces are made of bleached cotton cord, having metal tags at each end. The numbers run 0, 1, 2, and the lengths 8-4, 10-4, and 12-4. *See* LACES.

Row.—A term applied, in CROCHET, KNITTING, and NETTING, to the stitches or loops that begin at one end of a straight piece of work and end at the other.

Royal Cashmere.—A light cloth made for summer coating. It is both fine and narrow, and is composed of Saxon wool in worsted weft. *See* CASHMERE.

Ruche.—A French term, employed in needlework to denote a particular style of decorative arrangement of material, both in dressmaking and millinery—a kind of quilling; a plaited, or goffered strip of ribbon, net, lace, or other material, applied to a bodice, skirt, or head-dress. Of these Ruchings there are four descriptions, viz., the Feather, Twisted, and Gathered Ruches, and that which is known by two designations—the Fluted, or *Ruche à la Vieille* (see Fig. 708). This latter is used as a dress trimming, and resembles a single Box-plaited Flounce. To produce the desired effect, make a number of small Box-plaits, leaving the respective distances between each Plait and an equal amount of the Plaiting at the top and bottom of the Ruching loose beyond the respective stitchings, so as to form a sort of Frilling above and

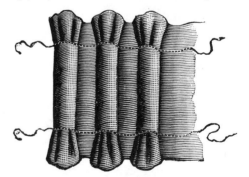

FIG. 708. RUCHE À LA VIEILLE.

below; bind both the edges of the material. A half-inch is the common width of each Plait, and this is the best size for Tarlatan, Muslin, and thin materials; but for Silk the Ruche flutings should measure from ½ inch to 1 inch. In Tarlatan or Grenadine, turn the edge down, so as just to be past where the stitches confining the plaits will be made; or snip out the raw edges in small points, TACK several strips together, and cut through all at once. Silk needs a book muslin lining as wide as the Ruche when made, including the headings, but no wider, as the silk alone folds over the edges of the muslin, to the depth required for the headings, which should never be more or less than the width of the fluting employed at the same time. The same proportion must be maintained as that, in length and spacing, for Box plaits.

A Twisted Ruche is sometimes made on the straight,

but, for a separate trimming, looks best when on the bias. To make: Turn down the edges, and fold one of them in Plaits of about three-quarters of an inch in width, and let all respectively touch each other. Then make up the other edge in the same way, only turning the plaits in the opposite direction. This will give them a twist in the middle. Plissé Flounces may be stitched at about 1½ inches or 2 inches from the top, and the edge plaited to the opposite side, thus giving a kind of heading to the Flounces, and a spiral effect resembling a separate Twisted Ruche.

A Feather Ruche is produced by fringing-out silk, which must be unravelled the width way, or across the stuff, but not along the selvedge line, as the fringe would thus be too poor. Snip the depth the fringe is to be apart at every 2 inches, for, if further than that, the threads are not drawn nearly so fast, and, when the feathering is wide, the silk is liable to knot. These Ruches on the straight need to be fuller than crossway ones, and quite treble its own length must be allowed in estimating the quantity required for a given space.

A single Gathered Ruche is not often employed, as it is confined to crossway strips never more than 2 inches wide, pinked out at both edges, and gathered over a cord down the centre. The amount of fulness is not great, and is always the same; and whatever material is used, when cut on the cross for the Ruche, will be gathered up into the width of the material before it was cut. Cut an 18-inch material on the cross, and gather this piece, and it will be the correct fulness to place on an 18-inch space.

Ruck.—A very inelegant term as applied to the materials of women's dress, or needlework in general. It signifies the awkward and undesirable wrinkles, or unsightly folds of a small size, by which any material may become creased. Wrinkles or Rucks are produced either through bad cutting-out in the first instance, or through equally bad sewing.

Rucroc.—See RACROC.

Ruff.—An article of dress worn round the throat, and, in olden times, equally by men as by women. Some were made of muslin, of great width, either with a plainly hemmed edge, or bordered with lace, and much stiffened and goffered. These Ruffs may be seen in portraits by the Dutch masters. In the present day, very small Ruffs of muslin, tulle, or lace are worn, and by women only. Some few years ago, Ruffs of fur and of swansdown were used, instead of Boas, by children, and were tied round the throat by ribbon strings. They were adopted for the sake of economy.

Ruffle.—A frill worn round the wrist, made of silk, muslin, Cambric, or lace, or a combination of any of these materials. In the time of the Tudors they were much worn, both by men and women, and were called Handruffs. Strutt names them as being entered in an Inventory of Henry VIII.'s own wardrobe, where they are described as being made of " quilted black silks, ruffed at the hand, with strawberry leaves and flowers of gold, embroidered with black silk." Some were turned back over the arm; and in Elizabeth's time embroidered Ruffles were worn, bordered with rich lace. They appear in the portraits of Queen Katharine Parr, and in those of Mary and Elizabeth, by Holbein: and worn afterwards, in combination with armour, they looked exceedingly well, and softened the hardness of the lines. In the last century they were also in fashion, worn with velvet, red cloth, silk, satin, and embroidered coats by men, and an arrangement of lace round the neck and down the shirt front. Ruffles are still adopted by women for certain styles of evening costumes.

Rug.—A description of coarse, nappy, woollen carpet, covering only a portion of the floor, or used in a carriage. Rugs are not only produced in looms, but hand-made, by knitting, crochet, or ordinary needles. Woollen cloths, produced in great varieties of design and combinations of colours, are manufactured for travelling wraps and sofa coverings. Very beautiful floor Rugs are produced in the East—in Turkey, India, and Persia more especially.

Rumchunder Silks.—These are, as the name shows, Indian silk stuffs. They are manufactured in many varieties—plain, twilled, satin-faced, crape, and in double-warp weaving. The prices of these several kinds vary considerably, and they measure from 32 inches to 36 inches in width. They are all very beautiful in quality and make, and are of white and cream colour.

Run and Fell.—This is a description of needlework which comes under the denomination of Plain Sewing. It is a method sometimes adopted in lieu of Over-sewing, and employed in making seams, either in underlinen, or in the skirts and sleeves of dresses. To make a Fell: RUN two pieces of material together, having placed the raw edge of the piece nearest to the worker a little below that of the outer piece. Then open out the two now united, turn over the outer edge, and fold over both edges together. Then HEM them down, making the Hem as flat as possible.

Run Lace.—During the eighteenth century this description of lace was made in Northamptonshire, and appears to have been copied from foreign designs, probably from those of Lille. The lace ground, which is a Réseau Honeycomb, like Brussels Ground, was made upon the Pillow, and the design embroidered or run upon it afterwards with the needle, the thick parts being darned, and outlined with a thick thread or gimp. RUN LACE is now worked in Ireland upon a machine-made net; the pattern is placed under the net, and transferred, in outline, to the net, by lines RUN with a silky linen thread.

Runners.—The name by which the Bobbins that work across a pattern in Pillow Lace making are known.

Running.—A term used in needlework to denote the passing of a needle and thread in and out of the material to be sewn, at regular intervals, taking much smaller stitches than when Tacking (see Fig. 709), Runnings being made for permanent, and Tackings only for temporary use. Tucks in dresses and under-

FIG. 709. RUNNING.

clothing are always made by Running, which is also the stitch employed for making Gathers. The breadths of skirts are also Run together; the needles employed should be long and slender. When one breadth is gored, and the adjoining one is not, the former should be held next to the worker. If the Running were effected by means of a sewing machine, the gored breadth must be placed on the machine, and the straight one laid uppermost.

Running String. — This term may be employed instead of "drawing string," as it denotes the ribbon, tape, braid, or Bobbin, which is passed through a Hem, or double Running, by means of a bodkin. Running Strings are much employed for infants' and children's clothing, and for articles of women's underlinen; also in infants' hoods and bonnets, when the Running threads are drawn to pucker the material.

Russell.—A woollen cloth, first manufactured at Norwich. It resembles baize, but with knots over the surface. It was at one time known as "Brighton Nap." In the time of Henry VIII., certain Acts were passed for the protection of the manufacture of what were called Russells — a kind of worsted stuff, hot-pressed, or calendered, to give it the lustrous appearance of satin. Some mention of it was again made in the last century, when it was described as a sort of twilled Lasting, or a stout variety of Calimancoes, chiefly employed for petticoats and waistcoats. Subsequently, this textile was improved in character, and manufactured with a design as a dress material. It is now merged in the cloth called RUSSELL CORD.

Russell Cord.—A kind of corded Rep, employed for making summer coats, scholastic gowns, lawyers' bags, &c. It is a mixture of cotton and wool, the cord being of cotton; and it washes well. There are several kinds of Cords: Janus Cord is entirely of wool, as also is Persian Cord, both of which are used for women's dresses, the former being usually made in black, for mourning wear.

Russet. — A coarse kind of woollen homespun cloth, formerly worn by country people. It is otherwise called "Russeting," the colour being either grey, or of a reddish-brown hue, such as would be produced by a mixture of paint—two parts being red, and one part each of yellow and blue. From the resemblance in colour between this material, and a certain Devonshire apple, the latter derived its name of Russet. Peacham alludes to the costume of the peasantry in 1658:

Most of them wear Russet, and have their shoes well nailed.

Grey Russet is mentioned as

The ordinary garb of country folks.

Shakespeare adopts the term when he speaks of:

The morn in Russet mantle clad.

and Dryden likewise, in the passage:

Our summer such a Russet livery wears.

Russia Braids.—These are made respectively in two materials—Mohair and Silk. The former consist of two cords woven together, cut into short lengths, and sold by the gross pieces. The wide are in 36 yard lengths, and four pieces go to the gross. The numbers run from 0 to 8, and they may be had in colours and black. The silk is a Braid of similar make, and designed for Embroidery Work,

such as that on smoking caps. It is sold in skeins, six to the gross, each skein being supposed to contain 24 yards; but, when silk is dear, the skeins—while priced equally high—are reduced in quantity to 16 or 18 yards. It can be bought by the yard. *See* BRAID.

Russia Crash.—A coarse linen or hempen textile, derived from Russia, or made of Russian hemp. The width varies from 16 to 22 inches. It is very durable, the threads being rough and coarse in quality. It is sometimes employed as a foundation for Crewel Embroidery, and much for jack towels. It is sold unbleached, and is of a greyish brown colour.

Russia Duck.—This is a description of strong, coarse, linen Jean, made for trouserings, and having its origin in Russia; see also RAVENSDUCK, which seems to be very similar, if not altogether identical, to it. Both cloths so called have been manufactured at Dundee, and the adjoining districts, of superior workmanship, and equal in material.

Russia Leather.—Russia Leather may be recognised at once by its agreeable odour, if not by its colour. The leather is first steeped in an alkaline lye, and tanned with the cheapest bark in the country. It is then fulled, tanned a second time with birch bark, and dyed red, with the aromatic sanders-wood, or else of a drab colour. Afterwards it is rubbed over with the empyreumatic oil of the birch, and stamped, as a rule, with a small cross-barred pattern. A certain roughness is produced on the face, by pressure with an iron implement. This Leather is valuable on account of its being proof against the mould by which other kinds of Leather are injured, and against all attacks of insects. It is employed by boot and shoemakers, for travelling and other bags, for the binding of books, for straps, and many other articles; and shavings of it are valuable for use in the preservation of furs, and any materials liable to destruction by moth. Genuine Russia Leather may usually be known by dark, blackish looking spots, which are not regarded as blemishes.

Russia Musquash (*Fiber zibethicus*).—This animal is also known as the PEREWIASKA.

Russian Diaper.—This is a description of Diaper having a double diamond pattern of a larger size than that of the fine Irish kinds. *See* DIAPER.

Russian Embroidery.—This Embroidery is worked either upon hollands and washing materials, as trimming

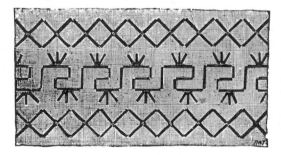

FIG. 710. RUSSIAN EMBROIDERY.

to children's dresses, or upon cloth or other dark foundations, for table borders, mantel borders, and cushions, in all Embroidery Stitches, made long, or diamond shape. When used for trimmings, it is worked upon bands of material in designs like that shown in Fig. 710, and the stitches are executed with ingrain cottons, Pearsall's washing silks, or Pyrenean wools. If both sides of the Embroidery are to be shown, work in Holbein Stitch and Point Sans Evers; if only one, in Point Russe. To work the Embroidery upon one side: Trace out the design upon holland, batiste, or écru-coloured linen, and work over all the outlines with POINT RUSSE STITCH, thus: Bring the needle up from the back of the work at the end of a line, and put it down at the other end of the line. Bring it out again at the end of the next line farthest away from the first made one, and put it down again close to the end of the first stitch. To work upon both sides, *see* HOLBEIN EMBROIDERY. The design shown in Fig. 710 is made with a line of stitches resembling battlements for the centre, and vandyke or diamonds as an edging. It is worked

line three times, in different shades of colour. Work the cross in the centre with two shades of filoselle, make the four small CROSS STITCHES with the lightest shade, the outline and centre cross with the darkest. When the work is finished, cut the canvas threads near the work, and pull them away singly, thus leaving the stitches upon the cloth. A brown cloth, with the work done with three shades of chestnut wool, and two of gold-coloured filoselle looks well, also an olive green cloth with peacock blue shades of wool, or a pale blue cloth with maroon wools shading to red silk or cinnamon-coloured silks.

Russian Lace.—This lace, although known on the Continent for many years, has never been much imported into England, and it was not until the International Exhibition of 1874, and the present, by the Duchess of Edinburgh, to the South Kensington Museum, of a collection of Russian Laces, that attention was drawn to its production. From these two sources we find that lace-

FIG. 711.   RUSSIAN EMBROIDERY.

entirely as described above, except that the three stitches forming the ornament to the battlements are made with SATIN STITCHES.

To work Fig. 711: This is intended for a table border, and is worked upon cloth, with canvas, and with Berlin wools and filoselle. Carefully frame some coarse Penelope canvas, and the cloth, in an EMBROIDERY FRAME. Take the darkest shade of wool, and work the outside line of the design, in POINT RUSSE, over three squares of the canvas, and in horizontal and upright lines alternately. Repeat with the next shade of wool for the second line, and with the lightest shade of wool for the third line. To work without a frame: STITCH the canvas and material together, and work in POINT DE CARREAU thus: Run a line, in a diagonal direction, up one side of the diamond, with the wool under four horizontal strands and over four upright strands alternately. Turn back and work down the line, filling up the spaces left uncovered. Repeat this

making is of very ancient origin in Russia, and that many of the designs still used are the same as made in early times; while the peculiarity and quaintness displayed in their execution is traceable, not to European influence, but to the ancient Oriental character of the Russian nation.

In the Cutworks and Drawn Works this influence is particularly detected, the threads that are retained being covered over, like those of Persian, Turkish, and Algerian Embroidery, with coloured silks, such as deep reds, bright yellows, dull coloured blues and greens, and with gold or silver threads interwrought with the design, and the linen left between the patterns in the Drawn Work embroidered with Satin and other stitches, in flower and geometrical designs worked with coloured silks. Bands of coloured silk brocades are frequently let into the lace, and are ornamented with embroidery, that produced at Jeletz being of animals with parti-coloured legs, two white, two blue, with red bodies in outline, and spots embroidered upon the body, in red, yellow, green, and bronze silks.

Darned Netting is also made in Russia. In some cases the meshes are made with silk or linen threads, and the darning executed in coloured silks; in others, the meshes are made of fine gold or silver wire, and the darning in silk.

Peter the Great protected the manufacture of Pillow Lace at Novgorod, and the lace made there was also made at Torjok; it is a kind of Tape, or Braid Lace, and is still manufactured in Russia. The pattern in it is outlined with Plain Braid, made with Cloth Stitch and Plain Edge, and the only variety to this outline consists in forming Hole Braid, also with a plain edge; but the peculiarity of the work consists of a Plaiting, or a single line of coloured silk thread, being worked in the centre of the braid, and following all the contours and turns. The Fillings are simple crossed threads, Plaitings, or Wheels, while the ground is either Plain Bars, or Réseau of Valenciennes pattern. The lace is executed with a small number of Bobbins, and is worked loosely and carelessly.

With the exception of the Cut, Drawn, and Darned Works, Russia has not produced any Needlepoints until the present century, when a lady founded a school at Moscow, under the patronage of the Czarevna, for the making of old Venice Point. This lace has been most successfully copied, and much of it is sold under the name of Point de Moscow. The stitches are all faithfully copied from old laces, also the Picots, or Brides Ornées, and Fleurs Volants. The thread used is fine, and of English make.

Russian Stitch.—*See* Crochet.

Russian Tapestry.—A material woven from hemp, designed for window curtains, having a decorative design, and a border of fringe. It is a durable article, and may be procured in various widths. The hemp of which it is made is said to be prepared with seal oil, and has a certain unpleasant odour in consequence; but this soon passes off on exposure to the air.

Russian Tapestry Work.—This is a strong and effective work, particularly suitable for ladies who have not much time to devote to fancy needlework. It is made with Russian Tapestry, woven as a border with two coloured threads, one forming a conventional design upon the other, which appears as a background to the pattern. The work consists in either outlining this conventional design, or filling it entirely in with coloured crewels. The Embroidery is done according to the design, and the colours chosen so as to contrast (without being too glaring) with the material threads. The best colours to use are two shades of peacock blue, two of ruby reds, two of olive greens, and two of old gold colours. The manner of working is as follows: Work the centre of the pattern on the material in outline, and in Crewel Stitch, outline each separate piece of it in that stitch with a line of dark and light blue crewels, or fill it entirely in with the light blue crewels in Crewel Stitch, and outline it with the dark shade. Work with the reds, greens, and yellows over detached pieces of the pattern in the same

way. For the border upon each side of the pattern, make vandyked lines with Cross Stitch of the darkest shades of the colours, or work Stars and Wheels with all the colours used in the centre.

S.

Sable (*Mustela zibellina*).—The fur of the Sable, an animal of the Weasel tribe, is one of the most beautiful and valuable of those imported to this country. The animal is a native of Siberia, although it is often called the Russian Sable. The fur is very dark and lustrous, and of great depth, and is in its highest perfection in winter. When prepared ready for making up, the skins measure 6 inches by 14 inches, and the best kinds are valued at from £6 to £20 a-piece. Although about 25,000 or 30,000 are annually collected in the Russian territories, only a small quantity, comparatively, are imported to this country. Other furs are known as "Sables." besides the real Siberian—viz., the Hudson's Bay, which is the *Mustela Canadensis*; the Baum, or Pine Marten (*M. Abietum*); the Sable of North America (*M. leucopus*); that of Tartary (*M. Sibirica*); of Japan (*M. melanopus*); and the Stone Marten (*M. Saxorum*), otherwise known as the French dyed Marten. The Hudson's Bay species ranks next in repute and value to the real Siberian; but all the varieties enumerated are inferior to it. In the reign of Henry VIII., no person under the rank of an Earl was permitted to wear the genuine Siberian Sable. Some brushes used by artists for painting are made from the tail of this animal.

Sabrina Work.—This work, which is a variety of Appliqué, first came into notice some fourteen years ago, and, though Crewel Work superseded it for some time, it has again become popular, and is capable of much artistic effect. It consists in cutting out, either from coloured velvets, velveteen, satin, silk, cloth, serge, or washing materials, whole or single petals of flowers, leaves, or conventionalised flower patterns, and affixing these pieces to coloured cloths or white linen backgrounds, with wide apart Buttonhole Stitches; while such parts of the design that are too small to allow of being cut out are worked, with Chain or Crewel Stitch, upon the material used as the background.

The work is used for quilts, table, mantel, and curtain borders, also for cushions and slippers, but looks better upon the first-mentioned large articles than upon the small ones. The whole beauty of it depends upon the selection of suitable patterns and appropriate colours, the execution being of the simplest description; but, with a judicious use of harmonies and slight contrasts together, good effects can be obtained without much labour. Gold-coloured backgrounds, with a pattern made with brown and yellow flowers and russet and green leaves; soft-coloured backgrounds, with designs in the same colour, but of several shades all darker than the background; blues shading to yellow, upon dark green backgrounds; pale blue background, with creamy white and pink designs; deep blue twill, with designs in shades of red cloth; dark grey oatmeal background, with either blue or red twill designs, will all be suitable combinations. To work: Select an outline crewel design composed of small leaves, fruit, or flowers, with tendrils, and, if it is an ironing design, and to be worked upon cloth, iron it off upon the material; or trace it out upon linen or oatmeal cloth, should it be required to wash. Cut out the various shapes of the pattern in cardboard, and lay these pieces down upon the colours that are to form the design. Cut these pieces out very carefully with sharp scissors, as upon their accuracy the neatness of the work depends. Prepare a number of pieces, and, though retaining the colour originally assigned to each, vary the shade of that colour where such a change would give more

cut out each flower and leaf separately, and many designs will allow the punches used by artificial flower makers to be employed instead of scissors for preparing the pieces. These punches are bought of the required shape, and are used as follows: Obtain a piece of lead, and upon it lay the material, in four or six layers, according to its thickness. Hold the punch in the left hand, over the material, strike it sharply down with a wooden mallet, and it will cut through the folds with the blow.

The design shown in Fig. 712 is intended as a mantelpiece or curtain border, and is a conventional flower pattern, taken from an Italian design of the seventeenth century.

FIG. 712. SABRINA WORK.

diversity to the design. For the leaves, choose dark yellow greens in preference to very light or blue green shades, but make them as varied in tint as possible. TACK the pieces down upon the foundation in their places, being guided by the traced design, and then BUTTONHOLE round each piece with wide apart stitches, and with Pearsall's washing silks or ingrain cotton, and in the colour that matches the piece so secured, Work the stems and connecting stalks, or tendrils of the design, with the same silks, and in CHAIN STITCH, and ornament the centres of the flowers with FRENCH KNOTS, or with SATIN STITCH.

When working a table border or quilt, it is tedious to

It can be worked, either with satin or velvet, upon cloth or satin sheeting, or with cloth upon grey oatmeal cloth. It is shown worked out in silk upon cloth. The colours should be varied according to the materials used, the ones described being only a guide. Select a medium shade of art blue cloth as foundation, cut out the lighter scrolls in a soft cinnamon shade of red silk, the darker scrolls in a deep rich red silk, the round flowers in light yellow pink silk; make the carnation of a deep shade of the same yellow pink, the leaves close to it in dark olive green, and the three balls in the same colour as the carnation. Work the connecting stems in CHAIN STITCH, and the small

MECHLIN LACE — RARE.

MODERN VALENCIENNES.

OLD VALENCIENNES — RARE.

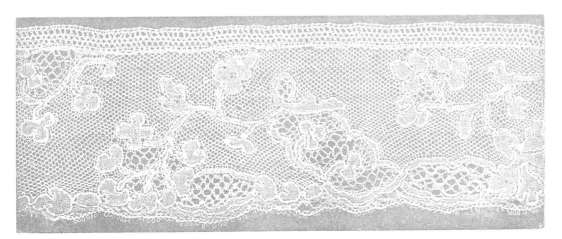

MECHLIN LACE — RARE.

rounds in SATIN STITCH, and surround each piece of silk with wide apart Buttonhole lines of silk matching it in shade.

Sac (Sack, or Sacque).—An old term, still in use, denoting a superfluous, but decorative, piece of a dress material, fastened to the shoulders at the back of the gown in wide, loose plaits, and descending to the ground, of such a length as to form a train. The gown itself is always complete without this appendage. Amongst others, Pepys speaks of a Sac, writing on 2nd March, 1669: "My wife this day put on first her French gown, called a Sac, which becomes her very well." It was introduced from France in the time of Charles II., died out, and was revived again *temp.* George I. Sir Walter Scott likewise alludes to it in the *Tapestried Chamber*: "An old woman, whose dress was an old-fashioned gown, which ladies call a Sacque—that is, a sort of robe, completely loose in the body, but gathered into broad plaits upon the neck and shoulders."

Sackcloth.—Large, coarse sheeting, employed for the wrapping up of bales, and the making of bags or sacks. In former times this term was used to denote a coarse haircloth, which was worn in token of penitence, mourning, or self-mortification.

Sacking.—A coarse description of flaxen or hempen textile, employed for bagging, and likewise for the bottoms of bedsteads. The manufacture is carried on chiefly in Ireland and at Dundee. Sacking is also known as "Burlap" and "Coffee-bagging." Cheap door mats and hearthrugs are made of Sacking, or Burlap, by embroidering in CROSS STITCH with coloured wool, as on Java Canvas. Leave a border outside the embroidery of two or three inches in depth, then ravel out a fringe, and make a second fringe of the wool drawn through the Sacking, which is to fall over that made of the Sacking. Lastly, sew the Rug upon some firm foundation, such as a piece of old Brussels carpet.

Saddle Cloths.—These are easily made, and are very useful presents to people who keep carriages. To make: Procure a piece of fine cloth—either dark blue, brown, or maroon, according to the colour of the carriage. Cut it 2 feet wide, and 7 to 8 inches long, curve it slightly inwards, to shape it to the horse's neck on one side, and round it at the ends, so that it is a little larger at the back than in the front. On the outside of this cloth, half an inch from the edge, trace a braiding pattern of 1 inch in width. Choose the pattern known as the Greek key, or one of small running scrolls; stitch firmly down to this the narrowest white or black silk braid procurable. Trace the monogram of the owner, in letters not more than 1½ inches long, upon the right-hand corner, at the back of the saddle cloth, above the braiding. Either COUCH down gold thread to cover their outlines, or work thickly over in SATIN STITCH, and in silk matching the braid. Should two Saddle Cloths be necessary, arrange one monogram on the right-hand side of the first one, and the other monogram on the left-hand side of the second one. Coronets or crests are sometimes worked instead of a monogram. The cloth must be lined with buckram

and stout black linen before it is completed; but this is better done at a saddler's than at home.

St. Andrew's Stitch.—*See* EMBROIDERY STITCHES.

Sam Cloth.—The ancient term for Sampler.

Sammal.—A woollen material employed in Ecclesiastical Embroidery.

Sampler.—Samplers, or, as they were first called, Sam Cloths, first came into use during the sixteenth century, on account of the great scarcity and high price of Lace pattern books; therefore, all the earliest laces, such as Cut Works, Drawn Threads, Reticellas, &c., were copied upon Sam Cloths by those who were not sufficiently rich to buy the pattern books, with the combined purpose of obtaining the design, and exhibiting the proficiency of the worker. At a later date, when lace was not so much made, and designs of all kinds were more abundant, Samplers were still worked, no longer with the object of perpetuating a pattern, but to exhibit the skill of the embroiderer; and no young lady's education, during the seventeenth and eighteenth centuries, was considered complete until she had embroidered in silks and gold thread a Sampler with a bordering of Drawn Work, and a centre filled with representations of animals, flowers, and trees, accompanied by verses appropriate to the undertaking. These Samplers were looked upon as such proofs of skill that they were preserved with much care, and many of those worked in the earlier part of the seventeenth century are still in a good state of preservation. Amongst the numbers exhibited, in 1881, at the Ancient Needlework Exhibition, the verses upon one worked in 1780 are quaint. They run as follows:

> Elizabeth Hide is my name,
> And with my needle I work the same,
> That all the world may plainly see
> How kind my parents have been to me.

To Make a Sampler: Take some Mosaic Canvas, of the finest make, and woven so that each thread is at an equal distance apart. Cut this 18 inches wide and 20 inches long, and measure off a border all round of 4 inches. For the border, half an inch from the edge, draw out threads in a pattern to the depth of half an inch, and work over these with coloured silk; then work a conventional scroll pattern, in shades of several colours, and in TENT STITCH, to fill up the remaining 3 inches of the border. Divide the centre of the Sampler into three sections. In the top section work a figure design. (In the old Samplers this was generally a sacred subject, such as Adam and Eve before the Tree of Knowledge.) In the centre section work an Alphabet in capital letters, and in the bottom an appropriate verse, the name of the worker, and the date.

(2) An oblong square of canvas, more or less coarse, upon which marking with a needle in Cross Stitch or otherwise is learned. Common canvas usually measures from 18 inches to 20 inches in width. In this case, cut off a piece of about 4 inches deep from one selvedge to the other. Then cut the remainder along the selvedge into three equal parts, so that each strip will be about 6 inches

in width. These strips must each be cut across into four parts, and this will make a dozen Samplers, 8 inches long and 6 inches wide respectively. This size will contain all the letters, large and small, besides numerals. As the raw edges of the canvas have to be turned in and sewn down by Hem Stitching, lay the fold down exactly to a thread; draw a thread or two under the hem, on each side respectively, and sew the end of the turn. To make the Hem Stitch, pass the needle under two threads and draw it, the point directed towards the worker. Then insert the needle back again, across the same thread, and out through the edge of the Hem. *See* MARKING.

Samples.—Trade patterns of every description of textile, arranged in graduated shades of colour, and attached to large cards, at one end of each little piece. They are all cut in oblong parallelograms—that is to say, the length is double that of the width of each. In this manner ribbon and men's cloths are frequently offered to the purchasers for sale, as are likewise samples of lace and frilling, ready plaited or quilled. Buttons, also, of a fancy description, short lengths of trimmings in braids, gimps and beads, and fringes of all kinds, are arranged on cards, sufficient being supplied of the goods having large patterns to show the whole design without any "repeat." Silks and woollen cloths are more generally made up into packages, and labelled with the name, price, and width of the material, and the name of either the manufacturer or of the firm where the goods are to be purchased. These Samples are sometimes disposed of for the making of Patchwork Quilts, or given away in charity for the same or a somewhat similar purpose.

Sanitary Clothing.—By this name under garments of pure undyed wool have been patented by Dr. Gustav Jaegar, of Stuttgart, also outer clothing and bedding; woollen stuffs being substituted for linen or calico sheets and pillow-cases; animal fibre being exclusively employed. *See* UNDERLINEN.

Sarcenet.—A name derived from Saracennet, given to indicate the Oriental origin of a thin kind of silk stuff, of a character superior, yet otherwise similar, to Persian, first used in this country in the thirteenth century. It can be obtained either plain or twilled, and in several colours, and is used for linings, being fine and very soft. The Silk Stuff known in the olden times as "Sendall" was said by Thynne, in his *Animadversions on Speght's Chaucer*, to be " A thynne stuffe lyke Sarcenett, and of a raw kynde of sylke or Sarcenet; but coarser and narrower than the Sarcenett now ys, as myselfe can remember." The scholastic dress, or costume of the doctor of physic, was described by Chaucer as being

. . . . lined with Taffata and Sendal.

Sarcenet Ribbons.—Ribbons of this description are much like piece Sarcenet of a superior quality, with plain edges. They are comparatively cheap, and suitable for caps.

Saree.—A cotton stuff, of Indian manufacture, worn by the natives as a wrapping garment; also the name of a long scarf of silk, or gauze, used in the same country.

Sashes.—A woven silk scarf, of thick and heavy quality, manufactured expressly for the use of officers, and finished with long fringe. Broad silk ribbons, worn as waist belts, by women, and children of both sexes, are also called Sashes. Those worn by officers in uniform are of a very handsome and peculiar make, and rich quality, being of thick woven silk, and having a deep fringe at each end. These military scarves are worn over one shoulder, and knotted at the waist under the other.

Satara.—A ribbed cloth, brightly dressed, lustred, and hot pressed.

Sateen.—A cotton textile, of satin make, glossy, thick, and strong, resembling Jean. It is chiefly employed for the making of stays, and sometimes for dresses and boots, and can be procured in black and white, and in various colours. It is twilled, and is superior to Jeans. There are not only Sateens of uni-colour, but figured varieties, in many combinations of colour, employed for women's gowns. The width measures from 27 inches to 1 yard.

Satin.—A silk twill, of very glossy appearance on the face, and dull at the back. Very usually seven out of every eight threads of the warp are visible; whereas, in other silk stuffs, each half of the warp is raised alternately. Its brilliancy is further augmented by dressing, it being rolled on hot cylinders. Some Satins are figured and brocaded, and amongst the best examples are those made in Spitalfields. A good quality Satin wears exceedingly well; the width runs from 18 inches to 22 inches. The lustre of Satin is produced by the irregular method in which the respective threads of the warp and weft are taken in connection with each other. Satin cannot be cleaned or dyed satisfactorily, as it is liable to become frayed. Strutt makes an allusion to it in an account of *Revels at Court, temp.* Henry VIII., when its usual colour was red. Dekker likewise speaks of it in Gull's *Hornbook*, 1609, as the dress material of the higher classes: " Though you find much Satin there, yet you shall likewise find many citizen's sons." Satinette is a thinner and cheaper description of the same stuff, but equally durable, and may be had in black and colours as a dress material. Its brilliancy is produced in the process of manufacture, without dress, or other artificial means.

Satin is of Chinese origin, the flowered kinds—those manufactured and imported into this country — being celebrated. It is also made at Lyons and Florence. Amongst other varieties may be mentioned the Indian Cuttanee Satin, which is a fine thick cotton-backed Satin, produced in stripes. There are three varieties of mixtures in colour — two each, in each variety. It is 27 inches in width, and is chiefly employed for upholstery, but is sometimes used by ladies for tea-gowns. There are also Satin Damasks, Satin de Lyons, Satin Foulards, Satin Merveilleux, Satin Sheeting, Satin Beige, Satin Sultan, and Satinette. These are all Silk textiles. There are others of mixed materials—such as the Satin de Bruges, which is a combination of silk and wool, made for upholstery. Sateen, which is a cotton stuff of Satin make; Satin striped Canvas, the former being of silk, and the Canvas of thread. Satin de Laine, composed of wool;

Satin Sultan, which has a mixture of wool with the silk, and is employed for mantles; and Satinet, an American cloth of Satin and wool.

Cyprus Satin is often mentioned in old inventories and account books, as, for instance, those of the Church-wardens of Leverton, near Boston, Lincolnshire, dated 1528: "For a yard of green sattyn of Sypryse, viijd.," which was probably employed in the repair of the Vestments. Also, in an inventory of the goods belonging to the Abbey of Peterborough, in 1539, it is said: "On Vestment of red, coarse Satten of Cyprus, with harts and knots." Satin proper was first introduced into this country from China. It represents the "Samite" of ancient times, which was frequently embroidered or interwoven with gold or silver threads:

> And in over-gilt Samite
> Y-clad she was by great délite.
> CHAUCER's *Romaunt of the Rose.*

It is likewise spoken of by Tennyson:

> An arm
> Rose up from out the bosom of the lake
> Clothed in white Samite.

Satin Cloth.—A French woollen material of Satin make, having a smooth face. It is employed for women's dresses, is produced in most colours, and is of stout quality and durable. The width measures from about 27 inches to 30 inches. It is otherwise known by its French name of SATIN DE LAINE.

Satin Damask.—A very costly silk material, varying in price according to the weight of silk, and the richness and elaboration of the design. In some examples it is enriched with gold threads, and may be procured of an exceedingly costly quality, having velvet flowers. The width varies from 28 inches to 32 inches.

Satin de Bruges.—This is a cloth of Satin make, having a smooth face. It is composed of a combination of silk and wool, and is designed for purposes of upholstery.

Satin de Laine.—A French textile of Satin make, but composed entirely of wool, and otherwise known as SATIN CLOTH. It is manufactured at Roubaix.

Satin de Lyons.—This description of rich silk has a gros grain back in lieu of a twill. *See* SATIN.

Satin Embroidery.—*See* EMBROIDERY IN SATIN STITCH.

Satinet.—An American cloth of mixed materials, both cheap and durable, and used by the labouring classes in that country as fustian and velveteen corduroy are employed in England. The warp of Satinet is of cotton, and the "filling-in" is composed mostly of the short, waste threads of woollen manufacture, combined with a sufficient quantity of long wool to permit of its being spun. It is woven in a peculiar way, so as to bring up the wool to the surface of the stuff; and is then heavily felted, so that the cotton should be entirely concealed.

Satin Foulards.—These are silk stuffs printed in various designs and colours, and measure from 24 inches to 25 inches in width.

Satin Lisse.—A French dress material made of cotton, but having a Satin-like lustre. It is lighter in substance than an English Sateen, and is twilled. For slight mourning it is very suitable, made up as a summer costume; and the small designs, floral and otherwise, with which it is covered, are pretty and elegant. It is produced in varieties of black, white, and violet or grey.

Satin Merveilleux.—This is a description of twilled Satin textile, of an exceedingly soft and pliable character, and having but little gloss. It is sold in different qualities, all of which measure 24 inches in width.

Satin Sheeting.—One of the "waste silk" materials, of Satin make on the face, and twilled cotton at the back, the chief substance of the material being of cotton. It is made in different degrees of fineness, runs to 54 inches in width, and is employed for purposes of embroidery, fancy, dress, and upholstery. Satin Sheeting is thicker in substance, coarser in the weaving, and less glossy, than the ordinary "cotton-backed Satin." It can be obtained in most beautiful shades of every colour, both new and old, and is made 22 inches in width. The Diapered Satin Sheeting is a comparatively new textile.

Satin Stitch.—*See* BERLIN WORK and EMBROIDERY STITCHES.

Satin-striped Canvas.—This is a fancy variety of Embroidery Canvas, having alternate stripes of Satin and plain thick Canvas, somewhat resembling the Java make. The Satin stripe has a horizontal cording, as the weft of flax runs through the silk stripe.

Satin Sultan.—A textile somewhat resembling Bengaline in the method of its manufacture, but having a Satin face. It is designed for mantles, measures 24 inches in width, and varies considerably in quality and price.

Satin Turk.—A peculiar description of silk textile made at Amiens; it is very durable, and is suitable as a dress material, being soft, not liable to much creasing, and less thick and stiff than Satin. It is also used for evening shoes, and waistcoats, and is about 27 inches in width.

Satin Veiné.—A French term, sometimes applied to the veins of leaves, or the tendrils of sprays worked in Embroidery and with Satin Stitch.

Saut de Lit.—One of the French terms employed to denote a dressing-gown, the extra covering put on immediately on rising from bed, and worn in the bedroom until the costume suitable for the breakfast-room be put on.

Saxon Embroidery.—The Anglo-Saxon ladies were celebrated for their outline Embroidery upon fine linen or silk before their Church needlework excited the envy of Pope Adrian IV. This outline work was formed of the richest material, and was remarkable as much for the delicacy of its workmanship as for the pure and symbolical character of its designs, which were chiefly taken from the emblems used by the early Christians to represent our Saviour, the Trinity, and the Unity of the Godhead. Thus, the Gammadion, the Triangle, and the Circle occur in this work, either combined or forming separate geometrical patterns, used for the wide borders upon priests' vestments or upon altar linen. The outlines and all the chief parts of the design are executed upon the surface of the material, and are made by laying down gold or silver threads, or thick silk threads, and Couching them to their places by a stitch brought from the back of the work on one side of the thread, and put down into the material on the other, and so securing it into its position. A few light stitches are worked directly on to the material as a finish to the chief lines, but they are always made subordinate to the Couched lines, to which much variety and richness are given by the use of the best and most varied materials. Fig. 713 is a specimen of Saxon Embroidery, taken from a quilt now in the South Kensington

FIG. 713. SAXON EMBROIDERY.

Museum. The subject is not ecclesiastical, as the quilt was not intended for Church uses, but it gives a fair idea of the manner in which this Embroidery was worked, and is a pattern that can be easily copied. To work: Trace the design upon fine linen (but only the outline) or white Surah silk, which back with holland. Put the material into an EMBROIDERY FRAME, COUCH gold thread round the outlines, and work the stitches that form the fillings to the leaves and flowers. These consist of Lines crossing each other diagonally and caught down with a stitch, and CROSS STITCH and DOUBLE STARS. Work the diagonal lines in green silk, lay them down on the material, and

secure them with a stitch made with red silk. Work the Cross Stitches in red silk, and the double Stars with red and green silk. Take a dark olive-green silk cord, and Couch this along every outline, sewing it to the material with a silk matching it in colour.

Saxony.—Cloth or flannel made of wool of the Merino sheep pastured on the loamy soil of Saxony, which is peculiarly favourable for the rearing of fine animals. Wool from the same breed pastured in Spain is much harsher in quality. The cloth is made in the West of England, and the flannel chiefly at Saddleworth, near Halifax. *See* FLANNEL.

Saxony Lace.—The making of Pillow Lace in Saxony dates from the sixteenth century, the art having been introduced from Flanders. Old authorities consider that it was introduced into Germany by Barbara Uttermann, the wife of a master miner at Annaberg, who founded a school for lace-making at that place in 1561; but modern writers look upon the religious emigrants as the probable sources of the industry, though all agree that during the life of Barbara Uttermann (1514 to 1575) lace-making became known in Germany, and continued to be a source of profit to that nation until the eighteenth century. Lace-making has much declined since that period, though lace still forms an article of manufacture. The best that is made resembles old Brussels, and obtains a good price; but the greatest sale is confined to a coarse Guipure Lace, known as Eternelle and Plaited Lace; and as it is one that any amateur with a little patience can make, the details are here given.

The materials required are a pillow and stand, lace patterns, bobbins, pins, thread, scissors, and Knitting needle; the bobbins and pillow differ from those used in Honiton Lace-making.

The pillow is oblong, the cover or bag for which make of twill 28 inches long and 8 inches wide. RUN this piece of material together, then make a wide HEM at the sides, to hold tape as a drawer. Draw up one side, but do not pull the material up close together; leave a round of 7 inches, into which TACK a piece of cardboard covered with twill. Fill up the cover with horsehair, bran, or wool, draw the second side together with the tape, and insert the cardboard to match the side first made. The white Cover Cloths for protecting the Lace are made like ordinary Cover Cloths. Cut a piece of strong linen 4½ inches wide, and long enough to go round the Cushion, and sew this round the Cover in the centre, to serve as a support to the lace and the pattern. The Cushion is not held upon the knee, but is fixed into a stand, which is from 28 inches to 30 inches high, so as to be within reach of a worker when sitting down. Make the stand either as an ordinary table with four legs, of a size just to hold the cushion, and elongate the four legs or supports above the table part to secure the Cushion between them; or make a table with two legs or supports like crutches, and secure these two upright pieces of wood into a strong foundation, while the fork or crutch of the upper part holds up the Cushion. The lace patterns are pricked out upon either Toile Ciré or Parchment, and do not differ from other Pillow Lace patterns. The Bobbins are

4½ inches long, and, after the thread is wound upon them, a thin metal shield is secured over it, to prevent its soiling when held in the hand. Ordinary large Bobbins can be used, but the sort sold expressly are the best. A great number are required. The pins are of brass, and finer than ordinary pins. No. 30 thread is used to commence upon, Nos. 50 and 60 being used for making ordinary lace, and No. 200 for fine lace. A Knitting needle is required to fasten the threads to when commencing the Lace, instead of tying the threads into a Knot, and pinning this Knot to the Cushion, as in Honiton Lace.

Before commencing to make any pattern, it is necessary to learn how the Bobbins are secured, increased, and decreased, and the manner of making the stitches. To adjust the Bobbins: Arrange the Cushion on the stand, and secure the pattern by pinning it down. Run the Knitting needle in across the Cushion where the pattern commences, push it into the material on the right side of the pattern, but leave it free on the left side. Take up each Bobbin separately, and fasten it to the Knitting needle thus: Hold the end of the thread in the right hand in front of the needle, with the left hand put the Bobbin under the needle, round it, and under the thread in the front, to form a secured loop; draw this up, and make another loop in the same way with the same Bobbin. Put on the required number of Bobbins in this manner.

To Cut off Threads.—Threads that have broken, and have been replaced by new ones, or threads no longer required in the pattern, are done away with as follows: Where they occur in Cloth Stitch or other parts of the Lace, tie them in a WEAVER'S KNOT, and pin them out of the way on the Cushion until some inches of the

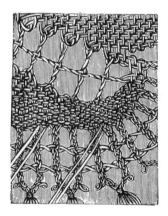

FIG. 714. SAXONY LACE—TO CUT OFF THREADS.

Lace beyond them have been made, then cut them away close to the Lace. Fig. 714 shows threads arranged for cutting away from Cloth Stitch. Where the threads are no longer required in the border of a pattern, they are formed into a little bunch thus: Take one thread and bind it well round the rest, then pull its end through the binding to secure it. Cut off the threads close, so that only a small bunch is made not larger than an ordinary PICOT. The bunches shown in Fig. 714 are purposely enlarged, in order that the manner of making them may be understood.

To Increase the Bobbins.—Bobbins are frequently added while the Lace is in progress, either for the purpose of increasing the Lace or when threads have been broken; they are adjusted as follows: Tie two threads together with a WEAVER'S KNOT, and hang these threads (which are

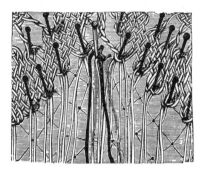

FIG. 715. SAXONY LACE—TO INCREASE THE BOBBINS.

coloured black in Fig. 715) over the pin which is placed in the hole nearest the part to be increased. Work in these new threads as they are reached in the proper course of the lace-making. Should the threads be added at the thick part of a pattern where Cloth Stitch is worked, after they have been woven in with the others the Knot that joins their ends together may be cut away; but should they be required in the ground or open parts of the Lace, this Knot must be retained.

The chief STITCHES are worked as follows:

Cloth Stitch, or Plain Dotting.—This Stitch is used

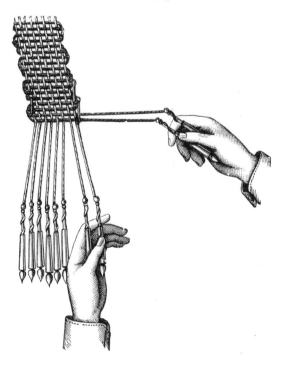

FIG. 716. SAXONY LACE—CLOTH STITCH OR PLAIN DOTTING.

for all the thick parts of the Lace, and closely resembles the ordinary Cloth Stitch of other laces. For the narrow piece, shown in Fig. 716, use ten Bobbins, of which allow eight to hang down the Pillow, using the other two to interlace in and out of the stationary threads. Hold two of the Hangers in the left hand, and take the Worker Bobbins in the right hand; put up a pin at the end of the Lace, twist the two workers together twice (see Fig. 716) so as to make an edge, leave one behind the pin, pass the other over the first Hanger in the left hand and under the second; take up the next two Hangers, and pass the Worker over and under them, and so continue until the other edge is reached. Then take the second Working Bobbin, and reverse the passing over and under until it reaches the other edge; here twist it together with the first Bobbin, stick in a pin at the edge, and then work them back. Keep the Hanging Bobbins in the left hand, so that the long lines down the Lace are evenly stretched.

Crossing.—A movement frequently resorted to when making this Lace, and worked as follows: Take up two Bobbins that lie close together, and move the one on the left hand over the right hand, and the one on the right hand under the left hand. A Crossing is shown in the Double Twist, Fig. 721.

Half Stitch, or Net Device.—This open Lattice Stitch is used for all the lighter parts of the design and is more difficult than Cloth Stitch, as the threads, while making it, are crossed. To work as shown in Fig. 717: Fasten on

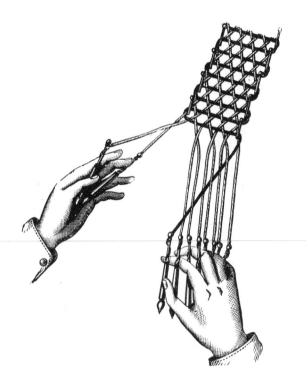

FIG. 717. SAXONY LACE—HALF STITCH OR NET DEVICE.

ten Bobbins, and use nine as Hanging or Passive Bobbins, and one as a Worker to form the Lace. Cross the Hangers one over the other, letting the left-hand Bobbins cross under the right-hand Bobbins (the left hand in the

illustration shows how the crossing is managed). Keep all the Hanging Bobbins in the hand. Stick a pin at the edge of the Lace, and pass the Worker Bobbin under and over each Bobbin, as in Cloth Stitch, until it reaches the other end. Do not draw it up close, but allow space for the crossing to show. Stick a pin in at the other edge, cross the Hanging Bobbins as before, and work back.

Lozenge.—Threads twisted together so as to form a thick and pointed diamond shape are much used in coarse Guipure Saxony Lace, and are called Lozenges. They are made generally with four Bobbins, as follows: Tie four Bobbins together, then hold three in the left hand but apart, as shown in Fig. 718, and take the fourth Bobbin in the right hand and pass it over, under, and over the three held down. This will bring it out upon the left side.

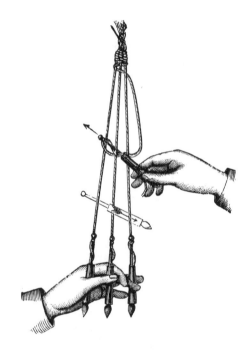

FIG. 718. SAXONY LACE—LOZENGE.

To return it, pass it under, over, and under the three held Bobbins (as shown by the white arrow in the engraving). Repeat these two lines until the length of the Lozenge is made. A small Lozenge takes twelve rows, a large one twenty, but no certain number of lines can be given, as all depends upon the thickness of the thread used. When the Lozenge is made, Knot the threads together, and proceed to make another if required.

Pin-sticking.—This is a movement that is required in all kinds of Pillow Lace making, and is used to form the design and to keep the various parts that are worked even and in their proper positions. The holes into which the Pins are put are all pricked upon the pattern. When one of these is reached, hold the Bobbins firmly in the left hand, take up a Pin in the right hand, and stick it firmly into its hole, keeping the threads in their right places on each side of the Pin. The manner of doing this is shown in Fig. 719.

Plaitings.—These are sometimes used to form the ground of the Lace. To make: Take four Bobbins and Plait them together until a pinhole is reached, divide them

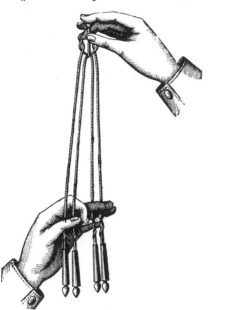

FIG. 719. SAXONY LACE—PIN STICKING.

at that place, and take two Bobbins from the Plait upon the other side of the pinhole. Cross the threads, and continue to Plait to the next pinhole; here divide the

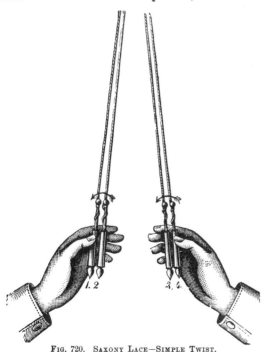

FIG. 720. SAXONY LACE—SIMPLE TWIST.

Bobbins, leave two and take up two, and continue the Plait to another pinhole, where divide again; work up the threads left at the pinholes in the same way.

Twists.—The Twists are of two kinds, Simple and Double, and are worked as follows: To form a *Simple Twist* as shown in Fig. 720. In the illustration the Bobbins that make the Twist are numbered from 1 to 4. Hold 1 and 2 in the left hand, 3 and 4 in the right hand. Simultaneously pass 2 over 1 with the left hand, and 4 over 3 with the right hand. The arrows in the engraving point in the direction of the Twist, which is not shown accom-

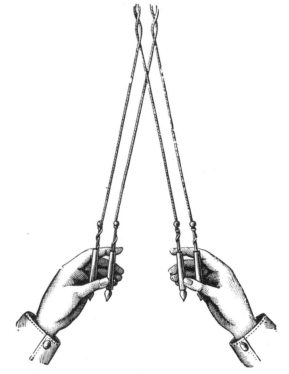

FIG. 721. SAXONY LACE—DOUBLE TWIST AND CROSSING.

plished, but with the Bobbins ready to make it; but the Twist made is shown in Fig. 721 in the first turn of the Double Twist. To form a *Double Twist*, the movement described in Simple Twist is repeated, and then the Bobbin marked 1 is moved over 2, and Bobbin marked 3 over Bobbin marked 4. Fig. 721 not only shows the Double Twist, but the manner of making a Crossing, the Bobbins being crossed after they are twisted.

Turn.—When the edge of the Lace is reached, or the thread turned in a contrary direction to that in which it started.

Wheels.—Form these by taking two Bobbins from the Lace wherever the upper lines of the Wheel are drawn. TWIST each couple together four times, then work the centre round of the Wheel in CLOTH STITCH; divide off the Bobbins into pairs again, Twist them four times, and work up into the lace where the lower lines of the Wheel end.

PATTERNS.—To work the Pattern shown in Fig. 722: Prick the pinholes where shown in the upper part, and hang fourteen Bobbins on to the Knitting needle. For the first row (indicated by two pinholes), commence on the left-hand side of the pattern. DOUBLE TWIST four of the eight left-hand Bobbins, and stick a pin in the right-hand hole; tie up two left-hand Bobbins, and take up, in addition to them, two right-hand Bobbins, SINGLE TWIST, CROSS, Single Twist, Cross, and stick a pin in the last hole of the second row (the one with three holes), tie up two left-

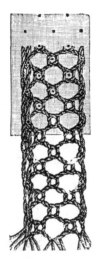

FIG. 722. SAXONY LACE.

hand Bobbins, take up the last two right-hand Bobbins in addition. Double Twist, Cross, Single Twist, Cross, tie up the two right-hand Bobbins, and take up, in addition, two left-hand Bobbins. Single Twist underneath the last pin, Cross, Single Twist, Cross. For the second row, commence on the left-hand side, take up ten Bobbins, Double Twist, Cross, stick a pin in the middle hole of the second row, Double Twist, Cross, tie up two left-hand Bobbins, take up

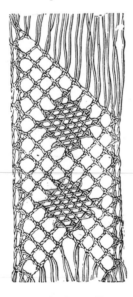

FIG. 723. SAXONY LACE.

two additional right-hand Bobbins, and repeat the work as before, stick a pin in the last hole of the third row. Work the double border with six outside Bobbins, and stick a pin in the last hole of the fourth row. For the third row, commence at the left-hand side row, take twelve Bobbins, work for three times as already described in the second row.

Stick a pin for the first pin in the first hole of the third row, and work the double border with six outside Bobbins. For the fourth row, commence at the left-hand side, take up all the Bobbins, work with the first four left-hand Bobbins the single border; repeat the work of the first row three times, and finish with the double border. Repeat for the rest.

The Pattern shown in Fig. 723 is simply made with Twists and Half Stitch. To work: Prick the design so that a pinhole is made in every open space. Work with Lace cotton No. 50, and hang on twenty-eight Bobbins. Commence at the left hand, make the double border with six Bobbins, and work the holes with DOUBLE TWISTS and CROSSINGS in the slant shown in the Pattern. For the second row, commence again at the left-hand side, and work the border and the holes until the diamond is reached, which work in the HALF STITCH or NET DEVICE. The threads arranged for working the diamond are shown at the bottom part of the engraving.

To work Fig. 724: Prick the Pattern with eight holes, hang on twenty Bobbins, and use lace thread No. 50. For the first row, form the left-hand border with six Bobbins, tie up four left-hand Bobbins, take the other two, and with two right-hand Bobbins TURN, CROSS, stick a pin, Turn, Cross again, tie up two left-hand Bobbins, take up two right-hand Bobbins, and repeat Turning, Crossing, and Pin-setting as before. Repeat alternately

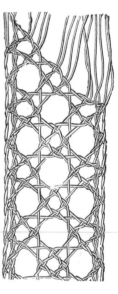

FIG. 724. SAXONY LACE.

until the first mesh of the first row is finished. For the second mesh, tie up two left-hand Bobbins, after having turned and crossed the last time in the first row, take up two right-hand Bobbins, Turn, Cross, stick a pin, as in the first row, tie up two right-hand Bobbins, take up two left-hand Bobbins, and repeat Turning, Crossing, and stick a pin, then tie up all these four Bobbins, and work with the four adjoining right-hand Bobbins, tie up two right-hand Bobbins, take up two left-hand Bobbins, and repeat. Turn and Cross to commence the third mesh, work this like the first, and finally work the right-hand border line. The second row contains the same meshes, only differently arranged, and is worked accordingly.

In the design given in Fig. 725, the pricked pattern of which is shown in Fig. 726, Detail A, the stitches used are Cloth Stitch, Half Stitch, or Net Device, the diamond-shaped hole, explained in Fig. 723, and the mesh shown in Fig. 724. Work with forty Bobbins, and with No. 40 thread. In the pricked pattern, the letter *a* shows where the Bobbins divide to work the slanting Cloth Stitch, the letters *d* and *c* give the side points of the diamond, and *b* the bottom point. Inside the large diamond at *b*, the square meshes shown in Fig. 725 are made; there are nine

Embroidery to signify a border of material, or work cut out after the pattern of a scallop shell's edge. It is more suitable for washing materials than a Vandyke border, the points of the latter being more easily frayed out. Sometimes a scallop edge is "pinked out," especially in silk, or in glazed calico; but in white stuffs it should be worked closely in BUTTONHOLE STITCH.

Scarves. — These are more or less long, straight, and comparatively narrow lengths of material designed for wear round the throat or the waist, or across one or both shoulders. They are generally made of a silk material, or else of lace; but also sometimes of woollen stuff, either woven or knitted. They may be had in every shade of

FIG. 725. SAXONY LACE.

FIG. 726. SAXONY LACE—DETAIL A.

of these, and they end at the letter *t*; and the points where the threads commence to make each separate one are indicated by the numerals 1, 2, 3, and 4. The small diamond upon each side of the large one is worked with Half Stitch, and is marked as to its points by the letters *l, m, n, o*. The border to the insertion is formed with six threads, like the borders already described. When an edging is made to Saxony Lace, form it with four threads, and plait together, carrying it along as a scalloped line; ornament this plait with the ordinary PICOTS or Loops that adorn the edges of other Pillow Laces.

Scallop Edge. — A term used in Dressmaking and

colour, in Tartan patterns, with brocaded, embroidered, or fringed ends. The Roman Silk Scarves, striped across the width, in combinations of various colours, are very handsome, and so are the embroidered Indian and Algerian.

Schleswig Pillow Lace.—Cutwork appears to have been made in Denmark from a very early period, and is still one of the occupations of Danish ladies. White Pillow Lace making was introduced into that country in the sixteenth century, when a manufactory was founded at Schleswig, and protected by heavy duties levied upon foreign laces. The early productions of Schleswig are a mixture of Flemish and Scandinavian designs, ornamented with the Stitches or Fillings that are usually found in Italian Laces, and are distinguished from Flemish Laces, to which they bear a great resemblance, by being worked in a very solid manner, and containing none of the lighter Plaitings or light parts of Brussels Lace. Much of it is still to be met with in English collections, having probably found its way there during the reign of Queen Anne, in the suite of her consort, Prince George of Denmark. The modern laces made in Denmark are copies from Lille and Saxony Laces, and are of a much lighter design than those of an earlier date; but the industry has not flourished since the commencement of the present century, except in the working of Tonder Lace, which is described under its own heading.

Scisseau.—The French word for Scissors.

Scissors.—Of this most essential appliance of a workbox there are great varieties in shape, size, and quality. They are classed respectively under the following description: The cast steel polished Shot Scissors, having shanks and bows of iron; Sheer Steel Scissors, comprising those in ordinary use, of which the blades only are hardened; and Lined Blades, which are made in large sizes, and almost entirely of iron, a strip of steel only being welded along the edge of the blades. Besides these, there are fancy varieties, the bow and shanks being leather-covered, or of gold or silver; Nail Scissors, having a file on each blade; Grape Scissors, with a groove on one blade, into which the other fits; Lamp Scissors, having a bend, bayonet-shaped, and other kinds, one of which, known as Buttonhole Scissors, is an important article in the workbox, and has a sharply-cut gap in the blades, for the purpose of accurately cutting a hole of certain invariable dimensions. Scissors are capable of much decoration by means of blueing, gilding, and studs of gold, as also by rich filigree work in the shanks, and embossed figures. The handles are sometimes made of mother-o'-pearl; but this plan is never satisfactory, as the cement loosens very quickly. The seat of the cutlery industry is at Sheffield. In Wilson's "*Rig Veda*" we find a passage which implies the use of Scissors, by the Ayrians, several centuries before Christ.

Sclavonic Embroidery. — Similar to Russian Embroidery.

Scotch Cambric.—A cotton textile, incorrectly called Cambric, fine in quality, rather starchy finished, and unglazed. Cotton Cambric is to be had of two kinds, that designed for dresses, either white or printed, and that to be used as French Cambric; the former is made in Lancashire, the latter at Glasgow. One variety is made of a mixture of cotton and flax, and is designed for handkerchiefs. Scotch cotton-made Cambric is employed for women's dresses. *See* Cambric.

Scotch Fingering.—A loose worsted yarn, much used for the knitting of stockings, cuffs, scarves, gaiters, and other articles. It is dyed in bright colours, and is sold by the spindle of six pounds.

Scrim.—This is a description of canvas, manufactured in several qualities. That especially for the use of paperhangers is made of Hemp and Jute. The Jute would dissolve if placed in water. The best quality is made entirely of Flax. Scrim is likewise used by gardeners for covering fruit trees. It measures from 36 to 40 inches in width. *See* Canvas.

Seal (*Phoca*).—Of this animal there are many varieties. They are natives of the western coasts of Scotland and Ireland, the shores of Labrador, Newfoundland, and Greenland. Some kinds supply leather (tanned and enamelled with black varnish) for women's shoes; others a beautiful fur, thick, soft, and glossy. The coarse hairs are removed, and the fur shaved, and dyed either a golden colour, or, more usually, a dark Vandyke brown, when it resembles a fine velvet. Medium-sized skins measure about 20 inches by 40 inches; when made into jackets, or used as trimmings, the fur should be turned in the cutting out, so as to lie upwards.

Sealskin Cloth.—The yarn used for this kind of cloth is the finest kind of Mohair, and the shade given in the dyeing is exactly similar to that of the real fur. It is manufactured in Yorkshire, and employed for women's outdoor jackets. This cloth must not be confounded with that called Silk Sealskin.

Seam.—A term used to denote the line of Over-sewing which connects the edges of two pieces of material together. The term is of Saxon derivation, and has always been retained in the English language.

Seaming.—A certain method adopted in Plain Sewing for uniting two pieces of material together, either by Over-sewing the selvedges, or by turning down two raw edges, the needle being passed through the folded edges very straight. When there is no selvedge, make a Fell on the wrong side; and, in the case of a gored skirt, either of a dress or under garment, hold the gored side with the raw edge next to the left-hand thumb, and take great care that, being cut on the bias, it does not become drawn or puckered.

In Over-sewing the seams of underclothing, place the two edges of material very evenly together, and keep them in position by means of pins inserted at regular distances. Hold the work very straight between the forefinger and thumb—not round the former, as in Hemming—and beware of slanting the needle, or the seam will become puckered. If one side of the material have a selvedge, and the other be cut on the cross (or diagonally), or have a raw edge, hold the latter nearest to you, under the thumb, as it will thus run less chance of being stretched.

Seaming Lace.—This term, with that of Spacing Lace, is continually mentioned in old Wardrobe Accounts of the sixteenth and seventeenth centuries, and does not intimate a particular kind of lace, but lace used for a certain purpose. It was the custom in those times to set apart the best and finest linen for such State occasions as births, deaths, or marriages, and the table linen and bed furniture so set apart were adorned with lace let in as an insertion wherever a seam in the linen appeared, and frequently where no seam was really needed. The lace chiefly used for this purpose was Cut Work, as, being made of linen, it accorded best with the rest of the article; but in England, Hollie Point was frequently substituted for Cut Work; and upon the Continent, the least costly of the various native productions. There is still preserved a sheet ornamented with Cut Work that was once in the possession of Shakespeare, and large quantities of linen adorned with Cut Work are constantly met with in Swedish or Danish families of consideration.

Seam Stitch.—*See* KNITTING.

Seamstress.—A term employed to denote a woman who seams or sews; a needlewoman whose department in her particular art is to perform Plain Sewing, as distinguished from dress or mantle making, and from decorative Embroidery.

Sea Otter Fur.—The Sea Otter (*Enhydra Marina*) is a species of the genus *Lutra*. It yields the most costly of all furs, the colour of which is a silver-grey, tipped with black; the fur is splendidly thick, soft, and shining, and exceedingly velvet-like to the touch. The Sea Otter is larger than the species frequenting rivers, and is found in the North Pacific, from Kamschatka to the Yellow Sea on the Asiatic coast, and from Alaska to California on the American coast. Only about a tenth part of the skins taken are exported to this country. The Russians, Japanese and Chinese, prize the fur greatly, and it is one of the most costly in the English market. *See* OTTER.

Seating.—A textile made of hair, of satin make, designed for upholstering purposes, such as the seats and backs of chairs, sofas, and cushions. *See* HAIR CLOTH.

Seed Embroidery.—A work practised in Germany, but not much known in England. It is formed by making flowers and buds with various seeds, and connecting these together with stems and stalks of Chenille, and working the leaves in Chenille. The seeds used for the work are those of the Indian corn, pumpkin, and cucumber, for large flowers, and canary and aster for the small. These seeds are pierced at each end with a carpet needle, and attached by these holes to the material. To work: Select a Crewel Work design of single flowers, such as daisies, sunflowers, or marigolds, and seeds that match the size of the petals, also Chenilles of various shades of green, and sewing and purse silk matching the flowers. Trace the design upon white or pale coloured blue satin, back it with holland, and frame it in an EMBROIDERY FRAME. Pierce the seeds at the top and bottom, and sew them to their places, either as flat petals, when lay them flat upon the satin, and secure with a stitch, made in sewing silk, at each of their ends; or as raised petals, when place them upright upon the satin, sew them together, and then down to the material. Having placed the seeds, work the centres of the flowers in FRENCH KNOTS with the purse silk, and the stems, stalks, and leaves in the green Chenille and in SATIN STITCH. The Embroidery is used for sachets, hand bags, and fire-screens. Necklaces and bracelets are made of melon or pumpkin seeds, by threading them upon fine silk, and forming them into balls, chains, tassels, and other devices.

Seerhand Muslin.—This is a description of cotton fabric somewhat resembling Nainsook and Mull, being a kind of intermediate quality as compared to them. It is particularly adapted for a dress material, as it preserves its clearness after being washed.

Self-Coloured.—A term employed in reference to textiles, to signify that the dye is of one colour only, and other-

wise indicated by the term uni-coloured. It is sometimes employed to signify, either that the stuff is of its natural colour, in the raw material, or that it has not been dyed since it left the loom.

Selvedge.—The firmly finished edge of any textile, so manufactured as to preclude the ravelling out of the weft. It is sometimes spelt Selvage. The excellence of the make of the cloth is shown by the even quality of the Selvedge. In flannels it is grey, pink, or violet-coloured, and varies in depth. Black silks likewise have coloured Selvedges. In "The Boke of Curtasye," of the fourteenth century, we find it mentioned:

> The over nape schall dowbulle be layde
> To the utter side the *selvage* brade.

Semé.—A French term denoting "sewn," and having reference to the small dot-like patterns (as distinguished from "Running" ones) embroidered on any textile; otherwise called Powderings.

Semes.—An ancient term applied to Embroidery that is worked as if it was thrown or cast upon the background in detached sprays and bunches, instead of being designed in a connected pattern. The word is derived from the French *semer*, "to sow, or sprinkle."

Serge.—A loosely woven, very durable, twilled material, of which there are several varieties, distinguished by some additional name; the warp is of worsted, and the woof of wool. It is dyed in every colour, besides being sold in white and black. Serges may be had in either silk or wool. Some of those made of the latter material are smooth on both sides of the cloth, others are only smooth on one side and woolly on the other, while varieties are manufactured rough and woolly on both sides. All these kinds of Serge are employed for women's dress, and the stoutest in quality for purposes of upholstery. Amongst the most serviceable, as well as the warmest kind, is that manufactured, under Government auspices, solely for the use of the Royal Navy; but this can only be obtained by favour, for private use, from the captain of some man-of-war, who may chance to have more in stock than is required for immediate use amongst his crew. It is dyed in a more permanent way than that sold in the shops, and is very much warmer and heavier. Ordinary Serge is made like Sateen, one side being woolly and the other smooth, the longest wool being used for the warp, which is more twisted than the woof. There are a great many varieties of cloth known as Serge—viz., French Flannel Serge, composed of long wool, and somewhat of the appearance of Indian Cashmere; the Serge de Berri, is a French-made, woollen stuff, produced in the province of which it bears the name; Serge Cloth is smooth on one side and rough on the other; Witney Serges are hairy throughout; Silk Serge is employed in the making of costly mantles; Serge Ribbon Sashes are soft, tie easily, do not crease, and may be washed; and Pompadour Flannel Serges, so designated on account of the small floral designs with which they are decorated; they are 29 inches in width. Serge varies in width in its several varieties of make and material. The coarse and heavy kinds, employed for upholstery, are of double width, whether of wool or silk; that of the ordinary woollen dress Serges runs from about 30 inches to a yard; Silk Serges are narrower. One variety of the last-named is used by tailors for the lining of coats. Though the twill is fine, it is of stout make, and can be had both in black and colours.

Serge de Berri.—This is a French woollen textile, employed as a dress material, and is produced in the province of which it bears the name. *See* SERGE.

Setting-in Gathers.—A phrase employed in reference to Plain Sewing, to perform which proceed as follows: Halve and quarter the band, and the material to be gathered, placing a small pin at each spot where these divisions are to be indicated, which is at the same time to secure the band and the full portion of material together. Hold the work so as to keep the left thumb on the junction of the Gathers and the band. As the latter is double, insert the raw edge of the former between the two sides of the band. Take up one ridge only of the gathering with the needle at a time, and proceed with great regularity, so as to form what will have the appearance of a neat Hemming Stitch. When the back of the band has to be secured to the gathers, endeavour to work as neatly as before, so as not to draw them awry, nor to show through any stitches taken at the back on the front or right side. Before commencing to sew in the Gathers, they must be stroked into their respective places in very even succession. *See* STROKING.

Setting-up Lace.—This is only required when Raised Pillow Lace flowers are made, and consists of sewing the raised petals to their right positions, and then stiffening them so as to stand upright. To work: Wash the hands in warm water, then shake the lace out upon a piece of tissue paper; take the finest possible needle, and, with lace thread, adjust the petals by sewing them down; make a small knot in the thread, fasten down lightly to the lace any back petals, running the thread from one petal to the other at the back of the lace; fasten inner petals by curving them inwards, or irregularly, according to design, and sew on to the lace any loose butterflies or other portions that have been made separately. To fasten off the thread, make a loop, and pass the needle through it, then draw it up, and cut the thread close. To finish or stiffen the flowers: Boil a quarter of an ounce of rice in a pint of water, and when cold strain it, and with a camel-hair brush paint over with it the inside of the parts in relief. When making a bold curve in the Raised Work, dip an ivory knitting needle into the rice water, and apply that to the lace; only damp the lace with the mixture, never make it wet.

Sew and Fell.—The process of Felling is effected by Running and Felling, and Sewing and Felling. To do the latter, fold one of the raw edges of the cloth on the wrong side, over the other raw edge; and thus form a Hem, after the manner of RUNNING and FELLING.

Sewing.—A comprehensive term, signifying stitchery of all plain kinds performed with a needle, by which means garments, or articles of upholstery, are made and mended. The word Working is frequently employed to signify Sewing, although one of general application to every kind of manual and intellectual labour. The word Stitching may be used, like Sewing, as a generic term, to denote any description of work with a needle. In Wilson's *Rig Veda*, II., p. 288, we find the words: "May she sew the work with a needle that is not capable of being cut or broken . . . of which the stitches will endure." *Sivan* is the term for the verb to sew, or sewing. Twenty-two centuries ago the Buddhists wore made, or sewn, dresses, in lieu of mere wrappings.

In Pillow Lace making, what are called Sewings are frequently required, either to join on fresh Bobbins to the pattern at certain places, or to secure one part of the lace to another. Sewings are called Plain Rope and Return Rope, and in Lace instructions, the word "Sew" is generally given as an abbreviation.

To make a *Plain Sewing*: Stick a pin into the pinhole above the one where the Sewing is to be made, to keep the work firm. Insert a crochet hook into the vacant pinhole, and under the twisted strand of the lace, draw one of the working threads through in a loop, pass the second working Bobbin through this loop, tail foremost, and pull the loop down. Take out the pin put in to secure the lace, and put it into the pinhole, and continue the work. Sewing with a Needle Pin: This is done where there are a long series of Sewings to be made, and when the securing pin of the lace upon the cushion is likely to interfere with their making. Stick a securing pin into the hole below the pinhole to be sewn to, so that there will be a vacant hole, lay one of the working threads across this space, and hold the Bobbin in the left hand. Insert the Needle Pin into the lowest strand, and insinuate the thread underneath it, which is done by holding the thread tightly down with the forefinger. Directly it is held, slacken the thread, bring the Needle Pin over, keep the thread under the point, then give a little sharp flick, and the thread will come through in a loop; draw this loop farther through, and hold it with the Needle Pin, and put the next Bobbin through it. Take out the securing pin, put it into the pinhole, and continue the lace.

Return Rope.—The same as Rope Sewing.

Rope Sewing.—To make: Lift all the Bobbins but one pair; pass this pair round the others. Sew to the next hole, pass the pair round again, sew to the next hole from the last Sewing, and continue until the spot is reached for the work to re-commence.

Sewing Cotton.—Cotton thread, which may be had on reels of 25 to 1000 yards in measure. The latter are much in requisition. The better class are known as "six cords," of which there is a large variety of makes, glazed and unglazed, the most saleable lengths running from 200 to 300 and 400 yards. Reel as well as Ball Sewing Cotton can be had in every variety of colour, and the ingrain marking cotton in red and blue.

Sewing Machines.—Appliances by which needlework may be executed more rapidly, and with greater regularity than by hand. The first invented and introduced into England was that by Elias Howe, a mechanic, of Massachusetts, in 1841. It was then employed for staymaking only; the needle imitated the action of the hand, and passed entirely through the material. The second kind of machine was of French invention, and made a Chain Stitch. Amongst those of the greatest repute, besides that invented by Howe, the following should be named—viz., Wheeler and Wilson's Silent Automatic Tension Machine, Wilcox and Gibbs' Automatic Machine, Grover and Baker's, Singer's, Thomas's, the Florence, and the Wanzer. There are several varieties of these Machines, including those producing Lock Stitch or Chain Stitch, and those respectively worked by hand or by treadle, and by one or both feet. The hand-worked Machine is naturally more portable than that which has a treadle. Amongst the latest improvements in Sewing Machines, that distinguished as the "Vertical Feed" should be named, which will sew elastic materials of many thicknesses, which needs no basting, and which will not pucker one side of the material sewn. Another is the White Sewing Machine, which does not need an ordinary needle, and has a self-setting description of needle, and self-threading shuttle of its own.

Sewing Silks.—Of silk thread employed for plain or Fancy Needlework there are three classes—viz., that for Plain Sewing, that for Knitting, and the third for Embroidery. Amongst those used for Plain Sewing there are the following: The China Silk, which is very fine, and of a pure white, and is much used by glove-makers; a coarser kind, of two or three-cord twist, employed in staymaking. The Light Dyes, or coloured Sewing Silks, may be had in all shades, and fine in quality, and are sold in skeins of from fifty to eighty in the ounce, and also on small reels; those sold in skeins are the cheapest. Machine Silks are sold by the gross, and by their weight on reels, the latter containing from 30 to 200 yards. These are to be had both in black and in colours. Floss Silk, or Soie Platte, is to be had in raven-black, China, and all colours; it is sold twisted into hanks, and used for darning silk stockings. Filoselle, otherwise called Spun Silk, or Bourre de Soie, is the portion of ravelled silk thrown aside in the filature of the cocoons, which is carded and spun like cotton. This is employed both for Plain Sewing, in the darning of stockings and silk vests, and likewise for Embroidery. Tailors' Twist, a coarse silk thread, of which a number together are wound on reels, each bearing two ounces, the numbers running from 1 to 8; also to be had in small reels containing a single thread of 12 yards. They are in many shades of colour. For Knitting there are many varieties, amongst which is the Ice Silk, which may be had of both two and four-fold strands, and is produced in very beautiful shades of several colours. Crochet Silk, or Soie Mi-serré, which is only half tightened in the twisting, as its name denotes. It is flexible, glossy, and peculiarly suited to Crochet work. Purse, or Netting Twist, which may be had of various sizes and qualities, and designed especially for purse-making, although likewise employed for the purposes of Embroidery. The principal kinds of Silk employed for Fancy Work and Embroidery are the white Dacca Silk, or Soie Ovale, and Mitorse Silk. The former is sold in large skeins, varying in degrees of fineness, and employed in flat Embroideries, and likewise in some kinds of Raised Work. It is also used in working on fine canvas, and can be had in a variety of colours. It will bear sub-division of the strands when too coarse for the work required, and is

sold done up into knotted skeins. The latter, Mitorse Silk, which is only half twisted, somewhat resembles Floss Silk, but is of a superior quality, and is more suitable for purposes of Embroidery. Also what is called Three Cord, is closely twisted silk, resembling Bullion, and likewise used for Embroidery. Sewing Silks are sold on cards, reels, and skeins, singly, or by the ounce; that for machine use on larger reels than the other kinds, and in longer lengths.

Shadow Stitch.—*See* HALF STITCH.

Shalloons.—A loosely woven worsted stuff, thin, short-napped, and twilled, used by tailors for coat linings, and also for dresses. It is woven from Lincolnshire and Yorkshire Long Staple Wool, of the finest qualities, twilled on both sides, and mostly dyed red. It is the staple manufacture of Halifax, whence upwards of 10,000 pieces are annually exported to Turkey and the Levant. It is made in various colours, and the width varies from 32 inches to 36 inches. This stuff was originally manufactured at Châlons, whence the name is derived. There is a very fine variety called "Cubica."

In blue *Shalloon* shall Hannibal be clad.—DEAN SWIFT.

Shantung Pongee Silk.—This is a soft, undyed, and undressed Chinese washing silk, and much resembles the Indian goods of the same character, but is somewhat duller in colour. The various qualities are uniformly of 19 inches in width, and differ respectively in price very considerably for the piece of 20 yards. Shantung is the name of the province in which the silk is manufactured. It is much employed in this country as a dress material.

Shap-faced.—A term employed to denote that the plush or velvet cloth is faced with the short ends of waste silk, the back of the material being of cotton.

Sharps.—A description of needles in common use among sempstresses for ordinary Plain Sewing. *See* NEEDLES.

Shawl Materials.—These are a mixture of silk and wool, the silk being thrown to the top; the patterns are copied from the Oriental damassé designs. These materials are employed for the partial making and trimming of dresses, and measure from 23 inches to 24 inches in width, the prices varying very considerably. Real shawls made of goat's hair, thick and warm in make and quality, are also sold for cutting up into dresses and mantles.

Sheep's Wool.—The peculiar substance called wool is, in a great degree, the product of cultivation. It is produced, not only on sheep, but on the Llama, and the Thibet and Angora goat. The coat produced on all other animals can only be described either as fur or hair. All the varieties of the sheep owe their origin to the Argali, which has a coat of wool next to the skin, supplemented by a longer growth of hair. In the States of Barbary, the South of Italy, Sicily, and Portugal, the wool of a once remarkably fine wool-bearing breed of sheep has greatly deteriorated through neglect. In Spain it was produced in high perfection when the product was carefully cultivated. Sheep's wool takes a year in completing its full growth, after which the animal changes its coat, which, if not sheared, will fall off *en masse*, leaving a short crop of the new soft wool in its place. That which is shorn from the living animal is called "Fleece," and that which is pulled off by the fellmonger after death is called "Pelt," which is very inferior to the former, and will not take a good dye, being harsher and weaker, and is generally too short to be worked without an admixture of longer wools. It is also known as "Skin Wool," and is commonly used for flannels, serges, and such kinds of stuff as need little, if any, milling. The manufacturers classify sheep's wool into two kinds—the long, or "combing" wool, and the short, or "clothing" wool. The former varies in length from 3 to 8 or 10 inches; the latter from 3 to 4 inches. Of this clothing wool all cloth is made, its shortness rendering it fit for carding (effected with a comb of fine short teeth) and spinning into yarn, and for the subsequent felting. The long, or "combing" wool, is prepared on a comb with long steel teeth; it is combed out straight, opening the fibres like flax, either by hand or machinery. This is made into crape, poplin, bombazines, carpets, and the finer sorts of worsted goods. These two classes of wool are likewise described as the long, or short "stapled" wool, and by this term the separate locks into which the wool is naturally divided are designated, each of which comprises a certain number of fibres or curly hairs. The longer kinds of the fleece (or superior) wool are employed for hosiery yarns, or for hand-yarn for the warps of serges, and other cloths, which have a warp of "combed" and a woof of "carded" wool. In the fleece of a single English sheep there are some eight or ten varieties in degrees of fineness, known respectively by different names, and applicable for the manufacture of various textiles. Thus the wool is sorted with much care. Its softness is of equal importance to its fineness, and in this silky characteristic that of the English sheep is inferior to the Indian, or to the Peruvian and Chilian Llama. No Merino sheep, however fine, yields so soft a wool as the Indian, of which Cashmeres are made. Not only the breed of the sheep, but the district in which they are reared, influences the quality. The counties of Leicestershire and Lincolnshire, and the districts of Teeswater and Dartmoor, produce a greater length of "combing" wool than elsewhere, the staple being sometimes a foot in length. Dorsetshire, Herefordshire, and the South Downs produce our short-stapled variety, and those grown on the Cheviot Hills give a wool of considerable softness, though not otherwise of the first quality.

Sheep's wool in its natural state is of a white, grey, or brownish-black colour. Of the latter coarse cloths are made, undyed. The white is selected for dyeing in bright colours. The soft wool of lambs is extensively employed in the manufacture of hats, on account of its felting quality. That of dead lambs, having less of the felting properties, is used for hosiery and soft flannels, and is called "skin-lambswool." The lambs of certain breeds of sheep, natives of the North of Europe, have such fine skins that they are dressed as furs, are very costly, and held in much esteem as articles of wear, or for trimmings of outdoor apparel, by wealthy Russians and others.

Our Australian wools are very fine, the Spanish Merino sheep having been imported there. The staple is long and the quality soft, and it is excellent for combing and spinning. The Shetland Islands also produce a breed of sheep bearing remarkably fine and delicate wool. (See SHETLAND WOOL.) Saxon wool, much employed in this country, is of a very superior quality, and is produced by the Spanish Merino breed, introduced by the late King of Saxony. This Spanish variety of wool is considered the finest in Europe, and is of remote Eastern origin, introduced into Italy, and thence, by the Romans, into Spain. Comparatively little of this wool is now employed in England, the Australian and Saxon sufficiently supplementing our own breeds. *See* WOOLLEN CLOTHS.

Sheetings.—Stout cloths made of different widths for bed linen—both plain and twilled, bleached and unbleached—and constituting one of those manufactures classified under the name "Piece Goods." They are made in Wigans, Croydons, and double warps, from 2 to 3 yards wide. Those of linen are named Scotch and Barnsley bleached, loom Dowlas, and loom Scotch, the widths of which are known distinctively by the number of inches they measure. Also the Irish, union Irish, which is mixed with cotton; Lancashire linen, union Lancashire, Russia, and imitation Russia. The respective widths of these run from $\frac{7}{8}$ths to $\frac{1}{4}$ths. The strongest coarse Sheeting is the Russia, which may be had of various widths, from an ell to 2½ yards. Bolton Sheeting, otherwise called Workhouse Sheeting, is of calico, and is sold in pairs of sheets. They should each measure from 2½ yards to 3 yards for ordinary beds. The width for a single bed is about 66 inches, that for a double one from 78 inches to 3 yards.

Shell Couching.—*See* COUCHING.

Shetland Point Lace.—A work known in Italy as Trina de Lana, where it is used much more than in England. It is a Needle-made Lace, composed of Shetland wool instead of fine Lace cotton, and therefore of sufficiently coarse texture to form babies' shawls, quilts, or scarves, and other objects that require to be both light and warm yet ornamental. The Lace is made either with white or black Shetland wool, from designs selected from old Flat Needle-made Points, which are enlarged, and then worked out by being formed of some of the simplest of the many Point Lace stitches. The cordonnet of the Buttonholed outline of flat Points is replaced by a line of Chain Stitch, which serves as a stay to the stitches that fill in the design. To work as shown in Fig. 727: Enlarge the design to twice its size, then trace out outlines of the parts that are to be filled in upon blue wrapping paper, from which remove any stiffness by crumpling it up and smoothing it out flat. Take the Shetland wool, thread a darning needle with it, and surround the pattern with a line of CHAIN STITCH. Let this Chain Stitch be quite distinct from the blue paper, and perfectly connected stitch to stitch. Then connect these lines of stitches together for the ground of the Lace by filling in the open spaces between the design with CORDED BARS, which occasionally vary with WHEELS. Fill in the design with lines of plain BUTTONHOLES, or with POINT DE BRUXELLES, LATTICE, or POINT DE GRECQUE. Form the FOOTING of the Lace with a line of Chain Stitch, the outer edge with the same Chain Stitch line, and enrich with POINT DE VENISE edging and Wheels, ornamented with PICOTS. Shetland

Point Lace looks particularly well when worked over a baby's shawl and edged with the pattern shown in Fig. 727; the design for the centre of the shawl should be detached sprigs, joined by Corded Bars.

Shetland Wool.—As sold in the shops, this is a yarn much employed for the knitting of shawls, and the weaving of stockings of the finest quality. The yarn is exceedingly soft, and has only two threads. It is to be had in oleander (a new pink), white, black, slate, brown, azurine, scarlet, violet, buff, coral, purple, partridge, gas blues and greens, and ingrain, and is sold by the pound or ounce. Wool of this kind is not produced in England proper. It is thicker than Pyrenean wool, and softer than both it and the Andalusian, not being so tightly twisted. It is employed for the knitting of shawls, hoods, jackets, and shoes for infants. The sheep producing it are of small size, and run

piece of narrow cardboard, and put it into a little bag, which pin down to the Pillow out of the way of the Bobbins. To avoid constant shifting when working very narrow lace, prick two pieces of PASSEMENT at the same time with the same design, and fasten them on to the Pillow so that no break intervenes, or prick as long a pattern as the Pillow will allow, taking care that the ends will correspond, and allow of the design being continued.

Ship Ladder Stitch.—See *Ladder Stitch,* EMBROIDERY STITCHES.

Shirred.—A word employed by Americans, derived by them from the old German *Schirren,* and employed to signify an irregular GAUGING. Shirrings are close Runnings, or cords, inserted between two pieces of cloth, as the lines of indiarubber in Shirred Braces or Garters, or the drawing and puckering up any material. See French

FIG. 727. SHETLAND POINT LACE.

wild all the year over the hills until—the ground being covered with snow—they descend to the seashore and feed on weed. The staple of these sheep is longer than that of the Merino, and their skins are much employed as Furs. The breed goes by the name of Beaver Sheep, and the wool produced is of various colours—viz., black, brown, grey, and white.

Shifting Pillow Lace. — The pattern upon which Pillow Lace is worked rarely exceeds a few inches in length; therefore, when working a lace edging or insertion, the lace, while in progress, has constantly to be taken off the pillow and re-adjusted on to the pattern. To shift: Work the lace to the edge of the pattern, take up all the pins, but leave those in the last part of the work still sticking into the lace, and then stick these into the top part of the pattern, so that the working can be continued at the proper place. Roll up the finished lace on to a

term *Coulissé*; also Reeve, borrowed from the nautical term to "Reef" a sail, to gather up in small folds.

Shirt.—A man's linen or calico under-garment, the name having reference to its being of a "short" length. It was worn in Saxon times by both sexes, of the same form, and by the same name. Under the Normans, the nobility wore them embroidered. In the fourteenth century, Silk Shirts were worn by some, and also those of fine Holland and Cambric. Shirts decorated with either embroidery or gold, silver, or silk, were prohibited by a Sumptuary Law, in the reign of Henry VIII., to all persons under the rank of knighthood. Mr. David Anderson, damask manufacturer, of Deanside Brae, made a shirt entirely in the loom, without any kind of needlework, and sent it to Dr. Cupar, as a specimen for the Hunterian Museum, Glasgow. The neck, wristbands, and shoulder-straps were of double cloth, and neatly stitched; the buttonholes properly worked with the appropriate stitch, the buttons sewn on, the gussets inserted, and a ruffle added. On the breast the Glasgow arms were woven, and the motto, "Let Glasgow flourish," beneath which were the words: "Woven and presented by David Anderson." See *Shirt*, under CUTTING OUT.

Shirtings.—These are otherwise called Fancy Cotton Shirtings, and consist of cotton cloths manufactured after the same manner as Ginghams, only that they bear somewhat of a resemblance to flannel in the looseness and fluffiness of the threads. Shirtings are classified in the trade as one of those manufactures denominated "Piece Goods," and are made in pieces of 36 yards in length, and from 36 inches to 45 inches in width. Pretty and serviceable dresses are sometimes made of the same description of cotton cloth, which has been sized and glazed. They may be had in stripes and fancy designs in various colours,

mantles of Queen Elizabeth is described by Paul Heutzner (1602) as being of "bluish silk, Shot with silver threads." In the present day, there are not only Shot Silk Stuffs but Shot Alpacas, and mixtures of two different materials employed for women's gowns. Shakespeare alludes to this description of weaving in a Silk Stuff:

> The tailor make thy doublet of changeable Taffeta, for thy mind is a very opal.—*Twelfth Night.*

Shuttle.—An appliance made of wood, used in the process of weaving for shooting the thread of the woof, which is wound upon it, between the threads of the warp. Also *see* TATTING.

Sicilian Embroidery.—An effective and easy work, formed with muslin, thin cambric, and braid, and used for trimmings to washing dresses, or for teacloths and ornamental linen. The work is sometimes called Spanish

FIG. 728. SICILIAN EMBROIDERY.

chiefly in pink, blue, and violet. Women's cuffs and collars are made largely in these Shirting Cloths. There are also ZEPHYR SHIRTINGS.

Shoddy.—Cloth made either of the flue and fluff thrown off from other woollen stuffs in the process of weaving, mixed with long hair from new wool; or else of old garments torn into fibres, or cut up into small pieces, and re-spun. It differs from what is known as "Mungo" in being of an inferior quality, and producing a coarse kind of cloth.

Shot Stuffs.—Textiles of various materials, made to change in colour according to the different positions in which they are viewed, and therefore of the lights and shades upon them. This is effected by a particular method adopted in the weaving, and the intermixture of a weft and warp respectively of different colours. In the sixteenth century they were called "Chaungeantries," and were mixtures of silk, "sailtrie," or linen yarn. One of the

Embroidery, and is intended to imitate Embroidery upon muslin; but as no stitches, with the exception of Buttonhole, are worked, it is much more quickly formed than true Embroidery. It consists in tracing out a modern Point Lace design, and Tacking muslin, and then thin cambric, over the design, the outlines of which are marked out with a thick braid, known as Spanish Braid. Both the materials are retained in those parts of the work that are intended as the pattern parts, but the cambric is cut away beyond the braid from the ground, and only the muslin left, while the raw edges of the cambric are concealed by the braid being sewn down to the muslin foundation. Wheels, Eyeletholes, and Ladder Stitch are worked when open spaces lighten the design, and then both materials are cut from underneath these stitches, and the raw edges Buttonholed round, while the edge of the pattern is formed with scalloped or

RUN LACE.

IMITATION BRUSSELS.

straight lines of Buttonhole. To work as shown in Fig. 728: This pattern is reduced in size, and can be made larger if required. Two widths of braid are used in it, either white or écru coloured, and muslin and cambric matching the braids in tint. Trace out the design upon stiff paper, and fill in the parts that form the pattern with black ink, so that they may be visible through the materials that cover them, or TACK down the muslin and cambric upon brown paper, and trace the design upon the cambric when it is secured. Take the narrower braid, and sew it along the top of the pattern, so as to form the FOOTING. Stitch it down securely upon both sides, then Tack the wider braid on to the design with a tacking thread, and when in position, OVERCAST it to the material upon the side where both cambric and muslin are to be retained. Cut the round holes for the WHEELS and make them, drawing the Braid round the circle thus formed, and cut away both materials and make the LADDER STITCH where indicated; BUTTONHOLE the edge of the materials over in those places. Cut away the cambric underneath the other edge of the broad braid, and Overcast the braid to the muslin. The edge of the pattern is made with both materials; Buttonhole in small scallops round the extreme edge, and ornament this place with PICOTS; then form the wide scallops with a line of Buttonhole, turn its outer edge to the interior of the design, and cut the cambric away beyond these scallops leaving only the muslin.

Sicilienne.—A description of fine Poplin, made of silk and wool, and especially employed for the making of mantles. It varies in width, and may be had from 24 inches to 56 inches in width.

Sienna Point.—One of the names by which DARNED NETTING is known in Italy.

Silesia.—A fine brown Holland, originally made in the German province of Silesia, and now produced in England. It is glazed for roller window blinds, and may be had in various widths, from 28 inches to 90 inches.

Silk.—The fine, glossy, soft thread spun by the *Bombyx mori*, or silkworms, so as to form a pale yellow or amber-coloured receptacle, called a cocoon, within which the caterpillar, in a chrysalis form, lies during its transformation into a butterfly. It is the strongest and most durable, as well as the most beautiful of all fibres for the manufacture of textiles. Our chief supplies are derived from China, India, Italy, and the Levant. An attempt has likewise been made to produce silk in Australia, and so far as it has been procured, it is of a rich and superior kind; the breed of silkworms recently discovered in Switzerland has been imported to that Colony, as it is free from the disease so long contributing to deteriorate the cocoons. The use of raw silk for spinning and weaving dates back —so far as records of the Chinese Empire exist to demonstrate—to some 2700 years before Christ, when the Empress See-ling-Shee herself unravelled the fibres of the cocoons. and was the first to weave it into a web. The derivation of silk from the cocoons of the silkworm, and the manner in which the material was produced, remained a secret with the Chinese until the time of Justinian, A.D. 555, and it

was at this time that the two Persian monks—who were Christian missionaries—became acquainted with the use of the silkworms, learned the art of working the fibres into textiles, and, at the desire of the Emperor, contrived to secrete some of the eggs of the caterpillars in a hollow cane, and brought them to Constantinople in safety. It is to these two missionaries that we owe all the various breeds of the insect, which, in course of time, became naturalised in various parts of Europe. Alexander the Great was the first to introduce both the silk and a knowledge of its use, in the West. For 200 years after the age of Pliny, the employment of silk stuffs as dress materials was confined to women.

Silk Boot Laces.—These laces are to be had in both flat and round form. The former are produced in lengths, respectively of 6-4 and 8-4, and are sold in boxes containing one gross each. The latter, otherwise called "Aiguilette," are round, are not twisted, but woven, and have tags. They are also sold in boxes of one gross each; the lengths being the same as those of the flat laces.

Silk Braid.—This Braid is also called Russia Silk Braid. Silk Braid is employed for purposes of Embroidery, and is used for men's smoking caps, slippers, &c. It can be had in very bright colours, and consists of two cords woven together; it is sold in skeins, six to the gross. Each skein should measure 24 yards in length, but they are rarely found to contain more than 16 or 18 yards.

Silk Canvas or Berlin.—This description of canvas is of a very even and delicate make, and is especially designed to obviate the necessity of grounding designs in Embroidery. The silks usually employed for this Canvas are Chenille and Floss. It is to be had in most colour the white, black, claret, and primrose, being the most in vogue. Different qualities are sold. It is made in widths varying from half an inch to 1½ yards. The threads are formed of fine silk wound round a cotton fibre. *See* CANVAS.

Silk Cotton.—Silken fibres which envelope the seeds of a tree of the genus *Bombax*. It is a native of Asia, Africa, and America. The fibres are smooth and elastic, but too short to be eligible for spinning, and is especially employed for the stuffing of cushions. It is imported into this country, from the East Indies, under the name of "Mockmain." The Silk Cotton is enclosed within the capsules containing the seed, which is embedded in it.

Silk Damask.—A silk woven stuff manufactured after the peculiar method originated at Damascus, whence the name. The Flemings introduced the art of producing designs of every description in the process of weaving the cloth, into this country in the sixteenth century. At that time it was very costly, and dresses made of it were only worn upon State occasions, by women of high position. Silk Damask is now superseded as a dress material by what is called Broché Silk, having a design thrown upon the face in satin. As a material for purposes of upholstery, hangings, curtains, furniture coverings, &c., Silk Damask is as much employed as ever. It is very thick and rich in appearance, and is the costliest of all stuffs used for these purposes. It can be had in every

M M M

description of colour and shade of the same. The chief seat of the industry is at Lyons, where it is produced by means of the "Jacquard Loom."

Silk Dress Laces.—These consist of a narrow silk braid, dyed in various colours, and chiefly employed for evening dresses. They are made in lengths of 5-4 and 6-4, and may be purchased singly or by the gross.

Silk Imperial Braid.—A very narrow woven fancy Braid, having a kind of Pearl edge. It is made in all varieties of colour, and also of mixed colours, such as green and gold. It is sold by the skein, and is employed for purposes of Embroidery.

Silk Mantle Cords.—These Cords may be had in various colours and sizes, are heavy made in quality, and very much in use. The numbers are 1, 1½, 2, 2½, 3, and 4; the numbers 1, 2, and 3, are those chiefly in request. There are four pieces to the gross of 36 yards each, and they may be had in black and in colours.

Silk Sealskin.—This is a very beautiful patent textile, composed of Tussar Silk, and made in imitation of Sealskin Fur; and is designed for mantles, jackets, hats, waistcoats, and trimmings, and sold at one-fourth the price of the real fur. It measures 52 inches in width, and is a costly material dyed brown or golden colour. In making it up the nap should be turned so as to lie upwards to produce the lights and shades upon it, after the manner in which the real skin of the seal is always worn.

Silk Serge.—A stout twilled silk textile of fine make, and employed for the lining of men's coats. It is to be had in various colours as well as in black. The ordinary width of this material measures 24 inches.

Silk Spray Embroidery.—A variety of Embroidery with Satin Stitch, and one that is used to ornament dress trimmings with, as it is capable of being transferred from one background to another. The work consists in embroidering upon fine lawn or holland a spray of flowers in silk or filoselle in their natural tints, cutting away the holland round the spray and arranging that upon net, silk, or velvet as it is required. To work: Trace upon holland or lawn, sprays of flowers from designs intended for Embroidery with SATIN STITCH, and frame in an EMBROIDERY FRAME. Work the leaves of the design in Satin Stitch from the centre vein of the leaf to the edge, and use a light and dark green on the two sides; work the centre vein of the leaf in a darker shade of green to that used in the other part, and surround the leaf with an outline worked in BUTTONHOLE STITCH, so as to raise it slightly above the Satin Stitch centre. Work the Buttonholes as short stitches and not too close together, make all the leaves thus, only varying the shades of green used in them. For the flowers, slightly pad them with wool, and then work them in long Satin Stitches from their centre to their edge with Floss silk in shades of colour matching the natural hue of the flowers. Surround the flowers like the leaves with a Buttonhole Edge, and fill in their centres with FRENCH KNOTS. Work the stalks that connect the flowers and leaves together with double rows of CHAIN STITCH. Before removing the work from the Frame, make some strong starch, and spread it

over the back, and when that is dry, cut out the sprays from the holland, carefully cutting round the Buttonhole Edgings of leaves and flowers. TACK, with fine stitches, these sprays on to the material they are intended to ornament. The sprays are also worked with crewels instead of silks, or with crewels mixed with filoselles, and when this is done the Embroidery is formed of large bold flowers, such as sunflowers, pæonies, and carnations, and is used for curtain and table borders, or to scatter over a quilt.

Silk Stuffs.—Silk yarn is woven into a great variety of textiles in England and elsewhere, which may be referred to under their respective headings; as well as in thread more or less twisted, for the purpose of sewing and of embroidery. Prior to the sixth century, all silk stuffs were brought to Europe from Bokhara, by the former inhabitants of those parts—the "Seres"—from which its Latin name *serica* was derived. The variety of textiles made of the fibres of the silkworms' cocoons is very extensive, and varies with the several countries in which they are produced, whether India, China, Japan, Turkey, Great Britain, France, or Italy, in each of which nationalities the varieties are also many and beautiful. Some are dyed in ingrain colours, so that they may be washed with impunity. Some are watered, others brocaded, woven with a pile, forming either velvet or plush, or produced with a combination of velvet and plain silk, or velvet and Satin. There are Watered Silks, Moirés, Satins, Satinettes, Satin Turks, Taffetas, Gauzes, Persians, Stockingette Silks, Poplins, which are combined with wool; and corded Silk Cloths, unmixed with any other substance—as the Paris Cords. Besides these there are ribbons of every variety and quality, and Silk Canvas for purposes of Embroidery. In the Middle Ages the manufacture of Silk Stuffs made great progress in Europe. The trade spread from Italy to France and Spain, where it was introduced at an early period by the Moors; and we read that some silk textiles were purchased for our Henry II. The manufacture of these stuffs in England dates from the time of the immigration of the French refugees, at the revocation of the Edict of Nantes, when a manufactory was established at Spitalfields; and the introduction of the throwing machine, by Sir Thomas Lombe, completely established the industry in this country. The first silk manufactory at Derby was opened by him in the year 1717; but silk stockings were first produced in England in the time of Queen Elizabeth, for whose use they were specially made.

In the selection of a black silk, it should be tested by holding it up to the light and looking through it, so that the evenness of the rib may be seen. It should then be crushed together in the hand, and suddenly released, when it should spring out as quickly, leaving no crease. This spring is called the *verve*, of which poor silk stuffs have little or none, and those adulterated with jute are also deficient in this characteristic. Pure silk does not stiffen when wetted, and the black dye should have a slight tinge of green when the light is seen through it. Stiff silks do not wear well, as they cannot be pure; the softer the texture, the purer the silk. Another mode of testing the quality is to ravel out the weft.

Silk Tassels.—These may be had in several varieties, both of quality, make, colour, and size. Some are of Chenille, others of twisted silk, the upper portion, where the several strands are confined together, being made on a foundation of wood turned for the purpose, round which the silk is wound. There are also loosely-made Tassels attached to a heading of knotted silk, or band of gimp, and Silk Tassels made for purses, some of purse, others of plain sewing silks. *See* TASSELS.

Silk Warp.—A mixed material of silk and wool combined. It is exceedingly fine and delicate in texture, has a grey ground, rayed with scarlet or black stripes, of either two or three threads in width, and is manufactured in widths of 32 inches. Silk Warp is made for shirting of a superior description, for use in hot climates.

Silk-woven Elastic Cloth. — *See* STOCKINGETTE CLOTH and ELASTIC CLOTH.

Silver Lace.—*See* GOLD LACE.

Single Crochet.—*See* CROCHET, page 125.

Single Diamonds.—*See* MACRAMÉ.

Skein.—A term signifying a length of any kind of yarn, whether of silk, wool, linen, thread, or cotton, wound off a hank, doubled and knotted. Skeins weigh either an ounce, or half an ounce, with the exception of sewing silk and Berlin lambswool, which are lighter. Braid may also be purchased made up in skeins.

Skirt Braids.—These are made of Alpaca and Mohair, and are cut into lengths of sufficient quantity for a dress, and tied up for sale in knots. The numbers so cut are 29, 41, and 53, in the " super " and "extra " heavy sorts. The lengths vary from 4 to 5 yards, but gross pieces may also be procured.

Skirting.—Strong thick woollen, worsted, cotton, or mixed fabrics, woven of certain dimensions, so as to be suitable in length and width for women's underskirts, and to preclude the necessity of making gores and seams. Amongst the several varieties there are the Felt Skirtings in dark grey and heather, at 72 inches in width; Prairie Skirtings is a comparatively new material, as is Striped Skirtings, made of silk and wool combined, with cross-over stripes, and in wide widths. Besides these, other varieties might be enumerated, the number of which is always augmenting with each successive season.

Skirt Linings.—These are of various materials, selected to suit the dress for which they are designed. Instead of following the usual plan adopted in reference to the lining of a bodice, cut out the skirt first and TACK it upon the lining. For black velveteen silecia, striped or checked, is the best suited; for a pale-coloured silk the silecia should be of plain white; for dark stuffs and quilted petticoats figured Silecias are preferable. In this case make a facing of alpaca to cover the lining at the lower part of the skirt of half a foot or rather more in depth. Owing to a spring, as well as the stiffness in alpaca, it is to be recommended for use in the same way round the extreme edge of long dresses and trains, 10 inches in depth, more especially, because the dress is less likely to roll the wrong side upwards when the wearer turns round; besides that, a light-coloured lining becomes so quickly soiled when sweeping the ground. The lining of a heavy poplin or woollen dress should be restricted to a mere facing of about 10 or 12 inches in depth. When there are trimmings or flounces extend the lining upwards as high as the top of the trimming, but so that all the stitches shall be concealed underneath them. If the skirt be gored, cut the lining to fit the gores exactly, as otherwise the skirt will set stiffly over the triangular plaits that will have to be made. As a rule, alpaca and silecia are the principal materials in use for Skirt Linings, and more especially the former. When the breadths of a dress have been cut out, pin the raw sides of each flatly together at the bottom, and fold the skirt in half on a table, so as to expose half of the front, and half of the back breadth, the hem being towards you. Then lay the lining muslin with one selvedge up the folded edge of the skirt front, the torn part of the muslin being at the hem; and slope off the right-hand corner of the muslin even with the dress. Measure the depth of the facing, placing pins at the upper part to mark it; and cut off by them. Next lay the piece so cut on the top of the remainder of the muslin, in exactly the same position, and it will be found that the hollowed-out upper part of the first gives very nearly the proper curve for the lower part of the second. The two pieces, when joined by the selvedges in front, will extend nearly half round the skirt. The rest is taken piece by piece in the same way; the selvedges are always joined together, although they lie very slantingly after the first, where the skirt front was straight. When the middle of the back width is reached, allow about 1 inch for joinings, and cut off what is not wanted in a line with the folded skirt, so that the centre join there will set upright, like the front. But, owing to the increase of slope as the muslin nears the back, the join will neither be exactly on the straight, nor on the cross of the muslin. If alpaca be used, the joins must be opened and pressed flat before the lining is sewn into the skirt. The material employed for mourning called Paramatta should have a lining of black mull muslin.

Skunk Fur (*Mephitis Americana*).—This animal is a native of British America, and the fur, which is imported by the Hudson Bay Company, is of a dark brown colour, rather long in the hair, and rough; and two yellowish white stripes run from the head to the tail. The animal is allied to the polecat, and the odour is strong and disagreeable, forming an almost insuperable objection to a very warm and handsome fur. Those who wear it should expose it as much as possible to the outer air.

Slanting Gobelin.—*See* BERLIN WORK.

Slanting Hole Braid.—*See* BRAIDS.

Slanting Stitch.—*See* CROCHET, page 125.

Slashes or Panes.—A term used by tailors and dressmakers, to signify a vertical cutting in any article of dress. intended to expose to view some other garment worn beneath it, of a contrasting colour. Sometimes the latter is only an artificially-produced effect, pieces of stuff of a different material being sewn under the Slashings.

Sir Walter Scott speaks of "a gray jerkin, with scarlet cuffs and slashed sleeves." These Slashes are otherwise called "Panes"; Coryat, author of *Crudities*, writing in the year 1611, observes: "The Switzers wear no coates, but Doublets, and hose of Panes, intermingled with red and yellow, and some with blew, trimmed with long puffes to yellow and blew Sarcenet rising up between the Panes."

Sleeves.—The portion of any garment which covers the arms, in whole or in part. In Sleeves, as in shoes, boots, and head-dresses, the most ridiculous freaks of Fashion have been exhibited. We read that William the Conqueror brought over extravagant styles in dress, as exemplified more especially in the Sleeves of the dresses, which increased to absurdity in the reign of William Rufus. They were then widened at the wrists, and hung down beyond the hands, as far as to the knees, like those of the Chinese. These were succeeded, under the Plantagenets, by some of more natural proportions; but "Bag Sleeves," large and ungainly, were introduced under Henry VI., and Slashed and Laced ones followed these. In the reign of Henry VII. they were separate articles of dress, worn as ornaments by the knights and others, and could be put on, and taken off at pleasure. They were of enormous dimensions, opening almost up to the shoulder on the inside, and cut and embroidered, in deep tongue-like scallops, of nearly a foot in length. The fact that Sleeves were often separate from the rest of the dress explains the facility afforded for, the giving and receiving of a Sleeve, as a love token between a Knight and his Mistress, which was worn thenceforth in his helmet. Puffed and Tied Sleeves, called the "Virago Sleeve," and those tight in the arm, and increasing in width to the shoulder, there rising high above it, were in vogue in *temp.* Queen Elizabeth, and afterwards of James I. and of Charles II. Under Cromwell large turned-up square cuffs, to close straightly cut sleeves, were universal. Within our own times the varieties worn have been considerable, including those filled out at the top of the arm with wadded circular cushions; and the *Jigôt*. They are nowadays sometimes so short as to extend only 2 inches or 3 inches in depth, from the junction with them of the bodice armhole; others are long and confined to the wrist with a band. There are some that are opened as far as from the inner bend of the elbow, and depend widely from the joint on the outside. Some are cut closely to fit the arm, others are puffed at the shoulder and elbows, or at the shoulder only. They are plain-cut, or gauged, and trimmed according to the current fashion of the time. But whatever that fashion may be, more length must be allowed in the sleeve at the shoulder—above the arm—by 2 inches than underneath the arm; the upper or outer part of the sleeve must be cut in a convex circular form, and the inside concave, and an inch allowed everywhere for turning-in the raw edges. When the sleeve is to be sewn into the armhole high up on the shoulder, make the rounding at the top large. Many of those now in fashion are cut on the bias, and to make them thus, fold the material over to the necessary dimensions indicated by the pattern, and lay the latter with the straight part of the outside seam on the straight fold, and so cut out the sleeve. Then join the sides on the inside of the arm, and extend the outer seam from the elbow to the wrist only. Should the Sleeves be tightly fitting, make three very small plaits at the point of the elbow, on the outer side, before regulating the cutting and adjustment of the wrist. Cut the inner (or under) part of the sleeve a little narrower from the top to just below the elbow. Stitch the sleeves all the way down the outer and inner seams. A method much adopted by dressmakers is, to place the right sides of the material together, and the right sides of the lining together also, then to stitch them all at once, and turn them right side out, which is the means of concealing the stitches and raw edges. When the sleeve is to be sewn into the armhole, place the point at the extreme length of the sleeve, about 1½ inches below the shoulder seam of the bodice.

Slip Stitch.—*See* CROCHET (page 125), GUIPURE D'ART, and KNITTING.

Slot.—An inelegant term, employed in the eastern counties of England to denote a casing formed either by a double Running, or by a Hem, for the reception of a ribbon or tape, to be used as a Running-string, for drawing the article into small gathers; or to close the opening of a bag.

Small Dots.—In Needlemade Laces small dots are often made over a net-patterned ground to enrich it, or to edge parts of the design. The Dots made in Alençon Grounds are distinguished by being formed of Buttonhole centres and surrounded by a tiny raised cord edged with horsehair, but form ordinary dots either with rounds of BUTTONHOLE or with OVERCAST, or twist the thread five times round the needle and then pull the needle through; the twists will remain upon the work as a small raised knob.

Smock.—An old English name for shift or chemise. The term is now obsolete in refined society, excepting in the use of quotations from old writers, by whom it was employed. The word shift, used in the sense of a woman's inner garment, has also fallen into disuse, and the French term *chemise* adopted in its place.

Smock Linen.—The linen of which our peasants' Smockfrocks are made, which is a strong even green linen, employed also for articles designed for embroidery.

Snowflake.—A term employed to denote a particular method of weaving woollen cloths, by which process small knots are thrown upon the face, as in Knickerbocker Cloths, which have the appearance, when white or light in colour, of a sprinkling of snow. *See* KNICKERBOCKERS.

Socks.—These woven or knitted articles of wear belong to the class of goods called "Hosiery." They are short stockings, such as worn by men, instead of stockings In Mediæval times they were made of Fustian; and such we find were worn by Edward IV. And it would seem that in those early times they were employed as extras, to be worn over long stockings. Elizabeth of York (1502) was charged "For ij yerdes of white fustyan, for Queen, xiij^d." Also "To Thomas Humberston, hosyer, for the cloth & making of vij. payre sokkes for the Queene's grace, at vj. the payere."—*Privy Purse Expenses of Elizabeth of York.*

Amongst our modern varieties of Socks there are those of silk—including the description known as spun silk—produced in a great variety of colours besides white and black. In cotton, white unbleached, and in colours; with fancy patterns stripes, "Heather," and combinations of two colours; in Worsted, white, black, and coloured; in lambs-wool, white, black, and coloured; in Shetland, lambswool and yarn, mixed; in Angola and Vigonia, white, black, and coloured; in Fleecy, having a smooth face and a thick warm nap inside; in Gauze, remarkably thin, and suitable for wear under silk; made of cotton and worsted. Men's Hose are to be had in various sizes, known respectively as Boys', Youths', Men's, Slender-men's, Men's Out-size, Gouty Hose, and Fishermen's Hose. The best sorts have a double thickness of woven material at the heels and toes, and while in both knitting and weaving many varieties of make are to be had, Socks are always knit or woven after a more elastic pattern at the top, for about 2 inches in depth, to render them more tightly-fitting round the leg. *See* also KNITTING STOCKINGS.

Soie Mi-serré.—This kind of sewing silk is also known as crochet silk, and its French name denotes that the twist is but half tightened, *mi'* being a contraction of *à moitié serré*, or "half tightened or drawn." It is a coarse kind of the silk twist known as Cordonnet, differing in the method of twisting. It is more glossy than the sorts employed for netting and for purse making on account of the comparative looseness of its make, and is, on the same account, more suitable for Crochet work, being very soft and flexible.

Soie Platte.—The French name for floss silk. It is thicker than the Dacca silk, or Soie Ovale, and is employed for all descriptions of tapestry work, for adding lustre to certain portions, such as designs of gems. It is also used in grounding embroideries on canvas. English floss silk is superior to the French, and is made in several degrees of fineness, so that it can be adapted to the canvas selected, whether coarse or fine; it may be had in any colour and shade desired.

Solomon's Bar.—*See* MACRAMÉ.

Solomon's Knot.—*See* MACRAMÉ.

Sorrento Edging.—Used in modern Point Lace. To work: Make a BUTTONHOLE STITCH the eighth of an inch long, and secure it with a tight Buttonhole Stitch upon it. Then make another Buttonhole half the length of the first, and secure that. Continue alternately to the end of the row.

Sorrento Lace.—Used in modern Point Lace. To make: Work successive rows of SORRENTO EDGING, and make the short BUTTONHOLE STITCHES fall always above the longer ones. To vary the stitch as shown in Fig. 729: First row—Commence at a corner and work from right to left, and make a loose Buttonhole Stitch. Second row—Work two loose Buttonhole Stitches, then one into the braid, and fasten off. Third row—Twist the needle in and out every loose stitch, and draw the thread tight, fasten

to the braid. Fourth row—Work two loose Buttonhole Stitches into the first loop, but not over the straight thread. Then one Buttonhole Stitch into the next loop, and alternate these stitches to the end of the row. Fifth

FIG. 729. SORRENTO LACE.

row—Work a single loose Buttonhole into every other stitch. Sixth row—Commence as in the second row, and continue all the rows until the space is full.

Another way, and as shown in Fig. 730: Commence at

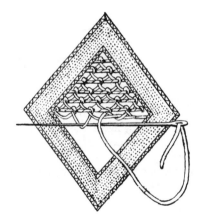

FIG. 730. SORRENTO LACE.

the point of the lace, and take a single thread across from right to left. Second row—Work one BUTTONHOLE STITCH over the straight thread, and fasten to the braid. Third row—Twist the needle in and out every loop, draw tight, and fasten to the braid. Fourth row—Work a Buttonhole Stitch into every loop, and take up the single thread with it. Fifth row—Twist the thread back and fasten to the braid. Then commence again and work the same as the second row, and continue the rows until the space is filled.

Soutache Braids.—These are very narrow silk braids, varying a little in their several widths, and having an open-work centre. They are produced in many colours, and employed for embroidery and the braiding of mantles, dresses, &c., and are likewise known as RUSSIAN BRAIDS.

Spaced Braid.—This braid is made in various patterns in imitation of lace stitches. The spaces or divisions into which the two patterns are severally woven are alternately thick, or close and narrow, and comparatively wide and open. The form consists merely of a little plain band connecting the open pearl-edged and lace-like braid. This latter space measures about half an inch in length, and the connecting and very narrow band about a third of an inch. Spaced Braid is made of cotton, and employed for the embroidery of white articles of wear, or other use.

Spaced Braid Work.—A variety of Modern Point Lace, but made without fancy stitches and with braids outlined with cord. The peculiarity of the work consists in the braids that are used being woven not as a plain and straight surface, or one continually repeated design, but in an irregular manner imitating various lace stitches. Thus in one space the threads will be closely woven and give the look of Buttonhole worked closely together, while in another the braid will appear like a number of loose and open loops such as are used in Sorrento Lace Stitch. The effect of the work depends upon the judicious adjustment of these thick and open parts of the braid, so that they carry out the idea of the pattern. To work: Select a design such as is used in MODERN POINT when worked with fancy stitches. Trace this out upon pink calico, and back the calico with brown paper; TACK the braid to the design, so that its thick and close parts should principally form the connecting stems or parts of the design, and its light and more open braid the flowers and more ornamental parts; OVERCAST the braid securely down with fine lace thread, as in Modern Point, and work BARS to connect the various parts. Make the Bars of BUTTONHOLE lines ornamented with PICOTS. Fill in any centre spaces in the pattern that the braid leaves exposed with WHEELS. Then take a fine lace cord and Overcast it on the braid so that it follows every curve made, and place it on the outer edge of the braid, not the inner edge. Put the cord on carefully and rather tight, but not so as to draw the braid up. Finish the work with a line of plain braid to form a FOOTING by which to sew the lace on to material, and for the other edge sew on the looped edging used as a finish to Modern Point Lace.

Spacing Lace.—_See_ SEAMING LACE.

Spangles (called in French _Pailettes_).—These are usually small tin plates, silvered or gilded, having a perforation in the centre. Some are flat, and others concave in form, and vary much in price. Flat Spangles are extensively used in theatrical and fancy costumes.

Spanish Embroidery.—A modern work, and closely resembling Darning on Muslin. The Embroidery is executed for washing purposes upon mull muslin with darning cotton, and for dress trimmings upon black or coloured net with filoselles. It is easily executed, and merely consists of filling in the pattern with lines of Herringbone Stitches, but it looks well for children's aprons when worked upon white materials, and for ball trimmings when made upon coloured nets. To work: Select or draw a pattern composed of leaves and tendrils arranged as continuous sprays, and one in which the leaves are narrow and with pointed terminations, such as flags and carnations, or where the leaves used are grape or ivy leaves. Trace this upon pink calico, back it with brown paper, and TACK the muslin to the pattern. Commence to work from the extreme point of a leaf, and carry a line of close and even HERRINGBONE STITCHES from the point to the base of the leaf. Work from every point to the base in this manner until that leaf is filled in, and work all the rest in the same way. Then, to form the veins of the leaves, HEM STITCH down the centre of each over the Herringboning to the point or points, giving a separate line of stitches for each point. Work the stems, stalks, and tendrils that complete the pattern by doubling the filoselle or darning cotton, and going over them with a RUN line. Unpick the material from the work, and make the right side that which is not worked on, the stitches showing through the thin foundation. _See_ SICILIAN EMBROIDERY for another kind of Spanish Embroidery.

Spanish Guipure.—One of the names given to SPANISH LACE, also to HONITON, IRISH, or POINT CROCHET.

Spanish Lace.—Lace was made in Spain from the fifteenth century, the earlier kinds of it, such as Cut Works, Lacis, and gold and silver lace, being all manufactured there; but the Spanish Laces that have become the most celebrated are the gold and silver laces known as Point d'Espagne, the Blonde Laces, and the Spanish or Rose Points. The laces of Spain, with the exception of Point d'Espagne, were not so widely known on the Continent as those made in Italy, Flanders, and France, until the dissolution of the Spanish religious houses in 1830, as the finer laces were not used in that country as articles of daily wear, and all the magnificent Needlemade fine laces were absorbed for the adornment of the churches. When the vast hoards possessed by each religious establishment were brought to light, it was perceived that Venetian and Italian Points were rivalled, by those made in Spain, from the earliest part of the seventeenth century down to the eighteenth. Point d'Espagne was made as far back as the middle of the fifteenth century, and the best and earliest workers are believed to have been Jews, as, after their expulsion from Spain, in 1492, the lace produced was not so good. However, in the seventeenth century it enjoyed a very high reputation, and was extensively used, not only in its own country, but in France and Italy. The earliest banner of the Inquisition, still in existence at Valladolid, is trimmed with Point d'Espagne, and that lace is still made in small quantities. Point d'Espagne is made with gold and silver threads, upon which a pattern is embroidered in coloured silks.

Silk Blonde Laces are made in Catalonia, and particularly in Barcelona. They are either white or black blondes, and the patterns are of thick heavy work, upon light Réseau Grounds. The mantillas worn by the Spanish ladies are the chief articles of manufacture, the black blonde mantilla being used for afternoon wear, and the white blonde for evening or State occasions.

Spanish Point, or Spanish Guipure à Bride, or Rose Point, is a Needle Lace, in the making of which infinite variety and patience is displayed. In design and execution it is so similar to the Venetian Points that the best judges cannot always distinguish between the two, although there are some slight differences. This resemblance can be accounted for by the lace being made in both countries almost exclusively by the members of religious houses, who were transferred at the will of their superior from one

is joined together with a fine Bride Ground. These were worked just when the lace was declining, and only differ in design from other Point Laces, the stitches and manner of workmanship being the same. The Raised Spanish Points with those of Venice are distinguished by the thick Cordonnet that surrounds the outline of the design and

FIG. 731. SPANISH OR ROSE POINT.

country to the other. The Spaniards and Italians both believe themselves to be the original inventors of Needle Point. The Italians claim it as coming to them through the Greeks who took refuge in Italy from religious

the principal parts of the interior, and also by the Brides connecting the parts being ornamented with Couronnes rather than Picots, and more elaborate than those used in the Venetian Points.

The piece of lace shown in Fig. 731 is a piece of Rose Raised Point that belonged to Queen Elizabeth, and one

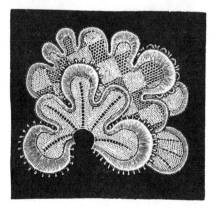

FIG. 732. SPANISH POINT—DETAIL.

FIG. 733. SPANISH POINT—DETAIL.

which exhibits the beauty of this lace, and is also capable of being copied. To make: Trace the pattern with white paint upon dark green linen or Toile Ciré, which TACK to stiff paper and keep in the hand to stitch the pieces of lace to as worked. Then trace upon separate pieces of Toile Ciré portions of the design of a size such as are shown in Figs. 732 and 733. Trace the outlines only of these, and

persecutions in their own land. The Spaniards assert that they learnt it from the Moors of Granada and Seville. Some of the Spanish Points are not raised, but are formed with a pattern worked out in Buttonhole Stitches, which prick with pinholes placed at stated intervals, as shown in Fig. 734 (which is the crescent shaped flower), as follows: Tack the Toile Ciré on to a double fold of green linen, take a needle and prick out the outline with two holes close together, then a space, and then two holes. Follow the out-

FIG. 734. SPANISH POINT—OUTLINE.

line of the thick raised part of the pattern in this manner, and make as many holes upon the inside line as upon the outside. Rub a little white paint into the holes to see them better. Make the FIL DE TRACE (*see* Fig. 735, which is of the stalk connecting the flower shown in

FIG. 735. SPANISH POINT—FIL DE TRACE.

Fig. 732, and the crescent) round these holes with Mecklenburgh thread, No. 12. Secure it to the back, and bring it up to the front of the pattern in the first of the small holes, and put it down again to the back in the second, so that it makes a small stitch upon the right side of the pattern. Tie the cotton together at the back, and then take No. 7 Mecklenburgh thread and run it round the outline and through the small stitches made with the coarse thread. The pattern is now prepared for the stitches to fill in between the raised CORDONNET. These are made of BUTTONHOLE and in the varieties of that stitch already described in POINT LACE. The ones shown in Fig. 731 can be copied from that pattern or any others inserted that the worker may prefer, as long as not more than six or seven different stitches are used over one piece of lace, and that the chief part of the filling in is done with close and even rows of Buttonhole. Having worked the inside of the detached piece of lace, proceed to surround it with

a flat or raised Cordonnet, or sew it to another piece of lace, and join them together by working the Cordonnet over them. In the pattern of lace given in Fig. 731, the inside pieces are all worked separately, and joined to the outside by the heavy Cordonnets that appear surrounding the centres: thus, work the two wings and small circle outside the pine-shaped crescent, on the right

FIG. 736. SPANISH POINT—DETAIL.

side of the lace, on one piece of Toile Ciré, and the crescent centre on another, take them both off the Toile Ciré and lay them upon the large pattern, run in the filling for the raised part, and join the two together with the Buttonhole that covers it. Work the large Rose at the top of the pattern, and shown in Fig. 736, in pieces, and put together. Commence with the five centre leaves,

FIG. 737. SPANISH POINT—DETAIL.

work in plain Buttonhole with a row of open stitches down the centre of each leaf, which make by missing three stitches in the centre of every row. Sew these pieces together, and make a small padded crescent to fit their centre. Work the two small leaves of the five forming the outside with Buttonhole, leaving three stitches in every row, as shown in the pattern, so that an open Diamond is formed; repeat this stitch in the half of the leaves on each side of the smallest leaves, and then work the other entirely in thick Buttonhole, except for the open square in the centre. Work the middle leaf in one piece, but alter the stitches where shown in the illustration. Join these various parts together with a raised Cordonnet, which trim with FLEURS VOLANTS. In the spray, shown in Fig. 737, use the same fillings as those used in the outer leaves of the Rose; work the narrow raised Cordonnet before taking the lace off the Toile Ciré. Work the thick raised Cordonnet when the piece is attached to the one nearest it in the design. For the crescent in the centre: Wind soft Moravian cotton round a pencil, and when the pad thus made is thick enough slip it off, and catch it lightly together; lay it down in its place, and Buttonhole it thickly over, and then trim it with SPINES. Work two BUTTONHOLE BARS in the centre of it, and trim with Spines; work these at the back of the crescent after it is taken off the Toile Ciré, and before it is placed in its right position. The other separate parts of the pattern are worked in a similar manner to those already described. For the raised Cordonnets surrounding each flat part proceed as follows: For the narrow and only slightly raised lines, run soft Moravian thread along their outlines and in their centre, and then Buttonhole this thread carefully over; for the highly raised parts, make a pad of Moravian thread, as shown in Fig. 738. Take the

FIG. 738. SPANISH POINT—RAISED CORDONNET.

stitches from point to point of the outline until there are sufficient to raise it well above the surface, and then increase the pad at the inside of the Cordonnet, and at the centre, so that these parts are well raised above the outside and the ends. Then cover the whole pad with an even row of Buttonhole Stitches, as shown partly worked in Fig. 738. Work now the lace-like edge that trims the Cordonnet. These are made of loops resembling Couronnes and Spines, and are known as Fleurs Volants or Pinworks. Much of the beauty of the lace depends upon these lace-like edges, and no labour should be spared to bring them to perfection. For the Couronnes: Make a loop upon the edge of the lace, return the thread from the spot it started from, and work Buttonholes over these two threads with PICOTS to trim the outer edge of the Buttonhole line. For the Spines: Make a tiny loop, and pin it

out upon the Toile Ciré, in a straight line from the edge of the lace, take the thread up to the pin and cover it and the loop with a line of Buttonholes until the edge is again reached. Make Bars ornamented with Picots where required, and where shown in Fig. 738, to keep the lace together, and when the lace is quite finished, rub over every raised part with a small ivory AFICOT, so as to polish and smooth the threads.

Spanish Lace—Imitation.—A lace made in imitation of the hand-made and raised Spanish Points. It is formed of fine linen, fine linen cord, and lace cotton, and is worked as follows: Trace out the design shown in Fig. 739 upon

FIG. 739. SPANISH LACE—IMITATION.

white or écru-coloured linen, and back this with brown paper for a foundation. Commence the work by forming the ground. Work this over the linen, but be careful that no stitch of the ground takes up the linen beneath it. Make the ground with one of the lace stitches used in hand-made Point Lace, and described under that heading. The one shown in the illustration is POINT DE VENISE, but POINT DE FILLET or POINT DE TULLE can be used equally well. The ground finished, lay along the stems of the pattern and round every outline of leaf or flower a fine white cord. Tack the cord down so as to keep it in position, and BUTTONHOLE it down upon the linen with fine lace thread either of white or écru colour. Every stitch of the Buttonhole must take in the linen material as well as the lace ground. Finally unpick the work from the brown paper, turn it, and cut away the linen from the back of the ground along the lines of Buttonholes, and only retain the material where it is surrounded with Buttonhole and forms the thick parts of the pattern.

Spider Couching.—*See* COUCHING.

Spider Stitch.—*See* GUIPURE D'ART.

Spider Wheel.—*See* CATHERINE WHEEL.

Spindle.—One of the attachments or appliances belonging to a sewing machine. It is also an apparatus used for making thread and yarn. It consists of a round stick of turned wood like a broomstick, tapering at the ends. The distaff was stuck into the spinster's waist-belt, and at the other end the flax, cotton, or wool was wound, and from this she drew a few strands at a time, and attached them to the spindle, which was set revolving by striking it frequently, and so both twisting the thread and winding it into a ball. The spindle in modern machine-spinning forms a part of a complicated apparatus. The spindle and distaff were for many ages the only appliances used for the making of thread. The simple method of turning the spindle by striking it was superseded by the adoption of a wheel and band, which appliance was called a "one-thread wheel." This has long been employed in India, and in Europe also for making cotton, flax, and wool; but various kinds of wheels are found to be necessary for the spinning of different sorts of yarn. *See* SPINNING WHEELS.

Spines.—These are also called Pinworks, and are used to trim the raised Cordonnets that surround Spanish and Venetian Point Lace, and also other kinds of Point Lace. The Spines are long straight points that stick out from the edge of the Cordonnet. To work: Secure the thread into the CORDONNET, then make a tiny loop one-sixteenth of an inch and pin this out from the lace by sticking a pin into it and drawing it out with the pin straight from the lace. Run the thread up to the pin and put it round it, then BUTTONHOLE over the loop and the last thread until the lace is again reached. Another way: Secure the thread into the Cordonnet, then twist it six or eight times round the needle, and draw the needle through; push the loops thus made on the thread up to the lace edge, and secure them.

Spinning.—A method by which the fibres of plants and the hair of animals were formed from short and entangled filaments into long and secure threads strong enough not to break when woven together, and of a continuous thickness. This art dates from the first efforts of civilisation, but no record of its invention is preserved. Reference is made to it in the Divine writings by Moses, proving, at the smallest computation, that it existed some 1500 years before Christ. Amongst the Ancient Greeks the invention was ascribed to Minerva. From the very earliest ages it was the duty of women to prepare these threads, and either weave them into garments or sell them for the same purpose; and it is curious to notice that the same spindle and distaff that is represented upon Egyptian monuments, in use, is still as met with in some of the remotest parts of Scotland, although these ancient implements were much modified and improved before hand Spinning succumbed to modern machinery. The art of Spinning consists in drawing out from a bundle of wet yarn, hemp, or wool, a number of small threads and twisting them together, so that they form an unbroken and continuous line of firmly-twisted material. This was first effected only by the spindle, which was twirled round in the hand and even thrown in the air, while the threads were pulled out of it by the hand, and twisted together by the action of the spindle. An improvement was made to this by winding the thread as spun upon the distaff, a long thin piece of wood.

The spinning wheel succeeded to the spindle and distaff, which was driven by the foot, and left the hands of the spinner at liberty to guide the flax, which she drew towards her, having previously wetted from the spindle, which was mounted on the wheel, and which twisted the thread by a treadle.

The distaff was introduced into England in the fifteenth century, by an Italian. It was superseded by a spinning wheel, invented at Nuremburg, in 1530; then by the spinning-jenny, invented by Hargreaves, a Lancashire cotton spinner, in 1764, and by means of which the spinster could make eight threads at once. Fifteen years later, the mule jenny replaced it, by which no less than eighty threads could be simultaneously produced, instead of one only, as in the primitive use of the distaff. In the process of Spinning by means of the mule jenny the several threads are opened, cleansed, twisted, and then wound off upon reels.

Spinning Wheels.—These appliances have long been adopted for the purpose of turning the spindle, round which the yarn is wound, instead of the ancient method of striking it perpetually, to keep it in motion. What was designated a "one thread wheel," was first invented; and has long been employed in India, as well as for cotton, flax, and wool spinning in Europe. Various descriptions of yarn require different kinds of wheels for their respective spinning. That for flax is turned by a treadle, moved by the foot; a catgut cording passes round in a groove in the rim of the wheel, over the pulley of the spindle on which the thread is wound. The wheel for cotton and wool spinning is of a different kind from that for flax. The spindle is made of iron, placed horizontally upon the extremity of a wooden frame, supported on legs. Upon this there stands a wheel, round which, and the spindle likewise, a band passes. Worsted is spun more after the manner of Flax. Spinning wheels were universally employed on the Continent of Europe and in this country until the year 1764, when a wonderful series of mechanical inventions were adopted by all the weaving manufactories, and left the pretty spinning wheels of the olden times to decorate the cottages of the peasantry, and supply the artists with a charming object, to break the hard straight lines in his sketch. *See* SPINNING, &c.

Spinster.—One who spins, an occupation followed by women from times of the remotest antiquity, and in all civilised nations. Thus the work so designated became a sort of characteristic of the sex; and as unmarried women used in some parts to spin the yarn of all the linen required for their *trousseaux*, and for their household—when they should commence their own housekeeping—they were given the name of Spinster, which came in course of time to denote a single woman.

Split Stitch.—*See* EMBROIDERY STITCHES.

Spools.—A word employed to signify reels, but more in use in Ireland than in England. They are made in wood stained black, brown, or red, of many different sizes; and some may now be had of gigantic dimensions, respectively containing, it is said, cotton, which unwound, would reach a mile in length. There is a hole—the Spool running lengthwise through the centre—to allow of their being fixed on a pin, upon which they can turn round, so as to give out the thread as required. Spools, or Reels are to be had of bone, ivory, and mother-o'-pearl, as well as of wood; and some are made like a succession of Spools made in one piece, the divisions being of use for the purpose of keeping the different colours of sewing silk respectively apart.

Spot Stitch.—*See* CROCHET, page 125.

Spotted Knitting.—*See* KNITTING.

Spotted Lace or Net.—A cotton textile, chiefly used for veils, or women's caps. Formerly the spots were worked upon the Net with a needle and thread, but now by machine. Some kinds are spotted with chenille, and others with beads, but these being heavy are apt to tear the Net. It is an inexpensive material.

Sprigs.—A term employed by Pillow Lace makers to denote detached pieces of lace, which are afterwards appliqué on to net foundations, or joined together so as to make a compact material. Sprigs are made in Honiton Lace, Brussels Lace, and Duchesse Lace, and need not be formed of flower sprays, but of some detached and small design.

Spun Silk.—This silk is very commonly called by two French names, *i.e.*, Filoselle and Bourre de Soie. It consists of that part of ravelled silk thrown on one side in the filature of the cocoons, which is subsequently carded, and then spun. The yarn has rather a rough and cotton-like appearance, but is very suitable for socks and stockings, being warm and durable. Handkerchiefs, shawls, and scarves, as well as a great variety of dress silks, are made of it, especially of Indian manufacture; and the peasants of Lombardy also employ it extensively for their home-made articles of dress. Spun Silk, or Filoselle may be had in white and black, in common, and in ingrain colours; and can be purchased retail, by the skein, or the pound. It may also be had in 1 ounce balls, for knitting and mending.

Square Crochet.—*See* CROCHET, page 126.

Square Netting.—*See* NETTING.

Square Plaitings.—*See* PLAITINGS.

Squirrel Fur (*Scuivus vulgaris*).—There are seven varieties of this Fur, which are prepared for the making of muffs, tippets, cuffs, linings, and trimmings, and consist respectively of the Black Russian, the Blue Siberian, the Razan-Siberian, Indian striped, English, American, and Flying Squirrels. These are all employed in their natural colours, which, according to the several varieties of the animal, are respectively grey, white, black, red, and of a bluish hue; the latter is the most highly valued, and is known as the *Petit Gris*. This description is obtained from Siberia. Inferior kinds are often dyed. Our chief supply of these skins is derived from Russia. They are light, warm, and durable. The tails of the animals are made into boas, and the hair is also extensively employed for artists' painting brushes. The fur on

the common squirrel's stomach is of a yellowish white, while that on the back is grey, the latter being the most in esteem. The skins, when prepared for making up into articles of wear, measure 4 inches by 8 inches in size.

Squirrel Lock.—The fur known by this name is that portion of the grey squirrels' fur that grows under the animal's body on the belly. It is of a yellowish white colour, and, being cut out with a bordering of the grey fur of the back, it has a pretty variegated appearance when made up. It is lighter in weight than the grey fur on the back, which should be remembered when purchasing a cloak lined with it. It measures 10 inches by 3 inches in size.

Stamped Plush.—This variety of Plush is manufactured in strips of about 4 or 5 inches in width, for borders to curtains and other articles of upholstery. It is also employed for purposes of Embroidery, and is to be had in various colours. *See* PLUSH.

Stamped Utrecht Velvet.—A textile similar to the plain kinds of this name, excepting in the designs stamped upon it. It is employed for furniture decorations, and also for purposes of Embroidery. *See* VELVET.

Stamped Velvet.—There are two kinds of Velvet which have the effect of being stamped, although only one of them has a pattern produced by stamping. This latter, or real Stamped Velvet, which is of comparatively inferior quality, has a silk face and a cotton back. It is woven with a silk pile, and, by means of heated stamping irons, formed into various designs; it is so pressed as to make the portions between those that are raised appear as if of satin make. The superior Velvet, known as Velvet Broché, has a design in silk pile, woven into the web, and not stamped. Stamped Velvet is employed for the making of dress bodices and trimmings.

Stamped Velveteen.—A material used for Embroidery, and likewise employed for women's dress. It is 27 inches in width. *See* VELVETEEN.

Stamped Velvet Work.—A modern Embroidery that is both effective and easy, and which has arisen from the use in the present day of stamped velvet for furniture trimmings. The Embroidery consists of giving a certain prominence to the pattern stamped upon the velvet by outlining its edges with gold or silver thread or filoselle, and filling in some of the chief parts with Satin Stitch worked with filoselle. To work: Select a velvet of a deep ruby, olive green, peacock blue, or salmon shade, with a pattern stamped upon it that is bold and geometrical. Take some Japanese gold thread and lay it down along the outer lines of the pattern. COUCH this thread to the material with silk matching it in colour, bring the silk up from the back of the work, put it over the gold thread and back into the velvet, so that it makes a short stitch over the thread, and thus secures it. Work round all the principal outlines with the gold thread, but fill in minor lines with filoselle of a contrasting shade to the velvet, and with CREWEL STITCH. Having finished the outline, take two light-coloured filoselles, one a shade lighter than the velvet, and the other a shade darker, and with these cover with SATIN STITCH the extreme centre of a stamped flower or geometrical design, using the filoselles alternately. The stamped pattern should not be too much filled in with stitches, as if they are overdone the work will look heavy. Stamped Velvet Work is used for cushions, handkerchief and glove cases.

Stamping.—This is a method adopted for producing a pattern on cotton, silk, or woollen stuffs, having a stiff raised pile on the face. It is effected by hot irons pressed on the material by a machine. There are stamped velvets used for dresses and trimmings made of a combination of silk and cotton, and there are stamped woollen stuffs, having a pile—such as the Utrecht velvets, employed for purposes of upholstery.

Star. — *See* BERLIN WORK, GUIPURE D'ART, and MACRAMÉ.

Star Braid.—A kind of Braid designed for Fancy Embroidery, made in blue and red, and having a white star. It is 1½ inches in width, and these stars are woven at successive intervals of an inch apart. It is very smoothly woven, and is much employed for covers of chair backs, strips being united together in suitable lengths in Crochet Work. An arrangement of narrow white cotton Braid is also made so as to form an openwork trimming. It is folded into the form of conventional stars, which are sewn in position in their centres; sometimes a smaller Star is worked in embroidery cotton, white or coloured. It is sold by the yard in shops, for the trimming of children's dresses; and a narrower make of the same sort of trimming is produced for edgings.

Star Ground.—This is a lace ground, made with a needle, and one that is often used to connect sprays of lace made on the Pillow. To work, as shown in Fig. 740:

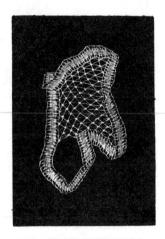

FIG. 740. STAR GROUND.

TACK the sprays to be connected on to coloured paper, right side uppermost, which back with brown paper, use Lace thread No. 9, and a fine, long, and pointless needle. Commence on the left hand, at the space of one pinhole down the side of the work. Make a BUTTONHOLE STITCH

at the distance of one-eighth of an inch from the commencement, and fasten it into the lace; then make a second Buttonhole Stitch, close to the first, thus: Put the needle up through the lace from behind, and bring it down under the thread. Repeat these two stitches one-eighth of an inch apart, and so on to the end of the row. Work down the side to the next pinhole, carry the thread from that pinhole across to the pinhole on the opposite side, fasten it there, work down to the next pinhole, and then repeat two stitches in each loop of the last row, working over the stretched thread, and so securing it.

Star Netting.—*See* NETTING.

Statute Galloons.—These are narrow cotton or silk ribbons, employed for the binding of flannels. They are made in five widths, known respectively as the twopenny, fourpenny, sixpenny, eightpenny, and tenpenny, the first named three being those most in request. They are sold in four pieces of 36 yards each to the gross.

Stay Bindings.—These Bindings are of twilled cotton, and may be had in white, grey, drab, black, blue, red, and buff colour. They are sold by the gross in lengths of 12-12, 8-18, or 6-24; and the widths run ⅜, ½, and ⅝ inch; or from No. 10 up to 30.

Stay Cord.—This Cord is to be had made of cotton and of linen, for the purpose of lacing stays, and it is sold either by the gross yards, or sufficient for a single pair.

Stay Hooks.—These Hooks are more or less employed for the purpose of keeping the petticoats or the skirt of a gown in its proper place, the band or yoke of any or all of these being passed under the Hook, and so held down securely, or else a hole is worked in them through which the Hook passes. They are sewn on the busk of the stays, the point turned downwards, and may be had plated, of white metal, brass, or japanned, measuring about an inch in length. Stay Hooks should only be employed to keep the skirt of the gown in its right place, as all the underskirts should be worn beneath, that is, inside the Stays.

Stay Laces.—These are otherwise called Stay-cord, and are made of both cotton and linen; and silk Staylaces, made of a flat braid, are also to be had. The first are sold by the gross yards, and also in small lengths, and are always supplied with the Stays in the shops, and by the makers. The latter, known as Paris Silk Stay Laces, are likewise sold with the best kinds of Stays. The numbers are 1, 2, and 3; the lengths 6-4, 8-4, 10-4, 12-4, 14-4, 16-4, and 20-4.

Stays.—These are otherwise known as Corsets, which latter name has been adopted from the French. They consist of a low bodice, without sleeves or shoulder-straps, made of either jean, satin, or coutille, which latter is a French material of slighter make than jean. They are more or less supplied with casings, to contain either strips of whalebone or steel, which are placed in various directions, according to the discretion of the several makers, the better to keep the garment from wrinkles, so as to form both a support to the wearer, and a firm foundation on which to fit the bodice of a gown. Some Stays are made to open not only at the back and front, but at the hips and bosom,

They may be had in white, black, red, blue, and grey colours; and sometimes consisting of one colour, are stitched and embroidered with another. They are laced at the back and fastened in front by means of two steel busks, one provided with metal buttons and the other with metal loops. Some of these busks, which have quite superseded the old whalebone and wooden ones, formerly in use when Stays were only open at the back, are of equal width throughout; but others are widened below the waist into what is called a Spoonbill. Steel busks are to be had for sewing under the narrow double busks of the Stays to preserve them from being broken when the wearer may stoop, which is of frequent occurrence when she is a stoutly-built person. There are no less than 300 different makes of Stays, which are given out to private houses to be made by the great manufacturers. French Corsets are largely imported into this country.

Stay Tape.—This is more properly called STAY BINDING.

Stem Stitch.—This stitch is largely used to form the stems, tendrils, curves, and raised parts in Honiton and other Pillow Lace making. There are three kinds of Stem Stitch—Beginner's Stem, Buckle Stem, and Stem Stitch proper.

To work *Beginner's Stem*: This stitch is used to form the stalks of leaves, or to carry the Bobbins at the back of the lace from one part to another. Divide the Bobbins into three and plait them together in a three plait, until the length required is made.

To work *Buckle Stem*: Buckle Stem differs from Stem Stitch by being worked with a Plain Edge upon both sides, and a row of open work down its centre, instead of being quite thick and solid; it is used for working the main stem of a spray of flowers, where that stem is to be rather broad. Hang on eight pairs of Bobbins where the main stem commences, four pairs for Hangers and four pairs for Workers. For the first row: Work from left to right into the middle, that is, across two Hanging pairs of Bobbins; Twist the Workers once, and also the next pair (which will now become the fourth Working pair, make a stitch, Twist both pairs once again—the Twists make the centre holes). Continue to work across to the other side with the first pair, make a Plain Edge with them, bring them back into the middle, Twist once, and leave them. Take up the fourth working pair, work to the left edge, back into the middle, and Twist once. There are now two pairs of Workers in the middle and both twisted, make a stitch with these pairs, Twist once, then again work to the edges and back into the middle.

Stem Stitch.—This stitch is not only used for Stem, but it forms the circles inside flowers, and frequently the Raised Work at the side of leaves, and in other parts of the pattern. The little trefoil shown in Fig. 741 is formed entirely of Stem Stitch, and will, therefore, if made, enable the worker to thoroughly master this stitch. To work: Hang on six pairs of Bobbins at the end of the stem (four or five pairs are used if the stem is to be very fine, but ordinary stems are made with six pairs). Prick the pinholes that form the Plain Edge upon one side of the Stem; it

is on the stitch at the other edge that the variation is made, the rest of the work being simply CLOTH STITCH and PLAIN EDGE. Give three TWISTS to the outside pair, and put them on one side; with the next pair work across in Cloth Stitch until the last pair is reached, then make a stitch and a half or TURNING STITCH, as follows: Work a Cloth Stitch, give each pair one twist to the left, put the middle left hand Bobbin over the middle right hand Bobbin, lift the two pairs with each hand, and give them a little pull to make the inner edge firm; put aside the inner pair and work back with the other to the pins, where make the Plain Edge with the pair which have been first put aside. Stem Stitch must always be more or less of a curve, and the pinholes on the outside, so that it is sometimes necessary to turn the Plain Edge from the right to the left hand in the course of the work, but the Turning Stitch never varies. The innermost Bobbin works backwards and forwards, but the second one of the pair at this part remains stationary. In working round sharp curves slant the pins outwards and run one

FIG. 741. TREFOIL IN STEM STITCH.

down to its head here and there; three or four upright pins will hold the lace steady except where the Stem is almost straight, then a greater number of upright pins are required. Knots are passed away in Stem Stitch, and extra threads cut away six rows after they are discontinued. When the circle round the inside of the flower shown in Fig. 741 is worked, the work will come across the Stem, and there a SEWING must be made before the Plain Edge; then make the Plain Edge Stitch, and continue the work as before round the first petal, there make another Sewing, but slightly different to the one first made. In the first place it was made with the inner pair of Bobbins, but on this occasion the Turning Stitch is dispensed with work straight across, sew to the nearest pinhole but to the outside edge instead of the strand across, work straight back, and continue Stem Stitch round the middle petal. At the end of the middle petal make a Sewing like the last, but at the end of the third where the work is finished off, make two Sewings. Then tie the threads inside the last pair, tie up two or three more pairs, and cut off quite close. Also *see* EMBROIDERY STITCHES.

Stephanie Lace.—A modern lace, worked by hand, in imitation of Venetian Point. It was exhibited at the Lace Exhibition at Brussels in 1880, and called by that name after the Princess Stephanie. It is worked as detailed in SPANISH and VENETIAN POINTS.

Stiletto.—A small sharply-pointed instrument, otherwise called a PIERCER forming one of the necessary appliances of a workbox. It is like a very small dagger or *Stylus*, only round instead of flat in the blade, and graduated to a point. Stilettoes may be had entirely of silver, steel, bone, mother-o'-pearl, or ivory, or else mounted in silver if of mother-o'-pearl, or mounted in the latter if of steel. The best are of steel. It is employed for making eyeletholes in dressmaking, staymaking, Embroidery, and for other purposes, and with the advantage of the preservation from tearing of the material, to which a cutting of the tissue would render it liable.

Stirrup.—*See* NETTING.

Stitchery.—The art of Needlework, for which Stitchery is a synonymous term; it is of Anglo-Saxon origin.

Stitches.—Under this term all the various ways of putting a needle into a material, or forming a solid fabric out of thin threads of linen, silk, or wool, are described; and the word is used not only to denote the manner by which one fabric is connected to another, or embellished by another, but by which thin threads are joined together, so as to make a material more or less solid. The ornamental stitches formed by the sewing needle for the purposes of Embroidery comprise all kinds of Embroidery with wools, silks, or crewels, upon solid foundations, Berlin Work upon open canvas, and all Needlemade laces. The same term is used to designate the various modes by which articles of clothing or upholstery are made and mended, by means of needles of various descriptions, and silk, woollen, flax, cotton, hair, gold or silver thread, either worked by hand or in a machine. The various stitches, together with the modes of their application, are fully described under their several heads.

Stitching.—This is one of the varieties in Plain Sewing, and is a method by which two pieces of material are very firmly sewn together. To work in this style: RUN two pieces of cloth together, and turn them so as to leave the raw edges inside, and out of sight. Then commence to

FIG. 742. STITCHING.

make a kind of double Running, but only taking one stitch at a time. When one has been taken, and the needle drawn out, replace it in the spot where it was previously inserted, bringing it out beyond the spot where it was last drawn out. Thus there will be a line of stitches respectively touching one another (Fig. 742), and no spaces left between

them as in Running. The Stitching should be made at a little distance, within the edge formed, at the union of the two pieces of cloth; and they should be of uniform length, and the horizontal line of perfect evenness. This description of work may be executed with a Sewing Machine.

Stockingette Cloth.—This textile is otherwise known as Jersey, or Elastic Cloth, varying respectively in their widths, though differing little otherwise. Elastic Cloth measures 24 inches in width, Jersey Cloth 30 inches, and Stockingette may be had up to 2 yards in width.

Stockings.—Elastic coverings for the feet and legs, extending upwards above the knee, and woven in a loom, knitted by hand, or made in a stocking machine. In the early Anglo-Saxon and Mediæval times they were not elastic, but simply cut out of some woven textile which was embroidered or plain, of costly silk, woollen, fustian, or cotton cloth, according to the condition in life of the wearer. Previously to the time of Henry VIII. knitted silk stockings were unknown in England. According to Stowe, the King himself "did wear only cloath hose, or hose cut out of ell broad taffaty; or that by great chance there came a pair of Spanish silke-stockings from Spaine." The same writer notes that Sir Thomas Gresham gave the King "a great present" in a "payre of long Spanish silk stockings," from which country they were originally introduced. According to the same authority, Queen Elizabeth's "silk woman, Mistress Mountague," presented her with "a payre of blacke knit silk stockings for a new year's gift." It appears that these so well pleased the Queen that she told her "silk woman" she would "henceforth wear no more Cloth Stockings." Stocking knitting was thenceforth practised in this country and elsewhere; but the stocking loom was invented by William Lee, of Woodborough, near Nottingham, in 1589, when the Queen was in her decline. Her successor, King James, did not patronise the art, and thus Lee established his manufactory at Rouen, under the patronage of Henri IV. and his Minister Sully. But he was proscribed under the excuse of his being a Protestant, through the means taken by the jealous inhabitants of that manufacturing city, and had to conceal himself in Paris. Some of his workmen, however, escaped to England, and planted the first stocking manufactories in the counties of Leicester, Nottingham, and Derby.

For the production of "ribbed stockings" we are indebted to Jedidiah Strutt, 1758; and to Arkwright for the spinning machine for the manufacture of cotton Stockings. The method of stocking-weaving is an art distinctly differing from that of cloth-weaving. In the former, instead of two threads, viz., the warp and the woof, the whole fabric consists of one continuous thread, formed into a series of loops in successive rows, those of each row being drawn respectively through their several predecessors. The yarn of which this peculiar cloth is woven is also spun after a different method from that of other yarn, as two rows are united to form one thread, which is called "double-spun twist." Very numerous varieties are manufactured, both in make, patterns, combinations of material and of colour, quality in every description of material, and of size, both in knitted and in woven Stockings. Of silk hose there are the fine silk and spun silk, plain, embroidered, open-worked, and with clocks (or clox) in white, black, colours, and mixtures of colours, and also silk with cotton feet, or cotton tops from half way up the calf of the leg. In those of spun silk, partially cotton feet and tops may like-wise be had. There are Shetland Stockings, which are peculiarly soft and fine; others of Angola and Vigonia, in colours white and black; of lambswool, also, in colours, white and black; of merino; in ditto of gauze (a combina-tion of cotton and worsted) which are exceedingly thin and worn under silk; of Lisle thread, in white, black, and all colours, and likewise of commoner thread; of worsted, grey, black, and speckled; and of unbleached cotton, of various degrees of fineness, some being very fine and having silk clocks, the best descriptions being known as "Balbriggan"; and of fleecy, having a smooth face and a thick nap inside, very warm, and suitable for invalids. They are all made in a variety of sizes, viz., infants', children's, girls', maids', slender women's (a size which may be worn by persons of tall stature and full propor-tions, who have small feet), women's full size, and women's large or "out-size." Stocking-knitting frames for hand-work are much employed; and there are likewise small Stocking-knitting machines for home use, if required. *See* SOCKS, and also KNITTING STOCKINGS.

Stocking Yarn.—This is Cotton thread, and is spun softer and looser than either Mule or Water Twist. Two threads are afterwards doubled together, and then slightly twisted round each other.

Stone Marten (*Mustela saxorum*).—This fur is much esteemed throughout Europe. The fur underneath the body is of a bluish white, the top hairs being of a dark brown. The throat is usually of a pure white, by which it is distinguished. The French excel in dyeing this fur, on which account it is called French Sable. It is also dyed in this country, the excellent qualities of the skin adapt-ing it to a great variety of purposes. *See* SABLE.

Straight Holes.—These are made in Pillow Lace, and are described in BRAIDS under the heading of *Hole Braid.*

Strand Ground.—This ground is used to connect sprays of Honiton Lace, and is formed of irregular Bars made on the Pillow and with two Bobbins. To work: TACK the sprays right side downwards on to blue paper, and commence the ground. SEW a pair of Bobbins on to one edge of a spray, TWIST these Bobbins until they form a rope, and carry them across to a piece of lace opposite to the one they started from. Sew them to this lace, Twist the threads, carry them down to where a new bar is to be made, Sew them to the lace, Twist them until they form a bar of the necessary length, and attach them to a piece of lace on the opposite side. Make the Bars irregular, and when they cross one another in the grounding Sew them together, and when starting them from the lace edges always twist them down to a fresh point of departure, instead of cutting them off,

as being at the back of the work the twisted threads will not show.

Strasbourg Work.—*See* ROMAN WORK.

Straw Braids or Plaits.—These are made after various methods, and of many qualities of straw, according to the country or soil in which the wheat or grass is grown, and the national fancy of the several countries where the industry is carried on. Its chief seat in England is Bed-fordshire. There are two sorts of straw, known respectively as the Red Lammas, and the White Chittein, which are grown in the Midland and Southern counties, and are produced best in a light but rich soil. There are Plaits also, made at Luton, and elsewhere, of Rye-straw, grown in the Orkney Islands, and fabricated in imitation of the Tuscan.

The principal plait made in this country is called the Dunstable, which is made of two split straws, of which the insides are placed together so as only to show the outside of each in the plaiting. Straw-plaiting is an industry carried on by women and children in their own private homes, after the manner of the Devonshire Lace-making. The edges of the several plaits are laid successively over that of the next in order, and coiled round and round, thus forming a ridge, and as our straw is strong and thick in quality, the hats, bonnets, and other articles, such as baskets and chair-seats, are of a heavier description than any made of foreign straw.

Straw Braids are made in very long lengths, and are sewn together by means of long thin Needles, called STRAWS. The straw is split when used in Embroidery on silk or velvet, the latter is found most suitable; when for introduction into worsted work for carriage bags or baskets. Rushes are likewise used for men's and women's hats and bonnets, and also for baskets. There are several kinds of straw in use for such purposes. Of our own straw manufactures immense cargoes are exported to all parts of the world, some of the whole straw, some split, and of both superior and of inferior quality, the plaits or made-up articles of the latter being of very trifling cost. There are large importations of articles made of Straw Plaits, and interlacings from Swiss manufactories, and much, also, from Japan, and the south of France, of a very delicate character, dyed in a variety of colours. Very pretty cabinets, boxes, and cardcases, as well as many other articles of use, are decorated with a covering of coloured Straw-work, much resembling Mosaic work. In the Cantons of Argau, Fribourg, and Appenzell, the manufacture of Straw Plaits for hat making, and fancy kinds of Plaits, some round as well as flat, together with tassels and flowers and other trimmings, have been brought to great perfection. In Appenzell the embroidered straw bonnets are very handsome. The industry is of a peculiar and creditable description in Fribourg; but, perhaps, that of Argau may still rank as the first in Switzerland, as it did at the time of our English Exhibition in 1851. Taking a comprehensive view of the industry of all nations in Straw Plaiting, that of Leghorn and the various districts of Tuscany may be regarded as holding the first place in order of merit in the manufacture of bonnets.

Those of Leghorn are plaited in one piece; the Tuscan are made flat—without any twist forming a ridge, after the English method—and sewn together successively. These two Italian kinds excel all others both in beauty and durability, and in the variety of designs executed. The straw is of a beautiful buff colour, being the stalks of a very fine and peculiar description of wheat. There is a delicate Straw Plait produced in Brazil for hat and bonnet making, formed of a species of grass, which is very light in weight, and all made in one piece, like that of Leghorn.

The origin of Straw Plaiting is of somewhat recent date in England, only going back about one hundred and thirty, or forty years, but it has now reached a high state of perfection. The industry is also carried on with considerable success in Germany and Lombardy.

Straw Cotton.—This is a wiry kind of thread, starched and stiff, produced chiefly in the neighbourhoods of Dunstable and Luton. The numbers run from 10 to 100, and the cotton is exclusively made for use in the manufacture of straw goods. It is but little sold in the retail trade.

Straw Embroidery.—This work is used for ball dress trimmings, or to ornament an entire net dress. It consists in tacking upon black Brussels silk net, or yellow coloured net, leaves, flowers, corn, butterflies, &c., that are stamped out of straw, and connecting these with thick lines made of yellow filoselle. The leaves are stamped in eight different shapes, of which three are shown in Fig. 743,

FIG. 743. STRAW EMBROIDERY.

and the flowers and butterflies can also be bought in different sizes. These straw leaves, &c., are bought at Messrs. Barnards, or Catts. To work: Trace out upon white linen a Running pattern of leaves, flowers, &c., back this with brown paper, and TACK on to it a strip of black or coloured net. Take some filoselle, matching the straw leaves in colour, divide it in half, and RUN with it, or work in ROPE STITCH, all the stems and tendrils in the pattern. Then slightly gum the straw leaves and flowers to their places, and afterwards stitch them into their positions with a few stitches down their centres, made with fine silk.

Straws.—These are needles of a particular description, employed in hat and bonnet making. They are long and slight, as compared with those commonly used in Plain Sewing and Embroidery. *See* NEEDLES.

Streak Stitch.—In hand-made laces the veins of leaves or flowers are made with an open line, that is sometimes designated Streak Stitch. It is formed thus: Trace the shape of the leaf or flower, and draw a line down its centre with a pencil, fill in the leaf with close BUTTONHOLE STITCHES, but when the pencil line is reached in each line of Buttonhole, miss over three stitches before working the next Buttonhole. This will leave an open line down the leaf, and give the appearance of a vein. It is also another name for the CLOTH STITCH used in Pillow Laces.

Strengthening.—*See* KNITTING.

Stretch Needlework.—*See* EMBROIDERY.

String Netting.—This particular kind of work is made to cover glass bottles or other perishable articles that are often used, the network formed by the string protecting the more fragile object that it covers. To work, as shown in Fig. 744: Procure some fine but good twine, and a

FIG. 744. STRING NETTING.

carpet needle, through which the twine can be threaded. Take the bottle and tie a piece of twine tightly round its neck, close to the stopper; carry it down the side of the bottle, and tie it round the bottom of the bottle, then up the opposite side, and round the neck again, and down to the bottom. Thread the twine, and work from the bottom of the bottle to the neck. Make a row of close BUTTONHOLE STITCHES over the loop to commence with, and then work rows of loose Buttonholes, with a return thread, back to where each row commenced, round and round the bottle, so that they enclose it in a tightly-fitting case, until the neck is reached. OVERCAST the loops of string round the neck, and plait up a piece of string to hold the bottle by.

String Rugs.—These are made from odds and ends of coarse Berlin or fleecy wool, which are either knitted up with string or worked into coarse canvas in loops. *To Work with String:* Take the largest pair of bone knitting needles, balls of strong twine, and balls made of the various lengths of wool, tied together so as to make a long length. CAST ON thirty-six stitches of twine, and KNIT a row in PLAIN KNITTING. In the next row put the needle through the stitch to be knitted, then wind the wool (having first secured its end) three times round two fingers of the left

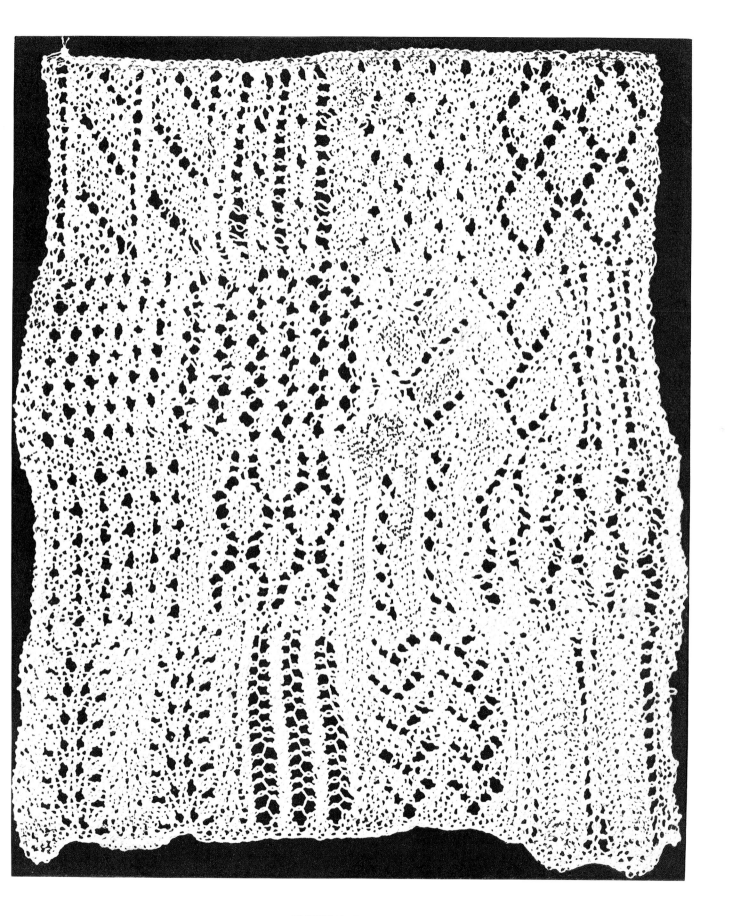

KNITTING SAMPLER.

hand, pass the needle round these threads, and Knit them with the stitch. Repeat for every stitch. Knit the next row plain, and repeat the plain and looped row until the length required for the rug is obtained. Work as many strips as will make the width of the rug sew them together, and line with coarse sacking.

To make upon Canvas: Select strong and firmly woven sacking, and cover the whole of it with a number of tufts of wool. Cut the wool up into lengths of 4 inches; take three of these lengths, double them, and fold them together. Make a hole in the canvas with a large stiletto, push the ends of the wool through this hole, and tie them all together in a knot at the back of the canvas. Continue to insert these loops, and secure them until the canvas is quite filled up, then line it with a piece of sacking.

Stroking.—A term of Saxon origin, used in reference to Needlework to denote the disposing of small gathers formed in linen or calico, in regular order and close succession respectively. It is effected by drawing the point of a blunt needle from the top of each gather, where it is

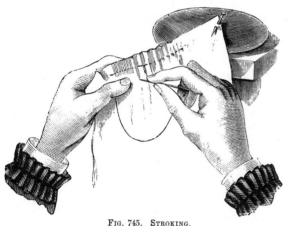

FIG. 745. STROKING.

attached to a band or yoke downwards, after the manner indicated in Fig. 745, which shows the process as adopted in the case of a Running. To make: Draw up the fulness on the Running thread, and secure it round a pin to the left, and with the needle or a pin stroke down the several gathers, placing the thumb of the left hand upon each successively, and proceeding from left to right. *See* SETTING-IN GATHERS.

Stuffs. — This term is one of general significance, and may be applied to any woven textile, whether of gold, silver, cotton, hair, thread, silk, or wool, but it more especially denotes those of worsted, made of long or "combing wool," such as Callimancoes, Camlets, Florenteens, Lutestrings, Merinoes, Moreens, Plaids, Shalloons, Tammies, &c. Stuffs are distinguished from other woollen cloths by the absence of any nap or pile, and having little or no tendency to shrink nor curl when damp, nor to felt in the process of weaving. They are woven either plain or twilled, with spots or designs of various kinds, but in all the thread is laid bare, the superfluous fibres of hair being singed off by means of a red-hot

iron. After the process of weaving and singeing, they are tightly rolled, soaked in hot water, and boiled, then scoured, stocked, or milled, and the moisture pressed out between rollers. They are then passed through a mordant and dyed. To dry them, they are rolled round iron cylinders filled with steam, and, lastly, placed in Bramah's hydraulic presses.

Style Cashmere. — A name which originated from Cross and Tent Stitch, being largely used in Persia in Embroideries upon open canvas materials. It is sometimes applied to Berlin woolwork.

Sunn.—The fibre of the *Crotalaria juncea*, grown in various parts of Hindostan. The strongest, whitest, and most durable species of Sunn is produced at Comercolly. Although called the "Indian Hemp," it is a perfectly different plant from the *Cannabis sativa*, from which Hemp is obtained. Under the name of "Sane" it is named in many Sanscrit books, but by that of "Sunn" it is known in most parts of India. It is probably the earliest of the distinctly mentioned fibres of that country, and in the Hindoo *Institutes of Menu* it is stated that the sacrificial thread of the Rajpoot is ordered to be made of Sunn, cotton being reserved for the Brahmins. It is much cultivated throughout the whole of India, and is employed for sacking, cordage, &c. It is also largely imported to this country.

Surah Silk.—A fine soft twilled silk stuff, employed for dresses, and especially for those of brides and young ladies. It is distinguished from a foulard by its greater softness and flexibility, which preserves it from creasing; and it has no dressing or glaze, like the former. It is to be had in silver-grey and white, and in various light colours of a delicate tint, and measures 26 inches in width. It bears an Indian name, and is probably of Indian origin, but is imported from France, where it is manufactured.

Swansdown.—The breast of the Wild Swan, composed of exceedingly fine soft fluffy white feathers, like down. The bird abounds in Iceland, Lapland, and in the eastern parts of Europe and Asia. The Swanskins imported to this country are employed for tippets, boas, ruffs, muffs, and trimmings for opera cloaks and infants' dress. The skins measure 10 inches, by 24 inches, and are imported into England from Dantzic and the Baltic.

Swanskin, or Swansdown Calico.—A description of calico stuff, one side of which is fluffy, the fibres being pulled to the surface and forming a nap, and somewhat resembling Swansdown feathers. It is much used for underclothing, especially by labourers and persons suffering from rheumatism, for which latter, as cotton holds moisture, it is not as suitable as any woollen textile. It is tightly and closely woven, similar to "Cricketing," but of a commoner description of quality, and may be had both white and unbleached. In America it is sometimes employed in lieu of flannel. There is also a cloth called Swanskin, a very thick and closely-woven textile made of wool, and much employed by sailors and labourers; it is likewise used by laundresses for ironing cloths.

o o o

Swedish Drawn Work.—*See* TONDER LACE.

Swedish Pillow Lace.—The nuns at Wadstena are believed to have been the founders of lace-making in Sweden, and claim to have been taught the art by their founderess, St. Bridget, who died in 1335, but they more probably learnt it from Spanish and Italian nuns during the first part of the sixteenth century. The Wadstena Lace has attained great celebrity in Sweden, and until the suppression of the monasteries, the nuns retained the secret of making it. It was made with gold and silver threads netted or knitted together at first, and finally plaited together. Cutwork and Darned Netting were also made in Sweden from a very early date, and the first, under the title of Hölesom, is still worked by Swedish ladies, who adorn their linen and their houses with it; but the gold-plaited laces have quite disappeared, and the only Pillow Lace now made in Sweden consists of a coarse Torchon Lace resembling the Torchon makes of lace in Bedfordshire, Buckinghamshire, and Germany, made by peasants in the neighbourhood of the convent of Wadstena, and being of no value is only used in Sweden for common purposes.

Swedish Work.—A kind of weaving much practised in Sweden, and useful for making braids of various colours, string straps, and narrow ribbon borders. It is worked in

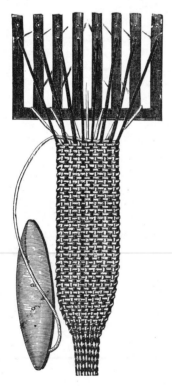

FIG. 746. SWEDISH WORK.

a small frame, shaped like a comb, and with two sets of threads to form the woof, while the warp is made by a thread wound upon a very thin shuttle, passed backwards and forwards, and in and out of the stationary threads. To work as shown in Fig. 746: Choose two colours of silk

thread; for the upper threads let it be red, for the lower white. Wind eight red threads separately up into balls, and pass their ends through the holes made for them in the upper part of the frame. Wind up seven white threads separately in balls, and pass their ends through the gaps in the comb at the lowest part. Tie the red and white threads together in the front of the frame, and pull them out long enough to use. Arrange a lead cushion at the back of the frame, and to this attach the red and white threads securely, pin them down exactly one thread over the other, and at a distance of a foot from the frame, with all the threads perfectly stretched. To keep the red threads divided from the white, put a wooden knitting needle between them on the cushion and a small wedge of wood, a little nearer the comb. Upon a very thin Shuttle wind the warp thread, which make either of black silk or of a deep blue, or colour according to fancy. Attach this to the knot that joins all the threads together, and hold in the left hand; pass it for the first row underneath the red threads between them and the white, and for the second row bring it to the front of the work over a red thread, under a white, over a red thread, under a white, and by so doing bring the white threads forward; for the third row pass the Shuttle through the threads, dividing the red from the white, and so again bringing the red uppermost. Repeat the first and second row to the end of the work. As the threads become used up, alter the frame, push it as far back as it will go first, and afterwards unwind more threads from the balls at the back, being careful always to secure these tightly. First fasten the braid as it is made to the waist, to prevent the trouble of holding it, and then wind it up out of the way. The edge of the braid will be made quite secure, as there being more threads in the upper than the lower line, the warp thread will always twine round a red one at each side.

Fig. 747 is woven in the same manner as Fig. 746, but the threads arranged for the upper and under threads

FIG. 747. SWEDISH WORK.

of the woof are the same as to colour. When the work is finished, DARN the long lines into the braid, passing over five rows and under two. Make these Darned lines of various shades of contrasting colours.

In Fig. 748 the upper holes in the frame are used, as well as the set through which the threads are passed, as in Fig. 746, and these double lines of upper threads are worked up in the weaving as follows : In the return, or second row, pass the Shuttle over two threads, one from

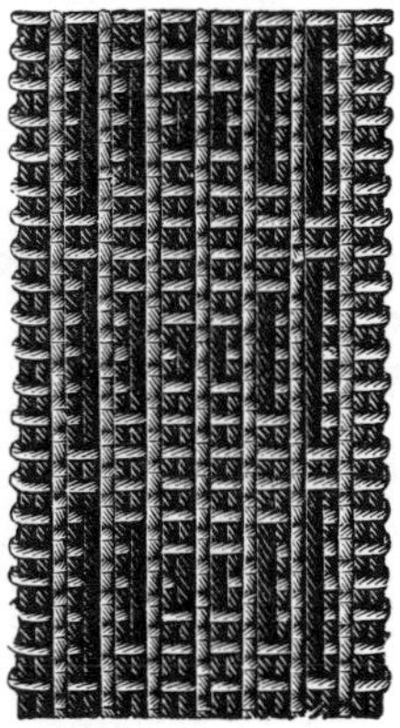

FIG. 748. SWEDISH WORK.

the upper line and one from the double line, then bring up one thread from the lowest line, and put the Shuttle under that, and then over two threads of the upper lines, as before. Darn in the long dark lines when the braid is made.

Swiss Cambric.—This is a cotton material, manufactured at Zurich and St. Gall for a long period before muslins (of which Swiss Cambric is one of the varieties), was produced in England ; but, when made in our looms, we obtained a great advantage over the weavers in Switzerland, owing to our inventions in the art, which were subsequently adopted by them. Swiss Cambric is only to be had in white ; it is a description of Victoria Lawn, and is chiefly employed for frillings, flounces of petticoats and dresses, and also for infants' wear. It measures about 1 yard in width. *See* MUSLIN.

Swiss Darning.—The method of reproducing Stocking-web by means of a darning needle and a thread of yarn worked double. *See* DARN.

Swiss Embroidery.—This Embroidery is the same as is known as Broderie Anglaise, Irish Work, and Madeira Work. It consists of working upon fine linen or thin muslin patterns in Satin Stitch and other Embroidery Stitches with white Embroidery cotton. During the first half of the present century the peasants of Switzerland were celebrated for the beauty and delicacy of the work they produced, but since white Embroidery has been made by machinery, the Swiss Embroidery has obtained but little sale, and the work is dying out as a trade manufacture. For a description of the work *see* BRODERIE ANGLAISE.

Swiss Lace.—Lace was manufactured in Switzerland during the sixteenth century, and some curious pattern books, printed during that time for the use of Swiss lace-makers, are still in the possession of the Antiquarian

Society at Zurich. These patterns are only of narrow Plaited Pillow Laces or of Knotted Thread Laces, and, although Cutworks and Darned Netting were also made, Swiss Laces obtained no celebrity until the revocation of the Edict of Nantes filled Switzerland with Protestant refugees, many of whom were lacemakers, and who established at Nuremberg a lace manufactory, and smuggled the lace there made into France. The lace was an imitation of Brussels Pillow Lace, which was considered quite equal to the real ; also of Point d'Espagne Wire Lace, made with gold or silver threads, and Lille Lace. The manufactory continued to flourish until the end of the last century, but since then the lacemakers have not been able to compete with cheaper manufactures, and the trade has disappeared.

Swiss Lace—Imitation.—This is a machine-made textile, employed in upholstery for window curtains, wall paper preservers, behind washstands, and for short blinds. The chief seat of the industry is Neufchâtel, but imitations of it are produced at Nottingham, made of coarse cotton. Some new kinds have been produced in broad stripes, alternately coloured with designs, and white of the ordinary open-work description. The Swiss Lace produced at Nottingham is very inexpensive, and varies in width ; it may be had to suit the largest windows.

Swiss Muslin.—Muslin was manufactured at St. Gall and Zurich long prior to the production of the textile in England. It is a coarse description of buke or book muslin, much used for curtains, made with raised loose work in various patterns, and also plain. It measures from about 30 inches to a yard in width.

Swiss Patchwork.—*See* RAISED PATCHWORK.

T.

Tabaret.—A stout satin-striped silk, employed for furniture hangings, and much resembling Tabbinet, but is superior to it in quality. It has broad alternate stripes of satin and watered material, differing from each other respectively in colour ; blue, crimson, or green satin stripes are often successively divided by cream-coloured Tabby ones. *See* TABBY.

Tabbinet.—A name for poplin of rich character, the warp being of silk, the weft of wool, and so called because the surface is " tabbied " or watered. Sometimes a pattern is introduced into it. It is chiefly used for window curtains and other upholstery purposes. It is a more delicate description of textile than what is called Tabby, and was at one time very extensively manufactured in Ireland. One variety is woven in diaper patterns.

Tabby.—A coarse kind of Taffeta, thick, glossy, and watered by pressure between the rollers of a cylinder, and the application of heat and an acidulous liquor. It is manufactured after the manner of Taffeta, but is thicker and stronger. The name is derived from the verb "to Tabby," or to wave or water. The beautiful description of silk called *Moiré* is a Tabby; and worsted stuffs, such as moreen, are likewise Tabbies.

Table Linen.—Tablecloths, table napkins, tray ditto, damask slips, damask d'oyleys, and five o'clock teacloths are all included under this denomination. Tablecloths may be had of various dimensions, and either in single or double damask. They may be had from 2 yards square, or 2 yards by 2½ yards, or else of 2½ yards by 3, 3½, 4, 4½, 5, 5½, up to 8 yards in length, so as to dine from six to twenty persons; also, in due proportions, up to 10 yards in length. Tablecloths may also be had of 3 yards square in double damask, advancing half a yard up to 10 yards; also the same, in a finer quality, may be had of 3½ yards square, or manufactured expressly in any dimensions required. There are also altar cloths, and other linen, made expressly for ecclesiastical purposes. Damask slips to match any of the Tablecloths named may be had of 22 inches in width, up to 27 inches. Five-o'-clock tea-cloths, with d'oyleys to match them, are made in white damask with coloured borders, and checked in crossbars of ingrain colours; also in drab, and in coffee colour. Dinner napkins are to be had in single and double damask, of three-quarters of a yard square, also of three-quarters of a yard by seven-eighths, also of seven-eighths by 1 yard. Damask d'oyleys are manufactured in a round, oval, or square form. Tray cloths, of 1½ yards square, and 1 yard by 1¼ yards. Servants' hall and kitchen Tablecloths may be had both in diaper and damask, of either 1¾ yards in width, or of 2 yards. Men servants' thumb waiting napkins may be had 18 inches square; pastry napkins, 22 inches square; fish napkins, 22 inches square; and breakfast napkins, of damask, double damask, and with a small spot pattern, of several dimensions. All these are produced in the best Irish linen manufactories, and the sizes are generally about the same as those produced in England. There are also bleached Barnsley and Scotch diaper cloths.

Tablier.—The French term to signify an apron, or protective covering for the front of a dress; it is tied or buttoned round the waist, and sometimes extends upwards over the front of the bodice.. *See* En Tablier.

Tabs.—A term denoting the square-cut loosely hanging border-trimming of a bodice or skirt, and consisting of a succession of regularly recurring cuts of an inch, or 2 or 3 inches in depth, the three raw edges of each pendant square of material being bound round, usually with a piece of the same material, cut on the bias. Tabs are sometimes made on flounces. In making a Battlemented trimming, Tabs are first made, and then every second Tab is cut out, leaving the appearance of architectural battlements. Also loops of ribbon, or of strong twilled and striped tape attached to the fronts and backs of boots at the top, with which they are pulled on the foot are called Tabs. They are likewise made of leather, and nailed on carriage window sashes, for the purpose of raising, or letting them down, and to the lids of desks for the same purpose.

Tacking.—A term synonymous with Basting, and employed n needlework to designate small stitches taken through two pieces of material, at wide and regular intervals. It is most securely effected by working from left to right, and designed to keep the two portions of stuff in place, preparatory to their being permanently sewn together. Paper patterns directing the cutting out of a garment, or for embroidery, are thus Tacked or "Basted" on; but simple Running from right to left suits best for this purpose. An inferior kind of thread is sufficiently good for the purpose of Tacking, as the use made of it is only temporary. To Tack an article of wear or other use: Lay the dress (for instance) on the table, and the lining upon it, and take up a small piece, through both materials, with the needle, of about one-eighth of an inch at a time, each stitch at about an inch apart, successively, and work from left to right, as above directed.

Taffeta, or Taffety.—A thin glossy silk, of a wavy lustre, the watering process being of the same nature as that for Tabby. It is to be had in all colours, some plain others striped with silk, gold, and silver, and likewise chequered and flowered, the different kinds being distinguished by the names of the localities where they are made, such as the English, Lyons, Tours, Florence, and China Taffetas. The latter is made in various descriptions, and used for apparel, amongst which there is one that is so pliant, as well as thick, that it shows no creases after pressure, and will also bear washing. Our own Taffeta was used in the sixteenth century for costly articles of dress, and in the next century for pages, and for doublets. In Stubbes's *Anatomy of Abuses*, published in 1583, he speaks of all persons dressing alike, indiscriminately, in "silks, velvets, satens, damaskes, taffeties, and suche like, notwithstanding that they be both base by birthe, meane by estate, and servile by calling; and this I count a greate confusion, and a general disorder; God be merciful unto us!" He adds that the ladies wore "taffatie of ten, twenty, or forty shillynges a yard." These were of silk, and those worn by pages early in the seventeenth century were also of a thin description. Our modern home-made Taffeta is of a stout thick make, and usually black. Long silk gloves, extending up towards the elbow, are of this description of material. Taffeta was first imported into England in the fourteenth century. There were also several English made varieties produced, such as the Armesin-Taffeta, the Ell-broad Taffeta, and the Tuft-Taffeties, having a raised pile, and of different widths. Besides these, foreign varieties were imported, such as the Alamode and Lustring black Lyons Taffetas, and others from Avignon, Florence, and Spain, each respectively known by the places where they were manufactured. According to *Chambers's Cyclopædia* (1741), these stuffs were to be had in every colour, and every kind of design, some being striped with gold or silver. The sort described by Ben Jonson (1610) was very delicate in texture:

> . . . . My shirts
> I'll have of Taffeta-Sarsnet, soft and light
> As cobwebs.
> 　　　　　　　　　　*—The Alchemist.*

We also find an allusion to this stuff made by Shakespeare :

> Beauties no richer than rich Taffata ;

and again—

> Taffata phrases, silken terms precise,
> Three-pil'd hyperboles.
>
> —*Love's Labour Lost.*

An imitation of Taffeta was made in the sixteenth century, composed of linen. According to Planché, silk Taffeta was called Tafta in Brittany.

Taille.—A French term denoting the waist or figure.

Tailors' Buttonholes.—These Buttonholes are made after the ordinary method adopted in Plain Sewing, but precede the usual work by laying a piece of fine black cord all round the hole, exactly at its raw edge, and there BASTE or OVERCAST, to keep it in the right position while the Buttonhole Stitch is performed over it. *See* BUTTONHOLE STITCH and the accompanying illustration, Fig. 749.

thread, but leaving a loop at every stitch, instead of drawing it tight. Continue so doing through every loop, round and round, till the hole be filled.

Another variety of this stitch will be seen in Fig. 751,

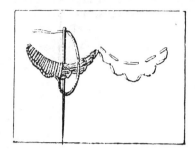

FIG. 751. DECORATIVE BUTTONHOLE STITCH.

as applied to decorative trimmings. The chain, or linked portion of the stitch is made round the outer

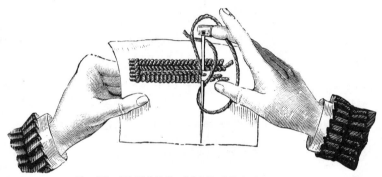

FIG. 749. TAILORS' COAT BUTTONHOLES.

There are two other varieties of Buttonhole Stitch besides Tailors' Buttonholing ; one is the Open Buttonhole Stitch, which is employed to fill in a hole in a

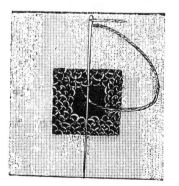

FIG. 750. OPEN BUTTONHOLE STITCH.

tight glove, when there is no piece of kid of the same colour which can be used as a patch. *See* Fig. 750.

To produce this kind of Network, which resembles in appearance a piece of chain armour, insert the needle at the edge of the hole, passing it in downwards, and pointing towards yourself, through the loop formed by the

edge of any article of wear, or other use, so as to form a secure border outside the raw edge, whether of cambric muslin or of flannel. It is also employed to produce small designs on the material, irrespective of any use but that of decoration.

To work the decorative Buttonhole Stitch : Make several runnings within the outer and inner outlines, to be covered, as indicated in the illustration, so as to make a thickness over which to work, and then insert the needle at the outer edge of the inner outline (traced in Embroidery cotton) and passing it straight down at the back, bring it out again outside the outer outline through the loop formed by the thread. If it be intended to form an edging for the border of any article, finish the Embroidery Work before the cutting away of the straight raw edge of the material, but not very close to the work.

Tailors' Twist.—A coarse silk thread, made of several threads twisted together, wound on reels, of 2 ounces in weight each. The numbers used by tailors run from 1 to 8. There are also small reels containing a single thread of 12 yards, equivalent to 1 yard of twelve threads. By this arrangement dealers can keep a larger supply of shades at a smaller cost.

Take in.—*See* KNITTING.

Tambour Cotton.—This is a description of sewing cotton, suitable—as the name indicates—for embroidering the Tambour muslins, and is likewise employed by tailors for the purpose of Basting. It is to be had in skeins, sold in half bundles of 5 pound each. The numbers are 12, 14, 16, 18, 20, 24, 30, 36, and 40. It is also sold in balls of a variety of sizes.

Tambour Lace.—This Lace, chiefly worked in Ireland, where it is known as Limerick Lace, but also at Islington, Coggleshall, and Nottingham. The lace known as Tambour only differs from Tambour Work by the ground that it is made upon, which in the lace is either of black or white Nottingham Net. Since machinery has produced Tambour Lace, the making of the real lace has declined.

Tambour Muslin.—This is a muslin embroidered by hand on a small frame, called a Tambour—a name adopted for it in consequence of the resemblance formed to a Tambourine, when the muslin is stretched over it. Tambour Muslins are of open make, and clear and semi-transparent in texture. The designs produced on them are various, some being in spots, some in small sprigs, and others in long running patterns like delicate wreaths. It may be executed by means of a sewing machine, the work being composed of Chain Stitch. In former times, evening dresses were made of this muslin, but now curtains only. The widths run from 27 inches, to 30 inches, and the muslin is sold in lengths of 12 yards.

Tambour Needles.—These Needles resemble those employed for Crochet Work, and known also as Shepherds' Hooks. They are, however, smaller, and invariably of steel, and are very commonly made of the length of a medium-sized sewing needle. A small handle of suitable size is sold with it, into which it is securely fixed by means of a small thumb screw, and can be released at pleasure, should it be broken. This handle, which is made of ivory, bone, or wood, is hollow, and the opposite end can be unscrewed to supply a receptacle for a small stock of needles.

Tambour Stitch.—*See* CROCHET, page 126.

Tambour Work.—This Embroidery is of Eastern origin, and was worked in China, Persia, India, and Turkey, long before it became known in England, and up to the present date it is still largely employed in the East, and the work there executed is much appreciated from the beautiful colours employed and the labour expended upon it. Until the middle of the last century, Tambour Work, except in Turkey and the Levant, was not known in Europe, but at that time it was introduced into Saxony and Switzerland, where it was worked only upon white muslin and cambric with white thread, and used to ornament dresses, curtains, caps, borders, and all varieties of white trimmings. The peasants of these countries soon excelled in the Embroidery, and their Tambour Work was not only eagerly bought on the continent but large quantities of it were shipped to the East, whence the work originally came. In England, Tambour Work (the name of which is derived from the French, and means a drum, in allusion to the shape of the frame used), or Tambouring, upon white materials with white thread, became an article

of manufacture sixty years ago, and gave employment to the poorer classes in Middlesex, Nottingham, and Ireland, but since the introduction of machinery, and the facility with which the stitch is executed by its means, to make it by hand is no longer profitable. For many years English and Continental workers only embroidered in this work upon crêpe, muslin, and fine cambric, it being considered indispensable that the left hand manipulating under the material to form the Tambour Stitch must be visible to correctly form the design, but when this was found unnecessary, the embroideries with gold thread and many coloured silks upon fine cloth, and other thick materials, were produced, and were successful. Since Chain Stitch has taken the place of Tambour Stitch, the left hand is released, and the material if solid, does not require framing, which is a great saving of time, as the Embroidery is done much more quickly when held in the hand than when stretched in a Frame.

The materials required are Frames, netting silks of all colours, gold thread, known as Passing, white Embroidery cotton, and muslin, cambric, crêpe, cloth, satin or serge.

The old *Tambour Frames* consist of two hoops shaped like the top of a drum, and made either of iron or wood. These hoops are covered with velvet, and fit closely one into the other. The material is stretched upon the smaller hoop, which is then fitted into the larger, and the work thus held cannot become slack. The round hoops are no longer used, except for fine muslin or crêpe, which would tear if lashed to the tapes of an ordinary square Embroidery Frame. For all other materials the ordinary Embroidery Frame is used, and the material attached to it in the usual method.

The real Tambour Stitch, which is now superseded by Chain Stitch, is made as follows : A Tambour needle, which resembles a Crochet needle but not quite so hooked at the tip, is used. Frame the material, and attach the thread to the under side. Put the Tambour needle with the right hand through to the back of the frame at the commencement of one of the traced lines. Hold the thread in the left hand under the line, catch hold of the thread with the hook, and bring it through to the front of the work as a loop. Only allow enough thread to come through to make the loop, which retain on the hook. Put the hook again through the material to the back of the frame, one-tenth of an inch beyond the first puncture. Let it take up the thread there, and pull it up as a loop to the front, and let the first made loop slide over the second and down upon the traced line. With a little practice the stitches can be made with marvellous rapidity. The only things to observe is that the loops follow the outline of the design, are the same distance apart, and that the thread making them is always evenly stretched.

Chain Stitch, used at present in Tambour Work, is the ordinary Chain Stitch described in EMBROIDERY STITCHES.

To Work upon Crêpe : Trace the design, frame it in a Tambour Frame, outline the pattern with CHAIN STITCH worked in gold thread, and then mark out this with an inner Chain Stitch line, made with coloured netting silk.

To Work upon Muslin, Cambric, and Net : Trace the design upon the material, frame it in a Tambour Frame, and then work in CHAIN STITCH with Embroidery cotton.

FIG. 752. TAMBOUR WORK.

Select this cotton so that it is coarser than the threads of the material, as if of the same texture it becomes absorbed and does not stand out sufficiently.

To Work upon Thick Materials : Trace the design upon the material, which either frame in an Embroidery Frame or hold in the hand. Work over in CHAIN STITCH every outline of leaf, flower, or petal with netting silk of a colour matching its shade, and to fill in, work a straight line of Chain Stitch down the centre of the leaf or petal, and then lines of Chain Stitch from the outline to the centre. For the stalks, work two or three rows of Chain Stitch, according to their thickness. Geometrical patterns will only require their outlines, indicated by two lines of Chain Stitch worked close together. These lines should be of two shades of one colour, the darkest outside, or the outside line of gold or silver thread, and the inside of a bright silk.

To work Fig. 752 : This is worked upon dark navy blue cloth, with three shades of ruby coloured netting silk and one of pale blue. Trace the design, and outline all the chief parts of it, such as the rosette and the flowers, with CHAIN STITCH in the darkest shade of ruby. For the scrolls and tendrils, outline them in the second shade of ruby, and in Chain Stitch. Then work a second Chain Stitch line inside the first in the lightest shade of ruby. Work the POINT LANCÉ STITCHES in the darkest shade of ruby, also the filled-in SATIN STITCH, and make the FRENCH KNOTS and the little edging stitches with the pale blue silk.

Tamis.—A worsted cloth, manufactured expressly for straining sauces. It is sold at oil shops.

Tammies.—These stuffs are composed of a union of cotton and worsted, the warp being like Buntings, made of worsted; yet, unlike the latter, they are plain, highly glazed, and chiefly used for upholstery. They are a kind of Scotch Camlet, and are otherwise called "Durants." They are twilled, with single warps, and are usually coarser than twilled Bombazets, and may be had in most colours. Their width varies from 32 inches, to 72 inches, and are mostly used for women's petticoats, curtains, and for window blinds.

Tape Lace.—The Braid and Tape Laces, or Guipures of the seventeenth and eighteenth centuries comprise most of the coarse Pillow Laces made in Italy, Spain, and Flanders, and are endless in variety of design and ground, although all retain the leading characteristics of the design, appearing to consist of plain or ornamental braids or tapes arranged so as to form patterns, and connected together with either Bride or Réseau Grounds. The earliest Tape Laces are made with Bride Ground and simple Cloth Stitch, but gradually these were superseded by very elaborate designs worked as part of the braid-like patterns, and connected by open meshed grounds. The stitches used in Tape Laces are given in BRAID WORK, and the manner of working the lace in GUIPURE LACE.

Tape Measures.—These Tapes are employed in trade, as well as for home use, for the measurement of dress and upholstery materials of all kinds. They are painted, and marked with figures and lines to indicate measurements from a quarter of an inch to 36 inches in length. Those in general use are wound up in small circular brass or boxwood boxes, by means of a little projecting handle or nut. They may also be had in coloured ribbon, with a case made in ivory, mother-o'-pearl, bone, or of some shell, having like those before named a pin running through the centre, on which it is wound.

Tapes.—Narrow bands of linen or cotton, employed as strings. They are of various makes, and are known as Star; India (or Chinese), which is of superior strength, and may be had either soft or sized, and cut in any lengths, and sold in large quantities, the numbers running from 00 to 12; the Imperial, a firmly made superior article, in numbers from 11 to 151; Dutch, of good, fine quality of linen, numbered as the Imperial; Frame, a stout half-bleached linen, and also made with a mixture of cotton; Filletings, a very heavy unbleached Holland, Nos. 3¼ to 10, and sold in various lengths; Stay, which is striped and narrow, employed by tailors to bind buttonholes and selvedges; Pink, made of cotton, numbers 16, 24, and 32,

Greece it was introduced into the Roman Empire. By Latin writers it is called Tapes or Tapete—a word derived from the Greek, and signifying an outer covering of any kind; from this its present name comes. After the break-up of the power of Rome, the making of Tapestry seems to have been discontinued in Europe until the time of the Holy Wars, when the Crusaders found it still practised and used by the Saracens. The manufacture was re-established by them in Europe, and the work for some time was known as Opus Saracenium, or Saracenic, and the maker called Saracens. Up to the sixteenth century Tapestry was worked either by the hand upon close cord-like canvas, and was really embroidery with coloured worsteds, silks, and gold thread, or was made in a loom in a manner that was neither true, weaving, nor embroidery, but a combination of both, it being formed with a warp of cords stretched in a frame and worked over with short threads of coloured worsteds, threaded upon

Fig. 753. TAPESTRY.

cut in any length, or to be had very long on reels, it is used in law offices, and known as Red Tape; Pro Patria, a fine linen of similar make to Dutch, and of the same numbers. Bobbin Tape is made in cotton and linen, either round or flat, the sizes running in uneven numbers from 5 to 21, inclusive. The Indian Tape is twilled, and rather stiff. The Dutch plain, and does not easily knot; but it is less durable than the former. Tapes are loom-woven, after the manner of ribbons; many improvements having in recent years been invented in the machinery employed. Tapes are named by Chaucer:

> The Tapes of hire white Volupere,
> Were or the same suit of hire colere.
> *The Miller's Tale.*

Tapestry.—The making of Tapestry originated in the East, whence it spread to Egypt, and was there largely practised, and by the Egyptians taught to the Israelites. The art was known to the Greeks in the time of Homer, who makes frequent mention of it in his *Iliad*, and from

needles which filled in the design, without the cross threads or weft of true weaving. This manner of working Tapestry is alluded to in the Old Testament, in the verse, "I have woven my bed with cords."

From the time of its introduction into Europe until its final decay, Tapestry formed a very important item in the expenditure of the wealthy, it being used to hang round the walls of palaces and churches, and to lay down as coverings to the floors upon State occasions, when it took the place of the ordinary rush-strewn floor. Every monastery possessed a loom, and the work was reckoned among the accomplishments of the monks, who decorated the sanctuary with hangings, and worked altar-cloths and coverings. The first manufactories of any size established on the Continent were at Arras, in Flanders, Antwerp, Brussels, Liège, and other cities; but the work produced at Arras soon became so famous that the name of that town superseded the name of the work it executed, and for many years Tapestry, wherever made, was known as Arras. Thus, Canon Rock mentions that the Tapestry hangings given to the choir of Canterbury Cathedral by Prior Goldston (1595), though probably made by the monks of that establishment, are spoken of in the description of them as Arras Work. France soon entered the field in rivalry of Flanders, Henry IV. founding in 1606, the celebrated manufactory of Gobelin, which was re-modelled by the Minister Colbert, in the time of Louis XIV., and then became celebrated as a royal manufactory, and one that exists in the present day. The name Gobelin comes from the first artist who set up his looms in Paris, and who was a native of Flanders. His property known as the Hôtel de Gobelins, was purchased by the Crown. The first Tapestry manufactory was established in this country in 1509, by one William Sheldon. This he did, with the co-operation of a master Tapestry maker, Robert Hicks at Barcheston, in Warwickshire. The second attempt to

A species of the same description of manufacture is called Moquette Tapestry, and is of recent date. It is of wool, designed to imitate the genuine Tapestry, and much resembling Utrecht Velvet. The fine kinds are employed for table-cloths, and the thick for carpets. It has a long close pile, and is chiefly woven in floral devices.

Tapestry worked by the needle, as illustrated in Fig. 753, differs but slightly from Embroidery. The stitches are made to lie close together, so that no portion of the foundation is visible, and each stitch is worked over only one cord of the foundation. The Stitches are Tent and Satin Stitch, with the outlines of the design followed by a gold thread, Couched to the surface. The labour of working large pieces for hangings by this method is great, particularly as every design is shaded and worked with colours matching the natural tints of the objects

Fig. 754. TAPESTRY.

establish the industry on a large scale in England was made at Mortlake, Surrey, about a hundred years later, by Francis Crane, at whose death the manufactory was closed, after having enjoyed the warm patronage of James I., Charles I., and Charles II. The work was assisted by foreign artists and workmen, and a small manufactory was instituted at Soho, London, as also at Fulham and Exeter. The manufacture then ceased in this country, until re-established by Her Majesty the Queen, at Windsor, where it is carried on with great success from designs executed by good artists, and particularly from those of the late E. M. Ward, R.A., under the patronage of H.R.H. the Duke of Albany and H.R.H. the Princess Louise, Marchioness of Lorne.

represented. The designs are drawn upon the canvas, but the colouring of them is left to the taste of the worker.

Fig. 754 represents Tapestry made upon a loom. The work that is generally recognised as true Tapestry was made either with an upright or with a horizontal frame. When using the latter, the pattern was placed beneath the cords, and the worker executed it upon the wrong side This make is the one revived at Windsor, and is executed as follows: A double warp of strong white thread is stretched and worked with treadles. Upon a roller beneath the warp, but close to it is the coloured pattern. The worker takes a reel of coarse crewel wool, depresses one of the warp line of threads, runs the wool into the space

P P P

where the colour is required, and brings it out again. He then by a movement of the treadle, brings the depressed warp line above the one first uppermost, and returns his colour through the intermediate space. The threads as worked, are pushed tightly together with a carding instrument, and all the ends of wool are left upon the surface of the work. In this process the worker never sees the right side of the Tapestry until it is taken out of the frame. With the high frame, although the worker cannot see what he is doing while manipulating the threads, he can pass to the back of the frame and there inspect it if required.

Tapestry Cloth.—This material is a description of Rep made in linen, and unbleached; it measures 28 inches in width, and is employed as a foundation for painting in the style of Tapestry.

Tapestry Stitch.—*See* EMBROIDERY STITCHES.

Tape Work.—A modern work, and one that is generally combined with Crochet or Tatting. It consists of forming rosettes with broad or binding tape, and uniting these rosettes with Crochet or Tatting as antimacassars, mats, or other drawing-room ornaments. The materials required are soft untwilled Tape, known as Chinese or Binding

FIG. 755. TAPE WORK.

Tape, the width depending upon the size of the rosette to be made; the widths most used are half an inch to an inch: Crochet cotton, and Tatting cotton of medium sizes.

To work the rosette shown in Fig. 755: Take a piece of Chinese Tape 1 inch in width; cut it to a length of 13 inches, fold it in half-quarters, eighths, and sixteenths, so that sixteen lines are formed down its width. Crease these well to render them visible; sew the two ends

together neatly with RUNNING and FELLING, and take a thread and run it in as a Vandyke line, as shown in Fig. 756, Detail A, from the bottom to the top of the tape, so that each point is upon one of the sixteen lines. Draw the tape together by means of this line, but not quite close, and fasten off the thread securely. Take a Crochet hook and Arden's Crochet cotton (No. 16), and finish off the rosette with Crochet. For the outside, pull out the points, and commence to work at the bottom of one of them. Make 4 CHAIN, †, a PICOT (made with 5 Chain drawn together by putting the hook back into the

FIG. 756. TAPE WORK—DETAIL A.

first made of the five), 1 Chain, 1 TREBLE, into the place where the Crochet commenced, 3 Chain, 1 Treble into the top part of the point, *, 1 Chain, a Picot, 1 Chain; repeat from * twice; 1 Treble into the top of the Treble first worked on the point to make the crossbar; 1 Treble into the point side by side with the first Treble, 3 Chain, 1 Treble into the hollow or lower part of the point, 1 Chain, and repeat from † until the circle is complete; then fasten the first 3 Chain to the last, and tie and cut off the cotton. For the centre: Work 1 DOUBLE CROCHET and 1 Chain between every centre point, catching the Double Crochet into the top of the point.

To make an *Antimacassar*: Work thirty-six of these rosettes and join them by the following small Crochet rosette: Make a CHAIN of 10 stitches, which join up, and work 16 DOUBLE CROCHET into it. Second round —1 Chain and 1 Treble into every second stitch on the first round. Third round—1 TREBLE *, 1 Chain, 1 PICOT; repeat twice from *, 1 Treble into the same stitch as the first Treble, 6 Chain; repeat from the commencement, and work this over every Treble in the second round.

Rosettes can be made entirely of tape. They are cut and sewn up, and run with a Vandyke line as previously described, but are drawn together quite in the centre. Unite them by sewing together at the points, and use the following small Tatted Circle to fill in spaces left between the uniting points. To work the Tatted Circle: Make a loop, work 4 DOUBLE, 1 PURL, *, 1 Double, 1 Purl; repeat from * four times, 5 Double; draw the loop up as an oval and work a second, but in this omit the first Purl and join the work to the last Purl on the first row instead; repeat until eight ovals are made. The number of ovals will depend upon the size of the cotton used and can be varied. Join the Rosettes to the Tatted Circles at their Purls.

Another Description of Tape Work is made by simply joining Vandyke braid to form insertions, like the one shown in Fig. 757. To work: Take Vandyke braid of a narrow width, and sew three of the points close together upon one side of it, and sew together the next three points upon the opposite side. Continue to sew these points together alternately at each side until the length of the insertion is obtained. Make three lengths of tape in this way, and then join them. For the edge,

FIG. 757. TAPE WORK.

work in Crochet 3 CHAIN, 1 SINGLE, join to the point nearest to the one commenced at; then 4 Chain over the hollow, 1 Single, join to the points; repeat from the commencement, and work both sides alike. This last kind of Tape Work when executed with narrow braid, instead of tape, is known as Mignardise Crochet, and is described under that heading in Crochet, page 111.

Tape Lace Work.—In this work the solid parts are made with narrow tape, drawn up into scallops or points, as previously described, and the open parts with Lace Stitches. To work: Take fine braid, a quarter of an inch in width, either white or coloured; cut off 12 inches, which sew up and run as described before, and make twelve points upon both sides. Draw these only slightly together and sufficient to form an open rosette. Take Lace cotton and fill in the centre of this rosette with a series of rounds in POINT DE BRUXELLES. Connect each Point de Bruxelles in the first row to a point of the rosette; work into the loops of the first row for the second, and work three to four rows, gradually lessening the size of the loops, so as to draw to a centre. Enclose this rosette with straight lines of tape. Make these by Running the Vandyke lines upon the tape as before, and drawing them up, but leave as long straight lines. Sew these to the rosettes at the top and bottom, and the rosettes together in the centre of the work; fill in all spaces left between the tapes with ENGLISH WHEELS and ORNAMENTAL BARS.

Tapisserie.—The French term for Tapestry, and for any description of hangings, the word *Tapis* denoting a carpet. *See* TAPESTRY.

Tapisserie d' Auxerre.—This Embroidery consists of working with Berlin single wool in Satin Stitches upon net. It is used to form antimacassars, or to stretch upon a frame in front of fire grates. The designs are chiefly of stars, circles, diamonds, and other geometrical figures. To work: Select a rather open and stiff hexagonal net, either of black or white, divide this off into squares before commencing the work, so that the designs may be evenly embroidered. Take a black or white thread, so as to

contrast with the net, and run it into one row of the net. Miss thirty meshes and run in another line, and repeat until the net is marked out with horizontal lines of thread, then run lines across the horizontal ones to form perfect squares upon the net. Mark out upon paper the outline of the diamond or cross to be worked, and see that it fits into one or several squares, hold this under the net, and make SATIN STITCHES upon the net with single Berlin wool, so as to fill in the figure; move the paper pattern and work in the design until all the squares are full, varying the colours of the wool. Finish off by drawing out the threads from the net that made the squares.

Tarlatan.—A thin gauze-like muslin, much stiffened, and so called from the chief centre of the manufacture, Tarare, in France. It may be had in various colours, and is much used for evening dresses. It was originally an Indian manufacture, which was copied in Europe. The width of Tarlatan is very considerable, measuring from $1\frac{1}{2}$ yards to 2 yards in width.

Tartan.—A term denoting the chequered pattern peculiar to the Scotch national costume, the varieties in the colours, combinations of the same, and the dimensions of the squares in each pattern, distinguishing one Clan from another. There are also Fancy Tartans, which, together with those of Scotch origin, are produced in silk and stuff dress materials, woollen shawls, handkerchiefs, ribbons, stockings, and socks. Tartan woollen stuffs were introduced from Normandy in the eleventh century, and are commonly called Plaids, the material and the chequered patterns and combinations of colours, being usually confounded together under the name Plaid. Before the sixteenth century there is no record of the *Tartan* being the distinctive costume of the Scottish Clans, as it was common to many nations besides. Its use in Scotland, as such, was prohibited by Act of Parliament in 1747, and the Grey Shepherds' Mauds were manufactured instead; the Act was repealed in 1782.

Tassel.—Tassels are used as a finish to embroidered cushions. To make: Take some of the silks or wools used in the embroidery, selecting the greatest number from the shade chiefly used in the work. Wind these round a piece of cardboard 3 or 4 inches wide, and when enough has been wound to make a thick Tassel, push the whole off the card. Thread a wool needle with some silk, twist this round the wound wool half an inch from the top, secure it with a stitch; push the needle up through the top of the Tassel, and fasten the Tassel on to the material with it, and then cut the ends of wool apart that are at the bottom. There are also Tassels which are machine-made, pendant tufts of silk, wool, cotton, thread, or gold and silver cord, sometimes attached to the end of cords, or to a gimp or braid heading, following one another in a row. They are sold separately, or as a trimming by the yard; they may be had in every colour and combination of colours, to suit any article of dress or upholstery, and are made in Chenille, fine silk thread, and silk twist. The worsted sorts are chiefly used for furniture decorations, but are also manufactured in fine qualities for dress.

Blind Tassels are made of unbleached thread, as well as of worsted in white, scarlet, green, and other colours.

Tassel Stitch.—*See* EMBROIDERY STITCHES.

Tatted Lace.—*See* TATTING.

Tatting.—The precise date of the first introduction of Tatting cannot be determined, as, for many years, it did not take any prominent position in the arts of the day, but it has been practised for more than a hundred years, and is a reproduction of the Ragusa Gimp Laces and Knotted Laces of the sixteenth century, of which Knot Work was the first imitation. Knot Work is made over a cord, with the cotton forming it wound upon a netting needle, but in Tatting the stitches are made over a thread, and the thread wound upon a Shuttle small enough to allow of its being passed easily backwards and forwards over and under the thread it is forming the stitches upon.

The English name of Tatting, taken from the word Tatters, indicates the fragile piece-meal nature of the work, as does the French name of Frivolité; but however fragile and lace-like in appearance, it is exceedingly strong, and capable of bearing much rough usage. Unlike Crochet and Knitting, where each stitch is slightly dependent on its neighbour, and one becoming unfastened endangers the rest, the stitches of Tatting are isolated as far as their strength goes, being composed of knots and remaining separate knots, and are very difficult to undo when once formed. The work consists of so few stitches that it is extremely simple, and requires neither thought nor fixed attention when once the nature of the stitch has been mastered, a glance, or the feel of it passing through the fingers, being sufficient for an experienced Tatter. It also has the advantage of being very portable, and can be worked at for a few minutes and put down again without becoming disarranged, which is an impossibility with many descriptions of lace.

For many years Tatting was made as a succession of Knots over a loop of its own thread, which was then drawn up and the stitches on it formed into an oval by being drawn together. These ovals had the appearance of Buttonholes, and were only connected by the little piece of plain thread that was missed after one oval was made and before the next loop was formed. To connect them at all tightly a needle and thread were used, and they were sewn together at their widest part. Two great improvements to Tatting have been made within the last fifteen years; first, the introduction of the lace loops known as Picots, and called Purls in Tatting, which trim the edges of real lace and add much to its lightness; and secondly, the use of a second thread or Shuttle, which enables straight lines and scallops to be worked, as well as the original ovals. The Purls worked round the edge of the ovals and straight lines serve to soften their thick look, and they also are used to connect the various parts, the thread being drawn through a Purl and secured with a knot (where a join is to be made), while the lace is in progress, instead of having recourse to a needle and thread. The second thread or Shuttle enables the Tatter to execute elaborate designs that were quite impossible when only one thread was used. The two threads are tied together, and the first is used to form a loop and make an oval, while on the second the first thread forms the stitches, and leaves them upon it without drawing it up; it is then in a position to make a loop and work an oval if required, and to continue forming stitches upon the second thread whenever the pattern so directs, thus making the work twice as ornamental, and enabling large and wide designs to be formed.

There are two ways of working with the double threads, the one most used is made by winding the first thread upon the Shuttle and securing it to that, while the second thread is either left attached to the skein or wound upon the second Shuttle and remains passive, all the stitches being formed upon it with the first thread, which forms loops of itself and covers them, so as to make ovals where required. In the second plan, invented by Mrs. Mee, the working thread is not detached from the skein, and so joins in it are obviated—and these must be frequent when it is wound upon a small Shuttle and detached from the skein. In this second plan, the second thread attached to the skein is placed above the one wound upon the Shuttle, when both are held in the left hand, and is put round the fingers of that hand so as to form a loop upon which the knots are formed by the Shuttle thread. As the knots are really made from the loop, the waste all comes from that thread. When an oval has to be made, as the loop will not draw up, a crochet needle is used to draw the foundation thread up as a loop close to the last piece of completed lace, and the Shuttle being put through this loop, as in an ordinary join, forms the stitches into an oval.

The Stitch or Knot of Tatting is formed with two movements—sometimes only one of these movements is made—and the stitch so made is known as Half Stitch, but the Whole or Double Stitch is the one almost universally used. It is very simple, but depends upon the position of the hands. Hold the shuttle horizontally in the right hand, between the first finger and thumb, and rather backwards, and let the thread fall from it from the inner part of the right side; pass the other end of the thread, after making the loop (when only one thread is used) over the left hand. Slip the Shuttle under the loop thread, which let pass between it and the first finger of the right hand and back between it and the thumb, and bring it quickly out between the first and second fingers of the left hand. Drop the loop from the last fingers of the left hand, but retain that finger and thumb upon it, give a slight jerk, so as to make the twist just formed transfer itself from the Shuttle thread to the loop, which it should be a part of; put back the left fingers into the loop and stretch it out, and draw the knot up close to the thumb while the Shuttle thread is tightened with the right hand. Bring the Shuttle back over the left hand with its thread hanging downwards, and pass the loop under the Shuttle between the thumb and Shuttle, and back between the first finger and Shuttle, drop the loop, jerk, and draw up as before; when enough stitches have been formed, draw the loop up so that they form an oval. The difficulties of the beginner consists in keeping the thread falling from the Shuttle in its right place, making the knot upon the right thread, giving the proper jerk, turning the stitches to the outside of the oval, and leaving too much or too little space between the drawn up ovals. The fingers at first also seem to be always in the way, and the Purls made too small; but, after a little practice, all these difficulties disappear, and there are no others to contend with.

The STITCHES and TERMS used in TATTING are as follows:—

Double Stitch.—This stitch is the one most used in Tatting. It is made with two loops or knots, and requires two movements of the Shuttle. The first part of the stitch, when used without the second part, is called Half, or Single Stitch. To work: Make a loop of the thread as shown in Fig 758, letter *a*, hold its join between the first finger and thumb of the left hand and the loop over all the fingers; let the unattached end of the thread fall

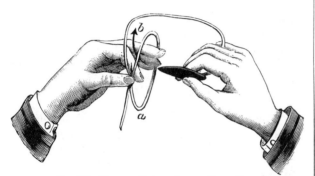

FIG. 758. TATTING, DOUBLE STITCH—FIRST PART.

downwards, and the end attached to the Shuttle arrange upwards (*see* Fig. 758, letter *b*), and let it pass over the knuckles of the left hand, so as to be out of the way of the loop and not interfere with the Shuttle while making the knot. Hold the Shuttle flat between the thumb and first finger of the right hand, and let the end of the thread come from the inner part of the side that is towards the fingers of the right hand; let it pass under the first two, but over and caught by the little finger. Put the Shuttle into the loop (as shown by the arrow in Fig. 758), between the first and second fingers of the left hand, and while pushing the Shuttle out towards the

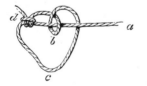

FIG. 759. TATTING, DOUBLE STITCH—FIRST KNOT.

left hand; let the loop thread pass over the Shuttle and between it and the first finger of the right hand; then bring the Shuttle back towards the right hand, and let the loop thread pass back under the Shuttle, between it and the thumb. Do not take the right thumb and the first finger off the Shuttle during this movement, only raise

them to allow of the passage of the loop thread. Draw the last three fingers of the left hand out of the loop, but keep the first finger and thumb still on the join; pull the thread attached to the Shuttle tight with a jerk, and by so doing let the Half Stitch or Knot just made be formed of the loop and held by the Shuttle thread. (*see* Fig. 759, where *a* is the Shuttle thread, *b* the stitch made but not tightened, *c* the loop, and *d* a completed stitch). Draw the stitch tight by putting the left hand fingers back into the loop and extending them. Keep the knot thus made close to the thumb of the left hand, and complete the Double thus: The thread attached to the Shuttle will now be hanging downwards, and not over the left hand. Keep the thumb and the first finger on the loop and the other fingers in the loop as before. Hold the Shuttle as before, but rather forward (*see* Fig. 760), but put it over the left hand and

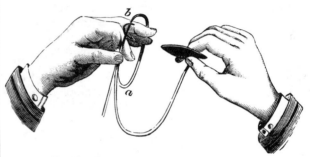

FIG. 760. TATTING, DOUBLE STITCH—SECOND PART.

beyond the loop; push it backwards into the loop *a* (as shown by the arrow *b* in Fig. 760) between the first and second finger of the left hand, and let the loop thread pass under the Shuttle between it and the right hand thumb, and then back to the left over the Shuttle, between it and the first finger. Never lose hold of the Shuttle during this movement, only raise the fingers to allow of the loop passing under them. Take the left hand fingers out of the loop as before, retaining hold with the thumb and first finger; pull the Shuttle thread with a jerk, so that the knot formed is

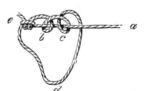

FIG. 761. TATTING, DOUBLE STITCH—SECOND KNOT.

made of the loop thread and runs upon the Shuttle thread (*see* Fig. 761, in which *a* is the Shuttle thread, *c* is the new knot not tightened, *d* the loop, *b* the first half of the knot tightened, and *e* a completed stitch). Put the fingers of the left hand into the loop again, and draw the knot tight by extending them; hold the stitches down as made, and keep them close together. The error likely to be made in the stitch is that the knot is formed of the Shuttle thread, and not of the loop. This is detected in two ways—first from the look of the stitch made, and secondly, the loop will not pull up or open out, but remains firm. The loop thread when the stitches are properly made can be drawn up quite close by being pulled, or can be enlarged to any size. A Double Stitch can be made upon a straight piece of thread, instead of a loop, if the thread is held in the left hand between the thumb and forefinger, and caught round the third finger.

English Stitch.—A name sometimes given to the second half of *Double Stitch*

French Stitch.—A name sometimes given to *Half Stitch.*

Half Stitch.—This stitch is also known as Single. It is not so much used in Tatting as the Double, but it is occasionally required. It is the first part of the DOUBLE, and is worked thus: Make a loop with the thread, which hold at its join between the thumb and first finger of the left hand, and let the loop pass round all the fingers. Pass the end of the thread attached to the Shuttle over the left hand out of the way of the loop. Hold the Shuttle flat between the thumb and first finger of the right hand, and let the thread proceed from it from the inner part of the outside of the Shuttle, that is, towards the fingers of the right hand. Let the thread pass underneath the hand until it reaches the little finger; bring it out here, and let that finger tighten, or loosen it at pleasure. Put the Shuttle into the loop between the first and second fingers of the left hand, and while pushing the Shuttle towards that hand, let the loop thread pass over the Shuttle and between it and the first finger of the right hand. Then bring the Shuttle back towards the right hand, and let the loop thread pass back between the Shuttle and the right thumb. Keep hold of the Shuttle, and only raise the thumb and finger so that the thread may pass beneath them. Draw the left hand fingers out of the loop, but keep hold of it with the thumb and first finger. Pull the thread attached to the Shuttle tight with a jerk, and by so doing, let the knot formed by the movements be made of the loop thread, and see that it runs upon the Shuttle thread. Tighten this by putting the left hand fingers again into the loop, and extending them. The loop that is formed is shown in Fig. 758, *a* being the tight Shuttle thread, *c* the loose loop, *b* the knot made and not drawn tight. The position of the hands to commence the stitch is shown in Fig. 759.

Join.—There are two ways of joining Tatting, both of which are frequently required in the same pattern. In one, the Purls are used to attach circles and ovals, and in the other, straight lines of Tatting are made with the aid of a second thread between the ovals and circles formed with the first thread.

To Join with the Purls: Make a loop, and upon it form stitches until the PURL upon an already finished piece of Tatting is reached, to which the piece in progress is to be attached. Take the Tatting pin, or an ordinary pin or Crochet hook, pass it through the Purl, and with it pull the loop through the Purl, where it is beyond the stitches, taking care that the loop thread is not twisted as it passes through. Draw it through until it will admit of the Shuttle, and pass the Shuttle through it and then

straighten out the loop thread again. If the loop thread has been twisted when put through the Purl, the stitches will not run upon it and cannot be drawn up. If it has been correctly drawn through, the stitches will run upon the loop in the ordinary manner.

To Join with Two Threads: When two threads are used, sometimes both are wound upon Shuttles, at others only the first, or working thread, is attached to a Shuttle, and the second left attached to the reel. It is immaterial which course is pursued, but, in the explanation, the "first thread" indicates the one that does the work, and is wound upon a Shuttle; and the "second thread" the one used to make the lines that join the pattern made with ovals and circles, without the necessity of breaking the thread. To work: Knot the two threads together, make a loop with the first thread, and work upon it with the first thread. Draw it up, and continue to work ovals or circles with the first thread, until the desired number is finished. Draw this up tight, pick up the second thread, hold it between the thumb and first finger of the left hand with the work already made, and keep it as a straight line by catching it down with the third finger. Open the first and second fingers with the thread extended between them, wide enough for the Shuttle to pass, and work a stitch with the first thread in the usual way. Drop the second thread, as the loop is dropped while making the stitch, and give the first thread the customary jerk, so that the knot is formed of the straight thread. Work stitches until the length of the line required is completed; then drop the second thread, and continue the pattern with the first.

Josephine Knot.—This Knot is used in Tatting as an ornament to break the line of a straight piece of thread when the work is done with one thread only. It is made as follows: Make a loop, and upon it work five to seven HALF STITCHES, according to the thickness of the thread used; commence to draw the loop up, but before it is quite drawn up, put the Shuttle through it, then draw it quite close, and a lump or thick knot will be formed.

Loop.—All the Tatting that is made with the help of one thread only is formed upon a loop. After the required number of stitches are made the loop is drawn together, and an oval or circle thus formed. To work: Make a loop over the left hand, hold the join between the first finger and thumb, and let the end of the thread attached to the Shuttle be upwards, and pass it over the left hand out of the way of the loop. Make the required number of stitches, then drop the loop, and hold the stitches lightly and firmly in the left hand, and gradually draw the loop together by pulling the thread attached to the Shuttle. Pull this until the first and last stitch upon the loop meet.

Picot.—A name sometimes applied to denote a *Purl*.

Pin and Ring.—The instrument shown in Fig. 762 is used in Tatting for two purposes, one to draw loops of cotton up with so as to connect various parts of the design, and the other to work the Purl with. The ring is put round the little finger of the right hand, so that the pin can be used without moving the ring. This instrument is not a necessity to Tatting, an ordinary black-headed pin answering as well.

FIG. 762. TATTING PIN AND RING.

Purl.—The Purls in Tatting are sometimes called loops, which rather confuses the worker between them and the loop upon which the circles and ovals in Tatting are made. Purls are the small loops that stand out from the edge of any part of the design and trim it, giving to it the appearance of the Picots made in Needle Laces; they are also used to pass the thread through when two parts of a pattern have to be joined. They are made in two ways, of which the following is the easier: Make a stitch, and allow one-eighth of an inch of thread on both the loop and the Shuttle thread before commencing the next stitch, when the stitches are drawn close by the loop being pulled up, the piece of Shuttle thread between them will stand out beyond them as a small loop. When making a number of Purls, always divide them with a stitch, and be careful to leave the same length of thread for each Purl.

Another way: Take a knitting needle or big pin, according to the size required for the Purl, make a stitch, then pass the thread round the needle and make another stitch close up to the needle. When the knitting needle is withdrawn, the thread that went round it forms the Purl. This plan is more tedious than the one first given, but the Purls made by it are sure to be of the same size.

Shuttle.—The Shuttle is the instrument used in Tatting to wind the cotton upon. It is shown in Fig. 763, and is made of three pieces of bone, ivory, and mother-o'-pearl or tortoiseshell. Of the three pieces two are oval, flat on the inside, and convex on the outer, and these are

FIG. 763. TATTING SHUTTLE.

joined together with a small short thick piece of ivory, through which a hole is bored. The Shuttle can be obtained of three sizes: No. 1 is used for very fine Tatting, No. 2 for the ordinary description of work, and No. 3 for coarse.

In selecting a Shuttle, see that the two brass pins that keep it together do not protrude upon the outside, as they are then apt to entangle the thread while working, and prevent the stitches being easily made. Also take care that the points are close. To fill the Shuttle: Pass the end of the thread through the hole bored in the centrepiece of the Shuttle, and then secure it by a knot; wind the cotton upon the Shuttle by passing it alternately through the two ends, but do not put too much cotton on at once, or the points will gape open at the ends.

Single Tatting.—See HALF STITCH.

Stitches.—The number of Stitches in Tatting are very limited. They comprise Double Stitch, Half Stitch or Single Tatting, Josephine Knot, and Purl.

Tatting with Two Shuttles.—Tatting with Two Threads or Shuttles is a modern invention, and one that has done much to render the work like real lace. Before it was invented all the Tatting that could be done had to be made upon a loop of the only thread used, and then drawn up. This produced any amount of circles and ovals, but as these were only connected with a line of plain thread, the designs they formed were poor, and mainly consisted of Stars, Trefoils, and Rosettes, worked separately, and joined together at the Purls. By the introduction of a second thread, scalloped and straight lines

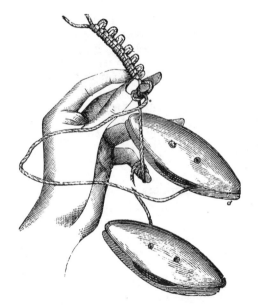

FIG. 764. TATTING WITH TWO SHUTTLES.

can be worked between the ovals and circles, and this is an immense improvement to the work, as the designs are intricate and much more serviceable, and the wearisome joining of separate pieces is greatly avoided. To work with two Shuttles: Wind thread upon both Shuttles, which latter should be of different colours, to distinguish between them. Knot the two threads together, and hold both between the finger and thumb of the left hand. Make a loop, and work with the first Shuttle, as in ordinary Tatting for ovals and circles, but when a straight line between these is shown in the pattern

take up the second thread and catch it round the little
finger of the left-hand to keep it out in a straight line
from the thumb (*see* Fig. 764). Then with the first Shuttle
or thread make the usual stitches, using the second thread
instead of a loop, and dropping it, so that the knot is
formed of it, and stretching it out again over the hand, so
that the knot is tightened. Work upon the straight
thread the number of stitches required, and leave them
without drawing them up as a loop, but draw them
together by pulling the shuttle thread. Then to make
ovals, drop the second thread, and work only with the
first, but be careful to commence the oval close to the
stitches upon the second thread, so that no space is left
between the stitches. Continue to work upon the second
thread when any straight parts of the pattern are required,
and tie it up and fasten it off when no longer wanted. It
is not necessary to attach this thread to a second Shuttle,
as it makes no stitches; it is quite sufficient to leave it
fastened to the reel. Fig. 764 shows a straight line, ornamented with Purls made with the two threads as follows:
Tie the two threads together, and hold both in the left
hand between the thumb and first finger; wind the thread
from the second Shuttle round the little finger, and open
the hand out; then make 1 DOUBLE, 1 PURL, alternately,
upon the straight thread. The illustration shows a Purl
just made, and the first Half of the Double.

Another Way to work with two Shuttles: Tie the
two threads together, and wind up upon the Shuttles, but
let one of the Shuttle threads be still attached to the skein.
In working, always use this as the foundation thread, and
keep it stretched across the fingers of the left hand, or as
a loop, so that as the knots are really formed upon the
foundation thread the thread used most is from the skein.
As the foundation thread will not allow of being drawn
up like an ordinary loop when making an oval, draw the
stitches together with the help of the pin, and form a
small loop, as in *Join*, through which pass the Shuttle.
By using this plan of working, the knots formed by
joining lengths of thread are avoided.

The following selection of TATTING PATTERNS will be
found useful:

Diamond.—The Diamond shown in Fig. 765 is used,
when worked with coarse cotton, to make pincushion
covers, or parts of an antimacassar, and when worked with
fine cotton, for caps or trimmings. For coarse work, use
Walter and Evans' Crochet cotton, No. 1; for fine Tatting,
cotton No. 40. Use two Shuttles, and work the four
corners of the diamond singly. First corner—Make a
loop, work upon it 7 DOUBLE, 1 PURL, 1 Double, 1 Purl
1 Double, 1 Purl, 1 Double, 6 Double, draw the loop up,
and make another close to it, on which work 6 Double,
fastened to the last Purl of first loop; 4 Double, 1 Purl,
2 Double, 1 Purl, 2 Double, 6 Double, draw the loop up,
and make another loop close to it, and upon that work
6 Double, fastened on the last Purl of preceding loop; 4
Double, 1 Purl, 1 Double, 1 Purl, 8 Double. Take up the
second Shuttle, fasten the thread to the end of the thread
at the first loop, throw the thread of the first Shuttle over
the fingers of the left hand, and work with the first thread

upon the second thread. Work 5 Double, and then a circle
made with the first thread only, make a loop, upon which
work 8 Double, fastened on the last Purl of the last of
the loops worked close together; 5 Double, 1 Purl, 5
Double, 1 Purl, 4 Double, 1 Purl, 6 Double, draw the loop
up, and so make the circle, then work over the thread of
the second Shuttle 5 Double, 1 Purl, 1 Double, 1 Purl, 3
Double, 1 Purl, 1 Double, 1 Purl, 5 Double; make a loop
with the first thread, and upon it work with the first
thread a circle thus, 6 Double, 1 Purl, 4 Double, 1 Purl, 5
Double, 1 Purl, 5 Double, fasten to the first Purl made on
the loop made first of the three together; 8 Double, draw
the circle up and work upon the second thread with the
first, 5 Double, fasten the thread so as to form a circle with
the stitches worked on the second thread, and then cut off.
The engraving shows the three little loops made first at
the extreme point of the corner, and the two circles
fastened to these, and upon each side of the large loop
which is made gradually upon the second thread. Work
the four corners as described, and then the centre of the

FIG. 765. DIAMOND TATTING.

design. This consists of four leaves, which touch each
other at their base. To work a leaf: Make a loop, 3
Double, 1 Purl, 2 Double, 1 Purl, 1 Double, 1 Purl, 1
Double, 1 Purl, 2 Double, 1 Purl, 3 Double, and draw up.
Work all the leaves thus, and join them as worked to
the first Purl made upon the preceding leaf, omitting
that Purl in the newly made leaf. Work the oval circles
which connect the corners to the centre as follows: Fasten
the thread to the Purl of a corner, make a loop, work 7
Double, 1 Purl, 8 Double, fasten the thread into a Purl of
another corner opposite to the one on the first corner, work
8 Double, 1 Purl, 7 Double, and draw up the loop, fasten
the thread through the same Purl of the first corner that
it was first fastened to, carry it on to the next Purl of the
same corner, and fasten it to that, then work an oval
circle as before, and continue until the 4 oval circles on
that side are made, then fasten the thread on the two cross
Purls of the centre pattern, and work 4 oval circles on
the other side of the corner, connecting a new or third
corner with them to the design. Work the 8 oval circles

ROMAN WORK.

RICHELIEU GUIPURE.

VENETIAN EMBROIDERY.

still remaining as described, connecting the last or fourth corner into the design with them. When the diamond is completed, draw two threads on each side of each corner pattern, along the lines made at the top and bottom of the oval circles, to strengthen the lines there made, and so that they stand out boldly.

D'Oyley.—The pattern shown in Fig. 766 can be used for a D'Oyley if worked with fine Tatting cotton (No. 60) and the smallest Shuttle; or for an antimacassar when

the work thus: For the twelfth and fourteenth ovals—Make a loop, work 1 Double, 1 Purl, 9 Double, 1 Purl, 9 Double, 1 Purl, 1 Double. For the sixteenth and eighteenth ovals—Make a loop, work 3 Double, 1 Purl, * 1 Double, 1 Purl, repeat from * thirteen times, 3 Double. Work the twentieth and twenty-second ovals like the twelfth and fourteenth, and in the twenty-first oval join in the middle Purl to the thirteenth, fifteenth, seventeenth, and nineteenth ovals, and repeat from the first oval. Repeat until

Fig. 766. TATTED D'OYLEY.

worked with Crochet cotton. A fourth part of the round is shown, and the Tatting is made with one thread and in four pieces, which are joined with a needle and thread and finished with Ornamental Wheels inserted into the centres of the Tatted Circles. To work: Commence in the centre of the D'Oyley, and work the eleven little ovals that are close together first, these are all made alike and the work reversed between each. First oval—Make a loop, upon which work 1 DOUBLE, 1 PURL, 6 Double, 1 Purl, 6 Double, 1 Purl, 1 Double; draw the loop up, reverse the work, make a second loop, and work as before; join every alternate oval in the first and last Purl, omitting those Purls in the making of the new ovals. When the tenth oval is reached, work to the centre Purl, and then join on to the eighth and sixth, fourth and second ovals. Proceed with the work after the eleven ovals are made with the same kind of ovals, reversing them as before, but increase the size of those ovals that come to the outside of

eight patterns or points are made, then take a piece of stiff paper, cut it out in a circle the size of a D'Oyley, lay the Tatting upon it, join the first and last oval and any ovals that touch in the engraving and have not been joined in the work, and gather together as a centre two ovals from each pattern, which connect and draw up by an Ornamental WHEEL made with a needle and thread. Leave the Tatting on the paper and add the fresh work to it as made. The next round will consist of the double scallops that connects the first part of the work to the stars. This scallop is more clearly defined in the engraving in the lower scallops beneath the stars than in the upper ones, as it is there not drawn up so much, both rounds being alike. Commence by working the oval under the one which is attached to the large outside oval at the right of the pattern for the oval; make a loop, work 1 Double, 1 Purl, 6 Double, 1 Purl, 6 Double, 1 Purl, 1 Double, and draw up; go on working and reversing the ovals, and join the three inside ovals; continue until sixteen small ovals are made, join the sixteenth oval to the fourteenth, twelfth, tenth, and eighth ovals, and when working the eighteenth and twentieth ovals join them in the centre, Purl to the sixth and fourth ovals respectively. Join the twenty-second and twenty-fourth ovals together at the middle Purl, and join the twenty-sixth and twenty-eighth ovals with a long Purl to the middle Purl of the two highest of the large Purls in the centre of an outside oval on the last round (*see* Fig. 766). Join the thirtieth oval to the last four inside ovals, and repeat the pattern until all the scallops are made, and then fasten off. The third round is composed of Stars; these are worked separately and joined to the last Round and to each other as the Purls that touch are made. Make each Star with twenty-four ovals; work these alternately for the outside oval. Make a loop, work 1 Double, 1 Purl, 8 Double, 1 Purl, 8 Double, 1 Purl, 1 Double, draw the loop up. For the inside oval: Make a loop, work 1 Double, 1 Purl, 7 Double, 1 Purl, 7 Double, 1 Purl, 1 Double. Join every alternate oval in the first and last Purl, omitting that Purl at the join on the new oval; when the twelve inside ovals are made, draw the centre Purls on them together into a Circle, and make an Ornamental Wheel with a needle and thread inside the Circle. Work the last round of the Tatting as a double scallop, and like the second round, except that in each oval make 8 Double instead of 6 Double, so as to make the ovals larger.

Edging.—(Block Pattern.) Work in Arden's No. 18 Crochet cotton for a three-quarter inch border. The pattern is done with two threads, and it is important that when the first or shuttle one is used, its first stitch is made quite up to the last stitch formed with the under thread, and, when the latter is taken over the fingers for working the first stitch is made close to the root of the loop made with the shuttle cotton. Commence on the second, or under thread; put this round the fingers, and on it make 5 Double, 1 Purl, 5 Double, 1 Purl, 4 Double. Drop the under thread, †, make a loop with the shuttle thread, and on it work 5 Double, join to the first Purl upon the under thread, 5 Double, 1 Purl, 5 Double, 1 Purl, 5 Double, draw up the loop, take up the under thread, and work 4 Double on it. Drop it, make a loop with the shuttle thread, and work 5 Double: join to the last Purl of first loop, *, 2 Double, 1 Purl, repeat from * seven times, work 5 Double. Draw the loop up, make a third loop like the second one, and close to it, and join it to the last Purl on the second loop. Take up the under thread, work 4 Double, drop it, and with the shuttle thread make the fourth loop, thus: 5 Double, join to the last Purl on the third loop, 5 Double, 1 Purl, 5 Double, 1 Purl, 5 Double, draw the loop up. Put the under thread round the fingers, work 4 Double, join to the Purl last made on the under thread before the first loop was commenced, and, still using the same thread work 5 Double, join to the last Purl on the fourth loop, work 5 Double, 1 Purl, 5 Double, 1 Purl, 4 Double. Drop the under cotton, and commence with the shuttle thread to repeat the pattern from †; but after the second group of 5 Double, join to the Purl in the middle of fourth loop, instead of making a Purl.

(2). Work the edging illustrated in Fig. 767 with Walter and Evans's Tatting cotton No. 40, or Crochet cotton, No. 20. Two threads are required, and the work is made in two pieces, the first consisting of the ovals and connecting line, the second of the single oval and line forming the border. To work the Ovals: Tie the two

FIG. 767. TATTING—EDGING (NO. 2).

threads together, *, make a loop upon the shuttle thread, and upon it work 8 DOUBLE, 1 PURL, 4 Double, 1 Purl, 4 Double. Draw this up, and close to it make another loop, upon which work 4 Double; join to the last Purl on the first oval, 4 Double, 1 Purl, 2 Double, 1 Purl, 4 Double, 1 Purl, 4 Double. Draw up, and work close to the 2 ovals a third. Make a loop, work 4 Double, join to the last Purl on the second oval, 4 Double, 1 Purl, 8 Double. Draw this oval up, and tighten all the ovals; then pick up the under or second thread, and upon it work 10 Double. Drop the second thread, and work the three lower ovals with the first thread. In the first oval make a loop, work 8 Double, 1 Purl, 1 Double, 1 Purl, 3 Double, 1 Purl, 4 Double; draw up. Work the second oval, make a loop, work 4 Double, join to the last Purl on the preceding oval, 5 Double, 1 Purl, 5 Double, 1 Purl, 4 Double. Draw up, and work the third oval. Make a loop, work 4 Double, join to the last Purl on the second oval, 3 Double, 1 Purl, 1 Double, 1 Purl, 8 Double. Draw up all the ovals close together, and work on the second thread 10 Doubles. Then repeat the pattern from *, but, instead of the first Purl upon the first oval, join the work to the last Purl upon the third oval. Do this also when the first oval of the bottom set of ovals is reached. For the border: Tie two threads together, and work the single oval with the first thread, the connecting line with the two threads. For the oval make a loop, and on it work 6 Double, join the oval to the Purl left upon the last oval of the three bottom ovals, work 4 Double, join the oval to the Purl left upon the first oval of the next group of three, work 6 Double. Draw up and pick up the under thread, upon which work 8 Double, and connect to the top Purl on the second oval of the group of three, work 8 Double, drop the second thread, and work the single oval with the shuttle thread. Repeat the border from the commencement. Sew the edging to the material by attaching the border line to it.

(3) Work the Edging shown in Fig. 768 with Walter and Evans' Tatting cotton, No. 40, or Crochet cotton, No 20. It is made with two threads, the three ovals being formed on the first thread, and the line connecting them

with both the threads. To work : Tie the two threads together, and for the first Oval make a loop with the thread on the Shuttle and work on it 4 DOUBLE, 1 PURL, 4 Double, 1 Purl, 4 Double, 1 Purl, 4 Double ; draw up tight, and work the next oval quite close to the first. Make a loop, work 4 Double, join to the last Purl upon the first oval, work 9 Double, 1 Purl, 4 Double ; draw up. Work the the third oval like the first, but omit the first Purl, and join to the second oval instead. Draw the three ovals well together, and tie the two threads together ; turn the ovals downwards, and upon the under or second thread work 4

FIG. 768. TATTING—EDGING (NO. 3).

Double, join to the last Purl on the third oval; work 1 Purl, 4 Double, 1 Purl, 8 Double. Turn the work, and repeat the three ovals made with the shuttle thread, join the first to the straight line by passing the thread round the straight line after the first 4 Double is worked, and omit the Purl there. Then work 4 Double and join to the third loop of the first group of ovals, work the rest of the first oval and the others as already described, and repeat the ovals and the connecting line to the end of the Edging. Sew the Edging on to the material with the help of the Purls upon the connecting line.

(4) *Pointed.*—This Edging is useful for trimming ladies' underclothing. It is worked with two threads, and is made by working five ovals divided from each other with curved lines, which are joined in the centre, while the ovals are arranged in a pyramidal form, two upon each side and one as a point. Each group of five ovals is connected by a straight line of stitches. To work : Use Walter and Evans' Crochet cotton, No. 10, and the medium-sized Shuttle. Knot the two threads together, and work upon the second thread, *, 12 DOUBLE, 1 PURL, 3 Double, *, then make a loop with the first thread and work an oval of 4 Double, 1 Purl, 2 Double, then 1 Purl and 1 Double five times, 6 Double (make the Purls of a good size); draw the loop up, pick up the second thread, and work on it 3 Double, 1 Purl, 3 Double ; drop the second thread, and make an oval like the last, but join it to the last Purl upon the first oval, instead of making the first Purl ; draw the oval up and take up the second thread, upon this work 3 Double, drop the second thread and make the third oval like the second, but work 1 Double, 1 Purl, seven instead of five times ; draw it up, and work 3 Double upon the second thread. Work the fourth oval like the second, then 3 Double upon the second thread, join to the Purl last made upon the second thread and work 3 Double. Make the fifth oval like the second oval, work 3 Double upon the second thread, and join to the first oval made on it ; then work 9 Double, 1 Purl, 3 Double ; repeat the pattern from *, but in making the second point join the fourth and fifth ovals of the last point to the centre Purl of the first and second new ovals, and omit those Purls in them.

(5) *Scalloped.*—The Scalloped Edging in Fig. 769 is represented with only one Scallop formed, and without the Crochet line that completes the Edging, and that is worked to sew the Edging to a foundation. The work is so represented, as it shows the Tatting more clearly, and as the Scallop is frequently joined to an insertion, the Crochet line would then be superfluous. To work : Use Walter and Evans' Boar's Head cotton, No. 14. Commence with the ring in the centre ; make a LOOP, work 1

FIG. 769. TATTING—SCALLOPED EDGING (NO. 5).

Double, 1 Purl, * 2 Double, 1 Purl, repeat from * ten times, 1 Double, draw the loop up, and Twist the thread into the first Purl on the ring. To make the outside edge : Leave half an inch of cotton, and then work the oval; make a loop, work 5 Double, 1 Purl, * 1 Double, 1 Purl, repeat from * four times, 5 Double, draw the loop up, leave the same length of cotton as before, and join it to the next Purl on the centre ring and repeat the oval. Make six ovals, joining each to the one preceding it, and to the Purl on the centre ring.

(6) *Simple Double Thread.* — Work with Arden's Crochet cotton, No. 18, and with two threads. Tie the two threads together, make a loop with the first or shuttle thread, work 5 Double, 1 Purl, 6 Double, 1 Purl, 5 Double, draw the loop up, and turn it upside down under the left finger and thumb, then upon the under or second thread close to the loop, work 5 Double, 1 Purl, 5 Double, × turn the work upright and with the shuttle thread make a loop, work 5 Double, join to the last Purl on the first loop, *, work 2 Double, 1 Purl, repeat from * seven times, work 5 Double, draw the loop up, and close to it, upon the under thread work 5 Double, 1 Purl, 5 Double ; make a loop with the shuttle thread and work 5 Double, join to the last Purl of the last loop, work 6 Double, 1 Purl, draw the loop up, and on the under thread work 5 Double, 1 Purl, 5 Double. Repeat the pattern from ×. Work a CROCHET CHAIN as a foundation to this Edging.

(7) *Simple Single Thread.* — Work with Arden's cotton No. 18, or with Walter and Evans' No. 50, and with one thread. × Make a loop, upon it work 5 DOUBLE, 1 PURL, *, 2 Double, 1 Purl, repeat from * five times, work 5 Double. Draw the loop up ; × turn the loop upside down and place it under the finger and thumb, make a loop one-eighth of an inch beyond the first one, and on it work 5 Double, 1 Purl, 5 Double, and draw up. Reverse the work, make a loop one-eighth of an inch from the last made, and repeat the first loop, joining it to the last Purl on the second loop after the first 5 Double instead of working the Purl. Repeat the pattern from ×. Connect the smaller row of loops with a CROCHET CHAIN,

which take from Purl to Purl, and keep these at equal distances apart. Use this Chain as the foundation to the Edging.

(8) See *Lappet.*

Ground Work.—The design shown in Fig. 770 is intended to be used when Tatting in large pieces, such as veils, caps, scarves, and other articles where a ground resembling net is required. The design, if used for a veil, should be worked either in cotton No. 100, or in the finest black machine silk; if for large articles, in stouter silk or thread. To work: Cut out upon a sheet of paper, the shape of the article to be made, and Tat backwards and forwards in rows, regulating the length of the rows by the paper pattern. Commence at the widest part of the material.

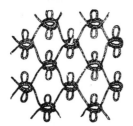

FIG. 770. TATTING—GROUND WORK.

First row, first oval—Make a loop, work 3 DOUBLE, 1 PURL, 3 Double, 1 Purl, 3 Double, 1 Purl, 3 Double, draw up, leave half an inch of cotton, then repeat the oval; work to the end of the row in this manner, being careful always to leave the same length of thread between each oval. Second row—Make a loop and commence an oval, join the second Purl of the oval in progress to the centre of the half inch of cotton left between the ovals in the first row, and finish the oval. Continue these rows of ovals until the article is finished, and where any extra breadth is required, make the threads between the ovals longer; where a slight contracting is needed, make the threads between them shorter.

Insertions. — The patterns given for these Tatting Insertions are chiefly used for trimming underclothing. They can either be sewn to a Tatted Edging when finished, or can be turned into an Edging by a line of Crochet in Chain Stitch being worked along one of their edges, to which it is attached by the Purls at the edge of the design.

(1) To work Fig. 771: In this pattern, only one thread is used. For a coarse Insertion, such as is shown,

FIG. 771. TATTING—INSERTION (No. 1).

use Walter and Evans' Crochet cotton, No. 10; for a finer make, Tatting cotton, No. 30. To work the first oval—

Make a loop, work upon it 5 DOUBLE, 1 PURL, *, 1 Double, 1 Purl, repeat from * four times, 5 Double, draw the loop up, leave a quarter of an inch of cotton, reverse the work, and make the second oval as the first. For the third oval—Repeat the directions, but join the new oval to the first one after the first 5 Double. For the fourth oval—Repeat the directions, but join it to the second oval after the first 5 Double of the new oval is made. Repeat for the whole length.

(2) The pattern shown in Fig. 772 is in two pieces, and worked with Walter and Evans' Crochet cotton, No. 10; two threads are required. To work: Fill the Shuttle with the first thread, make a loop with it, and on it work for the first circle 10 DOUBLE, 1 PURL, 10 Double. Draw the loop up, put the second thread round the left hand, and work upon it with the first thread, 8 Double, 1 Purl, 8 Double. Second oval: Make a loop, work 10 Double, join to the Purl of the first oval, 10 Double: draw the loop up, repeat from the commencement until the length required is made, then re-commence to make the other side of the Insertion. First oval—Make

FIG. 772. TATTING—INSERTION (No. 2).

a loop with the first thread, 10 Double, join to the Purl which connects the first and second ovals of the first piece, work 10 Double, draw the loop up. Take up the second thread, and upon it work with the first thread 8 Double, 1 Purl, 8 Double. Second oval—Make a loop, work 10 Double, join to the same Purl as the first oval was joined to, work 10 Double, and draw the loop up. Repeat the work from the commencement, and join the next two ovals to the Purl which connects the third and fourth ovals worked on the first piece. Repeat until the right length is made, and then make the outside lines. Crochet 7 CHAIN, 1 DOUBLE CROCHET, into the Purl upon the second thread, 7 Chain, 1 Double Crochet into the next Purl upon the second thread, and repeat for both lines.

(3) To work Fig. 773: Use Walter and Evans' Crochet cotton No. 50, and use two threads. Work the insertion in two pieces. Commence by tying the two threads together, and work with the cotton in the right hand over that in the left hand. Commence with the first thread, working upon the second and without a loop, 1 PLAIN, 1 PURL, (turn the Purl downwards), 1 Plain, 6 DOUBLE, 1 Purl, *, 6 Double, 1 Purl, 1 Plain. Turn these stitches all downwards from the first, 6 Double, then turn the work so as to bring the upper edge downwards, and work 6 Double, which fasten on to the last Purl

turned downwards with the right hand thread, thus forming an upward loop. Turn the work downwards,

FIG. 773. TATTING—INSERTION (NO. 3).

draw the thread in the right hand underneath the one in the left hand, and work 6 Double, 1 Purl, 6 Double, turned upwards. Fasten these stitches to the first down-

Lappet.—In working the designs shown in Fig. 774, where is given the size of the Lappet, use Tatting cotton No. 50 and two Shuttles or threads. The Lappet is worked in four pieces and joined. The pieces consist of the large and small Rosette that make the centre, the insertion surrounding them, and the edging round the insertion. To work : Commence with the largest Rosette. Wind the cotton upon two Shuttles and knot the two ends together with the first thread. Make a loop, and work upon it 10 DOUBLE, 1 long PURL, 10 Double; draw up the loop and turn it downwards, *; close to it work upon the second thread with the first thread the scallop that connects the six centre loops of the Rosette together, make the scallop with 8 Double, 1 Purl, 8 Double. Turn the work, and close to the scallop work a loop as already described, but join this

FIG. 774. TATTING—LAPPET (NO. 1).

ward Purl. The first part of border is now completed ; turn it downwards, and work 8 Double, 1 Purl, 8 Double, 1 Purl, 1 Plain. Turn the work downwards, and work 6 Double, which fasten on to the last Purl, turned up. Repeat the work from *, and continue until the first piece is made the length required. Then work the second piece, and fasten it to the first at the Purls between the 8 Doubles, which are repeated twice in every pattern.

(4) See *Lappets* Nos. 1 and 2.

loop to the first one made, instead of making a Purl in it. Repeat from * four times, so as to make five with the first loop, six loops and five scallops. Then work another scallop and fasten both the ends of the thread on to the second thread over which the first scallop was worked, where the scallop joins the first loop. The inner round of the rosette completed, work the outside round. Commence where the first round left off and work upon the second thread with the first thread, * 6 Double, 1

Purl, 5 Double; fasten to the Purl of the scallop on the first round, and then continue with 5 Double, 1 Purl, 6 Double; fasten to the thread between two scallops of the preceding round. Repeat from * five times. For the small Rosette, work like the first round of the large Rosette.

The Insertion.—This is worked in two pieces; the half which touches the edging is worked first, and as follows: Unite the two Shuttles by knotting the threads, *, work with the first thread, make a loop, and upon it work 8 Double, 1 long Purl, 8 Double, draw the loop up, turn it downwards, and close to it and upon the second thread with the first, make a scallop with 6 Double, 1 Purl, 6 Double. Turn the work, and close to the scallop work a loop, but fasten this second loop to the first one instead of making a Purl upon it. Turn the work, make another scallop, and repeat from * fifteen times, but make the two scallops at the lowest part of the Lappet (where shown in the illustration) longer than the others with 8 Double instead of 6. After working the last scallop, fasten the threads to the first loop of the Insertion, and cut them off. Work the second half of the Insertion like the first part, but join the loops to those made in the first half and omit the Purls. Work the scallops with 5 Double, 1 Purl, 5 Double, as they are smaller than the ones first made.

For the Edging.—Tie the two threads together, make a loop with the first thread and work upon it 8 DOUBLE, 1 PURL, 1 Double, draw the loop up; turn the work, make another loop, work upon it 2 Double, *, 1 Purl, 1 Double; repeat from * eight times; work 2 double, draw up; fasten this loop to the preceding one, so that both loops meet. Turn the work, and work over the second thread with the first thread 9 Double to form the scallop between the loops; repeat from * to the end of the Edging.

Make up the Lappet as follows: TACK the different pieces in their right positions on to a piece of stiff paper, join the Rosettes together, and to the Purls upon the inner scallops by passing a thread alternately through a Purl upon the Rosette and upon the scallop, and CORD this thread, so as to make it strong enough. Tack the outer Purls of the Insertion to the part of the Lappet, where it is connected with the muslin, and then BUTTON-HOLE the edge of the muslin over, taking up the Purls in their positions with the Buttonholes. Work the long line that connects the Insertion with the Edging with two threads, make Doubles upon the second thread with the first, and connect the Purls upon the outer edge of the Insertion, and the Purls of the inner loop of the Edging to the straight line of Doubles. Work 7 Double between each Purl, and connect the Purls of Edging and Insertion, except at the extreme point of the Lappet, there work 6 Double, and connect a Purl from the Edging, *, 6 Double, and connect the two Purls, 6 Double, and connect a Purl from the Edging; repeat from * twice, and then continue to connect the two Purls as at first.

(2) Work the Lappet illustrated in Fig. 775 with Tatting cotton, No. 100 for fine trimmings, No. 50 for caps or cravat ends, and No. 20 for coarse work. It is worked with two threads or Shuttles, and in three pieces—

the graduated ovals inclosing the centre of the design, the edging, and the centre. To work the Ovals: Commence with the smallest, which is at the top of the Lappet. Make a loop, and on it work 3 DOUBLE, 1 PURL, 7 Double, 1 Purl, 7 Double, 1 Purl, 3 Double. Draw the loop up, and then close to it work a second oval with 3 Double, join the oval on to the last Purl of the one preceding it, work 8 Double, 1 Purl, 8 Double, 1 Purl, 3 Double. Draw the loop up, miss one-fifth of an inch on the thread, and work a third oval, thus: Make a loop, work 4 Double, fasten to the preceding oval, work 9 Double, 1 Purl, 9 Double, 1 Purl, 4 Double. Repeat this third oval four times, but in the fourth oval work 10 Double instead of 9; in the fifth, 11 Double instead of 9; and in the sixth, 12 Double instead

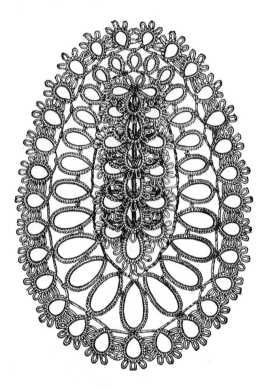

FIG. 775. TATTING—LAPPET (NO. 2)

of 9. Work the seventh oval like the sixth. Slightly increase the distance between each oval as they become larger. Eighth oval—Work 5 Double, join to the preceding oval, work 13 Double, 1 Purl, 13 Double, 1 Purl, 5 Double. Ninth oval—As eighth, but work 14 Double instead of 13 Double. Tenth oval—Work 6 Double, join to the preceding oval, work 15 Double, 1 Purl, 15 Double, 1 Purl, 6 Double. Eleventh and twelfth ovals—As tenth, but work 16 Double in them, instead of 15 Double. Thirteenth oval—Work 6 Double, join to the preceding circle, work 17 Double, 1 Purl, 17 Double, 1 Purl, 6 Double. Repeat these ovals backwards from the twelfth to the second, and then join the first and the twenty-fifth oval.

Form the Edging with a row of small graduated circles joined to the outer Purl of the ovals. Fasten the thread to the first oval, make a loop, and work on it 3 DOUBLE, 1 PURL, * 2 Double, 1 Purl, repeat from * five times, work 1 Purl, 3 Double (make the Purls rather long), draw the loop up, and fasten on the thread to the top Purl of next oval. Work the second circle like the first, but omit the first Purl, and fasten the circle to the last Purl on the first circle. Third circle—Work like the second. Fourth and Fifth circles—Like the second, but work the fourth with 4 Double instead of 3 Double, and the fifth with 5 Double instead of 3 Double. Sixth to ninth circle—Work 5 Double, join to the preceding circle, *, work 2 Double, 1 Purl, repeat from * six times, work 5 Double. Tenth to fourteenth circle—5 Double, join to the preceding circle, *, work 2 Double, 1 Purl, repeat from * seven times, work 5 Double. Fifteenth circle—Work 5 Double, join to the preceding circle, *, work 2 Double, 1 Purl, repeat from * eight times, work 5 Double. Work the circles backwards from the fourteenth to the second for the other side of the Lappet, and fasten the twenty-ninth circle to the first, and the Purls of the scallops to the circles during the working, as shown in the illustration.

The Centre is composed of six pieces, each piece containing five circles of three different sizes. For the first and smallest set of circles—Make a loop, work .5 DOUBLE, 1 PURL, *, 3 Double, 1 Purl, repeat from * five times, work 5 Double. Draw up this circle, and make two others like it, omitting the first Purl in them, and joining them at that place to the preceding circle. Fasten the thread to the first circle, so as to join the three circles close together, and work two little circles close to this join. Make these of 6 Double, 1 Purl, 6 Double. Leave an interval of thread, and commence the second set of five circles. Work this like the first. For the third set work as before, but enlarge the three biggest circles composing it with an extra Purl and 2 Double, and enlarge the two small circles with an extra 2 Double upon each side of the Purl. For the fourth, fifth, and sixth sets of circles work as before, but enlarge each of them every time with an extra Purl and 2 Double, worked to the three largest circles, and an extra 2 Double worked upon each side of the Purl in the two smallest circles. Arrange these pieces so that they overlap each other, as shown in Fig. 775. BUTTONHOLE over the thread upon which they were worked, so as to make it firm, and give a stitch here and there to keep the circles in their right places. Then CORD a thread over the thread upon which the ovals are made, and connect this to the outer Purls upon the centre pattern and to the Purl made in every one of the small circles.

Medallion.—(1) The round shown in Fig. 776 is one much used in Tatting, as with it several articles can be formed; thus, if worked with coarse Crochet cotton No. 12 and a large Shuttle, it will make medallions for Antimacassars, while if worked with fine cotton it forms pincushion covers and mats. To work for a pincushion: Use Walter and Evans' Boar's Head cotton, No. 14, and a small Shuttle. Make the eighteen outside ovals and the small dots before the six ovals forming the centre. First dot —Make a loop, work 2 DOUBLE, * 1 PURL, 2 Double,

repeat from * twice; draw the loop up and turn this dot down under the left thumb. First oval—Make a loop, work 4 Double, *, Purl, 2 Double; repeat from * four times, work 2 Double, and draw close. Reverse the work. Second dot—Make a loop, work 2 Double, join to the last Purl of the previous dot, work 2 Double, *, 1 Purl, 2 Double; repeat from * once and draw close. Second oval—Make a

FIG. 776. TATTING—MEDALLION (No. 1).

loop, work 4 Double, join to the last Purl of the oval, work 2 Double, *, 1 Purl, 2 Double; repeat from * three times, work 2 Double, draw close and reverse the work. Repeat the second dot and the second oval until eighteen dots and ovals are formed, then break off, but leave an end of cotton. To work the centre, First oval—Make a loop, work 8 Double, join to the Purl of the first dot, work 8 Double, and draw up. Work six ovals like the instructions, and join an oval to every third dot. When they are made, fasten off, and then attach the two threads together, so as to join the medallion. An ordinary sized pincushion will require nine of these medallions.

When making a pincushion of the Tatted medallions, the centre, as a variety, can be a Crochet instead of a Tatted medallion. The Crochet medallion shown in Fig. 777 is suitable. To work: Use the same cotton that

FIG. 777. CROCHET MEDALLION TO INSERT INTO TATTING.

is employed in the Tatting. First round—Begin in the centre and make an 8 CHAIN, which join as a round; into this round work 16 DOUBLE CROCHET. Second round—Work 1 Double Crochet, 10 Chain, turn, work a SLIP STITCH in each of the 10 Chain. Work round the the stem thus made in Double Crochet, working three stitches in one to turn the point, miss one stitch upon the preceding row, work 2 Double Crochet, and repeat from * seven times, so as to form the eight raised petals. Third round—Work at the back of the last round behind the petals, make a petal between each of those on the last row, 1 Double Crochet at the back of each, and cut off the cotton when the round is finished. Fourth round— Work 2 Double Crochet at the point of each petal, and 5 Chain between each point. Fifth round—*, Work 2 TREBLE over the first 2 Double Crochet, 5 Chain, 2 Double Crochet in the centre of the last 5 Chain, and 5 Chain; repeat from * to the end of the round. Sixth round—1 Double Crochet in the centre of the last 5 Chain, *, 5 Chain, 1 Treble in the centre of the next 5 Chain, 5 Chain, 1 Slip Stitch in the top of the Treble Stitch, 6 Chain, 1 Slip Stitch in the same place, 5 Chain, another Slip Stitch in the same place, 5 Chain, 1 Double Crochet in the centre of the next 5 Chain, repeat from * 15 times so as to make 16 points.

(2) The small medallion shown in Fig. 778 can be enlarged by using coarse cotton, or worked with fine cotton of the size given in the previous one. It is used to fill up spaces left by larger medallions when making pincushions and antimacassars. Two threads or Shuttles are required to make the design. To work: Commence with the thread from the first Shuttle and make 9 DOUBLE

FIG. 778. TATTING—MEDALLION (NO. 2).

with it upon the thread from the second Shuttle; then take the first thread and work three ovals with it close together for each oval; make a loop, work 7 Double, 1 PURL, 7 Double, and draw up. Pick up the second thread and work over it with the first thread, 9 Double, join to the thread before the first 9 Double, and repeat from the commencement. Work eight points and join the first oval of each point to the last oval of the preceding point.

(3) The small medallion shown in Fig. 779 is particularly useful for joining large pieces of work or

FIG. 779. TATTING—MEDALLION (NO. 3).

medallions. It is worked with Walter and Evans' Boar's Head cotton, No. 14, and with one Shuttle. To

work: Commence with the single oval on the right side of the figure, make a loop, *, work 2 DOUBLE, 1 PURL, and repeat from * eight times; draw up the loop, and work another oval in the same way; leave very little cotton between the two ovals and join them in the first and last Purl Stitches. Leave a quarter of an inch of cotton and work another oval, join it to the last made in the fourth Purl Stitch of each oval, work a fourth oval, and join it to the preceding oval; in the first Purl Stitch work a fifth oval as the last, knot the cotton into the middle of the thread left between the second and third ovals, and leave the cotton so that the next oval will be exactly opposite the second oval; work the last oval, and join it to the preceding one in the fourth Purl, and to the first oval in the last Purl; then fasten off.

(4) The design shown in Fig. 780 is a simple double oval, and is used for the same purpose as the last pattern. It should be worked in the same cotton as the other part of the article it is intended to join. First oval—Make a

FIG. 780. TATTING—MEDALLION (NO. 4).

loop, work 4 DOUBLE, 1 PURL, * 2, Double, 1 Purl; repeat from * nine times, work 4 Double, draw up the loop close, and commence the second oval, which completes the figure. Join to the rest of the work at the centre Purl of both ovals.

Tatting and Tapework Mat.—Small mats are very useful for drawing room purposes. They can be made entirely of medallions, such as are shown in Fig. 776, joined, or with Rosettes of Tatting and Rosettes of Tapework. To form the Tatting Rosette: Use shuttle No. 3, and fine Tatting cotton, No. 60 or 80. The Rosette is made of large and small ovals, the large ones form the outside of the Rosette, and the small are turned towards the centre part. Make a loop and work 5 DOUBLE, 1 PURL, 5 Double for the small oval; draw up and turn the oval down under the left thumb. For the large oval miss one-eighth of an inch of thread, make a loop, work 5 Double, 1 Purl, *, 1 Double, 1 Purl; repeat from * six times, work 6 Double, join the oval up, and reverse the work. Miss one-eighth of an inch of thread and work the small oval as before; then repeat the large oval, but instead of working the first Purl, join to the last Purl of the first made large oval. Work twelve large and twelve small ovals, then fasten off and make the centre, thus: Make a loop, work 1 Double, join on to the Purl in the first small oval, 1 Double, join to the Purl in the second oval, and continue to work a Double and join until all the small ovals are joined on; then draw the loop up and tie the thread firmly before cutting it off. Make ten Rosettes for a small mat, twelve or fourteen for larger mats. To make up the small mat, join nine Rosettes, leave seven of the large ovals in a Rosette free, join the eighth to the eighth of another Rosette, and the twelfth to a Rosette upon the opposite side. Take tape three-quarters of an inch wide and make a Rosette with it, as shown in TAPEWORK, make 8 Tape Rosettes, join them together and to the Tatted Rosettes between Purls 8 and 12. Then take the Tatted Rosette that is left and put it into the circle left inside the Tape Work and join it to it.

Tatting Combined with Crochet and Lace Stitches.— The description of Tatting shown in Fig. 781 is used for trimmings, and is worked with a Crochet Edging, and with Tatted Circles joined with Lace Stitches, worked upon the thread left between the Tatted Circles. Work with Tatting cotton No. 50. Commence the work with the circles. Make a loop, upon which work 13 DOUBLE; draw the loop up, miss two-thirds of an inch of thread and make a second circle like the first, and repeat for the length required for the row, always leaving the same sized piece of thread between the circles. Fasten a second row

FIG. 781. TATTING—CROCHET AND LACE.

of circles to the first row, thus: Work a circle as before on the thread one-third of an inch from the first row, miss the same distance after the circle is worked, and fasten the thread to the second circle on the preceding row and repeat to the end. To fasten the thread to the already made circles, draw it through them so as to form a loop, and put it through the loop thus made. Make the third row of circles like the second, one-third of an inch of thread between the new circles and the ones on the second row. Finish the centre part of the Tatting with a line of thread without circles, fasten this to each circle, leaving two-thirds of an inch between each.

To work the Edging: Fasten the thread to the first row of the circles in the centre of the thread, miss a tiny bit of thread, and work the small Josephine Knot thus: Make a loop, work 5 SINGLE upon it, and draw the loop up quite tight, putting the thread downwards between the loop. Leave a tiny bit of thread and work a circle, make a loop, work 3 DOUBLE, 1 PURL, 2 Double, and 5 Purl, divided by 2 Double, 2 Double, 1 Purl, 3 Double, draw up; miss a tiny bit of thread and work another Josephine Knot,

then miss the same amount of thread; make a small loop and upon it work 8 Double, then turn, and make a loop, upon which work 3 Double, 9 Purl, divided by 2 Double, 3 Double; draw up this loop, and join it to the last made small loop. Break off the cotton, connect it with the other side of the small loop to the centre part of the thread left in the first row, and repeat the edging from *, only omitting the second Purl of the first circle, and joining it to the last Purl on the preceding circle, as shown in the illustration. Make the upper edging of CROCHET. First row—Connect the cotton to the centre part of the thread left in the third row of the centre with a DOUBLE CROCHET, *, work 5 CHAIN and 1 Double Crochet into the centre part of the thread between the next two circles; repeat to the end of the row. Second row—1 TREBLE into every other Chain in the first row.

To work the Lace Stitches: TACK the work upon a piece of stiff paper, and upon each side of the thread left between the circles work POINT DE GRECQUE, each stitch an equal distance apart. Work the same stitch along the two edging lines.

To Wash Coarse Tatting.—Put it in a saucepan with a lather of soap and cold water, and leave it until the water boils; then rinse it, and, if it looks yellow, pass it through blue water; when nearly dry, pull it out and iron it, placing a handkerchief between it and the iron.

To Wash Fine Tatting.—Take an ordinary wine bottle and sew several folds of flannel upon it. To this flannel TACK the Tatting, taking care to stretch out the design so as to keep it in its right positions. Make a lather with curd soap and thoroughly rub this into the Tatting; then put the bottle into a saucepan and boil it. Rinse the soap well away from it, and when it is nearly dry, untack it from the flannel, stretch it out, and lay a handkerchief over it, and then iron it. Open out all the Purls with a Pin.

Tatting.—A description of stout matting of Indian manufacture, is employed for doorways, and kept wet. The native name for this textile is *Tattie*, whence our word Tatting is derived.

Tatting Shuttle.—This kind of appliance resembles somewhat a Netting Needle in the mode of its employment, and reception of the cotton or cord; but instead of a long narrow and pointed form, it is of a flattish, and of rather an oval shape, a little pointed at the ends. It consists of two sides, united in the centre by a piece of the same material, whether of ivory, bone, or wood. The thread is wound round this central part of the Shuttle.

Taunton.—A description of broadcloth, so called from the town in Somersetshire where it was originally manufactured.

Tent Stitch.—A stitch employed in Tapestry Work and in fine Embroideries. It is produced by crossing over one strand of canvas in a diagonal direction, sloped from right to left, and resembles the first half taken in Cross Stitch. When beads are sewn upon canvas this stitch is employed. *See* BERLIN WORK and EMBROIDERY STITCHES.

Terry Velvet.—A textile made entirely of silk, and having fine ribs or cords on the best side. Inferior kinds are made with a cotton back. Chiefly used for trimmings, particularly for children's garments; and can be had in most colours. It is not to be recommended in black. Although called velvet, it has not the nap or pile, that is a distinguishing characteristic of such a textile. When employed as a trimming, it is cut on the bias. The width of the material is about 27 inches.

Tête de Bœuf.—*See* Embroidery Stitches.

Tête de Mores.—A very narrow Guipure Lace made in the sixteenth century, but now obsolete.

Textile.—A generic term, signifying any stuff manufactured in a loom, of whatever material, produced by weaving the products of the animal, or vegetable worlds, into cloth, webs, or any other make of fabric, for clothing, upholstery, or other use. Textiles may be produced in wool, hair, fur, silk, cotton, flax, hemp, mallow, the filaments of leaves and barks, and the coating of pods and tree-wool; also a fine silk thread, the chief manufacture of which is carried on at Palermo, spun by, and procured from, the *Pinna marina*, a large mussel, found on the coast of Italy. The Textile made of this silk was known by the name of Byssus by the ancients. A kind of vegetable silk is procured from the Paper-Mulberry tree of Japan, and a strong cloth from Hop-stalks in Sweden; Nets and Fringes from mulberry fibres in Louisiana, as also fine cloth from the same tree in Otaheiti. In France a cloth is made from the fibres of the pine-apple, and one from the stalks of nettles. In Yorkshire, as elsewhere in England, a fine firm russet-coloured cloth is produced from the cotton-grasses. Textiles are also made of very fine gold and silver wire.

Thibet Cloth.—A stuff made of coarse goat's hair. Also a fine description of woollen cloth, used for making women's dresses; it is a kind of Camlet.

Thickset.—This is a description of fustian, employed for men's dress, of the working class. Like velveret, it is a kind of cotton velvet.

Thimble.—An appliance fitted as a guard to the top of the right-hand middle finger, and for the purpose of pressing a needle through any material to be sewn. The name is derived from the Scotch *Thummel*, from *Thumbbell*, a bell-shaped shield, originally worn on the thumb; the practice is still maintained among sailors. The Dutch have the credit of the invention; and in 1695 one John Lofting came over from Holland, and established a manufactory of Thimbles at Islington. They are of two forms, the closed, or ordinary bell-shaped, and the open, such as employed by tailors and upholsterers. They are made in gold, silver, plated steel, brass, celluloid, bone, ebony, ivory, steel, brass-topped, &c., and are pitted with little cells to receive the blunt end of the needle. Thimbles are made in various sizes; and all common sorts are sold by the gross, but may be purchased singly. Gold thimbles are sometimes set round with

turquoises and other gems. Those made of ebony, ivory, and celluloid are very suitable for embroidery and lace work. The former are known by the name of "Nuns' Thimbles." Those of brass and steel are used by tailors and upholsterers, and by the working class in general. In England Thimbles are made by means of moulds, and then of a stamping and punching machine. In the fourteenth century our Thimbles were made of leather, and in the present day a leather band worn round the hand, and having a thicker part for the hollow of the palm, is employed by shoemakers. Thimbles were called Fingerlings so long as they were made of leather; and when, in the fourteenth century, they were superseded by metal, the name Thimble was adopted. There are two allusions made to Thimbles by Shakespear—one in *King John* and another in the *Taming of the Shrew*. In the former we read—

> Your ladies and pale visag'd maids,
> Like amazons, come tripping after drums;
> Their thimbles into armed gauntlets change,
> Their needles into lances.
> —*King John.*

> And that I'll prove upon thee,
> Though thy little finger be armed in a Thimble.
> —*Taming of the Shrew.*

Thorns.—Used in Needlepoints to decorate the Cordonnets and raised parts of the lace. *See* Spines.

Thread.—This is a comprehensive term denoting the finest description of manufactured fibre, or filaments, of whatever material it may be composed, for the purpose of needlework. In the manufacture of it several strands are doubled and twisted in a frame, the yarn being moistened with a paste of starch, which has been passed over flannel, to absorb the superfluous moisture. The yarns are then brought together by rollers, slightly compressed, and twisted together; and the thread is made up in hanks, skeins, balls, or wound on reels. Silk twist is made up in hard round bars, of about 5 or 6 inches in length. Thread is, however, a term which is distinctively applied to Flax; thus, Thread or Lisle thread stockings, or gloves, are only made of fine Linen Thread. Fine gold and silver wire, flattened, or cotton, silk, wool, and worsted yarns prepared for needlework are all called Thread in trade. A yard measure of cotton Sewing Thread contains 54 inches; of the real Linen Thread, 90 inches; of Worsted, 35 inches. Silk Sewing Thread is usually twisted in lengths of from 50 to 100 feet, with hand reels, somewhat similar to those employed in rope making. The manufacture of white Sewing Thread, known as Ounce Thread—to distinguish it from different kinds of coloured and white Thread then made in Aberdeen and Dundee—was begun about 1750, having been introduced into this country from Holland in 1725, and carried on for a long time privately in the family of a lady, who first learned the secret, and began the trade. This Ounce Thread had been originally called Nuns' Thread or Sisters' Thread, so designated because it was spun by the Nuns of Flanders and Italy. The earliest mention of Thread is in connection with Paris, Cologne, Bruges, and Lisle, in the fifteenth century, and subsequently in the seventeenth century at Coventry. At the present day the largest quantity is made in Scotland.

When flax is spun for weaving, it is termed Yarn, and when two of these strands are twisted together for sewing, it is called Sewing Thread or Twist. Amongst the various makes are the strong Stitching Thread; the much-twisted Wire Thread, used by bonnet-makers; the Shrewsbury, in various colours, and sold in pound papers, for strong coarse work; the Scotch, in all colours and thicknesses, and the Lace Thread. Ordinary Linen Thread, is to be had unbleached, black, and drab, and in soft satin finish. It is sold by the dozen pounds, done up in half-ounce knots, and also in small skeins; when sold in small quantities, it should be by the number of skeins. Carpet Thread is a heavy-made three-cord, and may be had in unbleached, black, drab, yellow, red, brown, and green; in soft and satin finish. Flourishing Thread is used for repairing table linen, and for this purpose the most useful sizes are 4, 5, and 6. It is also used for Embroidery on linen and flannel, not only on account of its flossy appearance, but as it does not shrink when washed.

Thread Canvas.—This textile is manufactured from hemp, and is woven in the usual sizes and widths. A fine description made of flax is also to be procured.

Threader.—*See* NEEDLE-THREADER.

Thread Lace.—Also known as Dentelle de Fil. The term is applied indifferently to all laces made with flax thread to distinguish them from laces made with gold and silver or cotton threads, whether of the Pillow or Needle. Laces made with flax are much superior to those of cotton, as the latter stiffens and becomes thick when cleaned, while the former always retains its flexibility and clearness. Much of the beauty of the lace depends upon the fineness of the thread employed in its make, and the supremacy of the laces of Flanders over those of France was partly owing to the flax grown in Brabant being of superior quality. This was steeped in the River Lys, whose waters were unusually clear, and then spun in a dark and damp cellar, the thread breaking if exposed either to warmth or light. Mechlin, Lille, and Brussels Lace are all made of this flax thread, and frequently costs £240 a pound, while the thread used for Honiton Lace, until a recent period, was obtained from Antwerp at a high price.

Three Cord.—*See* BRAID or TWIST.

Thrown Silk.—Raw hanks of silk, consisting of two or more strands, tossed and swung to and fro in the process of being doubled, twisted, and reeled; and so transformed from roughly assorted hanks, as imported into this country, into a suitable condition for the use of the weaver. Thrown Silk is otherwise known as Organzine. Those employed in throwing the raw silk are called Throwsters. When thrown, the strands are twisted in a contrary direction to that in which the strands, or singles, are twisted.

Thrums.—The waste fringe-like ends of thread, cut off by weavers from the cloth in process of weaving, or the fringed edge of the material. It also signifies a thick nap on a woven textile. A description of hat was worn in the time of Queen Elizabeth having a long pile-like shaggy fur, which was called a "silk thrummed hat," and to it allusion is made by Quarles:

> Are we born to thrum caps or pick straw?

Likewise we find the word and its signification employed in connection with it in *Midsummer Night's Dream*:

> Come, sisters, come;
> Cut thread, and thrum.

Ticking.—A strong material made both in linen and cotton, for the purpose of making mattresses, feather beds, pillows, and bolsters; and is usually woven in stripes of blue and white, or pink and white. It is also used for window and door blinds, and for this purpose can be procured in other stripes of fancy colour. Ticking is of Jean make, or basket-woven. It measures from about 32 inches to a yard wide. When employed in making feather or down pillows the cloth sack should be well rubbed with beeswax on the wrong side, after the sewing up of one end and the two sides, before being filled with the feathers. Ticking is much used as a foundation for Silk Embroidery, as the lines or stripes in the cloth render the work easy, and contribute to the formation of the various designs. *See* TICKING WORK.

Ticking Work.—A modern Embroidery worked in imitation of the bright and elaborate embroideries executed in Arabia, Persia, and Turkey, and one which reproduces the gorgeous colouring for which they are celebrated, without the same amount of labour being expended. The work is intended to be bright and therefore is formed of bright colours, but these are selected with a due regard to their contrasts, and care is taken that they are such as would be found in Eastern embroideries, and not those obtained from aniline dyes, such as gas green, mauve, magenta, and startling blues. The work is used for summer carriage rugs, garden chairs, banner screens, couvrepieds, parasol covers, and such small articles as mats, bags, and cushions, and it is made with ordinary blue and white Ticking, or white and grey Ticking, or with French Ticking, which is woven with bright lines of red and orange colours, instead of being only of subdued tints. Besides the Ticking, which is used as a foundation, bright coloured ribbons, braids, and ribbon velvet, varying from half an inch to an inch in width, are required; also narrow gold braids and purse silk of many colours. For very narrow work, such as is required for needlecases and other small articles, what is known as Breton ribbon and China ribbon are used, as these are woven in quarter inch widths. The braids or ribbons are sewn down at intervals upon the Ticking, following the lines woven in it, so as to allow of the foundation appearing between them; they are then secured either with narrow gold braid stitched down to each edge, or they are edged with lines of stitches worked in the purse silks, and finished off in the centre with Embroidery Stitches. The Ticking left exposed is also embellished with Embroidery Stitches, and there is no limit to the variety of stitches or colour that can be blended together in one piece of work. Black velvet and dark velvets add considerably to the effect by their use, as do the gold braids and gold twist, but odd lengths of

FIG. 782. TICKING WORK (No. 1).

ribbon and braid will make very good patterns of Ticking Work.

Fig. 782 shows the general effect of a number of lines of Ticking covered with fancy stitches, and Figs. 783 and 784

(1) To work Fig. 782, Select a grey and white Ticking, and to cover up the grey lines sew on a dark blue

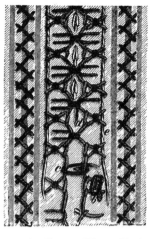

FIG. 783. TICKING WORK (No. 2).

velvet strip, then a maroon or ruby velvet strip, a dark green ribbon or braid, a scarlet braid, a bronze braid, a

FIG. 784. TICKING WORK (No. 3).

give some of the combinations of stitches that can be worked upon one or several pieces of silk or braid.

blue braid and a scarlet braid, edge each of these upon both sides with a narrow silk braid of an old gold colour (not yellow). Work upon the velvet strips in old gold silk with FRENCH KNOTS, and work SATIN STITCH made as a cross. Work a line of HERRINGBONE STITCH in pale blue silk upon the white lines of Ticking between the velvets, which repeat between the green and scarlet braid and the blue and scarlet braid; work the eight pointed stars in scarlet black silk, and make the black silk stars upon the scarlet and braid.

(2) To work Fig. 783 : This pattern is worked upon Ticking woven in narrow lines; the centre part made upon a coloured braid an inch and a half in width, and the side lines over the Ticking lines. Work the side lines in scarlet silk and in HERRINGBONE STITCH, and for the centre commence at the line marked *a* in the illustration. Make two long BUTTONHOLE STITCHES, one-eighth of an inch apart, and then two more of the same length, with a loose loop between, at the distance of half an inch from the first two. Repeat these two Buttonholes down one side, and then upon the other side, and make the long loops always opposite each other. Fasten the thread off securely, and commence again at the spot marked *b*. OVERCAST the two Buttonholes at that place together, and then run the needle under the work to *c*, where Over-

(4) To work Fig. 785 : This is a variety of Ticking Work into which Chain Stitch is introduced, and is worked with three shades of one colour. Make the dark narrow lines of gold or black braid of the narrowest width Work vandyke lines between them, which unite in the centre with a CROSS STITCH with the darkest colour; work the scroll in CHAIN STITCH in the lightest colour, and the outer line of the pine-shaped patterns in the darkest colour. Fill their centres with FRENCH KNOTS, and make in the medium colour, the three stitches together with SATIN STITCH, in a colour matching the Chain Stitch.

(5) The design shown in Fig. 786 is intended to be worked over Ticking woven with the ordinary sized

FIG. 786. TICKING WORK (NO. 5.)

narrow lines. To work: Lay down upon the blue lines

FIG. 785. TICKING WORK (No. 4).

cast the two long loops (one from each side) together. Then make the two lines upon each side of this centre spot with SATIN STITCH, and work the two Buttonholes together above the *c*. Repeat to the end of the row. Take a different coloured silk or thread, and work in the centre of the pattern a line of TÊTE DE BŒUF STITCHES, putting one stitch into each vacant spot, as shown by the letter *d*. With the same coloured silk, RUN the outer lines of the pattern marked *e*, and secure these lines by passing them through the two Buttonhole Stitches. Use three coloured silks for this design, two in the centre pattern and one for the Herringbone.

(3) To work Fig. 784 : This is worked either upon bright French ticking or upon broad ribbon of a bright colour. The scroll designs upon each side of the centre match each other in colour; work them in POINT RUSSE and FRENCH KNOTS. Work the scroll in bronze silk, and the wreath in gold coloured silk. For the centre, which is upon the white part of the Ticking, make the vandyke lines edging it in blue, red, and green, the sprays in red, and the rosette, and diamond, in deep ruby, with pale blue lines as centres.

in the Ticking, black, scarlet, green, blue, and golden brown braids alternately, and over these work Stars and FRENCH KNOTS with yellow filoselle. Work a double vandyke line in filoselle of shades matching the braids over the white lines in the Ticking; make each line of vandyke with one CHAIN STITCH, as shown in the illustration.

(6) The design given in Fig. 787 is an Embroidery pattern that is used to work over the brightly woven lines of French Ticking. To work: Trace the outline upon

FIG. 787. TICKING WORK (NO. 6).

a band of orange or red colour, and work with brown filoselle and with POINT RUSSE. Use only one coloured filoselle for each strip of Embroidery, but change that colour in every strip.

(7) Fig. 788 is an Embroidery pattern worked out with fine braid and Embroidery Stitches, and is used to cover the broad lines of the brightly woven French Ticking. To work: Trace the design and STITCH over the chief outlines the very narrowest black braid, between the lines of braid in the long ovals. Make FRENCH KNOTS in filoselle, and between the lines of braid surrounding the circle, make a double curved line of CHAIN STITCHES in filoselle. Work the centre flower in SATIN STITCH and French Knots, and in natural colours. Work the wreath passing over the long ovals and the lines forming diamonds in their centres in filoselle contrasting in shade to the Ticking, and fasten down each point of the diamond with a CROSS STITCH of black filoselle.

Tied Work.—A work not much practised in England, and introduced from the Continent, where it is used to make fringes to Crochet and Knitting, or for white and dark materials, according to the fringe being made with white cotton, or black or coloured worsteds and silks. The implements required for the work are long narrow frames made with broad pieces of wood placed from 3 to 6 inches apart, a Netting Mesh and needle, and skeins of silk, worsted, or cotton. The frames used for Tied Work require a row of brass hooks fastened along the inner edge of the upper piece, and the outer edge of the lower piece of wood; these hooks are placed half an inch apart and arranged upon the upper and lower wood so as to be opposite to each other. To work: NET with a half inch Mesh five rows of Netting the length required for the fringe. In the fifth row wind the thread twice round the Mesh to make those loops double the length of the other rows. Sew the knots of the first row of Netting on to a piece of narrow black or white braid, opening them out so that the loops are properly stretched. Fasten this piece of braid with drawing pins to the top of the frame quite at the edge, and see that each knot is above and between the row of hooks upon the lower edge of the top part of the frame, and fasten the row of hooks into the second row of knots, and fasten the last row of knots (those belonging to the long loops) over the hooks on the bottom part of the frame, thus leaving the Netting rows well stretched and tight between the two parts of the frame. Take a skein of silk or worsted, cut it once across, divide the strands so as to obtain a tolerable thickness (too many will make the fringe heavy, too few poor, so that no exact number of strands can be given, as the number depends upon the material used). Fasten one end of these strands tightly to the first top hook, carry the skein down to the hook on the lower part of the frame, beyond the one underneath the top hook, twist it backwards round this, and take it up to the top again, miss a hook, and pass it over the next one; bring it down to the bottom again, miss a hook, and twist it backwards round the next hook. Repeat for the length of the frame and there secure the skein to prevent that part of it wound round the hooks from slipping, and so that the work can be continued. Take a second skein and repeat the winding, using up the hooks not covered the first time. Thread a darning needle wtih a piece of worsted or silk, and make with it a good knot under the first hook on the top line. Draw together both sides of the skein that went over the hook with this

FIG. 788. TICKING WORK (No. 7).

knot, and wind the thread several times round so as to make a good knot, and secure it into the Netting Knot. Run the needle and thread to the Netting Knot on the second netting row, and make a knot there of the skeins that cross at that place, run the thread diagonally down to the Netting Knot on the third row, beyond the one first secured on the second row, and make a knot there with the two skeins that cross at that place. Repeat these knots, always working up and down the netting rows diagonally, and carefully securing each knot made with the threaded needle to the knot beneath it belonging to the Netting. When the work is finished, cut the worsted knots made on the second, third, and fourth rows, but be careful not to cut the netted foundation. Cut the first, second, and third rows of knots both above and below them, and fluff up the little balls of wool thus left in the same way as in DAISY MATS; for the fourth row leave only the already cut piece above the fourth knot; cut the worsted secured to the hooks on the lower part of the frame, so as to make tassels as a finish. Any length of this Tied Work can be made as long as the new strands or skeins are always added at the lower hooks, where as that part forms the tassels, the join will not interfere with the strength of the fringe.

Tiffany.—A thin description of semi-transparent silk textile, resembling gauze. It is of French manufacture.

Tiffeny.—A description of muslin, of open make, and a pale écru colour. It is of double width, and is employed for Needle Embroidery.

Tinsel.—A term used to signify a thin and loosely-woven material, formed partly or entirely of gold and silver threads, and introduced into embroidery; but chiefly employed for theatrical purposes. The dress of the harlequin is composed entirely of tinsel. We find allusions to this bright and sparkling material in some of our classical authors. Tinsel can be purchased in thin sheets for application to Net, Gauze, and Velvet; or for the wrappers of bonbons and crackers. The use of Tinsel was limited in the reign of Henry VIII. to certain ranks amongst the nobility, and according to a sumptuary law, "No man under the State of an erle were in his apparel of his body or horse, any cloth of gold or silver, or tinceld satin."

Tinsel Embroidery.—This is worked upon net, tulle, and thin muslin materials, and is an imitation of the Turkish Embroideries with gold thread upon crepe. The patterns are in outline, and consist of geometrical or arabesque designs, which should be simple, and with lines rather wide apart. To work: Trace the design upon pink calico, which back with brown paper, and upon this TACK the net. Take the very narrowest tinsel, thread it on to a wool needle, and work it backwards and forwards along the outlines. Put it in below a line, and bring it out above it in a slanting direction to the right, slant it again, and put it in below the line, and press it down with the thumb, so that it rather overlays itself, and forms the line as a series of VANDYKE STITCHES. Work in floss silk and in SATIN STITCH such parts of the pattern that are too small for the tinsel lines. Tinsel can be used instead of

gold thread in embroideries upon velvet, brocade, and silk, but as it soon tarnishes, the latter is the best to employ for good work.

Tippet or Cape.—An article of dress, worn alike by men and women. It is circular in form, and covers the shoulders, extending from around the throat to below the shoulders, and sometimes to the waist, and even longer. Tippets are usually made of the same material as the coat or dress, or else of fur. Those of Fur are much worn by women, especially of the upper classes, and by coachmen and footmen over their out-of-door livery great-coats. Sometimes several cloth capes are worn with ulsters, especially by coachmen.

Tissues.—A comprehensive term, including all textiles composed of threads interlaced by means of a shuttle. But there is also one particular fabric especially so designated. It is a species of cloth, woven either with gold and silver strands, or else with some of varied colours. It may be made of silk, and shot with gold and silver. We find entries in the household bills of Henry VIII. of both descriptions of this material—"broad and narrow silver Tissue," and "crimson Tissue;" for in olden times it was the distinctive name of a particular textile. Ben Jonson speaks of a—

Cloth of bodkin, or Tissue;

and earlier still, Chaucer makes allusion to it in *Troilus and Cressida*:

His helm to hewen was in twenty places
That by a tissue hong, his back behind.

Milton and Dryden both mention it. The latter describes its character as—

A robe of tissue, stiff with golden wire.

Tobines.—A stout twilled silk textile, much resembling Florentine, employed for women's dresses. It is to be had in all colours, and is very durable.

Toe.—*See* KNITTING STOCKINGS.

Toile.—A French term, signifying linen cloth. It is also the name given in France to distinguish the pattern in lace from the ground. The pattern is so called from its flat linen-like appearance.

Toile Cirée.—The French name for oil-cloth, or oilsilk.

Toile Colbert.—This is a loosely woven canvas material, identical with that employed in the Turkish and Algerian Embroideries imported to this country, and sold in the fancy-work shops. It is an inferior description of material.

Toile d'Alsace.—This is a description of linen cloth made for a dress material, and closely resembling that known as Toile de Vichy. It is imported from France.

Toile Damascene.—The French name for Embroidery executed upon damask, or honeycomb canvas, similar to towelling embroidery.

Toile de Religeuse.—This cloth is otherwise known as *Toile de Nonne*, or Nuns' Cloth.

Toile de Vichy.—A linen cloth, usually produced in stripes of two colours—blue and white or pink and white—like striped grass. It is employed as a summer dress material, and is to be had in ready-made costumes, as well as by the yard. It is a French material, and measures a yard in width.

Toile Satinée.—This material is of a cotton-like foulard. It is soft, and is produced in all colours, and printed in a great variety of patterns. It measures about 30 inches in width. Toile Satinée may also be had in plain colours.

Toilet Covers.—These small cloths, made for the covering of dressing-tables, are usually manufactured of marcella or picqué. They are also to be had in damask, of various dimensions, finished with common fringe, and also by the better kinds of fringe, which are knotted (*see* TOILET FRINGES.) These Covers may be bought by the yard also if desired.

Toilet Fringes.—These are of various descriptions—the "bullion," "scarlet and white loop," "bobbin-loop," "open," "plain," "black and white head," and "star;" all made of white cotton, and sold in pieces containing 36 yards each. As indicated by their name, they are used to trim toilet covers. The widths of these fringes vary from three-quarters of an inch, to 2 inches.

Toilinette.—A cloth composed of silk, cotton, and woollen yarn, the warp being of the former two combined and the weft of the latter. It is employed for making waistcoats for men, and is a kind of German quilting.

Tonder Lace.—This is lace worked in Tonder and in North Schleswig, and is of two kinds, one being made upon the Pillow and of native design, although freely copied from Italian, Flemish, and Scandinavian patterns. These Tonder Laces are heavy and solid in appearance, and require a close inspection before the beauty of their workmanship can be discovered, and they are almost entirely free from the plaited and braided parts that add so much to the effect of other laces. The second description of lace made at Tonder, and known as Tonder Muslin, is Drawn Work, similar to Broderie de Nancy. In this lace, Needlepoints and Pillow Laces are imitated with the greatest accuracy by the threads of the material being drawn out, re-united, and divided so as to follow all the intricacies of a flower or arabesque design. No lace stitches, such as are known as Fillings, are added, and no Embroidery Stitches, as are found in Indian Work and Dresden Point, but a raised or thin Cordonnet frequently marks out the outline of the chief parts of the patterns.

Tongue Shaped.—A term used by dressmakers, in reference to the decoration of border trimming, by means of cutting out in that form.

Torchon Ground.—This stitch is used either for a Pillow Lace Ground, or to fill in the centres of flowers instead of the Plaitings in many varieties of lace. Being rather large, it requires a certain amount of space, and the real beauty of the design consists in its regularity. Therefore great attention should be paid to the pricking of the parchment pattern. To work Fig. 789: Obtain some Point paper, such as is used for tracing out Berlin patterns upon, put a piece of parchment underneath it and folds of flannel. Sketch out the groundwork of the design with a fine tracing pen upon the Point paper, guided by the lines in making the points of the diamonds, and prick the five holes each diamond requires through to the parchment with a large pin. Put the parchment pattern on to the Pillow, and hang on two pairs of Bobbins at *a*, two pairs at *b*, make a CLOTH STITCH with the two pairs at *a*. TWIST each pair three times, and put up a pin between them. Leave them and take up the two pairs at *b*; make a Cloth Stitch with them, and TWIST each pair three times; put up a pair of Bobbins between them, make a Cloth Stitch with the four centre Bobbins, Twist each pair three times, put in a pin between the two pairs, and make a Cloth Stitch close up to the pin to enclose it. Take the centre pair to the right and make a Cloth Stitch with the pair next to them on the right. Twist each pair three times, put up a pin, and leave them. Take the pair of centre Bobbins to the left and make a Cloth Stitch with the pair to the left, Twist each pair three times, and put up a pin between them. Take the

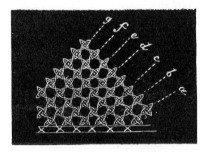

FIG. 789. TORCHON GROUND.

four centre Bobbins and make a Cloth Stitch.* Put up two pairs of Bobbins at *c*, make a Cloth Stitch, Twist each pair three times, put up a pin between them, take the nearest pair of Bobbins from the last diamond marked *b*, make a Cloth Stitch with one of the pairs from *c*, Twist each pair three times, and set up a pin between them. Repeat from * for the point not marked with a letter in the illustration. Take up the four centre Bobbins of *c*, make a Cloth Stitch, and Twist each pair thrice, and put up a pin between them; enclose the pin with a Cloth Stitch, take up the pair of *c* Bobbins nearest the pair of *b* Bobbins, and work a Cloth Stitch. Twist each pair three times, and put up a pin between them, and enclose the pin with a Cloth Stitch. Take the other pair of *c* Bobbins nearest to the unmarked Bobbins, make a Cloth Stitch, Twist each pair three times, and put up a pin between them, which enclose with a Cloth Stitch. Repeat for *d*, *e*, *f*, and *g* points. This ground can be worked either with fine or coarse thread, and the three Twists given to the Bobbins can be altered to one or two Twists, according to the thread used. The rest of the pattern is not altered.

MODERN DRAWN WORK

RUG WORK FORMED WITH COUCHING AND CROSS STITCH

Torchon Lace.—A simple thread lace that was at one time known as Beggars' Lace, and at another as Gueuse Lace. It is worked upon a Pillow and resembles Saxony Lace, the patterns being of the simplest, and formed with a loose thick thread, while the ground is a coarse Réseau ground. This lace was made in the seventeenth century, and from that time has been largely used on the Continent for common purposes. It is still worked on the Continent and in England, but much of the cheap Torchon Lace now sold is made by machinery.

Torjok Lace.—*See* RUSSIAN LACE.

Tournure.—The French term employed to denote the general outline and appearance of a person or costume. It is also used to signify a Bustle, or arrangement of

lengths; linen diaper and damask, to supply a thinner and softer kind of towel; linen having borders in blue or red, and decorated with designs and fringes; Turkish Bath Towelling, with or without a long nap; cotton towels in honeycomb pattern, with coloured striped borders, cotton diapers, Russian, and other kinds. For kitchen use there is the Linen Crash for roller towels; and Russia Crash, coarse and very durable, the widths running from 16 inches to 22 inches; and the White Loom Towelling for best kitchen use. Forfar Towels are coarse, heavy, and of unbleached flax, of 32 inches to 75 inches in width, and suitable for rough kitchen service. Dowlas Towelling, half bleached, with round threads like Russia Crash, but not so coarse, runs from 25 inches to

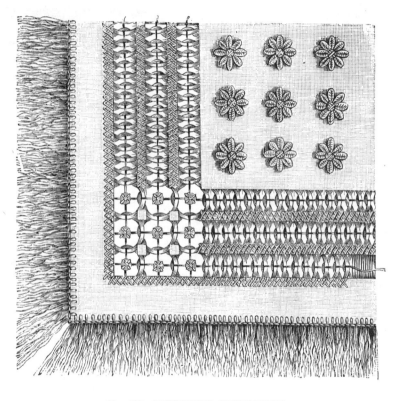

FIG. 790. TOWELLING EMBROIDERY.

puffed out crinoline, or wire, worn for the purpose of distending the back of a skirt, from the waist, and extending more or less downwards, according to the current fashion.

Tow.—This is a preparation of the fibres of flax. After the latter have been "hackled," they are divided into two sorts; the short and coarse are called Tow, and the long and fine make, Line Tow; which latter is prepared and spun on machines like cotton.

Towelling.—Every description of cloth designed for towels, whether of linen or cotton, sold singly or by the yard, is called by this name. For bed-room use there is Huckaback—the medium quality to be had at one shilling a yard—manufactured in linen, cotton, or a mixture of both, and may be cut from the piece or sold in towel

30 inches in width. In the accounts of Henry VIII.'s wardrobe expenses there is a mention made of "certeyne pieces of diaper for table cloths and towelles," as also still earlier in those of Edward IV. Ailesham, in Lincolnshire, was celebrated for fine linen napery as far back as the fourteenth century. Both Towelling, Glass and Tea Cloths, as well as Linen Damask, are employed for the purposes of Embroidery. Glass Cloths having red and blue stripes are especially so used.

Towelling Embroidery.—A modern work so named from the foundation being of thick materials, such as Java Canvas, Honeycomb, and white or stone coloured linens, such as could be used for Towels. The work consists of making handsome borders of Drawn Work, and ornamenting the plain squares left between the drawn threads and the centre of the material with Stars made with Satin Stitch and lines of Herringbone, Chain, or Feather Stitches worked either in filoselle, single Berlin wool, double crewels, or ingrain cottons. The embroidery is used for table-cloths, antimacassars, toilet cloths, bed pockets, mats, and for the ornamental towel so frequently suspended in front of the useful towels in a bedroom. To work, as shown in Fig. 790: Select a rather strong and coarse linen material, cut it to the size required, including a space of two inches for the fringe. At the end of this space make a line of wide apart BUTTONHOLE STITCHES. Leave an inch of material, and draw out threads beyond it to the depth of half an inch, leave a quarter of an inch of material, and draw out another half inch of threads, leave a quarter of an inch of material and draw out another half inch of threads. Draw out the threads in this manner along the four sides of the material; at each corner the only threads left will be those belonging to the undrawn parts of the material. Great care must be taken in cutting the threads, particularly at the corners, as a wrong cut of the scissors will spoil the whole work. Protect the corners at their edges with a close and narrow line of Buttonhole, worked with fine cotton, so as not to show in the design. Take a bright coloured filoselle or wool, and work a line of CROSS STITCH with it round the outer edge of the drawn threads, and fill in the spaces left between them with the same lines of Cross Stitches. Take a piece of fine Crochet cotton and make with it the pattern formed of the threads left in the material where the rest have been drawn away. Fasten the Crochet cotton securely at one of the corners, carry it across the first open space, divide in half the few threads between this and the next open space, take the last half upon the needle, and twist them over the first half, draw up the needle and cotton, and repeat to the end of that corner. When the threads are reached that are close together, divide them off into sets of eight threads, and take the last four first upon the needle, and twist them over the first four. Repeat until every space of drawn threads is worked over. Work small WHEELS over the open squares left at the corners. Fill in the centre of the design with stars made with coloured filoselle. Finish by drawing out the threads to form a fringe.

Fig. 791 is a pattern in Holbein Stitch used to em-

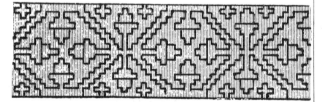

FIG. 791. TOWELLING EMBROIDERY.

broider the centres of Towelling Embroidery. To work: Trace out the design upon fine linen, or count the threads during the progress of the work in coarse materials. Use fine purse silk or Pearsall's washing silk, and work entirely in HOLBEIN STITCH.

When working Towelling Embroidery for nightgown cases omit the Drawn thread border and the fringe, and work a border with single Cross Stitches close together before commencing a pattern. The simplest design is to cover the centre with six pointed stars, made in a wool of a bright shade, and to connect these together with long lines of SATIN STITCH worked in a darker shade of wool.

Tracery. — Honiton Pillow Lace making is often enriched with Tracery, which is a kind of raised work, formed over a background of Cloth and Half Stitch. Its use gives to the patterns a very handsome effect, but, of course, increases the difficulty of the work. In Fig. 792

FIG. 792. TRACERY.

this Tracery is illustrated, and the butterfly is worked as follows: Commence at the tail, hang on eight pairs of Bobbins and two Gimp Bobbins, work in CLOTH STITCH, crossing the gimps at the narrow part, and tie and cut them off when the head is finished. Add two more pairs of Bobbins and work each of the antennæ with five pairs, finish the tips with two SEWINGS, then tie and cut off. Hang on five pairs of Bobbins at the small ring on the lower wing of the butterfly, work round it, join where it touches, then work down the body, add another pair of Bobbins, and work STEM STITCH round the inside edge of the lower wing. Sew to the body for the first three rows, work round the wing to the body again, sew once, and carry the Tracery round the oval in the upper wing, then round the inner edge of the wing to the spot where it is joined to the lower one. Sew as the Tracery is crossed and hang on four more pairs of Bobbins, so as to have five upon each side for the CUCUMBER PLAITINGS, which are made as follows: Work a row of Stem on each side, and when the working pairs come into the middle again, make a Cucumber Plaiting; when finished, turn Bobbin No. 2 back over the Pillow and keep it there with a pin. Work the Stem rows with Bobbins No. 3 and 4, so that the Cucumber Plaiting will not pull when Bobbins No. 1 and 2 are again used. Make four of these plaitings, joining the little ring to the edge as passed. Cut off five pairs of Bobbins and bring the remaining ones back in a VANDYKE tracery, then tie and cut off. Fasten on ten pairs of Bobbins for the Cucumber Plaitings in the upper wing, which work, and then fill up the rest of the space with two Vandyke Traceries, that cross each other, or with LONG PLAITINGS. Having finished the wings, work the background. Hang on eight pairs of Bobbins to the upper end of the large wing of the butterfly, and work in HALF STITCH; sew to each side, and add a pair of Bobbins to each Sewing for six turns. As there will be most holes on the lower side of the wing, occasionally sew twice into the same hole on the upper side. Cut off three or four pairs of Bobbins as the narrowing down the body proceeds, then turn and fill in the lower wing, adding Bobbins as required, and sew securely before cutting off. Hang on five pairs of Bobbins near the head, and work the open edge with PEARLS.

Cross Tracery.—The two arms of the Cross are commenced at the same time from different sides, are brought down to meet in the middle and are carried once more to the side. Two Twists have, therefore, to be attended to. In doing a cross it is always best to put a pin into the middle hole so as to mark it, and when working over a large space to Twist thrice instead of twice. The number of Bobbins used is altered to the space to be filled. To work a Cross Tracing over ten passive pairs of Bobbins without counting those that form the outside edge: First row—Work 1 CLOTH STITCH, TWIST (which means Twist the Workers twice, the Passive pairs on each side once), work 8, Twist, work 1. Second row—Work 2, Twist, work 6, Twist, work 2. Third row—Work 3, Twist, work 4, Twist, work 3. Fourth row—Work 4, Twist, work 2, Twist, work 4. Fifth row—Work 5, Twist, stick a pin, work 5. Sixth row—Work 4, Twist, work 2, Twist, work 4. Seventh row—Work 3, Twist, work 4, Twist, work 3. Eighth row—Work 2, Twist, work 6, Twist, work 2. Ninth row—Work 1, Twist, work 8, Twist, work 1.

Vandyke Tracery.—This Tracery is worked much in the same way as Cross Tracery, and forms a zig-zag device on the open parts of leaves and other spaces. It is illustrated in the lower wings of the Butterfly (Fig. 792). It is not marked out with pins, but formed with Twists, and unless great attention is paid to it, will not work out satisfactorily. The Working Bobbins in it are Twisted twice as they pass to and fro, and the Passive Bobbins on each side of the strand thus formed, once. The pattern is made by varying the place of the Twist. To make a Vandyke Tracery across ten Passive Pairs of Bobbins without counting those that form the outside edge which are worked as usual. First row—Begin from the inner side, work 2 CLOTH STITCHES, TWIST (which means Twist the workers twice, the passive pair on each side of the workers once), work 8. Second row—Work 7, Twist, work 3. Third row—Work 4, Twist, work 6. Fourth row—Work 5, Twist, work 5. Fifth row—Work 6, Twist, work 4. Sixth row—Work 3, Twist, work 7. Seventh row—Work 8, Twist, work 2. The point of the Vandyke is now reached. Eighth row—Work 3, Twist, work 7. Ninth row—Work 6, Twist, work 4, Tenth row—Work 5, Twist, work 5. Eleventh row—Work 4, Twist, work 6. Twelfth row—Work 7, Twist, work 3. Another point having thus been made, repeat the Tracery from the first row.

Tram.—A kind of doubled silk yarn of inferior raw silk, in which two or more thicknesses have been slightly twisted together. It is wound, cleaned, doubled, and thrown so as to twist in one direction only. Tram is employed for the weft or cross-threads of Gros de Naples velvets, flowered silk stuffs, and the best varieties of silk goods in general. Tram is also known by the name of Shute.

Transfer Embroidery.—In old needlework it frequently happens that the material upon which the embroidery is placed, and which forms its ground, becomes soiled and worn out, while the embroidery itself is still fresh and good. To transfer Embroidery: Trace the outline of the pattern upon the new material, which frame in an EMBROIDERY FRAME. Procure narrow silk cords, dyed exactly to match the colours used in the embroidery, or use gold cord, edge the Embroidery by stitching a line of cord down to it, then paste tissue paper at the back of the old material, and when that is perfectly dry, cut out the embroidery, leaving but the sixteenth of an inch of material beyond it. Lay the Embroidery upon the traced outlines in the Frame and pin it well down, and stitch it down in its proper lines with fine waxed silk, securing the little edging of old material to the new. Take a second cord like the first, and COUCH this upon the outline, so as to hide the small edging of old material. Work upon the new material tendrils, sprays, rays, and other pieces of the embroidery that could not be transferred. Some people prefer to put the two cords on after the Embroidery is laid upon the new material, but the first method is the best.

Transfer Lace.—Laces made with detached sprays, such as Brussels, Honiton, and Point Duchesse, and laid upon net foundations, are easily transferred to new grounds. To transfer: Carefully unpick the tacking stitches that secure the lace to the net, make a design of the lace upon calico, and back this with brown paper, lay the sprigs of lace face downwards upon the pattern, and keep them in place with a few light tacking stitches. Then lay over them some of the finest and best Brussels cream coloured net, and tack this to the margin of the pattern. Thread a needle with the finest cream lace thread, and OVERCAST round the outline of every part of the lace, and thus secure it to the net. Unpick the lace very carefully from the pattern.

Travail au Metier.—*See* FRAME WORK.

Treble Crochet.—*See* CROCHET, page 127.

Treble Diamonds.—*See* MACRAMÉ LACE.

Treble Star.—*See* MACRAMÉ LACE.

Treble Stitch.—*See* CROCHET, page 127.

Trefoils.—These are much used as edgings in Honiton Lace, and are made in various ways. To work the Close Trefoil shown in Fig. 793: Prick the pattern and hang on six pairs of Bobbins. Commence at the upper part of the left hand lower leaf of the first Trefoil, and work down it in HALF STITCH, make a PEARL EDGE to the point of contact with the next pattern of Trefoil, turn the Pillow, and work the other half of the leaf in CLOTH STITCH, SEWING every row in the middle except the first, which is secured by taking up the Runners or Working pair of Bobbins, that lie idle at the pins. Work the middle leaf

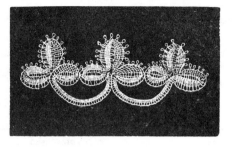

FIG. 793. TREFOILS—CLOSE.

of the pattern like the first leaf, but make the Cloth Stitch before the Half Stitch and put a Pearl Edge to both sides, and lastly, work the third leaf; work the lower side first in Cloth Stitch, and put a Pearl Edge to the upper part. The number of Pinholes in the centre of the leaves is not so great as those upon the outside, a false Pinhole is, therefore, made at the top. Work STEM STITCH with an open edge upon one side to the next pattern, and then repeat the three leaves.

To work the open Trefoil shown in Fig. 794: Prick the

the bottom of each petal on the outside edge, where the work turns. Work round the centre petal entirely with Pearl Edge on one side and Plain upon the other, and Sew twice to the inner circle. For the third petal work until seven Pearls have been made on the outer edge, and then work both edges Plain, and where the Pearls leave off TWIST the outside pair of Bobbins three times before making the first stitch. As the leaf narrows, cut off a pair of Bobbins and connect to the leaf at the nearest place, and when the inner circle is reached, Sew to it, and then make a ROPE SEWING down it to the next leaf; here disentangle the Bobbins and commence on the leaf. Hang on two pairs of Bobbins in addition if the leaf is worked in Half Stitch; three pairs if in Cloth Stitch. Work down the leaf, connect to the nearest petal of the Trefoil at the point of contact, and at the bottom of the leaf cut off two or three pairs of Bobbins. Make Stem Stitch for two pinholes, and repeat from the beginning; the only difference being that in the following Trefoils, at the third petal, Sew twice to the Trefoil preceding it. If the Trefoil Edge is to be repeated beyond the four Trefoils given, move the Bobbins thus: Turn the flap of the COVER CLOTH over them, pin the doubled cloth tightly upon each side and to the pillow, so that the threads are a little slack, take out all the pins from the finished lace, but leave those at the last part still in the lace. Detach the cloth containing the Bobbins from the lower end of the pattern and fasten it down again at the

FIG. 794. TREFOILS—OPEN.

Pattern and hang on ten pairs of Bobbins at the end of the first leaf, work it in CLOTH STITCH with an open edge upon each side; when it is complete cut off four pairs of Bobbins and commence the Trefoil at the inner circle. Work this in STEM STITCH, SEW as the circle is crossed, and commence the first petal of the Trefoil; work this in Cloth Stitch, hang on two pairs of Bobbins in successive rows, and make false Pinholes where required. The edge will be an open or PLAIN EDGE until the point where the first Trefoil touches the next is passed, at which place work the outer edge as a right-hand PEARL. Work a PEARL EDGE on one side and a plain upon the other to the end of the first petal, when Sew twice to the inner circle. Make plain and not pearl the lowest hole at

upper end, pin the last made Trefoil and leaf down on the first one of the pattern, putting the pins in half way; undo the Bobbins and continue the work.

Another description of Open Trefoil, and one used for the sprigs in Lace, and not for the edging, is illustrated in STEM STITCH.

Treille.—One of the names by which the Réseau Grounds of Pillow and Needle Laces are distinguished from the Toile or pattern they surround. The value of many laces is decided by the thickness or fineness of the thread used in the Treille, and the number of Twists given to the Bobbins when making it.

Trellis Work.—An Embroidery of recent date, resembling Strasbourg Embroidery or Roman Work, by being cut away from its background, but made with coloured instead of plain materials. It is intended to represent a climbing plant trailing over trellis work, and for this reason only plants that climb can be used, such as honeysuckles, passion flowers, roses. The materials required are American gold cloth, Sateens of green shades and whole colours, and coloured cretonnes of flower patterns, and filoselles. The Trellis is made with the gold cloth, the leaves and sprays of the design with the green sateen, and the flowers and buds with the cretonne, while the whole is finished with Embroidery worked with the filoselles. The work is used for summer fire screens or for mantel boards or cushions. To work: Frame two pieces of strong linen one over the other in an EMBROIDERY FRAME. Trace the design through upon this, and retain the design to cut the leaves and flowers from. Cut out long strips of gold cloth half an inch wide and lay these over the linen in diagonal lines, so as to form an open diamond-pattern Trellis Work. BASTE the cloth to the linen to keep it in position, but take the basting stitches right over the cloth from side to side, so as not to prick it with a needle. Cut out the leaves and stems from the sateen cloth, varying their shades of colour as much as the material will allow. Place the leaves, &c., upon the linen, and keep them in their right positions by pasting them down, as in Cretonne Work (APPLIQUÉ, BRODERIE PERSE). Cut the flowers and the buds from the chintz and paste them to the linen. Bring the leaves and flowers over the Trellis Work, and give them the appearance of twining about it. Leave the work stretched in the frame until the paste is dry, then take it out, and with filoselle silk, matching the tints of the leaves and flowers, BUTTONHOLE round their edges, so as to secure them to the linen foundation. Mark out the veins of the leaves with CREWEL STITCH, and the centres of the flowers with FRENCH KNOTS, and heighten the colouring of the flowers by adding in SATIN STITCH some lines of light filoselle. Buttonhole round the edges of the Trellis Work with Buttonhole Stitch in two shades of old gold, so that one side of the lines is darker than the other. When the Embroidery is finished, cut away the linen from the back where it has not been connected to the pattern by being caught by the Buttonholes.

Tresse.—A French term for Braid.

Tricotage.—A French term for Knitting.

Tricot Stitch.—*See* CROCHET, page 128.

Triellis d'Allemagne.—One of the names given to Netting, but generally meaning the head nets made in Germany in this work.

Trimmings.—A term of general application to ready-made decorations, varying in material, form, and method of manufacture. Those in Muslin are made in Edgings, Flounces, Insertions, and Scollops. They are made in pieces of from 24 yards, to 36 yards, and in short lengths; but may be bought by the yard. Quillings and Ruches of ribbon, net, and tarlatan, Plaitings of any material for dresses, fringes, spangles, beads, gimps, and braids of every colour, or mixture of colours, in

cotton, silk, and worsted, and every description of lace, are all to be included under the term Trimmings. They may also be had in strips of fur of all kinds, and in arrangements of flowers and feathers.

Trina de Lana.—*See* SHETLAND POINT LACE.

Trolle Kant.—An old Flemish lace no longer manufactured, but of great beauty. The flower or Toilé of the lace was usually made with Cloth Stitch, which was completely surrounded with a raised thread, while the grounds used were Trolly, Plaited, and Net, all being frequently employed upon the same piece of lace. The name of this lace has been corrupted into Trolly and given to a coarse English lace.

Trolly Laces.—These are Pillow Laces, made in Normandy, in Flanders, and in Buckinghamshire, and Devonshire. The distinguishing feature of these laces is their ground, which is an imitation of the Antwerp Trolly Net or Point de Paris Ground, and is made with twists, while the pattern is outlined with a thick thread like that used in the old Flemish Laces, and known as Trolle Kant. The lace is still made in Buckinghamshire, Northampton, and Devonshire, but like other pillow laces has declined since the introduction of machine made imitations.

Trouserings.—This is a term of general significance, denoting a great variety of cloths, specially made for the use which the name indicates, such as varieties of broadcloth, tartans, drills, &c.

Tucks.—These are parallel folds of material, lying either horizontally, or perpendicularly on any article of dress, of whatever material, either for shortening a garment, or for the purpose of ornamentation. These folds, or Tucks, are sometimes graduated, when several of them follow each other successively; and at other times they are made of respectively differing sizes. When about to make them, first measure the cloth accurately, to ascertain how many Tucks of a given size may be made. Fold it from selvedge to selvedge, and press the fold sufficiently firmly so as to form a crease, following a single thread to ensure perfect straightness. Turn down the folded portion to the depth desired, and then make a very close and delicate RUNNING along the double inner fold. Do not take more than three stitches at a time on the needle, when Running. When many Tucks are to be made parallel with each other, as in the case of infants' clothing, shirts, and underlinen in general, make the measurements by means of a piece of cardboard, cut exactly of the right width, and correct any unevenness in the folding before making the Runnings.

When Tucks are to be made in crape, the difficulty of the needlewoman is increased, and the method of making them is somewhat more complicated, as they require to be lined, and the material itself proves troublesome of management. The size of Tucks in crape varies from 2 inches in width to the depth of what are worn on a widow's skirt. Formerly they were made, like those of other materials, simply doubled in an ordinary fold of itself only; now they are lined. Employ mull-muslin for a good and new crape, but if the latter be of poor quality, or a piece that has been re-calendered, use book-muslin. For wear on a gored skirt, cut the crape from the straight way, across from selvedge to selvedge, not on the bias, as for an old-fashioned "all round" skirt. Then proceed to join the front and side gores of the skirt together. Lay it on the table with the hem towards you, and the roll of crape across it, with the selvedge to the hem. Then pin it down flat, cut off the pieces that come lower than the skirt, at the edge of the last gores, so that the crape may be the same distance from the hem at the sides, as in the middle of the front gore, and allow half an inch for the Running and Turning up with the muslin; and when completed, let the Tuck be quite 1 inch above the hem, as it so quickly frays out, if permitted to touch the ground. When the extreme edge is cut into the right shape, take the yard measure and place pins as far up the crape, measuring from the edge first cut, as the trimming is to be, allowing an additional quarter of an inch for Running it on the dress; then cut off by this pin guide. After this, treat the train in the same way, using the curvature just left by hollowing the top of the front Tuck for the middle of the back breadth, to economise the slope, if it be a long train. By laying on the trimming in this way, there will be a join at each side of the train, but it does not show at that point in gored or demi-trains, and it is a very great improvement to avoid making conspicuous joins, or triangular overlapping plaits, so as to make a straight flounce follow a bend.

Crape is sold in 23 inches, 42 inches, and 60 inches widths, therefore it is very easy to judge which will be most advantageous for dividing into one, two, or three Tucks, according to the degree of mourning demanded. When crape trimmings are taken from the straight way of the stuff, so are the muslin linings; and if the crape be cut crosswise, so must be the muslin. Proper unglazed cotton, called crape cotton, must be used in the making of mourning, as glacé thread would be perceptible on dull black stuffs. In Running the crape and muslin edges together on the wrong side, a quarter of an inch in, hold the former towards you, and do not pull against the muslin. Neither should project beyond the other. Draw the cotton fairly, but not tightly; and set the stitches tolerably closely. Then, when the two are turned right side out, for the seam to be between them, draw the muslin up about a quarter of an inch beyond the crape, so that the extreme edge of the Tuck shall be really double crape for a quarter of an inch. This, and the inner turning, uses up the half inch which was mentioned in reference to the cutting. TACK the upper edge of the crape a quarter of an inch in on the muslin with white cotton, in stitches of the same length in front as behind; as those at the back will serve as a mark for running the Tuck upon the skirt afterwards. A white Basting ought to be previously Run on the foundation, at the height the trimming should reach; the least irregularity in the arrangement of these Tucks is apparent, when devoid of any heading, and to attempt it while working on the inside of a Tuck, on a gored skirt, without an accurate white cotton line on both, would prove a great mistake. This plain mounting is most suitable for deep mourning, but otherwise cording, or

one-eighth of an inch fold standing upwards may head the Tucks; and then this cord or fold can be put on the skirt first, and be used as the guide line for sewing on the Tuck, instead of a Running of white cotton.

Fancy folds and rouleaux may sometimes serve as a suitable finish to Tucks, and by some are made in one with them. But it is better to make them separately, and to lay them on the raw edge of the flounce. Take care in this case to match the rouleau, and the flounce or Tuck, in the diagonal slope of the crape and the grain of the two pieces. If that of the Tuck slope from right to left, and that of the trimming the contrary way, the effect will be very bad.

Tulle.—A fine Silk Net, manufactured in the Jacquard looms, and which is a wide description of the material called blonde, which is employed for quillings. It is a silk bobbin-net, the manufacture of which in this country commenced at Nottingham. It originated in France, where it was called after the town in which it was first produced, Point de Tulle. A variety of the same delicate textile is known as Tulle Bruxelles. Tulle may be had in black and white, and in every colour, and is about a yard wide. It is employed for veils, bonnets, and dress trimmings, and is made both with spots of different dimensions, and varying in closeness one to the other; and also plain.

Tulle Embroidery.—This is a very simple kind of Embroidery, worked with floss silks upon fine black or white Tulle, and used for trimmings to ball dresses and other light fabrics. To work: Select an easy outline Crewel Work or Embroidery pattern, trace this out upon pink calico and TACK the Tulle on to the calico. Thread a fine darning needle with floss silk and RUN this along so as to trace the pattern out with a run line. DARN the floss silk into the Tulle to fill in any parts of the design that are thick, and work two to three Run lines close together to make stalks or any prominent lines. To work as shown in Fig. 795: Work upon black tulle, and with

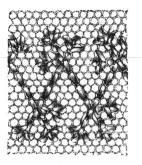

FIG. 795. TULLE EMBROIDERY.

crimson floss silk. RUN the floss silk diagonally across the tulle to form the chief lines of the pattern, and work the rest with short SATIN STITCHES.

To work Fig. 796: Use white tulle and blue filoselle. Twist the filoselle several times in and out the tulle to form the diamonds, and work the centre of the device by darning the filoselle into the tulle.

FIG. 796. TULLE EMBROIDERY.

To work Fig. 797: Trace the design upon a piece of pink calico, lay the black tulle material upon it, and work

FIG. 797. TULLE EMBROIDERY.

over the traced lines with SATIN STITCH, using a bright floss silk of a yellow shade.

Tunisian Crochet. — One of the names given to Tricot. *See* CROCHET, page 128.

Turgaux. — The French term for fluted plaitings. *Turgaux d'Orgue* signify wide flutings, resembling the pipes of an organ, whence its name.

Turkey Red. — A cotton cambric, of a bright scarlet colour of indelible dye, made both twilled and plain. It was originally imported from Turkey, whence its name. The art of dyeing this red was practised in the Middle Ages in the East; in the course of the last century it was introduced into France by Greek dyers, and imported thence by Frenchmen, who founded the first manufactory in this country. It is now made in Glasgow and in Lancashire, and is much employed for trimmings and linings, the colour being proof against any amount of washing.

The method of dyeing this cloth is as follows: The bleached yarn is soaked in oil, then dipped in carbonate of soda, and exposed to the action of the air and of steam in a hot room. It is then passed through a solution of nut-galls and a red mordant successively, and is thus ready for dyeing. To effect this it is boiled for two or three hours in a vessel containing madder-root, or *munjeet*, and, lastly, it is boiled in a solution of soap.

Turkey Red Handkerchiefs. — These can be had already hemmed, in sizes measuring from 18 inches by 18 inches to 28 inches by 28 inches; the price varying to a considerable extent, according to their quality.

Turkish Embroidery. — The Turks, although not so celebrated as the Persians, East Indians, and Japanese for their needlework, have the same true appreciation of design, and fondness for brilliant colouring harmoniously blended, as other Asiatic nations. Their braiding with

gold thread upon cloth is as well-known as the Indian Braiding, as is also their Patchwork or Appliqué Work done with cloth or silk; and besides these they are known for their embroideries with silk and gold thread upon thin gauze-like materials. At the present time attention has been peculiarly directed to this particular class of their work, vast quantities of it having been exported to England and France. This work is done upon Toile Colbert, a thin open canvas material far inferior in value to the elaborate Embroidery of which it forms the background, but in Turkey labour is cheap, and the price of materials considerable, so the workers who earn a scanty living have to obtain the least expensive. The patterns for Turkish Work are all arabesque or of conventionalised flower designs, the silks used are known as raw silks dyed with vegetable dyes, and gold thread or tinsel. The stitches differ from those employed in ordinary European embroideries by being worked very much at the fancy of the worker as to place and uniformity. The stitches most used are Rope Stitch most elaborately twisted, Satin Stitch made with short stitches, Point de Riz, Cross Stitch, Tent Stitch, Herringbone worked so closely that no ground appears between the stitches; also lines of thread thrown across the space and covered with Tent Stitch, while threads are drawn out in a design and Overcast over so as to form small open squares as the centre to a flower or pine-shaped arabesque. The silks used in the two stitches that make a Cross Stitch are frequently of different colours, and the stitches themselves are rarely worked in straight rows, but oblique or following the curves of the pattern, sometimes half of them will start from one side of the piece of the design being worked, and slant to the centre, to be met by others slanting in an opposite direction, these latter being executed in a different kind of stitch to those first made; in fact, there is no rule to the filling in of any of the designs, beyond the employment in the colouring of large quantities of dull yellow and a kind of cinnamon red, with smaller proportions of blue, green, and orange. The borderings to most of the Embroidery upon Canvas are made with Drawn Work, whose threads are Overcast or Buttonholed over with silks of different shades, and are never left visible. The best way to make up this Embroidery for use (the ground being generally dirty and coarse) is to cut out the design from the background, arrange it upon STAMPED plush or brocaded silk, slightly OVERCAST the edges to those materials, and cover the Overcasting and the raw edge with a line of gold thread COUCHED down. Very handsome table covers, mantel-boards, and cushions can thus be obtained without much additional labour.

Turkish Embroidery upon Cloth. — This is executed in a variety of colours, and with gold thread and floss or raw silk. To work as shown in Fig. 798, which is the half of a tablecloth or coverlet: Cut out the centre of the pattern shown by the horizontal lines out of a fine carmine red cloth, embroider with SATIN STITCH the arabesque design upon it with pale green silk and black silk arranged, as shown in the illustration, and then outline every part of the Embroidery with two lines of gold thread, which COUCH down upon the material with gold silk. Make the background of the outer part of the tablecloth of fine black cloth, and conceal the join by working it over with pale green silk, and outlining that with gold thread. Embroider the scroll upon the black cloth with bright red, blue, and green, outlining every part with gold

FIG. 798. TURKISH EMBROIDERY.

thread. For the border either cut out the ovals from light red cloth and Couch them on to the background with gold thread, or work them in ROPE STITCH and outline them with yellow silk cord; make the lines enclosing them like those in the centre.

The Turks also embroider with gold thread upon gauze and crape, and also with gold threads upon morocco, and in this latter work they frequently insert gold coins, and execute the minutest designs without spoiling the delicate thread they use.

Turkish Lace.—The lace made in Turkey is limited to one description, and is not made for the market, but in the harems, for the use of the ladies of the harem. It is a species of Tambour and Crochet Work, made with a needle and with silk of various colours. It is called Oyah Lace.

Turkish Towels.—These are cotton cloths, having a long nap, cut or uncut. Some are all white, some unbleached, and others are bordered with ingrain red stripes, with stripes across from selvedge to selvedge, or cross-bars throughout. They have fringes at each end. Turkish Towelling may also be had by the yard, and has latterly been employed for women's bathing dresses, &c. See TOWELLINGS.

Turned Row.—See KNITTING.

Turn Heel.—See KNITTING STOCKINGS.

Turnhout Lace.—The lace made in this place is Mechlin Lace.

Turning Scallops.—In Pillow Laces it frequently happens that the pattern is formed of open petals or scallops that are wider upon their outside curve than upon

their inner. This form of the pattern necessitates more pinholes being pricked upon the outer curve than upon the inner, and in order to keep the threads working backwards and forwards across the lace, and thus forming it, secured at each curve, it is necessary that false pinholes shall be arranged upon the inner curve so as to keep the outer and inner edges level with each other.

To Turn a Scallop: Work across to the inside, TWIST thrice and stick a pin, but instead of completing the edge, work back with the same pair of Bobbins, and when the inside is again reached take out the pin and re-stick it in the same hole, then finish the plain inside edge with the idle pair. Repeat until the scallop has been rounded.

To Turn a Scallop in Stem Stitch: Use six pair of Bobbins. In making these scallops the last two holes of the scallop belong equally to the scallop upon each side. Work round the first scallop until these holes are reached, stick a pin in the first and complete the plain edge, then lay back by the pins the outside pair. Work across, and as the pins are again reached twist the Hanging or Passive pair of Bobbins lying next them thrice, and make the PLAIN EDGE with these, but do not twist the Worker or Runner pair which is left at the pins, work across, SEW to the inner part of the design, turn the pillow, work back to the pins where the untwisted pair is lying, do not touch the pins, but work across and back with this pair, and when the pins are again reached take out the second one, Sew to the hole, re-stick the pin, and work another row of STEM STITCH. All this is done without Twisting, the work having arrived at the second scallop, here twist the outside pair, and stick a pin, and finish the Plain Edge with the pair put away.

Turning Stitch.—See TURN STITCH.

Turn Stitch.—Also known as Turning Stitch, and used in Honiton and other Pillow Laces at the end of a row. It is made with a Cloth Stitch and a half Cloth Stitch as follows: Work a CLOTH STITCH, give each pair of Bobbins one TWIST to the left, put the middle left hand Bobbin over the middle right; lift the two pairs with each hand, and give them a little pull.

Turn Stitch.—See KNITTING.

Turquoise Silk.—This silk is likewise known as Gros de Suez. It is a description of material made for bonnets and trimmings, which measures from 18 inches to 22 inches in width.

Tuscan Straw Work.—Finely plaited straw of wheat, having a delicate and slender stalk, and golden hue; growing in Tuscany, and manufactured into circular "flats," for hat and bonnet, mat and basket making, in the neighbourhoods of Florence, Pisa, and Sienna. The "tress" is sometimes formed of seven or nine straws, but generally of thirteen; and, being tied at one end, it is plaited by hand, till a length of about 20 yards is made. The hat when completed is made of but one piece.

Tussore Silks.—These are of Indian manufacture, and are all "wild" and raw silks, plain made, and without any cord or woven patterns, although some are stamped or printed in England from Indian blocks. They are sold by the piece of 9½ yards, are 34 inches in width, and vary much in price. They are produced by the larva of the *Antheræa mylitta* of Linnæus, while the cultivated silk fibres come from the *Bombyx mori.* These silks in their un-bleached state are of a darkish shade of fawn colour, unlike the golden and white hues of that produced by the mul-berry-fed worms. The particular characteristic of the Tussar silk fibre is that it is flat, while that spun by the *Bombyx mori* is round. The silk textile made from the former is strong, yet light in wear, soft to the touch, and very suitable for summer costumes, and will bear both cleaning and washing. The silks of this description are respectively known by a variety of names; that previously given is the French application, but the native names are Tussar, Tussah, and Tasar; it is the most important of the wild silks of India.

Tweed.—A woollen cloth woven of short lengths of wool, and lightly felted and milled, the yarn being dyed before woven. It is soft, flexible, and durable, being un-mixed with either shoddy or cotton. Tweed of the finest quality is made of Saxony and Australian wools, while the common sorts are of the Danish and South American sheep. It is manufactured at Selkirk, Hawick, and Jed-burgh, in the neighbourhood of the Tweed—whence its name. There is also a variety produced by a very peculiar method of manufacture, called the Harris Tweed, having its origin in the island after which it is called. It is a homespun material in diagonal weaving, undyed, and of a kind of warm sand colour. Others of older date are distinguished by the names Cheviot, Glengarry (which is mottled), Scotch, and Waterproof Tweeds; they may be had either checked or plain, and their average widths run to about 48 inches. In former times they were known as Tweel. *See* TWILL.

Twill, or Tweed.—A term descriptive of a certain process in weaving, *i.e.*, passing the weft thread across diagonally, so forming small ribs, the weft going over one, and under two warp threads alternately, or else over one, and under three or more, which method is reversed on its return. The threads are generally doubled one way. In plain weaving it would pass over one and under the next in succession. All stuffs, whether of silk, woollen, or cotton, are stronger when of this make.

Twist.—This term is used when one Bobbin has to be turned over another, and a twist together thus given to the threads. In Pillow Lace directions the worker is con-stantly told to Twist once, twice, or three times, as the case may be. To make a Twist: Lift the pair of Bobbins in the hand and hold them loosely, Twist them over each other with a rapid motion of the forefinger and thumb, and then give them a pull.

A description of cotton yarn made in several varieties, and also of sewing silk, is known as Twist, such as Purse Twist and Tailors' Twist, also Gold and Silver Twist, employed for purposes of Embroidery. The Silk Sewing Twist is sold in balls, hanks, and reels, in all colours. Of the cotton-yarn Twist there are three kinds, viz., the Green, Mule, and Water, of which the numbers run from 20 to 100.

Twisted Bar.—*See* MACRAMÉ LACE.

Twisted Chain.—A name by which the Ridge or Twisted Bar in Macramé is sometimes called, it is also used instead of Rope Stitch, *see* EMBROIDERY STITCHES, and RIDGE BAR, MACRAMÉ.

Twisted Net.—The ordinary kind is of cotton, which was machine made early in the present century, and before that by hand. It is composed of three threads; one pass-ing from right to left, and the other proceeding the opposite way, while the third winds about them both, in a serpentine course, intertwisting so as to form regular openings, which in the best qualities appear rather elongated in the direc-tion of the selvedge. The common kinds are used as linings and foundations. The Brussels is the best, and may be had in widths of 2 yards, for dresses. The meshes in this quality are extra twisted. Fancy sprigs and spotted patterns may be had in net, from 18 inches to 33 inches wide.

Twist Stitch.—*See* EMBROIDERY STITCHES.

Tying Bobbins.—When making Pillow Lace the Bobbins used are first tied together in pairs, and then knotted together in greater or smaller numbers, according to the width of the lace and the Bobbins required to make it. When any part of the lace is finished and the Bobbins have to be cut off, the Bobbins are first secured together by a movement known as Tying-up. Take the two out-side Bobbins, turn their tails to one another, and tie them by passing one over, one under, the opposite thread and draw through. Do this twice; take two other Bobbins and repeat, and then cut away the Bobbins that are not required.

U.

Ulster.—A loose overcoat, worn by men and women, the breadths of which are cut straight, and confined at the waist by a belt of the same material. Sometimes Ulsters are made of thick tweed; a double-faced cloth of uni-colour, and a plaid inside; or of other warm woollen cloth; and also of alpaca of different colours, for summer wear. Ulsters are well furnished with pockets, and some-times have either a hood or cape of the same stuff.

Umbrella.—An appliance made to give shelter to the person when exposed to the rain, and for which a variety of textiles are expressly made, and rendered waterproof. Amongst these are certain twilled, or plainly-woven silk stuffs, to be had in several colours; also in alpaca, gingham, Orleans cloth, and dyed calico. There are many varieties in the construction of umbrella frames, as also in the sticks and handles; and the ribs may be either of whalebone or metal. Umbrellas were employed by the Anglo-Saxons, of which an illustration may be seen in Harleian MSS., in which a figure wearing some description of hat, a cloak, tight-sleeved tunic, and boots to the ankle, is followed by a bare-headed attendant, who holds over him an Umbrella, or Sunshade, having a handle with a joint, the stick slanting obliquely from the centre. But the use of this appliance is of far more remote antiquity. The Chinese have employed it from time immemorial, and there, as in various Oriental countries, it is used as an article of State, rather than a mere shelter from the sun. Illustrations of those in use in the ancient metropolis of Persia (Persepolis) may be seen on the ruined walls. Umbrellas are also represented on the ruins of Nineveh (1,200 years before Christ). Dr. Layard states that "on the later bas-reliefs a long piece of embroidered linen or silk, falling from one side like a curtain, appears to screen the King completely from the sun." He also observes, in reference to the Ninevitish illustrations, that "the Parasol was reserved exclusively for the Monarch, and is never represented as borne over any other person." In Eastern lands they were and are very handsome; composed of silk, and decorated with an openwork border, with tassels, and a flower on the top of the stick. In ancient Greece and Rome they were also employed as a mark of distinction, as well as a shelter from the sun; but they were not of so decorative a character, being made of leather or skin.

On occasions, however, when the Veil could not be spread over the roof of the Amphitheatre, women, and effeminate men used to shield themselves from the sun by these rude Umbrellas, or *Umbraculum* of the period. Amongst the ancient Greeks the Dayshade, or *Skiadeion* was employed at a certain Festival (the Panathenia) by the Athenian maidens, held over them by the daughters of the aliens.

In later times, they have been in use all over Europe, and much employed in ecclesiastical processions, and in the Regalia of the Pope. The State Umbrella of the native Princes of India continues to be employed, the handle of which is of gold or silver, and the silk cover splendidly decorated and embroidered with gold and silver thread. Only in the last century was its use adapted to shield the person from the inclemency of the weather. The first man who made a practice of carrying one was Jonas Hanway, and in the *Statistical Account of Glasgow*, by Dr. Cleland, it is said that about the year 1781-2 Mr. John Jamieson, surgeon, brought with him an Umbrella, on his return from Paris, which was the first seen in the city, and attracted universal attention. When first introduced as a protection from the rain in England, their use by men was regarded as very effeminate.

Those first made in England were exceedingly coarse and heavy, and by no means a decorative article of use. They were covered with oilsilks, and were not easily opened when wet; the frames were made of rattan canes, split and dried. Afterwards whalebone replaced them, and a ring attached to a narrow ribbon was employed to draw the folds together. We find a mention of the article in one of Ben Jonson's comedies, in 1616, and in Beaumont and Fletcher's *Rule a Wife and have a Wife* (1640):

> Are you at ease ? Now is your heart at rest ?
> Now you have got a shadow—an umbrella,
> To keep the scorching world's opinion
> From your fair credit. . . .

When selecting a Silk Umbrella, it is as well to hold it up to the light and look through it, to judge of the evenness of the grain and the shade of the black dye, which in the best black silks will have a greenish hue when the light is seen through them. When wet, they should not be placed near the fire, and neither shut up nor stretched open, but left to hang in loose folds in some dry place. A silk case drawn over them when travelling is a good protection against injury, but the continual drawing on and off of a case will rub and wear out the folds. Large oiled cotton yellow Umbrellas are still in use amongst the Italian peasantry, and enormous specimens of a bright red colour are employed as tents to cover fruit, flower stalls, &c., in the streets of Continental towns, and have a very picturesque effect.

Umritzur Cashmere.—A peculiar manufacture of Cashmere, having a kind of zigzag chevron pattern, produced in the weaving, instead of a twill. It is made in every variety of Indian colour, and is exceedingly soft and warm. The width measures 26 inches, and it is sold in pieces of about 9 yards each.

Unbleached Thread Tassels.—These are employed, amongst others, for Window Blind Tassels. *See* TASSELS.

Underlinen.—This is a comprehensive term, applied almost to every article worn beneath the external garments, or at night, both of men and women. Underlinen is made of a variety of materials, although the several articles of wear come under the general denomination of Underlinen. These may be made of silk, stockingette, spun silk, lawn, cambric, merino, flannel, longcloth, Norwegian pine wool, elastic cotton cloth, &c. The several articles of Underclothing, such as shirts, chemises, drawers, nightdresses for men and women, "combination" garments, square-cut and high petticoat bodices, knickerbockers, white petticoats, and infants' clothing, comprising the barrow, petticoat, shirt, and stays, are all described under CUTTING OUT; as also FRILLS and LININGS, for all measurements and placing. In the great ready-made Underlinen manufactories, where the several articles are all hand-made, the cloth, of whatever quality, is folded in immense blocks, in appropriate lengths and widths, of which a certain thickness is laid on a long table to be cut out *en masse*. In the centre of this table there is a hollow space, occupied by a steam-propelled circular tape saw, without teeth, like the blade of a knife, which turns rapidly round, and the folded cloth—sufficient for some three hundred or upwards of shirts, or other articles—is pressed against it, and turned according to the outline pencilled on the top layer of cloth, when the whole is cut sharply through; the pieces taken out of the neck and other places are cut into cuffs and collars. The plain sewing is then executed by hand, and with such extreme cleanliness, that it is not washed, but passes at once into the hands of the ironers. The several smoothing irons are heated by gas, introduced into the hollow of each through a tube and lighted. Thus greater expedition in the work is obtained.

There is a new description of Underlinen, made on the system of Professor Gustav Jaeger, M.D., of Stuttgart, and patented by the Messrs. Benger, in this country,

America, and most of the kingdoms of Europe. The material is pure wool, woven after the method of stockingette cloth, and is designed to clothe the body from the throat to the extremities, including the feet. The shirts and chemises can be had separately from the drawers; but "combinations" are also produced. This description of Underlinen is called the "Normal" wool Underclothing. In substance it is light, fine, and smooth, and is made both for summer and winter wear.

The Underlinen of the institution, called the "Rational Dress Society," forms a portion of what is called the "Hygienic Wearing Apparel," and the new improvements which this Society is endeavouring to introduce, in lieu of the ever-changing fashions, are patronised by the National Health Society. Amongst other changes in the style of outward apparel, this Rational Dress Society advocates, and produces stays without whalebones, under-petticoats and skirts divided in the form of leggings, called dual, or divided skirts; and stockings, manufactured like gloves, or digitated, which is very clumsy, and not likely to meet with favour. *See* CUTTING OUT.

Undyed Cloths.—These woollen cloths are produced both for trouserings and suitings, in greys, drabs, and buffs, of various shades.

Undyed Stockingette Cloth.—This description of elastic cloth may be had in single, double, and treble width. *See* STOCKINGETTE CLOTH.

Union Cord.—A round white cord, made for stay-laces, of firm quality, being composed of both linen and cotton thread. The combination of the two substances is supposed to improve the quality of the cord, the cotton supplying a degree of pliability and softness, and the linen thread the requisite firmness and strength.

Union Cord Braid.—This kind of Braid consists of two or more cords woven together of Mohair or worsted, also called Russia Braid. It may be had in black, or in colours; the numbers run 0 to 8. It is cut into short lengths, and sold by the gross pieces, each gross containing four pieces. The wider lengths measure 36 yards.

Union Diaper.—This cloth is made of a combination of linen and cotton thread; but in the method of weaving, and the small diamond-shaped designs, of two or three varieties, it in all respects resembles linen diaper.

Unions.—Stout materials composed of a mixture of linen and cotton, much dressed and stiffened, and chiefly used for linings, and window blinds. There are imitations made of cotton. The width is regulated by inches, and the sizes required to fit the various widths of window frames are always to be had. In procuring Union Cloths for window blinds, it is advisable to purchase inferior kinds, well glazed, as they do not bear washing satisfactorily, and when soiled should be replaced by new ones.

Unwinding Bobbins.—All workers of Pillow Lace, until they become thoroughly acquainted with the art, will experience great trouble with their Bobbins, either in keeping them disentangled and straight down the Pillow, or in keeping them the same length, which requires continual unwinding and settling.

To Unwind a Bobbin so that the thread hanging from it is to be longer: Tighten it, and slowly turn the Bobbin to the left; if the thread will then unwind, nothing more is needed, but should it not do so, raise the HALF HITCH of thread that keeps the Bobbin thread secure, lift this off over the head of the Bobbin, unwind the length required, and then make the Half Hitch again.

To Shorten or Wind up the Thread: Lift the Bobbin with the left hand, hold it horizontally, raise the Half Hitch with a pin, and keep it raised until sufficient thread is wound up, when drop it over again into its old position.

Upholstery.—A term, by which every description of textile employed in the making and covering of furniture is designated. Varieties of silk, velvet, horse-hair, reps, chintz, leather, cloth, moreen, Utrecht velvet, cretonnes, muslin, dimity, and cotton, are all included under the name of Upholstery Cloths or Stuffs.

Upholstery Cotton.—A coarse description of sewing cotton, made in scarlet, crimson, blue, green, yellow, drab, and brown, to suit the colours of furniture coverings and curtains.

Utrecht Velvet.—A very strong and thick material composed of worsted, but of velvet make, having a raised deep pile, and sometimes a cotton back. It may be had in all colours, and is used by upholsterers and coach-builders. It derives its name from the town in Holland to which it owes its origin. There is an imitation made, which is woven in wool, and is called Banbury Plush.

V.

Valenciennes Lace.—The beauty of this Pillow Lace and its solidity has earned for it the name of "belles et eternelle Valenciennes," and a fame extending from 1650 to the present time. The first manufacture of Valenciennes was in the city of that name, which, though originally one of the towns of Hainault had been transferred by treaty to France. When first the lace was made it had to contend for public favour with the beautiful Needlepoints of Italy, and those of Alençon and Brussels; but Louis XIV. encouraged its growth and it soon attained celebrity as a lace useful for ordinary occasions and for all descriptions of trimmings, being especially used for the ruffles then so much worn. It attained its greatest celebrity between the years 1720 and 1780, and in Valenciennes alone 14,000 workers were employed in its manufacture, while in the surrounding villages it was also made. The number of these workers, however, declined, and during the French Revolution the ones that remained were dispersed, fleeing to Belgium from their persecutors, and giving a trade to that nation, which it has made most flourishing. In Belgium there are six centres for Valenciennes lace making, Alost, Ypres, Bruges, Ghent, Menin, and Courtrai, and the work they produce has individual marks by which it can be separately known. The distinguishing characteristics of this lace are that it is a flat lace, with ground and pattern worked simultaneously with the same thread, and no different kind of thread is introduced to outline the pattern or to work any part of it. It is worked in one piece and by one person, unlike Brussels Lace, which passes through many hands. So much depends in the lace upon the whole fabric being made by the same person, that it always commands a higher price when this can be certified; and in the old days, when the manufactory was carried on in Valenciennes, the difference could be detected between lace worked in the town and lace worked out of the town, although made by the same person. This difference arose from the peculiarly damp climate of Valenciennes, which was favourable to the smooth passing backwards and

it resembles the finest cambric, upon grounds varied in several ways in one piece; sometimes these grounds resemble minute circles, surrounded by another circle, and pierced with numerous pinholes; at others they are formed of small squares, each containing five pinholes, while some patterns have twisted and plaited grounds of great beauty. Fig. 799 represents an old Renaissance pattern. These Flemish designs were gradually changed, and the patterns became much simpler, while the grounds, instead of being close, were formed of hexagon and octagon meshes, and what is known as the Dotted style introduced, in which the design is small, and is thrown as powderings over the ground, instead of taking up the greater part of the work. This style has been somewhat altered in the laces lately made at Ypres through the exertions of Felix Brunfaut, who has designed con-

FIG. 799. VALENCIENNES—OLD.

forwards of the Bobbins, and the lace being there formed in underground rooms. From these circumstances the lace made in the town was known as Vraie Valenciennes, and commanded a much higher price than that made in the surrounding villages and in Flanders, which was known as Fausse Valenciennes and Bâtarde. The flax employed was of the finest quality, but in the oldest specimens it has a slightly reddish tinge, while the number of Bobbins used (300 being required for a piece 2 inches in width, and 12,000 being often in use together,) and the labour required in forming the lace made it most expensive, a yard of a flounce or a pair of broad ruffles frequently taking a year to execute, although the work was continued for fourteen hours of the day.

The earliest patterns of Valenciennes are of great beauty; they consist of conventionalised scrolls and flower designs, made in thick Cloth Stitch so that

nected patterns and bouquets of flowers far superior to those worked during the Dotted period; but Valenciennes Lace of the present day cannot compete in its graceful arrangements of pattern, evenness of work, and variety of ground, with the old Vraie Valenciennes. In each town where it is worked the ground is made differently; in Alost the ground is square-meshed, and is made by the Bobbins being twisted five times, which adds to the solidity of the lace, although the patterns from this town are inferior. In Ypres the ground is square-meshed; the Bobbins twisted four times, and the lace made of the widest and most expensive kind. In Ghent the ground is square-meshed, and the Bobbins only twisted two and a half times; the lace is there made only in narrow widths, but is of good quality. In Courtrai and Menin the grounds are square, and twisted three and a half times; the lace produced is among the cheapest manufactured·

In Bruges the grounds are circular, and the Bobbin twisted three times; this lace is the one most imported to England.

The Valenciennes Lace which is now manufactured is not nearly so elaborate as that of earlier date, and the narrow widths are quite within the power of an amateur to make. To work as shown in Fig. 800: In this design the manner of pricking the pattern is shown as a continuation of the lace. The pattern requires 130 Bobbins, five of which form the Engrelure, and the rest the ground and the thick part or pattern. The ground is formed of Twists, and is the same as is used in some of the Mechlin

pinhole, Twist them three times, divide them, cross, set up a pin, leave one right hand and one left-hand Bobbin

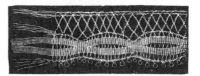

FIG. 802. VALENCIENNES LACE EDGING.

at the pinhole. * Twist one right and one left-hand Bobbin together thrice to the next pinhole, here stick a pin, Twist

FIG. 800. VALENCIENNES LACE EDGING—MODERN.

Laces. To work the ground which is shown enlarged in Fig. 801: For each mesh four Bobbins are required. Hang on two Bobbins at each pinhole at the top of the pattern, and seven at the FOOTING. Work the Footing by twisting four of the Bobbins together, leave two, which carry

the two Bobbins from the right hand down to this pin, divide them. Cross, and repeat from*. The illustration shows the manner of working the ground in diagonal lines. Work in CLOTH STITCH for the thick parts of the design, and hang on extra Bobbins, which cut off when no longer required, and run through as shown, where possible. To work Fig. 802: This narrow edging is very simple; it is worked with the ground already explained, and with Cloth Stitch and a PEARL EDGE. The pricked pattern is shown

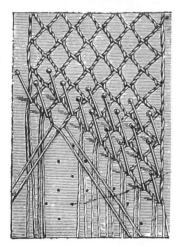

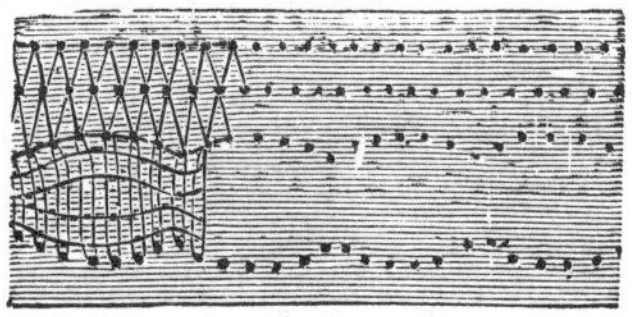

FIG. 801. VALENCIENNES TWISTED GROUND.

through the three other Bobbins belonging to the Footing, and which remain hanging straight down through the length of the work. TWIST the two Bobbins taken from the Footing three times, take the two Bobbins from the next

FIG. 803. VALENCIENNES LACE EDGING—DETAIL A.

in Fig. 803, Detail A. Use fine Lace thread, No. 300, and forty-four Bobbins, six of which are required for the double Footing. To work: Make the ground with three Twists to each pair of Bobbins, cross, and set up a pin; work the thick part in Cloth Stitch, Twist two Bobbins for the edge to it on the inner side, and use four Bobbins for the outside Twist.

To Work a Valenciennes Plaited Ground: The ground shown in Fig. 804 is one of the original Valenciennes Ground, and is more difficult to execute than the simple Twist; it is, however, much more durable. To work: Eight Bobbins are required for each mesh; plait four of these together down on the left side to a Pinhole, and four on the right, set up a pin, and cross a pair of threads as

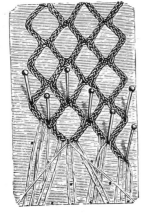

FIG. 804. VALENCIENNES PLAITED GROUND.

shown in the illustration, take two of the original Bobbins, and two from the other side, and plait them together.

Valentia.—A mixed material, having a cotton warp, or a cotton and silk warp, for the silk pattern, and a worsted weft of British wool. Valentias are produced at Spital-fields, and many are showy in appearance. They are manufactured for waistcoats, and are very similar to TOILINETTES.

Vandyke Albisola Point.—An Italian Lace worked in the sixteenth century, but now obsolete.

Vandyke Couching.—*See* COUCHING.

Vandykes.—This term is descriptive of a particular pointed form cut as a decorative border to collars and other portions of wearing apparel, and to the trimmings of dress skirts and bodices. It may be described as the form called chevron. The style owes its name to the great painter, who immortalised it in his portraits, and it may be seen in those of Charles I. and men of his time.

Vandyke Stitch.—*See* EMBROIDERY STITCHES.

Vandyke Tracing.—*See* TRACERY.

Veils.—These articles, chiefly worn with hats and bonnets for the protection of the face, may be had of lace, net, spotted net, gauze, tulle, and crape. They may be purchased ready made, cut, woven, or Pillow-made in shapes, or purchased by the yard. The gauze material sold for Veils, for country, travelling, or sea-side wear, may be had in blue, brown, grey, green, and black. Large white muslin and coloured cotton Veils may still be seen at Genoa. In Spain they are made of lace in large squares, covering the head, and lying over the shoulders. In Lima the Veils cover one eye. Brides wear them of great size, made of white lace, and covering them from the crown of the head to the knees. The widths of gauze for Veiling measures from half a yard to three-quarters in width; some being worn so long, especially in very cold countries, as to take 2 yards of material. The ordinary size would take three-quarters of a yard. Spotted net is about half a yard in width, and for an ordinary Veil three-quarters of a yard would be sufficient. Eastern Veils are worn very large, covering the forehead and bound round the mouth.

Vellum.—The skins of calves, kids, and lambs prepared for the purposes of engrossing, book binding, and illumination. Vellum is a superior kind of parchment. For the method of preparing Vellum, *see* PARCHMENT, which, as well as Vellum, is employed in the process of making certain Laces and Embroideries.

Velours.—The French term signifying Velvet. It also denotes a special description of furniture, carpet velvet, or plush, partly of linen and partly of double cotton warps and mohair yarn wefts, manufactured in Prussia.

Velouté.—The French name for a description of Velvet Lace, employed as a trimming.

Velveret.—An inferior sort of Velvet, employed for trimmings, the web of which is of cotton, and the pile of silk. The cotton makes it stiff; and when black, its inferiority to velvet, as in Thickset, is especially remarkable, as it does not keep its colour equally well. It is not to be recommended for a dress or jacket material, owing to its stiffness, and tendency to crease; besides which, the cotton which forms a part of its substance does not retain the blackness of the dye.

Velvet.—A closely-woven silk stuff, having a very thick, short pile or nap on the right side, formed by putting a portion of the warp threads over a needle, more or less thick, so as to regulate the quality of the Velvet; and, when the needle is removed, by passing a sharp steel instrument through the long opening it has left, to cut all the loops that had been formed. This nap always lies in one direction, and thus it must only be brushed that way, and that with either a piece of Velvet or cloth. The finest qualities of this material are made at Genoa and Lyons. When required for the purpose of trimmings, it should be cut diagonally. There are inferior sorts made with a cotton back. Others consist of a mixture throughout of silk and cotton, called velveteen, of which there are many qualities, and which may be had in all colours, and also brocaded. There are also Cotton Velvets, produced in various colours, and having small chintz patterns. According to Planché, in his *History of British Costume*, Velvet, under the Latin name of *Villosa*, or the French *Villuse*, is stuff mentioned during the thirteenth century. Shakespeare, in the *Taming of the Shrew*, and *à propos* of a saddle, speaks of

One girt, six times pieced, and a woman's cruppe of Velure.

And in *Henry IV.*,

I have removed Falstaff's horse, and he frets like a gummed velvet.

Also in *Measure for Measure*, the First Gentleman replies to Lucio,

An thou the velvet; thou art good velvet,
Thou'rt a three piled piece, I warrant thee.
I had as lief be a list of an English Kersey,
As be piled, as thou art piled, of a French velvet.

The large northern cities of Italy (especially Genoa) were the first to excel in the manufacture of Velvet. The French followed in acquiring a great proficiency in this branch of silk-weaving, and at the Revocation of the Edict of Nantes, the French silk weavers introduced the art into this country, and established it at Spitalfields.

Velvet Cloth.—A plain cloth with a gloss, employed in Ecclesiastical Embroidery.

Velvet Cloths.—These are beautifully soft and warm descriptions of cloth, suitable for ladies' jackets. They may be had both checked and striped, as well as in plain uniform colours.

Velveteen.—A description of fustian, made of twilled cotton, and having a raised pile, and of finer cotton, and better finish than the latter. It is made in claret, blue, green, and violet colour. Rain drops do not spot it, but the heat of a fire is injurious to the dye. It is a thick, heavy material, useful for winter dresses, children's clothing, women's outdoor jackets, and men's coats.

Velvet Flowers.—These, as well as the leaves, are cut by means of a punch for purposes of Appliqué Embroidery, when the stems can be worked in gold bullion. When to be thus employed, paste a piece of thin paper at the back of the velvet before it is cut out into the desired forms, and cut through both, otherwise the edges will become frayed. Flower making, including those of Velvet for wear on bonnets and the trimmings of evening dresses, is an art which has latterly been brought to great perfection.

Velvet Ribbons.—Of these there are many varieties, the plain, black, and coloured, plain Terry, figured, and embossed plush, and Tartan, both fancy and original checks. *See* RIBBONS.

Velvet Work.—From the nature of this material but few Embroidery Stitches can be executed upon it. It is, however, largely used in Church Embroideries as a background for altar cloths and hangings. The chief parts of the Embroidery are then worked upon linen stretched in a frame and transferred to the velvet when finished, and only tendrils, small scrolls, and tiny rounds worked as a finish to the Embroidery upon the velvet. For this description of work *see* CHURCH EMBROIDERY.

Another Way: The second kind of Velvet Work is made with embossed velvet, and is very effective and easy. It consists of outlining with gold thread the embossed flowers and arabesques, and filling in the centre of such parts with Satin Stitch worked in coloured filoselles. To work: Select a deep and rich toned piece of embossed velvet, and COUCH along every outline of the embossing two threads of Japanese gold thread. Then take two shades of green filoselle, and vein any of the leaves of the design with CREWEL STITCH and a pale shade of filoselle of the same colour as the velvet, and fill in the centres of any flowers or geometrical figures with long SATIN STITCHES.

Another Way: Frame the velvet and back it with holland. Trace out the design to be worked on the velvet with the help of white chalk, and work it over with floss silk. Bring the floss silk up from the back of the material, and put it down again to the back, making a long SATIN

STITCH. Make as few stitches as the pattern will allow of, as from the nature of the material they are difficult to work; ornament parts of the work with gold or silver thread or silk cords Couched down with silks matching them in shade.

Another Way: This is really Velvet Appliqué, and consists in cutting out of various coloured pieces of velvet, leaves, flowers, and scroll work, and attaching them to silk or satin backgrounds. To work: Back the pieces of velvet with brown holland, which paste evenly on them; lay a paper design of the right size over these pieces, and carefully cut them to the right shapes. Frame the satin or silk background after having backed it with linen, and arrange the pieces of velvet upon it as they should be laid. First TACK them slightly down to the foundation with tacking threads, to judge of their effect, and, when that is decided, OVERCAST each piece carefully to the foundation. To conceal these Overcast Stitches, COUCH down upon them either two lines of gold thread, or one of silk cord and one of gold thread, and work stalks and tendrils upon the background in SATIN STITCH; finish off the centres of the flowers with FRENCH KNOTS.

Venetian Bar.—This is used in modern Point Lace. To work Fig. 805: Work the first row from right to left

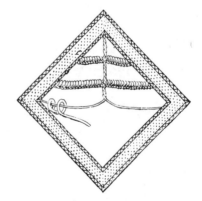

FIG. 805. VENETIAN BAR.

in SORRENTO BAR. Second row—Work a number of close BUTTONHOLE STITCHES on the lines thrown across the space. Third row—Work from right to left like the first row, and return with Buttonhole Stitch as before. Continue these two lines to the end of the space. For Fig. 806: Take the thread from left to right across the

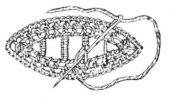

FIG. 806. VENETIAN BAR.

space, and work over it in Buttonhole Stitches. Work a number of these bars, a little distance apart, until the space is filled.

Venetian Carpets.—These are manufactured both in England and Scotland. They are composed of a worsted warp, traversed by a woollen weft, and arranged in stripes of different colours, the shoot being invisible, in consequence of its very dark colour. By a peculiar interchange of the two threads the production of the design on both sides of the stuff is accomplished. The pattern is necessarily a simple "diced" one, and the carpets are durable as well as thick, and suitable for bedrooms and nurseries.

Venetian Embroidery.—This is work resembling Roman Work and Strasbourg Embroidery, but is lighter than either in effect, on account of the introduction of Lace Stitches in some of the parts where the material is cut

BRUXELLES, HERRINGBONE, POINT DE GRECQUE, and other POINT LACE STITCHES, and vein the heavier leaves with lines of ROPE STITCH. Having finished the whole of the Embroidery, carefully cut away the linen that is not secured by the Buttonhole lines from underneath the Buttonhole Bars, and the Lace Stitches. Use a very sharp and small pair of scissors, and cut with the utmost care.

Another Way: In this second description of Venetian Embroidery the work is formed upon Brussels net, and is an imitation of lace. To work: Trace a lace design of some arabesque and running pattern upon pink calico, which back with brown paper. Then TACK net over it, and with a needle and fine thread RUN the outlines of the

FIG. 807. VENETIAN EMBROIDERY.

away. The work is done upon strong linens, hollands, and batiste, and is used for furniture trimmings, such as mantel and table borders, banner screens, and curtain borders. To work as shown in Fig. 807: Trace the outlines of the pattern upon écru-coloured linen, and RUN these outlines with thread both on their scalloped and plain side. Work them over with BUTTONHOLE lines, made of silk matching the linen in colour, and while doing so connect the various parts with plain Buttonhole Bars. Be careful that the lines of Buttonhole always turn their edges as shown in the illustration, as should they be made otherwise they will not secure the design when the material is cut away. Take some fine écru silk and fill in the parts of the design that are intended to imitate light and open flowers and leaves with WHEELS, POINT DE

design on the net. Work these over with lines of BUTTONHOLES, made with various coloured floss silks or filoselles, and work a scalloped Buttonhole edging. Cut the net away from the outside of the edging, and work in the centres of flowers or other centres to the outlines with a few long SATIN STITCHES. Use more than one shade of colour on each piece of lace, but let them blend together, and only use the soft shades of yellow, pink, blue, salmon, and green, and no dark or vivid colours.

Venetian Guipure.—One of the names given to Venetian Point, the word Guipure originally meaning lace made either of silk or thread upon parchment. *See* VENETIAN LACE.

Venetian Lace.—The Venetians dispute with the Spaniards the invention of Needlemade laces, considering

GENOA PLAITED LACE, WITH BORDER OF DRAWN WORK (RARE).

GREEK LACE, OF RETICELLA PATTERN.

that they obtained the rudiments of the art from the Saracens settled in Sicily before the Spaniards became acquainted with it. It is difficult to decide which nation has the superior claim, particularly as lace was in early times almost exclusively made in convents, and the nuns were not always of the same nationality as the people amongst whom they lived; but there seems to be no doubt that both Needle and Pillow Laces were made in Italy in the fifteenth century, although they attained their greatest renown during the sixteenth and seventeenth centuries, being then used at most of the Continental Courts, and rivalling for many years the productions of Flanders.

The laces made in Venice during the sixteenth and seventeenth centuries included Reticellas (Punto à Reticella), Cutwork (Punto Tagliato), Flat Venetian Point (Punto in Aria), Raised Venetian Point (Punto à Fogliami), Macramé (Punto à Groppo), Darned Netting (Punto à Maglia), Drawn Work (Punto Tirato), and Burano or Argentella Point, a grounded Venetian Lace. Of these numerous kinds the flat and raised Venetian Points were not worked before 1600, but they gradually superseded the others, and though very costly, became the universal decoration for all occasions of dress, besides being largely used for ecclesiastical purposes; and it was not until the middle of the seventeenth century that their fame at all declined. In 1654 Colbert prohibited the exportation of the Venetian Laces into France in order that the lace manufactories he had founded in Alençon and Argentan might be protected, and these same laces, although at first only intended to imitate Venetian Points, developed into something lighter and finer and soon became the fashion; the fine Needlepoints made at Brussels also shared in this change of taste, and were worn by the nobles of the Italian and French Courts, in preference to the heavier Venice Points. Under these adverse circumstances, the making of Venetian Points was discontinued, and at present the manufacture is quite extinct.

The Venetian flat Needlepoints, made when the lace was declining, are difficult to distinguish from the Spanish flat Points, but their patterns are generally lighter and finer. They are connected with Brides that do not run straight from one part of the pattern to another, but are irregular and broken up into several short Bars, each of which are trimmed with two plain Picots and not with Couronnes. The Venice Raised Points are extremely rich and varied as to their designs, which are either arabesque or conventionalised scrolls and flowers. They are sometimes worked in coloured silks, such as purple, yellow, and cream. They are distinguished by their Bride grounds, highly raised Cordonnets, solid stalks, and chief parts being worked in high relief, surrounded by Fleurs Volants, sometimes three rows deep; while many lace stitches known as Fillings are introduced into the various parts of the pattern, so that the effect of the lace is less solid and heavy and more running than the Raised Spanish Points. To work these Needlepoints: Draw the pattern upon detached pieces of parchment, outline with a FIL DE TRACE, and OVERCAST with BUTTONHOLE STITCHES, either padded or flat; to make the raised or flat Cordonnet, trim this with PICOTS, and fill with fancy stitches the spaces surrounded by the Cordonnets; TACK each separate piece when finished to a tracing of the whole design and secure by BRIDES ORNÉES, make the raised work separately and then attach to the flat parts. For the detailed manner of making the lace *see* SPANISH LACES.

The grounded Venetian Lace known as Burano or Argentella Point was made long after the disappearance of the Venetian Raised and flat Points. It resembled both Brussels and Alençon Laces, but was distinguished from them by its extreme flatness and absence of all raised parts, the lines of Buttonhole that surrounded the Fillings being as flat as those stitches, and the designs, consisting chiefly of powderings, either shaped as circles, ovals, or small sprays thrown upon the net-patterned ground. By many critics, Burano Point is considered superior to Needlemade Brussels Lace, from the whiteness of its thread and the great delicacy of its designs. It was made in Burano at the beginning of the present century, but is now obsolete.

Imitation Venice Points.—An imitation of the celebrated Venice raised and flat Points has lately been worked by ladies with much success. The design is all drawn upon one piece of linen, and the raised outlines made by working over a linen cord. The rest of the lace follows the old manner of making. To work as shown in Fig. 808: Trace the design upon Toile Ciré or thin Parchment, obtain some of Catt's fine linen cord and slightly TACK this to the Toile Ciré, marking out with it all the outlines of the thick parts of the lace. Take fine Mecklenburgh thread, No 20, and fill in the parts surrounded with the cord chiefly in rows of thick BUTTONHOLE STITCHES, but also with *Point de Brabançon* and *Point de Grecque* (*see* POINT LACE) Make in the process of the work the BARS that connect the detached parts of the pattern; make these with BUTTONHOLE Bars, ornamented with PICOTS, SPINES, and COURONNES. Cover the cord over with even rows of Buttonholes with the same fine thread, and ornament the raised CORDONNET thus made with Picots. Make the edge of the lace with a cord covered with Buttonholes, and with loops covered over with Buttonholes and trimmed with Picots.

Venetian Long Stitch Embroidery.—This is an old-fashioned description of Worsted Work, in which the design is worked with coloured worsteds or crewels upon open canvas, such as Toile Colbert, or upon net, or white silk canvas, the ground being left exposed. To work: Select an arabesque or geometrical Worsted Work pattern containing several colours but with little shading. Frame the canvas or net in an EMBROIDERY FRAME, so as to keep it well stretched, and work the design upon it in LONG STITCH. Let each Long Stitch pass over four, five, six, eight, or ten squares of the material one way, but only cover one square the other way (a square being two warp and two woof threads); arrange the length of these stitches according to the space one shade of colour has to cover, and make their greatest length either across the width of the material or perpendicular, according to the shading required. In shading the designs use the old-fashioned colours and not those obtained from aniline dyes.

Venetians.—A heavy kind of tape or braid, resembling double Londons. They are employed more especially for Venetian blinds, whence the name. The colours are ingrained, and the widths run half an inch, 1¼ inches, and 1½ inches. Another kind of braid or tape is made for Venetian blinds—thread webs, in white, unbleached blue, and green; sold in lengths of from 18, 24, to 36 **yards**; the widths running from 1 inch to 1½ inches.

shown in Drawn Work, but instead of being Overcast or Buttonholed over with plain linen thread, fine purse silks of various shades of colour are used, as in the Oriental Embroideries. *See* DRAWN WORK.

Venice Point.—*See* VENETIAN LACES.

Vest.—A generic term, signifying a garment, but adopted to denote a special article of wear, as in the case of the word vestment. A Vest now means a waistcoat, or a closely-fitting elastic article of underclothing, worn by both sexes, with or without long sleeves, and with either a high or low neck. It is worn inside a shirt or chemise,

FIG. 808. VENETIAN POINT—IMITATION.

Venetian Stitch.—A term sometimes applied to close rows of Buttonholes as Fillings in Needlepoint Laces, as this particular stitch is the one most used in Venetian Points. To work: Fasten the thread to the right side of the place to be filled in, and take it across to the left, cover it with a line of close and even BUTTON-HOLES and secure to the right side; fasten the thread again to the left side and work it over with Buttonholes, working each new stitch into the rib of the stitch above it in the first line. Repeat the second line until the space is filled.

Venezuelan Drawn Work.—The lace that is made at Venezuela is remarkable for its beauty. It resembles the Oriental Drawn Thread Work and the Italian and Swedish Drawn Works. The work is executed upon cambric or linen, and the threads are drawn away and divided, as

and is to be had in spun silk, merino, lambswool, cotton, or gauze, the latter of silk, or a union of silk and cotton, or silk and wool. These latter may be worn all the year round, and do not shrink when washed. Cotton vests are to be had both bleached and unbleached; are strong and thick. Vests may be had both hand-made, and machine-made; the trade in the former is extensively carried on by Scotchwomen, who knit them at a reasonable charge. Vests, as well as other under-garments, may be had woven of the Norwegian Pine Wool in its natural colour. This material is strongly to be recommended for persons exposed to a damp or very changeable climate, as it contains very curative properties in cases of rheumatism, a strong essential oil being procured from the bark of this pine for application to affected parts.

Vêtement.—The French term, signifying a garment.

Victoria Crape.—A comparatively new description of crape, composed entirely of cotton. It is made in different widths, from 1 to 2 yards, like ordinary crape. In appearance it is like silk crape, and is very inexpensive, but it is not economical to the purchaser, as it does not wear at all well.

Victoria Frilling.—This is a description of cotton cambric Frilling, produced at Coventry, for the purpose of trimming bed, and underlinen. Its distinctive characteristic consists in the fact that the drawing cord is woven into the fabric, which is an advantage in every respect. Victoria Frilling may be had in three different widths for bed linen, viz., of 2 inches, 2½ inches, and 3 inches. It is also made for the trimming of underlinen as narrow as half an inch. It is a patent manufacture.

Victoria Lawn.—This is a description of muslin, semi-transparent, and employed as a lining for skirts of dresses. It is rather stiff, and may be had in black and white, and is also used for frillings, and for petticoats worn under clear muslin dresses. It was at one time employed for evening dresses.

Vicuna Cloth.—This beautiful cloth is made from the wool of the vicuna, which is a species of the llama of Peru and Chili. It is employed as a dress material, and is very soft in texture; and is produced in neutral colours, measuring 29 inches in width.

Vienna Cross Stitch.—See *Persian Cross Stitch*, Embroidery Stitches.

Vigogne.—A delicate all wool textile, twilled, and produced in neutral colours—greys, lavenders, and steel—as well as black. The widths run from 45 inches to 48 inches, according to the quality; the commoner kinds have a small *Armure* pattern woven in them. Vigogne is the French name for the wool of the Peruvian sheep, or for a woollen stuff of the finest Spanish wool. It is very suitable as a summer dress material, for which it is designed.

Volant.—The French term denoting either a flounce, or a frill; both of which are descriptions of dress trimmings.

Vraie Réseau.—This term indicates that the Network ground to either Needlepoint or Pillow Laces has been either worked with a Needle or with Bobbins. Before the introduction of machine-made net, all the grounds of lace were worked in this way, but since then the lace flowers or pattern has been Appliqué on to the machine net, except when especial orders for the Vraie Réseau or real ground is given, as the costliness of the thread used and the time the real ground takes to manufacture more than trebles the price of the lace. Two of the Vraie Réseau Grounds are shown enlarged in Valenciennes Lace, but there are a great many varieties both of the plaited and twisted net patterns, besides the Dame Joan, Trolly, Torchon, Star, Point de Paris, and Italian, all of which are described under their own headings. The term Vraie Réseau is often given exclusively to the ground used in Brussels Lace, but in reality all the lace grounds made without the assistance of machinery are Vraie Réseau.

W.

Wadding.—Wadding, as sold in the shops, is carded cotton wool; bleached, unbleached, slate-coloured, and black, cut into sheets of various sizes, and sold by the gross, but it is also manufactured in lengths of 12 yards, for quilting. It is placed between the outer material and the lining of any garment; if not quilted, it is necessary to attach it to the linings, or it is apt to form into lumps. It has latterly been regarded as preferable to flannel or domett for shrouds, for which the bleached Wadding is employed. The French name for Wadding is *Ouate*, which was that originally given to the downy tufts found in the pods of the plant called *Apocynum*, imported from Egypt and Asia Minor. To make Wadding, a lap or fleece, prepared by the carding machine, is applied to tissue paper by means of a coat of size, which is made by boiling the cuttings of hareskins, and adding alum to the gelatinous solutions. When two laps of cotton are glued with their faces together, they form the most downy kind of Wadding.

Waistcoatings.—These are fancy textiles made of worsted and cotton, or worsted only, or of silk in which there is a pattern, worked in the loom; differently coloured yarns being employed. The name by which these cloths are known explains the use to which they are applied. Huddersfield is the chief seat of the industry.

Wamsutta Calicoes.—Various descriptions of cloth made at New Bedford, Massachusetts, and known as Wamsuttas. One of them is a double warp cotton sheeting, which may be had in Manchester, where there is a depôt. The Wamsutta Mills produce some 12,000 miles of sheeting and shirting, or 20,000,000 square yards of cotton cloth every year. They were opened in the year 1846, and the annual consumption of cotton is about 19,000 bales. The cotton chiefly employed is what is called in the markets "benders," because raised within the bends of the Mississipi river, where the rich soil produces a peculiarly strongly-fibred variety. The strength of these yarns is tested by a machine, eighty threads together being steadily stretched by means of a screw, to prove their endurance, until they part, and the breaking weight is indicated on a dial. Thus, according to the results of this daily test, the yarn produced in these mills is claimed to be 20 per cent. stronger than the standard for "super extra" wearing yarn, according to the tables laid down in English books; and every piece of cloth is examined by a committee of inspectors before it is allowed to leave the mills. Not only are bleached and brown sheetings and shirtings, both heavy and fine, produced at Wamsutta, but also muslin and cambric muslin, for underclothing.

Warp.—This term is employed by weavers to denote the threads that run longitudinally from end to end of a textile, and are crossed by the weft, otherwise called the woof. The Warp passes through the treadles and reed, and the Weft, otherwise called the Woof, which is wound round the shuttle, crosses it.

Warp Stitch.—*See* EMBROIDERY STITCHES.

Washing Lace.—*See* LACE.

Wash-leather.—An imitation of chamois leather, made of split sheeps' skins, from which gloves and linings for waistcoats, bodices, and petticoats are produced. The skins go through a process of oiling and aluming, and when thoroughly prepared for use, may be washed until worn out, without losing their buff colour. Wash-leather is formed into regimental belts, and into gloves for both sexes; it is employed for household purposes, such as the cleaning of plate and of brasses. It also goes by the name of Buff Leather.

Watered.—This term, as applied to any kind of textile, signifies that a wavy pattern has been impressed upon it, which has not been woven into its texture. The method of producing it is, to place two pieces of material together lengthwise, and to pass them between two cylindrical metal rollers, into the hollow within one of the latter a heated iron is introduced. Thus, as the two pieces of stuff will not exactly coincide in their respective positions with the rollers, one portion will be subjected to a greater degree of pressure than another, resulting in the wave-like pattern desired.

Watered Linings.—These cloths may be had both in linen or cotton, in cream, slate, and dove colour, and are chiefly employed for the lining of men's coats. The width is 38 inches. *See* LININGS.

Watered Twist.—Cotton thread, manufactured for the weaving of calicoes by means of water mills. It is spun hard, and is much twisted. Arkwright's water mill was the first ever erected. He set up the works at Cromford, Derbyshire, employing the Derwent as the water power. This kind of machine employed used to be called "water-spinning" machines, and thus the name of the cloth produced was Water Twist, but had no reference to the process called "watering."

Watered Woollen Cloths.—These are new materials, produced at Bradford, for women's dresses. They are soft and undressed, and are to be had in black. For the method of watering *see* WATERED.

Waterproofed Fabrics.—An extensive variety of textiles rendered impervious to moisture, without thereby being injured in their texture or colour. They may be had in thick and thin woollen cloths; in silk, alpaca, and in what is called "Macintosh;" but the latter, being air tight, as well as waterproof, is a very unwholesome article for wear, and is only suitable for hot water bottles, air cushions, water beds, &c.

Waterproofed Zephyr Tweed.—This is a very light material, employed for summer wear, and rendered waterproof. It measures 55 inches in width, and is suitable for wear as a dust cloak, as well as in rain. It can be had in different shades of drab and grey.

Wavy Couching.—*See* COUCHING.

Weaver's Knot.—*See* KNOTS.

Weaving.—The method by which the web of every kind of textile is produced, and of which there are many varieties. Plain Weaving signifies that the warp and weft intersect each other in regular order, crossing at right angles, and producing a simple web of uniform face and construction. Tweeling, that every thread of the weft passes under one, and over two or more threads of the weft. Twilled silk yarn is called Satin, twilled cotton is fustian or jean, and twilled wool is Kerseymere or serge. This tweeling may be executed on both sides of the material, as in shalloon; and this method of weaving may be so diversified, by various dispositions of the loom, as to produce stripes and decorative designs, such as those exhibited in damask, diaper, and dimity. Pile Weaving is the method by which velvets are produced, a third series of short threads being employed, besides those of the warp and weft, and introduced between the two latter, being doubled under the weft, so as to form loops. These are afterwards cut to form the "pile," and, when uncut, they present an appearanc elike Terry Velvet. When pile weaving is adopted in the production of cotton cloth, the result may be seen in fustians, corduroys, &c. Figure Weaving is another and beautiful method of Weaving, by which designs—either of different materials, or colours—are introduced in the warp or weft. To effect this, the threads are so disposed as that certain colours shall be concealed, whilst others are drawn to the front, and they must change places from time to time, according to the necessity for their re-introduction, in carrying out and completing the design. In producing stripes, a variety of dissimilar threads may be arranged in the warping, and so left without change; or the threads of the warp and those of the weft may be of different colours respectively, which will produce that changeable hue on the cloth which is known by the term "shot." The Jacquard loom is the most perfect kind of "draw-loom" yet produced, to carry out Figure Weaving in its most beautiful and intricate varieties; and damasks in silk, linen, cotton, and wool are now wholly manufactured by it. Stockingette or Elastic Cloth Weaving is another form of the art, which is very distinct from those branches already named. Instead of a foundation consisting of two threads—the warp and weft—there is but one continuous thread employed for the whole web. This single thread is formed into a perpetually successive series of loops, and the loops of one row are drawn through those of its predecessor. Stockingette Cloth is produced in imitation of knitting; and, besides the large looms in which it is manufactured wholesale, there are hand-worked machines, in which small articles may be woven—such as stockings, scarves, and vests. Ribbons are woven in the same way as ordinary cloth.

The power-loom, which succeeded the hand-loom, was invented by the Rev. Dr. Edmund Cartwright in 1757. Horrocks' loom was afterwards produced, and Monteith's in 1798; and the "Jacquard," invented in 1752, has been greatly improved in England since the time it was first introduced. Hand Weaving is now confined to cloth produced in gaols by the felons. Weaving is an art of the most remote antiquity, and of Eastern origin. In this country it can be traced back to the Anglo-Saxons and early Britons. In London the weavers formed one of the most ancient of the Guilds, and were called the *Telarii.* The domestic title, "wife," is derived from the verb "to weave," as she was distinguished so much in olden times by her labours with the distaff. The Saxon for weave was *wefan,* and the German is *weben,* whence, in the same way, *weih*—a woman, one who works at the distaff and makes a web—is derived. King Alfred, when speaking in his will of his descendants, distinguishes the sexes as those respectively of the "spindle side," and the "spear side;" and this idea may be seen exemplified on many graves in Germany, which are severally distinguished by the effigies of spears and spindles. In reference to Queen Anne, Dryden speaks of "a distaff on the throne." This adoption of the name "wife," from the art of weaving, is a natural sequence to that of giving the name "spinster" to an unmarried woman—the girl is supposed to spin the yarn for her future clothing, which she is to wear woven into webs for garments, as a wife.

Webbing.—This is a strong thick tape woven in a peculiar way; usually striped in blue and white, or pink and white, and may be had from 2 to 3 inches in width. It is made of hemp thread, and designed for the support of sofa squabs, and bedding, being nailed to the wooden framework at both ends and sides, and interlaced successively in and out, at regular distances apart. It is also employed for the stands of butlers' trays and trunks, for trunk-lid supports and trunk trays; and also for girths, &c. The various kinds are known as Manchester, and Holland, black or red, and stay tapes. The term "Webbing" is also used to signify Warp as prepared for the weaver.

Webbing (Elastic).—A preparation of indiarubber inclosed in silk, mohair, or cotton. Their respective widths are given according to the number of cords, from one to sixteen, or upwards. The narrow single cords are to be had in two lengths of 72 yards to the gross; the wider makes are in four pieces, containing 36 yards each, and are generally sold by the gross. These goods should not be kept in air-tight parcels, or they will lose their elasticity. Webbings are produced of appropriate dimensions for belts, the sides of boots, known as "spring sides," and narrow frilled cotton ones, employed for underlinen.

Weft.—The yarns or threads running across the length of the cloth, that is, from selvedge to selvedge, in a web. The Weft is also known by the name of Woof, and is wound round the shuttles during the process of weaving, while the Warp is extended in many successive threads, and passes through the treadles and reed.

Weldbores.—This is a description of woollen cloth manufactured at Bradford, Yorkshire.

Welsh Flannels.—Welsh-made flannels are of a bluish shade, and have a broad grey selvedge on both sides. They somewhat resemble the Lancashire Flannels, and measure from 30 to nearly 36 inches in width. There are also Patent Welsh Flannels, which are very fine and of superior texture, but are not very durable and

are made for infants' clothing. Wales is the country where Flannel was originally made. Much is still produced by hand labour from the fleeces of the flocks on the native mountains, and is of peculiar quality and finish; but the most extensive manufacture of Flannels, not only in England, but in the whole world, is in Lancashire, especially in the neighbourhood and town of Rochdale, where the greatest variety of widths, finish, and substance is produced, in the thin gauze, medium, thick, double raised, and Swanskin.

Welted.—This term signifies the ribbing of any material, by the insertion of wadding between it and the lining, and Run in parallel lines. It is of the same nature as Quilting, only that the Runnings do not cross each other so as to make a diamond pattern. Stays are Welted to stiffen them, in places where whalebones would be objectionable; black petticoats are sometimes Welted, to make them stand out, after the style of hoops.

Welting.—See *Ribbing* in KNITTING.

Welts.—These are the rounds of Ribbing worked in Stocking Knitting as the commencement to a stocking, and are intended to keep the top of that article from rolling up.

Whalebone.—This bone is taken from the upper jaw of the whale, and is utilised for umbrella frames; it is also very extensively employed by staymakers and dressmakers. For the use of the former it is cut into suitable lengths, the widths varying between three-sixteenths and 1½ inches. It is sold by the pound. For the use of dressmakers it is also prepared, neatly cut into lengths, and sold by the gross sets, or in small quantities. The price of Whalebone fluctuates much, being dependent on the success of the whalers. Steels, cut in lengths, and sold in calico covers, have greatly superseded the use of Whalebone both for the stay and dressmaking trades. About 1¾ tons of the bone are produced in the mouth of one whale, of 16 feet long, the ordinary value of which is about £160 per ton. This bone forms a kind of fringe or strainer, in the mouth of the Baleen whale, acting as a net to retain the small fish, on which the creature preys, which, when his jaws are open, are washed in and out. This bone takes the place of teeth, and consists of numerous parallel *laminæ,* descending perpendicularly from the palate. In a whale of 60 feet long the largest piece of Baleen would be 12 feet in length. To prepare Whalebone for use, immerse it for twelve hours in boiling water, before which it will be found too hard for the purposes of manufacture.

Wheatear Stitch.—*See* EMBROIDERY STITCHES.

Wheeling.—A description of yarn used for charitable purposes. It may be had in all colours.

Wheels.—These are required in all descriptions of ornamental needlework, and in Pillow and Needle Laces. They are made in a variety of forms, from the simple Wheel formed of Corded Bars, to the most elaborate device. To work Wheels used in Needlemade Laces and

Embroidery, and as shown in Fig. 809: This design illustrates a Wheel wherein the centre of the material is retained. Trace a circle upon the material, and RUN threads round the tracing to the thickness of a quarter of

FIG. 809. WHEEL.

an inch. BUTTONHOLE over these threads with a close and even line of Buttonholes, as shown in Fig. 810, Detail, and turn the Buttonhole edge to the outside. Work a line of POINT DE VENISE as an edging to the Buttonholes.

FIG. 810. WHEEL—DETAIL.

To work the Wheel shown in Fig. 811: This Wheel is chiefly used in Embroideries and in Point Lace. Outline the circle, Run a thread round it, and BUTTONHOLE over the thread with close Buttonholes, turning the edge of the Buttonholes to the inside. Work upon that edge a row of

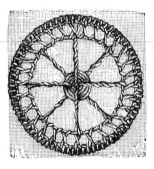

FIG. 811. WHEEL.

loose POINT DE BRUXELLES into every other Buttonhole. Run a thread into these loops, so as to draw them together into a circle, and make BARS across the open space left in the centre of Wheel. Commence at 1 in Fig. 812, Detail, and cross to 2, CORD the line to the centre of the

Wheel, then take the thread to 3, and Cord back, and so follow all the numerals, always Cording the thread back to the centre. When the lines are all made, fill the centre of the Wheel up by passing the thread over and under the

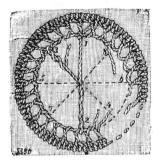

FIG. 812. WHEEL—DETAIL.

threads for five rounds, and then finish by Cording the thread up 1, which has been left uncorded in order to bring it back.

To Work an Open Wheel: This Wheel is formed with Corded Bars, which are many or few, according to the size of the space to be filled.

Fig. 813 shows a Wheel worked with four Bars; Fig. 814, a wheel worked with eight Bars; and Fig. 815, one worked

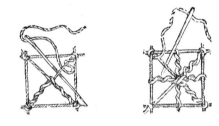

FIG. 813. WHEEL.   FIG. 814. WHEEL.

with thirteen Bars. They are all worked alike. Fasten the thread to the corner of the space, and take it across to the opposite corner. CORD it back to the centre, and carry it to the angle on the other side. Cord it back to the centre, and take it to the last angle, Cord back and fill

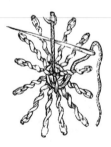

FIG. 815. WHEEL.

up the rest of the space with the same kind of lines, always returning to the centre; fill that in with rounds of thread worked over and under the lines, and where these are sufficient, Cord the thread up the first line that was made.

To work Fig. 816: This open Wheel is much more elaborate than the others, and is chiefly used in fine Embroidery or Lace Work. Run a line of thread round the space, and cover it with a close row of BUTTONHOLES. Turn the edges to the inside, make a tiny loop in the centre of the Wheel, which cover with a round of Buttonholes, and TACK this down with tacking threads to keep it

FIG. 816. WHEEL.

steady; work a round of open Buttonholes with six loops, and continue to work in rounds with close Buttonholes where the spokes of the Wheel come, and loose Buttonholes to divide them. Finish the spaces between the spokes with a Vandyked CORDED BAR, but take the spokes in lessening rows of close Buttonhole down to the edge of the Wheel. Finish by taking the tacking thread out of the centre, and cutting the material away underneath if there is any.

To work Fig. 817: This Wheel is of the same kind as

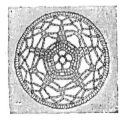

FIG. 817. WHEEL.

the last. Enclose the circle with a round of BUTTONHOLE, and then make POINT DE BRUXELLES loops round; work a second round of Point de Bruxelles, and gradually thicken with closer stitches where the spokes come; then work three rows of close Buttonhole, and finish with a circle of six Buttonhole Stitches.

To Make a Pillow Lace Wheel:—Prick a pattern with holes, eighteen holes to the inch and a quarter of an inch wide. Hang on twelve pairs of Bobbins, work in the pins right and left six times, take the four centre Bobbins and TWIST the pair to the left three times. Take the pair to the left and work it to the left-hand pin, and Twist the pair now nearest the centre pair three times, put up a pin in the centre between the two pairs of twisted Bobbins, make a CLOTH STITCH to enclose the pin, and Twist the two pairs three times, leave them, take up the pair of Bobbins behind the left-hand pin, work in the pin, and work across to the pair of centre Bobbins nearest the

left hand, Twist the working pair three times, make a CLOTH STITCH, Twist each pair three times, and carry back the pair nearest the left hand to the left-hand pin, putting a pin between the two pairs to the left. Take up the right-hand Bobbins behind the right-hand pin and work in the pin; bring the Worker Bobbins to the pair of centre Bobbins nearest the right-hand pin, Twist the workers three times, and make a Cloth Stitch with the right-hand centre pair, Twist each pair three times, and take back the pair nearest the right hand to the right-hand pin; having put a pin between the twisted Bobbins in the centre, take up the four centre Bobbins, make a Cloth Stitch and Twist each pair three times, put up a pin between the twisted pairs. The pins will be in the form of a small diamond and the design will form a Star with an open hole in the centre and six small ones round it.

Wheel Stitch.—*See* EMBROIDERY STITCHES.

Whipcord Couching.—Similar to Wavy Couching. *See* COUCHING.

Whipping.—A term used in needlework, denoting a method of drawing up a piece of frilling of any fine material into gathers, by means of sewing loosely over a delicately rolled edge of the same. To work: Hold the cambric with the wrong side towards you, and insert the needle at the back of the proposed roll, not through, but just below it. Secure firmly the end of the thread there, at the extreme right. Then hold the cambric in the left hand, close to where the roll should begin; and damping the thumb, roll the material over towards you, very closely and finely, first passing the thumb upwards, and then downwards. As soon as space is made for the setting of two or three stitches, make them, inserting the needle at the back as before, and at very regular distances apart; the thread should be drawn a little at first, to test its capability for running easily, when required as a drawing string, and then drawn a little from time to time. The second part of the work is to adjust the frilling in equal proportions to the article for which it is intended. To do this, it is essential that the cambric frill be "halved and quartered," and even divided into smaller spaces; pins are inserted to mark the several measurements. The article to be trimmed must be marked with pins in the same way, and when ready for the drawing of the string, place each centre, and each quarter, one against the other, the Frilling next to you; secure them to each other by means of pins, one being now sufficient at each division of the material, the corresponding pin may be removed. The article and its trimming will thus be equally divided, and there will be no greater fulness in one quarter than in another. This done, adjust the Whipping evenly in each compartment, and secure the needle end of the loose drawing thread temporarily, by twisting it round the top and end of a pin several times. Then hold the two pieces of pinned material between the thumb and forefinger of the left hand; keeping the work very flat, lying along the finger. Take up every Whip, or portion of the roll, between the stitches, in sewing the two parts together and insert the needle in a slanting direction, that the thread may exactly lie in the folds of the Whipping.

White Embroidery.—*See* EMBROIDERY.

White Wolf Skins (*Canis oxidentalis*).—The fur of wolf skins is very thick, warm, and durable, the tail bushy and handsome, but the skin of the white wolf of northern latitudes is the most valuable, and rarest of any of the varieties known. The hair is long, and tipped with a darker colour. Wolf skins are made into carriage and sofa rugs, and mats for the hearths, &c.

Whole Stitch.—A name sometimes applied to the Cloth Stitch of Pillow Lace. *See* CLOTH STITCH.

Widen.—*See* KNITTING.

Widow's Lawn.—This material can only be procured in certain shops, and for Widows' Weeds. It is a linen muslin, very clear, and even in make, 52 inches in width.

Widows' Weeds.—This is a comprehensive term, denoting the whole mourning apparel of a widow; of which the broad flat fold of crape, extending backwards over the top of the bonnet, and falling straight down the back; the peculiarly shaped muslin cap, with very long broad muslin strings, which are never tied; and the broad muslin cuffs, thinner in the centre than at the two borders, form the most remarkable features. The custom for widows to wear a peculiar style of cap is of Roman origin, and the wearing of their "weeds" was compulsory for a period of ten months. See the *Epistles of Seneca*, 65. The term "Weeds" was used in the Middle Ages to signify an entire dress. In such a sense it is employed in Ritson's *Ancient Popular Poetry*, in which the cloak, or complete suit is denoted by it, viz.:

He cast on him his Royal weed;

and, again, in reference to Ecclesiastical vestments:

His cope, and scapelary,
And all his other weed.

The poet Spenser speaks of "lowly shepherds' Weeds"; and Milton of "Palmers' Weeds." Also, as a badge of sorrow, he says:

In a mourning weed, with
Ashes upon her head, and tears
Abundantly flowing, &c.

Width.—A term employed in dressmaking, synonymously with that of Breadth; meaning the several lengths of material employed in making a skirt, which—according to the fashion of the day—is composed of a certain number, gored or otherwise. The term Breadth is more generally in use.

Wigans.—These consist of a description of calico, so named after the place of its manufacture. In quality they are soft, warm, and finished; but are stout and heavy, and are employed for many purposes. They are made for sheetings, amongst other purposes, and measure from 2 to 3 yards in width.

Wild Rose Border.—The design shown in Fig. 818 is one made in Honiton Lace. To work: Commence at the flower, and work the centre round of that in STEM STITCH, with five pair of Bobbins, Sewing each row to the edge of the round. Make the petals alternately in CLOTH and HALF STITCH, with eight pair of Bobbins and a GIMP. Work down the flower stem to the knot of the next pattern with six pair of Bobbins and in Stem Stitch, make the knot and work in Stem Stitch to the leaves. Make the small leaf touching the flower first, carry Stem up the side and return, making Cloth Stitch with eight pair of Bobbins, connect to the flower with a SEWING. Work the large leaf on the opposite side in the same way, and with ten pair of Bobbins. Cut off four pair when they reach the leaf stem, and work in Stem Stitch to the last leaf, cut off a pair, and take the Stem Stitch down the middle of that leaf; here hang on two pair of Bobbins, turn the pillow, and work down one side in Cloth Stitch, RAISED WORK and PEARL EDGE. At the bottom of the leaf cross the leaf stem, cut off a pair of Bobbins, turn the Pillow, and work the other half of the leaf in Half Stitch and PLAIN EDGE. Cut off a pair of Bobbins at the tip, and work the centre fibre of the leaf touching the last made one, and when the bottom of it is reached, turn the Pillow, work down one side in Half Stitch and Plain Edge, turn the pillow and work the other in Cloth Stitch and Pearl Edge. When finished, work the stalk in Stem Stitch to the next flower with six

FIG. 818. WILD ROSE BORDER.

pair of Bobbins, the recut off the Bobbins. In working the stalks, make the Pearls to the inner side, and not to the outer, as shown in the illustration, as they would be lost when the lace is sewn to a foundation. Fasten on six pair of Bobbins, and work the two lower leaves in Cloth Stitch, with Pearls upon the edge towards the flowers, and connect them at the tips; and, lastly, work the four middle leaves with Raised Work, and join each to the main stalk, and work them in pairs. Work the centre of the Rose in CUCUMBER PLAITINGS.

Wilton Carpets.—Carpets of this description are rather expensive, in consequence of the large amount of material demanded, and the slow process of the weaving. Nearly 3000 threads of yarn are employed on a web of linen, only 27 inches wide. Wilton Carpets much resemble Brussels in the manner of manufacture; the surface yarn being worked on a linen web, the designs raised entirely from the warp, and the yarn is carried over wires, more or less fine, which, when withdrawn, leave a series of loops. These wires are sharp, and cut through them in their removal, leaving a velvet pile. In the manufacture of Brussels carpets the wires are round, and are not designed to cut the pile, but to leave the loops intact, after the style of Terry velvet. The original seat of the industry was at Axminster, Devonshire, but is now at Wilton, near Salisbury. Inferior imitations are made in Yorkshire, and in Scotland.

Wimple.—An article of Mediæval dress, now only retained in conventual houses by the Nuns. It is a neck-cloth, which sometimes is drawn across the chin, as well as up the sides of the face and temples, meeting the band which tightly covers the forehead, passing straight across it just above the eyebrows. It is made of linen, but formerly it was sometimes made of silk. Wimples may be seen on monumental effigies of many of our early Queens, abbesses, nuns, and great ladies.

In Chaucer's *Romaunt of the Rose*, this ancient, and still existing article of dress is mentioned, viz.:

> Wering a vaile instead of wimple,
> As nounes don in their abbey.

Winseys.—These are made of two descriptions—all wool, and of wool and calico. They are very durable, and are used by the poorer class of people. There is a quantity of oil in the common qualities, accompanied by a disagreeable odour.

Wire Ground.—This ground is sometimes used in Brussels Lace; it is made of silk, with its net-patterned meshes partly raised and arched, and is worked separately from the design, which is sewn on to it when completed.

Wire Ribbon.—A narrow cotton ribbon or tape, used for the purposes of millinery, into which three or four fine wires are woven, It is sold in packets, which respectively contain twelve pieces, of 12 yards each, eight of 18, or six of 24 yards.

Witch Stitch.—*See* EMBROIDERY STITCHES.

Wool.—This is the soft curled or crisped species of hair or fur, of which the coat or fleece of the sheep consists. It is also to be found on other animals. There are two classes of wool, the short and the long stapled; the short, not exceeding 4 inches, keeps the name of wool; the long, which measures from 6 to 10 inches, is prepared for weaving in a different manner, and is combed and made into worsted stuffs. The longest length of staple obtained has been 20 inches. The long-stapled wool sheep of England are of four breeds: those of Dishley, in Leicestershire, Lincolnshire, of Teeswater, and Dartmoor, those of Lincolnshire sometimes growing wool a foot in length. The average weight of these fleeces is reckoned from 8 to 10 pound. Our short-stapled sheep are those of Dorsetshire, Herefordshire, and the Southdowns. The manufacture of woollen cloth is commenced by cleaning the wool, which is a long process of boiling, &c. It is then dyed, sprinkled over with olive oil, and beaten with rods. It then passes through a scribbling engine, to separate the fibres into light flakes, called "laps," thence through the carding engine; after that through the slubbing or roving machine, to make the wool into the soft loose thread, which is subsequently spun into yarn and made into cloth. Milling and fulling then follow, by which a length of 40 yards, and 100 inches in width, would be reduced to the proper thickness of ordinary superfine cloth, by shrinking it to some 30 yards long and 60 inches wide.

The manufacture of woollen cloth by the ancient Britons is demonstrated by their presence in the Tumuli or Barrows already opened; and it is a matter of historical record that not its use alone, but its manufacture, is connected with the names of the highest ladies in the land. In the spinning of wool King Alfred's mother was distinguished for her skill, and Edward I., while he wisely arranged to "settle his sons at schole," set his daughters to "wollwerke." In the reign of Edward III. the export of wool from England was made a felony, and the exportation of the woollen yarn forbidden under a penalty of forfeiture.

Woollen-backed Satin.—A very serviceable make of Satin, chiefly employed for jackets and mantles, and which, owing to the mixture of wool with the silk, does not form creases in its wear. It is 24 inches in width.

Woollen Cord.—This is one of the varieties of corduroy. It has a warp of cotton and a weft of wool, and is cut after the same manner as cotton cord—another description of the same class of textile—but the face is wholly woollen, whence its name. It is suitable for men's riding breeches or trousers, and is both warm and strong.

Woollen Matelassé.—This description of cloth is manufactured exactly after the manner of silk Matelassé, and is chiefly employed for the making of mantles, being a thick material, of handsome appearance, and satisfactory in wear. It has much the appearance of being quilted in the form of leaves, flowers, and other devices. The width measures from about 1½ yards to 2 yards.

Woollen Textiles.—These are spun from the soft, curly, short-stapled woollen yarn, which varies in length from 3 inches, to 4 inches, and is the only kind employed for making cloth. The term cloth, like stuff, has a general significance, and is applied to textiles composed of every kind of material, but is of more particular application to goods made from short stapled wool. Amongst those made from it are broad cloth, kerseymere, pelisse cloths, frieze bearskin, bath coating, duffil, tweed, hodden grey, plush, flannel (of many descriptions), domett, baize, and blanketing.

Woollen Yarn.—All wool is distinguished by this name which has not passed through the process of combing, whether by hand or machinery, Lambswool fingering is sent out by the manufacturers in ½ pounds, consisting of eight skeins, of 1 ounce weight each; but the correctness of the weight cannot be relied upon. They are from two to ten fold, are supplied in 3 pound, 6 pound, and 12 pound packages. The fleecy wools are produced in a great variety of colours. Lambswool yarn of a superior quality may be had in white, grey, drab, and other colours, in 3 pound, 6 pound, and 12 pound parcels, the numbers running from 0½ to 4. Smaller quantities may be purchased. Berlin lambswools are dyed in every description of colour; the numbers run from 0½ to 4. They are supplied in parcels of 3 pound, 6 pound, and 12 pound, may be had of single and double thickness, and by weight or skein, according to the requirements of the purchaser. There is also the Leviathan wool, which is composed of many strands, and is full and soft, and designed for Embroidery on canvas of considerable coarseness; the Lady Betty wool, in black, white, and scarlet, sold by weight or skein; the Eider Yarn, which is peculiarly delicate and glossy, and employed for hand-made shawls and scarves; the Andalusian, a tightly twisted wool, about the thickness of single Berlin; the Shetland wool, which is finer than the latter; the Pyrenean, which is of a still finer description; and Zephyr wool, which is remarkably thin and fine. Wool mendings, sometimes incorrectly called Angola, consist of a mixture of wool and cotton, and may be had in small skeins, or on cards, or reels, in many shades of colour. *See* WOOL.

Wool Needles.—These are short and thick, with blunt points, and long eyes, like those of darning needles. They are sometimes called tapestry needles. *See* NEEDLES.

Wool Velours.—A description of very soft, thick, and close-grained flannel, having much nap, and is employed for making dressing jackets, and French peignoirs, and peasants' or maid servants' short loose square cut jackets, having pockets on each side. It is made in many colours and patterns, and chiefly striped like Ribbongrass.

Woolwork Flowers.—These are flowers made by winding wool round wire foundations so that they stand erect and can be used as detached bouquets, or placed simply round the borders of mats. The flowers that are suitable are convolvulus, poppy, Marguerite daisy, geranium, and lily of the valley. The materials required are netting Meshes from half an inch to 1½ inches in width, pieces of thin wood, round in shape, 2 inches in diameter, with a small hole in the centre and with scalloped edges, the same thin pieces of wood shaped as squares of 2¼ inches, very tiny cap wire, and single Berlin wool matching the colouring of the flowers.

To Work a Convolvulus: Take a round shaped piece of wood and in every scallop round its edge lay down a line of fine wire, bringing all the ends of the wire to the back of the wood through the centre hole, where twist them together and cut off. Thread a wool needle with white wool, fasten the wool in the hole in the centre of the wood, and pass it round and round in circles between the wires and the wood, as each wire is reached make a stitch over it so as to enclose it, then carry the wool along to the next wire and make a stitch over that, and so continue to work round after round, each one slightly larger than the other, until half the rosette is covered. Fasten off the white wool, and continue the work with pale blue wool instead, which carry up nearly to the edge of the rosette; cut the wires at the back, close to the edge and turn these pieces so as to secure them into the edge of the flower, which will assume a trumpet shape as soon as released: Curve the edge of the convolvulus over, make very short stamens, by covering wire with yellow wool, which insert into the flower centre, and then wind

green wool round the ends of wire left in the centre of the flower to form the stalk.

To Work a Daisy: Take a netting Mesh three-quarter of an inch wide, some white wool and fine wire, wind the wool round the Mesh and secure it with the wire (as described for making the poppy) forty-eight times, then take the wool off the Mesh, the wire this time will form the bottom of the petals. To form the top, tie together with a little knot every loop in sets of three. Take a round piece of brown velvet the size of the centre of a Marguerite, which line with buckram, and work a number of FRENCH KNOTS upon it with yellow filoselle, sew round this the bottom or wired part of the petals, and arrange so that it is twice encircled with the wire and so that the petals from each round come alternately.

To Work a Geranium: The petals of this flower are so small that it does not require a wooden foundation. Take a piece of fine wire, and bend it into a heart shape without the indent in the centre, half an inch in length. Fasten a doubled piece of wool up the centre of this, and work over this foundation with soft shades of rose colour wool. Thread a wool needle, fasten it to the top of the petal, pass it in between the doubled wool and over the wire on the right side, in and out through the doubled wool and over the wire on the left side; continue this form of plaiting until the wire is entirely concealed with a close and thick line of stitches. Make five petals in this manner, join them by twisting the ends of the wire together, and cover that by winding green wool round the end. A primrose is made in the same manner as a geranium, but with the petals more indented in the centre, and with pale lemon coloured wool.

To Work a Lily of the Valley: Make the petals with a wire outline, pointed in the centre and wide in the middle, work them over with white wool, as described in the geranium, turn their edges over, and make up four of them as a flower. Arrange them along a stalk to form a lily spray, and make small round buds of twisted white wool for the top part of the spray.

To Make the Leaves: These are all made upon wire like the geranium, the only alteration being in the shape the wire is bent into.

To Make the Stamens: Cover straight pieces of wire with yellow wool, and turn the end of the wire round so as to thicken the top part.

To Work a Poppy: Take a netting Mesh 1½ inches in width, some deep scarlet wool, also some fine wire, and cover with red silk. Wind the wire upon two small pieces of wood or cardboard to keep it from getting entangled, and leave a piece of it in the centre, double it, and leave 2 inches of it hanging, and also 2 inches of the scarlet wool, which wind once loosely round the Mesh over one of the wires (which open out again) at the edge of the Mesh; lay the other wire over the wool where it has gone over the first wire, and thus secure it. Wind the wool loosely round the Mesh again, this time over the second wire, and lay the first wire over the wool. Wind the wool twenty times round the Mesh, each time securing it with the wires alternately over and under it; then take it off the Mesh. The part where the twisted wires are will be the top of the petal; run a wire through the other end of the petal, and draw the loops there up quite tightly with it, then bring the piece of doubled wire down to the bottom of the petal and the piece beyond the loops on the other side, and twist them both in to the bottom part. Make four of these petals, and either put into the centre of them the dried head of a small poppy, or make a knob of green wool on the top of a piece of wire and put that in.

To Work a Rose: Take a piece of thin wood 2¼ inches square and make a hole in it in the centre, and one at each edge, through these pass fine wires, which lay across the centre, and make quite tight. Take wool of the right shade of rose colour, and commencing at the centre, wind it carefully round and round under the crossed wires, but never attached to them; keep them flat and evenly laid by holding them down with the left thumb. When sufficient rounds have been made, thread the wool on to a fine darning needle and draw it through the centre of the petal, from the outside edge at one part to the opposite outside edge, so as to secure the rounds of wool, and to make the cleft in the centre of the rose leaf; then take the petal off the woodwork by undoing the wires. A finished petal is shown in Fig. 819. Make a dozen petals in this way, six of which

FIG. 819. WOOLWORK FLOWERS—ROSE PETAL.

should be large, and the others rather small. Make the centre of the rose with loops of yellow thread, run a wire through them, tie them up tight a quarter of an inch from the wire; cut them off a little beyond the tie, and comb the wool out beyond the tie so as to make it fluffy. Sew the petals to the centre, and wind green wool round as a stalk.

The best way of making up Woolwork Flowers is to KNIT a quantity of moss with various shades of green wool, put it round a centre of black velvet, and insert the flowers into the moss. When an urn stand has to be made, by Buttonholing with dark wool over rounds of window cord, a thicker centre to the mat is made than by knitting.

Worcesters.—These are woollen cloths, named after the place where they had their origin, as far back, at least,

as the fourteenth century. It appears that Worcester cloth was considered so excellent that its use was prohibited to the Monks by a Chapter of the Benedictine Order, held in 1422. Bath was equally famous for the cloth manufactured there by the Monks of the Bath Abbey from the middle of the fourteenth century.

Work.—A generic and very comprehensive term, often applied to the accomplishments of the needle, whether of Plain Sewing, or of Embroidery.

Taylor thus speaks of Queen Katharine of Arragon:—

> Although a Queen, yet she her days did pass
> In working with the needle curiously.
> *The Needle's Excellency.*

> * * * My soul grows sad with troubles;
> Sing, and disperse 'em, if thou can'st: leave working.
> *Henry VIII.*, Act 3.

> * * * I'll have the work ta'en out,
> And give 't Iago. *Othello.*

> Work Tibet, work Annot, work Margerie,
> Sew Tibet, knit Annot, spin Margerie.
> Let us see who will win the victory.

NICHOLAS UDALIS, "Work Girls' Song" in *Royster Doyster.*

Workhouse Sheeting.—This is a coarse twilled and unbleached cloth, employed for sheeting and likewise for bedroom curtains, embroidered with Turkey red and worked in crewels. It is very much utilised for purposes of embroidery, and is of the ordinary width for sheeting.

Work over Cord.—A term sometimes used in Church Embroidery to denote basket, whipcord, and other Couchings that are made over laid threads.

Worsted.—A class of yarn, well twisted and spun, of long staple wool, varying in length from 3 inches to 10 inches, which, after being cleansed, is combed, to lay the fibres parallel before it is spun, and afterwards wound on reels, and twisted into hanks. The wool was originally thus treated and prepared at Worsted, in Norfolk, whence its name, the manufacture having received a great impetus through Edward III., and his Queen Philippa of Hainault, who introduced a great number of woollen manufacturers from the Netherlands, who settled at Norwich, York, Kendal, Manchester, and Halifax; although it was first established in England in the reign of Henry I., when some Dutchmen, escaping from an inundation, came over and settled at Norwich. In the reign of Queen Elizabeth, a fresh immigration of Flemings took place, who likewise settled at Norwich, and also at Colchester and Sandwich, bringing with them great improvements. Textiles called "stuffs" are, properly speaking, those composed of Worsted, although frequently used as a comprehensive term applied to all fabrics alike. The principal stuffs made of this fine long-fibred wool include moreen, lasting, Denmark satins, rateen, merino, damask, bombazet, tammies, callimanco, shalloon, cubica, serge, plaid, camlet, mousseline de laine, challis, shawls, carpets, crapes, poplins, and hosiery. These are stiffer and more rough than woollen-made fabrics. Cotton warps are often introduced into them, which impair their durability; but, when combined with silk, as in poplins and Bombazines, it is otherwise. The term Worsted Stuffs applies equally to those made of combed wool, combining cotton or silk, which are not "fulled" (like woollen cloth), as to those entirely of Worsted. The manufacture of Worsted stuffs, although very ancient, has only reached its present state of excellence within the last fifty years. According to tradition, we owe the invention of the wool-comb to St. Blaise, and the anniversary of his canonisation (3rd Feb.) used for centuries to be kept as a gala day at Bradford. The Flemish refugees who escaped from the tyranny of the Duke of Alva (1570), settling in Yorkshire, made Halifax for many years the seat of the Worsted industry, which became famous for its damasks, lastings, and other such goods. The first spinning machinery was set up at Bradford in 1790, in a private house, and, five years later, the first manufactory was built. In the year 1834, the union of a cotton warp with Worsted was made, and in 1836 the wool of the Peruvian alpaca was introduced, and, at about the same time, that of mohair of goats' hair of Asia Minor. *See* WOOL.

Worsted Bindings.—These are employed by upholsterers and saddlers, produced in a variety of colours, and can be procured in various lengths to the gross: 6-18, 9-16, or 6-24. The several widths have been designated "double London," "shoe," "double shoe," "extra quality."

Worsted Braids.—These Braids vary in width and make, are employed as dress trimmings, and produced in various colours, though chiefly in black. The numbers run 53, 57, 61, 65, 69, 73, 77, 81, 85, 89, 93, 97, 101. They are sold in 36 yard lengths, four pieces to the gross, or a shorter piece if desired. Many Braids that are called mohair or alpaca, are really of Worsted. There are also Waved Worsted Braids, sold in knots, containing from 4 to 5 yards each. The numbers run 13, 17, and 21, and the Braid is by the gross pieces. It is employed for the trimming of children's dresses. Skirt Braids, said to be of mohair and alpaca, and called Russia Braids, are many of them made of Worsted. They consist of two cords woven together, cut into short lengths, and sold by the gross pieces. The wider ones are in 36 yard lengths, four pieces to the gross. The numbers run from 0 to 8, and the Braid may be had in black or colours.

Worsted Damasks.—These are thick cloths, to be had in many varieties of excellence for the purposes of upholstery. They are produced in all colours, and the widths are suitable for curtains, &c. The chief seat of the industry is at Halifax.

Worsted Fringes.—These are made in very extensive varieties of length and pattern. They run generally from 2½ inches to 4 inches in depth, and the several varieties are classified under three descriptions—viz., Plain-head, Plain-head and Bullion, and Gymp-head. They may be had in all colours and degrees of richness. There are also Worsted Fringes designed for dress,

which are called fancy fringes, and are made of worsted or silk, from half an inch in width to 2 or 3 inches. Worsted tassels, if required for dress or furniture, may be had to match any of these fringes.

Worsted Work.—This needlework, once known as Opus Pulvinarium, then as Cushion Style, and Worsted Work is now generally entitled Berlin Work, a name given to it when coloured patterns and Berlin Wools were first used in its manufacture. The origin of Worsted Work is very ancient, it being undoubtedly known and practised in the East before it was introduced into Europe from Egypt, but it is difficult to trace an account of it, from the practice of ancient writers classing all descriptions of needlework under one heading, until the latter end of the thirteenth century, when the various methods of Embroidery were distinguished and classed with great accuracy, and what was then known as Cushion Style, was especially mentioned as being used for kneeling mats, cushions, and curtains in cathedrals, and occasionally upon sacred vestments, as can still be seen on the narrow hem of the Sion Cope (date 1225), now in the South Kensington Museum. Like all other works of art during the Middle Ages, it was chiefly practised in convents and nunneries, and used for the adornment of sacred objects, but as the nuns were the only instructors in those days, noble ladies were sent to them to learn to work as well as to read, and beguiled many tedious hours by adorning their homes with specimens of their skill. Worsted Work, distinguished from Embroidery by being made upon a foundation of loosely woven canvas that requires to be thoroughly covered instead of being worked upon materials that can be left visible, was in favour after the Reformation, and much of it worked by Anne Boleyn, Mary Queen of Scots and her ladies, is still in existence. In the time of Queen Anne, and Queen Mary, silk Embroideries and Crewel Work were more fashionable, but in the reign of George III. much Worsted Work was done, that executed by the Duchess of York for Oatlands Park being particularly noticeable, from the designs, colouring, and workmanship, being her own. The Linwood Exhibition of Worsted Work during the earlier part of the present century, consisting of sixty-four full length pieces, deserves notice, as these were all executed by one lady (Miss Linwood), who copied the designs from oil paintings, upon a canvas, known as Tammy, and worked them out in Worsteds that were especially dyed to suit the required shades,

When it is remembered that before the year 1804 all designs for Worsted Work had to be drawn by hand and coloured according to the taste of the worker, and that the Worsteds used were harsher and coarser than those now employed, some idea of the labour of the work then, as compared with what it is at present, can be gathered. It was to remedy this, that a printer at Berlin produced a series of designs copied from pictures and printed upon Point paper, so that each stitch was plainly visible; these were coloured by hand with due regard to the real colouring of the pictures they represented, and afterwards worked out in Tent Stitch upon very fine canvas with fine Worsteds and Silks. Shortly afterwards, a large and coarser canvas began to be substituted for the fine, and Cross Stitch instead of Tent Stitch; and finally, the Worsteds were superseded by Berlin Wool, and the good patterns by large unwieldly flower, or impossible animal designs, which, coupled with their execution in the brightest colours producable, was the death blow to Worsted Work from an artistic point of view. For the last twenty years, and since the public mind has become more alive to the beauty and fitness of needlework for decorative purposes, these abominations have been justly discarded; but they must not be confounded with the work itself, which, when executed in fine stitches upon fine canvas, in soft and harmonious colouring and correct designs, is as capable of embodying an artist's idea as other needlework mediums. The design shown in Fig. 820

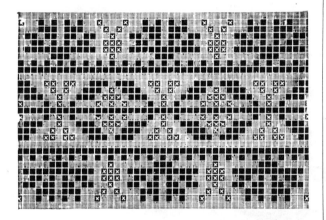

FIG. 820. WORSTED WORK.

is an arabesque pattern, worked with three shades of Berlin wool, the darkest of which is shown by the dark squares, the next by the squares filled with crosses, and the lightest by the check pattern squares. To work: Fill in the dark squares with CROSS STITCH and with deep ruby-coloured wool, the check squares with pale olive green wool, and the squares filled with crosses with pale blue filoselle. For manner of working, *see* BERLIN WORK.

Worsted Yarns.—There are many varieties in these yarns, such as Worsted, for carpet mending, which is very coarse, and may be had in many bright colours, and sold in paper bags, wound in balls; the bags containing from 3 to 6 pounds each. Also Hank Worsted for knitting stockings, dyed in various colours—white, black, speckled, grey, scarlet, &c., and sold by the half dozen or dozen pounds, made up in ½ pound skeins. Also Fingering Worsted, sent out in ½ pounds by the manufacturers, comprising eight skeins, of 1 ounce weight each. It may be bought in small quantities in retail shops. Also Scotch Fingering, which is a loosely spun yarn, produced in very bright colours, and sold by the spindle of 6 pounds. Scotch Fingering is much employed for the knitting of children's gaiters, stockings, scarves,

and mittens. Ordinary Fingering Worsted is sent out by the manufacturers in ½ pounds, or eight skeins, each skein being considered an ounce in weight. There are also Worsted balls, sold for the purpose of mending. These can be had in black and white, speckled and grey, made up in balls of 3, 4, or 6 "drams" each, and sold in bags containing 3 pounds, 6 pounds, or 12 pounds weight of yarn.

Wristbands. — These form an important part of a shirt, and the method of making them should, therefore, be known. Although some portion of the garment may be of calico the breast, collar, and cuffs or wristbands must always be of linen. They must consist of three pieces of material, two of linen, and one of thin calico. To work: Cut the wristbands by a thread, the selvedge way of the linen, lay all the triple thickness together, and as the calico must be placed between the other two, lay it outside them, and the two pieces of linen together, when commencing to work. RUN all neatly together on the wrong side, and then turn over one of the linen sides, so that the running and raw edges shall be turned in. Press the edge to make it lie flat, and then draw a thread in the linen, on the side farthest from the ridge made by the portions folded over on the inside. Compare the band with that of another shirt, to regulate the measurement for the drawing of the thread, as the Hemstitching should always be made at a certain depth from the edge. TACK the opposite side and the two ends, to secure them in their right positions, and then stitch the band where the thread has been drawn. The ends of the band will have to be treated in the same way —a thread drawn and a stitching made. The shape of these wristbands, as well as of collars, changes continually, thus a pattern should be obtained, and if the corners have to be rounded, or any new slopings be required, they must be so cut before the first Tacking is made. Great care will be needed where any curve has to be made, as no thread can be drawn in such a case. The method of making a shirt collar is precisely the same as of making a cuff; and while the exact form must depend on the current fashion, these general directions apply to all.

Y.

Yak Crochet.—*See* CROCHET, page 118.

Yak Lace.—This is a coarse Pillow Lace, made in Buckinghamshire and Northampton, in imitation of Maltese Silk Guipure. The material used is obtained from the fine wool of the Yak. The patterns are all simple, and are copied from the geometric designs of real Maltese Lace. They are connected with plaited Guipure Bars, ornamented with Purls, that form part of the pattern, being worked with the same threads and at the same time. The thick parts of the design are worked in Cloth Stitch and Plaitings.

Yak Lace has been most successfully imitated in Crochet (*see* Fig. 821); it is there worked in Maltese thread, and in black, white, or écru colours, according to taste. To work the pattern given, *see* CROCHET directions, page 119.

Besides the Yak Lace made with Crochet, an imitation of it is formed with the needle upon a foundation of coarse grenadine, which is afterwards cut away, the work closely resembles the lace made upon the Pillow. It can be used for dress and furniture trimmings, though it will not wash. The materials required are strong and rather coarse black, coloured, or white grenadine, or tarlatan, Mohair yarn matching the grenadine in colour, strips of cartridge paper, and prepared linen, such as is known as carbonised linen, as shown in Fig. 822. Trace the design, which can be taken from the finished scallop on the left hand side of the

dine between each stitch, until the space is filled in; then return over the lines with a second thread, and CORD every one. This Run foundation is shown in the right hand leaves of the illustration. Take a good long thread and work in the long lines. For the leaves there will be five long lines required, for the scallop four, and for the Footing two. DARN each of these lines in and out of the short threads, taking up one and leaving the next, as in ordinary Darning, and where a BAR has to be made to connect the leaves to each other or to the Footing, or the scallops to the centre star, make it as a CORDED BAR with the thread as it is working, as joins of all kinds must be avoided wherever possible, and fresh threads taken in in the darning. Cord the long lines in the Footing, like the Bars, but the other long lines will not require this unless the thread used is very thin. Work the stars in the centre of the pattern so that they

FIG. 821. YAK LACE—IMITATED IN CROCHET.

illustration upon the carbonised linen, back the pattern with calico, and lay the grenadine over it, which TACK down quite evenly upon it. Take the cartridge paper, and from it cut out the straight line that forms the FOOTING, the leaves surmounting the scallop, and the scallop. Lay these bits of paper down upon the grenadine, and stitch them down to it by a securing line in their centres. (They are used to keep the stitches worked over them from taking up the grenadine, where it has to be cut away.) Now commence to work. Take an Embroidery needle with a blunt point, thread the Mohair upon it, and work in all the short up and down lines in the lace first, and which form the foundation for the long lines. Run a thread across a space and let it take up two strands of the grenadine beyond the cartridge paper, bring it to the other side and let it take up two strands of the grenadine there, work backwards and forwards in this way, leaving only one strand of grena-

are connected to the leaves and the scallops. Make them in GENOA STITCH thus: Carry along their length four lines of thread, and then DARN over them thickly, drawing the stitches in tight at the points of the star and loosening them in the centre. Make a loop of thread, for the scalloped edge, which secure into one of the short lines on the scallop, miss the next short line, and make a second loop into the third; continue to the end of the pattern, and make the loops larger at the broad part of the scallop than at the narrow. Cord this line of loops, and run a plain thread through them, which also Cord. Having finished the work, cut away the tacking threads, and so release the lace from the pattern; then carefully cut away the grenadine from the back of the stitches, and leave them without any support.

Yard.—A measure of length employed for every description of textile or material for personal wear, upholstery, &c., or for needlework. One yard equals 3 feet or 36 inches, and is the standard of British and American measurement. The cloth yard in old English times was of the length of the arrows employed both in battle, and for the chase.

Yarn.—This term signifies thread spun from fibres of any description, whether of flax, hemp, cotton, silk, or wool.

Yarn Measure.—A hank of worsted yarn is generally estimated in England at 560 yards, or seven "leas" of 80 yards each. Linen yarn is estimated by the number of "leas" or "cuts," each of 3 yards, contained in 1 pound weight. In Scotland it is estimated by the number of rounds in the spindle, or 48 "leas." Thus, No. 48 in England, is called 1 pound yarn in Scotland. One hank of cotton yarn is 840 yards, and a spindle of 18 hanks is 15,120 yards.

Yaws.—A vulgar term denoting the thin places in cloth.

cotton, and at very low prices, for petticoat skirts. Yokes, such as employed in dress, are copied from those made of wood, and worn on the shoulders by those who carry pails of either water or milk.

Yokohama Crape.—This is a very fine, close make of Crape, otherwise known as Canton Crape, employed especially for mantle-making, but also for the trimming of dresses. It is made in two widths, measuring respectively 25 inches and 2 yards. There is much more substance in it than in ordinary Crape, and it is not transparent, like the latter. The Yokohama is the costliest of all descriptions of Crape, and the most durable in wear.

Yorkshire Flannels.—These Flannels have a plain selvedge, and are superior to those made in Lancashire. They are made in the natural colour of the wool, so that they are improved in appearance by washing, contrary to the ordinary rule.

FIG. 822. YAK LACE—IMITATION.

Yokes.—These are headings, or shaped bands, into which plaitings or gatherings of garments are sewn, and which are so cut as to fit either the shoulders or the hips, and from which the rest of the bodice, nightdress, dressing gown, or the skirt is to depend. The Yoke of a shirt or nightdress is sometimes called a neckpiece, and is always made of double material, like that of a skirt. Of whatever the cloth may consist, one rule applies to all Yokes, viz., that the straight way of the stuff should be placed at the centre of the Yoke, whether that centre be at the back of the shoulders or forming a sort of stomacher at the front of the skirt. This rule holds good for those made of crape likewise, which must be so folded as that there shall be no seam made. Woven Yokes may now be purchased in all colours, made of

Ypres Lace.—The lace made at Ypres is Valenciennes Lace. *See* VALENCIENNES LACE.

Z.

Zante Lace.—This lace is similar to the Greek Reticellas. It is still to be purchased in the Ionian Isles, but the manufacture of it has long been discontinued.

Zephyr Cloth.—A fine, thin, finely spun woollen cloth, made in Belgium, thinner than tweed, and employed for women's gowns. Shawls also are made of this material, the wool being fine, and loosely woven, and very light in its weight. It can be dyed in very brilliant colours, and resembles a Kerseymere.

Zephyr Ginghams or Prints.—These are pretty delicate textiles, resembling a cotton batiste, designed for summer wear, and produced in pale but fast colours, which bear washing. They are to be had in pink and blue, and measure from 32 inches to a yard in width.

Zephyr Merino Yarn.—The term employed by the wool staplers of Germany to signify what is usually called German or Berlin.

Zephyr Shirting.—This is a kind of gauze flannel, having a silk warp. It is manufactured for use in hot climates, and is a superior description of cloth. The ground-work is grey, shewing the threads of white silk, and there is a pattern formed of narrow stripes, either of black or of pink, running the lengthway of the stuff. Zephyr Shirting measures 32 inches in width.

Zulu Cloth. — A closely woven cloth, twill-made, designed for Crewel Embroidery or Outline Work, the closeness of the weaving facilitating the drawing of the designs.